D1288757

Dear West Customer:

West Academic Publishing has changed the look of its American Casebook Series®.

In keeping with our efforts to promote sustainability, we have replaced our former covers with book covers that are more environmentally friendly. Our casebooks will now be covered in a 100% renewable natural fiber. In addition, we have migrated to an ink supplier that favors vegetable-based materials, such as soy.

Using soy inks and natural fibers to print our textbooks reduces VOC emissions. Moreover, our primary paper supplier is certified by the Forest Stewardship Council, which is testament to our commitment to conservation and responsible business management.

The new cover design has migrated from the long-standing brown cover to a contemporary charcoal fabric cover with silver-stamped lettering and black accents. Please know that inside the cover, our books continue to provide the same trusted content that you've come to expect from West.

We've retained the ample margins that you have told us you appreciate in our texts while moving to a new, larger font, improving readability. We hope that you will find these books a pleasing addition to your bookshelf.

Another visible change is that you will no longer see the brand name Thomson West on our print products. With the recent merger of Thomson and Reuters, I am pleased to announce that books published under the West Academic Publishing imprint will once again display the West brand.

It will likely be several years before all of our casebooks are published with the new cover and interior design. We ask for your patience as the new covers are rolled out on new and revised books knowing that behind both the new and old covers, you will find the finest in legal education materials for teaching and learning.

Thank you for your continued patronage of the West brand, which is both rooted in history and forward looking towards future innovations in legal education. We invite you to be a part of our next evolution.

Best regards,

Louis H. Higgins
Editor in Chief, West Academic Publishing

CASES AND MATERIALS

on

ARBITRATION LAW AND PRACTICE

Fifth Edition

■ ■ ■

By

Thomas E. Carbonneau

Orlando Distinguished Professor of Law
Faculty Director, Arbitration Institute
Penn State University

AMERICAN CASEBOOK SERIES®

WEST®

A Thomson Reuters business

Mat #40828265

© West, a Thomson business, 2007
© 2009 Thomson Reuters
   610 Opperman Drive
   St. Paul, MN 55123
   1–800–313–9378
Printed in the United States of America

ISBN: 978–0–314–91142–1

To my daughter:
Sara Lucille Carbonneau
"Lou"

*

PREFACE

Arbitration occupies a dominant place in the U.S. legal system. Its significance and stature are unquestioned. Only the foolhardy would ignore its existence and impact upon the legal process. It has become, in effect, the primary means for resolving civil disputes.

Arbitration now exceeds its traditional range of application by a very substantial margin. Its use is no longer relegated to commercial relationships and contract disputes between merchants. Its jurisdictional reach extends to the purchase of securities and other consumer transactions. It is the remedy by which employment disputes are resolved. It also governs controversies that involve federal rights created by congressional statutes, the regulation of commerce, and fundamental civil liberty guarantees. Few, if any, disputes are deemed inarbitrable.

The most controversial question in the current law of arbitration centers upon the validity and enforceability of arbitration agreements. There appears to be resistance among some courts to the enforcement of adhesionary arbitration agreements, especially in the consumer and employment areas. This development is most pronounced among the state and federal courts in California. There, arbitration agreements are more frequently voided on the basis of unconscionability or for a lack of mutuality. These courts, it seems, have concluded that procedural fairness must be guaranteed in unilateral contracts for arbitration. Courts in other jurisdictions have periodically invoked the costs of arbitration and their distribution among the contracting parties to nullify arbitration agreements. No matter the basis, opposition to arbitration agreements is confined to a relatively insignificant minority of courts. Their reluctance to enforce arbitration agreements is an uncharacteristic judicial position. In the vast majority of cases, courts give full effect to arbitration agreements.

Arbitral awards or judgments are also generally favored by courts and enforced. Vacatur or nullification is a rare result. The Federal Arbitration Act (FAA) codifies a policy that sustains the recourse to arbitration. It limits the judicial supervision of arbitral awards to procedural matters that are vital to the legitimacy of adjudication. Moreover, courts have interpreted the narrow grounds for review restrictively. Recent practice, however, has somewhat eroded the policy of near automatic enforcement of awards by developing "opt-in" provisions for judicial merits review, an action to clarify awards, and enhancing the evident partiality ground for vacatur with a regime of arbitrator disclosure. Because of the new emphasis upon disclosure, partiality in either neutral and party-appointed arbitrators has become the most effective means for challenging awards.

Opt-in provisions are an off-shoot of the principle of freedom of contract. In many respects, they constitute a wayward development. Freedom of contract is at the very heart of U.S. arbitration law; it provides that parties are free to agree to arbitration and to establish the protocol for, or design of, their arbitration. Even though the governing statute limits judicial supervision to matters procedural, opt-in provisions permit parties to agree to the *de novo* judicial review of arbitral awards. This development not only compromises the status of the law and the functionality of arbitration, but it has also divided the federal circuits. With the U.S. Supreme Court decision in *Hall Street Associates*, parties have lost this option in FAA arbitration.

The action to clarify awards—despite its practical value—is likely to have a pernicious effect because it will eventually service the ends of adversarial representation. Under the decisional law, it is a common law doctrine that allows courts to remand an award to the arbitral tribunal to have opaque determinations explained or clarified. As a result, losing parties have already asked courts and tribunals to "clarify" arbitral determinations that go against their interests. The procedure then introduces full blown appeal into the arbitral process by the back door.

Challenging the neutrality of arbitrators and their determinations with this level of intensity is ominous. It underscores the tension in arbitration law between the protection of rights and the functionality of the adjudicatory process. It highlights the difficulty of providing simultaneously for due process in and access to adjudication. The U.S. Supreme Court has nonetheless been unwavering and unequivocal over the last forty years in its support for arbitration. During that period, it has decided more than thirty arbitration cases and articulated a judicial doctrine that admits of no qualifications to the right to arbitrate. All but matters of criminal liability falls within the purview of arbitration. Moreover, the arbitrator is the sovereign decider of the merits, the procedure, and even jurisdiction.

At this stage in the development of the U.S. Supreme Court's decisional law on arbitration, it is clear that the Court is using the FAA as a stepping stone to elaborating a judicial doctrine on arbitration. The Court has added significantly to the content of the legislation. For example, FAA § 2— unquestionably the key provision of the Act both historically and doctrinally— establishes that the surrender of judicial remedies by contract does not violate public policy and thereby validates arbitration agreements as a legitimate exercise of contract freedom. Nonetheless, in the Court's rulings, arbitration agreements are not simply contracts. In the words of Justice Black, when he reacted critically to the majority's endorsement of the separability doctrine in his dissent in *Prima Paint Corp. v. Flood & Conklin Mfg. Co*, 388 U.S. 395, 87 S. Ct. 1801. 18 L.Ed.2d 1270 (1967), they are "super" contracts, "[e]levate[d]—above all other contractual provisions." Glossing the FAA, the Court has made arbitration agreements nothing less than the means for correcting the dysfunctional provision of adjudicatory services in American society.

The Court has altered the governing legislation in other respects. The federal preemption doctrine, pieced together by the Court over a number of cases, has been instrumental to the creation and maintenance of the "strong federal policy on arbitration." It guaranteed that a set of uniformly favorable principles to arbitration would apply in all United States jurisdictions. In establishing the doctrine, the Court literally rewrote the express content of the FAA, extending the statute's application to state courts and legislatures. Federal preemption also allowed the Court to "promulgate" an implied federal right to arbitrate. The case law nevertheless acknowledged that several FAA provisions were directed to federal district courts and that the governing legislation did not create federal question jurisdiction. These would-be anomalies did not impede the Court's policy on arbitration. Federalization of the law is well-established; since *Dobson*, 513 U.S. 265 (1995), and *Doctor's Associates, Inc.*, 517 U.S. 681 (1996), it is essentially unquestioned. An expansive view of interstate commerce governs and states cannot enact laws restricting—directly or indirectly—arbitration agreements.

The Court has exhibited singular determination in upholding the federal policy on arbitration. It admits of no exceptions to settled views and demands compliance to them regardless of logic, legal tradition, or intrinsic truth. In this regard, the Court is more perspicacious than it is single-minded or arbitrary. It is generally acknowledged that exceptions, additions, or modifications to legal rules, once recognized, mutate over time and progressively swallow up or transform the original rule. The U.S. law of arbitration would not be as cohesive, viable, or effective were it riddled with the twists and turns of qualification. The campaign for federalization was waged to create a disciplined, uniform, and unambiguous regulation of arbitration. After all, the goal that is contemplated is nothing less than the building a workable system of civil adjudication and justice in U.S. society.

While there are misgivings, debates, and controversies, arbitration—despite imperfections—is in a golden era. The Court sustains every aspect of the operation of the arbitral process in both the domestic and transborder sphere. Doctrine is adapted to achieve the objectives of policy; everything is sacrificed to bring about an accessible form of adjudicatory justice. The judicial support not only is consistent, but it also is unequivocal. As a consequence, arbitration has expanded its range to new dispute areas and its scope of application beyond contract itself. With the extension of the contract to nonsignatory parties and the deference paid to adhesionary agreements, arbitral clauses implied at law may soon become a new feature of the U.S. court doctrine on arbitration. The critique, and possibly impairment, of arbitration can only effectively proceed from the legislative branch. It is to it that forces antagonistic to arbitration have directed their primary efforts.

These course materials convey a comprehensive picture of the arbitral process. In particular, they seek to provide legal professionals with the knowledge and understanding necessary to participate effectively in counseling on arbitration, the drafting of arbitration agreements, conducting arbitral proceedings, and managing court actions relating to arbitration. The principles, rules, and procedural structures that are described are basic to the law of arbitration and apply to all systems of arbitration.

The chapters describe the various stages of an arbitration, define the issues that are vital to its operation, assess the legal doctrines and concepts that regulate it, and point to critical doctrinal and practical developments. In some respects, the availability of recourse to arbitration has changed the face of traditional law-making and lawyering. Arbitration dislodges the application and activity of the traditional judicial process. Although arbitration is effective and valuable, it is hardly without drawbacks. Lawyers and clients need to assess the remedy and make a judgment about its transactional viability for them. The materials point to problems that are likely to arise in the practice of arbitration law and propose a framework for elaborating solutions.

The volume begins with a presentation of essential terms and definitions. It then introduces the basic statutory law in the area (the FAA and the RUAA). Thereafter, it addresses the major themes in the decisional law on arbitration: federalization, contractualism, and arbitrability. It investigates particular applications of the arbitral remedy (traditional and nontraditional), *e.g.*, labor and employment, securities, consumer, and maritime arbitration. The issues that relate to the enforcement of arbitral awards are thoroughly outlined and discussed. Finally, in terms of domestic arbitration, the most recent and difficult problems of practice are identified and treated comprehensively.

The consideration of international commercial arbitration is equally complete and thorough. It begins with an evaluation of the contributions of the international commercial arbitration process to the conduct of transborder commerce and the harmonization of law and legal procedure. The central significance of the 1958 New York Arbitration Convention is highlighted in terms of the language of the treaty and the decisional law that underlies it.

The presentation emphasizes the importance of practical problems and underscores the fragility of existing rules and the need for professionals in the field to be analytically rigorous as well as creative in their approach to problems. The text that follows seeks to educate through a comprehensive presentation of relevant and timely information, the rigorous analytical evaluation of that data, and the identification of the practical implications of the "findings of fact" and "conclusions of law."

Copyright Acknowledgments

The author is most grateful to Jason Reimer for his editorial assistance and contribution. He is also indebted to Sherry Miller, Mary Beth Aber, and Lisa Woltz for their word processing services.

The author gratefully acknowledges the copyright permissions granted by the following organizations:

1. The Virginia Law Review Association and Fred B. Rothman & Co. to reprint excerpts from Cohen & Dayton, *The New Federal Arbitration Law*, 12 VA. L. REV. 265, 281 (1926);

2. The Tulane Law Review Association to reprint excerpts from Carbonneau, *Arbitral Justice: The Demise of Due Process in American Law*, 70 TUL. L. REV. 1945 (1996) (Originally published by the Tulane Law Review Association. All rights reserved.);

3. The American Review of International Arbitration to reprint excerpts from Carbonneau, *"A-Legality" and Arbitration: The German Supreme Court Joins the Fray*, 4 AM. REV. INT'L ARB. 217 (1993) and Carbonneau, *Beyond Trilogies ...*, 6 AM. REV. INT'L ARB. 1 (1995);

4. Transnational Publishers, Inc. to reprint excerpts from Carbonneau, *Darkness and Light in the Shadows of International Arbitral Adjudication*, in FACT-FINDING BEFORE INTERNATIONAL TRIBUNALS 153 [Eleventh Sokol Colloquium] (R. Lillich ed. 1991) (Reprinted with permission of Transnational Publishers, Inc.);

5. Juris Publishing, Inc. to reprint a variety of articles from the *World Arbitration and Mediation Report*.

*

Summary of Contents

———

TABLE OF CONTENTS

———

*

TABLE OF CASES

The principal cases are in bold type. Cases cited or discussed in the text are in roman type. References are to pages. Cases cited in principal cases and within other quoted materials are not included.

*

CASES AND MATERIALS
on
ARBITRATION
LAW AND PRACTICE

Fifth Edition

*

CHAPTER ONE

AN INTRODUCTION

■ ■ ■

1. WHAT IS ARBITRATION?

Arbitration is a private, generally informal, and nonjudicial trial procedure for adjudicating disputes. It functions as an alternative to judicial litigation by providing binding determinations through presumably less expensive, more efficient and expert, and nonetheless fair proceedings. Although it can engender settlements, arbitration is not intended to operate as a means for achieving dispute resolution directly through party agreement. Arbitration is neither negotiation nor mediation. The parties confer upon the arbitrators' full legal authority to adjudicate disputes, *i.e.*, to render a final disposition on the matters submitted that can be enforced through coercive legal means. Party agreement sets the process in motion, but it does not dictate the outcome. Once the parties entrust the arbitral tribunal with the authority to rule, they—subject to a possible settlement—relinquish control of the dispute and of its resolution to the arbitrators.

The recourse to arbitration is consensual. The parties to a transaction or other relationship agree by contract to submit existing or prospective disputes to arbitration. The agreement to arbitrate is the centerpiece of the process—both in terms of legal doctrine and from a practical vantage point. The parties have the freedom—the legal right—to engage in arbitration and to make specific provisions for the implementation and operation of their arbitration. By entering into a contract of arbitration, the parties voluntarily abandon their right to judicial relief and, in effect, create a private system of adjudication that presumably is better adapted to their transactional needs.

T. CARBONNEAU, THE LAW AND PRACTICE OF ARBITRATION ch. 1(1) (3d ed. 2009).

In *AMF v. Brunswick Corp.*, national competitors for the manufacture of electronic bowling equipment entered into a litigation settlement which provided that any future disputes regarding comparative advertising claims would be submitted to a neutral third-party for an advisory opinion. The U.S. District Court for the Eastern District of New York enforced the procedure for a third-party opinion under the Federal Arbitration Act (FAA). The court reasoned that, because the FAA did not define the term "arbitration," any submission to a third-party constituted an agreement to arbitrate. The court stated that no "magic words such as 'arbitrate'... [were] needed to obtain benefits of the Act [the FAA]."

1

Moreover, the term "arbitration" "eludes easy definition" and could be synonymous with mediation and conciliation. Accordingly, the FAA "provided for [the] enforcement of agreements to 'settle' disputes...."

On the basis of this flexible and somewhat whimsical construction of the FAA, the court compelled AMF and Brunswick to have recourse to their agreed-upon ADR procedure (the non-binding advisory opinion). Despite its title, content, and legislative history, the FAA—in the court's view—was not just an arbitration statute, but legislation broadly applicable to all forms of alternative dispute resolution (ADR).

AMF INC. v. BRUNSWICK CORP.

621 F.Supp. 456 (E.D. N.Y. 1985).

(footnote omitted)

[...]

WEINSTEIN, Chief Judge.

In this case of first impression, AMF Incorporated seeks to compel Brunswick Corporation to comply with their agreement to obtain a non-binding advisory opinion in a dispute over the propriety of advertising claims. For reasons indicated below, the agreement to utilize an alternative dispute resolution mechanism must be enforced.

I. FACTS

AMF and Brunswick compete nationally in the manufacture of electronic and automatic machinery used for bowling centers. In earlier litigation before this court, AMF alleged that Brunswick had advertised certain automatic scoring devices in a false and deceptive manner. Brunswick responded with counterclaims regarding advertisements for AMF's pinspotter, bowling pins and automatic scorer. In 1983 the parties ended the litigation with a settlement agreement filed with the court. Any future dispute involving an advertised claim of "data based comparative superiority" of any bowling product would be submitted to an advisory third party, the National Advertising Division ("NAD") of the Council of Better Business Bureaus, to determine whether there was experimental support for the claim.

[...]

In March and April 1985, Brunswick advertised its product, Armor Plate 3000, in a trade periodical called Bowler's Journal.... [T]he advertisement ... detail[s] the advantages of Armor Plate; and ... strongly suggests that research supports the claim of durability as compared to wood lanes.

[...]

AMF, disputing the content of the advertisement, sought from Brunswick the underlying research data.... Brunswick replied that having undertaken the expense of research it would not make the results available to AMF. Thereupon AMF informed Brunswick that it was invoking ... the settlement agreement and requested that Brunswick provide substantiation to an independent third party. Brunswick responded that its advertisement did not fall within the terms of the agreement. AMF now brings this action to compel Brunswick to submit its data to the NAD for nonbinding arbitration.

[. . .]

III.   LAW

A.   *Arbitration*

1.   *The Act*

AMF characterizes the settlement agreement as one subject to the Federal Arbitration Act.... The Act provides for enforcement of agreements to "settle" disputes arising after the agreement was entered into. In relevant part it reads:

> A written provision in ... a contract evidencing a transaction involving commerce to settle by arbitration a controversy thereafter arising out of such contract or transaction, or the refusal to perform the whole or any part thereof ... shall be valid, irrevocable, and enforceable, save upon such grounds as exist at law or in equity for the revocation of any contract.

... The issue posed is whether "a controversy" would be "settled" by the process set forth in the agreement.

Brunswick argues that the parties did not contemplate the kind of arbitration envisaged by the Act because the opinion of the third party is not binding on AMF and Brunswick and the agreement cannot settle the controversy. Arbitration, Brunswick argues, must present an alternative to litigation; that is, it must provide "a final settlement of the controversy between the parties."

Arbitration is a term that eludes easy definition. One commentator has pointed out that "difficulty with terminology seems to have persisted throughout the entire development of arbitration.".... He suggests that arbitration has become "synonymous with 'mediation' and 'conciliation.' ".....

The Federal Arbitration Act, adopted in 1925, made agreements to arbitrate enforceable without defining what they were. Contemporary cases provide a broad description of arbitration: "[a] form of procedure whereby differences may be settled." ... At no time have the courts insisted on a rigid or formalistic approach to a definition of arbitration.

Case law following the passage of the Act reflects unequivocal support of agreements to have third parties decide disputes—the essence of arbitration. No magic words such as "arbitrate" or "binding arbitration" or "final dispute resolution" are needed to obtain the benefits of the Act....

[. . .]

An adversary proceeding, submission of evidence, witnesses and cross-examination are not essential elements of arbitration.... The Second Circuit has set a standard of "fundamental fairness" in arbitration; rules of evidence and procedure do not apply with the same strictness as they do in federal courts....

Arbitration is a creature of contract, a device of the parties rather than the judicial process. If the parties have agreed to submit a dispute for a decision by a third party, they have agreed to arbitration. The arbitrator's decision need not be binding in the same sense that a judicial decision needs to be to satisfy the constitutional requirement of a justiciable case or controversy....

2. *Application of the Act to the Facts*

Under the circumstances of this case, the agreement should be characterized as one to arbitrate. Obviously there is a controversy between the parties—is there data supporting Brunswick's claim of superiority. Submission of this dispute will at least "settle" that issue, even though the parties may want to continue related disputes in another forum.

It is highly likely that if Brunswick's claims are found by NAD to be supported that will be the end of AMF's challenge to the advertisement. Should the claims not be found to be supported, it is probable that Brunswick will change its advertising copy. Viewed in the light of reasonable commercial expectations the dispute will be settled by this arbitration. That it may not end all controversy between the parties for all times is no reason not to enforce the agreement.

The mechanism agreed to by the parties does provide an effective alternative to litigation, even though it would not employ an adversary process. That the arbitrator will examine documents *in camera* and *ex parte* does not prevent recognition of the procedure as arbitration since the parties have agreed to this special practice in this unique type of dispute. Courts are fully familiar with the practice since prosecutorial and business secrets often require protection by *ex parte* and *in camera* proceedings during the course of a litigation.

In a confidential-submission scheme, such as the one agreed to here, adversarial hearings cannot take place. But this fact does not militate against application of the Act. Rather it supports arbitration since the special arbitrator may be more capable of deciding the issue than is a court which relies so heavily on the adversary process. Moreover, the particular arbitrator chosen by these parties is more capable than the courts of finding the faint line that separates data supported claims from puffery in the sometimes mendacious atmosphere of advertising copy.

[. . .]

The alternative dispute resolution (ADR) procedure agreed upon in the settlement is designed to reduce the acrimony associated with protracted litigation and to improve the chances of resolving future advertising disputes. This form of ADR is designed to keep disputes of this kind out of court.

The value of this settlement agreement lies largely in the particular experience and skill of the NAD as a resolver of disputes. In the fourteen years since its formation, the NAD has developed its own process of reviewing complaints of deceptiveness, coupling relative informality and confidentiality with safeguards to ensure procedural fairness. . . . To these advantages of the special ADR system designed by the parties is added the unique ability of the NAD to decide what is fair in advertising. A judge might make this inquiry, but ultimately it would have to defer to the very expertise that NAD offers without resort to the courts.

General public policy favors support of alternatives to litigation when these alternatives serve the interests of the parties and of judicial administration. Here AMF and Brunswick agreed in June 1983 that a special ADR mechanism would serve them better than litigation. Such decisions are encouraged by no less an observer than the Chief Justice of the United States. In his words, ADR devices are often superior to litigation "in terms of cost, time, and human wear and tear." . . .

As suggested by the "Plan for Court–Annexed Arbitration, United States District Court, Eastern District of New York," effective January 1, 1986, the specific policy of this court is to enforce ADR agreements. In most instances they reduce the need for court trials and save clients' time and money.

A remedy at law would be inadequate since it could only approximate the skilled, speedy and inexpensive efforts available by way of specific performance. A lawsuit would deny AMF the practical specialized experience that the parties agreed to have available for an examination of data-based comparative advertising. A court decision and an NAD decision would have different effects on the parties' reputations within the bowling products industry. In short, a remedy at law falls short of providing many of the advantages of specific performance.

[. . .]

IV. CONCLUSION

[. . .]

AMF's petition to compel the submission of data pursuant to Paragraph 9 of the settlement agreement of June 30, 1983 is enforceable under the Federal Arbitration Act and pursuant to this court's equity jurisdiction.

[. . .]

So Ordered.

NOTES AND QUESTIONS

1. The decision in *AMF v. Brunswick Corp.* illustrates the dangers of disregarding conventional logic and rationality in the articulation of judicial policy. The sole and transparent objective of the "discussion" and manipulation of ideas is to achieve the result the court finds desirable in the case. With all due respect to Judge Weinstein and his office, the *trompe l'oeil* does not even approximate Cardozo in *Palsgraf* or *Allegheny College*. It is mere spin, unabashedly presented and intellectually unsustainable. It is a flawed construction of the applicable statute. Simply stated, the FAA does not contain any of the definitional indeterminacy that the court attributes to it. Moreover, the court's duty to enforce court-annexed arbitration schemes has no bearing on the meaning and content of the FAA. All of these statements in support of the conclusion are deliberately inapposite and distortive. It appears that the court believes it must falsify the law to achieve a noble end and that all can be sacrificed to achieve that objective.

2. Is a "super" FAA realistic? What does the court seek to accomplish? In your view, is it being analytically rigorous and sound or engaging in practical politics? What are the likely consequences of the adopted methodology?

3. Is the *AMF v. Brunswick Corp.* court correct or plainly wrong? Does it distort well-recognized concepts of arbitration law to enforce the parties' contract provision? What is the purpose of undertaking this exercise? Could the issue have been resolved more simply and accurately—for example, purely on the basis of contract law?

4. How would you define arbitration and why? Is the court right to see difficulty in defining the concept of arbitration?

5. Unfortunately, *AMF v. Brunswick Corp.* now has a substantial and—thankfully—mixed progeny. For example, in *Harrison v. Nissan Motor Corp. in U.S.A.*, 111 F.3d 343 (3d Cir. 1997), the U.S. Court of Appeals for the Third Circuit issued a ruling at odds with the opinion in *AMF v. Brunswick Corp.* There, Harrison filed suit and alleged defects in the car she purchased from Nissan. Nissan moved to dismiss the suit because the consumer had not had recourse to the "informal dispute resolution procedure provided by Nissan pursuant to the Pennsylvania Automobile Lemon Law." Nissan's motion for dismissal was denied. Nissan appealed. Harrison argued that the FAA was inapplicable to the informal ADR procedure. The FAA did not govern non-binding arbitration.

Although *AMF v. Brunswick Corp.* might be the leading precedent, the *Harrison* court concluded that the ADR mechanism in the instant case was not arbitration as contemplated under the FAA. Moreover, as an apparent concession to the opinion in *AMF v. Brunswick Corp.*, non-binding arbitration did not present a high probability of resolving the parties' dispute. Further, the court acknowledged that the FAA did not define the term "arbitration." Nonetheless, "the essence of arbitration" was its adjudicatory character: in arbitration, the parties agree to "arbitrate through to completion"; arbitration "does not occur until the process is completed and the arbitrator makes a decision." Finally, in the court's view, the drafters of the Lemon Law should—and easily could—have used the word "arbitration" if they intended the ADR procedure in the statute to be governed by the FAA.

6. In *Wolsey, Ltd. v. Foodmaker, Inc.*, 144 F.3d 1205 (9th Cir. 1998), the U.S. Court of Appeals for the Ninth Circuit proposed a different answer to the question of what processes fall within the ambit of the FAA. It held that a provision for nonbinding American Arbitration Association (AAA) arbitration was enforceable under FAA § 2.

In 1991, Wolsey contracted with Foodmaker to obtain the right to develop "Jack in the Box" restaurants in Hong Kong and Macau. The contract contained a dispute resolution provision, establishing a three-step process by which to resolve all disputes: (1) a senior executive officer meeting; (2) non-binding AAA arbitration; and (3) litigation in federal court. In March 1994, Wolsey alleged fraudulent inducement and initiated the dispute resolution process. After meeting with the senior executives of Foodmaker, he filed a demand for AAA arbitration. The arbitral tribunal ruled in favor of Wolsey, but Foodmaker did not comply with the non-binding award. Wolsey filed suit in federal court, alleging new claims based upon statutory law. These claims had not been advanced in the AAA arbitration. Foodmaker, therefore, moved to compel arbitration. The district court denied the motion; Foodmaker appealed to the Ninth Circuit.

The Ninth Circuit has been less than hospitable toward arbitration. Like other courts in California, it readily finds problems with arbitration agreements and does not hesitate to invalidate arbitration agreements on the basis of unconscionability. In the instant case, however, it determined that, despite the Development Agreement's reference to "non-binding" arbitration, an order to compel arbitration could be issued. The court relied on case law "reflect[ing] unequivocal support of agreements to have third parties decide disputes—the essence of arbitration. No magic words such as 'arbitrate' or 'binding arbitration' or 'final dispute resolution' [were] needed to obtain the benefits of the [FAA].... If the parties [had] agreed to submit for a decision by a third party, they have agreed to arbitration." Referring to the "presumption in favor of arbitrability created by the FAA," the Ninth Circuit underscored that, in *Moses H. Cone Memorial Hosp. v. Mercury Constr. Corp.*, 460 U.S. 1 (1983), the U.S. Supreme Court held that "arbitration need not be binding in order to fall within the scope of the Federal Arbitration Act."

The court's determination was somewhat ironic and its reasoning unconvincing. Its principal contribution seems to have been to undercut arbitration's essential defining characteristics. Do you agree with this assessment of the court's ruling? Do you agree with the court's position?

7. The U.S. District Court for the Eastern District of New York's holding in the area transgresses even more radically the actual content and underlying purpose of the FAA. In *CB Richard Ellis, Inc. v. American Environ. Waste Management*, 1998 WL 903495 (E.D.N.Y. 1998) (unrep. in F. Supp.2d), it held that the FAA governs a contractual provision for the submission of disputes to mediation. In *CB Richard Ellis, Inc.*, American Environmental agreed to remove waste from commercial properties managed by CB. The contract contained a general clause for the mediation of disputes.

When disputes arose, one party filed a judicial action, while the other party alleged that the disagreements should first be submitted to mediation.

The court addressed the question of whether the parties were—pursuant to their contract—obligated to mediate their differences before filing a court action. The court stated that the FAA controlled the determination because, in part, "[b]oth sides agree[d] that the [FAA]...govern[ed]" such questions. Why party provision or acquiescence should be so vital to the FAA's scope of application remains unclear. Moreover, the court referred to the circuit precedent, namely, *AMF v. Brunswick Corp.* According to the court, the reference in FAA § 2 to the "settlement" of disputes by arbitration allowed the provision (hence the legislation) to cover not only arbitration agreements, but also clauses for the mediation of disputes and other forms of ADR. You should assess the court's reasoning. What is its likely impact upon the drafting of arbitration agreements and counseling on arbitration? Is it likely to change the way courts think about arbitration? Does it alter your evolving sense of arbitration?

8.   The majority of U.S. courts, it seems, actually read the FAA before they apply it. They, therefore, implement it as enacted, not as it could have been passed or amended. In *Heritage Building Systems, Inc.*, 185 S.W.3d 539 (Tex. Ct. App. 2006), the court intimated that the FAA was not an all-purpose ADR statute by holding that, when parties have agreed to arbitrate disputes, it is improper to compel mediation under the FAA at the request of only one of the parties. Presumably, a mutual agreement to proceed to mediation would have been enforceable—not on the basis of the FAA, but rather as a matter of contract. The Seventh Circuit reached such a conclusion in *Omni Tech Corp. v. MPC Solutions Sales LLC*, 432 F.3d 797 (7th Cir. 2005). There, the court held that a written agreement to submit disputes to an accounting firm for a binding determination did not constitute an arbitration agreement. Like other types of ADR references, the agreed-upon procedure was enforceable under contract law. The arbitration statute simply was not applicable. Similarly, the Tenth Circuit, in *Salt Lake Tribune Publishing Co., L.L.C. v. Management Planning, Inc.*, 390 F.3d 684 (10th Cir. 2004), held that an appraisal procedure, not intended by the parties to be final and binding in all circumstances, did not sufficiently resemble "classic arbitration" to be arbitration.

In *McGowan v. Progressive Preferred Ins. Co.*, 274 Ga.App. 483, 618 S.E.2d 139 (2005), a Georgia court of appeals held that a provision for a binding appraisal in an insurance contract was not governed by the state arbitration act because, unlike an arbitral proceeding, an appraisal does not determine any facts other than value. It does not address liability or serve as an alternative forum to courts.

Finally, in *Lindsay v. Lewandowski*, 139 Cal.App.4th 1618, 43 Cal.Rptr.3d 846 (2006), a California court of appeals refused to enforce a settlement provision because the reference to "binding mediation," a material term, was confusing and ultimately incomprehensible. The court noted that the word "mediation" had been crossed out and replaced with "arbitration" in other parts of the agreement. It concluded that "about the only thing that is clear is that parties did not regard binding mediation as the equivalent of arbitration." Even if the agreement were enforced, the court asserted that it would be unclear whether the rules of arbitration, court-ordered mediation, mediation confidentiality, or some combination of all of them applied.

Nonetheless, there are instances of legitimate interface between arbitration and mediation. For example, in *Stewart v. Covill & Basham Construction, L.L.C.*, 317 Mont. 153, 75 P.3d 1276 (2003), the parties' contract provided for binding AAA arbitration. When the homeowner failed to make timely payments, the company proposed mediation prior to binding arbitration. The company's written proposal for mediation specifically stated that, if the efforts to mediate were unsuccessful, the parties would go to binding arbitration. The court held that the company did not waive its contractual right to compel arbitration when it proposed and participated in an unsuccessful mediation.

The parties' agreement can link the two mechanisms, making the resort to one process a condition precedent to recourse to the other. In *Kemiron Atlantic, Inc. v. Aquakem Int'l, Inc.*, 290 F.3d 1287 (11th Cir. 2002), the Eleventh Circuit held that a failure to request mediation, which the contract established was a necessary precursor to arbitration, precluded the instant enforcement of the arbitration agreement. "[T]he parties agreed to conditions precedent before arbitration [could] take place and, by placing those conditions in the contract, the parties clearly intended to make arbitration a dispute resolution mechanism of last resort.... Because neither party requested mediation, the arbitration provision ha[d] not been activated and the FAA [did] not [for the time being] apply." The decision applies the principles of freedom of contract: Court enforcement of contracts as written and agreed-to by the parties. The circumstances nonetheless could be construed as a possible waiver of the condition precedent.

The First Circuit has ruled in a related vein. In *HIM Portland, LLC v. DeVito Builders, Inc.*, 317 F.3d 41 (1st Cir. 2003), the court determined that "[w]here contracting parties condition an arbitration agreement upon the satisfaction of some condition precedent, the failure to satisfy the specified condition will preclude the parties from compelling arbitration and staying [judicial] proceedings under the FAA."

9. In light of the foregoing, you should finalize your evaluation of the definitional controversy surrounding arbitration. Draft a memorandum advising the supervising partner on the interface between arbitration and alternative dispute resolution. How alike and different are arbitration, negotiation, and mediation? Is arbitration more akin to a court proceeding?

* * *

An Illustration and Application

Does TV judging constitute arbitration? Is *Judge Judy* or *Judge Joe Brown* an arbitrator, an actor, or an actual judge? What attributes or characteristics induce you to the conclusion you reach? Otherwise stated: Is adjudication for entertainment arbitration?

Consider in this context the following case from *The People's Court* show. The claimant in *Kabia v. Koch*, 186 Misc.2d 363, 713 N.Y.S.2d 250 (N.Y. City Civ. Ct. 2000), Idris Kabia, accused "Judge" Edward I. Koch of libel and slander for reportedly calling him a "kidnapper" during the taping of an episode of "The People's Court." Koch sought summary judgment pursuant to the "arbitration agreement" signed by Kabia along with his agreement to participate in the program.

Prior to his appearance on the television show, Kabia filed an action in small claims court. The producer of The People's Court offered to have him resolve his dispute on the television program. Both Kabia and his son, the defendant, signed an "Agreement to Arbitrate." The agreement provided that the arbitrator's decision would be final and binding. Further, the arbitrator, producers, and the staff could not be held liable for any claims resulting from the recording or editing of the program. The agreement also exempted all parties from liability for derogatory, injurious, or defamatory statements made during the show. The People's Court agreed to pay any award that was rendered or to pay each participant $250 in the event of no award. Kabia and his son participated in a televised proceeding. The judge did not render an award. Kabia cashed the $250 check he was given for his participation.

In addressing the merits, the court examined a prior case which held that The People's Court was not a recognized form of arbitration because the losing party did not pay the award. The court declined to follow the precedent, stating that "nowhere in McKinney's Practice Commentaries, Black's Law Dictionary or case law does it state that an arbitration agreed to by both parties, in writing, fails to be an arbitration under [New York State law] because the award or judgment is paid by a third party." To uphold the conclusion that The People's Court constituted a valid and legitimate form of arbitration, the court invoked the public policy favoring arbitration and the narrow grounds upon which an award could be vacated or modified. It ruled that, "The People's Court proceeding...was an arbitration proceeding in accordance with...New York State public policy, which encourages arbitration." As a result, the taping of the television program represented a valid form of arbitration and was subject to the federal rules of arbitration.

Arbitrators who participated in a contractually agreed-upon arbitration proceeding were entitled to absolute immunity. The court reasoned that, "although not judges, arbitrators exercise judicial functions and are protected from civil liability for acts done in the exercise of judicial functions whether general or special damages are sought." In the court's view, Koch's statements fell within the range of protected conduct. It, therefore, dismissed the case against him with prejudice.

NOTES AND QUESTIONS

1. Under U.S. law, arbitrators enjoy the same immunity as judges. There is, therefore, no arbitrator malpractice, unless the arbitrator fails or refuses to render a decision. In the latter circumstance, the arbitrator is in breach and subject to contract liability. *See Morgan Phillips, Inc. v. JAMS/Endispute, LLC*, 140 Cal.App.4th 795, 44 Cal.Rptr.3d 782 (2006). The reasons for

arbitral immunity—applying both to arbitrators and arbitral institutions or service-providers that administer arbitrations—are to guarantee objective decision-making and to avoid vexatious litigation. In other national jurisdictions, arbitrators are generally held to a reckless disregard standard. Liability can only be imposed for conduct that is so unthinking that it constitutes a reckless disregard of the parties' interest. Although the immunity in these countries is qualified, arbitrators benefit from very substantial protection. *See* J. LEW, ed., THE IMMUNITY OF ARBITRATORS (Lloyds of London Press 1996). Finally, it is unlikely that the parties can alter the governing rule by contract because they would be unlikely to find a candidate willing to serve as their arbitrator.

2.　The factor that makes the question of defining arbitration difficult in *Kabia v. Koch* is entertainment. Can you describe the impact of that factor on the court's reasoning and result? What other considerations play a role and compete with the *sui generis* entertainment factor?

3.　Is the risk of losing vital to participation in a true adjudicatory or arbitral process? Is that risk absent in *Kabis v. Koch*? Does the risk of loss still apply? What risks, beyond financial loss, could a party face?

4.　If *The People's Court* is indeed arbitration or a form of arbitration, what rules of arbitral procedure are applicable? Moreover, all these television shows have a clerk of court or a bailiff character. This feature adds to versimilitude of the presentation. "Actual" arbitrations and arbitrators do not have such a personage. Do these factors make any difference? Is the essence of arbitration a mock court? Why or why not?

2.　WHY CHOOSE ARBITRATION?

Prior to the U.S. Supreme Court's modern advocacy for arbitration, arbitration was relegated to specialized trades and business sectors—maritime transactions; cotton, textile, garment, and diamond trades; cargo or other delivery specifications conformity: In a word, the work of arbitration took place in the mundane shadows of commerce. The Court progressively expanded the remedy to international commercial transactions, commerce generally, employment disputes, and consumer transactions.

Arbitration responds well to commercial practices and conflicts. First, arbitration is reputed to be confidential—a private adjudicatory process. Arbitral proceedings are not open to the public and awards generally are not published. Unless the parties to the arbitration agree to disclose information or one party does so unilaterally, or a court commands that information be divulged, business associates, competitors, and clients have no knowledge of the dispute, the proceedings, or the outcome. The recourse to arbitration, therefore, allows commercial parties to maintain a competitive position despite transactional problems.

Second, arbitral adjudication tends to be more flexible and less adversarial and protracted than its judicial counterpart. The reduction of litigious obfuscation results in an economy of time and money. Arbitral tribunals usually consist of a sole arbitrator or of three-member panels.

Juries are not a component of the arbitral process. The commercial experience of the tribunal lessens the significance of legal precedent, eliminates the need for complex rules of evidence, and minimizes the need for discovery, the use of experts, and other informational trial procedures. The possibility of tactical litigious warfare, therefore, is also attenuated. As a general matter, the arbitral tribunal is bound to provide the arbitrating parties with a fair and reasonable opportunity to be heard, to admit and weigh the pertinent evidence, and to decide the matters submitted in a rational and timely fashion. Procedural informality, placing trust in the arbitrators' professional capabilities, and allowing commercial equity to trump jural rules are the hallmarks of commercial arbitration.

Third, the parties to the arbitration have the right to select the arbitrators. The designated arbitrators ordinarily have considerable experience in the relevant business sector. Their commercial expertise allows them to reach accommodative determinations that reflect a consensus in the trade. By choosing to arbitrate, therefore, business parties avoid inexpert judges who may be prone to impose legalistic solutions upon commercial problems.

As a general matter, the parties select an uneven number of arbitrators to avoid a deadlock in reaching a determination—one arbitrator is usually agreed upon for smaller matters and a three-member panel is selected to preside over larger, more complex cases. When a three-member panel is to be chosen, each party names its arbitrator and the two party-appointed arbitrators name a third arbitrator, known as the neutral, who acts as the chair of the panel. It is generally assumed that the party-appointed arbitrators, although they may be required or expected to act impartially, will favor the designating party's case, leaving the neutral arbitrator to cast the deciding vote. The settled expectation has been that a party-designated arbitrator will represent its party's interest in the deliberations. This situation sometimes leads to "arbitrations-within-arbitrations," in which the party-appointed arbitrators make their case to the neutral arbitrator. It can also raise vacatur issues in terms of "evident partiality" if full disclosure is not made. These circumstances obviously give the appointment of the neutral arbitrator a great deal of importance.

In international business, the neutrality as to nationality of arbitral proceedings and awards is a fourth factor that contributes to the "business appeal" of arbitral adjudication. Most international business parties deem the reference to arbitration indispensable in multinational commercial ventures. It eliminates the conflicts associated with the assertion of national court jurisdiction, the choice of applicable law, and the enforcement of foreign judgments. Arbitration also tempers the juridical disparities between different legal traditions and systems. In the context of international business transactions, arbitration functions as a *de facto* transborder legal system, providing the global commercial community with an adjudicatory process free of national bias and parochial laws and practices and able to dispense sensible commercial justice.

Finally, it should be underscored that the less adversarial tenor of arbitral proceedings contributes to arbitration's "business appeal." Business relationships can generally be preserved or salvaged once the dispute is resolved. In arbitration, commercial parties are not forced "to declare war on the other side"; rather, they can make their case and let a neutral expert decide the matter. In effect, arbitration functions as a type of "in-house" adjudicatory process through which the usages of a specialized community are applied to the resolution of disputes among the community's constituent members.

NOTES AND QUESTIONS

1. A few practical points: You should realize that arbitration is **private** adjudication. Courts and the public rule of law may never surface in the process at all. If they do, they generally will have a limited role. Your clients must understand that the contractual reference to arbitration is **binding**. When you sign or acquiesce to an agreement to arbitrate disputes, you will proceed to arbitration and will be bound by the result. Appeal is exceedingly limited. For all intents and purposes, arbitration is final.

2. Is the privatization of adjudication through arbitration in the best interests of society? Why and why not? The rise of arbitration is directly related to the problem of managing judicial resources. The weight of the criminal docket has made civil justice inaccessible—inaccessibility as measured by dockets, costs, delays, and the protracted character of judicial proceedings. Why is arbitration more accessible? How does it resolve the unavailability of adjudication?

3. The principal and principled aspect of the recourse to arbitration is to trade efficiency and functionality against rights protection. If an adjudicatory process fails to work because it is overly protective of rights, its social worth is only theoretical. In the end, its inability to operate efficiently leads to no rights protection at all. It never achieves finality or achieves it at an exorbitant cost of both time and money.

4. In your view, when should functionality prevail over rights protection? Is the choice the same in commercial matters as in employment or consumer matters?

3.   HOW DOES ARBITRATION WORK?

Arbitration is a trial process. It is a framework of procedural rules for conducting private adjudications. Although it has proven itself to be highly effective, it is not a panacea. To parse Justice Stevens in *Mitsubishi Motors Corp. v. Soler Chrysler–Plymouth, Inc.*, 473 U.S. 614 (1985), arbitration is not a formula for universal justice. In reality, arbitration does not even supply the perfect procedural equation for all forms of commercial adjudication. In some instances, arbitration can provide a better, or the best, procedural protocol, but it is nothing more or less than an alternative remedy—one of several mechanisms for achieving the final and binding resolution of disputes. Like adversarial trials or party-negotiated settlements, arbitration has advantages and disadvantages. In each case, the choice of remedial relief—whether to pursue traditional litigation, arbitration, or structured negotiation—must be made on the basis of an understanding of the mechanisms, the circumstances of the dispute, and the capacity of the mechanisms to respond to these circumstances.

Parties generally engage in arbitration to achieve quicker results. To hasten relief, arbitrating parties forgo discovery, the protection of appeal, and trust arbitrators to provide due process. In agreeing to arbitrate disputes, the parties, therefore, may compromise their basic legal rights. The benefit of the bargain for expedient private adjudication carries with it the possibility that party expectations of procedural and substantive fairness will be irretrievably frustrated.

The marketplace for arbitrator services may provide some protection against disappointing or unprofessional arbitrators. Deficient arbitrators are unlikely to be hired for subsequent arbitrations. There is, however, no ignoring the "private character" of arbitral adjudication. There is no public certification of arbitrators. Arbitrator malpractice does not exist. Trust in the professionalism of arbitrators and arbitral institutions is a major part of the process.

The arbitration agreement may be the best means for addressing potential abuse in arbitral proceedings. In their agreement, the parties can require the arbitrators to conduct an adversarial proceeding—complete with pre-trial discovery, the use of party-appointed expert witnesses, and the exercise of the right of cross-examination—and to follow legal precedent. The arbitrators' failure to follow these requirements would constitute a ground for challenging and vacating the award. The parties could also provide for a general right of judicial appeal of all rulings made in the arbitration. The 1986 Netherlands arbitration statute contains a provision authorizing, for example, the use of appellate arbitral tribunals and recent U.S. decisional law endorses, in part, such a procedure, as well as the contractual right to seek judicial review of the merits of arbitral awards. At this point, however, the parties have come nearly full circle to their original point of departure. They are basically providing for a "judicialized" arbitral proceeding. The modification lessens considerably the "alternative" value of arbitral adjudication and its viability as different means of conducting adjudication. The process still provides adjudicator expertise and greater adjudicatory access, but loses its flexibility and adaptiveness.

Complex arbitration provisions also create transactional costs. Anticipating the procedural character of the arbitral proceedings or other aspects of the process (the type of relief that is available, the format of the award, the power of the arbitrators to conduct on-site inspections) creates a "front-end load" to the transaction. The negotiations will be longer, more involved, and more difficult; legal representation will be more significant and expensive; and the transaction itself may be frustrated as a result. Such agreements are more difficult to implement and more likely to become pathological.

NOTES AND QUESTIONS

1. What is, in your assessment, the most distinctive feature of the arbitral trial? Why? How does it make arbitration more desirable? What aspect of arbitral adjudication should be eliminated and why? What procedural device, if any, should replace that aspect?

2. Some argue that the judicial trial is built upon distrust while its arbitral counterpart is anchored in trust. Do you agree? In the clash of interests, is trust inevitably naïve? What safeguards are indispensable notwithstanding the trust? How might these safeguards be included? Does the bargain for arbitration include the possibility of irretrievable loss?

3. What does "pathology" mean in terms of arbitration? Does it go to the process or the agreement or both? How can it be best avoided?

4. Explain what is meant by a "judicialized" arbitration. What are the advantages and disadvantages of judicialization? In such a framework, should the arbitrators be lawyers? Why or why not?

5. What are the principal trade-offs in arbitration? What do you ultimately surrender and gain? Do those trade-offs make arbitration worthwhile?

* * *

The Stages of the Arbitral Trial

Assuming an agreement to arbitrate exists in a valid contractual form, the arbitral proceeding usually takes place in accordance with the rules of an administering arbitral institution, like the American Arbitration Association (AAA), the National Arbitration Forum (The Forum), or the International Chamber of Commerce (ICC). The institutional rules provide the framework for the operation of the various stages of the arbitral process: (1) the constitution of the arbitral tribunal; (2) the establishment of the submission to arbitration or the tribunal's terms of reference; (3) the selection of an arbitral trial procedure; (4) the conduct of the proceedings; (5) the closure of the proceedings; (6) the tribunal's deliberations; and (7) the rendering of an award.

Threshold Matters

Following receipt of a demand for arbitration, the administering arbitral institution notifies the other party of the demand and requests that the parties nominate arbitrators pursuant to their agreement. The supervising institution can supply the parties, if necessary, with lists of arbitrators. Once the arbitral tribunal is constituted, the parties can enter into a submission to arbitrate. The submission establishes the specific elements of the parties' disagreement and the arbitral tribunal's authority to rule—its jurisdiction. Under some arbitral laws and procedures, the parties need not enter into a submission; the parties and the arbitrators simply meet to establish the matters to be arbitrated (a pre-hearing conference).

In ICC practice, the description of the parties' dispute constitutes the arbitrators' terms of reference. The terms of reference constitute a critical phase of ICC arbitrations. The arbitral tribunal has no authority to adjudicate beyond the stipulations contained in the terms of reference (unless the parties provide otherwise). To facilitate matters, ICC arbitrators, with party approval, sometimes establish the terms of reference during the course of the proceedings. In all forms of arbitration, the arbitrators' failure to rule upon a submitted claim or a ruling on a matter not submitted can result in the vacatur of the award or parts of it. Given its jurisdictional and adjudicatory significance, the content of the submission or of the terms of reference (or of the result of the pre-hearing conference) can be hotly disputed and difficult to establish.

The designated arbitrators must agree to serve as the arbitrator and accept the statement of claims before the arbitration can proceed. The arbitrators are obligated to disclose any conflict of interest or other matter that might impair their ability to rule in an impartial manner. The arbitrators can refuse to serve on the panel or can disqualify themselves. The parties can attempt to disqualify an arbitrator through an action before the supervising arbitral institution or a court of law. Assuming none of these actions is undertaken, the arbitral institution, with the participation of the arbitral tribunal and the parties, chooses the venue for the arbitration. The parties pay the required deposits and administrative fees, and the tribunal sets a time for the initial hearing.

Depending upon the complexity of the matter and the disposition of the arbitrating parties, an arbitration can be conducted on a purely documentary basis. In an "arbitration on the documents," the parties provide the administering arbitral institution with a statement of their position and allegations. They also supply the institution with their exhibits and other supporting evidence. The arbitral tribunal rules on the basis of the submitted materials. Arbitrations can also consist of a documentary record with an abbreviated hearing or of a set of elaborate hearings that include pre-trial procedures and testimonial evidence. Actual proceedings can be as varied as the type of parties involved and the circumstances of the transaction. The character of the proceeding is generally determined by the arbitration agreement or by the parties' ability to agree once a dispute arises. If no contractual disposition exists and the parties are unable to agree, the arbitral tribunal—along with the administering arbitral institution—decides such matters.

The Hearings

As to the hearings, the parties generally expect to have a reasonably fair and flexible proceeding. The arbitrators usually have sufficient procedural authority to thwart strident adversarial debates and trial tactics that unnecessarily lengthen the proceedings. The parties want to be heard and to make their case. They then want the arbitral tribunal to decide.

There is a convergence between standard trial practices in arbitration and the mode of trial that applies in continental European civil law systems. In these systems, the civil jury trial is unknown. Procedure constitutes an incidental part of legality. A judge or a bench of judges is at the center of the trial process and is entrusted with the responsibility of conducting trial proceedings. The trial is not a single dramatic event, but rather a series of meetings between the court and the parties. The litigants' obligation is to state their claims and allegations. The judge conducts the investigation of the facts and decides what evidence is relevant. Documentary evidence is more significant than testimonial accounts. There is no right to conduct pre-trial discovery by the parties, to engage in cross-examination, to call expert witnesses, or to conduct a direct examination of witnesses. Civil law trials are not party- or lawyer-driven proceedings. The court must hear the parties and allow them to respond to the opposing side's allegations. Adversarial debate is a feature of the process, but not its central and all-consuming characteristic.

The typical arbitral trial generally tracks this civilian model of adjudication. Arbitral systems usually do not include a right to pre-trial discovery. Ordinarily, parties are required to exchange document and witness lists prior to the commencement of the proceedings. The arbitral tribunal has the authority to decide whether proffered evidence is relevant and to evaluate the admitted evidence. While the arbitrating parties have the right to be heard, neither side can abuse its adjudicatory rights by manufacturing specious arguments, issues, and evidence—thereby tactically prolonging the proceeding for litigious advantage. Traditional arbitral proceedings thereby share with the civilian trial the discipline of a functional adjudicatory process that mediates between the need for fairness and the need for efficiency.

Evidence and Witnesses

During an arbitral proceeding, the parties make their case through the means described in the document and witness lists. In most arbitral systems, the parties' agreement to arbitrate implies a duty to arbitrate in good faith. Failing to respond to tribunal requests in a timely fashion, attempting to create delay by presenting too many lay or expert witnesses, pursuing the other side's witnesses too stridently, or refusing to comply with the tribunal's specific requests for documentary information—all potentially constitute a breach of the good faith obligation. The arbitral tribunal determines whether noncomplying party conduct amounts to a breach, and the tribunal can then take the breach into account in its final award. This procedure reinforces the arbitral tribunal's authority and demands that the parties abide by the spirit and letter of their agreement to arbitrate.

The right to notification and full disclosure are strictly enforced during the arbitral proceeding. Direct, *ex parte* communications between the arbitrators and one of the parties are not permitted. All communications are directed to a case manager at the supervising arbitral institution who then supplies both the arbitral tribunal and the other side with the information. This system avoids any appearance of partiality and maintains the integrity and fairness of the process. During the proceeding, the tribunal can rule on jurisdictional questions and other matters such as the attachment of assets in the form of interim awards. Such rulings are like a final award. Their enforcement can require judicial proceedings.

When the parties have completed their presentation of evidence and witnesses and summarized their respective positions, the arbitral tribunal closes the proceedings and adjourns to deliberate. At this stage, new information can be admitted only with the tribunal's permission. Admission of new information also requires that the opposing party be given an opportunity to respond. The tribunal's deliberations are conducted in secret. Its eventual ruling can be reached by simple majority vote. Especially in domestic practice, arbitral tribunals render awards without issuing an opinion or reasons. The award usually follows a standard format: A statement of the facts, the issues, the parties' respective positions, and a disposition of the matters submitted. The exclusion of an explanation for the result in domestic practice is intended to discourage challenges against the award, specifically the possible judicial review of the merits of the arbitral determination. The administering arbitral institution sends the award to the parties usually within thirty days of the closure of the proceedings.

The Award

The rendering of a final award triggers the final payment of outstanding institutional and arbitrator fees from the money placed on deposit by the parties. The administering arbitral institution may withhold the award until all fees and costs have been paid. The costs of the arbitration generally are shared equally by the parties. Each party is responsible for its attorney's fees, unless the agreement contains a "loser-pays-all" provision. The implementation of such a provision may require the arbitral tribunal to reconvene and to rule upon whether there is a "loser" and, if not, how the costs should be apportioned. Alternately, the arbitral tribunal may exercise its discretion to distribute the costs of the proceeding. The parties can comply voluntarily with the terms of the award or seek to have the award enforced or challenged through legal means. In this type of legal proceeding, the award can be converted to a judicial judgment in an enforcement action. The grounds for challenging arbitral awards are restrictive and narrow. Courts rarely vacate arbitral awards. In fact, the challenging party may risk Rule 11 sanctions if its opposition to the award is found to be perfunctory or designed primarily to postpone the day of reckoning.

Possible Problems

Arbitrations do not always run as smoothly as the description of their procedures indicates. Parties who are opposed to participating in an arbitration can create a host of problems to thwart the process. They can challenge the arbitral tribunal's jurisdiction by alleging that the arbitration agreement is an invalid contract, nonexistent, or fails to cover the dispute in question. Also, a party can simply refuse to appear at the proceedings, decline to nominate an arbitrator, or ignore the directives of the supervising arbitral institution. In addition, a party can create disagreement about the procedures to be followed in the arbitral proceeding or the power of the arbitral tribunal—for example, whether the arbitral tribunal can award punitive damages, whether experts can appear and how they are to be qualified, or whether the arbitrators can order attachments during the proceedings to secure the payment of the eventual award. Further contention can be generated regarding matters of administrative detail such as whether the place of arbitration is equally convenient for both parties or how the costs of the arbitration and arbitrator fees are to be apportioned.

NOTES AND QUESTIONS

1. Structuring the arbitral trial may become a significant activity in the legal representation that is afforded to clients. Lawyers will eventually develop protocols that reconcile conflicting trial traditions. Attention will also be devoted to the composition of the arbitral tribunal and of the qualifications and experience of arbitrators. Counseling may extend to prospective arbitrators. They need to assess whether they should accept their appointment and how they should effectuate their entry into the process.

2. In regard to the arbitral hearings, are there features of the judicial trial that you will not abandon to institutional dispositions or arbitrator discretion? Can you explain your choices or decisions? Does a "selective" recourse to arbitration indicate a distrust of, or a lack of commitment to, the arbitral process? Is the incorporation of procedural limitations into the arbitration agreement likely to make it more difficult to hire arbitrators or to find a willing service-provider? Is there a greater risk that the agreement may fail and collapse under the weight of *sui generis* provisions?

3. U.S. attorneys who are new to the arbitral process and procedure always express concern about the availability of discovery. They then want to be able to control the appearance and number of witnesses, as well as preserve their prerogative to engage in cross-examination. Does this attitude demonstrate professionalism or an inability to adapt? Might professional inadaptability be good? Should it be addressed in the arbitration agreement? If so, how? Are lawyers trained in other legal systems and traditions any less likely to resist change from what is for them the tried and true? Is there an intrinsic standard for measuring justice? If so, can you provide a glimpse of it?

4. What assessment do you reach of the civilian trial? What are its principal qualities? Its primary drawbacks? Why do you think it was initially so suitable as a model for arbitral hearings? Was it simply a question of which lawyers initially endorsed arbitration? Is a "mix and match" approach sensible or likely to lead to perverse and unworkable hybrids?

5. Devise a functional system of arbitral due process. Focus upon the core elements and how they could be effectively implemented.

4. THE IMPACT OF ARBITRATION

The ascendancy of arbitration has altered the manner in which lawyers practice law. As noted in the *Introduction (supra),* negotiating and writing contracts for arbitration, representing clients in arbitral proceedings, and advocating in award enforcement actions are an integral part of contemporary law firm work. Practicing lawyers must be able to draft sophisticated arbitration agreements that are responsive to the client's transactional needs. These contracts must intermediate between the need to maintain the principle of legality, the integrity and functionality of the dispute resolution process, and the client's concern for economy, fairness, and finality.

Arbitration's enhanced presence in law practice and transactional settings has also generated a sometimes intemperate debate among commentators about fairness in contract and the comparable worth of public and private justice. Additionally, arbitration's new day has had a ricochet impact upon the remedial mechanism itself. Its chief characteristics are or can be adjusted in light of the circumstances of application. What was both possible and desirable in self-contained and self-regulating commercial sectors can be impractical and even untoward in more commonplace dealings between parties of disparate status and standing.

Technical expertise and flexible procedures are not as key to the provision of justice in social justice settings. In fact, they may have an opposite effect. Courts have emphasized the importance of how arbitration is selected or imposed and how protective the designated process is of legal rights. While it retains its essential character, arbitration in consumer and employment matters differs in a number of respects from arbitration in commercial, labor, maritime, and construction cases. For example, privacy in commercial arbitration has the effect of preserving competitive advantage and trade secrets, whereas in consumer and employment matters it can be seen as a camouflage for illegality and overreaching. Further, the elasticity of determination and the use of arbitrator discretion can invite or be seen as undermining statutory rights and regulatory policies.

The Earlier Status and Role

Traditionally, contracting parties who agreed to arbitrate subscribed to a private adjudicatory process that contained flexible and adapted procedures. It generally was a mandatory part of their trade association and was included in their membership. As part of their admission to the association, parties agreed to a standard arbitration process to resolve disputes. Self-governance avoided unwanted intrusions and misguided interference. In a purely transactional setting, parties could agree to arbitration either in the form of *ad hoc* arbitration or institutional arbitration. In the former, the parties provided for the management and administration of the arbitration, while—in the latter—they delegated those tasks to an arbitral service-provider. Institutional arbitration came with a cost, but also with the benefit of experience and professional standards. Parties could also require that arbitrators rule according to law or decide the case pursuant to more commercially-adapted standards. Further, they could authorize the arbitrators to rule in equity. Awards rendered through established arbitral institutions presented fewer problems of enforcement. Freedom of contract even allowed the contracting parties to vary the institutional rules—essentially to craft a customized procedure. Such modifications might, however, convert an institutional arbitration into an *ad hoc* proceeding, without a reduction in costs.

The Newer Form of Arbitration

Contemporary arbitration raises critical questions about the function of adjudication and the purpose of dispute resolution. As the foregoing makes clear, its scope of application has expanded considerably in the last several decades—especially in the resolution of international commercial disputes and in the domestic operation of the U.S. legal system. From an obscure status—that of an "inside" remedy in specialized areas (like labor and commerce)—it has emerged as an adjudicatory procedure viable in almost any dispute circumstance.

Greater recourse to arbitration challenges traditional notions of adjudicatory fairness and due process. Most arbitration agreements are enforceable and can apply to regulatory matters—from securities regulation and antitrust to civil rights. When business entities impose arbitration upon clients and consumers in a unilateral contract, these parties are deprived, without their consent, of their right to a constitutionally-sanctioned judicial proceeding. Forced and unknowing participation in the arbitral process contradicts the tenet of voluntary recourse to arbitration. Moreover, it can entail the abridgement of rights. This, in conjunction with the federal courts' nearly absolute "hands-off" supervisory policy, allows arbitration to close itself off to external scrutiny and to function with nearly complete independence. The integrity of the process is dependent upon the arbitrators and, to a lesser extent, upon legal counsel.

The Courts' Disposition

The federal decisional law seeks to maintain the systemic autonomy of arbitration, recognizing it as an indispensable part of arbitration's institutional viability. In effect, the courts have removed any real vitality to the already narrow statutory grounds for policing arbitral awards. The aggressive judicial protection of arbitration is meant to eliminate dilatory strategies and tactics. As a consequence, a consumer who fails to read or understand the standard language of a purchase contract from a manufacturer or who is forced to arbitrate in order to buy goods or services may be left without any protection against an unruly or incompetent (or perhaps even a partial) arbitrator. Arbitration can only coexist with a docile judiciary. Courts may have been difficult to access, but now the legal doctrine on arbitration makes them even more distant. Arbitration is the gateway or portal to the consumer economy and employment. The U.S.

Supreme Court's rulings on securities arbitration—*Shearson/American Express, Inc. v. McMahon*, 482 U.S. 220 (1987), *Rodriguez de Quijas v. Shearson/American Exp., Inc.*, 490 U.S. 477 (1989)—and *Securities Industry Ass'n v. Connolly*, 883 F.2d 1114 (1st Cir. 1989), made clear that acquiescence to arbitration is the passport to goods, services, and employment. Arbitral tribunals have become the new courts of law for civil litigation.

Conclusions

The "reconstruction" of civil justice through arbitration may be a beneficial event. Despite some adversarialization, the arbitral procedure has remained adaptable and resilient. The arbitral, legal, and judicial processes may be responding as effectively as possible to new contingencies, and providing—in times of radical economic and political restructuring—a means of maintaining a fundamental rule of law within American society. Overburdened courts—saddled with criminal proceedings—are unable to provide sufficient justice services to civil litigants. Arbitration supplies timely access, legal representation, fair hearings, and a final and binding decision.

The Bill of Rights may now require its beneficiaries to be more creative and self-reliant. Arbitration may satisfy the domestic need for adjudicatory services in the same way that it fashioned a rule of law for the international business community. There, arbitration made commercial justice possible in circumstances dominated by the conflict of jurisdiction, law, and enforcement regimes. Arbitration provided a system of adjudication that transcended national boundaries. Although the parties, interests, and disputes differ, arbitration may be able to guide domestic systems to a suitable redefinition of civil justice. If the movement toward alternative, privatized justice has done nothing else, it has placed enormous responsibility on the shoulders of the legal profession and given it the opportunity to participate in a wholesale but quiet redefinition of law and adjudicatory legitimacy.

NOTES AND QUESTIONS

1. Why is the reference to arbitration sometimes "coerced"? Is the use of coercion a good idea? Is it inescapable?

2. How much "adversarialization" can arbitration tolerate before it mutates into a different, less useful and effective process? What kind of accommodation could be reached between arbitration and adversarial representation? Why might those accommodations work?

3. If the volume of arbitration cases is as considerable as has been suggested, what are the most likely effects upon the practice of law? What changes is the surge to arbitration likely to entail? Does it make law practice more or less attractive?

4. What burdens does the wholesale redefinition of law and adjudication through arbitration place upon the legal profession? Who really supervises the operation of the arbitral process?

CHAPTER TWO

BASIC CONCEPTS

■ ■ ■

The law of arbitration is comprised of basic concepts and doctrines. Understanding these notions is essential to the evaluation of arbitral agreements, the arbitral process, and the judicial litigation pertaining to the process.

1. FREEDOM OF CONTRACT

The primary rule that governs the law, practice, and regulation of arbitration in the United States is the doctrine of freedom of contract. In *Volt Info. Sciences, Inc. v. Board of Trustees of Leland Stanford Junior Univ.*, 489 U.S. 468 (1989), a leading case in U.S. arbitration law, the U.S. Supreme Court held that:

> ...The FAA does not require parties to arbitrate when they have not agreed to do so...nor does it prevent parties who do agree to arbitrate from excluding certain claims from the scope of their arbitration agreement.... It simply requires courts to enforce privately negotiated agreements to arbitrate, like other contracts, in accordance with their terms.... Arbitration under the Act is a matter of consent, not coercion, and parties are generally free to structure their arbitration agreements as they see fit....

Freedom of contract allows the parties to the arbitration agreement to write their own rules of arbitration—in effect, to have the agreement to arbitrate establish the law of arbitration for their particular transaction. The parties, therefore, are the ultimate sovereigns in the process— superior to the State and any institutional administrator in the provision of rules. They are the law-givers for their transaction—customizing the process to their needs, eliminating unsuitable rules and techniques, and providing procedural devices that achieve fairness, finality, and functionality.

The parties, for example, might believe that formal evidentiary rules are necessary to a fair arbitral trial or that arbitrators are bound to apply legal rules or that the proceedings must be conducted in complete confidentiality to protect trade secrets or their commercial advantage or reputation. In the parties' view, a suitable adjudicatory framework must maintain the right to pre-trial discovery, call witnesses, question them directly, and engage in cross-examination. In other words, the parties can define the basic structures and content of the arbitral trial.

Obviously, freedom of contract privileges the position of the economically stronger and more sophisticated party. Some states, in particular California, afford protection to the weaker party against the oppression of the stronger party. California courts often invoke the law of unconscionability to invalidate fundamentally unfair arbitration agreements. Freedom of contract, therefore, can be rendered ineffectual where power relationships are uneven. Freedom of contract also places a burden upon the parties to craft their agreement, requiring that they have a sufficient knowledge of arbitration law, arbitral procedure, and the various facets of their transaction. Finally, it places a "front-end load" on the parties' dealings, demanding that they negotiate the contract and come to a basic agreement about the implicated matters.

Mastrobuono v. Shearson Lehman Hutton, Inc., 514 U.S. 52 (1995), is another landmark arbitration case. There, the Court appeared to qualify the freedom of contract principle with the objectives of the federal policy favoring arbitration. Parties were free to establish the modalities of their arbitration as long as their dispositions supported the effective reference to arbitration. In other words, freedom of contract was fully operative only if it resulted in the submission of disputes to arbitration.

NOTES AND QUESTIONS

1. How would you characterize the Court's concept of freedom of contract in *Volt*? Does it leave any room for "public interest considerations"? Are any limits placed upon the parties' right to enter into and establish the content of their agreements? The Court does not appear to take into account the setting for arbitration; therefore, the rule applies to all forms of arbitration. Is this a desirable circumstance? In *Volt*, as you will ascertain shortly, the Court concluded that the contracting parties had agreed to a governing law of arbitration that rescinded their agreement to arbitrate. Is that result a sensible application of the principle of freedom of contract? Can it provide for fully self-destructive results?

2. In constructing a model arbitration agreement for clients, what elements of the judicial trial, if any, would you retain in prospective arbitral proceedings? Why? In these hybrid frameworks, how likely is it that fealty to arbitration can be maintained? What traits of arbitration cannot be altered or amended? Why?

3. Is lawyer and client customization likely or realistic? Isn't it possible only in circumstances in which both lawyers and clients are highly sophisticated and experienced and fully lucid about the particular transaction? Does the exercise of contract privilege become perfunctory in nearly all situations and lead inevitably to the adoption of a standard arbitral clause? Would it be reasonable to conclude that freedom of contract is an empty rhetorical promise? If so, why does the court put so much store in the concept?

4.   Is the approach in *Mastrobuono* a better use of judicial rule-making authority? Are the results more credible and practical? What impact does the holding have upon prospective arbitration agreements?

2.   ARBITRATION AGREEMENTS

A contract for arbitration can take one of two forms: the submission or the arbitral clause. The **submission** is an arbitration agreement in which the parties agree that an existing dispute shall be submitted to arbitration. The **arbitral clause**, also known as the compromissory clause, is a contract under which the parties agree to submit future disputes to arbitration. Although there is some laxity in the application of these requirements, a contract for arbitration, in either form, must be in writing and must satisfy the usual requirements for contract validity.

The arbitral clause is the primary form of an arbitration agreement and usually contains simple, standard language providing for the submission of disputes to arbitration: "[A]ny dispute arising under this contract shall be submitted to arbitration under the rules of [an arbitral institution]." Ordinarily, the arbitral clause appears as a provision within a larger contract; it, however, can take the form of a separate agreement. When it is materially separated from the principal agreement, the arbitral clause must identify the contractual relationship to which it applies. In any event, in terms of legal theory, the arbitral clause is always distinct from the main contract. Under the separability doctrine, the arbitral clause has an autonomous legal identity. The nullity of the main contract, therefore, does not invalidate the agreement to arbitrate, unless the moving party establishes—to the satisfaction of the arbitrators or a court—that the nullity also affects the arbitration provision.

How do you decide which it goes to?

Once a dispute arises in a transaction governed by an arbitral clause, the parties usually enter into a submission agreement. That agreement defines the specific elements of the dispute, confers jurisdiction upon the arbitral tribunal, and initiates the arbitral proceedings. It should be underscored that a valid arbitration agreement that has not been mutually rescinded by the parties divests the courts of jurisdiction to entertain any matter covered by the agreement, even when a resulting award is incapable of coercive legal enforcement or the arbitral proceeding is delayed.

The **terms of reference** are a feature of ICC arbitration and roughly equivalent to a submission to arbitration. The terms of reference are critical to the arbitration process and to the validity of the eventual award. They define the parties' disagreement and invest the arbitrators with the authority to rule upon the specifically defined dispute(s). In a word, they establish the arbitral tribunal's jurisdiction to adjudicate; the tribunal can only rule upon those disputes that the parties have actually submitted to arbitration. Although the parties may have other conflicts, the tribunal does not have the legal right to rule upon any other matter(s), unless the parties so agree and provide. Finally, the terms of reference

even if related?

require that the parties arrive at a mutually acceptable definition of their disagreement. Although merely identifying a problem is different from taking a position on it, establishing the terms of reference may itself generate some level of disagreement and delay the recourse to arbitration.

NOTES AND QUESTIONS

1. Given the strength of the federal policy on arbitration and the commercial origins of arbitration, evidencing the existence of an arbitration agreement through a writing is a requirement that has been construed liberally. The rules of contract formation are read with a view to achieving the objectives of the federal policy supporting arbitration. *See Asia Pacific Indus. Corp. v. Rainforest Café, Inc.*, 380 F.3d 383 (8th Cir. 2004) (favorable statement regarding possible use of arbitration made in a letter of response constituted a binding agreement to arbitrate). Some courts do not require that the agreement be signed in order to be effective. *See Tinder v. Pinkerton Sec.*, 305 F.3d 728 (7th Cir. 2002). Moreover, a properly-worded email can constitute a valid and enforceable employment arbitration agreement. *See Campbell v. General Dynamics Govt. Sys. Corp.*, 407 F.3d 546 (1st Cir. 2005). The failure to read an agreement does not render it unenforceable; an "opportunity to read" the document is sufficient to validate the contract. *See Pennington v. Frisch's Restaurants, Inc.*, 147 Fed. Appx. 463 (6th Cir. 2005); *Royal Ins. Co. of Am. v. BHRS, L.L.C.*, 333 F. Supp.2d 1293 (S.D. Fla. 2004). There is, therefore, a wide judicial tolerance for imperfectly executed or deficiently formed agreements to arbitrate. This approach testifies to the wisdom and truth of Justice Holmes' adage to the effect that the life of the law is experience, not logic.

2. In the Nineteenth and early Twentieth Centuries, Latin American and other civilian legal systems that disfavored arbitration provided that the submission agreement was the only valid form of contract for arbitration. Can you explain how that practice thwarted party recourse to arbitration? Can you also surmise what the basis for the opposition to arbitration in these and other legal systems?

3. In contemporary U.S. law, problems with the enforcement of the agreement to arbitrate arise principally in the context of consumer transactions and employment disputes. Should the adhesionary character of an arbitral clause prevent or impair its enforcement? Why or why not? How does your view square with the federal policy on arbitration?

4. Assess the significance of declaring that arbitration agreements are separable. Is there any practical value to such a rule? Is it a meaningless technicality? Why or why not?

5. The current practice has modified the process of establishing the content of the submission or the terms of reference. Rather than have the parties define their dispute at the outset of the process, arbitrators in some cases have taken on the task of establishing the terms of the parties' disagreement. The arbitrators fulfill their new responsibility during the course of the proceeding as positions are elaborated, additional facts come to

light, and evidence is introduced. Is this a better approach? Is it legal? How can it be validated? What does it reveal about the ethos of arbitration?

3. ARBITRABILITY

The question of arbitrability is a significant consideration in the law of arbitration. It establishes which disputes can be lawfully submitted to arbitration. The question of whether a dispute can be submitted to arbitration is usually expressed as a defense to the enforcement of the arbitral agreement or award. A ruling that a dispute is inarbitrable can prevent an arbitration from taking place or continuing or result in the vacatur or nonenforcement of a rendered award. Arbitrability, therefore, represents a limit upon the parties' right to engage in arbitration and upon the arbitrators' authority to rule. The inarbitrability defense can take one of two forms: Inarbitrability can arise because of the subject matter of the dispute or because the agreement to arbitrate is a deficient contract.

Under subject-matter inarbitrability, the recourse to arbitration is prohibited as a matter of law. It is a universal principle of contract law that parties are free to enter into any contract as long as it does not violate public policy. There is a point, however, at which even private commercial conduct implicates the public interest. When a commercial dispute affects public policy, most arbitration laws provide that it is inarbitrable because of its subject matter. To some extent, subject-matter inarbitrability is a subset of the public policy exception to arbitration.

One of the most difficult problems of arbitrability is determining whether disputes involving the government regulation of commercial activity—such as antitrust laws or restrictions on the sale of securities— can be submitted to arbitration. The traditional view had been that allegations of predatory conduct, conspiracies to fix prices, or fraudulent brokerage practices are so intertwined with the larger social interest that such claims cannot be submitted to privatized justice. Such litigation involves questions of the authority to implement regulatory policy, the social significance of individual transactions, and whether arbitrators (like judges) have the independence to rule on divisive regulatory policy matters. With the U.S. Supreme Court decision in *Mitsubishi Motors Corp. v. Soler Chrysler–Plymouth,* Inc., 473 U.S. 614 (1985), the federal judiciary progressively rejected the traditional view and held that statutory claims, regardless of whether they arose in international or domestic contracts, could be submitted to arbitration. In fact, under U.S. law, most, if not all, statutory rights can be adjudicated through arbitration.

Disputes also can be deemed inarbitrable on the basis of contract considerations. Here, the application of the arbitrability doctrine does not involve public policy; the subject matter of the dispute is not an obstacle to arbitration. Parties invoking this defense might allege that the dispute in question is not covered by the arbitration agreement. Therefore, they cannot be compelled to arbitrate simply because they have not agreed to do so. The parties may have restricted the scope of their arbitral agreement to disputes relating to matters of contract delivery and payment. All other disagreements or conflicts arising between them would first be submitted to mediation and then (if necessary) to judicial litigation before a court of competent jurisdiction. Disputes relating to the payment of royalties or conformity of goods to technical specifications would not fall within the agreed-upon reference to arbitration. They would be inarbitrable as a matter of contract. The parties, however, could submit these disagreements to arbitration by modifying their current agreement or entering into a submission agreement when a dispute arises.

Inarbitrability as a result of contract also can arise in circumstances in which the agreement to arbitrate cannot be established or is flawed as a contract. The limitation on arbitration here does not arise from the scope of the arbitration agreement, but rather from whether it exists and if it is viable as an agreement. It should be noted that, under the separability doctrine, the alleged contractual deficiency must directly implicate the arbitration clause itself. Moreover, the failure to follow the requirements of the arbitration agreement as to the constitution of the arbitral tribunal or procedure can result in a ruling of contract inarbitrability. The agreed-upon provisions for arbitration cannot be ignored without mutual party acquiescence.

A number of critical questions accompany the application of the subject-matter and contract inarbitrability defenses. A court that entertains a defense to arbitration based upon subject-matter inarbitrability must determine which subject matters are vital to the public interest. Ordinarily, because such a case involves statutory rights, courts will refer to the enabling legislation. The question then becomes one of determining whether the statute contains a nonwaiver of rights provision that is sufficiently clear to prohibit party recourse to arbitration. If neither party objects to the arbitration of a dispute that is inarbitrable because of its subject matter, it is conceivable that the arbitration could go forward. The arbitral tribunal, however, could object to its own jurisdiction. Alternatively, the administering arbitral institution or a government agency that is aware of the proceeding might oppose the proceeding. Also, the party that does not prevail could change its mind and challenge the enforcement of the award once the proceeding is terminated, although such conduct would raise an estoppel problem.

Claims of contract inarbitrability raise questions of party intent and contract interpretation. The court hearing a motion to resist arbitration or to challenge an award on this basis must determine, through the ordinary canons of contract interpretation, the scope of the parties' reference to arbitration. State contract law applies. Generally, a broad reference to arbitration encompasses contract disputes (performance, delivery, excuse, conformity to specifications, frustration of purpose and impossibility, warranties, and language interpretation) and disputes involving rights established by public law regulations (rights acquired under tax, securities, bankruptcy, antitrust, or civil rights legislation). Most courts have held that parties must specifically exclude disputes they do not want to arbitrate if they have broadly agreed to arbitrate disputes.

NOTES AND QUESTIONS

1. Does the arbitrability of statutory rights represent a trespass by arbitration into the public domain—an intrusion into the realm of public jurisdiction? Are contract and statutory disputes indistinguishable? Should the submission of statutory claims to arbitration be accompanied by a requirement that arbitrator determinations on statutory matters be written and reasoned according to law? Would "qualified" subject-matter arbitrability of statutory disputes be a better approach? How extensively should arbitrators consider judicial interpretations of the relevant statute when they are confronted with statutory and contractual questions to decide?

2. What public policies apply to arbitration? Is arbitration itself a public policy? Is it the supreme public policy? Why should it trump or engulf the political regulation of commerce and the implementation of civil liberty guarantees? Is the suggested conflict more theoretical than real? How would you identify and define the public domain?

3. When is an agreement to arbitrate likely to be unenforceable as a contract? What deficiencies might lead to invalidity? What contract formation matters are particularly relevant to arbitration? Other than manifest abuse of right through overreaching or coercion, should the validity of an arbitration agreement be determined by the fairness of the arbitral procedure it establishes? When would an arbitral procedure be deemed fair legally? What would the federal policy on arbitration provide on this score?

4. Why should a general, "garden variety" reference to arbitration presume the arbitrability of statutory claims? Given the impact on public policy, should the presumption be reversed? Why not have freedom of contract prevail and allow parties to determine the arbitrability of statutory matters on a case-by-case basis?

5. Assess the inter-relationship, if any, between public policy, freedom of contract, and subject-matter inarbitrability.

4. THE SEPARABILITY DOCTRINE AND *KOMPETENZ–KOMPETENZ*

These concepts are intended to protect the jurisdictional authority of arbitral tribunals and the autonomy of the arbitral process. Prior to their incorporation in the law of arbitration, a party bent on delay would oppose the arbitration by alleging that the principal contract was void—usually, for reasons of public policy. Because the agreement to arbitrate was generally included in the main contract, it suffered the fate of the other contract provisions. In a word, the parties were not bound to arbitrate because the agreement to arbitrate was arguably invalid. The mere allegation of the invalidity of the main contract, therefore, gave the courts jurisdiction to decide whether a valid contract of arbitration existed.

Judicial intervention delayed the arbitration and impeded the implementation of the agreed-upon recourse to arbitration. Dilatory tactics flourished in such a setting.

The separability doctrine provides that the agreement to arbitrate is separate from, and independent of, the main contract. Therefore, allegations of contractual invalidity made against the main contract do not necessarily affect the arbitral clause. The challenging party must establish that the alleged invalidity bears directly upon the arbitral clause. Otherwise, the reference to arbitration remains in effect. The critical inquiry then centers upon whether a court or the arbitral tribunal should decide the impact of the allegation upon the arbitral clause.

At this juncture, the separability doctrine works in tandem with *kompetenz-kompetenz*. The *kompetenz-kompetenz* doctrine, also known as jurisdiction to rule on jurisdictional challenges, provides that the arbitral tribunal has the authority to decide on its own authority to rule. Otherwise stated, the arbitrators can decide whether an arbitration agreement exists or is valid (the basis of arbitrators' authority to adjudicate) and what the agreement establishes in terms of arbitrability and the arbitral process (the scope of the arbitrators' adjudicatory authority as provided by the agreement to arbitrate). The arbitral tribunal, therefore, can rule on whether there is a flaw in the main contract that affects the validity of the arbitral clause. The tribunal also can decide claims that the dispute in question is not covered by the arbitral clause. The tribunal's rulings on jurisdictional matters are subject to judicial scrutiny either at the time of pronouncement (when they are rendered in the form of an interim award) or at the enforcement stage of the process (when the rulings are part of the final award). Ordinarily, recourse to the courts on jurisdictional matters occurs at the end of the process when there is the least likelihood of reversal.

NOTES AND QUESTIONS

1. The availability of separability and *kompetenz-kompetenz* reflects how favorably disposed a law or legal system is to arbitration. The two doctrines not only countermand delaying strategies, but also empower arbitrators to exercise judge-like powers to define their own jurisdiction. Lax and delayed judicial supervision gives the arbitrators basically unfettered jurisdictional authority.

2. How likely is it that arbitrators will find flaws in their jurisdictional investiture when the finding of flaws results in their loss of lucrative work? Courts have no financial stake in such determinations. Are they not then in a better position to reach a determination on jurisdiction? Why does the governing legal standard head in the opposite direction?

3. Should parties, who have some skepticism about the ability of arbitrators to decide these issues, be allowed to eliminate *kompetenz-kompetenz* by contract? In these circumstances, can the power of contract outdo the authority of statutes? Are arbitrations exclusively one-off events with no bearing on

systemic policies or even other arbitrations? Would a provision for the judicial determination of arbitral jurisdiction constitute a violation of public policy?

4. An unusual feature of the U.S. law on arbitration is that it does not recognize or incorporate the *kompetenz-kompetenz* doctrine. FAA § 3 provides that jurisdictional issues pertaining to arbitration (whether a valid agreement exists and whether a dispute is covered by the agreement) shall be decided by a federal district court in the context of determining whether a judicial proceeding should be stayed pending arbitration. Under *First Options of Chicago, Inc. v. Kaplan*, 514 U.S. 938 (1995), the contracting parties can agree, however, to delegate the determination of jurisdictional questions to the arbitrators. *Kompetenz-kompetenz*, therefore, is available by a contractual provision. Is this a suitable way in which to "codify" the availability of the doctrine? What does the FAA's failure to provide for *kompetenz-kompetenz* say about the statute's underlying gravamen? Does the parties' ability to provide for it by contract undermine the statutory regime?

5. THE ARBITRATORS' ADJUDICATORY POWERS

The basic rule of U.S. arbitration law is that arbitrators (as a matter of law) possess the remedial authority necessary to adjudicate the dispute at hand. Borrowed from labor arbitration cases, the rule has been applied by the courts to all forms of arbitrations, including proceedings for consumer and employment arbitration. The U.S. law on arbitration also provides that arbitrators have the authority to award punitive damages and attorney's fees. If the parties want to restrict the authority of arbitrators, they must specifically so state in the arbitration agreement. The authorization to rule generally presumes the ability to award all types of relief.

Arbitral tribunals can award pre-and post-judgment interest. They can issue orders for provisional relief. These orders take the form of interim awards that involve the attachment of property, the garnishment of wages, or other measures to secure the enforceability of the final award. Such orders have no coercive legal effect unless a court converts the interim award into a judicial judgment. Court action is necessary especially when the order may affect the conduct or rights of a nonarbitrating party (the source of salary or revenue or the custodian of property). U.S. federal courts generally are favorably disposed to confirming orders for interim relief in aid of arbitration. The enforcement of interim measures is critical to the viability of arbitration. The inability to secure payment would make the proceedings risky and perhaps pointless.

The arbitrators also have the authority to issue orders for the production of evidence by an arbitrating party. When the party refuses to comply, the arbitral tribunal can seek to have its injunction enforced by a court or—under some arbitration systems—can simply take the party's refusal to comply into account in the final award. Ordinarily, the arbitrators' power to order the production of evidence and to enjoin conduct applies only to the parties to the arbitration. U.S. arbitration law is an exception to the rule. Under the FAA, arbitrators can compel nonarbitrating parties to produce evidence or to appear at the proceeding or both. Some federal courts have sought to restrict the arbitrators' subpoena powers in regard to third parties in light of the lack of a privity foundation for their exercise of power.

Arbitrators ordinarily must rule according to law. Freedom of contract, however, allows parties to agree to another decisional predicate. They can require the arbitrators to rule according to equity or as amiable compositors. The latter status empowers the arbitrators to disregard an unjust legal result once they have established how the law would resolve the dispute. They can then substitute a determination they find "right and just" for the inequitable outcome. Amiable composition places ultimate reliance upon the knowledge, ability, and experience of the arbitrators to articulate a sensible resolution to the dispute. It also reflects basic adjudicatory reality: Decision-makers come to a conclusion that they believe to be fair and interpret the law and the contract accordingly. There is no doubt, however, that the concept of amiable composition affords the arbitrators considerable (perhaps untoward) discretionary authority.

Finally, arbitrators can be empowered to rule on yet a third decisional basis. In addition to law and some form of equity, the arbitral tribunal can be expressly authorized to decide matters according to its technical expertise and knowledge. This standard applies to arbitrations in which the application of law is essentially irrelevant and the matters in issue involve scientific, engineering, or other specialized knowledge.

NOTES AND QUESTIONS

1. Arbitrators appear to have nearly unrestricted remedial powers. They are able to decide with little fear of reversal or admonishment. The marketplace for arbitrator services and party provision in the contract for arbitration are the only sources of meaningful limitations. What aspects of this subject are important to you? Why? How would you address your concerns in the arbitration agreement? What client interest might be at stake in these circumstances?

2. When should arbitrators be allowed to issue injunctions? Must they follow the standard legal requirements? Are their determinations subject to judicial supervision? Does the federal policy on arbitration influence your thinking on this matter? Is any restriction—no matter its purpose—reprehensible? Is it fair or in the public interest for injunctive relief to be more readily available and easier of access in arbitration?

3. Why would FAA § 7 allow arbitrators to subpoena nonarbitrating parties? Why should an ordinary citizen be subject to the authority of a private arbitrator? Should FAA § 7 survive a project of statutory revision? How would you rewrite the provision? Would you keep it as part of the statute?

4. How should arbitrators rule? Why?

6. ENFORCEMENT OF AWARDS

The statutory grounds for judicial supervision of arbitral awards are quite limited and exclude the judicial review of the merits of awards. The received wisdom is that the parties have bargained for a single adjudication. Appellate relief is limited to flagrant procedural abuses that constitute a denial of justice. Under FAA § 10, the parties are entitled to proceedings that are free of corruption, in which they are heard by disinterested arbitrators who decide only the matters submitted to them pursuant to the stipulations of the agreement. Moreover, they must be given notice of the proceedings and be treated equally and fairly in terms of making their case through documents, witnesses, other evidence, and the presentation of arguments.

Arbitrators can only rule upon the disputes that are actually submitted to them in the reference to arbitration. A ruling on a matter that is not submitted constitutes an excess of arbitral authority and can bring about the vacatur of the award (if the excessive ruling is inseparable from the other rulings in the award) or a partial enforcement of the award (if the excessive ruling can be severed from the other parts of the award). Excess of authority can also include unwarranted procedural rulings or the failure to follow the agreement or institutional rules.

The arbitral tribunal must conduct the proceedings in such a manner as to allow the parties a fair and reasonable opportunity to present their case and to respond to the allegations made against them. An adequate process must be observed, but the rule of fairness need not thwart the arbitrators' authority to conduct the proceeding, their ability to rule, or the efficiency of the hearing. An "abbreviated" form of due process establishes a functional balance between the rule of law, the guarantee of legal rights, and the means for their implementation.

Awards also are subject to judicial scrutiny under the non-statutory or common law grounds. These grounds, added by the decisional law to the statutory provision, permit judicial review of the merits of awards. The latter is impliedly excluded by the statute. The decisional import allows awards to be assessed by court for manifest disregard of the law, irrational rulings, or violation of statutory public policy.

In several recent cases, courts have held that arbitrating parties have the contractual right to provide for a merits review of arbitral awards. The parties, in effect, can increase the standard of review that applies to their arbitration. The federal circuits are divided on the legitimacy of the practice. A minority believe that such "opt-in" provisions for judicial review are a valid exercise of contract rights, whereas the majority of federal appellate courts either reject the practice on jurisdictional grounds or allow it only with substantial restrictions.

NOTES AND QUESTIONS

1. The enforcement of awards is critical to the viability of the arbitral process. If arbitrator determinations were not enforceable at law, there would be little, if any, incentive to proceed with arbitration. The process would become contaminated with dilatory tactics and merely be a preliminary bout to litigation. Coercive enforcement is necessary only in the event that voluntary compliance does not take place. The action is either to confirm or vacate the award.

2. By and large, the judicial policy favoring arbitration dominates the regime of enforcement. The vast majority of actions for vacatur fail. There is almost an absence of judicial protection from arbitrator error or incompetence. Is such a policy and practice a good idea? Why do you think the courts adopted such a position? Is it somehow commanded by the statute? Why would FAA § 10 exist if it were not or almost never to apply? Do and should courts merely "rubber stamp" what arbitrators decide, especially on the law? Does perfunctory judicial supervision lessen the dignity of the courts? Why not provide for the automatic enforcement of awards?

3. You should think about how to define the various statutory and non-statutory grounds for vacatur. When might arbitrators exceed their powers or manifestly disregard the law? How much do they need to disclose to avoid a challenge of the award for "evident partiality"? Must actual bias be established to constitute the latter? Why are public policy violations restricted to matters of statutory public policy? When does an arbitral ruling become irrational?

4. Assess the significance of the development of "opt-in" provisions for the heightened judicial review of arbitral awards. The provision simply surfaced in a contract between a U.S. and Japanese company that went to litigation before the U.S. Ninth Circuit. It resulted from practice, not legislation or the judicial or academic imagination. What might have induced parties to agree to more judicial scrutiny of arbitrator rulings on the law? While it creates another layer of protection, does the reference to courts contribute to disabling the arbitral process? Why agree to arbitration if you believe the process is dangerous or arbitrators incompetent? Do courts have a monopoly on the construction and application of law?

5. You should construct arguments for and against "opt-in" provisions from the judicial point of view. Why are most federal courts less than enthusiastic about the development? Such agreements, it seems, are completely in line with the core concept of freedom of contract.

7. CONSOLIDATION AND CLASS ACTIONS

The U.S. Federal Rules of Civil Procedure provide for consolidation as a procedural device intended to enhance the efficiency of federal judicial administration. Under its power to consolidate proceedings, a federal court can join the litigation of several different but related cases into a single proceeding in order to avoid duplicative litigation and inconsistent results. The cases must involve disputes arising from the same factual core and must generate very similar, if not identical, questions of law.

The application of the judicial power of consolidation to arbitral proceedings raised both practical and doctrinal problems. Court-ordered consolidation of separate arbitral proceedings creates issues about the boundaries of the contract for arbitration. In effect, courts rewrite material provisions of the agreement and force parties to arbitrate with parties who were not included in the original agreement. Parties, therefore, are bound by an implied duty to arbitrate imposed by an entity outside the boundaries of the contract. Court consolidation violates the parties' autonomy and their sovereign authority over their transaction. The court intrudes upon a private transaction for no public reason.

It can also result in multiple arbitrators, possibly several different supervising arbitral institutions and institutional rules, clashing provisions on applicable law and trial procedures, and a need to reconcile conflicts between the various submissions to arbitration. In effect, consolidating different arbitral proceedings can generate an administrative nightmare that ultimately requires the court to intrude further into the arbitral process and literally to rewrite the terms of the relevant arbitration agreements. The availability of consolidation can also invite party use of dilatory tactics to frustrate the recourse to arbitration.

The U.S. Court of Appeals for the Second Circuit, which initiated the practice of arbitral consolidation, reconsidered its position, holding that consolidation was an exceptional remedy and that its availability was constrained by the parties' freedom of contract. Nonetheless, parties should make some provision for consolidation in their agreement to shield themselves from marauding judicial support for arbitration. An express provision stating that consolidation is excluded or possible only with the mutual consent of the parties should eliminate the prospect of unwarranted judicial interference. Parties should also consider whether the affected arbitrators should be consulted or their consent required to effectuate consolidation, and—if consolidation proceeds—whether the arbitrators should submit a plan for the reorganization of the arbitrations.

Most courts and commentators align class actions in arbitration with consolidation. Both procedures involve the exercise of judicial authority. Further, they are designed to achieve the aggregation of related claims into a single proceeding for the purpose of efficiency, economy of adjudicatory resources, and consistency of determination. The central question is whether courts can certify classes in arbitration or order classwide arbitrations when the arbitration agreement is silent on the matter. The U.S. Supreme Court has recently ruled that the determination is to be made by the arbitrator. Once a court finds that an arbitration agreement exists, all other matters are to be decided by the arbitrator. The interpretation of the contract is a sovereign activity of the arbitrator. *See Green Tree Fin. Corp. v. Bazzle*, 539 U.S. 444 (2003).

Class action waivers have created a great deal of discussion among commentators. If an agreement to arbitrate is adhesionary and unilaterally imposed upon a weaker party, the view is that any accompanying reduction of rights is illegal. Stronger parties—like manufacturers and employers—can exclude class action relief in arbitration agreements and eliminate some litigation leverage against themselves. Despite the protestations, courts generally uphold arbitration agreements with class action waivers or—at worse—sever them and enforce the remainder of the agreement. The ideological discord is especially in evidence in consumer and employment arbitration. A minority of courts invalidate arbitration agreements because they contain a class action waiver.

NOTES AND QUESTIONS

1. Who benefits disproportionately from class action litigation? Why is that the case? Can arbitration reduce the disproportionate benefits? Which party in the litigation cast of characters makes the most money? Do class action lawsuits have an impact upon regulatory policies? Are they simply another cost of doing business imposed by the legal profession?

2. Are class action waivers in adhesionary arbitration agreements nothing other than a naked power grab by corporate parties? Why should the law of arbitration and the federal policy on arbitration be used to condone such patently unfair tactics? Is it conceivable that the implicated corporate parties are performing a public service by pruning adjudicatory systems of undesirable and counterproductive litigation?

3. Consolidation is now part of the transborder law on arbitration. The 1986 Dutch statute on arbitration, for example, allows the courts to order consolidation, as do a number of other foreign jurisdictions. When is consolidation likely to be invoked by courts? Why? In which transactional circumstances are uniformity of result and the efficient use of resources most likely to be challenged? You should identify commercial relationships that involve integrated and interdependent transactions. Maritime transactions, for instance, involve a variety of parties: the supplier, the buyer, the owner of the vessel, the renter of the vessel, an insurer, and a reinsurer. Consolidation appears to be tailor-made for these types of transactions; in fact, the rules of the Society of Maritime Arbitrators state that use of the rules implies that the parties have agreed to consolidation and even third-party presence at the arbitration.

4. When might consolidation be useful in other forms of arbitration? Why?

5. What motivates the courts' use of consolidation in connection with arbitration? Is it an example of judicial hostility to arbitration? If not, does it nonetheless indicate a possible systemic danger in the relationship between courts and the arbitral process? Does the latter testify to the wisdom of a policy of unequivocal support for arbitration?

Given the "deregulatory" approach to arbitration, the key to a successful arbitration resides primarily in the choice of the arbitrator(s). The selection of an institutional administrator and of a neutral venue or situs for arbitration also are important. The arbitrators, however, will conduct the proceedings, evaluate the evidence and arguments, and render a final and binding decision on the matters submitted. Moreover, how the arbitrators will reason individually and collectively and settle on a resolution of the dispute are critical to the interests of the parties. Selecting arbitrators who are able to perform their duties responsibly; master the case, the evidence, and the other adjudicatory tasks; and come to a fair, effective, and commercially adapted ruling is a fundamentally important aspect of the process.

8. ARBITRAL INSTITUTIONS

Trade associations, chambers of commerce, commodity groups, and industrial organizations supervise and administer arbitrations. For example, the diamond trade and textile merchants have their own arbitration procedure. The Better Business Bureau offers a framework for administering arbitrations. Members of trade or industry groups are usually required to arbitrate disputes with other group members if the disputes involve association business. Transactional parties can choose to arbitrate on their own (*ad hoc* arbitration) or under the administration of an arbitral institution (institutional arbitration). There are a number of well-known arbitral institutions that supervise arbitrations.

The American Arbitration Association (AAA), a non-profit organization founded in the 1920s and headquartered in New York City with regional offices throughout the United States, supervises a large number of labor, commercial, construction, and securities arbitrations. The AAA also provides commercial mediation services. It administers more than 100,000 ADR cases annually. Its administrative fee is generally reasonable and is established according to a sliding scale based on the amount in controversy. In 1997, the AAA established the Center of International Dispute Resolution and published new rules on international arbitration.

The National Arbitration Forum (The Forum) was founded in 1986 by a group of lawyers, judges, and mediators to provide technologically-sophisticated ADR services that complied with established rules of law. It provides both arbitration and mediation services through panels of neutrals who are former judges, lawyers, and industry experts. In arbitral proceedings, neutrals assess the facts and apply the settled law; in fact, they are sworn to apply the known law and agreed-upon rules. Parties are afforded procedural rights consistent with those available in judicial proceedings. Forum arbitral proceedings include the right to discovery.

JAMS (originally the Judicial Arbitration and Mediation Service) was established in Orange County, California in 1979. It merged with Endispute in 1994; the latter had been formed in 1981 on the east coast. JAMS/Endispute had offices in Washington, D.C., Chicago, Illinois, Los Angeles and San Francisco, California. In 1999, after a group of forty-five JAMS/Endispute neutrals and managers bought the company from institutional investors, JAMS/Endispute renamed itself JAMS. The company is now known as JAMS The Resolution Experts; the initials are no longer an abbreviation. JAMS consists of two hundred full-time neutrals who are highly trained and experienced professionals. They have demonstrated their ability to adjudicate cases and to help parties settle their differences. Many are former judges, justices, and lawyers. JAMS provides all types of ADR services and covers a wide range of disputes (from bankruptcy and class action to health care and intellectual property ending with real estate and toxic torts).

The International Chamber of Commerce (ICC) is perhaps the most visible and well-known provider of institutional arbitral services for international arbitrations. Its headquarters are located in Paris, France; ICC arbitrations, however, can be and are held everywhere in the world. The ICC administers approximately 500–600 arbitrations annually. ICC rules give the ICC some supervisory authority over ICC arbitrations. The ICC Court of Arbitration supervises ICC awards prior to their official rendition. The court's function is largely administrative; it has no true legal jurisdictional authority over the dispute or the parties.

Administrative costs for ICC arbitrations also are established according to a sliding scale based upon the amount in controversy. Although the fee schedule has been revised recently to lessen the expense of ICC arbitrations, the administrative costs remain high. A recently published study, however, indicates that attorney's fees represent nearly three-quarters of the cost of an international arbitration. The ICC also provides mediation services for commercial disputes. An ICC arbitral award carries considerable weight with most national courts both in the developed and developing world. There is also a high rate of voluntary compliance with ICC awards among arbitrating parties.

The London Court of International Arbitration (LCIA) is quite similar to the ICC and competes with it for arbitration business. It does a lesser business than the ICC, supervising approximately 125–150 arbitrations annually. London itself has a long-standing reputation as a venue for international arbitration; in excess of 10,000 arbitrations take place in London every year in a variety of areas (*e.g.*, maritime, insurance, and commodities). The professional infrastructure and English language make London an attractive venue for holding arbitral proceedings between U.S. and foreign parties. The liberalization and modernization of the English arbitration law in 1996 should further enhance the business of arbitration in London. LCIA arbitration is less costly than its ICC counterpart because the LCIA charges an hourly fee for its services. Like the other arbitral institutions, the LCIA has a relatively new set of institutional rules on international commercial arbitration. The rules came into effect in January 1998 and improve the process of LCIA arbitration by limiting dilatory tactics and the possibility of procedural disruption of the proceedings by disgruntled parties. Arbitrators are given somewhat greater authority in the conduct of proceedings.

In 1965, the Convention on the Settlement of Investment Disputes between States and Nationals of Other States (the "ICSID Convention" or "Washington Convention") established an international form of arbitration for dealing with investment disputes between foreign investors and host States. The ICSID arbitral process (also known as "World Bank" arbitration) is intended to be an entirely autonomous and self-contained dispute resolution framework. The national courts of the contracting States cannot entertain challenges to ICSID arbitral proceedings or awards; the only course of action allowed to national courts is to recognize and enforce ICSID awards. In other words, national courts must recognize an ICSID award as binding and enforce it as if it were a final judgment of a court of the requested State. The exclusive remedial recourse against an ICSID award lies within the ICSID framework itself; an award can be subject to interpretation, revision, and annulment through an internal appellate procedure. ICSID arbitrations are administered by the International Centre for Settlement of Investment Disputes, an international organization created under the ICSID Convention.

Although the Convention has been ratified by one hundred and fifty-five States (including the United States), the utility and efficacy of ICSID arbitration had been under question. Prior to the emergence of bilateral investment treaties (BITs) and the reference to ICSID arbitration in the NAFTA treaty, the number of submitted cases since 1966, when the Convention entered into force, had been less than overwhelming—fewer than forty cases. Only twenty-six actual decisions had been rendered. Also, considerable controversy had been generated as a result of the annulment of two ICSID awards in the mid–1980s through the internal *ad hoc* committee review procedure (*Klöckner*, ICSID Case No. ARB/81/2, *reprinted in* 1 J. INT'L ARB. 145 [1984], and *Amco Asia*, ICSID Case No. ARB/81/1, *reprinted in* 1 J. INT'L ARB. 601 [1986]). Moreover, sovereign immunity from execution appears to be unresolved or at least unsettled under ICSID. According to Article 55 of the Convention, "nothing" in the Convention "shall be construed as derogating from the law in force in any Contracting State relating to immunity of that state or of any foreign state from execution." The ICSID Secretariat, however, indicated several years ago that this provision has never hindered or prevented the enforcement of an ICSID award.

BITS and NAFTA have altered considerably the position and operation of ICSID in the marketplace for transborder arbitral services. There are more than one hundred pending cases, and more than one hundred cases have been concluded. ICSID administers both Convention and non-Convention arbitral proceedings. The latter are done through its Additional Facility. The Additional Facility Rules cover commercial transactions that have some features of an investment dispute and fact-finding proceedings. The Secretary–General can also act as an appointing authority for arbitrators for *ad hoc* arbitrations.

These major arbitral institutions, with the exception of ICSID, are completely private organizations. They are not subject to government regulation or any other form of public scrutiny or certification. Their reputation and business are dependent entirely upon market factors. All of these organizations are highly regarded and exercise considerable influ-

ence in the field of arbitration. The institutions publish their own litera-
ture, have their own rules for the conduct of arbitrations, provide lists of
arbitrators, and have case managers who facilitate the administration of
arbitral proceedings.

NOTES AND QUESTIONS

1.   One of the critical considerations in terms of institutional arbitration
is whether parties should hire a service-provider to administer their arbitration or conduct an *ad hoc* arbitration. The advantage to *ad hoc* arbitration is
the avoidance of institutional fees and possibly intrusive authority. The
parties and the arbitrators (and possibly the courts) are the only strategic
players in the process. The disadvantages are the loss of the institution's
imprimatur and its professional guidance and services. It also places the
administrative burdens upon the parties and their counsel. That burden can
become particularly difficult and heavy in the event of extensive or irreconcilable disagreement. Only the courts an resolve an impasse.

2.   In light of the foregoing considerations, which approach to the administration of arbitrations would you favor? What factors influence your decision? How would you explain your choice to clients? Does the use of a service-
provider constitute a form of insurance against certain risks? Is the premium
excessive?

3.   What are the basic differences between the AAA, The Forum, and
JAMS? Do they have unique properties or features? Do you have a sense of
when you would have recourse to one institution and not another? Explain
your thinking.

4.   How are the international service providers different from their
domestic counterparts? Do they have special capabilities? Are monopolies a
problem in this sector of the service economy? If you were advising a U.S.
corporation that was contracting with a foreign company, which—if any—of
the institutions would you use? Why?

9.   A–NATIONAL ARBITRATION

The theory underlying "a-national arbitration" provides that transborder commercial arbitrations are completely outside the domestic regulatory reach of national laws and courts. It thereby provides for the
eventual exercise of absolute authority by arbitrators and the assertion of
absolute autonomy for the arbitral process. Whatever constraints and
limitations apply to arbitration in domestic law cannot impinge upon
international arbitral agreements, proceedings, or awards. Transborder
arbitrations are subject solely to the normative restraints contained in
international conventions on arbitration or that exist as a matter of
customary international arbitral practice. Courts at the place of arbitration can only assist arbitral proceedings (designate arbitrators, compel a
party to arbitrate, order the production of evidence, or enforce rulings for
interim relief) and courts at the place of enforcement can supervise

awards only on a limited statutory basis. In effect, the transborder arbitral process is, *de facto,* an autonomous and self-regulating international system of adjudication.

In contrast, the concept of *lex loci arbitri* (law of the place of arbitration) argues for the continued vitality of national law in the regulation of transborder arbitration. When the parties designate a particular country as the place of arbitration—whether by happenstance, for the sake of convenience, on the basis of personal whim, or because of the location's neutrality in relation to the parties and the transaction—they enter that State's territory and subject themselves and the arbitration to the State's laws. The local disposition on arbitration cannot be ignored or suspended simply because the proceedings are international in character. Local courts must apply the restrictions of domestic law to the arbitration if the national legislation so requires. Under this view, the legitimacy of an adjudicatory process depends upon the will of a sovereign—not the individual will of private parties. The lawfulness of an adjudicatory determination, even privately rendered, arises from the operation of law, not the parties' consent. Territorial sovereignty mandates local regulation of transborder arbitrations.

National legal authority can affect transborder arbitrations in a number of ways. For example, the domestic arbitration statute might require arbitral tribunals to be constituted in a particular fashion or mandate the use of certain trial procedures in arbitration. If the parties have agreed upon a nonconforming process and they are unable to modify their agreement, local courts—upon the motion of the party resisting arbitration or on their own—could compel compliance or declare the agreement to arbitrate void and nullify the arbitration. The local law of arbitration, therefore, can allow domestic courts to negate an agreement to arbitrate or nullify an award even though the award is intended for enforcement in another jurisdiction. Negative local action can make the agreement or award unenforceable elsewhere.

There is little justification for allowing the rules of a particular locality to thwart a transborder arbitration on an international basis when the national jurisdiction has no interest in the arbitral proceeding or award and the arbitration is connected to it only for reasons of neutrality, convenience, or infrastructure. States that espouse the pursuit of a strong supervisory role through their courts are likely to be excluded from the lucrative business of acting as venues for arbitrations. Transborder arbitral proceedings do not call into question the core concerns of domestic legality. The objective of these proceedings is to achieve commercial justice in an international setting, not resolve civil liberty debates or engage in the politics of regulation. Moreover, the basic uniformity of national laws on arbitration renders the concerns of the proponents of the *lex loci arbitri* rather anodyne.

The *lex mercatoria* or international law merchant represents yet another development that reinforces the a-national character of transborder arbitration. International arbitrators not only adjudicate international commercial disputes, but they also have elaborated a common law of international contracts and business transactions in their rulings. Moreover, when international arbitrators rule on statutory rights and claims, they become *de facto* international legislators. International arbitral awards, therefore, constitute legal precedent that can bind subsequent arbitrators and even courts. Despite their private jurisdictional authority, international arbitrators occupy a unique position for articulating international commercial law principles. The practical objective of their contractual mission allows them to craft functional decisional predicates for international commercial disputes.

NOTES AND QUESTIONS

1. What elements of analysis distinguish an international arbitration from its domestic counterpart? Should the nationality of the implicated parties be a significant consideration? What about the subject matter of the transaction or the place of contract performance? Does it matter where the arbitral proceedings are held?

2. Can the parties themselves simply declare that their transaction and arbitration are international in character? How? What factors should be considered in reaching a determination on this question?

3. Is there any meaningful consequence or distinction between engaging in an international as opposed to a domestic arbitration? Are regulatory interests affected by the difference of form?

4. When should national interests prevail over international arbitration? Why is it so important to avoid the reach of domestic law? Should countries not have a right to regulate conduct and events that take place within their own borders? Is "globalism" an ugly phenomenon or reality?

5. What definition would you propose of the State authority to legislate and make rules for regulating conduct and activities? When might such authority have an extraterritorial impact?

6. How do international or domestic arbitrators achieve or acquire law-making authority?

10. MODERN LEGISLATION ON ARBITRATION

In the United States, the U.S. Arbitration Act (Federal Arbitration Act [FAA]) governs matters of arbitration. There is also a Uniform Arbitration Act or law for states. At the international level, the U.N. Commission on International Trade Law (UNCITRAL) published a Model Law on International Commercial Arbitration and the U.N. Convention on the Recognition and Enforcement of Foreign Arbitral Awards (the 1958 New York Arbitration Convention). Both instruments are very popular and create a transborder standard on arbitration. These statutes contain a number of common features. Current legal systems generally sustain the privatization of adjudication through arbitration (at least in regard to international business disputes) and agree upon a deregulatory approach to arbitration both domestically and internationally.

Modern legislative enactments on arbitration generally are characterized by a favorable policy toward arbitration and contain the following substantive provisions: (1) Express language recognizing both arbitration agreements (the submission and the arbitral clause) as valid contracts. The recourse to arbitration represents a lawful exercise of the parties' contractual rights. As a consequence, arbitration agreements can be challenged only on traditional contract grounds (*e.g.*, duress, adhesion, unconscionability, and a failure or inadequacy of consideration). Forgoing judicial relief, as a matter of law, does not constitute a violation of public policy. Moreover, freedom of contract is instrumental to arbitration. (2) Clear recognition of the legal effect of a valid contract of arbitration: An arbitration agreement divests the courts of jurisdiction to rule upon disputes validly submitted to arbitration—unless the parties agree mutually (expressly or impliedly) to rescind the agreement to arbitrate. (3) Provisions of law establishing a duty on courts to cooperate with the arbitral process and to assist its operation by naming arbitrators, compelling arbitration, or enforcing arbitrator rulings. (4) Limited and narrow grounds for the judicial supervision of awards that establish a strong presumption of the enforceability of awards. Other than flagrant abuses by the arbitrators that amount to a denial of justice, courts can refuse to enforce awards only for violations of minimum due process guarantees (notice of the proceeding and the right to be heard) or because the arbitrators failed to respect the arbitration agreement. (5) Finally, most contemporary statutory regulations of arbitration acknowledge and legitimate the emergence of "a-national" arbitration in the sphere of international commercial dispute resolution. As noted in the preceding section, under this concept, arbitral proceedings and awards are completely detached from the potential restrictions of national law and need only comply with the customary norms of transborder arbitration.

NOTES AND QUESTIONS

1.   Statutory regimes are important. They provide legislative commands, policies, and direction. A cooperative judiciary, however, is just as, if not more, essential to the rule of law in a given area. The FAA would never have come to symbolize such a strongly favorable policy toward arbitration had the courts not advocated on behalf of the process. Any able judge can find ways to undermine statutory provisions and frustrate regulatory objectives.

2.   Does legislation favoring arbitration represent an abdication of responsibility? Are political institutions declaring adjudicatory insolvency and admitting failure? Is the privatization of adjudicatory proceedings essential to the proper operation of modern society?

3.   You should notice that the legislative recognition of the contract validity of arbitration agreements eventually lead to the judicial proclamation

that contract freedom principles dominated the law of arbitration. Is this an acceptable development in the construction of the law? The two statements, positioned side-by-side, seem to say different, opposite, and even incompatible things. How do you assess this circumstance?

4. Why should courts take a "hands off" approach to arbitration?

5. Draft a statute on arbitration that you find acceptable and necessary. Explain your choices.

* * *

Rights Protection Versus Functionality Illustrated

Once arbitration is invoked, can it maintain, despite the informality of its procedures and its reliance upon arbitrator discretion, a sufficient commitment to the protection of legal rights? Will the arbitral process undergo a transformation as a result of its new role? When the rights invoked in arbitration are created by statute, are special procedures warranted in the arbitral proceedings or before the courts? Should such proceedings be open to the public, be conducted by arbitrators with special expertise in the implicated statutory area, require the writing of a detailed opinion on why a statutory claim was dismissed or how it was decided, and involve a higher level of judicial supervision of the merits of the arbitral awards that are rendered? What becomes of the regulatory laws when their content is applied and interpreted by arbitrators in unpublished and perhaps unreasoned or ill-reasoned decisions? If lawyer participation is the source of legal legitimacy in the evolving arbitral framework, how is the work and role of lawyers to be defined and evaluated? Can the systemic autonomy of arbitration and the protection of the public interest both be maintained?

These questions have no easy or evident answers. Even in international commerce, where arbitration is clearly necessary and dominant, the expansion of arbitral functions challenges the foundation of law-making authority and the viability of standard legal operations. Sovereignty yields to the requirements of commerce and hence of arbitration, but the acquiescence (even here) is uneasy and characterized by a lack of predictability and possible inconsistency. The movement toward "judicialized" arbitration is especially disturbing because the participation of lawyers— in particular, U.S.-trained lawyers—shifts the balance in arbitral procedure from autonomy and functionality to procedural integrity and rectitude. There is some possibility that arbitration may not survive the success of its own development.

11. HYPOTHETS

The following hypothetical circumstances are meant to provide an opportunity for identifying and evaluating the basic issues and legal rules of U.S. arbitration law. The hypothets anticipate many of the issues that will be considered by the case law as well as the radical character of the rulings in the area. You should allow the content of these problems to guide your reading of the materials. Construct an assessment of the issues before and after your reading of the court opinions. What fundamental problems of legality do these circumstances raise? What problems do they raise for the prospective client? What practical solutions might be achieved?

I.

"A" is a diamond dealer and retailer in Lansing, Michigan. He has been involved in the diamond trade for more than twenty years and is a long-time member of the Diamond Exchange of New York City. Membership in that organization is necessary for admission to the trade. The Exchange is the entity through which all wholesale diamond transactions take place in the United States. Exclusion from the Exchange means exclusion from the business. As part of its conditions for admission, the Diamond Exchange requires that its members agree to resolve all transactional disputes between themselves or with the Exchange through the Exchange's arbitration process. The arbitration of disputes is standard practice within the trade.

Arbitral tribunals under the Exchange's rules consist of a member of the Exchange's Executive Committee who serves as the chair and two members of the Exchange who are appointed by the chair. Members asked to serve as arbitrators cannot refuse the appointment unless they are implicated in the dispute or have another serious reason for refusing the appointment. An unjustified refusal can result in a suspension or loss of membership. All arbitral proceedings take place in New York City at the Exchange. According to the Exchange's rules, the arbitral tribunal must meet informally with all of the parties to discuss preliminary matters, conduct hearings, question the parties, and come to a determination within fifteen days of the initial meeting. The arbitrating parties can only be represented by another member of the Exchange. The chair of the arbitral tribunal decides all procedural matters relating to the proceedings. On these matters, the chair need not consult the other members of the tribunal. The tribunal can demand whatever information it deems necessary to its decision and can exclude whatever information it believes irrelevant. The parties are allowed a maximum of fifteen hours in which to make their case and may present only material documents and a limited number of witnesses—three character witnesses and three other witnesses. The arbitral tribunal rules according to standard trade practices and its decision is final and binding. The parties specifically waive the right of recourse against the award, including any action for judicial supervision or review.

"A" has been accused by another member of the Exchange of breaching a handshake deal for the purchase of diamonds. She alleges that "A" failed to provide payment within the designated time and refused to honor fully their agreement. All Exchange business among members is done on a handshake basis; the sanction for a violation of the oral promise to pay or to deliver is exclusion from the Exchange. Reinstatement is not possible and the banishment has worldwide consequences. In a word, the violating member is completely excluded from the diamond business.

Assume that the arbitral tribunal finds "A" in violation of the Exchange's rules of conduct and issues an award excluding "A" from the Exchange. "A" brings an action before a Michigan federal district court alleging that the award is unenforceable because the arbitrators failed to take into account and properly examine all of the evidence and decided the matter in an arbitrary and capricious fashion. "A" also alleges that the award and the Exchange's arbitral procedure are unconstitutional because they have deprived him of his property without due process of law. In addition, "A" brings a defamation action against his accuser and the Exchange before the same Michigan court.

1.   There are a host of problems that arise in these facts ranging from the propriety of the Michigan court's jurisdiction to the enforceability of the arbitral award. For purposes of the arbitration analysis, you should focus upon the following questions: What type of arbitration took place at the Exchange? What rationale and purpose underlie this type of arbitration? How does it differ from standard forms of arbitration? Does it represent a lawful use of the contractual right to engage in arbitration? Is it a contractual form of arbitration? The arbitral procedure gives the chair and the arbitral tribunal unlimited authority in the conduct of the proceedings. Can this type of trial procedure ever pass constitutional muster? What makes it so unfair? Does the composition of the tribunal and the method of arbitrator selection strike you as equally and as fundamentally unfair?

2.   Assume that the tribunal renders an award that states that " 'A' has been found in violation of the Exchange's Prime Directive, Rule Number One in the recited circumstances and is expelled from the Exchange." In light of its brevity, what sort of judicial recourse is possible against the award? How does "A" substantiate the allegations of procedural unfairness? Verbatim records or transcripts are not a customary part of arbitral proceedings. Should the federal district court in Michigan even entertain "A" 's claims? What arguments can be made for and against court action in these circumstances? What effect does the defamation action have on those facts and the grounds for judicial review? Finally, what advice would you have provided "A" when "A" agreed to arbitration as part of the requirements of membership?

II.

"B" contacts several moving companies to solicit bids on transporting personal household goods and furnishings from California to New York. ABC moving company presents "B" with the best price and also boasts of a high quality record in the secure transport of goods. The company's competitive bid reflects lower rates for the insurance of the goods against damage while in transit and upon delivery. The insurance rates are lower because of the company's safety record and because customers must agree to take all disputed insurance claims to arbitration. The standard clause in the contract reads: "Any dispute arising between the transport company and the undersigned customer pertaining to the performance and execution of this agreement shall be submitted to arbitration under the rules of the American Arbitration Association. Disputes between the customer and the insurance carrier are included in this broad reference to arbitration."

1. "B" seeks your advice on this matter. Would you advise "B" to accept or to reject the contract? How would you justify whichever response you give? Do problems exist in the language of the arbitral clause? Is this a lawful form of arbitration? Why and why not?

2. Should "B" 's status or the character of the dispute have any bearing upon the enforceability of the arbitral clause once "B" signs the contract? Would you propose a counteroffer to the moving company's boilerplate language? Why? What language might a reasonable counter include?

3. Assume that, upon delivery, a member of the working crew loses control of the refrigerator and it falls upon "B" 's pedigree dog and kills it. The falling appliance also smashes a rare and very valuable vase. "B" claims that the crew had been drinking beer at the time of the incident and was reckless in its conduct. "B" wants compensation for pain and suffering and emotional loss, as well as for the loss of property. Is this dispute part of the contractual reference to arbitration? Should it be? Why and why not? If the arbitrators have jurisdiction, how should they decide the matter(s)?

III.

Identify and evaluate the various components of the following transactions (type of transaction, relationship of actors, interests involved, potential problem areas, and the like). Would you recommend the recourse to arbitration in any of these circumstances? What factors and considerations motivate your recommendation? How might you persuade the other side to arbitrate or forgo arbitration? What provisions should a good arbitration agreement include in these circumstances and why? Do any of these circumstances implicate the public policy exception to enforcement?

1. A local law firm wants to associate and eventually merge with an out-of-state law firm. The merger would involve the creation of a new partnership. Provisions pertaining to partnership profit share, collections policy, administrative staff, advertising, and client generation need to be worked out. Together, the two firms have 250 associate lawyers and 50 partners. The objective of the merger is to service a group of mutual multistate clients and to establish a dominant presence in regional commercial litigation.

2. An individual invents and manufacturers in his home (with the members of his family) a special process for imprinting tee-shirts. The products that result from the process are distinctive in terms of color,

texture, and permanence of the imprint. They also contain unique designs. A broker approaches the individual to establish a supply contract with a large product distributor. The broker also intimates that her distributor-customer might be interested in the purchase of the process if the supply arrangement works out satisfactorily. The supply contract eventually anticipates the production and sale of a considerable volume of tee-shirt items.

3. ABC company, a family-owned-and-operated venture, is seeking to raise capital through a private offering of its stock. It hires a local accountant to supervise and conduct the sale of its shares. The proceeds raised are intended to finance the expansion of the business and the replacement of outdated machinery and office equipment. The anticipated additional revenue will also be used to augment owner salaries. The sale is confined to current management, employees, and relatives or friends of the owners. The ownership percentage is carefully calculated so that the three principal owners remain the majority stockowners, with the majority of shares evenly divided between them. The fourth owner has opposed the private offering and has fewer shares than her three colleagues. Also, the three majority owners intend to borrow money from the company to pay for their new shares.

IV.

A recent business school graduate is seeking employment with a Fortune 500 brokerage house in a junior executive capacity with the sales department. The candidate is female, black, and gay. She is an adamant and vociferous proponent of minority rights. The company personnel office is very impressed with the candidate's academic credentials and performances—both of which are outstanding. The company is willing to pay her top dollar and to place her in an accelerated program. There is a nine-month probationary period at a modest apprenticeship salary. Thereafter, the negotiated renumeration kicks in, as well as substantial benefits (including both medical/dental and retirement). An offer of employment is made but it is contingent upon the candidate's express acceptance of, and subscription to, an arbitration agreement. The arbitral clause provides:

> The employee agrees that any and all disputes that arise pertaining to her recruitment, application and interviewing for employment, actual employment, and termination of employment and beyond shall be submitted to arbitration. Similarly, the employer agrees to submit all grievances that it may have against the employee to arbitration, except for injunctive relief for non-compete violations and workmen's compensation claims. The employer shall bear the costs of the arbitration. The resulting arbitral award shall be final and binding. The agreement to arbitrate prevents either party from bringing or participating in class action litigation in regard to covered claims. The parties' agreement applies to contract, regulatory, statutory, and jurisdictional disputes. The American Arbitration Association (AAA) Rules for employment arbitration shall apply. The arbitration agree-

ment and the arbitral proceedings shall be governed by New York state law.

1. What feature of the arbitral clause are important from a contract formation perspective? Is the arbitration agreement a bilateral contract? Does it reflect the parties' intent? If so, how? Is there consideration?

2. What is the agreement's scope of application? Why is that factor important?

3. What are regulatory disputes? What are jurisdictional disputes?

4. Is there an employment contract other than the arbitral clause? Is the candidate likely to be an "at will" employee?

5. What allegations are likely to surface in the event of termination during the probational period? Should such controversies be heard exclusively before courts? Why and why not?

6. Is the arbitral clause fair? Why and why not? What features of the agreement promote either conclusion?

7. Is the class action waiver related to costs and *vice versa*?

CHAPTER THREE

U.S. STATUTES ON ARBITRATION

■ ■ ■

1. THE PERIOD OF "HOSTILITY"

In the nineteenth century, U.S. law contained provisions that were hostile to arbitration. Such hostility was characteristic of the policy in most legal systems of the period. Judges were unwilling to surrender the privilege of conducting adjudications and to have private individuals not schooled in the law preside over trials. Arbitration, in their view, was makeshift justice. Courts were reluctant to compel parties to arbitrate. In the words of Mr. Justice Story,

> ... [w]hen ... [courts] are asked to ... compel the parties to appoint arbitrators whose award shall be final, they necessarily pause to consider whether such tribunals possess adequate means of giving redress, and whether they have a right to compel a reluctant party to submit to such a tribunal, and to close against him the doors of the common courts of justice, provided by the government to protect rights and to redress wrongs.

Tobey v. County of Bristol, 23 F. Cas. 1313, 1320–21 (C.C. D. Mass. 1845) (No. 14,065).

In order to be legally binding, the reference to arbitration, therefore, had to be accompanied by continuous voluntary party participation in the arbitral proceeding. Unlike English courts, which reviewed the merits of awards through the case-stated procedure, courts in the United States would readily enforce awards once they were rendered. Their attack on arbitration centered upon the agreement to arbitrate, in particular the arbitral clause. Under U.S. law, the arbitral clause was subject to unilateral rescission at any time prior to the rendition of an award. The submission agreement could also be avoided prior to the rendering of an award, but, because it was entered into after a dispute arose, it represented a firmer and more considered waiver of judicial relief.

NOTES AND QUESTIONS

1. Assess the rationale that Justice Story advances for exempting arbitral agreements—as opposed to awards—from the process of coercive legal enforcement. Does the distinction between agreements and awards on this

basis make sense—from a doctrinal point of view, from a practical vantage point?

2. Can arbitral autonomy be achieved and maintained under these circumstances? If the parties adhere to their agreement to arbitrate until the arbitral tribunal rules, the arbitral process does result in a final and binding determination. Is that discretionary party allegiance to the arbitration agreement sufficient to make arbitral adjudication a functional remedy? As part of your appraisal of *Tobey v. County of Bristol*, you should consider the trade-offs that are involved in the elaboration of a rule of arbitral enforcement.

3. From a practical and strategic perspective, what impact should the rule of *Tobey v. County of Bristol* have upon the conduct of arbitrating parties? What would you advise your client during the proceeding under the *Tobey* regime if you believed that the tribunal was likely to rule against him or her in the award? Doesn't the *Tobey* rule undermine any meaningful recourse to arbitration?

4. In anticipation of the U.S. Supreme Court's rulings in *Wilko v. Swan*, 346 U.S. 427 (1953), and *Rodriguez de Quijas v. Shearson/American Express, Inc.*, 490 U.S. 477 (1989), what opinion do you believe Mr. Justice Story had of arbitration as a mechanism for justice? Did he articulate a truly negative opinion of arbitration? What practical historical circumstances and characteristics of the then-contemporary legal system do you think influenced the perception of arbitration in *Tobey*? Have these circumstances and characteristics changed sufficiently to warrant a different systemic view of arbitration?

5. Assess the principle of freedom of contract (discussed in Chapter Two) in light of the opinion in *Tobey*.

6. Finally, in an earlier part of his opinion, Mr. Justice Story notes that arbitration agreements are not "against public policy." He further states that courts "have and can have no just objection to these domestic forums, and will enforce . . . their awards when fairly and lawfully made, without hesitation or question." What does this excerpt add to your understanding of the *Tobey* doctrine? Were U.S. courts at this time really bent on discouraging and undermining party recourse to private arbitral justice? What final evaluation do you reach of the *Tobey* doctrine?

2. THE UNITED STATES ARBITRATION ACT OF 1925

The United States Arbitration Act, more commonly known as the Federal Arbitration Act or the FAA, is a landmark piece of legislation that ended the era of would-be judicial hostility to arbitration in the United States. In many respects, it is a precocious example of a modern arbitration statute; enacted in 1925, it anticipates the central provisions of more contemporary statutes by some thirty to fifty years. It legitimizes arbitration agreements and establishes a presumption in favor of their enforceability. It also restricts the role of courts and provides limited grounds for the judicial supervision of awards. The objective of the Act was to rehabilitate arbitration as an adjudicatory mechanism and to give it the systemic autonomy it needed to function effectively as a remedial process. The FAA retains its original language in its current form; supplementary provisions, which coincide with and reinforce the original language and legislative intent, were added in 1970, 1988, and 1990.

The United States Arbitration Act

§ 1. "Maritime Transactions" and "Commerce" Defined: Exceptions to Operation of Title

"Maritime transactions," as herein defined, means charter parties, bills of lading of water carriers, agreements relating to wharfage, supplies furnished vessels or repairs of vessels, collisions, or any other matters in foreign commerce which, if the subject of controversy, would be embraced within admiralty jurisdiction; "commerce," as herein defined, means commerce among the several States or with foreign nations, or in any Territory of the United States or in the District of Columbia, or between any such Territory and another, or between any such Territory and any State or foreign nation, or between the District of Columbia and any State or Territory or foreign nation, but nothing herein contained shall apply to contracts of employment of seamen, railroad employees, or any other class of workers engaged in foreign or interstate commerce.

§ 2. Validity, Irrevocability, and Enforcement of Agreements to Arbitrate

A written provision in any maritime transaction or a contract evidencing a transaction involving commerce to settle by arbitration a controversy thereafter arising out of such contract or transaction, or the refusal to perform the whole or any part thereof, or an agreement in writing to submit to arbitration an existing controversy arising out of such a contract, transaction, or refusal, shall be valid, irrevocable, and enforceable, save upon such grounds as exist at law or in equity for the revocation of any contract.

§ 3. Stay of Proceedings Where Issue Therein Referable to Arbitration

If any suit or proceedings be brought in any of the courts of the United States upon any issue referable to arbitration under an agreement in writing for such arbitration, the court in which suit is pending, upon being satisfied that the issue involved in such suit or proceeding is referable to arbitration under such an agreement, shall on application of one of the parties stay the trial of the action until such arbitration has been had in accordance with the terms of the agreement, providing the applicant for the stay is not in default proceeding with such arbitration.

§ 4. Failure to Arbitrate under Agreement; Petition to United States Court Having Jurisdiction for Order to Compel Arbitration; Notice and Service Thereof; Hearing and Determination

A party aggrieved by the alleged failure, neglect, or refusal of another to arbitrate under a written agreement for arbitration may petition any United States district court which, save for such agreement, would have jurisdiction under Title 28, in a civil action or in admiralty of the subject matter of a suit arising out of the controversy between the parties, for an order directing that such arbitration proceed in the manner provided for in such agreement. Five days' notice in writing of such application shall be served upon the party in default. Service thereof shall be made in the manner provided by the Federal Rules of Civil Procedure. The court shall hear the parties, and upon being satisfied that the making of the agreement for arbitration or the failure to comply therewith is not in issue, the court shall make an order directing the parties to proceed to arbitration in accordance with the terms of the agreement. The hearing and proceedings, under such agreement, shall be within the district in which the petition for an order directing such arbitration is filed. If the making of the arbitration agreement or the failure, neglect, or refusal to perform the same be in issue, the court shall proceed summarily to the trial thereof. If no jury trial be demanded by the party alleged to be in default, or if the matter in dispute is within admiralty jurisdiction, the court shall hear and determine such issue. Where such an issue is raised, the party alleged to be in default may, except in cases of admiralty, on or before the return day of the notice of application, demand a jury trial of such issue, and upon such demand the court shall make an order referring the issue or issues to a jury in the manner provided by the Federal Rules of Civil Procedure, or may specially call a jury for that purpose. If the jury find[s] that no agreement in writing for arbitration was made or that there is no default in proceeding thereunder, the proceeding shall be dismissed. If the jury find[s] that an agreement for arbitration was made in writing and that there is a default in proceeding thereunder, the court shall make an order summarily directing the parties to proceed with the arbitration in accordance with the terms thereof.

§ 5.   Appointment of Arbitrators or Umpire

If in the agreement provision be made for a method of naming or appointing an arbitrator or arbitrators or an umpire, such method shall be followed; but if no method be provided therein, or if a method be provided and any party thereto shall fail to avail himself of such method, or if for any other reason there shall be a lapse in the naming of an arbitrator or arbitrators or umpire, or in filling a vacancy, then upon the application of either party to the controversy the court shall designate and appoint an arbitrator or arbitrators or umpire, as the case may require, who shall act under the said agreement with the same force and effect as if he or they had been specifically named therein; and unless otherwise provided in the agreement the arbitration shall be by a single arbitrator.

§ 6.   Application Heard as Motion

Any application to the court hereunder shall be made and heard in the manner provided by law for the making and hearing of motions, except as otherwise herein expressly provided.

§ 7.   Witnesses Before Arbitrators; Fees; Compelling Attendance

The arbitrators selected either as prescribed in this title or otherwise, or a majority of them, may summon in writing any person to attend before them or any of them as a witness and in a proper case to bring with him or them any book, record, document, or paper which may be deemed material as evidence in the case. The fees for such attendance shall be the same as the fees of witnesses before masters of the United States courts. Said summons shall issue in the name of the arbitrator or arbitrators or a majority of them and shall be signed by the arbitrators, or a majority of them, and shall be directed to the said person and shall be served in the same manner as subpoenas to appear and testify before the court; if any person or persons so summoned to testify shall refuse or neglect to obey said summons, upon petition the United States court in and for the district in which such arbitrators, or a majority of them, are sitting may compel the attendance of such person or persons before said arbitrator or arbitrators, or punish said person or persons for contempt in the same manner provided by law, for securing the attendance of witnesses or their punishment for neglect or refusal to attend in the courts of the United States.

§ 8. Proceedings Begun by Libel in Admiralty and Seizure of Vessel or Property

If the basis of jurisdiction be a cause of action otherwise justifiable in admiralty, then, notwithstanding anything herein to the contrary the party claiming to be aggrieved may begin his proceeding hereunder by libel and seizure of the vessel or other property of the other party according to the usual course of admiralty proceedings, and the court shall then have jurisdiction to direct the parties to proceed with the arbitration and shall retain jurisdiction to enter its decree upon the award.

§ 9. Award of Arbitrators; Confirmation; Jurisdiction; Procedure

If the parties in their agreement have agreed that a judgment of the court shall be entered upon the award made pursuant to the arbitration, and shall specify the court, then at any time within one year after the award is made any party to the arbitration may apply to the court so specified for an order confirming the award, and thereupon the court must grant such an order unless the award is vacated, modified, or corrected as prescribed in sections 10 and 11 of this title. If no court is specified in the agreement of the parties, then such application may be made to the United States court in and for the district within which such award was made. Notice of the application shall be served upon the adverse party, and thereupon the court shall have jurisdiction of such party as though he had appeared generally in the proceeding. If the adverse party is a resident of the district within which the award was made, such service shall be made upon the adverse party or his attorney as prescribed by law for service of notice of motion in an action in the same court. If the adverse party shall be a nonresident, then the notice of the application shall be served by the marshal of any district within which the adverse party may be found in like manner as other process of the court.

§ 10. Same; Vacation; Grounds; Rehearing

(a) In any of the following cases the United States court in and for the district wherein the award was made may make an order vacating the award upon the application of any party to the arbitration—

1. Where the award was procured by corruption, fraud, or undue means.

2. Where there was evident partiality or corruption in the arbitrators, or either of them.

3. Where the arbitrators were guilty of misconduct in refusing to postpone the hearing, upon sufficient cause shown, or in refusing to hear evidence

pertinent and material to the controversy; or of any other misbehavior by which the rights of any party have been prejudiced.

4. Where the arbitrators exceeded their powers, or so imperfectly executed them that a mutual, final, and definite award upon the subject matter submitted was not made.

5. Where an award is vacated and the time within which the agreement required the award to be made has not expired the court may, in its discretion, direct a rehearing by the arbitrators.

(b) The United States district court for the district wherein an award was made that was issued pursuant to section 580 of title 5 may make an order vacating the award upon the application of a person, other than a party to the arbitration, who is adversely affected or aggrieved by the award, if the use of arbitration or the award is clearly inconsistent with the factors set forth in section 572 of title 5.

§ 11. Same; Modification or Correction; Grounds; Order

In either of the following cases the United States court in and for the district wherein the award was made may make an order modifying or correcting the award upon the application of any party to the arbitration:

(a) Where there was an evident material miscalculation of figures or an evident material mistake in the description of any person, thing, or property referred to in the award.

(b) Where the arbitrators have awarded upon a matter not submitted to them, unless it is a matter not affecting the merits of the decision upon the matter submitted.

(c) Where the award is imperfect in matter of form not affecting the merits of the controversy.

The order may modify and correct the award, so as to effect the intent thereof and promote justice between the parties.

§ 12. Notice of Motions to Vacate or Modify; Service; Stay of Proceedings

Notice of a motion to vacate, modify, or correct an award must be served upon the adverse party or his attorney within three months after the award is filed or delivered. If the adverse party is a resident of the district within which the award was made, such service shall be made upon the adverse party or his attorney as prescribed by law for service of notice of motion in an action in the same court. If the adverse party shall be a nonresident then the notice of the application shall be served by the marshal of any district within which the adverse party may be found in like manner as other process of the court. For the purposes of the motion any judge who might make an order to stay the proceedings in an action brought in the same court may make an order, to be served with the notice of motion, staying the proceedings of the adverse party to enforce the award.

§ 13. Papers Filed with Order on Motions; Judgment; Docketing; Force and Effect; Enforcement

The party moving for an order confirming, modifying, or correcting an award shall, at the time such order is filed with the clerk for the entry of judgment thereon, also file the following papers with the clerk:

(a) The agreement; the selection or appointment, if any, of an additional arbitrator or umpire; and each written extension of the time, if any, within which to make the award.

(b) The award.

(c) Each notice, affidavit, or other paper used upon an application to confirm, modify, or correct the award, and a copy of each order of the court upon such an application.

The judgment shall be docketed as if it was rendered in an action.

The judgment so ordered shall have the same force and effect, in all respects, as, and be subject to all the provisions of law relating to, a judgment in an action; and it may be enforced as if it had been rendered in an action in the court in which it is entered.

§ 14. Contracts Not Affected

This title shall not apply to contracts made prior to January 1, 1926.

§ 15. Inapplicability of the Act of State doctrine

Enforcement of arbitral agreements, confirmation of arbitral awards, and execution upon judgments based on orders confirming such awards shall not be refused on the basis of the Act of State doctrine.

§ 16. Appeals

(a) An appeal may be taken from—

(1) an order—

(a) refusing a stay of any action under section 3 of this title,

(b) denying a petition under section 4 of this title to order arbitration to proceed,

(c) denying an application under section 206 of this title to compel arbitration,

(d) confirming or denying confirmation of an award or partial award, or

(e) modifying, correcting, or vacating an award;

(2) an interlocutory order granting, continuing, or modifying an injunction against an arbitration that is subject to this title; or

(3) a final decision with respect to an arbitration that is subject to this title.

(b) Except as otherwise provided in section 1292(b) of title 28, an appeal may not be taken from an interlocutory order—

(1) granting a stay of any action under section 3 of this title;

(2) directing arbitration to proceed under section 4 of this title;

(3) compelling arbitration to proceed under section 206 of this title;

(4) refusing to enjoin an arbitration that is subject to this title.

* * *

The FAA is presented below by individual section followed by relevant commentary. You should assess each section and evaluate its significance as a provision of law and for its impact upon the U.S. law of arbitration. Isolate the fundamental components of each section and identify the section's underlying purpose. What role does the content of the section play in the regulatory framework and in the practical operation of arbitration?

9 U.S.C. §§ 1–16 (1996)

§ 1. "Maritime Transactions" and "Commerce" Defined: Exceptions to Operation of Title

"Maritime transactions," as herein defined, means charter parties, bills of lading of water carriers, agreements relating to wharfage, supplies furnished vessels or repairs of vessels, collisions, or any other matters in foreign commerce which, if the subject of controversy, would be embraced within admiralty jurisdiction; "commerce," as herein defined, means commerce among the several States or with foreign nations, or in any Territory of the United States or in the District of Columbia, or between any such Territory and another, or between any such Territory and any State or foreign nation, or between the District of Columbia and any State or Territory or foreign nation, but nothing herein contained shall apply to contracts of employment of seamen, railroad employees, or any other class of workers engaged in foreign or interstate commerce.

Commentary

Section One defines the FAA's scope of application, *i.e.*, it identifies the circumstances in which the federal law of arbitration applies. According to the U.S. Supreme Court in *Prima Paint Corp. v. Flood & Conklin Mfg. Co.*, 388 U.S. 395 (1967), the FAA is "a congressional directive" to the federal courts, instructing them on how they should rule on issues of arbitration law. These remarks anticipate the federalism problems that will eventually arise. The judicial resolution of those federalism problems will enhance substantially the FAA's scope of application. As the opinion in *Southland Corp. v. Keating*, 465 U.S. 1 (1984), and the later decision in *Allied-Bruce Terminix Cos., Inc. v. Dobson*, 513 U.S. 265 (1995), demonstrate, the current rule is that the FAA is binding in federal question cases, diversity cases in which state law applies, and upon state courts ruling in state law cases that can be linked to interstate commerce. In other words, the FAA—in reality—is the national law of arbitration.

Under Section One, the FAA applies to maritime and commercial matters that are part of interstate commerce or which involve foreign commerce. The U.S. Supreme Court in *Citizens Bank v. Alafabco*, 539 U.S. 52 (2003), took an expansive view of interstate commerce. There, the Court held that commercial lending had a broad impact on the U.S. economy. Moreover, by enacting the FAA, Congress invoked its widest powers under the Commerce Clause. As a result, the FAA applied to transactions "in commerce" and "in the flow" of interstate commerce. It also appears from the language of Section One that the FAA does not apply to the resolution of disputes that arise from employment contracts or relationships. Presumably, the special rights of recourse that might have been available to workers in specialty areas of foreign or interstate commerce could be undermined by the use of arbitration. *Gilmer v. Interstate/Johnson Lane Corp.*, 500 U.S. 20 (1991), directly challenged the exclusion of employment contracts from the purview of the federal legislation on arbitration. There, the Court upheld an arbitral clause that was said to govern disputes arising out of a stock broker's employment contract, notwithstanding the language of Section One.

In 2001, the U.S. Supreme Court issued its landmark ruling in *Circuit City Stores, Inc. v. Adams*, 532 U.S. 105 (2001), holding that the employment contract exclusion in FAA § 1 only applied to the employment contracts of interstate transportation workers. Employers, therefore, could require all other employees to submit employment-related disputes to arbitration. Accordingly, the strong federal policy in favor of arbitration generally applied to the enforcement of arbitration agreements in employment relationships.

According to the Court, the FAA was enacted by Congress to eliminate the "hostility of American courts to the enforcement of arbitration agreements" and thereby to compel "judicial enforcement of a wide range of written arbitration agreements." Section 2 of the FAA, the Court further stated, provided for the enforceability of any "written provision in any maritime transaction or a contract evidencing a transaction involving commerce to settle by arbitration a controversy thereafter arising out of such contract or transaction." The Court had interpreted Section 2 as "implementing Congress' intent to exercise its commerce power to the full." Section 1, therefore, only exempted "contracts of employment of seamen, railroad employees, or any other class of workers engaged in foreign or interstate commerce" from the FAA's scope of application.

Because its holding was derived from a textual analysis of the statute, the Court stated that it "need not assess the legislative history of the exclusion provision." That legislative history became "problematic" when "sources...removed from the full Congress" were consulted. Furthermore, the Court saw no contradiction in its position that Congress would exempt from the scope of the statute only workers over whom it had jurisdiction in 1925, namely, seamen and railroad workers, and yet intend the Act to apply to workers over whom—pursuant to its limited Commerce Clause power—it had no control. "It is reasonable to assume that Congress excluded 'seamen' and 'railroad employees' from the FAA for the simple reason that it did not wish to unsettle...dispute resolution schemes covering certain workers."

Justices Stevens, Ginsburg, Breyer, and Souter dissented. In their dissenting opinions, the Justices explained that the FAA was originally intended to allow the arbitration of commercial and maritime disputes, and that there was no legislative intent to have the FAA govern in employment matters. The FAA was a "response to the refusal of courts to enforce commercial arbitration agreements, which were commonly used in the maritime context." The original bill, in fact, was drafted by the Committee on Commerce, Trade, and Commercial Law of the American Bar Association (ABA). A sponsor of the bill stated that the FAA intended "to give an opportunity to enforce an agreement [to arbitrate] in commercial contracts and admiralty contracts." The bill was originally opposed by representatives of organized labor, primarily the International Seamen's Union of America, "because of their concern that...[it] might authorize federal judicial enforcement of arbitration clauses in employment contracts."

It should be underscored that the FAA's legislative history makes clear that it was not intended to be a source of new substantive legal rights. In the words of one of its proponents, the FAA provides for the enforcement of ordinary contractual rights in areas of specialized commercial activity:

> This bill simply provides for one thing, and that is to give an opportunity to enforce an agreement in commercial contracts and admiralty contracts an agreement to arbitrate, when voluntarily placed in the document by the parties to it. It does not involve any new principle of law except to provide a simple method by which the parties may be brought before the court in order to give enforcement to that which they have already agreed to.... It does nothing more than that. It creates no new legislation, grants no new rights, except a remedy to enforce an agreement [to arbitrate] in commercial contracts and in admiralty contracts.

65 *Cong. Rec.* 1931 (1924) (statement of Rep. Graham). Congress considered the FAA as a means by which commercial parties could gain access to a private adjudicatory remedy through the exercise of their contract rights. It allowed the federal courts to give effect to those agreements. It was deemed a procedural enactment that created a statutory mechanism for enforcing arbitral agreements and awards:

> The principal support for the Act came from trade associations dealing in groceries and other perishables and from commercial and mercantile groups in the major trading centers.... Practically all who testified in support of the bill ... explained that the bill was designed to cover contracts between people in different states who shipped, bought, or sold commodities....

Prima Paint Corp. v. Flood & Conklin Mfg. Co., 388 U.S. 395, 409 n.2 (1967) (Black, J., dissenting).

This historical background demonstrates the enormous distance that separates the FAA's original meaning and purpose at the time of enactment from its current version in the decisional law. The courts have extended the reach of the FAA far beyond the adjudication of specialized commercial claims and have given the right to arbitrate not only a substantive character, but a constitutional stature as well. Moreover, the courts viewed the federalism questions that arose in connection with the

FAA as an opportunity to transform the legislation into a substantive law enactment. What began as a procedure for special interests became a cornerstone remedy of civil litigation.

§ 2. Validity, Irrevocability, and Enforcement of Agreements to Arbitrate

A written provision in any maritime transaction or a contract evidencing a transaction involving commerce to settle by arbitration a controversy thereafter arising out of such contract or transaction, or the refusal to perform the whole or any part thereof, or an agreement in writing to submit to arbitration an existing controversy arising out of such a contract, transaction, or refusal, shall be valid, irrevocable, and enforceable, save upon such grounds as exist at law or in equity for the revocation of any contract.

Commentary

Section Two is—historically and doctrinally—the centerpiece provision of the FAA. It establishes the legal validity of arbitration agreements. Section Two recognizes both the arbitral clause and the submission agreement as lawful forms of contract. Neither agreement violates public policy. Arbitral agreements are "valid, irrevocable, and enforceable"—a statement that clearly repudiates the past judicial practice of upholding arbitration agreements only once the arbitral tribunal had rendered an award. Merchants can decide for themselves whether to forgo the courts. An agreement to arbitrate can only be challenged on standard contract formation grounds, *i.e.*, the failure of consideration, adhesion, or unconscionability.

Challenging arbitration agreements for contract deficiencies, however, has not been very successful. The policy support for arbitration permits a great deal of latitude in the definition of contract validity. Unilateral and adhesionary contracts for arbitration are often enforced.

In *Harris v. Green Tree Financial Corp.*, 183 F.3d 173 (3d Cir. 1999), the U.S. Court of Appeals for the Third Circuit upheld a broad arbitration clause that granted only one of the contracting parties—the stronger one—the right to litigate certain claims. The court stated that "the mere fact Green Tree retains the option to litigate some issues in court, while the Harrises must arbitrate all claims does not make the arbitration agreement unenforceable. We have held repeatedly that inequality in bargaining power, alone, is not a valid basis upon which to invalidate an arbitration agreement." The court determined that the agreement was not unconscionable.

The California state Supreme Court has taken a particularly active role in policing the validity of arbitration agreements. It endorsed a far more expansive concept of unconscionability than the Third Circuit, emphasizing the need for a fully bilateral obligation to arbitrate. That position has influenced a number of other courts.

In *Armendariz v. Foundation Health Psychcare Services, Inc.*, 24 Cal.4th 83, 99 Cal.Rptr.2d 745, 6 P.3d 669 (2000), the California high court held that certain minimum requirements were necessary to create a legally enforceable arbitration agreement. The minimum requirements focused upon the parties' disparity of position and the possible compromise of the weaker party's rights. Under California law, an arbitration agreement imposed by the stronger party is unconscionable if it does not guarantee an arbitral process that protects discovery rights, provides a written decision that makes court review possible, impartial arbitrators, full damage relief, and limited costs. In particular, the obligation to arbitrate disputes must be mutual—equally applicable to both parties.

There can be little doubt that *Armendariz* states a position that is the polar opposite of its counterpart in *Harris*. It might be subject to federal preemption because it arguably has a negative bearing upon the validity of arbitration agreements. It nonetheless states a standard for minimum arbitral due process in settings in which parties are uneven and negotiation of the agreement is unavailable.

The form in which the arbitration agreement is presented has generated litigation. Courts, for example, have wrestled with the question of whether a provision for arbitration in an employee handbook constitutes a valid agreement to arbitrate. Some courts merely require that an agreement to arbitrate be physically discernable; others demand that employers provide some means to effectuate acknowledgement and/or rejection; and yet others seek an explicit and affirmative consent by the employee to the waiver of judicial process. *See, e.g., Leodori v. CIGNA Corp.*, 175 N.J. 293, 814 A.2d 1098, *cert. denied*, 540 U.S. 938 (2003). "Handbook" agreements generally are upheld unless they significantly and abusively compromise the legal rights of the employee. Moreover, it is clear that state contract law cannot target or disable arbitration contracts in particular.

The "in writing" requirement is generally construed flexibly by courts. For example, arbitration agreements need not be signed in order to be effective. Email transmissions can serve as a valid agreement to arbitrate as long as they contain the necessary language. Illiteracy does not constitute a defense to enforceability as long as there was an opportunity to read the agreement. The federal policy in favor of arbitration attenuates the rigor of contract formation requirements. *See, e.g., Asia Pacific Indus. Corp. v. Rainforest Café, Inc.*, 380 F.3d 383 (8th Cir. 2004); *Edwards v. Blockbuster, Inc.*, 400 F.Supp.2d 1305 (E.D. Okla. 2005).

A broad arbitral clause subjects all disputes related to the agreement to arbitration and any doubts are resolved in favor of arbitration. *See MedCam Inc. v. MCNC*, 414 F.3d 972 (8th Cir. 2005). A "presumption of arbitrability ... can be overcome only if it may be said with positive assurance that the arbitral clause is not susceptible to the interpretation that it covers the asserted dispute." *Orange Cty. Choppers, Inc. v. Goen Techn. Corp.*, 374 F.Supp.2d 372 (S.D.N.Y. 2005). A broad clause also covers disputes that the parties did not anticipate at the time of contracting or that were created by operation of law rather than the agreement. *See Masco Corp. v. Zurich Am. Ins. Co.*, 382 F.3d 624 (6th Cir. 2004) (when a broad arbitral clause exists, only express provisions excluding a particular dispute or the most commanding evidence will remove a dispute from the forum of arbitration).

A line of cases has developed in the decisional law under FAA § 2 addressing the question of whether an arbitration agreement between private parties could displace the authority and jurisdiction of government agencies to investigate and pursue remedies on behalf of aggrieved claimants. For example, in *Equal Employment Opportunity Commission v. Kidder, Peabody & Co., Inc.*, 156 F.3d 298 (2d Cir. 1998), the U.S. Court of Appeals for the Second Circuit affirmed a district court ruling that an arbitration agreement between an employer and employee precluded the Equal Employment Opportunity Commission (EEOC) from seeking purely monetary relief for the employee under the Age Discrimination in Employment Act (ADEA) in federal court. In its ruling, the court stated that "to allow the EEOC to recover monetary damages would frustrate the purpose of the [Federal Arbitration Act] (FAA) because an employee, having signed the agreement to arbitrate, could avoid arbitration by having the EEOC file in the federal forum seeking back pay on his or her behalf."

In contrast, the U.S. Court of Appeals for the Sixth Circuit held, in a split decision in *Equal Employment Opportunity Commission v. Frank's Nursery & Crafts, Inc.*, 177 F.3d 448 (6th Cir. 1999), that the EEOC was not required to arbitrate a Title VII statutory action—even though the employee signed an arbitration agreement. Given the broad grant of powers by the U.S. Congress to the EEOC, the Sixth Circuit concluded that the provisions of the FAA, preclusion principles, and waiver rules could not be used to treat an EEOC right of action as identical to an employee's own private right of action.

In *EEOC v. Waffle House, Inc.*, 534 U.S. 279 (2002), the U.S. Supreme Court held that an agreement between an employer and an employee to arbitrate workplace disputes did not bar the EEOC from obtaining either injunctive or victim-specific relief. The EEOC had brought suit in state court seeking injunctive relief and back pay, reinstatement, and damages on behalf of an employee who had been discharged after he had a seizure at work. The EEOC asserted a claim under Title I of the Americans with Disabilities Act on behalf of the employee, who was not a party to the suit. The Court held in a 6–3 ruling that the EEOC was not barred from seeking either injunctive or victim-specific relief for the employee.

The Court began by stating that the EEOC had the same authority under the ADA that it had under the Civil Rights Act, namely, the authority to bring injunctive actions to force employers to halt unlawful employment practices. The Court also stated that the FAA "does not mention enforcement by public agencies" and "does not purport to place any restriction on a nonparty's choice of judicial forum." The ADA "clearly makes the EEOC the master of its own case and confers on the agency the authority to evaluate the strength of the public interest at stake." According to the Court, it is both the EEOC's "province" to select a forum and to decide how public resources should be used to obtain victim-specific relief.

The Court reaffirmed the independent power of the EEOC to investigate and bring its own enforcement actions under Title VII and the ADA. It determined that, because of its independent power, the EEOC was not bound by an arbitration agreement signed by an employee, nor was it limited in its discretion as to what remedies it would seek on behalf of an employee. Just because an employee agreed to arbitrate disputes did not mean that the EEOC, acting upon that employee's allegations of discrimination, was bound by the agreement.

In all likelihood, the opinion will have only a minor impact upon the vast majority of employees who file discrimination cases with the EEOC. As noted by the Court itself, "the EEOC only files suit in a small fraction of the charges that employees file...." In "year 2000, the EEOC received 79,896 charges of employment discrimination...[and] only filed 291 lawsuits and intervened in 111 others." The Court further recognized that "the EEOC files less than two percent of all antidiscrimination claims in federal court." Thus, "permitting the EEOC access to victim-specific relief in cases where the employee has agreed to binding arbitration, but has not yet brought a claim in arbitration, will have a *negligible* effect on the federal policy favoring arbitration." And, it remains "an open question whether a settlement or arbitration judgment would affect the validity of the EEOC's claim or the character of relief the EEOC may seek."

In his dissent, Justice Thomas argued that, if an employee agreed to arbitration, the EEOC was bound by that agreement because the EEOC could do "on behalf of an employee that which an employee has agreed not to do for himself," namely, to seek monetary relief before a court. Justice Thomas further contended that, while "the EEOC has the statutory right to *bring* suit, it has no statutory entitlement to *obtain* a particular remedy." Thus, "whether a particular remedy is 'appropriate' in any given case is a question for a court and not for the EEOC." Because the employee had waived his right to obtain relief in a judicial forum by signing an arbitration agreement, the EEOC was precluded from seeking victim-specific relief in a judicial forum.

The question of whether a contracting party waives its right to demand the arbitration of contract disputes by participating in judicial proceedings regarding those disputes is an issue that has surfaced with greater frequency in the decisional law on arbitration. It arose initially in cases involving international commercial arbitration. There, the question was whether a party seeking interim relief from a court in aid of arbitration breached the arbitration agreement by engaging in such conduct. Any recourse to the courts prior to the rendition of the award and its enforcement could be seen as a violation of the promise to arbitrate. In contemporary practice, arbitration agreements in international contracts contain a provision stating that seeking interim relief from the courts does not violate the obligations under the agreement to arbitrate. Moreover, Article 9 of the UNCITRAL Model Law on Arbitration confirms that practice by providing: "It is not incompatible with an arbitration agreement for a party to request, before or during arbitration proceedings, from a court an interim measure of protection and for a court to grant such measure."

In the domestic setting, the question remains relatively novel and not fully decided in terms of specific issues. How does the language of the FAA direct or encourage the courts to rule on this matter? Does the judicial policy underlying the FAA provide a clearer, better, or more accurate answer than the express language of the statute? From the perspective of legal regulation, when should estoppel arguments become relevant or controlling in arbitration law for purposes of enforcing the agreement to arbitrate? Otherwise stated: When should a contracting party's conduct be deemed so antagonistic to the contract provisions that the party should be deprived of its right to compel arbitration or the enforcement of an arbitral award?

Judicial determinations appear to turn on how extensive the recourse was to courts and judicial procedures and whether the party's conduct prejudiced or burdened significantly the other party. In fact, prejudice to the opposing party is the "touchstone" of waiver for the right to arbitrate. Factors to be considered include: the timeliness of the motion to arbitrate, the degree to which the party seeking arbitration has contested the merits in court, extent of motion practice, assent to court orders, and the depth of discovery. *See Hoxworth v. Blinder, Robinson & Co.*, 980 F.2d 912 (3d Cir. 1992).

For example, the California Court of Appeal for the Second District held in *Davis v. Continental Airlines, Inc.*, 59 Cal.App.4th 205, 69 Cal. Rptr.2d 79 (1997), that the defendants waived their right to arbitration by unreasonably delaying their motion to compel arbitration until after engaging in extensive discovery with the plaintiff. The court held that the defendants waived their right to compel arbitration. It quoted *Christensen v. Dewor Developments*, 33 Cal.3d 778, 191 Cal.Rptr. 8, 661 P.2d 1088 (1983), stating that "although the burden of proof is heavy on the party seeking to establish waiver, which should not lightly be inferred in light of public policy favoring arbitration, a determination by a trial court that the right to compel arbitration has been waived ordinarily involves a question of fact, which is binding on the appellate court if supported by substantial evidence." The court held that the trial court's finding of a waiver was supported by substantial evidence. The court indicated that a waiver may be found when a party seeking arbitration "has (1) previously taken steps inconsistent with an intent to invoke arbitration, (2) unreasonably delayed in seeking arbitration, or (3) acted in bad faith or with willful misconduct." The court further stated that "mere participation in litigation is not enough" to constitute a waiver and that the party seeking to establish a waiver "must show that some prejudice has resulted from the other party's delay in seeking arbitration."

A Texas court of appeals held in *Vireo P.L.L.C. v. Cates,* 953 S.W.2d 489 (Tex. Ct. App. 1997), that a "plaintiff who sues on an arbitrable claim unconditionally, without having initiated arbitration of the claim or demanding specific performance of the arbitration agreement, creates in the defendant a right of election—the defendant may insist or not upon arbitration, as he chooses." The court further stated that, if the defendant does not insist upon arbitration, the contracting parties have "mutually repudiated the arbitration covenant as a matter of law and waived any right thereunder."

§ 3. Stay of Proceedings Where Issue Therein Referable to Arbitration

If any suit or proceedings be brought in any of the courts of the United States upon any issue referable to arbitration under an agreement in writing for such arbitration, the court in which suit is pending, upon being satisfied that the issue involved in such suit or proceeding is referable to arbitration under such an agreement, shall on application of one of the parties stay the trial of the action until such arbitration has been had in accordance with the terms of the agreement, providing the applicant for the stay is not in default proceeding with such arbitration.

Commentary

Section Three of the FAA outlines the legal effects of an arbitration agreement that is "valid, irrevocable, and enforceable" under Section Two. A valid agreement to arbitrate divests the courts of jurisdiction to entertain the dispute. A federal court cannot assume jurisdiction over a dispute that is properly the subject of an arbitration agreement. When the court is notified of the existence of an arbitration agreement, it can engage in only two types of inquiry: (1) whether the agreement to arbitrate is a valid contract (a Section Two scrutiny); and (2) whether the dispute in question is covered by ("referable to") arbitration (a Section Three scrutiny that amounts to a determination of the question of contractual inarbitrability). Once this scrutiny has been exercised, the court is obligated by statute to stay the court proceeding "until such arbitration has been had in accordance with the terms of the agreement. . . ."

Recent case law has endorsed an unequivocal approach to granting stays under FAA § 3 that is fully in compliance with the "strong federal policy in favor of arbitration." The principal, and to some extent preemptory, element of a petition for a stay is the existence of a valid agreement to arbitrate disputes. According to one federal district court, there is "little reason to require that an arbitration be commenced by a defendant against itself before a stay [of a court proceeding] can be ordered." Provided there is an enforceable contract of arbitration, a judicial action can be stayed even though no arbitral proceeding has been initiated. As "long as a written agreement to arbitrate exists[,] there is no specific requirement that arbitration actually be pending before a stay of litigation can be granted." The opinion represents a liberal interpretation of FAA § 3's requirement that "the party applying for the stay is not in default in proceeding with such arbitration." *See Sims v. Montell Chrysler, Inc.*, 317 F.Supp.2d 838 (N.D. Ill. 2004).

Even a non-signatory party can secure a stay under FAA § 3. In *Waste Mgmt., Inc. v. Residuos Indus. Multiquim, S.A. de C.V.*, 372 F.3d 339 (5th Cir. 2004), the Fifth Circuit held that FAA § 3 allows nonsignatories to an arbitration agreement to seek a mandatory stay of litigation in favor of a pending arbitration to which they are not a party, provided the litigation includes an issue referable to arbitration under the agreement. The basic test for granting such a stay is "whether proceeding with the litigation [would] destroy the signatories' right to a meaningful arbitration." There are three factors to consider: (1) the arbitrated and litigated disputes must involve the same operative facts; (2) the claims asserted in the arbitration and litigation must be "inherently inseparable"; and (3) the litigation must have a "critical impact" on the arbitration.

It should be noted that, under the arbitration laws of most national jurisdictions, challenges to the contractual validity of the arbitration agreement and to its scope of application would be referred to the arbitral tribunal. As stated earlier, this procedure reflects the application of the separability and *kompetenz-kompetenz* doctrines. U.S. arbitration law does not recognize the principle of *kompetenz-kompetenz*. Jurisdictional challenges, therefore, require a court proceeding under the language of Sections Two and Three. Judicial recourse on these grounds invites the use of dilatory tactics and can cause a year or two delay in the arbitral proceeding. This omission in the FAA underscores the early date of its enactment and suggests a need to revise and update the legislation.

Despite such gaps, however, the FAA remains a highly functional regulatory scheme. In fact, the federal decisional law has recently remedied the *kompetenz-kompetenz* lacuna to some extent. In its ruling in *First Options of Chicago, Inc. v. Kaplan*, 514 U.S. 938 (1995), the U.S. Supreme Court affirmed the power of the courts to rule on jurisdictional challenges under Sections Two and Three of the FAA, but also held that the parties could agree to submit such jurisdictional disputes to the arbitral tribunal. Such contractual grants of authority to arbitrators are likely to become a standard feature of both boilerplate and negotiated arbitration agreements.

Two aspects of the language of Section Three need to be underscored. The reference at the outset of the provision to actions "brought in any of the courts of the United States" confirms that the FAA is directed exclusively to the federal courts. There is no hint of a Congressional intent to establish rules for state courts or to elaborate rules of federal law that supersede state provisions. Also, the last clause of the section states that a party moving to stay a judicial trial on the ground of the existence of a valid arbitration agreement that encompasses the dispute submitted to the court must "not [be] in default in proceeding with such arbitration." The party seeking to avoid a lawsuit on the basis of the existence of an arbitration agreement must act diligently to maintain its rights. To conserve its right to arbitrate disputes, a party must invoke the process in a timely manner. If neither party invokes the agreed-upon arbitral mechanism, the agreement to arbitrate is rescinded by conduct—at least for purposes of the dispute in question. In effect, the parties are estopped from blocking judicial jurisdiction in the matter.

Finally, both Sections Two and Three fail to provide a defense to the enforcement of arbitration agreements and awards on the basis of the subject matter of the dispute. In fact, the FAA contains no mention whatsoever of the subject-matter inarbitrability defense—not even in Section Ten, which regulates the enforcement of awards. The absence of the defense strongly suggests that the enactment is procedural in character. There was no need to refer to subject matter considerations in any of the FAA provisions because other, more substantive statutes would supply the appropriate limits on the right to arbitrate. Moreover, the FAA is intended to apply to interstate maritime and commercial transactions. There was, therefore, no need to delimit the reach of legislation that already circumscribed itself. It applied only to typical commercial disputes.

The Act also fails to integrate public policy into its regulation of arbitral agreements and awards. The courts added an equivalent common law ground in their decisional law, but the legislation itself contains no mention of public policy. As with subject-matter inarbitrability, it may have been the expectation of Congress that other, more substantive statutes would define the role of public policy in arbitration on a subject-matter-by-subject-matter basis, thereby maintaining the FAA's procedural focus. However explained, the lack of reference in the FAA to subject-matter inarbitrability and public policy remains puzzling if for no other reason than they are standard concepts in most laws of arbitration. Their exclusion may have invited the decisional law to embark upon the curtailment of both defenses. At present, neither defense has a vital presence in the U.S. law of arbitration. Arbitration is now lawfully applied to all types of disputes, ranging from the standard commercial and maritime conflicts to disputes about statutory rights and consumer claims, with little mention of the impact of this wide jurisdiction upon the public interest.

* * *

In *Arthur Andersen LLP*, the Court addressed the issue of whether non-signatory parties are entitled to relief under FAA §§ 3 and 16.

ARTHUR ANDERSEN LLP v. CARLISLE
___ U.S. ___, 129 S.Ct. 1896, 173 L.Ed.2d 832 (2009).

JUSTICE SCALIA delivered the opinion of the Court.

Section 3 of the Federal Arbitration Act (FAA) entitles litigants in federal court to a stay of any action that is "referable to arbitration under an agreement in writing." ... Section 16(a)(1)(A), in turn, allows an appeal from "an order ... refusing a stay of any action under section 3." We address in this case whether appellate courts have jurisdiction under § 16(a) to review denials of stays requested by litigants who were not parties to the relevant arbitration agreement, and whether § 3 can ever mandate a stay in such circumstances.

I

Respondents Wayne Carlisle, James Bushman, and Gary Strassel set out to minimize their taxes from the 1999 sale of their construction-equipment company. Arthur Andersen, LLP, a firm that had long served as their company's accountant, auditor, and tax adviser, introduced them to Bricolage Capital, LLC, which in turn referred them for legal advice to Curtis, Mallet–Prevost, Colt & Mosle, LLP. According to respondents, these advisors recommended a "leveraged option strategy" tax shelter designed to create illusory losses through foreign-currency-exchange options. As a part of the scheme, respondents invested in various stock warrants through newly created limited liability corporations (LLCs), which are also respondents in this case. The respondents LLCs entered into investment-management agreements with Bricolage, specifying that "[a]ny controversy arising out of or relating to this Agreement or the br[ea]ch thereof, shall be settled by arbitration conducted in New York, New York, in accordance with the Commercial Arbitration Rules of the American Arbitration Association." ...

As with all that seems too good to be true, a controversy did indeed arise. The warrants respondents purchased turned out to be almost entirely worthless, and the Internal Revenue Service (IRS) determined in August 2000 that the "leveraged option strategy" scheme was an illegal tax shelter. The IRS initially offered conditional amnesty to taxpayers who had used such arrangements, but petitioners failed to inform respondents of that option. Respondents ultimately entered into a settlement program in which they paid the IRS all taxes, penalties, and interest owed.

Respondents filed this diversity suit in the Eastern District of Kentucky against Bricolage, Arthur Andersen and others [footnote omitted] (all except Bricolage and its employees hereinafter referred to as petitioners), alleging fraud, civil conspiracy, malpractice, breach of fiduciary duty, and negligence. Petitioners moved to stay the action, invoking § 3 of the FAA and arguing that the principles of equitable estoppel demanded that respondents arbitrate their claims under their investment agreements with Bricolage. [Footnote omitted.] The District Court denied the motions.

Petitioners filed an interlocutory appeal, which the Court of Appeals for the Sixth Circuit dismissed for want of jurisdiction. ... We granted *certiorari*. ...

II

Ordinarily, courts of appeals have jurisdiction only over "final decisions" of district courts. 28 U.S.C. § 1291. The FAA, however, makes an exception to that finality requirement, providing that "an appeal may be taken from ... an order ... refusing a stay of any action under section 3 of this title." 9 U.S.C. § 16 (a)(1)(A). By that provision's clear and unambiguous terms, any litigant who asks for a stay under § 3 is entitled to an immediate appeal from denial of that motion regardless of whether the litigant is in fact eligible for a stay. Because each petitioner in this case explicitly asked for a stay pursuant to § 3, ... the Sixth Circuit had jurisdiction to review the District Court's denial.

The courts that have declined jurisdiction over § 3 appeals of the sort at issues here have done so by conflating the jurisdictional question with the merits of the appeal. They reason that because stay motions premised on equitable estoppel seek to expand (rather than simply vindicate) agreements, they are not cognizable under §§ 3 and 4, and therefore the relevant motions are not actually "under" those provisions. ... The dissent makes this step explicit, by reading the appellate jurisdictional provision of § 16 as "calling for a look-through" to the substantive provisions of § 3. ...Jurisdiciton over the appeal, however, "must be determined by focusing upon the category of order appealed from, rather than upon the strength of the grounds for reversing the order." *Behrens v. Pelletier*, 516 U.S. 299, 311, 116 S. Ct. 834, 133 L. Ed. 2d 773 (1996).[1] The jurisdictional statute here unambiguously makes the underlying merits irrelevant, for even utter frivolousness of the underlying request for a § 3 stay cannot turn a denial into something other than "an order ... refusing a stay of any action under section 3." ...

Respondents argue that this reading of § 16(a) will produce a long parade of horribles, enmeshing courts in fact-intensive jurisdictional inquiries and permitting frivolous interlocutory appeals. Even if these objections could surmount the plain language of the statute, we would not be persuaded. Determination of whether § 3 was invoked in a denied stay request is immeasurably more simple and less factbound than the threshold determination respondents would replace it with: whether the litigant was a party to the contract (an especially difficult question when the written agreement is not signed). It is more appropriate to grapple with that merits question after the court has accepted jurisdiction over the case. Second, there are ways of minimizing the impact of abusive appeals. Appellate courts can streamline the deposition of meritless claims and even authorize the district court's retention of jurisdiction when an appeal

---

1. Federal courts lack subject matter jurisdiction when an asserted federal claim is "so insubstantial, implausible, foreclosed by prior decisions of this Court, or otherwise completely devoid of merit as not to involve a federal controversy." *Steel Co. v. Citizens for Better Environment*, 523 U.S. 83, 89, 118 S. Ct. 1003, 140 L. Ed. 2d 210 (1998) (quoting *Oneida Indian Nation of N.Y. v. County of Oneida*, 414 U.S. 661, 666, 94 S. Ct. 772, 39 L. Ed. 2d 73 (1974)). Respondents have not relied upon this line of cases as an alternative rationale for rejection of jurisdiction, and there are good reasons for treating subject-matter jurisdiction differently, in that respect, from the appellate jurisdiction here conferred. A frivolous federal claim, if sufficient to confer jurisdiction, would give the court power to hear related state-law claims, see 28 U.S.C. § 1367; no such collateral consequences are at issue here. And while an insubstantial federal claim can be said not to "aris[e] under the Constitution, laws, or treaties of the United States," § 1331, insubstantiality of the merits can hardly convert a judge's "order ... refusing a stay" into an "order ... refusing" something else. But we need not resolve this question today.

is certified as frivolous. ....And, of course, those inclined to file dilatory appeals must be given pause by courts' authority to "award just damages and single or double costs to the appellee" whenever an appeal is "frivolous." ...

III

Even if the Court of Appeals were correct that it had no jurisdiction over meritless appeals, its ground for finding this appeal meritless was in error. We take the trouble to address that alternative ground, since if the Court of Appeals is correct on the merits point we will have awarded petitioners a remarkably hollow victory. We consider, therefore, the Sixth Circuit's underlying determination that those who are not parties to a written arbitration agreement are categorically ineligible for relief.

Section 2—the FAA's substantive mandate—makes written arbitration agreements "valid, irrevocable, and enforceable, save upon such grounds as exist at law or in equity for the revocation of a contract." That provision creates substantive federal law regarding the enforceability of arbitration agreements, requiring courts "to place such agreements upon the same footing as other contracts." ... Section 3, in turn, allows litigants already in federal court to invoke agreements made enforceable by § 2. That provision requires the court, "on application of one of the parties,"[2] to stay the action if it involves an "issue referable to arbitration under an agreement in writing." ...

Neither provision purports to alter background principles of state contract law regarding the scope of agreements (including the question of who is bound by them). Indeed § 2 explicitly retains an external body of law governing revocation (such grounds "as exist at law or in equity").[3] And we think § 3 adds no substantive restriction to § 2's enforceability mandate. "[S]tate law," therefore, is applicable to determine which contracts are binding under § 2 and enforceable under § 3 "*if* that law arose to govern issues concerning the validity, revocability, and enforceability of contracts generally." ... Because "traditional principles" of state law allow a contract to be enforced by or against nonparties to the contract through "assumption, piercing the corporate veil, alter ego, incorporation by reference, third-party, beneficiary theories, waiver and estoppel," ... the Sixth Circuit's holding that nonparties to a contract are categorically barred from § 3 relief was error.

---

2. Respondents do not contest that the term "parties" in § 3 refers to parties to the litigation rather than parties to the contract. The adjacent provision, which explicitly refers to the "subject matter of a suit arising out of the controversy between the parties," 9 U.S.C. § 4, unambiguously refers to adversaries in the action, and "identical words and phrases within the same statute should normally be given the same meaning." ... Even without benefit of that canon, we would not be disposed to believe that the statute allows a party to the contract who is not a party to the litigation to apply for a stay of the proceeding.

3. We have said many times that federal law requires that "questions of arbitrability ... be addressed with a healthy regard for the federal policy favoring arbitration." ... Whatever the meaning of this vague prescription, it cannot possibly require the disregard of state law *permitting* arbitration by or against nonparties to the written arbitration agreement.

Respondents argue that, as a matter of federal law, claims to arbitration by nonparties are not "referable to arbitration *under* an agreement in writing," 9 U.S.C. § 3 (emphasis added), because they "seek to bind a signatory to an arbitral obligation *beyond* that signatory's strictly contractual obligation to arbitrate." ... Perhaps that would be true if § 3 mandated stays only for disputes between parties to a written arbitration agreement. But that is not what the statute says. It says that stays are required if the claims are "referable to arbitration under an agreement in writing." If a written arbitration provision is made enforceable against (or for the benefit of) a third party under state contract law, the statute's terms are fulfilled.[4]

Respondents' final fallback consists of reliance upon *dicta* in our opinions, such as the statement that "arbitration ... is a way to resolve those disputes but only those disputes that the parties have agreed to submit to arbitration," ... and the statement that "[i]t goes without saying that a contract cannot bind a non-party." ... The former statement pertained to *issues* parties agreed to arbitrate, and the latter referred to an entity (the Equal Employment Opportunity Commission) which obviously had no third-party obligations under the contract in question. Neither these nor any of our other cases have presented for decision the question whether arbitration agreements that are otherwise enforceable by (or against) third parties trigger protection under the FAA.

Respondents may be correct in saying that courts' application of equitable estoppel to impose an arbitration agreement upon strangers to the contract has been "somewhat loose." ... But we need not decide here whether the relevant state contract law recognizes equitable estoppel as a ground for enforcing contracts against third parties, what standard it would apply, and whether petitioners would be entitled to relief under it. These questions have not been briefed before us and can be addressed on remand. It suffices to say that no federal law bars the State from allowing petitioners to enforce the arbitration agreement against respondents and that § 3 would require a stay in this case if it did.

* * *

We hold that the Sixth Circuit had jurisdiction to review the denial of petitioners' request for a § 3 stay and that a litigant who was not a party to the relevant arbitration agreement may invoke § 3 if the relevant state contract law allows him to enforce the agreement. The judgment of the Court of Appeals for the Sixth Circuit is reversed, and the case is remanded for further proceedings consistent with this opinion.

It is so ordered.

---

4. We thus reject the dissent's contention that contract law's long-standing endorsement of third-party enforcement is "a weak premise for inferring an intent to allow third parties to obtain a § 3 stay." ... It seems to us not weak at all, in light of the terms of the statute. There is no doubt that, where state law permits it, a third-party claim is "referable to arbitration under an agreement in writing." It is not our role to conform an unambiguous statute to what we think "Congress probably intended." ...

DISSENT

JUSTICE SOUTER, with whom THE CHIEF JUSTICE and JUSTICE STEVENS join, dissenting.

Section 16 of the Federal Arbitration Act (FAA) authorizes an interlocutory appeal from the denial of a motion under § 3 to stay a district court action pending arbitration. The question is whether it opens the door to such an appeal at the behest of one who has not signed a written arbitration agreement. Based on the longstanding congressional policy limiting interlocutory appeals, I think the better reading of the statutory provisions disallows such an appeal, and therefore respectfully dissent.

Section 16(a) of the FAA provides that "[a]n appeal may be taken from . . . an order . . . refusing a stay of any action under section 3 of this title." . . . The Court says that any litigant who asks for and is denied a § 3 stay is entitled to an immediate appeal. . . . The majority's assumption is that "under section 3" is merely a labeling requirement, without substantive import, but this fails to read § 16 in light of the "firm congressional policy against interlocutory or 'piecemeal' appeals." . . .

The right of appeal is "a creature of statute," . . . and Congress has granted the Federal Courts of Appeals jurisdiction to review "final decisions," 28 U.S.C. § 1291. "This insistence on finality and prohibition of piecemeal review discourage undue litigiousness and leaden-footed administration of justice." . . . Congress has, however, "recognized the need of exceptions for interlocutory orders in certain types of proceedings where the damage of error unreviewed before the judgment is definitive and complete . . . has been deemed greater than the disruption caused by intermediate appeal." . . . Section 16 functions as one such exception, but departures from "the dominant rule in federal appellate practice," . . . are extraordinary interruptions to the normal process of litigation and ought to be limited carefully.

An obvious way to limit the scope of such an extraordinary interruption would be to read the § 16 requirement that the stay have been denied "under section 3" as calling for a look-through to the provisions of § 3, and to read § 3 itself as offering a stay only to signatories of an arbitration agreement. It is perfectly true that in general a third-party beneficiary can enforce a contract, but this is a weak premise for inferring an intent to allow third parties to obtain a § 3 stay and take a § 16 appeal. While it is hornbook contract law that third parties may enforce contracts for their benefit as a matter of course, interlocutory appeals are a matter of limited grace. Because it would therefore seem strange to assume that Congress meant to grant the right to appeal a § 3 stay denial to anyone as peripheral to the core agreement as a nonsignatory, it follows that Congress probably intended to limit those able to seek a § 3 stay.

Asking whether a § 3 movant is a signatory provides a bright-line rule with predictable results to aid courts in determining jurisdiction over § 16 interlocutory appeals. And that rule has the further virtue of mitigating the risk of intentional delay by savvy parties who seek to frustrate litigation by gaming the system. Why not move for a § 3 stay? If granted, arbitration will be mandated, and if denied, a lengthy appeal may wear down the opponent. The majority contends . . . "that there are ways of minimizing the impact of abusive appeals." Yes, but the sanctions suggested apply to the frivolous, not to the far-fetched; and as the majority's opinion concludes, such an attenuated claim of equitable estoppel as petitioners raise here falls short of the sanctionable.

Because petitioners were not parties to the written arbitration agreement, I would hold they could not move to stay the District Court proceedings under § 3, with the consequence that the Court of Appeals would have no jurisdiction under § 16 to entertain their appeal. I would accordingly affirm the judgment of the Sixth Circuit.

Notes and Questions

1. Would you characterize *Arthur Andersen LLP* as an opinion that is favorable to arbitration? Why? If not, why not?

2. What rights do nonsignatory parties have in relation to the FAA?

3. What doctrinal relationship exists between FAA § 3 and FAA § 16?

4. Does the majority opinion only support the federal policy on arbitration or does it also give effect to the interests of justice? Are the latter two factors synonymous?

5. Does the dissent confound or enlighten the matter? Why?

6. What is the dissent's primary rationale?

§ 4. Failure to Arbitrate under Agreement; Petition to United States Court Having Jurisdiction for Order to Compel Arbitration; Notice and Service Thereof; Hearing and Determination

A party aggrieved by the alleged failure, neglect, or refusal of another to arbitrate under a written agreement for arbitration may petition any United States district court which, save for such agreement, would have jurisdiction under Title 28, in a civil action or in admiralty of the subject matter of a suit arising out of the controversy between the parties, for an order directing that such arbitration proceed in the manner provided for in such agreement. Five days' notice in writing of such application shall be served upon the party in default. Service thereof shall be made in the manner provided by the Federal Rules of Civil Procedure. The court shall hear the parties, and upon being satisfied that the making of the agreement for arbitration or the failure to comply therewith is not in issue, the court shall make an order directing the parties to proceed to arbitration in accordance with the terms of the agreement. The hearing and proceedings, under such agreement, shall be within the district in which the petition for an order directing such arbitration is filed. If the making of the arbitration agreement or the failure, neglect, or refusal to perform the same be in issue, the court shall proceed summarily to the trial thereof. If no jury trial be demanded by the party alleged to be in default, or if the matter in dispute is within admiralty jurisdiction, the court shall hear and determine such issue. Where such an issue is raised, the party alleged to be in default may, except in cases of admiralty, on or before the return day of the notice of application, demand a jury trial of such issue, and upon such demand the court shall make an order referring the issue or issues to a jury in the manner provided by the Federal Rules of Civil Procedure, or may specially call a jury for that purpose. If the jury find[s] that no agreement in writing for arbitration was made or that there is no default in proceeding thereunder, the proceeding shall be dismissed. If the jury find[s] that an agreement for arbitration was made in writing and that there is a default in proceeding thereunder, the court shall make an order summarily directing the parties to proceed with the arbitration in accordance with the terms thereof.

Commentary

Section Four authorizes the federal courts to compel party compliance with the agreement to arbitrate. It also implies that the federal courts have a duty to assist the arbitral process when the exercise of coercive legal authority is necessary to the operation of the process. Along with Section Two, this provision expressly reverses the former judicial hostility to arbitration. It commands courts to take an active role in sustaining the contractual recourse to arbitration. One of the parties to the arbitration agreement must invoke the court's jurisdiction and authority by establishing the existence of a written agreement to arbitrate and demonstrating the other party's failure to abide by the contract. Furthermore, the court with proper jurisdiction is the court that would have had jurisdiction over the matter had the parties not agreed to arbitration.

The remainder of the provision is quite complex. Despite the intricacy of the language, the applicable regime appears to be that, before the requested court can issue an order compelling a party to arbitrate, it must ascertain that an arbitration agreement, in fact, does exist. Once the existence of the agreement is established, the requested court must determine whether the recalcitrant party's refusal to comply is unwarranted in the circumstances. The party allegedly in breach of the agreement has the right to request a jury trial on both issues (except in California).

The statement of the applicable procedure appears excessive for an arbitration statute. It reveals a preoccupation with achieving legal procedural regularity in the disposition of issues arising in arbitration law. This feature of the statute is also in evidence in other provisions of the FAA, confirming its status as a set of directives to the federal courts, but also raising questions about the suitability of the statutory approach to the regulation of arbitration. Guaranteeing compliance with constitutional standards of legality in an action to compel arbitration is perhaps unnecessary and counterproductive. Providing for the possible jury determination of the relevant issues invites the type of delay that can frustrate the recourse to arbitration. A court determination of the issues would advance the interests of arbitration without compromising the basic rights of the parties—especially in specialized commercial sectors. The FAA's regulatory focus, in some respects, gives arbitration a secondary status. The chief objective is not to establish a set of rules for the operation of the arbitral process, but rather to integrate arbitration into the substantive and procedural design of the legal system.

§ 5. Appointment of Arbitrators or Umpire

If in the agreement provision be made for a method of naming or appointing an arbitrator or arbitrators or an umpire, such method shall be followed; but if no method be provided therein, or if a method be provided and any party thereto shall fail to avail himself of such method, or if for any other reason there shall be a lapse in the naming of an arbitrator or arbitrators or umpire, or in filling a vacancy, then upon the application of either party to the controversy the court shall designate and appoint an arbitrator or arbitrators or umpire, as the case may require, who shall act under the said agreement with the same force and effect as if he or they had been specifically named therein; and unless otherwise provided in the agreement the arbitration shall be by a single arbitrator.

Commentary

Section Five adds further content to the duty of the courts to assist and cooperate with arbitral proceedings. At the request of one of the parties, a court can nominate an arbitrator when the parties cannot agree upon the designation or one party refuses to comply with its contractual obligation to name an arbitrator. The provision gives the principle of freedom of contract proper recognition: The parties, through their agreement, control the procedure for nominating arbitrators. It is only in circumstances in which freedom of contract fails, *i.e.*, when the agreement is silent and no agreement can be reached subsequently or when there is a refusal to comply with the agreed-upon procedure, that the court can intervene (at the request of a party) and remedy the stalemate. While the agreement to arbitrate eliminates judicial authority to rule on the dispute, coercive judicial power surrounds the operation of the arbitral process. When the contractual rule of law fails, the courts can guarantee the enforcement of contractual obligations. Court-designated arbitrators have the same status and authority as party-appointed arbitrators.

Section Five makes no mention of the possible role administering arbitral institutions might play in naming an arbitrator on behalf of a party or initiating a court proceeding to nominate an arbitrator. The development of arbitral practice has made such procedures commonplace. Once again, the omission indicates that, even though the FAA is a viable arbitration statute, some of its content needs to be aligned with the contemporary development of arbitral practice. Finally, Section Five adopts a rebuttable preference for a sole arbitrator. From a practical perspective, such a preference facilitates judicial supervision and the efficiency of arbitration. Designating one or two members of a three-member panel along with a neutral arbitrator would require more extensive court intervention and further construction of the arbitration agreement.

§ 6. Application Heard as Motion

Any application to the court hereunder shall be made and heard in the manner provided by law for the making and hearing of motions, except as otherwise herein expressly provided.

Commentary

Section Six establishes equivalency between court proceedings relating to arbitration and any other action filed before the federal courts. Motions pertaining to arbitral proceedings shall not be subject to any extraordinary administrative requirements. The statute, however, reserves the right to amend ordinary court procedures, presumably to advance the interests of the arbitral process.

§ 7. Witnesses Before Arbitrators; Fees; Compelling Attendance

The arbitrators selected either as prescribed in this title or otherwise, or a majority of them, may summon in writing any person to attend before them or any of them as a witness and in a proper case to bring with him or them any book, record, document, or paper which may be deemed material as evidence in the case. The fees for such attendance shall be the same as the fees of witnesses before masters of the United States courts. Said summons shall issue in the name of the arbitrator or arbitrators or a majority of them and shall be signed by the arbitrators, or a majority of them, and shall be directed to the said person and shall be served in the same manner as subpoenas to appear and testify before the court; if any person or persons so summoned to testify shall refuse or neglect to obey said summons, upon petition the United States court in and for the district in which such arbitrators, or a majority of them, are sitting may compel the attendance of such person or persons before said arbitrator or arbitrators, or punish said person or persons for contempt in the same manner provided by law, for securing the attendance of witnesses or their punishment for neglect or refusal to attend in the courts of the United States.

Commentary

Section Seven gives arbitrators unique evidence-gathering powers. The adjudicatory authority of the arbitrators extends to nonarbitrating parties who can be ordered to appear and testify or to comply with requests for documents or other evidentiary elements. The language of Section Seven is unequivocal: "[t]he arbitrators ... may summon ... *any* person...." (Emphasis added). Therefore, when the FAA governs the arbitral proceeding, arbitrators have the same subpoena powers as a court of law. If the third party refuses to comply with the order, the arbitral tribunal can petition the appropriate federal court to compel the party to comply, under penalty of the court's power to impose sanctions for contempt. In issuing its order, the arbitral tribunal must satisfy ordinary notification requirements and a majority of the arbitrators must sign the order.

Granting arbitrators subpoena power over third-parties generally is a unique conferral of power. The drafters of the FAA intended to give the arbitrators the tools necessary to engage in effective record-building. Arbitrators could not decide without thorough access to, and understanding of, the facts. Despite its practical utility in the gathering of evidence, the ability of arbitrators to enjoin third-parties violates the contractual foundation of arbitration. The affected third-parties never agreed to participate in the arbitration and, because the arbitration is a private and consensual proceeding, there is no legal basis upon which to subject them to the arbitrators' adjudicatory authority, except for the language of Section Seven. The provision implies that arbitration implicates the public interest—a position that is manifestly inconsistent with the contractual definition of arbitral adjudication in Section Two. Such extensive powers may have made sense within the confines of specialized commercial communities, but—once the reach of the arbitral process is extended and given more general application—providing for the exercise of arbitral powers beyond the arbitrating parties, even for the exclusive purpose of evidence-gathering, should be reconsidered.

The federal courts are divided on the question. The Third Circuit, in *Hay Group, Inc. v. E.B.S. Acquisition Corp.*, 360 F.3d 404 (3d Cir. 2004), held that FAA § 7 conferred limited subpoena powers on arbitrators and did not give them the authority to compel nonparties to comply with prehearing discovery requests. In *Stolt-Nielsen S.A. v. Celanese AG*, 430 F.3d 567 (2d Cir. 2005), the Second Circuit held that FAA § 7 should be broadly construed to allow arbitrators to subpoena any evidence that was material to the case. Arbitrators could compel nonparties to testify and produce documents at both preliminary and final hearings.

§ 8. Proceedings Begun by Libel in Admiralty and Seizure of Vessel or Property

If the basis of jurisdiction be a cause of action otherwise justifiable in admiralty, then, notwithstanding anything herein to the contrary the party claiming to be aggrieved may begin his proceeding hereunder by libel and seizure of the vessel or other property of the other party according to the usual course of admiralty proceedings, and the court shall then have jurisdiction to direct the parties to proceed with the arbitration and shall retain jurisdiction to enter its decree upon the award.

Commentary

Section Eight deals with maritime litigation and the seizure of assets for the satisfaction of claims. It essentially transposes the jurisdictional rules from the judicial to the arbitral setting. The presence of the "res" is necessary to the assertion of arbitral jurisdiction and the accompanying judicial supervision of the process.

§ 9. Award of Arbitrators; Confirmation; Jurisdiction; Procedure

If the parties in their agreement have agreed that a judgment of the court shall be entered upon the award made pursuant to the arbitration, and shall specify the court, then at any time within one year after the award is made any party to the arbitration may apply to the court so specified for an order confirming the award, and thereupon the court must grant such an order unless the award is vacated, modified, or corrected as prescribed in sections 10 and 11 of this title. If no court is specified in the agreement of the parties, then such application may be made to the United States court in and for the district within which such award was made. Notice of the application shall be served upon the adverse party, and thereupon the court shall have jurisdiction of such party as though he had appeared generally in the proceeding. If the adverse party is a resident of the district within which the award was made, such service shall be made upon the adverse party or his attorney as prescribed by law for service of notice of motion in an action in the same court. If the adverse party shall be a nonresident, then the notice of the application shall be served by the marshal of any district within which the adverse party may be found in like manner as other process of the court.

Commentary

Section Nine establishes that a party, within one year of the rendering of the award, may apply to a court for an order confirming the award. The provision recites the standard requirements for court jurisdiction and for effectuating the enforcement procedure. The provision takes the principle of contractual freedom into account: The parties may choose the court that will issue the order confirming the award prospectively in their agreement. Judicial confirmation of the award begins the process of coercive enforcement of the award against the noncomplying party.

In *Photopaint Techn., LLC v. Smartlens Corp.*, 335 F.3d 152 (2d Cir. 2003) the Second Circuit held that the FAA establishes a one-year statute of limitations for the judicial confirmation of arbitral awards. Even though FAA § 9 was written in the conditional tense, it should be interpreted as being imperative. The Fourth and Eighth Circuits, however, read the provision as permissible, allowing confirmations beyond the one-year time period. The conflict in interpretation has created a split in the federal circuits on this matter. A rigorous rule on the proscription of confirmation actions could have a negative impact upon arbitration by making it less effective and more expensive. It could also be argued that a one-year prescriptive rule enhances the finality and efficacy of the arbitral process.

§ 10. Same; Vacation; Grounds; Rehearing

(a) In any of the following cases the United States court in and for the district wherein the award was made may make an order vacating the award upon the application of any party to the arbitration—

1. Where the award was procured by corruption, fraud, or undue means.

2. Where there was evident partiality or corruption in the arbitrators, or either of them.

3. Where the arbitrators were guilty of misconduct in refusing to postpone the hearing, upon sufficient cause shown, or in refusing to hear evidence pertinent and material to the controversy; or of any other misbehavior by which the rights of any party have been prejudiced.

4. Where the arbitrators exceeded their powers, or so imperfectly executed them that a mutual, final, and definite award upon the subject matter submitted was not made.

5. Where an award is vacated and the time within which the agreement required the award to be made has not expired the court may, in its discretion, direct a rehearing by the arbitrators.

(b) The United States district court for the district wherein an award was made that was issued pursuant to section 580 of title 5 may make an order vacating the award upon the application of a person, other than a party to the arbitration, who is adversely affected or aggrieved by the award, if the use of arbitration or the award is clearly inconsistent with the factors set forth in section 572 of title 5.

Commentary

Section Ten articulates the grounds upon which a federal district court with appropriate jurisdiction can refuse to confirm and enforce an arbitral award. The action, known as "vacatur" of the award, renders the award unenforceable by coercive legal means. The basis for denying legal effect to an arbitral award is quite limited. In the main, it centers upon significant procedural deficiencies. The paucity of grounds and their narrowness reflect the FAA's liberal regulatory policy. The spirit of that policy has been reinforced by the decisional law. Any one of the four grounds in Section Ten could have become a significant obstacle to the enforcement of awards. The courts could have broadly construed the words "undue means," "evident partiality," "misconduct," or "imperfect execution of powers" and conducted a relatively rigorous scrutiny of awards. Federal courts have engaged in a modest and undemanding review of awards that sometimes borders on the perfunctory. A nearly irrebuttable presumption exists in the federal case law that arbitral awards, once rendered, are legally enforceable.

As to the statutory grounds themselves: they are only four in number; they avoid any reference to a substantive basis for review (thereby, impliedly eliminating the possibility of a merits review of awards); they expressly relegate judicial scrutiny to violations of basic procedural fairness; and they indicate, by their number and content, a statutory policy favoring the enforcement of awards. Parties can obtain judicial relief from an award only when the arbitral trial was manifestly unfair and arbitrator abuse characterized the proceeding. Arbitral proceedings must conform to the minimum guarantees of due process: the right to receive notice, to be heard, and to have the arguments presented considered by the tribunal.

Grounds (a) and (b): The presence of wholesale illegitimacy, such as bribery, threats of violence, or other forms of intimidation, will invalidate an award. In all likelihood, the determination in the award reflects the corruption of the process through "undue means," rather than a disinterested evaluation of the evidence and the arguments. In *Superadio Ltd. Partnership v. Winstar Radio Productions, LLC*, 446 Mass. 330, 844 N.E.2d 246 (2006), the Massachusetts Supreme Judicial Court held that "undue means" under the Massachusetts arbitration law meant "underhanded, conniving, or unlawful" behavior that is similar to corruption or fraud.

Grounds (c) and (d): The arbitrators also must avoid slightly more technical violations of their adjudicatory mandate. Their conduct of the proceedings cannot "prejudice" the right of either party to a fair hearing. They cannot rule on matters not submitted and must provide the parties with a ruling that resolves the dispute. The decisional law liberally construes these statutory requirements. Arbitrators are not required to conduct proceedings in a judicial manner, but rather need to satisfy basic procedural standards. The vast majority of awards are enforceable because most arbitrators are capable of conducting proceedings that satisfy minimal requirements of professional adjudication.

Ground (e): In those rare instances in which an award is vacated, the court can order the arbitrators to rehear the matter and render another award, provided the arbitration agreement has not lapsed and the court believes a rehearing serves the best interest of the parties and justice. Resubmission of the matter to the original arbitrators obviates the need to begin the adjudicatory process anew. The resubmission procedure, however, also signifies that corrective judicial supervision not only is exceptional and limited to significant procedural flaws, but its impact may be relegated to a reconsideration of the matter by the arbitrators. The courts' function then is to preserve whenever and however possible the parties' reference to arbitration. The content of Section Ten, therefore, guarantees the systemic autonomy of the arbitral process by strictly limiting judicial supervision and by having the courts safeguard the results of the process.

Section Ten impliedly eliminates the judicial review of the merits of awards because it contains no grounds for conducting the supervision of awards on that basis and its list of grounds for review is presumably exhaustive. Moreover, the provision contains no reference to the subject-matter inarbitrability defense or the public policy exception to the enforcement of arbitral awards. Apparently, U.S. domestic arbitral awards cannot be challenged on a substantive law basis. The absence of these grounds makes the domestic U.S. law of arbitration rather unique. As noted earlier, it is likely that the limitation in Section One of the statute's scope of application to maritime and commercial matters implies a subject-matter inarbitrability defense and that Congress intended to delineate the subject matter and public policy limits on arbitration in other statutes that addressed directly the subject matter deemed inapposite for arbitral adjudication.

The decisional law has added several common law grounds for effectuating the judicial supervision of arbitral awards. They include: "manifest disregard of the law"; violations of public policy; and capricious, arbitrary, or irrational arbitral determinations. Most of these grounds overlap with each other and are interpreted by the courts in a distinctly restrictive manner. They arose primarily in the special setting of labor and, to a lesser extent, maritime arbitration and gradually were interpreted to have a more general application. Their existence in the decisional law contradicts the statutory language and purpose of Section Ten and the judicial policy favoring arbitration. They continue to function in part because of inertia and the general judicial confusion that surrounds their implementation. Suffice it to say that it is difficult to challenge an award on any of these common law bases, even on the ground of public policy violations.

§ 11.   Same; Modification or Correction; Grounds; Order

In either of the following cases the United States court in and for the district wherein the award was made may make an order modifying or correcting the award upon the application of any party to the arbitration:

(a) Where there was an evident material miscalculation of figures or an evident material mistake in the description of any person, thing, or property referred to in the award.

(b) Where the arbitrators have awarded upon a matter not submitted to them, unless it is a matter not affecting the merits of the decision upon the matter submitted.

(c) Where the award is imperfect in matter of form not affecting the merits of the controversy.

The order may modify and correct the award, so as to effect the intent thereof and promote justice between the parties.

Commentary

Section Eleven makes possible the enforcement of awards that contain formalistic errors. It substantiates the view that the FAA intends to foster the reference to arbitration, establish a supportive bond between the judicial and arbitral processes, and eliminate the dilatory undermining of the arbitral process. Under Section Eleven, U.S. federal courts, upon the request of one of the parties, have the power to modify or correct awards for inadvertent technical errors that might preclude enforcement. The rationale for the provision is a general "interests of justice" justification. The errors in question must be "evident" and unrelated to the merits of the determination. The provision has not become a source of litigious obfuscation.

Ground (b) of Section Eleven recognizes implicitly a severance procedure that is commonplace in arbitration laws. In circumstances in which arbitrators exceed their authority and rule on matters not submitted to arbitration, the court may enforce that part of the award that is valid by severing it from those portions that represent an illicit exercise of adjudicatory authority. The award then is partially enforced. As noted in ground (b), severance of the award is possible only when the various parts of the award are not interrelated or interdependent.

In 2000, the U.S. Supreme Court held that the FAA's venue provisions, §§ 9–11, were permissive in character. They allowed motions to confirm, vacate, or modify an arbitration award to be brought either in the district where the award had been rendered or in any district proper under the general venue statute. *See Cortez Byrd Chips, Inc. v. Bill Harbert Constr. Co.*, 529 U.S. 193 (2000).

The general venue statute provides for venue in a diversity action in "a judicial district in which a substantial part of the events or omissions giving rise to the claim occurred, or a substantial part of property that is the subject of the action is situated." 28 U.S.C. § 1391(a)(2). The Court explained that "the three venue sections of the FAA [were] best analyzed together, owing to their contemporaneous enactment and the similarity to their pertinent language."

The Court warned that "[e]nlightenment [would] not come merely from parsing the language [of the statute]." Instead, the Court looked to the statute's legislative history:

> When the FAA was enacted in 1925, it appeared against the backdrop of a considerably more restrictive general venue statute than the one current today. At the time, the practical effect of 28 U.S.C. § 112(a) was that a civil suit could usually be brought only in the district in which the defendant resided. The statute's restrictive application was all the more pronounced due to the courts' general inhospitality to forum selection clauses. Hence, even if an arbitration agreement expressly permitted [an] action to be brought in the district in which arbitration had been conducted, the agreement would probably prove to be in vain. The enactment of the special venue provisions in the FAA thus had an obviously liberalizing effect, undiminished by any suggestion, textual or otherwise, that congress meant simultaneously to foreclose a suit where the defendant resided. Such a consequence would have been as inexplicable in 1925 as it would be passing strange 75 years later.

The Court stated that interpreting the FAA venue provisions to require motions to confirm, vacate, or modify the award only in the district where the arbitration took place "would be more clearly at odds with both the FAA's 'statutory policy of rapid and unobstructed enforcement of arbitration agreements,' or with the desired flexibility of parties in choosing a site for arbitration." The Court pointed out that "[a]lthough the location of the arbitration may well be the residence of one of the parties, or have some other connection to a contract at issue, in many cases the site will have no relation whatsoever to the parties or the dispute." The Court further explained that "parties may be willing to arbitrate in any inconvenient forum, say, for the convenience of the arbitrators, or to get a panel with special knowledge or experience, or as part of some compromise, but they might well be less willing to pick such a location if any future court proceedings had to be held there." The Court was concerned that the flexibility to make those types of practical choices would be "inhibited by a venue rule mandating the same inconvenient venue if someone later sought to vacate or modify the award."

The Court also noted that a restrictive interpretation of the venue provisions would put them in "needless tension" with FAA § 3 which "provides that any court in which an action 'referable to arbitration under an agreement in writing' is pending 'shall on application of one of the parties stay the trial of the action until such arbitration has been had in accordance with the terms of the agreement.' " The Court explained that the existing precedent gives "a court with the power to stay the action under § 3...the further power to confirm any ensuing arbitration award." Under a restrictive interpretation of the venue provisions, if an arbitration were held outside the district of that litigation, a subsequent proceeding to confirm, modify, or vacate the award could not be brought in the district of the original litigation, a result that the Court found unacceptable.

Finally, the Court held that a restrictive "interpretation would create anomalous results in the aftermath of arbitrations held abroad." FAA §§ 204, 207, and 302 "together provide for liberal choice of venue for actions to confirm awards subject to the 1958 Convention on the Recognition and Enforcement of Foreign Arbitral Awards and the 1975 Inter–American Convention on International Commercial Arbitration. But reading §§ 9–11 to restrict venue to the site of the arbitration would preclude any action under the FAA in courts of the United States to confirm, modify, or vacate awards rendered in foreign arbitrations not covered by either convention." The Court noted that "[a]lthough such actions would not necessarily be barred for lack of jurisdiction, they would be defeated by restrictions on venue, and anomalies like that are to be avoided when they can be." The Court admitted that "[t]here have been, and perhaps there still are, occasional gaps in the venue laws, [but] Congress does not in general intend to create venue gaps, which take away with one hand what Congress had given by way of jurisdictional grant with the other. Thus, in construing venue statutes it is reasonable to prefer the construction that avoids leaving such gaps."

The Court concluded by explaining that "[a]ttention to practical consequences...points away from the restrictive reading of §§ 9–11 and confirms the view that the liberalizing effect of the provisions in the day of their enactment was meant to endure through treating them as permitting, not limiting, venue choice today." Therefore, the Court held that the permissive view of FAA venue provisions prevailed.

Finally, it should be noted that U.S. courts have recognized a common law right to seek the clarification of awards from rendering tribunals. The action is intended to respond to circumstances in which the court of confirmation simply does not understand what the tribunal determined. Rather than vacate an incomprehensible award for "indefiniteness," the court remands the award to the arbitrators for clarification. There is no authorization for the procedure in the statute and FAA § 11 seems, in fact, to prohibit it. It contradicts the *functus officio* doctrine and it can permit courts to conduct a merits review of awards and to force arbitrators to adopt a judicial disposition of the dispute. In the context of adversarial representation, it is likely to cause delays and increased costs. Although it is intended to be pragmatic, the action to clarify may well undermine the autonomy of arbitration. *See Hardy v. Walsh Manning Securities, L.L.C.*, 341 F.3d 126 (2d Cir. 2003); *Office and Professional Employees Int'l Union, Local 471 v. Brownsville Gen. Hosp.*, 186 F.3d 326 (3d Cir. 1999).

§ 12. Notice of Motions to Vacate or Modify; Service; Stay of Proceedings

Notice of a motion to vacate, modify, or correct an award must be served upon the adverse party or his attorney within three months after the award is filed or delivered. If the adverse party is a resident of the district within which the award was made, such service shall be made upon the adverse party or his attorney as prescribed by law for service of notice of motion in an action in the same court. If the adverse party shall be a nonresident then the notice of the application shall be served by the marshal of any district within which the adverse party may be found in like manner as other process of the court. For the purposes of the motion any judge who might make an order to stay the proceedings in an action brought in the same court may make an order, to be served with the notice of motion, staying the proceedings of the adverse party to enforce the award.

§ 13. Papers Filed with Order on Motions; Judgment; Docketing; Force and Effect; Enforcement

The party moving for an order confirming, modifying, or correcting an award shall, at the time such order is filed with the clerk for the entry of judgment thereon, also file the following papers with the clerk:

(a) The agreement; the selection or appointment, if any, of an additional arbitrator or umpire; and each written extension of the time, if any, within which to make the award.

(b) The award.

(c) Each notice, affidavit, or other paper used upon an application to confirm, modify, or correct the award, and a copy of each order of the court upon such an application.

The judgment shall be docketed as if it was rendered in an action.

The judgment so ordered shall have the same force and effect, in all respects, as, and be subject to all the provisions of law relating to, a judgment in an action; and it may be enforced as if it had been rendered in an action in the court in which it is entered.

§ 14.   Contracts Not Affected

This title shall not apply to contracts made prior to January 1, 1926.

Commentary

Sections Twelve, Thirteen, and Fourteen state that the FAA applies to contracts made after January 1, 1926, and they deal with the technical requirements for filing various motions. They are generally self-explanatory.

§ 15.   Inapplicability of the Act of State doctrine

Enforcement of arbitral agreements, confirmation of arbitral awards, and execution upon judgments based on orders confirming such awards shall not be refused on the basis of the Act of State doctrine.

Commentary

Section Fifteen is inappositely situated in the domestic section of the U.S. law of arbitration. It regulates the impact of the Act of State doctrine upon the enforcement of arbitral agreements and awards. Act of State applies primarily, if not exclusively, in the transborder context, more than likely when a U.S. national or entity alleges that it is aggrieved by the conduct of a foreign State that has taken place within the state's territorial borders. Act of State functions as an objection to U.S. judicial jurisdiction in much the same manner as sovereign immunity. Under the latter, it is alleged that the foreign State cannot be sued before national courts because of its status as a foreign State: It is immune from suit because it is sovereign. Under the former, the foreign State cannot be held accountable for its conduct before a U.S. court because its actions took place within its own territory and were undertaken to further the public interest of the foreign nation. The matter is nonjusticiable because it implicates U.S. foreign policy interests and thereby the constitutional separation of powers doctrine under which the Executive Branch has exclusive authority over the diplomatic interests of the United States.

Unlike Sovereign Immunity, Act of State is unique to U.S. law; it arose and is embedded in U.S. constitutional considerations. It has received the steadfast support of the U.S. Supreme Court. It arises in cases that involve state conduct roughly equivalent to the exercise of eminent domain powers in the domestic setting. The state has allegedly confiscated foreign investor property for a public purpose (giving rise under international law to a duty to provide some form of compensation).

Although it could have an impact upon the domestic enforcement of transborder agreements and awards, the doctrine clearly has little, if anything, to do with the enforcement of domestic arbitration agreements and awards. Assuming the provision functions in the international context, it establishes a very useful rule, reflecting the received wisdom of transborder arbitration practice. In effect, neither Sovereign Immunity nor the Act of State doctrine should be used to frustrate the recourse to arbitration or the enforcement of awards. Once a State agrees to arbitrate, it is deemed to have waived its sovereign right not to be sued. It has agreed to adjudicate its disputes before the arbitral tribunal, and U.S. courts will enforce that implied contractual waiver of immunity under the Foreign Sovereign Immunities Act. Moreover, the State's action, allegedly done for a public purpose within its territory, will not allow it to escape its contractual obligation to arbitrate or to be bound by an arbitral award. As long as the dispute is covered by the agreement to arbitrate, its public law character will not hinder the conduct of the arbitration or frustrate the viability of the award. Nationalizing foreign investor property will not terminate the obligation to arbitrate disputes.

It should be noted that the provisions of Section Fifteen also apply to judicial judgments confirming arbitral awards. When a party refuses to comply with the award rendered by the arbitral tribunal, the other party will seek judicial confirmation of the award and its compulsory enforcement. The request to confirm the award will be opposed by an action for vacatur. If the award is confirmed, the court issues a judgment for the execution of the award. In effect, the award is transformed into a judicial judgment and, at this stage, is no longer an arbitral award. Section Fifteen makes clear that the Act of State doctrine, although it could preclude the enforcement of an ordinary judicial judgment, cannot be used to challenge a judicial judgment that provides for the enforcement of an arbitral award.

§ 16.   Appeals

(a) An appeal may be taken from—

(1) an order—

    (a) refusing a stay of any action under section 3 of this title,

    (b) denying a petition under section 4 of this title to order arbitration to proceed,

    (c) denying an application under section 206 of this title to compel arbitration,

    (d) confirming or denying confirmation of an award or partial award, or

    (e) modifying, correcting, or vacating an award;

(2) an interlocutory order granting, continuing, or modifying an injunction against an arbitration that is subject to this title; or

(3) a final decision with respect to an arbitration that is subject to this title.

(b) Except as otherwise provided in section 1292(b) of title 28, an appeal may not be taken from an interlocutory order—

(1) granting a stay of any action under section 3 of this title;

(2) directing arbitration to proceed under section 4 of this title;

(3) compelling arbitration to proceed under section 206 of this title;

(4) refusing to enjoin an arbitration that is subject to this title.

Commentary

Section Sixteen was enacted in 1988. Together, Sections Fifteen and Sixteen constitute the most recent amendments to the domestic provisions of the FAA—an effort by Congress to modernize somewhat the 1925 legislation by adding provisions that reflect contemporary developments in arbitration law. Despite the relative complexity of its language, Section Sixteen makes a simple and straightforward point: It confirms and gives legislative stature to the decisional law creation of an "emphatic federal policy favoring arbitration." In essence, under the provision, the right of interlocutory appeal exists against any court order that is antagonistic to the pursuit of arbitration, *e.g.*, an order refusing to stay a judicial proceeding in favor of arbitration or refusing to compel arbitration. There is, however, no right of appeal against an interlocutory order that supports the recourse to arbitration. The order of a federal court, for example, that confirms the parties' right and obligation to proceed with arbitration is final.

On the one hand, the dichotomy of regimes clearly favors the interests of arbitration and aligns itself with the FAA policy to legitimate and support arbitration. The gravamen of Section Sixteen also furthers the establishment of a bond of cooperation between the judicial and arbitral processes. One commentator describes the significance of Section Sixteen in these terms:

> It is a pro-arbitration statute designed to prevent the appellate aspect of the litigation process from impeding the expeditious disposition of an arbitration. Its inherent acknowledgment is that arbitration is a form of dispute resolution designed to save the parties time, money, and effort by substituting for the litigation process the advantages of speed, simplicity, and economy associated with arbitration. Its theme is that judicial involvement in the process should be kept to the barest minimum to avoid undermining those goals.

D. Siegel, *Practice Commentary*, Title 9 Arbitration U.S. Code Ann. 1996 Cum. Ann. Pocket Pt. 306 (1996).

On the other hand, the blatant use of a double standard and the heavy-handed restriction of rights against arbitration, characteristic features of the contemporary U.S. decisional law on arbitration, undermine the regulatory integrity of the legislation. It is one thing to safeguard arbitration against outright juridical bias and to proclaim the right of contractual recourse to arbitration within specialized and self-regulating communities and demand federal judicial compliance with that policy. It is, however, quite another matter to exempt arbitration from ordinary legal rules, especially when it reaches more widely into the community. Arbitration's need for systemic autonomy and independence from judicial intervention does not require a complete elimination of legal restrictions.

The law may have had to favor arbitration to protect it from the prejudice of the courts, but, once arbitration attained lawful standing, the protective treatment itself became abusive. It distorts the necessary balance between the functional autonomy of the arbitral process and the safeguarding of legal rights.

The substance of Section Sixteen appears to confirm that the sin of would-be judicial antipathy toward arbitration can never be fully expiated. The penance must be constantly reaffirmed, and the price of redemption escalates whenever any thought of rights protection is entertained. Not only is the sin of judicial hostility to be avoided, but any semblance or reminder of it, no matter how pale or remote, also must be cast aside, lest the legal system return inexorably to its sinful ways. The literalism of this theology forces the legal system to divest itself of any sense of regulatory equilibrium, to engage in overly zealous rule-making, and to abandon its primary mission of rights protection.

In early December 2000, the U.S. Supreme Court handed down its opinion in *Green Tree Financial Corp.-Alabama v. Randolph*, 531 U.S. 79 (2000). In its opinion, the Court—through the late Chief Justice Rehnquist—addressed a number of issues of contemporary arbitration law, including a matter involving the exercise of judicial review with respect to arbitral awards. In that regard, the Court held that, when a district court compels the parties to arbitrate their differences and dismisses all claims brought before it by the litigation, that determination constitutes a "final decision" under FAA § 16(a)(3) and it is subject to appeal under the FAA statutory provision.

The Court summarized the procedural history of the litigation in the following terms:

> The Court of Appeals for the Eleventh Circuit. . .held that it had jurisdiction to review the District Court's order because that order was a final decision. . . . The Court of Appeals looked to § 16 of the Federal Arbitration Act (FAA), 9 U.S.C. § 16, which governs appeal from a District Court's arbitration order, and specifically § 16(a)(3), which allows appeal from "a final decision with respect to an arbitration that is subject to this title." The Court determined that a final, appealable order within the meaning of the FAA is one that disposes of all the issues framed by the litigation, leaving nothing to be done but execute the order. The Court of Appeals found the District Court's order within that definition.
>
> [. . .]
>
> We granted *certiorari*. . ., and we now affirm the Court of Appeals with respect to the [jurisdictional question]. . . .

Part II of the Court's opinion was a unanimous disposition. In some respects, however, it could be seen as the most controversial segment of the Court's opinion. In reaching its determination, the Court does not appear to reinforce the federal policy in favor of arbitration; it disregards the lower court distinction between "embedded" and "independent" pro-

ceedings in defining 'finality'; and it advances a generally strained interpretation of that term.

First, the Court took exception with the petitioners' construction of
FAA § 16 as "generally permit[ting] immediate appeal of orders hostile to
arbitration, whether the orders are final or interlocutory, but bars appeal
of interlocutory orders favorable to arbitration." Prior to *Green Tree*, as
noted earlier, it was generally acknowledged that FAA § 16 was a pro-
arbitration provision that created a double standard expressly favoring
arbitration. The petitioners were entirely correct in their assessment of
the provision: it was meant to delay the reconsideration of judicial
holdings in favor of arbitration and to subject unfavorable dispositions to
immediate review. For reasons which go unstated and are difficult to
determine, the Court refused to recognize that feature of FAA § 16 and
chose to give the provision a more ordinary and even-handed application:

> Section 16(a)(3), however, preserves immediate appeal of any "final deci-
> sion with respect to an arbitration," regardless of whether the decision is
> favorable or hostile to arbitration. And as petitioners and respondent agree,
> the term "final decision" has a well-developed and longstanding meaning.
> It is a decision that "ends the litigation on the merits and leaves nothing
> more for the court to do but execute the judgment"...Because the FAA
> does not define "a final decision with respect to an arbitration" or otherwise
> suggest that the ordinary meaning of "final decision" should not apply, we
> accord the term its well-established meaning....

Second, the Court also disregarded the longstanding distinction between "embedded" and "independent" proceedings in determining whether court action in regard to arbitration is "final":

> We disagree [with petitioners' position]. It does not appear that, at the time
> of § 16(a)(3)'s enactment, the rules of finality were firmly established in
> cases like this one, where the District Court both ordered arbitration and
> dismissed the remaining claims. We also note that at that time, Courts of
> Appeals did not have a uniform approach to finality with respect to orders
> directing arbitration in "embedded" proceedings. The term "final decision,"
> by contrast, enjoys a consistent and longstanding interpretation. Certainly
> the plain language of the statutory text does not suggest that Congress
> intended to incorporate the rather complex independent/embedded distinc-
> tion, and its consequences for finality, into § 16(a)(3). We therefore con-
> clude that where, as here, the District Court has ordered the parties to
> proceed to arbitration, and dismissed all the claims before it, that decision
> is "final" within the meaning of § 16(a)(3), and therefore appealable.

Third, the Court concluded that "final decision" under FAA § 16
means the termination of litigation with regard to the issues brought
before the court. That an action to vacate, confirm, or modify the award
may be brought once the compelled arbitration is completed did not alter
the Court's view that the lower court action with respect to the arbitration was final:

> The District Court's order directed that the dispute be resolved by arbitra-
> tion and dismissed respondent's claims with prejudice, leaving the court

nothing to do but execute the judgment. That order plainly disposed of the entire case on the merits and left no part of it pending before the court. The FAA does permit parties to arbitration agreements to bring a separate proceeding in a district court to enter judgment on an arbitration award once it is made (or to vacate or modify it), but the existence of that remedy does not vitiate the finality of the District Court's resolution of the claims in the instant proceeding....The District Court's order was therefore "a final decision with respect to an arbitration" within the meaning of § 16(a)(3), and an appeal may be taken....

FAA § 16(a)(3) governs the appeals process against court orders relating to arbitration. The statutory provision upholds the federal policy in favor of arbitration by prohibiting interlocutory relief against court orders that stay litigation pending arbitration. While a dismissal of the judicial proceeding constitutes a final order, a stay merely "administratively close[s]" the case and amounts to a postponement. *See South Louisiana Cement, Inc. v. Van Aalst Bulk Handling, B.V.*, 383 F.3d 297 (5th Cir. 2004). *See also Jeffers v. D'Alessandro*, 169 N.C.App. 455, 612 S.E.2d 447 (2005) (slip copy) (order to compel arbitration is not a "final judgment" and cannot be certified for appeal). Thereafter, the court either will assist the arbitrators in the conduct of the arbitral proceedings when it is requested or entertain a petition to confirm or vacate the resulting award. Upon confirming the award for purposes of enforcement, the court, in effect, has dismissed the court action. An order to that effect would be subject to appeal under FAA § 16. The appeal, however, may be foreclosed by *res judicata* because of the confirmation of the award.

The *Rooker–Feldman* doctrine is relevant to FAA § 16. It is intended to prevent "a party losing in state court from seeking what in substance would be appellate review of the state judgment [in the lower federal courts] based on the losing party's claim that the state judgment itself violate[d] the loser's federal rights." It originated in *Rooker v. Fidelity Trust Co.*, 263 U.S. 413 (1923) and *District of Columbia Court of Appeals v. Feldman*, 460 U.S. 462 (1983). It is meant to discourage forum-shopping and the relitigation of cases based on a strained federal rights argument. It works *in tandem* with FAA § 16 in that it generally precludes reconsideration of an order to compel arbitration. The preclusion of appeal under *Rooker-Feldman* obviously is not temporary or merely delayed. Moreover, it applies to the jurisdictional divide between state and federal courts, rather than to the exercise of appellate jurisdiction among federal courts on arbitration matters. *Rooker-Feldman* is a bar when a party challenges the application of law in a state court litigation, but not when the challenge is directed to the constitutionality of the state law that was applied in the proceeding before the state court.

Pieper v. American Arbitration Association, 336 F.3d 458 (6th Cir. 2003), *cert. denied*, 540 U.S. 1182 (2004), demonstrates the standard application of the doctrine. After being compelled to arbitrate by an Ohio state court, Pieper filed suit before a federal district court alleging that "the dispute was not properly subject to arbitration and seeking injunctive relief that would bar [the] AAA from beginning the arbitration hearings." The federal court concluded that it lacked subject matter jurisdiction to engage in the appellate review of state court proceedings. On appeal, the ruling was upheld because "under the *Rooker-Feldman* doctrine[,]" the lower federal court "was without jurisdiction to grant relief" because *Rooker-Feldman* "generally prohibits federal courts from reviewing state-court judgments."

Despite the clarity of its application in the foregoing case, *Rooker-Feldman* raises a number of unresolved issues that indicate it may not work in concert with FAA § 16 in all circumstances. When a state court denies a motion to compel arbitration, federal law would command inter-locutory recourse to an appellate court. Does *Rooker-Feldman* foreclose recourse to the lower federal courts in this instance? Does that mean that recourse to federal appellate courts also is precluded? These circumstances also raise the possible arguments that either the state court applied a state law contrary to the FAA—which, therefore, should be preempted—or the state court misconstrued the applicable law such that it denied the affected party its federal right to arbitrate under FAA § 2. The latter argument assumes that FAA § 2 does in fact create such a right and some sort of accompanying federal question jurisdiction. The case law acknowl-edges the "anomalies," but has not proposed any resolution of the issue.

These unprovided-for complications at least raise the question of whether *Rooker-Feldman* is intended only to have a pro-arbitration effect, allowing state court determinations favorable to arbitration to escape lower federal court scrutiny. The doctrine was articulated in a federalism-jurisdictional context and not in circumstances of support for or compli-ance to the federal policy on arbitration. It is difficult to imagine how state court proceedings that prevent the recourse to arbitration under state law would not result in an action before federal courts. The issue, however, has yet to receive a full airing in the decisional law.

NOTES AND QUESTIONS

1. In what sense does the FAA typify the common law approach to the enactment of statutory law? Does the statute convey a complete picture of the arbitral process? Is the portrait of arbitration that emerges from the legisla-tion sufficient for purposes of advising a client on the decision of whether to arbitrate? What other knowledge might be necessary or useful to accomplish this task? The commentary characterizes the FAA as a document that principally intermediates between the arbitral process and the fundamental aspects of the U.S. legal process and gives primary attention to legal consider-ations rather than the regulation of arbitration. Is that a fair and realistic assessment of the statute?

2. At the time of its enactment and for some years beyond, the FAA was seen as a procedural enactment. As the analysis of the FAA demonstrates (in Section One), even proponents of the legislation argued that it created "no new rights" but for the enforcement mechanism in Section Ten. Do you

agree? How would you argue that the FAA establishes a federal right to arbitrate? If such a right exists, does it have constitutional standing? Does arbitration raise federal-question jurisdiction? Is the contractual right to arbitrate equivalent to First Amendment rights or federal statutory rights attributed to securities investors? How might such a right be vindicated, if at all, in diversity litigation before the federal courts or before state courts when state law governs a case sounding in interstate commerce?

3. You should pay particular attention to Section One and the FAA's scope of application. Try to discover what makes the FAA a federal law enactment. Also, isolate those features of Section One that restrict the reach of the FAA to specialized commercial communities. Do you agree that the FAA originated as special interest legislation, meant to allow arbitration to function in remote sectors of society? Does a fair reading of the text of the FAA or of the character of arbitral adjudication support a wider reach to the remedy? What might justify an "unfair" reading? In articulating your responses, consider the following view of the function of arbitration from Cohen & Dayton, *The New Federal Arbitration Law*, 12 Va. L. Rev. 265 (1926):

> Not all questions arising out of contracts ought to be arbitrated. It is a remedy peculiarly suited to the disposition of the ordinary disputes between merchants as to questions of fact—quantity, quality, time of delivery, compliance with terms of payment, excuses for non-performance, and the like. It has a place also in the determination of the simpler questions of law—the questions of law which arise out of these daily relations between merchants as to the passage of title, the existence of warranties, or the questions of law which are complementary to the questions of fact which we have just mentioned.

Id. at 281, *cited in Prima Paint Corp. v. Flood & Conklin Mfg. Co.*, 388 U.S. 395, 409 n.13 (1967) (Black, J. dissenting).

4. The two critical provisions of the FAA are Sections Two and Ten which deal with the arbitral agreement and award. Why are these provisions indispensable to the regulatory framework? You should assess critically the grounds for the vacatur of awards and arrive at an assessment of their viability as grounds for exercising judicial scrutiny. Also, what other provisions of the FAA appear significant to you and for what reasons?

3. THE UNIFORM LAW FOR STATES

In August 2000, the National Conference of Commissioners on Uniform State Laws (NCCUSL) "approved and recommended for enactment in all the states" the Uniform Arbitration Act (2000). The vote was nearly unanimous (Alabama abstained and the Michigan and Rhode Island state delegations were absent).

The Uniform Arbitration Act was originally promulgated in 1955. It had not been revised since 1956. The Uniform Arbitration Act of 1956 was adopted in forty-nine jurisdictions. These jurisdictions included the District of Columbia, Puerto Rico, and the U.S. Virgin Islands. Only four states did not enact some version of the uniform law: Alabama, Georgia,

Mississippi, and West Virginia. Some states were counted among the adopting jurisdictions because their enacted law on arbitration was modeled upon the FAA and "substantially similar" to the uniform law.

A number of the adopting states enacted special arbitration provisions in addition to the uniform law. These provisions related to and promoted international commercial arbitration. The laws generally were modeled upon or inspired by the UNCITRAL Model Law on International Commercial Arbitration. Such laws are in force in the following state jurisdictions: California, Colorado, Connecticut, Florida, Georgia, Hawaii, Illinois, Maryland, North Carolina, Ohio, Oregon, and Texas.

The work of modernizing the uniform legislation began in 1996 with the creation of a NCCUSL drafting committee. The need for revisions was spurred by the rapid pace and dramatic character of developments in the field of arbitration. Despite the high quality of the existing uniform law, the increased scope of application for arbitration and the greater sophistication of arbitral doctrine demanded a more elaborate uniform legislative framework.

As approved, the Uniform Arbitration Act (2000) incorporates principles and concepts that were developed in the contemporary case law on arbitration—e.g., on arbitrator disclosure and impartiality and the awarding of punitive damages and attorney's fees. In the final analysis, however, the RUAA (2000) is not ready-made for immediate and unqualified adoption in any state jurisdiction. The 1955 version of the uniform law had been such a document. Because it constituted a fully comprehensive statement of regulatory principles on arbitration, the 1956 Act represented a substantial improvement over the narrow procedural focus of the FAA. The successor law, however, is simply not in the same qualitative league in terms of content, organization, and drafting methodology. The new law suffers from severe deficiencies in language. Simply and pointedly stated, the statute is poorly drafted. To any attorney schooled in civil-law methodology or who understands the importance of clear and accessible legislation, the 2000 version is a very approximative and problematic statutory statement. Not only are many of its provisions inelegantly rendered, but the inadequacies of language also give rise to ambiguities and confusion about the rule that is being propounded.

In addition, the drafting committee appears to have addressed a number of controversial developments in the law either by taking a side on the question or by determining that it should not take any action at all—leaving it to judges or legislatures to craft an eventual rule. This approach is not only inconsistent, but it is also likely to invite controversy. It does not represent the type of balanced consideration that generates credible characterizations of the emerging law. By overstepping the bounds of its authority in this manner, the drafting committee, in effect, compromised the persuasiveness of all of its recommendations and the objectives of its mission.

In a word, the Uniform Arbitration Act (2000) stands as a missed opportunity at a critical time in the history of arbitration law to write a significant, perhaps landmark, piece of legislation on arbitration. Thus far, the UAA (2000) has been adopted in twelve states (Alaska, Colorado, Hawaii, Nevada, New Jersey, New Mexico, North Carolina, North Dakota, Oklahoma, Oregon, Utah, and Washington). In 2002, it was introduced in fourteen state legislatures, including Arizona, Connecticut, Indiana, Minnesota, New Jersey, Ohio, and Vermont. It has been approved by the American Bar Association and endorsed by the American Arbitration Association, the National Academy of Arbitrators, and the National Arbitration Forum.

Uniform Arbitration Act (2000)

(SELECTED PROVISIONS)

[. . .]

SECTION 4. EFFECT OF AGREEMENT TO ARBITRATE; NONWAIVABLE PROVISIONS.

(a) Except as otherwise provided in subsections (b) and (c), a party to an agreement to arbitrate or to an arbitration proceeding may waive or, the parties may vary the effect of, the requirements of this [Act] to the extent permitted by law.

(b) Before a controversy arises that is subject to an agreement to arbitrate, a party to the agreement may not:

(1) waive or agree to vary the effect of the requirements of Section 5(a), 6(a), 8, 17(a), 17(b), 26, or 28;

(2) unreasonably restrict the right under Section 9 to notice of the initiation of an arbitration proceeding;

(3) unreasonably restrict the right under Section 12 to disclosure of any facts by a neutral arbitrator; or

(4) waive the right under Section 16 of a party to an agreement to arbitrate to be represented by a lawyer at any proceeding or hearing under this [Act], but an employer and a labor organization may waive the right to representation by a lawyer in a labor arbitration.

(c) A party to an agreement to arbitrate or arbitration proceeding may not waive, or the parties may not vary the effect of, the requirements of this section or Section 3(a), (c), 7, 14, 18, 20(c) or (d), 22, 23, 24, 25(a) or (b), 29, 30, 31, or 32.

NOTES AND QUESTIONS

1. What principle of U.S. arbitration law is illustrated by the content of Section 4(a)? What qualifications are introduced in regard to the basic principle? When can parties establish their own rules of arbitration?

2. State and explain the content of Section 4(b)(1). What provisions of the law are imperative or mandatory? How easy or difficult is it to answer the

foregoing question? What do you think of the drafting techniques used here and elsewhere in the statute?

3.   Compare Section 4(b)(1) and 4(b)(4) in terms of drafting technique. Which provision is clearer and more accessible? Why? Also, explain the significance of the distinction in Section 4(b)(4).

4.   Compare and explain the distinctions that are made in Section 4(b) and (c). What are these provisions meant to say? Can it be stated in plain English?

SECTION 6.   VALIDITY OF AGREEMENT TO ARBITRATE.

(a) An agreement contained in a record to submit to arbitration any existing or subsequent controversy arising between the parties to the agreement is valid, enforceable, and irrevocable except upon a ground that exists at law or in equity for the revocation of a contract.

(b) The court shall decide whether an agreement to arbitrate exists or a controversy is subject to an agreement to arbitrate.

(c) An arbitrator shall decide whether a condition precedent to arbitrability has been fulfilled and whether a contract containing a valid agreement to arbitrate is enforceable.

(d) If a party to a judicial proceeding challenges the existence of, or claims that a controversy is not subject to, an agreement to arbitrate, the arbitration proceeding may continue pending final resolution of the issue by the court, unless the court otherwise orders.

NOTES AND QUESTIONS

1.   Assess Section 6(a). What is an "agreement contained in a record"? Is this an obtuse way of defining the "in-writing" requirement for arbitration agreements? Does it promote understanding to state that the term "means information that is inscribed on a tangible medium or that is stored in an electronic or other medium and is retrievable in perceivable form"? Is this English or the caricature of a definition? How would you define the "in-writing" requirement?

2.   Does Section 6(b) reject or ignore *First Options of Chicago, Inc. v. Kaplan*, 514 U.S. 938 (1995), and its recognition of *kompetenz-kompetenz* by party provision?

3.   Under Section 6, courts—it appears—have exclusive authority to decide questions of contract inarbitrability, namely, "whether an agreement to arbitrate exists or [whether] a controversy is subject to an agreement to arbitrate." Arbitrators, it seems, are only empowered to decide matters that follow in the wake of the resolution of the central issue of arbitrability, *i.e.*, "whether a condition precedent to arbitrability has been fulfilled and whether a contract containing a valid agreement to arbitrate is enforceable." In a word, courts decide jurisdiction and arbitrators interpret the contract.

Section 6(b) and (c) fail to acknowledge that the parties can agree to authorize the arbitrators to rule on matters of contract inarbitrability. By omitting any reference to this possibility, the drafters misrepresented the current law. *First Options of Chicago, Inc. v. Kaplan*, 514 U.S. 938 (1995), established that contracting parties can empower arbitrators to decide questions of contract inarbitrability. To the extent that Section 6(c) suggests otherwise (as it appears to do), it is inaccurate.

The *Reporter's Notes* provide an explanation for the statutory language. As to the issue of the impact of the *Kaplan* decision upon judicial and arbitral authority to decide, the Reporter provides the following commentary:

> 2.   Section 6(b) and (c) reflect the decision of the Drafting Committee to include language in the RUAA [the Revised Uniform Arbitration Act] that incorporates the holdings of the vast majority of state courts and the law that has developed under the FAA that, in the absence of an agreement to the contrary, issues of substantive arbitrability, *i.e.*, whether a dispute is encompassed by an agreement to arbitrate, are for a court to decide and issues of procedural arbitrability, *i.e.*, whether prerequisites such as time limits, notice, laches, estoppel, and other conditions precedent to an obligation to arbitrate have been met, are for the arbitrators to decide....
>
> In particular it should be noted that Section 6(b) which provides for courts to decide substantive arbitrability is subject to waiver under Section 4(a). This approach is not only the law in most States, as noted above, but also follows Supreme Court precedent under the FAA that if there is no agreement to the contrary, questions of substantive arbitrability are for the courts to decide. *First Options of Chicago, Inc. v. Kaplan*, 514 U.S. 938 (1995). Some arbitration organizations, such as the American Arbitration Association in its rules on commercial arbitration disputes, provide that arbitrators, rather than courts, make the initial determination as to substantive arbitrability....

Do these statements absolve the codification of its deficiencies? Why did the drafters resort to such an arcane and opaque method of establishing rules? Why make the text of a proposed law on such an important topic so inaccessible?

4.   Section 6(c) is also cast in cumbersome and opaque language. The *Reporter's Notes* explain that it establishes the decisional domain of the arbitrator. Once arbitrators are properly invested with the authority to rule, they decide all matters relating to the contract and its interpretation. They also make decisions regarding the proceedings. Can you provide an explanation of the distinction being made by the Reporter between "procedural" and "substantive" arbitrability? How is the distinction reflected in the text of the statute?

5.   As to Section 6(d), the Reporter rightly provides that: "Section 6(d) follows the practice of the American Arbitration Association and most other arbitration organizations that if arbitrators are appointed and either party challenges the substantive arbitrability of a dispute in a court proceeding, the arbitrators in their discretion may continue the arbitration hearings unless a court issues an order to stay the arbitration or makes a final determination that the matter is not arbitrable."

A clearer and more useful statement of the law on matters of inarbitrability might have read as follow:

> Challenges to the validity and enforceability of the arbitration agreement can be brought on the ground that the subject matter of the dispute is inarbitrable as a matter of law or because the agreement to arbitrate allegedly is deficient as a contract or, if a valid contract, does not cover the dispute in question.
>
> (i) The legislature ordinarily decides whether nonjudicial recourse (like arbitration) can be had to resolve disputes that arise under a statute or other enactment. Statutory language that prohibits nonjudicial recourse should be clear and express, making the legislature's intent unmistakable. In particular, it should establish whether the nonwaiver of judicial remedies applies to the rights or remedies or both that are created or made available under the statute. Whenever possible, ambiguities in the statute should be construed to favor the recourse of arbitration.
>
> (ii) Contract problems with regard to the reference to arbitration can arise as to the existence or scope of the arbitration agreement. If no agreement exists or if the agreement is contractually flawed to the point of unenforceability, the reference to arbitration is excluded. If the dispute is beyond the governing arbitral clause's scope of application, arbitration becomes available only through a submission.
>
> (iii) Unless the parties' agreement provides otherwise, courts decide matters of contract inarbitrability. If the parties provide to the contrary in their agreement, these issues can be resolved by the arbitrators.

How do you assess the promulgated statutory text and the preceding provision?

SECTION 8. PROVISIONAL REMEDIES.

(a)   Before an arbitrator is appointed and is authorized and able to act, the court, upon [motion] of a party to an arbitration proceeding and for good cause shown, may enter an order for provisional remedies to protect the effectiveness of the arbitration proceeding to the same extent and under the same conditions as if the controversy were the subject of a civil action.

(b)   After an arbitrator is appointed and is authorized and able to act:

(1)   the arbitrator may issue such orders for provisional remedies, including interim awards, as the arbitrator finds necessary to protect the effectiveness of the arbitration proceeding and to promote the fair and expeditious resolution of the controversy, to the same extent and under the same conditions as if the controversy were the subject of a civil action, and

(2)   a party to an arbitration proceeding may move the court for a provisional remedy only if the matter is urgent and the arbitrator is not able to act timely or the arbitrator cannot provide an adequate remedy.

(c) A party does not waive a right of arbitration by making a [motion] under subsection (a) or (b).

NOTES AND QUESTIONS

1. Section 8 responds to a problem that arose in the contemporary practice of arbitration and for which most institutional rules now provide a solution. Once a demand for arbitration is filed, an answer follows and the parties must begin the process of naming arbitrators. In the interval, prior to the constitution of the arbitral tribunal, problems may arise regarding securing evidence and enforcement assets. Institutional rules generally provide for the appointment of an interim arbitrator. The Uniform Law addresses these problems through motions to the courts. Which method is preferable? What practical problems can be associated with each approach?

2. Explain the function of interim or provisional relief in arbitration.

3. What is the purpose and meaning of Section 8(c)?

SECTION 10. CONSOLIDATION of Separate Arbitration Proceedings.

(a) Except as otherwise provided in subsection (c), upon [motion] of a party to an agreement to arbitrate or to an arbitration proceeding, the court may order consolidation of separate arbitration proceedings as to all or some of the claims if:

(1) there are separate agreements to arbitrate or separate arbitration proceedings between the same persons or one of them is a party to a separate agreement to arbitrate or a separate arbitration proceeding with a third person;

(2) the claims subject to the agreements to arbitrate arise in substantial part from the same transaction or series of related transactions;

(3) the existence of a common issue of law or fact creates the possibility of conflicting decisions in the separate arbitration proceedings; and

(4) prejudice resulting from a failure to consolidate is not outweighed by the risk of undue delay or prejudice to the rights of or hardship to parties opposing consolidation.

(b) The court may order consolidation of separate arbitration proceedings as to some claims and allow other claims to be resolved in separate arbitration proceedings.

(c) The court may not order consolidation of the claims of a party to an agreement to arbitrate if the agreement prohibits consolidation.

NOTES AND QUESTIONS

1. Section 10 seeks to codify new principles of arbitration law. It provides rules on the "[c]onsolidation [o]f [s]eparate [a]rbitration [p]roceedings." Like the previous sections, the provision addresses an important aspect of the contemporary U.S. arbitration law. The critical issue pertaining to consolidation in arbitration is whether party consent is necessary to allow

courts to join separate, but related arbitrations. The interplay between *Nereus* and *Boeing* made that much of the law evident. *See Compania Espanola de Petroleos, S.A. v. Nereus Shipping, S.A.*, 527 F.2d 966 (2d Cir. 1975), *cert. denied*, 426 U.S. 936 (1976); *Government of the United Kingdom of Great Britain v. Boeing, Co.*, 998 F.2d 68 (2d Cir. 1993). It is difficult to understand why the provision is not anchored in the clear majority view that mutual party consent is a requisite to consolidation. Instead, mutual party provision on the matter is positioned as an exception to the general proposition that courts can consolidate arbitrations upon the request of *one* of the arbitrating parties. A string of conditions accompanies the statement of the courts' authority to consolidate.

2. What do you make of Section 10(a)(1)? How do you interpret the distinction between "separate agreements to arbitrate" and "separate arbitration proceedings"? Is it meaningful? Is it necessary? Who are the "third" people? What conditions are the drafters attempting to create? Are they trying to establish that the judicial consolidation of separate arbitrations is possible only if the affected parties are parties to an existing arbitration agreement or proceeding? Why did they not just say that?

3. Consolidation raises doctrinal and administrative problems. Why does Section 10 not even recognize these aspects of the process? How would you revise the provision to incorporate these aspects?

4. Section 10(a)(2) and (3) state clearly the settled law on consolidation. There must be a common nexus of facts and issues between the arbitrations and the submission of these related claims to different tribunals would create the possibility of conflicting determinations. Paragraph (4), however, appears to state that the use of judicial consolidation depends upon whether the court concludes that consolidation is less harmful than nonconsolidation in terms of delay and the protection of the rights of the party opposing consolidation. The rule attributes very broad discretion to the courts in ordering consolidation. Does giving such power to the courts contribute to the autonomy of the arbitral process? Is judicial intermeddling likely in light of the wide reach of the rule? Why are courts supreme in matters of arbitral consolidation and not elsewhere in the arbitral process? Is the rule a fair reflection of the position of the decisional law?

5. Section 10(b) allows for the partial consolidation of claims. Partial consolidation has not been a significant aspect of the case law on or the practice of arbitration—and perhaps for good reason. Although the proposed rule establishes an additional option in matters of consolidation, it is difficult to assess or appreciate its practical utility. In fact, it is likely to generate a number of problems: It increases the use of judicial discretion when existing court options already are too numerous; it further complicates an already complex and controversial procedure; and it is likely to create jurisdictional debates and onerous problems of administration. The wisdom that underlies this provision is, to say the least, questionable.

The *Reporter's Notes* provide the following justification for the consolidation provisions that appear in the UAA (2000):

> As in the judicial forum, consolidation effectuates efficiency in conflict resolution and avoidance of conflicting results. By agreeing to include an

arbitration clause, parties have indicated that they wish their disputes to be resolve in such a manner. In many cases, moreover, a court may be the only practical forum within which to effect consolidation. . . . Furthermore, it is likely that in many cases one or more parties, often non-drafting parties, will not have considered the impact of the arbitration clause on multiparty disputes. By establishing a default provision which permits consolidation (subject to various limitations) in the absence of a specific contractual provision, Section 10 encourages drafters to address the issue expressly and enhances the possibility that all parties will be on notice regarding the issue.

6.   There is no doubt that consolidation is a highly practical device that can remedy the deficiencies of duplicative litigation. That benefit, however, does not respond to the critical concern and necessary doctrinal limit that contracting parties *agree* to when they agree to arbitrate their disputes. Arbitration agreements do not ordinarily come with jurisdictional presumptions of expansive application that allows them to be stretched beyond their stated scope of application. Courts may be the best vehicles for achieving the benefits of consolidation, but arbitration should and must remain, according to a now classical expression, a "matter of consent. . .not coercion." *See Volt Info. Sciences, Inc. v. Board of Trustees of Leland Stanford Junior Univ.*, 489 U.S. 468 (1989). Further, the Reporter's commentary seems to be saying that, by establishing an overly aggressive statutory rule on consolidation, parties will have a stronger incentive to address the matter of consolidation themselves in their agreement to avoid the rule's application. This peculiar rationalization for the rule and its content is unlikely to persuade anyone.

Finally, the UAA (2000) should adopt a position on consolidation that "embodies the fundamental principle of judicial respect for the preservation and enforcement of the terms of agreements to arbitrate." ". . . [T]he legitimate expectations of contracting parties [should] limit the ability of courts to consolidate proceedings."

SECTION 12.   DISCLOSURE BY ARBITRATOR.

(a) Before accepting appointment, an individual who is requested to serve as an arbitrator, after making a reasonable inquiry, shall disclose to all parties to the agreement to arbitrate and arbitration proceeding and to any other arbitrators any known facts that a reasonable person would consider likely to affect the impartiality of the arbitrator in the arbitration proceeding, including:

(1) a financial or personal interest in the outcome of the arbitration proceeding; and

(2) an existing or past relationship with any of the parties to the agreement to arbitrate or the arbitration proceeding, their counsel or representatives, a witness, or another arbitrator.

(b) An arbitrator has a continuing obligation to disclose to all parties to the agreement to arbitrate and arbitration proceeding and to any other arbitrators any facts that the arbitrator learns after accepting appointment which a reasonable person would consider likely to affect the impartiality of the arbitrator.

(c) If an arbitrator discloses a fact required by subsection (a) or (b) to be disclosed and a party timely objects to the appointment or continued service of the arbitrator based upon the fact disclosed, the objection may be a ground under Section 23(a)(2) for vacating an award made by the arbitrator.

(d) If the arbitrator did not disclose a fact as required by subsection (a) or (b), upon timely objection by a party, the court under Section 23(a)(2) may vacate an award.

(e) An arbitrator appointed as a neutral arbitrator who does not disclose a known, direct, and material interest in the outcome of the arbitration proceeding or a known, existing, and substantial relationship with a party is presumed to act with evident partiality under Section 23(a)(2).

(f) If the parties to an arbitration proceeding agree to the procedures of an arbitration organization or any other procedures for challenges to arbitrators before an award is made, substantial compliance with those procedures is a condition precedent to a [motion] to vacate an award on that ground under Section 23(a)(2).

NOTES AND QUESTIONS

1.   Section 12 establishes rules on a subject area that has become of critical practical significance in the U.S. law of arbitration—"[d]isclosure[s] [b]y [a]rbitrator[s]." By and large, the provision is more limpid than the rules in the foregoing Sections. Moreover, the proposed rules are relatively standard and uncontroversial. At the outset, in Section 12(a), the drafters establish a basic duty of disclosure (which is central to arbitrator impartiality and the enforceability of the award). Prospective arbitrators have a duty to disclose to the arbitrating parties, the administering arbitral institutions, and to the other arbitrators personal, professional, financial, or other information that might affect their ability to decide disputes in an impartial fashion.

2.   The duty has several elements: It applies before the arbitrator accepts the appointment as an arbitrator, requires the prospective arbitrator to engage in "a reasonable inquiry," and involves a disclosure to the arbitrating parties and other arbitrators. The disclosures consist of "any known facts" that a "reasonable person" might think could affect an individual's ability to assess the submitted matters impartially. Under the rule, prospective arbitrators then must disclose two basic types of information: An interest ("financial or personal") in the outcome of the matter, and relationships ("existing or past") with any individual involved in the arbitration ("parties to the agreement to arbitrate or the arbitration proceeding, their counsel or representative, witnesses, or other arbitrators"). According to Section 12(b), the obligation to disclose facts material to impartiality continues after the initial appointment (presumably, throughout the proceeding). The same elements are used to define the scope of the duty.

3.   How would you advise prospective arbitrators about what constitutes "a reasonable inquiry"? What is meant by a "known fact[ ]"? Is there a proximate cause dilemma to determining what facts or circumstances might affect impartiality? What does the "reasonable person" standard mean in this context? Is it likely that a rule of disclosure will result inevitably in overdis-

closure? Should the rule be the same for neutral and party-designated arbitrators?

4. The rule of disclosure does not seem to arise from a situation of actual abuse, but rather it appears to be intended to be a preventive measure. It can create administrative burdens and delay the recourse to arbitration. It also may generate challenges to awards if disclosure standards are overly rigorous or ill-defined.

If the goal was to strengthen the integrity of arbitration, there were more practical and effective methods to guarantee the professionalism and disinterest of the arbitrators. Institutional rules, for example, could require that party arbitrators be chosen from a pool of neutrals established by the institutions. Institutional administrators could set arbitrator compensation and conduct their own examination of arbitrators on their lists. Also, all tribunals could consist of a sole arbitrator appointed by the institutional administrator or a court. If the real issue is that parties cannot be trusted to appoint objective arbitrators, the function of appointment should be shifted to another actor within the process.

It should be noted that the tradition of partisan arbitrators has not undermined or compromised other forms of arbitration. Labor arbitrators generally are perceived as favoring the union member-worker over management; this circumstance explains the high frequency of awards that apply reinstatement remedies. In addition, maritime arbitrators are appointed on the basis of whether they favor the interests of the ship owner, the party leasing the vessel, the owner of the cargo that was transported, or the insurers who are implicated in the property loss. These forms of arbitration continue to be dominant despite the usage of partisan arbitrators.

If you were asked to advise a would-be czar of adjudication, how would you assess the development of the regime of arbitrator disclosure? Is it necessary or in the best interest of arbitration?

5. Despite its positive attributes, Section 12 could be improved in a number of respects. In places, it suffers from the drawbacks that plague the entire statute. Word choice generally is poor; the syntax is sometimes awkward to the point of confusion; and the statement of the rule can itself become an obstacle to communicating the meaning of the intended regulation. Section 12 could be rewritten to read:

Arbitrator Impartiality—The Duty of Disclosure and the Disqualification of Arbitrators

The Arbitrator's Duty to be Impartial and to Disclose Information Pertaining to Impartiality. All arbitrators must be impartial. Prospective arbitrators must disclose to the arbitrating parties and to the other arbitrators information that affects or might affect their ability to rule in an impartial fashion.

Prior to accepting their appointment, arbitrators must take stock of their business, financial, and personal interests and review their past and existing social and business associations and relationships. They must then disclose facts that might be likely to affect their ability to be impartial or which might create an appearance of partiality if the circumstances were not disclosed. The information should be communicated to the administering institution which will convey it to the parties and the arbitral tribunal. In fulfilling this obligation, prospective arbitrators must exercise due diligence and the professional care that is incumbent upon individuals who exercise arbitral functions and participate in the arbitral process. Finally, arbitrators are held to the duty to investigate and to disclose throughout the arbitral proceeding.

Based upon the investigation and disclosure, arbitrators can withdraw or reject the offer of appointment or can disqualify or recuse themselves. Moreover, a nominating party can refuse to finalize an appointment or can revoke its appointment of an arbitrator at the outset of the proceeding. An objection to the continued service of an arbitrator at a later stage of the proceeding shall be submitted to the arbitral tribunal. The tribunal shall decide whether the objection has been made in good faith and whether removal of the challenged arbitrator is warranted.

In the event that an arbitrator is disqualified and removed by the tribunal, that arbitrator is entitled to reasonable compensation for services rendered, provided such services were of reasonable professional quality. The arbitral tribunal shall determine the amount of any compensation that is owed and shall direct the parties to provide funds for such compensation. Moreover, the tribunal shall—in consultation with the administering agency—provide for the appointment of a replacement arbitrator. Replacement arbitrators shall be appointed in the same basic manner as the original arbitrators and shall have the same authority as the original arbitrators. The parties, however, can agree to proceed with a truncated tribunal.

Neutral arbitrators are held to a very high standard of impartiality. As a consequence, they must satisfy the duty of investigation and disclosure with utmost care. Even minor failures in this regard can result in the neutral arbitrator's removal. Removal of a neutral arbitrator must be done through the joint action of the remaining members of the arbitral tribunal and the administering institution. It may also involve a court action.

In the event that the tribunal concludes that the challenge to an arbitrator was motivated by bad faith and/or by an intent to delay or sabotage the arbitration, it may impose sanctions upon the party who acted in bad faith.

When an arbitrator fails to disclose information that is reasonably available and that information has a clear bearing upon the question of arbitrator impartiality, the tribunal can presume that the arbitrator is partial and, as a result, can disqualify the arbitrator.

Evident partiality discovered and established after the award is rendered can result in the vacatur or nonenforcement of the award.

If the parties so provide, these provisions can be supplemented or replaced by institutional or other rules pertaining to arbitrator disqualification.

Compare the suggested provision with its promulgated counterpart in the statute. What are the principal differences? Do the suggested emendations constitute an improvement? Do they make matters worse? Why? When should the failure to disclose or inadequate disclosure lead to the vacatur of the award? Are there less draconian remedies, like remand or the reformation of the submission? Should all disclosure issues be settled at the head of the process?

6. The *Reporter's Notes* add the following explanations for the statutory language and content of Section 12:

[. . .]

The problem of arbitrator partiality is a difficult one because consensual arbitration involves a tension between abstract concepts of impartial justice and the notion that parties are entitled to a decision-maker of their own choosing, including an expert with the biases and prejudices inherent in particular worldly experience. Arbitrating parties frequently choose arbitrators on the basis of prior professional or business associations, or pertinent commercial expertise. . . . The competing goals of party choice, desired expertise and impartiality must be balanced by giving parties "access to all information which might reasonably affect the arbitrator's partiality." . . . Other factors favoring early resolution of the partiality issues by informed parties are legal and practical limitations on post-award judicial policing of such matters.

[. . .]

A greater number of other courts, mindful of the tradeoff between impartiality and expertise inherent in arbitration, have placed a higher burden on those seeking to vacate awards on grounds of arbitrator interests or relationships. . . .

2. In view of the critical importance of arbitrator disclosure to party choice and perceptions of fairness and the need for more consistent standards to ensure expectations in this vital area, the Drafting Committee determined that the RUAA should set forth affirmative requirements to assure that parties should have access to all information that might reasonably affect the potential arbitrator's neutrality. . . .

The Drafting Committee decided to delete the requirement of disclosing "any" financial or personal interest in the outcome or "any" existing or past relationship and substituted the terms "a" financial or personal interest in the outcome or "an" existing or past relationship. The intent was not to include de minimis interests or relationships. For example, if an arbitrator owned a mutual fund which as part of a large portfolio of investments held some shares of stock in a corporation involved as a party in an arbitration, it might not be reasonable to expect the arbitrator to know of such investment and in any event the investment might be of such an insubstantial nature so as not to reasonably affect the impartiality of the arbitrator.

3. The fundamental standard of Section 12(a) is an objective one: disclosure is required of facts which a reasonable person would consider likely to affect the arbitrator's impartiality in the arbitration proceeding. . . . The Drafting Committee adopted the "reasonable person" test with the intent of making clear that the subjective views of the arbitrator or the parties are not controlling. However, parties may agree to higher or lower standards for disclosure under Section 4(b)(3) so long as they do not

"unreasonably restrict" the right to disclosure and also may establish mechanisms for disqualification. . . .

Section 12(a) requires an arbitrator to make a "reasonable inquiry" prior to accepting an appointment as to any potential conflict of interests. The extent of this inquiry may depend upon the circumstances of the situation and the custom in a particular industry. For instance, an attorney in a law firm may be required to check with other attorneys in the firm to determine if acceptance of an appointment as an arbitrator would result in a conflict of interest on the part of that attorney because of representation by an attorney in the same law firm of one of the parties in another matter.

Once an arbitrator has made a "reasonable inquiry" as required by Section 12(a), the arbitrator will be required to disclose only "known facts" that might affect impartiality. The term "knowledge" (which is intended to include "known") is defined in Section 1(5) to mean "actual knowledge."

[. . .]

5.   Special problems are presented by tripartite panels involving "party-arbitrators"—that is, in situations such as where each of the arbitrating parties selects an arbitrator and a third, neutral arbitrator is jointly selected by the party-arbitrators. . . . In some such cases, it may be agreed that the party-arbitrators are not regarded as "neutral" arbitrators, but are deemed to be predisposed toward the party which appointed them. . . . However, in other situations even the party arbitrators may have a duty of neutrality on some or all issues. The integrity of the process demands that party-arbitrators, like other arbitrators, disclose pertinent interests and relationships to all parties as well as other members of the arbitration panel. It is particularly important for the neutral arbitrator to know the interest of the party arbitrator, for example, if the party arbitrator is being paid on a contingent-fee basis. Thus, Section 12(a) and (b) apply to party arbitrators but under a "reasonable person" standard for someone in the position of a party and not a neutral arbitrator.

[. . .]

Do these remarks lessen the possible apprehensions about the rule of disclosure? Do they convince you that disclosures are necessary and beneficial to arbitration? After reading these remarks, can you better advise prospective arbitrators?

Section 14. Immunity of Arbitrator; Competency to Testify; Attorney's Fees and Costs.

(a) An arbitrator or an arbitration organization acting in that capacity is immune from civil liability to the same extent as a judge of a court of this State acting in a judicial capacity.

(b) The immunity afforded by this section supplements any immunity under other law.

(c) The failure of an arbitrator to make a disclosure required by Section 12 does not cause any loss of immunity under this section.

(d) In a judicial, administrative, or similar proceeding, an arbitrator or representative of an arbitration organization is not competent to testify, and may not be required to produce records as to any statement, conduct, decision, or ruling occurring during the arbitration proceeding, to the same extent as a judge of a court of this State acting in a judicial capacity. This subsection does not apply:

(1) to the extent necessary to determine the claim of an arbitrator, arbitration organization, or representative of the arbitration organization against a party to the arbitration proceeding; or

(2) to a hearing on a [motion] to vacate an award under Section 23(a)(1) or (2) if the [movant] establishes prima facie that a ground for vacating the award exists.

(e) If a person commences a civil action against an arbitrator, arbitration organization, or representative of an arbitration organization arising from the services of the arbitrator, organization, or representative or if a person seeks to compel an arbitrator or a representative of an arbitration organization to testify or produce records in violation of subsection (d), and the court decides that the arbitrator, arbitration organization, or representative of an arbitration organization is immune from civil liability or that the arbitrator or representative of the organization is not competent to testify, the court shall award to the arbitrator, organization, or representative reasonable attorney's fees and other reasonable expenses of litigation.

NOTES AND QUESTIONS

1. Section 14 has fewer problems than other statutory sections, but its overall quality remains mixed. Both its content and presentation could be substantially improved. As a preliminary matter, it seems peculiar to group the topics of arbitrator immunity, arbitral confidentiality, and attorney's fees together. They are not generally associated with one another. Moreover, each topic appears to receive abbreviated consideration. Because of their importance in arbitral practice, these topics should command a larger presence in the framework of the uniform law.

2. As to specific features, Section 14(a) establishes that arbitral immunity is equivalent to the immunity enjoyed by state judges when they act in their judicial capacity. Why is this a sound rule? What does it say about arbitration and the arbitral process from a regulatory perspective? Is there a downside to the statement? Do all states provide judges with full or nearly full immunity? What consequences might flow upon arbitration law if they do not? Could limited or perfunctory immunity generate "back door" federalism issues? How?

The immunity extends to "[a]n arbitrator or an arbitration organization." Expanding the reach of the immunity to cover arbitral institutions at least raises an issue of policy. The proposed rule reflects the current practice of the institutions themselves. Whether a self-proclaimed exemption from professional malpractice laws should be integrated into the uniform law remains a matter of debate. The wholesale incorporation of a nearly absolute institutional privilege appears to be unwise on its face—although there are powerful arguments for its inclusion. The drafters, therefore, could have created a separate and more limited form of immunity for arbitral institutions that would have nonetheless provided protection from disappointed parties who were intent upon subverting the process. What type of limited immunity might have been adopted? Is limited immunity workable? Can the administration of arbitrations survive without immunity?

3. A few linguistic details in Section 14(a), (b), and (c) call for additional comment. The phrase "arbitration organization" is used instead of the more usual "arbitral institution." No explanation is provided for the change in word usage, although Section 1 of the Act defines the new phrase. That definition, however, is not very helpful. It is too generalized to provide any real clarification. An illustration of what constitutes an "[a]rbitration organization" might have made the new term more understandable. Moreover, the phrase "[a]n arbitrator or an arbitration organization acting in such capacity" is not only awkward, but it is also ungrammatical. "Capacity" cannot be equated with the prior objects—"arbitrator" and "arbitration organization." It would have been correct and stylistically acceptable to state: "arbitrators or arbitral institutions acting in their [arbitral] capacity." Rigorous use of language is hardly inapposite in a statutory context.

4. Section 14(d) (1) and (2) appear to establish a rule of confidentiality for arbitral proceedings. They create a privilege that shields both arbitrators and agents of the administering arbitral institution from orders that they testify or produce documents regarding the arbitration. The privilege applies to orders emanating from either judicial or administrative or even other types of tribunals. It is the same privilege enjoyed by state court judges in the exercise of their official capacities. The privilege does not apply when the tribunal is adjudicating a claim between an arbitrator, the supervising arbitral institution, or an agent of the institution *and* one of the arbitrating parties or in circumstances in which the award is being challenged and a serious basis for vacatur exists.

Although the first exception above is stated in language that is broad and imprecise, it appears reasonable to conclude that it relates to circumstances in which an arbitrating party allegedly owes money to an arbitrator or to the administering arbitral institution. The collection of a debt requires proof of its existence and of the party's failure to pay. The privilege of confidentiality yields to evidentiary needs here in part because the delinquent party should not be protected from accountability. The exception, however, does not gauge its impact upon the autonomy of the arbitral process. To some extent, it also invites dilatory tactics by allowing a party to undermine the confidentiality of the process by withholding payment of its share of the costs and fees. In addition, it is not clear from current practice that the nonpayment of arbitral fees and costs constitute a problem sufficient to justify an exception to the rule of confidentiality. The institutional practice of requiring deposits at the beginning and replenishing them throughout the arbitration appears to have been effective (up-to-now) in dealing with such issues.

5. Eliminating confidentiality for purposes of vacatur reflects standard practice. In fact, once a challenge to an award has been lodged and goes to decision, there is little that is not eventually known about the arbitration, the arbitral proceedings, and the arbitral award. Requiring the challenging party to establish a *prima facie* basis for vacatur effectively reduces the prospect that the arbitration will be rehearsed in public for purposes of enforcement. What constitutes a *prima facie* ground and how it should be established are unresolved questions. The underlying objective, however, is clear—to require the party seeking vacatur to have a serious reason for challenging the award. Otherwise, the rule of confidentiality remains intact and fully functional. When confidentiality is operative, it becomes nearly impossible to constitute a record of the arbitration. As a consequence, the vacatur action—in all probability—will fail.

6. Arbitral confidentiality, expressed as "competency to testify," touches upon a number of vital issues of arbitration law. Section 14 of the uniform law takes an enlightened position on these matters. In contrast to the recommendation made in Section 14(d)(2), it has been standard practice to allow parties to challenge the confirmation of the award upon any of the stated statutory grounds. In effect, the exercise of that right meant that whatever transpired in the arbitration and led to the award would be divulged in order to allow the court to evaluate the challenger's petition. The party's right to lodge an action to vacate an award, in effect, gave the court the authority to review *de novo* the arbitral award and process. The exercise of such review authority obviously breached arbitral autonomy and contradicted the judicial policy in favor of arbitration. Through the device of confidentiality, the drafters of the uniform law created an ingenious means by which to circumvent the standard vacatur practice and to enhance the autonomy and functionality of arbitration.

Moreover, through Section 14(d), arbitration gains the type of confidentiality protection that generally had been available only for mediation (given the perceived need for unreserved party participation in that process). A guarantee of confidentiality, extended to include arbitral institutional actors, adds to the attractiveness of arbitration as a dispute resolution process. Under current practice, courts have assumed a highly interventionist posture in such matters. Arbitral actors and proceedings are fully vulnerable to external demands for information. The privilege that has been created proposes to remedy this feature of judicial practice.

7. Section 14(3) reinforces the underlying policy (announced in various places in Section 14) of limiting judicial recourse in regard to arbitration. It provides for the award of penalties against parties who unsuccessfully challenge the immunity or testimonial privilege of an arbitrator, an arbitral institution, or the institution's agents. The cause of action must involve and advance an issue already determined by the statute, namely, that the arbitrator is immune from adjudicatory malpractice liability and incompetent to testify. When the claim can be resolved simply by reference to the statute, the court must award the other party attorney's fees and other costs. It is curious that the drafters did not use the adjective "frivolous" or the phrase "the failure to state a cause of action" to describe the circumstances that were contemplated by the statutory provision. Instead, they chose to use a cumbersome restating technique that renders the provision awkward to read and

difficult to understand. The restating technique, however, makes the provision very precise. The precision that the drafters attempted to integrate into the uniform law, however, sometimes seems more characteristic of and more appropriate for a contract document or an instructional manual than a statute.

8. Finally, the reference to attorney's fees in the title of the section is misleading (at least, initially). The topic of the attribution of attorney's fees is a relatively unsettled question in U.S. arbitration law. It should not appear in the title of a section unless that section contains controlling rules on the matter. The topic of attorney's fees is addressed in Section 21(b), the title of which, ironically, does not reveal that it addresses that issue.

9. The *Reporter's Notes* add the following explanations for the statutory language and content in Section 14:

[. . .]

Arbitral immunity has its origins in common law judicial immunity and in most jurisdictions tracks it directly. The key to this identity is the "functional comparability" of the role of arbitrators and judges. . . .

In addition to the grant of immunity from a civil action, arbitrators are also generally accorded immunity from process when subpoenaed or summoned to testify in a judicial proceeding in a case arising from their service as arbitrator. . . . This full immunity from any civil proceedings is what is intended by the language in Section 14(a).

2. Section 14(a) also provides to an entity acting as an arbitration organization the same immunity as is provided to an individual acting as an arbitrator. Extension of judicial immunity to those arbitration organizations is appropriate to the extent that they are acting "in certain roles and with certain responsibilities" that are functionally comparable to those of a judge. . . . This immunity to neutral arbitration organizations is because the duties that they perform in administering the arbitration process are the functional equivalent of the comparable role and responsibility of judges in administering the adjudication process in a court of law. There is substantial precedent for this conclusion. . . .

Also the provision draws no distinction between neutral arbitrators and advocate arbitrators. Both types of arbitrators are covered by this provision.

10. A possible rewriting of Section 14 might read as follows:

Section 14. Arbitrator Immunity.

Arbitrators are immune from any form of civil liability in the performance of their adjudicatory functions as arbitrators. Arbitrator immunity is like the civil immunity enjoyed by state court judges when the latter act in their official capacity, except that arbitrator immunity is generally unqualified.

Arbitrators do not cease to be immune because they failed to disclose information under Section 12, they have been disqualified or removed, or the award they rendered was not enforceable.

A person who disregards the civil immunity of an arbitrator and files a civil action for damages, alleging that the arbitrator failed to properly exercise his/her functions as an arbitrator, is subject to paying the arbitrator's attorney's fees and costs for the litigation, if the court rules that the arbitrator is immune from suit under the applicable statute.

Arbitral institutions who administer arbitrations enjoy a more limited qualified immunity. These institutions are immune from civil liability in the performance of their functions, provided the breach of their professional duty does not reach a level of gross negligence, wanton disregard, or recklessness.

Section [14–1]. Confidentiality of the Proceedings.

Parties engage in arbitration with a view to resolving their disputes privately. In order to maintain the confidentiality of arbitration, arbitrators and agents of arbitral institutions cannot be compelled to testify about or produce documents concerning the arbitration by a court of law or an administrative or other tribunal. Moreover, information that such parties may voluntarily communicate is not admissible in such proceedings.

Post-award disclosures of otherwise confidential information regarding the arbitration can result in the assessment of civil liability against an arbitrator or an arbitral institution. Arbitral immunity is not applicable in these circumstances. Such disclosures also constitute a breach of the ethical standards that apply to arbitrators and arbitral institutions. Other participants in the arbitration are encouraged to maintain the confidentiality of the proceedings. Wherever possible, contracts or arbitral rulings should provide for the assessment of penalties for the violation of arbitral confidentiality by these other parties.

The rule of arbitral confidentiality does not apply to actions for the payment of fees and other costs brought by an arbitrator or an arbitral institution against a party to the arbitral proceedings. In an action for the vacatur of an award, a record of the arbitral proceedings can only be constituted if the party opposing the award establishes *prima facie* a serious basis for possible vacatur. Otherwise, the rule of confidentiality applies to any information pertaining to the arbitration.

Attempts to undermine the rule of confidentiality by bringing actions that violate its requirements shall result in the award of attorney's fees and court costs.

Section [14–2]. Arbitrating Party Immunity.

Parties who participate in an arbitration are entitled to the same immunity from civil liability that litigating parties enjoy in a court proceeding that takes place under state law. This immunity, whether absolute or qualified, does not exempt them from the obligation to arbitrate in good faith or the sanctions that could be imposed by the arbitrators for the breach of that duty. At all times during the arbitration, unless the parties' agreement provides otherwise, the parties are subject to the authority of the arbitral tribunal. Moreover, the parties remain responsible for the payment of arbitral fees and costs.

Section [14–3]. Extraordinary Sanctions.

Whenever party conduct undermines arbitrator immunity or arbitral confidentiality and the party's conduct is particularly egregious and threatens the functionality of the arbitral process, a court can award punitive damages in addition to attorney's fees and costs to discourage such behavior.

Section [14–2] and [14–3] add new elements to the content of Section 14 that were not included by the drafting committee. The provision of immunity to arbitrators and arbitral institutions logically raises the question of whether an immunity privilege should be extended to the arbitrating parties. Immunity would apply to arbitrating party conduct during the arbitral proceedings, in particular as to the advocacy undertaken by the parties. The proposed rule acknowledges that a duty to arbitrate in good faith exists and applies to the parties and to the proceedings. The protection of the right to advocate would not necessarily conflict with that duty. Also, allowing for party advocacy (as established, defined, and regulated by state law) would not exempt the arbitrating parties from the authority of the arbitral tribunal or financial liability for arbitral fees and costs.

Proposed Section [14–3] is basically self-explanatory. It provides additional support for the rules of immunity and confidentiality by increasing possible sanctions for violations. Despite the controversial character of punitive damages in domestic law, their availability could reinforce the functional operation of the arbitral process. If flagrant violations of express rules are not discouraged, they are likely to become standard practice. The resolution of such matters could be left to the discretion of a reconstituted arbitral tribunal, but the procedural difficulty and delay of so doing argues strongly for court disposition of these issues. Judicial action undertaken to sustain the arbitral process as established by the parties should not be seen as interference.

SECTION 15. ARBITRATION PROCESS.

(a) An arbitrator may conduct an arbitration in such manner as the arbitrator considers appropriate for a fair and expeditious disposition of the proceeding. The authority conferred upon the arbitrator includes the power to hold conferences with the parties to the arbitration proceeding before the hearing and, among other matters, determine the admissibility, relevance, materiality and weight of any evidence.

(b) An arbitrator may decide a request for summary disposition of a claim or particular issue:

(1) if all interested parties agree; or

(2) upon request of one party to the arbitration proceeding if that party gives notice to all other parties to the proceeding, and the other parties have a reasonable opportunity to respond.

(c) If an arbitrator orders a hearing, the arbitrator shall set a time and place and give notice of the hearing not less than five days before the hearing begins. Unless a party to the arbitration proceeding makes an objection to lack or insufficiency of notice not later than the beginning of the hearing, the party's appearance at the hearing waives the objection. Upon request of a party to the arbitration proceeding and for good cause shown, or upon the arbitrator's own initiative, the arbitrator may adjourn the hearing from time to time as necessary but may not postpone the hearing to a time later than that fixed by the agreement to arbitrate for making the award unless the parties to the arbitration proceeding consent to a later date. The arbitrator may hear and decide the controversy upon the evidence produced although a party who was duly notified of the arbitration proceeding did not appear. The court, on request, may direct the arbitrator to conduct the hearing promptly and render a timely decision.

(d) At a hearing under subsection (c), a party to the arbitration proceeding has a right to be heard, to present evidence material to the controversy, and to cross-examine witnesses appearing at the hearing.

(e) If an arbitrator ceases or is unable to act during the arbitration proceeding, a replacement arbitrator must be appointed in accordance with Section 11 to continue the proceeding and to resolve the controversy.

NOTES AND QUESTIONS

1.   Section 15 deals with the "[a]rbitration [p]rocess." This heading is not altogether accurate because the provision, overall, addresses the arbitrator's authority to conduct the arbitral proceeding. The phrase "arbitration process" connotes something larger than the proceedings themselves. A more accurate title, therefore, could have been used.

2.   The content of Section 15 is characteristic of the compositional approach used throughout the new uniform law: In essence, the content of the section articulates rules in arcane legalese, and thereby generates propositions that are awkward to the point of being incomprehensible. The most striking feature of Section 15 is its conceptual disarray; there is no discernible organizational order to the elaboration or positioning of the various rules. The content of these rules also lacks cohesion and balance—minor matters are linked to broader policy concerns for no discernible reason or objective. Propositions refer indiscriminately to fundamental procedural concerns and the incidents that flow from the micro-management of the arbitral process. This approach and its consequences are simply not commensurate with the goal of drafting a model statute—one that will seriously affect law practice and the protection of rights for some time to come. Do you agree with this assessment? Is it a fair [and balanced] evaluation? Do you think the new uniform is helpful to the practice of law in the area of arbitration? Is the RUAA a statute or a "how to" manual? Which framework is more workable in practice: The RUAA or the FAA?

3.   The *Reporter's Notes* provide a number of clarifications to the content of Section 15. Compared to the actual statutory text, these notes represent a much clearer expression of the objective that underlies the statutory language and of the law it is meant to articulate:

> 1.   Section 15 is a default provision and under Section 4(a) is subject to the agreement of the parties. Section 15(a) is intended to give an arbitrator wide latitude in conducting an arbitration subject to the parties' agreement and to determine what evidence should be considered. It

should be noted that the rules of evidence are inapplicable in an arbitration proceeding except that an arbitrator's refusal to consider evidence material to the controversy which substantially prejudices the rights of a party are grounds for vacatur under Section 23(a)(3). . . .

2. As the use of arbitration increases, there are more cases that involve complex issues. In such cases arbitrators are often involved in numerous pre-hearing matters involving conferences, motions, subpoenas, and other preliminary issues. Although the present UAA makes no specific provision for arbitrators to hold pre-hearing conferences or to rule on preliminary matters, arbitrators likely have the inherent authority to do such. Numerous cases have concluded that in arbitration proceedings, procedural matters are within the province of the arbitrators. . . .

Additionally, many arbitration organizations whose rules may govern particular arbitration proceedings provide for pre-hearing conferences and the ruling on preliminary matters by arbitrators. . . .

Section 15(a) is intended to allow arbitrators broad powers to manage the arbitration process both before and during the hearing. This section makes the authority of arbitrators to hold prehearing conferences explicit and is meant to provide arbitrators with the authority in appropriate cases to require parties to clarify issues, stipulate matters, identify witnesses, provide summaries of testimony, to allow discovery, and to resolve preliminary matters. However, it is also the intent of Section 15(a) not to encourage either extensive discovery or a form of motion practice. While such methods as discovery or prehearing conferences may be appropriate in some cases, these should only be used where they 'aid in the fair and expeditious disposition of the arbitration proceeding.' The arbitrator should keep in mind the goals of an expeditious, less costly, and efficient procedure. . . .

[. . .]

Section 15(b) is intended to allow arbitrators to decide a request for summary disposition but only after a party requesting summary disposition gives appropriate notice and opposing parties have a reasonable opportunity to respond. . . .

4. Despite the Committee's intent and the Reporter's clarifications, problems remain. The proposed language tracks, to some degree, the major subject-matter themes of Section 15, but it also departs from the content of the section in a number of significant respects. First, in Section 15(a), the drafters underscore the arbitrator's power to order pre-hearing conferences. In fact, under Section 15(a), the arbitrator's procedural powers are three-fold: (1) to conduct "fair and expeditious" hearings; (2) to hold pre-hearing conferences with the parties; and (3) to rule on evidentiary matters (those matters pertaining to the "admissibility, relevance, materiality, and weight" of the evidence). The order and organization of the provision again is chaotic and makes it difficult to isolate and understand its basic focus. Section 15(c) is an excellent illustration of how to micro-manage the arbitration process through a variety of unrelated statements that, it seems, are simply grouped together by happenstance. The final statement in Section 15(c) appears to "come out of the blue" and to invite court interference with the arbitral

process. The lack of context and cohesion in the provision, in effect, makes it difficult to assess the import of the various statements.

5. Section 15(d), (e), and (f) are generally acceptable rules of arbitral regulation; it is, however, difficult to place them logically under the rubric "Arbitration Process." They appear to relate to different facets of the proceedings or procedure. For example, the appointment of a replacement arbitrator in Section 15(f) could be integrated with a section on arbitrator appointment or could stand on its own. There also are interpretative problems that accompany the looseness of the organization. In Section 15(d), reference is made to the essential components of the arbitral trial triggered by the arbitrator under Section 15(c). It is difficult to understand why this section was not presented as a centerpiece provision on arbitral due process. Instead, it is buried inside an already disorganized section and conveys the impression that it is the standard that applies exclusively to would-be evidentiary hearings. Finally, Section 15(e) provides for adjudication by majority rule in arbitrations governed by the statute. The rule propounded reflects standard practice, but—once again—it does not directly implicate the management of the arbitral proceedings. Rather, it establishes the predicate for legitimate decision-making in arbitration.

6. A rewritten Section 15 might read as follows:

Section 15. Arbitrator Authority to Conduct the Proceedings.

The arbitral tribunal must conduct the arbitral proceedings in a fair and expeditious manner. In particular, the tribunal must provide the parties with an opportunity to be heard and to respond to the allegations made by the other side.

As to matters of procedure, unless the parties' agreement or the applicable institutional rule provide otherwise, the tribunal has the authority to establish the time and place of the hearings. In exercising this authority, the tribunal must give reasonable notice to the parties. Adjournments of the proceedings are at the tribunal's discretion, but must be granted when requested by a party and good cause is shown. Moreover, the tribunal may order pre-hearing conferences to decide evidentiary matters. The tribunal can also engage in the summary disposition of issues if all of the parties so request or if one party makes such a request with reasonable notice to the other parties.

In granting adjournments, the tribunal must remain mindful of any time-limits that have been established in regard to the arbitration. All arbitrators must be present at the proceedings. The tribunal, however, may rule on the basis on the evidence presented even when parties—who have been duly-notified—fail to appear and to present their case. Objections to the arbitrators' determination of procedural matters must be made in a timely fashion. Entering an appearance or participating in the proceedings without indicating an opposition to the determination can constitute a waiver of the right to make an objection.

[. . .]

SECTION 17. WITNESSES; SUBPOENAS; DEPOSITIONS; DISCOVERY.

(a) An arbitrator may issue a subpoena for the attendance of a witness and for the production of records and other evidence at any hearing and may administer oaths. A subpoena must be served in the manner for service of subpoenas in a civil action and, upon [motion] to the court by a party to the arbitration proceeding or the arbitrator, enforced in the manner for enforcement of subpoenas in a civil action.

(b) In order to make the proceedings fair, expeditious, and cost effective, upon request of a party to or a witness in an arbitration proceeding, an arbitrator may permit a deposition of any witness to be taken for use as evidence at the hearing, including a witness who cannot be subpoenaed for or is unable to attend a hearing. The arbitrator shall determine the conditions under which the deposition is taken.

(c) An arbitrator may permit such discovery as the arbitrator decides is appropriate in the circumstances, taking into account the needs of the parties to the arbitration proceeding and other affected persons and the desirability of making the proceeding fair, expeditious, and cost effective.

(d) If an arbitrator permits discovery under subsection (c), the arbitrator may order a party to the arbitration proceeding to comply with the arbitrator's discovery-related orders, issue subpoenas for the attendance of a witness and for the production of records and other evidence at a discovery proceeding, and take action against a noncomplying party to the extent a court could if the controversy were the subject of a civil action in this State.

(e) An arbitrator may issue a protective order to prevent the disclosure of privileged information, confidential information, trade secrets, and other information protected from disclosure to the extent a court could if the controversy were the subject of a civil action in this State.

(f) All laws compelling a person under subpoena to testify and all fees for attending a judicial proceeding, a deposition, or a discovery proceeding as a witness apply to an arbitration proceeding as if the controversy were the subject of a civil action in this State.

(g) The court may enforce a subpoena or discovery-related order for the attendance of a witness within this State and for the production of records and other evidence issued by an arbitrator in connection with an arbitration proceeding in another State upon conditions determined by the court so as to make the arbitration proceeding fair, expeditious, and cost effective. A subpoena or discovery-related order issued by an arbitrator in another State must be served in the manner provided by law for service of subpoenas in a civil action in this State and, upon [motion] to the court by a party to the arbitration proceeding or the arbitrator, enforced in the manner provided by law for enforcement of subpoenas in a civil action in this State.

1. The *Reporter's Notes* provide the following clarifications on Section 16:

> 1. The Drafting Committee considered but rejected a proposal to add "or any other person" after "an attorney." A concern was expressed about incompetent and unscrupulous individuals, especially in securities arbitration, who hold themselves out as advocates.

> 2. This section is not intended to preclude, where authorized by law, representation in an arbitration proceeding by individuals who are not licensed to practice law either generally or in the jurisdiction in which the arbitration is held.

2. The content of Section 17 corresponds to its title. The drafting improvement, however, does not progress much further. The "rag-tag" order and the lack of composition that prevail elsewhere in the uniform law quickly take over the content of this section. Given their subject-matter inter-relationship, Section 17 could easily have been merged with Section 15. The sections, in effect, both deal with the arbitrator's power to conduct arbitral proceedings. Indeed, the rationale for having two separate sections of the uniform law address the same subject-matter is far from clear.

3. Section 17(a), (d), (f), and (g) address, in relevant part, the arbitrator's power to issue subpoenas for purposes of evidence-gathering in the form either of documents or the testimony of witnesses. It is not clear, except by implication, that the arbitrator's authority to issue subpoenas applies to both arbitrating and nonarbitrating parties. The FAA articulates a clearer position on that matter. The phrase: "An arbitrator may issue a subpoena for the attendance of a witness...." implies that the arbitrator's subpoena powers extend to non-arbitrating third-parties. It, however, would make for a more comprehensible and workable rule to state directly that:

> Arbitrators possess the authority to issue subpoenas for the purpose of evidence-gathering. They can issue subpoenas to the arbitrating parties or third-parties. The subpoena power is meant to provide a means by which arbitrators can secure both documentary and testimonial evidence that would otherwise be inaccessible but which the arbitrators deem necessary to the proceeding and, possibly, to the determination of the dispute. In the event that the subpoenaed party refuses to comply, the arbitrator can file a motion to compel enforcement before a court of competent jurisdiction.

4. Section 17 (a) further provides that an arbitrator can use the subpoena power to gather evidence "at any hearing." It is unclear why the drafters used such an open-ended phrase, but surely they must have intended to allow for coercive evidence-gathering by arbitrators in any arbitral proceeding in which an arbitrator sits as a member of an arbitral tribunal. Further, the administration of oaths is included in the arbitrator's procedural powers. Does this mean that the law of perjury now applies in an arbitral setting? Institutional rules do not address this matter. Is the contemplated oath-taking then mere window dressings or, at best, a type of individual psychological compulsion? Does the provision simply allow arbitrators to do what they want or is

this a matter now for the arbitration agreement? In the final analysis, would you agree that a law so unclear and riddled with ambiguities should not serve as the model statute in an area that is as dynamic and vital as arbitration?

5. The remainder of the provision deals with the deposition of witnesses, conduct of discovery, and issuance of protective orders related to privileged information. The statute seems to give arbitrators a great deal of authority in the conduct of such matters. It appears that arbitrators decide what is procedurally "appropriate" with a view to making the arbitral "proceeding fair, expeditious, and cost effective." The latter phrase is used three times in the provision and may have some general regulatory and doctrinal significance, although there is no express indication to that effect in the statute. Section 17(g) addresses the jurisdictional problems that might arise in an interstate arbitral context and seems to provide for the type of judicial assistance that would proceed from the application of full faith and credit principles. The exact meaning and objective of the provision are again difficult to discern without the assistance of the *Reporter's Notes*.

6. The *Reporter's Notes* provide for the following clarifications of the various matters addressed:

1. Presently, UAA Section 7 provides an arbitrator only with subpoena authority for the attendance of witnesses and production of documents at the hearing (RUAA Section 17[a]) or to depose a witness who is unable to attend a hearing (RUAA Section 17[b]). Section 17(b) allows an arbitrator to permit a hearing deposition only where it will insure that the proceeding is "fair, expeditious, and cost effective." This standard is also required in Section 17(c) concerning prehearing discovery and in Section 17(g) regarding the enforcement of subpoenas or discovery orders by out-of-state arbitrators. Note that Section 17(a) and (b) are not waivable under Section 4(b) because they go to the inherent power of an arbitrator to provide a fair hearing by insuring that witnesses and records will be available at an arbitration proceeding.

[. . .]

3. The approach to discovery in Section 17(c) is modeled after the Center for Public Resources (CPR) Rules for Non–Administered Arbitration of Business Disputes, R. 10 and United Nations Commission on International Trade Law (UNCITRAL) Arbitration Rules, Arts. 24(2), 26. The language follows the majority approach under the case law of the UAA and FAA that, unless the contract specifies to the contrary, the discretion rests with the arbitrators whether to allow discovery. The purpose of the discovery procedure in Section 17(c) is to aid the arbitration process and ensure an expeditious, efficient and informed arbitration, while adequately protecting the rights of the parties. Because Section 17(c) is waivable under Section 4, the provision is intended to encourage parties to negotiate their own discovery procedures. Section 17(d) establishes the authority of the arbitrator to oversee the prehearing process and enforce discovery-related orders in the same manner as would occur in a civil action, thereby minimizing the involvement of (and resort of the parties to) the courts during the arbitral discovery process.

At the same time, it should be clear that in many arbitrations discovery is unnecessary and that the discovery contemplated by Section 17(c) and (d) is not coextensive with that which occurs in the course of civil litigation under federal or state rules of civil procedure. Thus, the parties could decide to eliminate or limit discovery in their arbitration agreement.

[. . .]

5. The simplified, straightforward approach to discovery reflected in Section 17(c)-(e) is premised on the affirmative duty of the parties to cooperate in the prompt and efficient completion of discovery. The standard for decision in particular cases is left to the arbitrator. The intent of Section 17, similar to Section 8(b) which allows arbitrators to issue provisional remedies, is to grant arbitrators the power and flexibility to ensure that the discovery process is fair and expeditious.

6. In Section 17 most of the references involve "parties to the arbitration proceeding." However, sometimes arbitrations involve outside, third parties who may be required to give testimony or produce documents. Section 17(c) has been changed so that the arbitrator should take the interests of such "affected persons" into account in determining whether and to what extent discovery is appropriate and Section 17(b) has been broadened so that a "witness" who is not a party can request the arbitrator to allow that person's testimony to be presented at the hearing by deposition if that person is unable to attend the hearing.

7. The Drafting Committee has made clear in Section 17(d) that if an arbitrator allows discovery, the arbitrator has the authority to issue subpoenas for a discovery proceeding such as a deposition. . . .

[. . .]

The Drafting Committee decided that the present approach of courts to safeguard the rights of third parties while insuring that there is sufficient disclosure of information for a full and fair hearing is adequate. Further development in this area should be left to case law because (1) it would be very difficult to draft a provision to include all the competing interests when an arbitrator issues a subpoena or discovery order against a nonparty [*e.g.*, courts seem to give lesser weight to nonparty's claims that an issue lacks relevancy as opposed to nonparty's claims that a matter is protected by privilege]; (2) state and federal administrative laws allowing subpoenas or discovery orders do not make special provisions for nonparties; and (3) the courts have protected well the interests of nonparties in arbitration cases.

10. Section 17(g) is intended to allow a court in State A (the State adopting the RUAA) to give effect to a subpoena or any discovery-related order issued by an arbitrator in an arbitration proceeding in State B without the need for the party who has received the subpoena first to go to a court in State B to receive an enforceable order. This procedure would eliminate duplicative court proceedings in both State A and State B before a witness or record or other evidence can be produced for the arbitration proceeding in State B. . . .

[. . .]

SECTION 20. CHANGE OF AWARD BY ARBITRATOR.

(a) On [motion] to an arbitrator by a party to an arbitration proceeding, the arbitrator may modify or correct an award:

   (1) upon a ground stated in Section 24(a)(1) or (3);

   (2) because the arbitrator has not made a final and definite award upon a claim submitted by the parties to the arbitration proceeding; or

   (3) to clarify the award.

(b) A [motion] under subsection (a) must be made and notice given to all parties within 20 days after the movant receives notice of the award.

(c) A party to the arbitration proceeding must give notice of any objection to the [motion] within 10 days after receipt of the notice.

(d) If a [motion] to the court is pending under Section 22, 23, or 24, the court may submit the claim to the arbitrator to consider whether to modify or correct the award:

   (1) upon a ground stated in Section 24(a)(1) or (3);

   (2) because the arbitrator has not made a final and definite award upon a claim submitted by the parties to the arbitration proceeding; or

   (3) to clarify the award.

(e) An award modified or corrected pursuant to this section is subject to Sections 19(a), 22, 23, and 24.

NOTES AND QUESTIONS

   1. Section 20 permits the clarification of an award upon remand to the rendering tribunal. Who determines when clarification is in order: The court in an action to confirm or vacate, a party to the action, a third-party (like the administering arbitral institution)? What is the basis for seeking a clarification? When does a lack of clarity exist? When is it sufficient for a remand? What result if the rendering tribunal cannot be reconstituted or refuses to act because it believes the award is clear or for some other reason?

   2. What happens if the rendering tribunal renders another award that is, in the court's or party's view, just as unclear?

   3. Can a lack of clarity be distinguished from dissatisfaction with the result? How?

   4. Is clarification different from correction, vacatur, and appeal? Explain.

SECTION 21. REMEDIES; FEES AND EXPENSES OF ARBITRATION PROCEEDING.

(a) An arbitrator may award punitive damages or other exemplary relief if such an award is authorized by law in a civil action involving the same claim and the evidence produced at the hearing justifies the award under the legal standards otherwise applicable to the claim.

(b) An arbitrator may award reasonable attorney's fees and other reasonable expenses of arbitration if such an award is authorized by law in a civil action involving the same claim or by the agreement of the parties to the arbitration proceeding.

(c) As to all remedies other than those authorized by subsections (a) and (b), an arbitrator may order such remedies as the arbitrator considers just and appropriate under the circumstances of the arbitration proceeding. The fact that such a remedy could not or would not be granted by the court is not a ground for refusing to confirm an award under Section 22 or for vacating an award under Section 23.

(d) An arbitrator's expenses and fees, together with other expenses, must be paid as provided in the award.

(e) If an arbitrator awards punitive damages or other exemplary relief under subsection (a), the arbitrator shall specify in the award the basis in fact justifying and the basis in law authorizing the award and state separately the amount of the punitive damages or other exemplary relief.

NOTES AND QUESTIONS

1. Section 21 is innovative by comparison to other statutory frameworks. It accurately reflects the contemporary status of remedial relief in U.S. arbitration law. It authorizes arbitrators to award both punitive damages and attorney's fees. They may also order relief that they believe is "just and appropriate under the circumstances." The statutory text provides for sensible limitations on the arbitrators' discretion to award damages. How does this compare to the power granted under the FAA?

2. The source of limitations, however, is unclear. Does the law or party agreement establish the qualifications in Section 21(a), (b), and (c)? What sanction can be imposed if the arbitrator misapplies the law on damages? How or can the arbitrator misapplication of law be distinguished from excess of authority or manifest disregard?

3. Does Section 21(e) imply that there is a procedure for the judicial review of the merits of arbitrator determinations on punitive damages?

4. What result if the law chosen by the parties or the law of the place or seat of the arbitration allows punitive damages but the law of the place of enforcement prohibits them or allows them on a more restrictive basis? Which law governs in these circumstances? Why? Is full faith and credit or federal preemption relevant?

SECTION 22. CONFIRMATION OF AWARD.

After a party to an arbitration proceeding receives notice of an award, the party may make a [motion] to the court for an order confirming the award at which time the court shall issue a confirming order unless the award is modified or corrected pursuant to Section 20 or 24 or is vacated pursuant to Section 23.

SECTION 23. VACATING AWARD.

(a) Upon [motion] to the court by a party to an arbitration proceeding, the court shall vacate an award made in the arbitration proceeding if:

(1) the award was procured by corruption, fraud, or other undue means;

(2) there was:

(A) evident partiality by an arbitrator appointed as a neutral arbitrator;

(B) corruption by an arbitrator; or

(C) misconduct by an arbitrator prejudicing the rights of a party to the arbitration proceeding;

(3) an arbitrator refused to postpone the hearing upon showing of sufficient cause for postponement, refused to consider evidence material to the controversy, or otherwise conducted the hearing contrary to Section 15, so as to prejudice substantially the rights of a party to the arbitration proceeding;

(4) an arbitrator exceeded the arbitrator's powers;

(5) there was no agreement to arbitrate, unless the person participated in the arbitration proceeding without raising the objection under Section 15(c) not later than the beginning of the arbitration hearing; or

(6) the arbitration was conducted without proper notice of the initiation of an arbitration as required in Section 9 so as to prejudice substantially the rights of a party to the arbitration proceeding.

(b) A [motion] under this section must be filed within 90 days after the [movant] receives notice of the award pursuant to Section 19 or within 90 days after the [movant] receives notice of a modified or corrected award pursuant to Section 20, unless the [movant] alleges that the award was procured by corruption, fraud, or other undue means, in which case the [motion] must be made within 90 days after the ground is known or by the exercise of reasonable care would have been known by the [movant].

(c) If the court vacates an award on a ground other than that set forth in subsection (a)(5), it may order a rehearing. If the award is vacated on a ground stated in subsection (a)(1) or (2), the rehearing must be before a new arbitrator. If the award is vacated on a ground stated in subsection (a)(3), (4), or (6), the rehearing may be before the arbitrator who made the award or the arbitrator's successor. The arbitrator must render the decision in the rehearing within the same time as that provided in Section 19(b) for an award.

(d) If the court denies a [motion] to vacate an award, it shall confirm the award unless a [motion] to modify or correct the award is pending.

SECTION 24. MODIFICATION OR CORRECTION OF AWARD.

(a) Upon [motion] made within 90 days after the [movant] receives notice of the award pursuant to Section 19 or within 90 days after the [movant] receives notice of a modified or corrected award pursuant to Section 20, the court shall modify or correct the award if:

> (1) there was an evident mathematical miscalculation or an evident mistake in the description of a person, thing, or property referred to in the award;

> (2) the arbitrator has made an award on a claim not submitted to the arbitrator and the award may be corrected without affecting the merits of the decision upon the claims submitted; or

> (3) the award is imperfect in a matter of form not affecting the merits of the decision on the claims submitted.

(b) If a [motion] made under subsection (a) is granted, the court shall modify or correct and confirm the award as modified or corrected. Otherwise, unless a motion to vacate is pending, the court shall confirm the award.

(c) A [motion] to modify or correct an award pursuant to this section may be joined with a [motion] to vacate the award.

NOTES AND QUESTIONS

Sections 23 and 24 are basically comparable to the corresponding grounds in the FAA. Can you improve them in some fashion? Are they clear and free of ambiguity? Are they economically drafted and presented?

[...]

* * *

Omitted Issues

The Drafting Committee determined that the new uniform law should not address three issues in contemporary arbitration law. To varying degrees, these issues have stretched the operative principles of that law to their outer limits: First, the validity and enforceability of adhesionary arbitration contracts in the consumer and employment areas; second, the use of so-called "opt-in" provisions for the expanded review of awards, in which parties agree as part of the recourse to arbitration that a court should review on the merits any legal ruling rendered by the arbitrators or the award should be subject to review by a second, internal arbitral body; and, third, whether the manifest disregard of the law ground for the vacatur of awards and the public policy exception to enforcement should be statutorily codified. Do you agree with the policy and rationale that was adopted by the drafters? In reaching your assessment, consider the following excerpts.

I.

Adhesionary Contracts

The drafters provided an Official Comment on the question of whether adhesionary and unconscionable arbitration agreements are enforceable contracts. The Official Comment reads in part:

> As a result of concerns over fairness in arbitration involving those with unequal bargaining power, organizations and individuals involved in employment, consumer and health-care arbitration have determined common standards for arbitration in these fields.
>
> [. . .]
>
> The Drafting Committee determined to leave the issue of adhesion contracts and unconscionability to developing law because (1) the issue of unconscionability reflects so much the substantive law of the States and not just arbitration, (2) the case law, statutes, and arbitration standards are rapidly changing, and (3) treating arbitration clauses differently from other contract provisions would raise significant preemption issues under the Federal Arbitration Act. However, it should be pointed out that a primary purpose of Section 4 which provides that some sections of the RUAA are not waivable is to address the problem of contracts of adhesion in the statute while taking into account the limitations caused by federal preemption.
>
> Because an arbitration agreement effectively waives a party's right to a jury trial, courts should ensure the fairness of an agreement to arbitrate, particularly in instances involving statutory rights which provide claimants with important remedies. Courts should determine that an arbitration process is adequate to protect important rights. Without these safeguards, arbitration loses credibility as an appropriate alternative to litigation.

II.

Expanded Review of Awards

The "opt-in" provisions for the expanded review of awards reportedly generated significant discussions within the Drafting Committee. That committee eventually voted by a majority to exclude from Section 23 a provision allowing for expanded judicial review of awards by contract or agreements for the review of awards by appellate arbitral tribunals. Recognizing that such provisions provided certain advantages, the *Reporter's Notes* described the reasoning which led to their exclusion:

> . . . Paramount is the assertion that permitting parties a 'second bite at the apple' on the merits effectively eviscerates arbitration as a true alternative to traditional litigation. An opt-in section in the RUAA might lead to the routine inclusion of review provisions in arbitration agreements in order to assuage the concerns of parties uncomfortable with the risk of being stuck with disagreeable arbitration awards that are immune from judicial review. The inevitable post-award petition for vacatur would in many cases result in the negotiated settlement of many disputes due to the specter of vacatur litigation the parties had agreed would be resolved in arbitration.

This line of argument asserts further that an opt-in provision would virtually ensure that, in cases of consequence, losers will petition for vacatur, thereby robbing commercial arbitration of its finality and making the process more complicated, time-consuming and expensive. Arbitrators would be effectively obliged to provide detailed conclusions of law and if the parties agree to judicial review for errors of fact, findings of fact in order to facilitate review. In order to lay the predicate for the appeal of unfavorable awards, transcripts would become the norm and counsel would be required to expend substantial time and energy making sure the record would support an appeal. Finally, the time to resolution in many cases would be greatly lengthened, as well as increasing the prospect of re-opened proceedings on remand following judicial review.

At its core, arbitration is supposed to be an alternative to litigation in a court of law, not a prelude to it. It can be argued that parties unwilling to accept the risk of binding awards because of an inherent mistrust of the process and arbitrators are best off contracting for advisory arbitration or foregoing arbitration entirely and relying instead on traditional litigation.

The third argument raised in opposition to an opt-in provision is the prospect of a backlash of sorts from the courts. The courts have blessed arbitration as an acceptable alternative to traditional litigation, characterizing it as an exercise in freedom of contract that has created a significant collateral benefit of making civil court dockets more manageable. They are not likely to view with favor parties exercising the freedom of contract to gut the finality of the arbitration process and throw disputes back into the courts for decision. It is maintained that courts faced with that prospect may well lose their recently acquired enthusiasm for commercial arbitration.

...The decision not to include in the RUAA a statutory sanction of either expanded judicial review or of internal, arbitral review of the "opt-in" device effectively leaves the issue of the legal propriety of this means for securing review of awards to the developing case law under the FAA and state arbitration statutes. Consequently, parties remain free to agree to contractual provisions for internal arbitral or judicial review of challenged awards, on whatever grounds and based on whatever standards they deem appropriate. . . .

III.

Codifying the Common–Law Grounds for Vacatur

As to the non-codification of the two common-law grounds for challenging the validity of awards, the *Reporter's Notes* state:

5. There are reasons for the RUAA not to embrace these two standards. The first is presented by the omission from the FAA of either standard. Given that omission, there is a very significant question of possible FAA preemption of a such a provision in the RUAA, should the Supreme Court or Congress eventually confirm that the four narrow grounds for vacatur set out in Section 10(a) of the federal act are the exclusive grounds for vacatur. The second reason for not including these vacatur grounds is the dilemma in attempting to fashion unambiguous, "bright line" tests for these two standards. The case law on both vacatur

grounds is not just unsettled but also is conflicting and indicates further evolution in the courts.

Conclusions

It is difficult to envisage the Uniform Arbitration Act (2000) as a successful statutory framework. One distinguished arbitration expert has described it in part as passing the "doing no harm" test. *See* James H. Carter, *Uniform Law Commissioners Adopt Revised UAA*, 5–3 ADR CURRENTS 1, 11 (2000). *See also* AMERICAN ARBITRATION ASSOCIATION, DISPUTE RESOLUTION TIMES 1 (July–September 2000). Even a modestly positive assessment seems questionable. In some respects, the new uniform law adopts the character and tonality of a procedural manual, rather than a statute. It contains too much "legalese" in word and structure and its pursuit of would-be precision often renders the propounded rules distorted and conceptually inaccessible. The lack of compositional clarity and misguided doctrinal content are present in too many provisions.

In the final analysis, how do you evaluate UAA (2000) as a statutory text? Does it contribute to the golden age of arbitration law? Does it codify universal propositions for the legal regulation of arbitration? Are the *Reporter's Notes* a better statement of prospective legal rules on arbitration?

CHAPTER FOUR

ARBITRATION AND FEDERALISM

■ ■ ■

1. INTRODUCTION: INITIAL STEPS TOWARD "FEDERALIZATION"

The FAA was enacted during the era of *Swift v. Tyson*, 41 U.S. (16 Pet.) 1 (1842). The latter decision provided that federal courts hearing state law cases on a diversity basis were bound by state court opinions only when the cases before them involved state constitutions or statutes. When such laws were not involved, the federal courts were free to devise their own rules of decision independently of state court rulings. *Erie R.R. Co. v. Tompkins*, 304 U.S. 64 (1938), overruled *Swift v. Tyson*, providing that "there is no general federal common law," and that "Congress has no power to declare substantive rules of common law applicable in a state, whether they be local in their nature or general, whether they be commercial law or a part of the law of torts." 304 U.S. at 78. In effect, *Erie* reversed the prior doctrine by requiring federal courts, in cases of diversity jurisdiction, to apply state law except when the controversy was governed by the U.S. Constitution or an Act of Congress.

Viewing the enactment of the FAA from the perspective of *Erie*, the question became whether the federal law on arbitration—providing for the enforceability of arbitration agreements—was merely a set of procedural regulations or a unique piece of legislation that created substantive rights and was therefore binding upon the federal courts in all cases. More specifically, in a diversity of citizenship case involving purely state interests, could the provisions of the FAA dislodge the application of a less favorable or perhaps antagonistic (but otherwise controlling) state statute or decisional law?

Under *Erie*, the displacement of applicable state law on arbitration could be seen as a preemptive application of general federal common law. Although clearly protective of federalism principles, such an interpretation could have fragmented any national consensus on arbitration and undermined the FAA's clear mandate to make arbitration an autonomous and viable alternative adjudicatory process. In this setting, another view of the federalism issue, progressively elaborated in the court construction of the FAA in diversity cases, could be advanced. Because *Erie* mandates the application of state law in all diversity cases except those in which the U.S. Constitution or federal legislation is controlling, the courts could deem that the FAA was applicable as a federal enactment, holding—in effect—that the FAA represents more than the enactment of merely procedural regulations and that it actually creates substantive rights. According to a distinguished scholar in the area, "[t]o be consistent with *Erie*, a court creating federal common law need only ground its authority to do so on some federal enactment other than the diversity grant." Field, *The Scope of Federal Common Law*, 99 HARV. L. REV. 881, 888 (1986).

In this regard, the decision in *Prima Paint Corp. v. Flood & Conklin Mfg. Co.*, 388 U.S. 395 (1967), has landmark significance. The Court upheld the Second Circuit's view that: "[A]rbitration clauses as a matter of federal law are 'separable' from the contracts in which they are embedded, and...where no claim is made that fraud was directed to the arbitration clause itself, a broad arbitration clause will be held to encompass arbitration of the claim that the contract itself was induced by fraud." 388 U.S. at 402, 404.

Prima Paint also is noteworthy for the U.S. Supreme Court's definition of the FAA's systemic stature and underlying legislative purpose. In *Prima Paint*, the Court underscored the primary intent and ultimate objective of the federal legislation on arbitration, and it expressed its judicial resolve to give full effect to both these aspects of the Act in relevant litigation. The Court further stated that the question in *Prima Paint* "was not whether Congress may fashion federal substantive rules to govern questions arising in simple diversity cases,...[but] whether Congress may prescribe how federal courts are to conduct themselves with respect to subject matter over which Congress plainly has power to legislate." 388 U.S. at 405. In other words, *Prima Paint* did not involve the issue of federalism and states' rights, but whether Congress could provide substantive directives to the federal courts in areas in which Congress had specific legislative powers. The Court, in effect, answered the federalism question by implication while appearing to disregard it: Congress could create federal law where it had legislative authority to act. Therefore, in diversity cases in which questions arose regarding the validity of the recourse to arbitration, the federal courts were under an obligation to apply the relevant federal legislation in the area. The only limitation upon the application of federal law in this area appeared to be that the contracts in question containing arbitration clauses must affect interstate commerce.

In *Prima Paint*, the Court articulated what was to become a fundamental tenet of its evolving decisional law on arbitration: That the FAA's purpose to provide for the enforceability of arbitration agreements was manifest, and that objective—buttressed by the reference to contractual freedom—must be given effect in the federal decisional law whenever possible. In the Court's own language, "[i]n so concluding, we not only honor the plain meaning of the statute but also the unmistakably clear congressional purpose that the arbitration procedure, when selected by the parties to a contract, be speedy and not subject to delay and obstruction in the courts." 388 U.S. at 404. Challenges to the validity of arbitration agreements on the basis of state law, therefore, were seen primarily as a dilatory tactic—an attempt to defeat the effect of the arbitration agreement and to frustrate the clear purpose of the federal legislation.

The federal courts grappled earlier with the federalism question in two cases. In *Bernhardt*, the U.S. Supreme Court took an *"Erie-*sensitive" position, holding that the FAA was a federal procedural enactment that could not dislodge the application of state law in federal diversity cases. Allowing claims to be submitted to arbitration through the federal courts in diversity cases might lead to adjudicatory outcomes not otherwise available under state law. The undermining of state law would violate the directive in *Erie*.

In *Robert Lawrence*, the U.S. Second Circuit Court of Appeals advanced a different view of the FAA's status, declaring that it represented the enactment of federal substantive law on arbitration agreements under the constitutional powers of the U.S. Congress. The federal law was applicable in both state and federal courts and also controlled in diversity cases. Judge Medina, in *Robert Lawrence*, anticipates prophetically more than forty years of subsequent litigation on arbitration.

Finally, in *Citizens Bank v. Alafabco, Inc.*, 539 U.S. 52 (2003), the U.S. Supreme Court adopted a broad definition of "interstate commerce" that extended the reach of the FAA. It stated that the FAA covered a "written provision in any ... contract evidencing a transaction involving commerce." The term "involving commerce" was the functional equivalent of the more common term "affecting commerce," an interpretation that generally signaled the broadest possible exercise of Congress' Commerce Clause power. According to the Court, the FAA provides for the enforcement of arbitration agreements within the full reach of the Commerce Clause and, therefore, encompasses a wide range of activities. A "cramped view" of the Congress' power under the Commerce Clause was not proper. That power could be exercised in individual cases without showing any specific effect on interstate commerce as long as the economic activity in question represented a general practice subject to federal control.

BERNHARDT v. POLYGRAPHIC CO. OF AMERICA

350 U.S. 198, 76 S.Ct. 273, 100 L.Ed. 199 (1956).

(footnotes omitted)

MR. JUSTICE DOUGLAS delivered the opinion of the Court.

This suit, removed from a Vermont court to the District Court on grounds of diversity of citizenship, was brought for damages for the discharge of petitioner under an employment contract. At the time the contract was made petitioner was a resident of New York. Respondent is a New York corporation. The contract was made in New York. Petitioner later became a resident of Vermont, where he was to perform his duties under the contract, and asserts his rights there.

The contract contains a provision that in case of any dispute the parties will submit the matter to arbitration under New York law by the American Arbitration Association, whose determination "shall be final and absolute." After the case had been removed to the District Court, respondent moved for a stay of the proceedings so that the controversy could go to arbitration in New York. The motion alleged that the law of New York governs the question whether the arbitration provision of the contract is binding.

The District Court ruled that under *Erie R.R. Co. v. Tompkins*,...the arbitration provision of the contract was governed by Vermont law and that the law of Vermont makes revocable an agreement to arbitrate at any time before an award is actually made. The District Court therefore denied the stay. The Court of Appeals reversed. The case is here on a petition for certiorari which we granted because of the doubtful application by the Court of Appeals of *Erie R.R. Co. v. Tompkins*.

A question under the United States Arbitration Act,...§§ 1, 3, lies at the threshold of the case...No maritime transaction is involved here. Nor does this contract evidence "a transaction involving commerce" within the meaning of § 2 of the Act. There is no showing that petitioner while performing his duties under the employment contract was working "in" commerce, was producing goods for commerce, or was engaging in activity that affected commerce, within the meaning of our decisions.

[T]he larger question presented here...is [] whether arbitration touched on substantive rights, which *Erie R.R. Co. v. Tompkins* held were governed by local law, or was a mere form of procedure within the power of the federal courts or Congress to prescribe. Our view is that § 3, so read, would invade the local law field. We therefore read § 3 narrowly to avoid that issue. We conclude that the stay provided in § 3 reaches only those contracts covered by §§ 1 and 2.

The question remains whether, apart from the Federal Act, a provision of a contract providing for arbitration is enforceable in a diversity case.

[. . .]

... We deal here with a right to recover that owes its existence to one of the States, not to the United States. The federal court enforces the state-created right by rules of procedure which it has acquired from the Federal Government and which therefore are not identical with those of the state courts. Yet, in spite of that difference in procedure, the federal court enforcing a state-created right in a diversity case is in substance "only another court of the State." The federal court therefore may not "substantially affect the enforcement of the right as given by the State." If the federal court allows arbitration where the state court would disallow it, the outcome of litigation might depend on the courthouse where suit is brought. For the remedy by arbitration, whatever its merits or shortcomings, substantially affects the cause of action created by the State. The nature of the tribunal where suits are tried is an important part of the parcel of rights behind a cause of action. The change from a court of law to an arbitration panel may make a radical difference in ultimate result. Arbitration carries no right to trial by jury that is guaranteed both by the Seventh Amendment and by Ch. 1, Art. 12th, of the Vermont Constitution. Arbitrators do not have the benefit of judicial instruction on the law; they need not give their reasons for their results; the record of their proceedings is not as complete as it is in a court trial; and judicial review of an award is more limited than judicial review of a trial—all as discussed in *Wilko v. Swan*. We said in the *York* case that "The nub of the policy that underlies *Erie R.R. Co. v. Tompkins* is that for the same transaction the accident of a suit by a non-resident litigant in a federal court instead of in a State court a block away should not lead to a substantially different result." ... There would in our judgment be a resultant discrimination if the parties suing on a Vermont cause of action in the federal court were remitted to arbitration, while those suing in the Vermont court could not be.

[. . .]

The judgment of the Court of Appeals is reversed and the cause is remanded to the District Court for proceedings in conformity with this opinion.

Reversed and remanded.

[. . .]

NOTES AND QUESTIONS

1. From a historical and doctrinal perspective, the Court's reasoning pertaining to the impact of procedural remedies upon substantive determinations is a critical facet of the opinion. Justice Douglas refers favorably to *Wilko v. Swan*, 346 U.S. 427 (1953), in his discussion of arbitration and he will deliver an eloquent dissent in *Scherk v. Alberto–Culver Co.*, 417 U.S. 506 (1974).

2. The view that arbitrators will not rule in the same manner as judges or that the submission of claims to arbitration, in all probability, will lead to results different from a judicial determination is in direct opposition to the Court's "new wave" position that arbitration is "a mere form of trial" which has no impact upon substantive legal rights. This position was articulated initially in *Mitsubishi Motors Corp. v. Soler Chrysler–Plymouth, Inc.*, 473 U.S. 614 (1985), and has become a staple of the federal decisional law on arbitration.

3. Which view is correct? Does Justice Douglas' description of arbitration constitute disparagement and express hostility about the process? Is it a realistic and accurate assessment? Would Justice Douglas' position on arbitration remain the same if federalism and states' rights were not involved in the litigation? What rights warrant the depreciation of arbitration? Which ones do not?

ROBERT LAWRENCE CO. v. DEVONSHIRE
FABRICS, INC.

271 F.2d 402, 402–05, 407, 409–10 (2d Cir. 1959).

(footnotes omitted)

MEDINA, Circuit Judge.

Devonshire Fabrics, Inc. (Devonshire) appeals from an order denying its motion for a stay of proceedings pending arbitration pursuant to the United States Arbitration Act, 9 U.S.C. § 3.

Plaintiff in this action, Robert Lawrence Company, Inc. (Lawrence) is seeking damages for allegedly fraudulent misrepresentations made by Devonshire inducing it to purchase and pay for a quantity of woolen fabric. The transaction out of which this case arose was initiated on August 4, 1955 when Lawrence, a Massachusetts corporation, ordered through its New York City office 36 pieces of a certain style of wool. Devonshire, a New York corporation, upon receipt of the order issued a confirmation which differed in several respects from the terms of the order. While the parties disagree as to which document embodies the final contract, each of the two documents contains the following provision for arbitration:

> Any complaint, controversy, or question which may arise with respect to this contract that cannot be settled by the parties thereto, shall be referred to arbitration. If the controversy concerns the condition or quality of merchandise it shall be referred to the Mutual Adjustment Bureau of the cloth and garment trades pursuant to the rules and regulations thereof. All other controversies shall be submitted to the American Arbitration Association.

Delivery of the goods, originally scheduled for October 1, 1955[,] was postponed at Lawrence's request until June 1956[,] when shipment to Boston was made. Lawrence paid the purchase price of $9,062.43 in July 1956. According to Lawrence, whose version of the fraud we must accept in the present posture of the case, certain latent defects were subsequently discovered and the merchandise proved not to be "first quality" as called for by the agreement. It is disputed whether Lawrence "rescinded" the contract or whether it waived its right to do so by later inconsistent acts.

The court below denied the stay of proceedings pending arbitration and held: "The question whether or not there is a valid agreement to arbitrate must be decided by the court prior to the issuance of a stay and cannot be submitted to arbitration 'as a controversy thereafter arising out of such contract' within section 2 . . . If the contract was fraudulent in its inception and therefore voidable at the option of the plaintiff and plaintiff has disaffirmed such contract, then there is no valid agreement to arbitrate which would justify a stay."

I

[. . .]

The case involves questions left open by the Supreme Court in *Bernhardt v. Polygraphic Co. of America....* The basic inquiry must be whether the validity and interpretation of the arbitration clause of the contract in this case is governed by Federal Law, *i.e.*, the federal Arbitration Act, or by local Law. ...[T]he exclusion of diversity cases [from the FAA] would emasculate the federal Arbitration Act...[and] we find a reasonably clear legislative intent to create a new body of substantive law relative to arbitration agreements affecting commerce or maritime transactions. Thus we think we are here dealing not with state-created rights but with rights arising out of the exercise by the Congress of its constitutional power to regulate commerce and hence there is involved no difficult question of constitutional law under *Erie*.

[. . .]

[W]e think the text of the Act and the legislative history demonstrate that the Congress based the Arbitration Act in part on its undisputed substantive powers over commerce and maritime matters. To be sure much of the Act is purely procedural in character and is intended to be applicable only in the federal courts. But Section 2['s] declaring that arbitration agreements affecting commerce or maritime affairs are "valid, irrevocable, and enforceable" goes beyond this point and must mean that arbitration agreements of this character, previously held by state law to be invalid, revocable or unenforceable, are now made "valid, irrevocable, and enforceable." This is a declaration of national law equally applicable in state or federal courts. This conclusion flows directly from the realization by the Congress that nothing of significance would have been accomplished without tapping these substantive sources of power. It is these that put teeth into the statute and make it accomplish the salutary and beneficial ends the Congress had in mind.

[. . .]

We, therefore, hold that the Arbitration Act in making agreements to arbitrate "valid, irrevocable, and enforceable" created national substantive law clearly constitutional under the maritime and commerce powers of the Congress and that the rights thus created are to be adjudicated by the federal courts whenever such courts have subject matter jurisdiction, including diversity cases, just as the federal courts adjudicate controversies affecting other substantive rights when subject matter jurisdiction over the litigation exists. We hold that the body of law thus created is substantive not procedural in character and that it encompasses questions of interpretation and construction as well as questions of validity, revocability and enforceability of arbitration agreements affecting interstate commerce or maritime affairs, since these two types of legal questions are inextricably intertwined.

In the case before us there can be little doubt that the transaction in question relates to an interstate shipment of goods and involves "commerce" within the meaning of Sections 1 and 2. We, therefore, find federal law as derived from the Arbitration Act to be controlling.

II

[. . .]

We now turn to the decision of this case and the formulation of the principles of federal substantive law necessary for this purpose.

The District Court held that there could be no finding of an "agreement to arbitrate" until it was judicially resolved whether or not there was fraud in the inception of the contract as alleged by Lawrence. But surely this is an oversimplification of the problem. For example, it would seem to be necessary to answer the following questions before we can decide to affirm or reverse the order appealed from: (1) is there anything in the Arbitration Act or elsewhere to prevent the parties from making a binding agreement to arbitrate any disputes thereafter arising between them, including a dispute that there had been fraud in the inception of the contract; (2) is the exception of Section 2, "save upon such grounds as exist at law or in equity for the revocation of any contract[,]" applicable if such an agreement to arbitrate has been made and the only fraud charged is fraud in inducing the purchase of the goods, rather than fraud in connection with the making of the agreement to arbitrate; (3) did the parties in the case before us make a binding agreement to arbitrate; and (4) is the arbitration clause broad enough to cover the charge of fraud?

That the Arbitration Act envisages a distinction between the entire contract between the parties on the one hand and the arbitration clause of the contract on the other is plain on the face of the statute. Section 2 does not purport to affect the contract as a whole. On the contrary, it makes "valid, irrevocable, and enforceable" only a "written provision in any maritime transaction or a contract evidencing a transaction involving commerce to settle by arbitration a controversy thereafter arising out of such contract or transaction"; and Section 3 provides for the granting of a stay in any suit or proceeding in the federal courts "upon an issue referable to arbitration under an agreement in writing for such arbitration."

[. . .]

Finally, any doubts as to the construction of the Act ought to be resolved in line with its liberal policy of promoting arbitration both to accord with the original intention of the parties and to help ease the current congestion of court calendars. Such policy has been consistently reiterated by the federal courts and we think it deserves to be heartily endorsed...

It would seem to be beyond dispute that the parties are entitled to agree, should they desire to do so, that one of the questions for the arbitrators to decide in case the controversy thereafter arises, is whether or not one of the parties was induced by fraud to make the principal contract for the delivery of the merchandise. Surely there is no public policy that would stand as a bar to an agreement of such obvious utility, as is demonstrated by the facts of this case. The issue of fraud seems inextricably enmeshed in the other factual issues of the case. Indeed, the difference between fraud in the inducement and mere failure of performance by delivery of defective merchandise depends upon little more than legal verbiage and the formulation of legal conclusions. Once it is settled that arbitration agreements are "valid, irrevocable, and enforceable" we know of no principle of law that stands as an obstacle to a determination by the parties to the effect that arbitration should not be denied or postponed upon the mere cry of fraud in the inducement, as this would permit the frustration of the very purposes sought to be achieved by the agreement to arbitrate, *i.e.* a speedy and relatively inexpensive trial before commercial specialists.

[. . .]

NOTES AND QUESTIONS

1. Despite the court's attempts to distinguish *Robert Lawrence* from *Bernhardt*, the opinion in *Robert Lawrence* advances a radically different view of the systemic standing of the FAA and of the federalism issues it generates.

2. Do you agree that the FAA constitutes a "declaration of national law that applies in both state and federal courts"? How can such a statement be justified? Do you believe Justice Douglas would agree? The *Robert Lawrence* court seems to state that Section Two of the FAA is a substantive provision that creates federal rights. What rights does it create? Does the text of the statute justify that interpretation? Do cases involving the application of Section Two raise a federal question?

3. *Robert Lawrence* is a very modern opinion on arbitration, despite the date of its rendition. On the question of fraud, it invokes the freedom of contract doctrine to resolve the jurisdictional question (much like the Court in *First Options of Chicago, Inc. v. Kaplan*, 514 U.S. 938 [1995]) and it, in another place, refers to the salutary effect of arbitration upon the management of court dockets. Do you agree with the court's interpretation of FAA § 3 and its view that fraud in the inducement is equivalent to defective performance for purposes of determining the contractual validity of the arbitration agreement?

PRIMA PAINT CORP. v. FLOOD & CONKLIN MFG. CO.

388 U.S. 395, 87 S.Ct. 1801, 18 L.Ed.2d 1270 (1967).

(footnotes omitted)

MR. JUSTICE FORTAS delivered the opinion of the Court.

[. . .]

On October 7, 1964, respondent, Flood & Conklin Manufacturing Company, a New Jersey corporation, entered into what was styled a "Consulting Agreement," with petitioner, Prima Paint Corporation, a Maryland corporation. This agreement followed by less than three weeks the execution of a contract pursuant to which Prima Paint purchased F &

C's paint business. The agreement took into account the possibility that Prima Paint might encounter financial difficulties, including bankruptcy, but no corresponding reference was made to possible financial problems which might be encountered by F & C. The agreement stated that it "embodies the entire understanding of the parties on the subject matter." Finally, the parties agreed to a broad arbitration clause, which read in part:

> "Any controversy or claim arising out of or relating to this Agreement, or the breach thereof, shall be settled by arbitration in the City of New York, in accordance with the rules then obtaining of the American Arbitration Association * * *."

The first payment by Prima Paint to F & C under the consulting agreement was due on September 1, 1965. None was made on that date. Seventeen days later, Prima Paint did pay the appropriate amount, but into escrow. It notified attorneys for F & C that in various enumerated respects their client had broken both the consulting agreement and the earlier purchase agreement. Prima Paint's principal contention...was that F & C had fraudulently represented that it was solvent and able to perform its contractual obligations, whereas it was in fact insolvent and intended to file a petition...[for bankruptcy]...shortly after execution of the consulting agreement. Prima Paint noted that such a petition was filed by F & C on October 14, 1964, one week after the contract had been signed. F & C's response, on October 25, was to serve a "notice of intention to arbitrate." On November 12, three days before expiration of its time to answer this "notice," Prima Paint filed suit in the United States District Court for the Southern District of New York, seeking rescission of the consulting agreement on the basis of the alleged fraudulent inducement. The complaint asserted that the federal court had diversity jurisdiction.

Contemporaneously with the filing of its complaint, Prima Paint petitioned the District Court for an order enjoining F & C from proceeding with the arbitration. F & C cross-moved to stay the court action pending arbitration. F & C contended that the issue presented—whether there was fraud in the inducement of the consulting agreement—was a question for the arbitrators and not for the District Court....

The District Court granted F & C's motion to stay the action pending arbitration, holding that a charge of fraud in the inducement of a contract containing an arbitration clause as broad as this one was a question for the arbitrators and not for the court. For this proposition it relied on *Robert Lawrence Co. v. Devonshire Fabrics, Inc....* The Court of Appeals for the Second Circuit dismissed Prima Paint's appeal....It held that the contract in question evidenced a transaction involving interstate commerce; that under the controlling *Robert Lawrence Co.* decision a claim of fraud in the inducement of the contract generally—as opposed to the arbitration clause itself—is for the arbitrators and not for the courts; and that this rule—one of "national substantive law"—governs even in the face of a contrary state rule. We agree, albeit for somewhat different reasons, and we affirm the decision below.

[. . .]

In *Bernhardt v. Polygraphic Co.,* . . . this Court held that the stay provisions of § 3, invoked here by respondent F & C, apply only to the two kinds of contracts specified in §§ 1 and 2 of the Act, namely those in admiralty or evidencing transactions in "commerce." Our first question, then, is whether the consulting agreement between F & C and Prima Paint is such a contract. We agree with the Court of Appeals that it is . . . . The consulting agreement was inextricably tied to . . . [the] . . . interstate transfer and to the continuing operations of an interstate manufacturing and wholesaling business. There could not be a clearer case of a contract evidencing a transaction in interstate commerce.

Having determined that the contract in question is within the coverage of the Arbitration Act, we turn to the central issue in this case: whether a claim of fraud in the inducement of the entire contract is to be resolved by the federal court, or whether the matter is to be referred to the arbitrators . . . .

With respect to cases brought in federal court involving maritime contracts or those evidencing transactions in "commerce," we think that Congress has provided an explicit answer. That answer is to be found in § 4 of the Act, which provides a remedy to a party seeking to compel compliance with an arbitration agreement. Under § 4, with respect to a matter within the jurisdiction of the federal courts save for the existence of an arbitration clause, the federal court is instructed to order arbitration to proceed once it is satisfied that "the making of the agreement for arbitration or the failure to comply [with the arbitration agreement] is not in issue." Accordingly, if the claim is fraud in the inducement of the arbitration clause itself—an issue which goes to the "making" of the agreement to arbitrate—the federal court may proceed to adjudicate it. But the statutory language does not permit the federal court to consider claims of fraud in the inducement of the contract generally. Section 4 does not expressly relate to situations like the present in which a stay is sought of a federal action in order that arbitration may proceed. But it is inconceivable that Congress intended the rule to differ depending upon which party to the arbitration agreement first invokes the assistance of a federal court. We hold, therefore, that in passing upon a § 3 application for a stay while the parties arbitrate, a federal court may consider only issues relating to the making and performance of the agreement to arbitrate. In so concluding, we not only honor the plain meaning of the statute but also the unmistakably clear congressional purpose that the arbitration procedure, when selected by the parties to a contract, be speedy and not subject to delay and obstruction in the courts.

There remains the question whether such a rule is constitutionally permissible. The point is made that, whatever the nature of the contract involved here, this case is in federal court solely by reason of diversity of citizenship, and that since the decision in *Erie R.R. Co. v. Tompkins*, federal courts are bound in diversity cases to follow state rules of decision in matters which are "substantive" rather than "procedural," or where the matter is "outcome determinative." ... The question in this case, however, is not whether Congress may fashion federal substantive rules to govern questions arising in simple diversity cases. Rather, the question is whether Congress may prescribe how federal courts are to conduct themselves with respect to subject matter over which Congress plainly has power to legislate. The answer to that can only be in the affirmative. And it is clear beyond dispute that the federal arbitration statute is based upon and confined to the incontestable federal foundations of "control over interstate commerce and over admiralty." ...

In the present case no claim has been advanced by Prima Paint that F & C fraudulently induced it to enter into the agreement to arbitrate "[a]ny controversy or claim arising out of or relating to this Agreement, or the breach thereof." This contractual language is easily broad enough to encompass Prima Paint's claim that both execution and acceleration of the consulting agreement itself were procured by fraud. Indeed, no claim is made that Prima Paint ever intended that "legal" issues relating to the contract be excluded from arbitration, or that it was not entirely free so to contract. Federal courts are bound to apply rules enacted by Congress with respect to matters—here, a contract involving commerce—over which it has legislative power.

Affirmed.

[...]

Mr. Justice Black, with whom Mr. Justice Douglas and Mr. Justice Stewart join, dissenting.

The Court here holds that the United States Arbitration Act, as a matter of federal substantive law, compels a party to a contract containing a written arbitration provision to carry out his "arbitration agreement" even though a court might, after a fair trial, hold the entire contract—including the arbitration agreement—void because of fraud in the inducement. The Court holds, what is to me fantastic, that the legal issue of a contract's voidness because of fraud is to be decided by persons designated to arbitrate factual controversies arising out of a valid contract between the parties. And the arbitrators who the Court holds are to adjudicate the legal validity of the contract need not even be lawyers, and in all probability will be nonlawyers, wholly unqualified to decide legal issues, and even if qualified to apply the law, not bound to do so. I am by no means sure that thus forcing a person to forgo his opportunity to try his legal issues in the courts where, unlike the situation in arbitration, he may have a jury trial and right to appeal, is not a denial of due process of law. I am satisfied, however, that Congress did not impose any such procedures in the Arbitration Act. And I am fully satisfied that a reasonable and fair reading of that Act's language and history shows that both Congress and the framers of the Act were at great pains to emphasize that nonlawyers designated to adjust and arbitrate factual controversies arising out of valid contracts would not trespass upon the courts' prerogative to decide the legal question of whether any legal contract exists upon which to base an arbitration.

I.

[. . .]

. . . The lower courts, relying on the Second Circuit's decision in *Robert Lawrence Co. v. Devonshire Fabrics, Inc.*, . . . held that, as a matter of "national substantive law," the arbitration clause in the contract is "separable" from the rest of the contract and that allegations that go to the validity of the contract in general, as opposed to the arbitration clause in particular, are to be decided by the arbitrator, not the court.

The Court today affirms this holding for three reasons, none of which is supported by the language or history of the Arbitration Act. First, the Court holds that because the consulting agreement was intended to supplement a separate contract for the interstate transfer of assets, it is itself a "contract evidencing a transaction involving commerce," the language used by Congress to describe contracts the Act was designed to cover. But in light of the legislative history which indicates that the Act was to have a limited application to contracts between merchants for the interstate shipment of goods, and in light of the express failure of Congress to use language making the Act applicable to all contracts which "affect commerce," the statutory language Congress normally uses when it wishes to exercise its full powers over commerce, I am not at all certain that the Act was intended to apply to this consulting agreement. Second, the Court holds that the language of § 4 of the Act provides an "explicit answer" to the question of whether the arbitration clause is "separable" from the rest of the contract in which it is contained. Section 4 merely provides that the court must order arbitration if it is "satisfied that the making of the agreement for arbitration * * * is not in issue." That language, considered alone, far from providing an "explicit answer," merely poses the further question of what kind of allegations put the making of the arbitration agreement in issue. Since both the lower courts assumed that but for the federal Act, New York law might apply and that under New York law a general allegation of fraud in the inducement puts into issue the making of the agreement to arbitrate (considered inseparable under New York law from the rest of the contract), the Court necessarily holds that federal law determines whether certain allegations put the making of the arbitration agreement in issue. And the Court approves the Second Circuit's fashioning of a federal separability rule which overrides state law to the contrary. The Court thus holds that the Arbitration Act, designed to provide merely a procedural remedy which would not interfere with state substantive law, authorizes federal courts to fashion a federal rule to make arbitration clauses "separable" and valid. And the Court approves a rule which is not only contrary to state law, but contrary to the intention of the parties and to accepted principles of contract law—a rule which indeed elevates arbitration provisions above all other contractual provisions. As the Court recognizes, that result was clearly not intended by Congress. Finally, the Court summarily disposes of the problem raised by *Erie R.R. Co. v. Tompkins*,...recognized as a serious constitutional problem in *Bernhardt v. Polygraphic Co.*,...by insufficiently supported assertions....

II.

...The language of...sections [2 and 3] could not, I think, raise doubts about their meaning except to someone anxious to find doubts. They simply mean this: [A]n arbitration agreement is to be enforced by a federal court unless the court, not the arbitrator, finds grounds "at law or in equity for the revocation of any contract." Fraud, of course, is one of the most common grounds for revoking a contract. If the contract was procured by fraud, then, unless the defrauded party elects to affirm it, there is absolutely no contract, nothing to be arbitrated. Sections 2 and 3 of the Act assume the existence of a valid contract. They merely provide for enforcement where such a valid contract exists. These provisions were plainly designed to protect a person against whom arbitration is sought to be enforced from having to submit his legal issues as to validity of the contract to the arbitrator. The legislative history of the Act makes this clear. Senator Walsh of Montana, in hearings on the bill in 1923, observed, "The court has got to hear and determine whether there is an agreement of arbitration, undoubtedly, and it is open to all defenses, equitable and legal, that would have existed at law * * *." Mr. Piatt, who represented the American Bar Association[,] which drafted and supported the Act, was even more explicit: "I think this will operate something like an injunction process, except where he would attack it on the ground of fraud." ...Mr. Cohen, the American Bar Association's draftsman of the bill, assured the members of Congress that the Act would not impair the right to a jury trial, because it deprives a person of that right only when he has voluntarily and validly waived it by agreeing to submit certain disputes to arbitration. The court and a jury are to determine both the legal existence and scope of such an agreement. The members of Congress revealed an acute awareness of this problem. On several occasions they expressed opposition to a law which would enforce even a valid arbitration provision contained in a contract between parties of unequal bargaining power. Senator Walsh cited insurance, employment, construction, and shipping contracts as routinely containing arbitration clauses and being offered on a take-it-or-leave-it basis to captive customers or employees. He noted that such contracts "are really not voluntarily (*sic*) things at all" because "there is nothing for the man to do except to sign it; and then he surrenders his right to have his case tried by the court * * *." He was emphatically assured by the supporters of the bill that it was not their intention to cover such cases. The significant thing is that Senator Walsh was not thinking in terms of the arbitration provisions being "separable" parts of such contracts, parts which should be enforced without regard to why the entire contracts in which they were contained were agreed to.

The issue for him was not whether an arbitration provision in a contract was made, but why, in the context of the entire contract and the circumstances of the parties, the entire contract was made. That is precisely the issue that a general allegation of fraud in the inducement raises: Prima contended that it would not have executed any contract, including the arbitration clause, if it were not for the fraudulent representations of F & C. Prima's agreement to an arbitration clause in a contract obtained by fraud was no more "voluntary" than an insured's or employee's agreement to an arbitration clause in a contract obtained by superior bargaining power.

Finally, it is clear to me from the bill's sponsors' understanding of the function of arbitration that they never intended that the issue of fraud in the inducement be resolved by arbitration. They recognized two special values of arbitration: (1) the expertise of an arbitrator to decide factual questions in regard to the day-to-day performance of contractual obligations, and (2) the speed with which arbitration, as contrasted to litigation, could resolve disputes over performance of contracts and thus mitigate the damages and allow the parties to continue performance under the contracts. Arbitration serves neither of these functions where a contract is sought to be rescinded on the ground of fraud. On the one hand, courts have far more expertise in resolving legal issues which go to the validity of a contract than do arbitrators. On the other hand, where a party seeks to rescind a contract and his allegation of fraud in the inducement is true, an arbitrator's speedy remedy of this wrong should never result in resumption of performance under the contract. And if the contract were not procured by fraud, the court, under the summary trial procedures provided by the Act, may determine with little delay that arbitration must proceed. The only advantage of submitting the issue of fraud to arbitration is for the arbitrators. Their compensation corresponds to the volume of arbitrations they perform. If they determine that a contract is void because of fraud, there is nothing further for them to arbitrate. I think it raises serious questions of due process to submit to an arbitrator an issue which will determine his compensation. . . .

III.

With such statutory language and legislative history, one can well wonder what is the basis for the Court's surprising departure from the Act's clear statement which expressly excepts from arbitration "such grounds as exist at law or in equity for the revocation of any contract." Credit for the creation of a rationalization to justify this statutory mutilation apparently must go to the Second Circuit's opinion in *Robert Lawrence Co. v. Devonshire Fabrics, Inc.* . . . In that decision Judge Medina undertook to resolve the serious constitutional problem which this Court had avoided in *Bernhardt* by holding the Act inapplicable to a diversity case involving an intrastate contract. That problem was whether the Arbitration Act, passed 13 years prior to *Erie R.R. Co. v. Tompkins* . . . , could be constitutionally applied in a diversity case even though its application would require the federal court to enforce an agreement to arbitrate which the state court across the street would not enforce. *Bernhardt's* holding that arbitration is "outcome determinative[]"...and its recognition that there would be unconstitutional discrimination if an arbitration agreement were enforceable in federal court but not in the state court...posed a choice of two alternatives for Judge Medina. If he held that the Arbitration Act rested solely on Congress' power, widely recognized in 1925 but negated in *Erie*, to prescribe general federal law applicable in diversity cases, he would be compelled to hold the Act unconstitutional as applied to diversity cases under *Erie* and *Bernhardt*. If he held that the Act rested on Congress' power to enact substantive law governing interstate commerce, then the *Erie-Bernhardt* problem would be avoided and the application of the Act to diversity cases involving commerce could be saved.

The difficulty in choosing between these two alternatives was that neither, quite contrary to the Court's position, was "clear beyond dispute" upon reference to the Act's legislative history. As to the first, it is clear that Congress intended the Act to be applicable in diversity cases involving interstate commerce and maritime contracts, and to hold the Act inapplicable in diversity cases would be severely to limit its impact. As to the second alternative, it is clear that Congress in passing the Act relied primarily on its power to create general federal rules to govern federal courts. ...Finally, there are clear indications in the legislative history that the Act was not intended to make arbitration agreements enforceable in state courts or to provide an independent federal-question basis for jurisdiction in federal courts apart from diversity jurisdiction. The absence of both of these effects—which normally follow from legislation of federal substantive law—seems to militate against the view that Congress was creating a body of federal substantive law.

Suffice it to say that Judge Medina chose the alternative of construing the Act to create federal substantive law in order to avoid its emasculation under *Erie* and *Bernhardt*. But Judge Medina was not content to stop there with a holding that the Act makes arbitration agreements in a contract involving commerce enforceable in federal court even though the basis of jurisdiction is diversity and state law does not enforce such agreements. The problem in *Robert Lawrence*, as here, was not whether an arbitration agreement is enforceable, for the New York Arbitration Act, upon which the federal Act was based, enforces an arbitration clause in the same terms as the federal Act. The problem in *Robert Lawrence*, and here, was rather whether the arbitration clause in a contract induced by fraud is "separable." Under New York law, it was not: general allegations of fraud in the inducement would, as a matter of state law, put in issue the making of the arbitration clause. So to avoid this application of state law, Judge Medina went further than holding that the federal Act makes agreements to arbitrate enforceable: he held that the Act creates a "body of law" that "encompasses questions of interpretation and construction as well as questions of validity, revocability and enforceability of arbitration agreements affecting interstate commerce or maritime affairs."...

Thus, 35 years after the passage of the Arbitration Act, the Second Circuit completely rewrote it. Under its new formulation, § 2 now makes arbitration agreements enforceable "save upon such grounds as exist at *federal* law for the revocation of any contract." And under § 4, before enforcing an arbitration agreement, the district court must be satisfied that "the making of the agreement for arbitration, as a *matter of federal law*, is not in issue." And then when Judge Medina turned to the task of "the formulation of the principles of federal substantive law necessary for this purpose,"...he formulated the separability rule which the Court today adopts—not because § 4 provided this rule as an "explicit answer," not because he looked to the intention of the parties, but because of his notion that the separability rule would further a "liberal policy of promoting arbitration."...

Today, without expressly saying so, the Court does precisely what Judge Medina did in *Robert Lawrence*. It is not content to hold that the Act does all it was intended to do: make arbitration agreements enforceable in federal courts if they are valid and legally existent under state law. The Court holds that the Act gives federal courts the right to fashion federal law, inconsistent with state law, to determine whether an arbitration agreement was made and what it means. Even if Congress intended to create substantive rights by passage of the Act, I am wholly convinced that it did not intend to create such a sweeping body of federal substantive law completely to take away from the States their power to interpret contracts made by their own citizens in their own territory.

[...]

IV.

...The plain purpose of the Act as written by Congress was this and no more: Congress wanted federal courts to enforce contracts to arbitrate and plainly said so in the Act. But Congress also plainly said that whether a contract containing an arbitration clause can be rescinded on the ground of fraud is to be decided by the courts and not by the arbitrators. Prima here challenged in the courts the validity of its alleged contract with F & C as a whole, not in fragments. If there has never been any valid contract, then there is not now and never has been anything to arbitrate. If Prima's allegations are true, the sum total of what the Court does here is to force Prima to arbitrate a contract which is void and unenforceable before arbitrators who are given the power to make final legal determinations of their own jurisdiction, not even subject to effective review by the highest court in the land. That is not what Congress said Prima must do. It seems to be what the Court thinks would promote the policy of arbitration. I am completely unable to agree to this new version of the Arbitration Act, a version which its own creator in *Robert Lawrence* practically admitted was judicial legislation. Congress might possibly have enacted such a version into law had it been able to foresee subsequent legal events, but I do not think this Court should do so.

I would reverse this case.

NOTES AND QUESTIONS

1. Some forty years after its enactment, through the litigation in *Prima Paint*, the FAA generated a substantial controversy in the U.S. Supreme Court regarding the meaning of the legislation, the purview of its application, and its impact in the context of federal diversity jurisdiction. The majority and dissenting opinions in *Prima Paint* are irretrievably at odds on all of these issues and employ different methodologies to sustain their views. Which reading of the FAA—its scope and content—do you find generally more persuasive? Why? Is it fair to say that the majority engages in proclaiming rules simply by fiat while the dissenting opinion has the discipline of logical textual interpretation and the support of the statute's legislative history? Could the majority's methodology be seen as more politically astute and creative, adapting the FAA to the evolving realities of federalism, litigation, and the arbitral process? Is this type of adaptation a legitimate judicial function?

2. The central issue in *Prima Paint* involves the consideration of several allied issues which contributes to the complexity of the determination and to the vigorous debate between the majority and dissenting opinions. The primary question in *Prima Paint* is whether a party's allegation of contractual fraud—specifically, fraud in the inducement of the agreement—might void both the main contract and the arbitral clause. If the claim has any credibility, *i.e.*, states a *prima facie* case, jurisdiction over the parties' dispute should be redirected to the courts, because the arbitral tribunal has no legal basis upon which to exercise its adjudicatory authority. The foundation of its authority, the arbitral clause, is suspect and, therefore, inoperative (at least, temporarily). If the court ruling on the matter finds the claim of fraud in the inducement to be unfounded, presumably the reference to arbitration would be reinvigorated and the arbitral tribunal would assert jurisdiction over the resolution of the other contract disputes.

Prima Paint, therefore, raises a threshold jurisdictional issue. Does the claim of contractual invalidity vest jurisdiction with the courts or the arbitral tribunal to rule upon the impact of that claim upon the agreement to arbitrate? A party seeking to frustrate the agreement to arbitrate or complicate the determination of the matter could simply allege that the contract is void for any number of reasons. Under the contract theory of arbitral adjudicatory authority, the judicial process would always intervene to decide this initial question, thereby creating an opportunity at least to delay the arbitration and to undermine the autonomy of the arbitral mechanism.

The majority's answer to this dilemma, between the legal doctrine propounding the necessity of a valid contractual reference to arbitration and the policy favoring arbitral independence, is the separability doctrine. As in many other legal systems, the policy to foster arbitration overrides the law—here, by proclaiming that the arbitral clause is a separate contract that stands on its own. Allegations of contractual deficiency must be directed specifically at the clause itself; the deficiency of the main agreement does not necessarily impinge upon the arbitration agreement. The separability doctrine heightens the adverse party's burden of proof, makes dilatory objections less likely, and avoids the reference to the courts by maintaining the arbitral tribunal's jurisdiction.

Is there any textual support in the FAA for the separability doctrine? Does state contract law provide a better doctrinal foundation for separability? Is the separability doctrine sufficient to address the jurisdictional problem that has been raised? Who decides on its application to the facts of the case?

3. Why does the FAA apply in *Prima Paint*? What role does state law play? Is the "congressional command" a sufficient response to the federalism issue? Why or why not? Is the selection of a particular law "outcome determinative"? Does federalism or arbitration win?

4. In *Prima Paint*, does the FAA, as legislative history indicates, remain a mere procedural enactment that regulates or validates the process of arbitration in specialized commercial sectors? If there is indeed substantive content to the FAA, what federal rights does it create and for whom? Can you provide any explanation for the Court's apparently imperative need to restrict state jurisdiction and state legislative authority in the area of arbitration? Is this a return to *Swift* for purposes of the law of arbitration? What remains of state power in this area? In 1967, there was surely much less of a perception of a litigation crisis than today. Why would the Court be bent on consecrating a federally established national policy on arbitration based upon such a seemingly modest 1925 Congressional enactment?

5. *Prima Paint* not only announces the federal policy surge toward arbitration, but indicates as well the pattern of the Court's decision-making in the area. In almost every subsequent Court decision on arbitration (*Kaplan* is an exception), the majority opinion is accompanied by a dissent. The majority opinion advocates an unequivocal determination in favor of arbitration and depreciates significantly applicable rules of law that might hinder its underlying policy objective. Logic and accuracy do not restrict the majority reasoning. The dissent, usually undertaken by a well-respected and scholarly member of the Court (Black in *Prima Paint*, Douglas in *Scherk*, Stevens in *Mitsubishi* and *Vimar*, Thomas in *Terminix* and *Mastrobuono*, for example), emphasizes the legal dimension of the issue raised, consults comprehensively the legislative history, and accurately portrays the law in the area.

Criticism of the respective approaches notwithstanding, there is an unmistakable legislative quality to the content of the majority opinions that makes short shrift of legal analysis, while the dissents generally constitute persuasive lawyers' briefs on behalf of the role and integrity of law. Throughout its evolution, the U.S. decisional law on arbitration appears to have functioned on the basis of a dialectic opposition between policy and law, beginning with *Prima Paint* and continuing through *Scherk*, *McMahon*, *Terminix*, *Mastrobuono*, and *Vimar*.

The structure and content of the debate within the Court about arbitration raise a host of questions about law and policy: Which side of the Court has the better approach to legal regulation generally and, more specifically, in regard to arbitration? Does the underlying intent of the FAA justify the Court's recourse to policy? Do the needs of judicial administration? Why is the avoidance of law necessary in the majority rulings and what is the likely impact upon the institution of arbitration? Is the societal interest in arbitration and its availability truly more important than federalism? You should give some thought to these questions; they are at the core of the contemporary American law of arbitration. Integrate them into the debate about rights protection (the function of law and the legal system) and arbitral autonomy.

6. Justice Black's dissenting opinion warrants its own analysis. It, too, announces the future, but on the opposing side. Do you agree with Justice Black that arbitrators are "wholly unqualified to decide legal issues" and their mission is "to adjust and arbitrate factual controversies"? Do these remarks smack of judicial hostility to arbitration? Might the majority be right to take its unequivocal policy position to ward off any rise in the judicial antipathy toward arbitration? What view of arbitration and its form of adjudication is commanded by the statute? Does Justice Black's assertion conflict with the statutory definition of arbitration?

It is clear that Justice Black disagrees with the majority on all the significant issues raised in the *Prima Paint* litigation. In his view, the separability doctrine has a dubious origin, places arbitration agreements in a privileged position that exempts them from the legal requirements of contract validity, and should not be allowed to permit arbitral fact-finders to rule on legal questions. Moreover, principles of general federal common law that are vaguely attached to federal statutory enactments like the separability doctrine should not displace the application of state law in a diversity context especially when the transaction in question eludes the federal statute's scope of application. The majority opinion constitutes an untoward "mutilation" of the statute.

Given this disagreement, assess the following excerpts from Justice Black's dissent:

i) "The Court thus holds that the Arbitration Act, designed to provide merely a procedural remedy which would not interfere with state substantive law, authorizes federal courts to fashion a federal rule to make arbitration clauses 'separable' and valid."

ii) "The only advantage of submitting the issue of fraud to arbitration is for the arbitrators."

iii) "Fraud, of course, is one of the most common grounds for revoking a contract. If the contract was procured by fraud,...there is absolutely no contract, nothing to be arbitrated."

iv) "The language of...[the FAA]...could not, I think, raise doubts about...[its] meaning except to someone anxious to find doubts."

7. Finally, Justice Black's dissent raises concerns about the statutory basis for the federal separability doctrine. Although the Court relies on Section Four of the FAA as the statutory anchor for the doctrine, there is, as Justice Black opines, little in the content of the provision to justify that interpretation. Moreover, simply applying the separability doctrine, no matter what the statutory or federalism objections might be, does not directly or

indirectly create jurisdiction in the arbitral tribunal to rule on the validity of the arbitral clause. The legal system needs to further recognize and grant arbitrators the power to rule on jurisdictional challenges that proceed from allegations that there is either no arbitration agreement or a defective one. Neither the FAA nor the case law gives effect to the *kompetenz-kompetenz* doctrine which is the necessary corollary of separability. In fact, Section Three of the FAA appears to give courts the exclusive power to determine whether a valid arbitration exists, and—as a consequence—whether there is a legal basis for the arbitral tribunal's exercise of adjudicatory authority.

Isn't that the point?

Does the federal separability doctrine imply that arbitrators have jurisdiction to rule on jurisdiction? How does that square with the language of Section Three? Is there a gap in the law? Does it matter? You should consider the holding in *First Options v. Kaplan, infra,* in evaluating these questions.

8.   The vitality of the separability doctrine was recently reaffirmed by the U.S. Supreme Court in *Buckeye Check Cashing, Inc. v. Cardegna,* 546 U.S. 440 (2006). There, it made clear that the separability doctrine was as essential part of U.S. arbitration law and dictated practice in both state and federal courts: "We reaffirm today that, regardless of whether the challenge is brought in federal or state court, a challenge to the validity of the contract as a whole, and not specifically to the arbitration clause, must go to the arbitrator." The Court made evident the settled law on the question:

> . . . [A]s a matter of substantive federal arbitration law, an arbitration provision is severable from the remainder of the contract. . . . [U]nless the challenge is to the arbitration clause itself, the issue of the contract's validity is considered by the arbitrator in the first instance. . . . [T]his arbitration law applies in state as well as federal courts.

The Court concluded that Florida public policy and contract law, and even its concept of criminal culpability, did not overwhelm separability or federal preemption: "We simply reject[] the proposition that the enforceability of the arbitration agreement turn[s] on the state legislature's judgment concerning the forum for enforcement of the state-law cause of action." Additionally, the Court declared that separability arose from FAA § 2, as well as §§ 3 and 4, thereby making it fully enforceable in state courts.

At the outset of its opinion, the Court made a distinction between different types of challenges that could be lodged against arbitration agreements. It recognized two types of challenges: (1) *Southland*-like challenges and (2) challenges to the "contract as a whole." In a footnote, the Court identified a third type of challenge, *i.e.,* whether a contract (presumably, of arbitration) was entered into by the parties. These brief statements constitute a rudimentary outline of the jurisdictional doctrine of *kompetenz-kompetenz* and principles of arbitration law that are recognized as basic law in other, like-minded jurisdictions, like France and England.

It appears that the Court was establishing a distinction between subject matter and contractual inarbitrability and elaborating the basis for a challenge on either ground. *Southland* challenges involve the application of statutes that provide for the exclusive resolution of dispute through courts. When the parties agreed to arbitrate such disputes, courts must decide whether the arbitration agreement is effective in light of the statutory subject matter barrier to arbitration. The consideration of that question inexorably leads to another which is even more decisive: Whether the "blocking" statute's jurisdictional exclusivity (if it is state legislation) is preempted by federal law under FAA § 2.

The Court's two additional statements in this matter relate to inarbitrability based on contract, rather than subject matter. They represent the traditional basis upon which to bring jurisdictional challenges to the arbitral tribunal in most legal systems. Arbitrator authority to rule can be challenged on the basis that the parties never entered into an arbitration agreement. The Court recognized this ground in the footnote. A challenge can also be brought on the basis that a contract to arbitrate exists, but is deficient in formation and unenforceable. Finally, a party could argue that the agreement to arbitrate is good as a contract, but it does not apply or extend to the controversy at hand. In some legal systems, the tribunal's right to rule can be opposed because, although the arbitral clause is fully enforceable and applicable, it has not been correctly applied according to its terms in the litigation in question. In other words, the instituted arbitration deviates from the agreed-upon provisions in the contract that relate, presumably, to material matters.

It would be useful to have a complete and systemic statement from the Court on these issues, rather than haphazard and elliptical statements periodically given in various cases. The lack of clarity and structure creates uncertainties and ambiguities in practice and litigation. The situation is the consequence of court-made law that adds a great deal of content to the controlling statute. A revision of the FAA should address such critical issues and provide a full framework of rules to govern them. For a recent application of *Buckeye, see Rubin v. Sona Int'l Corp.*, 457 F.Supp.2d 191 (S.D.N.Y. 2006) (Westlaw reg. req.) (court rejects the distinction between void and voidable contracts and holds that the arbitrator decides the enforceability of an arbitration agreement, "unless the challenge is to the arbitration clause itself").

CITIZENS BANK v. ALAFABCO, INC.

539 U.S. 52, 123 S.Ct. 2037, 156 L.Ed.2d 46 (2003).

Per Curiam.

The question presented is whether the parties' debt-restructuring agreement is "a contract evidencing a transaction involving commerce" within the meaning of the Federal Arbitration Act (FAA).... As we concluded in *Allied-Bruce Terminix Cos. v. Dobson*, 513 U.S. 265, 115 S.Ct. 834, 130 L.Ed.2d 753 (1995), there is a sufficient nexus with interstate commerce to make enforceable, pursuant to the FAA, an arbitration provision included in that agreement.

I

Petitioner The Citizens Bank—an Alabama lending institution—seeks to compel arbitration of a financial dispute with respondents Alafabco, Inc.—an Alabama fabrication and construction company—and its officers. According to a complaint filed by respondents in Alabama state court, the dispute among the parties arose out of a series of commercial loan transactions made over a decade-long course of business dealings. In 1986, the complaint alleges, the parties entered into a quasi-contractual relationship in which the bank agreed to provide operating capital necessary for Alafabco to secure and complete construction contracts. That relationships began to sour in 1998, when the bank allegedly encouraged Alafabco to bid on a large construction contract in Courtland, Alabama, but refused to provide the capital necessary to complete the project. In order to compensate for the bank's alleged breach of the parties' implied agreement, Alafabco completed the Courtland project with funds that would otherwise have been dedicated to repaying existing obligations to the bank. Alafabco in turn became delinquent in repaying those existing obligations.

On two occasions, the parties attempted to resolve the outstanding debts.... The debt-restructuring arrangement included an arbitration agreement covering " 'all disputes, claims, or controversies.' " That agreement provided that the FAA " 'shall apply to [its] construction, interpretation, and enforcement.' " ... Alafabco defaulted on its obligations under the renewal notes and sought bankruptcy protection in federal court in September 1999.

In return for the dismissal of Alafabco's bankruptcy petition, the bank agreed to renegotiate the outstanding loans in a second debt-restructuring agreement....

Within a year of the December 1999 debt restructuring, Alafabco brought suit ... against the bank.... Invoking the arbitration agreements, the bank moved to compel arbitration of the parties' dispute. The Circuit Court ordered respondents to submit to arbitration in accordance with the arbitration agreements.

The Supreme Court of Alabama reversed.... Because there was no showing "that any portion of the restructured debt was actually attributable to interstate transactions; that the funds comprising that debt originated out-of-state; or that the restructured debt was inseparable from any out-of-state projects," ... the court found an insufficient nexus with interstate commerce to establish FAA coverage of the parties' dispute.

[...]

II

The FAA provides that a "written provision in any maritime transaction or a contract *evidencing a transaction involving commerce* to settle by arbitration a controversy...." (emphasis added). The statute further defines "commerce" to include "commerce among the several States." § 1.... [P]etitioner contends that the decision below gives inadequate breadth to the "involving commerce" language of the statute. We agree.

We have interpreted the term "involving commerce" in the FAA as the functional equivalent of the more familiar term "affecting commerce"—words of art that ordinarily signal the broadest permissible exercise of Congress' Commerce Clause power. *Allied-Bruce Terminix Cos.*, 513 U.S., at 273–274, 115 S.Ct. 834. Because the statute provides for "the enforcement of arbitration agreements within the full reach of the Commerce Clause," *Perry v. Thomas*, 482 U.S. 483, 490, 107 S.Ct. 2520, 96 L.Ed.2d 426 (1987), it is perfectly clear that the FAA encompasses a wider range of transactions than those actually "in commerce"—that is, "within the flow of interstate commerce," *Allied-Bruce Terminix Cos.*, *supra*, at 273, 115 S.Ct. 834 (internal quotation marks, citation, and emphasis omitted).

The Supreme Court of Alabama was therefore misguided in its search for evidence that a "portion of the restructured debt was actually attributable to interstate transactions" or that the loans "originated out-of-state" or that "the restructured debt was inseparable from any out-of-state projects." ... Such evidence might be required if the FAA were restricted to transactions actually " 'in commerce,' " ... but, as we have explained, that is not the limit of the FAA's reach.

Nor is application of the FAA defeated because the individual debt-restructuring transactions, taken alone, did not have a "substantial effect on interstate commerce." ... Congress' Commerce Clause power "may be exercised in individual cases without showing any specific effect upon interstate commerce" if in the aggregate the economic activity in question would represent "a general practice ... subject to federal control.". ...

This case is well within our previous pronouncements on the extent of Congress' Commerce Clause power. Although the debt-restructuring agreements were executed in Alabama by Alabama residents, they nonetheless satisfy the FAA's "involving commerce" test for at least three reasons. First. Alafabco engaged in business throughout the southeastern United States using substantial loans from the bank that were renegotiated and redocumented in the debt-restructuring agreements. Indeed, the gravamen of Alafabco's state-court suit was that it had incurred " 'massive debt' " to the bank in order to keep its business afloat, and the bank submitted affidavits of bank officers establishing that its loans to Alafabco had been used in part to finance large construction projects in North Carolina, Tennessee, and Alabama.

Second, the restructured debt was secured by all of Alafabco's business assets, including its inventory of goods assembled from out-of-state parts and raw materials. If the Commerce Clause gives Congress the power to regulate local business establishments purchasing substantial quantities of goods that have moved in interstate commerce, ... it necessarily reaches substantial commercial loan transactions secured by such goods.

Third, were there any residual doubt about the magnitude of the impact on interstate commerce caused by the particular economic transactions in which the parties were engaged, that doubt would dissipate upon consideration of the "general practice" those transactions represent. ...
No elaborate explanation is needed to make evident the broad impact of

commercial lending on the national economy or Congress' power to regulate that activity pursuant to the Commerce Clause....

The decision below therefore adheres to an improperly cramped view of Congress' Commerce Clause power....

Accordingly, the petition for writ of certiorari is granted, the judgment of the Supreme Court of Alabama is reversed, and the case is remanded for further proceedings and not inconsistent with this opinion.

It is so ordered.

NOTES AND QUESTIONS

1. How does the Court's construction of interstate commerce fit into the federal policy in favor of arbitration?

2. Is there any commercial or consumer transaction that does not fit into the Court's broad view of interstate commerce? When might an arbitration clause not be protected by the FAA?

3. What does "broad impact" upon the national economy mean? Does it mean that local actors, involved in local business, can still have some sort of effect upon interstate or national commerce and their arbitration agreements would therefore be subject to the FAA? What sort of standard is that?

4. Is this a close case? Why or why not? What power to regulate commerce is left to the state?

2.   THE FEDERALISM TRILOGY

The full implications of the ruling in *Prima Paint* on federalism and the status of the FAA were elaborated by the courts over time. In this context, the U.S. Supreme Court decided three cases in the mid–1980s that clarified the policy underlying its arbitration doctrine and confirmed the consequences of that doctrine on federalism. The Court's rulings in *Moses H. Cone Memorial Hospital v. Mercury Constr. Corp.*, 460 U.S. 1 (1983), *Southland Corp. v. Keating*, 465 U.S. 1 (1984), and *Dean Witter Reynolds v. Byrd*, 470 U.S. 213 (1985), made clear that the Court viewed the FAA as having a fundamental Congressional objective. The Court would uphold that objective regardless of state law.

* * *

Moses H. Cone involved a contract dispute between a North Carolina hospital and an Alabama building contractor. The contract for the construction of additions to the hospital's main building provided that disputes would be resolved by the architect within a specified period of time. If the dispute went unresolved, it would be submitted to binding arbitration. When a dispute arose over costs and could not be resolved, the hospital filed an action before a North Carolina court seeking, in part, a declaratory judgment that there was no right to arbitrate "under the contract due to waiver, latches, estoppel, and failure to make a timely demand for arbitration." 460 U.S. at 7. The building contractor then filed an action before the federal district court to compel arbitration under Section Four of the FAA. The district court stayed the action pending resolution of the hospital's suit in state court. On appeal, the Fourth Circuit reversed the stay and issued instructions to compel arbitration. The U.S. Supreme Court upheld the appellate opinion.

MOSES H. CONE MEMORIAL HOSP. v. MERCURY CONSTRUCTION CO.

460 U.S. 1, 103 S.Ct. 927, 74 L.Ed.2d 765 (1983).

(footnotes omitted)

JUSTICE BRENNAN delivered the opinion of the Court.

[. . .]

III

We turn now to the principal issue to be addressed, namely the propriety of the District Court's decision to stay this federal suit out of deference to the parallel litigation brought in state court. *Colorado River Water Conservation District v. United States*, 424 U.S. 800 (1976), provides persuasive guidance in deciding this question.

A

[. . .]

. . .[T]he decision whether to dismiss a federal action because of parallel state-court litigation does not rest on a mechanical checklist, but on a careful balancing of the important factors as they apply in a given case, with the balance heavily weighted in favor of the exercise of jurisdiction. The weight to be given to any one factor may vary greatly from case to case, depending on the particular setting of the case. *Colorado River* itself illustrates this principle in operation. By far the most important factor in our decision to approve the dismissal there was the "clear federal policy. . .[of] avoidance of piecemeal adjudication of water rights in a river system" as evinced in the McCarran Amendment. We recognized that the Amendment represents Congress's judgment that the field of water rights is one peculiarly appropriate for comprehensive treatment in the forums having the greatest experience and expertise, assisted by state administrative officers acting under the state courts. In addition, we noted that other factors in the case tended to support dismissal, the absence of any substantial progress in the federal-court litigation; the presence in the suit of extensive rights governed by state law; the geographical inconvenience of the federal forum; and the Government's previous willingness to litigate similar suits in state court.

[. . .]

. . .As we shall now explain, we agree with the Court of Appeals that the District Court in this case abused its discretion in granting the stay.

IV

Applying the *Colorado River* factors to this case, it is clear that there was no showing of the requisite exceptional circumstances to justify the District Court's stay.

The Hospital concedes that the first two factors mentioned in *Colorado River* are not present here. There was no assumption by either court of jurisdiction over any res or property, nor is there any contention that the federal forum was any less convenient to the parties than the state forum. The remaining factors, avoidance of piecemeal litigation, and the order in which jurisdiction was obtained by the concurrent forums, far from supporting the stay, actually counsel against it.

A

There is no force here to the consideration that was paramount in *Colorado River* itself, the danger of piecemeal litigation.

The Hospital points out that it has two substantive disputes here, one with Mercury, concerning Mercury's claim for delay and impact costs, and the other with the Architect, concerning the Hospital's claim for indemnity for any liability it may have to Mercury. The latter dispute cannot be sent to arbitration without the Architect's consent, since there is no arbitration agreement between the Hospital and the Architect. It is true, therefore, that if Mercury obtains an arbitration order for its dispute, the Hospital will be forced to resolve these related disputes in different forums. That misfortune, however, is not the result of any choice between the federal and state courts; it occurs because the relevant federal law requires piecemeal resolution when necessary to give effect to an arbitration agreement. Under the Arbitration Act, an arbitration agreement must be enforced notwithstanding the presence of other persons who are parties to the underlying dispute but not to the arbitration agreement. If the dispute between Mercury and the Hospital is arbitrable under the Act, then the Hospital's two disputes will be resolved separately, one in arbitration, and the other (if at all) in state-court litigation. Conversely, if the dispute between Mercury and the Hospital is not arbitrable, then both disputes will be resolved in state court. But neither of those two outcomes depends at all on which court decides the question of arbitrability. Hence, a decision to allow that issue to be decided in federal rather than state court does not cause piecemeal resolution of the parties' underlying disputes. Although the Hospital will have to litigate the arbitrability issue in federal rather than state court, that dispute is easily severable from the merits of the underlying disputes.

B

The order in which the concurrent tribunals obtained and exercised jurisdiction cuts against, not for, the District Court's stay in this case. The Hospital argues that the stay was proper because the state-court suit was filed some 19 days before the federal suit. In the first place, this argument disregards the obvious reason for the Hospital's priority in filing. An indispensable element of Mercury's cause of action under § 4 for an arbitration order is the Hospital's refusal to arbitrate. That refusal did not occur until less than a day before the Hospital filed its state suit. Hence, Mercury simply had no reasonable opportunity to file its § 4 petition first. Moreover, the Hospital succeeded in obtaining an *ex parte* injunction from the state court forbidding Mercury from taking any steps to secure arbitration. Mercury filed its § 4 petition the same day that the injunction was dissolved.

That aside, the Hospital's priority argument gives too mechanical a reading to the "priority" element of the *Colorado River* balance. This factor, as with the other *Colorado River* factors, is to be applied in a pragmatic, flexible manner with a view to the realities of the case at hand. Thus, priority should not be measured exclusively by which complaint was filed first, but rather in terms of how much progress has been made in the two actions. *Colorado River* illustrates this point well. There, the federal suit was actually filed first. Nevertheless, we pointed out as a factor favoring dismissal "the apparent absence of any proceedings in the District Court, other than the filing of the complaint, prior to the motion to dismiss." Here, the opposite was true. It was the state-court suit in which no substantial proceedings (excepting only the abortive temporary injunction) had taken place at the time of the decision to stay. In the federal suit, by contrast, the parties had taken most of the steps necessary to a resolution of the arbitrability issue. In realistic terms, the federal suit was running well ahead of the state suit at the very time that the District Court decided to refuse to adjudicate the case.

This refusal to proceed was plainly erroneous in view of Congress's clear intent, in the Arbitration Act, to move the parties to an arbitrable dispute out of court and into arbitration as quickly and easily as possible. The Act provides two parallel devices for enforcing an arbitration agreement: a stay of litigation in any case raising a dispute referable to arbitration, 9 U.S.C. § 3, and an affirmative order to engage in arbitration, § 4. Both of these sections call for an expeditious and summary hearing, with only restricted inquiry into factual issues. Assuming that the state court would have granted prompt relief to Mercury under the Act, there still would have been an inevitable delay as a result of the District Court's stay. The stay thus frustrated the statutory policy of rapid and unobstructed enforcement of arbitration agreements.

C

[. . .]

The basic issue presented in Mercury's federal suit was the arbitrability of the dispute between Mercury and the Hospital. Federal law in the terms of the Arbitration Act governs that issue in either state or federal court. Section 2 is the primary substantive provision of the Act, declaring that a written agreement to arbitrate "in any maritime transaction or a contract evidencing a transaction involving commerce . . . shall be valid, irrevocable, and enforceable, save upon such grounds as exist at law or in equity for the revocation of any contract.''

Section 2 is a congressional declaration of a liberal federal policy favoring arbitration agreements, notwithstanding any state substantive or procedural policies to the contrary. The effect of the section is to create a body of federal substantive law of arbitrability, applicable to any arbitration agreement within the coverage of the Act. In *Prima Paint Corp. v. Flood & Conklin Mfg. Corp.*, [w]e held that the language and policies of the Act required the conclusion that the [contractual] fraud issue was arbitrable. Although our holding in *Prima Paint* extended only to the specific issue presented, the courts of appeals have since consistently concluded that questions of arbitrability must be addressed with a healthy regard for the federal policy favoring arbitration. We agree. The Arbitration Act establishes that, as a matter of federal law, any doubts concerning the scope of arbitrable issues should be resolved in favor of arbitration, whether the problem at hand is the construction of the contract language itself or an allegation of waiver, delay, or a like defense to arbitrability.

[W]e emphasize that our task in cases such as this is not to find some substantial reason for the exercise of federal jurisdiction by the district court; rather, the task is to ascertain whether there exist "exceptional" circumstances, the "clearest of justifications," that can suffice under *Colorado River* to justify the surrender of that jurisdiction. Although in some rare circumstances the presence of state-law issues may weigh in favor of that surrender,...the presence of federal-law issues must always be a major consideration weighing against surrender.

D

Finally, in this case an important reason against allowing a stay is the probable inadequacy of the state-court proceeding to protect Mercury's rights. We are not to be understood to impeach the competence or procedures of the North Carolina courts. Moreover, state courts, as much as federal courts, are obliged to grant stays of litigation under § 3 of the Arbitration Act. It is less clear, however, whether the same is true of an order to compel arbitration under § 4 of the Act. We need not resolve that question here; it suffices to say that there was, at a minimum, substantial room for doubt that Mercury could obtain from the state court an order compelling the Hospital to arbitrate. In many cases, no doubt, a § 3 stay is quite adequate to protect the right to arbitration. But in a case such as this, where the party opposing arbitration is the one from whom payment or performance is sought, a stay of litigation alone is not enough. It leaves the recalcitrant party free to sit and do nothing, neither to litigate nor to arbitrate. If the state court stayed litigation pending arbitration but declined to compel the Hospital to arbitrate, Mercury would have no sure way to proceed with its claims except to return to federal court to obtain a § 4 order, a pointless and wasteful burden on the supposedly summary and speedy procedures prescribed by the Arbitration Act.

[...]

Affirmed.

JUSTICE REHNQUIST, with whom THE CHIEF JUSTICE and JUSTICE O'CONNOR join, dissenting.

In its zeal to provide arbitration for a party it thinks deserving, the Court has made an exception to established rules of procedure. The Court's attempt to cast the District Court's decision as a final judgment fails to do justice to the meaning of the word "final," to the Act of Congress that limits the jurisdiction of the courts of appeals, or to the district judges who administer the laws in the first instance.

If the District Court had not stayed the proceeding, but had set a trial date two months away, there would be no doubt that its order was interlocutory, subject to review only by mandamus or pursuant to 28 U.S.C. § 1292(b). This would be true even though § 4 of the Arbitration Act provides that "the court shall proceed summarily" to trial, because an order setting a trial date only guides the course of litigation, and does not, of its own force, dispose of it on the merits. Such an order is tentative; that is, it is subject to change at any time on the motion of a party or by the court, sua sponte.

The order the District Court actually entered is no more final. It delayed further proceedings until the completion of pending litigation in the state courts. This order was also tentative; it was subject to change on a showing that the state proceedings were being delayed, either by the Hospital or by the court, or that the state courts were not applying the federal act, or that some other reason for a change had arisen. This order did not dispose of the case on the merits. If the state court had found that there was no agreement to arbitrate within the meaning of the Federal Arbitration Act, the District Court would have been bound by that finding. But res judicata or collateral estoppel would apply if the state court reached a decision before the District Court in the absence of a stay. The likelihood that a state court of competent jurisdiction may enter a judgment that may determine some issue in a case does not render final a federal district court's decision to take a two day recess, or to order additional briefing by the parties in five days or five months, or to take a case under advisement rather than render an immediate decision from the bench. Such a possibility did not magically change that character of the order the district judge entered in this case.

Section 1291 of the Judicial Code is a Congressional command to the federal courts of appeals not to interfere with the district courts' management of ongoing proceedings. Unless the high standards for a writ of mandamus can be met, or the district court certifies an interlocutory appeal pursuant to § 1292(b), Congress has directed that the district courts be permitted to conduct their cases as they see fit.

[. . .]

Furthermore, I am not as certain as is the Court that by staying this case the District Court resolved "an important issue." An issue should not be deemed "important" for these purposes simply because the court of appeals or this Court thinks the appellant should prevail. The issue here was whether the factual question whether there was an agreement to arbitrate should be adjudicated in a state or federal court. Unless there is some reason to believe that the state court will resolve this factual question wrongly, which the Court quite rightly disclaims,...I do not see how this issue is more important than any other interlocutory order that may place a litigant at a procedural disadvantage.

For these reasons, I do not believe the District Court's order was appealable. Interlocutory orders are committed by statute to the judgment of the District Courts, and this Court ill-serves the judges of those courts and the overwhelming majority of litigants by devising exceptions to the statute when it believes a particular litigant has been wronged.

Given my view of appealability, I do not find it necessary to decide whether the District Court's order was proper in this case. I am disturbed, however, that the Court has sanctioned an extraordinary departure from the usual and accepted course of judicial proceedings by affirming the Court of Appeals decision on an issue that was not decided in the District Court.

The Court of Appeals ordered the District Court to enter an order compelling arbitration, even though that issue was not considered by the District Court. This Court has maintained the difference between appellate jurisdiction and original jurisdiction at least since *Marbury v. Madison* ("It is the essential criterion of appellate jurisdiction that it revises and corrects the proceedings in a case already instituted."). I do not understand how the Court can say that the Court of Appeals had discretion to perform a non-appellate act.

The Court relies on 28 U.S.C. § 2106, which provides that a court of appeals:

> may affirm, modify, vacate, set aside or reverse any judgment, decree, or order of a court lawfully brought before it for review, and may remand the case and direct the entry of such appropriate judgment, decree, or order, or require such further proceedings to be had as may be just under the circumstances.

This statute does not grant the courts of appeals authority to constitute themselves as trial courts. Section 4 of the Arbitration Act gives the Hospital a right to a jury trial. By deciding that there were no disputed issues of fact, the Court of Appeals seems to have decided a motion for summary judgment that was not before it. This is the kind of issue that district judges decide every day in the ordinary course of business. It is not the kind of issue that Courts of Appeals determine.

There was no reason to believe that the District Court would not have acted promptly to resolve the dispute on the merits after being reversed on the stay. That judges of a court of appeals believe they know how a case should be decided is no reason for them to substitute their own judgment for that of a district judge without regard to the normal course of appellate procedure.

The judgment below should be vacated and the case remanded to the Court of Appeals with directions to dismiss the appeal for want of jurisdiction. Failing that, even if the Court is correct that the stay order was an error, the judgment should be reversed, insofar as it decides the question of arbitrability, and remanded to the district court for further proceedings under the Arbitration Act.

NOTES AND QUESTIONS

1. According to the majority opinion, what is the essential purpose of the FAA? What sections of the FAA support the Court's interpretation of the gravamen of the legislation? Is the FAA still special interest legislation or has arbitration acquired a more prominent remedial function in the legal system?

2. Why should the state court be denied jurisdiction in the circumstances of *Moses H. Cone*? Even if a federal court lawfully asserted jurisdiction, wouldn't state law control the contract and the merits of the litigation? What if the parties have provided for state court jurisdiction and/or the application of state law in their contract? Would or should that factor change the outcome?

3. How do you interpret the Court's reference to "a body of federal substantive law of arbitrability" in defining the content of Section Two? What meaning does the Court appear to attach to the concept of "arbitrability"?

4. On the one hand, the majority states that the FAA creates "a body of federal substantive law of arbitrability, applicable to any arbitration agreement within the coverage of the Act." On the other hand, it also claims that "state courts, as much as federal courts, are obliged to grant stays of litigation under § 3 of the Arbitration Act." Are these two statements consistent? Does this mean the state courts must apply the FAA and disregard the provisions of state law on arbitration? What impact does this have on federalism concerns?

5. A considerable portion of the dissenting opinion appears in the foregoing materials. Can you describe the essence of Justice Rehnquist's objection to the majority opinion? Would it be a fair reading of the dissent to characterize its content as "anti-arbitration"? Does the dissent provide any elucidation of the reasons for the later enactment of Section Sixteen of the FAA?

6. At footnote 32, 460 U.S. at 26, in the opinion (not reproduced *supra*), the court makes the following observation:

> The Arbitration Act is something of an anomaly in the field of federal-court jurisdiction. It creates a body of federal substantive law establishing and regulating the duty to honor an agreement to arbitrate, yet it does not create any independent federal-question jurisdiction.

The observation is significant on a number of grounds: First, the Court no longer debates whether the FAA is a procedural or substantive enactment. Despite the clear legislative history to the contrary, the Court recognizes that the FAA is the vehicle for the creation of new federal rights. The basic right appears to be the right to engage in, or provide for, arbitration with a corollary duty upon the courts to enforce the contractual promise to arbitrate. Ascertaining when this right becomes enforceable by federal and state courts seems to be the essential question in *Moses H. Cone* and subsequent cases. Is it a right of constitutional magnitude? Must there be a separate basis for the application of federal law?

Second, relatedly and as significantly, the Court characterizes the FAA as an "anomaly" for jurisdictional purposes. The Act, the Court continues, does not create "federal-question jurisdiction" for purposes of litigation involving arbitration. The observation gains importance in relation to the later decisional law. Indeed, the most recent cases pose the question, albeit critically in dissent, of whether the Court's construction of the FAA has not, in effect, resulted in the creation of federal-question jurisdiction for purposes of arbitration. *See Terminix* and *Mastrobuono* (Thomas, J., dissenting), *infra*. Such a result challenges fundamental principles of federalism, the legislative history of the statute, and the express language of Section One.

Further in the same footnote, given the would-be anomalous lack of federal-question jurisdiction, the Court declares that "there must be diversity of citizenship or some other independent basis for federal jurisdiction" before a federal court can issue an order to compel arbitration under Section Four of the Act in a diversity case governed by state law. The answer begs the question: Under *Erie*, diversity of citizenship is a sufficient basis for asserting federal court jurisdiction, but not for applying federal law. Diversity alone should not compel or authorize a federal court to apply the FAA, unless the statute and the right to arbitrate have constitutional dimensions.

In a related and more recent ruling, the U.S. Court of Appeals for the Second Circuit held that, where a petitioner complains principally and in good faith that an arbitral award was rendered in manifest disregard of federal law, a substantial federal question is presented and the federal courts have jurisdiction to entertain the petition for vacating the award. *See Greenberg v. Bear, Stearns & Co.*, 220 F.3d 22 (2d Cir. 2000). In its reasoning, the court stated that arbitration questions did not themselves confer subject matter jurisdiction on federal courts for reviewing an award. Federal question jurisdiction existed when the complaint "establishe[d] either that federal law create[d] a cause of action or that plaintiff's right to relief necessarily depend[ed] on [the] resolution of substantial question[s] of federal law." The Federal Arbitration Act (FAA) does not confer subject matter jurisdiction on the federal courts even though it creates a federal substantive law of arbitration. Because federal question jurisdiction does not arise simply because a claim is brought under the FAA, there must be an independent basis of jurisdiction that allows federal courts to entertain petitions to vacate arbitral awards.

The court wrote: "We hold that where, as here, the petitioner complains principally and in good faith that the award was rendered in manifest disregard of federal law, a substantial federal question is presented and the federal courts have jurisdiction to entertain the petition. In contrast to grounds of review that concern the arbitration process itself—such as corruption or abuse of power—review for manifest disregard of federal law necessarily requires the reviewing court to do two things: first, determine what the federal law is, and second, determine whether the arbitrator's decision manifestly disregarded that law. This process so immerses the federal court in questions of federal law and their proper application that federal question subject matter jurisdiction is present."

"Where the arbitrators' alleged manifest disregard of federal law forms a key part of the petitioners' complaint about the award, the federal questions thereby presented are substantial enough to support federal jurisdiction...."

At another point in footnote 32, 460 U.S. at 26, the *Moses Cone* Court states:

> [A]lthough enforcement of the Act is left in large part to the state courts, it nevertheless represents federal policy to be vindicated by the federal courts where otherwise appropriate.

This statement contravenes fundamental federalism principles. What happened to the position in *Prima Paint* that the FAA stood as a Congressional directive to the federal courts on matters of arbitration? Can the view that state courts are primarily responsible for the practical enforcement of the FAA ever be reconciled with the language of Section One? The position that the FAA is binding upon state courts has now crept into the Court's decisional law and will be underscored and consecrated in later opinions. *See*, in particular, *Terminix, infra.*

In footnote 34, 460 U.S. at 26, the Court articulates a basis for integrating state courts into the arbitration regime established by the FAA. First, because of the operation of common law principles, most state courts, in the Court's view, have agreed voluntarily to be bound by the stay provision in Section Three of the Act. State court practice eliminates any need to clarify the allegedly ambiguous jurisdictional reference in Section Three to actions brought "in any of the courts of the United States." Whether the state court precedent is either so voluminous or so clear on the question is certainly debatable, but the Court's discovery of ambiguity in the language of Section Three is strained at best and contradicts its reading of the provision in *Prima Paint* (not to mention the legislative history of the statute).

Second, and this reasoning gets to the nub of the federalism question and more readily explains the motivation of the holding, the Court observes that a disparity in the enforcement of arbitration agreements among the federal and state courts would undermine the Congressional intent underlying the FAA. This practical rationale is persuasive in some respects, but it is hardly a solution to the federalism issue and state rights problems that are generated by the Court's holding. In advancing this justification, the Court refers to "Congress's intent to mandate enforcement of all covered arbitration agreements." 460 U.S. at 27. If "covered...agreements" include all those clauses that are the subject of litigation before the federal and state courts, then the FAA applies to any and all agreements to arbitrate. And, the law of arbitration has been federalized.

In 2009, the Court decided another "anomaly" case, addressing the lack of federal jurisdiction in the FAA. It adopted a liberal standard for determining whether a case involved federal law, the so-called "look through" doctrine.

The dissent, however, made a much stronger case for an even more liberal method for establishing federal jurisdiction under the FAA in particular cases.

VADEN v. DISCOVER BANK

___ U.S. ___, 129 S.Ct. 1262, 173 L.Ed.2d 206 (2009).

JUSTICE GINSBURG delivered the opinion of the Court.

Section 4 of the Federal Arbitration Act, 9 U.S.C. § 4, authorizes a United States district court to entertain a petition to compel arbitration if the court would have jurisdiction, "save for [the arbitration] agreement," over "a suit arising out of the controversy between the parties." We consider in this opinion two questions concerning a district court's subject-matter jurisdiction over a § 4 petition: Should a district court, if asked to compel arbitration pursuant to § 4, "look through" the petition and grant the requested relief if the court would have federal-question jurisdiction over the underlying controversy? And if the answer to that question is yes, may a district court exercise jurisdiction over a § 4 petition when the petitioner's complaint rests on state law but an actual or potential counterclaim rests on federal law?

The litigation giving rise to these questions began when Discover Bank's servicing affiliate filed a complaint in Maryland state court. Presenting a claim arising solely under state law, Discover sought to recover past-due charges from one of its credit cardholders, Betty Vaden. Vaden answered and counterclaimed, alleging that Discover's finance charges, interest, and late fees violated state law. Invoking an arbitration clause in its cardholder agreement with Vaden, Discover then filed a § 4 petition in the United States District Court for the District of Maryland to compel arbitration of Vaden's counterclaims. The District Court had subject-matter jurisdiction over its petition, Discover maintained, because Vaden's state-law counterclaims were completely preempted by federal banking law. The District Court agreed and ordered arbitration. Reasoning that a federal court has jurisdiction over a § 4 petition if the parties' underlying dispute presents a federal question, the Fourth Circuit eventually affirmed.

We agree with the Fourth Circuit in part. A federal court may "look through" a § 4 petition and order arbitration if, "save for [the arbitration] agreement," the court would have jurisdiction over "the [substantive] controversy between the parties." We hold, however, that the Court of Appeals misidentified the dimensions of "the controversy between the parties." Focusing on only a slice of the parties' entire controversy, the court seized on Vaden's counterclaims, held them completely preempted, and on that basis affirmed the District Court's order compelling arbitration. Lost from sight was the triggering plea—Discover's claim for the balance due on Vaden's account. Given that entirely state-based plea and the established rule that federal-court jurisdiction cannot be invoked on the basis of a defense or counterclaim, the whole "controversy between the parties" does not qualify for federal-court adjudication. Accordingly, we reverse the Court of Appeals' judgment.

I

This case originated as a garden-variety, state-law-based contract action: Discover sued its cardholder, Vaden, in a Maryland state court to recover arrearages amounting to $10,610.74, plus interest and counsel fees.[1] Vaden's answer asserted usury as an affirmative defense. Vaden also filed several counterclaims, styled as class actions. Like Discover's complaint, Vaden's pleadings invoked only state law: Vaden asserted that Discover's demands for finance charges, interest, and late fees violated Maryland's credit laws. . . . Neither party invoked—by notice to the other or petition to the state court—the clause in the credit card agreement providing for arbitration of "any claim or dispute between [Discover and Vaden]."[2] . . .

Faced with Vaden's counterclaims, Discover sought federal-court aid. It petitioned the United States District Court for the District of Maryland for an order, pursuant to § 4 of the Federal Arbitration Act (FAA or Act), . . . compelling arbitration of Vaden's counterclaims.[3] Although those counterclaims were framed under state law, Discover urged that they were governed entirely by federal law, specifically, § 27(a) of the Federal Deposit Insurance Act (FDIA), 12 U.S.C. § 1831d(a). Section 27(a) prescribes the interest rates state-chartered, federally insured banks like Discover can charge, "notwithstanding any State constitution or statute which is hereby preempted." This provision, Discover maintained, was completely preemptive, i.e., it superseded otherwise applicable Maryland law, and placed Vaden's counterclaims under the exclusive governance of the FDIA. On that basis, Discover asserted, the District Court had authority to entertain the § 4 petition pursuant to 28 U.S.C. § 1331, which gives federal courts jurisdiction over cases "arising under" federal law.

The District Court granted Discover's petition, ordered arbitration, and stayed Vaden's prosecution of her counterclaims in state court pending the outcome of arbitration. . . . On Vaden's initial appeal, the Fourth Circuit inquired whether the District Court had federal-question jurisdiction over Discover's § 4 petition. To make that determination, the Court of Appeals instructed, the District Court should "look through" the § 4

---

1. Discover apparently had no access to a federal forum for its suit against Vaden on the basis of diversity-of-citizenship jurisdiction. Under that head of federal-court jurisdiction, the amount in controversy must "excee[d] . . . $75,000." 28 U.S.C. § 1332(a).

2. Vaden's preference for court adjudication is unsurprising. The arbitration clause, framed by Discover, prohibited presentation of "any claims as a representative or member of a class." . . .

3. Section 4 reads, in relevant part:

"A party aggrieved by the alleged failure, neglect, or refusal of another to arbitrate under a written agreement for arbitration may petition any United States district court which, save for such agreement, would have jurisdiction under title 28, in a civil action or in admiralty of the subject matter of a suit arising out of the controversy between the parties, for an order directing that such arbitration proceed in the manner provided for in such agreement." 9 U.S.C. § 4.

petition to the substantive controversy between the parties. . . . The appellate court then remanded the case for an express determination whether that controversy presented "a properly invoked federal question.". . .

On remand, Vaden "concede[d] that the FDIA completely preempts any state claims against a federally insured bank.". . . Accepting this concession, the District Court expressly held that it had federal-question jurisdiction over Discover's § 4 petition and again ordered arbitration. . . . In this second round, the Fourth Circuit affirmed, dividing 2 to 1. . . .

Recognizing that "a party may not create jurisdiction by concession,". . . the Fourth Circuit majority conducted its own analysis of FDIA § 27(a), ultimately concluding that the provision completely preempted state law and therefore governed Vaden's counterclaims. [Footnote omitted.] . . .

We granted *certiorari* in view of the conflict among lower federal courts on whether district courts, petitioned to order arbitration pursuant to § 4 of the FAA, may "look through" the petition and examine the parties' underlying dispute to determine whether federal-question jurisdiction exists over the § 4 petition. . . . [Footnote omitted.] . . .

As this case shows, if the underlying dispute is the proper focus of a § 4 petition, a further question may arise. The dispute brought to state court by Discover concerned Vaden's failure to pay over $10,000 in past-due credit card charges. In support of that complaint, Discover invoked no federal law. When Vaden answered and counterclaimed, however, Discover asserted that federal law, specifically § 27(a) of the FDIA, displaced the state laws on which Vaden relied. What counts as the underlying dispute in a case so postured? May Discover invoke § 4, not on the basis of its own complaint, which had no federal element, but on the basis of counterclaims asserted by Vaden? To answer these questions, we first review relevant provisions of the FAA . . . and controlling tenets of federal jurisdiction.

II

In 1925, Congress enacted the FAA "[t]o overcome judicial resistance to arbitration," . . . and to declare " 'a national policy favoring arbitration' of claims that parties contract to settle in that manner." . . . To that end, § 2 provides that arbitration agreements in contracts "involving commerce" are "valid, irrevocable, and enforceable." . . . [Footnote omitted.] Section 4—the section at issue here—provides for United States district court enforcement of arbitration agreements. Petitions to compel arbitration, § 4 states, may be brought before "any United States district court which, save for such agreement, would have jurisdiction under title 28 . . . of the subject matter of a suit arising out of the controversy between the parties." . . . [Footnote omitted.]

The "body of federal substantive law" generated by elaboration of FAA § 2 is equally binding on state and federal courts. . . . "As for jurisdiction over controversies touching arbitration," however, the Act is "something of an anomaly" in the realm of federal legislation: It "bestow[s] no federal jurisdiction but rather requir[es] [for access to a federal forum] an independent jurisdictional basis" over the parties' dispute. ...[Footnote omitted.] Given the substantive supremacy of the FAA, but the Act's nonjurisdictional cast, state courts have a prominent role to play as enforcers of agreements to arbitrate. ...

The independent jurisdictional basis Discover relies upon in this case is 28 U.S.C. § 1331, which vests in federal district courts jurisdiction over "all civil actions arising under the Constitution, laws, or treaties of the United States." Under the longstanding well-pleaded complaint rule, however, a suit "arises under" federal law "only when the plaintiff's statement of his own cause of action shows that it is based upon [federal law]." ... Federal jurisdiction cannot be predicated on an actual or anticipated defense: "It is not enough that the plaintiff alleges some anticipated defense to his cause of action and asserts that the defense is invalidated by some provision of [federal law]." ...

Nor can federal jurisdiction rest upon an actual or anticipated counterclaim. We so ruled, emphatically, in *Holmes Group*, 535 U.S. 826. Without dissent, the Court held in *Holmes Group* that a federal counterclaim, even when compulsory, does not establish "arising under" jurisdiction. [Footnote omitted.] Adhering assiduously to the well-pleaded complaint rule, the Court observed, *inter alia*, that it would undermine the clarity and simplicity of that rule if federal courts were obliged to consider the contents not only of the complaint but also of responsive pleadings in determining whether a case "arises under" federal law.... [Footnote omitted.]

A *complaint* purporting to rest on state law, we have recognized, can be recharacterized as one "arising under" federal law if the law governing the complaint is exclusively federal. ...Under this so-called "complete preemption doctrine," a plaintiff's "state cause of action [may be recast] as a federal claim for relief, making [its] removal [by the defendant] proper on the basis of federal question jurisdiction." ... [Footnote omitted.] A state-law-based *counterclaim*, however, even if similarly susceptible to recharacterization, would remain nonremovable. Under our precedent construing § 1331, as just explained, counterclaims, even if they rely exclusively on federal substantive law, do not qualify a case for federal-court cognizance.

III

Attending to the language of the FAA and the above-described jurisdictional tenets, we approve the "look through" approach to this extent: A federal court may "look through" a § 4 petition to determine whether it is predicated on an action that "arises under" federal law; in keeping with the well-pleaded complaint rule as amplified in *Holmes Group*, however, a federal court may not entertain a § 4 petition based on the contents, actual or hypothetical, of a counterclaim.

A

The text of § 4 drives our conclusion that a federal court should determine its jurisdiction by "looking through" a § 4 petition to the parties' underlying substantive controversy. We reiterate § 4's relevant instruction: When one party seeks arbitration pursuant to a written agreement and the other resists, the proponent of arbitration may petition for an order compelling arbitration in

> "any United States district court which, save for [the arbitration] agreement, would have jurisdiction under title 28, in a civil action or in admiralty of the subject matter of a suit arising out of the controversy between the parties."
> 9 U.S.C. § 4.

The phrase "save for [the arbitration] agreement" indicates that the district court should assume the absence of the arbitration agreement and determine whether it "would have jurisdiction under title 28" without it.... Jurisdiction over what? The text of § 4 refers us to "the controversy between the parties." That phrase, the Fourth Circuit said, and we agree, is most straightforwardly read to mean the "substantive conflict between the parties." ... [Footnote omitted.]

The majority of Courts of Appeals to address the question, we acknowledge, have rejected the "look through" approach entirely.... The relevant "controversy between the parties," Vaden insists, is simply and only the parties' discrete dispute over the arbitrability of their claims. She relies, quite reasonably, on the fact that a § 4 petition to compel arbitration seeks no adjudication on the merits of the underlying controversy. Indeed, its very purpose is to have an arbitrator, rather than a court, resolve the merits. A § 4 petition, Vaden observes, is essentially a plea for specific performance of an agreement to arbitrate, and it thus presents principally contractual questions: Did the parties validly agree to arbitrate? What issues does their agreement encompass? Has one party dishonored the agreement?

Vaden's argument, though reasonable, is difficult to square with the statutory language. Section 4 directs courts to determine whether they would have jurisdiction "save for [the arbitration] agreement." How, then, can a dispute over the existence or applicability of an arbitration agreement be the controversy that counts?

The "save for" clause, courts espousing the view embraced by Vaden respond, means only that the "antiquated and arcane" ouster notion no longer holds sway.... The "save for" clause, as comprehended by proponents of the "ouster" explanation, was designed to ensure that courts would no longer consider themselves ousted of jurisdiction and would therefore specifically enforce arbitration agreements....

We are not persuaded that the "ouster" explanation of § 4's "save for" clause carries the day. To the extent that the ancient "ouster" doctrine continued to impede specific enforcement of arbitration agreements, § 2 of the FAA, the Act's "centerpiece provision," ... directly attended to the problem. Covered agreements to arbitrate, § 2 declares, are "valid, irrevocable, and enforceable, save upon such grounds as exist at law or in equity for the revocation of any contract." Having commanded that an arbitration agreement is enforceable just as any other contract, Congress had no cause to repeat the point.... [Footnote omitted.]

In addition to its textual implausibility, the approach Vaden advocates has curious practical consequences. It would permit a federal court to entertain a § 4 petition only when a federal-question suit is already before the court, when the parties satisfy the requirements for diversity-of-citizenship jurisdiction, or when the dispute over arbitrability involves a maritime contract.... [Footnote omitted.] Vaden's approach would not accommodate a § 4 petitioner who *could* file a federal-question suit in (or remove such a suit to) federal court, but who has not done so. In contrast, when the parties' underlying dispute arises under federal law, the "look through" approach permits a § 4 petitioner to ask a federal court to compel arbitration without first taking the formal step of initiating or removing a federal-question suit—that is, without seeking federal adjudication of the very questions it wants to arbitrate rather than litigate....

B

Having determined that a district court should "look through" a § 4 petition, we now consider whether the court "would have [federal-question] jurisdiction" over "a suit arising out of the controversy" between Discover and Vaden.... As explained above, § 4 of the FAA does not enlarge federal-court jurisdiction; rather, it confines federal courts to the jurisdiction they would have "save for [the arbitration] agreement." ... Mindful of that limitation, we read § 4 to convey that a party seeking to compel arbitration may gain a federal court's assistance only if, "save for" the agreement, the entire, actual "controversy between the parties," as they have framed it, could be litigated in federal court. We conclude that the parties' actual controversy, here precipitated by Discover's state-court suit for the balance due on Vaden's account, is not amenable to federal-court adjudication. Consequently, the § 4 petition Discover filed in the United States District Court for the District of Maryland must be dismissed.

[...]

In holding that Discover properly invoked federal-court jurisdiction, the Fourth Circuit looked beyond Discover's complaint and homed in on Vaden's state-law-based defense and counterclaims. Those responsive pleadings, Discover alleged, and the Fourth Circuit determined, were completely preempted by the FDIA.... The Fourth Circuit, however, misapprehended our decision in *Holmes Group*. Under the well-pleaded complaint rule, a completely preempted counterclaim remains a counterclaim and thus does not provide a key capable of opening a federal court's door. ...

[. . .]

The dissent would have us treat a § 4 petitioner's statement of the issues to be arbitrated as the relevant controversy even when that statement does not convey the full flavor of the parties' entire dispute. Artful dodges by a § 4 petitioner should not divert us from recognizing the actual dimensions of that controversy. The text of § 4 instructs federal courts to determine whether they would have jurisdiction over "a suit arising out of *the* controversy between the parties"; it does not give § 4 petitioners license to recharacterize an existing controversy, or manufacture a new controversy, in an effort to obtain a federal court's aid in compelling arbitration. [Footnote omitted.]

Viewed contextually and straightforwardly, it is hardly "fortuit[ous]" that the controversy in this case took the shape it did. . . . Seeking to collect a debt, Discover filed an entirely state-law-grounded complaint in state court, and Vaden chose to file responsive counterclaims. Perhaps events could have unfolded differently, but § 4 does not invite federal courts to dream up counterfactuals when actual litigation has defined the parties' controversy. [Footnote omitted.]

As the dissent would have it, parties could commandeer a federal court to slice off responsive pleadings for arbitration while leaving the remainder of the parties' controversy pending in state court. That seems a bizarre way to proceed. In this case, Vaden's counterclaims would be sent to arbitration while the complaint to which they are addressed—Discover's state-law-grounded debt-collection action—would remain pending in a Maryland court. When the controversy between the parties is not one over which a federal court would have jurisdiction, it makes scant sense to allow one of the parties to enlist a federal court to disturb the state-court proceedings by carving out issues for separate resolution. [Footnote omitted.]

Furthermore, the presence of a threshold question whether a counterclaim alleged to be based on state law is totally preempted by federal law may complicate the dissent's § 4 inquiry. This case is illustrative. The dissent relates that Vaden eventually conceded that FDIA § 27(a), not Maryland law, governs the charges and fees Discover may impose. . . . But because the issue is jurisdictional, Vaden's concession is not determinative. . . . The dissent simply glides by the preemption issue, devoting no attention to it, although this Court has not yet resolved the matter.

In sum, § 4 of the FAA instructs district courts asked to compel arbitration to inquire whether the court would have jurisdiction, "save for [the arbitration] agreement," over "a suit arising out of the controversy between the parties." We read that prescription in light of the well-pleaded complaint rule and the corollary rule that federal jurisdiction cannot be invoked on the basis of a defense or counterclaim. Parties may not circumvent those rules by asking a federal court to order arbitration of the portion of a controversy that implicates federal law when the court would not have federal-question jurisdiction over the controversy as a whole. It does not suffice to show that a federal question lurks somewhere inside the parties' controversy, or that a defense or counterclaim would arise under federal law. Because the controversy between Discover and Vaden, properly perceived, is not one qualifying for federal-court adjudication, § 4 of the FAA does not empower a federal court to order arbitration of that controversy, in whole or in part. [Footnote omitted.]

Discover, we note, is not left without recourse. Under the FAA, state courts as well as federal courts are obliged to honor and enforce agreements to arbitrate.... Discover may therefore petition a Maryland court for aid in enforcing the arbitration clause of its contracts with Maryland cardholders.

True, Maryland's high court has held that §§ 3 and 4 of the FAA prescribe federal-court procedures and, therefore, do not bind the state courts.[4] But Discover scarcely lacks an available state remedy. Section 2 of the FAA, which does bind the state courts, renders agreements to arbitrate "valid, irrevocable, and *enforceable*." This provision "carries with it duties [to credit and enforce arbitration agreements] indistinguishable from those imposed on federal courts by FAA §§ 3 and 4." ... Notably, Maryland, like many other States, provides a statutory remedy nearly identical to § 4. See Md. Cts. & Jud. Proc. Code Ann. § 3–207 (Lexis 2006) ("If a party to an arbitration agreement ... refuses to arbitrate, the other party may file a petition with a court to order arbitration.... If the court determines that the agreement exists, it shall order arbitration. Otherwise it shall deny the petition."). See also Walther v. Sovereign Bank, 386 Md. 412, 424, 872 A.2d 735, 742 (2005) ("The Maryland Arbitration Act has been called the 'State analogue ... to the Federal Arbitration Act.' The same policy favoring enforcement of arbitration agreements is present in both our own and the federal acts." (internal quotation marks and citation omitted)). Even before it filed its debt-recovery action in a Maryland state court, Discover could have sought from that court an order compelling arbitration of any agreement-related dispute between itself and cardholder Vaden. At no time was federal-court intervention needed to place the controversy between the parties before an arbitrator.

* * *

For the reasons stated, the District Court lacked jurisdiction to entertain Discover's § 4 petition to compel arbitration. The judgment of the Court of Appeals affirming the District Court's order is therefore reversed, and the case is remanded for further proceedings consistent with this opinion.

It is so ordered.

CHIEF JUSTICE ROBERTS, with whom JUSTICE STEVENS, JUSTICE BREYER, and JUSTICE ALITO join, concurring in part and dissenting in part.

---

4. This Court has not decided whether §§ 3 and 4 apply to proceedings in state courts ... and we do not do so here.

I agree with the Court that a federal court asked to compel arbitration pursuant to § 4 of the Federal Arbitration Act should "look through" the dispute over arbitrability in determining whether it has jurisdiction to grant the requested relief. But look through to what? The statute provides a clear and sensible answer: The court may consider the § 4 petition if the court "would have" jurisdiction over "the subject matter of a suit arising out of the controversy between the parties." . . .

The § 4 petition in this case explains that the controversy Discover seeks to arbitrate is whether "Discover Bank charged illegal finance charges, interest and late fees." . . . Discover contends in its petition that the resolution of this dispute is controlled by federal law—specifically § 27(a) of the Federal Deposit Insurance Act (FDIA), 12 U.S.C. § 1831d(a) (setting forth the interest rates a state-chartered, federally insured bank may charge "notwithstanding any State constitution or statute which is hereby preempted"). Vaden agrees that the legality of Discover's charges and fees is governed by the FDIA. [Asterisk omitted.] A federal court therefore "would have jurisdiction . . . of the subject matter of a suit arising out of the controversy" Discover seeks to arbitrate. That suit could be an action by Vaden asserting that the charges violate the FDIA, or one by Discover seeking a declaratory judgment that they do not.

The majority is diverted off this straightforward path by the fortuity that a complaint happens to have been filed in this case. Instead of looking to the controversy the § 4 petitioner seeks to arbitrate, the majority focuses on the controversy underlying that complaint, and asks whether "the *whole* controversy," as reflected in "the parties' state-court filings," arises under federal law. . . . [Emphasis added by dissent.] Because that litigation was commenced as a state-law debt-collection claim, the majority concludes there is no § 4 jurisdiction.

This approach is contrary to the language of § 4, and sharply restricts the ability of federal courts to enforce agreements to arbitrate. The "controversy" to which § 4 refers is the dispute alleged to be subject to arbitration. The § 4 petitioner must set forth the nature of that dispute— the one he seeks to arbitrate—in the § 4 petition seeking an order to compel arbitration. Section 4 requires that the petitioner be "aggrieved" by the other party's "failure, neglect, or refusal . . . to arbitrate under a written agreement for arbitration"; that language guides the district court to the specific controversy the other party is unwilling to arbitrate.

[. . .]

There is no reason to suppose "controversy" meant the controversy subject to arbitration everywhere else in the FAA, but something quite different in § 4. The issue is whether there is jurisdiction to compel arbitration to resolve a controversy; why would the pertinent controversy for assessing jurisdiction be anything other than the same one asserted to be subject to arbitration?

The majority looks instead to the controversy the state-court litigation seeks to resolve. This produces the odd result of defining "controversy" more broadly than the § 4 petition itself. Discover's petition does not seek to arbitrate its state-law debt-collection claims, but rather Vaden's allegation that the fees Discover has been charging her (and other members of her proposed class) violate the FDIA.... The majority does not appear to question that there would be federal jurisdiction over a suit arising out of the subject matter of that dispute. The majority finds no jurisdiction here, however, because "a federal court could not entertain Discover's state-law debt-collection claim." ... There is no jurisdiction to compel arbitration of a plainly federal controversy—the FDIA dispute—because there is no jurisdiction to compel arbitration of the debt-collection dispute. But why Discover should have to demonstrate federal jurisdiction over a state-court claim it does not seek to arbitrate is a mystery....

The majority's approach will allow federal jurisdiction to compel arbitration of *entirely* state-law claims. Under that approach the "controversy" is not the one the § 4 petitioner seeks to arbitrate, but a broader one encompassing the "whole controversy" between the parties.... If that broader dispute involves both federal and state-law claims, and the "originating" dispute is federal, ... a party could seek arbitration of just the state-law claims. The "controversy" under the majority's view would qualify as federal, giving rise to § 4 jurisdiction to compel arbitration of a purely state-law claim.

Take this case as an example. If Vaden had filed her FDIA claim first, and Discover had responded with a state-law debt-collection counterclaim, that suit is one that "could be litigated in federal court." ... As a result, the majority's approach would seem to permit Vaden to file a § 4 petition to compel arbitration of the entirely state-law-based debt-collection dispute, because that dispute would be part and parcel of the "full flavor[ed]," "originating" FDIA controversy.... Defining the controversy as the dispute the § 4 petitioner seeks to arbitrate eliminates this problem by ensuring that the *actual dispute* subject to arbitration is federal.

The majority's conclusion that this controversy "is not one qualifying for federal-court adjudication," ... stems from its mistaken focus on the existing litigation. Rather than ask whether a court "would have" jurisdiction over the "subject matter" of "a" suit arising out of the "controversy," the majority asks only whether the court *does* have jurisdiction over the subject matter of a *particular* complaint. But § 4 does not speak of actual jurisdiction over pending suits; it speaks subjunctively of prospective jurisdiction over "the subject matter of a suit arising out of the controversy between the parties." ... The fact that Vaden has chosen to package the FDIA controversy in counterclaims in pending state-court litigation in no way means that a district court "would [not] have" jurisdiction over the "subject matter" of "a suit" arising out of the FDIA controversy. A big part of arbitration is avoiding the procedural niceties of formal litigation; it would be odd to have the authority of a court to compel arbitration hinge on just such niceties in a pending case.

By focusing on the sequence in which state-court litigation has unfolded, the majority crafts a rule that produces inconsistent results. Because Discover's debt-collection claim was filed before Vaden's counterclaims, the majority treats the debt-collection dispute as the "originating controversy." ... But nothing would have prevented the same disagreements between the parties from producing a different sequence of events. Vaden could have filed a complaint raising her FDIA claims before Discover sought to collect on any amounts Vaden owes. Because the "originating controversy" in that complaint would be whether Discover has charged fees illegal under federal law, in that situation Discover presumably *could* bring a § 4 petition to compel arbitration of the FDIA dispute. The majority's rule thus makes § 4 jurisdiction over the same controversy entirely dependent upon the happenstance of how state-court litigation has unfolded. Nothing in § 4 suggests such a result.

The majority glosses over another problem inherent in its approach: In many if not most cases under § 4, no complaint will have been filed.... What to "look through" to then? The majority instructs courts to look to the "full-bodied controversy." ... But as this case illustrates, that would lead to a different result had the state-court complaint not been filed. Discover does not seek to arbitrate whether an outstanding debt exists; indeed, Discover's § 4 petition does not even allege any dispute on that point.... A district court would therefore not understand the § 4 "controversy" to include the debt-collection claim in the absence of the state-court suit. Under the majority's rule, the FDIA dispute would be treated as a "controversy" qualifying under § 4 before the state suit and counterclaims had been filed, but not after.

The far more concrete and administrable approach would be to apply the same rule in all instances: Look to the controversy the § 4 petitioner seeks to arbitrate—as set forth in the § 4 petition—and assess whether a federal court would have jurisdiction over the subject matter of a suit arising out of that controversy. The controversy the moving party seeks to arbitrate and the other party will not would be the same controversy used to assess jurisdiction to compel arbitration.

The majority objects that this would allow a court to "hypothesiz[e] discrete controversies of its own design," ... in an apparent effort to find federal jurisdiction where there is none. Not so. A district court entertaining a § 4 petition is required to determine what "a suit" arising out of the allegedly arbitrable controversy would look like. There is no helping that, given the statute's subjunctive language. But that does not mean the inquiry is the free-form one the majority posits.

To the contrary, a district court must look to the specific controversy—the concrete dispute that one party has "fail[ed], neglect[ed], or refus[ed]" to arbitrate—and determine whether *that* controversy would give rise to a suit under federal law. District courts do that sort of thing often enough; the exercise is closely analogous to the jurisdictional analysis in a typical declaratory judgment action.... Looking to the specific controversy outlined in Discover's § 4 petition (whether its fees violate the FDIA), it hardly requires "dream[ing]" to conceive of a lawsuit in which Vaden would claim the FDIA has been violated and Discover would claim it has not. . . .

Nor would respondents' approach allow a § 4 petitioner to simply "recharacterize" or "manufacture" a controversy to create federal jurisdiction. . . . All of the established rules of federal jurisdiction are fully applicable in scrutinizing whether a federal court would have jurisdiction over a suit arising out of the parties' underlying controversy.

[. . .]

Accordingly, petitioners may no more smuggle state-law claims into federal court through § 4 than they can through declaratory judgment actions, or any other federal cause of action. To the extent § 4 brings some issues into federal court in a particular case that may not be brought in through other procedural mechanisms, it does so by "enlarg[ing] the range of remedies available in the federal courts[,] . . . not extend[ing] their jurisdiction." . . .

[. . .]

The correct approach is to accord § 4 the scope mandated by its language and look to "a suit," arising out of the "subject matter" of the "controversy" the § 4 petitioner seeks to arbitrate, and determine whether a federal court would have jurisdiction over such a suit.

The majority concludes by noting that state courts are obliged to honor and enforce agreements to arbitrate. . . . The question here, however, is one of remedy. It is a common feature of our federal system that States often provide remedies similar to those under federal law for the same wrongs. We do not, however, narrowly construe the federal remedies—say federal antitrust or civil rights remedies—because state law provides remedies in those areas as well. . . .

* * *

Discover and Vaden have agreed to arbitrate any dispute arising out of Vaden's account with Discover. Vaden's allegations against Discover have given rise to such a dispute. Discover seeks to arbitrate that controversy, but Vaden refuses to do so. Resolution of the controversy is governed by federal law, specifically the FDIA. There is no dispute about that. In the absence of the arbitration agreement, a federal court "would have jurisdiction . . . of the subject matter of a suit arising out of the controversy between the parties," 9 U.S.C. § 4, whether the suit were brought by Vaden or Discover. The District Court therefore may exercise jurisdiction over this petition under § 4 of the Federal Arbitration Act.

NOTES AND QUESTIONS

1. What dispute divides the parties and which one of them wants to submit to arbitration? Is it debt collection or the charging of questionable fees? Can you segregate these disputes? If so, how? Are they conjoined? If so, what result? Is the majority or dissent more persuasive on this matter? Why?

2. Is Discover Bank's filing in state court a "scarlet letter" for jurisdictional purposes? Explain your answer and your sense of the question.

3. Evaluate the majority's claim, in footnote 4, that the plaintiff's motivation to conduct the litigation in a judicial forum is "unsurprising." What impact does this factor have, if any, upon the majority's determination?

4. Is the majority opinion a brief for states rights? If so, how and in what specific respects? Does it tout the federal policy in favor of arbitration? Where, in the opinion, is such a position evident?

5. What definition of federal jurisdiction does the majority espouse under the FAA? How is the dissent's concept on this score different?

6. What is the "look through" doctrine for purposes of FAA § 4? How do the majority and dissent's positions differ on this matter? Is "look through" a favorable-to-arbitration concept? In what way(s)? When would it frustrate the policy on arbitration?

7. How does FAA § 2 provide a resolution or lessening of the tension between the majority and dissenting opinions?

8. How might the Court fill the federal question gap in the FAA? Is recognizing a would-be anomaly sufficient or should a firmer stance be adopted? What might the latter provide?

* * *

Southland Corp. v. Keating, decided a year later, provides some clarification as to the direction and motivation of the Court's decision-making on matters of arbitration. The consequences upon federalism concerns are just as staggering, but the basis for asserting federal authority is more evident. 465 U.S. 1 (1984). The issue in *Keating* centered upon the constitutionality of a section of the California Franchise Investment Law (CAL. CORP. CODE § 31512 (West 1977)) which had been interpreted to require exclusive judicial adjudication of claims brought under the statute. Keating's claim, brought on behalf of Seven–Eleven franchisees against Southland Corporation (the Seven–Eleven franchiser) alleged, among other things, that Southland had breached its fiduciary duty and violated the disclosure requirements of the California Franchise Investment Law. After the trial court held the nonwaiver provisions of the Franchise Investment Law valid, the California court of appeals determined that, if the Franchise Investment Law rendered arbitration agreements unenforceable, it conflicted with the provisions of the FAA and was, therefore, invalid under the Supremacy Clause of the U.S. Constitution. 109 Cal.App.3d 784, 167 Cal.Rptr. 481, 493–94 (1980). The California Supreme Court interpreted the investment law provision to require exclusive judicial adjudication of claims brought under the statute; it held that claims asserted under the investment law were inarbitrable; and it further concluded that the California statute did not contravene the federal legislation on arbitration. 31 Cal.3d 584, 604, 183 Cal.Rptr. 360, 645 P.2d 1192 (1982).

The U.S. Supreme Court determined that the federal legislation created a duty not only upon the federal courts, but also upon the state courts to apply the federal policy on arbitration embodied in the FAA. "In enacting section 2 of the Federal Act, Congress declared a national policy favoring arbitration and withdrew the power of the states to require a judicial forum for the resolution of claims which the contracting parties agreed to resolve by arbitration." 465 U.S. 1, 10 (1984). Agreeing with the essential reasoning of the California appellate court opinion, the Court further held that, "in creating a substantive rule applicable in state as well as federal courts, Congress intended to foreclose state legislative attempts to undercut the enforceability of arbitration agreements. We hold that § 31512 of the California Franchise Investment Law violates the supremacy clause." *Id.* at 16.

SOUTHLAND CORP. v. KEATING

465 U.S. 1, 104 S.Ct. 852, 79 L.Ed.2d 1 (1984).

(footnotes omitted)

CHIEF JUSTICE BURGER delivered the opinion of the Court.

This case presents the questions (a) whether the California Franchise Investment Law, which invalidates certain arbitration agreements covered by the Federal Arbitration Act, violates the Supremacy Clause and (b) whether arbitration under the Federal Act is impaired when a class-action structure is imposed on the process by the state courts.

[. . .]

III

. . . [T]he California Franchise Investment Law provides:

Any condition, stipulation or provision purporting to bind any person acquiring any franchise to waive compliance with any provision of this law or any rule or order hereunder is void. . . .

The California Supreme Court interpreted this statute to require judicial consideration of claims brought under the State statute and accordingly refused to enforce the parties' contract to arbitrate such claims. So interpreted the California Franchise Investment Law directly conflicts with § 2 of the Federal Arbitration Act and violates the Supremacy Clause.

In enacting § 2 of the Federal Act, Congress declared a national policy favoring arbitration and withdrew the power of the states to require a judicial forum for the resolution of claims which the contracting parties agreed to resolve by arbitration.... Congress has thus mandated the enforcement of arbitration agreements.

We discern only two limitations on the enforceability of arbitration provisions governed by the Federal Arbitration Act: they must be part of a written maritime contract or a contract "evidencing a transaction involving commerce" and such clauses may be revoked upon "grounds as exist at law or in equity for the revocation of any contract." We see nothing in the Act indicating that the broad principle of enforceability is subject to any additional limitations under State law....

The Federal Arbitration Act rests on the authority of Congress to enact substantive rules under the Commerce Clause. In *Prima Paint Corp. v. Flood & Conklin Manufacturing Co.*, the Court examined the legislative history of the Act and concluded that the statute "is based upon...the incontestable federal foundations of 'control over interstate commerce and over admiralty.'" The contract in *Prima Paint*, as here, contained an arbitration clause. One party in that case alleged that the other had committed fraud in the inducement of the contract, although not of the arbitration clause in particular, and sought to have the claim of fraud adjudicated in federal court. The Court held that, notwithstanding a contrary state rule, consideration of a claim of fraud in the inducement of a contract "is for the arbitrators and not for the courts[ ]".... The Court relied for this holding on Congress' broad power to fashion substantive rules under the Commerce Clause.

... The statements of the Court in *Prima Paint* that the Arbitration Act was an exercise of the Commerce Clause power clearly implied that the substantive rules of the Act were to apply in state as well as federal courts. As Justice Black observed in his dissent, when Congress exercises its authority to enact substantive federal law under the Commerce Clause, it normally creates rules that are enforceable in state as well as federal courts.

In *Moses H. Cone Memorial Hospital v. Mercury Construction Corp.*, we reaffirmed our view that the Arbitration Act "creates a body of federal substantive law" and expressly stated what was implicit in *Prima Paint*, *i.e.*, the substantive law the Act created was applicable in state and federal courts....

Although the legislative history is not without ambiguities, there are strong indications that Congress had in mind something more than making arbitration agreements enforceable only in the federal courts. The House Report plainly suggests the more comprehensive objectives:

> "The purpose of this bill is to make valid and enforceable agreements for arbitration contained *in contracts involving interstate commerce* or within the jurisdiction or [sic] admiralty, or which may be the subject of litigation in the Federal courts."

This broader purpose can also be inferred from the reality that Congress would be less likely to address a problem whose impact was confined to federal courts than a problem of large significance in the field of commerce. The Arbitration Act sought to "overcome the rule of equity, that equity will not specifically enforce any arbitration agreement." The House Report accompanying the bill stated:

> "The need for the law arises from...the jealousy of the English courts for their own jurisdiction.... This jealousy survived for so lon[g] a period that the principle became firmly embedded in the English common law and was adopted with it by the American courts. The courts have felt that the precedent was too strongly fixed to be overturned without legislative enactment...."

Surely this makes clear that the House Report contemplated a broad reach of the Act, unencumbered by state law constraints. As [has been] stated "the purpose of the act was to assure those who desired arbitration and whose contracts related to interstate commerce that their expectations would not be undermined by federal judges, or...by state courts or legislatures." Congress also showed its awareness of the widespread unwillingness of state courts to enforce arbitration agreements and that such courts were bound by state laws inadequately providing for [arbitration]. The problems Congress faced were therefore twofold: the old common law hostility toward arbitration, and the failure of state arbitration statutes to mandate enforcement of arbitration agreements. To confine the scope of the Act to arbitrations sought to be enforced in federal courts would frustrate what we believe Congress intended to be a broad enactment appropriate in scope to meet the large problems Congress was addressing.

Justice O'Connor argues that Congress viewed the Arbitration Act "as a procedural statute, applicable only in federal courts." If it is correct that Congress sought only to create a procedural remedy in the federal courts, there can be no explanation for the express limitation in the Arbitration Act to contracts "involving commerce." For example, when Congress has authorized this Court to prescribe the rules of procedure in the Federal Courts of Appeals, District Courts, and bankruptcy courts, it has not limited the power of the Court to prescribe rules applicable only to causes of action involving commerce. We would expect that if Congress, in enacting the Arbitration Act, was creating what it thought to be a procedural rule applicable only in federal courts, it would not so limit the Act to transactions involving commerce. On the other hand, Congress would need to call on the Commerce Clause if it intended the Act to apply in state courts. Yet at the same time, its reach would be limited to transactions involving interstate commerce. We therefore view the "involving commerce" requirement in § 2, not as an inexplicable limitation on the power of the federal courts, but as a necessary qualification on a statute intended to apply in state and federal courts.

Under the interpretation of the Arbitration Act urged by Justice O'Connor, claims brought under the California Franchise Investment Law are not arbitrable when they are raised in state court. Yet it is clear beyond question that if this suit had been brought as a diversity action in a federal district court, the arbitration clause would have been enforceable. The interpretation given to the Arbitration Act by the California Supreme Court would therefore encourage and reward forum shopping. We are unwilling to attribute to Congress the intent, in drawing on the comprehensive powers of the Commerce Clause, to create a right to enforce an arbitration contract and yet make the right dependent for its enforcement on the particular forum in which it is asserted. And since the overwhelming proportion of all civil litigation in this country is in the state courts, we cannot believe Congress intended to limit the Arbitration Act to disputes subject only to federal court jurisdiction. Such an interpretation would frustrate Congressional intent to place "[a]n arbitration agreement...upon the same footing as other contracts, where it belongs."

In creating a substantive rule applicable in state as well as federal courts, Congress intended to foreclose state legislative attempts to undercut the enforceability of arbitration agreements. We hold that § 31512 of the California Franchise Investment Law violates the Supremacy Clause.

IV

The judgment of the California Supreme Court denying enforcement of the arbitration agreement is reversed; as to the question whether the Federal Arbitration Act precludes a class action arbitration and any other issues not raised in the California courts, no decision by this Court would be appropriate at this time. As to the latter issues, the case is remanded for further proceedings not inconsistent with this opinion.

It is so ordered.

JUSTICE STEVENS, concurring in part and dissenting in part.

The Court holds that an arbitration clause that is enforceable in an action in a federal court is equally enforceable if the action is brought in a state court. I agree with that conclusion. Although Justice O'Connor's review of the legislative history of the Federal Arbitration Act demonstrates that the 1925 Congress that enacted the statute viewed the statute as essentially procedural in nature, I am persuaded that the intervening developments in the law compel the conclusion that the Court has reached. I am nevertheless troubled by one aspect of the case that seems to trouble none of my colleagues.

For me it is not "clear beyond question that if this suit had been brought as a diversity action in a Federal District Court, the arbitration clause would have been enforceable." The general rule prescribed by § 2 of the Federal Arbitration Act is that arbitration clauses in contracts involving interstate transactions are enforceable as a matter of federal law. That general rule, however, is subject to an exception based on "such grounds as exist at law or in equity for the revocation of any contract." I believe that exception leaves room for the implementation of certain substantive state policies that would be undermined by enforcing certain categories of arbitration clauses.

The exercise of State authority in a field traditionally occupied by State law will not be deemed preempted by a federal statute unless that was the clear and manifest purpose of Congress. . . .

The limited objective of the Federal Arbitration Act was to abrogate the general common law rule against specific enforcement of arbitration agreements, and a state statute which merely codified the general common law rule, either directly by employing the prior doctrine of revocability or indirectly by declaring all such agreements void, would be preempted by the Act. However, beyond this conclusion, which seems compelled by the language of § 2 and case law concerning the Act, it is by no means clear that Congress intended entirely to displace State authority in this field. Indeed, while it is an understatement to say that "the legislative history of the. . .Act. . .reveals little awareness on the part of Congress that state law might be affected," it must surely be true that given the lack of a "clear mandate from Congress as to the extent to which state statutes and decisions are to be superseded, we must be cautious in construing the act lest we excessively encroach on the powers which Congressional policy, if not the Constitution, would reserve to the states." . . .

The textual basis in the Act for avoiding such encroachment is the provision of § 2 which provides that arbitration agreements are subject to revocation on such grounds as exist at law or in equity for the revocation of any contract. The Act, however, does not define what grounds for revocation may be permissible, and hence it would appear that the judiciary must fashion the limitations as a matter of federal common law. . . . The existence of a federal statute enunciating a substantive federal policy does not necessarily require the inexorable application of a uniform federal rule of decision notwithstanding the differing conditions which may exist in the several States and regardless of the decisions of the States to exert police powers as they deem best for the welfare of their citizens. . . .

A contract which is deemed void is surely revocable at law or in equity, and the California legislature has declared all conditions purporting to waive compliance with the protections of the Franchise Disclosure Act, including but not limited to arbitration provisions, void as a matter of public policy. Given the importance to the State of franchise relationships, the relative disparity in the bargaining positions between the franchiser and the franchisee, and the remedial purposes of the California Act, I believe this declaration of State policy is entitled to respect.

. . .We have exercised such judgment in other cases concerning the scope of the Arbitration Act, and have focused not on sterile generalization, but rather on the substance of the transaction at issue, the nature of the relationship between the parties to the agreement, and the purpose of the regulatory scheme. . . . Surely the general language of the Arbitration Act that arbitration agreements are valid does not mean that all such agreements are valid irrespective of their purpose or effect. . . .

We should not refuse to exercise independent judgment concerning the conditions under which an arbitration agreement, generally enforceable under the Act, can be held invalid as contrary to public policy simply because the source of the substantive law to which the arbitration agreement attaches is a State rather than the Federal Government. I find no evidence that Congress intended such a double standard to apply, and I would not lightly impute such an intent to the 1925 Congress which enacted the Arbitration Act.

A state policy excluding wage claims from arbitration...or a state policy of providing special protection for franchisees, such as that expressed in California's Franchise Investment Law, can be recognized without impairing the basic purposes of the federal statute. Like the majority of the California Supreme Court, I am not persuaded that Congress intended the pre-emptive effect of this statute to be "so unyielding as to require enforcement of an agreement to arbitrate a dispute over the application of a regulatory statute which a state legislature, in conformity with analogous federal policy, has decided should be left to judicial enforcement."...

Thus, although I agree with most of the Court's reasoning and specifically with its jurisdictional holdings, I respectfully dissent from its conclusion concerning the enforceability of the arbitration agreement. On that issue, I would affirm the judgment of the California Supreme Court.

JUSTICE O'CONNOR, with whom JUSTICE REHNQUIST joins, dissenting.

[. . .]

Today, the Court takes the facial silence of § 2 as a license to declare that state as well as federal courts must apply § 2. In addition, though this is not spelled out in the opinion, the Court holds that in enforcing this newly-discovered federal right state courts must follow procedures specified in § 3. The Court's decision is impelled by an understandable desire to encourage the use of arbitration, but it utterly fails to recognize the clear congressional intent underlying the FAA. Congress intended to require federal, not state, courts to respect arbitration agreements.

I

The FAA was enacted in 1925. As demonstrated below,... Congress thought it was exercising its power to dictate either procedure or "general federal law" in federal courts. The issue presented here is the result of three subsequent decisions of this Court.

In 1938 this Court decided *Erie Railroad Co. v. Tompkins. Erie* denied the federal government the power to create substantive law solely by virtue of the Article III power to control federal court jurisdiction. Eighteen years later the Court decided *Bernhardt v. Polygraphic Co. Bernhardt* held that the duty to arbitrate a contract dispute is outcome-determinative, *i.e.* "substantive," and therefore a matter normally governed by state law in federal diversity cases.

Bernhardt gave rise to concern that the FAA could thereafter constitutionally be applied only in federal court cases arising under federal law, not in diversity cases. In *Prima Paint Corp. v. Flood & Conklin Mfg. Co.*, we addressed that concern, and held that the FAA may constitutionally be applied to proceedings in a federal diversity court. The FAA covers only contracts involving interstate commerce or maritime affairs, and Congress "plainly has the power to legislate" in that area. . . .

Nevertheless, the *Prima Paint* decision "carefully avoided any explicit endorsement of the view that the Arbitration Act embodied substantive policies that were to be applied to all contracts within its scope, whether sued on in state or federal courts." Today's case is the first in which this Court has had occasion to determine whether the FAA applies to state court proceedings. One statement on the subject did appear in *Moses H. Cone Memorial Hospital v. Mercury Construction Corp.*, but that case involved a federal, not a state, court proceeding; its dictum concerning the law applicable in state courts was wholly unnecessary to its holding.

II

The majority opinion decides three issues. First, it holds that § 2 creates federal substantive rights that must be enforced by the state courts. Second, though the issue is not raised in this case, the Court states that § 2 substantive rights may not be the basis for invoking federal court jurisdiction under 28 U.S.C. § 1331. Third, the Court reads § 2 to require state courts to enforce § 2 rights using procedures that mimic those specified for federal courts by FAA §§ 3 and 4. The first of these conclusions is unquestionably wrong as a matter of statutory construction; the second appears to be an attempt to limit the damage done by the first; the third is unnecessary and unwise.

[. . .]

One rarely finds a legislative history as unambiguous as the FAA's. That history establishes conclusively that the 1925 Congress viewed the FAA as a procedural statute, applicable only in federal courts, derived, Congress believed, largely from the federal power to control the jurisdiction of the federal courts.

In 1925 Congress emphatically believed arbitration to be a matter of "procedure." At hearings on the Act congressional subcommittees were told: "The theory on which you do this is that you have the right to tell the Federal courts how to proceed." The House Report on the FAA stated: "Whether an agreement for arbitration shall be enforced or not is a question of procedure. . . ." On the floor of the House Congressman Graham assured his fellow members that the FAA

"does not involve any new principle of law except to provide a simple method . . . in order to give enforcement. . . . It creates no new legislation, grants no new rights, except a remedy to enforce an agreement in commercial contracts and in admiralty contracts."

A month after the Act was signed into law the American Bar Association Committee that had drafted and pressed for passage of the federal legislation wrote:

> "The statute establishes a procedure in the Federal courts for the enforcement of arbitration agreements.... A Federal statute providing for the enforcement of arbitration agreements does relate solely to procedure in the Federal courts.... [W]hether or not an arbitration agreement is to be enforced is a question of the law of procedure and is determined by the law of the jurisdiction wherein the remedy is sought. That the enforcement of arbitration contracts is within the law of procedure as distinguished from substantive law is well settled by the decisions of our courts."

Since *Bernhardt*, a right to arbitration has been characterized as "substantive," and that holding is not challenged here. But Congress in 1925 did not characterize the FAA as this Court did in 1956. Congress believed that the FAA established nothing more than a rule of procedure, a rule therefore applicable only in the federal courts.

If characterizing the FAA as procedural was not enough, the draftsmen of the Act, the House Report, and the early commentators all flatly stated that the Act was intended to affect only federal-court proceedings....

Yet another indication that Congress did not intend the FAA to govern state court proceedings is found in the powers Congress relied on in passing the Act. The FAA might have been grounded on Congress's powers to regulate interstate and maritime affairs, since the Act extends only to contracts in those areas. There are, indeed, references in the legislative history to the corresponding federal powers. More numerous, however, are the references to Congress's pre-*Erie* power to prescribe "general law" applicable in all federal courts. At the congressional hearings, for example: "Congress rests solely upon its power to prescribe the jurisdiction and duties of the Federal courts." And in the House Report:

> The matter is properly the subject of Federal action. Whether an agreement for arbitration shall be enforced or not is a question of procedure to be determined by the law court in which the proceeding is brought and not one of substantive law to be determined by the law of the forum in which the contract is made....

[...]

The foregoing cannot be dismissed as "ambiguities" in the legislative history....

B

The structure of the FAA itself runs directly contrary to the reading the Court today gives to § 2. §§ 3 and 4 are the implementing provisions of the Act, and they expressly apply only to federal courts. § 4 refers to the "United States district court[s]," and provides that it can be invoked only in a court that has jurisdiction under Title 28 of the United States Code. As originally enacted, § 3 referred, in the same terms as § 4, to "courts [or court] of the United States." There has since been a minor amendment in § 4's phrasing, but no substantive change in either section's limitation to federal courts.

[. . .]

IV

The Court . . . rejects the idea of requiring the FAA to be applied only in federal courts partly out of concern with the problem of forum shopping. The concern is unfounded. Because the FAA makes the federal courts equally accessible to both parties to a dispute, no forum shopping would be possible even if we gave the FAA a construction faithful to the congressional intent. In controversies involving incomplete diversity of citizenship there is simply no access to federal court and therefore no possibility of forum shopping. In controversies with complete diversity of citizenship the FAA grants federal court access equally to both parties; no party can gain any advantage by forum shopping. Even when the party resisting arbitration initiates an action in state court, the opposing party can invoke FAA § 4 and promptly secure a federal court order to compel arbitration. . . .

Ironically, the FAA was passed specifically to rectify forum shopping problems created by this Court's decision in *Swift v. Tyson* . . . . By 1925 several major commercial states had passed state arbitration laws, but the federal courts refused to enforce those laws in diversity cases. The drafters of the FAA might have anticipated *Bernhardt* by legislation and required federal diversity courts to adopt the arbitration law of the state in which they sat. But they deliberately chose a different approach. As was pointed out at congressional hearings, an additional goal of the Act was to make arbitration agreements enforceable even in federal courts located in states that had no arbitration law. The drafters' plan for maintaining reasonable harmony between state and federal practices was not to bludgeon states into compliance, but rather to adopt a uniform federal law, patterned after New York's path-breaking state statute, and simultaneously to press for passage of coordinated state legislation. The key language of the Uniform Act for Commercial Arbitration was, accordingly, identical to that in § 2 of the FAA.

In summary, forum shopping concerns in connection with the FAA are a distraction that do not withstand scrutiny. The Court ignores the drafters' carefully devised plan for dealing with those problems.

V

Today's decision adds yet another chapter to the FAA's already colorful history. In 1842 this Court's ruling in *Swift v. Tyson* set up a major obstacle to the enforcement of state arbitration laws in federal diversity courts. In 1925 Congress sought to rectify the problem by enacting the FAA; the intent was to create uniform law binding only in the federal courts. In *Erie* (1938), and then in *Bernhardt* (1956), this

Court significantly curtailed federal power. In 1967 our decision in *Prima Paint* upheld the application of the FAA in a federal court proceeding as a valid exercise of Congress's Commerce Clause and Admiralty powers. Today the Court discovers a federal right in FAA § 2 that the state courts must enforce. Apparently confident that state courts are not competent to devise their own procedures for protecting the newly discovered federal right, the Court summarily prescribes a specific procedure, found nowhere in § 2 or its common law origins, that the state courts are to follow.

Today's decision is unfaithful to congressional intent, unnecessary, and, in light of the FAA's antecedents and the intervening contraction of federal power, inexplicable. Although arbitration is a worthy alternative to litigation, today's exercise in judicial revisionism goes too far. I respectfully dissent.

NOTES AND QUESTIONS

1. In her dissent, Justice O'Connor describes the history of the FAA and how it contributes to the federalism debate. Prior to 1925, the federal courts were obligated under the rule of *Swift v. Tyson* to apply general federal common law in diversity cases. At that time, there were few state statutes on arbitration and no federal legislation on the topic. Only states with significant commercial activity, like New York, had enacted legislation in the area. Accordingly, in the absence of federal laws, federal courts sitting in diversity cases refused to enforce agreements to arbitrate. The FAA was intended to remedy that problem within the context of *Swift v. Tyson*. By creating a statutory mechanism for the enforcement of arbitration agreements and awards, the FAA allowed the federal courts to uphold the party reference to arbitration. The same result would apply regardless of whether the litigation took place in New York state court or before a federal district court. The FAA was intended to allow the community of merchants to resolve their disputes through the customary mechanism of arbitration despite *Swift v. Tyson*, the absence of federal law, or the lack of state legislation.

Erie changed considerably the setting in which the FAA was to function. The goal of finding a basis for federal court action now was obsolete. The objective became a competition for primacy between the federal and state law in diversity cases. Should the FAA yield to state laws on arbitration that might not espouse the same disposition on arbitration? *Erie* clearly dictated the primacy of state law. Once the context of application for the FAA shifted from remedying a gap in the *Swift* doctrine to an *Erie* problem of the competing jurisdiction of substantive law, the institutional standing of the FAA was transformed. The FAA was no longer a procedural enactment, but rather the vehicle of substantive federal rights. It represented Congress' power over the federal courts and the Congressional exercise of Commerce Clause power over interstate commerce. It was not special interest legislation, but rather a statement of federal policy on arbitration.

These circumstances explain the considerable distance traveled between the enactment of the FAA and the rulings in *Prima Paint* and *Keating*. The FAA's legislative history describes the enactment of an entirely different statute from the one described in modern case law. Once the FAA was integrated into the *Erie* debate, it became a different statutory regime, legislation whose application far exceeded the express language of its provisions or its original intent. With *Keating*, the FAA not only was binding upon the federal courts in diversity cases (that much already was clear in *Prima Paint*) and binding upon state courts in cases touching upon interstate commerce (*Moses H. Cone*), but it also literally vacated the power of states to enact statutes that contradicted, directly or indirectly, the federal policy on arbitration. In effect, the U.S. law on arbitration had been federalized. The Court restricted state legislative rights to guarantee the "unobstructed enforcement" of arbitration agreements.

Does the foregoing discussion coincide with the majority or the dissent's sense of the FAA's origins and purpose? Does it coincide with your evaluation of the FAA? Has the decisional law wrongfully used its judicial powers of decision? Or was the "adaptation" of the FAA necessary and inevitable, and, therefore, justified?

2. What is the precedential significance of *Bernhardt v. Polygraphic Co.* in the evolution of the Court's decisional law on arbitration in light of *Keating*? According to Justice O'Connor's dissent, "*Bernhardt* held that the duty to arbitrate a contract dispute is...'substantive'...and therefore a matter normally governed by state law in federal diversity cases." The word substantive means that the issue is "outcome-determinative." What does this view of *Bernhardt* add to the federalism debate on arbitration? Is arbitration truly substantive? Isn't arbitration a mere form of trial; a choice of remedy? You should revisit these questions after examining the majority opinions in *Mitsubishi*, *McMahon*, and *Rodriguez*, *infra*.

3. In *Robert Lawrence Co. v. Devonshire Fabrics, Inc. (supra)*, the Second Circuit stated that the FAA was "a declaration of national law equally applicable in state or federal court." How does that observation fit into the federalism trilogy and the reasoning in *Keating*? Do you think the *Keating* Court subscribes to that statement? Why?

4. Does Justice O'Connor believe that the decision in *Prima Paint* was correctly decided? In terms of law and policy, is *Prima Paint* distinguishable from the reasoning in *Keating*? What views does Justice O'Connor have on *Moses H. Cone*? Why does she appear more tolerant of those decisions than other precedents on arbitration?

5. How might one argue that Justice Stevens, while advocating for the continued operation of state authority in the arbitration area, is also making the case for the inarbitrability defense? What is Justice Stevens referring to when he speaks about the exercise of good judgment in evaluating the scope of the FAA? Do you agree that the case law has focused on "sterile generalizations," rather than considered analysis? What plan does Justice Stevens articulate for the peaceful coexistence of arbitration and state legislative authority? You should compare Justice Stevens' writing here with his opinions in *Mitsubishi*, *McMahon*, and *Mastrobuono*, *infra*.

6. The majority opinion is quite straightforward: A provision in a state statute that mandates the resolution of statutory disputes exclusively through the courts is unconstitutional because it contravenes the provisions of the

FAA. The FAA is controlling because it reflects the exercise of Congressional authority over interstate commerce and, under the Supremacy Clause, that power overrides state authority.

The Court makes a variety of noteworthy contentions in the footnotes of the opinion. In footnote 10, the Court states: "In holding that the Arbitration Act preempts a state law that withdraws the power to enforce arbitration agreements, we do not hold that §§ 3 and 4 of the Arbitration Act apply to proceedings in state courts. The Federal Rules do not apply in such state court proceedings." On what basis does the Court discriminate between the applicability of the various provisions of the federal statute? Can Sections Two and Three be separated on a substantive basis? What substantive or procedural role remains for the states in the area of arbitration in light of this decision?

In footnote 11: "If we accepted this analysis [Justice Stevens' argument for the peaceful coexistence of arbitration and state legislative authority], states could wholly eviscerate congressional intent to place arbitration agreements 'upon the same footing as other contracts' ... simply by passing statutes such as the Franchise Investment Law. We have rejected this analysis because it is in conflict with the Arbitration Act and would permit states to override the declared policy requiring enforcement of arbitration agreements." Is the Court's distrust of states warranted? Why is compromise untenable? Is there an element of exaggeration to the Court's position? With Chief Justice Burger on the Court, does an ADR rationale creep into the case law and work with the *Erie* problem to undermine the protection of legal rights?

7.   To acquire a proper sense of the implications of the *Keating* opinion and of the reasoning in *Volt Information Sciences* that follows, *infra*, read these excerpts from the Court's opinion in *Perry v. Thomas*, 482 U.S. 483 (1987). *Perry v. Thomas* was decided after *Keating* but before *Volt*. In *Perry*, plaintiff Thomas filed suit against his former employer and two of its employees in California state court to collect commissions on the sale of securities. Thomas refused to honor the arbitral clause in his broker registration form and defendants filed a motion to compel arbitration under the FAA in both state and federal court. Thomas alleged that § 229 of the California Labor Code authorized him to maintain a legal action for wages despite the agreement to arbitrate, arguing that "the state's interest in protecting wage earners outweighed the federal interest in uniform dispute resolution." 482 U.S. at 486. Pursuant to the precedent in *Merrill Lynch, Pierce, Fenner & Smith, Inc. v. Ware*, 414 U.S. 117 (1973), the California courts denied the motion to compel arbitration. They read *Ware* to provide that § 229 was not pre-empted by the FAA. The Court reversed the decision:

[...]

In *Ware*, which also involved a dispute between a securities broker and his former employer, we rejected a Supremacy Clause challenge to § 229 premised in part on the contention that, because the 1934 Act had empowered the NYSE to promulgate rules and had given the SEC authority to review and modify these rules, a private agreement to be bound by the arbitration provisions of NYSE Rule 347 was enforceable as a matter of federal substantive law, and pre-empted state laws requiring resolution of the dispute in court. But the federal substantive law invoked in *Ware* emanated from a specific federal regulatory statute governing the securities industry, the 1934 Act. We examined the language and policies of the 1934 Act and found "no Commission rule or regulation that specifie[d] arbitration as the favored means of resolving employer-employee disputes,"...or that revealed a necessity for "nationwide uniformity of an exchange's house-keeping affairs."...The fact that NYSE Rule 347 was outside the scope of the SEC's authority of review militated against finding a clear federal intent to require arbitration.... Absent such a finding, we could not conclude that enforcement of California's § 229 would interfere with the federal regulatory scheme....

By contrast, the present appeal addresses the pre-emptive effect of the Federal Arbitration Act, a statute that embodies Congress' intent to provide for the enforcement of arbitration agreements within the full reach of the Commerce Clause. Its general applicability reflects that "[t]he preeminent concern of Congress in passing the Act was to enforce private agreements into which parties had entered...."...We have accordingly held that these agreements must be "rigorously enforce[d]."...This clear federal policy places § 2 of the Act in unmistakable conflict with California's § 229 requirement that litigants be provided a judicial forum for resolving wage disputes. Therefore, under the Supremacy Clause, the state statute must give way.

The oblique reference to the Federal Arbitration Act in footnote 15 of the *Ware* decision, 414 U.S., at 135, cannot fairly be read as a definitive holding to the contrary. There, the Court noted a number of decisions as having "endorsed the suitability of arbitration to resolve federally created rights."...Footnote 15 did not address the issue of federal pre-emption of state-created rights. Rather, the import of the footnote was that the reasoning, and perhaps result, in *Ware* might have been different if the 1934 Act "itself ha[d] provided for arbitration."...

Our holding that § 2 of the Federal Arbitration Act preempts § 229 of the California Labor Code obviates any need to consider whether our decision in *Byrd* would have required severance of Thomas' ancillary claims for conversion, civil conspiracy, and breach of fiduciary duty from his breach-of-contract claim. We likewise decline to reach Thomas' contention that Perry and Johnston lack "standing" to enforce the agreement to arbitrate any of these claims, since the courts below did not address this alternative argument for refusing to compel arbitration. However, we do reject Thomas' contention that resolving these questions in appellants' favor is a prerequisite to their having standing under Article III of the Constitution to maintain the present appeal before this Court. As we perceive it, Thomas' "standing" argument simply presents a straightforward issue of contract interpretation: whether the arbitration provision inures to the benefit of appellants and may be construed, in light of the circumstances surrounding the litigants' agreement, to cover the dispute that has arisen between them. This issue may be resolved on remand; its status as an alternative ground for denying arbitration does not prevent us from reviewing the ground exclusively relied upon by the courts below.

III

The judgment of the California Court of Appeal is reversed, and the case is remanded for further proceedings not inconsistent with this opinion.

It is so ordered.

JUSTICE STEVENS, dissenting.

Despite the striking similarity between this case and *Merrill Lynch, Pierce, Fenner & Smith, Inc. v. Ware*, the Court correctly concludes that the precise question now presented was not decided in *Ware*. Even though the Arbitration Act had been on the books for almost 50 years in 1973, apparently neither the Court nor the litigants even considered the possibility that the Act had pre-empted state-created rights. It is only in the last few years that the Court has effectively rewritten the statute to give it a pre-emptive scope that Congress certainly did not intend. *See Southland Corp. v. Keating*. . . . [B]ecause I share Justice O'Connor's opinion that the States' power to except certain categories of disputes from arbitration should be preserved unless Congress decides otherwise, I would affirm the judgment of the California Court of Appeal.

JUSTICE O'CONNOR, dissenting.

The Court today holds that § 2 of the Federal Arbitration Act requires the arbitration of appellee's claim for wages despite clear state policy to the contrary. This Court held in *Southland Corp. v. Keating* that the Act applies to state court as well as federal court proceedings. Because I continue to believe that this holding was "unfaithful to congressional intent, unnecessary, and in light of the [Act's] antecedents and the intervening contraction of federal power, inexplicable," I respectfully dissent.

Even if I were not to adhere to my position that the Act is inapplicable to state court proceedings, however, I would still dissent. We have held that Congress can limit or preclude a waiver of a judicial forum, and that Congress' intent to do so will be deduced from a statute's text or legislative history, or "from an inherent conflict between arbitration and the statute's underlying purposes." . . . As Justice Stevens has observed, the Court has not explained why state legislatures should not also be able to limit or preclude waiver of a judicial forum. . . .

. . . [T]here can be little doubt that the California Legislature intended to preclude waiver of a judicial forum; it is clear, moreover, that this intent reflects an important state policy. Section 229 of the California Labor Code specifically provides that actions for the collection of wages may be maintained in the state courts "without regard to the existence of any private agreement to arbitrate."

In my view, therefore, even if the Act applies to state court proceedings, California's policy choice to preclude waivers of a judicial forum for wage claims is entitled to respect. Accordingly, I would affirm the judgment of the California Court of Appeal.

482 U.S. at 490–95.

* * *

Dean Witter Reynolds v. Byrd is the final segment of the federalism trilogy. *Byrd* involved a dispute between a customer and the Dean Witter Reynolds securities brokerage firm. Byrd filed a complaint against Dean Witter Reynolds in a U.S. district court, claiming jurisdiction based on the existence of a federal question as well as diversity of citizenship, alleging violations of the U.S. Securities Act of 1934 and of various state law provisions relating to securities regulation. The broker-dealer contract, however, contained an arbitration agreement. Based upon that agreement, Dean Witter filed a motion to sever the pendant state claims and compel arbitration, staying arbitration pending the resolution of the federal court action. Both at the federal trial and appellate levels, the motion to sever the pendant state claims and compel arbitration was denied because of the "intertwining" doctrine, barring the arbitration of state law claims that are factually inseparable from claims under the federal securities act. According to the appellate court reasoning, the intertwining doctrine maintained the federal courts' "exclusive jurisdiction over the federal securities claim" by preventing the earlier arbitral determination of the state claim to bind the federal proceeding through collateral estoppel. Also, "by declining to compel arbitration, the courts avoid bifurcated proceedings and perhaps redundant efforts to litigate the same factual question twice."

Despite the persuasiveness of this reasoning, the U.S. Supreme Court reversed the decision, holding that the pendant state claims should be compelled to arbitration. In a unanimous opinion, the Court stated that "the Act leaves no place for the discretion by a district court, but instead mandates that district courts *shall* direct the parties to proceed to arbitration on issues as to which an arbitration agreement has been signed." The Court emphasized the underlying controlling Congressional intent of the federal legislation on arbitration, namely, "that the purpose behind the act's passage was to ensure judicial enforcement of privately made agreements to arbitrate and [we] therefore reject the suggestion that the overriding goal of the FAA was to provoke the expeditious resolution of claims."

DEAN WITTER REYNOLDS, INC. v. BYRD

470 U.S. 213, 105 S.Ct. 1238, 84 L.Ed.2d 158 (1985).

(footnotes omitted)

JUSTICE MARSHALL delivered the opinion of the Court.

The question presented is whether, when a complaint raises both federal securities claims and pendent state claims, a Federal District Court may deny a motion to compel arbitration of the state-law claims despite the parties' agreement to arbitrate their disputes. . . .

I

In 1981, A. Lamar Byrd sold his dental practice and invested $160,000 in securities through Dean Witter Reynolds Inc., a securities broker-dealer. The value of the account declined by more than $100,000 between September 1981 and March 1982. Byrd filed a complaint against Dean Witter in [federal court], alleging a violation of the Securities Exchange Act of 1934 and of various state-law provisions....

[...]

III

The Arbitration Act provides that written agreements to arbitrate controversies arising out of an existing contract "shall be valid, irrevocable, and enforceable, save upon such grounds as exist at law or in equity for the revocation of any contract." 9 U.S.C. § 2. By its terms, the Act leaves no place for the exercise of discretion by a district court, but instead mandates that district courts shall direct the parties to proceed to arbitration on issues as to which an arbitration agreement has been signed. §§ 3, 4. Thus, insofar as the language of the Act guides our disposition of this case, we would conclude that agreements to arbitrate must be enforced, absent a ground for revocation of the contractual agreement.

It is suggested, however, that the Act does not expressly address whether the same mandate, to enforce arbitration agreements, holds true where, as here, such a course would result in bifurcated proceedings if the arbitration agreement is enforced. Because the Act's drafters did not explicitly consider the prospect of bifurcated proceedings, we are told, the clear language of the Act might be misleading. Thus, courts that have adopted the view of the Ninth Circuit in this case have argued that the Act's goal of speedy and efficient decisionmaking is thwarted by bifurcated proceedings, and that, given the absence of clear direction on this point, the intent of Congress in passing the Act controls and compels a refusal to compel arbitration. They point out, in addition, that in the past the Court on occasion has identified a contrary federal interest sufficiently compelling to outweigh the mandate of the Arbitration Act...and they conclude that the interest in speedy resolution of claims should do so in this case....

We turn, then, to consider whether the legislative history of the Act provides guidance on this issue. The congressional history does not expressly direct resolution of the scenario we address. We conclude, however, on consideration of Congress' intent in passing the statute, that a court must compel arbitration of otherwise arbitrable claims, when a motion to compel arbitration is made.

The legislative history of the Act establishes that the purpose behind its passage was to ensure judicial enforcement of privately made agreements to arbitrate. We therefore reject the suggestion that the overriding goal of the Arbitration Act was to promote the expeditious resolution of claims. The Act, after all, does not mandate the arbitration of all claims, but merely the enforcement, upon the motion of one of the parties, of privately negotiated arbitration agreements. The House Report accompanying the Act makes clear that its purpose was to place an arbitration agreement "upon the same footing as other contracts, where it belongs" and to overrule the judiciary's long-standing refusal to enforce agreements to arbitrate. This is not to say that Congress was blind to the potential benefit of the legislation for expedited resolution of disputes.... Nonetheless, the passage of the Act was motivated, first and foremost, by a congressional desire to enforce agreements into which parties had entered, and we must not overlook this principal objective when construing the statute, or allow the fortuitous impact of the Act on efficient dispute resolution to overshadow the underlying motivation. Indeed, this conclusion is compelled by the Court's recent holding in *Moses H. Cone Memorial Hospital v. Mercury Construction Corp.* in which we affirmed an order requiring enforcement of an arbitration agreement, even though the arbitration would result in bifurcated proceedings....

We therefore are not persuaded by the argument that the conflict between two goals of the Arbitration Act, enforcement of private agreements and encouragement of efficient and speedy dispute resolution, must be resolved in favor of the latter in order to realize the intent of the drafters. The preeminent concern of Congress in passing the Act was to enforce private agreements which parties had entered, and that concern requires that we rigorously enforce agreements to arbitrate, even if the result is "piecemeal" litigation, at least absent a countervailing policy manifested in another federal statute... By compelling arbitration of state-law claims, a district court successfully protects the contractual rights of the parties and their rights under the Arbitration Act.

IV

It is also suggested, however, and some Courts of Appeals have held, that district courts should decide arbitrable pendent claims when a nonarbitrable federal claim is before them, because otherwise the findings in the arbitration proceeding might have collateral-estoppel effect in a subsequent federal proceeding. This preclusive effect is believed to pose a threat to the federal interest in resolution of securities claims, and to warrant a refusal to compel arbitration. Other courts have held that the claims should be separately resolved, but that preclusive effect warrants a stay of arbitration proceedings pending resolution of the federal securities claim....

We believe that the preclusive effect of arbitration proceedings is significantly less well settled than the lower court opinions might suggest, and that the consequence of this misconception has been the formulation of unnecessarily contorted procedures. We conclude that neither a stay of proceedings, nor joined proceedings, is necessary to protect the federal interest in the federal-court proceeding, and that the formulation of collateral-estoppel rules affords adequate protection to that interest.

Initially it is far from certain that arbitration proceedings will have any preclusive effect on the litigation of nonarbitrable federal claims. Just last Term, we held that neither the full-faith-and-credit provision of 28 U.S.C. § 1738, nor a judicially fashioned rule of preclusion, permits a federal court to accord res judicata or collateral-estoppel effect to an unappealed arbitration award in a case brought under 42 U.S.C. § 1983. *McDonald v. West Branch*, 466 U.S. 284 (1984). The full-faith-and-credit statute requires that federal courts give the same preclusive effect to a State's *judicial proceedings* as would the courts of the State rendering the judgment, and since arbitration is not a judicial proceeding, we held that the statute does not apply to arbitration awards. The same analysis inevitably would apply to any unappealed state arbitration proceedings. We also declined, in *McDonald*, to fashion a federal common-law rule of preclusion, in part on the ground that arbitration cannot provide an adequate substitute for a judicial proceeding in protecting the federal statutory and constitutional rights that § 1983 is designed to safeguard. We therefore recognized that arbitration proceedings will not necessarily have a preclusive effect on subsequent federal-court proceedings.

Significantly, *McDonald* also establishes that courts may directly and effectively protect federal interests by determining the preclusive effect to be given to an arbitration proceeding. Since preclusion doctrine comfortably plays this role, it follows that neither a stay of the arbitration proceedings, nor a refusal to compel arbitration of state claims, is required in order to assure that a precedent arbitration does not impede a subsequent federal-court action. The Courts of Appeals that have assumed collateral-estoppel effect must be given to arbitration proceedings have therefore sought to accomplish indirectly that which they erroneously assumed they could not do directly.

The question of what preclusive effect, if any, the arbitration proceedings might have is not yet before us, however, and we do not decide it. The collateral-estoppel effect of an arbitration proceeding is at issue only after arbitration is completed, of course, and we therefore have no need to consider now whether the analysis in *McDonald* encompasses this case. Suffice it to say that in framing preclusion rules in this context, courts shall take into account the federal interests warranting protection. As a result, there is no reason to require that district courts decline to compel arbitration, or manipulate the ordering of the resulting bifurcated proceedings, simply to avoid an infringement of federal interests.

Finding unpersuasive the arguments advanced in support of the ruling below, we hold that the District Court erred in refusing to grant the motion of Dean Witter to compel arbitration of the pendent state claims. Accordingly, we reverse the decision of the Court of Appeals insofar as it upheld the District Court's denial of the motion to compel arbitration, and we remand for further proceedings consistent with this opinion.

[. . .]

NOTES AND QUESTIONS

1. Justice White, in his concurring opinion, raises the difficult issue of the arbitrability of statutory rights—here, rights acquired under the provi-

sions of the Securities Exchange Act of 1934. The question will be addressed in detail in subsequent sections of the materials, but it is fair to conclude, as does the Court, that the issue was not properly before the Court in *Byrd*. As the later rulings in *McMahon* and *Rodriguez* illustrate, the question of the arbitrability of securities claims under the federal securities legislation involves the extension or restriction of the doctrine established in *Wilko v. Swan*, 346 U.S. 427 (1953), *infra*. The Court in *Byrd* appears open to the proposition that statutory rights, securities claims in particular, can be submitted to arbitration. What aspects of the Court's opinion presage that disposition? Is the determination that statutorily created rights are arbitrable an inevitable development in the decisional law? Does such a ruling advance the interests of arbitration and comport with its adjudicatory gravamen? Why then would such a ruling be necessary?

2. Focus upon the "intertwining doctrine" and its function in the protection of legal rights and in the administration of justice. Doesn't the rationale for the doctrine preclude the arbitration of the implicated claims?

3. Assess the role that Justice Marshall attributes to ADR in the operation of the FAA. In light of his statements, what appears to be the primary motivation for the enactment of the FAA?

4. How does consideration of *res judicata* and collateral estoppel become involved in the holding of the case? Do you think withholding *res judicata* effect from arbitral awards contributes to the adjudicatory autonomy of the arbitral process? What would or should a federal court do when a party to a litigation presents an arbitral award that disposes of the dispute on the basis of state or foreign law? What result if the arbitral tribunal applied federal law but in an area of law where federal courts disagree?

5. What remains of Justice Black's view in *Prima Paint* and of Justice Stevens' position in *Keating* that there could be a logical, rational, and substantively sound reconciliation of arbitration policy with the traditional values and function of the legal system? The federalism trilogy, *Moses H. Cone, Keating*, and *Byrd*, leaves little doubt about its ultimate contribution: It effectively federalizes the domestic U.S. law of arbitration. The Court discovers in the FAA a "strong federal policy supporting arbitration" and a Congressional command to the courts to enforce it. It employs a triple constitutional reference to expand the reach of the FAA and to achieve a uniform national legal position on arbitration: A broad view of interstate commerce under the Commerce Clause, the dominance of federal law under the Supremacy Clause, and the constitutional power of the Congress to direct the conduct of the federal courts. As a result, the FAA is binding upon federal courts in diversity cases and upon state courts ruling on matters that have some linkage to interstate commerce. The FAA also overrides the legislative authority of states to regulate arbitration given the supremacy of federal law. In effect, all statutes and litigation in the United States that implicate arbitration must conform to the provisions and underlying policy of the FAA.

From *Prima Paint* to the federalism trilogy, the Court supports the autonomy of the arbitral process at the price of substantially undermining, if not eradicating, state authority in the area. The Court's decisional law emphasizes the FAA's mandate and the need to eliminate judicial hostility to arbitration. There is a judicial duty to recognize and give effect to arbitration agreements. The Court's pronouncements also add content to the FAA and heighten its systemic standing. The Court is determined to achieve a cohesive and coherent national law and policy on arbitration. The two cases that follow first cast doubt on the process of federalization (*Volt*) and then unequivocally confirm the federalization of the American law of arbitration (*Terminix*).

3.   A NOTE OF DISSONANCE

Volt Information Sciences involved a contractual agreement between Stanford University and Volt Information Sciences, Inc., one of several contractors working on a large construction project on the Stanford campus. Its contract, to install a system of electrical conduits, contained standard provisions on dispute resolution and choice-of-law, respectively providing for arbitration and the application of local law. A dispute arose between Volt and Stanford regarding compensation for extra work allegedly performed by the contractor. Volt demanded arbitration and Stanford initiated a legal action in which it sued Volt for breach of contract and fraud and also sought indemnification from two other contractors not bound by an arbitration agreement. The California courts denied Volt's motion to compel arbitration and ordered a stay of the arbitral proceeding. According to state procedural law, California courts have discretion to stay arbitral proceedings pending the resolution of related litigation against third parties not bound by the arbitration agreement. The purpose of the provision is to avoid conflicting rulings on the same matter by different tribunals:

> Section 1281.2 (c) [of the CAL. CIV. PROC. CODE ANN. (West 1982)] provides, in pertinent part, that when a court determines that "[a] party to the arbitration agreement is also a party to a pending court action or special proceeding with a third party, arising out of the same transaction or series of related transactions and there is a possibility of conflicting rulings on a common issue of law or fact [,] . . . the court (1) may refuse to enforce the arbitration agreement and may order intervention or joinder of all parties in a single action or special proceeding; (2) may order intervention or joinder as to all or only certain issues; (3) may order arbitration among the parties who have agreed to arbitration and stay the pending court action or special proceeding pending the outcome of the arbitration proceeding; or (4) may stay arbitration pending the outcome of the court action or special proceeding." 489 U.S. at 471, n.3.

The question before the U.S. Supreme Court was two-fold: Had the parties in *Volt* intended to have California law govern not only the contract, but also any ensuing arbitration and, if so, was the applicable law valid under the Supremacy Clause of the Federal Constitution given that the application of state law resulted in a stay of the arbitration proceeding? In turn, these issues engendered a more wide-ranging, albeit circuitous, question: Could party intent be used to defeat the agreed-upon recourse to arbitration? In other words, although the parties agreed to resolve their contractual disputes through arbitration, they would have expressly provided for the application of a state law that could, upon the exercise of judicial discretion, undermine that intent.

California state courts held that the choice-of-law clause (mandating the application of local law) also governed the arbitration agreement. Because California law applied and its procedural law allowed courts to stay arbitral proceedings in circumstances of "intertwining" arbitral and legal proceedings, Volt's request to compel arbitration could lawfully be denied. This determination permitted state law to frustrate the rationale of and predominate over the FAA. In practical terms, it simply provided Stanford, the noncomplying party, with a loophole by which to avoid arbitration.

In prior rulings, primarily in the federalism trilogy, the Court held unequivocally that state legislation could not block the recourse to arbitration. The aim of promoting adjudicatory efficiency in these cases was not a sufficiently significant concern to override the FAA's policy mandate. The content of prior rulings would have predicted an espousal by the majority of the basic approach and content of the dissenting opinion. In arguing for a reversal, the dissenting justices emphasized the state law's detrimental impact upon and inconsistency with the provisions of the FAA and its objectives. State law, after all, was being used to thwart agreed-upon recourse to arbitration.

With an impressive 6 to 2 majority, the Court nonetheless held in *Volt* that the parties' contractual intent was clear (or, at least, the state court's interpretation of it could not be challenged) and that the intent to have state law govern could effectively defeat the agreement to arbitrate. The Court's previous preoccupation with elaborating legal rules uniformly favorable to arbitration was nowhere to be found. Now, the Court was of the view that the FAA meant to have arbitration agreements enforced as written. According to the Court, parties who expressly agree to arbitrate disputes also can agree, by implication from a choice-of-law provision, to undo that agreement whenever a court decides to exercise its discretion to stay arbitral proceedings under state procedural law. Because the dissent represented the views of the Court's two most liberal members, ideological differences appear to be at the heart of the determination. Rather than a statement on arbitration law, *Volt* seems to reflect the majority's adherence to the concept of sanctity of contract which, in turn, acts as a vehicle for expressing a particular concept of the role of government and of the place of the individual in society.

VOLT INFORMATION SCIENCES, INC. v. BOARD OF TRUSTEES OF LELAND STANFORD JUNIOR UNIVERSITY

489 U.S. 468, 109 S.Ct. 1248, 103 L.Ed.2d 488 (1989).

(footnotes omitted)

[. . .]

CHIEF JUSTICE REHNQUIST delivered the opinion of the Court.

Unlike its federal counterpart, the California Arbitration Act, Cal. Civ. Proc. Code Ann. § 1280 *et seq.* (West 1982), contains a provision allowing a court to stay arbitration pending resolution of related litigation. We hold that application of the California statute is not pre-empted by the Federal Arbitration Act in a case where the parties have agreed that their arbitration agreement will be governed by the law of California.

[. . .]

Appellant devotes the bulk of its argument to convincing us that the Court of Appeal erred in interpreting the choice-of-law clause to mean that the parties had incorporated the California rules of arbitration into their arbitration agreement.... Appellant acknowledges, as it must, that the interpretation of private contracts is ordinarily a question of state law, which this Court does not sit to review. But appellant nonetheless maintains that we should set aside the Court of Appeal's interpretation of this particular contractual provision for two principal reasons.

Appellant first suggests that the Court of Appeal's construction of the choice-of-law clause was in effect a finding that appellant had "waived" its "federally guaranteed right to compel arbitration of the parties' dispute," a waiver whose validity must be judged by reference to federal rather than state law. This argument fundamentally misconceives the nature of the rights created by the FAA....

...§ 4 of the FAA does not confer a right to compel arbitration of any dispute at any time; it confers only the right to obtain an order directing that "arbitration proceed in the manner provided for in [the parties'] agreement." Here the Court of Appeal found that, by incorporating the California rules of arbitration into their agreement, the parties had agreed that arbitration would not proceed in situations which fell within the scope of Calif. Code Civ. Proc. Ann. § 1281.2(c) (West 1982). This was not a finding that appellant had "waived" an FAA-guaranteed right to compel arbitration of this dispute, but a finding that it had no such right in the first place, because the parties' agreement did not require arbitration to proceed in this situation. Accordingly, appellant's contention that the contract interpretation issue presented here involves the "waiver" of a federal right is without merit.

Second, appellant argues that we should set aside the Court of Appeal's construction of the choice-of-law clause because it violates the settled federal rule that questions of arbitrability in contracts subject to the FAA must be resolved with a healthy regard for the federal policy favoring arbitration.... These [cited] cases of course establish that, in applying general state-law principles of contract interpretation to the interpretation of an arbitration agreement within the scope of the Act...due regard must be given to the federal policy favoring arbitration, and ambiguities as to the scope of the arbitration clause itself resolved in favor of arbitration.

But we do not think the Court of Appeal offended the *Moses H. Cone* principle by interpreting the choice-of-law provision to mean that the parties intended the California rules of arbitration, including the § 1281.2(c) stay provision, to apply to their arbitration agreement. There is no federal policy favoring arbitration under a certain set of procedural rules; the federal policy is simply to ensure the enforceability, according to their terms, of private agreements to arbitrate. Interpreting a choice-of-law clause to make applicable state rules governing the conduct of arbitration, rules which are manifestly designed to encourage resort to the arbitral process, simply does not offend the rule of liberal construction set forth in *Moses H. Cone*, nor does it offend any other policy embodied in the FAA.

The question remains whether, assuming the choice-of-law clause meant what the Court of Appeal found it to mean, application of Cal. Civ. Proc. Code Ann. § 1281.2(c) is nonetheless pre-empted by the FAA to the extent it is used to stay arbitration under this contract involving interstate commerce. It is undisputed that this contract falls within the coverage of the FAA, since it involves interstate commerce, and that the FAA contains no provision authorizing a stay of arbitration in this situation. Appellee contends, however, that §§ 3 and 4 of the FAA, which are the specific sections claimed to conflict with the California statute at issue here, are not applicable in this state-court proceeding and thus cannot pre-empt application of the California statute. While the argument is not without some merit, we need not resolve it to decide this case, for we conclude that even if §§ 3 and 4 of the FAA are fully applicable in state-court proceedings, they do not prevent application of Cal. Civ. Proc. Code Ann. § 1281.2(c) to stay arbitration where, as here, the parties have agreed to arbitrate in accordance with California law.

The FAA contains no express pre-emptive provision, nor does it reflect a congressional intent to occupy the entire field of arbitration.... But even when Congress has not completely displaced state regulation in an area, state law may nonetheless be pre-empted to the extent that it actually conflicts with federal law, that is, to the extent that it "stands as an obstacle to the accomplishment and execution of the full purposes and objectives of Congress."...The question before us, therefore, is whether application of Cal. Civ. Proc. Code Ann. § 1281.2(c) to stay arbitration under this contract in interstate commerce, in accordance with the terms of the arbitration agreement itself, would undermine the goals and policies of the FAA. We conclude that it would not.

The FAA was designed "to overrule the judiciary's long-standing refusal to enforce agreements to arbitrate"...and to place such agreements " 'upon the same footing as other contracts' ".... While Congress was no doubt aware that the Act would encourage the expeditious resolution of disputes, its passage "was motivated, first and foremost, by a congressional desire to enforce agreements into which parties had entered."...Accordingly, we have recognized that the FAA does not require parties to arbitrate when they have not agreed to do so...nor does it prevent parties who do agree to arbitrate from excluding certain claims from the scope of their arbitration agreement. It simply requires courts to enforce privately negotiated agreements to arbitrate, like other contracts, in accordance with their terms. . . .

In recognition of Congress' principal purpose of ensuring that private arbitration agreements are enforced according to their terms, we have held that the FAA pre-empts state laws which "require a judicial forum for the resolution of claims which the contracting parties agreed to resolve by arbitration." . . . But it does not follow that the FAA prevents the enforcement of agreements to arbitrate under different rules than those set forth in the Act itself. Indeed, such a result would be quite inimical to the FAA's primary purpose of ensuring that private agreements to arbitrate are enforced according to their terms. Arbitration under the Act is a matter of consent, not coercion, and parties are generally free to structure their arbitration agreements as they see fit. . . . Where, as here, the parties have agreed to abide by state rules of arbitration, enforcing those rules according to the terms of the agreement is fully consistent with the goals of the FAA, even if the result is that arbitration is stayed where the Act would otherwise permit it to go forward. By permitting the courts to "rigorously enforce" such agreements according to their terms, . . . we give effect to the contractual rights and expectations of the parties, without doing violence to the policies behind the FAA.

The judgment of the Court of Appeals is *Affirmed*.

JUSTICE O'CONNOR took no part in the consideration or decision of this case.

JUSTICE BRENNAN, with whom JUSTICE MARSHALL joins, dissenting.

The litigants in this case were parties to a construction contract which contained a clause obligating them to arbitrate disputes and making that obligation specifically enforceable. The contract also incorporated provisions of a standard form contract prepared by the American Institute of Architects and endorsed by the Associated General Contractors of America; among these general provisions was § 7.1.1: "The Contract shall be governed by the law of the place where the Project is located." When a dispute arose between the parties, Volt invoked the arbitration clause, while Stanford attempted to avoid it (apparently because the dispute also involved two other contractors with whom Stanford had no arbitration agreements).

The Federal Arbitration Act requires courts to enforce arbitration agreements in contracts involving interstate commerce. . . . The California courts nonetheless rejected Volt's petition to compel arbitration in reliance on a provision of state law that, in the circumstances presented, permitted a court to stay arbitration pending the conclusion of related litigation. Volt, not surprisingly, suggested that the Supremacy Clause compelled a different result. The California Court of Appeal found, however, that the parties had agreed that their contract would be governed solely by the law of the State of California, to the exclusion of federal law. In reaching this conclusion the court relied on no extrinsic evidence of the parties' intent, but solely on the language of the form contract that the " 'law of the place where the project is located' " would govern.

This Court now declines to review that holding, which denies effect to an important federal statute, apparently because it finds no question of federal law involved. I can accept neither the state court's unusual interpretation of the parties' contract, nor this Court's unwillingness to review it. I would reverse the judgment of the California Court of Appeal.

I

Contrary to the Court's view, the state court's construction of the choice-of-law clause is reviewable for two independent reasons.

A

[. . .]

[T]he right of the parties to have their arbitration agreement enforced pursuant to the FAA could readily be circumvented by a state-court construction of their contract as having intended to exclude the applicability of federal law. It is therefore essential that, while according due deference to the decision of the state court, we independently determine whether we "clearly would have judged the issue differently if [we] were the state's highest court".

B

Arbitration is, of course, "a matter of contract and a party cannot be required to submit to arbitration any dispute which he has not agreed so to submit." . . . I agree with the Court that "the FAA does not require parties to arbitrate when they have not agreed to do so." . . . Since the FAA merely requires enforcement of what the parties have agreed to, moreover, they are free if they wish to write an agreement to arbitrate outside the coverage of the FAA. Such an agreement would permit a state rule, otherwise pre-empted by the FAA, to govern their arbitration. The substantive question in this case is whether or not they have done so. And that question, we have made clear in the past, is a matter of federal law.

[. . .]

The Court recognizes the relevance of the *Moses H. Cone* principle but finds it unoffended by the Court of Appeal's decision, which, the Court suggests, merely determines what set of procedural rules will apply. I agree fully with the Court that "the federal policy is simply to ensure the enforceability, according to their terms, of private agreements to arbitrate," . . . but I disagree emphatically with its conclusion that that policy is not frustrated here. Applying the California procedural rule, which stays arbitration while litigation of the same issue goes forward, means simply that the parties' dispute will be litigated rather than arbitrated. Thus, interpreting the parties' agreement to say that the California procedural rules apply rather than the FAA, where the parties arguably had no such intent, implicates the *Moses H. Cone* principle no less than would an interpretation of the parties' contract that erroneously denied the existence of an agreement to arbitrate.

While appearing to recognize that the state court's interpretation of the contract does raise a question of federal law, the Court nonetheless refuses to determine whether the state court misconstrued that agreement. There is no warrant for failing to do so. The FAA requires that a court determining a question of arbitrability not stop with the application of state-law rules for construing the parties' intentions, but that it also take account of the command of federal law that "those intentions [be] generously construed as to issues of arbitrability.". . . Thus, the decision below is based on both state and federal law, which are thoroughly intertwined. In such circumstances the state-court judgment cannot be said to rest on an "adequate and independent state ground" so as to bar review by this Court.

II

Construed with deference to the opinion of the California Court of Appeal, yet "with a healthy regard for the federal policy favoring arbitration," it is clear that the choice-of-law clause cannot bear the interpretation the California court assigned to it.

[. . .]

III

Most commercial contracts written in this country contain choice-of-law clauses, similar to the one in the Stanford–Volt contract, specifying which State's law is to govern the interpretation of the contract. . . . Were every state court to construe such clauses as an expression of the parties' intent to exclude the application of federal law, as has the California Court of Appeal in this case, the result would be to render the Federal Arbitration Act a virtual nullity as to presently existing contracts. I cannot believe that the parties to contracts intend such consequences to flow from their insertion of a standard choice-of-law clause. Even less can I agree that we are powerless to review decisions of state courts that effectively nullify a vital piece of federal legislation. I respectfully dissent.

NOTES AND QUESTIONS

1. The majority argues that the parties are bound by their contractual provisions as stipulated and that rigorous contract enforcement reinforces rather than undermines the consensual foundation of arbitration. The dissent addresses the case from the perspective of the federalism trilogy: State law in *Volt* undermines the right to arbitrate in a transaction involving interstate commerce, contravenes the provisions of the FAA, and is therefore unconstitutional under the Supremacy Clause.

In some measure, the disagreement between the various members of the Court exemplifies the clash between liberal and conservative ideologies. The majority stands upon the principle of *pacta sunt servanda* (party agreements must be observed) and refuses to relieve Volt of the burden of its errors in contractual strategy, while the dissent is willing to manipulate the sanctity of contract to achieve an outcome that achieves its brand of social justice and furthers the federal policy on arbitration. In this sense, the question of the FAA's legal status has little presence in the division that *Volt* creates in the Court. It is ancillary to the unstated but driving controversy about the function and meaning of legal rules, the judicial role in interpreting and applying law, and the ultimate mandate of judicial adjudication. Arguably, *Volt*, given the ideological substratum of the opinion and its position of dissonance in the decisional law, is not a ruling on arbitration at all, but rather a political colloquy within the Court on the larger questions that attend the operation of law.

2. A number of issues appear to have escaped the Court's attention. These issues arguably have some significance to the analysis and outcome, and they could have been used to reinforce the conclusions of either the majority or dissent. For example, the sophisticated business status of the parties could have sustained the majority's argument for the discipline of contract. By the same token, the boilerplate character of the choice-of-law clause would have added to the credibility of the dissent's position that the parties' intent was to arbitrate disputes and that the reference to a disabling state law was pure happenstance and of no, or of amendable, legal effect. In your view, are there other important elements or issues that fail to figure with deserved prominence in the Court's opinion? Why do you find these considerations vital? Why do you think the Court ignores them? Are some elements emphasized by the Court negligible?

3. The arbitral clause in *Volt* provided:

"All claims, disputes and other matters in question between the parties to this contract, arising out of or relating to this contract or the breach thereof, shall be decided by arbitration in accordance with the Construction Industry Arbitration Rules of the American Arbitration Association then prevailing unless the parties mutually agreed [sic] otherwise. This agreement to arbitrate ... shall be specifically enforceable under the prevailing arbitration law."

489 U.S. at 470, n.1.

What did the parties intend through the language of this provision? Did they agree to submit their transactional disputes to arbitration? Did they want California law to force them into judicial adjudication? What is the significance of the reference to the AAA rules? What is meant by the phrase "the prevailing arbitration law"? Does it refer to the California arbitration law, provided it either comports with the parties' intent to arbitrate their disputes or is in accord with the general disposition of the FAA on arbitration, or simply to the FAA standing alone? Is this provision an example of inadequate drafting skills even for a standard clause? Should the lawyer who wrote the provision be liable in malpractice when the client's intent to arbitrate is frustrated?

4. The binding character of party choice in contract and its impact upon the FAA's policy on arbitration are the doctrinal centerpiece of the *Volt*

opinion. The exercise of party choice, especially in contracts that include a reference to arbitration, can become a rather complex matter. The parties clearly have a legal right to choose the law that governs their contractual relationship. When they decide to arbitrate disputes, the parties also can choose a law to govern the procedural aspects of their arbitration. The law governing the contract and the law governing the arbitration can be the same law or a different law.

In *Volt*, the contractor adopted the standard practice of choosing the customer's law to govern the contract. No express choice-of-law was made as to the law governing the arbitration. The silence of the contract on this question was broken only by a reference to the AAA institutional rules of arbitration. Such rules do not constitute a law of arbitration. Party choice on the question, therefore, either was nonexistent or could be implied from and equated with the choice-of-law provision as to the contract. The Court chooses to use the methodology of implication to select California arbitration law as the law governing the arbitration. The silence of the clause as to the arbitral choice-of-law, however, could also mean that the parties simply omitted to choose a law governing the arbitration. It could also be addressed by holding that a sophisticated business party should reasonably be expected to write a complete contract. The gap in the arbitration agreement could be filled in a number of ways. Any one of the following laws could be selected as the governing law of arbitration. The arbitration law at the place of arbitration because it is the law of the territorial venue. The arbitration law at the likely place of the enforcement of the award because the award will affect local assets. The arbitration law at the place where lawsuits are filed in connection with the arbitration because the ruling court is most familiar with its own law. The arbitration law of the place that has the greatest connection with the designated institutional rules of arbitration to facilitate familiarity, enforcement, and sound decision-making. A uniform statutory law or common law of arbitration in order to promote the harmony of laws and to avoid giving choice-of-law an outcome determinative effect. Or, the FAA when federal courts can be implicated in the matter through diversity or federal-question jurisdiction because the statute is favorable to arbitration.

This list of possible options may not be exhaustive. It illustrates the dangers of not exercising party choice in a transactional setting and the difficulty of providing a remedy when gaps are left in the contract. How would you resolve the choice-of-law problem in *Volt*? Who should make the determination as to which law of arbitration applies when the agreement is silent? What factors should influence the choice? What assumptions might be useful in filling the gap? Should the choice-of-law as to contract always be an influential factor or should silence on this specific question always be resolved in favor of the application of federal law?

5.   The *Volt* decision made commercial lawyers, large commercial law firms, and the arbitration bar in general shudder. Can you identify and explain the reasons for their reaction? Why should the opinion induce apprehension? What rationale might lurk in the fine points of the opinion? Is there any basis for considering *Volt* a decisional anomaly?

6. The reasoning and result in *Volt* could be tested by applying radical solutions to the issues in the case that reflect the contemporary judicial policy of always finding a means to sustain the reference to arbitration. For example, why couldn't Stanford's disputes with the two other contractors simply be joined or consolidated with the projected arbitration between Volt and Stanford? Why couldn't the California courts exercise their statutory discretion in that fashion? What are the likely legal and doctrinal objections? Shouldn't such objections succumb to the policy imperative underlying the FAA?

7. The majority opinion perceives no conflict between the provision in the California arbitration statute and the FAA. In fact, the majority believes that the statutory provision for the consolidation or stay of arbitral proceedings is in the best interest of justice. How does the majority reconcile this view with its holding in *Keating*? Is it plausible? In this regard, you should assess the Court's reasoning in footnote five of the opinion:

> [W]e think the California arbitration rules which the parties have incorporated into their contract generally foster the federal policy favoring arbitration.... [T]he FAA itself contains no provision designed to deal with the special practical problems that arise in multiparty contractual disputes when some or all of the contracts at issue include agreements to arbitrate. California has taken the lead in fashioning a legislative response to this problem, by giving courts authority to consolidate or stay arbitration proceedings in these situations in order to minimize the potential for contradictory judgments.

489 U.S. at 476 n.5.

Does this language simply ignore the problem and the fact that the California provision frustrates party recourse to arbitration?

8. In footnote six of the opinion, the Court states that the effect of *Keating*, and presumably of the other cases on arbitration, was to obligate state courts to apply Sections One and Two of the FAA, characterizing them as "substantive" provisions of the legislation. The Court, however, declares that the obligation never included Sections Three and Four, which refer expressly to the federal courts. Is the distinction persuasive? What are its practical implications? Does such a ruling provide for a cohesive doctrine on arbitration?

9. The relatively new doctrinal notion that causes a shift in the *Volt* Court's reasoning on arbitration is the view of contractualism: Under the FAA, arbitration agreements are enforceable according to their specific contract language. The emphasis of the decisional law moves from protecting the contractual right to arbitrate (the reversal of judicial hostility to arbitration) to the enforcement of stipulated obligations in the contract of arbitration (party autonomy). "[W]e have recognized that the FAA does not require parties to arbitrate when they have not agreed to do so." Even the dissent, in its footnote four, agrees with the new doctrinal emphasis:

> [T]he FAA does not pre-empt state arbitration rules, even as applied to contracts involving interstate commerce, when the parties have agreed to arbitrate by those rules to the exclusion of federal arbitration law. I would

not reach that question, however, because I conclude that the parties have made no such agreement.

Does the integration of the "contractualist" addendum in the Court's developing arbitration doctrine make sense in terms of the practical reality of commercial contracting or of the judicial enforcement of contracts? Would parties agree to arbitrate disputes and also agree that state law could surprise them into a nonagreement to arbitrate? Does the "contractualist" view respond to the conflict between federal and state law in *Volt*? Is it simply a means of conveniently sidestepping that issue? Why does contractualism appear to have the Court's unanimous support?

10. With *Volt*, conflicts and contradictions begin to surface in the Court's reasoning and rulings on arbitration both in terms of the federalism issue and in regard to the coherence of doctrine. The emphatic character of the Court's initial pronouncements on arbitration and federalism left little room for flexibility and the subtleties of exceptions. After *Volt*, how would you summarize the basic tenets of the Court's arbitration doctrine, especially as it relates to federalism and the standing of the FAA? Can you articulate a set of propositions that might predict the content of future rulings?

4. AFFIRMING THE FEDERALIZATION POLICY

Terminix v. Dobson, decided in 1995, aligns itself perfectly with the federalism trilogy, thereby reaffirming the judicial policy on federalization. In *Terminix*, an Alabama homeowner entered into a termite protection agreement with a local Terminix franchiser. The agreement contained a dispute resolution provision, which stated that "any controversy or claim" arising under the contract "shall be settled exclusively by arbitration." When the owner sold the home to another Alabama resident, the parties discovered that the house was swarming with termites, leading the new owner to file suit in state court against the seller and Terminix. The termite protection contract had been transferred to the new owner at the time of the sale. Terminix and its franchiser, however, objected to the assertion of jurisdiction by the state court on the basis of the arbitral clause in the contract and Section 2 of the FAA. On appeal, the Alabama Supreme Court upheld the trial court's refusal to stay the court action pending arbitration, stating that the federal law on arbitration was inapplicable to the transaction because the transaction's connection to interstate commerce was too slight. The U.S. Supreme Court disagreed and reversed the determination.

Throughout the majority opinion, Justice Breyer restates the basic propositions associated with the "hospitable" federal court "inquiry" into matters of arbitration. The primary purpose for the enactment of the FAA in 1925 was to purge the judiciary of its antiarbitration bias. The FAA's protection of arbitration from judicial prejudice applies wherever federal law can reach; in particular, the federal courts must apply the provisions of the FAA even when they exercise diversity jurisdiction over state litigation; state courts also must apply the FAA whenever a basis for applying federal law can be found, even in cases the merits of which are otherwise governed by state law. In effect, the Court stands firm on the federalization policy articulated in the federalism trilogy, in particular, *Southland Corp. v. Keating* ("we find it inappropriate to reconsider what is by now well-established law"). The Court holds fast to the notion that "the Federal Arbitration Act pre-empts state law" and that "state courts [let alone federal courts] cannot apply state statutes that invalidate arbitration agreements." The Court declares unequivocally: "[T]he Act does displace state law to the contrary."

ALLIED-BRUCE TERMINIX COS., INC. v. DOBSON

513 U.S. 265, 115 S.Ct. 834, 130 L.Ed.2d 753 (1995).

(footnotes omitted)

Justice Breyer delivered the opinion of the Court.

This case concerns the reach of § 2 of the Federal Arbitration Act. That section makes enforceable a written arbitration provision in "a contract *evidencing* a transaction *involving* commerce." Should we read this phrase broadly, extending the Act's reach to the limits of Congress' Commerce Clause power? Or, do the two underscored words, "involving" and "evidencing," significantly restrict the Act's application? We conclude that the broader reading of the Act is the correct one; and we reverse a State Supreme Court judgment to the contrary.

[. . .]

II

Before we can reach the main issues in this case, we must set forth three items of legal background.

First, the basic purpose of the Federal Arbitration Act is to overcome courts' refusals to enforce agreements to arbitrate. . . . The origins of those refusals apparently lie in " 'ancient times,' " when the English courts fought " 'for extension of jurisdiction, all of them being opposed to anything that would altogether deprive every one of them of jurisdiction.' " . . . American courts initially followed English practice. . . . When Congress passed the Arbitration Act in 1925, it was "motivated, first and foremost, by a . . . desire" to change this antiarbitration rule. . . . It intended courts to "enforce [arbitration] agreements into which parties had entered," . . . and to "place such agreements 'upon the same footing as other contracts' " . . . .

Second, some initially assumed that the Federal Arbitration Act represented an exercise of Congress' Article III power to "ordain and establish" federal courts. . . . In 1967 [in *Prima Paint*], however, this Court held that the Act "is based upon and confined to the incontestable federal foundations of 'control over interstate commerce and over admiralty.' " The Court considered the following complicated argument: (1) The

Act's provisions (about contract remedies) are important and often out-come-determinative, and thus amount to "substantive" not "procedural" provisions of law; (2) *Erie R.R. Co. v. Tompkins*...made clear that federal courts must apply state substantive law in diversity cases...; therefore (3) federal courts must not apply the Federal Arbitration Act in diversity cases. This Court responded by agreeing that the Act set forth substantive law, but concluding that, nonetheless, the Act applied in diversity cases because Congress had so intended. The Court wrote: "Congress may prescribe how federal courts are to conduct themselves with respect to subject matter over which Congress plainly has power to legislate."...

Third, the holding in *Prima Paint* led to a further question. Did Congress intend the Act also to apply in state courts? Did the Federal Arbitration Act pre-empt conflicting state antiarbitration law, or could state courts apply their anti-arbitration rules in cases before them, there-by reaching results different from those reached in otherwise similar federal diversity cases? In *Southland Corp. v. Keating*, this Court decided that Congress would not have wanted state and federal courts to reach different outcomes about the validity of arbitration in similar cases. The Court concluded that the Federal Arbitration Act pre-empts state law; and it held that state courts cannot apply state statutes that invalidate arbitration agreements....

We have set forth this background because respondents, supported by 20 state attorneys general, now ask us to overrule *Southland* and thereby to permit Alabama to apply its anti-arbitration statute in this case.... Nothing significant has changed in the 10 years subsequent to *Southland*; no later cases have eroded *Southland*'s authority; and, no unforeseen practical problems have arisen. Moreover, in the interim, private parties have likely written contracts relying upon *Southland* as authority. Fur-ther, Congress, both before and after *Southland*, has enacted legislation extending, not retracting, the scope of arbitration. *See, e.g.*, 9 U.S.C. § 15 (eliminating the Act of State doctrine as a bar to arbitration); 9 U.S.C. §§ 201–208 (international arbitration). For these reasons, we find it inappropriate to reconsider what is by now well-established law.

...We must decide in this case whether that Act used language about interstate commerce that nonetheless limits the Act's application, thereby carving out an important statutory niche in which a State remains free to apply its antiarbitration law or policy. We conclude that it does not.

III

The Federal Arbitration Act, § 2, provides that a

"written provision in any maritime transaction or *a contract evidencing a transaction involving commerce* to settle by arbitration a controversy there-after arising out of such contract or transaction...shall be valid, irrevoca-ble, and enforceable, save upon such grounds as exist at law or in equity for the revocation of any contract." 9 U.S.C. § 2 (emphasis added).

The initial interpretive question focuses upon the words "involving commerce."

[. . .]

After examining the statute's language, background, and structure, we conclude that the word "involving" is broad and is indeed the functional equivalent of "affecting."

[. . .]

Finally, a broad interpretation of this language is consistent with the Act's basic purpose, to put arbitration provisions on "the same footing" as a contract's other terms. . . . Conversely, a narrower interpretation is not consistent with the Act's purpose, for (unless unreasonably narrowed to the flow of commerce) such an interpretation would create a new, unfamiliar, test lying somewhere in a no-man's land between "in commerce" and "affecting commerce," thereby unnecessarily complicating the law and breeding litigation from a statute that seeks to avoid it.

[. . .]

IV

Section 2 applies where there is "a contract *evidencing a transaction* involving commerce." The second interpretive question focuses on the underscored words. Does "evidencing a transaction" mean only that the transaction (that the contract "evidences") must turn out, *in fact*, to have involved interstate commerce? Or, does it mean more?

[. . .]

We find the interpretive choice difficult, but for several reasons we conclude that the first interpretation ("commerce in fact") is more faithful to the statute than the second ("contemplation of the parties"). First, the "contemplation of the parties" interpretation, when viewed in terms of the statute's basic purpose, seems anomalous. That interpretation invites litigation about what was, or was not, "contemplated." Why would Congress intend a test that risks the very kind of costs and delay through litigation (about the circumstances of contract formation) that Congress wrote the Act to help the parties avoid? . . . .

Moreover, that interpretation too often would turn the validity of an arbitration clause on what, from the perspective of the statute's basic purpose, seems happenstance, namely whether the parties happened to think to insert a reference to interstate commerce in the document or happened to mention it in an initial conversation. After all, parties to a sales contract with an arbitration clause might naturally think about the goods sold, or about arbitration, but why should they naturally think about an interstate commerce connection?

Further, that interpretation fits awkwardly with the rest of § 2. That section, for example, permits parties to agree to submit to arbitration "an existing controversy arising out of" a contract made earlier. Why would Congress want to risk non-enforceability of this later arbitration agreement (even if fully connected with interstate commerce) simply because the parties did not properly "contemplate" (or write about) the interstate aspects of the earlier contract? The first interpretation, requiring only that the "transaction" in fact involve interstate commerce, avoids this anomaly, as it avoids the other anomalous effects growing out of the "contemplation of the parties" test.

Second, the statute's language permits the "commerce in fact" interpretation. That interpretation, we concede, leaves little work for the word "evidencing" (in the phrase "a contract evidencing a transaction") to perform, for every contract evidences some transaction. But, perhaps Congress did not want that word to perform much work. The Act's history, to the extent informative, indicates that the Act's supporters saw the Act as part of an effort to make arbitration agreements universally enforceable. They wanted to "get a Federal law" that would "cover" areas where the Constitution authorized Congress to legislate, namely "interstate and foreign commerce and admiralty."...Members of Congress, looking at that phrase, might have thought the words "any contract" standing alone went beyond Congress's constitutional authority. And, if so, they might have simply connected those words with the later words "transaction involving commerce," thereby creating the phrase that became law. Nothing in the Act's history suggests any other, more limiting, task for the language.

[...]

Finally, we note that an *amicus curiae* argues for an "objective" ("reasonable person" oriented) version of the "contemplation of the parties" test on the ground that such an interpretation would better protect consumers asked to sign form contracts by businesses. We agree that Congress, when enacting this law, had the needs of consumers, as well as others, in mind.... Indeed, arbitration's advantages often would seem helpful to individuals, say, complaining about a product, who need a less expensive alternative to litigation....

We are uncertain, however, just how the "objective" version of the "contemplation" test would help consumers. Sometimes, of course, it would permit, say, a consumer with potentially large damage claims, to disavow a contract's arbitration provision and proceed in court. But, if so, it would equally permit, say, local business entities to disavow a contract's arbitration provisions, thereby leaving the typical consumer who has only a small damage claim (who seeks, say, the value of only a defective refrigerator or television set) without any remedy but a court remedy, the costs and delays of which could eat up the value of an eventual small recovery.

In any event, § 2 gives States a method for protecting consumers against unfair pressure to agree to a contract with an unwanted arbitration provision. States may regulate contracts, including arbitration clauses, under general contract law principles and they may invalidate an arbitration clause "upon such grounds as exist at law or in equity for the revocation of any contract."... What States may not do is decide that a contract is fair enough to enforce all its basic terms (price, service, credit), but not fair enough to enforce its arbitration clause. The Act makes any such state policy unlawful, for that kind of policy would place arbitration clauses on an unequal "footing," directly contrary to the Act's language and Congress's intent....

For these reasons, we accept the "commerce in fact" interpretation, reading the Act's language as insisting that the "transaction" in fact "involve" interstate commerce, even if the parties did not contemplate an interstate commerce connection.

V

The parties do not contest that the transaction in this case, in fact, involved interstate commerce. In addition to the multistate nature of Terminix and Allied–Bruce, the termite-treating and house-repairing material used by Allied–Bruce in its (allegedly inadequate) efforts to carry out the terms of the Plan, came from outside Alabama.

Consequently, the judgment of the Supreme Court of Alabama is reversed and the case is remanded for further proceedings consistent with this opinion.

It is so ordered.

JUSTICE O'CONNOR, concurring.

I agree with the Court's construction of § 2 of the Federal Arbitration Act. As applied in federal courts, the Court's interpretation comports fully with my understanding of congressional intent. A more restrictive definition of "evidencing" and "involving" would doubtless foster prearbitration litigation that would frustrate the very purpose of the statute. As applied in state courts, however, the effect of a broad formulation of § 2 is more troublesome. The reading of § 2 adopted today will displace many state statutes carefully calibrated to protect consumers, *see, e.g.*, Mont. Code Ann. § 27–5–114(2)(b) (1993) (refusing to enforce arbitration clauses in consumer contracts where the consideration is $5,000 or less), and state procedural requirements aimed at ensuring knowing and voluntary consent, *see, e.g.*, U.S.C. Code Ann. § 15–48–10(a) (Supp.1993) (requiring that notice of arbitration provision be prominently placed on first page of contract). I have long adhered to the view... that Congress designed the Federal Arbitration Act to apply only in federal courts. But if we are to apply the Act in state courts, it makes little sense to read § 2 differently in that context. In the end, my agreement with the Court's construction of § 2 rests largely on the wisdom of maintaining a uniform standard.

I continue to believe that Congress never intended the Federal Arbitration Act to apply in state courts, and that this Court has strayed far afield in giving the Act so broad a compass.... [O]ver the past decade, the Court has abandoned all pretense of ascertaining congressional intent with respect to the Federal Arbitration Act, building instead, case by case, an edifice of its own creation. I have no doubt that Congress could enact, in the first instance, a federal arbitration statute that displaces most state arbitration laws. But I also have no doubt that, in 1925, Congress enacted no such statute.

Were we writing on a clean slate, I would adhere to that view and affirm the Alabama court's decision. But, as the Court points out, more than 10 years have passed since *Southland*, several subsequent cases have built upon its reasoning, and parties have undoubtedly made contracts in reliance on the Court's interpretation of the Act in the interim. After reflection, I am persuaded by considerations of *stare decisis* . . . to acquiesce in today's judgment. Though wrong, *Southland* has not proved unworkable, and, as always, "Congress remains free to alter what we have done." . . .

Today's decision caps this Court's effort to expand the Federal Arbitration Act. Although each decision has built logically upon the decisions preceding it, the initial building block in *Southland* laid a faulty foundation. I acquiesce in today's judgment because there is no "special justification" to overrule *Southland*. . . . It remains now for Congress to correct this interpretation if it wishes to preserve state autonomy in state courts.

JUSTICE SCALIA, dissenting.

[. . .]

. . . For the reasons set forth in Justice Thomas' opinion, which I join, I agree with the respondents (and belatedly with Justice O'Connor) that *Southland* clearly misconstrued the Federal Arbitration Act.

I do not believe that proper application of *stare decisis* prevents correction of the mistake. Adhering to *Southland* entails a permanent, unauthorized eviction of state-court power to adjudicate a potentially large class of disputes. Abandoning it does not impair reliance interests to a degree that justifies this evil. . . .

I shall not in the future dissent from judgments that rest on *Southland*. I will, however, stand ready to join four other Justices in overruling it. . . .

For these reasons, I respectfully dissent from the judgment of the Court.

JUSTICE THOMAS, with whom JUSTICE SCALIA joins, dissenting.

I disagree with the majority at the threshold of this case, and so I do not reach the question that it decides. In my view, the Federal Arbitration Act (FAA) does not apply in state courts. I respectfully dissent.

I

In *Southland Corp. v. Keating*, this Court concluded that § 2 of the FAA "appl[ies] in state as well as federal courts," . . . and "withdr[aws] the power of the states to require a judicial forum for the resolution of claims which the contracting parties agreed to resolve by arbitration". . . . In my view, both aspects of *Southland* are wrong.

A

Section 2 of the FAA declares that an arbitration clause contained in "a contract evidencing a transaction involving commerce" shall be "valid, irrevocable, and enforceable, save upon such grounds as exist at law or in equity for the revocation of any contract." ...On its face, and considered out of context, § 2 draws no apparent distinction between federal courts and state courts. But not until 1959, nearly 35 years after Congress enacted the FAA, did any court suggest that § 2 applied in state courts.... No state court agreed until the 1960's.... This Court waited until 1984 to conclude, over a strong dissent by Justice O'Connor, that § 2 extends to the States....

The explanation for this delay is simple: the statute that Congress enacted actually applies only in federal courts. At the time of the FAA's passage in 1925, laws governing the enforceability of arbitration agreements were generally thought to deal purely with matters of procedure rather than substance, because they were directed solely to the mechanisms for resolving the underlying disputes.... It would have been extraordinary for Congress to attempt to prescribe procedural rules for state courts.... And because the FAA was enacted against this general background, no one read it as such an attempt....

Indeed, to judge from the reported cases, it appears that no state court was even asked to enforce the statute for many years after the passage of the FAA. Federal courts, for their part, refused to apply state arbitration statutes in cases to which the FAA was inapplicable.... Their refusal was not the outgrowth of this Court's decision in *Swift v. Tyson*.... Rather, federal courts did not apply the state arbitration statutes because the statutes were not considered substantive laws.... In short, state arbitration statutes prescribed rules for the state courts, and the FAA prescribed rules for the federal courts.

It is easy to understand why lawyers in 1925 classified arbitration statutes as procedural. An arbitration agreement is a species of forum-selection clause: without laying down any rules of decision, it identifies the adjudicator of disputes. A strong argument can be made that such forum-selection clauses concern procedure rather than substance.... And if a contractual provision deals purely with matters of judicial procedure, one might well conclude that questions about whether and how it will be enforced also relate to procedure.

The context of § 2 confirms this understanding of the FAA's original meaning. Most sections of the statute plainly have no application in state courts, but rather prescribe rules either for federal courts or for arbitration proceedings themselves....

Despite the FAA's general focus on the federal courts, of course, § 2 itself contains no such explicit limitation. But the text of the statute nonetheless makes clear that § 2 was not meant as a statement of substantive law binding on the States. After all, if § 2 really was understood to "creat[e] federal substantive law requiring the parties to honor arbitration agreements," *Southland,* then the breach of an arbitration agreement covered by § 2 would give rise to a federal question within the subject-matter jurisdiction of the federal district courts. Yet the ensuing provisions of the Act, without expressly taking away this jurisdiction, clearly rest on the assumption that federal courts have jurisdiction to enforce arbitration agreements only when they would have had jurisdiction over the underlying dispute. In other words, the FAA treats arbitration simply as one means of resolving disputes that lie within the jurisdiction of the federal courts; it makes clear that the breach of a covered arbitration agreement does not itself provide any independent basis for such jurisdiction. Even the *Southland* majority was forced to acknowledge this point, conceding that § 2 "does not create any independent federal-question jurisdiction under 28 U.S.C. § 1331 or otherwise.". . . But the reason that § 2 does not give rise to federal-question jurisdiction is that it was enacted as a purely procedural provision. For the same reason, it applies only in the federal courts.

The distinction between "substance" and "procedure" acquired new meaning after *Erie.* . . . Thus, in 1956 [in *Bernhardt,*] we held that for *Erie* purposes, the question whether a court should stay litigation brought in breach of an arbitration agreement is one of "substantive" law. . . . But this later development could not change the original meaning of the statute that Congress enacted in 1925. Although *Bernhardt* classified portions of the FAA as "substantive" rather than "procedural," it does not mean that they were so understood in 1925 or that Congress extended the FAA's reach beyond the federal courts.

When Justice O'Connor pointed out the FAA's original meaning in her *Southland* dissent, . . . the majority offered only one real response. If § 2 had been considered a purely procedural provision, the majority reasoned, Congress would have extended it to all contracts rather than simply to maritime transactions and "contract[s] evidencing a transaction involving [interstate or foreign] commerce." Yet Congress might well have thought that even if it could have called upon federal courts to enforce arbitration agreements in every single case that came before them, there was no federal interest in doing so unless interstate commerce or maritime transactions were involved. This conclusion is far more plausible than *Southland*'s idea that Congress both viewed § 2 as a statement of substantive law and believed that it created no federal-question jurisdiction.

Even if the interstate commerce requirement raises uncertainty about the original meaning of the statute, we should resolve the uncertainty in light of core principles of federalism. . . . To the extent that federal statutes are ambiguous, we do not read them to displace state law. Rather, we must be "absolutely certain" that Congress intended such displacement before we give preemptive effect to a federal statute. . . . In 1925, the enactment of a "substantive" arbitration statute along the lines envisioned by *Southland* would have displaced an enormous body of state law: outside of a few States, predispute arbitration agreements either were wholly unenforceable or at least were not subject to specific performance. Far from being "absolutely certain" that Congress swept aside these state rules, I am quite sure that it did not.

B

Suppose, however, that the first aspect of *Southland* was correct: § 2 requires States to enforce the covered arbitration agreements and preempts all contrary state law. There still would be no textual basis for *Southland*'s suggestion that § 2 requires the States to enforce those agreements through the remedy of specific performance, that is, by forcing the parties to submit to arbitration. A contract surely can be "valid, irrevocable and enforceable" even though it can be enforced only through actions for damages. Thus, on the eve of the FAA's enactment, this Court described executory arbitration agreements as being "valid" and as creating "a perfect obligation" under federal law even though federal courts refused to order their specific performance. . . .

To be sure, §§ 3 and 4 of the FAA require that federal courts specifically enforce arbitration agreements. These provisions deal, respectively, with the potential plaintiffs and the potential defendants in the underlying dispute: § 3 holds the plaintiffs to their promise not to take their claims straight to court, while § 4 holds the defendants to their promise to submit to arbitration rather than making the other party sue them. Had this case arisen in one of the "courts of the United States," it is § 3 that would have been relevant. Upon proper motion, the court would have been obliged to grant a stay pending arbitration, unless the contract between the parties did not "evidenc[e] a transaction involving [interstate] commerce." . . . Because this case arose in the courts of Alabama, however, petitioners are forced to contend that § 2 imposes precisely the same obligation on all courts (both federal and state) that § 3 imposes solely on federal courts. Though *Southland* supports this argument, it simply cannot be correct, or § 3 would be superfluous.

[. . .]

II

[. . .]

. . . I see no reason to think that the costs of overruling *Southland* are unacceptably high. Certainly no reliance interests are involved in cases like the present one, where the applicability of the FAA was not within the contemplation of the parties at the time of contracting. In many other cases, moreover, the parties will simply comply with their arbitration agreement, either on the theory that they should live up to their promises or on the theory that arbitration is the cheapest and best way of resolving their dispute. In a fair number of the remaining cases, the party seeking to enforce an arbitration agreement will be able to get into federal court, where the FAA will apply. And even if access to federal court is impossible (because § 2 creates no independent basis for federal-question jurisdiction), many cases will arise in States whose own law largely parallels the FAA. Only Alabama, Mississippi, and Nebraska still hold all executory arbitration agreements to be unenforceable, though some other States refuse to enforce particular classes of such agreements. . . .

[. . .]

. . . In short, we have never actually held, as opposed to stating or implying in dicta, that the FAA requires a state court to stay lawsuits brought in violation of an arbitration agreement covered by § 2.

Because I believe that the FAA imposes no such obligation on state courts, and indeed that the statute is wholly inapplicable in those courts, I would affirm the Alabama Supreme Court's judgment.

NOTES AND QUESTIONS

1. Compare the circumstances in which the issue of the effect of a state statute arises in *Volt* and *Terminix*. Are the circumstances or the issues of litigation distinguishable in these two cases? Why does the Court arrive at markedly different conclusions in the two cases? What remains of state authority to legislate in the area of arbitration following *Terminix*? With which federalism cases is *Terminix* most similar?

2. The majority opinion recites and confirms the content of the law as it existed prior to *Volt*. It is significant that the Court perceived no conflict between *Volt* and *Terminix*; it, in fact, cites the language in *Volt* to sustain some of its reasoning in *Terminix*.

The majority also adds new elements to its analytical justification of its arbitration doctrine. First, it advances the view that the judicial policy on arbitration should be sufficiently straightforward to avoid creating complex and self-defeating judicial litigation on arbitration, "thereby unnecessarily complicating the law and breeding litigation from a statute that seeks to avoid it." 513 U.S. at 275. "Why would Congress intend a test that risks the very kind of cost and delay through litigation. . . that Congress wrote the Act to help the parties avoid." *Id.* at 278. Second, the majority undercuts the significance of the FAA's legislative history by questioning its utility and accuracy as a means of gauging the underlying intent of the statute, *e.g.*, "The Act's history, to the extent informative. . . ." *Id.* at 279. Third, the Court describes at some length the advantages of arbitration for achieving consumer protection, dismissing the need to protect consumers from unilateral agreements to arbitrate. *Id.* at 280–81.

What do these elements add to the debate about the federalization of the U.S. law of arbitration? How do they work to sustain the Court's view that the FAA dislodges the application of contrary state statutes and is binding upon state courts? Which of these rationalizations is the weakest? The most persuasive? Is the Court right at one level and wrong at another level?

As a final matter, what does the Court's disregard of legislative history indicate to you? If you were drafting the history of a bill for Congress, is there any way to make it more persuasive to the courts who might read it?

3. In her concurring opinion, Justice O'Connor refers to two state consumer protection laws that place restrictions on the validity of arbitration agreements. Are these provisions unconstitutional in light of the majority's reasoning? Would such a result reflect a fair reading of the FAA, of the FAA/*Erie* problem, of the case law in general, or of the case law without *Volt*?

4. Do you agree with Justice O'Connor that the federal law of arbitration is "an edifice of. . .[the Court's] own creation" and that the Court in its arbitration decisions "has strayed far afield"? Do you believe that the majority agrees with Justice O'Connor's evaluation? What type of law-making does the Court engage in if what Justice O'Connor says is true? Is this a proper foundation for the law of arbitration?

5. How do you assess and explain Justice O'Connor's "acquiescence" to the majority view? What role does *stare decisis* play here? Does she really concur or is her opinion a dissenting evaluation with no hope of ever being adopted by the Court? How does Justice O'Connor's "acquiescence" compare to the "evil" perceived by Justice Scalia?

6. Justice Thomas makes a number of highly persuasive points regarding the FAA's legislative history and the text of its provisions. Why do you think the majority is not persuaded? What really separates the majority from Justice Thomas' analytic reasoning and assessment of the statute and case law?

7. Evaluate Justice Thomas' criticism of the majority's position that Section Two of the FAA is a substantive provision binding upon state courts, while Sections Three and Four are merely procedural and govern only federal proceedings. What do Justice Thomas' criticisms indicate about the flaws in the majority's reasoning and general approach? On a related matter, is Justice Thomas correct to believe that, if Section Two were a substantive provision, it would create federal-question jurisdiction? Is this an indirect but logically inescapable effect of the case law? Explain.

8. Finally, assess Justice Thomas' statements regarding the cost of overruling *Keating*. Are these reasons more realistic than those advanced by the majority? In particular, you should note that there is nearly universal state law conformity with the provisions of the FAA. Does this make the federalism debate unnecessary or is the uniformity of law its consequence?

* * *

Doctor's Associates, Inc. v. Casarotto is the most recent U.S. Supreme Court ruling on the question of the supremacy of the FAA over state laws on arbitration. The 8 to 1 decision adds nothing new to the Court's doctrine on arbitration, but rather confirms the strength of the federalization development. Justice Thomas files a brief dissent based upon his position in *Terminix*. With *Casarotto*, the Court's stance on this question of arbitration law becomes completely unambiguous.

DOCTOR'S ASSOCIATES, INC. v. CASAROTTO

517 U.S. 681, 116 S.Ct. 1652, 134 L.Ed.2d 902 (1996).

JUSTICE GINSBURG delivered the opinion of the Court.

This case concerns a standard form franchise agreement for the operation of a Subway sandwich shop in Montana. When a dispute arose between parties to the agreement, franchisee Paul Casarotto sued franchisor Doctor's Associates, Inc. (DAI) and DAI's Montana development agent, Nick Lombardi, in a Montana state court. DAI and Lombardi sought to stop the litigation pending arbitration pursuant to the arbitration clause set out on page nine of the franchise agreement.

The Federal Arbitration Act declares written provisions for arbitration "valid, irrevocable, and enforceable, save upon such grounds as exist at law or in equity for the revocation of any contract." Montana law, however, declares an arbitration clause unenforceable unless "[n]otice that [the] contract is subject to arbitration" is "typed in underlined capital letters on the first page of the contract." Mont. Code Ann. § 27–5–114(4) (1995). The question here presented is whether Montana's law is compatible with the federal Act. We hold that Montana's first-page notice requirement, which governs not "any contract," but specifically and solely contracts "subject to arbitration," conflicts with the FAA and is therefore displaced by the federal measure.

I

Petitioner DAI is the national franchisor of Subway sandwich shops. In April 1988, DAI entered [into] a franchise agreement with respondent Paul Casarotto, which permitted Casarotto to open a Subway shop in Great Falls, Montana. The franchise agreement stated, on page nine and in ordinary type: "Any controversy or claim arising out of or relating to this contract or the breach thereof shall be settled by Arbitration...."...

In October 1992, Casarotto sued DAI and its agent, Nick Lombardi, in Montana state court, alleging state-law contract and tort claims relating to the franchise agreement. DAI demanded arbitration of those claims, and successfully moved in the Montana trial court to stay the lawsuit pending arbitration.

The Montana Supreme Court reversed. The Montana Supreme Court held that Mont. Code Ann. § 27–5–114(4) rendered the agreement's arbitration clause unenforceable. The Montana statute provides:

> "Notice that a contract is subject to arbitration...shall be typed in under-lined capital letters on the first page of the contract; and unless such notice is displayed thereon, the contract may not be subject to arbitration."

Notice of the arbitration clause in the franchise agreement did not appear on the first page of the contract. Nor was anything relating to the clause typed in underlined capital letters. Because the State's statutory notice requirement had not been met, the Montana Supreme Court declared the parties' dispute "not subject to arbitration."

[. . .]

The Montana Supreme Court read our decision in *Volt Information Sciences, Inc.* as limiting the preemptive force of § 2 and correspondingly qualifying *Southland* and *Perry.* As the Montana Supreme Court comprehended *Volt*, the proper inquiry here should focus not on the bare words of § 2, but on this question: Would the application of Montana's notice requirement "undermine the goals and policies of the FAA"? Section 27–5–114(4), in the Montana court's judgment, did not undermine the goals and policies of the FAA, for the notice requirement did not preclude arbitration agreements altogether; it simply prescribed "that before arbitration agreements are enforceable, they be entered [into] knowingly."

[. . .]

I

Section 2 of the FAA provides that written arbitration agreements "shall be valid, irrevocable, and enforceable, save upon such grounds as exist at law or in equity for the revocation of any contract." Repeating our observation in *Perry*, the text of § 2 declares that state law may be applied "if that law arose to govern issues concerning the validity, revocability, and enforceability of contracts generally." Thus, generally applicable contract defenses, such as fraud, duress or unconscionability, may be applied to invalidate arbitration agreements without contravening § 2.

Courts may not, however, invalidate arbitration agreements under state laws applicable only to arbitration provisions. By enacting § 2, we have several times said, Congress precluded States from singling out arbitration provisions for suspect status, requiring instead that such provisions be placed "upon the same footing as other contracts." Montana's § 27–5–114(4) directly conflicts with § 2 of the FAA because the State's law conditions the enforceability of arbitration agreements on compliance with a special notice requirement not applicable to contracts generally. The FAA thus displaces the Montana statute with respect to arbitration agreements covered by the Act.

The Montana Supreme Court misread our *Volt* decision and therefore reached a conclusion in this case at odds with our rulings. *Volt* involved an arbitration agreement that incorporated state procedural rules, one of which, on the facts of that case, called for arbitration to be stayed pending the resolution of a related judicial proceeding. The state rule examined in *Volt* determined only the efficient order of proceedings; it did not affect the enforceability of the arbitration agreement itself. . . .

Applying § 27–5–114(4) here, in contrast, would not enforce the arbitration clause in the contract between DAI and Casarotto; instead, Montana's first-page notice requirement would invalidate the clause. The "goals and policies" of the FAA, this Court's precedent indicates, are antithetical to threshold limitations placed specifically and solely on arbitration provisions. The State's prescription is thus inconsonant with, and is therefore preempted by, the federal law.

* * *

For the reasons stated, the judgment of the Supreme Court of Montana is reversed, and the case is remanded for further proceedings not inconsistent with this opinion.

It is so ordered.

Justice Thomas, dissenting.

For the reasons given in my dissent last term in *Allied-Bruce Terminix Cos. v. Dobson* I remain of the view that § 2 of the Federal Arbitration Act does not apply to proceedings in state courts. Accordingly, I respectfully dissent.

Notes and Questions

1. *Casarotto* makes the direction of the judicial policy on arbitration abundantly clear on questions of federalism. State law provisions cannot contravene the letter or spirit of the FAA as interpreted by the U.S. Supreme Court.

2. Justice Ginsburg states that arbitration agreements can be regulated by laws applying to all contracts; in effect, state laws cannot single out arbitration agreements for discriminating treatment.

3. Because arbitration agreements are contracts of adjudication, are they ordinary contracts? What room does this pronouncement leave to the states in terms of regulation?

4. If state law prohibits the enforcement of contracts that are against public policy, would a state law providing that public policy include protection against predispute waivers of judicial remedies in consumer transactions be invalid?

5. Finally, assess the Court's integration of the *Volt* decision as support for its result in *Casarotto*.

* * *

BUCKEYE CHECK CASHING, INC, v. CARDEGNA

546 U.S. 440, 126 S.Ct. 1204, 163 L.Ed.2d 1038 (2006).

Justice Scalia delivered the opinion of the Court.

We decide whether a court or an arbitrator should consider the claim that a contract containing an arbitration provision is void for illegality.

I

Respondents John Cardegna and Donna Reuter entered into various deferred-payment transactions with petitioner Buckeye Check Cashing (Buckeye), in which they received cash in exchange for a personal check in the amount of the cash plus a finance charge. For each separate transaction they signed a "Deferred Deposit and Disclosure Agreement" (Agreement), which included the following arbitration provisions:

"1. *Arbitration Disclosure* By signing this Agreement, you agree that if a dispute of any kind arises out of this Agreement or your application therefore or any instrument relating thereto, then either you or we or third-parties involved can choose to have that dispute resolved by binding arbitration as set forth in Paragraph 2 below. . . .

"2. *Arbitration Provisions* Any claim, dispute, or controversy . . . arising from or relating to this Agreement . . . or the validity, enforceability, or scope of this Arbitration Provision or the entire Agreement (collectively 'Claim'), shall be resolved, upon the election of you or us or said third-parties, by binding arbitration. . . . This arbitration Agreement is made pursuant to a transaction involving interstate commerce, and shall be governed by the Federal Arbitration Act ('FAA'), 9 U.S.C. Sections 1–16. The arbitrator shall apply applicable substantive law constraint [sic] with the FAA and applicable statutes of limitations and shall honor claims of privilege recognized by law. . . ." . . .

Respondents brought this putative class action in Florida state court, alleging that Buckeye charged usurious interest rates and that the Agreement violated various Florida lending and consumer-protection laws, rendering it criminal on its face. Buckeye moved to compel arbitration. The trial court denied the motion, holding that a court rather than an arbitrator should resolve a claim that a contract is illegal and void *ab initio*. The District Court of Appeal of Florida for the Fourth District reversed, holding that because respondents did not challenge the arbitration provision itself, but instead claimed that the entire contract was void, the agreement to arbitrate was enforceable, and the question of the contract's legality should go to the arbitrator.

Respondents appealed, and the Florida Supreme Court reversed, reasoning that to enforce an agreement to arbitrate in a contract challenged as unlawful " 'could breathe life into a contract that not only violates state law, but also is criminal in nature. . . .' " . . . We granted *certiorari*. . . .

II

A

To overcome judicial resistance to arbitration, Congress enacted the Federal Arbitration Act (FAA), 9 U.S.C. §§ 1–16. Section 2 embodies the national policy favoring arbitration and places arbitration agreements on equal footing with all other contracts:

[. . .]

Challenges to the validity of arbitration agreements "upon such grounds as exist at law or in equity for the revocation of any contract" can be divided into two types. One type challenges specifically the validity of the agreement to arbitrate. See, *e.g., Southland Corp.* v. *Keating*, 465 U.S.

1, 4–5 (1984) (challenging the agreement to arbitrate as void under California law insofar as it purported to cover claims brought under the state Franchise Investment Law). The other challenges the contract as a whole, either on a ground that directly affects the entire agreement (*e.g.*, the agreement was fraudulently induced), or on the ground that the illegality of one of the contract's provisions renders the whole contract invalid.[1] Respondents' claim is of this second type. The crux of the complaint is that the contract as a whole (including its arbitration provision) is rendered invalid by the usurious finance charge.

In *Prima Paint Corp.* v. *Flood & Conklin Mfg. Co.*, 388 U.S. 395 (1967), we addressed the question of who—court or arbitrator—decides these two types of challenges. The issue in the case was "whether a claim of fraud in the inducement of the entire contract is to be resolved by the federal court, or whether the matter is to be referred to the arbitrators." . . . Guided by § 4 of the FAA, [footnote omitted] we held that "if the claim is fraud in the inducement of the arbitration clause itself—an issue which goes to the making of the agreement to arbitrate—the federal court may proceed to adjudicate it. But the statutory language does not permit the federal court to consider claims of fraud in the inducement of the contract generally." . . . We rejected the view that the question of "severability" was one of state law, so that if state law held the arbitration provision not to be severable a challenge to the contract as a whole would be decided by the court. . . .

Subsequently, in *Southland Corp.*, we held that the FAA "created a body of federal substantive law," which was "applicable in state and federal courts." . . . We rejected the view that state law could bar enforcement of § 2, even in the context of state-law claims brought in state court. . . .

B

Prima Paint and *Southland* answer the question presented here by establishing three propositions. First, as a matter of substantive federal arbitration law, an arbitration provision is severable from the remainder of the contract. Second, unless the challenge is to the arbitration clause itself, the issue of the contract's validity is considered by the arbitrator in the first instance. Third, this arbitration law applies in state as well as federal courts. The parties have not requested, and we do not undertake, reconsideration of those holdings. Applying them to this case, we conclude that because respondents challenge the Agreement, but not specifically its arbitration provisions, those provisions are enforceable apart from the remainder of the contract. The challenge should therefore be considered by an arbitrator, not a court.

---

1. The issue of the contract's validity is different from the issue whether any agreement between the alleged obligor and obligee was ever concluded. Our opinion today addresses only the former, and does not speak to the issue decided in the cases cited by respondents (and by the Florida Supreme Court), which hold that it is for courts to decide whether the alleged obligor ever signed the contract . . . whether the signor lacked authority to commit the alleged principal . . . and whether the signor lacked the mental capacity to assent. . . .

In declining to apply *Prima Paint*'s rule of severability, the Florida Supreme Court relied on the distinction between void and voidable contracts. "Florida public policy and contract law," it concluded, permit "no severable, or salvageable, parts of a contract found illegal and void under Florida law." ... *Prima Paint* makes this conclusion irrelevant. That case rejected application of state severability rules to the arbitration agreement *without discussing* whether the challenge at issue would have rendered the contract void or voidable.... Indeed, the opinion expressly disclaimed any need to decide what state-law remedy was available.... Likewise in *Southland*, which arose in state court, we did not ask whether the several challenges made there—fraud, misrepresentation, breach of contract, breach of fiduciary duty, and violation of the California Franchise Investment Law—would render the contract void or voidable. We simply rejected the proposition that the enforceability of the arbitration agreement turned on the state legislature's judgment concerning the forum for enforcement of the state-law cause of action.... So also here, we cannot accept the Florida Supreme Court's conclusion that enforceability of the arbitration agreement should turn on "Florida public policy and contract law." ...

C

Respondents assert that *Prima Paint*'s rule of severability does not apply in state court. They argue that *Prima Paint* interpreted only §§ 3 and 4—two of the FAA's procedural provisions, which appear to apply by their terms only in federal court—but not § 2, the only provision that we have applied in state court. This does not accurately describe *Prima Paint*. Although § 4, in particular, had much to do with *Prima Paint*'s understanding of the rule of severability, ... this rule ultimately arises out of § 2, the FAA's substantive command that arbitration agreements be treated like all other contracts. The rule of severability establishes how this equal-footing guarantee for "a written [arbitration] provision" is to be implemented. Respondents' reading of *Prima Paint* as establishing nothing more than a federal-court rule of procedure also runs contrary to *Southland*'s understanding of that case. One of the bases for *Southland*'s application of § 2 in state court was precisely *Prima Paint*'s "reliance for [its] holding on Congress' broad power to fashion substantive rules under the Commerce Clause." ... *Southland* itself refused to "believe Congress intended to limit the Arbitration Act to disputes subject only to *federal-court* jurisdiction." ...

Respondents point to the language of § 2, which renders "valid, irrevocable, and enforceable" "a written provision in" or "an agreement in writing to submit to arbitration an existing controversy arising out of" a "contract." Since, respondents argue, the only arbitration agreements to which § 2 applies are those involving a "contract," and since an agreement void *ab initio* under state law is not a "contract," there is no "written provision" in or "controversy arising out of" a "contract," to which § 2 can apply. This argument echoes Justice Black's dissent in *Prima Paint:* "Sections 2 and 3 of the Act assume the existence of a valid contract. They merely provide for enforcement where such a valid contract exists." ... We do not read "contract" so narrowly. The word appears four times in § 2. Its last appearance is in the final clause, which allows a challenge to an arbitration provision "upon such grounds as exist at law or in equity for the revocation of any *contract*." (Emphasis added.) There can be no doubt that "contract" as used this last time must include contracts that later prove to be void. Otherwise, the grounds for revocation would be limited to those that rendered a contract voidable—which would mean (implausibly) that an arbitration agreement could be challenged as voidable but not as void. Because the sentence's final use of "contract" so obviously includes putative contracts, we will not read the same word earlier in the same sentence to have a more narrow meaning. [Footnote omitted.] We note that neither *Prima Paint* nor *Southland* lends support to respondents' reading; as we have discussed, neither case turned on whether the challenge at issue would render the contract voidable or void.

*   *   *

It is true, as respondents assert, that the *Prima Paint* rule permits a court to enforce an arbitration agreement in a contract that the arbitrator later finds to be void. But it is equally true that respondents' approach permits a court to deny effect to an arbitration provision in a contract that the court later finds to be perfectly enforceable. *Prima Paint* resolved this conundrum—and resolved it in favor of the separate enforceability of arbitration provisions. We reaffirm today that, regardless of whether the challenge is brought in federal or state court, a challenge to the validity of the contract as a whole, and not specifically to the arbitration clause, must go to the arbitrator.

The judgment of the Florida Supreme Court is reversed, and the case is remanded for further proceedings not inconsistent with this opinion.

It is so ordered.

JUSTICE ALITO took no part in the consideration or decision of this case.

JUSTICE THOMAS, dissenting.

I remain of the view that the Federal Arbitration Act (FAA), 9 U.S.C. § 1 *et seq.*, does not apply to proceedings in state courts.... Thus, in state-court proceedings, the FAA cannot be the basis for displacing a state law that prohibits enforcement of an arbitration clause contained in a contract that is unenforceable under state law. Accordingly, I would leave undisturbed the judgment of the Florida Supreme Court.

NOTES AND QUESTIONS

1. As noted earlier (*supra* at 140, note 8), *Buckeye Check Cashing* reaffirms *Prima Paint's* ruling on separability. The separability doctrine, in effect, allows challenges to the main contract to be decided by the arbitrator

and not a court. Can you explain how this result is achieved? What happens on the jurisdictional side if the party opposing arbitration alleges expressly that the contract vice or defect also affects the arbitral clause directly? Who would decide then and why? What function does separability perform? How did the doctrine originate?

2.   Evaluate the Florida state Supreme Court's position that the loan agreement's absolute voidness under state usury law rendered all its provisions, including the arbitral clause, completely unenforceable. For reasons of public policy, a usurious contract is an agreement that never existed. To what part(s) of this position does the majority opinion object? Commentators asserted that *Buckeye Check Cashing* reflected the Court's rejection of the distinction between void and voidable contracts, presumably for purposes of the enforcement of the arbitral clause. What is, however, the most significant doctrinal consequence of the Court's opinion? Does the arbitrator's right to rule trump the state right to regulate the legitimacy of consumer loans in its territory? Is this result what Justice Thomas objects to in his dissent?

3.   Examine how the majority uses *Prima Paint* and *Southland* to achieve the result in *Buckeye Check Cashing*. Are they both equally relevant to the determination in *Buckeye*? Do they respond to different aspects of the decision? What would be the implication of a ruling by the arbitrator that the loan agreement is governed by Florida law and is usurious and unenforceable?

4.   Under existing law, does a claim that the contract is an absolute nullity under the controlling state law for reason of a state public policy or public interest requirement amount to an abnegation of the entire contract? Why can the arbitrator still rule? Is it just the technicality that the complaint does not specifically target the arbitral clause? Or, is it a question of the arbitrator's right to rule on problems with the parties' contract? The arbitrator's authority to rule, however, does appear to be in jeopardy. It is being exercised on a potentially non-existent foundation? Is the ultimate consideration one of policy, the federal policy favoring arbitration? As long as an arbitral clause can be identified, the arbitrator will and must decide. What do you think?

5.   What elements of the federal doctrine on arbitration command the *Buckeye* outcome?

6.   Why does the federal separability doctrine apply in state courts?

7.   State contract law governs the validity of arbitral clauses as agreements—in effect, the Court would say, a *Southland* consideration. Given the latter and *Prima Paint*, along with *Allied Bruce Terminix* and *Doctor's Associates, Inc.*, what role does state law play in the law of arbitration? Is it an autonomous role?

PRESTON v. FERRER

___ U.S. ___, 128 S.Ct. 978, 169 L.Ed.2d 917 (2008).

JUSTICE GINSBURG delivered the opinion of the Court.

As this Court recognized in *Southland Corp.* v. *Keating*, 465 U.S. 1 (1984), the Federal Arbitration Act (FAA or Act) . . . establishes a national policy favoring arbitration when the parties contract for that mode of dispute resolution. The Act, which rests on Congress' authority under the Commerce Clause, supplies not simply a procedural framework applicable in federal courts; it also calls for the application, in state as well as federal courts, of federal substantive law regarding arbitration.... More recently, in *Buckeye Check Cashing, Inc.* v. *Cardegna*, 546 U.S. 440 (2006), the Court clarified that, when parties agree to arbitrate all disputes arising under their contract, questions concerning the validity of the entire contract are to be resolved by the arbitrator in the first instance, not by a federal or state court.

The instant petition presents the following question: Does the FAA override not only state statutes that refer certain state-law controversies initially to a judicial forum, but also state statutes that refer certain disputes initially to an administrative agency? We hold today that, when parties agree to arbitrate all questions arising under a contract, state laws lodging primary jurisdiction in another forum, whether judicial or administrative, are superseded by the FAA.

I

This case concerns a contract between respondent Alex E. Ferrer, a former Florida trial court judge who currently appears as "Judge Alex" on a Fox television network program, and petitioner Arnold M. Preston, a California attorney who renders services to persons in the entertainment industry. Seeking fees allegedly due under the contract, Preston invoked the parties' agreement to arbitrate "any dispute ... relating to the terms of [the contract] or the breach, validity, or legality thereof ... in accordance with the rules [of the American Arbitration Association]."...

Preston's demand for arbitration, made in June 2005, was countered a month later by Ferrer's petition to the California Labor Commissioner charging that the contract was invalid and unenforceable under the California Talent Agencies Act (TAA).... Ferrer asserted that Preston acted as a talent agent without the license required by the TAA, and that Preston's unlicensed status rendered the entire contract void. [Footnote omitted.]

The Labor Commissioner's hearing officer, in November 2005, determined that Ferrer had stated a "colorable basis for exercise of the Labor Commissioner's jurisdiction."... The officer denied Ferrer's motion to stay the arbitration, however, on the ground that the Labor Commissioner lacked authority to order such relief. Ferrer then filed suit in the Los Angeles Superior Court, seeking a declaration that the controversy between the parties "arising from the [c]ontract, including in particular the issue of the validity of the [c]ontract, is not subject to arbitration."... As interim relief, Ferrer sought an injunction restraining Preston from proceeding before the arbitrator. Preston responded by moving to compel arbitration.

In December 2005, the Superior Court denied Preston's motion to compel arbitration and enjoined Preston from proceeding before the arbitrator "unless and until the Labor Commissioner determines that . . . she is without jurisdiction over the disputes between Preston and Ferrer.". . . During the pendency of Preston's appeal from the Superior Court's decision, this Court reaffirmed, in *Buckeye*, that challenges to the validity of a contract providing for arbitration ordinarily "should . . . be considered by an arbitrator, not a court.". . .

In a 2–to–1 decision issued in November 2006, the California Court of Appeal affirmed the Superior Court's judgment. The appeals court held that the relevant provision of the TAA . . . vests "exclusive original jurisdiction" over the dispute in the Labor Commissioner.. . . *Buckeye* is "inapposite," the court said, because that case "did not involve an administrative agency with exclusive jurisdiction over a disputed issue.". . . The dissenting judge, in contrast, viewed *Buckeye* as controlling; she reasoned that the FAA called for immediate recognition and enforcement of the parties' agreement to arbitrate and afforded no basis for distinguishing prior resort to a state administrative agency from prior resort to a state court. . . .

The California Supreme Court denied Preston's petition for review. . . . We granted *certiorari* to determine whether the FAA overrides a state law vesting initial adjudicatory authority in an administrative agency. . . .

II

An easily stated question underlies this controversy. Ferrer claims that Preston was a talent agent who operated without a license in violation of the TAA. Accordingly, he urges, the contract between the parties, purportedly for "personal management," is void and Preston is entitled to no compensation for any services he rendered. Preston, on the other hand, maintains that he acted as a personal manager, not as a talent agent, hence his contract with Ferrer is not governed by the TAA and is both lawful and fully binding on the parties.

Because the contract between Ferrer and Preston provides that "any dispute. . . relating to the. . . validity, or legality" of the agreement "shall be submitted to arbitration.". . . Preston urges that Ferrer must litigate "his TAA defense in the arbitral forum." . . . Ferrer insists, however, that the "personal manager" or "talent agent" inquiry falls, under California law, within the exclusive original jurisdiction of the Labor Commissioner, and that the FAA does not displace the Commissioner's primary jurisdiction. . . .

The dispositive issue, then, contrary to Ferrer's suggestion, is not whether the FAA preempts the TAA wholesale. . . . The FAA plainly has no such destructive aim or effect. Instead, the question is simply who decides whether Preston acted as personal manager or as talent agent.

III

[. . .]

Section 2 "declare[s] a national policy favoring arbitration" of claims that parties contract to settle in that manner. . . . That national policy, we held in *Southland*, "appli[es] in state as well as federal courts" and "foreclose[s] state legislative attempts to undercut the enforceability of arbitration agreements.". . . The FAA's displacement of conflicting state law is "now well-established . . . and has been repeatedly reaffirmed." [Footnote omitted.]

A recurring question under § 2 is who should decide whether "grounds. . . exist at law or in equity" to invalidate an arbitration agreement. In *Prima Paint Corp.* v. *Flood & Conklin Mfg. Co.*, 388 U.S. 395, 403–404 (1967), we held that attacks on the validity of an entire contract, as distinct from attacks aimed at the arbitration clause, are within the arbitrator's ken.

The litigation in *Prima Paint* originated in federal court, but the same rule, we held in *Buckeye,* applies in state court. . . . The plaintiffs in *Buckeye* alleged that the contracts they signed, which contained arbitration clauses, were illegal under state law and void *ab initio*. . . . Relying on *Southland*, we held that the plaintiffs' challenge was within the province of the arbitrator to decide. . . .

Buckeye largely, if not entirely, resolves the dispute before us. The contract between Preston and Ferrer clearly "evidenc[ed] a transaction involving commerce,". . . and Ferrer has never disputed that the written arbitration provision in the contract falls within the purview of § 2. Moreover, Ferrer sought invalidation of the contract as a whole. In the proceedings below, he made no discrete challenge to the validity of the arbitration clause. . . . [Footnote omitted.] Ferrer thus urged the Labor Commissioner and California courts to override the contract's arbitration clause on a ground that *Buckeye* requires the arbitrator to decide in the first instance.

IV

Ferrer attempts to distinguish *Buckeye* by arguing that the TAA merely requires exhaustion of administrative remedies before the parties proceed to arbitration. We reject that argument.

A

The TAA regulates talent agents and talent agency agreements. "Talent agency" is defined, with exceptions not relevant here, as "a person or corporation who engages in the occupation of procuring, offering, promising, or attempting to procure employment or engagements for an artist or artists.". . . The definition "does not cover other services for which artists often contract, such as personal and career management (i.e., advice, direction, coordination, and oversight with respect to an artist's career or personal or financial affairs).". . . The TAA requires talent agents to procure a license from the Labor Commissioner.... "In furtherance of the [TAA's] protective aims, an unlicensed person's contract with an artist to provide the services of a talent agency is illegal and void."... [Footnote omitted.]

Section 1700.44(a) of the TAA states:

In cases of controversy arising under this chapter, the parties involved shall refer the matters in dispute to the Labor Commissioner, who shall hear and determine the same, subject to an appeal within 10 days after determination, to the superior court where the same shall be heard *de novo*.

Absent a notice of appeal filed within ten days, the Labor Commissioner's determination becomes final and binding on the parties.... [Footnote omitted.]

The TAA permits arbitration in lieu of proceeding before the Labor Commissioner if an arbitration provision "in a contract between a talent agency and [an artist]" both "provides for reasonable notice to the Labor Commissioner of the time and place of all arbitration hearings" and gives the Commissioner "the right to attend all arbitration hearings."... This prescription demonstrates that there is no inherent conflict between the TAA and arbitration as a dispute resolution mechanism....

Procedural prescriptions of the TAA thus conflict with the FAA's dispute resolution regime in two basic respects: First, the TAA, in § 1700.44(a), grants the Labor Commissioner exclusive jurisdiction to decide an issue that the parties agreed to arbitrate,... second, the TAA, in § 1700.45, imposes prerequisites to enforcement of an arbitration agreement that are not applicable to contracts generally....

B

Ferrer contends that the TAA is nevertheless compatible with the FAA because § 1700.44(a) merely postpones arbitration until after the Labor Commissioner has exercised her primary jurisdiction.... The party that loses before the Labor Commissioner may file for *de novo* review in Superior Court. See § 1700.44(a). At that point, Ferrer asserts, either party could move to compel arbitration under Cal. Civ. Proc. Code Ann. § 1281.2 (West 2007), and thereby obtain an arbitrator's determination prior to judicial review....

That is not the position Ferrer took in the California courts. In his complaint, he urged the Superior Court to declare that "the [c]ontract, including in particular the issue of the validity of the [c]ontract, *is not subject to arbitration*," and he sought an injunction stopping arbitration "unless and until, *if ever*, the Labor Commissioner determines that he/she has no jurisdiction over the parties' dispute." ... [[E]mphasis added.] Ferrer also told the Superior Court: "[I]f ... the Commissioner rules that the [c]ontract is void, Preston may appeal that ruling and have a hearing de novo *before this Court*."... [[E]mphasis added.]

Nor does Ferrer's current argument—that § 1700.44(a) merely postpones arbitration—withstand examination. Section 1700.44(a) provides for *de novo* review in Superior Court, not elsewhere. [Footnote omitted.] Arbitration, if it ever occurred following the Labor Commissioner's decision, would likely be long delayed, in contravention of Congress' intent "to move the parties to an arbitrable dispute out of court and into arbitration as quickly and easily as possible."... If Ferrer prevailed in the California courts, moreover, he would no doubt argue that judicial findings of fact and conclusions of law, made after a full and fair *de novo* hearing in court, are binding on the parties and preclude the arbitrator from making any contrary rulings.

A prime objective of an agreement to arbitrate is to achieve "streamlined proceedings and expeditious results."... That objective would be frustrated even if Preston could compel arbitration in lieu of *de novo* Superior Court review. Requiring initial reference of the parties' dispute to the Labor Commissioner would, at the least, hinder speedy resolution of the controversy.

Ferrer asks us to overlook the apparent conflict between the arbitration clause and § 1700.44(a) because proceedings before the Labor Commissioner are administrative rather than judicial.... Allowing parties to proceed directly to arbitration, Ferrer contends, would undermine the Labor Commissioner's ability to stay informed of potentially illegal activity... and would deprive artists protected by the TAA of the Labor Commissioner's expertise....

In *Gilmer* v. *Interstate/Johnson Lane Corp.*, 500 U.S. 20 (1991), we considered and rejected a similar argument, namely, that arbitration of age discrimination claims would undermine the role of the Equal Employment Opportunity Commission (EEOC) in enforcing federal law. The "mere involvement of an administrative agency in the enforcement of a statute," we held, does not limit private parties' obligation to comply with their arbitration agreements....

Ferrer points to our holding in *EEOC* v. *Waffle House, Inc.*, 534 U.S. 279, 293–294 (2002), that an arbitration agreement signed by an employee who becomes a discrimination complainant does not bar the EEOC from filing an enforcement suit in its own name. He further emphasizes our observation in *Gilmer* that individuals who agreed to arbitrate their discrimination claims would "still be free to file a charge with the EEOC."... Consistent with these decisions, Ferrer argues, the arbitration clause in his contract with Preston leaves undisturbed the Labor Commissioner's independent authority to enforce the TAA.... And so it may. [Footnote omitted.] But in proceedings under § 1700.44(a), the Labor Commissioner functions not as an advocate advancing a cause before a tribunal authorized to find the facts and apply the law; instead, the Commissioner serves as impartial arbiter. That role is just what the FAA-governed agreement between Ferrer and Preston reserves for the arbitrator. In contrast, in *Waffle House* and in the *Gilmer* aside Ferrer quotes, the Court addressed the role of an agency, not as adjudicator but as prosecutor, pursuing an enforcement action in its own name or reviewing a discrimination charge to determine whether to initiate judicial proceedings.

Finally, it bears repeating that Preston's petition presents precisely and only a question concerning the forum in which the parties' dispute will be heard.... "By agreeing to arbitrate a statutory claim, a party does not forgo the substantive rights afforded by the statute; it only submits to their resolution in an arbitral ... forum."... So here, Ferrer relinquishes no substantive rights the TAA or other California law may accord him. But under the contract he signed, he cannot escape resolution of those rights in an arbitral forum.

In sum, we disapprove the distinction between judicial and administrative proceedings drawn by Ferrer and adopted by the appeals court. When parties agree to arbitrate all questions arising under a contract, the FAA supersedes state laws lodging primary jurisdiction in another forum, whether judicial or administrative.

V

Ferrer's final attempt to distinguish *Buckeye* relies on *Volt Information Sciences, Inc.* v. *Board of Trustees of Leland Stanford Junior Univ.*, 489 U.S. 468 (1989). *Volt* involved a California statute dealing with cases in which "[a] party to [an] arbitration agreement is also a party to a pending court action ... [involving] a third party [not bound by the arbitration agreement], arising out of the same transaction or series of related transactions." Cal. Civ. Proc. Code Ann. § 1281.2(c) (West 2007). To avoid the "possibility of conflicting rulings on a common issue of law or fact," the statute gives the Superior Court authority, *inter alia*, to stay the court proceeding "pending the outcome of the arbitration" or to stay the arbitration "pending the outcome of the court action."...

Volt Information Sciences and Stanford University were parties to a construction contract containing an arbitration clause. When a dispute arose and Volt demanded arbitration, Stanford sued Volt and two other companies involved in the construction project. Those other companies were not parties to the arbitration agreement; Stanford sought indemnification from them in the event that Volt prevailed against Stanford. At Stanford's request, the Superior Court stayed the arbitration. The California Court of Appeal affirmed the stay order. Volt and Stanford incorporated § 1281.2(c) into their agreement, the appeals court held. They did so by stipulating that the contract—otherwise silent on the priority of suits drawing in parties not subject to arbitration—would be governed by California law.... Relying on the Court of Appeal's interpretation of the contract, we held that the FAA did not bar a stay of arbitration pending the resolution of Stanford's Superior Court suit against Volt and the two companies not bound by the arbitration agreement.

Preston and Ferrer's contract also contains a choice-of-law clause, which states that the "agreement shall be governed by the laws of the state of California.". . . A separate saving clause provides: "If there is any conflict between this agreement and any present or future law," the law prevails over the contract "to the extent necessary to bring [the contract] within the requirements of said law.". . . Those contractual terms, according to Ferrer, call for the application of California procedural law, including § 1700.44(a)'s grant of exclusive jurisdiction to the Labor Commissioner.

Ferrer's reliance on *Volt* is misplaced for two discrete reasons. First, arbitration was stayed in *Volt* to accommodate litigation involving third parties who were strangers to the arbitration agreement. Nothing in the arbitration agreement addressed the order of proceedings when pending litigation with third parties presented the prospect of inconsistent rulings. We thought it proper, in those circumstances, to recognize state law as the gap filler.

Here, in contrast, the arbitration clause speaks to the matter in controversy; it states that "any dispute . . . relating to . . . the breach, validity, or legality" of the contract should be arbitrated in accordance with the American Arbitration Association (AAA) rules. . . . Both parties are bound by the arbitration agreement; the question of Preston's status as a talent agent relates to the validity or legality of the contract; there is no risk that related litigation will yield conflicting rulings on common issues; and there is no other procedural void for the choice-of-law clause to fill.

Second, we are guided by our more recent decision in *Mastrobuono* v. *Shearson Lehman Hutton, Inc.*, 514 U.S. 52 (1995). Although the contract in *Volt* provided for "arbitration in accordance with the Construction Industry Arbitration Rules of the American Arbitration Association,". . . Volt never argued that incorporation of those rules trumped the choice-of-law clause contained in the contract. . . . Therefore, neither our decision in *Volt* nor the decision of the California appeals court in that case addressed the import of the contract's incorporation by reference of privately promulgated arbitration rules.

In *Mastrobuono*, we reached that open question while interpreting a contract with both a New York choice-of-law clause and a clause providing for arbitration in accordance with the rules of the National Association of Securities Dealers (NASD). . . . [Footnote omitted.] The "best way to harmonize" the two clauses, we held, was to read the choice-of-law clause "to encompass substantive principles that New York courts would apply, but not to include [New York's] special rules limiting the authority of arbitrators.". . .

Preston and Ferrer's contract, as noted, provides for arbitration in accordance with the AAA rules. . . . One of those rules states that "[t]he arbitrator shall have the power to determine the existence or validity of a contract of which an arbitration clause forms a part." . . . The incorporation of the AAA rules, and in particular Rule 7(b), weighs against inferring from the choice-of-law clause an understanding shared by Ferrer and Preston that their disputes would be heard, in the first instance, by the Labor Commissioner. Following the guide *Mastrobuono* provides, the "best way to harmonize" the parties' adoption of the AAA rules and their selection of California law is to read the latter to encompass prescriptions governing the substantive rights and obligations of the parties, but not the State's "special rules limiting the authority of arbitrators." . . .

* * *

For the reasons stated, the judgment of the California Court of Appeal is reversed, and the case is remanded for further proceedings not inconsistent with this opinion.

It is so ordered.

JUSTICE THOMAS, dissenting.

As I have stated on many previous occasions, I believe that the Federal Arbitration Act (FAA) . . . does not apply to proceedings in state courts. . . . Thus, in state-court proceedings, the FAA cannot displace a state law that delays arbitration until administrative proceedings are completed. Accordingly, I would affirm the judgment of the Court of Appeals.

NOTES AND QUESTIONS

1.   Judge Alex or Ferrer often chides the litigants that appear before him for their reprehensible behavior. *Ad hominem* attacks is too polite a term to describe some of his remonstrances. Here, the righteous judge is seeking to avoid paying his manager or talent agent based upon a technical provision of a California statute. It is not (it seems) that the representative did not render services, but rather than he lacked a license to render such services in a particular lawful capacity. Surely, Ferrer would be subject to a plea for restitutionary relief were his litigation strategy to work, unless his real claim was that the services were never rendered, unnecessary, defective, or otherwise worthless.

2.   The clash of state law with the FAA's basic aim and underlying policy is at the core of the litigation in *Preston v. Ferrer*. Why would arbitration be objectionable for either party? Why does Ferrer, in particular, object to the submission of the dispute to arbitration? What remedy does California state law command in these circumstances? What public interest consideration is being served (at least, arguably) by the state legislative framework? How is that objective intolerable to the federal interest?

3.   Could tolerance and mutuality be practiced in these circumstances? Why not allow the Labor Commissioner to decide on her jurisdiction first or have her decide the merits subject to arbitral or judicial appeal?

4.   How is the holding in *Buckeye Check Cashing* relevant to the reasoning and ruling in *Preston v. Ferrer*?

5.   How is the contract a transaction involving interstate commerce?

6. Assess the Court's distinction of the instant case from *EEOC v. Waffle House* and *Volt Info. Sciences, Inc.*

7. In the end, once parties have entered (or have been forced to enter) into an arbitration agreement, who decides disputes relating to the interpretation and validity of the contract or the arbitration agreement? Who decides contrary claims as to jurisdiction, especially as jurisdiction relates to the application of state law?

CHAPTER FIVE

FREEDOM OF CONTRACT, ARBITRATOR SOVEREIGNTY, AND STATUTORY ARBITRABILITY

■ ■ ■

1. THE FEDERAL DECISIONAL EDIFICE ON ARBITRATION

The U.S. Supreme Court has taken an active interest in promoting party recourse to arbitration and in protecting the autonomy and operation of the arbitral process. During its 1995 term, for example, the Court decided four arbitration cases. It continues to grant *certiorari* in arbitration cases on a relatively frequent basis. The Court's interest in arbitration has generated a large number of rulings (more than two dozen high court opinions thus far)—the type and number of pronouncements usually reserved for questions that significantly affect the legal system and civil liberties (*e.g.*, the racial composition of juries in criminal cases or the use of illegal substances as part of religious practices). To parse Justice O'Conner, the Court, in effect, has built an edifice of arbitration law of its own making. *See Allied–Bruce Terminix Cos. v. Dobson*, 513 U.S. 265 (1995) (O'Connor, Justice, concurring) ("[O]ver the past decade, the Court has abandoned all pretense of ascertaining congressional intent with respect to the Federal Arbitration Act, building instead, case by case, an edifice of its own creation...."). As previously noted, the decisional law has modified substantially the express language and stated purpose of the FAA.

In its rulings, the Court has federalized the law of arbitration, requiring the FAA to be applied by federal courts sitting in diversity of jurisdiction cases, and by state courts (and—in effect—state legislatures) whenever interstate commerce (in some form) is involved in the dispute. Despite the express language contained in FAA § 1, the courts have ruled that the FAA governs employment contracts and authorizes arbitration in various consumer areas (HMOs, banking and brokerage services, and the purchase of goods, like computers). This is significantly more than the limitation to commercial and maritime matters expressed in Section One.

Furthermore, the Court has repeatedly emphasized the significance of contract freedom in the U.S. law of arbitration, stating in various cases that "[a]rbitration under the Act is a matter of consent, not coercion . . . ." *Volt Info. Sciences, Inc. v. Board of Trustees of Leland Stanford Junior Univ.*, 489 U.S. 468, 479 (1989). As a result, the provisions contained in an arbitration agreement have the force of law for the parties' transaction. By contract, the parties can even reverse the effect of federalization by providing for the application of a state law to their arbitration, even though the transaction involves interstate commerce and the state law contains provisions that conflict with the FAA. The parties can also modify the terms of the FAA itself through a written stipulation. For instance, the Court in *First Options of Chicago, Inc. v. Kaplan*, 514 U.S. 938 (1995), ruled that the parties could confer *kompetenz-kompetenz* authority upon the arbitrators if they agreed to remove contract inarbitrability questions from the jurisdiction of the courts under FAA Section Three, and authorized the arbitrators to rule on such matters. The contract for arbitration, therefore, can be the decisive source of law in U.S. arbitral practice.

Section Two is the most significant provision of the FAA. It legitimizes the process of arbitral adjudication and provides that agreements to arbitrate are a lawful exercise of the parties' freedom of contract rights. Section Two further states that arbitration agreements are subject to the ordinary defenses to contract validity. In its elaboration of an "emphatic" federal policy "favoring arbitration," the Court has virtually eliminated the defense of adhesion to the enforceability of arbitration agreements. Arbitral clauses that are imposed unilaterally by an economically dominant party without any possibility of negotiation or modification (for example, an agreement to arbitrate all workplace disputes in a non-union employment contract which is imposed by the employer upon employees as a pre-condition to employment or continued employment) are valid and enforceable agreements. According to the Court's interpretation of Section Two, it seems that the bargain for arbitration is—as a matter of law—always beneficial for the parties to the transaction regardless of whether they are aware of the contract provision for arbitration or voluntarily agree to it.

Finally, the Court's rulings on arbitration have had another salient consequence. There is virtually no subject-matter inarbitrability defense to the enforcement of arbitral agreements and awards under U.S. law. The Court interprets the federal policy supporting arbitration as mandating a "hospitable" approach to questions of arbitrability. Accordingly, all disputes arising under a contract—whether statutory or contractual in character—can be submitted to arbitration. The FAA does not contain an express or even implied restriction on the type of dispute that can be lawfully submitted to arbitration. *See Shearson/Am. Express, Inc. v. McMahon*, 482 U.S. 220 (1987); *Rodriguez de Quijas v. Shearson/Am. Express, Inc.*, 490 U.S. 477 (1989). As the Court correctly observes, the content of individual statutes establishes whether Congress intended disputes arising under them to be resolved exclusively through judicial processes. In the vast majority of cases, the Court never finds any statement of congressional policy clear enough to prevent parties from submitting disputes to arbitration. Moreover, the parties' disagreement about a statutory matter, the Court observes, has no consequences beyond the boundaries of their particular transaction. The law is applied to purely individual conduct and has no systemic effect. Most, if not all, claims arising under regulatory laws that apply to commercial conduct (securities regulation, antitrust, and RICO), those pertaining to federal statutes that create individual rights (*e.g.*, ADA, ADEA, ERISA, and Family Medical Leave Act), and those that implicate civil rights legislation (Title VII of the Civil Rights Act of 1964 as amended by the Civil Rights Act of 1991) which involve the individual liberties and freedoms guaranteed by the Bill of Rights and the U.S. Constitution, can, therefore, be submitted to arbitration—despite their direct link to public policy matters.

2. CONTRACT FREEDOM

The opinion in *Volt Information Sciences v. Board of Trustees of Leland Stanford Junior University*, 489 U.S. 468 (1989), introduced and emphasized the role of contract freedom in the Court's doctrine on arbitration. The Court applied the freedom of contract principle in two subsequent cases. The first, *Mastrobuono v. Shearson Lehman Hutton, Inc.*, 514 U.S. 52 (1995), generated a strong, albeit solitary, dissent. To some degree, the decision in *Mastrobuono* contradicts the reasoning and the ruling in *Volt*, yet endorses its view of the significance of contract freedom in the law of arbitration. The second case, *First Options of Chicago, Inc. v. Kaplan*, 514 U.S. 938 (1995), a unanimous opinion, is also a significant decision. The Court defines with greater specificity the role of freedom of contract in arbitration and explores in greater detail the consequences of its position upon the legal regulation of arbitration.

Mastrobuono

Mastrobuono falls squarely within the orbit of the Court's federalization policy. Despite *Mastrobuono*'s factual and decisional similarity to *Volt*, the Court rules against the application of state law. In doing so, the Court places a qualification upon the freedom of contract principle articulated in *Volt*. In effect, after *Mastrobuono,* party choice as to state law will be fully respected only when the choice-of-law fosters the recourse to arbitration or when the parties have expressly recognized that the state law contains a restriction on the right to arbitrate and expressly agree that the restriction is applicable to their arbitration.

The plaintiffs in *Mastrobuono* opened a securities account with Shearson Lehman Hutton and signed a standard client's agreement. Paragraph thirteen of that agreement contained an arbitral clause under which the parties agreed to resolve disputes through NASD arbitration. It also provided for the application of New York law to the agreement. After closing the account, the plaintiffs filed suit alleging that Shearson personnel mishandled their funds. The brokerage company, however, prevailed on its motion to stay the court proceeding and to compel arbitration.

Thereafter, an arbitral tribunal awarded the plaintiffs $160,000 in compensatory damages and $400,000 in punitive damages. Shearson appealed, arguing that New York law governed the arbitral proceeding and that the rule in *Garrity v. Lyle Stuart, Inc.*, 40 N.Y.2d 354, 386 N.Y.S.2d 831, 353 N.E.2d 793 (1976), a landmark case, prohibited the arbitrators from awarding punitive damages. The U.S. Supreme Court granted *certiorari* to consider whether "a contractual choice-of-law provision may preclude an arbitral award of punitive damages that otherwise would be proper." The Court held in the negative, reversing the federal district court and Seventh Circuit Court of Appeals, which had held that the arbitral tribunal had no authority to award punitive damages given the provisions of the controlling New York law.

Through Justice Stevens, the majority opinion initially established that the reference to arbitration is a matter of contract choice. The purpose of the judicial implementation of the FAA is to enforce arbitration agreements as written. The Court cited language from *Volt* to sustain its interpretation of the federal legislation:

> "But it does not follow that the FAA prevents the enforcement of agreements to arbitrate under different rules than those set forth in the Act itself. Indeed, such a result would be quite inimical to the FAA's primary purpose of ensuring that private agreements to arbitrate are enforced according to their terms. *Arbitration under the act is a matter of consent, not coercion,* and parties are generally free to structure their arbitration agreements as they see fit. Just as they may limit by contract the issues which they will arbitrate... so too may they specify by contract the rules under which that arbitration will be conducted." 514 U.S. at 57 (emphasis added) (quoting *Volt*, 489 U.S. at 479).

The majority opinion in *Mastrobuono* then asserted that the doctrine in *Volt* sustained its determination.

MASTROBUONO v. SHEARSON LEHMAN HUTTON, INC.

514 U.S. 52, 115 S.Ct. 1212, 131 L.Ed.2d 76 (1995).

(footnotes omitted)

JUSTICE STEVENS delivered the opinion of the Court.

New York law allows courts, but not arbitrators, to award punitive damages. In a dispute arising out of a standard-form contract that expressly provides that it "shall be governed by the laws of the State of New York," a panel of arbitrators awarded punitive damages. The District Court and Court of Appeals disallowed that award. The question presented is whether the arbitrators' award is consistent with the central purpose of the Federal Arbitration Act to ensure "that private agreements to arbitrate are enforced according to their terms." *Volt Information Sciences, Inc.*...

[. . .]

II

Earlier this Term, we upheld the enforceability of a predispute arbitration agreement governed by Alabama law, even though an Alabama statute provides that arbitration agreements are unenforceable.... After determining that the FAA applied to the parties' arbitration agreement, we readily concluded that the federal statute pre-empted Alabama's statutory prohibition....

Petitioners seek a similar disposition of the case before us today. Here, the Seventh Circuit interpreted the contract to incorporate New York law, including the *Garrity* rule that arbitrators may not award punitive damages. Petitioners ask us to hold that the FAA pre-empts New York's prohibition against arbitral awards of punitive damages because this state law is a vestige of the " 'ancient' " judicial hostility to arbitration.... Petitioners rely on *Southland Corp. v. Keating*...and *Perry v. Thomas*..., in which we held that the FAA pre-empted two California statutes that purported to require judicial resolution of certain disputes. In *Southland*, we explained that the FAA not only "declared a national policy favoring arbitration," but actually "withdrew the power of the states to require a judicial forum for the resolution of claims which the contracting parties agreed to resolve by arbitration."...

Respondents answer that the choice-of-law provision in their contract evidences the parties' express agreement that punitive damages should not be awarded in the arbitration of any dispute arising under their contract. Thus, they claim, this case is distinguishable from *Southland* and *Perry*, in which the parties presumably desired unlimited arbitration but state law stood in their way. Regardless of whether the FAA pre-empts the *Garrity* decision in contracts not expressly incorporating New York law, respondents argue that the parties may themselves agree to be bound by *Garrity*, just as they may agree to forgo arbitration altogether. In other words, if the contract says "no punitive damages," that is the end of the matter, for courts are bound to interpret contracts in accordance with the expressed intentions of the parties—even if the effect of those intentions is to limit arbitration.

We have previously held that the FAA's pro-arbitration policy does not operate without regard to the wishes of the contracting parties. In *Volt Information Sciences, Inc.,*...the California Court of Appeal had construed a contractual provision to mean that the parties intended the California rules of arbitration, rather than the FAA's rules, to govern the resolution of their dispute.... Noting that the California rules were "manifestly designed to encourage resort to the arbitral process,"...and that they "generally foster[ed] the federal policy favoring arbitration,"...we concluded that such an interpretation was entirely consistent with the federal policy "to ensure the enforceability, according to their terms, of private agreements to arbitrate."... After referring to the holdings in *Southland*

and *Perry*, which struck down state laws limiting agreed-upon arbitrability, we added:

> "But it does not follow that the FAA prevents the enforcement of agreements to arbitrate under different rules than those set forth in the Act itself. Indeed, such a result would be quite inimical to the FAA's primary purpose of ensuring that private agreements to arbitrate are enforced according to their terms. Arbitration under the Act is a matter of consent, not coercion, and parties are generally free to structure their arbitration agreements as they see fit. Just as they may limit by contract the issues which they will arbitrate...so too may they specify by contract the rules under which that arbitration will be conducted." *Volt*, 489 U.S. at 479.

Relying on our reasoning in *Volt*, respondents thus argue that the parties to a contract may lawfully agree to limit the issues to be arbitrated by waiving any claim for punitive damages. On the other hand, we think our decisions in *Allied-Bruce*, *Southland*, and *Perry* make clear that if contracting parties agree to include claims for punitive damages within the issues to be arbitrated, the FAA ensures that their agreement will be enforced according to its terms even if a rule of state law would otherwise exclude such claims from arbitration. Thus, the case before us comes down to what the contract has to say about the arbitrability of petitioners' claim for punitive damages.

III

Shearson's standard-form "Client Agreement," which petitioners executed, contains 18 paragraphs. The two relevant provisions of the agreement are found in Paragraph 13. The first sentence of that paragraph provides, in part, that the entire agreement "shall be governed by the laws of the State of New York.".... The second sentence provides that "any controversy" arising out of the transactions between the parties "shall be settled by arbitration" in accordance with the rules of the National Association of Securities Dealers (NASD), or the Boards of Directors of the New York Stock Exchange and/or the American Stock Exchange.... The agreement contains no express reference to claims for punitive damages.

The choice-of-law provision, when viewed in isolation, may reasonably be read as merely a substitute for the conflict-of-laws analysis that otherwise would determine what law to apply to disputes arising out of the contractual relationship. Thus, if a similar contract, without a choice-of-law provision, had been signed in New York and was to be performed in New York, presumably "the laws of the State of New York" would apply, even though the contract did not expressly so state. In such event, there would be nothing in the contract that could possibly constitute evidence of an intent to exclude punitive damages claims. Accordingly, punitive damages would be allowed because, in the absence of contractual intent to the contrary, the FAA would pre-empt the *Garrity* rule....

Even if the reference to "the laws of the State of New York" is more than a substitute for ordinary conflict-of-laws analysis and, as respondents urge, includes the caveat, "detached from otherwise-applicable federal law," the provision might not preclude the award of punitive damages because New York allows its courts, though not its arbitrators, to enter such awards.... In other words, the provision might include only New York's substantive rights and obligations, and not the State's allocation of power between alternative tribunals. Respondents' argument is persuasive only if "New York law" means "New York decisional law, including that State's allocation of power between courts and arbitrators, notwithstanding otherwise-applicable federal law." But, as we have demonstrated, the provision need not be read so broadly. It is not, in itself, an unequivocal exclusion of punitive damages claims.

The arbitration provision (the second sentence of Paragraph 13) does not improve respondents' argument. On the contrary, when read separately this clause strongly implies that an arbitral award of punitive damages is appropriate. It explicitly authorizes arbitration in accordance with NASD rules; the panel of arbitrators in fact proceeded under that set of rules. The NASD's Code of Arbitration Procedure indicates that arbitrators may award "damages and other relief." NASD Code of Arbitration Procedure 3741(e) (1993). While not a clear authorization of punitive damages, this provision appears broad enough at least to contemplate such a remedy. Moreover, as the Seventh Circuit noted, a manual provided to NASD arbitrators contains this provision:

"B. Punitive Damages

"The issue of punitive damages may arise with great frequency in arbitrations. Parties to arbitration are informed that arbitrators can consider punitive damages as a remedy."...

Thus, the text of the arbitration clause itself surely does not support—indeed, it contradicts—the conclusion that the parties agreed to foreclose claims for punitive damages.

Although neither the choice-of-law clause nor the arbitration clause, separately considered, expresses an intent to preclude an award of punitive damages, respondents argue that a fair reading of the entire Paragraph 13 leads to that conclusion. On this theory, even if "New York law" is ambiguous, and even if "arbitration in accordance with NASD rules" indicates that punitive damages are permissible, the juxtaposition of the two clauses suggests that the contract incorporates "New York law relating to arbitration." We disagree. At most, the choice-of-law clause introduces an ambiguity into an arbitration agreement that would otherwise allow punitive damages awards. As we pointed out in *Volt*, when a court interprets such provisions in an agreement covered by the FAA, "due regard must be given to the federal policy favoring arbitration, and ambiguities as to the scope of the arbitration clause itself resolved in favor of arbitration."...

Moreover, respondents cannot overcome the common-law rule of contract interpretation that a court should construe ambiguous language against the interest of the party that drafted it....

[. . .]

We hold that the Court of Appeals misinterpreted the parties' agreement. The arbitral award should have been enforced as within the scope of the contract. The judgment of the Court of Appeals is, therefore, reversed.

It is so ordered.

JUSTICE THOMAS, dissenting.

In *Volt Information Sciences, Inc.,* . . . we held that the Federal Arbitration Act . . . simply requires courts to enforce private contracts to arbitrate as they would normal contracts—according to their terms. This holding led us to enforce a choice-of-law provision that incorporated a state procedural rule concerning arbitration proceedings. Because the choice-of-law provision here cannot reasonably be distinguished from the one in *Volt*, I dissent.

I

A

[. . .]

[In *Volt*], [w]e concluded that even if the FAA preempted the state statute as applied to other parties, the choice-of-law clause in the contract at issue demonstrated that the parties had agreed to be governed by the statute. Rejecting Volt's position that the FAA imposes a pro-arbitration policy that precluded enforcement of the statute permitting the California courts to stay the arbitration proceedings, we concluded that the Act "simply requires courts to enforce privately negotiated agreements to arbitrate, like other contracts, in accordance with their terms." . . . As a result, we interpreted the choice-of-law clause "to make applicable state rules governing the conduct of arbitration" . . . even if a specific rule itself hampers or delays arbitration. We rejected the argument that the choice-of-law clause was to be construed as incorporating only substantive law, and dismissed the claim that the FAA preempted those contract provisions that might hinder arbitration.

We so held in *Volt* because we concluded that the FAA does not force arbitration on parties who enter into contracts involving interstate commerce. Instead, the FAA requires only that "arbitration proceed in the manner provided for in [the parties'] agreement." . . . Although we will construe ambiguities concerning the scope of arbitrability in favor of arbitration, . . . we remain mindful that "as with any other contract, the parties' intentions control." . . . Thus, if the parties intend that state procedure shall govern, federal courts must enforce that understanding. "There is no federal policy favoring arbitration under a certain set of procedural rules; the federal policy is simply to ensure the enforceability, according to their terms, of private agreements to arbitrate." *Volt*. . . .

B

In this case, as in *Volt*, the parties agreed to mandatory arbitration of all disputes. As in *Volt*, the contract at issue here includes a choice-of-law clause. Indeed, the language of the two clauses is functionally equivalent: whereas the choice-of-law clause in *Volt* provided that "[t]he Contract shall be governed by the law of [the State of California]," the one before us today states, in Paragraph 13 of the Client's Agreement, that "[t]his agreement...shall be governed by the laws of the State of New York." New York law forbids arbitrators from awarding punitive damages...and permits only courts to award such damages. As in *Volt*, petitioners here argue that the New York rule is "anti-arbitration," and hence is pre-empted by the FAA. In concluding that the choice-of-law clause is ambiguous, the majority essentially accepts petitioners' argument. *Volt* itself found precisely the same argument irrelevant, however, and the majority identifies no reason to think that the state law governing the interpretation of the parties' choice-of-law clause supports a different result.

The majority claims that the incorporation of New York law "need not be read so broadly" as to include both substantive and procedural law, and that the choice of New York law "is not, in itself, an unequivocal exclusion of punitive damages claims." ...But we rejected these same arguments in *Volt*, and the *Garrity* rule is just the sort of "state rule[ ] governing the conduct of arbitration" that Volt requires federal courts to enforce.... "Just as [the parties] may limit by contract the issues which they will arbitrate, so too may they specify by contract the rules under which that arbitration will be conducted."... To be sure, the majority might be correct that *Garrity* is a rule concerning the State's allocation of power between "alternative tribunals,"...although *Garrity* appears to describe itself as substantive New York law. Nonetheless, *Volt* makes no distinction between rules that serve only to distribute authority between courts and arbitrators (which the majority finds unenforceable) and other types of rules (which the majority finds enforceable). Indeed, the California rule in *Volt* could be considered to be one that allocates authority between arbitrators and courts, for it permits California courts to stay arbitration pending resolution of related litigation....

II

The majority relies upon two assertions to defend its departure from *Volt*. First, it contends that "[a]t most, the choice-of-law clause introduces an ambiguity into an arbitration agreement."... We are told that the agreement "would otherwise allow punitive damages awards," because of Paragraph 13's statement that arbitration would be conducted "in accordance with the rules then in effect, of the National Association of Securities Dealers, Inc." It is unclear which NASD "rules" the parties mean, although I am willing to agree with the majority that the phrase refers to the NASD Code of Arbitration Procedure. But the provision of the NASD Code offered by the majority simply does not speak to the availability of punitive damages. It only states:

> "The award shall contain the names of the parties, the name of counsel, if any, a summary of the issues, including the type(s) of any security or product, in controversy, the damages and other relief requested, the

damages and other relief awarded, a statement of any other issues resolved, the names of the arbitrators, the dates the claim was filed and the award rendered, the number and dates of hearing sessions, the location of the hearings, and the signatures of the arbitrators concurring in the award." NASD Code of Arbitration Procedure § 41(e) (1985).

It is clear that § 41(e) does not define or limit the powers of the arbitrators; it merely describes the form in which the arbitrators must announce their decision. The other provisions of § 41 confirm this point.... The majority cannot find a provision of the NASD Code that specifically addresses punitive damages, or that speaks more generally to the types of damages arbitrators may or may not allow. Such a rule simply does not exist. The Code certainly does not require that arbitrators be empowered to award punitive damages; it leaves to the parties to define the arbitrators' remedial powers.

The majority also purports to find a clear expression of the parties' agreement on the availability of punitive damages in "a manual provided to NASD arbitrators."... But Paragraph 13 of the Client Agreement nowhere mentions this manual; it mentions only "the rules then in effect of the [NASD]." The manual does not fit either part of this description: it is neither "of the [NASD]," nor a set of "rules."

First, the manual apparently is not an official NASD document. The manual was not promulgated or adopted by the NASD. Instead, it apparently was compiled by members of the Securities Industry Conference on Arbitration (SICA) as a supplement to the Uniform Code of Arbitration, which the parties clearly did not adopt in Paragraph 13. Petitioners present no evidence that the NASD has a policy of giving this specific manual to its arbitrators. Nor do petitioners assert that this manual was even used in the arbitration that gave rise to this case. More importantly, there is no indication in the text of the Client's Agreement that the parties intended this manual to be used by the arbitrators.

Second, the manual does not provide any "rules" in the sense contemplated by Paragraph 13; instead, it provides general information and advice to the arbitrator, such as "Hints for the Chair."... The manual is nothing more than a sort of "how to" guide for the arbitrator. One bit of advice, for example, states: "Care should be exercised, particularly when questioning a witness, so that the arbitrator does not indicate disbelief. Grimaces, frowns, or hand signals should all be avoided. A 'poker' face is the goal."...

Even if the parties had intended to adopt the manual, it cannot be read to resolve the issue of punitive damages. When read in context, the portion of the SICA manual upon which the majority relies seems only to explain what punitive damages are, not to establish whether arbitrators have the authority to award them....

[...]

My examination of the Client Agreement, the choice-of-law provision, the NASD Code of Procedure, and the SICA manual demonstrates that the parties made their intent clear, but not in the way divined by the majority. New York law specifically precludes arbitrators from awarding punitive damages, and it should be clear that there is no "conflict," as the majority puts it, between the New York law and the NASD rules. The choice-of-law provision speaks directly to the issue, while the NASD Code is silent. Giving effect to every provision of the contract requires us to honor the parties' intent, as indicated in the text of the agreement, to preclude the award of punitive damages by arbitrators.

III

Thankfully, the import of the majority's decision is limited and narrow. This case amounts to nothing more than a federal court applying Illinois and New York contract law to an agreement between parties in Illinois. Much like a federal court applying a state rule of decision to a case when sitting in diversity, the majority's interpretation of the contract represents only the understanding of a single federal court regarding the requirements imposed by state law. As such, the majority's opinion has applicability only to this specific contract and to no other. But because the majority reaches an erroneous result on even this narrow question, I respectfully dissent.

NOTES AND QUESTIONS

1. The majority and dissenting opinions have dramatically different interpretations of the applicable precedent. For the majority, *Volt* sustains the result reached in *Mastrobuono*, while the dissent believes that the cases as decided cannot be reconciled. Which view of the decisional reality do you find more persuasive and why? How would you describe the holding in *Volt* and its relationship to *Mastrobuono*? Does an underlying conflict on policy or judicial construction provide a better explanation of the differing characterizations of the law? Is there an implied consumer protection issue involved in the debate?

2. What is the doctrinal status and content of the Court's contract freedom view of arbitration after the ruling in *Mastrobuono*?

3. In very strained reasoning, the Court stated that an independent "conflict-of-laws analysis" might point to the application of New York law, but would preclude the application of the New York bar on the award of punitive damages by arbitrators because the parties had not expressly decided to exclude such damages in their agreement, thereby making the state law provision subject to pre-exemption by the federalization policy. Moreover, even if the parties intended New York law to govern their contractual obligations, including their reference to arbitration, the choice of New York law would "include only New York's substantive rights and obligations, and not the state's allocation of power between alternative tribunals." Further, "[w]e think the best way to harmonize the choice-of-law provision with the arbitration provision is to read 'the laws of the State of New York' to encompass substantive principles that New York courts would apply, but not to include special rules limiting the authority of arbitrators. Thus, the choice-of-law provision covers the rights and duties of the parties, while the arbitra-

tion clause covers arbitration. . . ." The distinction is clear and imaginatively drawn, but acts only to justify a foregone conclusion.

4. Further, the Court argued that the reference in the agreement to NASD arbitration rules provided some justification for allowing the arbitrators to award punitive damages. Suffice it to state that the NASD Code of Arbitration Procedure, although it refers to the question of punitive damages in arbitration, does not establish a clear institutional rule on that score. As the Court itself admits, "[w]hile not a clear authorization of punitive damages, this provision appears broad enough at least to contemplate such a remedy." Finally, equity demands that the cost and burden of the contract ambiguity be shouldered by the party opposing the award of punitive damages when that party drafted the contract and created the ambiguity between the choice-of-law and arbitration provisions. "The reason for this rule is to protect the party who did not choose the language from an unintended or unfair result." And, "the choice-of-law clause introduces an ambiguity into an arbitration agreement that would otherwise allow punitive damages awards."

5. Justice Thomas' dissenting analysis is trenchant and comprehensive. How do you evaluate his response to the majority position that the choice of New York law did not include the allocation of power to alternative tribunals? Which side of the Court has the more accurate appraisal of the NASD Code of Arbitration Procedure and the SICA manual? Is there deliberate distortion on the part of the majority? Can its position be squared with the facts?

6. Finally, you should consider the general question of whether arbitrators can be authorized, by law or by contract, to award punitive damages. How would you support the *Garrity* rule and how would you argue against it? As a matter of public policy, should parties be able to contract about the right?

Kaplan

In *Kaplan*, the Court holds that courts rather than arbitral tribunals have jurisdiction to resolve questions of arbitrability (presumably, contract inarbitrability: Whether a contract of arbitration exists and covers a specific dispute or set of disputes), unless the agreement to arbitrate provides that the arbitral tribunal has the authority to decide the matter. To buttress its determination, the Court espouses expressly a contract freedom view of arbitration and of arbitration law in general, under which the contract of arbitration can basically function as a completely self-contained system of arbitration law. This view of arbitration reduces matters of arbitration and the public interest in adjudication to a question of contractual consent between the parties in individual cases.

The Kaplans were private investors and the owners of an investment company (MKI). They, individually, and MKI, as a separate business entity, incurred substantial losses during the October 1987 stock market crash and thereafter in other stock transactions. First Options, a brokerage firm that clears stock trades on the Philadelphia Stock Exchange, was their creditor. First Options, MKI, and the Kaplans entered into four "work out" agreements to repay the debts, only one of which (between

First Options and MKI) contained an arbitration agreement. When efforts to collect the debts failed, First Options filed a demand for arbitration against MKI and the Kaplans. The Kaplans refused to submit to arbitration and challenged the agreement to arbitrate. The arbitral tribunal nonetheless asserted jurisdiction and rendered an award against both MKI and the Kaplans. The question submitted to the Court was whether the arbitral tribunal had jurisdiction to adjudicate the disputes between First Options and the Kaplans.

The Court was unanimous in its resolution of the question. The Court's reasoning can be divided into three basic and inter-related parts. First, the Court—seemingly modifying, deserting, or forgetting its position that arbitration is a "mere form of trial"—acknowledges the "practical importance" of the arbitrability question to the party opposing arbitration, recognizing that arbitration involves the abandonment of the right to the judicial resolution of disputes. Second, it declares that the courts (rather than arbitral tribunals) have primary authority to resolve the arbitrability question, grounding its holding in and portraying its determination as a standard of review question. Finally, in a substantially, if not completely, contradictory corollary, the Court proclaims the contract of arbitration as the true source of final authority on the arbitrability question.

At the outset of the opinion, the Court describes the arbitrability question as a narrow concern, but concedes that it "has a certain practical significance." In particular, who decides whether there is a legal basis for compelling the parties to arbitrate can make "a critical difference" to the party resisting arbitration. By agreeing to arbitrate, a party abandons the right to obtain a judicial resolution of contractual disputes, even though some limited judicial supervision of arbitral awards is available. The Court now appears to believe that the waiver of rights gives the arbitrability question importance because it signifies that the parties, in effect, have chosen a form of justice other than judicial justice.

As a consequence, the Court concludes that the "emphatic federal policy" favoring arbitration does not govern the arbitrability question. In fact, on the threshold matter of arbitrability, the appropriate standard of review consists of a fully independent form of judicial review that replaces the normally "hospitable" federal court "inquiry" into issues of arbitration law. While all other arbitration questions are governed by the favorable federal policy, the Court believes that substantial unfairness would result if an unwilling, and—more importantly—an unobligated, party were forced to arbitrate. The Court creates a presumption that the arbitrability question is to be decided by the courts. To rebut the presumption, the party seeking to submit the arbitrability question to arbitration must submit persuasive evidence of the parties' agreement to have recourse to arbitration on the question of arbitrability. "Courts should not assume that the parties agreed to arbitrate arbitrability unless there is 'clear and unmistakable' evidence that they did so."

The two basic substantive segments of the *Kaplan* holding cannot coexist. On the one hand, the Court views arbitrability as a critical rights determination and mandates judicial disposition of the issue; on the other hand, it rules that the question, no matter how significant, can be reassigned to arbitral disposition through the vehicle of a private contract. At this point, none of the Court's complex reasoning on the standard of review question matters because arbitration clauses (especially adhesionary ones) will now routinely include a reference of arbitrability questions to the arbitral tribunal. In the consumer and commercial context, courts will simply be excluded from the jurisdictional phase of arbitration by party agreement. The power of a contract clearly trumps the judicial authority to supervise or decide any aspect of arbitration law.

FIRST OPTIONS OF CHICAGO, INC. v. KAPLAN

514 U.S. 938, 115 S.Ct. 1920, 131 L.Ed.2d 985 (1995).

(footnotes omitted)

JUSTICE BREYER delivered the opinion of the Court.

In this case we consider two questions about how courts should review certain matters under the [F]ederal Arbitration Act . . . : (1) how a district court should review an arbitrator's decision that the parties agreed to arbitrate a dispute, and (2) how a court of appeals should review a district court's decision confirming, or refusing to vacate, an arbitration award.

I

[. . .]

We granted *certiorari* to consider two questions regarding the standards that the Court of Appeals used to review the determination that the Kaplans' dispute with First Options was arbitrable. . . . First, the Court of Appeals said that courts "should independently decide whether an arbitration panel has jurisdiction over the merits of any particular dispute." . . . First Options asked us to decide whether this is so (*i.e.*, whether courts, in "reviewing the arbitrators' decision on arbitrability," should "apply a *de novo* standard of review or the more deferential standard applied to arbitrators' decisions on the merits") when the objecting party "submitted the issue to the arbitrators for decision." . . . Second, the Court of Appeals stated that it would review a district court's denial of a motion to vacate a commercial arbitration award (and the correlative grant of a motion to confirm it) "*de novo*." . . . First Options argues that the Court of Appeals instead should have applied an "abuse of discretion" standard. . . .

II

The first question—the standard of review applied to an arbitrator's decision about arbitrability—is a narrow one. To understand just how narrow, consider three types of disagreement present in this case. First, the Kaplans and First Options disagree about whether the Kaplans are personally liable for MKI's debt to First Options. That disagreement makes up the *merits* of the dispute. Second, they disagree about whether they agreed to arbitrate the merits. That disagreement is about the *arbitrability* of the dispute. Third, they disagree about *who should have the primary power to decide the second matter*. Does that power belong primarily to the arbitrators (because the court reviews their arbitrability decision deferentially) or to the court (because the court makes up its mind about arbitrability independently)? We consider here only this third question.

Although the question is a narrow one, it has a certain practical importance. That is because a party who has not agreed to arbitrate will normally have a right to a court's decision about the merits of its dispute (say, as here, its obligation under a contract). But, where the party has agreed to arbitrate, he or she, in effect, has relinquished much of that right's practical value. The party still can ask a court to review the arbitrator's decision, but the court will set that decision aside only in very unusual circumstances.... Hence, who—court or arbitrator—has the primary authority to decide whether a party has agreed to arbitrate can make a critical difference to a party resisting arbitration.

We believe the answer to the "who" question (*i.e.*, the standard-of-review question) is fairly simple. Just as the arbitrability of the merits of a dispute depends upon whether the parties agreed to arbitrate that dispute...so the question "who has the primary power to decide arbitrability" turns upon what the parties agreed about *that* matter. Did the parties agree to submit the arbitrability question itself to arbitration? If so, then the court's standard for reviewing the arbitrator's decision about that matter should not differ from the standard courts apply when they review any other matter that parties have agreed to arbitrate.... That is to say, the court should give considerable leeway to the arbitrator, setting aside his or her decision only in certain narrow circumstances.... If, on the other hand, the parties did not agree to submit the arbitrability question itself to arbitration, then the court should decide that question just as it would decide any other question that the parties did not submit to arbitration, namely independently. These two answers flow inexorably from the fact that arbitration is simply a matter of contract between the parties; it is a way to resolve those disputes—but only those disputes—that the parties have agreed to submit to arbitration....

We agree with First Options, therefore, that a court must defer to an arbitrator's arbitrability decision when the parties submitted that matter to arbitration. Nevertheless, that conclusion does not help First Options win this case. That is because a fair and complete answer to the standard-of-review question requires a word about how a court should decide whether the parties have agreed to submit the arbitrability issue to arbitration. And, that word makes clear that the Kaplans did not agree to arbitrate arbitrability here.

When deciding whether the parties agreed to arbitrate a certain matter (including arbitrability), courts generally (though with a qualification we discuss below) should apply ordinary state-law principles that govern the formation of contracts. . . . The relevant state law here, for example, would require the court to see whether the parties objectively revealed an intent to submit the arbitrability issue to arbitration. . . .

This Court, however, has (as we just said) added an important qualification, applicable when courts decide whether a party has agreed that arbitrators should decide arbitrability: Courts should not assume that the parties agreed to arbitrate arbitrability unless there is "clea[r] and unmistakabl[e]" evidence that they did so. In this manner the law treats silence or ambiguity about the question "*who* (primarily) should decide arbitrability" differently from the way it treats silence or ambiguity about the question "*whether* a particular merits-related dispute is arbitrable because it is within the scope of a valid arbitration agreement"—for in respect to this latter question the law reverses the presumption. . . .

But, this difference in treatment is understandable. The latter question arises when the parties have a contract that provides for arbitration of some issues. In such circumstances, the parties likely gave at least some thought to the scope of arbitration. And, given the law's permissive policies in respect to arbitration . . . one can understand why the law would insist upon clarity before concluding that the parties did not want to arbitrate a related matter. . . . On the other hand, the former question—the "who (primarily) should decide arbitrability" question—is rather arcane. A party often might not focus upon that question or upon the significance of having arbitrators decide the scope of their own powers. . . . And, given the principle that a party can be forced to arbitrate only those issues it specifically has agreed to submit to arbitration, one can understand why courts might hesitate to interpret silence or ambiguity on the "who should decide arbitrability" point as giving the arbitrators that power, for doing so might too often force unwilling parties to arbitrate a matter they reasonably would have thought a judge, not an arbitrator, would decide. . . .

On the record before us, First Options cannot show that the Kaplans clearly agreed to have the arbitrators decide (*i.e.*, to arbitrate) the question of arbitrability. . . .

[. . .]

We conclude that, because the Kaplans did not clearly agree to submit the question of arbitrability to arbitration, the Court of Appeals was correct in finding that the arbitrability of the Kaplan/First Options dispute was subject to independent review by the courts.

III

We turn next to the standard a court of appeals should apply when reviewing a district court decision that refuses to vacate . . . or confirms . . . an arbitration award. . . .

[. . .]

We believe...that the majority of Circuits is right in saying that courts of appeals should apply ordinary, not special, standards when reviewing district court decisions upholding arbitration awards. For one thing, it is undesirable to make the law more complicated by proliferating review standards without good reasons. More importantly, the reviewing attitude that a court of appeals takes toward a district court decision should depend upon "the respective institutional advantages of trial and appellate courts," not upon what standard of review will more likely produce a particular substantive result.... The law, for example, tells all courts (trial and appellate) to give administrative agencies a degree of legal leeway when they review certain interpretations of the law that those agencies have made.... But, no one, to our knowledge, has suggested that this policy of giving leeway to agencies means that a court of appeals should give extra leeway to a district court decision that upholds an agency. Similarly, courts grant arbitrators considerable leeway when reviewing most arbitration decisions; but that fact does not mean that appellate courts should give extra leeway to district courts that uphold arbitrators. First Options argues that the Arbitration Act is special because the Act, in one section, allows courts of appeals to conduct interlocutory review of certain antiarbitration district court rulings (*e.g.,* orders enjoining arbitrations), but not those upholding arbitration (*e.g.,* orders refusing to enjoin arbitrations).... But that portion of the Act governs the timing of review; it is therefore too weak a support for the distinct claim that the court of appeals should use a different standard when reviewing certain district court decisions. The Act says nothing about standards of review.

We conclude that the Court of Appeals used the proper standards for reviewing the District Court's arbitrability determinations.

[. . .]

The judgment of the Court of Appeals is affirmed.

It is so ordered.

NOTES AND QUESTIONS

1. *Kaplan* is a unanimous decision by the Court and represents a significant, albeit confusing, addition to the Court's case law on arbitration. Given the reasoning in *Kaplan* and in the prior case law, is it fair to say that the U.S. law on arbitration lacks a cohesive doctrinal architecture? The law appears to result from episodic doctrinal inventions in individual cases. Why has the court suddenly focused upon and developed this contract freedom view of arbitration? What does it add to the "edifice" of case law on the topic?

2. Despite its relative brevity, the opinion—in its presentation and definition of the issues and articulation of a solution—is a good example of judicial rhetoric. Justice Breyer relies heavily upon logic to articulate a justification for the result, but the text is profoundly disjointed. The reasoning

is opaque and confusing and—in the end—sustains an illogical determination. The opinion focuses upon an obtuse standard of review question and avoids assessing (perhaps deliberately) the significance of the question addressed to the law of arbitration.

3. First Options argued that appellate review of district court decisions on arbitration should be based upon the lax "abuse of discretion" standard. How might that standard be a suitable basis for judicial review in matters of arbitration? Why does the Court not agree?

4. At the outset of the opinion, the Court appears to imply a distinction between subject-matter and contract inarbitrability. From a doctrinal standpoint, is it appropriate to have the distinction turn on a question of the arbitration agreement's scope of application? Can or should the parties be able to exclude juridical principles and judicial functions entirely from their arbitration through the agreement to arbitrate? Should determining whether an arbitration agreement exists be a nondelegable judicial function? Why or why not? Under the *Kaplan* contract freedom view, could the parties to an agreement waive the application of Section Ten or any other provision of the FAA or of law? Could they require that awards be reviewed on the merits or *de novo*?

5. Do you agree with the Court that arbitration "is simply a matter of contract between the parties"? Is this an overstatement? What regulatory role remains for the law under this view?

6. Assess the implications of the following statement upon the law of arbitration. The statement is from the Court's discussion of appropriate standards of judicial review: "[I]t is undesirable to make the law more complicated by proliferating review standards without good reasons." Is the machinery of law and of rights protection simply too cumbersome to implement? How does the ADR philosophy fit into the statement?

7. The question of arbitrability is central to the legal regulation of arbitration. It involves, in some instances, determining whether a valid arbitration agreement exists and, if so, whether it covers the dispute in question. As the Court itself observes, the agreement's validity and scope of application establish the boundary between judicial and arbitral jurisdiction, between public and private adjudication, and represent the parties' willingness to waive their legal right to judicial relief. Given the importance of the choice, it would seem that the law should determine when it has been made.

In *Kaplan*, the Court had the opportunity to integrate the *kompetenz-kompetenz* doctrine into the U.S. law of arbitration. It does so indirectly by holding that arbitrators can rule upon the validity and scope of arbitration agreements, if the arbitration agreement authorizes them to rule on these matters. For all intents and purposes, the *Kaplan* holding amounts to an adoption of the *kompetenz-kompetenz* doctrine on an *ad hoc*, contract basis. It is, however, curious that the Court neither refers to the *kompetenz-kompetenz* doctrine nor acknowledges the relevance of Section Three of the FAA, which provides for court determination of contract inarbitrability questions.

Consideration is again diverted from the basic issues of arbitration law to the more traditional and familiar judicial question of the appropriate standard of review (as it applies to this particular question of arbitration law). Moreover, the Court does not draw an express distinction between subject-matter and contract inarbitrability, although both, one suspects given the tenor of the opinion, could be governed by the contract of arbitration. In effect, *Kaplan* proclaims that the contract of arbitration is the sovereign source of law between the parties in matters of arbitration.

8. In a subsequent case, *Maye v. Smith Barney, Inc.*, 897 F.Supp. 100, 105 n.3 (S.D.N.Y. 1995), a federal judge made the following observation about *Kaplan*:

> In some of its previous decisions, the Supreme Court held that a party's allegation that there had been fraud in the inducement of the entire contract, although the alleged fraud did not go to the arbitration clause in particular, was itself an issue to be resolved by the arbitrator.... It is somewhat unclear whether this rule is of continuing vitality in light of the holding in *First Options* that the question of whether the parties ever made an agreement to arbitrate is generally to be decided by the courts.

Is the suggestion accurate? Does *Kaplan* effectively overrule or render ineffective part of the holding in *Prima Paint*? What does the judge's observation say about the evolution and content of the Court's doctrine on arbitration? Is there some misunderstanding here that proceeds from the lack of a cohesive doctrinal architecture?

9. For a curious twist on the *First Options of Chicago, Inc.* doctrine, see *Awuah v. Coverall North Am. Inc.*, 554 F.3d 7 (2009). There, the court entertained the argument that "the arbitral forum [was] illusory" in the circumstances of a franchise agreement between Coverall and its Franchisees. The latter were mostly recent immigrants who had agreed to provide janitorial cleaning services. They were ill-educated, had poor linguistic skills, and very limited resources. They sued for a litany of contract claims and Coverall sought to compel arbitration pursuant to the franchise agreement. The question ostensibly before the court of appeals was who (a court of or an arbitrator) would decide whether the arbitration agreement was unconscionable.

The contract provided for arbitration under the AAA Rules. AAA Rule 7 (a) "codifies" *Kaplan* and generally the *kompetenz-kompetenz* doctrine by providing that arbitrators have the "power to rule on [their] own jurisdiction, including any objections with respect to the existence, scope or validity of the arbitration agreement."

The arbitration agreement also contained a severance provision, and severe limits on the arbitrator's power to modify the contract. It further provided that the parties would share the costs of arbitration and that the losing party would pay the winning party's attorney's fees. Moreover, class action arbitrations were barred.

The appellate court ruled that the arbitrator should decide whether the arbitral clause was sufficiently fair to be enforceable, *i.e.*, the arbitrator should rule on the unconscionability question. In other words, when the franchisees alleged that the agreement was unconscionable, the arbitrator was authorized by AAA Rule 7(a) to rule on the enforceability of the challenged agreement. The court, however, distinguished that question from the franchisees' claim that the arbitral forum was "illusory" on the basis of the exorbitant front-end and general costs of arbitration. The latter, the court asserted, created a question of whether the franchisees could have "access to the arbitrator." Relying on *Green Tree Fin. Corp. v. Randolph*, 531 U.S. 79 (2000), the court emphasized that the costs of the private remedy might foreclose plaintiff access to arbitration. Whether this was the case, *i.e.*, whether the provision for arbitration was illusory was a critical threshold consideration, separable from and anterior to unconscionability and the validity and enforceability of the arbitral clause, and was to be decided by the lower court.

Do you agree with the court's reasoning? Does it undermine or impair party prerogatives under *First Options of Chicago, Inc.* and the jurisdicational and decisional sovereignty of the arbitrator under *Howsam v. Dean Witter Reynolds, Inc.*, 537 U.S. 79 (2002) and *Green Tree Fin. Corp. v. Bazzle*, 539 U.S. 444 (2003)? The court quotes its prior ruling in *Kristian v. Comcast Corp.*, 446 F.3d 25, 37 (1st Cir. 2006), and contends that: "If arbitration prevents plaintiffs from vindicating their rights, it is no longer a 'valid alternative to traditional litigation.'" What does that statement mean and what does it do to AAA Rule 7(a)? Isn't the ruling a circumvention of the principle that arbitrators have the right to rule initially on their jurisdiction? It seems to bypass the arbitrator's authority and to restore judicial power over arbitration.

"Opt-in" Agreements

The *Kaplan* view of the significance of contract in determining the content of the law of arbitration has had a noticeable impact upon the development of the case law. In *Gateway Technologies, Inc. v. MCI*, the parties provided for the arbitration of subsequent disputes, but specified that "errors of law" committed by the arbitral tribunal "shall be subject to appeal." Despite this reference in the arbitral clause, the district court applied a "harmless error standard" of review, noting that its application of that standard would reflect "due regard for the federal policy favoring arbitration." The district court interpreted the provision in the arbitral clause as requiring a lesser form of judicial scrutiny of awards than "would be applied by an appellate court reviewing the actions of a trial court." Citing *Kaplan*, *Mastrobuono*, and *Volt Information Sciences*, the appellate court reversed the district court determination.

GATEWAY TECHNOLOGIES, INC. v. MCI TELECOMMUNICATIONS CORP.
64 F.3d 993, 996–97 (5th Cir. 1995).

[. . .]

II. DISCUSSION

A. *Standard of Review*

This court reviews the district court's confirmation of an arbitration award under a de novo standard. . . . As the Supreme Court recently explained [in *Kaplan*], this is not a special standard, but reflects the application of typical appellate principles. . . .

Usually, however, the district court's "review of an arbitration award is extraordinarily narrow." . . . In a proceeding to confirm or vacate an arbitration award, the Federal Arbitration Act. . . circumscribes the review of the court. . . .

In this case, however, the parties contractually agreed to permit expanded review of the arbitration award by the federal courts. Specifically, their contract details that "[t]he arbitration decision shall be final and binding on both parties, except that errors of law shall be subject to appeal.". . . Such a contractual modification is acceptable because, as the Supreme Court has emphasized, arbitration is a creature of contract and

> the FAA's pro-arbitration policy does not operate without regard to the wishes of the contracting parties. . . . '[I]t does not follow that the FAA prevents the enforcement of agreements to arbitrate under different rules than those set forth in the Act itself. Indeed, such a result would be quite inimical to the FAA's purpose of ensuring that private agreements to arbitrate are enforced according to their terms. Arbitration under the Act is a matter of consent, not coercion, and parties are generally free to structure their arbitration agreements as they see fit. Just as they may limit by contract the issues which they will arbitrate, so too may they specify by contract the rules under which that arbitration will be conducted.' *Mastrobuono*. . . (quoting *Volt Information Sciences, Inc*. . .).

. . . Because these parties contractually agreed to expand judicial review, their contractual provision supplements the FAA's default standard of review and allows for de novo review of issues of law embodied in the arbitration award.

The district court accordingly erred when it refused to review the "errors of law" de novo, opting instead to apply its specially crafted "harmless error standard." This choice apparently reflected the district court's unwillingness to enforce the parties' contract because "the parties have sacrificed the simplicity, informality, and expedition of arbitration on the altar of appellate review." Prudent or not, the contract expressly and unambiguously provides for review of "errors of law"; to interpret this phrase short of de novo review would render the language meaningless and would frustrate the mutual intent of the parties. When, as here, the parties agree contractually to subject an arbitration award to expanded judicial review, federal arbitration policy demands that the court conduct its review according to the terms of the arbitration contract. . . .

[. . .]

NOTES AND QUESTIONS

1. The ruling in *MCI*, in effect, provides that arbitrating parties have the legal right to modify Section Ten of the FAA by adding a basis for judicial review that is not part of that provision. Further, they may—by contract—

require the court to engage in a form of review that is otherwise legally impermissible and contravenes the gravamen of the federal policy on arbitration.

2. In *MCI*, the parties agreed to have the award reviewed on the merits for "errors of law." The contract, therefore, not only establishes the parties' rights and obligations, but also defines the courts' role and authority in regard to the supervision of the arbitration. What exactly does the phrase "errors of law" mean in terms of judicial review? Does it authorize *de novo* review? What if the tribunal miscited a case, paraphrased a rule while seeming to quote it, arguably misunderstood a controversial legal principle, or reversed law it thought wrong? What specific legal protections did the parties bargain for in their agreement? As a lawyer, how would you structure an arbitration agreement for your client with this in mind?

3. One wonders whether the implications of *Kaplan* extend to allowing the parties to waive the application of a particular provision of Section Ten or to entirely eliminate any form of judicial supervision.

4. Rather than adding content to Section Ten, is it legally permissible for arbitrating parties to stipulate that paragraph 1, 2, 3, or 4 of Section Ten or all of Section Ten will not apply to awards rendered in their arbitration? At that point, what utility does the FAA have in the regulation of arbitration? Under the *Kaplan-MCI* rule, don't private parties have greater authority to regulate arbitration than state legislatures or even the U.S. Congress? How do you think the original FAA-drafting Congress would react to the *Kaplan-MCI* rule?

5. It should be noted that, prior to *MCI*, the failure to comply with the provisions of the arbitral clause, when established, constituted a ground for vacatur of the award for "excess of arbitral authority."

* * *

In *Roadway Package*, the Third Circuit fully endorsed the position taken by the Fifth Circuit on opt-in provisions. In the court's view, there was little, if no, doubt as to the basic purpose of the FAA. *Volt*, along with *Kaplan*, had made the objective unmistakable.

ROADWAY PACKAGE SYSTEM, INC. v. KAYSER

257 F.3d 287 (3d Cir.), *cert. denied*, 534 U.S. 1020 (2001).

(footnotes omitted)

OPINION OF THE COURT

BECKER, Chief Judge.

This is an appeal from an order of the District Court vacating an arbitrator's award. Plaintiff Roadway Package System, Inc., (RPS) ships small packages for corporate clients. "Independent linehaul contractors," such as Defendant Scott Kayser, assist in its operations. RPS terminated Kayser's contract in 1998, alleging that he had failed to fulfill his obligations under the Linehaul Contractor Operating Agreement (LCOA), which governed their association. Kayser exercised his contractual right to demand arbitration and was awarded substantial damages. RPS then brought suit in the District Court for the Eastern District of Pennsylvania, asking the court to vacate the award. Applying the vacatur standards set forth in the Federal Arbitration Act (FAA), the District Court granted the motion on the grounds that the arbitrator exceeded the scope of his authority. We will affirm.

Kayser's appeal requires us to decide ... whether contracting parties may opt out of the FAA's default vacatur standards and fashion their own. Because the LCOA is a "contract evidencing a transaction involving commerce," ... the FAA governs the case.... [W]e first hold that the FAA permits parties to contract for vacatur standards other than the ones provided in the FAA. The FAA sets out "a substantive rule applicable in state as well as federal courts," ... but its rule is simply that courts must enforce the terms of private arbitration agreements.

[. . .]

II.

We must first decide whether the District Court properly applied the FAA's vacatur standards or whether it should have, as Kayser submits, used those laid out in the Pennsylvania Uniform Arbitration Act (PUAA).... We have no trouble in determining that this case is governed by the FAA. Subject to a few exceptions not implicated here, the statute applies to any "written provision in any ... contract evidencing a transaction involving commerce to settle by arbitration a controversy arising out of such contract or transaction." ... This language "extend[s] the Act's reach to the limits of the Congress' Commerce Clause power[.]"... The agreement to arbitrate in this case—one between citizens of different states and involving a contract for the delivery and pick up of packages that have been or will be shipped interstate—was unquestionably within Congress' power to reach under the Commerce Clause.

Our inquiry is not ended, however, simply because we have concluded that the FAA applies. Congress enacted the FAA "to overcome courts' refusals to enforce agreements to arbitrate."... The statute's ultimate purpose is to enforce the terms of private arbitration agreements.... Though the FAA generally embraces a "proarbitration policy," this policy "does not operate without regard to the wishes of the contracting parties."... Thus, if parties contract to arbitrate pursuant to arbitration rules or procedures borrowed from state law, the federal policy is satisfied so long as their agreement is enforced....

The foregoing does not mean that agreements specifying that arbitration will be conducted pursuant to state rules or procedures cease being subject to the FAA; it means simply that the FAA permits parties to "specify by contract the rules under which ... arbitration will be conducted."... When a court enforces the terms of an arbitration agreement that incorporates state law rules, it does so not because the parties have chosen to be governed by state rather than federal law. Rather, it does so because federal law requires that the court enforce the terms of the agreement....

... [W]e hold that parties may agree that judicial review of an arbitrator's decision will be conducted according to standards borrowed from state law. The FAA creates "a substantive rule applicable in state as well as federal courts," ... but *Volt* and *Mastrobuono* clarified that its rule is simply that courts must enforce the terms of arbitration agreements. We now join with the great weight of authority and hold that parties may opt out of the FAA's off-the-rack vacatur standards and fashion their own (including by referencing state law standards.)...

NOTES AND QUESTIONS

1. Do you agree with the court's characterization of the FAA § 10 grounds as "off-the-rack vacatur standards"? What does the court's statement imply? Is it an endorsement of absolute freedom of contract in arbitration?

2. Assess doctrinally and analytically the position that the FAA is a default framework for the regulation of arbitration. Is such a view sustainable?

3. Why does the FAA govern this transaction? Does the court's assessment persuade you? Explain your answer.

4. Is the court driven by logic, policy, or experience in this case?

* * *

Other federal circuits assumed a different position on the question. Their pronouncements constituted a brief in favor of the integrity of judicial jurisdiction and statutory law. For example, the Ninth Circuit—which initially subscribed to the contract freedom view—eventually concluded that that position was untenable in its absolute form.

KYOCERA CORP. v. PRUDENTIAL–BACHE TRADE SERVICES, INC.

341 F.3d 987 (9th Cir. 2003).

(footnotes omitted)

REINHARDT, Circuit Judge.

I. BACKGROUND

In 1984, Kyocera Corporation ("Kyocera"), Prudential–Bache Trade Corporation ("Prudential"), and the newly formed LaPine Technology Corporation ("LaPine") began a venture to produce and market computer disk drives. LaPine licensed its proprietary drive design to Kyocera, which manufactured the drives. Prudential's role was generally to stabilize the cash flow of the enterprise: in addition to financing LaPine's inventory and accounts receivable, Prudential purchased, through a subsidiary, the LaPine drives from Kyocera and resold the drives on credit to LaPine, which in turn marketed the drives to its customers.

By the summer of 1986, LaPine—which had never earned a profit—had fallen into serious managerial and financial difficulties. On August 13 and 21, 1986, Kyocera gave written notice that it considered LaPine and Prudential in default due to the failure to pay for delivered drives. Shortly thereafter, Kyocera, Prudential and LaPine began discussions regarding LaPine's reorganization and a restructuring of the relationship among the three companies.

The parties differ on the terms of the final agreement that resulted from the ensuing exchanges. In October and November of 1986, both a general "Definitive Agreement" and a subsidiary, more detailed "Amended Trading Agreement" were prepared. The primary dispute arises out of one term of the "Amended Trading Agreement": LaPine and Prudential claim that all parties agreed that Prudential would no longer purchase drives from Kyocera and resell them to LaPine, and that LaPine would instead purchase drives directly from Kyocera; Kyocera maintains that it never approved any such limitation of Prudential's role. When Kyocera refused to execute the "Amended Trading Agreement" as presented by LaPine and Prudential, LaPine notified Kyocera that it considered Kyocera in breach of contract. On May 7, 1987, LaPine instituted proceedings in federal district court, seeking damages and an injunction compelling Kyocera to continue supplying drives under the alleged terms of the contract.

On September 2, 1987, the district court granted Kyocera's motion to compel arbitration, and a panel of three arbitrators was convened. Arbitration proceeded in two phases. The arbitration panel first determined in "Phase I" that, under California law, Kyocera had entered into a contract by accepting LaPine and Prudential's version of the "Amended Trading Agreement," which required Kyocera to sell drives directly to LaPine. Again applying California law, the arbitrators then determined in "Phase II" that Kyocera breached this contract and that the breach was the proximate cause of damage to LaPine. On August 25, 1994, the arbitrators issued their final decision, unanimously awarding LaPine and Prudential $243,133,881 in damages and prejudgment interest against Kyocera.

Kyocera filed a motion in district court to "Vacate, Modify and Correct the Arbitral Award." The motion relied on the arbitration clause of the parties' "Definitive Agreement," which stated that:

> The arbitrators shall issue a written award which shall state the bases of the award and include detailed findings of fact and conclusions of law. The United States District Court for the Northern District of California may enter judgment upon any award, either by confirming the award or by vacating, modifying or correcting the award. The Court shall vacate, modify or correct any award: (i) based upon any of the grounds referred to in the Federal Arbitration Act, (ii) where the arbitrators' findings of fact are not supported by substantial evidence, or (iii) where the arbitrators' conclusions of law are erroneous.

Accordingly, Kyocera asserted that (i) there existed grounds for vacatur pursuant to the Federal Arbitration Act ("FAA") . . . (ii) the arbitration panel's factual findings were unsupported by substantial evidence, and (iii) the panel made various errors of law. LaPine and Prudential, in turn, moved to confirm the panel's award.

The district court denied Kyocera's motion and granted the motion of LaPine and Prudential. . . . The Court concluded that the Federal Arbitration Act granted federal courts the jurisdiction to review arbitration decisions only on certain enumerated grounds, and that private parties could not by contract enlarge this statutory standard of review. . . .

A. LaPine I

Kyocera timely appealed. It argued, almost exclusively, that the district court erred in applying only the Federal Arbitration Act standard, and not the broader contractual provisions for review. . . .

A divided panel of this court reversed the district court's determination that it was bound to apply only the statutory grounds for review, holding that federal court review of an arbitration agreement is not necessarily limited to the standards set forth in the Federal Arbitration Act. . . . Rather, the majority recognized that Supreme Court precedent required that private agreements to arbitrate be implemented on their own terms and according to their own procedural rules, and then extended that principle to provisions regarding the grounds on which federal courts may review arbitration proceedings. . . . The majority held that when parties resort to the use of an arbitral tribunal[,] . . . they may leave in place the limited court review provided by the FAA, or they may agree to remove that insulation and subject the result to a more searching court review of the arbitral tribunal's decision, for example a review for substantial evidence and errors of law. . . .

The majority then declined to review the district court's decision rejecting Kyocera's arguments under the statutory standard. Therefore, although we affirmed the district court's determination that Kyocera presented no basis for modifying the arbitral award on statutory grounds, . . . we remanded to allow the district court to apply the parties' contractually expanded standard of review of unsupported factual findings or errors of law. . . . No party requested en banc rehearing of our decision.

Judge Kozinski provided the deciding vote in LaPine I, although he noted in his tie-breaking concurrence that the question presented was "closer than most." . . . He recognized that although the Supreme Court cases "say that parties may set the time, place and manner of arbitration[,] none says that private parties may tell the federal courts how to conduct their business." . . . He further acknowledged that "[n]owhere has Congress authorized courts to review arbitral awards under the standard the parties here adopted." . . . Nevertheless, despite the fact that the private parties' agreed-upon standard of review was neither authorized by Congress nor compelled by the Supreme Court, Judge Kozinski concluded that the "supported by substantial evidence or erroneous legal conclusion" standard was sufficiently similar to the standard used in reviewing administrative and bankruptcy decisions, and the standard used in reviewing state court decisions on habeas corpus, to permit the district court to apply the contractual agreement's standard of review without difficulty. His decision would have been different, he stated, "if the agreement provided that the district judge would review the award by flipping a coin or studying the entrails of a dead fowl." . . .

Judge Mayer dissented. He stated simply and clearly that:

[w]hether to arbitrate, what to arbitrate, how to arbitrate, and when to arbitrate are matters that parties may specify contractually. . . . However, Kyocera cites no authority explicitly empowering litigants to dictate how an Article III court must review an arbitration decision. Absent this, they may not. Should parties desire more scrutiny than the Federal Arbitration Act authorizes courts to apply, "they can contract for an appellate arbitration panel to review the arbitrator's award[;] they cannot contract for judicial review of that award."

B. LaPine II

Given that LaPine I affirmed the district court's application of the statutory grounds for review, the court on remand reviewed the arbitration decision according to the non-statutory standards specified in . . . the "Definitive Agreement," addressing each arbitration phase separately. On April 4, 2000, the district court confirmed the arbitration panel's "Phase I" decision on contract formation. . . . The court held that the arbitrators' "conclusions are not only legally sound but they are amply supported by the undisputed facts." . . .

On October 2, 2000, the district court similarly confirmed most of the arbitrators' "Phase II" decision on contract breach and damages. However, the court "vacated" Finding of Fact number 135—which recited that LaPine achieved an operating profit in 1987 when in fact the accounting record showed an operating loss for that year—and "remanded" the case to the arbitral panel "for its consideration as to the effect, if any, of the vacation of Finding of Fact 135 on its damage award."

Although one panel member was deceased, the remaining two members of the arbitral panel issued a letter stating that the vacatur of Finding of Fact 135 had no effect on the damages award, because the panel's valuation methodology did not rely on actual profit figures for that year. On March 6, 2001, the district court confirmed the arbitrators' "Phase II" award, and on March 9, the court entered judgment in favor of Prudential and LaPine. Again, Kyocera timely appealed.

A three-judge panel of this court unanimously affirmed the district court's confirmation of the arbitral panel's award. . . . Kyocera timely filed a request for rehearing en banc, and on December 17, 2002, we granted that request. . . . We now affirm the district court's confirmation of the arbitral panel's award. In so doing, we correct the law of the circuit regarding the proper standard for review of arbitral decisions under the Federal Arbitration Act.

II. DISCUSSION

[. . .]

In this case, we need not speculate as to whether the arbitration panel properly applied complex California contract law to a complex factual dispute, because we conclude that Congress has explicitly prescribed a much narrower role for federal courts reviewing arbitral decisions. The Federal Arbitration Act ... enumerates limited grounds on which a federal court may vacate, modify, or correct an arbitral award. Neither erroneous legal conclusions nor unsubstantiated factual findings justify federal court review of an arbitral award under the statute, which is unambiguous in this regard. Because the Constitution reserves to Congress the power to determine the standards by which federal courts render decisions, and because Congress has specified the exclusive standard by which federal courts may review an arbitrator's decision, we hold that private parties may not contractually impose their own standard on the courts. We therefore review the arbitral panel's determination only on grounds authorized by the statute, and affirm the confirmation of the arbitration award.

[. . .]

B. The Grounds for Review

We now determine whether our decision in LaPine I, allowing private parties to impose on the federal courts a broader standard of review than the grounds authorized by statute, constitutes ... an error....

... [T]he Federal Arbitration Act allows a federal court to correct a technical error, to strike all or a portion of an award pertaining to an issue not at all subject to arbitration, and to vacate an award that evidences affirmative misconduct in the arbitral process or the final result or that is completely irrational or exhibits a manifest disregard for the law. These grounds afford an extremely limited review authority, a limitation that is designed to preserve due process but not to permit unnecessary public intrusion into private arbitration procedures.

Congress had good reason to preclude more expansive federal court review. Arbitration is a dispute resolution process designed, at least in theory, to respond to the wishes of the parties more flexibly and expeditiously than the federal courts' uniform rules of procedure allow.... Broad judicial review of arbitration decisions could well jeopardize the very benefits of arbitration, rendering informal arbitration merely a prelude to a more cumbersome and time-consuming judicial review process. Congress's decision to permit sophisticated parties to trade the greater certainty of correct legal decisions by federal courts for the speed and flexibility of arbitration determinations is a reasonable legislative judgment that we have no authority to reject.

Despite Congress's reasonable decision to adopt a narrow standard for judicial review of arbitration decisions, and despite the fact that Congress nowhere intimated that the federal courts were authorized to apply any other standard, the LaPine I panel concluded that private parties may contract for a more expansive (or less deferential) standard of review. The Third and Fifth Circuits agree with this conclusion.... These circuits generally emphasize that the purpose of the Federal Arbitration Act is to enforce the terms of private arbitration agreements, including terms specifying the scope of review of arbitration decisions.... In *Volt*, the Supreme Court determined that "[j]ust as [private parties] may limit by contract the issues which they will arbitrate, so too may they specify by contract the rules under which that arbitration will be conducted." ... The circuits mentioned above would expand *Volt* so as to provide that, just as the Federal Arbitration Act's default rules for how arbitration is to be conducted may be superceded by private contract, ... so too may the Act's statutory standards governing federal court review ... be superseded by private contract.

Three circuits [the Tenth, Seventh, and Eighth Circuits] appear to reject the proposition that private parties may dictate how federal courts shall conduct their proceedings....

These three circuits distinguished *Volt*'s holding that private parties' contractual agreements can alter the form and substance of the arbitration proceeding itself—a holding not contested here—from the question whether such agreements may alter statutorily prescribed federal court review of the proceeding....

We agree with the Seventh, Eighth, and Tenth Circuits that private parties have no power to determine the rules by which federal courts proceed, especially when Congress has explicitly prescribed those standards. Pursuant to *Volt*, parties have complete freedom to contractually modify the arbitration process by designing whatever procedures and systems they think will best meet their needs—including review by one or more appellate arbitration panels. Once a case reaches the federal courts, however, the private arbitration process is complete, and because Congress has specified standards for confirming an arbitration award, federal courts must act pursuant to those standards and no others. Private parties' freedom to fashion their own arbitration process has no bearing whatsoever on their inability to amend the statutorily prescribed standards governing federal court review. Even when Congress is silent on the matter, private parties lack the power to dictate how the federal courts conduct the business of resolving disputes.... A fortiori, private parties lack the power to dictate a broad standard of review when Congress has specifically prescribed a narrower standard.

We therefore overrule LaPine I, affirm the district court's 1995 conclusion, and hold that a federal court may only review an arbitral decision on the grounds set forth in the Federal Arbitration Act. Private parties have no power to alter or expand those grounds, and any contractual provision purporting to do so is, accordingly, legally unenforceable.

[. . .]

III. CONCLUSION

Private parties have no authority to dictate the manner in which the federal courts conduct judicial proceedings. That power is reserved to Congress—and when Congress is silent on the issue, the courts govern themselves. Here, because Congress has determined that federal courts are to review arbitration awards only for certain errors, the parties are powerless to select a different standard of review—whether that standard entails review by seeking facts unsupported by substantial evidence and errors of law or by "flipping a coin or studying the entrails of a dead fowl." . . . Private parties may design an arbitration process as they wish, but once an award is final for the purposes of the arbitration process, Congress has determined how the federal courts are to treat that award. We hold that the contractual provisions in this case providing for federal court review on grounds other than those set forth in the Federal Arbitration Act are invalid and severable. We further hold that Kyocera has shown no cause for relief under the standard provided in the Federal Arbitration Act. . . .

[. . .]

NOTES AND QUESTIONS

1. The *Kyocera* court seems to anchor its ruling in systemic and institutional considerations—in effect, power relationships between Congress, courts, and private parties. Which position—the Fifth or Ninth Circuit—is in the best interest of arbitration? Why?

2. In *Hughes Training, Inc. v. Cook*, 254 F.3d 588 (5th Cir. 2001), *cert. denied*, 534 U.S. 1172 (2002), the U.S. Supreme Court let stand a Fifth Circuit ruling that, when parties contract for a certain standard of review to govern the arbitration process, that standard governs the district court's review of the arbitration award. Moreover, that standard of review did not conflict with the FAA when the arbitration procedures, including the standard of review, were unambiguously incorporated into an employment agreement that stated, "the arbitration process 'shall be conducted in accordance with the [Employment Problem Resolution Procedures.]'" The Fifth Circuit held that "[i]t was not unfair for the arbitration agreement to include a standard of review that allowed the district court to assess the arbitrator's legal and factual conclusions." It noted, "Although the supplemental standard of review incorporated into the arbitration agreement benefited [the employer] in this instance, it was equally available to [the employee] had the award been unfavorable to her."

3. In *Puerto Rico Telephone Co., Inc. v. U.S. Phone Mfg. Corp.*, 427 F.3d 21 (1st Cir. 2005), the U.S. First Circuit adopted a middle-of-the-road position on the question of the validity and enforceability of opt-in agreements. The

contract involved in the litigation provided for AAA arbitration in Puerto Rico and further stated that Puerto Rican law governed the contract. The tribunal rendered an award for damages in the amount of $2.5 million. The defendant opposed the award and argued that, by selecting Puerto Rico as the arbitral venue and Puerto Rican law as the law of the contract, the parties had implicitly contracted for the application of the local arbitration statute that contained a higher standard of review against arbitral awards.

In its holding, the court made two essential points: First, ordinary (or "garden variety") factual or legal errors do not warrant judicial supervision or justify the judicial second-guessing of arbitrator rulings; second, and more germane to the issue of opt-in agreements, the mere inclusion of a generic choice-of-law in the contract was not a sufficient basis for requiring the application of the chosen state law as to the scope of review of arbitral awards. In effect, the judicial supervision standard in FAA § 10 could only be displaced by clear contract language providing for the application of a different standard.

In so holding, the court assessed the rulings of other federal circuits on the issue. Generally, the Ninth and Tenth Circuits prohibit the practice, followed closely by the Seventh and Eighth Circuits. These courts see such clauses as an intrusion upon federal jurisdictional authority and as having an undermining impact upon arbitration. The Third, Sixth, and now First Circuit give effect to private agreements to arbitrate and enforce opt-in provisions as long as they do not conflict with the strong federal policy on arbitration and contain specific and precise language providing for the displacement of the FAA standard.

4. In *Hoeft v. MVL Group, Inc.*, 343 F.3d 57 (2d Cir. 2003), the Second Circuit held that private parties cannot dictate the basis for the exercise of a federal court's authority to review an arbitral award. The court determined that review for manifest disregard of the law, although not an express part of FAA § 10, cannot be limited by the parties' agreement. The Second Circuit thereby joined the Seventh, Eighth, Ninth, and Tenth Circuits' position that "private parties have no power to determine the rules by which federal courts proceed" in the supervision of arbitral awards.

In *Hoeft*, a dispute arose over payment; the parties were unable to resolve it. The stock purchase agreement included special provisions to determine the amount of a deferred portion of the payment that MVL would make to the Hoefts in the following year. The amended stock purchase agreement included an arbitration clause that stated that, in the event that the parties disagreed on the amount of the payment and could not reach a resolution despite their reasonable best efforts, "such dispute shall be resolved by Stephen Sherrill, whose decision in such matters shall be binding and conclusive upon each of the parties hereto and shall not be subject to any type of review or appeal whatever."

Stephen Sherrill arbitrated the dispute and rendered an award in favor of the Hoefts for $1,402,565. When the Hoefts filed a motion to confirm the award, the award debtor responded with a motion to vacate the award on the grounds that Sherrill exceeded his powers and manifestly disregarded the law. The district court granted the motion to vacate the award stating that, although the arbitrator had not exceeded his powers, he had manifestly disregarded the law in calculating the amount owed.

On appeal, the Second Circuit concluded that parties "may not divest the courts of their statutory and common-law authority to review" arbitral awards under FAA § 10(a) or on the basis of the decisional law grounds. The Hoefts argued that contracting parties could exclude judicial review for manifest disregard of the law because it was not a part of the express statutory language. The court, however, reasoned that the decisional standard was just as vital to the supervision of arbitral awards as the statutory grounds. Moreover, although freedom of contract may be instrumental to arbitration, it did not encompass judicial review: "Unlike arbitration, however, judicial review is not a creature of contract, and the authority of the federal court to review an arbitration award ... does not derive from a private agreement." *See Insurance Corp. of Ireland v. Compagnie des Bauxites de Guinee*, 456 U.S. 694, 701 (1982). Federal courts are "not [the] rubber stamps" of contract stipulations; they cannot be deprived of their authority to review arbitral awards by private agreement. Referring to *Bowen v. Amoco Pipeline Co.*, 254 F.3d 925, 936 n.8 (10th Cir. 2001), the court concluded that: "[I]n the absence of clear authority to the contrary, parties may not interfere with the judicial process by dictating how the federal courts operate."

5.   The U.S. Court of Appeals for the Eighth Circuit also embraced a view of public judicial authority that made it impervious to contractual modifications. Such modifications could be effective only if the parties' intent and language were unmistakable. In *Schoch v. InfoUSA, Inc.*, 341 F.3d 785 (8th Cir. 2003), *cert. denied*, 540 U.S. 1180 (2004), InfoUSA bought Schoch's business and entered into a three-year employment agreement with Schoch. InfoUSA also granted Schoch the option to purchase 360,000 shares of InfoUSA stock. The options vested over a four-year period and could "be exercised for up to three months after termination of employment or consulting relationship." Schoch attempted to exercise his option to purchase shares. InfoUSA refused, claiming that Schoch's three-month period to exercise his option had already expired.

Both parties agreed to arbitrate the dispute. The arbitrator decided that Schoch's option had not expired and awarded him $1,632,000 in damages. The district court granted Schoch's motion to confirm the award. The Eighth Circuit affirmed on appeal.

InfoUSA opposed the arbitral award, asserting—*inter alia*—that a heightened standard of review applied. The Eighth Circuit, however, determined that the parties had not expressed "in crystal-clear language" their intent to have a heightened form of judicial scrutiny apply. Reiterating its reasoning in *UHC Management Co. v. Computer Sciences Corp.*, the Eighth Circuit stated, "It is not clear ... that parties have any say in how a federal court will review an arbitration award when Congress has ordained a specific, self-limiting procedure for how such a review is to occur [under the FAA].... Congress did not authorize *de novo* review of such an award on its merits; it commanded that when the exceptions do not apply, a federal court has no choice but to confirm." *UHC Management*, 148 F.3d 992, 997 (8th Cir. 1998). The court further stated that "if parties could contract for heightened judicial review, '[their] intent to do so must be clearly and unmistakably expressed.'"

6. Assess the following statement:

Invoking slogans (like freedom of contract) rather than articulating reasoned decisional predicates has its drawbacks as a judicial methodology. Reducing the governing law to a "fall-back" status is a radical statement in favor of self-regulation. It profoundly diminishes, and may in fact extinguish, the "theological" function of the law by making legal legitimacy depended upon the dynamic forces of the consuming marketplace. Despite its appeal as an efficient regulatory principle, absolute freedom of contract simply is not a good idea; it is not a proper basis for the legal regulation of arbitration. The descent to lower, and ever more economical, levels of legal regulation is a hazardous enterprise. Complete privatization challenges the civilizing function of law in society and its normative role. Protecting commercial arbitration from a history of irrational judicial hostility and using arbitration to remedy the severe inadequacies of the court system are comprehensible policy objectives. Even a judicial policy of substantial deference can make sense and express a necessary societal objective. Abandoning all manner of regulation and referring absolutely to contract, however, simply takes a policy of de-regulation to its illogical limits and imperils the strong societal interest in both adjudication and arbitration. It collapses the process of definition and the function of distinctions. It comes close to embracing absurdity as controlling truth.

HALL STREET ASSOCIATES, L.L.C., v. MATTEL, INC.

___ U.S. ___, 128 S.Ct. 1396, 170 L.Ed.2d 254 (2008).

JUSTICE SOUTER delivered the opinion of the Court.*

The Federal Arbitration Act (FAA or Act), 9 U.S.C. § 1 *et seq.*, provides for expedited judicial review to confirm, vacate, or modify arbitration awards. §§ 9–11 (2000 ed. and Supp. V). The question here is whether statutory grounds for prompt vacatur and modification may be supplemented by contract. We hold that the statutory grounds are exclusive.

I

This case began as a lease dispute between landlord, petitioner Hall Street Associates, L. L. C., and tenant, respondent Mattel, Inc. The property was used for many years as a manufacturing site, and the leases provided that the tenant would indemnify the landlord for any costs resulting from the failure of the tenant or its predecessor lessees to follow environmental laws while using the premises. . . .

Tests of the property's well water in 1998 showed high levels of trichloroethylene (TCE), the apparent residue of manufacturing discharges by Mattel's predecessors between 1951 and 1980. After the Oregon

---

* Justice Souter delivered the opinion of the Court. Justice Scalia joins all but footnote 7 of this opinion.

Department of Environmental Quality (DEQ) discovered even more pollutants, Mattel stopped drawing from the well and, along with one of its predecessors, signed a consent order with the DEQ providing for cleanup of the site.

After Mattel gave notice of intent to terminate the lease in 2001, Hall Street filed this suit, contesting Mattel's right to vacate on the date it gave, and claiming that the lease obliged Mattel to indemnify Hall Street for costs of cleaning up the TCE, among other things. Following a bench trial before the United States District Court for the District of Oregon, Mattel won on the termination issue, and after an unsuccessful try at mediating the indemnification claim, the parties proposed to submit to arbitration. The District Court was amenable, and the parties drew up an arbitration agreement, which the court approved and entered as an order. One paragraph of the agreement provided that

> "[t]he United States District Court for the District of Oregon may enter judgment upon any award, either by confirming the award or by vacating, modifying or correcting the award. The Court shall vacate, modify or correct any award: (i) where the arbitrator's findings of facts are not supported by substantial evidence, or (ii) where the arbitrator's conclusions of law are erroneous." . . .

Arbitration took place, and the arbitrator decided for Mattel. In particular, he held that no indemnification was due, because the lease obligation to follow all applicable federal, state, and local environmental laws did not require compliance with the testing requirements of the Oregon Drinking Water Quality Act (Oregon Act); that Act the arbitrator characterized as dealing with human health as distinct from environmental contamination.

Hall Street then filed . . . [a motion to vacate or correct the award] . . . on the ground that failing to treat the Oregon Act as an applicable environmental law under the terms of the lease was legal error. The District Court agreed, vacated the award, and remanded for further consideration by the arbitrator. The court expressly invoked the standard of review chosen by the parties in the arbitration agreement, which included review for legal error, and cited *LaPine Technology Corp. v. Kyocera Corp.*, 130 F.3d 884, 889 (CA9 1997), for the proposition that the FAA leaves the parties "free . . . to draft a contract that sets rules for arbitration and dictates an alternative standard of review." . . .

On remand, the arbitrator followed the District Court's ruling that the Oregon Act was an applicable environmental law and amended the decision to favor Hall Street. This time, each party sought modification, and again the District Court applied the parties' stipulated standard of review for legal error, correcting the arbitrator's calculation of interest but otherwise upholding the award. Each party then appealed to the Court of Appeals for the Ninth Circuit, where Mattel switched horses and contended that the Ninth Circuit's recent en banc action overruling *LaPine* in *Kyocera Corp. v. Prudential–Bache Trade Servs., Inc.*, 341 F.3d 987, 1000 (2003), left the arbitration agreement's provision for judicial review of legal error unenforceable. Hall Street countered that *Kyocera* (the later one) was distinguishable, and that the agreement's judicial review provision was not severable from the submission to arbitration.

The Ninth Circuit reversed in favor of Mattel in holding that, "[u]nder *Kyocera* the terms of the arbitration agreement controlling the mode of judicial review are unenforceable and severable." ... [footnote omitted]. . . .

... [W]e granted *certiorari* to decide whether the grounds for vacatur and modification provided by §§ 10 and 11 of the FAA are exclusive. . . . We agree with the Ninth Circuit that they are, but vacate and remand for consideration of independent issues.

II

Congress enacted the FAA to replace judicial indisposition to arbitration with a "national policy favoring [it] and plac[ing] arbitration agreements on equal footing with all other contracts." *Buckeye Check Cashing, Inc. v. Cardegna*, 546 U.S. 440, 443, 126 S. Ct. 1204, 163 L. Ed. 2d 1038 (2006). As for jurisdiction over controversies touching arbitration, the Act does nothing, being "something of an anomaly in the field of federal-court jurisdiction" in bestowing no federal jurisdiction but rather requiring an independent jurisdictional basis. *Moses H. Cone Memorial Hospital v. Mercury Constr. Corp.*, 460 U.S. 1, 25, n. 32, 103 S. Ct. 927, 74 L. Ed. 2d 765 (1983); see, *e.g.*, 9 U.S.C. § 4 (providing for action by a federal district court "which, save for such [arbitration] agreement, would have jurisdiction under title 28").[1] But in cases falling within a court's jurisdiction, the Act makes contracts to arbitrate "valid, irrevocable, and enforceable," so long as their subject involves "commerce." § 2. And this is so whether an agreement has a broad reach or goes just to one dispute, and whether enforcement be sought in state court or federal. . . .

The Act also supplies mechanisms for enforcing arbitration awards: a judicial decree confirming an award, an order vacating it, or an order modifying or correcting it. §§ 9–11. An application for any of these orders will get streamlined treatment as a motion, obviating the separate contract action that would usually be necessary to enforce or tinker with an

---

1. Because the FAA is not jurisdictional, there is no merit in the argument that enforcing the arbitration agreement's judicial review provision would create federal jurisdiction by private contract. The issue is entirely about the scope of judicial review permissible under the FAA.

arbitral award in court. [Footnote omitted.] § 6. Under the terms of § 9, a court "must" confirm an arbitration award "unless" it is vacated, modified, or corrected "as prescribed" in §§ 10 and 11. Section 10 lists grounds for vacating an award, while § 11 names those for modifying or correcting one. [Footnote omitted.]

The Courts of Appeals have split over the exclusiveness of these statutory grounds when parties take the FAA shortcut to confirm, vacate, or modify an award, with some saying the recitations are exclusive, and others regarding them as mere threshold provisions open to expansion by agreement.[2] ... We now hold that §§ 10 and 11 respectively provide the FAA's exclusive grounds for expedited vacatur and modification.

III

Hall Street makes two main efforts to show that the grounds set out for vacating or modifying an award are not exclusive, taking the position, first, that expandable judicial review authority has been accepted as the law since *Wilko v. Swan*, 346 U.S. 427, 74 S. Ct. 182, 98 L. Ed. 168 (1953). This, however, was not what *Wilko* decided....

The *Wilko* Court was explaining that arbitration would undercut the Securities Act's buyer protections when it remarked ... that "[p]ower to vacate an [arbitration] award is limited," ... and went on to say that "the interpretations of the law by the arbitrators in contrast to manifest disregard [of the law] are not subject, in the federal courts, to judicial review for error in interpretation." ... Hall Street reads this statement as recognizing "manifest disregard of the law" as a further ground for vacatur on top of those listed in § 10, and some Circuits have read it the same way.... Hall Street sees this supposed addition to § 10 as the camel's nose: if judges can add grounds to vacate (or modify), so can contracting parties.

But this is too much for *Wilko* to bear. Quite apart from its leap from a supposed judicial expansion by interpretation to a private expansion by contract, Hall Street overlooks the fact that the statement it relies on expressly rejects just what Hall Street asks for here, general review for an

---

2. The Ninth and Tenth Circuits have held that parties may not contract for expanded judicial review. See *Kyocera Corp. v. Prudential–Bache Trade Servs., Inc.*, 341 F.3d 987, 1000 (9th Cir.2003); *Bowen v. Amoco Pipeline Co.*, 254 F.3d 925, 936 (CA10 2001). The First, Third, Fifth, and Sixth Circuits, meanwhile, have held that parties may so contract. See *Puerto Rico Tel. Co. v. U.S. Phone Mfg. Corp.*, 427 F.3d 21, 31 (1st Cir. 2005); *Jacada (Europe), Ltd. v. International Marketing Strategies, Inc.*, 401 F.3d 701, 710 (CA6 2005); *Roadway Package System, Inc. v. Kayser*, 257 F.3d 287, 288 (CA3 2001); *Gateway Technologies, Inc. v. MCI Telecommunications Corp.*, 64 F.3d 993, 997 (CA5 1995). The Fourth Circuit has taken the latter side of the split in an unpublished opinion, see *Syncor Int'l Corp. v. McLeland*, 120 F.3d 262 (1997), while the Eighth Circuit has expressed agreement with the former side in *dicta*, see *UHC Management Co. v. Computer Sciences Corp.*, 148 F.3d 992, 997–998 (1998).

arbitrator's legal errors. Then there is the vagueness of *Wilko*'s phrasing. Maybe the term "manifest disregard" was meant to name a new ground for review, but maybe it merely referred to the § 10 grounds collectively, rather than adding to them. . . . Or, as some courts have thought, "manifest disregard" may have been shorthand for § 10(a)(3) or § 10(a)(4), the subsections authorizing vacatur when the arbitrators were "guilty of misconduct" or "exceeded their powers." . . . We, when speaking as a Court, have merely taken the *Wilko* language as we found it, without embellishment, . . . and now that its meaning is implicated, we see no reason to accord it the significance that Hall Street urges.

Second, Hall Street says that the agreement to review for legal error ought to prevail simply because arbitration is a creature of contract, and the FAA is "motivated, first and foremost, by a congressional desire to enforce agreements into which parties ha[ve] entered." . . . But, again, we think the argument comes up short. Hall Street is certainly right that the FAA lets parties tailor some, even many features of arbitration by contract, including the way arbitrators are chosen, what their qualifications should be, which issues are arbitrable, along with procedure and choice of substantive law. But to rest this case on the general policy of treating arbitration agreements as enforceable as such would be to beg the question, which is whether the FAA has textual features at odds with enforcing a contract to expand judicial review following the arbitration.

To that particular question we think the answer is yes, that the text compels a reading of the §§ 10 and 11 categories as exclusive. To begin with, even if we assumed §§ 10 and 11 could be supplemented to some extent, it would stretch basic interpretive principles to expand the stated grounds to the point of evidentiary and legal review generally. Sections 10 and 11, after all, address egregious departures from the parties' agreed-upon arbitration: "corruption," "fraud," "evident partiality," "misconduct," "misbehavior," "exceed[ing] . . . powers," "evident material miscalculation," "evident material mistake," "award[s] upon a matter not submitted;" the only ground with any softer focus is "imperfect[ions]," and a court may correct those only if they go to "[a] matter of form not affecting the merits." Given this emphasis on extreme arbitral conduct, the old rule of *ejusdem generis* has an implicit lesson to teach here. Under that rule, when a statute sets out a series of specific items ending with a general term, that general term is confined to covering subjects comparable to the specifics it follows. Since a general term included in the text is normally so limited, then surely a statute with no textual hook for expansion cannot authorize contracting parties to supplement review for specific instances of outrageous conduct with review for just any legal error. "Fraud" and a mistake of law are not cut from the same cloth.

That aside, expanding the detailed categories would rub too much against the grain of the § 9 language, where provision for judicial confirmation carries no hint of flexibility. On application for an order confirming the arbitration award, the court "must grant" the order "unless the award is vacated, modified, or corrected as prescribed in sections 10 and

11 of this title." There is nothing malleable about "must grant," which unequivocally tells courts to grant confirmation in all cases, except when one of the "prescribed" exceptions applies. This does not sound remotely like a provision meant to tell a court what to do just in case the parties say nothing else. [Footnote omitted.]

In fact, anyone who thinks Congress might have understood § 9 as a default provision should turn back to § 5 for an example of what Congress thought a default provision would look like:

> "[i]f in the agreement provision be made for a method of naming or appointing an arbitrator ... such method shall be followed; but if no method be provided therein, or if a method be provided and any party thereto shall fail to avail himself of such method, ... then upon the application of either party to the controversy the court shall designate and appoint an arbitrator...."

"[I]f no method be provided" is a far cry from "must grant ... unless" in § 9.

Instead of fighting the text, it makes more sense to see the three provisions, §§ 9–11, as substantiating a national policy favoring arbitration with just the limited review needed to maintain arbitration's essential virtue of resolving disputes straightaway. Any other reading opens the door to the full-bore legal and evidentiary appeals that can "rende[r] informal arbitration merely a prelude to a more cumbersome and time-consuming judicial review process," ... and bring arbitration theory to grief in post-arbitration process.

Nor is *Dean Witter,* ... to the contrary, as Hall Street claims it to be. *Dean Witter* held that state-law claims subject to an agreement to arbitrate could not be remitted to a district court considering a related, nonarbitrable federal claim; the state-law claims were to go to arbitration immediately.... Despite the opinion's language "reject[ing] the suggestion that the overriding goal of the [FAA] was to promote the expeditious resolution of claims," ... the holding mandated immediate enforcement of an arbitration agreement; the Court was merely trying to explain that the inefficiency and difficulty of conducting simultaneous arbitration and federal-court litigation was not a good enough reason to defer the arbitration,....

When all these arguments based on prior legal authority are done with, Hall Street and Mattel remain at odds over what happens next. Hall Street and its *amici* say parties will flee from arbitration if expanded review is not open to them.... One of Mattel's *amici* foresees flight from the courts if it is.... We do not know who, if anyone, is right, and so cannot say whether the exclusivity reading of the statute is more of a threat to the popularity of arbitrators or to that of courts. But whatever the consequences of our holding, the statutory text gives us no business to expand the statutory grounds. [Footnote omitted.]

IV

In holding that §§ 10 and 11 provide exclusive regimes for the review provided by the statute, we do not purport to say that they exclude more searching review based on authority outside the statute as well. The FAA is not the only way into court for parties wanting review of arbitration awards: they may contemplate enforcement under state statutory or common law, for example, where judicial review of different scope is arguable. But here we speak only to the scope of the expeditious judicial review under §§ 9, 10, and 11, deciding nothing about other possible avenues for judicial enforcement of arbitration awards.

[. . .]

Although we agree with the Ninth Circuit that the FAA confines its expedited judicial review to the grounds listed in 9 U.S.C. §§ 10 and 11, we vacate the judgment and remand the case for proceedings consistent with this opinion.

It is so ordered.

JUSTICE STEVENS, with whom JUSTICE KENNEDY joins, dissenting.

May parties to an ongoing lawsuit agree to submit their dispute to arbitration subject to the caveat that the trial judge should refuse to enforce an award that rests on an erroneous conclusion of law? Prior to Congress' enactment of the Federal Arbitration Act (FAA or Act) in 1925, the answer to that question would surely have been "Yes." [Footnote omitted.] Today, however, the Court holds that the FAA does not merely authorize the vacation [sic] [vacatur] or enforcement of awards on specified grounds, but also forbids enforcement of perfectly reasonable judicial review provisions in arbitration agreements fairly negotiated by the parties and approved by the district court. Because this result conflicts with the primary purpose of the FAA and ignores the historical context in which the Act was passed, I respectfully dissent.

Prior to the passage of the FAA, American courts were generally hostile to arbitration. They refused, with rare exceptions, to order specific enforcement of executory agreements to arbitrate. [Footnote omitted.] Section 2 of the FAA responded to this hostility by making written arbitration agreements "valid, irrevocable, and enforceable." . . . This section, which is the centerpiece of the FAA, reflects Congress' main goal in passing the legislation: "to abrogate the general common-law rule against specific enforcement of arbitration agreements," . . . and to "ensur[e] that private arbitration agreements are enforced according to their terms." . . . Given this settled understanding of the core purpose of the FAA, the interests favoring enforceability of parties' arbitration agreements are stronger today than before the FAA was enacted. As such, there is more—and certainly not less—reason to give effect to parties' fairly negotiated decisions to provide for judicial review of arbitration awards for errors of law.

Petitioner filed this rather complex action in an Oregon state court. Based on the diverse citizenship of the parties, respondent removed the case to federal court. More than three years later, and after some issues had been resolved, the parties sought and obtained the District Court's approval of their agreement to arbitrate the remaining issues subject to *de novo* judicial review. They neither requested, nor suggested that the FAA authorized, any "expedited" disposition of their case. Because the arbitrator made a rather glaring error of law, the judge refused to affirm his award until after that error was corrected. The Ninth Circuit reversed.

This Court now agrees with the Ninth Circuit's (most recent) interpretation of the FAA as setting forth the exclusive grounds for modification or vacation [sic] [vacatur] of an arbitration award under the statute. As I read the Court's opinion, it identifies two possible reasons for reaching this result: (1) a supposed *quid pro quo* bargain between Congress and litigants that conditions expedited federal enforcement of arbitration awards on acceptance of a statutory limit on the scope of judicial review of such awards; and (2) an assumption that Congress intended to include the words "and no other" in the grounds specified in §§ 10 and 11 for the vacatur and modification of awards. Neither reason is persuasive.

While § 9 of the FAA imposes a 1–year limit on the time in which any party to an arbitration may apply for confirmation of an award, the statute does not require that the application be given expedited treatment. Of course, the premise of the entire statute is an assumption that the arbitration process may be more expeditious and less costly than ordinary litigation, but that is a reason for interpreting the statute liberally to favor the parties' use of arbitration. An unnecessary refusal to enforce a perfectly reasonable category of arbitration agreements defeats the primary purpose of the statute.

That purpose also provides a sufficient response to the Court's reliance on statutory text. It is true that a wooden application of "the old rule of *ejusdem generis*" . . . might support an inference that the categories listed in §§ 10 and 11 are exclusive, but the literal text does not compel that reading—a reading that is flatly inconsistent with the overriding interest in effectuating the clearly expressed intent of the contracting parties. A listing of grounds that must always be available to contracting parties simply does not speak to the question whether they may agree to additional grounds for judicial review.

Moreover, in light of the historical context and the broader purpose of the FAA, §§ 10 and 11 are best understood as a shield meant to protect parties from hostile courts, not a sword with which to cut down parties' "valid, irrevocable and enforceable" agreements to arbitrate their disputes subject to judicial review for errors of law. [Footnote omitted.] § 2.

Even if I thought the narrow issue presented in this case were as debatable as the conflict among the courts of appeals suggests, I would rely on a presumption of overriding importance to resolve the debate and rule in favor of petitioner's position that the FAA permits the statutory grounds for vacatur and modification of an award to be supplemented by contract. A decision *"not to regulate"* the terms of an agreement that does not even arguably offend any public policy whatsoever, "is adequately justified by a presumption in favor of freedom." . . .

Accordingly, while I agree that the judgment of the Court of Appeals must be set aside, and that there may be additional avenues available for judicial enforcement of parties' fairly negotiated review provisions. . . . I respectfully dissent from the Court's interpretation of the FAA, and would direct the Court of Appeals to affirm the judgment of the District Court enforcing the arbitrator's final award.

JUSTICE BREYER, dissenting.

The question presented in this case is whether "the Federal Arbitration Act . . . *precludes* a federal court from enforcing" an arbitration agreement that gives the court the power to set aside an arbitration award that embodies an arbitrator's mistake about the law. . . . Like the majority [in *dicta*] and Justice Stevens, and primarily for the reasons they set forth, I believe that the Act does not *preclude* enforcement of such an agreement. . . .

At the same time, I see no need to send the case back for further judicial decisionmaking. The agreement here was entered into with the consent of the parties and the approval of the District Court. Aside from the Federal Arbitration Act itself, . . . respondent below pointed to no statute, rule, or other relevant public policy that the agreement might violate. The Court has now rejected its argument that the agreement violates the Act, and I would simply remand the case with instructions that the Court of Appeals affirm the District Court's judgment enforcing the arbitrator's final award.

NOTES AND QUESTIONS

1. Does the fact that the parties entered into the arbitration agreement during a legal proceeding make any difference to your analysis of its enforceability or the legal quality of its content? If the parties were truly interested in achieving finality, and ending their dispute, should they have instructed the court to choose an arbitrator and given the designated arbitrator absolute power to render an award that resolves the matter? Does the parties' qualified recourse to arbitration indicate a mixed commitment to the remedy and a possible solution? Should parties be free to choose a tepid recourse to arbitration?

2. At the outset of section II, the Court refers to *Buckeye Check Cashing* to acknowledge the federal stature of arbitration law in the United States. What significance attaches to the "national policy"? How did the policy become so national? Does it exceed "interstate and foreign commerce" limitations?

3. In the same section, the majority makes reference to the jurisdictional "anomaly" that attaches to the FAA. Can you explain what the reference means to the U.S. law of arbitration and how the "anomaly" has been addressed and whether it has been cured?

4. Do you agree with the majority that FAA § 9 is a 'totalitarian' text because it provides that "a court 'must' confirm [an award] ... 'unless' it is vacated, modified, or corrected ... ?" What arguments can be made on either side of the question? How does the majority use the statement to further its analysis?

5. The Court rules that FAA §§ 10 & 11 are the "exclusive" basis for the confirmation and vacatur of arbitral awards under the FAA. You should restate that conclusion, incorporating its necessary implications and consequences for the law of arbitration. Why does the majority never expressly assert that opt-in provisions for enhanced judicial review are invalid and unenforceable contracts? Does the omission portend a narrow holding? What factor narrows the holding? What aim does the majority attempt to achieve?

6. Evaluate Hall Street's use of *Wilko* to make its case. Would *Volt Info. Sciences, Inc.* have been a better anchor? Was a 'weak-kneed' approach the best that could be done in the circumstances? Was real thunder avoided and ignored?

7. Assess the Court's appraisal of manifest disregard of the law, especially its view that, "Maybe the term 'manifest disregard' was meant to name a new ground for review, but maybe it merely referred to the § 10 grounds collectively, rather than adding to them ... or ... [it] may have been shorthand for § 10 (a) (3) or § 10 (a) (4), the sections authorizing vacatur when the arbitrators were 'guilty of misconduct' or 'exceeded their powers.' " Is the statement groundless speculation or does it redefine manifest disregard and establish a new rule of law in its regard? Does the Court overstate the decisional law of the lower courts on the subject?

8. In its wake, *Hall Street Associates* has generated substantial judicial debate about the continued viability of manifest disregard of the law as a basis for challenging the enforceability of arbitral awards. The Court itself contributed to the discussion by reversing and remanding the Ninth Circuit decision in *Improv West Associates v. Comedy Club*, ___ U.S. ___, 129 S.Ct. 45 (2008). It asked the Ninth Circuit to reconsider its partial vacatur of an award for manifest disregard of the law in light of the ruling in *Hall Street Associates*. The Ninth Circuit upheld its prior determination, holding that manifest disregard remained a viable basis for the nullification of awards. *See* 553 F.3d 1277 (9th Cir. 2009) [the Ninth Circuit held that manifest disregard is merely a judicial gloss on FAA § 10 (a) (4)].

The courts, thus far, are divided on the question. Some have determined that *Hall Street Associates* sounded the death knell of manifest disregard. Citigroup Global Markets Inc. v. Bacon, 562 F.3d 349 (5th Cir. 2009) [in light of *Hall Street Associates,* "manifest disregard of the law as an independent, nonstatutory ground for setting aside an award must be abandoned and rejected."]; Hereford v. D.R. Horton, Inc., 2009 WL 104666 (Ala. Jan. 9, 2009); Robert Lewis Rosen Associates v. Webb, 566 F.Supp.2d 228 (S.D.N.Y. 2008). Yet other courts have concluded that manifest disregard remains part of the law of vacatur. Kashner Davidson Securities Corp. v. Mscisz, 531 F.3d 68 (1st Cir. 2008); Ramos–Santiago v. UPS, 524 F.3d 120 (1st Cir. 2008); Chase Bank USA, NA v. Hale, 859 N.Y.S.2d 342 (N.Y.Sup.2008); MasTec North America, Inc. v. MSE Power Systems, 581 F.Supp.2d 321 (N.D.N.Y. 2008); Stolt–Nielsen SA v. Animal Feeds Int'l Group, 548 F.3d 85 (2nd Cir.

2008) (*certiorari* granted on June 15, 2009) (asserting, in addition, that the FAA is more of a mechanism for enforcing the parties' agreement to arbitrate than a framework for judicial review); Coffee Beanery Ltd. v. WW L.L.C., 300 Fed.Appx. 415 (6th Cir. 2008) (unpub.) (*Hall Street Associates* only applies to contract expansions of the FAA grounds for vacatur!). You should evaluate the last two positions. What do they mean and how do you reconcile them with the ruling in *Hall Street*?

9. What is your view of the standing of manifest disregard after the ruling in *Hall Street Associates* ? Does it and should it continue to have a role in policing arbitral awards? Was its presence in the regulatory scheme always a misnomer or eccentricity? Formulate your opinion in light of the following commentary:

> However the ground originated, manifest disregard invites the courts to pass on the merits of arbitrator determinations. Although manifest disregard is invoked with some frequency in enforcement proceedings, it rarely results in the vacatur of awards. In those few cases in which it does, it ordinarily represents circumstances in which the court disagrees with the arbitrators' interpretation or application of law. No matter how episodic, such results conflict with the statutory policy and the decisional law, both of which prohibit the judicial re-evaluation of arbitrator rulings on the merits. Despite its generally perfunctory and sometimes controversial character, manifest disregard could play a role in legitimizing arbitrations involving statutory claims, especially those that address discrimination and civil liberties issues. The publication of redacted awards along with court supervision of arbitrator decisions on statutory claims would allow the law to grow and develop and give the arbitral adjudication of such claims greater transparency. In the final analysis, the contemporary function of manifest disregard is unsettled and subject periodically to variegated interpretations. Its present status demands future adjustments.

10. What remains of the contract freedom principle in arbitration after *Hall Street Associates*? Can parties still engage in the arbitration of their choosing? What "textual features" of the FAA constrain party autonomy? Why should FAA § 10 not be deemed a 'default' regulatory rule? Is there a public interest at play or is the Court attempting to protect arbitration from its critics? Is the FAA an enactment that sustains the rule of law in arbitration or arbitral freedom of contract? How does *Hall Street Associates* square with the Court's prior rulings on arbitration (*Dean Witter, Kaplan, Mastrobuono, Volt Info. Sciences, Rodriguez*)?

11. Address the first paragraph of section IV of the majority opinion. It is, by far, the most enigmatic pronouncement in the entire ruling. Is it *dicta*? Does it ignore the federal preemption doctrine? What are the other avenues for the confirmation or vacatur of arbitral awards?

12. In his dissent, Justice Stevens becomes the champion of contract freedom in arbitration. Evaluate his view that "the broader purpose of the FAA §§ 10 and 11 are best understood as a shield meant to protect parties from hostile courts, not a sword with which to cut down parties' 'valid,

irrevocable and enforceable' agreements to arbitrate their disputes subject to judicial review for errors of law." Is he right? Is his proposed rule a better means of regulating activity in arbitration? What does Justice Breyer add to the dissenting position?

3. ARBITRATOR SOVEREIGNTY

In *Howsam v. Dean Witter Reynolds, Inc.*, 537 U.S. 79 (2002), the U.S. Supreme Court held that a dispute over whether a National Association Securities Dealers (NASD) six-year eligibility requirement for submission precluded arbitration was a "question of arbitrability" that should be decided by an arbitrator, not the courts. Upon receiving investment advice from Dean Witter, Karen Howsam bought an interest in four limited partnerships. Subsequently, believing that Dean Witter had misrepresented the value of the partnerships, Howsam filed a demand for arbitration pursuant to the Client Service Agreement. The agreement contained an arbitration clause providing for the arbitration of all controversies arising out of a customer's accounts with the company. It allowed the client to select the arbitration forum.

Upon learning of Howsam's attempt to invoke arbitration, Dean Witter filed suit in federal district court asking that the dispute be declared ineligible for arbitration because it was more than six years old. NASD Code Section 10304 states that no dispute "shall be eligible for submission ... where six (6) years have elapsed from the occurrence or event giving rise to the ... dispute." The district court ruled that an arbitrator, not the court should interpret the NASD rule. Dean Witter appealed and the Tenth Circuit reversed. According to the appellate court, application of the NASD rule raised a question about the dispute's "arbitrability." Such questions should be resolved by a court, not the arbitrator. The U.S. Supreme Court granted Howsam's petition for *certiorari* because the lower federal courts "reached different conclusions about whether a court or an arbitrator primarily should interpret and apply this particular NASD rule."

In the Court's view, the question of whether parties have submitted a dispute to arbitration, *i.e.*, the "question of arbitrability," is "an issue for judicial determination unless the parties clearly and unmistakably provide otherwise." The phrase "question of arbitrability," however, only applies in limited circumstances "where contracting parties would likely have expected a court to decide the gateway matter, where they are not likely to have thought that they had agreed that an arbitrator would do so, and, consequently, where reference of the gateway dispute to the court avoids the risk of forcing parties to arbitrate a matter that they may well not have agreed to arbitrate."

Therefore, " 'procedural questions which grow out of the dispute and bear on its final disposition are presumptively not for the judge, but for an arbitrator to decide.' " Arbitrators should decide "allegation[s] of waiver, delay, or a like defense to arbitrability" because these issues do not raise the question of whether parties have agreed to submit a dispute to arbitration. Finally, the Court referred to the language of the Revised Uniform Arbitration Act of 2000 (RUAA) providing that an "arbitrator shall decide whether a condition precedent to arbitrability has been fulfilled." According to the commentary in the RUAA, "in the absence of an agreement to the contrary, issues of procedural arbitrability, *i.e.*, whether prerequisites such as time limits ... have been met, are for the arbitrator to decide."

Finding that the time limit rule "closely resembles the gateway questions that this court has found not to be questions of arbitrability," the Court ruled that the application of the NASD time-limit rule was a matter presumptively for the arbitrator, not the judge. Moreover, NASD arbitrators were "comparatively more expert about the meaning of their own rule" and consequently better able to apply it. Accordingly, aligning the "... decisionmaker with ... comparative expertise," better secures a "fair and expeditious resolution of the underlying controversy—a goal of arbitration systems and judicial systems alike."

HOWSAM v. DEAN WITTER REYNOLDS, INC.

537 U.S. 79, 123 S.Ct. 588, 154 L.Ed.2d 491 (2002).

BREYER, Justice.

This case focuses upon an arbitration rule of the National Association of Securities Dealers (NASD). The rule states that no dispute "shall be eligible for submission to arbitration ... where six (6) years have elapsed from the occurrence or event giving rise to the ... dispute." NASD Code of Arbitration Procedure § 10304 (1984) (NASD Code or Code). We must decide whether a court or an NASD arbitrator should apply the rule to the underlying controversy. We conclude that the matter is for the arbitrator.

I

The underlying controversy arises out of investment advice that Dean Witter Reynolds, Inc. (Dean Witter), provided its client, Karen Howsam, when, some time between 1986 and 1994, it recommended that she buy and hold interests in four limited partnerships. Howsam says that Dean Witter misrepresented the virtues of the partnerships. The resulting controversy falls within their standard Client Service Agreement's arbitration clause, which provides:

> "[A]ll controversies ... concerning or arising from ... any account ..., any transaction ..., or ... the construction, performance or breach of ... any ... agreement between us ... shall be determined by arbitration before any self-regulatory organization or exchange of which Dean Witter is a member."

The agreement also provides that Howsam can select the arbitration forum. And Howsam chose arbitration before the NASD.

To obtain NASD arbitration, Howsam signed the NASD's Uniform Submission Agreement. That agreement specified that the "present matter in controversy" was submitted for arbitration "in accordance with" the NASD's "Code of Arbitration Procedure." And that Code contains the provision at issue here, a provision stating that no dispute "shall be eligible for submission ... where six (6) years have elapsed from the occurrence or event giving rise to the ... dispute." NASD Code § 10304.

After the Uniform Submission Agreement was executed, Dean Witter filed this lawsuit in Federal District Court. It asked the court to declare that the dispute was "ineligible for arbitration" because it was more than six years old. And it sought an injunction that would prohibit Howsam from proceeding in arbitration. The District Court dismissed the action on the ground that the NASD arbitrator, not the court, should interpret and apply the NASD rule. The Court of Appeals for the Tenth Circuit, however, reversed.... In its view, application of the NASD rule presented a question of the underlying dispute's "arbitrability"; and the presumption is that a court, not an arbitrator, will ordinarily decide an "arbitrability" question. *See, e.g., First Options of Chicago, Inc. v. Kaplan,* 514 U.S. 938, 115 S.Ct. 1920, 131 L.Ed.2d 985 (1995).

The Courts of Appeals have reached different conclusions about whether a court or an arbitrator primarily should interpret and apply this particular NASD rule.... We granted Howsam's petition for *certiorari* to resolve this disagreement. And we now hold that the matter is for the arbitrator.

II

This Court has determined that "arbitration is a matter of contract and a party cannot be required to submit to arbitration any dispute which he has not agreed so to submit." ... Although the Court has also long recognized and enforced a "liberal federal policy favoring arbitration agreements," ... it has made clear that there is an exception to this policy: The question whether the parties have submitted a particular dispute to arbitration, *i.e.,* the *"question of arbitrability,"* is "an issue for judicial determination [u]nless the parties clearly and unmistakably provide otherwise." ... We must decide here whether application of the NASD time limit provision falls into the scope of this last-mentioned interpretive rule.

Linguistically speaking, one might call any potentially dispositive gateway question a "question of arbitrability," for its answer will determine whether the underlying controversy will proceed to arbitration on the merits. The Court's case law, however, makes clear that, for purposes of applying the interpretive rule, the phrase "question of arbitrability" has a far more limited scope.... The Court has found the phrase applicable in the kind of narrow circumstance where contracting parties would likely have expected a court to have decided the gateway matter, where they are not likely to have thought that they had agreed that an arbitrator would do so, and, consequently, where reference of the gateway dispute to the court avoids the risk of forcing parties to arbitrate a matter that they may well not have agreed to arbitrate.

Thus, a gateway dispute about whether the parties are bound by a given arbitration clause raises a "question of arbitrability" for a court to decide.... Similarly, a disagreement about whether an arbitration clause in a concededly binding contract applies to a particular type of controversy is for the court....

At the same time the Court has found the phrase "question of arbitrability" *not* applicable in other kinds of general circumstance where parties would likely expect that an arbitrator would decide the gateway matter. Thus " 'procedural' questions which grow out of the dispute and bear on its final disposition" are presumptively *not* for the judge, but for an arbitrator, to decide.... So, too, the presumption is that the arbitrator should decide "allegation[s] of waiver, delay, or a like defense to arbitrability." ... Indeed, the Revised Uniform Arbitration Act of 2000 (RUAA), seeking to "incorporate the holdings of the vast majority of state courts and the law that has developed under the [Federal Arbitration Act]," states that an "arbitrator shall decide whether a condition precedent to arbitrability has been fulfilled." RUAA § 6(c), and comment 2, 7 U.L.A. 12–13 (Supp.2002). And the comments add that "in the absence of an agreement to the contrary, issues of substantive arbitrability ... are for a court to decide and issues of procedural arbitrability, *i.e.,* whether prerequisites such as *time limits,* notice, laches, estoppel, and other conditions precedent to an obligation to arbitrate have been met, are for the arbitrators to decide." *Id.,* § 6, comment 2, 7 U.L.A., at 13 (emphasis added).

Following this precedent, we find that the applicability of the NASD time limit rule is a matter presumptively for the arbitrator, not for the judge. The time limit rule closely resembles the gateway questions that this Court has found not to be "questions of arbitrability." ... Such a dispute seems an "aspec[t] of the [controversy] which called the grievance procedures into play." ...

Moreover, the NASD arbitrators, comparatively more expert about the meaning of their own rule, are comparatively better able to interpret and to apply it. In the absence of any statement to the contrary in the arbitration agreement, it is reasonable to infer that the parties intended the agreement to reflect that understanding.... And for the law to assume an expectation that aligns (1) decision maker with (2) comparative expertise will help better to secure a fair and expeditious resolution of the underlying controversy—a goal of arbitration systems and judicial systems alike.

We consequently conclude that the NASD's time limit rule falls within the class of gateway procedural disputes that do not present what our cases have called "questions of arbitrability." And the strong pro-court presumption as to the parties' likely intent does not apply.

III

Dean Witter argues that, in any event, *i.e.,* even without an anti-arbitration presumption, we should interpret the contracts between the parties here as calling for judicial determination of the time limit matter. Howsam's execution of a Uniform Submission Agreement with the NASD in 1997 effectively incorporated the NASD Code into the parties' agreement. Dean Witter notes the Code's time limit rule uses the word "eligible." That word, in Dean Witter's view, indicates the parties' intent for the time limit rule to be resolved by the court prior to arbitration.

We do not see how that is so. For the reasons stated in Part II, *supra,* parties to an arbitration contract would normally expect a forum-based decision maker to decide forum-specific procedural gateway matters. And any temptation here to place special anti-arbitration weight on the appearance of the word "eligible" in the NASD Code rule is counterbalanced by a different NASD rule; that rule states that "arbitrators shall be empowered to interpret and determine the applicability of all provisions under this Code." NASD Code § 10324.

Consequently, without the help of a special arbitration-disfavoring presumption, we cannot conclude that the parties intended to have a court, rather than an arbitrator, interpret and apply the NASD time limit rule. And as we held in Part II, *supra,* that presumption does not apply.

IV

For these reasons, the judgment of the Tenth Circuit is *Reversed.*

Notes and Questions

1. How would you define a "gateway question" in light of the Court's opinion? How does the Court define the notion of "arbitrability"?

2. Who decides what circumstances or issues constitute a "gateway question" and a question of arbitrability. Why? Does the result favor or disfavor arbitration?

3. What is a "procedural question"? What impact does it have on the jurisdictional question?

4. Does freedom of contract play any role in the Court's ruling? What about the federal policy on arbitration?

* * *

Green Tree Fin. Corp. v. Bazzle, 539 U.S. 444 (2003), involved consolidated cases about loan contracts between Green Tree, homeowners, and purchasers of mobile homes. The arbitral clause in the loan agreements provided for the arbitration of all disputes "by one arbitrator selected by us with consent of you." Individual cases eventually were certified as a class and compelled to arbitration. The arbitral clause made no mention of classwide arbitration. On appeal, the South Carolina state Supreme Court held that, under state contract law, the silence of the agreement on classwide arbitration permitted the claims to be submitted to class action arbitration. The consideration of whether the agreement allowed for classwide arbitration created a number of divisions within the Court—four Justices formed a plurality; one Justice authored a concurring-dissenting opinion; and four Justices dissented. The split did not appear to reflect ideological opposition among the Justices. Rather, it indicated analytical disagreement about an important issue of arbitration law.

Justice Breyer authored the plurality opinion. In addressing the issue, the Court returned to an elusive concept of arbitrability that it originally propounded in *First Options of Chicago, Inc. v. Kaplan*, 514 U.S. 938 (1995). In *Kaplan*, the Court stated that courts decide the basic issues of arbitrability (whether there is a valid contract of arbitration that covers the question of litigation), unless the parties authorize the arbitrators to rule on these matters. The recent decision in *Howsam v. Dean Witter Reynolds, Inc.* confirmed this division of labor between the courts and arbitrators—unless the parties provide otherwise, the courts decide the threshold arbitrability matters, while the arbitrators rule upon issues that pertain to the implementation of the arbitration (*e.g.*, the application of a time-limit bar to the submitted claim). *Bazzle* now adds that the interpretation of the content of the arbitration agreement also falls within the sovereign decisional authority of the arbitrator. Simply stated, "Under the terms of the parties' contracts, the question—whether the agreement forbids class arbitration—is for the arbitrator to decide."

The impact of the plurality opinion upon the law of arbitration is generally favorable. The determination is not antagonistic to arbitration because it extends the reach of the arbitrator's discretion, limits the role of the courts in regard to the arbitral process, and enhances the systemic autonomy of arbitration. This appraisal is supported by the fact that the four dissenting Justices, as well as the concurring Justice, did not express animosity toward arbitration in their disagreement with the plurality.

The analytical division that separates the court into two camps centers upon the distinction between would-be substantive and procedural arbitrability. The late Chief Justice William Rehnquist authored the principal dissenting opinion. Advancing the view that *Kaplan* and *Howsam* are distinguishable, the dissent asserted that the courts must decide what the parties have agreed to in their agreement. The content of the agreement is not a mere matter of implementing the agreed-upon recourse to arbitration. The question in *Bazzle*, therefore, fell within the orbit of *Kaplan* and not *Howsam*: "I think that the parties' agreement as to how the arbitrator should be selected is much more akin to the agreement as to what shall be arbitrated, a question for the courts under *First Options*, than it is to 'allegations of waiver, delay, or like defenses to arbitrability,' which are questions for the arbitrator under *Howsam*." According to the dissent, the parties did not agree to classwide arbitration and the South Carolina state Supreme Court "imposed a regime that was contrary to the express agreement of the parties. . . ." The state court's failure to observe the parties' contract warranted the reversal of its decision.

The case also raised the outlines of a state law question. Justice Thomas dissented on the basis that the Federal Arbitration Act should not govern "a state court's interpretation of a private arbitration agreement." Late Chief Justice Rehnquist acknowledged that state contract law regulated contracts of arbitration, but emphasized that state laws that contravened federal law were subject to preemption. Finally, Justice Stevens—who concurred and ideally would have upheld the South Carolina state Supreme Court rather than remand the case—concluded that: "There is nothing in the Federal Arbitration Act that precludes ... [the] determinations by the Supreme Court of South Carolina." According to Justice Stevens, that court held "as a matter of state law that class-action arbitrations [were] permissible if not prohibited by the applicable arbitration agreement, and that the agreement between [the] parties [was] silent on the issue."

When the Court granted *certiorari* in *Bazzle*, the expectation was that it would decide the vexed question of classwide arbitration and begin the formal elaboration of a basic standard of fairness in consumer arbitration—including the possible unconscionability or limited validity of arbitration agreements in this setting. It is clear that—at least ostensibly—those matters did not occur to, let alone preoccupy, the Court. By ruling on a boundary-line issue—in effect, characterizing the class action question as an interpretation of a valid agreement to arbitrate and delegating the question to the arbitrator as a matter of procedural arbitrability (for the plurality) or by having a court interpret the content of the arbitration agreement to determine whether it excludes classwide arbitration (for the three-member dissent)—the Court stated that the fairness and legitimacy questions in consumer arbitration are a matter for the parties' contract and the ruling of the arbitrators. This conclusion reinforces the view, also stated in *Kaplan*, that the practice of arbitration should not be allowed to generate too much litigation about itself. The Court thereby substantially buttressed the independence and autonomy of arbitration.

GREEN TREE FIN. CORP. v. BAZZLE

539 U.S. 444, 123 S.Ct. 2402, 156 L.Ed.2d 414 (2003).

BREYER, Justice.

This case concerns contracts between a commercial lender and its customers, each of which contains a clause providing for arbitration of all contract-related disputes. The Supreme Court of South Carolina held (1) that the arbitration clauses are silent as to whether arbitration might take the form of class arbitration, and (2) that, in that circumstance, South Carolina law interprets the contracts as permitting class arbitration.... We granted *certiorari* to determine whether this holding is consistent with the Federal Arbitration Act....

We are faced at the outset with a problem concerning the contracts' silence. Are the contracts in fact silent, or do they forbid class arbitration as petitioner Green Tree Financial Corp. contends? Given the South Carolina Supreme Court's holding, it is important to resolve that question. But we cannot do so, not simply because it is a matter of state law, but also because it is a matter for the arbitrator to decide. Because the record suggests that the parties have not yet received an arbitrator's decision on that question of contract interpretation, we vacate the judgment of the South Carolina Supreme Court and remand the case so that this question may be resolved in arbitration.

I.

In 1995, respondents Lynn and Burt Bazzle secured a home improvement loan from petitioner Green Tree. The Bazzles and Green Tree entered into a contract, governed by South Carolina law, which included the following arbitration clause:

> "ARBITRATION—All disputes, claims, or controversies arising from or relating to this contract or the relationships which result from this contract . . . *shall be resolved by binding arbitration by one arbitrator selected by us with consent of you.* This arbitration contract is made pursuant to a transaction in interstate commerce, and shall be governed by the Federal Arbitration Act. . . . THE PARTIES VOLUNTARILY AND KNOWINGLY WAIVE ANY RIGHT THEY HAVE TO A JURY TRIAL, EITHER PURSUANT TO ARBITRATION UNDER THIS CLAUSE OR PURSUANT TO A COURT ACTION BY U.S. [SIC] [US] (AS PROVIDED HEREIN). . . . The parties agree and understand that the arbitrator shall have all powers provided by the law and the contract. These powers shall include all legal and equitable remedies, including, but not limited to, money damages, declaratory relief, and injunctive relief." . . . (emphasis added, capitalization in original).

Respondents Daniel Lackey and George and Florine Buggs entered into loan contracts and security agreements for the purchase of mobile homes with Green Tree. These agreements contained arbitration clauses that were . . . identical to the Bazzles' arbitration clause. . . .

At the time of the loan transactions, Green Tree apparently failed to provide these customers with a legally required form that would have told them that they had a right to name their own lawyers and insurance agents and would have provided space for them to write in those names. . . . The two sets of customers before us now as respondents each filed separate actions in South Carolina state courts, complaining that this failure violated South Carolina law and seeking damages.

In April 1997, the Bazzles asked the court to certify their claims as a class action. Green Tree sought to stay the court proceedings and compel arbitration. On January 5, 1998, the court both (1) certified a class action and (2) entered an order compelling arbitration. Green Tree then selected an arbitrator with the Bazzles' consent. And the arbitrator, administering the proceeding as a class arbitration, eventually awarded the class $10,935,000 in statutory damages, along with attorney's fees. The trial court confirmed the award, and Green Tree appealed to the South Carolina Court of Appeals claiming, among other things, that class arbitration was legally impermissible.

[. . .]

The South Carolina Supreme Court withdrew both cases from the Court of Appeals, assumed jurisdiction, and consolidated the proceedings. . . . That court then held that the contracts were silent in respect to class arbitration, that they consequently authorized class arbitration, and that arbitration had properly taken that form. We granted *certiorari* to consider whether that holding is consistent with the Federal Arbitration Act.

II

The South Carolina Supreme Court's determination that the contracts are silent in respect to class arbitration raises a preliminary question. Green Tree argued there, as it argues here, that the contracts are not silent—that they forbid class arbitration. And we must deal with that argument at the outset, for if it is right, then the South Carolina court's holding is flawed on its own terms; that court neither said nor implied that it would have authorized class arbitration had the parties' arbitration agreement forbidden it.

Whether Green Tree is right about the contracts themselves presents a disputed issue of contract interpretation. THE CHIEF JUSTICE believes that Green Tree is right; indeed, that Green Tree is so clearly right that we should ignore the fact that state law, not federal law, normally governs such matters and reverse the South Carolina Supreme Court outright. THE CHIEF JUSTICE points out that the contracts say that disputes "shall be resolved . . . by one arbitrator selected by us [Green Tree] with consent of you [Green Tree's customer]." And it finds that class arbitration is clearly inconsistent with this requirement. After all, class arbitration involves an arbitration, not simply between Green Tree and a *named customer,* but also between Green Tree and *other* (represented) customers, all taking place before the arbitrator chosen to arbitrate the initial, *named customer's* dispute.

We do not believe, however, that the contracts' language is as clear as THE CHIEF JUSTICE believes. The class arbitrator *was* "selected by" Green Tree "with consent of" Green Tree's customers, the named plaintiffs. And insofar as the other class members agreed to proceed in class arbitration, they consented as well.

Of course, Green Tree did *not* independently select *this* arbitrator to arbitrate its disputes with the *other* class members. But whether the contracts contain this additional requirement is a question that the literal terms of the contracts do not decide. The contracts simply say (I) "selected by us [Green Tree]." And that is literally what occurred. The contracts do not say (II) "selected by us [Green Tree] to arbitrate this dispute and no other (even identical) dispute with another customer." The question whether (I) in fact implicitly means (II) is the question at issue: Do the contracts forbid class arbitration? Given the broad authority the contracts elsewhere bestow upon the arbitrator, the answer to this question is not completely obvious.

At the same time, we cannot automatically accept the South Carolina Supreme Court's resolution of this contract-interpretation question. Under the terms of the parties' contracts, the question—whether the agreement forbids class arbitration—is for the arbitrator to decide. The parties agreed to submit to the arbitrator "*[a]ll* disputes, claims, or controversies arising from or relating to this contract or the relationships which result from this contract." And the dispute about what the arbitration contract in each case means (*i.e.,* whether it forbids the use of class arbitration procedures) is a dispute "relating to this contract" and the resulting "relationships." Hence the parties seem to have agreed that an arbitrator, not a judge, would answer the relevant question.... And if there is doubt about that matter—about the " 'scope of arbitrable issues' "—we should resolve that doubt " 'in favor of arbitration.' "...

In certain limited circumstances, courts assume that the parties intended courts, not arbitrators, to decide a particular arbitration-related matter (in the absence of "clea[r] and unmistakabl[e]" evidence to the contrary).... These limited instances typically involve matters of a kind that "contracting parties would likely have expected a court" to decide.... They include certain gateway matters, such as whether the parties have a valid arbitration agreement at all or whether a concededly binding arbitration clause applies to a certain type of controversy....

The question here—whether the contracts forbid class arbitration—does not fall into this narrow exception. It concerns neither the validity of the arbitration clause nor its applicability to the underlying dispute between the parties. Unlike *First Options,* the question is not whether the parties wanted a judge or an arbitrator to decide *whether they agreed to arbitrate a matter*..... Rather the relevant question here is what *kind of arbitration proceeding* the parties agreed to. That question does not concern a state statute or judicial procedures.... It concerns contract interpretation and arbitration procedures. Arbitrators are well situated to answer that question. Given these considerations, along with the arbitration contracts' sweeping language concerning the scope of the questions committed to arbitration, this matter of contract interpretation should be for the arbitrator, not the courts, to decide....

[...]

NOTES AND QUESTIONS

1. What is (if any) the "gateway question" in *Bazzle*?

2. Why does the South Carolina state Supreme Court take such a different position on the question of litigation?

3. Under current law, what is the function of the courts in regard to arbitration? When can courts intervene in the arbitral process?

4. Do you agree with the Court that the arbitrating parties bargain for this much arbitrator interpretation?

5.   Is this a salutary result for arbitration? Why or why not?

* * *

You should position *Pacificare* in relation to the holding in the two foregoing opinions. The Court, echoing to some extent the ruling in *Vimar Seguros y Reaseguros, S.A. v. M/V Sky Reefer*, 515 U.S. 528 (1995), appears to conclude that the issue is premature until it is decided by the arbitrator.

<h2 style="text-align:center">PACIFICARE HEALTH SYSTEMS, INC. v. BOOK</h2>

538 U.S. 401, 123 S.Ct. 1531, 155 L.Ed.2d 578 (2003).

(footnotes omitted)

Justice SCALIA delivered the opinion of the Court.

In this case, we are asked to decide whether respondents can be compelled to arbitrate claims arising under the Racketeer Influenced and Corrupt Organizations Act (RICO) ..., notwithstanding the fact that the parties' arbitration agreements may be construed to limit the arbitrator's authority to award damages under that statute.

I

Respondents are members of a group of physicians who filed suit against managed-health-care organizations including petitioners Pacifi-Care Health Systems, Inc., and PacifiCare Operations, Inc. (collectively, PacifiCare), and UnitedHealthcare, Inc., and UnitedHealth Group Inc. (collectively, United). These physicians alleged that the defendants unlawfully failed to reimburse them for health-care services that they had provided to patients covered by defendants' health plans. They brought causes of action under RICO, the Employee Retirement Income Security Act of 1974 (ERISA), and federal and state prompt-pay statutes, as well as claims for breach of contract, unjust enrichment, and in quantum meruit. . . .

Of particular concern here, PacifiCare and United moved the District Court to compel arbitration, arguing that provisions in their contracts with respondents required arbitration of these disputes, including those arising under RICO. . . . Respondents opposed the motion on the ground that, because the arbitration provisions prohibit an award of punitive damages, . . . respondents could not obtain "meaningful relief" in arbitration for their claims under the RICO statute, which authorizes treble damages. . . . *See Paladino v. Avnet Computer Technologies, Inc.*, 134 F.3d 1054, 1062 (C.A.11 1998) (holding that where a remedial limitation in an arbitration agreement prevents a plaintiff from obtaining "meaningful relief" for a statutory claim, the agreement to arbitrate is unenforceable with respect to that claim).

The District Court denied petitioners' request to compel arbitration of the RICO claims. . . . The court concluded that given the remedial limitations in the relevant contracts, it was, indeed, "faced with a potential Paladino situation ..., where the plaintiff may not be able to obtain meaningful relief for allegations of statutory violations in an arbitration forum." ... Accordingly, it found the arbitration agreements unenforceable with respect to respondents' RICO claims.... The Eleventh Circuit affirmed "for the reasons set forth in [the District Court's] comprehensive opinion," ... and we granted *certiorari*....

II

Petitioners argue that whether the remedial limitations render their arbitration agreements unenforceable is not a question of "arbitrability," and hence should have been decided by an arbitrator, rather than a court, in the first instance. They also claim that even if this question is one of arbitrability, and is therefore properly within the purview of the courts at this time, the remedial limitations at issue do not require invalidation of their arbitration agreements. Either way, petitioners contend, the lower courts should have compelled arbitration. We conclude that it would be premature for us to address these questions at this time.

[...]

... Two of the four arbitration agreements at issue provide that "punitive damages shall not be awarded [in arbitration]," ... one provides that "[t]he arbitrators ... shall have no authority to award any punitive or exemplary damages," ... and one provides that "[t]he arbitrators ... shall have no authority to award extra contractual damages of any kind, including punitive or exemplary damages." ... Respondents insist, and the District Court agreed, ... that these provisions preclude an arbitrator from awarding treble damages under RICO. We think that neither our precedents nor the ambiguous terms of the contracts make this clear.

Our cases have placed different statutory treble-damages provisions on different points along the spectrum between purely compensatory and strictly punitive awards.... [W]e have characterized the treble-damages provision of the False Claims Act ... as "essentially punitive in nature." ... [O]n the other hand, we explained that the treble-damages provision ... of the Clayton Act ... "is in essence a remedial provision." ... [W]e noted that "the antitrust private action [which allows for treble damages] was created primarily as a remedy for the victims of antitrust violations." And ... we stated that "it is important to realize that treble damages have a compensatory side, serving remedial purposes in addition to punitive objectives." Indeed, we have repeatedly acknowledged that the treble-damages provision contained in RICO itself is remedial in nature.... [W]e stated that "[b]oth RICO and the Clayton Act are designed to remedy economic injury by providing for the recovery of treble damages, costs, and attorney's fees." And ... we took note of the "remedial function" of RICO's treble-damages provision.

In light of our case law's treatment of statutory treble damages, and given the uncertainty surrounding the parties' intent with respect to the contractual term "punitive," the application of the disputed language to respondents' RICO claims is, to say the least, in doubt. And *Vimar* instructs that we should not, on the basis of "mere speculation" that an arbitrator might interpret these ambiguous agreements in a manner that casts their enforceability into doubt, take upon ourselves the authority to decide the antecedent question of how the ambiguity is to be resolved. 515 U.S., at 541, 115 S.Ct. 2322. In short, since we do not know how the arbitrator will construe the remedial limitations, the questions whether they render the parties' agreements unenforceable and whether it is for courts or arbitrators to decide enforceability in the first instance are unusually abstract. As in *Vimar*, the proper course is to compel arbitration.

The judgment of the Court of Appeals is reversed, and the case is remanded for further proceedings consistent with this opinion.

It is so ordered.

Justice THOMAS took no part in the consideration or decision of this case.

NOTES AND QUESTIONS

1. Does the opinion in *Pacificare* fit into the *Howsam-Bazzle* doctrine? If so, how?

2. Other than the reference to *Avnet*, it is curious that an agreed-upon arbitral limitation should lead to the unenforceability of the arbitration agreement. Should such a result be confined to circumstances of bargaining inequality between the parties? Or also when the parties are substantially uneven in terms of sophistication? Why should a restrictive reference to arbitration otherwise disturb the general agreement to arbitrate?

3. How do you assess the Court's position that the litigation is premature?

4. In your view, is the issue posed in *Pacificare* an arbitrability question or a gateway issue? If it involves interpreting the contract, is it always a gateway issue?

4. STATUTORY ARBITRABILITY

Like contractual inarbitrability, the question of subject-matter inarbitrability is of central importance to the law of arbitration. It defines the lawful adjudicatory role of arbitration. Should arbitration function primarily, if not exclusively, as a mechanism for resolving private contractual disputes (relating to performance, delivery, or payment)? Should its jurisdictional reach be expanded to include claims that arise in the context of contractual relationships and involve legal rights created by statute? Extending arbitration to the resolution of regulatory law claims blurs the jurisdictional boundary between judicial and arbitral adjudication, between the role of the law and the function of contract. In effect, arbitration gains, to some degree, a public law-making authority. It affects the relevant statutory framework and the underlying public interest by confining some part of its interpretation and implementation to a private adjudicatory process.

For example, a commercial transaction that results in a failure of timely payment or delivery can also implicate laws that are meant to curb economic monopolies. When the transaction contains an arbitral clause, should the law permit the arbitrators to rule both on the breach of contract claim and a counterclaim sounding in antitrust? Would a statutory command for exclusive judicial jurisdiction over the regulatory claim demand a severance of the arbitral and judicial litigation? A stay of arbitration pending the court action? If the claims are so inter-related that severance of the claims is not possible, should judicial or arbitral jurisdiction be favored?

The answers to these questions in the U.S. law of arbitration have been influenced by considerations of arbitral autonomy, the federal policy supporting arbitration, and the Court's decisional law in matters of international commercial arbitration. On the one hand, it can be argued, as a matter of basic doctrine, that some subject-matter limits must be imposed upon and are necessary to the process of arbitral adjudication. The marketplace may be a private arena, but it is also a stage upon which communitarian interests appear and have a role. Bankruptcies involve both the interests of creditors and the public's interest in the orderly dissolution of liability-ridden enterprises. The sale of securities is a private transaction done in the context of a financial market, the integrity of which is of critical importance to society at large. Commercial competition may enhance the profitability of private enterprises, but it also affects the position of consumers and the general operation of the American economic system. The public dimension of the issues raised by commercial conduct can sometimes warrant exclusive judicial jurisdiction.

On the other hand, the possibility of staying or bifurcating arbitral proceedings because of regulatory law claims can invite dilatory tactics and lessen substantially the adjudicatory effectiveness of arbitration. Parties can always manufacture a claim that enables them to shift the litigation to a court (at least, temporarily), thereby causing delay and greater expense (and perhaps frustrating the recourse to arbitration). In the absence of a clear and easily applicable rule for "intertwined" claims, a body of complex and difficult rules needs to be developed, placing greater stress upon the process. As Justice Breyer makes clear in *First Options v. Kaplan*, none of these consequences is desirable in the context of arbitration. Such rulings would eliminate the simplicity and clarity of the reference to arbitration, and they could transform the law of arbitration into a litigious, unworkable, and self-defeating body of principles. This approach would ultimately contravene the letter and spirit of the FAA, especially Section Two, and result in a deterioration of the system of alternative recourse. If the basic precepts of federalism cannot limit the federal policy on arbitration, it is unlikely that any other legal value or principle could thwart it.

Also, the Court's holdings in international arbitration cases have had a direct and profound impact upon the elaboration of a domestic rule of decision on subject-matter inarbitrability. In two significant cases, *Scherk v. Alberto–Culver Co.*, 417 U.S. 506 (1974), and *Mitsubishi Motors Corp. v. Soler Chrysler–Plymouth, Inc.*, 473 U.S. 614 (1985), the Court ruled that international arbitrators could rule upon statutory claims that arose in the performance of an international contract. At the time they were rendered, *Scherk* and *Mitsubishi* were expressly limited to matters involving transborder commercial arbitration. Their reasoning, however, began to creep into domestic arbitration cases. The Court eventually simply forgot about the international specificity of the holdings and integrated them into the domestic decisional law. As a result, precedent prohibiting the domestic recourse to arbitration for the adjudication of certain statutory claims was reversed, engendering a new interpretation of the domestic provisions of the FAA: Nothing in the Act prohibited the submission of statutory disputes to arbitration. Finally, as a result of its holdings in *Scherk* and *Mitsubishi*, the Court came to believe—or at least to state—that arbitration was a "mere form of trial," the use of which had no impact upon the disputed substantive rights. Therefore, the holdings in the international cases became the doctrinal foundation for the Court's elaboration of a domestic law rule that statutory claims could be submitted to arbitration.

The cases and case summaries that follow describe the effect of the U.S. Supreme Court's arbitration doctrine upon the subject-matter inarbitrability defense among the lower federal courts. To some extent, this section anticipates other developments in the course materials dealing with the arbitrability of statutory rights. In particular, the list of judicial determinations on the arbitrability of various statutory rights introduces a vital aspect of the law of securities arbitration as well as labor and employment arbitration. The present classification is more comprehensive of the rights addressed and provides a view of the debate to which the arbitrability of statutory rights question can give rise. The debate dimension of the area is not as evident either in the cases dealing with securities or employment arbitration. Finally, you should be aware throughout your assessment of these judicial rulings that they are the progeny of the international decisional law and its impact upon *McMahon* and *Rodriguez* as well as the ruling in *Gilmer*. That perspective will allow you to properly assess the inter-related doctrine that unites all these various areas of arbitration.

ERISA

PRITZKER v. MERRILL LYNCH, PIERCE, FENNER & SMITH, INC.

7 F.3d 1110 (3d Cir. 1993).

[. . .]

In this appeal, we revisit an issue which has commanded the attention of the Supreme Court and other courts of appeals since we last addressed it: whether claims of statutory violations of the Employee Retirement Income Security Act of 1974 . . . ("ERISA") are subject to arbitration pursuant to section 2 of the Federal Arbitration Act. . . . In *Barrowclough v. Kidder, Peabody & Co., Inc.*, 752 F.2d 923 (3d Cir. 1985), we held that statutory ERISA claims are not subject to arbitration. Since *Barrowclough*, however, Supreme Court decisions have substantially revised the rationale we relied upon there. We now hold that such claims are subject to arbitration under the FAA. We will, therefore, overrule *Barrowclough* insofar as it held that arbitration of statutory ERISA claims is precluded, and reverse the district court's order denying defendant's motion to compel arbitration of the plaintiffs' claims in this case. We also hold that the arbitration clauses in the agreements in question here should be read to include all of the named defendants even though only one defendant signed them. Accordingly, we will instruct the district court to order arbitration of the claims against the non-signatory defendants as well.[1]

[. . .]

. . . The arbitration clauses in the Cash Management Agreements state:

> It is understood that the following agreement to arbitrate does not consti-tute a waiver by the undersigned of the right to seek a judicial forum where such a waiver would be void under the Federal Securities Laws or the Employment Retirement Income Securities Act of 1974.

> The undersigned agrees, and by carrying an account for the under-signed you agree, that except as inconsistent with the foregoing sentence, all controversies which may arise between us, including but not limited to, any transaction or the construction, performance or breach of this or any other agreement between us, whether entered into prior, on or subsequent

---

1. We hold only that statutory ERISA claims are subject to arbitration under the FAA when the parties have executed a valid arbitration agreement encompassing the claims at issue. For a number of reasons (and the following list is not intended to be exhaustive), this opinion should not be read to require arbitration of statutory ERISA claims in all instances. First, our focus here is limited to arbitration under the FAA. We do not address, for example, labor or any other type of arbitration which may arise from the collective bargaining process or otherwise implicate the concerns we have previously expressed about a potential for conflict of interest. . . . Second, in contrast to this case, certain types of statutory ERISA claims may arise in such a fashion or may so implicate employees' rights that they come within the provision of the FAA which precludes arbitration of contracts of employment. . . . Finally, as explained further *infra*, the arbitration agreement must be valid and must encompass the ERISA claims at issue for the claims to be subject to arbitration rather than the judicial process.

to the date hereof, shall be determined by arbitration and shall be governed by the laws of the state of New York.

Any dispute hereunder shall be submitted to arbitration conducted under the provisions of the Constitution and Rules of the Board of Directors of the New York Stock Exchange, Inc., or pursuant to the Code of Arbitration Procedure of the National Association of Securities Dealers, Inc. as the undersigned may elect...

"[A]s a matter of contract, no party can be forced to arbitrate unless that party has entered an agreement to do so."... Thus, before it compels arbitration, a court should determine "that a valid agreement to arbitrate exists between the parties and that the specific dispute [comes] within the substantive scope of the agreement."... "Federal law applies when construing an arbitration clause when, as here, the motions pertaining to arbitration are brought pursuant to the [FAA]."...

[...]

In *Barrowclough*, a discharged stockbroker sued his former employer for improperly withholding deferred compensation benefits and for violating ERISA's reporting and fiduciary provisions. We held that while claims to establish or enforce rights to benefits under 29 U.S.C. § 1132(a) are subject to arbitration, claims based on violations of the substantive provisions of ERISA can be asserted in a federal court in spite of an arbitration agreement.... Our reasoning evolved from two cases in which the Supreme Court decided that statutory claims under Title VII of the Civil Rights Act...and the Fair Labor Standards Act...could be pursued in court after the employees asserting them had already proceeded through the labor arbitration process pursuant to their collective bargaining agreements. *See Alexander v. Gardner–Denver Co*. ...

At that time, we examined the text, structure and purpose of ERISA and concluded that statutory ERISA claims, over which federal courts have exclusive jurisdiction pursuant to 29 U.S.C. § 1132(e), must be brought in court rather than pursued in arbitration for three reasons. First, ERISA constituted a "complex and evolving body of federal law" requiring judicial interpretation to implement Congress' purpose of enforcing "minimum standards" to protect employee benefits.... Second, we found that the provisions of ERISA which afforded complainants broad access to the courts, as well as the absence of procedural barriers to ERISA lawsuits, suggested that Congress had intended that courts, not arbitrators, handle statutory claims.... Finally, we expressed concern that arbitrators might not be sufficiently trained to handle the complex legal issues presented by ERISA claims....

Merrill Lynch essentially argues that the precedential status of *Barrowclough* is relegated to obsolescence by subsequent Supreme Court decisions addressing the arbitrability of statutory claims under the FAA. In particular, Merrill Lynch directs our attention to *McMahon* and *Rodriguez*, in which the Court enforced agreements to arbitrate trading loss claims similar to those asserted by the Trustees in this case....

[. . .]

McMahon's analysis makes it clear that agreements to arbitrate statutory ERISA claims under the FAA may be enforceable. . . . When we apply *McMahon*'s reasoning to the facts before us, we have no doubt that the agreement to arbitrate must be upheld.

[. . .]

First . . . , under *McMahon*, if there is a "well-founded" claim that the agreements resulted from fraud or coercion, a party may not be compelled to arbitrate its claims. . . . The Trustees do not seriously attack the validity of the Cash Management Agreements or their respective arbitration clauses here. Although they repeatedly refer to the agreements they signed as "required clause[s] in a preprinted contract," we reject any insinuation that the clauses represent contracts of adhesion or "resulted from the sort of fraud or overwhelming economic power that would provide grounds 'for the revocation of any contract.' " . . . To the contrary, the record reveals no more than that the arbitration clauses were indeed part of pre-printed investment agreements and that the parties may have possessed unequal bargaining power when the agreements were signed. The Supreme Court has ruled, however, that agreements between securities dealers and investors are enforceable even though they may involve unequal bargaining power. . . .

Similarly, under *McMahon*, the Trustees might avoid arbitration if they could demonstrate that Congress intended to prevent a waiver of judicial remedies for statutory ERISA violations. They are unable to do so, however, because they have not identified a specific provision in ERISA's text which indicates that Congress intended to exempt statutory ERISA claims from the FAA.

As we have noted, in *Barrowclough*, we construed provisions in ERISA's statutory scheme which conferred exclusive jurisdiction on the federal courts to mean that the legislature intended to preclude arbitration of statutory ERISA claims. . . . In *McMahon* and *Rodriguez*, however, the Supreme Court twice rejected a similar inference drawn from the jurisdictional provisions of the federal securities laws. Instead, relying on *Mitsubishi Motors*, which held that claims under the federal antitrust laws were arbitrable despite provisions vesting exclusive jurisdiction in the federal courts, the *McMahon* Court held that claimants may waive the right to pursue securities claims exclusively in federal court by executing a valid compulsory arbitration agreement. . . . As the Court has repeatedly stated, such jurisdictional provisions speak only to the issue of which judicial forum is available, and not to whether an arbitral forum is unavailable. . . . In other words, such provisions do not constitute Congressional statements that statutory ERISA claims cannot be arbitrated.

[. . .]

. . . [W]e recognize that the *Barrowclough* panel was persuaded at least in part by concerns for the development of ERISA law, but these concerns have since been deemed insufficient to preclude arbitration. . . . As the Court noted in *Gilmer* in the age discrimination context, there is no reason to suspect that all ERISA claims will be subject to arbitration; judges will continue to issue decisions interpreting sections 404 and 406 of ERISA. Therefore, compelling arbitration of the Trustees' statutory ERISA claims will not stifle judicial development of the law.

[. . .]

Finally, in arguing that arbitration is inconsistent with ERISA's statutory purpose, the Trustees contend that since there is no assurance that arbitrators will follow court precedents, compulsory arbitration of ERISA claims frustrates the legislative goal of developing a consistent body of law. This argument has a familiar ring; it is a reiteration of the traditional distrust of arbitration on the ground that arbitrators cannot be relied upon to follow the law. The Court has uniformly rejected this position in its recent arbitration cases, however, and we will only briefly address the Trustees' contentions in this regard.

The Trustees make much of the fact that neither the American nor the New York Stock Exchanges require[s] that arbitrators give reasons for their decisions. The lack of such a requirement, the Trustees speculate, results in a stifling of the law's development, provides poor guidance for plan beneficiaries and fiduciaries and results in an inability to obtain effective appellate review. In *Gilmer*, however, the Court rejected similar claims, observing that the New York Stock Exchange arbitration rules provided for publication of written award summaries including the names of the parties, a statement of the issues and a description of the award. . . . For present purposes, we see no reason to distinguish between the ADEA claims at issue in *Gilmer* and the ERISA claims before us. Instead, we believe it is consistent with the Court's analysis in *Gilmer* to hold that an award summary need not state a rationale to avoid conflicts with the fundamental purposes of ERISA.

[. . .]

To recapitulate, we hold that statutory ERISA claims are subject to compulsory arbitration under the FAA and in accordance with the terms of a valid arbitration agreement. Where the parties to such a clause unmistakably intend to arbitrate all controversies which might arise between them, their agreement should be applied to claims against agents or entities related to the signatories. . . .

NOTES AND QUESTIONS

1.   The court's opinion in *Pritzker* relies heavily upon the U.S. Supreme Court's determinations in *McMahon* and *Gilmer*. The full significance of these decisions will become clearer when you have studied securities and employment arbitration in subsequent chapters. What importance does the *Pritzker* court attribute to them? How does it construe their holdings?

2.   Explain the significance of *McMahon* and *Gilmer* to the result reached in *Pritzker*.

3. In its discussion of *Barrowclough*, does the *Pritzker* court imply or seem to believe that the U.S. Supreme Court's recent rulings on arbitration means that *Gardner-Denver* is no longer good law?

4. How critical is the development of ERISA law to the determination?

5. Why does the *Pritzker* court find the statutory language in ERISA, which provides for exclusive judicial jurisdiction over rights, no longer controlling?

6. Was the arbitration clause in the Cash Management Agreement a contract of adhesion? Do you agree with the court's view of this matter? Why or why not? Is there another way to interpret that clause?

7. Why does stating that arbitrators do not follow law reflect a distrust of arbitration? Is this political correctness or a serious statement of analysis?

8. Finally, what limit does the court apply to the validity and enforceability of an arbitration agreement?

Bankruptcy

IN RE STATEWIDE REALTY CO.

159 B.R. 719 (Bankr. D.N.J. 1993).

[. . .]

The Federal Arbitration Act establishes a strong federal policy which favors arbitration, and which requires that agreements to arbitrate are rigorously enforced even where a party bound by such an agreement asserts a claim based on statutory rights. . . .

The controlling precedent in this circuit for a determination of whether the Bankruptcy Code provisions are in conflict with the arbitration clause is *Hays & Co. v. Merrill Lynch, Pierce, Fenner & Smith, Inc.*, 885 F.2d 1149 (3d Cir.1989). . . .

The court in *Hays* held that a trustee is bound by the terms of an arbitration clause to the same extent as the debtor would be, but that the trustee's Code § 544(b) claims are not subject to arbitration because they are not derivative of the debtor, and the trustee accordingly is not bound by the terms of the arbitration clause in the agreement. . . . Moreover, relying on *McMahon*, the *Hays* court held that the district court erred in its determination that it could exercise discretion to decline to enforce the arbitration clause. It found that the trustee did not meet its burden of demonstrating that the Bankruptcy Code provisions, policy or legislative history demonstrated any conflict with enforcement of an arbitration clause in a non-core proceeding brought by the trustee to enforce a claim of the estate in district court. . . . Furthermore, surveying the Supreme Court arbitration cases . . ., the Third Circuit concluded that it could "no longer subscribe to a hierarchy of congressional concerns that places bankruptcy law in a position of superiority over that [Arbitration] Act." . . . The Third Circuit reasoned in *Hays* that it was no longer good law to conclude that the policies of the Bankruptcy Code outweigh the policies of the Arbitration Act.

The reasoning of the *Hays* court has been followed in recent decisions in other jurisdictions. . . .

[. . .]

Guided by the foregoing analysis, the court finds that in the matter *sub judice*, the Debtor likewise fails to demonstrate that enforcement of the arbitration clause in the Management Agreement is contrary to the provisions or purpose of the Bankruptcy Code. The Debtor points to no Code provision, policy or portion of legislative history that demonstrates that arbitration should not be compelled.

[. . .]

The fact that the matter before the court is a core proceeding does not mean that arbitration is inappropriate. . . . The description of a matter as a core proceeding simply means that the bankruptcy court has the jurisdiction to make a full adjudication. However, merely because the court has the authority to render a decision does not mean it should do so. The discussion in *Hays* regarding core and non-core proceedings is not read by this court as suggesting that core proceedings may not be subject to arbitration. Rather, it appears that the *Hays* court sought to distinguish between actions derived from the debtor, and therefore subject to the arbitration agreement, and bankruptcy actions in essence created by the Bankruptcy Code for the benefit ultimately of creditors of the estate, and therefore not encompassed by the arbitration agreement.

[. . .]

In the present matter, in terms of efficiency, arbitration is perhaps better suited to resolve the disputes of all the parties. The former partners are presently in arbitration with Hilton International. The addition of the Debtor to the proceeding will enable all claims to be resolved in one forum. In any event, the factors of cost and expediency do not weigh mightily against arbitration. The fact that arbitration may not be as efficient or as expeditious has been held not to justify refusal to enforce arbitration clauses in itself, even in bankruptcy. . . .

As a general rule, the policy behind Chapter 11 Reorganization recognizes the expedient and economic resolution of business affairs. However, inquiry regarding conflict between the statutes should not be [so] broad as to swallow the policies of the Arbitration Act, especially when confirmation is not delayed by arbitration. . . . Following the reasoning of *Hays* in this case, the court cannot perceive any greater impact on the Bankruptcy Code in compelling arbitration than denying it. . . .

[. . .]

NOTES AND QUESTIONS

1. In the court's view, is there no public policy interest in the Bankruptcy Code or does the public policy interest in arbitration simply outweigh the public policy interest in bankruptcy?

2. What is the public's stake in bankruptcy and in arbitration? What do the relevant statutes provide? If you were a judge balancing those interests, where would you fall?

3. How do you assess the distinction between core and non-core proceedings? Should it make arbitration less or more likely?

4. Finally, assess the last paragraph of the reprinted opinion. Is the court saying that arbitrability is acceptable because privatization does not matter in that setting? If the recourse to arbitration is of no consequence, why not leave such matters in the jurisdiction of a public entity? Should arbitration always fully trump judicial recourse? Why can't the two processes be combined and work hand-in-hand? In your view, what is in the public interest after these two cases?

Several federal circuits have expanded the reach of arbitration in bankruptcy matters. They have lessened the significance of the previously central distinction between "core and non-core" matters and emphasized that the recourse to arbitration would be prohibited only if it jeopardized the objectives of the Bankruptcy Code. According to the U.S. Second Circuit, for example, bankruptcy courts do not have the discretion to override an arbitration agreement unless they find that the bankruptcy proceedings are based on provisions of the Bankruptcy Code that "inherently conflict" with the Arbitration Act or that the arbitration of the claim would "necessarily jeopardize" the objectives of the Bankruptcy Code. In *MBNA Am. Bank, N.A. v. Hill*, 436 F.3d 104 (2d Cir. 2006), the lower court had held that the consumer's claim that MBNA violated the automatic stay provision of the Bankruptcy Code was a "core" bankruptcy proceeding and the bankruptcy court was the most appropriate forum for resolving the dispute. The appellate court disagreed, holding that the bankruptcy court must enforce the arbitration agreement between debtor and creditor and ordering the class action to arbitration.

The Third Circuit has ruled in a similar vein. In *In re Mintze*, 434 F.3d 222 (3d Cir. 2006), it held that a bankruptcy court does not have the authority to deny enforcement to an otherwise valid arbitration agreement. In so holding, the court referred to *Hays and Co. v. Merrill Lynch, Pierce, Fenner & Smith, Inc.*, 885 F.2d 1149 (3d Cir. 1989). It stated that the "core/non-core" distinction had been vital to determining whether a bankruptcy court has jurisdiction to adjudicate fully the proceeding, but the court could refuse to enforce the arbitration agreement only if there was an inherent conflict between the objectives of the Arbitration Act and the Bankruptcy Code. The inherent conflict requirement applies to both core and non-core matters.

MINTZE v. AMERICAN GENERAL FIN. SERV., INC.

434 F.3d 222 (3d Cir. 2006).

ROTH, Circuit Judge.

[. . .]

III.

AGF argues that the Bankruptcy Court lacked the discretion to deny enforcement of the arbitration clause in the mortgage agreement. The District Court held, and Mintze contends, that the Bankruptcy Court had such discretion and that it was within its bounds of discretion when it ruled against AGF. . . .

A.

Bankruptcy proceedings are divided into two categories: core and non-core. . . . The distinction between the two categories is relevant because the type of proceeding may determine the ultimate authority of the bankruptcy court. In a core proceeding, a bankruptcy court has "comprehensive power to hear, decide and enter final orders and judgments." . . . In addition, the bankruptcy court can make findings of fact and conclusions of law. In contrast, the bankruptcy court's authority is significantly limited in non-core proceedings. In a non-core proceeding, the bankruptcy court is allowed only to make proposed findings of fact and proposed conclusions of law, which it submits to the district court. . . .

The core/non-core distinction does not, however, affect whether a bankruptcy court has the discretion to deny enforcement of an arbitration agreement. . . . It merely determines whether the bankruptcy court has the jurisdiction to make a full adjudication. Because this distinction does not affect whether the Bankruptcy Court had the discretion to deny arbitration, we will accept the parties' stipulation that the proceeding was a "core" proceeding for the purposes of deciding whether the Bankruptcy Court had discretion.

B.

[. . .]

The FAA has established a strong policy in favor of arbitration. . . . It requires rigorous enforcement of arbitration agreements. . . . By itself, the FAA mandates enforcement of applicable arbitration agreements even for federal statutory claims. . . .

The FAA's mandate can, however, be overridden. If a party opposing arbitration can demonstrate that "Congress intended to preclude a waiver of judicial remedies for the statutory rights at issue," the FAA will not compel courts to enforce an otherwise applicable arbitration agreement. . . . To overcome enforcement of arbitration, a party must establish congressional intent to create an exception to the FAA's mandate with respect to the party's statutory claims. . . .

Shortly after the Supreme Court decided *McMahon,* we applied its standard to a bankruptcy case that is similar to the present case. *See Hays,* 885 F.2d 1149. In *Hays,* we held that where a party seeks to enforce a debtor-derivative pre-petition contract claim, a court does not have the discretion to deny enforcement of an otherwise applicable arbitration clause. . . . *Hays* involved a trustee to the debtor's estate, bringing causes of action against a brokerage firm that managed two corporate accounts for the debtor. The complaints alleged federal and state securities violations, as well as some statutory claims created by the Bankruptcy Code. The *Hays* Court was presented with the question whether the Bankruptcy Code conflicts with the FAA "in such a way as to bestow upon a district court discretion to decline to enforce an arbitration agreement" with respect to the trustee's claims. Applying the *McMahon* standard, we said that

> the district court lacked the authority and discretion to deny enforcement of the arbitration clause *unless* [the trustee] had met its burden of showing that the text, legislative history, or purpose of the Bankruptcy Code conflicts with the enforcement of an arbitration clause in a case of this kind, that is, *a non-core proceeding brought by a trustee to enforce a claim of the estate in a district court.*

Hays, 885 F.2d at 1156–57 (emphasis added). We held that whether the *McMahon* standard is met determines whether the court has the discretion to deny enforcement of an otherwise applicable arbitration clause. . . . The starting point is *McMahon.* The Bankruptcy Court and District Court, however, applied the *McMahon* standard after determining that the Bankruptcy Court had the discretion to deny arbitration. Those courts applied *McMahon* to determine whether the Bankruptcy Court *should* have exercised its discretion, rather than to determine whether it had the discretion to exercise. This approach is not what is required by *McMahon* and *Hays.*

Mintze contends, and the District Court held, that our *Hays* decision primarily applies to non-core proceedings. . . .

We disagree with this interpretation—that the application of *Hays* is limited to non-core proceedings. First, *Hays* applied the Supreme Court's *McMahon* standard, which applies to all statutory claims subject to applicable arbitration clauses, not just to those claims arising in non-core bankruptcy proceedings. Second, the *Hays* decision did not seek to distinguish between core and non-core proceedings; rather, it sought to distinguish between causes of action derived from the debtor and bankruptcy actions that the Bankruptcy Code created for the benefit of the creditors of the estate. . . . Third, the two cases that the District Court cited from other circuits to support its holding that the Bankruptcy Court did not abuse its discretion, actually support the contention that *Hays* applies to *core* proceedings. The District Court cited *United States Lines* and *National Gypsum.* Both of these cases expressly state that a finding that a proceeding is a core proceeding does not automatically give a bankruptcy court the discretion to deny arbitration. Rather, those cases indicate that the *McMahon* standard must still be satisfied before a bankruptcy court has such discretion....

We find that the standard we articulated in *Hays* applies equally to core and non-core proceedings.... Where an otherwise applicable arbitration clause exists, a bankruptcy court lacks the authority and discretion to deny its enforcement, *unless* the party opposing arbitration can establish congressional intent, under the *McMahon* standard, to preclude waiver of judicial remedies for the statutory rights at issue.

IV.

We conclude that the Bankruptcy Court lacked the authority and the discretion to deny enforcement of the arbitration provision in the contract between Mintze and AGF. The FAA mandates enforcement of arbitration when applicable unless Congressional intent to the contrary is established. Mintze has failed to demonstrate through statutory text, legislative history, or the underlying purposes of the Bankruptcy Code that Congress intended to preclude waiver of judicial remedies for her claims....

NOTES AND QUESTIONS

1.   How is the opinion a pronouncement on jurisdiction?

2.   Does the FAA and the federal policy on arbitration have any authority in the court's reasoning?

3.   Why does the court abandon the distinction between "core" and "non-core" matters?

4.   Describe the objectives of the Bankruptcy Code. What public policy interests are considerations in the Code's objectives?

MBNA AM. BANK, N.A. v. HILL
436 F.3d 104 (2d Cir. 2006).

GIBSON, Circuit Judge.

[...]

II.

The Federal Arbitration Act establishes a "federal policy favoring arbitration agreements," ... and mandates the enforcement of contractual arbitration provisions. The Act provides that written agreements to arbitrate "shall be valid, irrevocable, and enforceable, save upon such grounds as exist at law or in equity for the revocation of any contract." ... A court has a duty to stay its proceedings if it is satisfied that the issue before it is arbitrable, and "[t]his duty ... is not diminished when a party bound by an agreement raises a claim founded on statutory rights." ...

However, as the Supreme Court acknowledged in *McMahon,* "[l]ike any statutory directive, the Arbitration Act's mandate may be overridden by a contrary congressional command." ... The party opposing arbitration has the burden of showing that Congress intended to preclude arbitration of the statutory rights at issue. Congressional intent can be deduced from the statute's text or legislative history, or from "an inherent conflict between arbitration and the statute's underlying purposes." ...

Disputes that involve both the Bankruptcy Code and the Arbitration Act often present conflicts of "near polar extremes: bankruptcy policy exerts an inexorable pull towards centralization while arbitration policy advocates a decentralized approach toward dispute resolution." ...

In resolving these conflicts, courts distinguish between claims over which bankruptcy judges have discretion to refuse arbitration and those that they must send directly to arbitration. Bankruptcy courts generally do not have discretion to refuse to compel arbitration of "non-core" bankruptcy matters, or matters that are simply "related to" bankruptcy cases.... As to these matters, the presumption in favor of arbitration usually trumps the lesser interest of bankruptcy courts in adjudicating non-core proceedings....

Bankruptcy courts are more likely to have discretion to refuse to compel arbitration of core bankruptcy matters, which implicate "more pressing bankruptcy concerns." ... However, even as to core proceedings, the bankruptcy court will not have discretion to override an arbitration agreement unless it finds that the proceedings are based on provisions of the Bankruptcy Code that "inherently conflict" with the Arbitration Act or that arbitration of the claim would "necessarily jeopardize" the objectives of the Bankruptcy Code.... This determination requires a particularized inquiry into the nature of the claim and the facts of the specific bankruptcy. The objectives of the Bankruptcy Code relevant to this inquiry include "the goal of centralized resolution of purely bankruptcy issues, the need to protect creditors and reorganizing debtors from piecemeal litigation, and the undisputed power of a bankruptcy court to enforce its own orders." ... If a severe conflict is found, then the court can properly conclude that, with respect to the particular Code provision involved, Congress intended to override the Arbitration Act's general policy favoring the enforcement of arbitration agreements.

In this case, Hill's claim under § 362(h) of the Bankruptcy Code is properly characterized as a "core" bankruptcy proceeding. Claims that clearly invoke substantive rights created by federal bankruptcy law necessarily arise under Title 11 and are deemed core proceedings.... So too are proceedings that, by their nature, could arise only in the context of a bankruptcy case.... Actions brought under 11 U.S.C. § 362(h) are therefore core proceedings because they derive directly from the Bankruptcy Code and can be brought only in the context of a bankruptcy case.

In addressing the question of whether Hill's core proceeding should be arbitrated, both the bankruptcy court and the district court provided thoughtful analysis and addressed the relevant competing interests. The bankruptcy court recognized that "Code § 362(h) presents a conundrum in the context of a conflict between the jurisdiction of bankruptcy courts and arbitral fora." The bankruptcy court concluded that its court was the most appropriate forum for Hill's claim because a section 362(h) cause of action is strictly a product of the Bankruptcy Code.... Moreover, at the time of the bankruptcy court's ruling, Hill's bankruptcy case was open and she continued to require the protection of the automatic stay. Finally, the bankruptcy court noted that automatic stay provisions are the equivalent of an injunctive order of the bankruptcy court.

The district court held that the bankruptcy court did not abuse its discretion by denying MBNA's motion. The district court recognized it as a close case, but ultimately was persuaded by the fact that a ruling on Hill's claim did not require the bankruptcy court to address the terms of the agreement between Hill and MBNA. Instead, the court would decide whether MBNA violated the automatic stay provision. The district court also emphasized that to allow arbitration to go forward would seriously jeopardize the objectives of the Code [since] automatic stay serves the same function as an injunction.

Although we reach the same conclusion as the lower courts that Hill's § 362(h) claim is a core proceeding, we hold that arbitration of her claim would not seriously jeopardize the objectives of the Bankruptcy Code because: (1) Hill's estate has now been fully administered and her debts have been discharged, so she no longer requires protection of the automatic stay and resolution of the claim would have no effect on her bankruptcy estate; (2) as a purported class action, Hill's claims lack the direct connection to her own bankruptcy case that would weigh in favor of refusing to compel arbitration; and (3) a stay is not so closely related to an injunction that the bankruptcy court is uniquely able to interpret and enforce its provisions.

First, and most importantly, arbitration of Hill's § 362(h) claim would not jeopardize the important purposes that the automatic stay serves: providing debtors with a fresh start, protecting the assets of the estate, and allowing the bankruptcy court to centralize disputes concerning the estate.... District courts have often reversed bankruptcy decisions refusing to compel arbitration of core bankruptcy matters and granted motions to arbitrate core claims on the grounds that arbitration would not interfere with or affect the distribution of the estate....

Hill's bankruptcy case is now closed and she has been discharged. Resolution of Hill's claim against MBNA therefore cannot affect an ongoing reorganization, and arbitration would not conflict with the objectives of the automatic stay. MBNA has reimbursed Hill for the $159.01 payment it extracted from her bank account, and Hill no longer requires the protection of the stay to ensure her fresh start.... Consequently, any damages that might be awarded on the § 362(h) claim would be Hill's personal property and would not be part of her bankruptcy estate.

These factors distinguish Hill's case from cases where appellate courts have held that bankruptcy courts had discretion to refuse to stay proceedings pending arbitration. In those cases, resolution of the arbitrable claims directly implicated matters central to the purposes and policies of the Bankruptcy Code. . . .

[. . .]

Notes and Questions

1. Explain bankruptcy law's "pull to centralization."

2. When is bankruptcy's interest "lesser"?

3. Are core issues still important in establishing a bankruptcy court's jurisdiction?

4. What role does congressional intent play in the arbitrability of statutory rights?

5. What is a core proceeding? When does it or should it influence the arbitrability determination?

6. How does an automatic stay in a bankruptcy case differ from an injunction, if at all?

7. Why does the court conclude that Hill's dispute with MBNA is arbitrable?

Antitrust Disputes

The U.S. District Court, District of Minnesota, held that a domestic antitrust claim is arbitrable. In *Hunt v. Up North Plastics, Inc.*, 980 F.Supp. 1046 (D. Minn. 1997), plaintiff filed suit on his own behalf and on behalf of a putative class of plaintiffs who purchased silage products from the defendants. He alleged that Up North, Ag–Bag, and Poly America, Inc. conspired to fix prices and allocate customers of silage products in violation of federal antitrust laws. Based on the arbitration clause in the sale invoices, Up North and Poly America moved to dismiss the class action.

The court granted Up North's and Poly America's motion. In doing so, it rejected Hunt's argument that domestic antitrust actions were inarbitrable. Although the Eighth Circuit had not yet expressly overruled *Helfenbein v. International Indus., Inc.*, 438 F.2d 1068 (8th Cir. 1971) (declaring that domestic antitrust violations are not subject to arbitration), the court explained that a number of recent decisions nevertheless undermined that holding.

The court asserted that the U.S. Supreme Court's decisions in *Mitsubishi Motors Corp. v. Soler Chrysler–Plymouth, Inc.*, 473 U.S. 614 (1985), which held that a foreign antitrust dispute is arbitrable, and *Shearson/American Express, Inc. v. McMahon*, 482 U.S. 220 (1987), which held that federal securities claims are arbitrable, "call into question the rationale of earlier cases exempting antitrust and other statutory claims from arbitration." It further stated that a number of other circuits—including the Ninth and Eleventh Circuit—have found domestic antitrust disputes arbitrable. And, lastly, it emphasized that the decision in *Swenson's Ice Cream Co. v. Corsair Corp.*, 942 F.2d 1307 (8th Cir. 1991), expressly states that, since the U.S. Supreme Court handed down its rulings in *Mitsubishi* and *Shearson/American Express,* the rule in *Helfenbein* "may no longer be a correct statement of the law." Consequently, the court held that the antitrust claim was arbitrable.

The prior law—stated in the opinion in *American Safety (infra)*—demonstrated a higher regard for the public interest, and placed a higher social value and legal significance upon antitrust regulation. Because the antitrust laws represented an expression of U.S. capitalism and economic organization, disputes arising under these statutes had to be resolved in a public forum by agents appointed to safeguard the public interest. The privatization of such matters was simply untenable in light of their impact upon the public interest. Is the public interest now different? Is antitrust no longer important? Why should privatization trump public law regulation? Are we dealing with "new paradigms"? If so, what are they?

AMERICAN SAFETY EQUIPMENT CORP. v. J.P. MAGUIRE & CO.

391 F.2d 821 (2d Cir. 1968).

(footnotes omitted)

FEINBERG, Circuit Judge:

These two appeals by American Safety Equipment Corp. (ASE) are from orders of the United States District Court for the Southern District of New York...which stayed, pending arbitration, two declaratory judgment actions by ASE.... The merits of these actions are not now directly in question, but the propriety of directing arbitration is. We conclude that the court should have decided itself at least some of the issues it referred to the arbitrators. Accordingly, we remand for further proceedings.

[. . .]

The basic question we must resolve is whether the district court erred in staying ASE's actions and ordering arbitration of ASE's antitrust allegations. . . .

[. . .]

. . . The basic issue was aptly phrased by this court fifteen years ago in *Wilko v. Swan*, 201 F.2d 439, 444 (2d Cir. 1953):

> We think that the remedy a statute provides for violation of the statutory right it creates may be sought not only in any "court of competent jurisdiction" but also in any other competent tribunal, such as arbitration, unless the right itself is of a character inappropriate for enforcement by arbitration * * *.

The question before us is whether the statutory right ASE seeks to enforce is "of a character inappropriate for enforcement by arbitration." . . .

[. . .]

A claim under the antitrust laws is not merely a private matter. The Sherman Act is designed to promote the national interest in a competitive economy; thus, the plaintiff asserting his rights under the Act has been likened to a private attorney-general who protects the public's interest. . . . Antitrust violations can affect hundreds of thousands—perhaps millions— of people and inflict staggering economic damage. . . . We do not believe that Congress intended such claims to be resolved elsewhere than in the courts. . . . [I]n fashioning a rule to govern the arbitrability of antitrust claims, we must consider the rule's potential effect. For the same reason, it is also proper to ask whether contracts of adhesion between alleged monopolists and their customers should determine the forum for trying antitrust violations. Here again, we think that Congress would hardly have intended that. . . .

. . . [T]he claim here is that the agreement itself was an instrument of illegality; in addition, the issues in antitrust cases are prone to be complicated, and the evidence extensive and diverse, far better suited to judicial than to arbitration procedures. Moreover, it is the business community generally that is regulated by the antitrust laws. Since commercial arbitrators are frequently men drawn for their business expertise, it hardly seems proper for them to determine these issues of great public interest. As Judge Clark said concerning the analogous situation in *Wilko v. Swan*, 201 F.2d at 445 (dissenting opinion):

> Adjudication by such arbitrators may, indeed, provide a business solution of the problem if that is the real desire; but it is surely not a way of assuring the customer that objective and sympathetic consideration of his claim which is envisaged by the Securities Act.

Appellee Hickok seems to argue that all these considerations are irrelevant because ASE does not seek damages, apparently conceding that a treble damage claim would not be arbitrable. We do not regard this distinction as significant if it is meant to persuade us that arbitrators rather than courts should declare whether contract provisions violate the Sherman Act. On the other hand, if Hickok is merely emphasizing that ASE's antitrust claims are actually being asserted as a defense to an action for royalties, we agree that questions of separability are present here, and we refer to them below. However, the problem of which forum should determine those questions remains; we believe it is governed by the same considerations discussed above.

We express no general distrust of arbitrators or arbitration; our decisions reflect exactly the contrary point of view. . . . Moreover, we do not deal here with an agreement to arbitrate made after a controversy has already arisen. . . . We conclude only that the pervasive public interest in enforcement of the antitrust laws, and the nature of the claims that arise in such cases, combine to make the outcome here clear. In some situations Congress has allowed parties to obtain the advantages of arbitration if they "are willing to accept less certainty of legally correct adjustment,"...but we do not think that this is one of them. In short, we conclude that the antitrust claims raised here are inappropriate for arbitration.

[...]

NOTES AND QUESTIONS

1. Is the submission of antitrust issues to international arbitrators the same as the submission of such claims to domestic arbitrators? What differences exist between the two sets of circumstances?

2. Of what relevance is the U.S. Supreme Court's view that arbitration is a mere form of trial that has no effect upon substantive rights in the context of the foregoing antitrust decisions?

3. What meaning do you attribute to the phrase: "A claim under the antitrust laws is not merely a private matter."? How would the court in *Hunt v. Up North Plastics* define "a private matter" or the public interest?

4. How persuasive do you find the opinion in *American Safety?*

5. Assume that an employer provides in the employee's employment contract that a reason for summary dismissal of any employee is "the employer's reasonable belief that the employee endorsed, supported, contributed to, encouraged, or had an abortion." The contract also contains an arbitration clause, making "any and all disputes" between the employee and the employer subject to arbitration. Further assume that an employee is dismissed because of the abortion clause. Are disputes pertaining to the termination arbitrable? Could a U.S. attorney intervene with a lawsuit on behalf of the employee?

Title VII

In *Paladino v. Avnet Computer Technologies, Inc.*, 134 F.3d 1054 (11th Cir. 1998), the U.S. Court of Appeals for the Eleventh Circuit affirmed the denial of a motion to compel the arbitration of a Title VII action. Handbook arbitration provisions that limited recovery to contract relief did not apply to Title VII. Additionally, the arbitral clause did not alert employees sufficiently to the arbitrability of statutory claims.

The clause provided that any employment claim would be decided by arbitration and the "arbitrator [was] authorized to award damages for breach of contract only, and shall have no authority whatsoever to make an award of other damages." The court determined that nonenforcement was consistent with *Brisentine v. Stone & Webster Engineering Corp.*, 117 F.3d 519 (11th Cir. 1997), in which the court held that a mandatory arbitration clause could not prevent the judicial litigation of a federal statutory claim unless: (1) the employee agreed individually to the contract containing the clause; (2) the agreement authorized the arbitrator to resolve federal statutory claims; and (3) the agreement gave the employee the right to insist on arbitration if the federal statutory claim was not resolved to his satisfaction by the grievance process.

In a brief concurrence, Circuit Judge Cox agreed that the motion to compel arbitration should be denied, but maintained that the arbitration clause did not cover Title VII claims at all. Because the clause deprived Paladino of any meaningful relief, Judge Cox asserted that the entire arbitration agreement was unenforceable.

NOTES AND QUESTIONS

1. The question of the arbitrability of Title VII claims is also relevant to employment arbitration. The purpose of the present consideration is to highlight the debate that underlies the question of the arbitrability of statutory rights. Title VII claims are based upon civil rights, guaranteed by the U.S. Constitution as well as federal legislation. Can an employer require that employees submit these claims to arbitration? Are arbitrators capable of resolving them?

2. The Eleventh Circuit seems to favor providing individuals with access to the courts to vindicate their statutory rights. Does the court in *Paladino* read the arbitration clause in the handbook accurately? What is the significance and function of the second clause in the arbitration agreement? Isn't it more than clear and self-evident that it is a limitation of damages provision? Why does the court hold differently?

3. Is it possible or legal for an employer to recognize the existence of a federal statute and a set of federal rights, to provide for the arbitration of all workplace claims (including statutory claims), and to limit the damages or remedies that can be awarded by the arbitral tribunal? Isn't the reference to arbitration already a compromise of the statute (1991 Civil Rights Act) because the statute contains a guarantee of a right to a jury trial? What real difference is there between front-end and back-end limitations?

4. Why is *Brisentine* relevant? There is no collective bargaining agreement in *Avnet*—only a handbook arbitration provision.

5. What is your assessment of the concurring opinion?

* * *

In *Coleman v. Houston Lighting and Power Co.*, 984 F.Supp. 576 (S.D Tex. 1997), the court held that employees covered by arbitral clauses in collective bargaining agreements nonetheless retained the right to pursue statutory employment discrimination claims in federal court. The right to pursue judicial relief was not qualified by any threshold requirements, like exhausting their remedies under the collective bargaining agreement.

Specifically, the Texas federal court held that a unionized worker did not waive his federal statutory rights under the ADA and Title VII by failing to exhaust the grievance and arbitration procedure contained in the CBA. The court concluded that the case was controlled by *Alexander v. Gardner–Denver Co.*, 415 U.S. 36 (1974). Despite *Gilmer v. Interstate/Johnson Lane Corp.*, 500 U.S. 20 (1991), the majority view "is that *Alexander* and its progeny remain good law and that statutory employment claims are independent of a collective bargaining agreement's grievance and arbitration procedures.''

The court added: "[T]his court concurs with the *Pryner* [*v. Tractor Supply Co.*, 109 F.3d 354 (7th Cir.), *cert. denied*, 522 U.S. 912 (1997)] court that '[t]he conservative reading of *Gilmer* is that it just pruned some dicta from *Alexander*—and it certainly cannot be taken to hold that collective bargaining agreements can compel the arbitration of statutory rights. That issue was not before the court or addressed by it.' Like the Seventh Circuit, this court 'is timid about declaring decisions by the Supreme Court overruled when the court has not said so.' Therefore, this court is of the view that *Alexander* remains good law where an employee's only obligation to arbitrate is contained in a collective bargaining agreement.''

NOTES AND QUESTIONS

1. *Coleman* addresses the arbitrability of Title VII rights and other civil rights in the context of a collective bargaining agreement, rather than an individual employment contract.

2. *Coleman* also raises the great debate between *Gilmer* and *Gardner-Denver*. This topic is addressed in the chapter on labor and employment arbitration.

3. Do you think that the same rule of law as to the arbitrability of Title VII claims should apply to the circumstances of collective bargaining and individual employment contracts? Why and why not? Why should Coleman or anyone else have a right to renege on their promise to arbitrate?

* * *

In *Mouton v. Metropolitan Life Insurance Co.*, 147 F.3d 453 (5th Cir. 1998), the plaintiff worked as a sales agent for Metropolitan Life Insurance Company. As a seller of mutual funds, he was required to be licensed by the NASD. In his U–4 Registration Form, the plaintiff agreed to "arbitrate any dispute, claim or controversy that [might] arise between me and my firm, or a customer, or any other person, that is required to be arbitrated under the rules, constitutions or by-laws of the NASD as may be amended from time to time.''

Mouton later testified against Metropolitan in a Title VII sexual harassment suit brought by a co-worker. At the time of his testimony, he was on disability leave. Mouton alleged that, when he returned to work, Metropolitan retaliated against him. The EEOC gave Mouton a right-to-sue letter and he filed a Title VII complaint against Metropolitan.

The district court found that a genuine issue of material fact existed, namely, whether the 1989 NASD Code mandated the arbitration of Title VII claims. The Code did not specifically require the arbitration of employment-related disputes. The court of appeals concluded that, in 1987, the NASD stated that employment disputes between its members and their registered representatives were subject to compulsory arbitration. Furthermore, when the Code was amended in 1993, the NASD explained that the inclusion of the new language in § 1 was intended to make clear that employer-employee disputes fell within the scope of the Code's arbitration provisions. The court determined that an arbitration clause need not specifically address employment-related disputes to mandate the arbitration of Title VII claims.

Mouton further contended that he could not be compelled to arbitrate his Title VII claim because he did not knowingly and voluntarily agree to waive his right to a judicial forum. The court responded: "Mouton agreed to arbitrate any dispute, claim, or controversy that may arise between himself and Metropolitan. We hold him to that agreement."

NOTES AND QUESTIONS

1. *Mouton* represents the majority position on the arbitrability of Title VII claims in the context of an individual employment contract. If the contract contains an arbitration agreement, statutory claims arising from the workplace setting generally will be arbitrable.

2. It is worth pondering one more time why the rule of application should be so different between collective bargaining and employment contract circumstances.

3. You should note that the arbitrability question is linked to the character of the arbitration agreement: The agreement is both broad and binding; therefore, the statutory claims are arbitrable.

4. How do you assess the court's interpretation of the 1993 amendment to the NASD Code?

5. Explain what is meant by resolving doubts about arbitrability in favor of arbitration.

6. In *14 Penn Plaza v. Pyett*, 556 U.S ___, 129 S.Ct. 1456 (2009), the U.S. Supreme Court made clear that claims relating to the Civil Rights Act of 1964 and 1991 could be submitted to arbitration in either labor agreements or private contracts (or employment relationships). Speaking for the majority, Justice Thomas integrated civil rights claims into the line of arbitrability opinions, beginning with *Mitsubishi* and including *McMahon*, *Rodriguez*, and *Gilmer*. As long as the submission is clear and unambiguous, these disputes can be resolved through arbitration. The waiver of the right to judicial process is seen as a procedural decision that has no impact upon the substantive guarantees of enabling statutes. Parties, therefore, are able to vindicate fully their statutory rights through the process of arbitral adjudication. Only Congress, in explicit legislative enactments, can remove statutory rights from the jurisdictional purview of arbitration. *14 Penn Plaza*, in effect, reverses the reasoning and ruling in *Gardner-Denver*.

Truth-in-Lending–Act Claims

In *Randolph v. Green Tree Financial Corp.-Alabama*, 178 F.3d 1149 (11th Cir. 1999), *aff'd in part, rev'd in part*, 531 U.S. 79 (2000), the U.S. Court of Appeals for the Eleventh Circuit held that Truth-in-Lending Act

(TILA) claims were inarbitrable when the arbitral remedy could not ensure the vindication of statutory rights.

The facts of the case involved the purchase of a mobile home, a financing agreement, and an arbitration clause contained in the latter contract. The plaintiff alleged that Green Tree's financial documents violated the TILA and that the TILA precluded the arbitration of disputes arising under its statutory framework. When Randolph filed her action before the district court, she also sought to certify a class of individuals who had entered into similar agreements with Green Tree. In response, Green Tree moved to compel arbitration and to stay or dismiss the court action. The district court denied the request for certification. It also ruled that the other issues raised in the complaint were subject to arbitration. It issued an order to compel arbitration and dismissed Randolph's claims with prejudice.

The appellate court considered whether the TILA precluded the enforcement of the arbitral clause in the agreement. It held that, because the arbitral clause failed to provide the minimum guarantees required to ensure that the plaintiff could vindicate her statutory rights under TILA, it was unenforceable. The court nonetheless acknowledged the strong federal policy favoring arbitration. It stated that inherent weaknesses in the procedural apparatus of the arbitration, in and of themselves, should not render an arbitral clause unenforceable. Some procedural flaws, however, present such barriers to the would-be litigants' exercise of their statutory rights that they render the agreement to arbitrate unenforceable. In such circumstances, the reference to arbitration defeats the remedial purpose of the statute. In *Paladino*, for example, the court held that forcing the plaintiff to bear the brunt of substantial arbitration costs combined with steep filing fees constituted a legitimate basis upon which to hold that arbitration did not comport with statutory intent.

Moreover, the arbitration clause in the instant case did not address the question of the distribution of filing fees and arbitration costs. The clause did not incorporate a standard set of rules (like those of the American Arbitration Association) that provide guidance on these matters. In the court's view, it was, therefore, possible that the parties would have to negotiate these issues before they could even proceed with arbitration. The court was disturbed by the fact that there was no guarantee that a successful plaintiff who received a modest award would not be saddled with the exorbitant arbitral costs:

> The arbitration clause in this case raises serious concerns with respect to filing fees, arbitrators' costs and other arbitration expenses that may curtail or bar a plaintiff's access to the arbitral forum, and thus falls within our holding in *Paladino*. This clause says nothing about the payment of filing fees or the apportionment of the costs of arbitration. It neither assigns an initial responsibility for filing fees or arbitrators' costs, nor provides for a waiver in cases of financial hardship. It does not say whether consumers, if they prevail, will nonetheless be saddled with fees and costs in excess of any award. It does not say whether the rules of the American Arbitration

Association, which provide at least some guidelines concerning filing fees and arbitration costs, apply to the proceeding, whether some other set of rules applies, or whether the parties must negotiate their own set of rules.

[. . .]

Accordingly, we conclude that the arbitration clause in this case is unenforceable, because it fails to provide the minimum guarantees required to ensure that Randolph's ability to vindicate her statutory rights will not be undone by steep filing fees, steep arbitrators' fees, or other high costs of arbitration. . . .

The court did not reach the issue of whether TILA precludes all arbitration agreements.

NOTES AND QUESTIONS

1. Does the opinion in *Randolph* betoken (as Justice Cardozo might have stated) a new standard for the determination of arbitrability questions? What might that new standard be? How does the reasoning in *Paladino* reflect that standard?

2. The U.S. Court of Appeals for the Third Circuit held that claims arising under the Truth–In–Lending Act ("TILA") and the Electronic Fund Transfer Act ("EFTA") were arbitrable even though class action relief may not be available in arbitration. In the court's assessment, the affected statutes were not enacted to guarantee access to class action procedures. *See Johnson v. West Suburban Bank*, 225 F.3d 366 (3d Cir. 2000), *cert. denied*, 531 U.S. 1145 (2001).

* * *

On an issue of first impression, the Third Circuit examined the statutory language, the legislative history, and the statutory purpose of both the TILA and the EFTA. It found that, while TILA contemplates class actions, it does not create a right to bring such suits. Rather, the statute creates civil liability for lenders who fail to give the required disclosures. The lender is subject both to actual and statutory damages. The court reasoned that "the right to proceed to a class action, insofar as the TILA is concerned, is a procedural one that arises from the Federal Rules of Civil Procedure." The TILA does not create a right to class action litigation. The court also found that "Congress did not address the role of arbitration in the legislative history" of the statute.

"Because nothing in the legislative history or the statutory text of the TILA clearly expresses congressional intent to preclude the ability of parties to engage in arbitration, Johnson must demonstrate that arbitration irreconcilably conflicts with the purposes of the TILA." Johnson unpersuasively argued, according to the court, that "class actions are central to TILA's purposes, because the statute's civil damages provisions are not remedial, but rather, given the frequent absence of actual damages, are designed to deter unfair credit practices." The court also found that plaintiffs who sign valid arbitration agreements and "lack the procedural right to proceed as part of a class . . . retain the full range of rights created by the TILA." Additionally, the court held that "when the right made available by a statute is capable of vindication in the arbitral forum, the public policy goals of that statute do not justify refusing to arbitrate." "While arbitrating claims that might have been pursued as part of class actions potentially reduces the number of plaintiffs seeking to enforce the TILA against creditors, arbitration does not eliminate plaintiff incentives to assert rights under the Act."

In assessing legislative intent in the various implicated statutes, the court stated that it was obligated to "give equal consideration to Congress' policy goals in enacting the FAA." "The statute was intended to overcome judicial hostility to agreements to arbitrate." Arbitration has some well-established advantages: "[I]t is usually cheaper and faster than litigation; it can have simpler procedural and evidentiary rules; it normally minimizes hostility and is less disruptive of ongoing and future business dealings among the parties; and it is often more flexible in regard to scheduling." Therefore, the congressional intent to promote arbitration carried with it equal, if not more, weight than the policy concerns argued by Johnson for the protection of class actions under the TILA.

McCarran–Ferguson Act

The McCarran–Ferguson Act (15 U.S.C. § 1012) establishes the generally preemptive effect of state law in the regulation of the business of insurance and the interpretation of insurance contracts. The statute provides (15 U.S.C. § 1012[b]): "No Act of Congress shall be construed to invalidate, impair, or supersede any law enacted by any state for the purpose of regulating the business of insurance . . . unless such Act specifically relates to the business of insurance." Insurance contracts can involve interstate commerce and contain arbitration agreements, thereby triggering the application of the FAA. When an insurance company becomes insolvent and the relevant contract provides for the arbitration of liquidation matters, does the FAA apply to the enforcement of the arbitration agreement or do state law provisions on liquidation requiring exclusive judicial recourse in such circumstances control?

There is no U.S. Supreme Court precedent directly on point. In *U.S. Dept. of Treasury v. Fabe*, 508 U.S. 491 (1993), the Court reversed a Sixth Circuit opinion on the status of an Ohio liquidation statute, but failed to clarify the relationship between the FAA and the McCarran–Ferguson Act. The circuits are split on the question. The Second and Ninth Circuits have held that the McCarran–Ferguson Act does not preclude the application of the FAA, while the Fifth, Sixth, and Tenth Circuits have held that the Act "reverse preempts" the FAA.

Consumer Remedies

In *Broughton v. Cigna Healthplans of California*, 21 Cal.4th 1066, 90 Cal.Rptr.2d 334, 988 P.2d 67 (1999), the Supreme Court of California held that claims for injunctive relief under the California Consumer Legal Remedies Act ("CLRA") were inarbitrable. The court found that this result was consistent with both the FAA and California law.

According to the U.S. Supreme Court, Section 2 of the FAA creates a federal policy in favor of arbitration. Moreover, the Court has consistently held that, by enacting Section 2, Congress withdrew the power of the states to require a judicial forum for the resolution of claims that the parties have agreed to resolve by arbitration. The Court also expanded the arbitrability of statutory rights, but—in doing so—recognized that certain controversies involving statutory rights may not be suitable for arbitration. For example, statutory claims are deemed inarbitrable when the governing statute provides exclusively for judicial remedies or there is an "inherent conflict" between arbitration and the purposes of the legislation.

The California Supreme Court reasoned that the key to finding an "inherent conflict" resided in identifying the nature of the remedy involved. Private remedies with an incidental public benefit were—in the court's view—fully arbitrable. When the primary purpose of a statutory remedy, however, was to prohibit conduct harmful to the general public, claims arising in the application of that remedy might be inhospitable to arbitration.

In the instant case, the court reasoned that two factors created an "inherent conflict" between arbitration and the underlying purpose of the CLRA. First, the CLRA was enacted to protect consumers against unfair and deceptive trade practices. It, therefore, allows courts to award actual damages, punitive damages, attorney's fees, and orders enjoining proscribed methods, acts, or practices. These damages are meant to benefit the plaintiff directly and have only an incidental public benefit in the sense of deterrence. The provision for injunctive relief, however, directly affects the public.

Second, the systemic and structural shortcomings of arbitration will likely diminish or frustrate the purposes of the CLRA. Specifically, arbitrators have no power to vacate or modify an injunction because (under California law) they lose their authority to adjudicate thirty days after service of the award. Public injunctions require an ongoing capacity to reevaluate the balance between the public interests and private rights involved. Moreover, when courts have affirmed the power of arbitrators over injunctions, they have acknowledged that the exercise of those powers require new arbitral proceedings. This is problematic because arbitrators generally are not subject to judicial review or bound by the prior decisions of other arbitrators ruling on the same case. Therefore, a series of arbitral hearings is an inadequate substitute for the continuity and consistency provided by a superior court proceeding in which the bench retains its jurisdiction until the dissolution of the injunction. Furthermore, the court recently held that an arbitral award does not have collateral estoppel effect in favor of third-parties, unless those parties so agree. *See Vandenberg v. Superior Court*, 21 Cal.4th 815, 88 Cal.Rptr.2d 366, 982 P.2d 229 (1999). In keeping with this decision, only parties to the arbitration proceeding would be able to enforce the injunction. As a consequence, other damaged parties seeking to enforce the injunction would have to relitigate the matter. Therefore, an arbitral injunction would be more difficult to enforce, and would be a less effective means of achieving the CLRA's goal of enjoining deceptive business practices.

Finally, superior court judges, as elected officials, are more appropriate watchdogs of the public interest. They are sworn to uphold the Constitutions of the United States and California, are locally elected, and may be recalled. They conduct public proceedings and their decisions can be reviewed by appellate courts. Moreover, they are subject to discipline by a public body. Arbitrators are not publicly accountable. Arbitral proceedings are private and are subject to minimal judicial scrutiny.

The court further stated that its decision on this question was not inconsistent with the FAA. According to the state court, the U.S. Supreme Court—although it restricted substantially the power of state legislatures to limit arbitration—has never specifically ruled on the issue of whether "a legislature may restrict a private arbitration agreement when [the agreement] inherently conflicts with a public statutory purpose that transcends private interest." Moreover, the court stated that its decision did not contravene the strong federal and state policies in favor of arbitration because it did not cast suspicion on arbitration as a method of dispute resolution. It merely recognized that arbitration is inappropriate in a narrow class of actions. The result thereby aligns itself with the U.S. Supreme Court's "inherent conflict" exception to arbitrability, and there is no evidence to suggest that the U.S. Congress ever intended arbitration to extend to the area of public injunction.

Moreover, in the court's view, its interpretation of the matter was consistent with the language of the controlling statute, which implied a distinction between arbitrable claims for damages and inarbitrable requests for injunctive relief. In *Gilmer*, the U.S. Supreme Court suggested that a statute, such as the ADEA, which promoted informal methods of "conciliation, conference, and persuasion," was consistent with arbitration and the implied arbitrability of claims. The CLRA promotes similar informal methods for resolving damages claims by requiring a thirty-day notice period and providing for a right-to-cure. If the alleged violator does not redress the matter on his/her own within the allotted time, the consumer may file an action. The legislature, however, did not enact similar provisions for injunctive relief. The difference in approach reflects the differing purposes behind the remedies. Damages are intended to repair private, individual wrongs and permit the use of informal methods to achieve that objective. Injunctive remedies are intended for the protection of the public and do not allow for the recourse to informal methods of dispute resolution which could compromise the statute's protective purpose. Thus, in keeping with the FAA, claims for personal relief in the form of damages under the CLRA remain fully arbitrable, while the public remedial function of the statute is implemented solely by the courts. Where a claim for damages and a claim for injunctive relief coexist, they should be bifurcated and resolved in separate forums.

Justice Chin disagreed with the majority's view and opined that all disputes under the CLRA are arbitrable. In his view, the U.S. Supreme Court has repeatedly held that state courts and legislatures may not limit the enforceability of arbitration agreements. The exceptions relied upon by the majority were intended to apply exclusively to legislation enacted by the U.S. Congress, not state legislatures. Therefore, the majority opinion was inconsistent with the FAA and unconstitutional. In keeping with the strong policy of enforcing arbitration agreements under California law, the majority had no power to presume that the state legislature did not intend to permit the arbitrability of requests for injunctive relief under the CLRA.

Legal Malpractice Claims and Fee Disputes

On February 20, 2002, the ABA Committee on Ethics and Professional Responsibility issued Formal Opinion 02–425. In that document, the committee addressed the ethical propriety of retainer agreements between attorneys and clients that contain arbitral clauses which require fee disputes and malpractice claims be submitted to arbitration. While the committee concluded that such contract provisions did not violate ethical standards, it conditioned their ethical acceptability upon a number of factors. First, the client's acceptance of the agreement to arbitrate such disputes must be based upon informed consent. Second, the effect of the arbitration agreement cannot be to limit or exclude the lawyer's liability exposure to the client:

> It is ethically permissible to include in a retainer agreement with a client a provision that requires the binding arbitration of fee disputes and malpractice claims provided that (1) the client has been fully apprised of the advantages and disadvantages of arbitration and has been given sufficient information to permit her to make an informed decision about whether to agree to the inclusion of the arbitration provision in the retainer agreement, and (2) the arbitration provision does not insulate the lawyer from liability or limit the liability to which she would otherwise be exposed under common and/or statutory law.

In explaining its position, the committee emphasized the distinction between fee disputes and professional malpractice claims. Many, if not most, bar associations have implemented arbitral procedures for addressing fee disputes. Rule 1.5 of the Model Rules of Professional Responsibility (MRPR) authorize "fee arbitration programs"; in fact, there are ABA Model Rules for Fee Arbitration. The MRPR, however, does not address instances in which the arbitral procedure applies to malpractice claims.

In particular, MRPR Rules 1.8(h) forbids lawyers from limiting their malpractice liability through contract unless such agreements are recognized at law as lawful and the subscribing client is represented independently. Moreover, a lawyer owes a client fiduciary duties that include "a duty to explain matters" under MRPR Rule 1.4(b). In terms of arbitration agreements in a professional services contract, the duty would oblige the attorney to explain effectively what arbitration is and its benefits and drawbacks. The explanation must be sufficient to allow the client to achieve "informed consent." Finally, the incorporation of an arbitral clause in a retainer agreement also implicates MRPR Rule 1.7(b) that addresses conflict of interest situations. According to the committee, Comment [6] to Rule 1.7 was particularly relevant; it provides: "If the probity of a lawyer's own conduct in a transaction is in serious question, it may be difficult or impossible for the lawyer to give a client detached advice."

Despite all of these misgivings, the committee concluded that agreements to arbitrate malpractice claims were ethically supportable. It aligned its reasoning to the judicial reasoning that ordinarily applies to matters of arbitration. That reasoning usually sustains the recourse to arbitration and is intended to eliminate any obstacles that might stand in the way of the reference to arbitration. For example, the committee stated that: "The mere fact that a client is required to submit disputes to arbitration rather than litigation does not violate Rule 1.8(h) [prohibiting the lawyer from limiting liability], even though the procedures implicated by various mandatory arbitration provisions can markedly differ from typical litigation procedures." It is difficult to understand when the evident differences between arbitral and judicial adjudication would be sufficient to trigger restraint in this area. Apparently, the unavailability of punitive damages in arbitration (as opposed to court proceedings) would be enough to mandate that the client be "independently represented in making the agreement."

The committee does not appear to appreciate the substantial conflict of interest that the unilateral incorporation of an arbitral clause in a retainer agreement represents. It cannot be rationally or plausibly argued that the attorney is not representing his/her own interest primarily and depriving the client of important procedural rights and protections against his/her lack of competence. Arbitration, in this and other settings, can serve no other purpose than limiting the lawyer's liability. There cannot be any fiduciary dimension to conduct that is manifestly self-serving and antagonistic to one side. It is nearly unthinkable that attorneys should attempt to deprive their clients of access to the courts and judicial proceedings.

HENRY v. GONZALEZ

18 S.W.3d 684 (Ct. App. Tx. 2000).

[. . .]

The record contains evidence, and the parties do not dispute, that an arbitration agreement existed between the parties, as it was contained within the attorney/client contract signed by Gonzalez. We have determined that Henry and Hearn's termination of the contract did not affect the validity of the internal arbitration agreement. Therefore, Henry and Hearn satisfied their burden of proof to establish their right to the remedy of arbitration. To overcome the application of the arbitration clause to him, Gonzalez was then required to establish some ground for revocation of the arbitration agreement. . . .

Gonzalez argues two grounds for revocation of the arbitration agreement: (1) the application of the arbitration clause to this case violates public policy, and; (2) fraudulent inducement. Gonzalez's public-policy contentions are unfounded because well established caselaw favors mandatory arbitration and holds that arbitration does not deny parties their right to a jury trial, as a matter of law. . . .

To the extent Gonzalez argues that he was fraudulently induced to sign the contract containing the arbitration clause due to his decreased mental capacity and the fact that the arbitration clause was not conspicuous, his argument fails. An allegation that the contract itself was fraudulently induced is a matter to be decided by the arbitrator. . . . Fraudulent inducement to sign the contract, thus, cannot support the trial court's order denying Henry and Hearn's motion to compel arbitration, as a matter of law.

To the extent Gonzalez argues he was fraudulently induced to agree to arbitration, his argument also fails. Although this question usually requires a fact determination by the trial court, Gonzalez had the burden to prove this issue, and under the "no evidence" standard of review, this court may determine whether the record contains any evidence to support the trial court's judgment. We hold that it does not. . . .

[. . .]

The matters in controversy fall within the scope of the arbitration agreement because the factual allegations forming the bases of the Gonzalezes' legal malpractice and breach of fiduciary duty causes of action necessarily arose from Henry and Hearn's representation of the Gonzalezes under the attorney/client contract. The Gonzalezes' DTPA cause of action falls within the scope of the arbitration agreement because the actions forming the basis of this cause of action related to "the providing of services" by Henry and Hearn to the Gonzalezes, necessarily related to that relationship, and were so factually interwoven with the contract that such action could not stand alone. . . .

We sustain Henry and Hearn's first, second, and third points of error. We need not reach the fourth point of error. Because the evidence shows that a valid arbitration agreement existed, no other ground exists to hold the arbitration agreement revocable, and the claims raised fell within the scope of this agreement, the trial court had no discretion but to compel arbitration. . . .

Dissenting opinion by: PHIL HARDBERGER, Chief Justice.

[. . .]

The legal and ethical implications of arbitration provisions in contracts between attorneys and their clients have been the subject of a number of articles. . . . The essence of these articles is that whatever public policy may be served by enforcing arbitration agreements is more than offset by the public policy of not allowing attorneys to take advantage of their clients. Trust is the essential ingredient in an attorney-client relationship. The great majority of clients are not even close to being in an equal bargaining position with their attorneys. They go to an attorney so the attorney can tell them what to do, not vice-versa.

In a serious personal injury case, such as this, clients are typically deeply in grief and overwhelmed by the circumstances that have come upon them. Pain and disability have entered their lives, and the breadwinner is no longer able to bring home wages for the family. As bills pour in, with no offsetting income, a true state of desperation exists. Are we then to allow attorneys, who represent such clients, to take away their rights to a jury should legal malpractice occur? I agree with the commentators in the cited articles and with the laws established in other jurisdictions that conclude that such a practice is against public policy. Certainly it should be against public policy in the absence of some additional protections for the client, which do not exist in the case.

The traditional advantages of arbitration may not be so advantageous in the context of a legal malpractice claim. For example, the savings of cost and time would likely be more of a disadvantage to the attorney alleged to have committed malpractice than to the client because the client's new attorney will typically be handling the claim on a contingency basis. . . .In addition, the ability to pursue the claim in court may provide the client with a bargaining advantage in negotiating with an attorney who seeks to avoid litigation and its potential negative publicity. . . .

More importantly, the fundamental fiduciary nature of the attorney-client relationship dictates against an attorney's ability to impose an arbitration condition on a client. Clients are often in vulnerable positions, requiring them to bestow a large amount of trust in their attorneys. "The client's vulnerability vis-à-vis the attorney is often exacerbated by the client's current legal situation. . . . He is neither expecting, nor emotionally prepared, to 'do battle' with his chosen attorney to protect his own rights." . . .Applying general contractual principles to an arbitration provision in the attorney-client context ignores the practical reality that in most instances the attorney and his or her client are not engaged in an arm's length transaction during their initial negotiations. . . .

Attorneys generally have a greater advantage over their clients in an arbitration setting. Attorneys are trained to conduct arbitration to the best advantage of their clients, in this case themselves. . . . Since one of the "selling points" of arbitration is the ability to proceed without an attorney, the client with the malpractice claim may not seek additional counsel, leaving the trained attorney with a distinct advantage. . . .

In a profession that is called upon to police itself, how can we justify allowing attorneys to take advantage of those who call upon their services? We cannot. Although the traditional contractual defenses, like unconscionability, may be available to clients who are taken advantage of, such a situation should never be allowed to arise. Clients who are in a weaker bargaining position may not be able to meet the burden of proving unconscionability.... This does not mean that the attorney would not have taken advantage of his or her client. It simply means that the legal definition of unconscionability, created by attorneys, is an uncertain road for an already burdened client.

Recognizing these public policy concerns, other states have prohibited or limited the inclusion of arbitration provisions in attorneys' engagement letters. For example, Pennsylvania has adopted a rule that permits an arbitration provision in an engagement letter only if: (1) the advantages and disadvantages are fully disclosed by the attorney; (2) the client is advised of his right to consult independent counsel and is given the opportunity to do so; and (3) the client's consent is in writing.... Both the District of Columbia and Michigan have taken a more restrictive approach and prohibit arbitration clauses in engagement letters unless the client has the advice of independent counsel.... Finally, Ohio has taken the most restrictive approach and simply prohibits pre-dispute arbitration agreements between attorneys and their clients.... Ohio reasons that requiring a client to hire a lawyer in order to hire a lawyer sends the wrong message....

Public policy mandates that some restrictions must be placed on an attorney's ability to include an arbitration provision in an engagement letter. Because no such restrictions were imposed in this case, I would conclude that the arbitration clause violates public policy and affirm the trial court's ruling. I respectfully dissent.

NOTES AND QUESTIONS

1. Despite the divisive nature of the debate on the question of the arbitrability of legal malpractice claims, courts are likely to reach the conclusion that such disputes are arbitrable. Such a conclusion would be in keeping with the forceful general trend in the area and would coincide with the determinations of various bar groups on the ethical propriety of arbitration agreements in retainer agreements.

2. It could be argued that the particular character of these claims warrants an adapted form of arbitration, the characteristics of which respond to the issues and interests that underlie these matters. While it appears contradictory to allow attorneys to deny their clients the traditional remedies typically available, there seems to be little basis for disallowing the arbitration of legal malpractice claims (given the strength of the policy in favor of arbitration) or for making special accommodations for these controversies inside the arbitration process. Notwithstanding the self-evident double standard, the breach of trust, and the contractual unfairness, this battle on subject-matter inarbitrability appears to be as likely of defeat as all the others.

3. Attorneys (and clients), therefore, must consider the content of a generally suitable agreement. In attempting to draft an arbitration clause or

contract, parties should understand the rules that generally apply to the crafting of arbitral agreements. The standard arbitration agreement is simple and economical as well as straightforward. It, however, only manages to get the parties to arbitration and to an arbitral institution. It is easy to enforce but offers no protection except to authorize the arbitrators and the arbitral institution to act in their discretion. An overly complex agreement obviously is much more difficult to negotiate and runs the risk of complicating enforcement or making enforcement impossible. It could become a pathological contract that creates stalemate, results in the useless expenditure of resources, and could lead to undesirable solutions. A balanced approach—one that intermediates between being binding and fair—is the best approach.

4.   In arriving at such an agreement, the parties should consider the following factors and aspects (stated roughly in order of importance):

1.   Scope or range of the agreement to arbitrate—what disputes do the parties agree to submit to arbitration—tort, contract, statutory, regulatory, jurisdictional;

2.   Appointment of arbitrators—who and how should the arbitrators be selected; are there specific qualifications; what is the desired number;

3.   Remedies and damages—what remedies are available in the arbitration—compensatory, punitive, and injunctive relief (a failure to exclude probably means that the relief is available); what about attorney's fees;

4.   Basis for arbitral rulings—do the arbitrators rule according to law, equity, amiable composition, technical expertise, or some combination of these factors;

5.   Type of arbitral trial—formal, informal, legal, flexible; what about cross-examination, expert witnesses, discovery, or time constraints;

6.   Content of the award—should reasons be supplied; within the award or apart from it;

7.   Allocation of arbitral costs and fees—determined by whom and on what basis;

8.   Standard of review—some federal circuits allow parties to provide for a merits review by courts of arbitral rulings on law;

9.   Selection of institutional rules;

10.   Selection of a law governing the general contract, the arbitration agreement, and the arbitration;

11.   Obligation to arbitrate in good faith;

12.   Potential liability of the arbitrator in the event of the vacatur of the award; waiver of fees if the award is set aside.

The agreement should be carefully crafted and worded.

CHAPTER SIX

FORMS OF ARBITRATION

■ ■ ■

Although arbitration possesses core characteristics, its use in different transactional settings creates distinctive forms of the remedy. Commercial arbitration is the most commonplace usage and traditional type of arbitration. There is a long-standing history of having recourse to arbitration to resolve business-to-business disputes. Maritime arbitration illustrates well that form of arbitration. Patterns—like the publication of maritime awards—have been established and the rules of arbitration have been adjusted to the transactional setting. For example, consolidation is recognized because maritime transactions involve numerous parties—the ship-owner, the renter, the cargo owner, and insurers. Arbitration remains arbitration and reflects the standard approach, but it acquires features and attributes that are particular to the area.

The expansion of arbitration's application to new transactional areas and to statutory claims has created even more distinctive forms of arbitration. For example, arbitration for years had been the acknowledged means of resolving inside-the-business securities disputes (*e.g.*, between brokerages and exchanges). The new form of securities arbitration has a different meaning and function. It applies to employee and customer disputes that lack any corporate character. This form of arbitration is no longer anchored in business practices and concerns, but involves disparate parties, individual interests, and possibly public law regulations. The tried and true model of business arbitration is hardly an apposite framework for dealing with discrimination claims that accompany termination or with an overreaching sales approach that entice individual investors to suffer the consequences of exaggerated market risk. The ethic of self-regulation can be applied to employees and customers but in a measured fashion that takes the specific needs of these participants into account. The necessary adjustments generate new forms of arbitration.

Securities arbitration overlaps with employment and consumer arbitration, both of which have become *sui generis* forms of arbitration. Employment arbitration is addressed in a subsequent chapter, while consumer arbitration is described and assessed in the present chapter. In all three forms of arbitration, unconscionability, costs, and fairness play a critical role. The question of the enforceability of the arbitration agreement is much more acute than in conventional commercial arbitration.

In the sections that follow, you should attempt to identify and explain the various "paradigms" of arbitration that emerge in each transactional situation. What aspects of the particular arbitral process make it traditional—a customary form of arbitration? What aspects make it unique? What would you add or subtract to better accommodate the competing interests? How is society represented, if at all, in the proceedings? Should it be? Why? Is arbitration always the better choice? Why and why not?

1. SECURITIES ARBITRATION

The evolution of the law toward a narrow subject-matter inarbitrability defense is perhaps best illustrated by the emergence of securities arbitration in the investor-consumer sector. The evolution of the law is progressive. There is a large temporal and doctrinal distance between *Wilko v. Swan*, 346 U.S. 427 (1953), and its related cases: *Shearson/American Express, Inc. v. McMahon*, 482 U.S. 220 (1987), and *Rodriguez de Quijas v. Shearson/American Express, Inc.*, 490 U.S. 477 (1989). The opening proposition, stated in *Wilko*, is that the 1933 Securities Act provides for exclusive judicial resolution of claims arising under the securities legislation as a limited exception to the FAA's policy on arbitration. The final proposition, articulated most clearly in *Rodriguez*, reverses the *Wilko* holding because it represents unlawful judicial hostility to arbitration. After *Rodriguez*, claims arising under either the 1933 Securities Act or the 1934 Securities Exchange Act can be submitted to arbitration in U.S. domestic law.

Wilko v. Swan

In *Wilko*, an investor lodged an action against a securities brokerage firm, claiming that the firm had violated Section 12(2) of the 1933 Act. The brokerage contract contained a dispute resolution clause providing for the submission of disputes to arbitration. Notwithstanding its view that the FAA embodied a strong congressional policy supporting arbitration, the Court deemed the arbitration agreement in *Wilko* to be unenforceable. The Court reasoned that the provision for arbitration countermanded the express policy of the 1933 Act prohibiting investors from waiving certain statutorily established rights, namely, the right to bring suit in any federal or state court, to select a forum from a wide choice of venue, to take advantage of the nationwide service of process provision, and to dispense with the amount in controversy requirement. Moreover, Section 12(2) of the Act expressly gave investors a cause of action to redress claims of misrepresentation against a seller of securities, requiring the defendant to prove its lack of scienter.

Therefore, despite a valid arbitration agreement, securities claims arising under the 1933 Act could not be submitted to arbitration. The Act's nonwaiver of rights provisions, in effect, manifested a congressional intent to create an exception to the FAA's validation of arbitration agreements. These circumstances were exceptional. The policy imperative underlying the 1933 Act took precedent over its counterpart in the FAA. Ordinarily, however, the FAA would have prevailed.

WILKO v. SWAN

346 U.S. 427, 74 S.Ct. 182, 98 L.Ed. 168 (1953).

(footnotes omitted)

MR. JUSTICE REED delivered the opinion of the Court.

[. . .]

The question is whether an agreement to arbitrate a future controversy is a "condition, stipulation, or provision binding any person acquiring any security to waive compliance with any provision" of the Securities Act which § 14 declares "void." We granted *certiorari* to review this important and novel federal question affecting both the Securities Act and the United States Arbitration Act. . . .

As the margin agreement in the light of the complaint evidenced a transaction in interstate commerce, no issue arises as to the applicability of the provisions of the United States Arbitration Act to this suit, based upon the Securities Act. . . .

In response to a Presidential message urging that there be added to the ancient rule of caveat emptor the further doctrine of "let the seller also beware," Congress passed the Securities Act of 1933. Designed to protect investors, the Act requires issuers, underwriters, and dealers to make full and fair disclosure of the character of securities sold in interstate and foreign commerce and to prevent fraud in their sale. To effectuate this policy, § 12(2) created a special right to recover for misrepresentation which differs substantially from the common-law action in that the seller is made to assume the burden of proving lack of scienter. The Act's special right is enforceable in any court of competent jurisdiction—federal or state—and removal from a state court is prohibited. If suit be brought in a federal court, the purchaser has a wide choice of venue, the privilege of nationwide service of process and the jurisdictional $3,000 requirement of diversity cases is inapplicable.

The United States Arbitration Act establishes by statute the desirability of arbitration as an alternative to the complications of litigation. The reports of both Houses on that Act stress the need for avoiding the delay and expense of litigation, and practice under its terms raises hope for its usefulness both in controversies based on statutes or on standards otherwise created. This hospitable attitude of legislatures and courts toward arbitration, however, does not solve our question as to the validity of petitioner's stipulation by the margin agreements to submit to arbitration controversies that might arise from the transactions.

Petitioner argues that § 14 ... shows that the purpose of Congress was to assure that sellers could not maneuver buyers into a position that might weaken their ability to recover under the Securities Act. He contends that arbitration lacks the certainty of a suit at law under the Act to enforce his rights. He reasons that the arbitration paragraph of the margin agreement is a stipulation that waives "compliance with" the provision of the Securities Act conferring jurisdiction of suits and special powers.

Respondent asserts that arbitration is merely a form of trial to be used in lieu of a trial at law, and therefore no conflict exists between the Securities Act and the United States Arbitration Act either in their language or in the congressional purposes in their enactment. Each may function within its own scope, the former to protect investors and the latter to simplify recovery for actionable violations of law by issuers or dealers in securities.

Respondent is in agreement with the Court of Appeals that the margin agreement arbitration paragraph...does not relieve the seller from either liability or burden of proof...imposed by the Securities Act. We agree that in so far as the award in arbitration may be affected by legal requirements, statutes or common law, rather than by considerations of fairness, the provisions of the Securities Act control. This is true even though this proposed agreement has no requirement that the arbitrators follow the law. This agreement of the parties as to the effect of the Securities Act includes also acceptance of the invalidity of the paragraph of the margin agreement that relieves the respondent sellers of liability for all "representation or advice by you or your employees or agents regarding the purchase or sale by me of any property. * * * "

The words of § 14...void any "stipulation" waiving compliance with any "provision" of the Securities Act. This arrangement to arbitrate is a "stipulation," and we think the right to select the judicial forum is the kind of "provision" that cannot be waived under § 14 of the Securities Act. While a buyer and seller of securities, under some circumstances, may deal at arm's length on equal terms, it is clear that the Securities Act was drafted with an eye to the disadvantages under which buyers labor. Issuers of and dealers in securities have better opportunities to investigate and appraise the prospective earnings and business plans affecting securities than buyers. It is therefore reasonable for Congress to put buyers of securities covered by that Act on a different basis from other purchasers.

When the security buyer, prior to any violation of the Securities Act, waives his right to sue in courts, he gives up more than would a participant in other business transactions. The security buyer has a wider choice of courts and venue. He thus surrenders one of the advantages the Act gives him and surrenders it at a time when he is less able to judge the weight of the handicap the Securities Act places upon his adversary.

Even though the provisions of the Securities Act, advantageous to the buyer, apply, their effectiveness in application is lessened in arbitration as compared to judicial proceedings. Determination of the quality of a commodity or the amount of money due under a contract is not the type of issue here involved. This case requires subjective findings on the purpose and knowledge of an alleged violator of the Act. They must be not only determined but applied by the arbitrators without judicial instruction on the law. As their award may be made without explanation of their reasons and without a complete record of their proceedings, the arbitrators' conception of the legal meaning of such statutory requirements as "burden of proof," "reasonable care" or "material fact"...cannot be examined. Power to vacate an award is limited. While it may be true, as the Court of Appeals thought, that a failure of the arbitrators to decide in accordance with the provisions of the Securities Act would "constitute grounds for vacating the award pursuant to section 10 of the Federal Arbitration Act," that failure would need to be made clearly to appear. In unrestricted submissions, such as the present margin agreements envisage, the interpretations of the law by the arbitrators in contrast to manifest disregard are not subject, in the federal courts, to judicial review for error in interpretation. The United States Arbitration Act contains no provision for judicial determination of legal issues such as is found in the English law. As the protective provisions of the Securities Act require the exercise of judicial discretion to fairly assure their effectiveness, it seems to us that Congress must have intended § 14...to apply to waiver of judicial trial and review.

[. . .]

Two policies, not easily reconcilable, are involved in this case. Congress has afforded participants in transactions subject to its legislative power an opportunity generally to secure prompt, economical and adequate solution of controversies through arbitration if the parties are willing to accept less certainty of legally correct adjustment. On the other hand, it has enacted the Securities Act to protect the rights of investors and has forbidden a waiver of any of those rights. Recognizing the advantages that prior agreements for arbitration may provide for the solution of commercial controversies, we decide that the intention of Congress concerning the sale of securities is better carried out by holding invalid such an agreement for arbitration of issues arising under the Act.

Reversed.

MR. JUSTICE JACKSON, concurring.

I agree with the Court's opinion insofar as it construes the Securities Act to prohibit waiver of a judicial remedy in favor of arbitration by agreement made before any controversy arose. I think thereafter the parties could agree upon arbitration. However, I find it unnecessary in this case, where there has not been and could not be any arbitration, to decide that the Arbitration Act precludes any judicial remedy for the arbitrators' error of interpretation of a relevant statute.

MR. JUSTICE FRANKFURTER, whom MR. JUSTICE MINTON joins, dissenting.

If arbitration inherently precluded full protection of the rights § 12(2) of the Securities Act affords to a purchaser of securities, or if there were no effective means of ensuring judicial review of the legal basis of the arbitration, then, of course, an agreement to settle the controversy by arbitration would be barred by § 14, the anti-waiver provision, of that Act.

There is nothing in the record before us, nor in the facts of which we can take judicial notice, to indicate that the arbitral system as practiced in the City of New York, and as enforceable under the supervisory authority of the District Court for the Southern District of New York, would not afford the plaintiff the rights to which he is entitled.

The impelling considerations that led to the enactment of the Federal Arbitration Act are the advantages of providing a speedier, more economical and more effective enforcement of rights by way of arbitration than can be had by the tortuous course of litigation, especially in the City of New York. These advantages should not be assumed to be denied in controversies like that before us arising under the Securities Act, in the absence of any showing that settlement by arbitration would jeopardize the rights of the plaintiff.

Arbitrators may not disregard the law. Specifically they are, as Chief Judge Swan pointed out, "bound to decide in accordance with the provisions of section 12(2)." On this we are all agreed. It is suggested, however, that there is no effective way of assuring obedience by the arbitrators to the governing law. But since their failure to observe this law "would constitute grounds for vacating the award pursuant to section 10 of the Federal Arbitration Act," ... appropriate means for judicial scrutiny must be implied, in the form of some record or opinion, however informal, whereby such compliance will appear, or want of it will upset the award.

We have not before us a case in which the record shows that the plaintiff in opening an account had no choice but to accept the arbitration stipulation, thereby making the stipulation an unconscionable and unenforceable provision in a business transaction. The Securities and Exchange Commission, as *amicus curiae*, does not contend that the stipulation which the Court of Appeals respected, under the appropriate safeguards defined by it, was a coercive practice by financial houses against customers incapable of self-protection. It is one thing to make out a case of overreaching as between parties bargaining not at arm's length. It is quite a different thing to find in the anti-waiver provision of the Securities Act a general limitation on the Federal Arbitration Act.

On the state of the record before us, I would affirm the decision of the Court of Appeals.

NOTES AND QUESTIONS

1. What concept of arbitration does Justice Reed advance on behalf of the majority? If his vision of arbitral adjudication does not necessarily evidence hostility or antipathy, could it be characterized as limited and

somewhat deprecatory? Is it fair to say that the majority in *Wilko* underestimates, or at least narrowly reads, the language and the policy of the FAA?

2.   Is Justice Reed correct in asserting that a buyer of securities gives up more legal rights in agreeing to arbitration than consumers of other goods and services? Where or what is the "public law dimension" of this case?

3.   Do you agree that arbitration represents a vehicle for achieving economy in litigation? Do both sides of the Court appear to share that view? Is it warranted by the text or legislative history of the FAA? Why hasn't it surfaced with greater force in prior opinions?

4.   Does *Wilko* involve commercial arbitration or consumer arbitration? Or consumer arbitration in a commercial context? Is there any real difference between these forms of arbitration and, if there is, why doesn't the Court make the distinction? What does the language of Section One of the FAA contribute to this discussion?

5.   You should analyze the rights protection argument that divides the majority and dissenting opinions. How does the availability of review and the quality of review factor into the rights protection analysis?

6.   Analyze carefully Justice Jackson's concurring opinion. What is he suggesting as a possible intermediary solution to the conflict between statutory policies? How does his position compare to Justice Black's view in *Prima Paint* and Justice Stevens' position in *Keating* as an attempt at reconciling divergent policies? What makes the "all-or-nothing" approach more attractive to the majority of the Court in all these cases?

7.   Do you find Justice Frankfurter's reasons for his confidence in securities arbitration reassuring? Do you believe that his characterization accurately reflects the actual operation of the arbitral remedy? Isn't he describing arbitration between brokers—inside-the-industry arbitration? Is that significant in terms of the result he reaches?

8.   You should note Justice Frankfurter's reference at the end of his opinion to unilateral arbitration agreements between the securities industry and its customers. He states that they would be unlawful and unenforceable. Assess his reasoning in the context of *McMahon* and *Rodriguez*, *infra*.

After *Wilko*, lower federal courts consistently held that claims arising under either the 1933 or 1934 Act were inarbitrable because of the public policy interest in securities investor protection. This assessment was grounded in the language of the Acts (the nonwaiver provisions), rather than the provisions of the FAA. The content of the FAA simply was not germane (*i.e.*, its lack of reference to subject-matter inarbitrability or the public policy defense) because its policy imperative was secondary to another Congressional objective as a matter of law. The opinion in *Scherk v. Alberto–Culver* (holding that 1934 Act claims were arbitrable in transborder contracts) did not alter the lower federal court position. The lower courts, it seems, took the core element of the *Scherk* decision seriously: Arbitrability for purposes of international contracts differed substantially from the concept of arbitrability that applied to domestic commercial transactions. Following *Scherk* (and contemporaneously with the later opinion in *Mitsubishi v. Soler*), however, the Court decided the federalism trilogy. *McMahon* reinforced the doctrine born of the federalism trilogy by integrating the reasoning of international arbitration cases into the domestic arbitration cases and by declaring that claims under the Exchange Act and the RICO statute could be submitted to arbitration.

Shearson/American Express, Inc. v. McMahon

As to the issue of the arbitrability of Exchange Act claims (a question which divided the Court 5–4), the majority opinion in *McMahon* begins with the view that a claim based upon statutorily established rights does not disrupt the ordinarily "hospitable" inquiry into the question of arbitrability. To defeat the implied presumption favoring the arbitrability of claims, the regulatory vehicle must contain, either in its language or legislative history, a congressional command mandating exclusive recourse to the courts for the vindication of claims. Moreover, the burden is upon the party opposing arbitration to establish the existence of such congressional intent.

The Court then advances a technical interpretation of the relevant provisions of the Exchange Act, arguing that the nonwaiver language of the Act applies exclusively to the substantive obligations under the legislation. Because the recourse to arbitration merely represents the selection of a different forum and remedial process, such an agreement—the Court would have us believe—has no impact upon the substantive statutory rights in question. The nonwaiver language, therefore, does not apply to the nonsubstantive provisions of the Act. The Court gives little significance either to the underlying purpose of the Exchange Act (to protect individual investors from overreaching by securities industry professionals) or to the possibility that arbitrators will construe the applicable law differently from judges, especially in light of the fact that the arbitral procedure in these circumstances is established and directed by the securities industry. In effect, the Court chooses to ignore the adhesionary character of the contract and the arbitration agreement, neglecting the evident need for consumer protection generated by the facts.

SHEARSON/AMERICAN EXPRESS, INC. v. MCMAHON
482 U.S. 220, 107 S.Ct. 2332, 96 L.Ed.2d 185 (1987).

(footnotes omitted)

JUSTICE O'CONNOR delivered the opinion of the Court.

This case presents two questions regarding the enforceability of predispute arbitration agreements between brokerage firms and their customers. The first is whether a claim brought under § 10(b) of the Securities Exchange Act of 1934 (Exchange Act) must be sent to arbitration in accordance with the terms of an arbitration agreement. The second is whether a claim brought under the Racketeer Influenced and Corrupt Organizations Act (RICO) must be arbitrated in accordance with the terms of such an agreement.

I

Between 1980 and 1982, respondents Eugene and Julia McMahon, individually and as trustees for various pension and profit-sharing plans, were customers of petitioner Shearson/American Express Inc. (Shearson), a brokerage firm registered with the Securities and Exchange Commission (SEC or Commission). Two customer agreements signed by Julia McMahon provided for arbitration of any controversy relating to the accounts the McMahons maintained with Shearson. The arbitration provision provided in relevant part as follows:

> "Unless unenforceable due to federal or state law, any controversy arising out of or relating to my accounts, to transactions with you for me or to this agreement or the breach thereof, shall be settled by arbitration in accordance with the rules, then in effect, of the National Association of Securities Dealers, Inc. or the Boards of Directors of the New York Stock Exchange, Inc. and/or the American Stock Exchange, Inc. as I may elect. . . ."

In October 1984, the McMahons filed an amended complaint against Shearson and petitioner Mary Ann McNulty, the registered representative who handled their accounts, in the United States District Court for the Southern District of New York. The complaint alleged that McNulty, with Shearson's knowledge, had violated § 10(b) of the Exchange Act and Rule 10b–5 by engaging in fraudulent, excessive trading on respondents' accounts and by making false statements and omitting material facts from the advice given to respondents. The complaint also alleged a RICO claim and state law claims for fraud and breach of fiduciary duties.

Relying on the customer agreements, petitioners moved to compel arbitration of the McMahons' claims pursuant to § 3 of the Federal Arbitration Act. The District Court granted the motion in part. . . . The court first rejected the McMahons' contention that the arbitration agreements were unenforceable as contracts of adhesion. It then found that the McMahons' § 10(b) claims were arbitrable under the terms of the agreement, concluding that such a result followed from this Court's decision in *Dean Witter Reynolds Inc. v. Byrd* and the "strong national policy favoring the enforcement of arbitration agreements." The District Court also held that the McMahons' state law claims were arbitrable. . . . It concluded, however, that the McMahons' RICO claim was not arbitrable "because of the important federal policies inherent in the enforcement of RICO by the federal courts.". . .

The Court of Appeals affirmed the District Court on the state law and RICO claims, but it reversed on the Exchange Act claims. . . . With respect to the RICO claim, the Court of Appeals concluded that "public policy" considerations made it "inappropriat[e]" to apply the provisions of the Arbitration Act to RICO suits. The court reasoned that RICO claims are "not merely a private matter." Because a RICO plaintiff may be likened to a "private attorney general" protecting the public interest, the Court of Appeals concluded that such claims should be adjudicated only in a judicial forum. It distinguished this Court's reasoning in *Mitsubishi Motors Corp. v. Soler*...concerning the arbitrability of antitrust claims, on the ground that it involved international business transactions and did not affect the law "as applied to agreements to arbitrate arising from domestic transactions."...

With respect to respondents' Exchange Act claims, the Court of Appeals noted that under *Wilko v. Swan*, claims arising under § 12(2) of the Securities Act of 1933 are not subject to compulsory arbitration. The Court of Appeals observed that it previously had extended the *Wilko* rule to claims arising under § 10(b) of the Exchange Act and Rule 10b–5. The court acknowledged that *Scherk v. Alberto–Culver Co*....and *Dean Witter Reynolds Inc. v. Byrd*...had "cast some doubt on the applicability of *Wilko* to claims under § 10(b)." The Court of Appeals nevertheless concluded that it was bound by the "clear judicial precedent in this Circuit," and held that *Wilko* must be applied to Exchange Act claims....

We granted *certiorari*, to resolve the conflict among the Courts of Appeals regarding the arbitrability of § 10(b) and RICO claims.

II

The Federal Arbitration Act...provides the starting point for answering the questions raised in this case. The Act was intended to "revers[e] centuries of judicial hostility to arbitration agreements"...by "plac[ing] arbitration agreements 'upon the same footing as other contracts.' " ...The Arbitration Act accomplishes this purpose by providing that arbitration agreements "shall be valid, irrevocable, and enforceable, save upon such grounds as exist at law or in equity for the revocation of any contract." The Act also provides that a court must stay its proceedings if it is satisfied that an issue before it is arbitrable under the agreement, § 3; and it authorizes a federal district court to issue an order compelling arbitration if there has been a "failure, neglect, or refusal" to comply with the arbitration agreement, § 4.

The Arbitration Act thus establishes a "federal policy favoring arbitration," *Moses H. Cone Memorial Hospital v. Mercury Construction Corp.*, requiring that "we rigorously enforce agreements to arbitrate." *Dean Witter Reynolds Inc. v. Byrd*.... This duty to enforce arbitration agreements is not diminished when a party bound by an agreement raises a claim founded on statutory rights. As we observed in *Mitsubishi Motors Corp. v. Soler Chrysler–Plymouth, Inc.,* "we are well past the time when judicial suspicion of the desirability of arbitration and of the competence of arbitral tribunals" should inhibit enforcement of the Act " 'in controversies based on statutes.' " ...Absent a well-founded claim that an arbitration agreement resulted from the sort of fraud or excessive economic power that "would provide grounds 'for the revocation of any contract,' " ...the Arbitration Act "provides no basis for disfavoring agreements to arbitrate statutory claims by skewing the otherwise hospitable inquiry into arbitrability."...

The Arbitration Act, standing alone, therefore mandates enforcement of agreements to arbitrate statutory claims. Like any statutory directive, the Arbitration Act's mandate may be overridden by a contrary congressional command. The burden is on the party opposing arbitration, however, to show that Congress intended to preclude a waiver of judicial remedies for the statutory rights at issue. If Congress did intend to limit or prohibit waiver of a judicial forum for a particular claim, such an intent "will be deducible from [the statute's] text or legislative history".

To defeat application of the Arbitration Act in this case, therefore, the McMahons must demonstrate that Congress intended to make an exception to the Arbitration Act for claims arising under RICO and the Exchange Act, an intention discernible from the text, history, or purposes of the statute. We examine the McMahons' arguments regarding the Exchange Act and RICO in turn.

III

When Congress enacted the Exchange Act in 1934, it did not specifically address the question of the arbitrability of § 10(b) claims. The McMahons contend, however, that congressional intent to require a judicial forum for the resolution of § 10(b) claims can be deduced from § 29(a) of the Exchange Act, which declares void "[a]ny condition, stipulation, or provision binding any person to waive compliance with any provision of [the Act]."

First, we reject the McMahons' argument that § 29(a) forbids waiver of § 27 of the Exchange Act. Section 27 provides in relevant part:

The district courts of the United States...shall have exclusive jurisdiction of violations of this title or the rules and regulations thereunder, and of all suits in equity and actions at law brought to enforce any liability or duty created by this title or the rules and regulations thereunder.

The McMahons contend that an agreement to waive this jurisdictional provision is unenforceable because § 29(a) voids the waiver of "any provision" of the Exchange Act. The language of § 29(a), however, does not reach so far. What the antiwaiver provision of § 29(a) forbids is enforcement of agreements to waive "compliance" with the provisions of the statute. But § 27 itself does not impose any duty with which persons trading in securities must "comply." By its terms, § 29(a) only prohibits waiver of the substantive obligations imposed by the Exchange Act. Because § 27 does not impose any statutory duties, its waiver does not constitute a waiver of "compliance with any provision" of the Exchange Act under § 29(a).

We do not read *Wilko v. Swan*...as compelling a different result. In *Wilko*, the Court held that a predispute agreement could not be enforced to compel arbitration of a claim arising under § 12(2) of the Securities Act. The basis for the ruling was § 14 of the Securities Act, which, like § 29(a) of the Exchange Act, declares void any stipulation "to waive compliance with any provision" of the statute. At the beginning of its analysis, the *Wilko* Court stated that the Securities Act's jurisdictional provision was "the kind of 'provision' that cannot be waived under § 14 of the Securities Act." ...This statement, however, can only be understood in the context of the Court's ensuing discussion explaining why arbitration was inadequate as a means of enforcing "the provisions of the Securities Act, advantageous to the buyer." ...The conclusion in *Wilko* was expressly based on the Court's belief that a judicial forum was needed to protect the substantive rights created by the Securities Act.... *Wilko* must be understood, therefore, as holding that the plaintiff's waiver of the "right to select the judicial forum"...was unenforceable only because arbitration was judged inadequate to enforce the statutory rights created by § 12(2).

Indeed, any different reading of *Wilko* would be inconsistent with this Court's decision in *Scherk v. Alberto–Culver Co.*... The Court reasoned that arbitration reduced the uncertainty of international contracts and obviated the danger that a dispute might be submitted to a hostile or unfamiliar forum. At the same time, the Court noted that the advantages of judicial resolution were diminished by the possibility that the opposing party would make "speedy resort to a foreign court." ...The decision in *Scherk* thus turned on the Court's judgment that under the circumstances of that case, arbitration was an adequate substitute for adjudication as a means of enforcing the parties' statutory rights. *Scherk* supports our understanding that *Wilko* must be read as barring waiver of a judicial forum only where arbitration is inadequate to protect the substantive rights at issue. At the same time, it confirms that where arbitration does provide an adequate means of enforcing the provisions of the Exchange Act, § 29(a) does not void a predispute waiver of § 27—*Scherk* upheld enforcement of just such a waiver.

The second argument offered by the McMahons is that the arbitration agreement effects an impermissible waiver of the substantive protections of the Exchange Act. Ordinarily, "[b]y agreeing to arbitrate a statutory claim, a party does not forgo the substantive rights afforded by the statute; it only submits to their resolution in an arbitral, rather than a judicial, forum." *Mitsubishi Motors Corp. v. Soler*.... The McMahons argue, however, that § 29(a) compels a different conclusion. Initially, they contend that predispute agreements are void under § 29(a) because they tend to result from broker overreaching. They reason, as do some commentators, that *Wilko* is premised on the belief "that arbitration clauses in securities sales agreements generally are not freely negotiated." ...According to this view, *Wilko* barred enforcement of predispute agreements because of this frequent inequality of bargaining power, reasoning that Congress intended for § 14 generally to ensure that sellers did not "maneuver buyers into a position that might weaken their ability to recover under the Securities Act."...

We decline to give *Wilko* a reading so far at odds with the plain language of § 14, or to adopt such an unlikely interpretation of § 29(a). The concern that § 29(a) is directed against is evident from the statute's plain language: it is a concern with whether an agreement "waive[s] compliance with [a] provision" of the Exchange Act. The voluntariness of the agreement is irrelevant to this inquiry: if a stipulation waives compliance with a statutory duty, it is void under § 29(a), whether voluntary or not. Thus, a customer cannot negotiate a reduction in commissions in exchange for a waiver of compliance with the requirements of the Exchange Act, even if the customer knowingly and voluntarily agreed to the bargain. Section 29(a) is concerned, not with whether brokers "maneuver[ed customers] into" an agreement, but with whether the agreement "weaken[s] their ability to recover under the [Exchange] Act." ...The former is grounds for revoking the contract under ordinary principles of contract law; the latter is grounds for voiding the agreement under § 29(a).

The other reason advanced by the McMahons for finding a waiver of their § 10(b) rights is that arbitration does "weaken their ability to recover under the [Exchange] Act." ...That is the heart of the Court's decision in *Wilko*, and respondents urge that we should follow its reasoning. *Wilko* listed several grounds why, in the Court's view, the "effectiveness [of the Act's provisions] in application is lessened in arbitration."...

...[T]he reasons given in *Wilko* reflect a general suspicion of the desirability of arbitration and the competence of arbitral tribunals...most apply with no greater force to the arbitration of securities disputes than to the arbitration of legal disputes generally. It is difficult to reconcile *Wilko*'s mistrust of the arbitral process with this Court's subsequent decisions involving the Arbitration Act....

Indeed, most of the reasons given in *Wilko* have been rejected subsequently by the Court as a basis for holding claims to be nonarbitrable. In *Mitsubishi*, for example, we recognized that arbitral tribunals are readily capable of handling the factual and legal complexities of antitrust claims, notwithstanding the absence of judicial instruction and supervision. Likewise, we have concluded that the streamlined procedures of arbitration do not entail any consequential restriction on substantive rights.... Finally, we have indicated that there is no reason to assume at the outset that arbitrators will not follow the law; although judicial scrutiny of arbitration awards necessarily is limited, such review is sufficient to ensure that arbitrators comply with the requirements of the statute....

The suitability of arbitration as a means of enforcing Exchange Act rights is evident from our decision in *Scherk*. Although the holding in that case was limited to international agreements, the competence of arbitral tribunals to resolve § 10(b) claims is the same in both settings. Courts likewise have routinely enforced agreements to arbitrate § 10(b) claims where both parties are members of a securities exchange or the National Association of Securities Dealers (NASD), suggesting that arbitral tribunals are fully capable of handling such matters. And courts uniformly have concluded that *Wilko* does not apply to the submission to arbitration of existing disputes...even though the inherent suitability of arbitration as a means of resolving § 10(b) claims remains unchanged....

Thus, the mistrust of arbitration that formed the basis for the *Wilko* opinion in 1953 is difficult to square with the assessment of arbitration that has prevailed since that time. This is especially so in light of the intervening changes in the regulatory structure of the securities laws. Even if *Wilko*'s assumptions regarding arbitration were valid at the time *Wilko* was decided, most certainly they do not hold true today for arbitration procedures subject to the SEC's oversight authority.

[...]

In the exercise of its regulatory authority, the SEC has specifically approved the arbitration procedures of the New York Stock Exchange, the American Stock Exchange, and the NASD, the organizations mentioned in the arbitration agreement at issue in this case. We conclude that where, as in this case, the prescribed procedures are subject to the Commission's § 19 authority, an arbitration agreement does not effect a waiver of the protections of the Act. While stare decisis concerns may counsel against upsetting *Wilko*'s contrary conclusion under the Securities Act, we refuse to extend *Wilko*'s reasoning to the Exchange Act in light of these intervening regulatory developments. The McMahons' agreement to submit to arbitration therefore is not tantamount to an impermissible waiver of the McMahons' rights under § 10(b), and the agreement is not void on that basis under § 29(a).

[...]

We conclude, therefore, that Congress did not intend for § 29(a) to bar enforcement of all predispute arbitration agreements. In this case, where the SEC has sufficient statutory authority to ensure that arbitration is adequate to vindicate Exchange Act rights, enforcement does not effect a waiver of "compliance with any provision" of the Exchange Act under § 29(a). Accordingly, we hold the McMahons' agreements to arbitrate Exchange Act claims "enforce[able]...in accord with the explicit provisions of the Arbitration Act."...

IV

Unlike the Exchange Act, there is nothing in the text of the RICO statute that even arguably evinces congressional intent to exclude civil RICO claims from the dictates of the Arbitration Act. This silence in the text is matched by silence in the statute's legislative history. The private treble-damages provision was added to the House version of the bill after the bill had been passed by the Senate, and it received only abbreviated discussion in either House.... There is no hint in these legislative debates that Congress intended for RICO treble-damages claims to be excluded from the ambit of the Arbitration Act....

Because RICO's text and legislative history fail to reveal any intent to override the provisions of the Arbitration Act, the McMahons must argue that there is an irreconcilable conflict between arbitration and RICO's underlying purposes. Our decision in *Mitsubishi Motors Corp. v. Soler*...already has addressed many of the grounds given by the McMahons to support this claim. In *Mitsubishi*, we held that nothing in the nature of the federal antitrust laws prohibits parties from agreeing to arbitrate antitrust claims arising out of international commercial transactions. Although the holding in *Mitsubishi* was limited to the international context,...much of its reasoning is equally applicable here. Thus, for example, the McMahons have argued that RICO claims are too complex to be subject to arbitration. We determined in *Mitsubishi*, however, that "potential complexity should not suffice to ward off arbitration."...Antitrust matters are every bit as complex as RICO claims, but we found that the "adaptability and access to expertise" characteristic of arbitration rebutted the view "that an arbitral tribunal could not properly handle an antitrust matter."...

Likewise, the McMahons contend that the "overlap" between RICO's civil and criminal provisions renders § 1964(c) claims nonarbitrable.... Yet § 1964(c) is no different in this respect from the federal antitrust laws. *Mitsubishi* recognized that treble-damages suits for claims arising under § 1 of the Sherman Act may be subject to arbitration, even though such conduct may also give rise to claims of criminal liability.... We similarly find that the criminal provisions of RICO do not preclude arbitration of bona fide civil actions brought under § 1964(c).

The McMahons' final argument is that the public interest in the enforcement of RICO precludes its submission to arbitration. *Mitsubishi* again is relevant to the question. In that case we thoroughly examined the legislative intent behind § 4 of the Clayton Act in assaying whether the importance of the private treble-damages remedy in enforcing the antitrust laws precluded arbitration of § 4 claims. We found that "[n]otwithstanding its important incidental policing function, the treble-damages cause of action...seeks primarily to enable an injured competitor to gain compensation for that injury."...Emphasizing the priority of the compensatory function of § 4 over its deterrent function, *Mitsubishi* concluded that "so long as the prospective litigant effectively may vindicate its statutory cause of action in the arbitral forum, the statute will continue to serve both its remedial and deterrent function."...

[...]

Not only does *Mitsubishi* support the arbitrability of RICO claims, but there is even more reason to suppose that arbitration will adequately serve the purposes of RICO than that it will adequately protect private enforcement of the antitrust laws. The special incentives necessary to encourage civil enforcement actions against organized crime do not support nonarbitrability of run-of-the-mill civil RICO claims brought against legitimate enterprises. The private attorney general role for the typical RICO plaintiff is simply less plausible than it is for the typical antitrust plaintiff, and does not support a finding that there is an irreconcilable conflict between arbitration and enforcement of the RICO statute.

In sum, we find no basis for concluding that Congress intended to prevent enforcement of agreements to arbitrate RICO claims. The McMahons may effectively vindicate their RICO claim in an arbitral forum, and therefore there is no inherent conflict between arbitration and the purposes underlying § 1964(c). Moreover, nothing in RICO's text or legislative history otherwise demonstrates congressional intent to make an exception to the Arbitration Act for RICO claims. Accordingly, the McMahons, "having made the bargain to arbitrate," will be held to their bargain. Their RICO claim is arbitrable under the terms of the Arbitration Act.

V

Accordingly, the judgment of the Court of Appeals for the Second Circuit is reversed, and the case is remanded for further proceedings consistent with this opinion.

It is so ordered.

JUSTICE BLACKMUN, with whom JUSTICE BRENNAN and JUSTICE MARSHALL join, concurring in part and dissenting in part.

I concur in the Court's decision to enforce the arbitration agreement with respect to respondents' RICO claims and thus join Parts I, II, and IV of the Court's opinion. I disagree, however, with the Court's conclusion that respondents' § 10(b) claims also are subject to arbitration.

Both the Securities Act of 1933 and the Securities Exchange Act of 1934 were enacted to protect investors from predatory behavior of securities industry personnel. In *Wilko v. Swan,*...the Court recognized this basic purpose when it declined to enforce a predispute agreement to compel arbitration of claims under the Securities Act. Following that decision, lower courts extended *Wilko*'s reasoning to claims brought under § 10(b) of the Exchange Act, and Congress approved of this extension. In today's decision, however, the Court effectively overrules *Wilko* by accepting the Securities and Exchange Commission's newly adopted position that arbitration procedures in the securities industry and the Commission's oversight of the self-regulatory organizations (SROs) have improved greatly since *Wilko* was decided. The Court thus approves the abandonment of the judiciary's role in the resolution of claims under the Exchange Act and leaves such claims to the arbitral forum of the securities industry at a time when the industry's abuses towards investors are more apparent than ever.

I

At the outset, it is useful to review the manner by which the issue decided today has been kept alive inappropriately by this Court. As the majority explains, *Wilko* was limited to the holding "that a predispute agreement could not be enforced to compel arbitration of a claim arising under § 12(2) of the Securities Act." ...Relying, however, on the reasoning of *Wilko* and the similarity between the pertinent provisions of the

Securities Act and those of the Exchange Act, lower courts extended the *Wilko* holding to claims under the Exchange Act and refused to enforce predispute agreements to arbitrate them as well.

In *Scherk v. Alberto–Culver Co.,*...the Court addressed the question whether a particular predispute agreement to arbitrate § 10(b) claims should be enforced. Because that litigation involved international business concerns and because the case was decided on such grounds, the Court did not reach the issue of the extension of *Wilko* to § 10(b) claims. The Court, nonetheless, included in its opinion dicta noting that "a colorable argument could be made that even the semantic reasoning of the *Wilko* opinion does not control the case before us." ...There is no need to discuss in any detail that "colorable argument," which rests on alleged distinctions between pertinent provisions of the Securities Act and those of the Exchange Act, because the Court does not rely upon it today. In fact, the "argument" is important not so much for its substance as it is for its litigation role. It simply constituted a way of keeping the issue of the arbitrability of § 10(b) claims alive for those opposed to the result in *Wilko*.

[...]

II

There are essentially two problems with the Court's conclusion that predispute agreements to arbitrate § 10(b) claims may be enforced. First, the Court gives *Wilko* an overly narrow reading so that it can fit into the syllogism offered by the Commission and accepted by the Court, namely, (1) *Wilko* was really a case concerning whether arbitration was adequate for the enforcement of the substantive provisions of the securities laws; (2) all of the *Wilko* Court's doubts as to arbitration's adequacy are outdated; (3) thus *Wilko* is no longer good law.... Second, the Court accepts uncritically petitioners' and the Commission's argument that the problems with arbitration, highlighted by the *Wilko* Court, either no longer exist or are not now viewed as problems by the Court. This acceptance primarily is based upon the Court's belief in the Commission's representations that its oversight of the SROs ensures the adequacy of arbitration.

A

I agree with the Court's observation that, in order to establish an exception to the Arbitration Act...for a class of statutory claims, there must be "an intention discernible from the text, history, or purposes of the statute." ...Where the Court first goes wrong, however, is in its failure to acknowledge that the Exchange Act, like the Securities Act, constitutes such an exception. This failure is made possible only by the unduly narrow reading of *Wilko* that ignores the Court's determination there that the Securities Act was an exception to the Arbitration Act. The Court's reading is particularly startling because it is in direct contradiction to the interpretation of *Wilko* given by the Court in *Mitsubishi Motors Corp. v. Soler,*...a decision on which the Court relies for its strong statement of a federal policy in favor of arbitration. In *Mitsubishi*, we viewed *Wilko* as holding that the text and legislative history of the Securities Act not general problems with arbitration established that the Securities Act constituted an exception to the Arbitration Act. In a surprising display of logic, the Court uses *Mitsubishi* as support for the virtues of arbitration and thus as a means for undermining *Wilko*'s holding, but fails to take into account the most pertinent language in *Mitsubishi*.

. . . The Court's misreading of *Wilko* is possible because, while extolling the policies of the Arbitration Act, it is insensitive to, and disregards the policies of, the Securities Act. This Act was passed in 1933, eight years after the Arbitration Act of 1925 . . . and in response to the market crash of 1929. The Act was designed to remedy abuses in the securities industry, particularly fraud and misrepresentation by securities-industry personnel, that had contributed to that disastrous event. . . . It had as its main goal investor protection, which took the form of an effort to place investors on an equal footing with those in the securities industry by promoting full disclosure of information on investments. . . .

The Court in *Wilko* recognized the policy of investor protection in the Securities Act. It was this recognition that animated its discussion. In reasoning that a predispute agreement to arbitrate § 12(2) claims would constitute a "waiver" of a provision of the Act, *i.e.*, the right to the judicial forum embodied in § 22(a), the Court specifically referred to the policy of investor protection underlying the Act. . . .

In the Court's view, the express language, legislative history, and purposes of the Securities Act all made predispute agreements to arbitrate § 12(2) claims unenforceable despite the presence of the Arbitration Act. . . .

Accordingly, the Court seriously errs when it states that the result in *Wilko* turned only on the perceived inadequacy of arbitration for the enforcement of § 12(2) claims. . . .

The Court's decision in *Scherk* is consistent with this reading of *Wilko*, despite the Court's suggestion to the contrary. . . . Indeed, in reading *Scherk* as a case turning on the adequacy of arbitration, the Court completely ignores the central thrust of that decision. . . . The *Scherk* Court relied on a crucial difference between the international business situation presented to it and that before the Court in *Wilko*, where the laws of the United States, particularly the securities laws, clearly governed the dispute. *Scherk*, in contrast, presented a multinational conflict-of-laws puzzle. In such a situation, the Court observed, a contract provision setting forth a particular forum and the law to apply for possible disputes was "an almost indispensable precondition to achievement of the orderliness and predictability essential to any international business transaction." . . . Accordingly, the *Scherk* decision turned on the special nature of agreements to arbitrate in the international commercial context.

In light of a proper reading of *Wilko*, the pertinent question then becomes whether the language, legislative history, and purposes of the Exchange Act call for an exception to the Arbitration Act for § 10(b) claims. The Exchange Act waiver provision is virtually identical to that of the Securities Act. More importantly, the same concern with investor protection that motivated the Securities Act is evident in the Exchange Act, although the latter, in contrast to the former, is aimed at trading in the secondary securities market.... We have recognized that both Acts were designed with this common purpose in mind. Indeed, the application of both Acts to the same conduct...suggests that they have the same basic goal. And we have approved a cumulative construction of remedies under the securities Acts to promote the maximum possible protection of investors....

In sum, the same reasons that led the Court to find an exception to the Arbitration Act for § 12(2) claims exist for § 10(b) claims as well. It is clear that *Wilko*, when properly read, governs the instant case and mandates that a predispute arbitration agreement should not be enforced as to § 10(b) claims.

B

Even if I were to accept the Court's narrow reading of *Wilko*, as a case dealing only with the inadequacies of arbitration in 1953, I do not think that this case should be resolved differently today so long as the policy of investor protection is given proper consideration in the analysis. Despite improvements in the process of arbitration and changes in the judicial attitude towards it, several aspects of arbitration that were seen by the *Wilko* court to be inimical to the policy of investor protection still remain. Moreover, I have serious reservations about the Commission's contention that its oversight of the SROs' arbitration procedures will ensure that the process is adequate to protect an investor's rights under the securities Acts.

[...]

Even those who favor the arbitration of securities claims do not contend, however, that arbitration has changed so significantly as to eliminate the essential characteristics noted by the *Wilko* Court. Indeed, proponents of arbitration would not see these characteristics as "problems," because, in their view, the characteristics permit the unique "streamlined" nature of the arbitral process. As at the time of *Wilko*, preparation of a record of arbitration proceedings is not invariably required today. Moreover, arbitrators are not bound by precedent and are actually discouraged by their associations from giving reasons for a decision. Judicial review is still substantially limited to the four grounds listed in § 10 of the Arbitration Act and to the concept of "manifest disregard" of the law....

The Court's "mistrust" of arbitration may have given way recently to an acceptance of this process, not only because of the improvements in arbitration, but also because of the Court's present assumption that the distinctive features of arbitration, its more quick and economical resolution of claims, do not render it inherently inadequate for the resolution of statutory claims. Such reasoning, however, should prevail only in the absence of the congressional policy that places the statutory claimant in a special position with respect to possible violators of his statutory rights. As even the most ardent supporter of arbitration would recognize, the arbitral process at best places the investor on an equal footing with the securities-industry personnel against whom the claims are brought.

Furthermore, there remains the danger that, at worst, compelling an investor to arbitrate securities claims puts him in a forum controlled by the securities industry. This result directly contradicts the goal of both securities Acts to free the investor from the control of the market professional. The Uniform Code provides some safeguards but despite them, and indeed because of the background of the arbitrators, the investor has the impression, frequently justified, that his claims are being judged by a forum composed of individuals sympathetic to the securities industry and not drawn from the public. It is generally recognized that the codes do not define who falls into the category "not from the securities industry." ...Accordingly, it is often possible for the "public" arbitrators to be attorneys or consultants whose clients have been exchange members or SROs. The uniform opposition of investors to compelled arbitration and the overwhelming support of the securities industry for the process suggest that there must be some truth to the investors' belief that the securities industry has an advantage in a forum under its own control....

More surprising than the Court's acceptance of the present adequacy of arbitration for the resolution of securities claims is its confidence in the Commission's oversight of the arbitration procedures of the SROs to ensure this adequacy. Such confidence amounts to a wholesale acceptance of the Commission's present position that this oversight undermines the force of *Wilko* and that arbitration therefore should be compelled because the Commission has supervisory authority over the SROs' arbitration procedures. The Court, however, fails to acknowledge that, until it filed an amicus brief in this case, the Commission consistently took the position that § 10(b) claims, like those under § 12(2), should not be sent to arbitration, that predispute arbitration agreements, where the investor was not advised of his right to a judicial forum, were misleading, and that the very regulatory oversight upon which the Commission now relies could not alone make securities-industry arbitration adequate. It is most questionable, then, whether the Commission's recently adopted position is entitled to the deference that the Court accords it.

The Court is swayed by the power given to the Commission by the 1975 amendments to the Exchange Act in order to permit the Commission to oversee the rules and procedures of the SROs, including those dealing with arbitration.... Subsequent to the passage of these amendments, however, the Commission has taken the consistent position that predispute arbitration agreements, which did not disclose to an investor that he has a right to a judicial forum, were misleading and possibly actionable under the securities laws. The Commission remained dissatisfied with the continued use of these arbitration agreements and eventually it proposed a rule to prohibit them, explaining that such a prohibition was not inconsistent with its support of arbitration for resolving securities disputes, particularly existing ones.... While emphasizing the Court's *Wilko* decision as a basis for its proposed rule, the Commission noted that its proposal also was in line with its own understanding of the problems with such agreements and with the "[c]ongressional determination that public investors should also have available the special protection of the federal courts for resolution of disputes arising under the federal securities laws." ...Although the rule met with some opposition, it was adopted and *remains in force today.*

Moreover, the Commission's own description of its enforcement capabilities contradicts its position that its general overview of SRO rules and procedures can make arbitration adequate for resolving securities claims. The Commission does not pretend that its oversight consists of anything other than a general review of SRO rules and the ability to require that an SRO adopt or delete a particular rule. It does not contend that its "sweeping authority"...includes a review of specific arbitration proceedings. It thus neither polices nor monitors the results of these arbitrations for possible misapplications of securities laws or for indications of how investors fare in these proceedings....

Finally, the Court's complacent acceptance of the Commission's oversight is alarming when almost every day brings another example of illegality on Wall Street. Many of the abuses recently brought to light, it is true, do not deal with the question of the adequacy of SRO arbitration. They, however, do suggest that the industry's self-regulation, of which the SRO arbitration is a part, is not functioning acceptably.

[...]

...Indeed, in light of today's decision compelling the enforcement of predispute arbitration agreements, it is likely that investors will be inclined, more than ever, to bring complaints to federal courts that arbitrators were partial or acted in "manifest disregard" of the securities laws.... It is thus ironic that the Court's decision, no doubt animated by its desire to rid the federal courts of these suits, actually may increase litigation about arbitration.

I therefore respectfully dissent in part.

JUSTICE STEVENS, concurring in part and dissenting in part.

Gaps in the law must, of course, be filled by judicial construction. But after a statute has been construed, either by this Court or by a consistent course of decision by other federal judges and agencies, it acquires a meaning that should be as clear as if the judicial gloss had been drafted by the Congress itself....

During the 32 years immediately following this Court's decision in *Wilko v. Swan*,...each of the eight Circuits that addressed the issue concluded that the holding of *Wilko* was fully applicable to claims arising under the Securities Exchange Act of 1934.... This long-standing interpretation creates a strong presumption, in my view, that any mistake that the courts may have made in interpreting the statute is best remedied by the Legislative, not the Judicial, Branch. The history set forth in Part I of JUSTICE BLACKMUN's opinion adds special force to that presumption in this case.

For this reason, I respectfully dissent from the portion of the Court's judgment that holds *Wilko* inapplicable to the 1934 Act. Like JUSTICE BLACKMUN, however, I join Parts I, II, and IV of the Court's opinion.

NOTES AND QUESTIONS

1.   The majority opinion limits the precedential value of *Wilko*, confining its holding to the 1933 Act, and effectively discredits its reasoning. According to the majority, rather than representing a statement of the importance of the policy of protecting investors from broker overreaching, *Wilko* symbolizes a general distrust of arbitration that conflicts with the Court's more recent pronouncements on arbitration. The *Wilko* decision, therefore, only bars arbitration where it is inadequate to protect the substantive statutory rights at issue. *Scherk* is seen as providing that, where arbitration is deemed (presumably by the courts) sufficient to protect the rights at issue, there is no bar to a waiver of a judicial forum. This reconstruction of precedents extends the doctrine, first articulated in *Scherk* and more forcefully stated in *Mitsubishi*, that the existence of statutory rights does not preclude the recourse to arbitration unless there is a legislative command that mandates judicial disposition of alleged violations. *McMahon*, in effect, ignores the special circumstances, express doctrinal content, and segregation of domestic and international considerations in the prior decisional law.

2.   *McMahon* similarly recasts the holding in *Mitsubishi*. A fair reading of *Mitsubishi* suggests that it establishes that antitrust claims are arbitrable in the context of international contracts. As in *Scherk*, the critical element is the fact that the dispute and the agreement to arbitrate are embedded in an international commercial transaction. If U.S. parties could frustrate the recourse to arbitration by alleging violations of domestic antitrust law, the stability of international commerce achieved with predictable dispute resolution through arbitration would be undermined. According to *McMahon*, however, *Mitsubishi* now stands for the proposition that the submission of statutory rights to arbitration does not represent an abandonment or elimination of those rights. Arbitral tribunals, like courts, are able to interpret and apply the governing statutory law. Resorting to the arbitral rather than judicial adjudication of statutory claims merely represents a choice of dispute resolution forum.

3.   As to the issue of the arbitrability of RICO claims, the Court in *McMahon* is unanimous in its view that such claims can be submitted to arbitration. While the RICO legislation could readily be seen as involving

matters of public policy, there is no express language in the statute or in its legislative history to indicate a congressional intent to preclude party selection of alternative, nonjudicial remedies. Accordingly, under the revamped understanding of *Mitsubishi*, the Court finds itself bound to conclude that RICO claims can be adjudicated through arbitration. The RICO statute does provide for civil claims, and arbitrators are able to assume jurisdiction over such disputes. Apparently, arbitral (like judicial) jurisdiction extends to the award of treble damages.

4. The majority and dissenting opinions render—once again—dichotomous evaluations of the issues and the governing law. The majority relies primarily upon a policy objective (sustaining the recourse to arbitration) and uses precedent, logic, and other devices of argumentation to uphold that objective. Although the result that is eventually reached is clear and unambiguous, its foundations are suspect and fragile. In a word, the distortive reasoning generates conceptual confusion because facts are misrepresented and the traditional means of justification are objectively unreliable. The dissent supplies an accurate and cogent account of the statutory language, its legislative history, and the prior case law. In the dissenting opinion, the rule of reason and rational evaluation inform and establish the proposed rule of law. Policy may influence the analysis, but it does not imprison the reasoning in circuitry and foregone conclusions. The approach is lawyerly and judicious, rather than legislative and rhetorical.

What is your assessment of the majority and dissenting approaches in the arbitration cases? Is there a consistent split between the two sides of the Court? If so, what does it imply about the U.S. law of arbitration and its elaboration? Can you devise a better approach or does the unequivocal character of the Court's position prevent any moderation?

5. In the majority opinion, Justice O'Connor, who dissented in *Byrd* and concurred with strong reservations in *Terminix*, outlines the basic principles of the current law on arbitration in Section II of the opinion. Do you believe that her description of the law is accurate not only in terms of its ultimate content, but also in regard to the law's progressive elaboration? In particular, do you agree with the statement that "[t]he Arbitration Act, standing alone, . . . mandates enforcement of agreements to arbitrate statutory claims"? Is this a fair reading of the FAA and the accompanying case law? Has the FAA ever stood alone in terms of its content or the establishment of legal rules?

6. Justice O'Connor refers to and cites the language of Sections 27 and 29(a) of the Exchange Act in Section III of the majority opinion. How do you evaluate her interpretation of those provisions? Does it reflect a plausible construction or are her views tendentious? Also, why didn't the *Scherk* Court emphasize that the legislation's nonwaiver provision applies only to the substantive provisions of the Act if that interpretation was so self-evident and clear in the statute?

7. The majority and dissent are absolutely at odds in terms of their assessment of the *Wilko* precedent as well as the *Scherk-Mitsubishi* addendum to *Wilko*. You should investigate the various facets of this disagreement, paying particular attention to the description of the gravamen of *Wilko* and of Congressional intent in the relevant statutes on both sides of the Court. Is the

majority simply adapting the law of arbitration creatively to new exigencies in the legal system which the dissent wants to frustrate by its attachment to by-gone history and institutional formalism? Is there another way to characterize the positions in this debate?

8.   There is no mention in any segment of *McMahon* either of consumer arbitration or subject-matter inarbitrability. Although arbitration has been commonplace in the securities industry, it applied previously to disputes between the exchanges, brokerage houses, and brokers. The form of securities arbitration at issue in *McMahon* is different in that it involves the integration of customers into the arbitral system. The facts indicate that the McMahons are quite sophisticated financial parties; nonetheless, they are clients of the securities industry and not participants in it. Shouldn't this factor have received greater presence in the Court's evaluation of the suitability of arbitration to resolve the securities disputes in question? Aren't the two types of arbitration implied by the circumstances of the case enormously different forms or usages of arbitration, subject to differing regulatory regimes and policy imperatives?

Also, the unilateral character of the arbitral clause should be under-scored. In most transactions for the purchase of securities, the broker pres-ents the buyer with a standard customer agreement that contains a boiler-plate provision for the arbitration of disputes. Every customer contract contains such an arbitral provision; in fact, buyers cannot purchase securities from any broker without agreeing to arbitrate disputes. This industry-wide practice makes arbitration the exclusive remedy for consumer complaints against brokers and for claims based upon the violation of securities law.

Again, these aspects of the transaction are not highlighted in the majority opinion. Do they have a direct bearing upon the legitimacy of arbitration in the context of securities disputes involving consumers? Aren't such agree-ments invalid under Section Two of the FAA? Why does the majority invoke the supervisory activities of the SEC in this context? Doesn't the dissent effectively refute the effectiveness of SEC supervision in terms of the opera-tion of the arbitral mechanism? How might the submission agreement con-tribute to a more legitimate form of securities arbitration involving investors?

It is rather astounding that the topic of subject-matter inarbitrability is never mentioned in the *McMahon* opinion. What the Court calls the "hospita-ble inquiry into arbitrability" is integrated into and arises from the view that the law of arbitration is a statement of congressional will and policy that is binding upon the courts. The notion that subject-matter inarbitrability is an established and functional part of arbitration law never explicitly enters into the Court's consideration of the question of the arbitrability of securities disputes. The doctrinal view that arbitration gains its adjudicatory legitimacy from the legal system and that the legal system has the authority to place limits upon the arbitral process is, if not ignored, certainly neglected. The thrust of the Court's decisional law is to find interpretative devices by which to eradicate any possible restriction on arbitral adjudication, from aggrandiz-ing the FAA's statutory purpose to eliminating state authority to regulate arbitration, and to having arbitration apply indiscriminately to contractual and statutory disputes. The *ad hoc* methodology and the uncompromising singularity of purpose have caused the U.S. law of arbitration to suffer. Judicial adjudication loses its identity because it has no mission that cannot be fulfilled by arbitration. Arbitration is discredited because it has no limit or boundary; no structural personality of its own except to be functional in all circumstances.

How would you assess the Court's failure to refer to the ordinary principles of arbitration law (subject-matter inarbitrability, in particular) in resolving arbitration cases? Does the content and framework of the FAA require the Court to embed its rulings principally in the constitutional and institutional aspects of the U.S. legal system? Is there a U.S. law of arbitration or more simply a federal judicial policy to support arbitration? Does the Court understand the arbitral process? If not, what is it deciding in these cases?

9.   It should be underscored that the Court is unanimous in its decision to allow for the arbitration of RICO claims. The RICO statute contains no mention of any dispute resolution restriction or prescription. According to the Court's reasoning, there is no statement, therefore, of a countervailing Congressional policy and the FAA can take effect unimpeded. Do you agree with this logic? Does the RICO statute not serve the public interest—in fact, a vital public interest? Are RICO claims meant to be settled in a private adjudicatory setting—away from the scrutiny of the public? What happens to the content of the statute if civil RICO claims can be submitted to arbitration? Does the unanimity in the decision express the Court's distaste for RICO and the litigation it generates? Does it indicate loyalty to the FAA's would-be objective or express a desire to manage federal court dockets by purging them of unwanted and undesirable litigation?

10.   Assess the following statement from Justice Blackmun's dissent: "It is thus ironic that the Court's decision, no doubt animated by its desire to rid the federal courts of these [investor] suits, actually may increase litigation about arbitration." 482 U.S. at 268. How might such a situation come about?

11.   The Court's holding and reasoning in *McMahon* generated a number of significant reactions. Within the arbitration community, applying securities arbitration to employment and consumer disputes appeared untoward. It created a need to adapt the traditional process to the needs of the new litigation. In the wake of *McMahon*, the American Arbitration Association (AAA) quickly developed a set of institutional rules tailored to securities arbitration. Previously, such cases had been governed by the rules for commercial arbitration. The alacrity of the AAA reaction indicated that the *McMahon* opinion was a source of new business for arbitral institutions and that arbitration in securities matters presented problems not normally associated with conventional arbitrations. With an increased volume of cases, new rules were needed to lessen the industry bias in prior procedures, account for the parties' disparity of position, and address the likelihood that most claims would raise questions of regulatory law.

When compared to their commercial counterpart, the AAA rules for securities arbitration differ in only a few, albeit fundamental, respects. First, in regard to the number of arbitrators on the tribunal, the commercial rules provide that generally only one arbitrator shall be appointed unless the parties provide otherwise or the AAA deems a plurality of arbitrators necessary. The securities arbitration rules require a panel of three arbitrators whenever a claim exceeds the relatively modest sum of $20,000. Second, the appointment of arbitrators is slightly more complicated under the rules for securities arbitration. The parties are given two lists of arbitrators—one listing arbitrators affiliated with the securities industry and the other nonaffiliated arbitrators. When the tribunal consists of three arbitrators, at least two must be nonaffiliated. If the arbitration is to be done by a sole arbitrator, that arbitrator must be nonaffiliated. Finally, in regard to the award, the rules for securities arbitration require arbitrators to "include a statement regarding the disposition of any statutory claims," whereas the rules for commercial arbitration mandate only that the award be in writing and signed by a majority of the arbitrators.

While the rules for securities arbitration are molded to the special character of these disputes, they may not alleviate the basic danger of having recourse to arbitration in a consumer and regulatory context. The practice of having three-member tribunals and a majority of nonaffiliated arbitrators may not sufficiently protect consumer interests. It may only provide a formalistic safeguard. Industry practice may still set applicable standards and the public interest may never be defined, elaborated upon, or referred to in this private adjudicatory process. Unlike judges, arbitrators may not have the sense of independence necessary to adopt minority, economically questionable, or otherwise "deviant" positions. Finally, mandating that securities arbitrators expressly acknowledge investor claims of statutory violations only provides superficial recognition of the disputes' public law character. The rules do not mandate a reasoned assessment of the claim, and appeal to a court is no more readily available in these arbitral circumstances than in others.

Although these alterations do not attenuate the juridical dilemma created by the Court's decision, they mitigate the harshness of the *McMahon* result. In *McMahon*, the Court was willing to have investor claims resolved through industry-controlled (SRO) arbitration procedures. By attempting to deal with disparities in position and the public law aspect of the cases, the new AAA rules at least are pointed in the direction of fairness and seek to protect the institution of arbitration from charges of glaring unsuitability and abuse. It bears reiterating, however, that these rules do not resolve the core problems raised by the arbitrability of securities claims: The adhesionary character of the arbitral compact, the economic and positional inequality of the parties, and the depreciation of the public interest in preventing individual investor fraud and broker overreaching in a sophisticated, volatile market.

Moreover, in its opinion, the *McMahon* Court looked to SEC supervision as a means of justifying its confidence in industry-controlled securities arbitration procedures. If unfairness and injustice surfaced, the Court seemed to reason, the Commission would be there to provide the necessary correction. "Black Monday" (October 19, 1987) demonstrated the fallacy of the Court's reasoning and made the underlying problems with securities arbitration transparent. Following the stock market collapse, an avalanche of investor claims were submitted to the industry-controlled (SRO) arbitral framework. Apparently, the SEC was unable to exercise its anticipated supervisory capabilities. The volume of pending cases and a growing public dissatisfaction with arbitral procedures led the Commission to consider asking for congressional legislation prohibiting mandatory predispute arbitration agreements in investor-broker contracts. It eventually resolved, however, merely to request a study of the problem. As indicated in the dissenting opinion, the depth of regulatory oversight from the Commission envisaged by the *McMahon* Court simply does not exist.

SEC inaction and public outcries of injustice with mandatory arbitration in securities cases may lead to legislative attacks upon the arbitral process. The *McMahon* opinion, in fact, gave rise to a determination in some legislative quarters to oppose the Court's reordering of fundamental juridical priorities. Massachusetts, for example, enacted legislation prohibiting the use of mandatory arbitration clauses in investor-broker contracts. Under the legislation, which took effect in January 1989, brokers were required to inform prospective clients of their legal right to judicial redress of their grievances. Moreover, brokers had to do business with investors who refused to agree to arbitrate. While the legislation was directed at consumer protection, it cast arbitration in an unfavorable light. Because the Massachusetts law arguably conflicted with the federal law on arbitration and the content of the Court's arbitral doctrine, it was attacked on constitutional grounds. The Massachusetts law was struck down at the federal district court level on the ground that it conflicted with the Supreme Court's "forceful endorsement of the arbitration process." This decision was upheld by the Court on appeal.

Do you believe that a legislative reversal of the judicial doctrine on arbitration is still likely? What factors might contribute to reinvigorating a legislative reconsideration? What arguments could be advanced to thwart the rise of arbitration in the resolution of consumer claims? Would the invalidation of the arbitral clause in this setting constitute an appropriate solution? What are the dangers of relying upon legislative solutions? What reasons would lead to a greater distrust in the area of consumer arbitration than in commercial arbitration?

Rodriguez v. Shearson/American Express, Inc.

Rodriguez de Quijas v. Shearson/American Express, Inc., 490 U.S. 477 (1989), completes the Court's undermining of the subject-matter inarbitrability defense in regard to statutory rights. The Court decides in this case that claims arising under the 1933 Securities Act are arbitrable, overruling and reversing *Wilko* because it embodied a would-be "outmoded presumption of disfavoring arbitration proceedings." Like *McMahon*, the facts of *Rodriguez* involved allegations of consumer fraud in an investor-broker contract for the purchase of securities. The plaintiffs, who had signed a standard contract containing an arbitration clause, claimed violations of both the 1933 Securities Act and the 1934 Securities Exchange Act. In *McMahon*, the Court ruled that 1934 Act claims could be submitted to arbitration; in *Rodriguez*, the issue of litigation was whether the 1933 Act claims should also be deemed arbitrable.

In a 5 to 4 decision, the *Rodriguez* Court used the principles articulated in *Mitsubishi* and *McMahon* to completely discredit the *Wilko* doctrine. The Court, through Justice Kennedy, made much of the fact that arbitration was "merely a form of trial" that did not affect the substantive rights in contest. Arbitral proceedings were an effective means of trial. Moreover, statutory rights did not occupy a privileged position; they, like contractual obligations, could be adjudicated through arbitration. Having recourse to arbitration resulted only in a waiver of the Act's procedural guarantees, not of the substantive statutory rights. The Act's nonwaiver provision applied only to the legislation's substantive provisions.

The majority opinion emphasized that *Wilko* was at odds with the Court's contemporary pronouncements on arbitration: "To the extent that *Wilko* rested on suspicion of arbitration as a method of weakening the protections afforded in the substantive law to would-be complainants, it has fallen far out of step with our current strong endorsement of the federal statutes favoring this method of resolving disputes." *Wilko* was imbued with " 'the old judicial hostility to arbitration' " and did not address the arbitrability question " 'with a healthy regard for the federal policy favoring arbitration' " mandated by the federalism trilogy. The ruling in *McMahon* dictated that *Wilko* could no longer stand as applicable law because the language of the 1933 and 1934 Acts pertaining to judicial remedies was identical: "Indeed, in *McMahon* the Court declined to read § 29(a) of the Securities Exchange Act of 1934, the language of which is in every respect the same as that in § 14 of the 1933 Act,...to prohibit enforcement of predispute agreements to arbitrate." Furthermore, an inconsistent interpretation of the provisions of the two acts would impair the functional harmony of the regulatory scheme for the sale of securities: "[T]he inconsistency between *Wilko* and *McMahon* undermines the essential rationale for a harmonious construction of the statutes, which is to discourage litigants from manipulating their allegations merely to cast their claims under one of the securities laws rather than another."

RODRIGUEZ DE QUIJAS v. SHEARSON/AMERICAN EXPRESS, INC.

490 U.S. 477, 109 S.Ct. 1917, 104 L.Ed.2d 526 (1989).

(footnotes omitted)

JUSTICE KENNEDY delivered the opinion of the Court.

The question here is whether a predispute agreement to arbitrate claims under the Securities Act of 1933 is unenforceable, requiring resolution of the claims only in a judicial forum.

I

Petitioners are individuals who invested about $400,000 in securities. They signed a standard customer agreement with the broker, which included a clause stating that the parties agreed to settle any controversies "relating to [the] accounts" through binding arbitration that complies with specified procedures. The agreement to arbitrate these controversies is unqualified, unless it is found to be unenforceable under federal or state law. The investments turned sour, and petitioners eventually sued respondent and its broker-agent in charge of the accounts, alleging that their money was lost in unauthorized and fraudulent transactions.

The District Court ordered all the claims to be submitted to arbitration except for those raised under § 12(2) of the Securities Act. It held that the latter claims must proceed in the court action under our clear holding on the point in *Wilko v. Swan*.... The Court of Appeals reversed, concluding that the arbitration agreement is enforceable because this Court's subsequent decisions have reduced *Wilko* to "obsolescence."...

II

The *Wilko* case, decided in 1953, required the Court to determine whether an agreement to arbitrate future controversies constitutes a binding stipulation "to waive compliance with any provision" of the Securities Act, which is nullified by § 14 of the Act. The Court considered the language, purposes, and legislative history of the Securities Act and concluded that the agreement to arbitrate was void under § 14. But the decision was a difficult one in view of the competing legislative policy embodied in the Arbitration Act, which the Court described as "not easily reconcilable," and which strongly favors the enforcement of agreements to arbitrate as a means of securing "prompt, economical and adequate solution of controversies."...

It has been recognized that *Wilko* was not obviously correct, for "the language prohibiting waiver of 'compliance with any provision of this title' could easily have been read to relate to substantive provisions of the Act without including the remedy provisions." ...The Court did not read the language this way in *Wilko*, however, and gave two reasons. First, the Court rejected the argument that "arbitration is merely a form of trial to be used in lieu of a trial at law." ...The Court found instead that § 14 does not permit waiver of "the right to select the judicial forum" in favor of arbitration...because "arbitration lacks the certainty of a suit at law under the Act to enforce [the buyer's] rights".... Second, the Court concluded that the Securities Act was intended to protect buyers of securities, who often do not deal at arm's length and on equal terms with sellers, by offering them "a wider choice of courts and venue" than is enjoyed by participants in other business transactions, making "the right to select the judicial forum" a particularly valuable feature of the Securities Act....

We do not think these reasons justify an interpretation of § 14 that prohibits agreements to arbitrate future disputes relating to the purchase of securities. The Court's characterization of the arbitration process in *Wilko* is pervaded by..."the old judicial hostility to arbitration." ...That view has been steadily eroded over the years.... The erosion intensified in our most recent decisions upholding agreements to arbitrate federal claims raised under the Securities Exchange Act of 1934...under the Racketeer Influenced and Corrupt Organizations (RICO) statutes...and under the antitrust laws. To the extent that *Wilko* rested on suspicion of arbitration as a method of weakening the protections afforded in the substantive law to would-be complainants, it has fallen far out of step with our current strong endorsement of the federal statutes favoring this method of resolving disputes.

Once the outmoded presumption of disfavoring arbitration proceedings is set to one side, it becomes clear that the right to select the judicial forum and the wider choice of courts are not such essential features of the Securities Act that § 14 is properly construed to bar any waiver of these provisions. Nor are they so critical that they cannot be waived under the rationale that the Securities Act was intended to place buyers of securities on an equal footing with sellers. *Wilko* identified two different kinds of provisions in the Securities Act that would advance this objective. Some are substantive, such as the provision placing on the seller the burden of proving lack of scienter when a buyer alleges fraud.... Others are procedural. The specific procedural improvements highlighted in *Wilko* are the statute's broad venue provisions in the federal courts; the existence of nationwide service of process in the federal courts; the extinction of the amount-in-controversy requirement that had applied to fraud suits when they were brought in federal courts under diversity jurisdiction rather than as a federal cause of action; and the grant of concurrent jurisdiction in the state and federal courts without possibility of removal....

There is no sound basis for construing the prohibition in § 14 on waiving "compliance with any provision" of the Securities Act to apply to these procedural provisions. Although the first three measures do facilitate suits by buyers of securities, the grant of concurrent jurisdiction constitutes explicit authorization for complainants to waive those protections by filing suit in state court without possibility of removal to federal court. These measures, moreover, are present in other federal statutes which have not been interpreted to prohibit enforcement of predispute agreements to arbitrate....

Indeed, in *McMahon* the Court declined to read § 29(a) of the Securities Exchange Act of 1934, the language of which is in every respect the same as that in § 14 of the 1933 Act to prohibit enforcement of predispute agreements to arbitrate. The only conceivable distinction in this regard between the Securities Act and the Securities Exchange Act is that the former statute allows concurrent federal-state jurisdiction over causes of action and the latter statute provides for exclusive federal jurisdiction. But even if this distinction were thought to make any difference at all, it would suggest that arbitration agreements, which are "in effect, a specialized kind of forum-selection clause,"...should not be prohibited under the Securities Act, since they, like the provision for concurrent jurisdiction, serve to advance the objective of allowing buyers of securities a broader right to select the forum for resolving disputes, whether it be judicial or otherwise. And in *McMahon* we explained at length why we rejected the *Wilko* Court's aversion to arbitration as a forum for resolving disputes over securities transactions, especially in light of the relatively recent expansion of the Securities and Exchange

Commission's authority to oversee and to regulate those arbitration procedures. . . .

Finally, in *McMahon* we stressed the strong language of the Arbitration Act, which declares as a matter of federal law that arbitration agreements "shall be valid, irrevocable, and enforceable, save upon such grounds as exist at law or in equity for the revocation of any contract." Under that statute, the party opposing arbitration carries the burden of showing that Congress intended in a separate statute to preclude a waiver of judicial remedies, or that such a waiver of judicial remedies inherently conflicts with the underlying purposes of that other statute. . . . But as Justice Frankfurter said in dissent in *Wilko*, so it is true in this case: "There is nothing in the record before us, nor in the facts of which we can take judicial notice, to indicate that the arbitral system . . . would not afford the plaintiff the rights to which he is entitled." . . . Petitioners have not carried their burden of showing that arbitration agreements are not enforceable under the Securities Act.

The language quoted above from § 2 of the Arbitration Act also allows the courts to give relief where the party opposing arbitration presents "well-supported claims that the agreement to arbitrate resulted from the sort of fraud or overwhelming economic power that would provide grounds 'for the revocation of any contract.' " . . . This avenue of relief is in harmony with the Securities Act's concern to protect buyers of securities by removing "the disadvantages under which buyers labor" in their dealings with sellers. Although petitioners suggest that the agreement to arbitrate here was adhesive in nature, the record contains no factual showing sufficient to support that suggestion.

adhesion
Response

III

. . . We now conclude that *Wilko* was incorrectly decided and is inconsistent with the prevailing uniform construction of other federal statutes governing arbitration agreements in the setting of business transactions. Although we are normally and properly reluctant to overturn our decisions construing statutes, we have done so to achieve a uniform interpretation of similar statutory language . . . and to correct a seriously erroneous interpretation of statutory language that would undermine congressional policy as expressed in other legislation. . . .

It also would be undesirable for the decisions in *Wilko* and *McMahon* to continue to exist side by side. Their inconsistency is at odds with the principle that the 1933 and 1934 Acts should be construed harmoniously because they "constitute interrelated components of the federal regulatory scheme governing transactions in securities." . . . In this case, for example, petitioners' claims under the 1934 Act were subjected to arbitration, while their claim under the 1933 Act was not permitted to go to arbitration, but was required to proceed in court. That result makes little sense for similar claims, based on similar facts, which are supposed to arise within a single federal regulatory scheme. In addition, the inconsistency between *Wilko* and *McMahon* undermines the essential rationale for a harmonious construction of the two statutes, which is to discourage litigants from manipulating their allegations merely to cast their claims under one of the securities laws rather than another. For all of these reasons, therefore, we overrule the decision in *Wilko*.

[. . .]

The judgment of the Court of Appeals is

Affirmed.

JUSTICE STEVENS, with whom JUSTICE BRENNAN, JUSTICE MARSHALL, and JUSTICE BLACKMUN join, dissenting.

The Court of Appeals refused to follow *Wilko v. Swan,* . . . a controlling precedent of this Court. As the majority correctly acknowledges, . . . the Court of Appeals therefore engaged in an indefensible brand of judicial activism. We, of course, are not subject to the same restraint when asked to upset one of our own precedents. But when our earlier opinion gives a statutory provision concrete meaning, which Congress elects not to amend during the ensuing 3 1/2 decades, our duty to respect Congress' work product is strikingly similar to the duty of other federal courts to respect our work product.

In the final analysis, a Justice's vote in a case like this depends more on his or her views about the respective lawmaking responsibilities of Congress and this Court than on conflicting policy interests. Judges who have confidence in their own ability to fashion public policy are less hesitant to change the law than those of us who are inclined to give wide latitude to the views of the voters' representatives on nonconstitutional matters. . . . As I pointed out years ago, *Alberto-Culver Co. v. Scherk*, there are valid policy and textual arguments on both sides regarding the interrelation of federal securities and arbitration Acts. . . . None of these arguments, however, carries sufficient weight to tip the balance between judicial and legislative authority and overturn an interpretation of an Act of Congress that has been settled for many years.

I respectfully dissent.

NOTES AND QUESTIONS

1. As with the *McMahon* and other arbitration opinions, the Court's reasoning in *Rodriguez* is calculated to achieve the objectives of policy. For example, the argument that arbitration is "merely a form of trial" with no impact upon substantive rights is hardly convincing. In the U.S. legal system, procedure is a primary ingredient of justice. In both theory and practice, arbitration is a reduced form of adjudication to which parties consent because they want to avoid the complexities of the legal process. Judicial and arbitral proceedings are two very different forms of achieving justice, responding to variegated adjudicatory goals. It is simply nonsense to equate them and disregard the well-settled view that party consent, knowingly and freely given, is at the core of arbitral adjudication's legitimacy.

Justice Kennedy's assessment of statutory rights and of the securities legislation is riddled with the misconceptions that attended the reasoning in

Mitsubishi and *McMahon*. Legal rights created by statute are not the equivalent of commercial contract claims. The latter address contract performance and the pecuniary interests of the contracting parties. Securities regulation responded to a financial catastrophe and was intended to eradicate fraud and overreaching against investors. Its mission was to stabilize the American financial marketplace. Statutory rights, such as those contained in the securities legislation, antitrust statutes, and RICO, implicate the public interest. They deal with the general welfare of society by affording individuals special protections and prohibiting conduct deemed reprehensible by the general mores. These statutes define basic precepts of community order and thereby rise to the level of public policy. As a consequence, they demand implementation and supervision by social institutions invested with public authority and exercising public responsibilities. Why affording this status to statutory rights, a status founded upon self-evident fact, should detract from the autonomy or legitimacy of arbitration is beyond logical comprehension. The threat of using statutory rights claims as a dilatory tactic can be averted by court supervision of the merits of statutory claims upon a motion to stay arbitration. Moreover, if *bona fide* statutory claims exist, they can be severed from the ordinary contract disputes, allowing the latter to proceed to arbitration. After all, "piecemeal" adjudication was permissible and, in fact, required in *Moses H. Cone*.

Justice Kennedy's discussion of the securities legislation is troubling for other reasons. The majority's view that the nonwaiver provision of the 1933 Act applies only to the substantive, and not procedural, rights contained in the Act misreads the legislation. Congress intended to buttress the investor's position by affording special remedies that minimized the investor's litigious burden. Qualifying such rights as merely procedural and waivable through adhesionary agreements begs the question and is an evident attempt to subvert the substantive guarantees proffered by the statute. Facilitating access to courts and minimizing evidentiary burdens are, in the American legal process especially, the most effective way to give content to substantive rights. Moreover, the majority's concurrent reading of the nonwaiver provisions of the 1933 and 1934 Acts is diametrically opposed to its interpretation of the same provisions in *Scherk*. In *Rodriguez*, the nonwaiver provisions are deemed identical, while, in *Scherk*, they are considered to contain completely different legislative commands thereby rendering in *Scherk* the 1934 Act claims (unlike 1933 Act claims) submissible to arbitration. Although legal significance may vary, the express language of statutes does not change over time without legislative amendment. The Court makes no reference to *Scherk* and offers no explanation for its drastic change of position.

The Court anchors its reasoning in the need to expunge judicial hostility to arbitration. The central issue of the American law of arbitration, however, is no longer one of legitimating arbitration, but rather establishing the basic boundaries, function, and identity of the process. As contractual freedom must not impinge upon the public order to remain workable in the legal order, so must arbitration acquire some essential contours and basic limitations. By invoking the danger of judicial hostility, the Court is battling a chimerical risk, an historical ghost that has ceased to influence the reality of the process.

In any event, a fair reading of *Wilko* should not lead to a construction of the opinion as a decision hostile to arbitration.

2.　Several of the Court's opinions in labor arbitration matters differ radically from the *McMahon-Rodriguez* view of the arbitrability of statutory rights. These cases establish a distinction between deferral to arbitration in the area of pure contract rights and interpretation and deferral to arbitration in the adjudication of statutory rights. The Court has refused to allow an arbitrator's award to preclude judicial action for claims based upon statutorily created rights contained in Title VII of the Civil Rights Act, the Fair Labor Standards Act, and Section 1983 of the Civil Rights Act. Here, recourse to arbitration under the provisions of a collective bargaining agreement does not preclude the employee from seeking judicial relief under state or federal law for the same claim. The employee, in effect, gets two bites at the apple. In these decisions, the Court finds arbitration to be an inadequate substitute for the courts in the protection of statutorily created rights, and grounds its reasoning expressly in a protection of rights rationale and in the need to preserve the courts' exclusive jurisdiction in such matters.

These decisions not only conflict with the NLRB's current policy of deferral to arbitration, but are also in marked contrast to the *Mitsubishi-McMahon-Rodriguez* appraisal of the significance of statutory rights in the commercial arbitration context. The issue will be addressed more specifically later, but you should consider the following questions: Why are the rights provided under the various statutes in the labor law context more significant than those contained in the Sherman Act, RICO, or the Securities Acts? How did the Court arrive at its prioritization of the importance of the rights involved? What elements distinguish the labor and commercial context and make the right to adjudicatory relief less important in the latter? The contrast in approach appears devoid of any rational basis.

3.　The dissent in *Rodriguez* grounds its criticism in a separation of powers argument and the need to have the Court respect legislative authority in establishing law. According to Justice Stevens, when the Court's "earlier opinion gives a statutory provision concrete meaning, which Congress elects not to amend during the ensuing 3 1/2 decades, our duty to respect Congress' work product is strikingly similar to the duty of other federal courts to respect our work product."

The dissent's reference to judicial respect for congressional prerogatives is perspicacious because it now appears that the only means of restoring balance and integrity to the American law of arbitration is through the exercise of legislative authority. *Rodriguez* confirms the Court's determination to eliminate any meaningful role for the subject-matter inarbitrability defense in the American law of arbitration. While such a position might be defensible in terms of international commercial arbitration, it is inapposite for any domestic regulation of arbitration because it produces an imbalance between private prerogatives and public duties and attributes to arbitration an adjudicatory task that it is ill-prepared and unsuited to perform. "Dumping" unwanted judicial caseloads into arbitral jurisdiction can only harm the arbitral process in the long run, especially when it requires arbitrators to rule upon socially significant issues that are regulated by statute. In the end, society may not only be riddled with an inefficient judicial process, but it may also have lost a workable alternative mechanism for specialty claims.

In keeping with the analysis of *McMahon*, do you think that the decision in *Rodriguez* should result in Congressional action to amend the provisions of the FAA to exclude *bona fide* claims based on statutory rights from the purview of arbitration and to prevent arbitrators from exercising public jurisdictional authority by prohibiting them, for example, from awarding punitive or treble damages? In addition, should some thought be given to adding a public policy exception to the statutory grounds for vacating awards? Such a provision could stand as a symbol of the dividing line between judicial and arbitral jurisdiction.

2.   CONSUMER ARBITRATION

Preliminary Phase: Terms and Conditions—
Arbitration "In the Box"

In *Hill v. Gateway 2000, Inc.*, 105 F.3d 1147 (7th Cir.), *cert. denied*, 522 U.S. 808 (1997), the Hills purchased a Gateway 2000 computer over the telephone. The box that arrived contained the computer and a list of terms and conditions that would govern the transaction unless the customer returned the computer within thirty days. One of these terms was an arbitration clause. The Hills kept the computer more than thirty days before complaining about its components and performance. They filed suit in federal court arguing, *inter alia*, that the product's shortcomings made Gateway a racketeer under RICO. Gateway asked the district court to enforce the arbitration clause; the judge refused, ruling that "[t]he present record is insufficient to support a finding of a valid arbitration agreement between the parties or that the plaintiffs were given adequate notice of the arbitration clause."

On appeal, the Seventh Circuit disagreed, holding that the arbitration agreement "in the box" was binding on the Hills. Relying primarily on *ProCD, Inc. v. Zeidenberg*, 86 F.3d 1447 (7th Cir. 1996) (holding that terms inside a box of software bind consumers who use the software after an opportunity to read the terms and to reject them by returning the product), the court concluded that, by keeping the computer for more than thirty days, the Hills accepted Gateway's offer—including the arbitration clause—thereby creating an enforceable contract. In so ruling, the Seventh Circuit rejected the Hills' argument that the arbitration clause did not stand out, stating that, under *Doctor's Associates, Inc. v. Casarotto*, 517 U.S. 681 (1996), the Federal Arbitration Act does not require that an arbitration clause be prominent in order to be enforceable.

In *Brower v. Gateway 2000, Inc.*, 246 A.D.2d 246, 676 N.Y.S.2d 569 (N.Y. App. Div. 1998). Tony Brower purchased a computer from Gateway 2000 (Gateway) through its direct-sales system. When it shipped purchased merchandise, Gateway included a copy of its "Standard Terms and Conditions Agreement" in the shipment. The agreement in question began with a "Note to Customer," providing in slightly larger print than the remainder of the document and in a box that spanned the width of the page: "This document contains Gateway 2000's Standard Terms and Conditions. By keeping your Gateway 2000 computer system beyond thirty (30) days after the date of delivery, you accept these Terms and Conditions." The relevant clause, entitled "DISPUTE RESOLUTION," read as follows:

> Any dispute or controversy arising out of or relating to this Agreement or its interpretation shall be settled exclusively and finally by arbitration. The arbitration shall be conducted in accordance with the Rules of Conciliation and Arbitration of the International Chamber of Commerce. The arbitration shall be conducted in Chicago, Illinois, U.S.A. before a sole arbitrator. Any award rendered in any such arbitration proceeding shall be final and binding on each of the parties, and judgment may be entered thereon in a court of competent jurisdiction.

Brower filed a class action lawsuit, alleging deceptive sales practices, including breach of warranty, breach of contract, fraud, and unfair trade practices. The allegations centered upon Gateway's representations and advertising promising "service when you need it," including around-the-clock free technical support, free software technical support, and certain on-site services. According to Brower, not only was he unable to avail himself of these services because it was virtually impossible to get through to a technician, but also Gateway continued to advertise its services notwithstanding numerous complaints and problems. The trial court dismissed the complaint, ruling that the arbitration agreement precluded its assertion of jurisdiction.

On appeal, Brower claimed that he had not bargained for or accepted arbitration and, therefore, the arbitration clause was a "material alteration" of a preexisting oral agreement. Under UCC 2–207(2), such a material alteration constitutes "proposals for addition to the contract" and becomes part of the contract only upon express acceptance. The court, however, concluded that the clause was outside the scope of UCC 2–207. It expressly recognized current business conduct: "Transactions involving 'cash now, terms later' have become commonplace, enabling the consumer to make purchases of sophisticated merchandise such as computers over the phone or by mail—and even by computer. Indeed, the concept of payment preceding the revelation of full terms is particularly common in certain industries, such as air transportation and insurance." In such circumstances, there is no contract until the consumer has retained the merchandise for more than thirty days and has presumably had the opportunity to examine the products and read the agreement. Therefore, because the consumer held the merchandise for the specified thirty days, an agreement had been reached.

Brower also argued that the arbitration clause was unenforceable because it was a contract of adhesion. It involved no choice or negotiation on the part of the consumer and had been presented on a "take-it-or-leave-it" basis. The court ruled, however, that, although the parties "clearly [did] not possess equal bargaining power, [that] factor alone [did] not invalidate the contract as one of adhesion." In fact, the consumer was not placed in a "take-it-or-leave-it" situation because the goods could be returned or purchased elsewhere. The inconvenience and exposure of returning the merchandise was a trade-off for the convenience and economy of shopping on the telephone or through the mail. The failure to read or understand the agreement did not invalidate the contract.

Brower also claimed that the arbitration agreement was unconscionable. It mandated recourse to an adjudicatory process that was unduly burdensome and costly to the individual consumer. Under the ICC's (International Chamber of Commerce) Rules of Conciliation and Arbitration, a claim of less than $50,000 required advance fees of $4,000. The filing fee alone exceeded the cost of the computer. Of the $4,000 advanced fee, $2,000 was a registration fee which was nonrefundable even if the consumer prevailed in the arbitration. Moreover, the travel costs were also disproportionate to the damages sought. Finally, the ICC Rules adopt the "loser pays" concept and would require the consumer to pay Gateway's legal fees if the former did not prevail.

Under New York law, unconscionability requires a showing that a contract is "both procedurally and substantively unconscionable when made," or "some showing of an absence of meaningful choice on the part of one of the parties together with contract terms which are unreasonably favorable to the other party." The court examined the contract formation process to determine if the consumer lacked a meaningful choice in entering into the contract. It took into account "such factors as the setting of the transaction, the experience and education of the party claiming unconscionability, whether the contract contained 'fine print,' whether the seller used 'high-pressured tactics' and any disparity in the parties' bargaining power." It concluded that none of these factors supported a finding of procedural unconscionability. The agreement itself, which was entitled in large print "STANDARD TERMS AND CONDITIONS AGREEMENT," consisted of only three pages, all of which appeared in the same size print. The contract was not "hidden" or "tucked away," nor was the option of returning the merchandise a "precarious" one. And, the word "standard" did not falsely convey to the consumer that the terms were standard within the industry.

The court did, however, determine that the arbitration agreement was substantively unconscionable. The cost of ICC arbitration was unreasonable in the setting of the transaction and would deter a consumer from invoking arbitration, the exclusively available remedy. "Barred from resorting to the courts by the arbitration clause in the first instance, the designation of a financially prohibitive forum effectively bars consumers from this forum as well; consumers are thus left with no forum at all in which to resolve a dispute."

1. How do the two reported cases differ? How are they alike? Which do you think makes more sense? Why? What basic rule of law emerges from them?

2. What is the basic rationale for the determination in *Hill*? Does that determination sustain contract fairness? Does it support the federal policy on arbitration? Why does the court decide the case the way it does?

3. Should there be a special rule for the validity of arbitration agreements in consumer transactions? If so, what would it provide? Would the rule be lawful under *Doctor's Associates, Inc.*?

4. Carefully assess the arbitral clause in *Brower*. Isolate its various features. How many camouflaged acts of unfairness exist? Can the agreement be viewed other than as unconscionable? If so, how? Is the unconscionability exclusively substantive?

5. How does disparity of position operate in both cases? How should it function generally in consumer arbitration?

6. Why does Brower bring a class action lawsuit? What impact does arbitration have upon that litigation strategy?

Intermediate Phase: Independent Administration— The Integrity of the Alternative

ENGALLA v. PERMANENTE MEDICAL GROUP, INC.

15 Cal.4th 951, 938 P.2d 903, 64 Cal.Rptr.2d 843 (1997).

(footnotes omitted)

[**Summary of the Facts.** Mr. Engalla immigrated to the United States in 1980 and had been employed since that time by the Oliver Tire & Rubber Co. as a certified public accountant. At the time of his hiring, Engalla enrolled in the company's health plan. The health benefits were offered through Kaiser Permanente. The Service Agreement for the Plan provided for the resolution of disputes through Kaiser's self-administered arbitration procedures. According to the California Supreme Court, the arbitration procedure was "designed, written, and mandated by Kaiser." Moreover, "[t]he fact that Kaiser . . . administer[ed] its arbitration program from an adversarial perspective [was] not disclosed to Kaiser members or subscribers."

According to the Service Agreement, in the event of a dispute, Kaiser and the subscriber were to designate an arbitrator within thirty days of service of the claim and the two party-designated arbitrators would name a neutral arbitrator within another thirty days. Subscribers agreed to pay a $150 fee for the costs of the arbitration. Kaiser documents described the arbitration program as fair to both parties, allowing employees to resolve disputes quickly and economically. The materials further represented that a hearing would ensue within several months of filing a demand for arbitration. An independent statistical analysis, however, revealed that nearly all Kaiser arbitrations experienced substantial delays; on average, the appointment of a neutral arbitrator alone took some twenty-two months (rather than the two months provided for in the Service Agreement).

In March 1986, Engalla sought treatment from Kaiser for respiratory problems. Tests revealed a possible abnormality in the right lung, but further examination of the condition was not undertaken. Prior radiological studies on Mr. Engalla had been lost, and the radiologist's recommendation for further examinations was ignored. Despite repeated visits by Mr. Engalla for respiratory problems, Kaiser personnel did not perform further diagnostic tests. Mr. Engalla was treated by a variety of Kaiser medical personnel (doctors, nurses, and physicians assistants) during this time; his condition was repeatedly diagnosed as allergies or a cold. In 1991, a radiological test was administered and revealed that Mr. Engalla had inoperable lung cancer.

At the end of May 1991, the Engallas filed a demand for arbitration, alleging negligent diagnosis of Mr. Engalla's condition by Kaiser physicians. Thereafter, Kaiser employees who administered the arbitration procedure engaged in a course of systematic delay. The Engalla's attorney requested expedited processing in light of Mr. Engalla's terminal condition. Kaiser responded to the attorney's repeated entreaties with less than timely and cooperative replies. A variety of procedural matters—the appointment of arbitrators and the scheduling of depositions—were delayed. Kaiser's obfuscation was especially evident in the appointment of a neutral arbitrator. Until the parties agreed upon a neutral, discovery could not be conducted and a hearing date could not be set. Kaiser acknowledged the appointment of a neutral arbitrator in late October 1991 nearly five months after the demand for arbitration and some three months beyond the sixty-day period provided for in the Service Agreement. Mr. Engalla died the next day. The Engallas then filed a lawsuit against Kaiser, claiming *inter alia* fraud as a defense to the enforcement of the arbitration agreement. Kaiser responded with a petition to compel arbitration.]

Mosk, Justice

[. . .]

After a hearing the trial court issued its order denying Kaiser's petition after making specific findings of fact on the issue of fraud both "in the inducement" and "in the application" of the arbitration agreement. The court further found that the arbitration agreement, as applied, was overbroad, unconscionable and a violation of public policy, inasmuch as Kaiser was arguing that the agreement could not be avoided on grounds of fraudulent inducement. The court further found that equitable considerations peculiar to this case required the invalidation of the arbitration provision.

The Court of Appeal reversed. It rejected the claim that Kaiser had defrauded the Engallas, finding *inter alia* that Kaiser's contractual representation of a 60–day time limit for the selection of arbitrators was not "a representation of fact or a promise by Kaiser because appointment of the neutral arbitrator requires the cooperation of and mutual agreement of the parties." ...The court further concluded there was no evidence of actual reliance on these representations nor evidence that the Engallas would have been any better off had their claims been submitted for judicial resolution rather than arbitration. The court also found that the availability of section 1281.6, which permits one of the parties to petition the court to appoint an arbitrator when the parties fail to agree on one, undermined the Engallas' claim that Kaiser's alleged deliberate delay in selecting arbitrators was a ground for avoiding the arbitration agreement. The court further rejected the claim that Kaiser's special relationship as Engalla's insurer or as a fiduciary in the administration of his health plan created any special duty to disclose the workings of its arbitration program. Finally, the court held the Engallas' waiver and unconscionability claims to be without merit. We granted review.

II. PROCEDURAL ISSUES

Before proceeding to the merits, we must address certain procedural and threshold matters. As both parties concede, California law is expressly incorporated into the arbitration agreement in question, and governs the adjudication of any disputes arising from that agreement.... California law incorporates many of the basic policy objectives contained in the Federal Arbitration Act, including a presumption in favor of arbitrability...and a requirement that an arbitration agreement must be enforced on the basis of state law standards that apply to contracts in general.... These policies guide our determination of the present matter.

The nature of the proceeding to resolve a petition to compel arbitration under California law was recently explained by this court in *Rosenthal v. Great Western Financial Securities Corporation*.... As we explain in that case, sections 1281.2 and 1290.2 create a summary proceeding for resolving these petitions.... The petitioner bears the burden of proving the existence of a valid arbitration agreement by the preponderance of the evidence, and a party opposing the petition bears the burden of proving by a preponderance of the evidence any fact necessary to its defense.... In these summary proceedings, the trial court sits as a trier of fact.... No jury trial is available for a petition to compel arbitration.

[. . .]

III. FRAUD IN THE INDUCEMENT OF THE ARBITRATION AGREEMENT

The Engallas claim fraud in the inducement of the arbitration agreement and therefore that "[g]rounds exist for the revocation of the agreement" within the meaning of section 1281.2, subdivision (b).... We construe section 1281.2, subdivision (b), to mean that the petition to compel arbitration is not to be granted when there are grounds for rescinding the agreement. Fraud is one of the grounds on which a contract can be rescinded. (Civ. Code, § 1689, subd. (b)(l).) In order to defeat a petition to compel arbitration, the parties opposing a petition to compel must show that the asserted fraud claim goes specifically "to the 'making' of the agreement to arbitrate," rather than to the making of the contract in general. . . . In the present case, the Engallas do allege, and seek to show, fraud in the making of the arbitration agreement.

[. . .]

Here the Engallas claim (1) that Kaiser misrepresented its arbitration agreement in that it entered into the agreement knowing that, at the very least, there was a likelihood its agents would breach the part of the agreement providing for the timely appointment of arbitrators and the expeditious progress towards an arbitration hearing; (2) that Kaiser employed the above misrepresentation in order to induce reliance on the part of Engalla and his employer; (3) that Engalla relied on these misrepresentations to his detriment. The trial court found evidence supporting those claims. We examine each of these claims in turn.

First, evidence of misrepresentation is plain. "[F]alse representations made recklessly and without regard for their truth in order to induce action by another are the equivalent of misrepresentations knowingly and intentionally uttered." . . . As recounted above, section 8.B. of the arbitration agreement provides that party arbitrators "shall" be chosen within 30 days and neutral arbitrators within 60 days, and that the arbitration hearing "shall" be held "within a reasonable time thereafter." Although Kaiser correctly argues that these contractual representations did not bind it to appoint a neutral arbitrator within 60 days, since the appointment of that arbitrator is a bilateral decision that depends on agreements of the parties, Kaiser's contractual representations were at the very least commitments to exercise good faith and reasonable diligence to have the arbitrators appointed within the specified time. This good faith duty is underscored by Kaiser's contractual assumption of the duty to administer the health service plan as a fiduciary.

Here there are facts to support the Engallas' allegation that Kaiser entered into the arbitration agreement with knowledge that it would not comply with its own contractual timelines, or with at least a reckless indifference as to whether its agents would use reasonable diligence and good faith to comply with them. . . . [A] survey of Kaiser arbitrations between 1984 and 1986 submitted into evidence showed that a neutral arbitrator was appointed within 60 days in only 1 percent of the cases, with only 3 percent appointed within 180 days, and that on average the neutral arbitrator was appointed 674 days almost 2 years after the demand for arbitration. . . . [T]he depositions of two of Kaiser's in-house attorneys demonstrate that Kaiser was aware soon after it began its arbitration program that its contractual deadlines were not being met, and that severe delay was endemic to the program. Kaiser nonetheless persisted in its contractual promises of expeditiousness.

Kaiser now argues that most of these delays were caused by the claimants themselves and their attorneys, who procrastinated in the selection of a neutral arbitrator. But Kaiser's counterexplanation is without any statistical support, and is based solely on anecdotal evidence related by Kaiser officials. Moreover, the explanation appears implausible in view of the sheer pervasiveness of the delays.... It is, after all, the defense which often benefits from delay, thereby preserving the status quo to its advantage until the time when memories fade and claims are abandoned. Indeed, the present case illustrates why Kaiser's counsel may sometimes find it advantageous to delay the selection of a neutral arbitrator. There is also evidence that Kaiser kept extensive records on the arbitrators it had used, and may have delayed the selection process in order to ensure that it would obtain the arbitrators it thought would best serve its interests. Thus, it is a reasonable inference from the documentary record before us that Kaiser's contractual representations of expeditiousness were made with knowledge of their likely falsity, and in fact concealed an unofficial policy or practice of delay.

The systemwide nature of Kaiser's delay comes into clearer focus when it is contrasted with other arbitration systems. As the Engallas point out, many large institutional users of arbitration, including most health maintenance organizations (HMOs), avoid the potential problems of delay in the selection of arbitrators by contracting with neutral third party organizations, such as the American Arbitration Association (AAA). These organizations will then assume responsibility for administering the claim from the time the arbitration demand is filed, and will ensure the arbitrator or arbitrators are chosen in a timely manner. Though Kaiser is not obliged by law to adopt any particular form of arbitration, the record shows that it did not attempt to create within its own organization any office that would neutrally administer the arbitration program, but instead entrusted such administration to outside counsel retained to act as advocates on its behalf. In other words, there is evidence that Kaiser established a self-administered arbitration system in which delay for its own benefit and convenience was an inherent part, despite express and implied contractual representations to the contrary.

A fraudulent state of mind includes not only knowledge of falsity of the misrepresentation but also an " 'intent to...induce reliance' " on it. It can be reasonably inferred in the present case that these misrepresentations of expeditiousness, which are found not only in the contract but in newsletters periodically sent to subscribers touting the virtues of the Kaiser arbitration program, were made by Kaiser to encourage these subscribers to believe that its program would function efficiently....

Kaiser also claims that the Engallas failed to demonstrate actual reliance on its misrepresentations.

[...]

In the present case, our assessment of the materiality of representations is somewhat complicated by the fact that the primary decision maker responsible for selecting the Kaiser health plan was not Engalla himself but his employer, Oliver Tire. The evidence shows that Engalla had little if any cognizance of the arbitration agreement, and that the form he signed to enroll in Kaiser merely stated that members' claims must be submitted to arbitration "[i]f the [health services plan] agreement so provides." On the other hand, Oliver Tire and its personnel employees were obviously aware of the arbitration provision and were responsible for scrutinizing the details of the health services plan before offering it to the company's employees. But this complication does not alter fundamentally our analysis of materiality. As we have recognized, an employer that negotiates group medical benefits for its employees acts as an agent for those employees during the period of negotiation.... An agency relationship is a fiduciary one, obliging the agent to act in the interest of the principal.... Accordingly, a material representation in this case is one that would have substantially influenced the health plan selection process of Oliver Tire, acting as an agent of its employees as a class.

Applying these principles to the present ease, we conclude that Kaiser's representations of expeditiousness in the arbitration agreement were not "so obviously unimportant" as to render them immaterial as a matter of law. We have recognized that expeditiousness is commonly regarded as one of the primary advantages of arbitration.... We have accordingly rejected, as a general proposition, the claim that arbitration agreements between an HMO and its participants are inherently one-sided in favor of the former. "The speed and economy of arbitration, in contrast to the expense and delay of a jury trial, could prove helpful to all parties...." ...The explicit and implicit representations contained in Kaiser's arbitration agreement serve to confirm to the reasonable potential subscriber that Kaiser has an efficient system of arbitration, in which what is lost in terms of jury trial rights would be gained in part by a swifter resolution of the dispute. If it is indeed the case that these representations were false, and concealed an arbitration process in which substantial delay was the rule and timeliness the rare exception, then we cannot say these misrepresentations were so trivial that they would not have influenced a reasonable employer's decision as to which among the many competing employee health plans it would choose for its employees.

Kaiser argues to the contrary that the existence of section 1281.6 negates any possible materiality that its misrepresentation of expeditiousness may have had. That section states in pertinent part that in the absence of an agreed method of appointing an arbitrator, "or if the agreed method fails or for any reason cannot be followed...the court, on petition of a party to the arbitration agreement, shall appoint the arbitrator." ...But the mere fact that there is a statutory remedy to expedite the arbitrator selection process does not necessarily render the reality of Kaiser's systematic delay irrelevant to the selection of a health plan. A party's success in having a section 1281.6 petition granted is not necessarily assured, nor is it costless, nor is it in accord with normal expectations of arbitration participants, who view arbitration as an alternative to the courts. " 'Typically, those who enter into arbitration agreements expect that their dispute will be resolved without necessity for any contact with the courts.' " . . . Given the reality that there exists a considerable number of roughly comparable group health plans . . . , a reasonable employer choosing a health plan for its employees may very well decline to select a plan with a dysfunctional arbitration system requiring court supervision.

Nor is there any evidence to conclusively rebut the inference of Oliver Tire's reliance on Kaiser's representations of expedition. Kaiser claims to the contrary that the company paid scant attention to the arbitration clause, focusing in particular on the statement of Theodomeir Roy, a personnel officer with Oliver Tire who advised the company in its selection of employee health plans, that he "would not be concerned if [the plan] didn't [have an arbitration clause]. And in fact if it did, as it has here, [we] sort of look with favor on it, thinking that it was an expeditious way to resolve disputes." Yet although Roy may have been indifferent to whether arbitration or some other effective dispute resolution mechanism was available, the evidence suggests he would have looked unfavorably on a system such as Kaiser is alleged to have actually had, which delayed the resolution of claims, required constant action by the claimant, and failed to adhere to its own contractual terms. There is therefore sufficient evidence to support the claim that Oliver Tire actually relied on Kaiser's misrepresentations.

We turn then to the question of injury. A defrauded party has the right to rescind a contract, even without a showing of pecuniary damages, on establishing that fraudulent contractual promises inducing reliance have been breached. . . . The rule derives from the basic principle that a contracting party has a right to what it contracted for, and so has the right "to rescind where he obtain[ed] something substantially different from that which he [is] led to expect." . . . It follows that a defrauded party does not have to show pecuniary damages in order to defeat a petition to compel arbitration. Of course, the Engallas cannot defeat a petition to compel arbitration on the mere showing that Kaiser has engaged generally in fraudulent misrepresentation about the speed of the arbitration process. Rather, they must show that in their particular case, there was substantial delay in the selection of arbitrators contrary to their reasonable, fraudulently induced, contractual expectations. Here, there is ample evidence to support the Engallas' contention that Kaiser breached its arbitration agreement by repeatedly delaying the timely appointment of an available party arbitrator and a neutral arbitrator.

To be sure, the mere fact that the selection of arbitrators extended beyond their 30– and 60–day deadlines does not by itself establish that Kaiser breached its arbitration agreement. It is, after all, the malpractice claimant in arbitration, like the plaintiff in litigation, who bears the primary responsibility of exercising diligence in order to advance progress towards the resolution of its claim . . . , and Kaiser is under no obligation to press for appointment of arbitrators when a claimant is himself dilatory. Nor is the contract breached when delay in the selection of arbitrators is the result of reasonable disagreements over arbitrator selection. Nonetheless, as explained above, Kaiser, by agreeing to 30– and 60–day periods for the appointment of arbitrators, committed itself to cooperate with reasonable diligence and good faith in the process of appointing the arbitrators within the specified times... Here, there is strong evidence that, despite a high degree of diligence on the part of Engalla's counsel in attempting to obtain the timely appointment of arbitrators, Kaiser lacked either reasonable diligence, good faith, or both, in cooperating on these timely appointments. Instead, the evidence shows that it engaged in a course of nonresponse and delay and added extracontractual conditions to the arbitration selection process, such as the requirement that the claimant name a party arbitrator first. Thus, strong evidence supports the conclusion that Kaiser did not fulfill its contractual obligations in this case to appoint arbitrators in a timely manner.

Nor does the presence of section 1281.6 excuse Kaiser's alleged misfeasance, as Kaiser contends. That section, as explained above, provides a statutory method for resolving breakdowns in the arbitrator selection process, and states in pertinent part that in the absence of an agreed method of appointing an arbitrator, "or if the agreed method fails or for any reason cannot be followed...the court, on petition of a party to the arbitration agreement, shall appoint the arbitrator." Kaiser contends that section 1281.6 is implicitly incorporated into the contract, which specifies that California law be followed. Yet the availability of section 1281.6 does not absolve Kaiser of its explicit and implicit contractual duties to timely select a neutral arbitrator and to not obstruct progress towards arbitration. All section 1281.6 provides is a remedy for the breach of those duties of which parties may avail themselves. As noted, this remedy compels claimants to go into superior court and seek specific performance of the arbitration agreement, forcing them to engage in at least some litigation in order to vindicate their rights and thereby violating the usual expectations of an arbitration agreement.... Nothing in the language of section 1281.6 compels a party to seek this remedy, nor does this language suggest that resort to section 1281.6 is a precondition to opposing successfully a petition to compel arbitration when the petitioning party has engaged in fraud. Rather, section 1281.6 appears to be simply a legislative means of implementing this state's policy in favor of arbitration by permitting parties to an arbitration contract to expedite the arbitrator selection process.

Of course, when a delay in the selection of arbitrators is the result of a reasonable and good faith disagreement between parties, or of some other reasonable cause, the remedy for such delay may indeed be a section 1281.6 petition rather than the abandonment of the arbitration agreement. But a party that imposes and administers its own arbitration program, that fraudulently misrepresents the speed of the arbitrator selection process so as to induce reliance, and that in fact engages in conduct forcing substantial delay, may not then compel arbitration by contending that the other party failed to resort to the court by filing a section 1281.6 petition.

In sum, we conclude there is evidence to support the Engallas' claims that Kaiser fraudulently induced Engalla to enter the arbitration agreement in that it misrepresented the speed of its arbitration program, a misrepresentation on which Engalla's employer relied by selecting Kaiser's health plan for its employees, and that the Engallas suffered delay in the resolution of its malpractice dispute as a result of that reliance, despite Engalla's own reasonable diligence. The trial court, on remand, must resolve conflicting factual evidence in order to properly adjudicate Kaiser's petition to compel arbitration.

IV.   WAIVER

The Engallas also claim the petition to compel arbitration should be denied on grounds of waiver. For reasons discussed below, we conclude that their waiver claims may have merit, but that the question of waiver must be determined by the trial court on remand.

Section 1281.2, subdivision (a), provides that a trial court shall refuse to compel arbitration if it determines that "[t]he right to compel arbitration has been waived by the petitioner." The Engallas argue that Kaiser's various dilatory actions constituted a waiver of its right to compel arbitration.

[. . .]

. . . [T]he question of waiver is one of fact, and an appellate court's function is to review a trial court's findings regarding waiver to determine whether these are supported by substantial evidence. The trial court in this case made no findings regarding the Engallas' waiver claim, focusing instead on their fraud claim, which has therefore been our primary focus as well. Given the summary-judgment-like posture of the present case, our sole task is to review the record to determine whether there are facts to support the Engallas' waiver claim. We conclude that the evidence of Kaiser's course of delay, reviewed extensively above, which was arguably unreasonable or undertaken in bad faith, may provide sufficient grounds for a trier of fact to conclude that Kaiser has in fact waived its arbitration agreement.

We emphasize, as we explained in our discussion of fraud, that the delay must be substantial, unreasonable, and in spite of the claimant's own reasonable diligence. When delay in choosing arbitrators is the result of reasonable and good faith disagreements between the parties, the remedy for such delay is a petition to the court to choose arbitrators under section 1281.6, rather than evasion of the contractual agreement to arbitrate. The burden is on the one opposing the arbitration agreement to prove to the trial court that the other party's dilatory conduct rises to such a level of misfeasance as to constitute a waiver . . . , and such waiver "is not to be lightly inferred" . . . . In this case, there is ample evidence that the claimant was diligent in seeking Kaiser's cooperation, and instead suffered from Kaiser's delay, a delay which was unreasonable or in bad faith. We leave it to the trial court to determine on remand whether waiver of the right to compel arbitration has in fact occurred.

V. UNCONSCIONABILITY

...[A]lthough the present contract has some of the attributes of adhesion, it did not, on its face, lack " 'minimum levels of integrity.' " ...The unfairness that is the substance of the Engallas' unconscionability argument comes essentially to this: The Engallas contend that Kaiser has established a system of arbitration inherently unfair to claimants, because the method of selecting neutral arbitrators is biased. They claim that Kaiser has an unfair advantage as a "repeat player" in arbitration, possessing information on arbitrators that the Engallas themselves lacked. They also argue that Kaiser, under its arbitration system, has sought to maximize this advantage by reserving for itself an unlimited right to veto arbitrators proposed by the other party. This method is in contrast to arbitration programs run by neutral, third party arbitration organizations such as the AAA, which give parties a very limited ability to veto arbitrators from its preselected panels.

Yet none of these features of Kaiser's arbitration program renders the arbitration agreement per se unconscionable. As noted above, section 1281.6 specifically contemplates a system whereby neutral arbitrators will be chosen directly by the parties. The alleged problem with Kaiser's arbitration in this case was not any defect or one-sidedness in its contractual provisions, but rather in the gap between its contractual representations and the actual workings of its arbitration program. It is the doctrines of fraud and waiver, rather than of unconscionability, that most appropriately address this discrepancy between the contractual representation and the reality. Thus, viewing the arbitration agreement on its face, we cannot say it is unconscionable.

VI. CONCLUSION AND DISPOSITION

For the foregoing reasons, the judgment of the Court of Appeal is reversed with directions to remand the case for proceedings consistent with this opinion.

GEORGE, C.J., and BAXTER, WERDEGAR and CHIN, JJ., concur.

KENNARD, Justice, concurring.

I concur in the majority opinion. I write separately to note that this case illustrates yet again the essential role of the courts in ensuring that the arbitration system delivers not only speed and economy but also fundamental fairness.

Unfairness in arbitration sufficiently extreme to justify court intervention can take many forms. As I have previously stated, in my view courts have the power to overturn an arbitrator's decision if it contains manifest error that causes substantial injustice.... It is also my view that arbitrators are limited to the same remedies that a court could award under the circumstances of the case, and that a court may overturn an arbitrator's award of relief that exceeds that limit. . . .

This case illustrates the role that courts play in maintaining the procedural fairness, as well as the substantive fairness, of arbitration proceedings. Procedural manipulations can be used by a party not only to delay and obstruct the proceedings, thereby denying the other party the speed and efficiency that are the arbitration system's primary justification, but also to affect the possible outcome of the arbitration. As to speed and efficiency, the Kaiser arbitration provision provides for appointment of a neutral arbitrator within a 60–day period. . . . In reality, a neutral arbitrator was appointed within 60 days in less than 1 percent of Kaiser's arbitrations; the appointment occurred within 180 days (3 times the contractual time period) in less than 3 percent of Kaiser's arbitrations. Indeed, the average time for appointment of a neutral arbitrator was 674 days, more than 11 times the contractual time period. The average time for a Kaiser-administered arbitration hearing to begin (not conclude) was 863 days or almost 30 months. . . . Although the comparison is not exact, it is instructive to compare the "speed" of Kaiser's arbitration process to the speed of judicial proceedings in Alameda County Superior Court, where this action was filed. During the 1993–1994 fiscal year that court disposed of 96 percent of its civil cases in less than 24 months.

By delaying arbitration in this case until after Wilfredo Engalla died, Kaiser also affected the potential outcome of his malpractice claims. Engalla's death reduced Kaiser's potential liability for noneconomic damages to $250,000 from the $500,000 potential liability it would have faced had the claims been arbitrated during Engalla's life. . . .

As the majority opinion makes clear, courts must be alert to procedural manipulations of arbitration proceedings and should grant appropriate relief when such manipulations occur. As here, such conduct may give rise to claims of fraud in the inducement of the arbitration agreement or claims that the manipulating party has waived its right to enforce the arbitration agreement. Moreover, if such conduct affects the arbitration award, it may form the basis for vacating the award as one "procured by corruption, fraud or other undue means". . . .

Finally, it is worth noting that new possibilities for unfairness arise as arbitration ventures beyond the world of merchant-to-merchant disputes in which it was conceived into the world of consumer transactions (like the health care agreement in this case) and nonunion employment relationships. In such cases, the assumption that the parties have freely chosen arbitration as a dispute resolution mechanism in a process of arm's-length negotiation may be little more than an illusion. Unlike the traditional model of arbitration agreements negotiated between large commercial firms with equal bargaining power, consumer and employment arbitration agreements are typically "take it or leave it" propositions, contracts of adhesion in which the only choice for the consumer or the employee is to accept arbitration or forgo the transaction. And the fact that the business organization imposing the arbitration clause is a repeat player in the arbitration system, while the consumer or employee is not, raises the potential that arbitrators will consciously or unconsciously bias their decisions in favor of an organization or industry that hires them regularly as an arbitrator.

Here, neither plaintiffs' decedent nor his employer was afforded an opportunity to accept or reject arbitration as the means of resolving disputes. Rather, Kaiser's standard health care agreement, which included the arbitration requirement, was presented on a "take it or leave it" basis.... There was no true bargaining involved here. Moreover, although Kaiser appears to have led its members to believe that Kaiser administered its arbitration system fairly and as a "fiduciary", in reality the opposite may have been true. Kaiser "administered" its arbitration system through its defense attorneys who appear to have manipulated the process to Kaiser's advantage.

Private arbitration may resolve disputes faster and cheaper than judicial proceedings. Private arbitration, however, may also become an instrument of injustice imposed on a "take it or leave it" basis. The courts must distinguish the former from the latter, to ensure that private arbitration systems resolve disputes not only with speed and economy but also with fairness.

BROWN, Justice, dissenting.

The intended target of the majority's wrath, the Permanente Medical Group, Inc., Kaiser Foundation Hospitals, and the Kaiser Foundation Health Plan (hereafter Kaiser) could not be more deserving. I write separately to represent the interests of the unintended victim of the majority's holding, private arbitration in California.

INTRODUCTION

Pursuant to the terms of a prior written agreement, the parties in this case submitted a medical malpractice dispute to private, or nonjudicial, arbitration. California law, like corresponding federal law under the United States Arbitration Act..., has long reflected a strong policy in favor of such arbitration.

As this court recently explained, "Title 9 of the Code of Civil Procedure,...as enacted and periodically amended by the Legislature, represents a comprehensive statutory scheme regulating private arbitration in this state.... Through this detailed statutory scheme, the Legislature has expressed a 'strong public policy in favor of arbitration as a speedy and relatively inexpensive means of dispute resolution.' ...Consequently, courts will 'indulge every intendment to give effect to such proceedings.' " ...Indeed, more than 70 years ago this court explained: "The policy of the law in recognizing arbitration agreements and in providing by statute for their enforcement is to encourage persons who wish to avoid delays incident to a civil action to obtain an adjustment of their differences by a tribunal of their own choosing.... 'Typically, those who enter into arbitration agreements expect that their dispute will be resolved without necessity for any contact with the courts.' ''. . .

Although the majority purports to "affirm the basic policy in favor of enforcement of arbitration agreements''. . ., it nonetheless concludes that "the governing statutes place limits on the extent to which a party that has committed misfeasance in the performance of such an agreement may compel its enforcement." . . . I cannot agree with the majority's interpretation of the governing statutory framework. In my view, except for seeking statutorily prescribed court assistance in the arbitrator selection process. . ., once a private arbitration is pending, a party must seek relief for its adversary's "misfeasance in the performance" in the arbitral forum, not in the courts. Make no mistake about it. The majority's decision to validate a party's unilateral withdrawal from a pending arbitration based on the conduct of its arbitration adversary will wreak havoc on arbitrations throughout the state. Therefore, I respectfully dissent.

FACTUAL AND PROCEDURAL BACKGROUND

Almost lost in the majority's exhaustive procedural summary is one key fact—namely, the arbitration process was already underway by the time the plaintiffs unilaterally withdrew. A brief review of the history of the arbitration is in order.

On May 31, 1991, pursuant to the terms of a "Group Medical and Hospital Services Agreement," Wilfredo Engalla, his wife, and their four children (hereafter the Engallas) demanded that Kaiser submit a medical malpractice dispute to binding private arbitration. On June 17, Kaiser submitted to the Engallas' arbitration demand. Two days later, the Engallas' counsel sent Kaiser the $150 check "required in order to initiate the arbitration proceeding."

The Engallas designated their party arbitrator on July 8, Kaiser designated its party arbitrator on July 17, and the parties confirmed their agreement on a neutral arbitrator on October 2. While the parties were in the process of designating arbitrators, they exchanged a number of discovery requests.

Thereafter, on October 28, the Engallas refused to continue with the pending arbitration. The reason the Engallas withdrew from the arbitration was that Kaiser declined to stipulate that Mrs. Engalla's separate loss of consortium claim survived her husband's death. It is this unilateral withdrawal from a pending arbitration that the majority's decision validates.

DISCUSSION

In evaluating both the Engallas' fraudulent inducement claim and their waiver claim, the majority focuses on Kaiser's performance during the course of the aborted private arbitration. According to the majority, the sine qua non of successful fraudulent inducement and waiver claims is unreasonable or bad faith delay by Kaiser. . . . Thus, the majority permits the fraudulent inducement claim to proceed because "there is strong evidence that, despite a high degree of diligence on the part of [the Engallas'] counsel in attempting to obtain the timely appointment of arbitrators, Kaiser lacked either reasonable diligence, good faith, or both, in cooperating on these timely appointments." . . . Likewise, the majority permits the waiver claim to proceed because "there is ample evidence that the [Engallas were] diligent in seeking Kaiser's cooperation, and instead suffered from Kaiser's delay, a delay which was unreasonable or in bad faith." . . .

Although the majority's desire to penalize Kaiser's obduracy is understandable, the consequences of validating a party's unilateral withdrawal from a pending arbitration based on the conduct of its arbitration adversary will reverberate far beyond the bad facts of the instant case. In stark contrast to the legislative response, which enhances the procedures for keeping a case in private arbitration . . ., the majority expands the procedures for removing a case from arbitration. The majority maintains that section 1281.2 compels its decision. . . . I cannot agree. That statute delineates certain narrow circumstances in which a trial court may uphold a party's "refus[al] to arbitrate." (§ 1281.2.) Nothing in section 1281.2 permits a party that has previously submitted a dispute to arbitration, and thereby agreed to arbitrate, to withdraw from that arbitration at some later date based on the unreasonable or bad faith delay of its adversary.

To construe section 1281.2 in the sweeping fashion advanced by the majority will seriously compromise the integrity of the arbitral process and will impose an unpredictable and unnecessary burden on our trial courts. It is well established that "contractual arbitration has a life of its own outside the judicial system." . . . "It is the job of the arbitrator, not the court, to resolve all questions needed to determine the controversy. . . . The arbitrator, and not the court, decides questions of procedure and discovery. . . . It is also up to the arbitrator, and not the court, to grant relief for delay in bringing an arbitration to a resolution." . . .

"This does not mean that a party to an arbitration proceeding has no remedy against dilatory tactics." . . . Rather, a party who has suffered as a result of such tactics may seek appropriate relief in the arbitral forum. . . .

Nor does the fact that the arbitrator selection process in a given private arbitration has not yet been completed preclude a party from obtaining appropriate relief. To the contrary, section 1281.6 provides a mechanism by which a party can seek limited assistance from the trial court in obtaining the appointment of an arbitrator or arbitrators. . . . "[O]nce there is an arbitrator appointed pursuant to section 1281.6, the party seeking to expedite the arbitration proceedings can apply to the arbitrator for [appropriate relief]." . . .

I do not share the majority's view that requiring a party to a private arbitration to file a section 1281.6 petition would "violat[e] the usual expectations of an arbitration agreement." . . . The majority's reliance on the statement in *Moncharsh* . . . that " '[t]ypically, those who enter into arbitration agreements expect that their dispute will be resolved without necessity for any contact with the courts' " ....is misplaced. *Moncharsh* did not hold that a party to a private arbitration would never have to have any contact with the courts but rather that "judicial intervention in the arbitration process [should] be minimized...." ...Indeed, the very paragraph of *Moncharsh* quoted by the majority emphasizes that title 9 of part 3 of the Code of Civil Procedure which includes section 1281.6—"represents a comprehensive statutory scheme regulating private arbitration in this state...."...

Section 1281.6 is the statutory remedy that our Legislature has provided for resolving disputes in the arbitrator selection process, thereby preventing such disputes from becoming occasions for avoiding private arbitration agreements. The statute's evident purpose is to facilitate, not to hinder, private arbitration. Requiring a party to employ a legislatively prescribed remedy simply cannot be deemed contrary to the "normal expectations of arbitration participants." ...In fact, the arbitration provision at issue in the present case specifically alerts the signatories that "[w]ith respect to any matter not herein expressly provided for, the arbitration shall be governed by California Code of Civil Procedure provisions relating to arbitration."

The inclusiveness of the language of section 1281.6 belies the notion that it contains some sort of ill-defined exception for unreasonable or bad faith delay.... By its own terms, the statute comes into play whenever "the agreed method [of appointing an arbitrator] fails or for any reason cannot be followed." ...If there were any doubt that the statutory remedy was intended to apply broadly, the Legislature has now put it to rest. Largely in response to this very case, the Legislature recently enacted Health and Safety Code section 1373.20, subdivision (a) (2), providing that for nonindependent arbitration systems such as Kaiser's "[i]n cases or disputes in which the parties have agreed to use a tripartite arbitration panel consisting of two party arbitrators and one neutral arbitrator, and the party arbitrators are unable to agree on the designation of a neutral arbitrator within 30 days after service of a written demand requesting the designation, it shall be conclusively presumed that the agreed method of selection has failed and the method provided in Section 1281.6 of the Code of Civil Procedure may be utilized." The new legislation also provides for attorney fees and costs against a party that "has engaged in dilatory conduct intended to cause delay in proceeding under the arbitration agreement."...

In this case, having previously submitted their dispute to private arbitration and having already completed the arbitrator selection process, the Engallas should have sought relief for Kaiser's dilatory conduct in the pending arbitration. For example, the Engallas could have presented their fraud and waiver claims directly to the arbitrators and requested that they not enforce the arbitration provision.... Likewise, the Engallas could have requested that the arbitrators sanction Kaiser's dilatory conduct by deeming Mrs. Engalla's separate loss of consortium claim to have survived her husband's death.... In fact, at oral argument, the Engallas' counsel conceded that this case could likely have remained in private arbitration if Mrs. Engalla's economic loss had been ameliorated.

The one thing the Engallas should not be permitted to do, however, is to circumvent the arbitrators altogether. The consequences of validating a party's unilateral withdrawal from a pending arbitration will be dramatic. Jurisdictional disputes will inevitably arise. Suppose, for example, that following the Engallas' unilateral withdrawal, Kaiser had elected to continue to pursue the pending arbitration and that the arbitrators had ultimately entered a default judgment in favor of Kaiser. Would that default judgment have been valid? Would the same have been true if the trial court had simultaneously entered a default judgment in favor of the Engallas in the pending litigation?

In addition, as the Engallas' counsel acknowledged at oral argument, if this court validates the Engallas' unilateral withdrawal, other parties to pending arbitrations will doubtlessly engage in the same conduct. Counsel's answer to this dilemma was that this court should "trust the trial courts." The majority's answer is to "emphasize...that the delay must be substantial, unreasonable, and in spite of the claimant's own reasonable diligence" and not "the result of reasonable and good faith disagreements between the parties."...

Neither answer is satisfactory. Under the majority's holding, which has all the precision of a "SCUD" missile, the resolution of fraudulent inducement and waiver claims will necessarily entail fact-intensive, case-by-case determinations.... The disruptive, time-consuming nature of these determinations is well illustrated by the facts of the present case, in which "[t]he Engallas ultimately had five months to complete discovery [on the petition to compel arbitration], during which time thirteen motions were filed and more than a dozen depositions were taken." ...Even assuring that the trial courts ultimately resolve all future claims correctly, the interim disruption to pending arbitrations will be simply intolerable.

CONCLUSION

"Great cases like hard cases make bad law. For great cases are called great, not by reason of their real importance in shaping the law of the future, but because of some accident of immediate overwhelming interest which appeals to the feelings and distorts the judgment. These immediate interests exercise a kind of hydraulic pressure which makes what previously was clear seem doubtful, and before which even well settled principles of law will bend." [Justice Holmes in *Northern Securities,* 193 U.S. 197, 400–01 (1904).].... Although legislators, practitioners, and courts have all expressed concern that disparities in bargaining power may affect the procedural fairness of consumer arbitration agreements, this case amply demonstrates why any solutions should come from the Legislature, whose ability to craft precise exceptions is far superior to that of this court.

However well-intentioned the majority and however deserving its intended target, today's holding pokes a hole in the barrier separating private arbitrations and the courts. Unfortunately, like any such breach, this hole will eventually cause the dam to burst. Ironically, the tool the majority uses to puncture its hole is the observation that " 'those who enter into arbitration agreements expect that their dispute will be resolved without necessity for any contact with the courts.' " ...Because I suspect that parties to private arbitrations will be having quite a bit more contact with the courts than they ever bargained for, I dissent.

NOTES AND QUESTIONS

1. *Engalla* is a very significant case—perhaps an opinion of fundamental significance in elaborating a regulatory policy on consumer arbitration in the HMO and other service areas. Its reasoning and rationale also have implications for the regulation of employment arbitration. The significance of the opinion is heightened by the fact that California is one of the most active and sophisticated ADR jurisdictions in the country, and that California courts have a longstanding acquaintance with and an elaborate decisional law on arbitration and ADR.

The majority opinion holds that an arbitration agreement can be defeated, albeit in exceptional circumstances, by allegations of fraud. The concurring opinion adds that the expansion of arbitration into consumer affairs warrants greater judicial supervision of this use of arbitration. Finally, the dissent opines that the problem in *Engalla* should have been resolved by the arbitrators or a court action assisting the arbitral process. The judicial intrusion recommended by the majority undermines the autonomy of arbitration and will wreck havoc in the arbitration system in California. Allowing parties to unilaterally withdraw from arbitration is antithetical to the process. Which analytical version of reality do you find most persuasive? Explain your reasoning specifically. How would you have ruled? Could all sides of the court be right? If so, what solution exists for the problems raised in the *Engalla* setting?

2. How does the majority opinion address and avoid the possible federalism problem that might be embedded in its determination? Do you find the court's approach convincing? Does it align its reasoning to the prior decisional law rulings?

3. Why is the determination of the validity or existence of an arbitration agreement submitted to the court and not a jury in California? What justification, if any, can you find in the FAA for that procedure? Is California law in breach of an FAA mandate?

4. The facts are particularly damning as to Kaiser, but is the description of the company's litigious conduct surprising? Isn't this what insurance companies do whenever they are engaged in adjudication? Why should this conduct be viewed as so reprehensible in this case?

5. Why does the majority reject the view that § 1281.6 provided a standard and unintrusive judicial remedy in the *Engalla* circumstances? Doesn't the federal policy on arbitration mandate the use of that procedure?

Isn't it likely to have been more effective than *Engallas'* present strategy? Do you agree with the majority that § 1281.6 is permissive, that its invocation violates in some respects the agreement to arbitrate, and that it is intended to be applied primarily when the parties disagree in good faith about the appointment of an arbitrator?

6. As to the court's assessment of the materiality of Kaiser's misrepresentation of its arbitral system, do you agree that Oliver Tire would have given substantial importance to the operation of Kaiser's arbitration system if it had been informed of the system's actual operation? Wouldn't the level of premiums and the benefit coverage be much more significant considerations for a company subscriber? What does this analysis suggest about the majority opinion and its underlying objectives?

7. What is the basis for and implications of the court's statement that Kaiser was under a duty of good faith cooperation with the arbitration process? Does or should such a duty apply only in self-administered arbitral systems?

8. Is the gravamen of *Engalla* fraud or adhesion? Is the court more concerned with Kaiser's "cloaking" of the true operation of its system and its obstructing conduct or with the fact that it established, designed, and administered an arbitral system that generously favored its interests over those of its subscribers? Is there a meaningful distinction between the two concepts in these circumstances? Do these considerations provide some explanation for the duty of good faith cooperation in arbitration? Isn't the court preoccupied with such transparent fundamental fairness that any determination other than sanctioning Kaiser would be unthinkable? If so, don't the circumstances of adhesion permit or lead to the type of abuse that occurred? The dissent and concurring opinions may be correct to view the *Engalla* opinion as announcing a radical change in the regulatory protocol that applies to consumer arbitration. What is your assessment?

Current Phase: Mutuality, Apportionment of Costs, Class Action Waivers

The "mutuality of the obligation to arbitrate" has become a critical aspect of the contemporary law of consumer arbitration. Arbitration agreements in the consumer setting are adhesion contracts—unilateral provisions for the arbitration of disputes. Courts sometimes hold such agreements unenforceable when they determine that the contract does not represent the weaker party's reasonable expectations or when they find the clause to be unduly oppressive and, therefore, unconscionable or against public policy.

A number of courts, however, avoid invalidating arbitration agreements even when they contain inequalities or other positional imbalances. To reach an assessment of enforceability, courts must distinguish between clauses that merely require the arbitration of disputes and those that limit the rights of the parties to recover. Moreover, according to U.S. Supreme Court precedent, arbitration is a mere substitution of forum, not a loss of rights. Other courts strictly enforce the obligation of mutuality: "neither party is bound unless both are bound."

Consumer arbitration agreements are vulnerable to challenge on a number of other grounds. The contemporary decisional law contains numerous cases on unconscionability, costs, and severance; the method of integrating arbitral clauses in consumer transactions; and the consequences of excluding class action relief. On the topic of unconscionability, the courts require, pursuant to the applicable state law, that a finding of unconscionability must satisfy both the procedural and substantive components of unconscionability. Arbitral clauses contained in consumer transactions are, by definition, procedurally unconscionable. Their terms are unilaterally imposed and presented on a take-it-or-leave-it basis by the economically superior party. The critical question, therefore, is whether the terms themselves oppress the weaker party. When they do through the deprivation of basic and fundamental rights, the arbitral clause is substantively unconscionable and becomes unenforceable.

Many of the unconscionability decisions overlap with the cases on the mutuality of the obligation to arbitrate. For example, when a builder required consumers to pay liquidated damages if they chose not to arbitrate, but did not subject himself to the same obligation, the failure of the arbitration agreement to disclose the potential costs of arbitration contributed to "the asymmetrical effects" of the provision. The California state courts especially have been active in policing consumer arbitration agreements for this type of unfairness or unconscionability.

Consideration of the cost of arbitration figures in the consumer arbitration decisions of other courts. The current position is that the party challenging the enforceability of the arbitration agreement on this basis must establish that the costs of the arbitration are prohibitive and preclude relief. The standard is applied on a case-by-case basis.

The decisional law also contains a number of refinements on the adjudication of unconscionability in consumer arbitration agreements. The party claiming unconscionability must provide proof of the claim. Moreover, unconscionable arbitral terms are not cured by the arbitral institutional rules incorporated into the arbitration agreement by reference.

Forum-selection provisions in consumer arbitration contracts has also divided courts. Some courts have addressed the issue through the prism of the holding in *Carnival Cruise Lines, Inc. v. Shute*, 499 U.S. 585 (1991). Other courts have avoided the *Shute* doctrine by holding that forum-selection clauses that are not effectively communicated or are calculated to discourage consumers from "pursuing legitimate claims" are unconscionable.

The failure to adhere strictly to contract formation formalities does not appear to render consumer arbitration agreements invalid. Courts have upheld arbitral clauses in a service contract that did not require a signature. Nursing home admission agreements have begun to include arbitral clauses. Their inclusion raises a number of issues: the patient's capacity to contract; a representative's capacity to contract on behalf of another party; and the arbitrability of tort disputes in light of the contract capacity issues.

Class action waivers in adhesionary consumer arbitration agreements have also divided the courts. Some courts have held that the FAA's plain language provides for the enforcement of arbitration agreements unless grounds for nonenforcement exist in state contract law. The position that class action waivers are "mutual obligations equally binding on both parties to the contract" has been adopted by the Third, Fourth, and Seventh Circuits. The waiver of class action relief need not be "knowing and voluntary." The right to bring a class action is "purely" procedural and does not affect the remedies that are available to the consumer. The lack of class action relief makes recovery less convenient but the consumer can still be made whole.

Other courts have taken an antagonistic position and emphasized the public importance of class action relief to consumer protection. These courts have held that adhesionary consumer contracts cannot explicitly ban class action litigation. If an arbitration agreement precludes class actions, it violates public policy because it requires consumers "to fight alleged improprieties at an exorbitant cost. Individual arbitration would be a small deterrent to companies certain that few proceedings [would] be instituted against them." In fact, "consumer class action litigation is of such public importance that public policy considerations allow class action arbitration even if an arbitration agreement does not explicitly so provide." Class action is too important to compromise because it may be the only means of redress.

The cases that follow illustrate these points of the contemporary doctrine. The courts suggest that the particular features of consumer arbitration may warrant adjustments to the standard law. They make clear that positional advantage, combined with the abridgement of rights, can subdue the federal judicial policy on arbitration. Nevertheless, the question remains: If access to adjudication is available, does the consumer have a better position and possibility in arbitration?

AAMES FUNDING CORP. v. SHARPE

2004 WL 2418284 (E.D. Pa. 2004) (not rep. in F.Supp.2d).

PADOVA, J.

[. . .]

I. BACKGROUND

... On or about January 10, 2000, First Choice solicited Plaintiff to enter into a home improvement contract for her home in Philadelphia. Plaintiff and her daughter thereafter executed a "proposal" for home improvement work in the amount of $5,640. Upon executing the contract, First Choice informed Plaintiff that someone from his office would be contacting her to arrange financing for the home improvement work. Two days later, Borso visited Plaintiff at her home to request all documentary information on her outstanding debts. Although Plaintiff never wanted a loan for anything but home improvements, Borso insisted that she would have to pay off any other outstanding debts in order to obtain the home improvement loan. Borso did not provide Plaintiff with a broker contract, did not identify himself as a broker, and did not explain that, as a mortgage broker, he would be paid by Plaintiff for arranging a loan.

On or about March 3, 2000, a settlement agent for Petitioner closed a loan at Plaintiff's home for a principal amount of $25,000 and at an interest rate of 11%. The settlement statement for the loan reflects the pay-off of Respondent's consumer loan, utility, and tax debts, as well as a $2,500 broker fee for Brookside. The settlement statement did not account for the $5,500 balance of the principal of the loan. Weeks later, First Choice's agent visited Plaintiff's home to inquire about the loan proceeds for the home improvement work. Plaintiff and her daughter advised First Choice that they never received the funds. . . .

On or about March 17, 2000, Plaintiff received three checks, $2,855 in cash payable to Plaintiff, $891 payable to PECO Energy, and $117 payable to CitiBank. . . . Plaintiff returned the checks to the sender because they did not represent the cash amount she was supposed to receive from the home improvement loan. First Choice, Borso, and/or Brookside never responded to inquiries from Plaintiff nor visited her at her home ever again. The $1,700 remainder of the principal remains unaccounted for and Plaintiff never received any home improvements. . . .

[. . .]

On September 13, 2004, Petitioner commenced the instant action against Respondent by filing a Petition to Compel Arbitration under § 4 of the FAA. . . . Petitioner maintains that Respondent is required to arbitrate her dispute against Petitioner pursuant to an arbitration agreement entered into by the parties. Under the arbitration agreement, Petitioner and Respondent are required to arbitrate "any and all" claims, with the exception of:

(i) foreclosure proceedings, whether by judicial action, power of sale, or any other proceeding in which a lien holder may acquire or convey title to or possession of any property which is security for this Transaction (including an assignment of rents or appointment of a receiver) or (ii) an application by or on behalf of the Borrower for relief under the federal bankruptcy laws or any other similar laws of general application for the relief of debtors, or (iii) any Claim where Lender seeks damages or other relief because of Borrower's default under the terms of a Transaction.

(Am.Pet., Ex. B.)

[. . .]

III. DISCUSSION

[. . .]

B. *Arbitrability*

Petitioner contends that Respondent is required to arbitrate the underlying dispute pursuant the agreement to arbitrate entered into by the parties in this action.... Before a reluctant party can be compelled to arbitrate, however, the court must "engage in a limited review to ensure that the dispute is arbitrable—*i.e.*, that a valid agreement to arbitrate exists between the parties and that the specific dispute falls within the substantive scope of that agreement." ... Federal law presumptively favors the enforcement of arbitration agreements....

Respondent contends that the arbitration agreement entered into by the parties in this case is void as unconscionable. Questions concerning the interpretation and construction of arbitration agreements are determined by reference to federal substantive law.... In interpreting such agreements, federal courts may apply state law pursuant to § 2 of the FAA.... Thus, generally applicable contract defenses may be applied to invalidate arbitration agreements without contravening the FAA.... A party challenging a contract provision as unconscionable generally bears the burden of proving that the provision is both procedurally and substantively unconscionable.... Procedural unconscionability pertains to the process by which an agreement is reached and the form of an agreement, including the use therein of fine print and convoluted or unclear language.... Substantive unconscionability refers to terms that unreasonably favor one party to which the disfavored party does not truly assent....

Respondent argues that the arbitration agreement is procedurally unconscionable as a contract of adhesion. An adhesion contract is defined as a "standard form contract prepared by one party, to be signed by the party in a weaker position, [usually] a consumer, who has little choice about the terms." ... Procedural unconscionability is generally established if the agreement at issue constitutes a contract of adhesion.... Petitioner does not dispute that the arbitration agreement at issue constitutes a contract of adhesion. Accordingly, Respondent has demonstrated that the agreement to arbitrate is procedurally unconscionable. Of course, "[a]n adhesion contract is not necessarily unenforceable," ... as Respondent must also demonstrate that the arbitration agreement is substantively unconscionable.

Respondent argues that the arbitration agreement is substantively unconscionable because it requires her to arbitrate the vast majority of her claims while allowing Petitioner to bring a foreclosure action in the courts. Respondent cites *Lytle v. CitiFinancial Services, Inc.,* 810 A.2d 643 (Pa. Super. Ct.2002), in support of her substantive unconscionability argument. *Lytle* involved a lender-borrower agreement which provided for arbitration of all claims by the parties, with the exception "[a]ny action to effect a foreclosure to transfer title to the property being foreclosed ... or [a]ny matter where all parties seek monetary damages in the aggregate of $15,000 or less in total damages (compensatory or punitive), costs and fees." ... The *Lytle* court noted that, in practice, the borrowers were required to arbitrate all disputes involving more than the modest sum of $15,000, while the lender remained free to enforce most of its substantive rights (*i.e.*, repayment of the debt and commencement of foreclosure proceedings) in court.... The court concluded that "under Pennsylvania law, the reservation by [a lender] of access to the courts for itself to the exclusion of the consumer creates a presumption of unconscionability, which in the absence of 'business realities' that *compel* inclusion of such a provision in an arbitration provision, renders the arbitration provision unconscionable and unenforceable under Pennsylvania law." ... (emphasis in original).

The Court concludes that the Respondent's reliance on the Pennsylvania Superior Court's decision in *Lytle* is unpersuasive. The Court is bound by the decision of the United States Court of Appeals for the Third Circuit in *Harris*, wherein the court rejected the borrowers' contention that an arbitration clause in a loan agreement was substantively unconscionable because it provided the lender with the option of litigating certain disputes, while providing no such choice to the borrowers.... The court concluded that "the mere fact that [the lender] retains the option to litigate some issues in court, while the [borrowers] must arbitrate all claims does not make the arbitration agreement unenforceable. We have held repeatedly that inequality in bargaining power, alone, is not a valid basis upon which to invalidate an arbitration agreement." ... ("It is of no legal consequence that the arbitration clause gives [the lender] the option to litigate arbitrable issues in court, while requiring the [borrowers] to invoke arbitration" because "mutuality is not a requirement of a valid arbitration clause").... The Court concludes, therefore, that the arbitration agreement entered into by Petitioner and Respondent is valid and enforceable. The Court further finds that the underlying dispute between Petitioner and Respondent falls within the broad scope of the arbitration agreement. Accordingly, Petitioner's Amended Petition to Compel Arbitration is granted.

[...]

NOTES AND QUESTIONS

1. What definition of unconscionability does the court adopt? Why? Do you feel that definition is consistent with other definitions from previous courts?

2. How is the decision in *Lytle* different from *Harris*? Is the latter more compelling? Why or why not?

3. Is the plaintiff deprived of rights by agreeing to arbitrate disputes?

4. What is the imbalance in the agreement? Why does it exist?

5. Is the acquiescence to *Harris* outdated?

PORPORA v. GATLIFF BUILDING COMPANY

160 Ohio App.3d 843, 828 N.E.2d 1081 (2005).

Moore, Judge.

Appellants, Gatliff Building Company and Randy Gatliff, appeal from a decision of the Medina County Court of Common Pleas, denying their motion to stay proceedings pending arbitration. We affirm.

I

Appellees, Michael and Lori Porpora, entered into a written contract with Gatliff Building Company for the construction of a home in Wadsworth, Ohio. The contract contained an arbitration clause. On December 22, 2003, appellees filed a complaint against appellants ... alleging claims of breach of contract, negligence, misrepresentation, fraud, and violations of the Ohio Consumer Sales Protection Act. On March 4, 2004, appellants filed a motion to stay the proceedings pending arbitration of the matter. Following a hearing, the trial court denied the motion on the ground that the arbitration clause was unconscionable.

[...]

II

[...]

Ohio's public policy encourages arbitration as a method to settle disputes.... An arbitration provision may, however, be unenforceable on grounds existing at law or in equity for the revocation of a contract.... One of those grounds is unconscionability. The party seeking to establish that an arbitration clause is unconscionable must show that the provision is both procedurally and substantively unconscionable.

Procedural unconscionability concerns the formation of the agreement and occurs when no voluntary meeting of the minds is possible.... In order to determine whether a contract provision is procedurally unconscionable, courts consider the relative bargaining positions of the parties, whether the terms of the provision were explained to the weaker party, and whether the party claiming that the provision is unconscionable was represented by counsel at the time the contract was executed. Additionally, when "there are strong indications that the contract at issue is an adhesion contract, and the arbitration clause itself appears to be adhesive in nature," there is "considerable doubt that any true agreement ever existed to submit disputes to arbitration." ...

Substantive unconscionability refers to the actual terms of the agreement. Contract terms are unconscionable if they are unfair and commercially unreasonable....

[...]

Procedural Unconscionability

At his May 18, 2004 deposition, Randy Gatliff, the president and owner of Gatliff Building Company, testified that since the company had been formed, each of its two standard construction contracts contained the arbitration clause that is at issue in this case. Gatliff also testified that he had never modified or removed the arbitration clause at the request of a customer and that if a customer was not willing to accept the language of the company's contract, he would instruct them to search for another home builder. Finally, Gatliff testified that he had not explained the arbitration clause to appellees and that he had not called their attention to the clause.

Appellees each executed an affidavit and attached those affidavits to their brief opposing appellants' motion to stay proceedings. In those affidavits, appellees stated that they were not represented by counsel when they executed the construction contract and that this was their first experience with a construction contract. Appellees further stated that no employee of Gatliff Building Company had offered them any information on arbitration or discussed the clause with them. Lastly, appellees stated that at the time they executed the agreement, they did not know what arbitration meant.

Randy Gatliff's own testimony characterizes the construction contract in general and the arbitration clause in particular as adhesive....

In light of all the foregoing facts and circumstances, we conclude that the arbitration clause in the construction contract between the parties is procedurally unconscionable.

Substantive Unconscionability

The arbitration clause contained in the construction contract between the parties reads as follows:

> All claims and disputes relating to this contract shall be subject to arbitration at the option of either the buyer or the contractor in accordance with the Arbitration Rules of the American Arbitration Association for the construction industry in effect at the time of the arbitration located in Medina County, Ohio. Written notice of demand for arbitration shall be filed with the other party to the contract and with the American Arbitration Association, within a reasonable time after the dispute has arisen. The buyer shall have no rights to seek or obtain arbitration until such time as the contractor has certified substantial completion in accordance with this agreement. An award in arbitration may be enforced and entered in a court of competent jurisdiction in the county in which the lot is located. Arbitration shall be mandatory for buyers and constitutes the sole method of buyer in seeking to enforce the provisions of this agreement.

The clause is skewed in favor of the contractor, imposing significant restrictions upon the buyer alone. First, the clause prohibits the buyer from initiating arbitration until the contractor has certified substantial completion. By forcing the buyer to wait to seek relief, this provision of the clause threatens to thwart the buyer's efforts to mitigate damages. Additionally, the clause provides that arbitration is the only method through which the buyer is permitted to enforce the contract provisions.

Among other consequences, this provision increases the financial hurdle the buyer must surmount in order to pursue a claim.

The clause does not disclose either the costs of arbitration or the fact that those costs are substantially higher than the costs associated with a regular court proceeding....

Appellees attached the AAA's published rules and procedures to their brief opposing appellants' motion to stay proceedings. Those rules reveal that the fees required to pursue a claim vary with the amount of damages alleged.... AAA Rule 50 does provide that the administrative fees may be deferred or reduced "in the event of extreme hardship on the part of any party." The rule makes clear, however, that such a deferral or reduction is entirely within the discretion of the AAA. Moreover, the rule does not provide for a waiver of the fees....

[...]

In light of all the foregoing facts and circumstances, we conclude that the arbitration clause in the construction contract between the parties is substantively unconscionable.

Given our determinations that the arbitration clause in the construction contract between the parties is both substantively and procedurally unconscionable, we conclude that the trial court did not err by determining that the clause was unconscionable, and both of appellants' assignments of error are overruled.

[...]

Judgment affirmed.

NOTES AND QUESTIONS

1. How do you assess the court's construction of the arbitral clause? Do you agree that some of its features are oppressive to the weaker party?

2. Would it be fair to say that the arbitral clause is customized to the circumstances of a home-building transaction? If so, why does customization become unlawful?

3. Does the situation reveal overreaching, coercion, or duress? Are the consumer's rights being compromised?

4. Is arbitration unfair to the consumer or is it in the consumer's best interest?

D.R. HORTON, INC. v. GREEN
120 Nev. 549, 96 P.3d 1159 (2004).

OPINION

PER CURIAM.

Appellant D.R. Horton, Inc., a real property developer, and respondents Michael Green, John Velickoff, and Tracy Velickoff (jointly the

Homebuyers) entered into home purchase agreements containing a mandatory binding arbitration provision. In the ensuing dispute over the provision's validity, the district court found that the arbitration clause was adhesive and unconscionable. On appeal, Horton argues that the district court erred in concluding that the arbitration clause was unenforceable. We disagree. We conclude that the clause is void as unconscionable and affirm the district court's order denying Horton's motion to compel arbitration.

FACTS AND PROCEDURAL HISTORY

The arbitration clause dispute arose from a construction defect controversy between the Homebuyers and Horton. These parties entered into home purchase agreements containing a mandatory arbitration provision. In each case, a two-page form sales agreement constituted the agreement between the parties. The agreement was printed in a very small font. The front page contained the sales price, other financial information, and the signature lines. A clause at the bottom in capitalized bold letters stated that: "PARAGRAPHS 10 THROUGH 27 CONSTITUTE A PART OF THIS CONTRACT."

The back page included, among other things, a limited warranty clause and a mandatory binding arbitration provision. The font size on the back page was smaller than the font utilized on the front page. The arbitration provision read as follows:

> 11.   THIS CONTRACT IS SUBJECT TO THE NEVADA ARBITRATION RULES GOVERNED UNDER NEVADA REVISED STATUTE CHAPTER 38 AND THE FEDERAL ARBITRATION ACT.
>
> Buyer and Seller agree that any disputes or claims between the parties, whether arising from a tort, this Contract, any breach of this Contract or in any way related to this transaction, including but not limited to claims or disputes arising under the terms of the express limited warranty referenced in Paragraph 10 of this Contract, shall be settled by binding arbitration under the direction and procedures established by the American Arbitration Association "Construction Industry Arbitration Rules" except as specifically modified herein or dictated by applicable statutes including the Nevada Revised Statute Chapter 38 and/or the Federal Arbitration Act. If Buyer does not seek arbitration prior to initiating any legal action, Buyer agrees that Seller shall be entitled to liquidated damages in the amount of ten thousand dollars ... ($10,000.00). Any dispute arising from this Contract shall be submitted for determination to a board of three (3) arbitrators to be selected for each such controversy. The decision of the arbitrators shall be in writing and signed by such arbitrators, or a majority of them, and shall be final and binding upon the parties. Each party shall bear the fees and expenses of counsel, witnesses and employees of such party, and any other costs and expenses incurred for the benefit of such party. All other fees and expenses shall be divided equally between Buyer and Seller.

With the exception of the paragraph title, which was in bold capital letters like the other contract headings, nothing drew special attention to this provision.

Green testified that he only read the first page of the document. He indicated that he did not read the second page because "it was all fine print" and Horton's agent told him that it was a standard contract. The Velickoffs indicated that they read both sides of the contract, including the arbitration provision. They testified, however, that they did not understand that the provision constituted a waiver of their right to a jury trial or that it impacted their statutory rights under NRS Chapter 40 involving construction defect claims. Neither Green nor the Velickoffs understood that they would be required to fund one-half of the expenses of the arbitration and that these expenses could be more costly than standard litigation.

[. . .]

After hearing arguments and conducting an evidentiary hearing, the district court denied Horton's motion to compel arbitration, essentially granting judgment in favor of the Homebuyers on the declaratory relief action. The district court ruled that the arbitration clause was adhesive and fell short of Nevada's standards regarding jury trial waivers. The district court also determined that the clause was procedurally and substantively unconscionable because, if enforced, it operated to waive the right to a jury trial without even mentioning that right, and it failed "to inform homeowners of the costs associated with arbitration and the substantial difference between arbitration fees and filing fees for suits filed under Chapter 40." The district court struck the arbitration clause, reasoning that absent such disclosures, the Homebuyers could not give an informed consent. This appeal followed.

DISCUSSION

[. . .]

Strong public policy favors arbitration because arbitration generally avoids the higher costs and longer time periods associated with traditional litigation. Nevertheless, courts may invalidate unconscionable arbitration provisions. "Generally, both procedural and substantive unconscionability must be present in order for a court to exercise its discretion to refuse to enforce a . . . clause as unconscionable." However, less evidence of substantive unconscionability is required in cases involving great procedural unconscionability. A clause is procedurally unconscionable when a party lacks a meaningful opportunity to agree to the clause terms either because of unequal bargaining power, as in an adhesion contract, or because the clause and its effects are not readily ascertainable upon a review of the contract. Procedural unconscionability often involves the use of fine print or complicated, incomplete or misleading language that fails to inform a reasonable person of the contractual language's consequences. As the Ninth Circuit has recognized, "substantive unconscionability focuses on the one-sidedness of the contract terms." (All citations omitted.)

The district court determined that the arbitration clause was unenforceable because the Homebuyers had no realistic bargaining opportunity; that is, the agreement was an adhesion contract. This finding is not supported by substantial evidence. In fact, the record demonstrates that it was possible to negotiate for deletion of the arbitration provision. Nevertheless, the district court also concluded that the provision was procedurally deficient because it failed to indicate that by agreeing to binding arbitration, the Homebuyers were giving up significant rights under Nevada law. The district court also considered the fact that the clause was in fine print and indistinguishable from many other contractual provisions, and thus its significance was downplayed. Finally, the district court found that Horton's sales agent referred to the contract as a form agreement containing standard language, leading the Homebuyers to believe that the clause was simply a formality that did not significantly affect their rights. Based upon these findings, the district court concluded that the arbitration provision was procedurally unconscionable.

[. . .]

The contracts Horton presented to the Homebuyers were difficult to read and the arbitration clause was on the back page. The signature lines, in contrast, were on the front page. Other than the fact that the paragraph headings relating to the arbitration provision were in bold capital letters, just like every other heading in the contracts, nothing drew attention to the arbitration provision. To the contrary, although the termite and drainage provisions were capitalized throughout, the body of the arbitration clause was not capitalized. Instead, it was in an extremely small font. As in *Burch,* the arbitration provision was inconspicuous. Thus, even if an individual read the contract, there was nothing to draw the reader's attention to the importance of the arbitration provision. This failure to highlight the arbitration agreement, together with the representations made by Horton's agent that these were standard provisions, are key features in the district court's finding of procedural unconscionability.

Finally, even if any home purchasers noticed and read the arbitration provision, as did the Velickoffs, they would not be put on notice that they were agreeing to forgo important rights under state law. In addition to the right to a jury trial, ... a construction defect claimant may recover attorney fees or other damages proximately caused by the construction defect controversy. In general, the right to request attorney fees would still exist in an arbitration proceeding because " '[b]y agreeing to arbitrate a statutory claim ..., a party does not forgo the substantive rights afforded by the statute; it only submits to their resolution in an arbitral, rather than a judicial, forum.' " However, the arbitration provision provides that each party is to bear its own attorney fees and expenses. While Horton did not have a duty to explain in detail each and every right that the Homebuyers would be waiving by agreeing to arbitration, to be enforceable, an arbitration clause must at least be conspicuous and clearly put a purchaser on notice that he or she is waiving important rights under Nevada law.

Our 1989 decision in *Tandy Computer Leasing v. Terina's Pizza* is relevant to our analysis of the arbitration provision in this case. In *Tandy Computer Leasing,* a computer equipment lessor brought an action in Texas against a family of Nevada pizza parlor owners. The lessor initiated the action in Texas pursuant to a forum selection clause in the lease agreement and subsequently sought to enforce the judgment in Nevada. We invalidated the forum selection clause, in part because of the lessor's failure to make the clause conspicuous. We noted that binding a consumer under such circumstances was unrealistic because [the] clause was buried on the very bottom of the back page of the lease agreement, in very fine print, in a paragraph labelled MISCELLANEOUS.... Nothing on the front page notifies the reader of the specific forum selection clause on the back page. The clause is not even in bold print.

In the instant case, the district court did not err in finding procedural unconscionability. The arbitration provision was inconspicuous, downplayed by Horton's representative, and failed to adequately advise an average person that important rights were being waived by agreeing to arbitrate any disputes under the contract. We conclude that the district court did not err in finding the arbitration clause to be procedurally deficient.

We now turn to the issue of substantive unconscionability. Two provisions of the agreement implicate substantive unconscionability: the $10,000 penalty for refusing to arbitrate, and the requirement that each party pay equally for the costs of arbitration.

Ting v. AT & T, a recent Ninth Circuit case applying California law, provides guidance in determining substantive unconscionability. In *Ting,* the Ninth Circuit invalidated, among other things, a contract provision requiring customers to split arbitration fees with AT & T. The Ninth Circuit held that "[w]here an arbitration agreement is concerned, the agreement is unconscionable unless the arbitration remedy contains a 'modicum of bilaterality.'" The court went on to say that:

> "[a]lthough parties are free to contract for asymmetrical remedies and arbitration clauses of varying scope ... the doctrine of unconscionability limits the extent to which a stronger party may ... impose the arbitration forum on the weaker party without accepting that forum for itself." (*Ting quoting Armendariz v. Foundation Health Psychcare,* 24 Cal.4th 83, 99 Cal.Rptr.2d 745, 6 P.3d 669, 692 (2000)).

Ting is similar to the case at bar. Here, the arbitration provision is one-sided because it contained a liquidated damages provision penalizing the Homebuyers if they chose to forgo arbitration but imposed no such penalty upon Horton. Although the one-sidedness of the provision is not overwhelming, it does establish substantive unconscionability, especially when considered in light of the great procedural unconscionability present in this case.

[...]

CONCLUSION

We conclude that the arbitration provision was procedurally and substantively unconscionable because it was inconspicuous, one-sided and failed to advise the Homebuyers that significant rights under Nevada law would be waived by agreeing to arbitration. While the absence of language disclosing the potential arbitration costs and fees, standing alone, may not render an arbitration provision unenforceable, the district court properly considered that as a factor in invalidating the provision. As the arbitration provision is unenforceable, we affirm the district court's order denying Horton's motion to compel arbitration.

NOTES AND QUESTIONS

1. Is there an implied message in the court's reasoning and result? Does the arbitral clause—either in its making or content—exhibit gross unfairness? Do you suspect that there is a "trigger mechanism" in the court's discussion?

2. What about the federal policy on arbitration? Should the opinion be deemed to violate FAA § 2 and be federally preempted? What arguments for and against that proposition can you make? What parts of the opinion might transgress the strictures of the federal policy? Which federal cases might be at play?

3. How are *Ting* and *Amendariz* relevant to the court's assessment of the facts and its ruling?

4. Are the rules for consumer arbitration different?

JONES v. CITIGROUP, INC.

38 Cal.Rptr.3d 461 (Ct. App. 2006).

OPINION

RYLAARSDAM, Acting P.J.

Defendants Citigroup, Inc., Citibank Federal Savings Bank, Citibank (South Dakota), N.A., and Citibank USA, N.A. appeal from an order denying their petition to compel arbitration of an unfair competition action filed by plaintiffs Rochelle Jones and Theresa Wilens.... They contend provisions of the applicable credit card agreements bar plaintiffs' class and private attorney general actions and require individual arbitration. Defendants argue the court erred by applying California rather than South Dakota law to find the ban on class and representative arbitrations unconscionable and that such a ban is not unconscionable. We agree plaintiffs have not shown procedural unconscionability and therefore the arbitration provision may be enforced. We remand for the superior court to issue a new order granting the petition to compel arbitration.

FACTS AND PROCEDURAL BACKGROUND

Plaintiffs filed an action, individually and as private attorneys general, ... alleging defendants ... fail[ed] to make required disclosures about finance charges and interest rates incurred when using a check drawn against a credit card account. The complaint alleges defendants recovered transaction fees and finance charges from credit card holders who used the so-called convenience checks. Jones also brought her claim on behalf of a putative class limited to California residents.

Defendants filed a motion to compel plaintiffs to arbitrate their claims on an individual basis and to stay the action based on a provision in the credit card agreements. In support of their motion, defendants submitted a declaration setting out the terms of the credit card agreements with plaintiffs. They provided the laws of South Dakota and the United States would govern. They also stated that defendants could "change this Agreement . . . at any time." . . .

The change in terms notice, or so-called bill stuffer, described the addition of a binding arbitration provision to the cardholder agreement. It stated that either defendants or plaintiffs "may, without the other's consent, elect mandatory, binding arbitration for any claim, dispute, or controversy between [them]." It also provided that all claims based on the current or a prior account or the relationship between the parties were subject to arbitration.

The change in terms notice also advised plaintiffs: "If you do not wish to accept the binding arbitration provision contained in this change in terms notice, you must notify us in writing within 26 days after the Statement/Closing date indicated on your [current] billing statement stating your non acceptance. . . . If you notify us by that time that you do not accept the binding arbitration provisions contained in this change in terms notice, you can continue to use your card(s) under your existing terms until the end of your current membership year or the expiration date on your card(s), whichever is later. At that time your account will be closed and you will be able to pay off your remaining balance under your existing terms." Neither plaintiff opted out of the arbitration agreement.

Included within the arbitration agreement was the following language: "Please read this provision of the agreement carefully. It provides that any dispute may be resolved by binding arbitration. Arbitration replaces the right to go to court, including the right to a jury and the right to participate in a class action or similar proceeding. In arbitration, a dispute is resolved by an arbitrator instead of a judge or jury. Arbitration procedures are simpler and more limited than court procedures." (Capitalization and bold omitted.)

[. . .]

The agreement stated it was governed by the Federal Arbitration Act. . . . It also provided that the "arbitrator will apply applicable substantive law consistent with the FAA. . . ." The agreement excluded small claims actions from arbitration.

Within approximately six months of the amendment to the agreement, Jones opened a second credit card account with defendants. The original agreement for the second account contained the arbitration provisions.

In opposing the motion to compel arbitration, plaintiffs did not file their own declarations or object to any portion of defendants' declaration. The court denied the motion, finding that "the exclusion of class and representative actions is unconscionable under California Law."

DISCUSSION

Defendants set out several arguments as to why the court erred in denying their motion to compel arbitration. These include its refusal to engage in a choice of law analysis with the conclusion South Dakota law would govern interpretation of the arbitration agreement; its failure to find the FAA controls and preempts application of California law to invalidate the arbitration provision based on unconscionability; and its failure to find the arbitration provision enforceable.

After the case was briefed and argued, the California Supreme Court rendered its decision in a case containing similar issues, *Discover Bank v. Superior Court* (2005) 36 Cal.4th 148, 30 Cal.Rptr.3d 76, 113 P.3d 1100 (*Discover*). We afforded the parties the opportunity to file supplemental briefs. *Discover* provides the framework for resolution of this case.

In *Discover* the court "conclude[d] that, at least under some circumstances, the law in California is that class action waivers in consumer contracts of adhesion are unenforceable, whether the consumer is being asked to waive the right to class action litigation or the right to classwide arbitration." (*Discover, supra,* 36 Cal.4th at p. 153, 30 Cal.Rptr.3d 76, 113 P.3d 1100.) In that case the defendant issued a credit card to the plaintiff. The cardholder agreement did not contain an arbitration provision. Subsequently, by using a change of terms notice included with the bill, the defendant amended the agreement to bar class action and private attorney general arbitrations. The amendment also provided that if a cardholder did not agree to arbitration, he or she was required to notify the bank and stop using the credit card; continued use of the card would be deemed acceptance of the amended terms.

Because there was a choice of law dispute that was remanded back to the appellate court for determination, the *Discover* court did not decide the enforceability of the ban on classwide arbitration at issue in its case. And it did "not hold that all class action waivers are necessarily unconscionable." (*Discover, supra,* 36 Cal.4th at p. 162, 30 Cal.Rptr.3d 76, 113 P.3d 1100.) Rather, it held that "when the waiver is found in a consumer contract of adhesion in a setting in which disputes between the contracting parties predictably involve small amounts of damages, and when it is alleged that the party with the superior bargaining power has carried out a scheme to deliberately cheat large numbers of consumers out of individually small sums of money, then, at least to the extent the obligation at issue is governed by California law, the waiver becomes in practice the exemption of the party 'from responsibility for [its] own fraud, or willful injury to the person of property of another.' ... Under these circumstances, such waivers are unconscionable under California law and should not be enforced." ... In other words, where a contract is both procedurally and substantively unconscionable under California law, it may be unenforceable.

To reach this conclusion, the court revisited the general rule that for a provision to be invalidated based on unconscionability, there must be both procedural and substantive unconscionability.... Procedural unconscionability results from surprise or oppression based on unequal bargaining power. Generally it arises from an adhesion contract drafted by the stronger party and that gives the weaker party only two choices, to accept the terms as presented or reject the contract....

In analyzing unconscionability, *Discover* discussed *Szetela v. Discover Bank* (2002) 97 Cal.App.4th 1094, 118 Cal.Rptr.2d 862 (*Szetela*) with approval. The facts in *Szetela* were similar to those in *Discover* in terms of how the amendment was presented to the cardholder. *Szetela* found procedural unconscionability based on the adhesive nature of a contract attempting to ban classwide arbitration.... *Discover* relied on *Szetela* for its holding about procedural unconscionability when it stated, "an element of procedural unconscionability is present" "when[ ] a consumer is given an amendment to its cardholder agreement in the form of a 'bill stuffer' that he would be deemed to accept if he did not close his account...." ... Similarly in *Aral v. Earthlink, Inc.* (2005) 134 Cal.App.4th 544, 36 Cal.Rptr.3d 229, relying on *Discover,* the court found "quintessential procedural unconscionability" because "the terms of the agreement were presented on a 'take it or leave it' basis ... with no opportunity to opt out." ...

Our case is different. Here, although the change was made in a "bill stuffer," plaintiffs were given an opportunity to opt out of arbitration. By giving written notice of their rejection of the amendment, they could continue to use their cards until the cards expired and then would be able to pay off their balances under the terms of their existing agreement without acceleration. This does not present the take it or leave it scenario described in *Discover* or *Szetela* as being procedurally unconscionable. Rather, it appears that defendant was cognizant of the oppressive nature of forcing a nonconsenting cardholder to either agree to arbitration or immediately cancel the account and took steps to avoid it.

Themselves relying on *Szetela,* plaintiffs contend the unilateral change in terms using a "bill stuffer" is "sufficient by itself to make the [a]rbitration [p]rovision procedurally unconscionable." But their claim they were put in a take it or leave it situation is refuted by the choice they were given to opt out of arbitration. And plaintiffs fail to acknowledge the different facts in *Szetela.*

Plaintiffs also seem to argue the means of its transmission rendered the amendment unconscionable, stating, "We have all seen what is typically stuffed in with our monthly credit card bills," and claiming the amendment "was probably buried in 'junk mail' that accompanies bills." We reject plaintiffs' attempt to go beyond the record. They filed no declaration in opposition to the motion to compel arbitration and so failed to offer any evidence about how the amendment was actually presented to them, whether they saw the change in terms notice, or whether it was, in fact, mixed in with junk mail. In addition, there is undisputed evidence that the inclusion of the amendment was prominently noted on the front of the bill itself. Moreover, *Discover* plainly does not say using "bill stuffers" as a means of amending an agreement is, per se, unconscionable. It focuses instead on the take it or leave it nature of the contractual modification. . . .

Nor does *Badie v. Bank of America* (1998) 67 Cal.App.4th 779, 79 Cal.Rptr.2d 273 support plaintiffs' argument. There, the appellate court refused to enforce an amendment adding an arbitration provision to an existing account by a change of terms notice. The primary basis for its decision was a determination that the original agreement was ambiguous as to whether it could be unilaterally amended to include such a provision. . . . The court did not rely on the principle of unconscionability.

In our case, by contrast, before the addition of the arbitration provision, the parties had already agreed defendant could "change this Agreement . . . at any time." California law specifically allows parties to agree to modify a contract. . . . "A written contract may expressly provide for modification. [Citation.] When a modification is in accordance with a provision authorizing and setting forth a method for its revision the rule that a contract in writing may be altered only by another written contract or an executed oral agreement has no application because there is no alteration. The modification is in accordance with the terms of the contract. [Citation.]" . . . The right to unilaterally add a term to the contract in and of itself does not offend California's public policy. And, of course, none of the arguments as to the propriety of amendments apply to Jones's second credit card agreement. It was never amended but contained the arbitration provision from its inception.

[. . .]

Further, because we decide the case on the ground there is no procedural unconscionability, we have no need to discuss any of the other arguments raised as to the issue of enforcement of the arbitration provision.

DISPOSITION

The order is reversed and the matter is remanded for the superior court to enter a new order granting appellants' motion to compel arbitration. In the interest of justice, the parties shall bear their own costs.

MOORE, J., Dissenting.

[. . .]

With regard to procedural unconscionability, the crux of the majority's argument turns on the factual distinction between this case and the facts in *Szetela v. Discover Bank* (2002) 97 Cal.App.4th 1094, 118 Cal. Rptr.2d 862 (*Szetela*). In that case, if the consumer did not accept the terms of the "bill stuffer" amendment to the cardholder agreement, the bank would immediately close the account, and the consumer would be permitted to pay off any balance under the existing terms.... Here, the plaintiffs may opt out of the arbitration agreement, and their accounts will remain open until the end of current membership year or until their current cards expire, at which time the defendants will close the account....

The majority believes that this is sufficiently distinguishable from *Szetela* and *Discover Bank v. Superior Court* (2005) 36 Cal.4th 148, 30 Cal.Rptr.3d 76, 113 P.3d 1100 (*Discover*). While in this case the defendants do allow the cardholder to continue using the account for a limited period of time, this does not, in my view, save the provision from procedural unconscionability. Ultimately, whether in a few months or several years, the cardholder is left in the same position—either accept the arbitration clause or forfeit the ability to use a credit card. It does indeed present "the terms of the agreement ... on a 'take it or leave it' basis ... with no opportunity to opt out." (*Aral v. Earthlink, Inc.* (2005) 134 Cal.App.4th 544, 557, 36 Cal.Rptr.3d 229.) The only difference here is that the consequences are less immediate, but they exist nonetheless. The short grace period is ultimately a distinction without a difference. In a relatively short amount of time, all of defendants' remaining customers will be bound by an arbitration clause, whether or not they want it.

As we noted in *Szetela,* such clauses are of no benefit to the consumer. Indeed, a clause prohibiting any form of collective representation "seriously jeopardizes customers' consumer rights by prohibiting any effective means of litigating Discover's business practices...."

[...]

NOTES AND QUESTIONS

1. Which factor is at the core of the court's determination: Federal policy on arbitration, consumer protection, contract formation rules, choice-of-law, or a combination? Why?

2. How persuasive do you find the distinction between the instant case and *Badie*?

3. In light of *Discover Bank*, how do you think the California state Supreme Court would have decided *Jones*?

4. Is this appellate court introducing a new ideology toward consumer arbitration?

5. What are the elements of essential fairness in a consumer arbitration agreement?

6. How significant is the consumer's right to class action relief?

MERCURIO v. WRIGHT MEDICAL TECHNOLOGY, INC.

402 F.3d 62 (1st Cir. 2005).

TORRUELLA, Circuit Judge.

Appellant Wright Medical Technology, Inc. ("Wright Medical"), a Tennessee corporation, appeals from the district court's refusal to enforce the forum selection clause in an arbitration provision that was part of a distribution agreement (the "Agreement") between Wright Medical and Ocean State Orthopedics, Inc. ("OSO"), a Rhode Island corporation. The district court affirmed a bankruptcy court's order that the arbitration of an underlying dispute regarding the Agreement take place in Rhode Island, contrary to the Agreement's plain language that the arbitration take place in Tennessee.

Because appellees have failed to show that the enforcement of the forum selection clause is unreasonable under the circumstances, we reverse the district court's decision. *See The Bremen v. Zapata Off–Shore Co.,* 407 U.S. 1, 15, 92 S.Ct. 1907, 32 L.Ed.2d 513 (1972) (a "forum [selection] clause should control absent a strong showing that it should be set aside"); *Silva v. Encyclopedia Britannica Inc.,* 239 F.3d 385, 386 (1st Cir.2001) ("The prevailing view towards contractual forum-selection clauses is that 'such clauses are prima facie valid and should be enforced unless enforcement is shown by the resisting party to be "unreasonable" under the circumstances.'") (quoting *The Bremen,* 407 U.S. at 10, 92 S.Ct. 1907).

I

Wright Medical manufactures and distributes medical supplies from its principal place of business in Tennessee. In September 1995, Wright Medical entered into the Agreement with OSO, whereby OSO became the exclusive distributor for Wright Medical products in Rhode Island. Appellee Gregory A. Mercurio, Jr., ("Mercurio"), was the president of OSO and signed the Agreement on its behalf.

Article 14 of the Agreement, entitled "Tennessee Contract," provides that it "shall be governed by and interpreted in accordance with the laws of the State of Tennessee." Article 16 of the Agreement, entitled "Arbitration of Disputes," is central to this appeal. It provides, in relevant part:

> *All disputes* arising in connection with this Agreement, *including the interpretation,* performance or non-performance of this Agreement, *shall* be settled *in Memphis, Tennessee,* USA, by arbitration in front of one Arbitrator. Such arbitrator shall be appointed by agreement of each of the parties. The arbitration procedures shall be held in accordance with the rules and procedures of The American Arbitration Association. _—Recital_

> Any such arbitration shall be conducted in the English language and *shall be governed by laws of the State of Tennessee. Judgment upon the*

Perfect?

Recital

award may be entered in any court of competent jurisdiction of the State of Tennessee. ([E]mphasis supplied).

In 1996, for reasons that are in dispute, Wright Medical terminated the Agreement. Thereafter, Wright Medical proceeded to appoint another distributor for its products in Rhode Island.

At some point not relevant to this appeal, Mercurio filed a voluntary petition in bankruptcy under Chapter 11 of the Bankruptcy Act ... and Peter J. Furness ("Trustee") became the trustee in bankruptcy.

Five years after termination of the Agreement, the Trustee, on behalf of Mercurio, commenced the present suit as an adversary proceeding against Wright Medical in the U.S. Bankruptcy Court for the District of Rhode Island. The substance of this action concerns an alleged breach of contract by Wright Medical in terminating the Agreement. Wright Medical moved the bankruptcy court to compel arbitration of that controversy pursuant to the terms of the Agreement. The bankruptcy judge granted this request, but ordered the arbitration to take place in Rhode Island rather than in Tennessee as stipulated in the Agreement.

The record is fairly sparse as to the reasoning of the bankruptcy court in bypassing the Agreement's unambiguous language in this respect.... Although we cannot fault the judge's laudable purpose, arbitration is a contractual matter in which, absent unusual circumstances not present in this case, the parties are entitled to the measure that they bargained for.

[...]

II

The " 'heavy burden of proof' ... required to set aside [a forum selection] clause on grounds of inconvenience," *Carnival Cruise Lines, Inc. v. Shute,* 499 U.S. 585, 595, 111 S.Ct. 1522, 113 L.Ed.2d 622 (1991), demands more of a litigant, however, than simply showing that another location would be more convenient. Were it otherwise, forum selection clauses would almost never be enforceable, for inconvenience to at least one of the parties is an almost forgone conclusion when dealing with a provision that requires litigating away from one's home turf. Yet these clauses are standard fare in today's multi-jurisdictional and international contractual relationships. At the time these contracts are entered into, the parties routinely, voluntarily, and knowingly agree to litigate and/or be bound by the decision of fora located in distant locations. Thus, something considerably more than the mere inconvenience of traveling to litigate in a different, even faraway foreign jurisdiction, is required to overcome a contractual agreement to do so. *Royal Bed & Spring Co. v. Famossul Industria e Comercio de Moveis Ltda,* 906 F.2d 45, 49 (1st Cir.1990) ("[A] showing of inconvenience as to a foreign forum would not be enough to hold a forum-selection clause unenforceable, especially if that inconvenience was known or contemplated by the parties at the time of their agreement."). The cost of such litigation alone cannot be enough to meet the "heavy burden" imposed upon the reneging party, who may now have second thoughts. *Cent. Contracting Co. v. Maryland Cas. Co.*, 367 F.2d 341, 344 (3d Cir.1966) ("Mere inconvenience or additional expense is not the test of unreasonableness since it may be assumed that the plaintiff received under the contract consideration for these things.").

The record in this case is bare of specific evidence regarding the extraordinary additional costs involved in litigating in Tennessee that were not foreseen by the contracting parties when they entered into the Agreement. OSO accepted some costs beforehand as a normal consequence of arbitrating in Tennessee. . . . With a distributorship in Rhode Island, the likelihood existed that witnesses and evidence would be located there rather than in Tennessee. OSO, however, chose to commit to Tennessee as the forum for dispute resolutions. The Trustee stands in the debtor's shoes and is not entitled to avoid the forum selected by OSO on mere allegations of inconvenience. . . .

The district judge's bare conclusion that the Trustee would be "deprived of his day in court" is unsupported by any evidence in the record. The Trustee was required to provide a *factual* record establishing the basis for his challenge to the forum selection clause. . . . We find no evidence in the record that would support the conclusion that requiring the parties to arbitrate their dispute in Tennessee would deprive the Trustee of his day in court.

We finish with language which should have a familiar ring by now:

> Courts must give effect to . . . freely negotiated forum selection clauses. . . . [The parties'] choice of arbitral forum should have been honored by the district court. Courts may not rewrite the parties' agreements and compel arbitration of their dispute in a forum which is not one of those enumerated in an arbitration agreement's forum selection clause.

[. . .]

The district court must order appellants to file their arbitration in Tennessee. The decision of the district court is reversed in part and the case is remanded for action consistent with this opinion.

Reversed in part and Remanded.

NOTES AND QUESTIONS

1. Is *Mercurio* a consumer case? Why and why not?

2. Is it an arbitration case? Can you distinguish forum selection clauses and arbitration agreements?

3. Does the court engage in practical politics? Why are exceptions to the underlying policy almost never made? Is there wisdom in the latter position?

4. Can the decision and reasoning in *Mercurio* be restricted to its facts? Why?

KRISTIAN v. COMCAST CORP.

446 F.3d 25 (1st Cir. 2006).

Lipez, Circuit Judge.

This appeal requires us to evaluate the enforceability of arbitration agreements that Comcast, a cable television provider, invoked against a group of its subscribers.... In [its] ruling, the district court did not have to reach a number of other issues raised by the subscribers in opposition to Comcast's demand for arbitration.

We disagree with the district court's interpretation of the arbitration agreements. Their language does have retroactive effect. This ruling requires us to address the other arguments raised by the subscribers against the enforceability of the arbitration agreements. We find that Comcast provided adequate notice of the arbitration agreements. However, we conclude that the provision of the arbitration agreements barring the recovery of treble damages is invalid as applied to the subscribers' federal antitrust claims because it prevents the vindication of a federal statutory right. Similarly, we conclude that the provisions of the arbitration agreements barring the recovery of attorney's fees and costs and barring class arbitration are invalid because they prevent the vindication of statutory rights under state and federal law. Nevertheless, the arbitration agreements contain savings clauses that provide for severance of these invalid provisions. With these provisions severed, the arbitration can go forward. Thus, we reverse the district court's ruling that the subscribers cannot be compelled to arbitrate their antitrust claims.

I.

[...]

... Plaintiffs Kristian and Masterman allege that Comcast engages in conduct that excludes, prevents, or interferes with competition, including Comcast's refusal to provide programming access to competitors either before or after Comcast merged with AT & T Broadband in 2002. Plaintiffs seek certification of class actions comprised of individuals who subscribed to Comcast cable services in the Boston area at anytime from December 1999 to the present.

When Plaintiffs first subscribed for cable services, none of their service agreements contained an arbitration provision. In 2001, Comcast began including an arbitration provision in the terms and conditions governing the relationship between Comcast and its subscribers. These terms and conditions are contained, in part, in notices that inform subscribers at the time of cable installation—and at least annually thereafter—of the terms and conditions governing their subscriptions ("Policies & Practices"). Comcast included the Policies & Practices with each Boston area subscriber's invoice as a billing stuffer during the November 2001 billing cycle.

[. . .]

II.

[. . .]

Pursuant to the arbitration agreements at issue, Comcast filed motions to compel arbitration in both cases. . . .

[. . .]

. . . As the district court's order refusing to compel arbitration applied to both the *Rogers* and *Kristian* complaints, the two cases have been consolidated for purposes of this appeal.

[. . .]

III.

As noted, the district court found that the arbitration agreements in the 2002/2003 Policies & Practices did not apply retroactively. Below, in relevant part, is the 2002/2003 arbitration language at issue, set forth in bold face as it appears in the agreements:

> IF WE ARE UNABLE TO RESOLVE INFORMALLY ANY CLAIM OR DISPUTE RELATED TO OR ARISING OUT OF THIS AGREEMENT OR THE SERVICES PROVIDED, WE HAVE AGREED TO BINDING ARBITRATION EXCEPT AS PROVIDED BELOW. YOU MUST CONTACT US WITHIN ONE (1) YEAR OF THE DATE OF THE OCCURRENCE OF THE EVENT OR FACTS GIVING RISE TO A DISPUTE . . . OR YOU WAIVE THE RIGHT TO PURSUE A CLAIM BASED UPON SUCH EVENT, FACTS OR DISPUTE.

> THERE SHALL BE NO RIGHT OR AUTHORITY FOR ANY CLAIMS TO BE ARBITRATED ON A CLASS ACTION OR CONSOLIDATED BASIS OR ON BASES INVOLVING CLAIMS BROUGHT IN A PURPORTED REPRESENTATIVE CAPACITY ON BEHALF OF THE GENERAL PUBLIC (SUCH AS A PRIVATE ATTORNEY GENERAL), OTHER SUBSCRIBERS, OR OTHER PERSONS SIMILARLY SITUATED UNLESS YOUR STATE'S LAWS PROVIDE OTHERWISE.

The district court focused its attention on the first sentence of the first paragraph, in particular the phrase "the services provided":

> The inclusion of the word "the" before "services provided" indicates to the Court that the services being discussed are those specifically provided under "this agreement." It is also noteworthy that "the services provided" is mentioned immediately after "this agreement" without any qualifying language whatsoever that would indicate that the services do not refer to the agreement itself. These two factors, acting in combination, lead the Court to believe that the phrase "*the* services provided" refers to specific services provided under the particular subscriber agreement at issue, and does not refer to services in a general sense.

The district court buttressed this interpretation of the arbitration clause with two other points.

First, the district court cited cases where certain contractual language meant retroactive effect. . . . The district court also cited cases where the arbitration provision explicitly addressed retroactivity. . . . Because the 2002/2003 arbitration agreements were not phrased like the agreements in any of the cases it cited, the district court found that the ambiguity of the agreements should be interpreted against Comcast in light of the policy of construing adhesion contracts strictly against the drafter. The district court expressly found that the arbitration agreements were contracts of adhesion. . . .

Second, the district court highlighted the presence of a statute of limitations provision found in the sentence immediately after the sentence containing the phrase "the services provided". In the district court's view, if the arbitration agreements had retroactive effect, the statute of limitations provision would act as a waiver of all disputes arising one-year prior to the arbitration provision in the 2002 Policies & Practices. Such a waiver would be a "significant departure from the parties' prior agreements, which did not even contain an arbitration provision." The district court stated that "there is no indication that the phrase 'the services provided' was intended to have such a dramatic effect on the parties' pre-existing contractual relationships."

We cannot agree with the district court's reading of the arbitration agreements. As an initial matter, the district court ignored a large number of cases where arbitration agreements contained language specifically *excluding* retroactive effect. For example, in *Security Watch, Inc. v. Sentinel Systems, Inc.,* 176 F.3d 369 (6th Cir.1999), the Sixth Circuit found no retroactivity in an arbitration clause that read " '[t]he parties shall follow these dispute resolution processes in connection with all disputes, controversies or claims ... arising out of or relating to the Products furnished pursuant to *this* Agreement or acts or omissions of Distributor or AT & T under *this* Agreement.' " *Id.* at 372 (emphasis added). In *Choice Security Systems, Inc. v. AT & T Corp.,* 141 F.3d 1149 (Table), 1998 WL 153254 (1st Cir. Feb. 25, 1998) (unpublished), we found no retroactivity in an arbitration provision that read "all disputes ... arising out of or relating to the products furnished pursuant to *this* Agreement." *Id.* at *1 (emphasis added). . . . In these cases, the language in the arbitration clause unmistakably limits arbitration to what is covered by the agreements—*e.g.,* "pursuant to this Agreement." These arbitration clauses do not contain the additional language found in the clauses at issue here—"any claim or dispute arising out of this agreement *or the services provided*"(emphasis added). Read most naturally, the phrase "or the services provided" covers claims or disputes that do not arise "out of this agreement" and hence are not limited by the time frame of the agreements.

In rejecting this natural reading, the district court, as noted, placed an undue amount of emphasis on the article "the" in the phrase "the services provided", which appears immediately after the reference to "this agreement". ("If we are unable to resolve informally any claim or dispute related to or arising out of the agreement or the services provided, we have agreed to binding arbitration except as provided below.") In effect, this reading adds to the phrase "the services provided" words of limitation—"under this agreement." There is no justification for rewriting the arbitration provision in this way. Additionally, because the word "services" is defined in the Policies & Practices, it is grammatically correct to include the definite article "the" before "services" in order to signify that "services" refer to "services" as defined in the text, rather than services in a general sense.

[. . .]

Furthermore, the district court incorrectly relied on the state contract principle requiring contracts of adhesion to be construed strictly against the drafter. Ordinarily, given the strong federal policy of resolving any doubts concerning arbitrability in favor of arbitration, any ambiguity created by the change in language from 2001 to 2002/2003 should be resolved in favor of finding arbitrability. *See Moses H. Cone Memorial Hospital v. Mercury Construction Corp.,* 460 U.S. 1, 24–25, 103 S.Ct. 927, 74 L.Ed.2d 765 (1983) ("[A]s a matter of federal law, any doubts concerning the scope of arbitrable issues should be resolved in favor of arbitration."). While the district court acknowledged this principle—as proffered by Comcast—in its discussion, it chose not to apply it. Instead, it concluded that "[i]n light of the fact that the subscriber agreements at issue in this case are unquestionably adhesion contracts, this Court considers it appropriate to hold the defendants to the words they chose to use in drafting the arbitration provisions."

To support this choice, the district court cited *Paul Revere Variable Annuity Ins. Co. v. Kirschhofer,* 226 F.3d 15 (1st Cir.2000). There, we acknowledged that "[o]ne important constraint is that the federal policy favoring arbitration does not totally displace ordinary rules of contract interpretation. Thus, numerous courts have employed the tenet of *contra proferentem* in construing ambiguities in arbitration agreements against the drafters." . . . The petitioners in *Paul Revere:*

> concede[d] that the *contra proferentem* tenet properly applies to such questions as whether a party has entered an arbitration agreement or whether an arbitration agreement is enforceable *vel non* [;] they nonetheless maintain[ed] that it ha[d] no application to questions touching upon the scope of an arbitration agreement.

. . . In response, we held that "generally speaking, the presumption in favor of arbitration applies to the resolution of scope questions. . . . A scope question arises when the parties have a contract that provides for arbitration of some issues and it is unclear whether a specific dispute falls within that contract." . . .

Here, Plaintiffs argue that the arbitration agreements are not enforceable as to their particular antitrust claims because the arbitration agreements do not apply retroactively. Plaintiffs concede that the arbitration agreements are generally valid. Put another way, Plaintiffs argue that their antitrust claims do not fall within the scope of the arbitration agreements as a result of non-retroactivity. Plaintiffs are in fact raising a scope question. . . . Where the federal policy favoring arbitration is in tension with the tenet of *contra proferentem* for adhesion contracts, and there is a scope question at issue, the federal policy favoring arbitration trumps the state contract law tenet. For this reason as well, the district court erred in ruling that the arbitration agreements did not apply retroactively to the antitrust claims of Plaintiffs.

Therefore, we conclude that the 2002/2003 arbitration agreements, like their 2001 predecessor, do have retroactive effect. Thus, we must address the other arguments advanced by Plaintiffs in opposition to the enforcement of the arbitration agreements.

[. . .]

V.

Plaintiffs contend that the 2002/2003 arbitration agreements should be invalidated because many of their provisions prevent Plaintiffs from vindicating their statutory rights. Plaintiffs' "vindication of statutory rights" arguments reflect "the presumption that arbitration provides a fair and adequate mechanism for enforcing statutory rights." *Rosenberg*, 170 F.3d at 14; *see also Mitsubishi Motors Corp. v. Soler Chrysler–Plymouth, Inc.*, 473 U.S. 614, 637, 105 S.Ct. 3346, 87 L.Ed.2d 444 (1985) ("[S]o long as the prospective litigant effectively may vindicate its statutory cause of action in the arbitral forum, the statute will continue to serve both its remedial and deterrent function.") Unless the arbitral forum provided by a given agreement provides for the fair and adequate enforcement of a party's statutory rights, the arbitral forum runs afoul of this presumption and loses its claim as a valid alternative to traditional litigation.

Plaintiffs assert that the arbitration agreements prevent them from vindicating their statutory rights because the agreements: (1) provide for limited discovery; (2) establish a shortened statute of limitations period; (3) bar recovery of treble damages; (4) prevent recovery of attorney's fees; and (5) prohibit the use of class mechanisms. Before undertaking our analysis of the five provisions in the arbitration agreements that Plaintiffs find objectionable, we must explain some preliminary considerations that inform the analysis of each of their vindication of statutory rights claims.

A. *"Questions of Arbitrability"*

i. *The Supreme Court trilogy*

a. *Howsam*

In analyzing a given vindication of statutory rights claim, we must first decide who the proper decision maker is for such a claim: an arbitrator or a court. The touchstone for deciding this question is *Howsam v. Dean Witter Reynolds, Inc.*, 537 U.S. 79, 123 S.Ct. 588, 154 L.Ed.2d 491 (2002). In *Howsam,* the Court "focuse[d] upon an arbitration rule of the National Association of Securities Dealers (NASD)" involving a six-year statute of limitations.... Dean Witter had asked the district court "to declare that the dispute was 'ineligible for arbitration' because it was more than six years old." ... The Supreme Court had to decide "whether a court or an NASD arbitrator should apply the [NASD's] rule to the underlying controversy," ...—the type of threshold decision we must make here for each of Plaintiffs' vindication of statutory rights claims.

The Court began its analysis with the observation that " 'arbitration is a matter of contract and a party cannot be required to submit to arbitration any dispute which he has not agreed so to submit.' "... The Court continued:

> Although the Court has also long recognized and enforced a liberal federal policy favoring arbitration agreements, it has made clear that there is an exception to this policy: The question whether the parties have submitted a particular dispute to arbitration, *i.e.*, the *"question of arbitrability,"* is an issue for judicial determination unless the parties clearly and unmistakably provide otherwise.

... This statement requires close scrutiny because it includes references to three distinct elements: (1) the federal policy favoring arbitration agreements, which has nothing to do with the intent of the parties that have entered into an arbitration agreement; (2) the exception to this policy—based on *the presumed intent* of the contracting parties—that the question of whether the parties have submitted a particular dispute to arbitration (the "question of arbitrability") is an issue for judicial determination; and (3) a clear and unmistakable expression of actual intent by the contracting parties that they want an arbitrator rather than a court to decide whether they have submitted a particular dispute to arbitration.

This second element, involving the presumed intent of the contracting parties favoring judicial determination of whether a particular dispute has been submitted to arbitration, is described by the Court as "the interpretive rule". The Court in *Howsam* had to decide "whether application of the NASD time limit provision falls into the scope of this ... interpretive rule." ... If the Court decided that the interpretive rule applied, a court would decide the applicability of the six-year statute of limitations. If the Court decided that the interpretive rule did not apply, the general policy favoring arbitration would govern, and the arbitrator would decide the applicability of the statute of limitations.

In rejecting the application of the interpretive rule to the dispute over the applicability of the statute of limitations, the Court explained that it would be wrong to view too broadly the presumption that the parties to an arbitration agreement intend that a court rather than an arbitrator will decide whether the parties have submitted a particular dispute to arbitration. As the Court explained:

> Linguistically speaking, one might call any potentially dispositive gateway question a "question of arbitrability," for its answer will determine whether the underlying controversy will proceed to arbitration on the merits. The Court's case law, however, makes clear that, for purposes of applying the interpretive rule [that a court rather than an arbitrator should decide whether the parties have submitted a particular dispute to arbitration], the phrase "question of arbitrability" has a far more limited scope. The Court

has found the phrase applicable in the kind of narrow circumstance where contracting parties would likely have expected a court to have decided the gateway matter, where they are not likely to have thought that they had agreed that an arbitrator would do so, and consequently, where reference of the gateway dispute to the court avoids the risk of forcing parties to arbitrate a matter that they may well not have agreed to arbitrate.

... The cornerstone here is an assumption about the intent of the contracting parties to an arbitration agreement, in "the kind of narrow circumstances where contracting parties would likely have expected a court to have decided the gateway matter." ... In these narrow circumstances, the gateway dispute poses a "question of arbitrability", meaning that a court, rather than an arbitrator, decides whether the parties have submitted the particular dispute to arbitration.

Howsam described two categories of disputes where we presume that *courts rather than arbitrators* should resolve the gateway dispute: (1) disputes "about whether the parties are bound by a given arbitration clause"; and (2) disagreements "about whether an arbitration clause in a concededly binding contract applies to a particular type of controversy." ... Examples of the former include whether an arbitration contract binds parties that did not sign the agreement; and whether an arbitration agreement survived a corporate merger and bound the subsequent corporation.... Examples of the latter include whether a labor-management layoff controversy was covered by the arbitration clause of a collective-bargaining agreement; and whether a clause providing for arbitration of various grievances covers claims for damages for breach of a no-strike agreement. *See AT & T Technologies, Inc. v. Comm. Workers of Am.*, 475 U.S. 643, 106 S.Ct. 1415, 89 L.Ed.2d 648 (1986)....

The Court also "found the phrase 'question of arbitrability' *not* applicable in other kinds of general circumstances where parties would likely expect that an arbitrator would decide the gateway matter." ... For example, " '[P]rocedural' questions which grow out of the dispute and bear on its final disposition" are presumptively *not* for the judge, but for an arbitrator to decide.... So too, the presumption is that the arbitrator should decide " 'allegation[s] of waiver, delay, or a like defense to arbitrability.' "... Citing the comments to the Revised Uniform Arbitration Act of 2000, the Court elaborated on this statement, stating:

> in the absence of an agreement to the contrary, issues of substantive arbitrability ... are for a court to decide and issues of procedural arbitrability, *i.e.* whether prerequisites such as time limits, notice, laches, estoppel, and other conditions precedent to an obligation to arbitrate have been met, are for the arbitrators to decide.

... Finally, the *Howsam* decision invoked the concept of comparative expertise:

> the NASD arbitrators, comparatively more expert about the meaning of their own rule, are comparatively better able to interpret and apply it. In the absence of any statement to the contrary in the arbitration agreement, it is

reasonable to infer that the parties intended the agreement to reflect that understanding. And for the law to assume an expectation that aligns (1) decisionmaker with (2) comparative expertise will help better to secure a fair and expeditious resolution of the underlying controversy....

... Based on this reasoning, the Court concluded that "the NASD's time limit rule falls within the class of gateway procedural disputes that do not present what our cases have called 'questions of arbitrability.' And the strong pro-court [as decision maker] presumption as to the parties' likely intent does not apply." ...

b. *Pacificare* and *Bazzle*

In the wake of *Howsam,* the Court decided two additional cases, *PacifiCare Health Systems, Inc. v. Book,* 538 U.S. 401, 123 S.Ct. 1531, 155 L.Ed.2d 578 (2003), and *Green Tree Financial Corp. v. Bazzle,* 539 U.S. 444, 123 S.Ct. 2402, 156 L.Ed.2d 414 (2003), that must also inform our analysis of the proper decision maker for the vindication of statutory rights claims before us. In *PacifiCare,* a group of physicians brought claims against a number of health-care management organizations ("HMOs"), including a RICO claim. The HMOs sought to compel arbitration.... The physicians opposed arbitration on the ground that they could not obtain "meaningful relief" in arbitration for their claims under the RICO statute, which authorizes treble damages, because the arbitration provision prohibited the awarding of punitive damages.... The HMOs asserted that there was no question of arbitrability, "and hence [the dispute] should have been decided by an arbitrator, rather than a court, in the first instance." ... They also asserted in the alternative that if there was a question of arbitrability, the remedial limitation at issue did not require invalidation of the arbitration agreements.... The Court ultimately reached neither of the HMOs' positions, concluding "that it would be premature for us to address these questions at this time." ... That was so because of a crucial ambiguity in the arbitration agreements.

The arbitration agreements at issue in *PacifiCare* explicitly prohibited the recovery of punitive damages, not treble damages.... This fact, coupled with existing precedent, convinced the Court that there was too much legal ambiguity to conclude that there was a question of arbitrability; as a result, the Court compelled arbitration. The Court reasoned that:

> since we do not know how the arbitrator will construe the remedial limitations, the questions whether they render the parties' agreements unenforceable and whether it is for courts or arbitrators to decide enforceability in the first instance are unusually abstract.... the proper course is to compel arbitration.

... Because the underlying meaning of the arbitration agreement was unclear with respect to the availability of treble damages, it was also unclear whether that agreement conflicted with the RICO statute. Since such a conflict might threaten the validity of the arbitration agreements, "we should not, on the basis of 'mere speculation' that an arbitrator might interpret these ambiguous agreements in a manner that casts their enforceability into doubt, take upon ourselves the authority to decide the antecedent question of how the ambiguity is to be resolved." . . . Given the presumption in favor of arbitration, a court should not foreclose the operation of that presumption by deciding that there is a question of arbitrability when there is the possibility that an arbitrator's decision in the first instance would obviate the need for judicial decision-making. . . .

In *Bazzle,* decided soon after *PacifiCare,* the Court once again confronted the significance of ambiguity in an arbitration agreement. *Bazzle* concerned "contracts between a commercial lender and its customers, each of which contains a clause providing for arbitration of all contract-related disputes." . . . The Supreme Court of South Carolina held that the arbitration clauses were silent as to whether arbitration could take place on a class basis, and that South Carolina law permitted class arbitration under those circumstances. . . . The Supreme Court was "faced at the outset with a problem concerning the contracts' silence. Are the contracts in fact silent, or do they forbid class arbitration?" . . . The lender asserted that the arbitration language prohibited class arbitration; the Court disagreed. It held that because the literal terms of the agreement did not resolve the class arbitration question, *i.e.,* the terms were ambiguous, the case "present[ed] a disputed issue of contract interpretation." . . . Drawing on *Howsam,* the Court noted that "the question here—does not fall into [the] narrow exception" described in *Howsam.* . . . That is, "[i]n certain limited circumstances, courts assume that the parties intended courts, not arbitrators, to decide a particular arbitration-related matter. . . . They include certain gateway matters, such as whether the parties have a valid arbitration agreement at all or whether a concededly binding arbitration clause applies to a certain type of controversy." . . . The contract interpretation question posed in *Bazzle* did not fall into this narrow exception:

> Rather the relevant question here is *what kind of arbitration proceeding* the parties agreed to. That question does not concern a state statute or judicial procedures. It concerns contract interpretation and arbitration procedures. Arbitrators are well situated to answer that question.

. . . In essence, the *Bazzle* court applied principles derived from *Howsam* and *PacifiCare.* From *Howsam,* it considered and rejected the interpretive rule (an exception to the federal policy favoring arbitration) that courts assume that the parties intended courts, not arbitrators, to decide certain arbitration-related matters. Confronted with a dispute about what the arbitration language meant with respect to the availability of class arbitration (an uncertainty analogous to the ambiguity addressed in *PacifiCare*), the Court concluded that an arbitrator, not a judge, should decide what kind of arbitration proceeding the parties had agreed to.

ii. Applying the "trilogy"

To reiterate, Plaintiffs assert that the arbitration agreements prevent them from vindicating their statutory rights in the following ways. The agreements: (1) provide for limited discovery; (2) establish a shortened statute of limitations period; (3) bar recovery of treble damages; (4) prevent recovery of attorney's fees; and (5) prohibit class arbitration. Comcast contends that none of these assertions raise a question of arbitrability.

We must first decide whether an arbitrator or a court should resolve each of the vindication of statutory rights claims, *i.e.*, whether a question of arbitrability is *actually* raised. That inquiry requires us to apply the principles we have culled from the Court's decisions in *Howsam, Pacifi-Care*, and *Bazzle*. Then, if a question of arbitrability is indeed raised by any of Plaintiffs' assertions, we must decide "the merits" of that assertion. By "the merits" we mean the question of whether the particular challenge raised by Plaintiffs to the arbitration agreements is a valid defense to the demand for arbitration. By "the merits" we do *not* mean the "underlying dispute," *i.e.*, Plaintiffs' antitrust claims against Comcast.

B. Howsam's *Clear Questions of Arbitrability*

We conclude that none of Plaintiffs' claims falls into either of the two categories of clear questions of arbitrability detailed in *Howsam*. Plaintiffs describe their position generally as follows: "the Policies & Practices as a whole is valid. However, as applied to our antitrust claims, the arbitration agreement contained therein prevents us from obtaining statutorily guaranteed relief; therefore, the arbitration clause is invalid as applied to our antitrust claims."

The two types of clear questions of arbitrability described by the Court in *Howsam* are: (1) disputes about whether the parties are bound by a given arbitration clause; and (2) disputes about whether an arbitration clause in a concededly binding contract applies to a particular type of controversy.... While earlier we categorized Plaintiffs' non-retroactivity claim as an argument about the "scope" of the arbitration agreements, their vindication of statutory rights claims do not fit into either of *Howsam's* categories. The examples provided by the *Howsam* court bear this out.... The former category concerns whether there is a binding arbitration agreement at all, *e.g.*, are non-signatories of an arbitration agreement bound by it? Here, there is no question that the Policies & Practices, which includes the arbitration provisions, establishes a valid contractual relationship between Comcast and each of its subscribers. Plaintiffs do not challenge generally the validity of the Policies & Practices, the requirement to arbitrate, or the five particular rules governing arbitration here. Rather, Plaintiffs rely on the specific circumstances of their case, *i.e.*, their antitrust claims, in challenging Comcast's demand for arbitration.

The second *Howsam* category also does not describe Plaintiffs' claims. That category involves disputes over whether a particular type of controversy is covered by a concededly valid arbitration agreement. Here, Plaintiffs do not assert that the arbitration provisions of the Policies & Practices do not apply to antitrust claims. Rather, Plaintiffs assert that arbitration subject to the provisions at issue shields Comcast from antitrust liability, and hence conflicts with the statutes providing for such liability.

In short, *Howsam's* two categories of clear questions of arbitrability do not tell us whether Plaintiffs have raised questions of arbitrability. Still, even without the benefit of a dispositive Supreme Court precedent, there are useful guides in the precedents we have discussed and in others.

C. Limited Discovery

The language in the arbitration agreements addressing discovery states that "Moreover, participating in arbitration may result in limited discovery." Plaintiffs contend that the language constraining discovery prevents them from obtaining the amount of discovery that they could expect to receive if discovery were conducted in the courts. But the Supreme Court has already foreclosed limited discovery as a ground for opposing the enforcement of an arbitration clause. In *Gilmer v. Interstate/Johnson Lane Corp.*, 500 U.S. 20, 111 S.Ct. 1647, 114 L.Ed.2d 26 (1991), the Supreme Court confronted this very argument in the context of an age discrimination arbitration dispute. The Court stated that "[i]t is unlikely, however, that age discrimination claims require more extensive discovery than other claims that we have found to be arbitrable, such as RICO and *antitrust* claims," and rejected the plaintiff's discovery argument. . . . Given this precedent, there is no need to decide anew whether limited discovery raises a question of arbitrability. It does not. Moreover, the Court's decision in *Gilmer* conforms to the interpretive principles the Court detailed in *Howsam, PacifiCare* and *Bazzle*. Any dispute over discovery would be procedural in nature, and therefore left for an arbitrator to resolve.

D. Limitations Period

The Clayton Act . . . and the Massachusetts Antitrust Act . . . provide a four-year limitations period for antitrust claims. In direct conflict with the statutory limitations period, the 2002/2003 arbitration agreements state that "you must contact us within one (1) year of the date of the occurrence of the event or facts giving rise to a dispute . . . or you waive the right to pursue a claim based upon such event, facts or dispute." Plaintiffs oppose arbitration of their antitrust claims based on the basis of this direct conflict between the antitrust statutes and the arbitration provisions.

It is tempting to rely on the precedent established in *Howsam*—where the Court ruled that an arbitrator is the proper decision maker for disputes concerning the applicability of the arbitrator's own time limits— to conclude that this conflict does not pose a question of arbitrability. . . . The temptation to rely on *Howsam* is buttressed by our own precedent, specifically *Marie v. Allied Home Mortgage Corp.*, 402 F.3d 1 (1st Cir. 2005). In *Marie,* we confronted a limitations clause contained in an arbitration agreement itself, rather than in the arbitrator's governing rules. . . . Here, we are also faced with a statute of limitations contained in a valid arbitration agreement. However, there is one significant difference between the situation we face and the circumstances in *Howsam* and *Marie,* which prevents us from simply applying here the rule established in those cases.

In both *Howsam* and *Marie,* the limitations period did not conflict with any other statute of limitations.... In *Howsam,* the question was whether the arbitrator's own time limit of six years applied to a dispute allegedly brought outside of the six-year window.... In *Marie,* the question was whether one of the parties had complied with the 60–day time limit set forth in the arbitration agreement.... In other words, in neither case was the statute of limitations in conflict with a statutory limitations period applicable to the particular claims at issue. Instead, in *Howsam* and *Marie* there were questions of whether a statute of limitations applied to a particular factual circumstance. That is a different type of question than the one we face here, which is whether a statute of limitations found in the arbitration agreement must yield to a statutorily mandated statute of limitations.

Nevertheless, we are not without some guidance from these decisions. In particular, in *Marie,* after noting that a dispute over a statute of limitations "is the sort of procedural prerequisite that is presumed to be for the arbitrator," we also explained that:

> While the time limit in *Howsam* was in the arbitrator's own rules rather than in the contract itself, this makes no difference. The arbitrator might be expected to have comparative expertise in determining the meaning of these sorts of contractual limitations provisions.... And ... *consideration of this kind of procedural provision may entangle the court in issues that go properly to the merits of the dispute, which are for the arbitrator.* ([E]mphasis added.)

... Comcast points out that both of Plaintiffs' complaints allege antitrust violations committed by Comcast before it promulgated the 2002/2003 Policies & Practices. But Comcast argues that the complaints are actually based on *ongoing* injury, rather than discrete events in the past. While Comcast raises this argument to challenge the view that it seeks retroactive application of the arbitration agreements, we can still consider the relevance of the ongoing injury inquiry to the question of arbitrability.

Ongoing injury has traditionally been understood to toll a statute of limitations under certain circumstances.... To determine: (1) whether Plaintiffs in fact suffer from an ongoing injury as a result of Comcast's allegedly illegal acts; and (2) whether such an injury, if it exists, tolls the statute of limitations contained in the Policies & Practices, would require an examination of the "merits of the case", *i.e.,* the facts, the province of the arbitrator.... Moreover, the statute of limitations defense is an affirmative defense.... Affirmative defenses often involve factual questions that *do* touch on the merits of a case. Indeed, *Howsam* placed " 'allegation [s] of waiver, delay, or a like defense to arbitrability' " squarely in the purview of the arbitrator.... For these reasons, we conclude that Plaintiffs' challenge to the statute of limitations contained in the 2002/2003 Policies & Practices does not raise a question of arbitrability.

[. . .]

VI.

[. . .]

For the reasons stated, the district court's holding that the arbitration clause in the 2002/2003 Policies & Practices, in its entirety, does not apply to Plaintiffs' antitrust claims is *reversed.* We *remand* for further proceedings not inconsistent with this opinion. The parties shall bear their own costs.

So ordered.

NOTES AND QUESTIONS

1. Distinguish between questions of arbitrability, gateway issues, and an interpretative rule. How do these concepts fit into the court's reasoning and into its view of the U.S. Supreme Court's decisional law on arbitration?

2. Which actor decides whether an arbitration agreement contains an ambiguity and which actor resolves the ambiguity?

3. Do you agree with the First Circuit's assessment of *PacifiCare*? How or what does it add to the U.S. Supreme Court's evolving decisional law on arbitration?

4. What does the court mean when it refers to a "scope" dispute? How does that concept fit into the *Howsam-Bazzle* decisional law?

5. How is *Kristian* a consumer arbitration case?

6. Is there a valid arbitration agreement between Comcast and its customers? Why? If so, what impact does it have on jurisdictional questions?

7. When is an arbitration agreement fair in a consumer setting? Who makes that determination?

8. Does subject-matter arbitrability play any role in the court's decision?

9. What is the function of a court in arbitration in light of *Howsam* and *Bazzle*?

10. Is it fair to speak of the arbitrator's decisional sovereignty?

* * *

Recent Rulings Antagonistic To Class Action Waivers

In *In re Am. Express Merchants Litigation*, 554 F.3d 300 (2d Cir. 2009), the Second Circuit invalidated a class action waiver because the waiver would have prevented a group of small merchants from pursuing their antitrust claims against American Express. The court made the rather extraordinary statement that enforcement of the waiver "would be incompatible with the federal substantive law of arbitration." You might want to try to explain what was meant by that statement, especially in light of the U.S. Supreme Court's interpretation of FAA § 2 and its creation of a federal judicial policy in favor of arbitration. The Second Circuit also referred to *Green Tree Fin. Corp.–Ala. v. Randolph*, 531 U.S. 79 (2000), emphasizing the importance of costs in upholding arbitration agreements between economically disparate parties. Although the allocation of costs is a consideration in assessing the validity of arbitration agreements, the *Randolph* Court was hardly enthusiastic about creating a possible means of challenging the enforceability of arbitral clauses on such a basis. Even though it identified relevant cases, the Second Circuit seems to have adjusted their significance to suit its own doctrinal ends. The ruling remains outside the established mainstream; it deviates from the acknowledged standard. It should, therefore, have limited precedential value.

Relatedly, in *Chalk v. T–Mobile USA, Inc.*, 560 F.3d 1087 (9th Cir. 2009), the Ninth Circuit held that a class action waiver in an arbitration agreement was substantively unconscionable under Oregon contract law, and, therefore, unenforceable. The court reiterated the basic tenets of the California view that such waivers prevented consumers with monetarily modest claims from being able to recover and vindicate their legal rights. The facts involved the purchase of a "pc card" to obtain wireless service. When a problem of compatibility eventually emerged with use, technical support from the manufacturer was unavailing and the retailer provide no useful assistance. The small individual losses demanded the aggregation of claims. While the court determined that there was no procedural unconscionability, it concluded that the agreement "unreasonably favored" the company and that it was "inherently one-sided" and "prevented individuals from vindicating their rights." The arbitration agreement provided that the class action waiver could not be severed. Therefore, the court concluded, the invalidity of the waiver rendered the entire agreement unenforceable.

On this subject, *Gentry v. Superior Court*, 42 Cal.4th 443, 64 Cal. Rptr.3d 773, 165 P.3d 556 (2007), is essentially controlling: "[A]lthough '[c]lass action and arbitration waivers are not, in the abstract, exculpatory clauses,'...such waivers can be exculpatory in practical terms because [they] can make it very difficult for those injured by unlawful conduct to pursue a legal remedy." The California state Supreme Court emphasized generally the "real world obstacles" to the "vindication of rights." It believed that a finding of unconscionability against class action waivers in arbitration agreements was sometimes warranted when modest individual claims could not be processed otherwise, members of the class could be retaliated against as individuals, and class standing allowed consumers to be better apprised of their legal rights. Do you agree with the reasoning and the conclusion the court reaches? Do these aspects of the opinion violate the federal policy underlying FAA § 2? Whose best interest does the remedy of class action serve? Lawyers, commercial competitors, or consumers? Should the trend in California and jurisdictions in the western United States be subject to federal preemption? Be that as it may, *Gentry* was followed in *Franco v. Athens Disposal Co., Inc.*, 171 Cal.App.4th 1277, 90 Cal.Rptr.3d 539 (2009).

Institutional Initiatives in Consumer Arbitration

In 1998, the Council of Better Business Bureaus, Inc. (CBBB) made public its position on binding, pre-dispute arbitration clauses in consumer contracts. The policy, adopted by the CBBB membership, acknowledged that arbitration often is a highly effective means of resolving disputes between businesses and consumers, but emphasized that ADR procedures, which restrict a consumer's access to courts, should be voluntary. Accordingly, the nation's 135 Better Business Bureaus agreed to arbitrate consumer-business disputes only when the contract gave the consumer fair notice of the consequences of agreeing to arbitration and when the customer formally acknowledges its acceptance of the arbitration clause.

According to the CBBB, "pre-dispute, binding arbitration clauses" have been used historically in contracts involving two business entities or in collective bargaining, where both sides are represented by sophisticated negotiators. In more recent years, however, these clauses are appearing more frequently in consumer product and service contracts. The CBBB believes that it is essential that parties enter into these agreements voluntarily, with a clear understanding of what disputes will be subject to the arbitration agreement, what arbitration will cost, and what rights are compromised in return for the opportunity to arbitrate.

The obligation to arbitrate has frequently been buried in the contract and/or drafted poorly. As a result, "in these cases, it is difficult to say that the consumer's agreement to arbitrate is voluntary. Indeed, it is often a complete surprise to consumers when a dispute later arises and they discover the lengthy documents they signed included one of these clauses." When businesses use a binding pre-dispute arbitration clause and name the Better Business Bureau as Provider, they will be required to follow the BBB policy for fair disclosure to consumers and give the BBB notice when they draft such contract provisions.

JAMS/ENDISPUTE (now JAMS), a nationally recognized private provider of dispute resolution services, also announced in 1998 a new policy designed to achieve greater fairness in the resolution of consumer disputes. The substance of the new policy is contained in a document entitled "Minimum Standards of Procedural Fairness" which applies to binding consumer arbitrations conducted by JAMS/ENDISPUTE. It is also reflected in the organization's new "Financial Services Arbitration Rules and Procedures" which apply to both consumer and commercial disputes.

The new policy governs agreements for financial services between customers and credit institutions. The rule changes ensure that: consumers receive adequate notice of the arbitration agreement, arbitral clause is equally binding upon the parties, choice of arbitration does not result in a loss of legal remedies, arbitrators are neutral and consumers participate in the selection of the arbitrators and are not discouraged from using legal counsel in the proceedings, and basic discovery remains available in the process. Finally, the allocation of costs for the arbitration must not preclude consumer access to the arbitral procedure. "JAMS/ENDISPUTE requires compliance with . . . [this] minimum set of standards of procedural fairness before accepting an assignment to arbitrate billing, lending, and banking or credit-services-related disputes between companies and individual consumers." The minimum standards, however, do not apply "to the use of arbitration in resolving disputes arising from commercial transactions between a lender and commercial borrowers or a company and commercial customers."

The National Consumer Disputes Advisory Committee of the American Arbitration Association, composed of seventeen of the nation's leading consumer affairs, business, government affairs, and alternative dispute resolution experts, developed a national *Due Process Protocol for Mediation and Arbitration of Consumer Disputes*. The development of the *Protocol* is in response to the pronounced trend toward incorporation of out-of-court conflict resolution processes in standardized agreements presented to consumers of goods and services. The *Consumer Due Process Protocol* includes a Statement of Fifteen Principles and is intended to protect the rights of consumers who are required to resolve disputes outside of court. The dispute can relate to the following types of transactions: banking, credit cards, financial services, home construction and improvements, insurance, communications, and the purchase and lease of motor vehicles and other personal property.

The American Arbitration Association announced in 1998 its endorsement of the *Consumer Due Process Protocol*. To ensure fairness and equity for consumer disputes resolved through mediation and arbitration, the American Arbitration Association has adopted the following policy:

> It is the policy of the American Arbitration Association to administer cases in accordance with the law. In following the law, the Association, as a matter of policy, will administer consumer dispute resolution programs that meet the standards outlined in the Consumer Due Process Protocol. If the Association determines that a consumer dispute resolution program on its face substantially and materially deviates from the minimum standards of the Consumer Due Process Protocol, the Association may decline to administer cases under that program.

The co-chair of the Advisory Committee stated: "The use of arbitration and mediation to resolve disputes between consumers and providers of goods and services is spreading rapidly as cost and delay in traditional court proceedings become more and more burdensome. . . . The role of the American Arbitration Association, an independent dispute resolution institution, in developing these standards is particularly appropriate because consumer arbitration is usually founded on contract terms specified by the seller of goods or services without any opportunity for negotiation or input from the consumer." Another co-chair stated that: "I would expect it to become a national standard for dispute resolution providers as mediation and arbitration grow as options for resolving disputes."

Finally, a consumer advocate stated: "I believe the Protocol takes an important step toward protecting the rights of consumers who are forced, typically without their knowledge or consent, to give up their right to bring a court action when they are harmed by a marketplace transaction.... While I firmly believe that it is improper to foreclose court access for consumers, especially through the use of small-print clauses in standardized form contracts, I am hopeful that the Protocol will place consumers on a more equal footing with providers than has been the case thus far."

Due Process Protocol for the Mediation and Arbitration of Consumer Disputes

—Statement of Principles—

Principle 1. Fundamentally–Fair Process

All parties are entitled to a fundamentally-fair ADR process. As embodiments of fundamental fairness, these Principles should be observed in structuring ADR Programs.

Principle 2. Access to Information Regarding ADR Program

Providers of goods or services should undertake reasonable measures to provide Consumers with full and accurate information regarding Consumer ADR Programs. At the time the Consumer contracts for goods or services, such measures should include: (1) clear and adequate notice regarding the ADR provisions, including a statement indicating whether participation in the ADR Program is mandatory or optional; and (2) reasonable means by which Consumers may obtain additional information regarding the ADR Program. After a dispute arises, Consumers should have access to all information necessary for effective participation in ADR.

Principle 3. Independent and Impartial Neutral; Independent Administration

1. **Independent and Impartial Neutral.** All parties are entitled to a Neutral who is independent and impartial.

2. **Independent Administration.** If participation in mediation or arbitration is mandatory, the procedure should be administered by an independent ADR Institution. Administrative services should include: the maintenance of a panel of prospective Neutrals, facilitation of Neutral selection, collection and distribution of [the] Neutral's fees and expenses, oversight and implementation of ADR rules and procedures, and monitoring of Neutral qualifications, performance, and adherence to pertinent rules, procedures[,] and ethical standards.

3. **Standards for Neutrals.** The Independent ADR Institution should make reasonable efforts to ensure that Neutrals understand and conform to pertinent ADR rules, procedures[,] and ethical standards.

4. **Selection of Neutrals.** The Consumer and Provider should have an equal voice in the selection of Neutrals in connection with a specific dispute.

5. **Disclosure and Disqualification.** Beginning at the time of appointment, Neutrals should be required to disclose to the Independent ADR Institution any circumstance likely to affect impartiality, including any bias or financial or personal interest which might affect the result of the ADR proceeding, or any past or present relationship or experience with the parties or their representatives, including past ADR experiences. The Independent ADR Institution should communicate any such information to the parties and other Neutrals, if any. Upon objection of the party to continued service of the Neutral, the Independent ADR Institution should determine whether the Neutral should be disqualified and should inform the parties of its decision. The disclosure obligation of the Neutral and procedure for disqualification should continue throughout the period of appointment.

Principle 4.   *Quality and Competence of Neutrals*

All parties are entitled to competent, qualified Neutrals. Independent ADR Institutions are responsible for establishing and maintaining standards for Neutrals in ADR Programs they administer.

Principle 5.   *Small Claims*

Consumer ADR Agreements should make it clear that all parties retain the right to seek relief in a small claims court for disputes or claims within the scope of its jurisdiction.

Principle 6.   *Reasonable Cost*

1. **Reasonable Cost.** Providers of goods and services should develop ADR programs which entail reasonable cost to Consumers based on the circumstances of the dispute, including, among other things, the size and nature of the claim, the nature of goods or services provided, and the ability of the Consumer to pay. In some cases, this may require the Provider to subsidize the process.

2. **Handling of Payment.** In the interest of ensuring fair and independent Neutrals, the making of fee arrangements and the payment of fees should be administered on a rational, equitable[,] and consistent basis by the Independent ADR Institution.

Principle 7.   *Reasonably Convenient Location*

In the case of face-to-face proceedings, the proceedings should be conducted at a location which is reasonably convenient to both parties with due consideration of their ability to travel and other pertinent circumstances. If the parties are unable to agree on a location, the determination should be made by the Independent ADR Institution or by the Neutral.

Principle 8.   *Reasonable Time Limits*

ADR proceedings should occur within a reasonable time, without undue delay. The rules governing ADR should establish specific reasonable time periods for each step in the ADR process and, where necessary, set forth default procedures in the event a party fails to participate in the process after reasonable notice.

Principle 9.   *Right to Representation*

All parties participating in processes in ADR Programs have the right, at their own expense, to be represented by a spokesperson of their own choosing. The ADR rules and procedures should so specify.

Principle 10.   *Mediation*

The use of mediation is strongly encouraged as an informal means of assisting parties in resolving their own disputes.

Principle 11.   *Agreements to Arbitrate*

Consumers should be given:

a) clear and adequate notice of the arbitration provision and its consequences, including a statement of its mandatory or optional character;

b) reasonable access to information regarding the arbitration process, including basic distinctions between arbitration and court proceedings, related costs, and advice as to where they may obtain more complete information regarding arbitration procedures and arbitrator rosters;

c) notice of the option to make use of applicable small claims court procedures as an alternative to binding arbitration in appropriate cases; and,

d) a clear statement of the means by which the Consumer may exercise the option (if any) to submit disputes to arbitration or to [the] court process.

Principle 12.   *Arbitration Hearings*

1. **Fundamentally-Fair Hearing.** All parties are entitled to a fundamentally-fair arbitration hearing. This requires adequate notice of hearings and an opportunity to be heard and to present relevant evidence to impartial decision-makers. In some cases, such as some small claims, the requirement of fundamental fairness may be met by hearings conducted by electronic or telephonic means or by a submission of documents. However, the Neutral should have discretionary authority to require a face-to-face hearing upon the request of a party.

2. **Confidentiality in Arbitration.** Consistent with general expectations of privacy in arbitration hearings, the arbitrator should make reasonable efforts to maintain the privacy of the hearing to the extent permitted by applicable law. The arbitrator should also carefully consider claims of privilege and confidentiality when addressing evidentiary issues.

Principle 13.   *Access to Information*

No party should ever be denied the right to a fundamentally-fair process due to an inability to obtain information material to a dispute. Consumer ADR agreements which provide for binding arbitration should establish procedures for arbitrator-supervised exchange of information prior to arbitration, bearing in mind the expedited nature of arbitration.

Principle 14. Arbitral Remedies

The arbitrator should be empowered to grant whatever relief would be available in court under law or in equity.

Principle 15. Arbitration Awards

1. **Final and Binding Award; Limited Scope of Review.** The arbitrator's award should be final and binding, but subject to review in accordance with applicable statutes governing arbitration awards.

2. **Standards to Guide Arbitrator Decision–Making.** In making the award, the arbitrator should apply any identified, pertinent contract terms, statutes, and legal precedents.

3. **Explanation of Award.** At the timely request of either party, the arbitrator should provide a brief written explanation of the basis for the award. To facilitate such requests, the arbitrator should discuss the matter with the parties prior to the arbitration hearing.

NOTES AND QUESTIONS

1.   How impartial and objective are the arbitral institutions' pronouncements on consumer arbitration? Are they likely to lose business because of their high-mindedness? Is consumer arbitration a source of lucrative business? What is the objective of the institutional position? Is the mandate created impossible to satisfy?

2.   How would you explain "arbitration" to the average client? Can you develop a colloquial definition? How would you address the rights protection dilemma in arbitration? What would you advise on discovery, expert witnesses, testimony, cross-examination, and the application of law?

3.   Assess the AAA Protocol rules on impartiality and disclosure. Must all arbitrators be free of any "leanings"? What about the institutional administrator? Are there minimal qualifications for arbitrators? How do they become part of an institutional list? When is disclosure sufficient?

4.   Should consumer arbitral tribunals be weighted in favor of the consumer? By number? By disposition? By law applicable? Is reverse unfairness a solution to disparity of position?

5.   When is a hearing "fundamentally fair"? Do the rules guide you on this matter? Can effective structural safeguards be created?

6.   How significant is the choice of arbitrators? How would you proceed on this aspect of the process?

7.   When is notice of the agreement to arbitrate adequate and when are costs reasonable? Do these two factors establish and define due process in

consumer arbitration? Can a fair process ever allay the injustice of an unfair agreement?

8. Are consumers entitled to reasoned determinations in the award? Why? How?

9. How does the AAA Protocol protect statutory rights and procedural recourse in the form of class litigation and the awarding of exemplary damages?

10. Does the content of the AAA Protocol assist you in drafting a standard agreement for the arbitration of consumer disputes?

3. MARITIME ARBITRATION

The use of arbitration to resolve maritime disputes illustrates how arbitration is traditionally applied in specialized sectors. The resolution of maritime disputes can involve the application of law and interpretation of contract provisions. The rules of maritime law, however, are generally well-settled. Moreover, most maritime disputes involve factual controversies that require knowledge of maritime practices and associated technical fields. Typically, disputes arise from standard contracts for the carriage of goods by sea or for the sale, purchase, or repair of vessels.

Characteristic disputes include questions of whether a vessel in a time charter arrangement was seaworthy at the time of delivery; whether vessel officers were negligent in the storage of cargo during loading or discharging operations; whether vessel equipment was suitable or efficient; problems relating to the application of safe port/safe berths clauses and to the determination of liability for stevedore damage to vessels; and issues relating to cargo contamination.

In the main, these disputes do not require significant legal expertise, but rather technical knowledge of vessels, navigation, the operation of machinery, and personnel duties. The reliance on standardized practices and the self-contained and technical character of the area (as well as other factors) make arbitration an appropriate mechanism for the resolution of maritime claims.

Arbitrations can be conducted exclusively on the basis of written submissions, a "documents-only" arbitration. Under this procedure, the parties can appoint two arbitrators who either issue a joint award based on their review of the documents submitted by the parties or, in the event they disagree, have recourse to an umpire who hears the arbitrators and decides the matter. The parties to a "documents-only" arbitration can also appoint three arbitrators who will decide the matter by a majority.

London—like New York City—is a traditional venue for maritime arbitration, despite the possibility that English courts can review arbitral awards on the merits. English court practice and the Arbitration Acts 1979 and 1996 have attenuated considerably the prospect of judicial review of the substance of awards. In particular, the 1996 Act, which codifies the recent decisional law, essentially eliminates court supervision of the substance of awards except for manifestly erroneous interpretations of the law that amount to a denial of justice. Although the near elimination of the merits review procedure may result in a less consistent and unstable maritime law, the autonomy of arbitration and London's attractiveness as a center of maritime arbitration will be enhanced.

The London Maritime Arbitrators' Association (LMMA) provides services for maritime arbitration, including a set of rules known as "The LMAA Terms." "Documents-only" arbitrations constitute a major part of the maritime arbitration business in London because of their speed, efficiency, and economy. Such arbitrations usually are conducted within a six to twelve month period of time.

The LMAA also provides for expedited arbitral procedures. Expedited arbitrations are analogous to a small claims proceeding and apply to maritime disputes that involve less than $25,000. The expedited procedure includes a sole arbitrator, strict time-limits for pleadings, limited oral testimony, and excludes any possibility of appeal. Further, the LMAA can assist the parties in reaching a negotiated settlement of their disputes through its mediation and conciliation services.

Ordinary arbitral proceedings may involve a long or short oral hearing procedure. Under the short procedure, lawyers for the parties present their case to the arbitral tribunal in a few hours, while—in the long procedure—the oral presentation can take several days. Major arbitration cases involve complicated trial procedures and participation of senior counsel. Hearings can last for weeks or months and require substantial technical expertise. The use of sole arbitrators is becoming more popular for reasons of speed and economy, but this procedure may not provide the necessary expertise for deciding complex maritime disputes.

The Society of Maritime Arbitrators, Inc. (SMA) was founded in 1963 by individuals involved in maritime arbitration in New York. The SMA is a non-profit organization. It does not administer arbitral proceedings, but has promulgated rules for the conduct of maritime arbitrations. In their most recent version (May 10, 1994) (revised September 15, 2003), these Rules are meant to foster greater dispute resolution efficiency in maritime arbitration. In 1999, responding to market demand, the SMA promulgated mediation rules which can be used alone or in tandem with SMA arbitration rules. The SMA has also promulgated a *Code of Ethics* for its members and maintains a Committee on Professional Conduct for investigative purposes. Its membership, from which parties can select their arbitrators, consists of approximately 130 commercial people (surveyors, engineers, brokers, stevedores, shipbuilders, insurers, vessel operators, agents, and other experts), who hold longstanding (at least 10 years) and prominent positions in their field. The SMA fulfills a number of other professional and educational functions, including the publication of SMA awards through its Award Service. The standard clause for SMA Arbitration reads as follows:

Should any dispute arise out of this Charter, the Matter in dispute shall be referred to three persons at New York, one to be appointed by each of the parties hereto, and the third by the two so chosen; their decision or that of any two of them shall be final, and for purpose of enforcing any award, this agreement may be made a rule of the Court. This Charter shall be governed by the Federal Maritime Law of the United States. The proceedings shall be conducted in accordance with the Rules of the Society of Maritime Arbitrators, Inc. (including Section 2—Consolidation). The arbitrators shall be members of the Society of Maritime Arbitrators, Inc.

See MARITIME ARBITRATION IN NEW YORK 1–3 (3d ed. 1994).

[The following documents, consisting of the SMA Arbitration Rules, the SMA Rules for Shortened Arbitration Procedures, and the SMA Code of Ethics, are reproduced with the permission of the Society of Maritime Arbitrations, Inc.]

I.

Maritime Arbitration Rules

SOCIETY OF MARITIME ARBITRATORS, INC.

PREAMBLE

INTERPRETATION AND APPLICATION OF RULES

The powers and duties of the Arbitrator(s) shall be interpreted and applied in accordance with these Rules and Title 9 of the United States Code. Whenever there is more than one Arbitrator, and a difference arises among them concerning the meaning or application of these Rules, the difference shall be resolved by majority vote or by an Umpire, where appropriate.

In all matters not expressly addressed in these Rules, the Arbitrators(s) shall act in the spirit of these Rules and make every effort to ensure that an award is legally enforceable.

[. . .]

I.   RULES APART OF THE ARBITRATION AGREEMENT

Section 1. Agreement of Parties

Wherever parties have agreed to arbitration under the Rules of the Society of Maritime Arbitrators, Inc., these Rules, <u>including any amendment</u>(s) in force on the date of the agreement to arbitrate shall be binding on the parties and constitute <u>an integral part of that agreement.</u>

Nevertheless, except for those Rules which empower the Arbitrators to administer the arbitration proceedings, the parties may mutually alter or modify these Rules.

Unless stipulated in advance to the contrary, the parties, by consenting to these Rules, agree that the Award issued may be published by the Society of Maritime Arbitrators, Inc. and/or its correspondents.

Section 2. Consolidation

The parties agree to consolidate proceedings relating to contract disputes with other parties which involve common questions of fact or law and/or arise in substantial part from the same maritime transactions or series of related transactions, provided all contracts incorporate SMA Rules.

Unless all parties agree to a sole Arbitrator, consolidated disputes are to be heard by a maximum of three Arbitrators to be appointed as agreed by all parties or, failing such agreement, as ordered by the Court.

II. TRIBUNALS

Section 3. Name of Tribunal

The "Panel" is any Tribunal created under the parties' agreement, to resolve disputes by arbitration under these Rules.

Section 4. Roster of Arbitrators

The SMA shall establish and maintain a roster of persons with qualifications to act as Maritime Arbitrators from which Arbitrators may be chosen.

Section 5. Office of Tribunal

Office of the Panel—Depending upon the number of Arbitrators, the office of the Panel shall be as follows:

(a) *Sole Arbitrator*—The home address or place of business of the sole arbitrator.

(b) *Two Arbitrators*—The home or business address of either of the Arbitrators, as decided by them.

(c) *Three Arbitrators*—The home or business address of the Arbitrator chosen by the other Panel members to act as Chairman of the Panel.

III. INITIATION OF THE ARBITRATION

Section 6. Initiation Under an Arbitration Agreement

Any party to an agreement for arbitration under SMA Rules may initiate an arbitration by giving written notice to the other party of its demand for arbitration and naming its chosen arbitrator.

In its demand for arbitration, the party initiating the process shall set forth the nature of the dispute, the amount of damages involved, if any, and the remedy sought.

The parties shall be free to amend or add to their claims until the proceedings are closed pursuant to Section 25.

Section 7. Fixing of Locality

The arbitration is to be held in the City of New York at a location chosen by the Panel, unless otherwise agreed by the parties.

The parties shall be given sufficient notice to enable them to appear or be represented at the proceedings.

IV. Appointment of Arbitrators

Section 8. Disqualification

No person shall serve as an Arbitrator who has or who has had a financial or personal interest in the outcome of the arbitration or who has acquired from an interested source detailed prior knowledge of the matter in dispute.

Section 9. Disclosure by Arbitrators of Disqualifying Circumstances

Prior to the first hearing or initial submissions, all Arbitrators are required to disclose any circumstance which could impair their ability to render an unbiased award based solely upon an objective and impartial consideration of the evidence presented to the Panel.

Such disclosure shall include close personal ties and business relations with any one of:

(a) the parties to the arbitration;

(b) other affiliates or associated companies of the parties;

(c) counsel for the parties;

(d) the other Arbitrators on the Panel.

No Arbitrator shall accept an appointment or sit on a Panel, where the Arbitrator or the Arbitrator's current employer has a direct or indirect interest in the outcome of the arbitration.

Upon receipt of the disclosure statement(s) from the Arbitrator(s), the parties may accept the Panel or challenge any (or all) of the Arbitrators.

If challenged, the grounds for it shall be made known to the Arbitrator(s), who may withdraw from the Panel and be replaced pursuant to Sections 13a and 13b as appropriate. However, if the challenged Arbitrator(s) consider(s) the challenge to be without merit and declines to withdraw, the arbitration shall proceed with due reservation of the challenger's right to seek recourse from the appropriate United States District Court after the Award has been issued.

Section 10. Direct Appointment by Parties

If the arbitration agreement specifies a method by which Arbitrators are to be appointed, that method shall be followed and in the event of a conflict, its terms shall prevail over this section of the Rules.

When requested by a party, the SMA shall submit its then current roster of members from which arbitrators may be appointed.

If a party fails to appoint its Arbitrator within the time frame specified in the arbitration agreement, the party demanding arbitration may resort to Section 5 of the Act.

If no such time frame is specified, the party demanding the arbitration shall give the other written notice that the appointment of its Arbitrator is made pursuant to Section 10 of these Rules which requires the other to appoint an arbitrator within twenty days of receipt of that notice, failing which the party demanding arbitration may appoint a second Arbitrator with the same force and effect as if that second Arbitrator were appointed by the other party. Any thus chosen second Arbitrator shall be a disinterested person with the same qualifications, if any, required by the arbitration agreement. If the arbitration agreement provides for three Arbitrators, the two so chosen shall appoint the third. Notwithstanding anything contained in this section to the contrary, if the party demanding arbitration seeks to compel the appointment of a second Arbitrator sooner than the stipulated twenty days, it is free to proceed under the Act.

Section 11. Appointment of Additional Arbitrator by Named Arbitrators

If the two party-appointed Arbitrators fail to appoint a third Arbitrator within a reasonable time, any party may petition the Court under the Act to make such an appointment after advising the Arbitrators.

Section 12. Notice of Appointment to Arbitrator(s)

Arbitrators may be appointed by the parties or their counsel, orally or in writing. If an oral appointment is made, it should be confirmed in writing as soon as practicable. The Chairman shall promptly notify the parties or their counsel that the Panel is complete and ready to proceed with the arbitration.

Section 13. Vacancies

If an Arbitrator is unable to serve, the vacancy shall be filled as follows:

(a) If the vacancy is created by a party-appointed Arbitrator, that party shall promptly name a replacement. The previously-selected Chairman will continue to serve in that capacity unless the two party-appointed Arbitrators choose a replacement Chairman before the hearings have commenced or, if the arbitration is conducted on documents alone, before the first submissions or documents are received by the Panel.

(b) If the office of Chairman becomes vacant, the two party-appointed Arbitrators shall appoint a replacement Chairman.

(c) Following the replacement of arbitrator(s), the arbitration shall resume on the existing record, unless the panel directs or the parties agree otherwise.

V. PROCEDURE FOR ORAL HEARING

Section 14. Representation

Any party has the option to be represented in the arbitration proceedings by counsel or any other duly-appointed representative.

Section 15. Stenographic Record

Unless otherwise agreed by the parties, a stenographic record of all hearings shall be arranged. The parties shall initially share the cost of the record, subject to final apportionment by the Arbitrator(s).

Section 16. Interpreters

If required, the party presenting shall furnish and initially pay for an interpreter. The interpreter shall be independent of both parties.

Section 17. Attendance at Hearings

Persons having a direct interest in the arbitration are entitled to attend hearings. The Panel has the power to compel witnesses to leave the hearing room during the testimony of other witnesses.

Section 18. Adjournments

The Panel may grant adjournments upon a showing of good cause. If all parties jointly request an adjournment, it shall be granted.

Section 19. Oaths

After the Panel has been accepted by the parties, each Arbitrator shall take the oath set forth in Appendix A hereto. If the arbitration is to be conducted without hearings, the Arbitrator(s) may make the oath in writing.

The Arbitrators shall require witnesses to testify under oath administered by any duly qualified person. . . . The form of oath may be amended to include an affirmation under penalty of perjury.

Section 20. Majority Decision

Whenever the Panel consists of more than one Arbitrator, the decision and award of the Arbitrators shall be by majority vote, where appropriate, unless a unanimous decision is required by the arbitration agreement. In cases where the arbitration clause calls for two party-appointed Arbitrators and an Umpire, should the two be unable to agree, they shall appoint an Umpire who shall take into account the reasons for their disagreement and adjudicate the matters in controversy as if he/she were sole Arbitrator.

Section 21. Order of Proceedings

If hearings are scheduled, the first hearing of the arbitration shall be at the time and place designated by the Chairman. The Chairman shall instruct each party or their counsel to deliver to each member of the Panel a statement identifying the other interested parties so that the Arbitrator(s) may determine whether grounds for voluntary withdrawal exist.

Each claimant should submit a pre-hearing statement of its position and claim.

At the first hearing, each party, or their counsel, may make an opening statement setting forth its position.

The arbitration proceeding shall be conducted in an orderly manner appropriate to judicial proceedings. Rules of evidence used in judicial proceedings need not be applied.

If it is not clear which party is the claimant, the Panel shall make the determination. Arbitrators shall apply burdens of proof and if by majority vote, the Panel concludes that the claimant has not made its case, no further evidence need be taken from the respondent, unless that respondent is asserting a counterclaim.

Copies of any documents, exhibits and accounts intended to be introduced at a particular hearing should be supplied to the other party or opposing counsel and to Panel members at least one week prior to the date of that hearing. Any fact or expert witness intended to testify before the Panel should likewise be identified at least one week in advance of the scheduled hearing date.

Following the presentation of all evidence, the parties may agree to present their arguments in a final oral hearing rather than in written briefs.

Section 22. Arbitration in the Absence of a Party

After a default has been established under the provisions of Section 4 of the Act or after the Panel has been completed pursuant to these Rules, the arbitration may proceed in the absence of the defaulting party, who, after due notice, failed to be present or failed to obtain an adjournment.

Section 23. Evidence

The parties may offer such evidence as they desire and shall produce such additional evidence as the Panel may deem necessary to an understanding and determination of the dispute. The Arbitrator(s) may subpoena witnesses or documents at their own initiative or at the request of any party....

The Panel shall be the judge of the relevancy and materiality of the evidence offered.

All evidence shall be taken in the presence of the Arbitrator(s) and of all the parties, except in the case of depositions or where any of the parties is absent without reasonable cause, in default, or has waived its right to be present or where submission of evidence by mail or in other form has been agreed by both parties.

The Panel has the power to direct that depositions be taken from witnesses who cannot testify in person.

All evidence submitted to the Panel, as well as all written communications between any party and the Panel, after it has been constituted, shall be submitted to all parties.

Section 24. Evidence by Affidavit

The Panel may receive evidence by affidavit and shall give such affidavits appropriate weight in light of any objections made by opponents.

Section 25. Closing of Proceedings

Upon completion of submission of evidence, the parties may submit briefs on an agreed schedule. If the parties cannot agree, the schedule shall be established by the Panel. Once all submissions are completed, the Chairman shall declare the proceedings closed.

Section 26. Reopening of Proceedings

Following the submission of briefs, the Panel may require the parties to provide clarifications concerning their claims or defenses and may order additional hearings for that purpose.

At any time prior to the issuance of an Award, hearings may be reopened on the application of any party provided the Panel agrees that good cause has been shown.

VI. Procedure for Other Than Oral Hearings

Section 27. Arbitration on Documents Alone

The parties, by written agreement, may submit their disputes to arbitration on documents alone. In such case, the Panel members shall make their disclosures in writing to all parties, pursuant to Section 9 and communicate the written oath ... to the parties. Thereafter, the parties shall make their submissions of documents and briefs, on such schedule as they agree. If the parties cannot agree, the Panel will establish the schedule....

VII. The Award

Section 28. Time

The Panel has the collective duty to issue awards not later than 120 days after the final evidence or brief has been received and the parties have been notified that the proceedings have been closed. Failure of the Panel to abide by this provision shall not be grounds for challenge of the Award.

Section 29. Form

The Award and the Arbitrator(s)' reasons for same shall be made in writing and signed either by the sole Arbitrator or Umpire or by a majority, if more than one, or by all, if unanimous. A partial or total dissent shall be signed by the dissenter and included with the majority Award.

Section 30. Scope

The Panel, in its Award, shall grant any remedy or relief which it deems just and equitable, including, but not limited to, specific performance. The Panel, in its Award, shall assess arbitration expenses and fees as provided in Sections 15, 36 and 37 and shall address the issue of attorneys' fees and costs incurred by the parties. The Panel is empowered to award reasonable attorneys' fees and expenses or costs incurred by a party or parties in the prosecution or defense of the case.

Any attorneys' fees or party costs awarded shall be quantified in the Award.

The Panel shall retain jurisdiction to modify the Award for the sole purpose of correcting obvious clerical and/or arithmetical errors.

Section 31. Award upon Settlement

Should the parties settle their dispute during the course of arbitration, the Panel may, upon the request of the parties, set forth the terms of the settlement in an Award.

Section 32. Delivery of Award to Parties

The parties accept that legal delivery of the Award may be accomplished:

(a) By mailing of the Award or a the copy thereof to the parties at their last known addresses or that of their counsel; or

(b) By personal service of the Award.

VIII.   SPECIAL PROVISIONS

Section 33. Waiver

Any party with knowledge that a provision of these Rules has been breached, but who continues with the arbitration without registering an official objection with the Panel shall be deemed to have waived any right to object.

Section 34. Time Periods

The parties may modify any period of time by mutual agreement and consent of the Panel. The Panel may extend or shorten any period of time established by the Rules upon a showing of good cause and shall notify the parties accordingly.

Section 35. Service of Documents

Wherever parties have agreed to arbitration under these Rules, they shall be deemed to have consented to service of any papers, notices or process necessary to initiate or continue an arbitration under these Rules or a court action to confirm judgment on the Award issued. Such documents may be served:

(a) By mail addressed to such party or counsel at their last known address; or

(b) By personal service.

Counsel for either party may be utilized by the Panel to implement subpoenas or other legal procedures instituted by the Panel. The expenses and fees for such services are to be allocated as the Panel members direct.

IX.   EXPENSES AND FEES

Section 36. Expenses

The expenses of witnesses shall be paid by the party producing or requiring the production of such witnesses subject to allocation by the Panel in its final Award.

Subject to final allocation in the Award, expenses incurred at the request of the Panel shall initially be borne equally by the parties. These include required travel and out-of-pocket expenses of the Panel members, the expense of producing witnesses requested by the Panel, or the cost of providing any proofs produced at the direct request of the Panel. The Panel may require an advance deposit for any sums it may reasonably have to expend.

The travel and living expenses of a party-appointed Arbitrator from outside the area named for the arbitration shall be borne by the party who appointed such Arbitrator.

Section 37. Arbitrator(s)' Fees

Each Panel member shall determine the amount of his/her compensation. When determining the fee, the Arbitrator(s) shall take into account the complexity, urgency and time spent on the matter.

At any time prior to issuance of the Award, the Panel may require that the parties post security for its estimated fees and expenses. Upon such request, each party shall promptly deposit the required amount into a segregated interest-bearing escrow account with the Chase Manhattan Bank, administered by the SMA. . . . Alternatively, such deposits may be held in any other escrow account or in any other manner, if agreed to by the Arbitrator(s).

If the dispute is settled during the course of the arbitration, a fee commensurate with work already performed in the arbitration is due to the Arbitrator(s).

Effective as of May 10, 1994; Revised September 15, 2003.

II.

RULES FOR SHORTENED ARBITRATION PROCEDURE OF
THE SOCIETY OF MARITIME ARBITRATORS, INC.

[. . .]

Supplement to the Arbitration Clause

"Notwithstanding anything contained herein to the contrary, should the sum claimed by each party not exceed U.S.$_____ (insert amount, exclusive of interest on the sum claimed, costs of the arbitration, and legal expenses), the dispute is to be governed by the 'Shortened Arbitration Procedure' of the Society of Maritime Arbitrators, Inc. (SMA) of New York, as defined in the Society's current Rules for such procedure, copy of which is attached hereto."

RULES FOR SHORTENED ARBITRATION PROCEDURE

1. Upon giving notice of a claim under these rules, the claimant shall nominate an arbitrator from the SMA roster to act as the sole arbitrator and simultaneously request the respondent's agreement. Failing a response by the respondent within 10 days of this initial nomination, the arbitrator so nominated shall become the sole arbitrator. The arbitrator shall promptly submit his/her disclosure statement to the parties, as required under Section 9 of the standard SMA Rules.

2. If the respondent does not agree to the nominated arbitrator as sole arbitrator, the respondent shall propose three other persons from the SMA roster to serve as sole arbitrator. Failing agreement on a sole arbitrator, either party may request that the President of the SMA appoint the sole arbitrator. This appointment shall be binding upon the parties.

3. Within 15 days of appointment, the arbitrator shall establish a written schedule for the prompt submission of the claimant's initial statement of claim with all supporting documents. The respondent shall submit its response and any counterclaim with all supporting documents within 20 days of receipt of claimant's submissions. In the event of a counterclaim, the first moving party shall respond within 20 days or sooner. At the arbitrator's discretion, the schedule may be varied by a few days. Short replies by both parties to each other's defenses may be exchanged consecutively or simultaneously, at the arbitrator's discretion.

4. The arbitration shall proceed on documents alone.

5. There shall be no discovery except as deemed necessary by the arbitrator.

6. The total items of dispute submitted by both parties under this procedure shall not number more than four, the combined total of which shall not exceed the figure agreed in the contract. At the arbitrator's sole discretion, a reasonable amendment to this limitation may be permitted.

7. The parties may be represented by attorneys or commercial advocates. An allowance towards legal expenses or time and expenses incurred by the parties in the prosecution or defense of the case may be awarded at the discretion of the arbitrator, but any such award shall not exceed $2,500.

8. The award shall be issued within 30 days of receipt of the final replies or the arbitrator's declaration that the proceeding is closed.

9. The fee and expenses of the arbitrator shall not exceed $1,500.

III.

NEW YORK SOCIETY OF MARITIME ARBITRATORS, INC. CODE OF ETHICS

1. Members shall be thoroughly familiar with and be guided by the Rules of the Society of Maritime Arbitrators.

2. Each member shall observe the highest standards of personal and professional conduct, free from impropriety or the appearance of impropriety. A member's personal behavior in the performance of his official duties should be beyond reproach.

3. Arbitrations shall be conducted with dignity and decorum and in such a manner as to reflect the importance and seriousness of the proceeding.

4. Before accepting appointment an arbitrator may only inquire as to the general nature of the dispute and the names of the parties and their

affiliates involved. A member shall not act as an Arbitrator in any proceeding in which he, his associates, or his relatives have a financial interest, or where his association with either the parties, counsel or other Arbitrators may give rise to an inference of bias without making a full disclosure of the relationship. A member shall not participate in a proceeding in which he has allowed others to inform him of details of the case before him prior to the first hearing.

5. No member shall confer with the party or counsel appointing him regarding the selection of a third Arbitrator.

6. Once the Panel is complete, all communications between the disputants or their counsel and the Panel shall be conducted through the Chairman. Neither of the other Arbitrators shall become involved in direct communication with either disputant or his counsel.

7. In the conduct of an arbitration, each member shall exercise care to remain absolutely impartial and always abide by principles of honesty and fair dealing. Since Arbitrators are obliged to render decisions, "compromise for compromise sake" should be avoided in favor of objective adjudication.

8. Once the proceedings start each member shall acquaint himself with all facts, arguments and discussions relative to the proceeding so that he may properly understand the dispute in arbitration.

9. During the deliberation process and prior to the award being finalized, the Arbitrators shall confer and jointly discuss the case in all its aspects. No discussion on the merits of the case is permitted at any time between Arbitrators unless all three are present.

10. Each member of this society shall be held accountable for his conduct as an Arbitrator. In case of complaint of misconduct of a member, he shall be given a hearing before the Committee on Professional Conduct, at which time the evidence of such alleged misconduct shall be presented to the member. He shall have the right of explaining or denying the alleged complaint to the Committee, which shall make such recommendations to the Board of Governors, as it deems advisable. All members agree to abide by the decision of a majority of the Board without right of appeal in any other forum whatsoever.

NOTES AND QUESTIONS

1. Do the SMA Rules improve the efficacy of arbitral adjudication? Which specific features of the 1994 Rules promote greater efficiency in maritime arbitration? What do arbitrating parties abandon in order to achieve that end? Is the exchange sound?

2. In what respects is SMA arbitration self-contained? Which specific provisions of the Rules point to that characteristic of the process? In your view, is SMA arbitration a legitimate form of dispute resolution? Could or should its procedural methodology be extended to other dispute areas? Would you advise your clients to use SMA arbitration?

3. What limit(s) do the Rules place on the party autonomy principle? Are these limit(s) necessary to the functionality of maritime arbitral proceedings? How do the Rules promote flexibility in the proceedings? Does the provision for flexibility contradict the restraint(s) placed upon party autonomy?

4. Is due process a preeminent concern of the Rules? Specifically assess the notice requirement and the rule of New York locality.

5. How do the Rules deal with the question of consolidation? Do they integrate the loser-pays-all rule? Do they require reasons with the award and allow dissents? What are "reasons"? Do they presume the publication of awards? How are vacancies addressed? Is a truncated or reduced tribunal possible?

6. In what matters would you require that the arbitrators reach a unanimous decision?

7. You should also evaluate the procedure for challenging arbitrators and for dealing with a refusal to appoint an arbitrator.

8. Describe the practical steps in instituting a maritime arbitral proceeding.

9. How do the rules guarantee or foster the impartiality of arbitrators?

10. How are deadlocks resolved?

11. How is the record constituted? Evidence gathered and evaluated?

12. What is an "award upon settlement"?

13. How is money handled during the proceeding?

14. How effective and sound are the Rules for the Shortened Arbitration Procedure?

15. Do you find the SMA Code of Ethics reassuring as a means of avoiding possible abuse or incompetence in SMA arbitrations?

CHAPTER SEVEN

LABOR AND EMPLOYMENT ARBITRATION

■ ■ ■

This chapter examines the use of arbitration for resolving workplace disputes. It also compares and contrasts a traditional and more contemporary use of arbitration. The U.S. Supreme Court favors both forms of arbitration and has elaborated a legal doctrine that sustains their operation. There are nonetheless a number of distinctions between the two forms of workplace arbitration—distinctions that have been meaningful in the decisional law.

Labor arbitration was established by the practice associated with collective bargaining agreements (CBA)—hence, the nomenclature of CBA arbitration. A union agrees to submit union member grievances to arbitration; when a worker lodges a complaint, the union must determine whether to take the claim to arbitration. The agreement to arbitrate is entered into by the union on behalf of its members. Therefore, individual statutory rights may not be subject to CBA arbitration if the union member has not personally agreed to the wavier of the judicial process for the adjudication of those rights.

Labor arbitrators are a well-defined group of adjudicators; their mission is to interpret the CBA and apply its provisions to individual claims. The law prohibits them from ignoring or exceeding the terms of the CBA in their rulings. Labor arbitrators must respect the contract and public policy.

CBA arbitration operates as a *quid pro quo* to the right to strike; it is an effective means of maintaining industrial peace and self-governance in the workplace. The U.S. Supreme Court has been an enthusiastic proponent of it since the early 1960s. The relevant legal doctrine continues to affirm the process and its independent operation.

Employment arbitration emerged in the 1990s, some thirty years after its labor counterpart. It does not involve unions and union representation; employees enter into arbitration agreements directly with the employer. The employee's acquiescence to the employer's arbitration provision is often a condition of employment or continued employment. The contracts for arbitration are generally adhesion agreements. Much of the litigation in the area involves the validity of the arbitration agreement, which usually is contained in an employee handbook. The distribution of costs and contract unconscionability have a significant presence in case law. Also, set asides and a lack of mutuality in the agreement can invalidate arbitration agreements. Employment arbitration raises serious challenges to the legitimacy of the recourse to arbitration between unequal parties. Its institution and longevity are not subject to serious question, but the likelihood of enforcement of the agreement is by no means guaranteed in some jurisdictions.

1. LABOR ARBITRATION

Labor arbitration is a highly sophisticated and *sui generis* form of arbitration. It is not governed by the FAA, but rather by the Labor Management Relations Act of 1947. Court rulings on commercial arbitration, however, have borrowed a number of elements from labor arbitration cases and generalized their holdings into broadly applicable statements of arbitration law. This is especially evident in the grounds for effectuating the judicial supervision of awards and in the elaboration of the doctrine of arbitral contractualism.

The first case, *Textile Workers Union of America*, introduces the basic framework of judicial rules applying to labor arbitration. The next three cases constitute the *Steelworkers Trilogy*. These celebrated decisions established the essence of the federal judicial doctrine on labor arbitration and consecrate the use of arbitration in the resolution of disputes that arise from collective bargaining agreements between unions and management. The *Steelworkers Trilogy* deals with the arbitrability of labor disputes and the enforcement of labor arbitration awards. Although it is not possible to convey a comprehensive sense of the practice of labor arbitration, arbitration has been instrumental in shaping U.S. labor-management relations and in elaborating the content of and implementing collective bargaining agreements. The remaining cases in this section— *AT&T Technologies* and *Misco*—summarize the basic principles of the judicial doctrine on labor arbitration and define the public policy exception to the enforcement of labor arbitral awards.

The recourse to arbitration in this setting makes the resolution of workplace disputes possible and effective. The several hundred thousand collective bargaining agreements that exist in the country generate a multitude of alleged violations on a daily basis. Resolving such disputes through court proceedings would literally overwhelm judicial dockets and demand that courts acquire specialized knowledge of the practices of the workplace. The system of labor arbitration provides a corps of professional labor arbitrators who not only dispose of the caseload in an efficient and timely manner, but who also have elaborated a type of *stare decisis* of labor arbitration. There is, for example, a basic consensus among labor arbitrators as to what constitutes just cause for dismissal, who bears the burden of proof in discipline cases, and how issues of seniority, promotions, and transfers are to be treated.

There are two types of labor arbitration. First, rights or grievance arbitration involves the interpretation or application of the terms and conditions of employment contained in the collective bargaining agreement. Rights arbitration is the more recent and more judicial form of labor arbitration. It is the form of labor arbitration that usually is referred to in the federal decisional law. Second, interest arbitration is the more legislative form of labor arbitration. It is used to establish the new terms and conditions of employment under a collective bargaining agreement. Historically, it was the original form of labor arbitration and constituted a substitute for strikes to resolve labor-management disagreements in the negotiation of new labor agreements. *See* M. ZIMNY, W. DOLSON, & C. BARRECA, LABOR ARBITRATION (1990); C. LACUGNA, AN INTRODUCTION TO LABOR ARBITRATION (1988). The following excerpts from the Court's opinions define the basic contours of the federal law on labor arbitration.

TEXTILE WORKERS UNION OF AMERICA v. LINCOLN MILLS OF ALABAMA

353 U.S. 448, 77 S.Ct. 912, 1 L.Ed.2d 972 (1957).

(footnotes omitted)

MR. JUSTICE DOUGLAS delivered the opinion of the Court.

Petitioner-union entered into a collective bargaining agreement in 1953 with respondent-employer, the agreement to run one year and from year to year thereafter, unless terminated on specified notices. The agreement provided that there would be no strikes or work stoppages and that grievances would be handled pursuant to a specified procedure. The last step in the grievance procedure—a step that could be taken by either party—was arbitration.

This controversy involves several grievances that concern work loads and work assignments. The grievances were processed through the various steps in the grievance procedure and were finally denied by the employer. The union requested arbitration, and the employer refused. Thereupon the union brought this suit in the District Court to compel arbitration.

The District Court concluded that it had jurisdiction and ordered the employer to comply with the grievance arbitration provisions of the collective bargaining agreement. The Court of Appeals reversed by a divided vote.... It held that, although the District Court had jurisdiction to entertain the suit, the court had no authority founded either in federal or state law to grant the relief....

The starting point of our inquiry is § 301 of the Labor Management Relations Act of 1947,...which provides:

> (a) "Suits for violation of contracts between an employer and a labor organization representing employees in an industry affecting commerce as defined in this chapter, or between any such labor organizations, may be brought in any district court of the United States having jurisdiction of the

parties, without respect to the amount in controversy or without regard to the citizenship of the parties."

(b) "Any labor organization which represents employees in an industry affecting commerce as defined in this chapter and any employer whose activities affect commerce as defined in this chapter shall be bound by the acts of its agents. Any such labor organization may sue or be sued as an entity and in behalf of the employees whom it represents in the courts of the United States. Any money judgment against a labor organization in a district court of the United States shall be enforceable only against the organization as an entity and against its assets, and shall not be enforceable against any individual member or his assets."

There has been considerable litigation involving § 301 and courts have construed it differently. There is one view that § 301(a) merely gives federal district courts jurisdiction in controversies that involve labor organizations in industries affecting commerce, without regard to diversity of citizenship or the amount in controversy. Under that view § 301(a) would not be the source of substantive law; it would neither supply federal law to resolve these controversies nor turn the federal judges to state law for answers to the questions. Other courts—the overwhelming number of them—hold that § 301(a) is more than jurisdictional—that it authorizes federal courts to fashion a body of federal law for the enforcement of these collective bargaining agreements and includes within that federal law specific performance of promises to arbitrate grievances under collective bargaining agreements.... That is our construction of § 301(a), which means that the agreement to arbitrate grievance disputes, contained in this collective bargaining agreement, should be specifically enforced.

From the face of the Act, it is apparent that § 301(a) and § 301(b) supplement one another. Section 301(b) makes it possible for a labor organization, representing employees in an industry affecting commerce, to sue and be sued as an entity in the federal courts. Section 301(b) in other words provides the procedural remedy lacking at common law. Section 301(a) certainly does something more than that. Plainly, it supplies the basis upon which the federal district courts may take jurisdiction and apply the procedural rule of § 301(b). The question is whether § 301(a) is more than jurisdictional.

[. . .]

Plainly the agreement to arbitrate grievance disputes is the *quid pro quo* for an agreement not to strike. Viewed in this light, the legislation does more than confer jurisdiction in the federal courts over labor organizations. It expresses a federal policy that federal courts should enforce these agreements on behalf of or against labor organizations and that industrial peace can be best obtained only in that way.

To be sure, there is a great medley of ideas reflected in the hearings, reports, and debates on this Act. Yet, to repeat, the entire tenor of the history indicates that the agreement to arbitrate grievance disputes was considered as *quid pro quo* of a no-strike agreement. And when in the

House the debate narrowed to the question whether § 301 was more than jurisdictional, it became abundantly clear that the purpose of the section was to provide the necessary legal remedies. . . .

It seems, therefore, clear to us that Congress adopted a policy which placed sanctions behind agreements to arbitrate grievance disputes, by implication rejecting the common-law rule. . . against enforcement of executory agreements to arbitrate. We would undercut the Act and defeat its policy if we read § 301 narrowly as only conferring jurisdiction over labor organizations.

The question then is, what is the substantive law to be applied in suits under § 301(a)? We conclude that the substantive law to apply in suits under § 301(a) is federal law, which the courts must fashion from the policy of our national labor laws. . . . The Labor Management Relations Act expressly furnishes some substantive law. It points out what the parties may or may not do in certain situations. Other problems will lie in the penumbra of express statutory mandates. Some will lack express statutory sanction but will be solved by looking at the policy of the legislation and fashioning a remedy that will effectuate that policy. The range of judicial inventiveness will be determined by the nature of the problem. . . . Federal interpretation of the federal law will govern, not state law. . . . But state law, if compatible with the purpose of § 301, may be resorted to in order to find the rule that will best effectuate the federal policy. . . . Any state law applied, however, will be absorbed as federal law and will not be an independent source of private rights.

[. . .]

Notes and Questions

1. You should pay particular attention to the Court's framing and characterization of the jurisdictional and federalism concerns in this case. They are of use in understanding the federalism issue in the context of commercial arbitration.

2. Is the court engaging in judicial legislation or crafting a rule that implements a congressional mandate? Identify language in the opinion, or lack thereof, that is the basis for either activity.

3. The Court's description of the legislative intent that underlies the Labor Management Relations Act is also significant. How does it compare to the Court's view of the legislative intent underlying the FAA?

UNITED STEELWORKERS OF AMERICA v. AMERICAN MANUFACTURING CO.

363 U.S. 564, 80 S.Ct. 1343, 4 L.Ed.2d 1403 (1960).

(footnotes omitted)

Opinion of the Court by Mr. Justice Douglas, announced by Mr. Justice Brennan.

This suit was brought by petitioner union in the District Court to compel arbitration of a "grievance" that petitioner, acting for one Sparks, a union member, had filed with the respondent, Sparks' employer. The employer defended on the ground (1) that Sparks is estopped from making his claim because he had a few days previously settled a workmen's compensation claim against the company on the basis that he was permanently partially disabled, (2) that Sparks is not physically able to do the work, and (3) that this type of dispute is not arbitrable under the collective bargaining agreement in question.

The agreement provided that during its term there would be "no strike," unless the employer refused to abide by a decision of the arbitrator. The agreement sets out a detailed grievance procedure with a provision for arbitration (regarded as the standard form) of all disputes between the parties "as to the meaning, interpretation and application of the provisions of this agreement."

The agreement reserves to the management power to suspend or discharge any employee "for cause." It also contains a provision that the employer will employ and promote employees on the principle of seniority "where ability and efficiency are equal." Sparks left his work due to an injury and while off work brought an action for compensation benefits. The case was settled, Sparks' physician expressing the opinion that the injury had made him 25% "permanently partially disabled." That was on September 9. Two weeks later the union filed a grievance which charged that Sparks was entitled to return to his job by virtue of the seniority provision of the collective bargaining agreement. Respondent refused to arbitrate and this action was brought. The District Court held that Sparks, having accepted the settlement on the basis of permanent partial disability, was estopped to claim any seniority or employment rights and granted the motion for summary judgment. The Court of Appeals affirmed...for different reasons. After reviewing the evidence it held that the grievance is "a frivolous, patently baseless one, not subject to arbitration under the collective bargaining agreement."...

Section 203(d) of the Labor Management Relations Act, 1947...states, "Final adjustment by a method agreed upon by the parties is hereby declared to be the desirable method for settlement of grievance disputes arising over the application or interpretation of an existing collective-bargaining agreement...." That policy can be effectuated only if the means chosen by the parties for settlement of their differences under a collective bargaining agreement is given full play.

A state decision that held to the contrary announced a principle that could only have a crippling effect on grievance arbitration. The case was *International Assn. of Machinists v. Cutler–Hammer, Inc....*. It held that "If the meaning of the provision of the contract sought to be arbitrated is beyond dispute, there cannot be anything to arbitrate and the contract cannot be said to provide for arbitration."... The lower courts in the instant case had a like preoccupation with ordinary contract law. The collective agreement requires arbitration of claims that courts might be unwilling to entertain. In the context of the plant or industry the grievance may assume proportions of which judges are ignorant. Yet, the agreement is to submit all grievances to arbitration, not merely those that a court may deem to be meritorious. There is no exception in the "no strike" clause and none therefore should be read into the grievance clause, since one is the *quid pro quo* for the other. The question is not whether in the mind of the court there is equity in the claim. Arbitration is a stabilizing influence only as it serves as a vehicle for handling any and all disputes that arise under the agreement.

The collective agreement calls for the submission of grievances in the categories which it describes, irrespective of whether a court may deem them to be meritorious. In our role of developing a meaningful body of law to govern the interpretation and enforcement of collective bargaining agreements, we think special heed should be given to the context in which collective bargaining agreements are negotiated and the purpose which they are intended to serve.... The function of the court is very limited when the parties have agreed to submit all questions of contract interpretation to the arbitrator. It is confined to ascertaining whether the party seeking arbitration is making a claim which on its face is governed by the contract. Whether the moving party is right or wrong is a question of contract interpretation for the arbitrator. In these circumstances the moving party should not be deprived of the arbitrator's judgment, when it was his judgment and all that it connotes that was bargained for.

The courts, therefore, have no business weighing the merits of the grievance, considering whether there is equity in a particular claim, or determining whether there is particular language in the written instrument which will support the claim. The agreement is to submit all grievances to arbitration, not merely those which the court will deem meritorious. The processing of even frivolous claims may have therapeutic values of which those who are not a part of the plant environment may be quite unaware.

The union claimed in this case that the company had violated a specific provision of the contract. The company took the position that it had not violated that clause. There was, therefore, a dispute between the parties as to "the meaning, interpretation and application" of the collective bargaining agreement. Arbitration should have been ordered. When the judiciary undertakes to determine the merits of a grievance under the guise of interpreting the grievance procedure of collective bargaining agreements, it usurps a function which under that regime is entrusted to the arbitration tribunal.

Reversed.

[. . .]

Mr. Justice Brennan, with whom Mr. Justice Harlan joins, concurring.

While I join the Court's opinions in Nos. 443, 360 and 538, I add a word in Nos. 443 and 360.

In each of these two cases the issue concerns the enforcement of but one promise—the promise to arbitrate in the context of an agreement dealing with a particular subject matter, the industrial relations between employers and employees. Other promises contained in the collective bargaining agreement are beside the point unless, by the very terms of the arbitration promise, they are made relevant to its interpretation. And I emphasize this, for the arbitration promise is itself a contract. The parties are free to make that promise as broad or as narrow as they wish, for there is no compulsion in law requiring them to include any such promises in their agreement. The meaning of the arbitration promise is not to be found simply by reference to the dictionary definitions of the words the parties use, or by reference to the interpretation of commercial arbitration clauses. Words in a collective bargaining agreement, rightly viewed by the Court to be the charter instrument of a system of industrial self-government, like words in a statute, are to be understood only by reference to the background which gave rise to their inclusion. The Court therefore avoids the prescription of inflexible rules for the enforcement of arbitration promises. Guidance is given by identifying the various considerations which a court should take into account when construing a particular clause—considerations of the milieu in which the clause is negotiated and of the national labor policy. It is particularly underscored that the arbitral process in collective bargaining presupposes that the parties wanted the informed judgment of an arbitrator, precisely for the reason that judges cannot provide it. Therefore, a court asked to enforce a promise to arbitrate should ordinarily refrain from involving itself in the interpretation of the substantive provisions of the contract.

To be sure, since arbitration is a creature of contract, a court must always inquire, when a party seeks to invoke its aid to force a reluctant party to the arbitration table, whether the parties have agreed to arbitrate the particular dispute. In this sense, the question of whether a dispute is "arbitrable" is inescapably for the court.

On examining the arbitration clause, the court may conclude that it commits to arbitration any "dispute, difference, disagreement, or controversy of any nature or character." With that finding the court will have exhausted its function, except to order the reluctant party to arbitration. Similarly, although the arbitrator may be empowered only to interpret and apply the contract, the parties may have provided that any dispute as to whether a particular claim is within the arbitration clause is itself for the arbitrator. Again the court, without more, must send any dispute to the arbitrator, for the parties have agreed that the construction of the arbitration promise itself is for the arbitrator, and the reluctant party has breached his promise by refusing to submit the dispute to arbitration.

In *American*, the Court deals with a request to enforce the "standard" form of arbitration clause, one that provides for the arbitration of "[a]ny disputes, misunderstandings, differences or grievances arising between the parties as to the meaning, interpretation and application of this agreement...." Since the arbitration clause itself is part of the agreement, it might be argued that a dispute as to the meaning of that clause is for the arbitrator. But the Court rejects this position, saying that the threshold question, the meaning of the arbitration clause itself, is for the judge unless the parties clearly state to the contrary. However, the Court finds that the meaning of that "standard" clause is simply that the parties have agreed to arbitrate any dispute which the moving party asserts to involve construction of the substantive provisions of the contract, because such a dispute necessarily does involve such a construction.

The issue in the *Warrior* case is essentially no different from that in *American*, that is, it is whether the company agreed to arbitrate a particular grievance. In contrast to *American*, however, the arbitration promise here excludes a particular area from arbitration—"matters which are strictly a function of management." Because the arbitration promise is different, the scope of the court's inquiry may be broader. Here, a court may be required to examine the substantive provisions of the contract to ascertain whether the parties have provided that contracting out shall be a "function of management." If a court may delve into the merits to the extent of inquiring whether the parties have expressly agreed whether or not contracting out was a "function of management," why was it error for the lower court here to evaluate the evidence of bargaining history for the same purpose? Neat logical distinctions do not provide the answer. The Court rightly concludes that appropriate regard for the national labor policy and the special factors relevant to the labor arbitral process, admonish that judicial inquiry into the merits of this grievance should be limited to the search for an explicit provision which brings the grievance under the cover of the exclusion clause since "the exclusion clause is vague and [the] arbitration clause quite broad." The hazard of going further into the merits is amply demonstrated by what the courts below did. On the basis of inconclusive evidence, those courts found that *Warrior...* was free completely to destroy the collective bargaining agreement by contracting out all the work.

The very ambiguity of the *Warrior* exclusion clause suggests that the parties were generally more concerned with having an arbitrator render decisions as to the meaning of the contract than they were in restricting the arbitrator's jurisdiction. The case might of course be otherwise were the arbitration clause very narrow, or the exclusion clause quite specific, for the inference might then be permissible that the parties had manifested a greater interest in confining the arbitrator; the presumption of arbitrability would then not have the same force and the Court would be somewhat freer to examine into the merits.

The Court makes reference to an arbitration clause being the *quid pro quo* for a no-strike clause. I do not understand the Court to mean that the application of the principles announced today depends upon the presence of a no-strike clause in the agreement.

MR. JUSTICE FRANKFURTER joins these observations.

NOTES AND QUESTIONS

1.   What doctrine of arbitration law does the Court announce in *American Manufacturing*? How is it related to the special circumstances of labor arbitration? Does it have a statutory justification or does it arise from a common law of arbitration?

2.   How persuasive is the Court's thesis regarding the "therapeutic" value of arbitrating "frivolous claims"?

3.   Does the lower court's determination amount to a judicial intrusion upon arbitral autonomy?

4.   You should compare and contrast the reasoning in *American Manufacturing* with its counterpart in *First Options of Chicago, Inc. v. Kaplan*. What evaluation do you reach of Justice Brennan's concurring opinion? How does he emphasize the policy perimeters of the Court's ruling? What meaning do you attribute to his statement that "[n]eat logical distinctions do not provide the answer"? What is Justice Brennan's point? In effect, do his remarks constitute a dissenting opinion?

UNITED STEELWORKERS OF AMERICA v. WARRIOR & GULF NAVIGATION CO.

363 U.S. 574, 80 S.Ct. 1347, 4 L.Ed.2d 1409 (1960).

(footnotes omitted)

Opinion of the Court by MR. JUSTICE DOUGLAS, announced by MR. JUSTICE BRENNAN.

[. . .]

We held in *Textile Workers v. Lincoln Mills* . . . that a grievance arbitration provision in a collective agreement could be enforced by reason of § 301(a) of the Labor Management Relations Act and that the policy to be applied in enforcing this type of arbitration was that reflected in our national labor laws. . . . The present federal policy is to promote industrial stabilization through the collective bargaining agreement. . . . A major factor in achieving industrial peace is the inclusion of a provision for arbitration of grievances in the collective bargaining agreement.

Thus the run of arbitration cases, illustrated by *Wilko v. Swan*, . . . becomes irrelevant to our problem. There the choice is between the adjudication of cases or controversies in courts with established procedures or even special statutory safeguards on the one hand and the settlement of them in the more informal arbitration tribunal on the other. In the commercial case, arbitration is the substitute for litigation. Here arbitration is the substitute for industrial strife. Since arbitration of labor disputes has quite different functions from arbitration under an ordinary commercial agreement, the hostility evinced by courts toward arbitration of commercial agreements has no place here. For arbitration of labor disputes under collective bargaining agreements is part and parcel of the collective bargaining process itself.

The collective bargaining agreement states the rights and duties of the parties. It is more than a contract; it is a generalized code to govern a myriad of cases which the draftsmen cannot wholly anticipate.... The collective agreement covers the whole employment relationship. It calls into being a new common law—the common law of a particular industry or of a particular plant....

A collective bargaining agreement is an effort to erect a system of industrial self-government. When most parties enter into a contractual relationship they do so voluntarily, in the sense that there is no real compulsion to deal with one another, as opposed to dealing with other parties. This is not true of the labor agreement. The choice is generally not between entering or refusing to enter into a relationship, for that in all probability pre-exists the negotiations. Rather it is between having that relationship governed by an agreed-upon rule of law or leaving each and every matter subject to a temporary resolution dependent solely upon the relative strength, at any given moment, of the contending forces. The mature labor agreement may attempt to regulate all aspects of the complicated relationship, from the most crucial to the most minute over an extended period of time. Because of the compulsion to reach agreement and the breadth of the matters covered, as well as the need for a fairly concise and readable instrument, the product of negotiations (the written document) is..."a compilation of diverse provisions: some provide objective criteria almost automatically applicable; some provide more or less specific standards which require reason and judgment in their application; and some do little more than leave problems to future consideration with an expression of hope and good faith." ...Gaps may be left to be filled in by reference to the practices of the particular industry and of the various shops covered by the agreement. Many of the specific practices which underlie the agreement may be unknown, except in hazy form, even to the negotiators. Courts and arbitration in the context of most commercial contracts are resorted to because there has been a breakdown in the working relationship of the parties; such resort is the unwanted exception. But the grievance machinery under a collective bargaining agreement is at the very heart of the system of industrial self-government. Arbitration is the means of solving the unforeseeable by molding a system of private law for all the problems which may arise and to provide for their solution in a way which will generally accord with the variant needs and desires of the parties. The processing of disputes through the grievance machinery is actually a vehicle by which meaning and content are given to the collective bargaining agreement.

Apart from matters that the parties specifically exclude, all of the questions on which the parties disagree must therefore come within the scope of the grievance and arbitration provisions of the collective agreement. The grievance procedure is, in other words, a part of the continuous collective bargaining process. It, rather than a strike, is the terminal point of a disagreement.

The labor arbitrator performs functions which are not normal to the courts; the considerations which help him fashion judgments may indeed be foreign to the competence of courts:

"A proper conception of the arbitrator's function is basic. He is not a public tribunal imposed upon the parties by superior authority which the parties are obliged to accept. He has no general charter to administer justice for a community which transcends the parties. He is rather part of a system of self-government created by and confined to the parties. . . ."

The labor arbitrator's source of law is not confined to the express provisions of the contract, as the industrial common law—the practices of the industry and the shop—is equally a part of the collective bargaining agreement[,] although [it is] not expressed in it. The labor arbitrator is usually chosen because of the parties' confidence in his knowledge of the common law of the shop and their trust in his personal judgment to bring to bear considerations which are not expressed in the contract as criteria for judgment. The parties expect that his judgment of a particular grievance will reflect not only what the contract says but, insofar as the collective bargaining agreement permits, such factors as the effect upon productivity of a particular result, its consequence to the morale of the shop, his judgment whether tensions will be heightened or diminished. For the parties' objective in using the arbitration process is primarily to further their common goal of uninterrupted production under the agreement, to make the agreement serve their specialized needs. The ablest judge cannot be expected to bring the same experience and competence to bear upon the determination of a grievance, because he cannot be similarly informed.

The Congress, however, has[,] by § 301 of the Labor Management Relations Act, assigned the courts the duty of determining whether the reluctant party has breached his promise to arbitrate. For arbitration is a matter of contract and a party cannot be required to submit to arbitration any dispute which he has not agreed so to submit. Yet, to be consistent with congressional policy in favor of settlement of disputes by the parties through the machinery of arbitration, the judicial inquiry under § 301 must be strictly confined to the question whether the reluctant party did agree to arbitrate the grievance or did agree to give the arbitrator power to make the award he made. An order to arbitrate the particular grievance should not be denied unless it may be said with positive assurance that the arbitration clause is not susceptible of an interpretation that covers the asserted dispute. Doubts should be resolved in favor of coverage.

We do not agree with the lower courts that contracting-out grievances were necessarily excepted from the grievance procedure of this agreement. To be sure, the agreement provides that "matters which are strictly a function of management shall not be subject to arbitration." But it goes on to say that if "differences" arise or if "any local trouble of any kind" arises, the grievance procedure shall be applicable.

Collective bargaining agreements regulate or restrict the exercise of management functions; they do not oust management from the performance of them. Management hires and fires, pays and promotes, supervises and plans. All these are part of its function, and absent a collective bargaining agreement, it may be exercised freely except as limited by public law and by the willingness of employees to work under the particular, unilaterally imposed conditions. A collective bargaining agreement may treat only with certain specific practices, leaving the rest to management but subject to the possibility of work stoppages. When, however, an absolute no-strike clause is included in the agreement, then in a very real sense everything that management does is subject to the agreement, for either management is prohibited or limited in the action it takes, or if not, it is protected from interference by strikes. This comprehensive reach of the collective bargaining agreement does not mean, however, that the language, "strictly a function of management," has no meaning.

"Strictly a function of management" might be thought to refer to any practice of management in which, under particular circumstances prescribed by the agreement, it is permitted to indulge. But if courts, in order to determine arbitrability, were allowed to determine what is permitted and what is not, the arbitration clause would be swallowed up by the exception. Every grievance in a sense involves a claim that management has violated some provision of the agreement.

Accordingly, "strictly a function of management" must be interpreted as referring only to that over which the contract gives management complete control and unfettered discretion. Respondent claims that the contracting out of work falls within this category. Contracting out work is the basis of many grievances; and that type of claim is grist in the mills of the arbitrators. A specific collective bargaining agreement may exclude contracting out from the grievance procedure. Or a written collateral agreement may make clear that contracting out was not a matter for arbitration. In such a case a grievance based solely on contracting out would not be arbitrable. Here, however, there is no such provision. Nor is there any showing that the parties designed the phrase "strictly a function of management" to encompass any and all forms of contracting out. In the absence of any express provision excluding a particular grievance from arbitration, we think only the most forceful evidence of a purpose to exclude the claim from arbitration can prevail, particularly where, as here, the exclusion clause is vague and the arbitration clause quite broad. Since any attempt by a court to infer such a purpose necessarily comprehends the merits, the court should view with suspicion an attempt to persuade it to become entangled in the construction of the substantive provisions of a labor agreement, even through the back door of interpreting the arbitration clause, when the alternative is to utilize the services of an arbitrator.

[. . .]

The judiciary sits in these cases to bring into operation an arbitral process which substitutes a regime of peaceful settlement for the older regime of industrial conflict. Whether contracting out in the present case violated the agreement is the question. It is a question for the arbiter, not for the courts.

Reversed.

[. . .]

NOTES AND QUESTIONS

1. Do you agree with the Court's description of the differences between labor and commercial arbitration? Has commercial arbitration evolved to occupy a similar status and perform a similar function? Do some of these would-be differences explain the practice of reasoned awards in labor matters?

2. Is the Court's characterization of *Wilko* fair and accurate? Does the Court's description of the function of the labor arbitrator sound like a description of the commercial arbitrator? Does that make sense to you conceptually? Why or why not?

3. You should pay particular attention to the Court's approach to and resolution of the arbitrability question because it also arises in the setting of commercial arbitration. Many of the essential points of the Court's reasoning are incorporated directly into the commercial arbitration cases. Is that proper? How different is a collective bargaining agreement from an ordinary commercial contract? Doesn't the system of commercial arbitration maintain the functionality of commerce?

UNITED STEELWORKERS OF AMERICA v. ENTERPRISE WHEEL AND CAR CORP.

363 U.S. 593, 80 S.Ct. 1358, 4 L.Ed.2d 1424 (1960).

(footnotes omitted)

Opinion of the Court by MR. JUSTICE DOUGLAS, announced by MR. JUSTICE BRENNAN.

[. . .]

The refusal of courts to review the merits of an arbitration award is the proper approach to arbitration under collective bargaining agreements. The federal policy of settling labor disputes by arbitration would be undermined if courts had the final say on the merits of the awards. As we stated in *United Steelworkers of America v. Warrior & Gulf Navigation Co.,* . . . the arbitrators under these collective agreements are indispensable agencies in a continuous collective bargaining process. They sit to settle disputes at the plant level—disputes that require for their solution knowledge of the custom and practices of a particular factory or of a particular industry as reflected in particular agreements.

When an arbitrator is commissioned to interpret and apply the collective bargaining agreement, he is to bring his informed judgment to bear in order to reach a fair solution of a problem. This is especially true when it comes to formulating remedies. There the need is for flexibility in meeting a wide variety of situations. The draftsmen may never have thought of what specific remedy should be awarded to meet a particular contingency. Nevertheless, an arbitrator is confined to interpretation and application of the collective bargaining agreement; he does not sit to dispense his own brand of industrial justice. He may of course look for guidance from many sources, yet his award is legitimate only so long as it draws its essence from the collective bargaining agreement. When the arbitrator's words manifest an infidelity to this obligation, courts have no choice but to refuse enforcement of the award.

The opinion of the arbitrator in this case, as it bears upon the award of back pay beyond the date of the agreement's expiration and reinstatement, is ambiguous. It may be read as based solely upon the arbitrator's view of the requirements of enacted legislation, which would mean that he exceeded the scope of the submission. Or it may be read as embodying a construction of the agreement itself, perhaps with the arbitrator looking to "the law" for help in determining the sense of the agreement. A mere ambiguity in the opinion accompanying an award, which permits the inference that the arbitrator may have exceeded his authority, is not a reason for refusing to enforce the award. Arbitrators have no obligation to the court to give their reasons for an award. To require opinions free of ambiguity may lead arbitrators to play it safe by writing no supporting opinions. This would be undesirable for a well-reasoned opinion tends to engender confidence in the integrity of the process and aids in clarifying the underlying agreement. Moreover, we see no reason to assume that this arbitrator has abused the trust the parties confided in him and has not stayed within the areas marked out for his consideration. It is not apparent that he went beyond the submission. The Court of Appeals' opinion refusing to enforce the reinstatement and partial back pay portions of the award was not based upon any finding that the arbitrator did not premise his award on his construction of the contract. It merely disagreed with the arbitrator's construction of it.

. . . Respondent's major argument seems to be that by applying correct principles of law to the interpretation of the collective bargaining agreement it can be determined that the agreement did not so provide, and that therefore the arbitrator's decision was not based upon the contract. The acceptance of this view would require courts, even under the standard arbitration clause, to review the merits of every construction of the contract. This plenary review by a court of the merits would make meaningless the provisions that the arbitrator's decision is final, for in reality it would almost never be final. This underlines the fundamental error which we have alluded to in *United Steelworkers of America v. American Manufacturing Co.* . . . As we there emphasized, the question of interpretation of the collective bargaining agreement is a question for the arbitrator. It is the arbitrator's construction which was bargained for; and so far as the arbitrator's decision concerns construction of the contract, the courts have no business overruling him because their interpretation of the contract is different from his.

[. . .]

NOTES AND QUESTIONS

1.   What is the basis for the judicial supervision of labor arbitral awards?

2.   Does the Court encourage labor arbitrators not to render opinions with their awards? Aren't reasoned awards essential to the self-contained character of the collective bargaining agreement and its arbitral system?

3.   What grounds of Section Ten might be relevant to the Court's analysis in this case if the FAA were applicable? How might public policy factor into this analysis? Does the specialty of labor arbitration call for a specific statutory regime or is a "hands-off" supervisory judicial approach sufficient?

4.   Finally, does commercial and labor arbitration continue to be different or similar? You should consider in particular the Court's constant reference to the underlying contract, namely, the collective bargaining agreement. The phrase appears in commercial arbitration cases as well. Do commercial arbitrations have any equivalent to the collective bargaining agreement? Are the functions of a labor and commercial arbitrator, therefore, substantially different?

AT & T TECHNOLOGIES, INC. v. COMMUNICATIONS WORKERS OF AMERICA

475 U.S. 643, 106 S.Ct. 1415, 89 L.Ed.2d 648 (1986).

(footnotes omitted)

JUSTICE WHITE delivered the opinion of the Court.

The issue presented in this case is whether a court asked to order arbitration of a grievance filed under a collective-bargaining agreement must first determine that the parties intended to arbitrate the dispute, or whether that determination is properly left to the arbitrator.

[. . .]

II

The principles necessary to decide this case are not new. They were set out by this Court over 25 years ago in a series of cases known as the *Steelworkers Trilogy*.... These precepts have served the industrial relations community well, and have led to continued reliance on arbitration, rather than strikes or lockouts, as the preferred method of resolving disputes arising during the term of a collective-bargaining agreement. We see no reason either to question their continuing validity, or to eviscerate their meaning by creating an exception to their general applicability.

The first principle gleaned from the *Trilogy* is that "arbitration is a matter of contract and a party cannot be required to submit to arbitration any dispute which he has not agreed so to submit." ...This axiom recognizes the fact that arbitrators derive their authority to resolve disputes only because the parties have agreed in advance to submit such grievances to arbitration....

The second rule, which follows inexorably from the first, is that the question of arbitrability—whether a collective-bargaining agreement creates a duty for the parties to arbitrate the particular grievance—is undeniably an issue for judicial determination. Unless the parties clearly and unmistakably provide otherwise, the question of whether the parties agreed to arbitrate is to be decided by the court, not the arbitrator....

The Court expressly reaffirmed this principle in *John Wiley & Sons, Inc. v. Livingston*.... The "threshold question" there was whether the court or an arbitrator should decide if arbitration provisions in a collective-bargaining contract survived a corporate merger so as to bind the surviving corporation.... The Court answered that there was "no doubt" that this question was for the courts. " 'Under our decisions, whether or not the company was bound to arbitrate, as well as what issues it must arbitrate, is a matter to be determined by the Court on the basis of the contract entered into by the parties.' ...The duty to arbitrate being of contractual origin, a compulsory submission to arbitration cannot precede judicial determination that the collective bargaining agreement does in fact create such a duty."...

The third principle derived from our prior cases is that, in deciding whether the parties have agreed to submit a particular grievance to arbitration, a court is not to rule on the potential merits of the underlying claims. Whether "arguable" or not, indeed even if it appears to the court to be frivolous, the union's claim that the employer has violated the collective-bargaining agreement is to be decided, not by the court asked to order arbitration, but as the parties have agreed, by the arbitrator. "The courts, therefore, have no business weighing the merits of the grievance, considering whether there is equity in a particular claim, or determining whether there is particular language in the written instrument which will support the claim. The agreement is to submit all grievances to arbitration, not merely those which the court will deem meritorious."...

Finally, it has been established that where the contract contains an arbitration clause, there is a presumption of arbitrability in the sense that "[a]n order to arbitrate the particular grievance should not be denied unless it may be said with positive assurance that the arbitration clause is not susceptible of an interpretation that covers the asserted dispute. Doubts should be resolved in favor of coverage." ...Such a presumption is particularly applicable where the clause is as broad as the one employed in this case, which provides for arbitration of "any differences arising with respect to the interpretation of this contract or the performance of any obligation hereunder...." In such cases, "[i]n the absence of any express provision excluding a particular grievance from arbitration, we think only the most forceful evidence of a purpose to exclude the claim from arbitration can prevail.". . .

This presumption of arbitrability for labor disputes recognizes the greater institutional competence of arbitrators in interpreting collective-bargaining agreements, "furthers the national labor policy of peaceful resolution of labor disputes and thus best accords with the parties' presumed objectives in pursuing collective bargaining." . . . The willingness of parties to enter into agreements that provide for arbitration of specified disputes would be "drastically reduced," however, if a labor arbitrator had the "power to determine his own jurisdiction. . . ." . . . Were this the applicable rule, an arbitrator would not be constrained to resolve only those disputes that the parties have agreed in advance to settle by arbitration, but, instead, would be empowered "to impose obligations outside the contract limited only by his understanding and conscience." . . . This result undercuts the longstanding federal policy of promoting industrial harmony through the use of collective-bargaining agreements, and is antithetical to the function of a collective-bargaining agreement as setting out the rights and duties of the parties.

With these principles in mind, it is evident that the Seventh Circuit erred in ordering the parties to arbitrate the arbitrability question. It is the court's duty to interpret the agreement and to determine whether the parties intended to arbitrate grievances concerning layoffs predicated on a "lack of work" determination by the Company. If the court determines that the agreement so provides, then it is for the arbitrator to determine the relative merits of the parties' substantive interpretations of the agreement. It was for the court, not the arbitrator, to decide in the first instance whether the dispute was to be resolved through arbitration.

The Union does not contest the application of these principles to the present case. Instead, it urges the Court to examine the specific provisions of the agreement for itself and to affirm the Court of Appeals on the ground that the parties had agreed to arbitrate the dispute over the layoffs at issue here. But it is usually not our function in the first instance to construe collective-bargaining contracts and arbitration clauses, or to consider any other evidence that might unmistakably demonstrate that a particular grievance was not to be subject to arbitration. The issue in the case is whether, because of express exclusion or other forceful evidence, the dispute over the interpretation of Article 20 of the contract, the layoff provision, is not subject to the arbitration clause. That issue should have been decided by the District Court and reviewed by the Court of Appeals; it should not have been referred to the arbitrator.

[. . .]

NOTES AND QUESTIONS

1. You should compare the contract freedom view advanced in *AT & T Technologies* with the one articulated in *First Options of Chicago, Inc. v.*

Kaplan. Unless the contract submits the question of arbitrability to the arbitrators, the courts have exclusive authority to decide the matter.

2. Can the principle articulated for labor arbitration also be applied in the context of commercial arbitration? Is the principle embedded in the special circumstances of labor arbitration? Does that factor make any significant difference?

3. Explain the Court's distinction between jurisdictional questions and a determination on the merits in labor arbitration cases. Does the line of distinction inevitably become blurred?

UNITED PAPERWORKERS INT'L UNION, AFL–CIO v. MISCO, INC.

484 U.S. 29, 108 S.Ct. 364, 98 L.Ed.2d 286 (1987).

(footnotes omitted)

JUSTICE WHITE delivered the opinion of the Court.

The issue for decision involves several aspects of when a federal court may refuse to enforce an arbitration award rendered under a collective-bargaining agreement.

[. . .]

[II]

[. . .]

A

Collective-bargaining agreements commonly provide grievance procedures to settle disputes between union and employer with respect to the interpretation and application of the agreement and require binding arbitration for unsettled grievances. In such cases, and this is such a case, the Court made clear almost 30 years ago that the courts play only a limited role when asked to review the decision of an arbitrator. The courts are not authorized to reconsider the merits of an award even though the parties may allege that the award rests on errors of fact or on misinterpretation of the contract. "The refusal of courts to review the merits of an arbitration award is the proper approach to arbitration under collective bargaining agreements. The federal policy of settling labor disputes by arbitration would be undermined if courts had the final say on the merits of the awards." . . . As long as the arbitrator's award "draws its essence from the collective bargaining agreement," and is not merely "his own brand of industrial justice," the award is legitimate. . . .

The reasons for insulating arbitral decisions from judicial review are grounded in the federal statutes regulating labor-management relations. These statutes reflect a decided preference for private settlement of labor disputes without the intervention of government: The Labor Management Relations Act of 1947. . . provides that "[f]inal adjustment by a method agreed upon by the parties is hereby declared to be the desirable method for settlement of grievance disputes arising over the application or interpretation of an existing collective-bargaining agreement." ...The courts have jurisdiction to enforce collective-bargaining contracts; but where the contract provides grievance and arbitration procedures, those procedures must first be exhausted and courts must order resort to the private settlement mechanisms without dealing with the merits of the dispute. Because the parties have contracted to have disputes settled by an arbitrator chosen by them rather than by a judge, it is the arbitrator's view of the facts and of the meaning of the contract that they have agreed to accept. Courts thus do not sit to hear claims of factual or legal error by an arbitrator as an appellate court does in reviewing decisions of lower courts. To resolve disputes about the application of a collective-bargaining agreement, an arbitrator must find facts and a court may not reject those findings simply because it disagrees with them. The same is true of the arbitrator's interpretation of the contract. The arbitrator may not ignore the plain language of the contract; but the parties having authorized the arbitrator to give meaning to the language of the agreement, a court should not reject an award on the ground that the arbitrator misread the contract.... So, too, where it is contemplated that the arbitrator will determine remedies for contract violations that he finds, courts have no authority to disagree with his honest judgment in that respect. If the courts were free to intervene on these grounds, the speedy resolution of grievances by private mechanisms would be greatly undermined. Furthermore, it must be remembered that grievance and arbitration procedures are part and parcel of the ongoing process of collective bargaining. It is through these processes that the supplementary rules of the plant are established. As the Court has said, the arbitrator's award settling a dispute with respect to the interpretation or application of a labor agreement must draw its essence from the contract and cannot simply reflect the arbitrator's own notions of industrial justice. But as long as the arbitrator is even arguably construing or applying the contract and acting within the scope of his authority, that a court is convinced he committed serious error does not suffice to overturn his decision. Of course, decisions procured by the parties through fraud or through the arbitrator's dishonesty need not be enforced. But there is nothing of that sort involved in this case.

B

The Company's position, simply put, is that the arbitrator committed grievous error in finding that the evidence was insufficient to prove that Cooper had possessed or used marijuana on company property.... No dishonesty is alleged; only improvident, even silly, fact-finding is claimed. This is hardly a sufficient basis for disregarding what the agent appointed by the parties determined to be the historical facts.

Nor was it open to the Court of Appeals to refuse to enforce the award because the arbitrator, in deciding whether there was just cause to discharge, refused to consider evidence unknown to the Company at the time Cooper was fired. The parties bargained for arbitration to settle disputes and were free to set the procedural rules for arbitrators to follow if they chose. Article VI of the agreement, entitled "Arbitration Procedure," did set some ground rules for the arbitration process. It forbade the arbitrator to consider hearsay evidence, for example, but evidentiary matters were otherwise left to the arbitrator....

. . . If we apply that . . . [statutory] standard here and assume that the arbitrator erred in refusing to consider the disputed evidence, his error was not in bad faith or so gross as to amount to affirmative misconduct....

C

[. . .]

A court's refusal to enforce an arbitrator's award under a collective-bargaining agreement because it is contrary to public policy is a specific application of the more general doctrine, rooted in the common law, that a court may refuse to enforce contracts that violate law or public policy. *W.R. Grace & Co. v. Rubber Workers*, 461 U.S. 757, 766 (1983). . . . That doctrine derives from the basic notion that no court will lend its aid to one who founds a cause of action upon an immoral or illegal act, and is further justified by the observation that the public's interests in confining the scope of private agreements to which it is not a party will go unrepresented unless the judiciary takes account of those interests when it considers whether to enforce such agreements. . . . In the common law of contracts, this doctrine has served as the foundation for occasional exercises of judicial power to abrogate private agreements.

In *W.R. Grace*, we recognized that "a court may not enforce a collective-bargaining agreement that is contrary to public policy," and stated that "the question of public policy is ultimately one for resolution by the courts." . . . We cautioned, however, that a court's refusal to enforce an arbitrator's *interpretation* of such contracts is limited to situations where the contract as interpreted would violate "some explicit public policy" that is "well defined and dominant, and is to be ascertained 'by reference to the laws and legal precedents and not from general considerations of supposed public interests.' " . . . In *W.R. Grace*, we identified two important public policies that were potentially jeopardized by the arbitrator's interpretation of the contract: obedience to judicial orders and voluntary compliance with Title VII of the Civil Rights Act of 1964. We went on to hold that enforcement of the arbitration award in that case did not compromise either of the two public policies allegedly threatened by the award. Two points follow from our decision in *W.R. Grace*. First, a court may refuse to enforce a collective-bargaining agreement when the specific terms contained in that agreement violate public policy. Second, it is apparent that our decision in that case does not otherwise sanction a broad judicial power to set aside arbitration awards as against public policy. Although we discussed the effect of that award on two broad areas of public policy, our decision turned on our examination of whether the award created any explicit conflict with other "laws and legal precedents" rather than an assessment of "general considerations of supposed public interests." . . . At the very least, an alleged public policy must be properly framed under the approach set out in *W.R. Grace*, and the violation of such a policy must be clearly shown if an award is not to be enforced.

[. . .]

NOTES AND QUESTIONS

1.   How significant is the public policy exception to the enforcement of labor arbitration awards? Where does it come from? Should it be applied to other types of arbitral awards? What types and on what basis? Does the public policy exception imply a review of the merits?

2.   There are other court rulings on labor arbitration cases that are relevant to understanding the Court's doctrinal activity in matters of commercial arbitration. As the prior materials explain, the Court has held that state statutory provisions that place restraints upon the parties' right to engage in arbitration are unconstitutional under the Supremacy Clause of the Federal Constitution. *See, e.g., Keating.* Moreover, the provisions of the FAA are applicable in both federal and state courts as long as there is a basis for the application of federal law. *See, e.g., Terminix.* The federal law on arbitration, in effect, dislodges or preempts the application of state arbitration laws, provided the litigation in question is not purely local. Moreover, the Court has interpreted widely the contractual reference to arbitration, deeming a general referral of disputes to arbitration to include statutory claims arising under federal regulatory law. *See, e.g., McMahon* and *Rodriguez.* The parties' agreement to arbitrate cannot be defeated by a claim that the parties' litigation involves the adjudication of federal statutory rights.

These determinations have a rough parallel in federal court decisions pertaining to the preemptive effect of Section 301 of the Labor Management Relations Act. In a recent case, the Court held that Section 301 of the Act was "a potent source of federal labor law" and disputes arising under or involving the interpretation of collective bargaining agreements should be governed by a unified and comprehensive body of federal law:

> [T]hough state courts have concurrent jurisdiction over controversies involving collective-bargaining agreements, . . . state courts must apply federal law in deciding those claims . . . and indeed any state-law cause of action for violation of collective-bargaining agreements is entirely displaced by federal law under § 301. . . . State law is thus "preempted" by § 301 in that only the federal law fashioned by the courts under § 301 governs the interpretation and application of collective-bargaining agreements.

United Steelworkers of America, AFL–CIO–CLC v. Rawson, 495 U.S. 362, 364 (1990).

The Court's preemption doctrine is designed to guarantee that collective bargaining agreements will be governed by a nationally uniform and consistent body of substantive law. Allowing employees to litigate employment-related claims in separate state law litigation involving the interpretation or application of collective-bargaining agreements, in all likelihood, would undermine the cohesion of the applicable law and eventually the stability of industrial relations. If a claim under state law involves the rights or duties established by a collective-bargaining agreement, it is preempted by federal law and the agreed-upon arbitral mechanism for dispute resolution. Otherwise, "the congressional goal of a unified federal body of labor-contract law would be subverted":

> [W]hen resolution of a state-law claim is substantially dependent upon analysis of the terms of an agreement made between the parties in a labor contract, that claim must either be treated as a § 301 claim . . . or dismissed as pre-empted by federal-contract law.

Allis-Chalmers Corp. v. Lueck, 471 U.S. 202, 220 (1985).

The Court, however, has found that some tort or contract claims based on state law are "independent" of, or not sufficiently "intertwined" with, the underlying labor agreement and do not involve the interpretation of the terms of the agreement even though the cause of action is factually "parallel" to a grievance procedure. *See Lingle v. Magic Chef, Inc., Norge Div.*, 486 U.S. 399 (1988). Reaching such a determination is, of course, the most difficult and elusive part of the Court's decisional law on statutory preemption in the labor context. When an employment-related right based on state law might be sufficiently independent of the collective-bargaining agreement to state an autonomous cause of action and avoid arbitration depends upon the interpretation of unforeseen variables in the specific case.

The lower federal courts, however, have generally applied the § 301 preemption doctrine in conformity with its intended "sweeping" character. They have held tortious interference with contract, negligent administration of drug testing, fraud, and breach of contract claims based on state law to be preempted. In keeping with the Court's disposition of the question in *Lingle v. Magic Chef*, claims based upon state or federal antidiscrimination laws appear more likely to avoid preemption.

For our purposes, the Court's intent to eliminate judicial or legal intrusion with the submission of labor disputes or employment claims to the agreed-upon arbitration procedure is most central. The § 301 preemption doctrine and the Court's straying from the *Alexander v. Gardner–Denver Co.* decisional law indicate a clear movement toward insulating the process of labor arbitration from the potentially undermining impact of parallel judicial litigation and the assertion of legal rights outside the confines of the underlying contract and its dispute resolution mechanism. The preoccupation with unitary resolution and exclusive pursuit of agreed-upon contractual rights may well be necessary to preserve the operation of the elaborate and long-standing process of labor arbitration, and thereby to maintain the framework for "industrial peace."

3. Is the approach and systemic disposition in labor arbitration decisions also necessary in the area of commercial arbitration? Is there an equivalency between the structure, operation, and purpose of these two forms of arbitration? Does labor arbitration exist for a public purpose, while commercial arbitration functions primarily to satisfy special interests? Is there any counterpart in commercial arbitration to the traditional antagonism between

unions and management? You should determine whether you believe the Court's federalism rulings and contractualist view of commercial arbitration have been influenced by its case law on labor arbitration. If there is some level of interface, do you believe that it is appropriate and sound? Why or why not? *See generally* 2 P. HARDIN, THE DEVELOPING LABOR LAW ch. 29, 1698–1706 (3d ed. 1992); P. SLOVAK, M. POSNER, & J. HIGGINS, JR., THE DEVELOPING LABOR LAW 1995 CUMULATIVE SUPPLEMENT ch. 29, 479–86 (3d ed. 1995).

2. EMPLOYMENT ARBITRATION

Introduction

The U.S. Supreme Court's decision in *Gilmer v. Interstate/Johnson Lane Corp.,* 500 U.S. 20 (1991), provided the impetus for the creation of a new form of arbitration, known as "employment" arbitration. In *Gilmer,* however, the agreement to arbitrate employment disputes was not technically part of the employment contract. In order to secure work as a stock broker, Gilmer signed a U–4 Registration Form with the New York Stock Exchange that required him to submit disputes with his employer to arbitration under the rules of the Exchange. The obligation to arbitrate claims against the employer, therefore, was implied and indirect. Accordingly, the Court in *Gilmer* never directly addressed the question of whether employment contracts containing mandatory, employer-imposed arbitral clauses constituted valid contractual references to arbitration under the FAA. Employers both inside and outside the securities industry nonetheless began inserting such clauses into standard employment contracts, usually as part of a company ADR process to handle workplace disputes.

Employment arbitration differs from traditional labor arbitration in that it applies to unrepresented or non-union employees. The agreement to arbitrate is not part of a collective bargaining agreement negotiated by union officials on behalf of unionized employees. Rather, the employer inserts arbitral clauses in individual employment contracts, usually as a pre-condition to employment. Therefore, the recourse to arbitration is mandatory and dictated by the employer. Such agreements also contain an express and comprehensive enumeration of the statutory claims that the employee agrees to submit to arbitration. This practice reflects, among other things, the employer's desire to avoid court litigation and to achieve an expeditious and final resolution of workplace disputes.

Studies indicate that the workplace has been generating more employee-initiated lawsuits; employment discrimination claims, in particular, have become more numerous. Also, jury awards in sexual harassment cases tend to be dramatic and generous to plaintiffs. ADR—in the form of arbitration—represents a means by which employers can reduce the cost of such litigation. Juries are not part of an arbitration, allowing seasoned experts to assess the evidence and decide. Moreover, arbitration is a private process; the likelihood of negative publicity, therefore, is much less than in a judicial proceeding. Arbitral hearings tend to be less formal and quicker with arbitrators rendering prompt awards. Finally, arbitrators usually are experts and are more likely to render predictable decisions.

Arbitration also has disadvantages. It is very difficult, if not next-to-impossible, to vacate an arbitral award; there is no meaningful appeal by which to correct evident legal or factual flaws. Discovery also is limited, and this factor may lead to serious gaps and disparities in the record. The "repeat player" phenomenon may give employers an unfair advantage in the adjudication of individual claims. Also, financial considerations (payment of all arbitrator fees by employers or the inability of employees to pay such fees) may compromise the integrity and impartiality of the process. The choice of arbitrators and the composition of the arbitral tribunal here are especially vital to the legitimacy and functionality of the process.

None of these considerations, however, resolves the essential questions: Whether arbitration should be imposed unilaterally upon employees by their employers either as a pre-condition to employment or after-the-fact in a modified employee handbook? Whether arbitrators should be authorized to resolve employee claims that pertain to federal statutory frameworks, including civil rights legislation? The gulf between the *Gilmer* doctrine (providing for the arbitrability of all claims in the employment context) and the *Gardner-Denver* holding (taking an unequivocal position in favor of the sanctity of statutory rights) appears to be wider than ever. The recent decision in *Wright v. Universal Maritime Serv. Corp.*, 525 U.S. 70 (1998), was at best a timid attempt by the U.S. Supreme Court at a modest compromise.

The development of employment arbitration has thus far generated the strongest challenge to the wisdom of the Court's endorsement of arbitration. Some lower state and federal courts have demonstrated serious reluctance to enforce these unilateral dispute resolution compacts, and members of the U.S. Congress proposed legislation to remedy the perceived inequities of these arbitration agreements. In litigation involving individual consumers and their relationship to corporate enterprises, there is now a more acute sense of the trade-offs implicated by the recourse to arbitration and ADR. Opposition is surfacing, but has yet to pose a serious threat to the majoritarian trend. In employment arbitration, the institutional development continues apace, while awaiting a specific pronouncement from the Court. In fact, various organizations have already developed practices and procedures to implement employment arbitration on a nationwide level.

The circumstances of employment arbitration raise a number of analytical questions. First, as to the law applicable and the interpretation and scope of the FAA itself: Does the exclusion of specific employment contracts in Section One of the FAA render the FAA and its accompanying decisional law inapplicable to employment arbitration? If so, should employment arbitration cases be treated as labor arbitration matters? Would the lack of a collective bargaining agreement and established arbitral practice (as well as the disparity of the parties' negotiating position) make analogous application inapposite? Should the courts then devise a general federal common law on employment arbitration that takes into account its special circumstances? Would such a law dislodge contrary state law in a diversity context or be mandated upon state courts? If rulings antagonistic to arbitration were possible in employment arbitration litigation, could such results coexist with the general federal policy on arbitration under the FAA? Assuming the courts read the employment contract exclusion in Section One narrowly, would or should the circumstances of employment arbitration lead to a more vigorous interpretation of contractual validity under Section Two? Even a modest judicial concern about the unfairness of the arbitration agreement could be seen as undermining the "emphatic federal policy" in favor of arbitration. Would or should employees coerced into arbitration be left without remedies under the FAA?

Second, there is a linkage between employment and labor arbitration. In *Gardner-Denver*, the Court held that unionized employees were not precluded from pursuing their statutory claims in a judicial forum despite an arbitration agreement and an arbitral proceeding under the collective bargaining agreement. The Court's decisional law pertaining to the preemptive effect of Section 301 of the Labor Management Relations Act has led it to stray from the *Gardner-Denver* doctrine. The Court's objective in precluding separate state court litigation regarding employee rights is to maintain a nationally-uniform law on the interpretation of collective bargaining agreements. What rule of law should govern in the circumstances of employment arbitration? Would or should the unilateral imposition and non-negotiable character of the arbitration agreement engender the application of a revitalized *Gardner-Denver* rule to redress *post facto* the imbalances of employment arbitration? Would the "double dip" allowed to employees make employment arbitration decidedly less attractive to employers because workplace disputes would involve an even more protracted dispute resolution system? Are the statutory rights at issue so critical—individually and collectively—that they warrant recourse to a commercially counterproductive and dysfunctional judicial process? As between the competing parties, should the employer or the employee be given the "procedural" upperhand? What is society's real stake in this debate—commercial efficiency or the protection of political rights?

Finally, employment arbitration compels revisiting the issue of the validity of arbitration agreements. Assuming that Section Two of the FAA or a similar common law doctrine applies, do arbitral clauses unilaterally imposed in employment contracts constitute lawful contractual waivers of judicial remedies in areas implicating fundamental rights? The Court has left little, if any, doubt that statutory and civil rights claims can be submitted to arbitration. The one-sided and economically-coercive character of employment arbitration agreements might generate a different judicial assessment of contractual validity under Section Two of the FAA. There is no longstanding experience, customary practice, or union representation associated with employment arbitration. It could also be argued that such contracts are a typical example of adhesionary contracts that prevail in many sectors of the national economy. Employees simply are placed in the same position as consumers. The perceived unfairness of the transactional circumstances are, therefore, neither unusual nor overwhelming.

As in many other settings, arbitration in the employment context can be readily justified by practical considerations of resource allocation. The dysfunctionality of the judicial process as a dispute resolution mechanism—in terms of costs, time, and disruption to commercial and individual interests—constitute the most compelling argument for arbitration and ADR. As noted earlier, employment discrimination suits are reputed to be on the rise and the EEOC has a staggering national backlog of cases. In these circumstances, employment arbitration or company-sponsored ADR frameworks may be the only realistic recourse available to employees. Court litigation is simply too expensive and too slow to provide employees with relief and the protection of their rights. In these circumstances, traditional legal values have little chance to survive, let alone triumph. Congressional legislation enacted to protect individual rights are often too distant from the reality of cases to have a direct effect upon the protection of rights. Arbitration and ADR provide employees with access to remedial mechanisms and expeditious results and allow employers to reduce litigation costs and to maintain the competitiveness of their enterprises in a globalized economy. In fact, there is considerable public and private support for employment arbitration. Professional groups are developing procedural protocols for employment arbitration, and the highly-regarded Dunlop Commission, established by the U.S. Departments of Commerce and Labor, endorsed and encouraged, in its 1994 report, the use of arbitration for the resolution of workplace disputes.

The argument for employment arbitration has substantial appeal. The progression of the arbitration industry in this new area, however, raises some reservations. A nagging suspicion and concern remain about the enthusiasm for arbitration and ADR. The unbounded exuberance steadfastly refuses to assess the larger societal interest in justice and to consider critically the long-term implications of the privatization of adjudication. Despite attempts to safeguard due process concerns in private justice processes, consumers, employees, and society at large are given a single option for second class justice. The EEOC and the NLRB now oppose pre-dispute arbitration agreements that might compromise employee rights under Title VII. The NASD and NYSE and other exchanges have excluded discrimination claims from mandatory inside-the-industry arbitration. How serious is U.S. society about integrating minorities, blacks, and women into the workplace if claims of racial discrimination and sexual harassment are submitted to private remedial mechanisms at the employer's choice? Are commands of political rights merely symbolic? Have we chosen to privilege functionality over other values in every sector of societal activity?

The Fountainhead Cases

ALEXANDER v. GARDNER-DENVER CO.

415 U.S. 36, 94 S.Ct. 1011, 39 L.Ed.2d 147 (1974).

(footnotes omitted)

Mr. Justice Powell delivered the opinion of the Court.

This case concerns the proper relationship between federal courts and the grievance-arbitration machinery of collective-bargaining agreements in the resolution and enforcement of an individual's rights to equal employment opportunities under Title VII of the Civil Rights Act of 1964.... Specifically, we must decide under what circumstances, if any, an employee's statutory right to a trial de novo under Title VII may be foreclosed by prior submission of his claim to final arbitration under the nondiscrimination clause of a collective-bargaining agreement.

I

In May 1966, petitioner Harrell Alexander, Sr., a black, was hired by respondent Gardner–Denver Co. (the company) to perform maintenance work at the company's plant in Denver, Colorado. In June 1968, petitioner was awarded a trainee position as a drill operator. He remained at that job until his discharge from employment on September 29, 1969. The company informed petitioner that he was being discharged for producing too many defective or unusable parts that had to be scrapped.

On October 1, 1969, petitioner filed a grievance under the collective-bargaining agreement in force between the company and petitioner's union.... No explicit claim of racial discrimination was made.

Under Art. 4 of the collective-bargaining agreement, the company retained 'the right to hire, suspend or discharge (employees) for proper cause.' Article 5, s 2, provided, however, that 'there shall be no discrimination against any employee on account of race, color, religion, sex, national origin, or ancestry,' and Art. 23, s 6(a), stated that '(n)o employee will be discharged, suspended or given a written warning notice except for just cause.' The agreement also contained a broad arbitration clause covering 'differences aris(ing) between the Company and the Union as to the meaning and application of the provisions of this Agreement' and 'any trouble aris(ing) in the plant.' Disputes were to be submitted to a multistep grievance procedure, the first four steps of which involved negotiations between the company and the union. If the dispute remained unresolved, it was to be remitted to compulsory arbitration. The company and the union were to select and pay the arbitrator, and his decision was to be 'final and binding upon the Company, the Union, and any employee or employees involved.' The agreement further provided that '(t)he arbitrator shall not amend, take away, add to, or change any of the provisions of this Agreement, and the arbitrator's decision must be based solely upon an interpretation of the provisions of this Agreement.' The parties also agreed that there 'shall be no suspension of work' over disputes covered by the grievance arbitration clause.

The union processed petitioner's grievance through the above machinery. In the final pre-arbitration step, petitioner raised, apparently for the first time, the claim that his discharge resulted from racial discrimination. The company rejected all of petitioner's claims, and the grievance proceeded to arbitration. Prior to the arbitration hearing, however, petitioner filed a charge of racial discrimination with the Colorado Civil Rights Commission, which referred the complaint to the Equal Employment Opportunity Commission on November 5, 1969.

At the arbitration hearing on November 20, 1969, petitioner testified that his discharge was the result of racial discrimination and informed the arbitrator that he had filed a charge with the Colorado Commission because he 'could not rely on the union.' The union introduced a letter in which petitioner stated that he was 'knowledgeable that in the same plant others have scrapped an equal amount and sometimes in excess, but by all logical reasoning I...have been the target of preferential discriminatory treatment.' The union representative also testified that the company's usual practice was to transfer unsatisfactory trainee drill operators back to their former positions.

On December 30, 1969, the arbitrator ruled that petitioner had been 'discharged for just cause.' He made no reference to petitioner's claim of racial discrimination. The arbitrator stated that the union had failed to produce evidence of a practice of transferring rather than discharging trainee drill operators who accumulated excessive scrap, but he suggested that the company and the union confer on whether such an arrangement was feasible in the present case.

On July 25, 1970, the Equal Employment Opportunity Commission determined that there was not reasonable cause to believe that a violation of Title VII of the Civil Rights Act of 1964...had occurred. The Commission later notified petitioner of his right to institute a civil action in federal court within 30 days. Petitioner then filed the present action in the United States District Court for the District of Colorado, alleging that his discharge resulted from a racially discriminatory employment practice in violation of s 703(a)(1) of the Act....

The District Court granted respondent's motion for summary judgment and dismissed the action.... The court found that the claim of racial discrimination had been submitted to the arbitrator and resolved adversely to petitioner. It then held that petitioner, having voluntarily elected to pursue his grievance to final arbitration under the nondiscrimination clause of the collective-bargaining agreement, was bound by the arbitral decision and thereby precluded from suing his employer under Title VII. The Court of Appeals for the Tenth Circuit affirmed *per curiam* on the basis of the District Court's opinion....

...We reverse.

II

Congress enacted Title VII of the Civil Rights Act of 1964...to assure equality of employment opportunities by eliminating those practices and devices that discriminate on the basis of race, color, religion, sex, or national origin.... Cooperation and voluntary compliance were selected as the preferred means for achieving this goal. To this end, Congress created the Equal Employment Opportunity Commission and established a procedure whereby existing state and local equal employment opportunity agencies, as well as the Commission, would have an opportunity to settle disputes through conference, conciliation, and persuasion before the aggrieved party was permitted to file a lawsuit. In the Equal Employment Opportunity Act of 1972,...Congress amended Title VII to provide the Commission with further authority to investigate individual charges of discrimination, to promote voluntary compliance with the requirements of Title VII, and to institute civil actions against employers or unions named in a discrimination charge.

Even in its amended form, however, Title VII does not provide the Commission with direct powers of enforcement. The Commission cannot adjudicate claims or impose administrative sanctions. Rather, final responsibility for enforcement of Title VII is vested with federal courts. The Act authorizes courts to issue injunctive relief and to order such affirmative action as may be appropriate to remedy the effects of unlawful employment practices.... Courts retain these broad remedial powers despite a Commission finding of no reasonable cause to believe that the Act has been violated.... Taken together, these provisions make plain that federal courts have been assigned plenary powers to secure compliance with Title VII.

In addition to reposing ultimate authority in federal courts, Congress gave private individuals a significant role in the enforcement process of Title VII. Individual grievants usually initiate the Commission's investigatory and conciliatory procedures. And although the 1972 amendment to Title VII empowers the Commission to bring its own actions, the private right of action remains an essential means of obtaining judicial enforcement of Title VII.... In such cases, the private litigant not only redresses his own injury but also vindicates the important congressional policy against discriminatory employment practices....

Pursuant to this statutory scheme, petitioner initiated the present action for judicial consideration of his rights under Title VII. The District Court and the Court of Appeals held, however, that petitioner was bound by the prior arbitral decision and had no right to sue under Title VII. Both courts evidently thought that this result was dictated by notions of election of remedies and waiver and by the federal policy favoring arbitration of labor disputes.... We disagree.

III

Title VII does not speak expressly to the relationship between federal courts and the grievance-arbitration machinery of collective-bargaining agreements. It does, however, vest federal courts with plenary powers to enforce the statutory requirements; and it specifies with precision the jurisdictional prerequisites that an individual must satisfy before he is entitled to institute a lawsuit.... There is no suggestion in the statutory scheme that a prior arbitral decision either forecloses an individual's right to sue or divests federal courts of jurisdiction.

In addition, legislative enactments in this area have long evinced a general intent to accord parallel or overlapping remedies against discrimination.... [T]he legislative history of Title VII manifests a congressional intent to allow an individual to pursue independently his rights under both Title VII and other applicable state and federal statutes. The clear inference is that Title VII was designed to supplement, rather than supplant, existing laws and institutions relating to employment discrimination. In sum, Title VII's purpose and procedures strongly suggest that an individual does not forfeit his private cause of action if he first pursues his grievance to final arbitration under the nondiscrimination clause of a collective-bargaining agreement.

In reaching the opposite conclusion, the District Court relied in part on the doctrine of election of remedies. That doctrine, which refers to situations where an individual pursues remedies that are legally or factually inconsistent, has no application in the present context. In submitting his grievance to arbitration, an employee seeks to vindicate his contractual right under a collective-bargaining agreement. By contrast, in filing a lawsuit under Title VII, an employee asserts independent statutory rights accorded by Congress. The distinctly separate nature of these contractual and statutory rights is not vitiated merely because both were violated as a result of the same factual occurrence. And certainly no inconsistency results from permitting both rights to be enforced in their respectively appropriate forums. The resulting scheme is somewhat analogous to the procedure under the National Labor Relations Act, as amended, where disputed transactions may implicate both contractual and statutory rights. Where the statutory right underlying a particular claim may not be abridged by contractual agreement, the Court has recognized that consideration of the claim by the arbitrator as a contractual dispute under the collective-bargaining agreement does not preclude subsequent consideration of the claim by the National Labor Relations Board as an unfair labor practice charge or as a petition for clarification of the union's representation certificate under the Act.... There, as here, the relationship between the forums is complementary since consideration of the claim by both forums may promote the policies underlying each. Thus, the rationale behind the election-of-remedies doctrine cannot support the decision below.

We are also unable to accept the proposition that petitioner waived his cause of action under Title VII. To begin, we think it clear that there can be no prospective waiver of an employee's rights under Title VII. It is true, of course, that a union may waive certain statutory rights related to collective activity, such as the right to strike.... These rights are con-

ferred on employees collectively to foster the processes of bargaining and
properly may be exercised or relinquished by the union as collective-
bargaining agent to obtain economic benefits for union members. Title
VII, on the other hand, stands on plainly different ground; it concerns not
majoritarian processes, but an individual's right to equal employment
opportunities. Title VII's strictures are absolute and represent a congressional command that each employee be free from discriminatory practices.
Of necessity, the rights conferred can form no part of the collective-
bargaining process since waiver of these rights would defeat the paramount congressional purpose behind Title VII. In these circumstances, an
employee's rights under Title VII are not susceptible of prospective
waiver. . . .

The actual submission of petitioner's grievance to arbitration in the
present case does not alter the situation. Although presumably an employee may waive his cause of action under Title VII as part of a voluntary
settlement, mere resort to the arbitral forum to enforce contractual rights
constitutes no such waiver. Since an employee's rights under Title VII
may not be waived prospectively, existing contractual rights and remedies
against discrimination must result from other concessions already made
by the union as part of the economic bargain struck with the employer. It
is settled law that no additional concession may be exacted from any
employee as the price for enforcing those rights. . . .

Moreover, a contractual right to submit a claim to arbitration is not
displaced simply because Congress also has provided a statutory right
against discrimination. Both rights have legally independent origins and
are equally available to the aggrieved employee. This point becomes
apparent through consideration of the role of the arbitrator in the system
of industrial self-government. As the proctor of the bargain, the arbitrator's task is to effectuate the intent of the parties. His source of authority
is the collective-bargaining agreement, and he must interpret and apply
that agreement in accordance with the 'industrial common law of the
shop' and the various needs and desires of the parties. The arbitrator,
however, has no general authority to invoke public laws that conflict with
the bargain between the parties[.]

[. . .]

IV

The District Court and the Court of Appeals reasoned that to permit
an employee to have his claim considered in both the arbitral and judicial
forums would be unfair since this would mean that the employer, but not
the employee, was bound by the arbitral award. In the District Court's
words, it could not 'accept a philosophy which gives the employee two
strings to his bow when the employer has only one.'. . . This argument
mistakes the effect of Title VII. Under the *Steelworkers* trilogy, an arbitral
decision is final and binding on the employer and employee, and judicial
review is limited as to both. But in instituting an action under Title VII,
the employee is not seeking review of the arbitrator's decision. Rather, he

is asserting a statutory right independent of the arbitration process. An employer does not have 'two strings to his bow' with respect to an arbitral decision for the simple reason that Title VII does not provide employers with a cause of action against employees. An employer cannot be the victim of discriminatory employment practices....

The District Court and the Court of Appeals also thought that to permit a later resort to the judicial forum would undermine substantially the employer's incentive to arbitrate and would 'sound the death knell for arbitration clauses in labor contracts.'... Again, we disagree. The primary incentive for an employer to enter into an arbitration agreement is the union's reciprocal promise not to strike.... It is not unreasonable to assume that most employers will regard the benefits derived from a no-strike pledge as outweighing whatever costs may result from according employees an arbitral remedy against discrimination in addition to their judicial remedy under Title VII. Indeed, the severe consequences of a strike may make an arbitration clause almost essential from both the employees' and the employer's perspective. Moreover, the grievance-arbitration machinery of the collective-bargaining agreement remains a relatively inexpensive and expeditious means for resolving a wide range of disputes, including claims of discriminatory employment practices. Where the collective-bargaining agreement contains a nondiscrimination clause similar to Title VII, and where arbitral procedures are fair and regular, arbitration may well produce a settlement satisfactory to both employer and employee. An employer thus has an incentive to make available the conciliatory and therapeutic processes of arbitration which may satisfy an employee's perceived need to resort to the judicial forum, thus saving the employer the expense and aggravation associated with a lawsuit. For similar reasons, the employee also has a strong incentive to arbitrate grievances, and arbitration may often eliminate those misunderstandings or discriminatory practices that might otherwise precipitate resort to the judicial forum.

V

Respondent contends that even if a preclusion rule is not adopted, federal courts should defer to arbitral decisions on discrimination claims where: (i) the claim was before the arbitrator; (ii) the collective-bargaining agreement prohibited the form of discrimination charged in the suit under Title VII; and (iii) the arbitrator has authority to rule on the claim and to fashion a remedy. Under respondent's proposed rule, a court would grant summary judgment and dismiss the employee's action if the above conditions were met. The rule's obvious consequence in the present case would be to deprive the petitioner of his statutory right to attempt to establish his claim in a federal court.

At the outset, it is apparent that a deferral rule would be subject to many of the objections applicable to a preclusion rule. The purpose and procedures of Title VII indicate that Congress intended federal courts to exercise final responsibility for enforcement of Title VII; deferral to arbitral decisions would be inconsistent with that goal. Furthermore, we have long recognized that 'the choice of forums inevitably affects the scope of the substantive right to be vindicated.'.... Respondent's deferral rule is necessarily premised on the assumption that arbitral processes are commensurate with judicial processes and that Congress impliedly intended federal courts to defer to arbitral decisions on Title VII issues. We deem this supposition unlikely.

Arbitral procedures, while well suited to the resolution of contractual disputes, make arbitration a comparatively inappropriate forum for the final resolution of rights created by Title VII. This conclusion rests first on the special role of the arbitrator, whose task is to effectuate the intent of the parties rather than the requirements of enacted legislation. Where the collective-bargaining agreement conflicts with Title VII, the arbitrator must follow the agreement. To be sure, the tension between contractual and statutory objectives may be mitigated where a collective-bargaining agreement contains provisions facially similar to those of Title VII. But other facts may still render arbitral processes comparatively inferior to judicial processes in the protection of Title VII rights. Among these is the fact that the specialized competence of arbitrators pertains primarily to the law of the shop, not the law of the land.... Parties usually choose an arbitrator because they trust his knowledge and judgment concerning the demands and norms of industrial relations. On the other hand, the resolution of statutory or constitutional issues is a primary responsibility of courts, and judicial construction has proved especially necessary with respect to Title VII, whose broad language frequently can be given meaning only by reference to public law concepts.

Moreover, the factfinding process in arbitration usually is not equivalent to judicial factfinding. The record of the arbitration proceedings is not as complete; the usual rules of evidence do not apply; and rights and procedures common to civil trials, such as discovery, compulsory process, cross examination, and testimony under oath, are often severely limited or unavailable.... And as this Court has recognized, '[a]rbitrators have no obligation to the court to give their reasons for an award.'.... Indeed, it is the informality of arbitral procedure that enables it to function as an efficient, inexpensive, and expeditious means for dispute resolution. This same characteristic, however, makes arbitration a less appropriate forum for final resolution of Title VII issues than the federal courts.

It is evident that respondent's proposed rule would not allay these concerns. Nor are we convinced that the solution lies in applying a more demanding deferral standard.... As respondent points out, a standard that adequately insured effectuation of Title VII rights in the arbitral forum would tend to make arbitration a procedurally complex, expensive, and time-consuming process. And judicial enforcement of such a standard would almost require courts to make *de novo* determinations of the employees' claims. It is uncertain whether any minimal savings in judicial time and expense would justify the risk to vindication of Title VII rights.

A deferral rule also might adversely affect the arbitration system as well as the enforcement scheme of Title VII. Fearing that the arbitral forum cannot adequately protect their rights under Title VII, some employees may elect to bypass arbitration and institute a lawsuit. The possibility of voluntary compliance or settlement of Title VII claims would thus be reduced, and the result could well be more litigation, not less.

We think, therefore, that the federal policy favoring arbitration of labor disputes and the federal policy against discriminatory employment practices can best be accommodated by permitting an employee to pursue fully both his remedy under the grievance-arbitration clause of a collective-bargaining agreement and his cause of action under Title VII. The federal court should consider the employee's claim *de novo*. The arbitral decision may be admitted as evidence and accorded such weight as the court deems appropriate.

The judgment of the Court of Appeals is reversed.

Reversed.

NOTES AND QUESTIONS

1. In comparison to more contemporary judicial decisions on arbitration, *Gardner-Denver* is a museum piece—both as to its reasoning and result. The Court gives primary importance to the objectives underlying the federal statute, attributes a unique character to the activity of the judicial branch of government, and actually states that arbitration is not necessarily suitable for the adjudication of all claims.

2. Under *Gardner-Denver,* the employee can either participate in collective-bargaining arbitration and then file a lawsuit or take the Title VII claim directly to court and forgo completely the grievance-arbitration machinery under the CBA. Which method would be better for an employee? Employer? Why?

3. How do you evaluate the Court's distinction regarding the source of rights? The arbitrator has jurisdiction to rule on contract but not statutory claims. What makes these rights so different in terms of importance? Are congressional objectives more central than workplace objectives?

4. Could a labor arbitrator rule on a Title VII claim if the employee (once the dispute arose) agreed to arbitrate the matter and to forgo all reference to judicial remedies? What result is mandated here by *Gardner-Denver*?

5. Does the opinion unnecessarily undermine arbitral autonomy? Why not have special labor arbitrators hear Title VII claims instead of having separate recourse to the courts?

6. Does *Gardner-Denver* share *Wilko*'s antagonism toward arbitration?

7. How should the reasoning in *Gardner-Denver* apply to a non-union setting involving an employment contract?

GILMER v. INTERSTATE/JOHNSON LANE CORP.

500 U.S. 20, 111 S.Ct. 1647, 114 L.Ed.2d 26 (1991).

(footnotes omitted)

JUSTICE WHITE delivered the opinion of the Court.

The question presented in this case is whether a claim under the Age Discrimination in Employment Act of 1967 (ADEA)...can be subjected to compulsory arbitration pursuant to an arbitration agreement in a securities registration application. The Court of Appeals held that it could...and we affirm.

I

Respondent Interstate/Johnson Lane Corporation (Interstate) hired petitioner Robert Gilmer as a Manager of Financial Services in May 1981. As required by his employment, Gilmer registered as a securities representative with several stock exchanges, including the New York Stock Exchange (NYSE).... His registration application, entitled "Uniform Application for Securities Industry Registration or Transfer," provided, among other things, that Gilmer "agree[d] to arbitrate any dispute, claim or controversy" arising between him and Interstate "that is required to be arbitrated under the rules, constitutions or by-laws of the organizations with which I register." ...Of relevance to this case, NYSE Rule 347 provides for arbitration of "[a]ny controversy between a registered representative and any member or member organization arising out of the employment or termination of employment of such registered representative."...

Interstate terminated Gilmer's employment in 1987, at which time Gilmer was 62 years of age. After first filing an age discrimination charge with the Equal Employment Opportunity Commission (EEOC), Gilmer subsequently brought suit in the United States District Court for the Western District of North Carolina, alleging that Interstate had discharged him because of his age, in violation of the ADEA. In response to Gilmer's complaint, Interstate filed in the District Court a motion to compel arbitration of the ADEA claim. In its motion, Interstate relied upon the arbitration agreement in Gilmer's registration application, as well as the Federal Arbitration Act.... The District Court denied Interstate's motion, based on this Court's decision in *Alexander v. Gardner–Denver Co.*...and because it concluded that "Congress intended to protect ADEA claimants from the waiver of a judicial forum." ...The United States Court of Appeals for the Fourth Circuit reversed, finding "nothing in the text, legislative history, or underlying purposes of the ADEA indicating a congressional intent to preclude enforcement of arbitration agreements." ...We granted *certiorari*...to resolve a conflict among the Courts of Appeals regarding the arbitrability of ADEA claims.

II

[...]

It is by now clear that statutory claims may be the subject of an arbitration agreement, enforceable pursuant to the FAA....

Although all statutory claims may not be appropriate for arbitration, "[h]aving made the bargain to arbitrate, the party should be held to it unless Congress itself has evinced an intention to preclude a waiver of judicial remedies for the statutory rights at issue." ...In this regard, we note that the burden is on Gilmer to show that Congress intended to preclude a waiver of a judicial forum for ADEA claims.... If such an intention exists, it will be discoverable in the text of the ADEA, its legislative history, or an "inherent conflict" between arbitration and the ADEA's underlying purposes.... Throughout such an inquiry, it should be kept in mind that "questions of arbitrability must be addressed with a healthy regard for the federal policy favoring arbitration."...

III

Gilmer concedes that nothing in the text of the ADEA or its legislative history explicitly precludes arbitration. He argues, however, that compulsory arbitration of ADEA claims pursuant to arbitration agreements would be inconsistent with the statutory framework and purposes of the ADEA. Like the Court of Appeals, we disagree.

A

Congress enacted the ADEA in 1967 "to promote employment of older persons based on their ability rather than age; to prohibit arbitrary age discrimination in employment; [and] to help employers and workers find ways of meeting problems arising from the impact of age on employment." ...To achieve those goals, the ADEA, among other things, makes it unlawful for an employer "to fail or refuse to hire or to discharge any individual or otherwise discriminate against any individual with respect to his compensation, terms, conditions, or privileges of employment, because of such individual's age." ...This proscription is enforced both by private suits and by the EEOC. In order for an aggrieved individual to bring suit under the ADEA, he or she must first file a charge with the EEOC and then wait at least 60 days.... An individual's right to sue is extinguished, however, if the EEOC institutes an action against the employer.... Before the EEOC can bring such an action, though, it must "attempt to eliminate the discriminatory practice or practices alleged, and to effect voluntary compliance with the requirements of this chapter through informal methods of conciliation, conference, and persuasion."...

As Gilmer contends, the ADEA is designed not only to address individual grievances, but also to further important social policies.... We do not perceive any inherent inconsistency between those policies, however, and enforcing agreements to arbitrate age discrimination claims. It is true that arbitration focuses on specific disputes between the parties involved. The same can be said, however, of judicial resolution of claims. Both of these dispute resolution mechanisms nevertheless also can further broader social purposes. The Sherman Act, the Securities Exchange Act of

1934, RICO, and the Securities Act of 1933 all are designed to advance important public policies, but, as noted above, claims under those statutes are appropriate for arbitration. "[S]o long as the prospective litigant effectively may vindicate [his or her] statutory cause of action in the arbitral forum, the statute will continue to serve both its remedial and deterrent function.". . .

We also are unpersuaded by the argument that arbitration will undermine the role of the EEOC in enforcing the ADEA. An individual ADEA claimant subject to an arbitration agreement will still be free to file a charge with the EEOC, even though the claimant is not able to institute a private judicial action. Indeed, Gilmer filed a charge with the EEOC in this case. In any event, the EEOC's role in combating age discrimination is not dependent on the filing of a charge; the agency may receive information concerning alleged violations of the ADEA "from any source," and it has independent authority to investigate age discrimination.... Moreover, nothing in the ADEA indicates that Congress intended that the EEOC be involved in all employment disputes. Such disputes can be settled, for example, without any EEOC involvement.... Finally, the mere involvement of an administrative agency in the enforcement of a statute is not sufficient to preclude arbitration. For example, the Securities Exchange Commission is heavily involved in the enforcement of the Securities Exchange Act of 1934 and the Securities Act of 1933, but we have held that claims under both of those statutes may be subject to compulsory arbitration....

Gilmer also argues that compulsory arbitration is improper because it deprives claimants of the judicial forum provided for by the ADEA. Congress, however, did not explicitly preclude arbitration or other nonjudicial resolution of claims, even in its recent amendments to the ADEA.... Moreover, Gilmer's argument ignores the ADEA's flexible approach to resolution of claims. The EEOC, for example, is directed to pursue "informal methods of conciliation, conference, and persuasion,". . .which suggests that out-of-court dispute resolution, such as arbitration, is consistent with the statutory scheme established by Congress. In addition, arbitration is consistent with Congress' grant of concurrent jurisdiction over ADEA claims to state and federal courts....

B

In arguing that arbitration is inconsistent with the ADEA, Gilmer also raises a host of challenges to the adequacy of arbitration procedures. Initially, we note that in our recent arbitration cases we have already rejected most of these arguments as insufficient to preclude arbitration of statutory claims....

Gilmer first speculates that arbitration panels will be biased.... [W]e note that the NYSE arbitration rules, which are applicable to the dispute in this case, provide protections against biased panels. The rules require, for example, that the parties be informed of the employment histories of the arbitrators, and that they be allowed to make further inquiries into the arbitrators' backgrounds.... In addition, each party is allowed one peremptory challenge and unlimited challenges for cause.... Moreover, the arbitrators are required to disclose "any circumstances which might preclude [them] from rendering an objective and impartial determination." ... The FAA also protects against bias, by providing that courts may overturn arbitration decisions "[w]here there was evident partiality or corruption in the arbitrators." ... There has been no showing in this case that those provisions are inadequate to guard against potential bias.

Gilmer also complains that the discovery allowed in arbitration is more limited than in the federal courts, which he contends will make it difficult to prove discrimination. It is unlikely, however, that age discrimination claims require more extensive discovery than other claims that we have found to be arbitrable, such as RICO and antitrust claims. Moreover, there has been no showing in this case that the NYSE discovery provisions, which allow for document production, information requests, depositions, and subpoenas,... will prove insufficient to allow ADEA claimants such as Gilmer a fair opportunity to present their claims. Although those procedures might not be as extensive as in the federal courts, by agreeing to arbitrate, a party "trades the procedures and opportunity for review of the courtroom for the simplicity, informality, and expedition of arbitration." ... Indeed, an important counterweight to the reduced discovery in NYSE arbitration is that arbitrators are not bound by the rules of evidence....

A further alleged deficiency of arbitration is that arbitrators often will not issue written opinions, resulting, Gilmer contends, in a lack of public knowledge of employers' discriminatory policies, an inability to obtain effective appellate review, and a stifling of the development of the law. The NYSE rules, however, do require that all arbitration awards be in writing, and that the awards contain the names of the parties, a summary of the issues in controversy, and a description of the award issued.... In addition, the award decisions are made available to the public.... Furthermore, judicial decisions addressing ADEA claims will continue to be issued because it is unlikely that all or even most ADEA claimants will be subject to arbitration agreements. Finally, Gilmer's concerns apply equally to settlements of ADEA claims, which, as noted above, are clearly allowed.

It is also argued that arbitration procedures cannot adequately further the purposes of the ADEA because they do not provide for broad equitable relief and class actions. As the court below noted, however, arbitrators do have the power to fashion equitable relief.... Indeed, the NYSE rules applicable here do not restrict the types of relief an arbitrator may award, but merely refer to "damages and/or other relief." ... The NYSE rules also provide for collective proceedings.... But "even if the arbitration could not go forward as a class action or class relief could not be granted by the arbitrator, the fact that the [ADEA] provides for the possibility of bringing a collective action does not mean that individual attempts at conciliation were intended to be barred." ... Finally, it should be remembered that arbitration agreements will not preclude the EEOC from bringing actions seeking class-wide and equitable relief.

C

An additional reason advanced by Gilmer for refusing to enforce arbitration agreements relating to ADEA claims is his contention that there often will be unequal bargaining power between employers and employees. Mere inequality in bargaining power, however, is not a sufficient reason to hold that arbitration agreements are never enforceable in the employment context. Relationships between securities dealers and investors, for example, may involve unequal bargaining power, but we nevertheless held in *Rodriguez de Quijas* and *McMahon* that agreements to arbitrate in that context are enforceable.... There is no indication in this case, however, that Gilmer, an experienced businessman, was coerced or defrauded into agreeing to the arbitration clause in his registration application. As with the claimed procedural inadequacies discussed above, this claim of unequal bargaining power is best left for resolution in specific cases.

IV

In addition to the arguments discussed above, Gilmer vigorously asserts that our decision in *Alexander v. Gardner–Denver Co.*.....and its progeny...preclude arbitration of employment discrimination claims. Gilmer's reliance on these cases, however, is misplaced.

In *Gardner-Denver*, the issue was whether a discharged employee whose grievance had been arbitrated pursuant to an arbitration clause in a collective-bargaining agreement was precluded from subsequently bringing a Title VII action based upon the conduct that was the subject of the grievance. In holding that the employee was not foreclosed from bringing the Title VII claim, we stressed that an employee's contractual rights under a collective-bargaining agreement are distinct from the employee's statutory Title VII rights:

> "In submitting his grievance to arbitration, an employee seeks to vindicate his contractual right under a collective-bargaining agreement. By contrast, in filing a lawsuit under Title VII, an employee asserts independent statutory rights accorded by Congress. The distinctly separate nature of these contractual and statutory rights is not vitiated merely because both were violated as a result of the same factual occurrence...."

We also noted that a labor arbitrator has authority only to resolve questions of contractual rights.... The arbitrator's "task is to effectuate the intent of the parties" and he or she does not have the "general authority to invoke public laws that conflict with the bargain between the parties." ...By contrast, "in instituting an action under Title VII, the employee is not seeking review of the arbitrator's decision. Rather, he is asserting a statutory right independent of the arbitration process." ...We further expressed concern that in collective-bargaining arbitration "the interests of the individual employee may be subordinated to the collective interests of all employees in the bargaining unit." ...

[. . .]

There are several important distinctions between the *Gardner-Denver* line of cases and the case before us. First, those cases did not involve the issue of the enforceability of an agreement to arbitrate statutory claims. Rather, they involved the quite different issue whether arbitration of contract-based claims precluded subsequent judicial resolution of statutory claims. Since the employees there had not agreed to arbitrate their statutory claims, and the labor arbitrators were not authorized to resolve such claims, the arbitration in those cases understandably was held not to preclude subsequent statutory actions. Second, because the arbitration in those cases occurred in the context of a collective-bargaining agreement, the claimants there were represented by their unions in the arbitration proceedings. An important concern therefore was the tension between collective representation and individual statutory rights, a concern not applicable to the present case. Finally, those cases were not decided under the FAA, which, as discussed above, reflects a "liberal federal policy favoring arbitration agreements." ... Therefore, those cases provide no basis for refusing to enforce Gilmer's agreement to arbitrate his ADEA claim.

V

We conclude that Gilmer has not met his burden of showing that Congress, in enacting the ADEA, intended to preclude arbitration of claims under that Act. Accordingly, the judgment of the Court of Appeals is *Affirmed*.

JUSTICE STEVENS, with whom JUSTICE MARSHALL joins, dissenting.

Section 1 of the Federal Arbitration Act (FAA) states:

"[N]othing herein contained shall apply to contracts of employment of seamen, railroad employees, or any other class of workers engaged in foreign or interstate commerce." ...

The Court today, in holding that the FAA compels enforcement of arbitration clauses even when claims of age discrimination are at issue, skirts the antecedent question whether the coverage of the Act even extends to arbitration clauses contained in employment contracts, regardless of the subject matter of the claim at issue. In my opinion, arbitration clauses contained in employment agreements are specifically exempt from coverage of the FAA. ...

I

[. . .]

Notwithstanding the apparent waiver of the issue below, I believe that the Court should reach the issue of the coverage of the FAA to employment disputes because resolution of the question is so clearly antecedent to disposition of this case. On a number of occasions, this Court has considered issues waived by the parties below and in the petition for certiorari because the issues were so integral to decision of the case that they could be considered "fairly subsumed" by the actual questions presented. . . .

[. . .]

II

The Court, declining to reach the issue for the reason that petitioner never raised it below, nevertheless concludes that "it would be inappropriate to address the scope of the § 1 exclusion because the arbitration clause being enforced here is not contained in a contract of employment. . . . Rather, the arbitration clause at issue is in Gilmer's securities registration application, which is a contract with the securities exchanges, not with Interstate." . . . In my opinion the Court too narrowly construes the scope of the exclusion contained in § 1 of the FAA.

There is little dispute that the primary concern animating the FAA was the perceived need by the business community to overturn the common-law rule that denied specific enforcement of agreements to arbitrate in contracts between business entities. . . . At the Senate Judiciary Subcommittee hearings on the proposed bill, the chairman of the ABA committee responsible for drafting the bill assured the Senators that the bill "is not intended [to] be an act referring to labor disputes, at all. It is purely an act to give the merchants the right or the privilege of sitting down and agreeing with each other as to what their damages are, if they want to do it. Now that is all there is in this." . . .

Given that the FAA specifically was intended to exclude arbitration agreements between employees and employers, I see no reason to limit this exclusion from coverage to arbitration clauses contained in agreements entitled "Contract of Employment." In this case, the parties conceded at oral argument that Gilmer had no "contract of employment" as such with respondent. Gilmer was, however, required as a condition of his employment to become a registered representative of several stock exchanges, including the New York Stock Exchange (NYSE). Just because his agreement to arbitrate any "dispute, claim or controversy" with his employer that arose out of the employment relationship was contained in his application for registration before the NYSE rather than in a specific contract of employment with his employer, I do not think that Gilmer can be compelled pursuant to the FAA to arbitrate his employment-related dispute. Rather, in my opinion the exclusion in § 1 should be interpreted to cover any agreements by the employee to arbitrate disputes with the employer arising out of the employment relationship, particularly where such agreements to arbitrate are conditions of employment.

My reading of the scope of the exclusion contained in § 1 is supported by early judicial interpretations of the FAA. As of 1956, three Courts of Appeals had held that the FAA's exclusion of "contracts of employment" referred not only to individual contracts of employment, but also to collective-bargaining agreements.... Indeed, the application of the FAA's exclusionary clause to arbitration provisions in collective-bargaining agreements was one of the issues raised in the petition for certiorari and briefed at great length in *Lincoln Mills* and its companion cases.... Although the Court decided the enforceability of the arbitration provisions in the collective-bargaining agreements by reference to § 301 of the Labor Management Relations Act,...it did not reject the Courts of Appeals' holdings that the arbitration provisions would not otherwise be enforceable pursuant to the FAA since they were specifically excluded under § 1....

III

Not only would I find that the FAA does not apply to employment-related disputes between employers and employees in general, but also I would hold that compulsory arbitration conflicts with the congressional purpose animating the ADEA, in particular. As this Court previously has noted, authorizing the courts to issue broad injunctive relief is the cornerstone to eliminating discrimination in society.... The ADEA, like Title VII of the Civil Rights Act of 1964, authorizes courts to award broad, class-based injunctive relief to achieve the purposes of the Act.... Because commercial arbitration is typically limited to a specific dispute between the particular parties and because the available remedies in arbitral forums generally do not provide for class-wide injunctive relief,...I would conclude that an essential purpose of the ADEA is frustrated by compulsory arbitration of employment discrimination claims. Moreover, as Chief Justice Burger explained:

> "Plainly, it would not comport with the congressional objectives behind a statute seeking to enforce civil rights protected by Title VII to allow the very forces that had practiced discrimination to contract away the right to enforce civil rights in the courts. For federal courts to defer to arbitral decisions reached by the same combination of forces that had long perpetuated invidious discrimination would have made the foxes guardians of the chickens."...

In my opinion the same concerns expressed by Chief Justice Burger with regard to compulsory arbitration of Title VII claims may be said of claims arising under the ADEA. The Court's holding today clearly eviscerates the important role played by an independent judiciary in eradicating employment discrimination.

IV

When the FAA was passed in 1925, I doubt that any legislator who voted for it expected it to apply to statutory claims, to form contracts between parties of unequal bargaining power, or to the arbitration of disputes arising out of the employment relationship. In recent years, however, the Court "has effectively rewritten the statute," and abandoned its earlier view that statutory claims were not appropriate subjects for arbitration. . . . Although I remain persuaded that it erred in doing so, the Court has also put to one side any concern about the inequality of bargaining power between an entire industry, on the one hand, and an individual customer or employee, on the other. . . . Until today, however, the Court has not read § 2 of the FAA as broadly encompassing disputes arising out of the employment relationship. I believe this additional extension of the FAA is erroneous. Accordingly, I respectfully dissent.

NOTES AND QUESTIONS

1.   In his dissent, Justice Stevens emphasizes that the contract in question is an employment contract and does not directly contain an arbitral clause. Does the obligation to arbitrate exist by ricochet as well as by adhesionary provision? Which parties agreed to arbitration? Is the agreement to arbitrate a valid contract? What does Section One of the FAA say about arbitral provisions in employment contracts?

2.   Would the existence of a submission agreement alter the reasoning or result in *Gilmer*? What concerns of legality and policy would the use of a submission address in the *Gilmer* facts? Would it address the most fundamental concern? What is the most fundamental concern in *Gilmer*?

3.   The majority addresses in some detail Gilmer's objections to the use of arbitration to adjudicate age discrimination claims. Evaluate the Court's statements and what they imply about the Court's attitude toward questions raised in arbitration litigation. Do you find any of the Court's statements reassuring in terms of the adjudication of political rights in arbitration?

4.   At the end of the majority opinion, Justice White characterizes the agreement to arbitrate as a set of "trade-offs" accepted by the employee and minimizes the "mere inequality of bargaining position" between the parties to the agreement. Are these statements an accurate reflection of the reality of the employment situation? Don't they make the contract and the circumstances of the transaction the exclusive vehicle of legal regulation? What is left of the role of law and basic fairness? Aren't these characterizations truly astounding and a radical departure from prior judicial practice?

5.   Focus upon the dissent's reference to the FAA's legislative history in terms of its application to labor matters and to the history of the arbitration of labor grievances at the end of Section II of the opinion. Doesn't the reference to these factors effectively refute the majority's absolute position on arbitration? Why doesn't the majority take this history into account? Does historical fact become irrelevant to the judicial decision-making in this area? In what other cases has the Court used legislative history in its rationale? Is it usually done in dissent, as in *Gilmer*? Is it fair to say that the Court has strayed quite far from its position in *Alexander v. Gardner–Denver Co.*? Do employees still have a "second bite at the apple"?

The Ruling in *Wright*

In 1998, the U.S. Supreme Court rendered its ruling in *Wright v. Universal Maritime Service Corp.*, 525 U.S. 70 (1998). In its opinion, delivered by Justice Scalia for a unanimous bench, the Court reversed a

Fourth Circuit ruling that a worker must first bring his ADA claim to collective bargaining arbitration before filing a lawsuit to vindicate his statutory rights.

Guided by its decision in *Austin v. Owens–Brockway Glass Container*, 78 F.3d 875 (4th Cir.), *cert. denied*, 519 U.S. 980 (1996), the Fourth Circuit had held that CBA provisions "to arbitrate employment disputes are binding upon individual employees even when the dispute involves a federal cause of action." Accordingly, "a failure to process a claim under the [labor] agreement precludes a court from exercising jurisdiction over the merits of the claim."

The Court saw Wright's claim as purely statutory, not contractual. The "presumption of arbitrability" did not apply because that presumption only involved claims that arose under the labor agreement. Moreover, a collective bargaining agreement's requirement to arbitrate statutory claims "must be particularly clear." The CBA's arbitration clause in this case was very general, providing for arbitration of "matters under dispute," with no explicit incorporation into the agreement of statutory antidiscrimination protections. The Court's conclusion was that the collective agreement "[did] not contain a clear and unmistakable waiver of the covered employee's right to a judicial forum for federal claims of employment discrimination."

The Court acknowledged the "tension" between *Alexander v. Gardner–Denver* and *Gilmer v. Interstate/Johnson Lane*. It, however, found it unnecessary to address and resolve any of the differences between the two lines of authority.

WRIGHT v. UNIVERSAL MARITIME SERVICE CORP.

525 U.S. 70, 119 S.Ct. 391, 142 L.Ed.2d 361 (1998).

(all emphasis in the original)

Justice Scalia delivered the opinion of the Court.

This case presents the question whether a general arbitration clause in a collective-bargaining agreement (CBA) requires an employee to use the arbitration procedure for an alleged violation of the Americans with Disabilities Act of 1990 (ADA)....

[. . .]

II

In this case, the Fourth Circuit concluded that the general arbitration provision in the CBA governing Wright's employment was sufficiently broad to encompass a statutory claim arising under the ADA, and that such a provision was enforceable. The latter conclusion brings into question two lines of our case law. The first is represented by *Alexander v. Gardner–Denver Co....* which held that an employee does not forfeit his right to a judicial forum for the claimed discriminatory discharge in violation of Title VII of the Civil Rights Act of 1964...if "he first pursues his grievance to final arbitration under the nondiscrimination clause of a collective-bargaining agreement." ...In rejecting the argument that the doctrine of election of remedies barred the Title VII lawsuit, we reasoned that a grievance is designed to vindicate a "contractual right" under a CBA, while a lawsuit under Title VII asserts "independent statutory rights accorded by Congress." ...The statutory cause of action was not waived by the union's agreement to the arbitration provision of the CBA, since "there can be no prospective waiver of an employee's rights under Title VII."... We have followed the holding of *Gardner-Denver* in deciding the effect of CBA arbitration upon employee claims under other statutes....

The second line of cases implicated here is represented by *Gilmer v. Interstate/Johnson Lane Corp....*, which held that a claim brought under the [ADEA]...could be subject to compulsory arbitration pursuant to an arbitration provision in a securities registration form. Relying upon the federal policy favoring arbitration embodied in the Federal Arbitration Act..., we said that "statutory claims may be the subject of an arbitration agreement, enforceable pursuant to the FAA."

There is obviously some tension between these two lines of cases. Whereas *Gardner-Denver* stated that "an employee's rights under Title VII are not susceptible of prospective waiver,"...*Gilmer* held that the right to a federal judicial forum for an ADEA claims could be waived. Petitioner and the United States as *amicus* would have us reconcile the lines of authority by maintaining that federal forum rights cannot be waived in union-negotiated CBAs even if they can be waived in individually executed contracts—a distinction that assuredly finds support in the text of *Gilmer....* Respondents and their *amici*, on the other hand, contend that the real difference between *Gardner-Denver* and *Gilmer* is the radical change, over two decades, in the Court's receptivity to arbitration, leading *Gilmer* to affirm that "questions of arbitrability must be addressed with a healthy regard for the federal policy favoring arbitration,"...; *Gilmer*, they argue, has sufficiently undermined *Gardner-Denver* that a union *can* waive employees' rights to a judicial forum. Although, as will appear, we find *Gardner-Denver* and *Gilmer* relevant for various purposes to the case before us, we find it unnecessary to resolve the question of the validity of a union-negotiated waiver, since it is apparent to us, on the facts and arguments presented here, that no such waiver has occurred.

III

In asserting the existence of an agreement to arbitrate the ADA claim, respondents rely upon the presumption of arbitrability this Court has found in § 301 of the Labor Management Relations Act, 1947 (LMRA)....

That presumption, however, does not extend beyond the reach of the principal rationale that justifies it, which is that arbitrators are in a better position than courts to *interpret the terms of a CBA....* The dispute in the present case, however, ultimately concerns not the application or interpretation of any CBA, but the meaning of a federal statute. The cause of action Wright asserts arises not out of contract, but out of the ADA, and is distinct from any right conferred by the collective-bargaining agreement.... To be sure, respondents argue that Wright is not qualified for his position as the CBA requires, but even if that were true he would *still* prevail if the refusal to hire violated the ADA.

Nor is the statutory (as opposed to contractual) focus of the claim altered by the fact that Clause 17 of the CBA recites it to be "the intention and purpose of all parties hereto that no provision or part of this Agreement shall be violative of any Federal or State Law."...As we discuss below in Part IV, this does not incorporate the ADA by reference. Even if it did so, however—thereby creating a contractual right that is coextensive with the federal statutory right—the ultimate question for the arbitrator would be not what the parties have agreed to, but what federal law requires; and that is not a question which should be *presumed* to be included within the arbitration requirement. Application of that principle is unaffected by the fact that the CBA in this case, unlike the one in *Gardner-Denver*, does not expressly limit the arbitrator to interpreting and applying the contract. The *presumption* only extends that far, whether or not the text of the agreement is similarly limited. It may well be that ordinary textual analysis of a CBA will show that matters which go beyond the interpretation and application of contract terms are subject to arbitration; but they will not be *presumed* to be so.

IV

Not only is petitioner's statutory claim not subject to a presumption of arbitrability; we think any CBA requirement to arbitrate ... must be particularly clear. In *Metropolitan Edison Co. v. NLRB*, 460 U.S. 693 (1983), we stated that a union could waive its officers' statutory right...to be free of antiunion discrimination, but we held that such a waiver must be clear and unmistakable....

We think the same standard applicable to a union-negotiated waiver of employees' statutory right to a judicial forum for claims of employment discrimination.... *Gardner-Denver* at least stands for the proposition that the right to a federal judicial forum is of sufficient importance to be protected against less-than-explicit union waiver in a CBA.... *Gilmer* involved an individual's waiver of his own rights, rather than a union's waiver of the rights of represented employees—and hence the "clear and unmistakable" standard was not applicable.

[...]

We hold that the collective-bargaining agreement in this case does not contain a clear and unmistakable waiver of the covered employees' rights to a judicial forum for federal claims of employment discrimination. We do not reach the question whether such a waiver would be enforceable. The judgment of the Fourth Circuit is vacated, and the case is remanded for further proceedings consistent with this opinion.

It is so ordered.

NOTES AND QUESTIONS

1. What does the U.S. Supreme Court achieve in *Wright*? Does the Court's reasoning successfully resolve the "tension" between *Gardner-Denver* and *Gilmer*? Does the "narrow" holding reflect a political failure within the Court? Do you agree that the Justices, in effect, failed to arrive at a real consensus?

2. Restate the Court's holding. Is the strained subtlety a means of expressing the indeterminacy of result?

3. Do federal courts distrust and even demean unions? The attitude toward unions in *Wright* converges with its counterpart in *Pryner*. Is the position a political or juridical statement?

4. The Fourth Circuit subsequently applied *Wright* in *Brown v. ABF Freight Systems, Inc.*, 183 F.3d 319 (4th Cir. 1999), *rev'g*, 997 F.Supp. 714 (E.D. Va. 1998). Ever faithful to systemic authority, that court held that an arbitration clause within a CBA lacked the requisite clarity to compel the arbitration of an ADA employment claim. In deciding *Brown*, the Fourth Circuit also took into account its recent decision in *Carson v. Giant Food, Inc.*, 175 F.3d 325 (4th Cir. 1999), in which it applied *Wright* and concluded that the CBA in question did not compel the arbitration of the appellee's statutory claims. With the benefit of both decisions, the court stated, "our task today is limited to determining whether the particular CBA in this case effectuates such a waiver. Before *Universal Maritime*, we may well have concluded that it does. In the face of that binding precedent, however, we are constrained to conclude that it does not." Further, "[I]n making that determination, however, we do not apply the usual interpretive presumption in favor of arbitration ... [r]ather, under the rule of *Universal Maritime*, we will not find an intent to arbitrate statutory claims absent a 'clear and unmistakable' waiver of an employee's 'statutory right to a judicial forum for claims of employment discrimination.'"

5. In *Carson*, the court explained that the requirement of a "clear and unmistakable" waiver can be satisfied in two ways: (1) such intent can be demonstrated through the drafting of an "explicit arbitration clause" pursuant to which the union agrees to submit all statutory employment-discrimination claims to arbitration; and (2) where the arbitration clause is "not so clear," employees might still be bound to arbitrate their federal claims if there is another provision in the CBA, like a nondiscrimination clause, that makes it unmistakably clear that the discrimination statutes at issue are part of the agreement.

6. In *Brown*, the Fourth Circuit found the arbitration clause contained in Article 37 insufficient to be sustained under *Universal Maritime*. The standard clause, submitting to arbitration "all grievances or questions of interpretation arising under...this Agreement," referred only to grievances arising under the Agreement, and "it cannot be read to require arbitration of those grievances arising out of alleged statutory violations." Moreover, the court opined, there was not another provision in the CBA which established

with the "requisite degree of clarity" that the discrimination statute (ADA claim) was part of the agreement. The nondiscrimination clause found in Article 37 did not make it "unmistakably clear" that it was incorporating federal statutory discrimination law.

The court stated, "[t]here is a significant difference, and we believe a legally dispositive one, between an agreement not to commit discriminatory acts that are prohibited by law and an agreement to incorporate, in toto, the antidiscrimination statutes that prohibit those acts....Rather, the parties must make 'unmistakably clear' their intent to incorporate in their entirety the 'discrimination statutes at issue', as we said in *Carson*." Moreover, "[t]he specific reference to the ADA in the second sentence of Article 37 which appellee contends confirms the ADA's explicit incorporation as part of the agreement we believe actually confirms our view that the preceding sentence does not constitute explicit incorporation of that statute into the agreement....Clearly, if the parties have already incorporated all federal statutory discrimination law into their contractual agreement, there would be no need to specify that individuals with a 'qualified disability under the ADA' were also covered."

7. Does the Fourth Circuit accurately interpret the ruling in *Wright*? What impact does *Wright* have upon the resolution of *Brown*?

8. Has the Fourth Circuit repudiated its decision in *Austin v. Owens–Brockway Glass Container, Inc.*, 78 F.3d 875 (4th Cir.), *cert. denied*, 519 U.S. 980 (1996)? *Austin* represented a categorical statement in favor of establishing the *Gilmer* holding as reigning doctrine and, concomitantly, of viewing *Gardner-Denver* as overruled and nullified. In the Fourth Circuit's reasoning, the effect of an arbitration agreement was clear and unmistakable—no matter the context of its application or impact on rights. Most federal courts found *Austin* too drastic in reasoning and result, despite its clarity. The court held in *Austin* that,

> [B]y agreeing to arbitrate a statutory claim, a party does not forgo the substantive rights afforded by the statute; it only submits to their resolution in an arbitral, rather than a judicial, forum.

> . . . *Gilmer* thus rejects the principal concern in *Alexander v. Gardner–Denver Co.* . . . that statutory arbitration is an "inappropriate forum" for the resolution of Title VII statutory rights....

> Emphasizing its support of arbitration as a method of dispute resolution, the *Gilmer* Court stated:

>> [A]ttacks on [the adequacy] of arbitration 'res[t] on suspicion of arbitration as a method of weakening the protections afforded in the substantive law to would-be complainants,' and as such, they are 'far out of step with our current strong endorsement of the federal statutes favoring this method of resolving disputes.' . . .

Elsewhere in *Austin*, the Fourth Circuit stated:

> In all of the cases, however, including the case at hand, the employee attempting to sue had made an agreement to arbitrate employment disputes. Whether the dispute arises under a contract of employment growing out of securities registration application, a simple employment contract, or

a collective bargaining agreement, an agreement has yet been made to arbitrate the dispute. So long as the agreement is voluntary, it is valid, and we are of opinion it should be enforced.

Evaluate the last statement. What is the court saying? Does it deny that there are different forms of arbitration that implicate different individual and policy interests?

14 PENN PLAZA LLC v. PYETT

556 U.S. ___, 129 S.Ct. 1456, 173 L.Ed.2d 398 (2009).

JUSTICE THOMAS delivered the opinion of the Court.

The question presented by this case is whether a provision in a collective-bargaining agreement that clearly and unmistakably requires union members to arbitrate claims arising under the Age Discrimination in Employment Act of 1967 (ADEA) . . . is enforceable. The United States Court of Appeals for the Second Circuit held that this Court's decision in *Alexander* v. *Gardner-Denver Co.*, 415 U.S. 36, 94 S. Ct. 1011, 39 L. Ed. 2d 147 (1974), forbids enforcement of such arbitration provisions. We disagree and reverse the judgment of the Court of Appeals.

I

Respondents are members of the Service Employees International Union, Local 32BJ (Union). Under the National Labor Relations Act (NLRA), 49 Stat. 449, as amended, the Union is the exclusive bargaining representative of employees within the building-services industry in New York City, which includes building cleaners, porters, and doorpersons. . . . In this role, the Union has exclusive authority to bargain on behalf of its members over their "rates of pay, wages, hours of employment, or other conditions of employment." . . . Since the 1930's, the Union has engaged in industry-wide collective bargaining with the Realty Advisory Board on Labor Relations, Inc. (RAB), a multiemployer bargaining association for the New York City real-estate industry. The agreement between the Union and the RAB is embodied in their Collective Bargaining Agreement for Contractors and Building Owners (CBA). The CBA requires union members to submit all claims of employment discrimination to binding arbitration under the CBA's grievance and dispute resolution procedures.

[. . .]

Petitioner 14 Penn Plaza LLC is a member of the RAB. It owns and operates the New York City office building where, prior to August 2003, respondents worked as night lobby watchmen and in other similar capacities. Respondents were directly employed by petitioner Temco Service Industries, Inc. (Temco), a maintenance service and cleaning contractor. In August 2003, with the Union's consent, 14 Penn Plaza engaged Spartan Security, a unionized security services contractor and affiliate of Temco, to provide licensed security guards to staff the lobby and entrances of its building. Because this rendered respondents' lobby services unnecessary, Temco reassigned them to jobs as night porters and light duty cleaners in other locations in the building. Respondents contend that these reassignments led to a loss in income, caused them emotional distress, and were otherwise less desirable than their former positions.

At respondents' request, the Union filed grievances challenging the reassignments. The grievances alleged that petitioners: (1) violated the CBA's ban on workplace discrimination by reassigning respondents on account of their age; (2) violated seniority rules by failing to promote one of the respondents to a handyman position; and (3) failed to equitably rotate overtime. After failing to obtain relief on any of these claims through the grievance process, the Union requested arbitration under the CBA.

After the initial arbitration hearing, the Union withdrew the first set of respondents' grievances—the age-discrimination claims—from arbitration. Because it had consented to the contract for new security personnel at 14 Penn Plaza, the Union believed that it could not legitimately object to respondents' reassignments as discriminatory. But the Union continued to arbitrate the seniority and overtime claims, and, after several hearings, the claims were denied.

In May 2004, while the arbitration was ongoing but after the Union withdrew the age-discrimination claims, respondents filed a complaint with the Equal Employment Opportunity Commission (EEOC) alleging that petitioners had violated their rights under the ADEA. Approximately one month later, the EEOC issued a Dismissal and Notice of Rights, which explained that the agency's " 'review of the evidence ... fail[ed] to indicate that a violation ha[d] occurred,' " and notified each respondent of his right to sue....

Respondents thereafter filed suit against petitioners in the United States District Court for the Southern District of New York, alleging that their reassignment violated the ADEA and state and local laws prohibiting age discrimination. [Footnote omitted.] Petitioners filed a motion to compel arbitration of respondents' claims pursuant to § 3 and § 4 of the Federal Arbitration Act (FAA), 9 U.S.C. §§ 3, 4. [Footnote omitted.] The District Court denied the motion because under Second Circuit precedent, "even a clear and unmistakable union-negotiated waiver of a right to litigate certain federal and state statutory claims in a judicial forum is unenforceable." ... Respondents immediately appealed the ruling under § 16 of the FAA, which authorizes an interlocutory appeal of "an order ... refusing a stay of any action under section 3 of this title" or "denying a petition under section 4 of this title to order arbitration to proceed." ...

The Court of Appeals affirmed.... According to the Court of Appeals, it could not compel arbitration of the dispute because *Gardner-Denver*, which "remains good law," held "that a collective bargaining agreement could not waive covered workers' rights to a judicial forum for causes of action created by Congress." ... The Court of Appeals observed that the *Gardner-Denver* decision was in tension with this Court's more recent decision in *Gilmer* v. *Interstate/Johnson Lane Corp.*, 500 U.S. 20 (1991), which "held that an individual employee who had agreed individually to waive his right to a federal forum *could* be compelled to arbitrate a federal age discrimination claim." [Emphasis in the original opinion.] ... The Court of Appeals also noted that this Court previously declined to resolve this tension in *Wright* v. *Universal Maritime Service Corp.*, 525 U.S. 70 (1998), where the waiver at issue was not "clear and unmistakable." ...

The Court of Appeals attempted to reconcile *Gardner-Denver* and *Gilmer* by holding that arbitration provisions in a collective-bargaining agreement, "which purport to waive employees' rights to a federal forum with respect to statutory claims, are unenforceable." ... As a result, an individual employee would be free to choose compulsory arbitration under *Gilmer*, but a labor union could not collectively bargain for arbitration on behalf of its members. We granted *certiorari*, 552 U.S. ___, 128 S. Ct. 1223 (2008), to address the issue left unresolved in *Wright*, which continues to divide the Courts of Appeals, [footnote omitted] and now reverse.

II

A

[...]

In this instance, the Union and the RAB, negotiating on behalf of 14 Penn Plaza, collectively bargained in good faith and agreed that employment-related discrimination claims, including claims brought under the ADEA, would be resolved in arbitration. This freely negotiated term between the Union and the RAB easily qualifies as a "conditio[n] of employment" that is subject to mandatory bargaining under § 159(a).... The decision to fashion a CBA to require arbitration of employment-discrimination claims is no different from the many other decisions made by parties in designing grievance machinery.[1]

Respondents, however, contend that the arbitration clause here is outside the permissible scope of the collective-bargaining process because it affects the "employees' individual, non-economic statutory rights." ... We disagree. Parties generally favor arbitration precisely because of the economics of dispute resolution.... As in any contractual negotiation, a union may agree to the inclusion of an arbitration provision in a collective-bargaining agreement in return for other concessions from the employer. Courts generally may not interfere in this bargained-for exchange. "Judicial nullification of contractual concessions ... is contrary to what

---

1. JUSTICE SOUTER claims that this understanding is "impossible to square with our conclusion in [*Alexander* v.] *Gardner-Denver* ... that 'Title VII ... stands on plainly different ground' from 'statutory rights related to collective activity': 'it concerns not majoritarian processes, but an individual's right to equal employment opportunities.'" ... (dissenting opinion) (quoting *Gardner-Denver* ... As explained below, however, JUSTICE SOUTER repeats the key analytical mistake made in *Gardner-Denver*'s *dicta* by equating the decision to arbitrate Title VII and ADEA claims to a decision to forgo these substantive guarantees against workplace discrimination.... The right to a judicial forum is not the nonwaivable "substantive" right protected by the ADEA.... Thus, although Title VII and ADEA rights may well stand on "different ground" than statutory rights that protect "majoritarian processes," ... the voluntary decision to collectively bargain for arbitration does not deny those statutory antidiscrimination rights the full protection they are due.

the Court has recognized as one of the fundamental policies of the National Labor Relations Act—freedom of contract." ...

As a result, the CBA's arbitration provision must be honored unless the ADEA itself removes this particular class of grievances from the NLRA's broad sweep.... It does not. This Court has squarely held that the ADEA does not preclude arbitration of claims brought under the statute....

In *Gilmer*, the Court explained that "[a]lthough all statutory claims may not be appropriate for arbitration, 'having made the bargain to arbitrate, the party should be held to it unless Congress itself has evinced an intention to preclude a waiver of judicial remedies for the statutory rights at issue.' " ... And "if Congress intended the substantive protection afforded by the ADEA to include protection against waiver of the right to a judicial forum, that intention will be deducible from text or legislative history." ... The Court determined that "nothing in the text of the ADEA or its legislative history explicitly precludes arbitration." ... The Court also concluded that arbitrating ADEA disputes would not undermine the statute's "remedial and deterrent function." ... In the end, the employee's "generalized attacks" on "the adequacy of arbitration procedures" were "insufficient to preclude arbitration of statutory claims," ... because there was no evidence that "Congress, in enacting the ADEA, intended to preclude arbitration of claims under that Act."
...

The *Gilmer* Court's interpretation of the ADEA fully applies in the collective-bargaining context. Nothing in the law suggests a distinction between the status of arbitration agreements signed by an individual employee and those agreed to by a union representative. This Court has required only that an agreement to arbitrate statutory antidiscrimination claims be "explicitly stated" in the collective-bargaining agreement. *Wright*, 525 U.S., at 80.... The CBA under review here meets that obligation. Respondents incorrectly counter that an individual employee must personally "waive" a "[substantive] right" to proceed in court for a waiver to be "knowing and voluntary" under the ADEA.... As explained below, however, the agreement to arbitrate ADEA claims is not the waiver of a "substantive right" as that term is employed in the ADEA.... Indeed, if the "right" referred to in § 626(f)(1) included the prospective waiver of the right to bring an ADEA claim in court, even a waiver signed by an individual employee would be invalid as the statute also prevents individuals from "waiv[ing] rights or claims that may arise after the date the waiver is executed." § 626(f)(1)(C).[2]

---

2. Respondents' contention that § 118 of the Civil Rights Act of 1991 ... precludes the enforcement of this arbitration agreement also is misplaced.... Section 118 expresses Congress' support for alternative dispute resolution: "Where appropriate and to the extent authorized by law, the use of alternative means of dispute resolution, including ... arbitration, is encouraged to resolve disputes arising under" the ADEA.... Respondents argue that the legislative history actually signals Congress' intent to preclude arbitration waivers in the collective-bargaining context. In particular, respondents point to a House Report that, in spite of the statute's plain language, interprets § 118 to support their position.... But the legislative history mischaracter-

Examination of the two federal statutes at issue in this case, therefore, yields a straightforward answer to the question presented: The NLRA provided the Union and the RAB with statutory authority to collectively bargain for arbitration of workplace discrimination claims, and Congress did not terminate that authority with respect to federal age-discrimination claims in the ADEA. Accordingly, there is no legal basis for the Court to strike down the arbitration clause in this CBA, which was freely negotiated by the Union and the RAB, and which clearly and unmistakably requires respondents to arbitrate the age-discrimination claims at issue in this appeal. Congress has chosen to allow arbitration of ADEA claims. The Judiciary must respect that choice.

B

The CBA's arbitration provision is also fully enforceable under the *Gardner-Denver* line of cases. Respondents interpret *Gardner-Denver* and its progeny to hold that "a union cannot waive an employee's right to a judicial forum under the federal antidiscrimination statutes" because "allowing the union to waive this right would substitute the union's interests for the employee's antidiscrimination rights." ... The "combination of union control over the process and inherent conflict of interest with respect to discrimination claims," they argue, "provided the foundation for the Court's holding [in *Gardner-Denver*] that arbitration under a collective-bargaining agreement could not preclude an individual employee's right to bring a lawsuit in court to vindicate a statutory discrimination claim." ... We disagree.

1

The holding of *Gardner-Denver* is not as broad as respondents suggest. The employee in that case was covered by a collective-bargaining agreement that prohibited "discrimination against any employee on account of race, color, religion, sex, national origin, or ancestry" and that guaranteed that "[n]o employee will be discharged ... except for just cause." ... The agreement also included a "multistep grievance procedure" that culminated in compulsory arbitration for any "differences aris[ing] between the Company and the Union as to the meaning and application of the provisions of this Agreement" and "any trouble aris[ing] in the plant." ...

The employee was discharged.... He filed a grievance with his union claiming that he was " 'unjustly discharged.' " ... Then at the final prearbitration step of the grievance process, the employee added a claim that he was discharged because of his race....

izes the holding of *Gardner-Denver*, which does not prohibit collective bargaining for arbitration of ADEA claims.... Moreover, reading the legislative history in the manner suggested by respondents would create a direct conflict with the statutory text, which encourages the use of arbitration for dispute resolution without imposing any constraints on collective bargaining. In such a contest, the text must prevail....

The arbitrator ultimately ruled that the employee had been " 'discharged for just cause,' " but "made no reference to [the] claim of racial discrimination." ... After obtaining a right-to-sue letter from the EEOC, the employee filed a claim in Federal District Court, alleging racial discrimination in violation of Title VII of the Civil Rights Act of 1964. The District Court issued a decision, affirmed by the Court of Appeals, which granted summary judgment to the employer because [of the submission to arbitration]....

This Court reversed the judgment on the narrow ground that the arbitration was not preclusive because the collective-bargaining agreement did not cover statutory claims.... Because the collective-bargaining agreement gave the arbitrator "authority to resolve only questions of contractual rights," his decision could not prevent the employee from bringing the Title VII claim in federal court "regardless of whether certain contractual rights are similar to, or duplicative of, the substantive rights secured by Title VII." ...

[...]

The Court's decisions following *Gardner-Denver* have not broadened its holding to make it applicable to the facts of this case. In *Barrentine* v. *Arkansas-Best Freight System, Inc.*, 450 U.S. 728 (1981), the Court considered "whether an employee may bring an action in federal district court, alleging a violation of the minimum wage provisions of the Fair Labor Standards Act, ... after having unsuccessfully submitted a wage claim based on the same underlying facts to a joint grievance committee pursuant to the provisions of his union's collective-bargaining agreement." ... The Court held that the unsuccessful arbitration did not preclude the federal lawsuit. Like the collective-bargaining agreement in *Gardner-Denver*, the arbitration provision under review in *Barrentine* did not expressly reference the statutory claim at issue....

McDonald v. *West Branch*, 466 U.S. 284 (1984), was decided along similar lines. The question presented in that case was "whether a federal court may accord preclusive effect to an unappealed arbitration award in a case brought under [42 U.S.C. § 1983]." ... The Court declined to fashion such a rule, again explaining that "because an arbitrator's authority derives solely from the contract, ... an arbitrator may not have authority to enforce § 1983" when that provision is left unaddressed by the arbitration agreement.... Accordingly, as in both *Gardner-Denver* and *Barrentine*, the Court's decision in *McDonald* hinged on the scope of the collective-bargaining agreement and the arbitrator's parallel mandate.

The facts underlying *Gardner-Denver*, *Barrentine*, and *McDonald* reveal the narrow scope of the legal rule arising from that trilogy of decisions. Summarizing those opinions in *Gilmer*, this Court made clear that the *Gardner-Denver* line of cases "did not involve the issue of the enforceability of an agreement to arbitrate statutory claims." ... Those decisions instead "involved the quite different issue whether arbitration of contract-based claims precluded subsequent judicial resolution of statutory claims. Since the employees there had not agreed to arbitrate their statutory claims, and the labor arbitrators were not authorized to resolve such claims, the arbitration in those cases understandably was held not to preclude subsequent statutory actions." ...[3] *Gardner-Denver* and its progeny thus do not control the outcome where, as is the case here, the collective-bargaining agreement's arbitration provision expressly covers both statutory and contractual discrimination claims.[4]

2

We recognize that apart from their narrow holdings, the *Gardner-Denver* line of cases included broad *dicta* that was highly critical of the use of arbitration for the vindication of statutory antidiscrimination rights. That skepticism, however, rested on a misconceived view of arbitration that this Court has since abandoned.

First, the Court in *Gardner-Denver* erroneously assumed that an agreement to submit statutory discrimination claims to arbitration was tantamount to a waiver of those rights.... For this reason, the Court stated, "the rights conferred [by Title VII] can form no part of the collective-bargaining process since waiver of these rights would defeat the paramount congressional purpose behind Title VII." ...

The Court was correct in concluding that federal antidiscrimination rights may not be prospectively waived, ... but it confused an agreement to arbitrate those statutory claims with a prospective waiver of the substantive right. The decision to resolve ADEA claims by way of arbitration instead of litigation does not waive the statutory right to be free from workplace age discrimination; it waives only the right to seek relief from a court in the first instance.... This "Court has been quite specific in holding that arbitration agreements can be enforced under the FAA without contravening the policies of congressional enactments giving employees specific protection against discrimination prohibited by federal law." ... The suggestion in *Gardner-Denver* that the decision to arbitrate statutory discrimination claims was tantamount to a substantive waiver of

---

3. JUSTICE SOUTER'S reliance on *Wright* v. *Universal Maritime Service Corp.*, 525 U.S. 70 (1998), to support its view of *Gardner-Denver* is misplaced.... *Wright* identified the "tension" between the two lines of cases represented by *Gardner-Denver* and *Gilmer*, but found "it unnecessary to resolve the question of the validity of a union-negotiated waiver, since it [was] apparent ... on the facts and arguments presented ... that no such waiver [had] occurred." ... And although his dissent describes *Wright's* characterization of *Gardner-Denver* as "raising a 'seemingly absolute prohibition of union waiver of employees' federal forum rights,'" ... it wrenches the statement out of context: "Although [the right to a judicial forum] is not a substantive right, see *Gilmer*, ... and *whether or not Gardner–Denver's* seemingly absolute prohibition of union waiver of employees' federal forum rights *survives Gilmer, Gardner–Denver* at least stands for the proposition that the right to a federal judicial forum is of sufficient importance to be protected against less-than-explicit union waiver in a CBA," ... [emphasis added by the majority opinion]. *Wright* therefore neither endorsed *Gardner-Denver's* broad language nor suggested a particular result in this case.

4. Because today's decision does not contradict the holding of *Gardner-Denver*, we need not resolve the *stare decisis* concerns raised by the dissenting opinions.... But given the development of this Court's arbitration jurisprudence in the intervening years, ... *Gardner-Denver* would appear to be a strong candidate for overruling if the dissents' broad view of its holding ... were correct....

those rights, therefore, reveals a distorted understanding of the compromise made when an employee agrees to compulsory arbitration.

In this respect, *Gardner-Denver* is a direct descendant of the Court's decision in *Wilko* v. *Swan*, 346 U.S. 427 (1953), which held that an agreement to arbitrate claims under the Securities Act of 1933 was unenforceable.... The Court subsequently overruled *Wilko* and, in so doing, characterized the decision as "pervaded by ... 'the old judicial hostility to arbitration.' " ... The Court added: "To the extent that *Wilko* rested on suspicion of arbitration as a method of weakening the protections afforded in the substantive law to would-be complainants, it has fallen far out of step with our current strong endorsement of the federal statutes favoring this method of resolving disputes." ... The timeworn "mistrust of the arbitral process" harbored by the Court in *Gardner-Denver* thus weighs against reliance on anything more than its core holding.... Indeed, in light of the "radical change, over two decades, in the Court's receptivity to arbitration," ... reliance on any judicial decision similarly littered with *Wilko's* overt hostility to the enforcement of arbitration agreements would be ill advised.[5]

Second, *Gardner-Denver* mistakenly suggested that certain features of arbitration made it a forum "well suited to the resolution of contractual disputes," but "a comparatively inappropriate forum for the final resolution of rights created by Title VII." ... According to the Court, the "factfinding process in arbitration" is "not equivalent to judicial factfinding" and the "informality of arbitral procedure ... makes arbitration a less appropriate forum for final resolution of Title VII issues than the federal courts." ... The Court also questioned the competence of arbitrators to decide federal statutory claims....

These misconceptions have been corrected. For example, the Court has "recognized that arbitral tribunals are readily capable of handling the factual and legal complexities of antitrust claims, notwithstanding the absence of judicial instruction and supervision" and that "there is no reason to assume at the outset that arbitrators will not follow the law." ... An arbitrator's capacity to resolve complex questions of fact and law extends with equal force to discrimination claims brought under the

---

5. JUSTICE STEVENS suggests that the Court is displacing its "earlier determination of the relevant provisions' meaning" based on a "preference for arbitration." ... But his criticism lacks any basis. We are not revisiting a settled issue or disregarding an earlier determination; the Court is simply deciding the question identified in *Wright* as unresolved.... And, contrary to JUSTICE STEVENS' accusation, it is the Court's fidelity to the ADEA's text—not an alleged preference for arbitration—that dictates the answer to the question presented. As *Gilmer* explained, nothing in the text of Title VII or the ADEA precludes contractual arbitration, ... and JUSTICE STEVENS has never suggested otherwise. Rather, he has always contended that permitting the "compulsory arbitration" of employment discrimination claims conflicts with his perception of "the congressional purpose animating the ADEA." ... The *Gilmer* Court did not adopt JUSTICE STEVENS' personal view of the purposes underlying the ADEA, for good reason: That view is not embodied within the statute's text. Accordingly, it is not the statutory text that JUSTICE STEVENS has sought to vindicate—it is instead his own "preference" for mandatory judicial review, which he disguises as a search for congressional purpose. This Court is not empowered to incorporate such a preference into the text of a federal statute.... It is for this reason, and not because of a "policy favoring arbitration," ... that the Court overturned *Wilko* v. *Swan*.... And it is why we disavow the antiarbitration *dicta* of *Gardner-Denver* and its progeny today.

ADEA. Moreover, the recognition that arbitration procedures are more streamlined than federal litigation is not a basis for finding the forum somehow inadequate; the relative informality of arbitration is one of the chief reasons that parties select arbitration. Parties "trad[e] the procedures and opportunity for review of the courtroom for the simplicity, informality, and expedition of arbitration." . . . In any event, "[i]t is unlikely . . . that age discrimination claims require more extensive discovery than other claims that we have found to be arbitrable, such as RICO and antitrust claims." . . . At bottom, objections centered on the nature of arbitration do not offer a credible basis for discrediting the choice of that forum to resolve statutory antidiscrimination claims.[6]

Third, the Court in *Gardner-Denver* raised in a footnote a "further concern" regarding "the union's exclusive control over the manner and extent to which an individual grievance is presented." . . . The Court suggested that in arbitration, as in the collective-bargaining process, a union may subordinate the interests of an individual employee to the collective interests of all employees in the bargaining unit. . . .

We cannot rely on this judicial policy concern as a source of authority for introducing a qualification into the ADEA that is not found in its text. Absent a constitutional barrier, "it is not for us to substitute our view of . . . policy for the legislation which has been passed by Congress." . . . Congress is fully equipped "to identify any category of claims as to which agreements to arbitrate will be held unenforceable." . . . Until Congress amends the ADEA to meet the conflict-of-interest concern identified in the *Gardner-Denver dicta*, and seized on by respondents here, there is "no reason to color the lens through which the arbitration clause is read" simply because of an alleged conflict of interest between a union and its members. . . . This is a "battl[e] that should be fought among the political branches and the industry. Those parties should not seek to amend the statute by appeal to the Judicial Branch." . . .

The conflict-of-interest argument also proves too much. Labor unions certainly balance the economic interests of some employees against the needs of the larger work force as they negotiate collective-bargain agreements and implement them on a daily basis. But this attribute of organized labor does not justify singling out an arbitration provision for disfavored treatment. This "principle of majority rule" to which respondents object is in fact the central premise of the NLRA. . . . It was Congress' verdict that the benefits of organized labor outweigh the sacrifice of individual liberty that this system necessarily demands. Respondents' argument that they were deprived of the right to pursue their ADEA claims in federal court by a labor union with a conflict of interest is therefore unsustainable; it amounts to a collateral attack on the NLRA.

---

6. Moreover, an arbitrator's decision as to whether a unionized employee has been discriminated against on the basis of age in violation of the ADEA remains subject to judicial review under the FAA. 9 U.S.C. § 10(a). "[A]lthough judicial scrutiny of arbitration awards necessarily is limited, such review is sufficient to ensure that arbitrators comply with the requirements of the statute." . . .

In any event, Congress has accounted for this conflict of interest in several ways. As indicated above, the NLRA has been interpreted to impose a "duty of fair representation" on labor unions, which a union breaches "when its conduct toward a member of the bargaining unit is arbitrary, discriminatory, or in bad faith." . . . This duty extends to "challenges leveled not only at a union's contract administration and enforcement efforts but at its negotiation activities as well." . . . Thus, a union is subject to liability under the NLRA if it illegally discriminates against older workers in either the formation or governance of the collective-bargaining agreement, such as by deciding not to pursue a grievance on behalf of one of its members for discriminatory reasons. . . . Respondents in fact brought a fair representation suit against the Union based on its withdrawal of support for their age-discrimination claims. . . . Given this avenue that Congress has made available to redress a union's violation of its duty to its members, it is particularly inappropriate to ask this Court to impose an artificial limitation on the collective-bargaining process.

In addition, a union is subject to liability under the ADEA if the union itself discriminates against its members on the basis of age. . . . Union members may also file age-discrimination claims with the EEOC and the National Labor Relations Board, which may then seek judicial intervention under this Court's precedent. . . . In sum, Congress has provided remedies for the situation where a labor union is less than vigorous in defense of its members' claims of discrimination under the ADEA.

III

Finally, respondents offer a series of arguments contending that the particular CBA at issue here does not clearly and unmistakably require them to arbitrate their ADEA claims. . . . But respondents did not raise these contract-based arguments in the District Court or the Court of Appeals. To the contrary, respondents acknowledged on appeal that the CBA provision requiring arbitration of their federal antidiscrimination statutory claims "is sufficiently explicit" in precluding their federal lawsuit. . . . In light of respondents' litigating position, both lower courts assumed that the CBA's arbitration clause clearly applied to respondents and proceeded to decide the question left unresolved in *Wright*. We granted review of the question presented on that understanding.

[. . .]

Respondents also argue that the CBA operates as a substantive waiver of their ADEA rights because it not only precludes a federal lawsuit, but also allows the Union to block arbitration of these claims. . . . Petitioners contest this characterization of the CBA . . . and offer record evidence suggesting that the Union has allowed respondents to continue with the arbitration even though the Union has declined to participate. . . . But not only does this question require resolution of contested factual allegations, it was not fully briefed to this or any court and is not fairly encompassed within the question presented. . . . Thus, although a substantive waiver of federally protected civil rights will not be upheld, ... we are not positioned to resolve in the first instance whether the CBA allows the Union to prevent respondents from "effectively vindicating" their "federal statutory rights in the arbitral forum." ... Resolution of this question at this juncture would be particularly inappropriate in light of our hesitation to invalidate arbitration agreements on the basis of speculation....

IV

We hold that a collective-bargaining agreement that clearly and unmistakably requires union members to arbitrate ADEA claims is enforceable as a matter of federal law. The judgment of the Court of Appeals is reversed, and the case is remanded for further proceedings consistent with this opinion.

It is so ordered.

JUSTICE STEVENS, dissenting.

JUSTICE SOUTER'S dissenting opinion, which I join in full, explains why our decision in *Alexander* v. *Gardner-Denver Co.*, 415 U.S. 36 (1974), answers the question presented in this case. My concern regarding the Court's subversion of precedent to the policy favoring arbitration prompts these additional remarks.

Notwithstanding the absence of change in any relevant statutory provision, the Court has recently retreated from, and in some cases reversed, prior decisions based on its changed view of the merits of arbitration. Previously, the Court approached with caution questions involving a union's waiver of an employee's right to raise statutory claims in a federal judicial forum. After searching the text and purposes of Title VII of the Civil Rights Act of 1964, the Court in *Gardner-Denver* held that a clause of a collective-bargaining agreement (CBA) requiring arbitration of discrimination claims could not waive an employee's right to a judicial forum for statutory claims.... The Court's decision rested on several features of the statute, including the individual nature of the rights it confers, the broad remedial powers it grants federal courts, and its expressed preference for overlapping remedies.... The Court also noted the problem of entrusting a union with certain arbitration decisions given the potential conflict between the collective interest and the interests of an individual employee seeking to assert his rights....

The statutes construed by the Court in the foregoing cases and in *Wilko* v. *Swan*, 346 U.S. 427 (1953), have not since been amended in any relevant respect. But the Court has in a number of cases replaced our predecessors' statutory analysis with judicial reasoning espousing a policy favoring arbitration and thereby reached divergent results. I dissented in those cases to express concern that my colleagues were making policy choices not made by Congress....

Today the majority's preference for arbitration again leads it to disregard our precedent. Although it purports to ascertain the relationship between the Age Discrimination in Employment Act of 1967 (ADEA), the

National Labor Relations Act, and the Federal Arbitration Act, the Court ignores our earlier determination of the relevant provisions' meaning. The Court concludes that "[i]t was Congress' verdict that the benefits of organized labor outweigh the sacrifice of individual liberty" that the system of organized labor "necessarily demands," even when the sacrifice demanded is a judicial forum for asserting an individual statutory right.... But in *Gardner-Denver* we determined that "Congress' verdict" was otherwise when we held that Title VII does not permit a CBA to waive an employee's right to a federal judicial forum. Because the purposes and relevant provisions of Title VII and the ADEA are not meaningfully distinguishable, it is only by reexamining the statutory questions resolved in *Gardner-Denver* through the lens of the policy favoring arbitration that the majority now reaches a different result. [Asterisk omitted.]

[...]

As was true in *Rodriguez de Quijas*, there are competing arguments in this case regarding the interaction of the relevant statutory provisions. But the Court in *Gardner-Denver* considered these arguments, including "the federal policy favoring arbitration of labor disputes," ... and held that Congress did not intend to permit the result petitioners seek. In the absence of an intervening amendment to the relevant statutory language, we are bound by that decision. It is for Congress, rather than this Court, to reassess the policy arguments favoring arbitration and revise the relevant provisions to reflect its views.

JUSTICE SOUTER, with whom JUSTICE STEVENS, JUSTICE GINSBURG, and JUSTICE BREYER join, dissenting.

The issue here is whether employees subject to a collective-bargaining agreement (CBA) providing for conclusive arbitration of all grievances, including claimed breaches of the Age Discrimination in Employment Act of 1967 (ADEA), ... lose their statutory right to bring an ADEA claim in court, § 626(c). Under the 35–year-old holding in *Alexander* v. *Gardner-Denver Co.* ..., they do not, and I would adhere to *stare decisis* and so hold today.

I

Like Title VII of the Civil Rights Act of 1964, ... the ADEA is aimed at " 'the elimination of discrimination in the workplace,' " ... and, again like Title VII, the ADEA "contains a vital element ... : It grants an injured employee a right of action to obtain the authorized relief".... "Any person aggrieved" under the Act "may bring a civil action in any court of competent jurisdiction for legal or equitable relief," 29 U.S.C. § 626(c), thereby "not only redress[ing] his own injury but also vindicat[ing] the important congressional policy against discriminatory employment practices,"....

Gardner-Denver considered the effect of a CBA's arbitration clause on an employee's right to sue under Title VII. One of the employer's arguments was that the CBA entered into by the union had waived individual employees' statutory cause of action subject to a judicial remedy for discrimination in violation of Title VII. Although Title VII, like the ADEA, "does not speak expressly to the relationship between federal courts and the grievance-arbitration machinery of collective-bargaining agreements," ... we unanimously held that "the rights conferred" by Title VII (with no exception for the right to a judicial forum) cannot be waived as "part of the collective bargaining process." ... We stressed the contrast between two categories of rights in labor and employment law. There were "statutory rights related to collective activity," which "are conferred on employees collectively to foster the processes of bargaining[, which] properly may be exercised or relinquished by the union as collective-bargaining agent to obtain economic benefits for union members." ... But "Title VII ... stands on plainly different [categorical] ground; it concerns not majoritarian processes, but an individual's right to equal employment opportunities." ... Thus, as the Court previously realized, *Gardner-Denver* imposed a "seemingly absolute prohibition of union waiver of employees' federal forum rights." ...[7]

We supported the judgment with several other lines of complementary reasoning. First, we explained that antidiscrimination statutes "have long evinced a general intent to accord parallel or overlapping remedies against discrimination," and Title VII's statutory scheme carried "no suggestion ... that a prior arbitral decision either forecloses an individual's right to sue or divests federal courts of jurisdiction." ... We accordingly concluded that "an individual does not forfeit his private cause of action if he first pursues his grievance to final arbitration under the nondiscrimination clause of a collective-bargaining agreement." ...

Second, we rejected the District Court's view that simply participating in the arbitration amounted to electing the arbitration remedy and waiving the plaintiff's right to sue. We said that the arbitration agreement at issue covered only a contractual right under the CBA to be free from discrimination, not the "independent statutory rights accorded by Congress" in Title VII. ... Third, we rebuffed the employer's argument that federal courts should defer to arbitral rulings. We declined to make the "assumption that arbitral processes are commensurate with judicial processes," ... and described arbitration as "a less appropriate forum for final resolution of Title VII issues than the federal courts." ...

Finally, we took note that "[i]n arbitration, as in the collective bargaining process, the interests of the individual employee may be subordinated to the collective interests of all employees in the bargaining unit," ... a result we deemed unacceptable when it came to Title VII claims. In sum, *Gardner-Denver* held that an individual's statutory right of freedom from discrimination and access to court for enforcement were beyond a union's power to waive.

---

7. *Gardner-Denver* also contained some language seemingly prohibiting even individual prospective waiver of federal forum rights ... an issue revisited in *Gilmer* v. *Interstate/Johnson Lane Corp.* ... and not disputed here.

Our analysis of Title VII in *Gardner-Denver* is just as pertinent to the ADEA in this case. The "interpretation of Title VII ... applies with equal force in the context of age discrimination, for the substantive provisions of the ADEA 'were derived *in haec verba* from Title VII,'" and indeed neither petitioners nor the Court points to any relevant distinction between the two statutes.... Given the unquestionable applicability of the *Gardner-Denver* rule to this ADEA issue, the argument that its precedent be followed in this case of statutory interpretation is equally unquestionable.... And "[c]onsiderations of *stare decisis* have special force" over an issue of statutory interpretation, which is unlike constitutional interpretation owing to the capacity of Congress to alter any reading we adopt simply by amending the statute.... Once we have construed a statute, stability is the rule, and "we will not depart from [it] without some compelling justification." ... There is no argument for abandoning precedent here, and *Gardner-Denver* controls.

II

The majority evades the precedent of *Gardner-Denver* as long as it can simply by ignoring it. The Court never mentions the case before concluding that the ADEA and the National Labor Relations Act, ... "yiel[d] a straightforward answer to the question presented," ... that is, that unions can bargain away individual rights to a federal forum for antidiscrimination claims. If this were a case of first impression, it would at least be possible to consider that conclusion, but the issue is settled and the time is too late by 35 years to make the bald assertion that "[n]othing in the law suggests a distinction between the status of arbitration agreements signed by an individual employee and those agreed to by a union representative." ... In fact, we recently and unanimously said that the principle that "federal forum rights cannot be waived in union-negotiated CBAs even if they can be waived in individually executed contracts ... assuredly finds support in" our case law, *Wright*, ... and every Court of Appeals save one has read our decisions as holding to this position ... ("an individual may prospectively waive his own statutory right to a judicial forum, but his union may not prospectively waive that right for him. All of the circuits to have considered the meaning of *Gardner-Denver* after *Gilmer*, other than the Fourth, are in accord with this view").

Equally at odds with existing law is the majority's statement that "[t]he decision to fashion a CBA to require arbitration of employment-discrimination claims is no different from the many other decisions made by parties in designing grievance machinery." ... That is simply impossible to square with our conclusion in *Gardner-Denver* that "Title VII ... stands on plainly different ground" from "statutory rights related to collective activity": "it concerns not majoritarian processes, but an individual's right to equal employment opportunities." ... ("[N]otwithstanding the strong policies encouraging arbitration, 'different considerations apply where the employee's claim is based on rights arising out of a statute designed to provide minimum substantive guarantees to individual workers' ") . . . .

When the majority does speak to *Gardner-Denver*, it misreads the case in claiming that it turned solely "on the narrow ground that the arbitration was not preclusive because the collective-bargaining agreement did not cover statutory claims." . . . That, however, was merely one of several reasons given in support of the decision, . . . and we raised it to explain why the District Court made a mistake in thinking that the employee lost his Title VII rights by electing to pursue the contractual arbitration remedy. . . . One need only read *Gardner-Denver* itself to know that it was not at all so narrowly reasoned, and we have noted already how later cases have made this abundantly clear. . . .

. . . Indeed, if the Court can read *Gardner-Denver* as resting on nothing more than a contractual failure to reach as far as statutory claims, it must think the Court has been wreaking havoc on the truth for years, since (as noted) we have unanimously described the case as raising a "seemingly absolute prohibition of union waiver of employees' federal forum rights." *Wright,* . . . .[8] Human ingenuity is not equal to the task of reconciling statements like this with the majority's representation that *Gardner-Denver* held only that "the arbitration was not preclusive because the collective-bargaining agreement did not cover statutory claims." . . .[9]

Nor, finally, does the majority have any better chance of being rid of another of *Gardner-Denver's* statements supporting its rule of decision, set out and repeated in previous quotations: "in arbitration, as in the collective-bargaining process, a union may subordinate the interests of an individual employee to the collective interests of all employees in the bargaining unit," . . . an unacceptable result when it comes to "an individual's right to equal employment opportunities." . . . The majority tries to diminish this reasoning, and the previously stated holding it supported, by making the remarkable rejoinder that "[w]e cannot rely on this judicial policy concern as a source of authority for introducing a qualification into the ADEA that is not found in its text." . . .[10] It is

---

8. The majority seems inexplicably to think that the statutory right to a federal forum is not a right, or that *Gardner-Denver* failed to recognize it because it is not "substantive." . . . But *Gardner-Denver* forbade union waiver of employees' federal forum rights in large part because of the importance of such rights and a fear that unions would too easily give them up to benefit the many at the expense of the few, a far less salient concern when only economic interests are at stake. . . .

9. There is no comfort for the Court in making the one point on which we are in accord, that *Gardner-Denver* relied in part on what the majority describes as "broad *dicta* that was highly critical of the use of arbitration for the vindication of statutory antidiscrimination rights." . . . I agree that *Gardner-Denver's* " 'mistrust of the arbitral process' . . . has been undermined by our recent arbitration decisions," . . . but if the statements are "*dicta,*" their obsolescence is as irrelevant to *Gardner-Denver's* continued vitality as their currency was to the case's holding when it came down; in *Gardner-Denver* itself we acknowledged "the federal policy favoring arbitration," . . . but nonetheless held that a union could not waive its members' statutory right to a federal forum in a CBA.

10. The majority says it would be "particularly inappropriate" to consider *Gardner-Denver's* conflict-of-interest rationale because "Congress has made available" another "avenue" to protect

enough to recall that respondents are not seeking to "introduc[e] a qualification into" the law; they are justifiably relying on statutory-interpretation precedent decades old, never overruled, and serially reaffirmed over the years.... With that precedent on the books, it makes no sense for the majority to claim that "judicial policy concern[s]" about unions sacrificing individual antidiscrimination rights should be left to Congress.

For that matter, Congress has unsurprisingly understood *Gardner-Denver* the way we have repeatedly explained it and has operated on the assumption that a CBA cannot waive employees' rights to a judicial forum to enforce antidiscrimination statutes.... And Congress apparently does not share the Court's demotion of *Gardner-Denver's* holding to a suspect judicial policy concern: "Congress has had [over] 30 years in which it could have corrected our decision ... if it disagreed with it, and has chosen not to do so. We should accord weight to this continued acceptance of our earlier holding." ...

III

On one level, the majority opinion may have little effect, for it explicitly reserves the question whether a CBA's waiver of a judicial forum is enforceable when the union controls access to and presentation of employees' claims in arbitration, ... which "is usually the case,".... But as a treatment of precedent in statutory interpretation, the majority's opinion cannot be reconciled with the *Gardner-Denver* Court's own view of its holding, repeated over the years and generally understood, and I respectfully dissent.

NOTES AND QUESTIONS

1. The significance of *14 Penn Plaza* can hardly be understated. It represents the reversal, in effect, of a major precedent in both arbitration law and civil rights, at the point at which the two converge. In some respects, it speaks to the end of an era and the beginning of another. Can you speculate as to the transition that is being arguably effectuated? How does the majority discredit the ruling in *Gardner-Denver*? Which policy is triumphant?

2. What did *Gardner-Denver* provide before it underwent a "make-over" at the hands of the majority? Justice Souter's dissenting opinion is particularly eloquent on this score. It is perhaps Justice Souter's most persuasive and analytically sophisticated writing on arbitration (or, more accurately, civil rights). As between the majority and Justice Souter's dissent, which opinion better achieves the best interest of the United States?

workers against union discrimination, namely, a duty of fair representation claim.... This answer misunderstands the law, for unions may decline for a variety of reasons to pursue potentially meritorious discrimination claims without succumbing to a member's suit for failure of fair representation.... More importantly, we have rejected precisely this argument in the past, making this yet another occasion where the majority ignores precedent.... And we were wise to reject it. When the Court construes statutes to allow a union to eliminate a statutory right to sue in favor of arbitration in which the union cannot represent the employee because it agreed to the employer's challenged action, it is not very consoling to add that the employee can sue the union for being unfair.

3. What in particular does Justice Stevens' dissent add to the debate?

4. What status does *Wright* have in the wake of *14 Penn Plaza*?

5. Do you agree with the majority's characterization of *Gardner-Denver*? Why and why not?

6. What law-making function does *Gilmer* now play in the arbitrability debate?

7. Do you believe that Justice Thomas and the other members of the majority (all conservatives) trust the labor unions? How would he (or they) answer that question? What about the union conflict-of-interest argument?

8. Is arbitration, once chosen, final, binding, and jurisdictionally exclusive in all contexts and circumstances after *14 Penn Plaza*?

9. Does *14 Penn Plaza* add fuel to the fire of the critics of arbitration and prepare a confrontation on the floor of the Congress that may foil the Court's "work product" on arbitration that has been in-the-making for forty years? How might the Court have taken that factor into account? Should or could it have?

10. Explain what Justice Souter means when he says at the end of his opinion, that "the majority [opinion]...may have little effect." Is the statement inconceivable?

11. How does each side of the Court use the notions of *stare decisis* and judicial restraint?

12. What do you make of the fact that Justice Powell authored the opinion in *Gardner-Denver* and Justice Thomas spoke for the majority in *14 Penn Plaza*?

The Employment Contract Exclusion

(FAA § 1)

As previously established, the U.S. Supreme Court addressed the problem of the employment contract exclusion (FAA § 1) in its landmark ruling in *Circuit City Stores, Inc. v. Adams*, 532 U.S. 105 (2001). The Court held that the so-called employment contract exclusion applies only to the employment contracts of workers directly involved in the interstate transport of good and services. Employers, therefore, could require—under the supportive umbrella of the FAA—all other employees to submit employment-related disputes to arbitration. The Court rejected and reversed the Ninth Circuit holding that the language in FAA § 1 exempted all employment contracts from the FAA's scope of application.

CIRCUIT CITY STORES, INC. v. ADAMS

532 U.S. 105, 121 S.Ct. 1302, 149 L.Ed.2d 234 (2001).

(footnotes omitted)

Justice Kennedy delivered the opinion of the Court.

Section 1 of the Federal Arbitration Act (FAA) excludes from the Act's coverage "contracts of employment of seamen, railroad employees, or any other class of workers engaged in foreign or interstate commerce." ... All but one of the Courts of Appeals which have addressed the issue interpret this provision as exempting contracts of employment of transportation workers, but not other employment contracts, from the FAA's coverage. A different interpretation has been adopted by the Court of Appeals for the Ninth Circuit, which construes the exemption so that all contracts of employment are beyond the FAA's reach, whether or not the worker is engaged in transportation. It applied that rule to the instant case. We now decide that the better interpretation is to construe the statute, as most of the Courts of Appeals have done, to confine the exemption to transportation workers....

In October 1995, respondent Saint Clair Adams applied for a job at petitioner Circuit City Stores, Inc., a national retailer of consumer electronics. Adams signed an employment application which included the following provision:

"I agree that I will settle any and all previously unasserted claims, disputes or controversies arising out of or relating to my application or candidacy for employment, employment and/or cessation of employment with Circuit City, *exclusively* by final and binding *arbitration* before a neutral Arbitrator. By way of example only, such claims include claims under federal, state, and local statutory or common law, such as the Age Discrimination in Employment Act, Title VII of the Civil Rights Act of 1964, as amended, including the amendments of the Civil Rights Act of 1991, the Americans with Disabilities Act, the law of contract and the law of tort."

App. 13 (emphasis in original).

Adams was hired as a sales counselor in Circuit City's store in Santa Rosa, California....

Two years later, Adams filed an employment discrimination lawsuit against Circuit City in state court, asserting claims under California's Fair Employment and Housing Act ... and other claims based on general tort theories under California law. Circuit City filed suit in the United States District Court for the Northern District of California, seeking to enjoin the state-court action and to compel arbitration of respondent's claims pursuant to the FAA.... The District Court entered the requested order. Respondent, the court concluded, was obligated by the arbitration agreement to submit his claims against the employer to binding arbitration. An appeal followed.

While respondent's appeal was pending in the Court of Appeals for the Ninth Circuit, the court ruled on the key issue in an unrelated case. The court held the FAA does not apply to contracts of employment.... In the instant case, following the rule announced in *Craft*, the Court of Appeals held the arbitration agreement between Adams and Circuit City was contained in a "contract of employment," and so was not subject to the FAA.... Circuit City petitioned this Court, noting that the Ninth Circuit's conclusion that all employment contracts are excluded from the

FAA conflicts with every other Court of Appeals to have addressed the question.... We granted *certiorari* to resolve the issue....

II

A

Congress enacted the FAA in 1925. As the Court has explained, the FAA was a response to hostility of American courts to the enforcement of arbitration agreements, a judicial disposition inherited from then-long-standing English practice.... To give effect to this purpose, the FAA compels judicial enforcement of a wide range of written arbitration agreements....

We had occasion in *Allied-Bruce* ... to consider the significance of Congress' use of the words "involving commerce" in § 2. The analysis began with a reaffirmation of earlier decisions concluding that the FAA was enacted pursuant to Congress' substantive power to regulate interstate commerce and admiralty... and that the Act was applicable in state courts and pre-emptive of state laws hostile to arbitration... Relying upon these background principles and upon the evident reach of the words "involving commerce," the Court interpreted § 2 as implementing Congress' intent "to exercise [its] commerce power to the full."...

The instant case, of course, involves not the basic coverage authorization under § 2 of the Act, but the exemption from coverage under § 1. The exemption clause provides the Act shall not apply "to contracts of employment of seamen, railroad employees, or any other class of workers engaged in foreign or interstate commerce."... Most Courts of Appeals conclude the exclusion provision is limited to transportation workers, defined, for instance, as those workers "actually engaged in the movement of goods in interstate commerce."... As we stated at the outset, the Court of Appeals for the Ninth Circuit takes a different view and interprets the § 1 exception to exclude all contracts of employment from the reach of the FAA. This comprehensive exemption had been advocated by *amici curiae* in *Gilmer*, where we addressed the question whether a registered securities representative's employment discrimination claim under the Age Discrimination in Employment Act of 1967 ... could be submitted to arbitration pursuant to an agreement in his securities registration application. Concluding that the application was not a "contract of employment" at all, we found it unnecessary to reach the meaning of § 1.... There is no such dispute in this case; while Circuit City argued in its petition for *certiorari* that the employment application signed by Adams was not a "contract of employment," we declined to grant *certiorari* on this point. So the issue reserved in *Gilmer* is presented here.

B

Respondent, at the outset, contends that we need not address the meaning of the § 1 exclusion provision to decide the case in his favor. In his view, an employment contract is not a "contract evidencing a transaction involving interstate commerce" at all, since the word "transaction" in § 2 extends only to commercial contracts.... This line of reasoning proves too much, for it would make the § 1 exclusion provision superfluous. If all contracts of employment are beyond the scope of the Act under the § 2 coverage provision, the separate exemption for "contracts of employment of seamen, railroad employees, or any other class of workers engaged in... interstate commerce" would be pointless.... The proffered interpretation of "evidencing a transaction involving commerce," furthermore, would be inconsistent with *Gilmer*... where we held that § 2 required the arbitration of an age discrimination claim based on an agreement in a securities registration application, a dispute that did not arise from a "commercial deal or merchant's sale." Nor could respondent's construction of § 2 be reconciled with the expansive reading of those words adopted in *Allied-Bruce*... If, then, there is an argument to be made that arbitration agreements in employment contracts are not covered by the Act, it must be premised on the language of the § 1 exclusion provision itself.

Respondent, endorsing the reasoning of the Court of Appeals for the Ninth Circuit that the provision excludes all employment contracts, relies on the asserted breadth of the words "contracts of employment of... any other class of workers engaged in... commerce." Referring to our construction of § 2's coverage provision in *Allied-Bruce*—concluding that the words "involving commerce" evidence the congressional intent to regulate to the full extent of its commerce power—respondent contends § 1's interpretation should have a like reach, thus exempting all employment contracts. The two provisions, it is argued, are coterminous; under this view the "involving commerce" provision brings within the FAA's scope all contracts within the Congress' commerce power, and the "engaged in... commerce" language in § 1 in turn exempts from the FAA all employment contracts falling within that authority.

This reading of § 1, however, runs into an immediate and, in our view, insurmountable textual obstacle. Unlike the "involving commerce" language in § 2, the words "any other class of workers engaged in... commerce" constitute a residual phrase, following, in the same sentence, explicit reference to "seamen" and "railroad employees." Construing the residual phrase to exclude all employment contracts fails to give independent effect to the statute's enumeration of the specific categories of workers which precedes it; there would be no need for Congress to use the phrases "seamen" and "railroad employees" if those same classes of workers were subsumed within the meaning of the "engaged in... commerce" residual clause. The wording of § 1 calls for the application of the maxim *ejusdem generis*, the statutory canon that "where general words follow specific words in a statutory enumeration, the general words are construed to embrace only objects similar in nature to those objects enumerated by the preceding specific words."... Under this rule of construction the residual clause should be read to give effect to the terms "seamen" and "railroad employees," and should itself be controlled and defined by reference to the enumerated categories of workers which are recited just before it; the interpretation of the clause pressed by respondent fails to produce these results.

. . . The application of the rule *ejusdem generis* in this case, however, is in full accord with other sound considerations bearing upon the proper interpretation of the clause. For even if the term "engaged in commerce" stood alone in § 1, we would not construe the provision to exclude all contracts of employment from the FAA. . . .

[. . .]

The Court's reluctance to accept contentions that Congress used the words "in commerce" or "engaged in commerce" to regulate to the full extent of its commerce power rests on sound foundation, as it affords objective and consistent significance to the meaning of the words Congress uses when it defines the reach of a statute. To say that the statutory words "engaged in commerce" are subject to variable interpretations depending upon the date of adoption, even a date before the phrase became a term of art, ignores the reason why the formulation became a term of art in the first place: The plain meaning of the words "engaged in commerce" is narrower than the more open-ended formulations "affecting commerce" and "involving commerce." . . . It would be unwieldy for Congress, for the Court, and for litigants to be required to deconstruct statutory Commerce Clause phrases depending upon the year of a particular statutory enactment.

In rejecting the contention that the meaning of the phrase "engaged in commerce" in § 1 of the FAA should be given a broader construction than justified by its evident language simply because it was enacted in 1925 rather than 1938, we do not mean to suggest that statutory jurisdictional formulations "necessarily have a uniform meaning whenever used by Congress." . . . As the Court has noted: "The judicial task in marking out the extent to which Congress has exercised its constitutional power over commerce is not that of devising an abstract formula." . . . We must, of course, construe the "engaged in commerce" language in the FAA with reference to the statutory context in which it is found and in a manner consistent with the FAA's purpose. These considerations, however, further compel that the § 1 exclusion provision be afforded a narrow construction. As discussed above, the location of the phrase "any other class of workers engaged in . . . commerce" in a residual provision, after specific categories of workers have been enumerated, undermines any attempt to give the provision a sweeping, open-ended construction. And the fact that the provision is contained in a statute that "seeks broadly to overcome judicial hostility to arbitration agreements," . . . which the Court concluded in *Allied-Bruce* counseled in favor of an expansive reading of § 2, gives no reason to abandon the precise reading of a provision that exempts contracts from the FAA's coverage.

In sum, the text of the FAA forecloses the construction of § 1 followed by the Court of Appeals in the case under review, a construction which would exclude all employment contracts from the FAA. While the historical arguments respecting Congress' understanding of its power in 1925 are not insubstantial, this fact alone does not give us basis to adopt, "by judicial decision rather than amendatory legislation,"...an expansive construction of the FAA's exclusion provision that goes beyond the meaning of the words Congress used. While it is of course possible to speculate that Congress might have chosen a different jurisdictional formulation had it known that the Court would soon embrace a less restrictive reading of the Commerce Clause, the text of § 1 precludes interpreting the exclusion provision to defeat the language of § 2 as to all employment contracts. Section 1 exempts from the FAA only contracts of employment of transportation workers.

C

As the conclusion we reach today is directed by the text of § 1, we need not assess the legislative history of the exclusion provision.... We do note, however, that the legislative record on the § 1 exemption is quite sparse....

[...]

We see no paradox in the congressional decision to exempt the workers over whom the commerce power was most apparent. To the contrary, it is a permissible inference that the employment contracts of the classes of workers in § 1 were excluded from the FAA precisely because of Congress' undoubted authority to govern the employment relationships at issue by the enactment of statutes specific to them. By the time the FAA was passed, Congress had already enacted federal legislation providing for the arbitration of disputes between seamen and their employers...When the FAA was adopted, moreover, grievance procedures existed for railroad employees under federal law...and the passage of a more comprehensive statute providing for the mediation and arbitration of railroad labor disputes was imminent.... It is reasonable to assume that Congress excluded "seamen" and "railroad employees" from the FAA for the simple reason that it did not wish to unsettle established or developing statutory dispute resolution schemes covering specific workers.

As for the residual exclusion of "any other class of workers engaged in foreign or interstate commerce," Congress' demonstrated concern with transportation workers and their necessary role in the free flow of goods explains the linkage to the two specific, enumerated types of workers identified in the preceding portion of the sentence. It would be rational for Congress to ensure that workers in general would be covered by the provisions of the FAA, while reserving for itself more specific legislation for those engaged in transportation.... Indeed, such legislation was soon to follow, with the amendment of the Railway Labor Act in 1936 to include air carriers and their employees....

III

Various *amici*, including the attorneys general of 22 States, object that the reading of the § 1 exclusion provision adopted today intrudes upon the policies of the separate States. They point out that, by requiring arbitration agreements in most employment contracts to be covered by the FAA, the statute in effect pre-empts those state employment laws which restrict or limit the ability of employees and employers to enter into arbitration agreements. It is argued that States should be permitted, pursuant to their traditional role in regulating employment relationships, to prohibit employees like respondent from contracting away their right to pursue state-law discrimination claims in court.

It is not our holding today which is the proper target of this criticism. The line of argument is relevant instead to the Court's decision in *Southland Corp. v. Keating*...holding that Congress intended the FAA to apply in state courts, and to pre-empt state antiarbitration laws to the contrary....

[...]

Furthermore, for parties to employment contracts[,]...there are real benefits to the enforcement of arbitration provisions. We have been clear in rejecting the supposition that the advantages of the arbitration process somehow disappear when transferred to the employment context....Arbitration agreements allow parties to avoid the costs of litigation, a benefit that may be of particular importance in employment litigation, which often involves smaller sums of money than disputes concerning commercial contracts. These litigation costs to parties (and the accompanying burden to the Courts) would be compounded by the difficult choice-of-law questions that are often presented in disputes arising from the employment relationship...and the necessity of bifurcation of proceedings in those cases where state law precludes arbitration of certain types of employment claims but not others. The considerable complexity and uncertainty that the construction of § 1 urged by respondent would introduce into the enforceability of arbitration agreements in employment contracts would call into doubt the efficacy of alternative dispute resolution procedures adopted by many of the Nation's employers, in the process undermining the FAA's proarbitration purposes and "breeding litigation from a statute that seeks to avoid it." ...The Court has been quite specific in holding that arbitration agreements can be enforced under the FAA without contravening the policies of congressional enactments giving employees specific protection against discrimination prohibited by federal law; as we noted in *Gilmer*, "by agreeing to arbitrate a statutory claim, a party does not forgo the substantive rights afforded by the statute; it only submits to their resolution in an arbitral, rather than a judicial, forum." ...

For the foregoing reasons, the judgment of the Court of Appeals for the Ninth Circuit is reversed, and the case is remanded for further proceedings consistent with this opinion.

It is so ordered.

JUSTICE STEVENS, with whom JUSTICE GINSBURG and JUSTICE BREYER join, and with whom JUSTICE SOUTER joins as to Parts II and III, dissenting.

JUSTICE SOUTER has cogently explained why the Court's parsimonious construction of § 1 of the Federal Arbitration Act (FAA or Act) is not consistent with its expansive reading of § 2. I join his opinion, but believe that the Court's heavy reliance on the views expressed by the Courts of Appeals during the past decade makes it appropriate to comment on three earlier chapters in the history of this venerable statute.

I

Section 2 of the FAA makes enforceable written agreements to arbitrate "in any maritime transaction or a contract evidencing a transaction involving commerce."... If we were writing on a clean slate, there would be good reason to conclude that neither the phrase "maritime transaction" nor the phrase "contract evidencing a transaction involving commerce" was intended to encompass employment contracts.

The history of the Act, which is extensive and well-documented, makes clear that the FAA was a response to the refusal of courts to enforce commercial arbitration agreements, which were commonly used in the maritime context....

[...]

Nevertheless, the original bill was opposed by representatives of organized labor, most notably the president of the International Seamen's Union of America, because of their concern that the legislation might authorize federal judicial enforcement of arbitration clauses in employment contracts and collective-bargaining agreements. In response to those objections, the chairman of the ABA committee that drafted the legislation emphasized at a Senate Judiciary Subcommittee hearing that "it is not intended that this shall be an act referring to labor disputes at all," but he also observed that "if your honorable committee should feel that there is any danger of that, they should add to the bill the following language, 'but nothing herein contained shall apply to seamen or any class of workers in interstate and foreign commerce.'"... Similarly, another supporter of the bill, then Secretary of Commerce Herbert Hoover, suggested that "if objection appears to the inclusion of workers' contracts in the law's scheme, it might be well amended by stating 'but nothing herein contained shall apply to contracts of employment of seamen, railroad employees, or any other class of workers engaged in interstate or foreign commerce.'"... The legislation was reintroduced in the next session of Congress with Secretary Hoover's exclusionary language added to § 1, and the amendment eliminated organized labor's opposition to the proposed law.

That amendment is what the Court construes today. History amply supports the proposition that it was an uncontroversial provision that merely confirmed the fact that no one interested in the enactment of the FAA ever intended or expected that § 2 would apply to employment contracts. It is particularly ironic, therefore, that the amendment has provided the Court with its sole justification for refusing to give the text of

§ 2 a natural reading. Playing ostrich to the substantial history behind the amendment.... ("We need not assess the legislative history of the exclusion provision"), the Court reasons in a vacuum that "if all contracts of employment are beyond the scope of the Act under the § 2 coverage provision, the separate exemption" in § 1 "would be pointless"...But contrary to the Court's suggestion, it is not "pointless" to adopt a clarifying amendment in order to eliminate opposition to a bill. Moreover, the majority's reasoning is squarely contradicted by the Court's approach in *Bernhardt* v. *Polygraphic Co. of America*...where the Court concluded that an employment contract did not "evidence 'a transaction involving commerce' within the meaning of § 2 of the Act," and therefore did not "reach the further question whether in any event petitioner would be included in 'any other class of workers' within the exceptions of § 1 of the Act."

The irony of the Court's reading of § 2 to include contracts of employment is compounded by its cramped interpretation of the exclusion inserted into § 1. As proposed and enacted, the exclusion fully responded to the concerns of the Seamen's Union and other labor organizations that § 2 might encompass employment contracts by expressly exempting not only the labor agreements of "seamen" and "railroad employees," but also of *"any other class of workers* engaged in foreign or interstate commerce." ... (emphasis added). Today, however, the Court fulfills the original—and originally unfounded—fears of organized labor by essentially rewriting the text of § 1 to exclude the employment contracts *solely* of "seamen, railroad employees, or any other class of *transportation* workers engaged in foreign or interstate commerce." ...In contrast, whether one views the legislation before or after the amendment to § 1, it is clear that it was not intended to apply to employment contracts at all.

[...]

III

Times have changed. Judges in the 19th century disfavored private arbitration. The 1925 Act was intended to overcome that attitude, but a number of this Court's cases decided in the last several decades have pushed the pendulum far beyond a neutral attitude and endorsed a policy that strongly favors private arbitration. The strength of that policy preference has been echoed in the recent Court of Appeals opinions on which the Court relies. In a sense, therefore, the Court is standing on its own shoulders when it points to those cases as the basis for its narrow construction of the exclusion in § 1. There is little doubt that the Court's interpretation of the Act has given it a scope far beyond the expectations of the Congress that enacted it....

It is not necessarily wrong for the Court to put its own imprint on a statute. But when its refusal to look beyond the raw statutory text enables it to disregard countervailing considerations that were expressed by Members of the enacting Congress and that remain valid today, the Court misuses its authority. As the history of the legislation indicates, the potential disparity in bargaining power between individual employees and large employers was the source of organized labor's opposition to the Act, which it feared would require courts to enforce unfair employment contracts. That same concern...underlay Congress' exemption of contracts of employment from mandatory arbitration. When the Court simply ignores the interest of the unrepresented employee, it skews its interpretation with it own policy preferences.

[. . .]

I respectfully dissent.

JUSTICE SOUTER, with whom JUSTICE STEVENS, JUSTICE GINSBURG, and JUSTICE BREYER join, dissenting.

Section 2 of the Federal Arbitration Act (FAA or Act) provides for the enforceability of a written arbitration clause in "any maritime transaction or a contract evidencing a transaction involving commerce," . . . while § 1 exempts from the Act's coverage "contracts of employment of seamen, railroad employees, or any other class of workers engaged in foreign or interstate commerce." Whatever the understanding of Congress's implied admiralty power may have been when the Act was passed in 1925, the commerce power was then thought to be far narrower than we have subsequently come to see it. As a consequence, there are two quite different ways of reading the scope of the Act's provisions. One way would be to say, for example, that the coverage provision extends only to those contracts "involving commerce" that were understood to be covered in 1925; the other would be to read it as exercising Congress's commerce jurisdiction in its modern conception in the same way it was thought to implement the more limited view of the Commerce Clause in 1925. The first possibility would result in a statutory ambit frozen in time, behooving Congress to amend the statute whenever it desired to expand arbitration clause enforcement beyond its scope in 1925; the second would produce an elastic reach, based on an understanding that Congress used language intended to go as far as Congress could go, whatever that might be over time.

In *Allied-Bruce Terminix Cos. v. Dobson* . . . we decided that the elastic understanding of § 2 was the more sensible way to give effect to what Congress intended when it legislated to cover contracts "involving commerce," a phrase that we found an apt way of providing that coverage would extend to the outer constitutional limits under the Commerce Clause. The question here is whether a similarly general phrase in the § 1 exemption, referring to contracts of "any...class of workers engaged in foreign or interstate commerce," should receive a correspondingly evolutionary reading, so as to expand the exemption for employment contracts to keep pace with the enhanced reach of the general enforceability provision. . . .

The number of courts arrayed against reading the § 1 exemption in a way that would allow it to grow parallel to the expanding § 2 coverage reflects the fact that this minority view faces two hurdles, each textually based and apparent from the face of the Act. First, the language of coverage (a contract evidencing a transaction "involving commerce") is different from the language of the exemption (a contract of a worker "engaged in...commerce"). Second, the "engaged in...commerce" catch-all phrase in the exemption is placed in the text following more specific exemptions for employment contracts of "seamen" and "railroad employees." The placement possibly indicates that workers who are excused from arbitrating by virtue of the catchall exclusion must resemble seamen and railroad workers, perhaps by being employees who actually handle and move goods as they are shipped interstate or internationally.

Neither hurdle turns out to be a bar, however. The first objection is at best inconclusive and weaker than the grounds to reject it; the second is even more certainly inapposite, for reasons the Court itself has stated but misunderstood.

[. . .]

The Court tries to deflect the anomaly of excluding only carrier contracts by suggesting that Congress used the reference to seamen and rail workers to indicate the class of employees whose employment relations it had already legislated about and would be most likely to legislate about in the future....This explanation, however, does nothing to eliminate the anomaly. On the contrary, the explanation tells us why Congress might have referred specifically to the sea and rail workers; but, if so, it also indicates that Congress almost certainly intended the catchall phrase to be just as broad as its terms, without any interpretive squeeze in the name of *ejusdem generis*.

The very fact, as the Court points out, that Congress already had spoken on the subjects of sailors and rail workers and had tailored the legislation to the particular circumstances of the sea and rail carriers may well have been reason for mentioning them specifically. But making the specific references was in that case an act of special care to make sure that the FAA not be construed to modify the existing legislation so exactly aimed; that was no reason at all to limit the general FAA exclusion from applying to employment contracts that had not been targeted with special legislation. Congress did not need to worry especially about the FAA's effect on legislation that did not exist and was not contemplated. As to workers uncovered by any specific legislation, Congress could write on a clean slate, and what it wrote was a general exclusion for employment contracts within Congress's power to regulate. The Court has understood this point before, holding that the existence of a special reason for emphasizing specific examples of a statutory class can negate any inference that an otherwise unqualified general phrase was meant to apply only to matters *ejusdem generis*. On the Court's own reading of the history, then, the explanation for the catchall is not *ejusdem generis*; instead, the explanation for the specifics is *ex abundanti cautela*, abundance of caution....

Nothing stands in the way of construing the coverage and exclusion clauses together, consistently and coherently. I respectfully dissent.

NOTES AND QUESTIONS

1. How does the opinion in *Adams* buttress the federal policy on arbitration? What new elements, if any, does it introduce into the Court's evolving arbitration doctrine?

2. Is inarbitrability an issue in *Adams*? Is separation of powers? What about the Commerce Clause?

3. What is the significance of legislative history? When can actual legislative history be "reversed" or ignored? Have you noticed a line of cases in which the Court ignores legislative history? What does this tell you?

4. What does the dissent emphasize? Is it right?

5. How do you interpret Justice Stevens' dissenting remark, "the Court is standing on its own shoulders when it points to those cases as the basis for its narrow construction of the exclusion. . . ."?

6. It is nice to see the majority and dissent flinging Latin phrases at each other (and the paraphrasing translations are greatly appreciated). What does the interpretation of the statute debate ultimately mean? Who is right? Does the original historical meaning control or should progressive circumstantial adaptation prevail? Is truth less important than practical policy in this context? How objective is the perception of necessity?

7. In subsequent litigation, the Ninth Circuit—perhaps to express its resistance to the U.S. Supreme Court's decision in *Adams*—held that the contract of a delivery driver who worked for a courier service was not covered by the FAA because it fell within the interstate transportation concept of the employment contract exclusion. A district court, therefore, could not compel arbitration. *See Harden v. Roadway Package Systems, Inc.*, 249 F.3d 1137 (9th Cir. 2001). *See also Palcko v. Airborne Express Inc.*, 372 F.3d 588 (3d Cir. 2004) (although an employment arbitration agreement could not be enforced under FAA § 1, the FAA did not preempt state law and the arbitration agreement could be enforced under state law).

8. As to *Adams*, on remand, the Ninth Circuit found the reference to arbitration flawed on another (more doctrinally acceptable) basis: It concluded that Circuit City's arbitration agreement was an unconscionable contract of adhesion and, therefore, unenforceable. As a result, the court reversed the order compelling Adams to arbitrate. The court found that, although federal policy favored arbitration, state contract defenses could still invalidate arbitration agreements. The Dispute Resolution Agreement (DRA) was procedurally unconscionable. Circuit City had greater bargaining power, drafted the contract, and made it a condition of employment. The court also found that the DRA forced employees to arbitrate claims against Circuit City, but did not require Circuit City to arbitrate its claims against employees. The court, therefore, determined that the DRA lacked the necessary mutuality of obligation.

9. The lack of mutuality was compounded by other restrictions: the limitation placed on available damages, the requirement that employees share the arbitration fees, and the strict one-year statute of limitations. Under current federal arbitration law, arbitrating parties must be given basically the same relief that would have been available in court. Moreover, an employee need not pay unreasonable costs and arbitrators' fees in order to engage in arbitration. *See Circuit City Stores, Inc. v. Adams*, 279 F.3d 889 (9th Cir. 2002).

Accord Circuit City Stores, Inc. v. Ahmed, 283 F.3d 1198 (9th Cir. 2002) (the court held that, if an employee is given a meaningful opportunity to opt out of an employer's binding arbitration program and fails to do so, the arbitration agreement is not procedurally unconscionable under California state contract law and the employee can be compelled to arbitrate). The Ninth Circuit focused upon whether the arbitration agreement was procedurally unconscionable. Determining that the agreement was not procedurally unconscionable, the court pointed out that "Ahmed was not presented with a contract of adhesion because he was given the opportunity to opt-out of the Circuit City arbitration program by mailing in a simple one-page form." Ahmed would have been allowed to keep his job if he had chosen not to participate in the arbitration program. The court further stated that the arbitration agreement "lacked any other indicia of procedural unconscionability" because the terms of the agreement were clearly spelled out in the written agreement. The court also noted that the employees had thirty days in which to opt-out and were encouraged to contact counsel or Circuit City representatives before deciding whether to participate in the program. Finally, the court, in refuting Ahmed's claim that he lacked the sophistication to be given a meaningful opportunity to opt-out of the arbitration program, emphasized the general rule that "one who signs a contract cannot [thereafter] complain of unfamiliarity with the language of the instrument."

10. Further, in the *Adam* court's view, the unconscionability rule did not discriminate against or single out arbitration agreements and, therefore, was a valid basis for refusing enforcement under the FAA. Also, the Ninth Circuit refused to sever the unconscionable provision. Finally, according to the court, "the arbitration agreement at issue here [is] virtually indistinguishable from the agreement the California Supreme Court found unconscionable in *Armendariz*...The provision does not require Circuit City [unlike its employees] to arbitrate its claims...Circuit City has offered no justification for this asymmetry, nor is there any indication that 'business realities' warrant the one-sided obligation. This unjustified one-sidedness deprives the DRA of the 'modicum of bilaterality' that the California Supreme Court requires for contracts to be enforceable under California law." *Adams*, 279 F.3d at 893–94.

11. In *Circuit City Stores, Inc. v. Mantor*, 335 F.3d 1101 (9th Cir. 2003), a more recent case, the Ninth Circuit held that an arbitration agreement between Circuit City Stores and an employee was procedurally unconscionable; that provisions of the agreement concerning statute of limitations, class actions, cost-splitting, and the employer's unilateral power to modify or terminate the agreement rendered the arbitration agreement substantively unconscionable; that the filing fee provision of the agreement was also

substantively unconscionable despite a waiver provision; and that the agreement was unenforceable in its entirety because the unconscionable provisions were not severable from the remainder of the agreement.

The main issue before the Ninth Circuit was whether the arbitration agreement was unconscionable under California contract law. The court noted that the FAA provides that arbitration agreements "shall be valid, irrevocable and enforceable" except when grounds "exist at law or equity for the revocation of any contract." The court also referred to *Ingle v. Circuit City Stores, Inc.*, 328 F.3d 1165, 1174 n.10 (9th Cir. 2003), in which it stated that federal law "does not supplant state law governing the unconscionability of adhesive contracts." Under California state contract law, unconscionability consists of a lack of meaningful choice in entering a contract or in negotiating its terms. As a result, the terms were unreasonably favorable to one party and oppressive to the other.

The Ninth Circuit held the arbitration agreement procedurally unconscionable because Mantor had no meaningful choice in accepting the arbitration agreement. The court found the terms of the arbitration agreement oppressive. Oppression, the court said, springs "from inequality of bargaining power [that] results in no real negotiation and an absence of meaningful choice." Circuit City had argued that the agreement was not oppressive because Mantor was given an opportunity to "opt-out" of the arbitration program. The court held that, although Mantor was given an "opt-out" form, Circuit City management impliedly and expressly pressured Mantor not to exercise his right. According to the court, when one of the parties possesses far greater bargaining power than the other or when the stronger party pressures, harasses, or compels the other party into entering into a contract, " 'oppression and therefore, procedural unconscionability, are present.' " In the court's view, "A meaningful opportunity to negotiate or reject the terms of a contract must mean something more than an empty choice. At a minimum, a party must have an actual, meaningful, and reasonable choice to exercise that discretion." Mantor had no meaningful choice because he could either participate in the arbitration program or lose his job.

The Ninth Circuit also held that the agreement was substantively unconscionable. Substantive unconscionability, the court said, concerns "the terms of the agreement and whether or not those terms are so one-sided as to shock the conscience." The court found the terms concerning the statute of limitations, class actions, cost-splitting, and the employer's unilateral power to modify or terminate the agreement substantively unconscionable. The Ninth Circuit also held that the Filing Fee/Waiver provision of Circuit City's arbitration agreement was substantively unconscionable. It held the fee waiver rule was "manifestly one-sided" and, therefore, unconscionable because it "(1) provides that an employee must pay an interested party 'for the privilege of bringing a complaint' and (2) assigns Circuit City, an interested party, the responsibility for deciding whether to waive the filing fee." Finally, the court refused to sever the unconscionable provisions. They were too numerous and severance would obligate the court to assume the role of "contract author rather than interpreter."

12. In *Al-Safin v. Circuit City Stores, Inc.*, 394 F.3d 1254 (9th Cir. 2005), the Ninth Circuit reaffirmed its long-standing negative evaluation of Circuit City's Dispute Resolution Rules and Procedures (DRRP) by holding a Circuit City arbitration agreement unconscionable and unenforceable under Washington state contract law. In so doing, it identified the provisions that could render an arbitration agreement unconscionable: Limitations on remedies and class actions, high costs for employees, binding employees exclusively to arbitration while allowing Circuit City to pursue disputes in court, and giving Circuit City the right to modify terms at will.

Under Washington state law, a contract clause need only be substantively unconscionable to be unenforceable. Substantive unconscionability refers to the terms themselves; by contrast, procedural unconscionability refers to how the agreement is negotiated and presented. The court of appeals concluded that Circuit City's DRRP "requires employees to forgo essential substantive and procedural rights and that clauses regarding coverage of claims, remedies, arbitration fees, cost-splitting, the statute of limitations, class actions, and modifications, render the agreement excessively one-sided and unconscionable."

In reaching this conclusion, the court relied upon its prior dispositions in *Ingle*, *Mantor*, and *Adams*. The cases involved the same Circuit City DRRP. Moreover, Washington and California law regarding substantive unconscionability were basically the same; each of them used a definition of substantively unconscionability that emphasized that the terms of the contract were so "one-sided" as to "shock the conscience." Additionally, Circuit City's DRRP did not meet *Gilmer*'s minimum requirements that arbitration agreements embody "basic procedural and remedial protections so that claimants can effectively pursue their statutory rights." Circuit City's agreement, the Ninth Circuit said, failed in this regard because it restricted remedies that would be available in a judicial forum.

The Allocation of Costs in Employment

Arbitration Agreements

Cost-splitting provisions can also make employment arbitration agreements suspect. The payment of costs by the employee creates a barrier to the accessibility of the arbitral remedy. Recent courts have generally found that even the partial allocation of costs to the employee can render the agreement substantively unconscionable. Once the defective provision is identified and combined with a lack of mutuality and the employer's unilateral ability to modify the terms of the agreement, severance is excluded as a means of salvaging the basic reference to arbitration.

In the California decisional law, the allocation of costs has special significance: "[A]n employee seeking to vindicate unwaivable [public law] rights may not be compelled to pay forum costs that are unique to arbitration." *Armendariz v. Foundation Health Psychcare Services, Inc.*, 24 Cal.4th 83, 99 Cal.Rptr.2d 745, 6 P.3d 669, 703 (2000). The contemplated rights are created by California legislation (*e.g.*, the Fair Employment and Housing Act [FEHA]). The California state Supreme Court in *Armen-*

dariz ruled that arbitration agreements that affect such rights "must be subject to particular scrutiny"; the decision in *Little v. Auto Stiegler, Inc.,* 29 Cal.4th 1064, 130 Cal.Rptr.2d 892, 63 P.3d 979 (2003), extended the *Armendariz* ruling to non-statutory rights. Moreover, even if an arbitration agreement satisfies the requirements in *Armendariz,* it could still be unconscionable. In *Abramson v. Juniper Networks, Inc.,* 115 Cal.App.4th 638, 9 Cal.Rptr.3d 422 (2004), a California court of appeal held an employment arbitration agreement involving unwaivable, nonstatutory public law rights unenforceable because the cost-sharing provision required the employee to pay half of the costs of arbitration. "When an employer imposes arbitration as a condition of employment, the arbitration agreement or arbitration process cannot generally require the employee to bear any *type* of expense that the employee would not be required to bear if he or she were free to bring the action in court."

In *Cole v. Burns Int'l Security Services,* 105 F.3d 1465 (D.C. Cir. 1996), the court held that the payment of arbitral costs by the employer was instrumental to the enforceability of a contract for the arbitration of workplace disputes. In fact, to render an otherwise unenforceable agreement valid, the employer was obligated to pay all of the costs for arbitration. The D.C. Circuit seemed to reason that contract unfairness was permissible as long as the culprit paid for it. The fact of the case indicate clearly the equity dilemma that was at the core of the litigation:

[. . .]

Clinton Cole used to work as a security guard at Union Station in Washington, D.C. for a company called LaSalle and Partners ("LaSalle"). In 1991, Burns Security took over LaSalle's contract to provide security at Union Station and required all LaSalle employees to sign a "Pre–Dispute Resolution Agreement" in order to obtain employment with Burns. The Pre–Dispute Resolution Agreement ("agreement" or "contract"), in relevant part, provides:

> In consideration of the Company employing you, you and the Company each agrees that, in the event either party (or its representatives, successors or assigns) brings an action in a court of competent jurisdiction relating to your recruitment, employment with, or termination of employment from the Company, the plaintiff in such action agrees to waive his, her or its right to a trial by jury, and further agrees that no demand, request or motion will be made for trial by jury.

> In consideration of the Company employing you, you further agree that, in the event that you seek relief in a court of competent jurisdiction for a dispute covered by this Agreement, the Company may, at any time within 60 days of the service of your complaint upon the Company, at its option, require all or part of the dispute to be arbitrated by one arbitrator in accordance with the rules of the American Arbitration Association. You agree that the option to arbitrate any dispute is governed by the Federal Arbitration Act, and fully enforceable. You understand and agree that, if the Company exercises its option, any dispute arbitrated will be heard solely by the arbitrator, and not by a court.

> This pre-dispute resolution agreement will cover all matters directly or indirectly related to your recruitment, employment or termination of employment by the Company; including, but not limited to, claims involving laws against discrimination whether brought under federal and/or state law, and/or claims involving co-employees but excluding Worker's Compensation Claims.
>
> The right to a trial, and to a trial by jury, is of value.
>
> YOU MAY WISH TO CONSULT AN ATTORNEY PRIOR TO SIGNING THIS AGREEMENT. IF SO, TAKE A COPY OF THIS FORM WITH YOU. HOWEVER, YOU WILL NOT BE OFFERED EMPLOYMENT UNTIL THIS FORM IS SIGNED AND RETURNED BY YOU.

...On August 5, 1991, Cole signed the agreement and began working for Burns.

In October 1993, Burns Security fired Cole. After filing charges with the Equal Employment Opportunity Commission, Cole filed the instant complaint in the United States District Court for the District of Columbia, alleging racial discrimination, harassment based on race, retaliation for his writing a letter of complaint regarding sexual harassment of a subordinate employee by another supervisor at Burns, and intentional infliction of emotional distress. Burns moved to compel arbitration of the dispute and to dismiss Cole's complaint pursuant to the terms of the contract.

The District Court found that the arbitration agreement clearly covered Cole's claims. The court also rejected Cole's suggestions (1) that the Pre–Dispute Resolution Agreement was excluded from coverage under the Federal Arbitration Act under 9 U.S.C. § 1, and (2) that the agreement was an unenforceable and unconscionable contract of adhesion. As a result, the trial court granted Burns Security's motion to compel arbitration and dismissed Cole's complaint....

* * *

After extensive discussion and reasoning, the court reaches its cryptic holding:

> In sum, we hold that Cole could not be required to agree to arbitrate his public law claims as a condition of employment if the arbitration agreement required him to pay all or part of the arbitrator's fees and expenses. In light of this holding, we find that the arbitration agreement in this case is valid and enforceable. We do so because we interpret the agreement as requiring Burns Security to pay all of the arbitrator's fees necessary for a full and fair resolution of Cole's statutory claims.

It seems that the court lacked confidence in its own determination. In her concurring-dissenting opinion, Judge LeCraft Henderson stated: "[I]f the majority believes that the arbitration agreement was reached under duress or that it is unconscionable, it should say so straight out and declare it unenforceable."

NOTES AND QUESTIONS

1. You should evaluate the pre-dispute resolution agreement imposed by Burns Int'l Security Services. The company's objective is to avoid jury trials and to maintain an option to avoid judicial litigation altogether. It includes an admonishment that prospective employees should agree to these conditions only upon the basis of informed consent. Is it possible, intellectually and practically, to describe this approach as anything but heavy-handed and overreaching? Is there any balance to the agreement or mutuality to the contemplated exchange? Why would the company seek to eliminate a prospective employee's litigation leverage as a plaintiff except to compromise the employee's rights and thereby foster its own? Is the provision relating to the jury trial a means of negating the 1991 amendment to Title VII that guaranteed the right to a jury trial? Does the agreement mean that individuals will be hired only if they agree to take the law and courts out of the employment relationship, if the employer so desires? Therefore, once you agree to work for the company, you abandon your status as a citizen. The agreement also states legal conclusions by providing that it is covered by the FAA and "fully enforceable." Is this a further indication that corporate enterprises have achieved sovereign autonomy in regard to their commercial operations and can act as independent legislative and executive authorities as long as they allude to arbitration?

2. Throughout its discussion, the court appears preoccupied with the parties' payment of arbitrator fees. In doing so, is the court advancing a legal value? Is it expressing in an indirect fashion its misgivings about the validity of the agreement? The court reasons that obliging employees to pay all or part of the arbitrators' fee would amount to a "*de facto* forfeiture of employee's statutory rights." Why should the payment of arbitrator fees be more significant in this regard than the agreement itself? Should the lawfulness of this new practice be determined by the allocation of a single cost of the process? While litigants do not pay judges' salaries directly, is that factor the most critical difference between arbitral and judicial adjudication?

On the one hand, the court states that "public law confers both substantive rights and a reasonable right of access to a neutral forum in which these rights can be vindicated." Is it not also true that the law expressly confers a right to a civil jury trial? Is the court's redefinition and depreciation of procedural rights designed to confirm its decision to adhere to precedent on arbitration? What does the allocation of the cost of arbitrator fees have to do with fundamental legal and political guarantees?

On the other hand, the court claims that "[t]he beneficiaries of public statutes are entitled to the rights and protections provided by law. Clearly, it would be unlawful for an employer to condition employment on an employee's agreement to give up the right to be free from racial or gender discrimination." Do the circumstances of employment arbitration create this situation? Why should the burdens of the agreement be more significant than the agreement itself? The court's reasoning is strained and formalistic, leaving substantial doubt that employee statutory rights can be vindicated. Is the court's emphasis upon the payment of arbitrator fees "too little, too late"?

3. The court expresses some level of confidence in the integrity of the arbitration process and arbitrators. The court implies that the availability of judicial review of awards legitimizes the arbitration agreement in *Cole*. How persuasive is that argument? It also admonishes arbitrators to adapt to their new functions in resolving workplace disputes, presumably because of the importance of the statutory rights that are at stake. It further states that it is "misguided to mourn" the U.S. Supreme Court's doctrine on the arbitrability of statutory rights. How do you interpret these remarks? What convictions and presumptions underlie the court's position?

In a more cogent assessment of the cost factor in *Shankle v. B–G Maintenance Management of Colorado, Inc.*, 163 F.3d 1230 (10th Cir. 1999), the U.S. Court of Appeals for the Tenth Circuit ruled that an arbitration agreement was unenforceable when it functioned as a condition of employment or of continued employment and required the employee to pay a prohibitively expensive part of the fees for arbitration. In the court's view, the agreement, as written, deprived the employee of any remedy by prohibiting recourse to the courts and by making arbitration unaffordable.

Matthew Shankle was a shift manager for B–G Maintenance Management of Colorado, Inc. B–G required Shankle to sign an arbitration agreement as a condition of continued employment. Under the agreement, the parties substituted arbitration for judicial recourse. In addition, the agreement provided that Shankle would pay half of the arbitrator's fee.

When B–G terminated Shankle, he filed a demand for arbitration. After receiving the arbitrator's fee arrangements, Shankle canceled the arbitration and filed suit under Title VII of the Civil Rights Act of 1964. B–G moved to compel arbitration, but the district court and the Tenth Circuit ruled that the arbitration agreement was invalid because it "actually prevent[ed] an individual from effectively vindicating his or her statutory rights." The court emphasized that, if an agreement prohibits the use of the judicial forum for a statutory claim, it must provide "an effective and reasonable alternative forum." Because so few employees could afford to pay their share of the fees, the use of arbitration was a limited, even useless remedy. The court dismissed B–G's claim that fee-splitting promoted neutrality. Even if fee-splitting did promote neutrality, that benefit was "substantially outweighed" by the restrictions placed on the employee's right of recourse.

The opinion in *Sobol v. Kidder, Peabody & Co., Inc.*, 49 F.Supp.2d 208 (S.D.N.Y. 1999), suggests a different assessment of costs. There, a female employee of Kidder alleged that she was pressured into resigning from Kidder Peabody by her supervisor. She claimed that the supervisor belittled her abilities, undermined her authority, and threatened to remove her as head of a department. She contended that the conduct violated the Equal Pay Act, Title VII, and the ADEA. The arbitral tribunal dismissed Sobol's claims and ruled that she was responsible for half of the arbitration fees. Sobol's share amounted to $25,650. The court upheld the award, ruling that NASD Rule 10205(c) gives the arbitrators the discretion to distribute the costs of the arbitration among the parties. The court stated that, because arbitration is generally less expensive than litigation, the assessment of half the fees neither discouraged arbitration nor offended public policy.

Also, in *Howard v. KPMG Peat Marwick*, 36 F.Supp.2d 183 (S.D.N.Y. 1999), *aff'd*, 173 F.3d 844 (2d Cir. 1999), a former female employee, filed a lawsuit against Peat Marwick alleging race and gender discrimination in the termination of her employment. The court granted Peat Marwick's motion to stay the judicial proceeding. Howard then filed a notice to arbitrate accompanied by a check in the amount of $150. The American Arbitration Association (AAA) responded, stating that the filing fee was $9,000. Howard then filed a motion requesting the court to compel Peat Marwick to pay all but $150 of the filing fee. The court directed Howard to exhaust the AAA's fee waiver mechanisms. The AAA changed the filing fee to $500—that amount was due immediately and the remaining $2,500 was deferred until the conclusion of the case.

The court held that the filing fee did not prevent Howard from vindicating her Title VII claims. The court noted that, in some cases, significant financial burdens can impede access to the arbitral forum and prevent the vindication of Title VII claims. Moreover, the court recognized that other courts have held that an employee cannot be forced to pay the arbitrators' fee, and that arbitration agreements are unenforceable when an employee is responsible for bearing some of the costs related to arbitration of Title VII claims.

Howard's willingness to pay $150 was based on the fact that that amount reflected the filing fee for initiating a civil suit under 28 U.S.C. § 1914. Neither *Gilmer* nor Title VII, however, provided that the fee for arbitration could not exceed the $150 filing fee for a civil suit. As long as there was an alternative forum for relief, the arbitration clause must be given effect. The court also concluded that Howard had the financial means of paying the $500 filing fee. The fee was not a barrier to relief. Finally, the allegation of remedial prohibition due to costs would not ripen until the $2,500 fee became due.

In late 2000, the U.S. Supreme Court rendered its decision in *Green Tree Financial Corp.-Alabama v. Randolph*, 531 U.S. 79 (2000). In its opinion, the Court—speaking through the late Chief Justice Rehnquist— addressed the impact of arbitral costs upon the validity of arbitration agreements. In contrast to the ruling in *Cole* and *Armendariz*, the Court held—in a divided segment of its opinion—that the fact that a consumer bears some of the costs of the arbitral process "alone is plainly insufficient to render [the arbitration agreement] unenforceable.... To invalidate the agreement would undermine the 'liberal federal policy favoring arbitration agreements'...[and] would conflict with [this Court's holdings, for example,]...that the party resisting arbitration bears the burden of proving that Congress intended to preclude arbitration of the statutory claims at issue.... Thus, a party seeking to invalidate an arbitration agreement on the ground that arbitration would be prohibitively expensive bears the burden of showing the likelihood of incurring such costs. Randolph did not meet that burden."

The members of the Court were quite divided on this issue. The ruling appears to have been decided by a slim 5 to 4 majority. The emerging view that argued that the allocation of the costs was a critical factor in determining the legitimacy of the reference to arbitration, as previously articulated in *Cole, Shankle*, and *Armendariz*, was clearly chilled by the holding in *Green Tree*. If the costs of arbitration were burdensome, the party being burdened did not get a pass, but rather needed to establish the existence and the extent of the financial burden. What was important to the majority of the Court in *Green Tree* was preserving the right to engage in arbitration, not to create and enlarge due process exceptions to it.

The concurring and dissenting opinions concluded that the lower court opinion should have been vacated and remanded for "closer consideration of the arbitration forum's [financial] accessibility." According to Justice Ginsburg, "As I see it, the case in its current posture is not ripe for [the majority's] disposition." Justice Ginsburg emphasized the disparity of position between the parties, the form contract presented on a take-it-or-leave-it basis, and Green Tree's position as a repeat player in arbitration. She concluded that "the Court...reached out prematurely to resolve the matter in the lender's favor."

GREEN TREE FINANCIAL CORP.-ALA. v. RANDOLPH

531 U.S. 79, 121 S.Ct. 513, 148 L.Ed.2d 373 (2000).

(footnotes omitted)

CHIEF JUSTICE REHNQUIST delivered the opinion of the Court.

In this case we first address whether an order compelling arbitration and dismissing a party's underlying claims is a "final decision with respect to an arbitration" within the meaning of § 16 of the Federal Arbitration Act, 9 U.S.C. § 16, and thus is immediately appealable pursuant to that Act. Because we decide that question in the affirmative, we also address the question whether an arbitration agreement that does not mention arbitration costs and fees is unenforceable because it fails to affirmatively protect a party from potentially steep arbitration costs. We conclude that an arbitration agreement's silence with respect to such matters does not render the agreement unenforceable.

I

Respondent Larketta Randolph purchased a mobile home from Better Cents Home Builders, Inc., in Opelika, Alabama. She financed this purchase through petitioners Green Tree Financial Corporation and its wholly owned subsidiary, Green Tree Financial Corp.-Alabama. Petitioners' Manufactured Home Retail Installment Contract and Security Agreement required that Randolph buy Vendor's Single Interest insurance, which protects the vendor or lienholder against the costs of repossession in the event of default. The agreement also provided that all disputes arising from, or relating to, the contract, whether arising under case law or statutory law, would be resolved by binding arbitration.

Randolph later sued petitioners, alleging that they violated the Truth in Lending Act (TILA) ... by failing to disclose as a finance charge the Vendor's Single Interest insurance requirement. She later amended her complaint to add a claim that petitioners violated the Equal Credit Opportunity Act ... by requiring her to arbitrate her statutory causes of action. She brought this action on behalf of a similarly situated class. In lieu of an answer, petitioners filed a motion to compel arbitration, to stay the action, or, in the alternative, to dismiss. The District Court granted petitioners' motion to compel arbitration, denied the motion to stay, and dismissed Randolph's claims with prejudice. The District Court also denied her request to certify a class.... She requested reconsideration, asserting that she lacked the resources to arbitrate and as a result, would have to forgo her claims against petitioners.... The District Court denied reconsideration.... Randolph appealed.

The Court of Appeals for the Eleventh Circuit first held that it had jurisdiction to review the District Court's order because that order was a final decision.... The Court of Appeals looked to § 16 of the Federal Arbitration Act (FAA) ... which governs appeal from a District Court's arbitration order, and specifically § 16(a)(3), which allows appeal from "a final decision with respect to an arbitration that is subject to this title." The Court determined that a final, appealable order within the meaning of the FAA is one that disposes of all the issues framed by the litigation, leaving nothing to be done but execute the order. The Court of Appeals found the District Court's order within that definition.

The court then determined that the arbitration agreement failed to provide the minimum guarantees that respondent could vindicate her statutory rights under the TILA. Critical to this determination was the court's observation that the arbitration agreement was silent with respect to payment of filing fees, arbitrators' costs, and other arbitration expenses. On that basis, the court held that the agreement to arbitrate posed a risk that respondent's ability to vindicate her statutory rights would be undone by "steep" arbitration costs, and therefore was unenforceable. We granted *certiorari* ... and we now affirm the Court of Appeals with respect to the first conclusion, and reverse it with respect to the second.

II

[...]

III

We now turn to the question whether Randolph's agreement to arbitrate is unenforceable because it says nothing about the costs of arbitration, and thus fails to provide her protection from potentially substantial costs of pursuing her federal statutory claims in the arbitral forum. Section 2 of the FAA provides that "[a] written provision in any maritime transaction or a contract evidencing a transaction involving commerce to settle by arbitration a controversy thereafter arising out of such contract . . . shall be valid, irrevocable, and enforceable, save upon such grounds as exist at law or in equity for the revocation of any contract." . . . In considering whether respondent's agreement to arbitrate is unenforceable, we are mindful of the FAA's purpose "to reverse the longstanding judicial hostility to arbitration agreements . . . and to place arbitration agreements upon the same footing as other contracts." . . .

In light of that purpose, we have recognized that federal statutory claims can be appropriately resolved through arbitration, and we have enforced agreements to arbitrate that involve such claims. . . . We have likewise rejected generalized attacks on arbitration that rest on "suspicion of arbitration as a method of weakening the protections afforded in the substantive law to would-be complainants." . . . These cases demonstrate that even claims arising under a statute designed to further important social policies may be arbitrated because " 'so long as the prospective litigant effectively may vindicate [his or her] statutory cause of action in the arbitral forum,' " the statute serves its functions. . . .

In determining whether statutory claims may be arbitrated, we first ask whether the parties agreed to submit their claims to arbitration, and then ask whether Congress has evinced an intention to preclude a waiver of judicial remedies for the statutory rights at issue. . . . In this case, it is undisputed that the parties agreed to arbitrate all claims relating to their contract, including claims involving statutory rights. Nor does Randolph contend that the TILA evinces an intention to preclude a waiver of judicial remedies. She contends instead that the arbitration agreement's silence with respect to costs and fees creates a "risk" that she will be required to bear prohibitive arbitration costs if she pursues her claims in an arbitral forum, and thereby forces her to forgo any claims she may have against petitioners. Therefore, she argues, she is unable to vindicate her statutory rights in arbitration. . . .

It may well be that the existence of large arbitration costs could preclude a litigant such as Randolph from effectively vindicating her federal statutory rights in the arbitral forum. But the record does not show that Randolph will bear such costs if she goes to arbitration. Indeed, it contains hardly any information on the matter. As the Court of Appeals recognized, "we lack . . . information about how claimants fare under Green Tree's arbitration clause." . . . The record reveals only the arbitration agreement's silence on the subject, and that fact alone is plainly insufficient to render it unenforceable. The "risk" that Randolph will be saddled with prohibitive costs is too speculative to justify the invalidation of an arbitration agreement.

To invalidate the agreement on that basis would undermine the "liberal federal policy favoring arbitration agreements."... It would also conflict with our prior holdings that the party resisting arbitration bears the burden of proving that the claims at issue are unsuitable for arbitration....We have held that the party seeking to avoid arbitration bears the burden of establishing that Congress intended to preclude arbitration of the statutory claims at issue.... Similarly, we believe that where, as here, a party seeks to invalidate an arbitration agreement on the ground that arbitration would be prohibitively expensive, that party bears the burden of showing the likelihood of incurring such costs. Randolph did not meet that burden. How detailed the showing of prohibitive expense must be before the party seeking arbitration must come forward with contrary evidence is a matter we need not discuss; for in this case neither during discovery nor when the case was presented on the merits was there any timely showing at all on the point. The Court of Appeals therefore erred in deciding that the arbitration agreement's silence with respect to costs and fees rendered it unenforceable.

The judgment of the Court of Appeals is affirmed in part and reversed in part.

It is so ordered.

JUSTICE GINSBURG, with whom JUSTICE STEVENS and JUSTICE SOUTER join, and with whom JUSTICE BREYER joins as to Parts I and III, concurring in part and dissenting in part.

I

I join Part II of the Court's opinion, which holds that the District Court's order, dismissing all the claims before it, was a "final," and therefore immediately appealable, decision.... On the matter the Court airs in Part III...—allocation of the costs of arbitration—I would not rule definitively. Instead, I would vacate the Eleventh Circuit's decision, which dispositively declared the arbitration clause unenforceable, and remand the case for closer consideration of the arbitral forum's accessibility.

II

The Court today deals with a "who pays" question, specifically, who pays for the arbitral forum. The Court holds that Larketta Randolph bears the burden of demonstrating that the arbitral forum is financially inaccessible to her. Essentially, the Court requires a party, situated as Randolph is, either to submit to arbitration without knowing who will pay for the forum or to demonstrate up front that the costs, if imposed on her, will be prohibitive....As I see it, the case in its current posture is not ripe for such a disposition.

The Court recognizes that "the existence of large arbitration costs could preclude a litigant such as Randolph from effectively vindicating her federal statutory rights in the arbitral forum."...But, the Court next determines, "the party resisting arbitration bears the burden of proving that the claims at issue are unsuitable for arbitration" and "Randolph did not meet that burden."...In so ruling, the Court blends two discrete inquiries: First, is the arbitral forum *adequate* to adjudicate the claims at issue; second, is that forum *accessible* to the party resisting arbitration.

Our past decisions deal with the first question, the *adequacy* of the arbitral forum to adjudicate various statutory claims....These decisions hold that the party resisting arbitration bears the burden of establishing the inadequacy of the arbitral forum for adjudication of claims of a particular genre....It does not follow like the night the day, however, that the party resisting arbitration should also bear the burden of showing that the arbitral forum would be financially inaccessible to her.

The arbitration agreement at issue is contained in a form contract drawn by a commercial party and presented to an individual consumer on a take-it-or-leave-it basis. The case on which the Court dominantly relies, *Gilmer*, also involved a nonnegotiated arbitration clause. But the "who pays" question presented in this case did not arise in *Gilmer*. Under the rules that governed in *Gilmer*—those of the New York Stock Exchange—it was the standard practice for securities industry parties, arbitrating employment disputes, to pay all of the arbitrators' fees....Regarding that practice, the Court of Appeals for the District of Columbia Circuit recently commented:

"In *Gilmer*, the Supreme Court endorsed a system of arbitration in which employees are not required to pay for the arbitrator assigned to hear their statutory claims. There is no reason to think that the Court would have approved arbitration in the absence of this arrangement. Indeed, we are unaware of any situation in American jurisprudence in which a beneficiary of a federal statute has been required to pay for the services of the judge assigned to hear her or his case."...

III

The form contract in this case provides no indication of the rules under which arbitration will proceed or the costs a consumer is likely to incur in arbitration. Green Tree, drafter of the contract, could have filled the void by specifying, for instance, that arbitration would be governed by the rules of the American Arbitration Association (AAA). Under the AAA's Consumer Arbitration Rules, consumers in small-claims arbitration incur no filing fee and pay only $125 of the total fees charged by the arbitrator. All other fees and costs are to be paid by the business party....Other national arbitration organizations have developed similar models for fair cost and fee allocation. It may be that in this case, as in *Gilmer*, there is a standard practice on arbitrators' fees and expenses, one that fills the blank space in the arbitration agreement. Counsel for Green Tree offered a hint in that direction....But there is no reliable indication in this record that Randolph's claim will be arbitrated under any consumer-protective fee arrangement.

As a repeat player in the arbitration required by its form contract, Green Tree has superior information about the cost to consumers of pursuing arbitration.... In these circumstances, it is hardly clear that Randolph should bear the burden of demonstrating up front the arbitral forum's inaccessibility, or that she should be required to submit to arbitration without knowing how much it will cost her.

As I see it, the Court has reached out prematurely to resolve the matter in the lender's favor. If Green Tree's practice under the form contract with retail installment sales purchasers resembles that of the employer in *Gilmer*, Randolph would be insulated from prohibitive costs. And if the arbitral forum were in this case financially accessible to Randolph, there would be no occasion to reach the decision today rendered by the Court. Before writing a term into the form contract, as the District of Columbia Circuit did ... or leaving cost allocation initially to each arbitrator, as the Court does, I would remand for clarification of Green Tree's practice.

The Court's opinion, if I comprehend it correctly, does not prevent Randolph from returning to court, post arbitration, if she then has a complaint about cost allocation. If that is so, the issue reduces to when, not whether, she can be spared from payment of excessive costs. Neither certainty nor judicial economy is served by leaving that issue unsettled until the end of the line.

For the reasons stated, I dissent from the Court's reversal of the Eleventh Circuit's decision on the cost question. I would instead vacate and remand for further consideration of the accessibility of the arbitral forum to Randolph.

NOTES AND QUESTIONS

1. The dissent, to some extent, makes the D.C. Circuit's ruling in *Cole* the centerpiece of its reasoning. Does the majority opinion contradict or embrace *Cole*? What could possibly be wrong with requiring proof of financial hardship? Is Justice Ginsburg right to think that Green Tree is a better source of the requisite information?

2. In your view, does the majority decide in favor of the lender prematurely? Is opposition in political ideology at work in that statement? Is political ideology present in the opinion explicitly or implicitly?

3. What role does the federal policy on arbitration play in the majority's opinion? In the dissent?

4. Subsequent lower court cases indicate that the *Green Tree* ruling has influenced the federal courts' approach to the assessment of costs upon the validity of arbitration agreements. For instance, the U.S. District Court for the Eastern District of Pennsylvania upheld an arbitration provision despite a loser-pays provision in regard to arbitral costs. It held that the loser-pays provision was enforceable and "did not deny plaintiff an effective and accessible forum." *See Goodman v. ESPE America, Inc.*, No. 00–CV–862, 2001 WL

64749, not reported, (E.D. Pa. 2001). (*See also Zumpano v. Omnipoint Communications*, 2001 WL 43781, not reported, (E.D. Pa. 2001) (arbitration agreement with fee-shifting provision and involving an employment discrimination claim is unenforceable only if plaintiff demonstrates that the arbitrator's fees and arbitral costs substantially deterred him from enforcing his statutory rights)). Moreover, the U.S. Fourth Circuit Court of Appeals held that a fee-splitting provision which divided the cost of arbitration between all parties did not *per se* render an arbitration agreement unenforceable. (*See Bradford v. Rockwell Semiconductor Sys., Inc.*, 238 F.3d 549 (4th Cir. 2001) (determining whether such a provision had an impact upon the validity of the arbitration agreement required a case-by-case analysis that focused upon the claimants' ability to pay arbitration fees and costs)).

5. At the end of its analysis, the Fourth Circuit in *Bradford* acknowledged that the federal circuits were divided on whether fee-splitting provisions were *per se* invalid. Both the Eleventh Circuit and the D.C. Circuit concluded that "fee-splitting provisions render arbitration agreements unenforceable because the cost of fee splitting deters or prevents employees from vindicating their statutory rights in arbitral forums." The First, Fifth, and Seventh Circuits, however, have refused to endorse that position. These courts prefer to assess the validity of fee-splitting provisions on a case-by-case basis. *See Perez v. Globe Airport Sec. Services, Inc.*, 253 F.3d 1280 (11th Cir. 2001), *reh'g and reh'g en banc denied* (Aug. 16, 2001). *But see LaPrade v. Kidder, Peabody & Co., Inc.*, 246 F.3d 702 (D.C. Cir. 2001) (court found that plaintiff misinterpreted *Cole* to provide "a virtually cost-free alternative to traditional court proceedings"; under *Cole*, an employee may be assessed reasonable forum fees because, even if the employee filed in federal court, he or she would still have to pay some costs; further, plaintiff failed to meet the burden of proof).

6. In comparing the two approaches, the Fourth Circuit turned to the various circuit interpretations of *Gilmer*. *Bradford*'s argument relied heavily upon the statement in *Cole* that, "under *Gilmer*, arbitration is supposed to be a reasonable substitute for a judicial forum. Therefore, it would undermine Congress' intent to prevent employees who are seeking to vindicate statutory rights from gaining access to a judicial forum and then require them to pay for the services of an arbitrator when they would never be required to pay for a judge in court." The Fourth Circuit adopted the Fifth Circuit's interpretation of *Gilmer*, that "the crucial inquiry under *Gilmer* is whether the particular claimant has an adequate and accessible substitute forum in which to resolve his statutory rights and that *Gilmer* does not call for the conclusion that fee-splitting in all cases deprives the claimant of such a forum." *See Williams v. Cigna Fin. Advisors, Inc.*, 197 F.3d 752 (5th Cir. 1999), *cert. denied*, 529 U.S. 1099 (2000); *Bradford*, 238 F.3d at 556.

7. Having endorsed the case-by-case analysis, the court found that the employee had "failed to demonstrate any inability to pay the arbitration fees and costs, much less prohibitive financial hardship, to support his assertion that the fee-splitting provision deterred him from arbitrating his statutory claims." The court, therefore, refused to invalidate the arbitration provision because of the fee-splitting requirement. The court invoked language in the *Green Tree* decision to justify its ruling, namely that "some showing of

individualized prohibitive expense would be necessary to invalidate an arbitration agreement on the ground that fee-splitting would be prohibitively expensive."

8. By contrast, the Sixth Circuit, in *Morrison v. Circuit City Stores, Inc.*, 317 F.3d 646 (6th Cir. 2003), held that the cost splitting provisions in two separate employment arbitration agreements were unenforceable. In so doing, the court articulated a new standard by which to address the cost issue when a case involved federal antidiscrimination statutes such as Title VII. It rejected the case-by-case approach under which the costs of arbitration and judicial litigation are compared or the impact of costs upon rights protection is assessed by the court after the plaintiff has engaged in arbitration. The Sixth Circuit held that "potential litigants must be given an opportunity, prior to arbitration on the merits, to demonstrate that the potential costs of arbitration are great enough to deter them and similarly situated individuals from seeking to vindicate their federal statutory rights in the arbitral forum." In the court's view, the focus should be upon a group of similarly situated individuals, rather than solely upon the plaintiff, in order to further the goal of the federal statutes to deter discrimination.

9. The Sixth Circuit's "similarly situated individuals" approach involves several steps of analysis. The court establishes the group of similarly situated plaintiffs by identifying similar "job description[s] and socioeconomic background[s]." In addition, it looks to the average costs of arbitration when determining whether a group of similarly situated people would be deterred from bringing their claims to arbitration. The court also compares the total arbitration costs to the costs of bringing the same claims to court. For example, while arbitrators' fees represent the additional expense of arbitration, court proceedings generally involve more depositions, interrogatories, and motions for discovery. The critical question is whether the total costs of arbitration might deter a group of similarly situated individuals from going to arbitration.

10. The court was not willing to discount the cost of arbitration when the arbitration agreement authorized the arbitrator to award attorney's fees to the prevailing party. Moreover, in considering whether a group of similarly situated individuals would be prevented from vindicating their statutory rights in an arbitral forum, the court indicated that higher-level employees, such as managers, would be more likely to have a cost-splitting provision enforced against them as compared to lower level employees.

11. Applying the "similarly situated individuals" approach to one of the cost-splitting provisions in the instant case, the court held that the provision was unenforceable. Although the cost-splitting provision gave Morrison the choice of paying either $500 or 3% of her yearly salary, whichever amount was greater, the court found that these costs were substantial enough to prohibit Morrison and similarly situated people from bringing their statutory claims to arbitration. The evidence indicated that Morrison earned approximately $54,060 annually; thus, she would have had to pay $1,622 within ninety days of the rendering of the arbitral award. The court felt that this amount was high enough to hinder Morrison and others from bringing a claim to arbitra-

tion. The court also noted that the average costs for the arbitration of employment discrimination claims were much higher than court costs.

12.   In a more recent case, the Third Circuit reached a similar conclusion and held that, under the *Randolph* standard, costs were established as prohibitive and prevented the plaintiff from effectively vindicating Title VII and ADEA rights. *See Spinetti v. Service Corp. Int'l*, 324 F.3d 212 (3d Cir. 2003).

13.   *Morrison's* socioeconomic measures of comparison were cited with approval in *Garrett v. Hooters–Toledo*, 295 F.Supp.2d 774 (N.D. Ohio 2003). There, the federal district court held that a cost-sharing provision was prohibitive and that the arbitration agreement reinforced the fundamental inequality between the parties. Moreover, in the event of mediation, Hooters alone choose the mediators.

14.   Recent federal and state court cases dealing with costs in arbitration have generally adopted the more rigorous view of costs articulated in *Cole* and *Shankle*. A federal district court in Colorado upheld the enforceability of an arbitration agreement but severed the provision for the allocation of arbitral costs. *Fuller and Williams v. Pep Boys*, 88 F.Supp.2d 1158 (D. Colo. 2000), involved discrimination claims under Title VII and 42 U.S.C. § 1981. The arbitral clause provided that the employer and employee would share equally the cost of any arbitration. Moreover, the parties would pay their own expenses and attorney's fees. Finally, the provision contained a severance clause. The court held that the cost-sharing arrangement was unlawful under *Shankle*, but used the severance clause to salvage the reference to arbitration.

15.   In a related, but more recent case, *Perez v. Hospitality Ventures–Denver LLC*, 245 F.Supp.2d 1172 (D. Colo. 2003), the same court again emphasized the importance of allocating arbitral costs and having a severance clause in agreements in which parties are unequal. In *Perez*, the court held an arbitration agreement in an employee handbook unenforceable because it required employees to split arbitral costs with the employer. Under the *Shankle* holding, fee-splitting provisions that prohibit employees from bringing claims in arbitration are illegal. Severability was not available because the agreement did not contain a severance clause. In the court's view, the contract did not represent a mutual agreement to arbitrate disputes, but rather a unilateral imposition of arbitration on the weaker party by the stronger party.

16.   Recent California court of appeal cases are in keeping with the federal decisions from Colorado. In *Fittante v. Palm Springs Motors, Inc.*, 105 Cal.App.4th 708, 129 Cal.Rptr.2d 659 (2003), the court held that the imposition of unreasonable costs on a party as a condition of access to the arbitral forum rendered that part of the arbitration agreement unconscionable. The unconscionable cost provision, however, could be severed and the remainder of the agreement enforced. Also, in *Abramson v. Juniper Networks, Inc.*, 115 Cal.App.4th 638, 9 Cal.Rptr.3d 422 (2004), the state appellate court held an employment arbitration agreement unenforceable because its cost-sharing provision required employees to pay half the costs of arbitration with regard to unwaivable, nonstatutory public law rights. According to the court, "when an employer imposes mandatory arbitration as a condition of employment the

arbitration agreement or arbitral process cannot generally require the employee to bear any *type* of expense that the employee would not be required to bear if he/she were free to bring the action in court."

The rulings were particularly significant because they applied and extended *Armendariz* to unjust termination claims. *Armendariz* involved unwaivable statutory rights and *Little v. Auto Stiegler, Inc.*, 29 Cal.4th 1064, 130 Cal. Rptr.2d 892, 63 P.3d 979 (2003), extended *Armendariz* to non-statutory rights. According to the court in *Abramson, Armendariz* and *Little* held that "an employee seeking to vindicate unwaivable rights may not be compelled to pay forum costs that are unique to arbitration." The *Abramson* court then decided that "the principle that arbitration costs may prevent arbitration claimants from effectively pursuing their public rights would apply with equal force to [wrongful termination] claims as to FEHA claims or to federal statutory claims."

✳Handbook Agreements

The decisional law on the validity and enforceability of employment arbitrations is expanding and acquiring greater definition. It is becoming clear, for example, that the agreement to arbitrate workplace disputes is a self-contained, autonomous contract that governs regardless of whether there is an underlying employment contract documenting the basic relationship between the employer and the employee. An employer and an at-will employee can agree in a written instrument to arbitrate disputes, including statutory discrimination claims, without converting the at-will employee to an employee under contract. The arbitral clause, therefore, stands on its own as a contract and does not affect, and is not affected by, the circumstances of employment. At times, the arbitral clause remains enforceable even though the employment agreement or relationship has expired. The employment arbitration agreement can govern all aspects of the association between the employer and the employee. The employment arbitration contract can take a variety of forms. In most circumstances, these contracts are far removed from the model of mutual, bilateral agreements. They generally are adhesionary contracts, unilaterally imposed by the employer.

* * *

Courts have addressed the use of employee handbooks by employers to create an obligation on the part of employees to submit workplace disputes to arbitration. Because some cases involved discrimination, some courts held that employee handbooks did not constitute binding agreements to arbitrate workplace disputes. Courts appear especially reluctant to deprive civil rights claimants of judicial recourse. In more recent cases, however, they affirmed the vitality of the *Gilmer* doctrine that all workplace disputes are arbitrable.

* * *

In *Towles v. United HealthCare Corp.*, 338 S.C. 29, 524 S.E.2d 839 (Ct. App. 1998), United sought to compel the arbitration of a former employee's claim pursuant to the Employee Handbook Acknowledgment Form that had been issued to the employee. The relevant portion of the Acknowledgment Form stated that "[a]rbitration is the final, exclusive and required forum for the resolution of all employment related disputes which are based on legal claim." The court of appeals held that the arbitration provision was a binding arbitration agreement that mandated the use of arbitration as the final and exclusive forum for resolving the employment dispute between Towles, the former employee, and United.

Towles raised a notice-based argument to challenge the enforceability of the Acknowledgment Form as an arbitration agreement. He argued that an employee handbook constituted a contract only if actual notice of the handbook's provisions was provided to the employee. The court rejected the contention, stating that precedent did "not focus on the need for actual notice when an employee handbook creates an employment contract, but rather holds that an employee must receive actual notice when an employer modifies an existing handbook." Further, the court stated that "the law does not impose a duty to explain a document's contents to an individual when the individual can learn the contents from simply reading the document."

The court then examined the Employee Handbook Acknowledgment Form. The court concluded that the Acknowledgment Form created a valid, binding contract requiring arbitration; it constituted a "specific communication of an offer" to Towles which "conditioned his acceptance of the Employment Arbitration Policy as part of his employment contract." Further, the court stated that Towle's continued employment with United amounted to a valid acceptance of the contractual offer.

* * *

In *Chanchani v. Salomon/Smith Barney, Inc.*, 2001 WL 204214 (S.D.N.Y. 2001) (unrep. op.), a U.S. district court in New York held that a dispute resolution clause contained in an employee handbook was enforceable even though the employee alleging discrimination had not returned the receipt form accompanying the clause. The plaintiffs, husband and wife, filed claims against Smith Barney alleging wrongful termination and employment discrimination. Pursuant to a dispute resolution clause contained in its Employee Handbook, Smith Barney moved to compel arbitration. The handbook was initially distributed in 1993. Updated versions containing receipt forms were handed out to employees thereafter on a yearly basis. The Chanchanis acknowledged receipt of the 1996 version by signing individual Employee Handbook Receipt Forms and returning them to Smith Barney. The forms affirmed that the Chanchanis had "reviewed the Handbook and agreed to 'comply with all the Policies and Procedures of the Company.'" Because the Chanchanis never signed the updated 1998 Receipt Form, however, they argued that they had not agreed to the terms of the provision and should not be forced to submit their claims to arbitration.

In addressing this matter, the court referred to the federal policy in favor of arbitration. It further stated that "courts in this district routinely uphold arbitration agreements contained in employee handbooks where, as here, the employee has signed an acknowledgment form." The Chanchanis argued, "notwithstanding this case law . . ., that the 1996 Employee Handbook policy [did] not constitute a binding agreement because Smith Barney 'disavowed' it by issuing the 'Interim Handbook.'" The court, however, had a different view, reasoning that "the subsequent handbook by its terms, superceded only 'conflicting' employment policies," and contained an arbitration clause identical to the clause issued in the year in which the Chanchanis had returned the receipt form. Furthermore, the FAA "does not require that the parties sign written acknowledgments of an arbitration agreement; it mandates only that the agreement itself be in writing." Because the Chanchanis continued to work at Smith Barney "after the promulgation of the [handbook], and never informed Smith Barney that they rejected its terms they [were] deemed [by the court] to have accepted its provisions."

* * *

The New Jersey state Supreme Court, however, refused to enforce an arbitration clause contained in an employee handbook. The employee failed to sign the "Employee Handbook Receipt and Agreement," which would have indicated his express intent to be bound by the terms of the handbook, including the arbitration provision. The court rejected the notion that an employee could impliedly consent to such an agreement and held that, for a waiver of rights provision to be valid, an express and unambiguous manifestation of intent on the part of an employee was needed.

In *Leodori v. CIGNA Corp.*, 175 N.J. 293, 814 A.2d 1098 (2003), Leodori brought suit against his employer alleging violations of the New Jersey Conscientious Employee Protection Act. Prior to his dismissal, Leodori had been employed as in-house counsel. In 1994, almost a year before Leodori began his employment, the company instituted an arbitration program for resolving employment disputes. A handbook was distributed to employees at several times. In 1998, the company distributed an updated handbook, containing specific language regarding arbitration. Two acknowledgment forms also accompanied this handbook—a receipt form and a second form entitled "Employee Handbook Receipt and Agreement." The former simply acknowledged that employees had received their copy of the July 1998 employee handbook. Leodori signed this form in September 1998. The latter form contained language reiterating that the employee had received the handbook, but also stated that employees agreed to two further provisions: (1) that their employment could be terminated at any time, and (2) that the employees would use CIGNA's internal and external dispute resolution procedures to resolve claims against the company rather than a court or government agency. Leodori did not sign this second form.

Leodori alleged that he was dismissed from his job because he engaged in whistleblowing. He filed a complaint in the New Jersey courts. The action was dismissed and then reinstituted. CIGNA appealed and the New Jersey state Supreme Court granted certifications.

In an unanimous decision, the high court affirmed the appellate ruling that Leodori be allowed to proceed in court. In reaching its decision, the court emphasized that state law could not impose more burdensome requirements for the formation of arbitration agreements than for the formation of other contracts. Also, a waiver of rights provision must clearly and unambiguously demonstrate that an employee has agreed to arbitrate any disputed claim.

To determine whether Leodori agreed to arbitrate his CEPA claims, the court asked two questions: (1) did the waiver of rights provision in the handbook clearly reflect an intention to arbitrate a CEPA claim; and, if so, (2) did the evidence indicate that Leodori clearly agreed to such a provision? The court found the language of the waiver of rights clause sufficient to include all applicable federal and state law claims, but not to compel arbitration.

The court thereby rejected CIGNA's contention that Leodori's receipt of the handbook and continued employment constituted an implied agreement to abide by the arbitration policy. The court held that an employee's implied consent to a waiver of rights provision was not sufficient and that a valid waiver only results from an "explicit, affirmative agreement that unmistakably reflects the employee's assent" to the waiver provision. The court concluded that, without Leodori's signature on the "Employee Receipt and Agreement," it could not enforce the arbitration provision unless it found some other affirmative assent on Leodori's part to be bound by the arbitration provision. While the court agreed with the company's assertion that Leodori was aware of the arbitration policy (as it was publicized in numerous documents distributed by the defendant), it stated that it could not find evidence that he intended to be bound by it. Absent such a finding, the court felt constrained to conclude that the record did not demonstrate that Leodori had surrendered his statutory rights knowingly and voluntarily.

CIGNA asserted that the court's holdings contradicted the FAA. The company also expressed concern that the court's decision would drastically alter an employer's ability to use arbitration agreements as a means of workplace dispute resolution. The court rejected both arguments stating that it was merely requiring employee acknowledgment in the form of a signature and that the employer obtain a clear indication of the intent to be bound by the employee. The resources necessary to fulfill these requirements were neither impractical nor excessive.

* * *

Similarly, a Pennsylvania superior court ruled that employees who sign an acknowledgment form are not bound by an arbitration agreement contained in an employee handbook when the totality of the circumstances makes clear that the agreement is unenforceable. In *Quiles v. Dollar Financial Group, Inc.*, 879 A.2d 281 (Pa. Super. Ct. 2005), Quiles sued Dollar for wrongful termination. Dollar sought arbitration pursuant to the company's Dispute Resolution Program described in the employee handbook. In addition, Dollar argued that Quiles signed the acknowledgment form, which stated "she had received...and carefully read this handbook...before signing below."

The court held that, because of the totality of the circumstances, Quiles had not "knowingly and voluntarily" accepted the terms of the agreement; thus, the contract was unenforceable. The court considered the following factors: Although the arbitration process was described in the employee handbook, Quiles never received or saw a copy of the handbook; Quiles and other employees were not provided with a copy of the handbook when they requested one; Quiles was from Puerto Rico and had difficulty with English; the acknowledgment form merely mentioned that the company had provisions relating to arbitration, but failed to provide a substantive explanation of the arbitration provision; and, lastly, Quiles was pressured into signing the form by her manager.

NOTES AND QUESTIONS

1.   Is there a presumption against the validity of handbook provisions? If so, can it be rebutted?

2.   Is there a controlling legal position on the handbook issue? If so, what is it? If not, what are the different views? How would you advise an employer?

3.   Can employee opposition and disaffection only be expressed effectively at the end of the process? Explain.

4.   Does unfairness lie in the agreement, in the circumstances of its making, or in the process? Can one remedy the other, even though all are deficient?

5.   Does *Leodori* provide real protection or is it simply requiring "hoop-jumping"?

6.   Articulate a judicial stance that balances effectively the law, policy, and all competing interests.

EDS Agreements: Avoiding the Mutuality Requirement

There are now a number of Ryan's Family Steak House cases. Each of them attempts to avoid the mutuality requirement of the obligation to arbitration by having employees sign a service agreement directly with a service-provider. In one of the initial cases, *Penn v. Ryan's Family Steak Houses, Inc.*, 269 F.3d 753 (7th Cir. 2001), the U.S. Court of Appeals for the Seventh Circuit ruled that an arbitration agreement entered into by an employee (at the behest of his employer) with an arbitration service provider was unenforceable because it contained an illusory promise under state contract law. In the court's assessment, "[t]he contract

[was]...hopelessly vague and uncertain as to the [service's] obligation....For all practical purposes, [the service's] promise under this contract 'makes performance entirely optional with the promisor.' " The contract also lacked consideration and mutuality of obligation and was, therefore, unenforceable.

The facts indicated that Ryan's entered into an agreement with Employment Dispute Services, Inc. (EDS), a specialized arbitration service-provider. The purpose of the contract was "to have EDS provide an arbitration forum for all employment-related disputes between Ryan's and its employees." Ryan's then required its prospective employees to enter into a contract with EDS to use its services exclusively to resolve any employment disputes that arose with Ryan's. The contract language emphasized that the contracting parties were the employee and EDS; Ryan's was described as "a third-party beneficiary of the contract."

Employers were the EDS' clients and paid its professional fees. Employees paid none of the fees for arbitration. According to the court's account of the record:

> EDS's sole business is apparently the provision of arbitration services for employment disputes according to this model: EDS contracts with employers to provide an arbitration forum for any claims the company's employees bring against it, and the companies that contract with EDS then require their employees to enter into separate contracts with EDS.

Despite a testimonial of EDS' Chair and co-owner describing the company's services as fair and neutral, the district court concluded that the EDS system "was inherently biased against employees." Employers not only constituted EDS' sole source of revenue, but they were "repeat players" who were familiar with the process, the arbitrators, and the system administrators. The court, therefore, denied EDS' petition to compel arbitration partially on this basis.

The lower court also expressed concern about EDS' ability to manipulate the arbitration process, especially in light of its control over arbitrator lists and the application of institutional rules. It viewed with equal circumspection the process' limited right of discovery (allowing essentially only one deposition per side in the proceeding) when most employment cases were fact-sensitive. Finally, the district court believed that the employee had not "knowingly waived" his right to a court hearing.

Penn, the employee, was a waiter in the Ryan's chain and had been fired after a few years of employment. He alleged that he had been fired in "retaliation for his complaints about...harassment" in the workplace. He filed a lawsuit against Ryan's, alleging a violation of the Americans with Disabilities Act (ADA) to which Ryan's responded with a motion to compel arbitration.

The Seventh Circuit upheld the district court's basic conclusion but for other reasons: "We agree with the district court that the arbitration contract Penn signed is unenforceable, although we reach that conclusion for different reasons." Judge Diane Woods took pains to emphasize that that determination conformed to the judicial policy that sustains and favors the recourse to arbitration:

> Arbitration has become a common tool in resolving employment disputes in recent years, and employers are increasingly requiring employees to sign contracts obligating them to arbitrate disputes as a condition of employment. The Supreme Court's recent decision in *Circuit City Stores, Inc. v. Adams*, 532 U.S. 105, 121 S.Ct. 1302, 149 L.Ed.2d 234 (2001), removes any lingering doubts as to whether these agreements are enforceable under the FAA.

The district court was mistaken in its unbalanced critique of the EDS arbitral system: "... [w]e are concerned that the district court placed too much weight on certain specifics of this system that, in and of themselves, do not distinguish it from many others that have passed muster...." The presumption in favor of the recourse to and adequacy of arbitration was very difficult, if not impossible, to rebut:

> The Supreme Court has repeatedly counseled that the FAA leaves no room for judicial hostility to arbitration proceedings and that courts should not presume, absent concrete proof to the contrary, that arbitration systems will be unfair or biased.

For Judge Wood, the issue did not center upon the merits of the EDS system, but rather upon the legal enforceability of the arbitration agreement between EDS and the employee. In her view, "Penn never entered into an enforceable contract to participate in [the EDS arbitral system]." The court concluded that there was a lack of mutuality of obligation between the parties, that EDS had agreed only to "an unascertainable, illusory promise," and that the contract lacked any basic detriment on EDS' part and was, therefore, devoid of consideration.

Although Judge Wood reached the right result while maintaining doctrinal integrity, her approach did minimize one aspect of the litigation: Ryan's and EDS' outrageous behavior. They undertook by private action to deny powerless people any possible access to justice. Judge Harlington Wood, Jr. refers to this in his concurring opinion:

> Penn was being hired as a waiter in a chain restaurant, not as a corporate executive. His employment was only to be "at will." Likely a substantial share of his income would be from tips. The agreement, the rules, the relationships between the parties, and the ramifications of the arbitration arrangement have now reached this court to sort out. Above his signature this agreement states that Penn signed it "knowingly and voluntarily." We doubt it could have been "knowingly" in view of its complexities, or even "voluntarily." Had he questioned its meaning and its complexities, it is doubtful Penn would have been hired. However, the agreement provided that Penn had the right to consult an attorney, but even if Penn could have afforded an attorney, the appearance of any attorney on the scene would doubtless have foreclosed any job opportunity. In Ryan's

eyes, Penn would look like a troublemaker. If he wanted the waiter's job, he would be trapped in an unfair situation until a court could unravel it.

The corporate behavior in *Penn* not only was a moral and ethical outrage, but it severely tarnished the image of arbitration. Arbitration is portrayed as a vehicle of abuse, overreaching, and injustice. Such a perverse use of arbitration, in the end, may deny society access to a remedial mechanism that provides a practical, economical, and expedient means to justice when no other remedy is available. This type of behavior is truly outside the law and demands the imposition of all available sanctions. What do you think?

WALKER v. RYAN'S FAMILY STEAK HOUSES, INC.

400 F.3d 370 (6th Cir. 2005).

(footnotes omitted)

OPINION

CLAY, Circuit Judge. Defendant Ryan's Family Steak Houses, Inc. appeals the ... order of the district court, denying its motion to dismiss and petition to compel arbitration, pursuant to the Federal Arbitration Act ... of [the] [plaintiffs'] claims for violations of the Fair Labor Standards Act.... For the reasons that follow, we AFFIRM.

I.

A. *Procedural History*

On November 12, 2002, Plaintiffs ... filed a self-styled "collective action" complaint for violations of the FLSA against ... Ryan's Family Steak Houses, Inc. ("Ryan's") in the United States District Court for the Middle District of Tennessee....

... [T]he district court denied Ryan's motion, holding that there was inadequate consideration for the arbitration agreements, the agreements had the hallmarks of unconscionable adhesion contracts, the agreements were not founded upon mutual assent, and Plaintiffs did not knowingly and voluntarily waive their constitutional right to a jury trial. The court also held that the arbitration forum provided for in the agreements is not able to provide for effective vindication of statutory claims and is an inappropriate substitute for the judicial forum. The court observed that the pool of arbitrators would be constituted in a biased manner and that the limited discovery available in the forum suggested structural bias in favor of the employer. The court further determined that the arbitration agreements appear to prohibit arbitration of class-based claims, which provides a powerful disincentive for employees to pursue individual claims of relatively low monetary value. Ryan's timely appealed.

B. *Substantive Facts*

Since 1996 or 1997, any individual who applies for employment with Ryan's has been presented with a 12–page application packet. The second page of the packet notifies the applicant that he or she is required to complete and sign the "Job Application Agreement to Arbitration of Employment–Related Disputes" (hereafter "Arbitration Agreement") in order to be considered for a position. Failure to sign and accept the Arbitration Agreement and its related rules and procedures purportedly terminates the job application process. After the one-page notice come five pages of single-spaced rules and procedures governing the arbitration procedure. Only after wading through the rules does the applicant get to the one-page job application for the positions of server, salad bar, dishwasher, frontline, hostess, meatcutter, cook, breadroom, or cashier. The two-page Arbitration Agreement, which the applicant must sign, then follows the application.

Plaintiffs cite several examples of applicants who were hired on the spot after a 15 to 20 minute interview, during which the hiring manager hurriedly presented them with various documents that they were instructed to sign in order to be considered for a job. The manager rarely explained the nature of the Arbitration Agreement to the applicants, nor were the applicants given the opportunity to take home and review any of the forms before signing or provided with copies of the executed Arbitration Agreement or rules. Consequently, many of the applicants do not even recall executing the agreements.

[. . .]

Unlike the typical pre-employment arbitration agreement which involves a contract between the applicant and his or her potential employer, Ryan's Arbitration Agreement is not between the applicant and Ryan's. Rather, it is between the applicant and Employment Dispute Services, Inc. ("EDSI"). EDSI is a South Carolina corporation whose sole business is the marketing and administration of the Employment Dispute Resolution Program. The program is a third-party arbitration system which was established in 1992 to provide employers and employees outside of the securities industry with a purportedly fair and expeditious means of resolving employment-related disputes. EDSI has contracts with a total of seven companies, including Ryan's.

The Arbitration Agreement that Plaintiffs executed explains that Ryan's (referred to therein as the "Company") had entered into a separate agreement with EDSI "to arbitrate and resolve any and all employment-related disputes between the Company's employees (and job applicants) and the Company." Although Plaintiffs were not provided with a copy of Ryan's separate agreement with EDSI, that agreement obligates EDSI to, *inter alia*, "administer and provide access to the EDSI alternative dispute resolution procedures and forum for all Company job applicants, employees, and the Company itself, as provided in the EDSI Rules and Procedures"; train managers and supervisors about the alternative dispute resolution program; and train managers and employees selected to serve as potential "adjudicators" in the program. Also, for an additional fee, EDSI will conduct "an employee relations audit (personnel polices and procedures, handbooks and other personnel forms), management training, and employee attitude surveys with recommended management respons- es." Ryan's agreement with EDSI is renewable from year to year, but Ryan's may cancel the contract with ten days' written notice.

By executing the Arbitration Agreement with EDSI, Plaintiffs agreed to (a) bring any employment disputes that he or she may have against Ryan's and that would otherwise be decided in a state or federal court only in EDSI's arbitral forum and (b) be bound by a final decision of the EDSI arbitration panel. The purported consideration for Plaintiffs' prom- ise to arbitrate is EDSI's agreement "to provide an arbitration forum, Rules and Procedures, and a hearing and decision based on any claim or dispute [that the applicant] may file or defend[.]" According to the agreement, Ryan's is a third party beneficiary of the agreement between Plaintiffs and EDSI, and Plaintiffs are third party beneficiaries of Ryan's agreement with EDSI. The agreement continues for the period of Plain- tiffs' employment with Ryan's, unless mutually terminated in writing by Plaintiffs and EDSI.

The 2000 version of EDSI's Employment Dispute Resolution Rules and Procedures—the most recent version of the rules—provides that the substantive rights and remedies in EDSI's arbitration forum are the same as are available in a federal or state court. The rules govern all legal disputes, claims, or causes of action that arise out of the employment or possible employment of all parties signatory to an employment dispute resolution agreement with EDSI. The rules govern both the claims of a "claimant" (*i.e.*, an applicant or employee) and any claims that a signatory defendant might bring against a claimant who has signed the Arbitration Agreement.

The rules further provide that a panel of three "adjudicators" re- solves arbitration claims and are chosen from three separate selection pools: (1) supervisors or managers of an employer signatory to an agree- ment with EDSI; (2) employees who are non-exempt from the wage and hour protections of the Fair Labor Standards Act; and (3) attorneys, retired judges, or other competent legal professional persons not associat- ed with either party. No individual who has been employed by an employ- er involved in the dispute can serve as an adjudicator.

EDSI provides the parties with a list of three potential adjudicators in each of the three selection pools. The parties have access to a schedule of the adjudicators' fees and their employment history for at least the previous five years, along with related biographical information. Potential adjudicators also are required to disclose any information which may preclude them from making an objective and impartial decision.

Once EDSI selects the pools of potential adjudicators, the claimant and the defendant alternately strike names from each of the three selection pools until one name from each pool remains. Any potential adjudicator may be struck for cause. As a matter of EDSI practice, if an adjudicator is removed from the pool for cause, EDSI provides another potential adjudicator.

Once arbitration proceedings commence, any party may serve a request for production of documents, and counsel for the parties have subpoena power. The rules also permit each party to schedule a deposition of one individual. A party may file a request for additional depositions, "but such requests are not encouraged and shall be granted in extraordinary fact situations and for good cause shown."

Under the 2000 version of the rules, EDSI reserves the right to modify or amend the Rules after the date the claimant signs the Arbitration Agreement. The claimant, however, has the right to have his or her dispute resolved pursuant to the rules that were in effect at the time the agreement was signed, unless he or she prefers the modified rules.

II.

Plaintiffs filed a self-styled class action under the FLSA, seeking unpaid wages and related penalties against Ryan's. Ryan's argues that Plaintiffs' action should not be in federal court at all and, pursuant to the FAA, moved to enforce the pre-employment arbitration agreements that Plaintiffs executed. For the reasons that follow, we hold that the district correctly refused to enforce Plaintiffs' arbitration agreements as unenforceable under Tennessee law.

[. . .]

In *Floss*, [211 F.3d 306 (6th Cir. 2000)], this Court addressed the propriety of virtually the identical arbitral scheme at issue in this case and, as in this case, applied Tennessee contract law. . . .

After voicing its concerns over EDSI's arbitrator selection process, the *Floss* Court held that the plaintiffs were not bound by their arbitration agreements because, as a matter of Tennessee law, EDSI had not provided adequate consideration for the plaintiffs' promise to submit any dispute that they may have with Ryan's to arbitration with EDSI. . . . According to the EDSI rules then in effect, EDSI had reserved the right to alter the applicable rules and procedures without any obligation to notify or receive the consent of the plaintiffs. . . . The Court held that EDSI's right to choose the nature of its performance rendered its promise "fatally indefinite" and, therefore, lacking in consideration. . . .

In response to the holding in *Floss*, EDSI amended its rules and the Arbitration Agreement in 2000. As under prior versions, the 2000 rules give EDSI the right to modify or amend the rules after the date the claimant signs the Arbitration Agreement. The rules, however, include the following additional language: "In the event these Rules and Procedures are modified after a Claimant has signed an Agreement, the claimant shall have the option to have his or her claim adjudicated under the Rules and Procedures that were in effect on the date the Agreement was signed or the Rules and Procedures that are in effect on the date their claim is filed with EDSI."

EDSI amended the Arbitration Agreement to be consistent with the revised rules. The Arbitration Agreement used to provide that any employment-related dispute would be brought only in EDSI's arbitration forum and under its rules and Procedures, "as modified from time to time." The new agreement omits the "as modified from time to time" language and adds the following: "However, should the EDSI Rules and Procedures be amended, I shall have the right to choose to have my employment-related dispute resolved under the Rules and Procedures that are in effect on the date I sign this Agreement or the Rules and Procedures in effect on the date I file a claim with EDSI."

Ryan's maintains that these linguistic changes to the rules and the agreement cure the consideration problem that the *Floss* court identified; they argue that EDSI's promise is not illusory because Plaintiffs can insist on the rules in effect at the time they entered into their Arbitration Agreements. Plaintiffs disagree, arguing that EDSI still maintains the right to modify or amend the rules without notice or consent.

We hold that Plaintiffs have the better argument because they signed the identical Arbitration Agreement at issue in *Floss*. Their agreements explicitly reserve EDSI the right to modify or amend the rules from time to time, without providing Plaintiffs the right to insist on the rules in effect at the time that they executed their respective agreements. Although the 2000 version of the rules purport[s] to afford Plaintiffs the right to enforce the rules in effect at the time of execution, Plaintiffs' agreements do not incorporate that right. Each of their agreements states that "My Agreement ... contains the entire understanding and agreement of the parties regarding these subjects" and that "My Agreement may not be altered or amended, except in writing signed by the President of EDSI and Me." There is no evidence in the record that any of Plaintiffs agreed in writing with the EDSI's President to adopt the 2000 version of the rules or that Plaintiffs provided any new consideration for EDSI's new promise to disregard (upon Plaintiffs' request) any post-execution amendments to its rules. Accordingly, as far as the named Plaintiffs are concerned, EDSI still retains the unfettered contractual right to alter or amend the rules and procedures, including the right to eliminate the rule added in 2000 that purports to give the claimant the right to enforce the rules and procedures that existed at the time that he or she executed the agreement. Therefore, Plaintiffs' Arbitration Agreements are no different from the agreements at issue, and held to be unenforceable, in *Floss* due to inadequate consideration from EDSI.

[. . .]

Adequate consideration cannot take the form of Ryan's promise to submit any claims it may have against Plaintiffs to EDSI's arbitral forum. As explained by one district court:

> EDSI is bound by its promise to Plaintiffs only to the extent that Ryan's is bound to submit to the forum, for without Ryan's consent EDSI can provide no benefit to Plaintiffs. EDSI/Ryan's Contract contains an escape clause

whereby Ryan's can cancel its Contract with EDSI on ten days notice. . . . This provision stands in clear contrast to the mutual termination clause found in the Arbitration Agreement, thus negating any consideration that Plaintiffs might be deemed to receive from EDSI's promise to provide the forum. Similarly, the ten-day escape clause eliminates consideration that might otherwise exist or flow from Plaintiffs' "third-party beneficiary" status, as alluded to in the Arbitration Agreement.

Geiger v. Ryan's Family Steak Houses, Inc., 134 F.Supp.2d 985, 1001 (S.D. Ind. 2001). Indeed, we question whether the agreement between EDSI and Ryan's even obligates Ryan's to submit to EDSI's arbitral forum at all. The EDSI/Ryan's agreement merely obligates EDSI (for a fee from Ryan's) to "*administer and provide access to* the EDSI alternative dispute resolution procedures and forum for all Company job applicants, employees, and the Company itself, as provided in the EDSI Rules and Procedures." . . . (emphasis added). Notably, the agreement does not *require* Ryan's to submit its employment claims to the EDSI forum. Thus, the Arbitration Agreements that Plaintiffs executed misrepresent the meaning of the EDSI/Ryan's agreement by stating that Ryan's "has entered into an agreement with [EDSI] to arbitrate and resolve any and all employment-related disputes between the Company's employees (and job applicants) and the Company." In truth, it is only the Ryan's applicant or employee who has agreed to bring any employment-related dispute exclusively in the EDSI arbitration forum. . . . Although the EDSI/Ryan's contract refers to EDSI's rules, and those rules govern any employment claim Ryan's may have against an applicant or employee, . . . the rules do not require Ryan's to submit to the EDSI forum to resolve its employment disputes. Even if the rules did so provide, Ryan's promise to submit to that forum would be "fatally indefinite" because (a) Plaintiffs' Arbitration Agreements reserve EDSI's right to modify those rules and (b) Ryan's exerts significant financial control over EDSI and, hence, the rules that supposedly bind Ryan's. . . .

[. . .]

The district court found that there was strong evidence that the Arbitration Agreements between Plaintiffs and EDSI did not result from a meeting of the minds in mutual assent. We agree.

It is well-settled under Tennessee law that a contract must result from a meeting of the minds of the parties in mutual assent to the terms. . . . Although the question of mutual assent involves largely an objective analysis, the parties' intent remains relevant, in particular the circumstances surrounding the formation of the contract. . . . The district court below held that Plaintiffs did not mutually assent with EDSI to the terms of their Arbitration Agreements because there is a question as to whether Plaintiffs were provided with the rules when they signed the contracts, conflicting evidence about whether Plaintiffs knew what they were signing at the time they executed the agreements, and evidence that Ryan's managers provided misleading information about the agreements and the arbitration process prior to execution. The court concluded that these facts overcome the general presumption under Tennessee law that a party is under a duty to learn the contents of a written contract before signing and, therefore, may not deny that a contract he or she admittedly has signed and that expresses the agreement that he or she made....

[. . .]

The district court held that Plaintiffs' Arbitration Agreements were unenforceable adhesion contracts. Under Tennessee law, an adhesion contract is "a standardized contract form offered to consumers of goods and services on essentially a 'take it or leave it' basis, without affording the consumer a realistic opportunity to bargain and under such conditions that the consumer cannot obtain the desired product or service except by acquiescing to the form of the contract." ... Here, Ryan's presented Plaintiffs with a standardized Arbitration Agreement at or around the time of applying for employment. Ryan's presented the agreements on a "take it or leave it" basis, because Plaintiffs had no opportunity to bargain over the agreements' terms and ostensibly would not be permitted to apply for employment without first agreeing to arbitrate.

We have some concerns about whether Plaintiffs demonstrated the final element of an adhesion contract: "the absence of a meaningful choice for the party occupying the weaker bargaining position." ... To find their Arbitration Agreements adhesive, the district court was required to cite "evidence that [Plaintiffs] would be unable to find suitable employment if [they] refused to sign [EDSI's] agreement." ... The court cited no such evidence.... Nevertheless, we note that the lack of such evidence may not be relevant to the agreements signed by Plaintiffs ... who were inter-viewed and hired without first executing their Arbitration Agreements. Arguably, because they already had been hired and were working when Ryan's presented them with the agreements, Ryan's may have terminated them had they refused to sign. Ryan's therefore had significantly more bargaining power over these Plaintiff-employees, who, unlike applicants, likely had forgone other employment opportunities and would have been severely disadvantaged by having to inform prospective employers that they were terminated shortly after their hire. In contrast to telling an applicant that he or she needs to sign the agreement or else do not bother applying, the threat of termination from one's current employment would appear to be sufficient in itself to demonstrate "the absence of a meaning-ful choice for the party occupying the weaker bargaining position." ... We need not remand to the district court to reexamine this issue, however, because the court correctly held that the Arbitration Agreements are unenforceable on other state law grounds. Accordingly, we affirm the court's denial of Ryan's motion to compel arbitration of Plaintiffs' claims.

III.

In addition to refusing to enforce Plaintiffs' arbitration agreements on state law grounds, the district court held that the agreements are unen-forceable because they do not allow Plaintiffs to effectively vindicate their rights under the FLSA. We agree for the reasons discussed below.

[. . .]

Even if there is no contract-based defense to the enforceability of an arbitration agreement, a court cannot enforce the agreement as to a claim if the specific arbitral forum provided under the agreement does not "allow for the effective vindication of that claim." . . . Generally, a party cannot avoid the arbitration process simply by alleging that the arbitration panel will be biased, because the FAA "protects against bias, by providing that courts may overturn arbitration decisions 'where there was evident partiality or corruption in the arbitrators.' " . . . However, the general rule prohibiting pre-arbitration challenges to an allegedly biased arbitration panel does not extend to an allegation that the arbitrator-selection process itself is fundamentally unfair. . . . In such a case, "the arbitral forum is not an effective substitute for a judicial forum," and, therefore, the party need not arbitrate first and then allege bias through post-arbitration judicial review.

The Arbitration Agreements and related rules and procedures at issue in this case demonstrate that EDSI's arbitral forum is not neutral and, therefore, the agreements are unenforceable. As previously described, under EDSI's rules, three "adjudicators" are selected from three separate selection pools to preside over the arbitration hearing. The first of these pools consists of supervisors and managers from another EDSI signatory company; the second consists of employees from another signatory; and the third contains attorneys, retired judges, and other "competent legal professional persons not associated with either party." Although dictum, language in *Floss* signaled this Court's extreme disapproval of this arbitrator selection mechanism:

> We have serious reservations as to whether the arbitral forum provided under the current version of the EDSI Rules and Procedures is suitable for the resolution of statutory claims. Specifically, the neutrality of the forum is far from clear in light of the uncertain relationship between Ryan's and EDSI. [Plaintiffs] Floss and Daniels suggest that EDSI is biased in favor of Ryan's and other employers because it has a financial interest in maintaining its arbitration service contracts with employers. Though the record does not clearly reflect whether EDSI, in contrast to the American Arbitration Association, operates on a for-profit basis, the potential for bias exists. In light of EDSI's role in determining the pool of potential arbitrators, any such bias would render the arbitral forum fundamentally unfair. . . .

[. . .]

The record in this case removes any of the uncertainties surrounding the relationship between Ryan's and EDSI that the Court noted in *Floss*. EDSI is clearly a for-profit business, and Ryan's annual fee accounted for over 42% of EDSI's gross income in 2002. Given the symbiotic relationship between Ryan's and EDSI, Ryan's effectively determines the three pools of arbitrators, thereby rendering the arbitral forum fundamentally unfair to claimants who are applicants or employees. . . .

The bias against employees and applicants is significantly enhanced by the lack of any criteria governing employees of signatory companies who are eligible to serve as adjudicators. There are no minimum educational requirements, potential arbitrators do not need to have any relevant experience as an adjudicator, and there is no explicit requirement that they be unbiased. Similarly, the rules do not require that the legal professionals who comprise the third pool possess either substantive or procedural knowledge of dispute resolution or of the employment law issues involved in the arbitration. The names of potential arbitrators for the legal professional pool purportedly are provided to EDSI by an unaffiliated company, Resolute Systems, Inc.; however, there is no information in the record regarding how Resolute Systems selects potential adjudicators for EDSI's program.

The bias is exacerbated by the lack of a protocol governing EDSI's selection of potential adjudicators from the three pools. The individuals in the supervisor and employee pools are neither randomly selected nor chosen by a disinterested person for their skills. Instead, all members of these two pools are chosen by the small number of employers who, like Ryan's, have signed alternative dispute resolution agreements with EDSI: Golden Corral Steak Houses, K & W Cafeterias, Papa John's Pizza, Sticky Fingers Restaurants, The Cliffs at Glass, Inc., and Wieland Investments, Inc. In addition, the rules do not prevent a supervisor of a signatory company from sitting on an adjudication panel with a non-supervisory employee from the same company, including someone whom the supervisor directly supervises. Further, EDSI has no policy in place that prohibits a signatory company from discussing the arbitration process or specific claims with its employee adjudicators or from attempting to improperly influence its employee adjudicators.

Finally, the limited discovery that the EDSI forum provides could significantly prejudice employees or applicants. The rules allow "just one deposition as of right and additional depositions only at the discretion of the (arguably biased) panel, with the express policy that depositions 'are not encouraged and shall be granted in extraordinary fact situations only for good cause shown.'"... We acknowledge that the opportunity to undertake extensive discovery is not necessarily appropriate in an arbitral forum, the purpose of which is to reduce the costs of dispute resolution. Indeed, when parties enter arbitration agreements at arms-length they typically should expect that the extent of discovery will be more circumscribed than in a judicial setting. But parties to a valid arbitration agreement also expect that neutral arbitrators will preside over their disputes regarding both the resolution on the merits and the critical steps, including discovery, that precede the arbitration award. A structural bias in the make-up of the arbitration panel, which would stymie a party's attempt to marshal the evidence to prove or defend a claim, can be just as prejudicial as arbitral bias in the final decision on the merits. Such is the case here, providing an additional basis to conclude that EDSI's and

Ryan's arbitration scheme does not allow for the effective vindication of Plaintiffs' FLSA claims.

IV.

For all the foregoing reasons, we AFFIRM the district court's holdings that state law contract defenses preclude enforcement of Plaintiffs' arbitration agreements and that Plaintiffs' arbitration agreements are unenforceable under the FAA because they do not allow for effective vindication of their FLSA claims.

NOTES AND QUESTIONS

1. Does Ryan's, in your view, engage in blatantly unfair conduct toward its employees? What, if any, is the corporate objective? Should corporate practice go in the opposite direction? Explain. Is this a modern version of having a "company store" policy?

2. What are the core elements of unfairness in Ryan's scheme for arbitration? Does the court forget anything in its list?

3. How is the contract adhesionary?

4. How might the Ryan's approach and agreement be made not oppressive?

5. Does the court take the federal policy on arbitration into account? If not, why not? If so, what impact does it have? What advice would you proffer to Ryan's?

6. Can Ryan's arbitration agreement and the process associated with it be rectified to yield an enforceable contract? How?

CHAPTER EIGHT

THE ENFORCEMENT OF ARBITRAL AWARDS

■ ■ ■

1. INTRODUCTION

The enforcement of arbitral awards is a critical part of the arbitration process. The reasons for this are self-evident: Without the ability to achieve enforcement, arbitration would lose its practical appeal. The arbitral process would be reduced to a preliminary, non-binding exercise, the cost of which in terms of time and money would preclude recourse. More delays and protracted proceedings at the enforcement stage would also eviscerate arbitration. By choosing arbitration, parties bargain for economical, expert, efficient, and enforceable private adjudication.

Federal court practice regarding the enforcement of domestic arbitral awards is in keeping with the dictates of the strong federal policy favoring arbitration. Most courts acknowledge a strong presumption in favor of enforcement. The presumption can be defeated in only those exceptional circumstances in which the arbitrators fail to provide the parties with basic adjudicatory due process. FAA § 10 articulates the statutory and common-law basis for the judicial supervision of arbitral awards. As construed by the courts, these grounds are neither rigorous nor demanding. Arbitrators must not be corrupt, exceed their powers, or ignore the parties' essential adjudicatory rights or the content of the arbitration agreement. The case law has added three common-law grounds to the statutory list: The award reflects a manifest disregard of the law, constitutes an arbitrary and capricious or irrational determination, or violates public policy. Somewhat paradoxically, the judicial elaboration of additional grounds for review has not created a greater likelihood of nullification of awards.

The FAA does not govern labor arbitration—at least, in a technical sense. The lack of a governing statutory regime obligated the courts to create a decisional basis for reviewing labor awards that also considered labor arbitrators' interpretation of collective bargaining agreements and federal labor statutes. "Manifest disregard of the law," along with the two other common-law grounds for review, satisfied these objectives. Courts could supervise the written rulings of labor arbitrators on matters of interpretation. The level of intended scrutiny, however, remained relatively superficial; the courts policed labor awards for gross deviations from the underlying contract or the applicable statute.

Problems emerged when the courts began to apply the grounds indiscriminately to all arbitral awards. It created confusion about the intended purpose of the nonstatutory basis for the supervision of arbitral awards. As a result, courts construed "manifest disregard" and the other nonstatutory grounds for review so narrowly that they generally have had little impact upon enforcement. For example, "manifest disregard" is established when arbitrators deliberately ignore what they have determined to be the applicable law and legal result in the case. The nonstatutory grounds also converge with the statutory basis for review. "Manifest disregard," for instance, overlaps with "excess of arbitral authority," and courts sometimes refer to both grounds simultaneously to justify their opinion in a given case.

Finally, the common-law grounds appear to authorize the courts to review the merits of arbitral determinations. FAA § 10 does not recognize merits review; in fact, such a practice contradicts the gravamen of the legislative provision and clashes with the judicial policy that underpins the statute. While a merits scrutiny may fit into the context of labor arbitration, it is completely inapposite for regulating the enforcement of awards that fall under the statutory regime of the FAA. Moreover, from a practical perspective, the review of commercial arbitration awards on the merits is difficult, if not impossible, to accomplish. The commonplace practice domestically has been to render awards without legal explanation or with only a limited explanation. Additionally, informal arbitral proceedings usually are not codified in a verbatim transcript.

Despite the tension between the statutory and common law grounds, the general result nonetheless is to uphold arbitrator determinations no matter the ground for recourse, the nature of the complaints, or the actual reasoning and construction. The circuits are split on a few issues of applicable doctrine, with some courts imposing more stringent demands on arbitrators and their use of decisional authority. By and large, however, clients, in arbitration, get finality and only "one bite at the apple."

The current framework has evolved and changed over time. It is increasing in sophistication and complexity. "Opt-in" provisions for merits review have emerged and generated a debate about their validity in the federal circuits. They pit absolute freedom of contract against the integrity of public authority. Additionally, arbitral tribunals now are expected to be fully impartial and dedicated completely to adjudicatory professionalism. Arbitrator disclosures, as a result, are a forefront issue in enforcement. Finally, at least one court has considered imposing sanctions for frivolous appeals against awards. These developments were introduced earlier, and will now be treated in greater detail in the materials.

NOTES AND QUESTIONS

1. The following sections give you the opportunity to assess the accuracy of the foregoing observations and determine whether the federal court practice on the enforcement of arbitral awards is sufficient, warranted, and reflects a proper exercise of judicial authority. Is a greater, more active judicial role warranted to protect the parties' legal rights? Should the courts pursue a perfunctory role? Does the expanded scope of arbitration in the resolution of civil disputes demand or justify greater court supervision of awards? You should also determine whether the actual court practice differs from the statutory statement of the basis for review.

2. Even though in many cases enforcement is the result, is some degree of judicial scrutiny of the merits necessary in order to reach even the foregone conclusion of enforceability? Does that practice violate the confidentiality of the arbitration especially when the award is cryptic or silent as to reasons for the determination? In these circumstances, does the disgruntled party, in effect, force the winning party to restate and defend part of the merits when an award is opposed upon any of the available grounds for review? Should the courts discourage this practice simply by upholding arbitral determinations on the basis of a facial scrutiny of the available record? What type of examination might constitute a facial scrutiny?

3. Does the adoption of the three "common-law" grounds for review invite more litigation and contravene the purpose and policy behind arbitration? In your view, what might constitute an irrational award? When should public policy prevent the enforcement of an award? Whenever arbitrators interpret or apply statutory law erroneously? Whenever a consumer is involved in the arbitration and loses? What is fair in these circumstances? What is systemically necessary?

4. Should there be a rule requiring reasoned opinions in all arbitrations? A verbatim transcript of the proceedings? Without either, how could the a court review the decision? How much reasoning is necessary to constitute an opinion?

5. Given the expanded adjudicatory reach of arbitration, should "manifest disregard" acquire the function of supervising awards that decide statutory claims? Would you eliminate judicial supervision entirely and create, for example, a special court or arbitral tribunal for reviewing and enforcing arbitral awards? How might the idea of denial of justice or of the public interest be integrated into the present scheme? If you were advising clients about the recourse to arbitration and they expressed concern about the lack of appeal, how might you use the arbitration agreement to address their concerns and still maintain the systemic autonomy of arbitration?

2. THE GENERAL POLICY

FINE v. BEAR, STEARNS & CO., INC.

765 F.Supp. 824, 827 (S.D.N.Y. 1991).

[. . .]

It is well-settled that a court's power to vacate an arbitration award must be extremely limited because an overly expansive judicial review of arbitration awards would undermine the litigation efficiencies which arbitration seeks to achieve. . . .

[. . .]

REMMEY v. PAINEWEBBER, INC.

32 F.3d 143, 146 (4th Cir. 1994), *cert. denied*, 513 U.S. 1112 (1995).

[. . .]

We must underscore at the outset the limited scope of review that courts are permitted to exercise over arbitral decisions. Limited judicial review is necessary to encourage the use of arbitration as an alternative to formal litigation. This policy is widely recognized, and the Supreme Court has often found occasion to approve it. . . .

A policy favoring arbitration would mean little, of course, if arbitration were merely the prologue to prolonged litigation. If such were the case, one would hardly achieve the "twin goals of arbitration, namely, settling disputes efficiently and avoiding long and expensive litigation." . . . Opening up arbitral awards to myriad legal challenges would eventually reduce arbitral proceedings to the status of preliminary hearings. Parties would cease to utilize a process that no longer had finality. To avoid this result, courts have resisted temptations to redo arbitral decisions. As the Seventh Circuit put it, "[a]rbitrators do not act as junior varsity trial courts where subsequent appellate review is readily available to the losing party." . . .

Thus, in reviewing arbitral awards, a district or appellate court is limited to determining " 'whether the arbitrators did the job they were told to do—not whether they did it well, or correctly, or reasonably, but simply whether they did it.' " . . . Courts are not free to overturn an arbitral result because they would have reached a different conclusion if presented with the same facts. . . .

[. . .]

* * *

In *Borop v. Toluca Pacific Securities Corp.*, 1997 WL 790588 (N.D. Ill. 1997), the court held that NASD arbitral awards are enforceable even though a party has not been represented effectively by counsel. Review for vacatur can only take place on the basis of the limited grounds in FAA §§ 10 and 11.

In an NASD arbitral proceeding, Borop alleged that his brokers, Toluca and Gucciardo, misrepresented the speculative character of securities and thereby induced him to enter into a high-risk transaction. The arbitral tribunal rendered an award in his favor. In a challenge to the award, Gucciardo contended that he had been denied effective counsel during the proceeding. His lawyer failed to appear at the hearing and to file an answer on his behalf.

Ruling upon a motion to confirm the award, the court recognized that confirmation was to be granted "unless the award is vacated, modified, or corrected as prescribed in Sections 10 and 11 of the FAA." FAA § 10 provides for the vacatur of awards on limited grounds (corruption, fraud, or undue means; evident partiality; procedural misconduct; or excess of arbitral authority). In the absence of a violation of Section 10, courts engage in a deferential standard of review. The court, therefore, granted the motion to confirm despite the alleged deficiencies of representation:

> Notwithstanding Gucciardo's unfortunate situation, the denial of effective counsel simply does not fall within the enumerated grounds in Section 10. . . . Furthermore, this Court is mindful that the Seventh Circuit has consistently refused to entertain claims of ineffective counsel as a basis of relief from an unfavorable result. . . .("Litigants whose lawyers fall asleep at crucial moments may seek relief from the somnolent agents; inexcusable inattention to the case [ ] does not justify putting the adversary to the continued expense and uncertainty of litigation."). . . .

* * *

NOTES AND QUESTIONS

1. The foregoing case excerpts and summary describe the general judicial policy of restrained review for arbitral awards and articulate the underlying policy rationale. As *Fine* demonstrates, the application of the policy usually results in the enforcement of awards. *Remmey* provides greater detail and, as a result, raises a number of questions.

2. Which term best characterizes the court's function in regard to arbitral awards? Is it a "process of review"? Would "judicial supervision" be more accurate? "Judicial confirmation"? Or is it an opportunity for losing parties to engage in the perfunctory or retaliatory exercise of their "rights"? Should sanctions be imposed in either of the latter settings? Why? How?

3. Would a less deferential approach better serve the interests of the parties, arbitration, and justice? Is the *Remmey* court exaggerating when it describes the judicial function as determining "whether the arbitrators did the job they were told to do"? What is the arbitrators' "job"? What "job" should the courts have? What is the basis of both "job descriptions"? Does a type of assumption of risk by the parties or benefit of the bargain theory explain the courts' perception of their systemic role in regard to arbitration? What should happen if the arbitrators truly misunderstand a central point of the applicable law? What result if they treat the parties equally, but engage in

a highly abbreviated procedure? Without a reasoned award, how could either be remedied, if they should be at all?

4. The following litigation attests to the increasing sophistication of the enforcement process. In *Green v. Ameritech Corp.*, 200 F.3d 967 (6th Cir. 2000), the court upheld an arbitral award despite claims that it did not satisfy the requirements established by the arbitration agreement. According to the plaintiffs, the arbitral award failed to set forth a full explanation as to each theory of the complaint as required by the arbitration agreement.

The parties proceeded to arbitration on a number of discrimination claims. All of the plaintiffs except Green settled within a few days. After the arbitral hearing, Green and Ameritech filed post-arbitration briefs. The arbitrator indicated that he hoped to meet with counsel for each party separately to attempt to have the parties settle. The parties did not settle. The arbitrator never rendered an award and did not contact the parties for almost a year. At that point, Green filed a motion to remove the arbitrator and appoint another or to reinstate the case to federal court, arguing that the arbitrator's failure to render an award breached the submission agreement.

Before the district court ruled on the motion, the arbitrator rendered an award in favor of the employer. The opinion described the plaintiff's claims, provided an account of the allegations of discrimination, and reached conclusions as to each claim. The arbitrator concluded that the plaintiff had not satisfied his burden of proof. Green filed an action to vacate the arbitral award because it deviated from the parties' agreement, was untimely, and in excess of the arbitrator's authority. In particular, it failed to comply with the requirement for an explanation of the decision.

The district court vacated the award for excess of authority because it did not provide a reasoned explanation as required by the parties' agreement. The appellate court disagreed. The Sixth Circuit determined that the award "explain[ed] the arbitrator's decision with respect to each theory advanced by each Plaintiff." Because the language was so general, the court was "left with little guidance as to how to determine whether the arbitrator explained his decision so as to meet the requirements of the agreement."

By ruling that the plaintiff failed to meet his burden of proof, the arbitrator had "explained" the result reached in the award. According to the court, "If parties to an arbitration agreement wish a more detailed arbitral opinion, they should clearly state in the agreement the degree of specificity required. In addition, the use of familiar legal terms would serve to ensure that reviewing courts have a standard to guide their analysis." Terms like "conclusions of law" and "finding of facts" would convey the demand for a formal judicial discussion of the facts and law. Such terminology would require the arbitrator to set forth the record and explain systematically the application of the law to the facts.

Even though the court upheld the award, it should be noted that the arbitrator's attempt to force the parties to settle or delay rendering an award could have been readily construed as misconduct. The AAA Rules, for example, are absolutely clear that an arbitrator is not to function as a mediator or participate in the parties' efforts to settle. Withholding the award until the parties resolved their own dispute appears to exceed even the arbitrator's wide discretion to fashion an appropriate remedy for the dispute. These deficiencies seem to constitute a more apposite basis for challenging the award than the would-be failure to provide a sufficient explanation of the result in the award.

3. IMPARTIALITY AND DISCLOSURES

COMMONWEALTH COATINGS CORP. v. CONTINENTAL CASUALTY CO.

393 U.S. 145, 89 S.Ct. 337, 21 L.Ed.2d 301 (1968).

Mr. Justice BLACK delivered the opinion of the Court.

At issue in this case is the question whether elementary requirements of impartiality taken for granted in every judicial proceeding are suspended when the parties agree to resolve a dispute through arbitration.

The petitioner, Commonwealth Coatings Corporation, a subcontractor, sued the sureties on the prime contractor's bond to recover money alleged to be due for a painting job. The contract for painting contained an agreement to arbitrate such controversies. Pursuant to this agreement petitioner appointed one arbitrator, the prime contractor appointed a second, and these two together selected the third arbitrator. This third arbitrator, the supposedly neutral member of the panel, conducted a large business in Puerto Rico, in which he served as an engineering consultant for various people in connection with building construction projects. One of his regular customers in this business was the prime contractor that petitioner sued in this case. This relationship with the prime contractor was in a sense sporadic in that the arbitrator's services were used only from time to time at irregular intervals, and there had been no dealings between them for about a year immediately preceding the arbitration. Nevertheless, the prime contractor's patronage was repeated and significant, involving fees of about $12,000 over a period of four of five years, and the relationship even went so far as to include the rendering of services on the very projects involved in this lawsuit. An arbitration was held, but the facts concerning the close business connections between the third arbitrator and the prime contractor were unknown to petitioner and were never revealed to it by this arbitrator, by the prime contractor, or by anyone else until after an award had been made. . . .

[FAA § 10] does authorize vacation of an award where it was 'procured by corruption, fraud, or undue means' or '(w)here there was evident partiality ... in the arbitrators.' These provisions show a desire of Congress to provide not merely for any arbitration but for an impartial one. It is true that petitioner does not charge before us that the third arbitrator was actually guilty of fraud or bias in deciding this case, and we have no reason, apart from the undisclosed business relationship, to suspect him of any improper motives. But neither this arbitrator nor the prime contractor gave to petitioner even an intimation of the close financial relations that had existed between them for a period of years. We have no doubt that if a litigant could show that a foreman of a jury or a judge in a court of justice had, unknown to the litigant, any such relationship, the judgment would be subject to challenge. This is shown beyond doubt by *Tumey v. State of Ohio*, 273 U.S. 510, 47 S.Ct. 437, 71 L.Ed. 749 (1927), where this Court held that a conviction could not stand because a small part of the judge's income consisted of court fees collected from convicted defendants. Although in *Tumey* it appeared the amount of the judge's compensation actually depended on whether he decided for one side or the other, that is too small a distinction to allow this manifest violation of the strict morality and fairness Congress would have expected on the part of the arbitrator and the other party in this case. Nor should it be at all relevant, as the Court of Appeals apparently thought it was here, that '(t)he payments received were a very small part of (the arbitrator's) income....' For in *Tumey* the Court held that a decision should be set aside where there is 'the slightest pecuniary interest' on the part of the judge, and specifically rejected the State's contention that the compensation involved there was 'so small that it is not to be regarded as likely to influence improperly a judicial officer in the discharge of his duty....' Since in the case of courts this is a constitutional principle, we can see no basis for refusing to find the same concept in the broad statutory language that governs arbitration proceedings and provides that an award can be set aside on the basis of 'evident partiality' or the use of 'undue means.' ... It is true that arbitrators cannot sever all their ties with the business world, since they are not expected to get all their income from their work deciding cases, but we should, if anything, be even more scrupulous to safeguard the impartiality of arbitrators than judges, since the former have completely free rein to decide the law as well as the facts and are not subject to appellate review. We can perceive no way in which the effectiveness of the arbitration process will be hampered by the simple requirement that arbitrators disclose to the parties any dealings that might create an impression of possible bias.

While not controlling in this case, Section 18 of the Rules of the American Arbitration Association, in effect at the time of this arbitration, is highly significant. It provided as follows:

Section 18. Disclosure by Arbitrator of Disqualification—At the time of receiving his notice of appointment, the prospective Arbitrator is requested to disclose any circumstances likely to create a presumption of bias or which he believes might disqualify him as an impartial Arbitrator. Upon receipt of such information, the Tribunal Clerk shall immediately disclose it to the parties, who if willing to proceed under the circumstances disclosed, shall, in writing, so advise the Tribunal Clerk. If either party declines to waive the presumptive disqualification, the vacancy thus created shall be filled in accordance with the applicable provisions of this Rule.

And based on the same principle as this Arbitration Association rule is that part of the 33d Canon of Judicial Ethics which provides:

33. Social Relations.

. . . (A judge) should, however, in pending or prospective litigation before him be particularly careful to avoid such action as may reasonably tend to awaken the suspicion that his social or business relations or friendships, constitute an element in influencing his judicial conduct.

This rule of arbitration and this canon of judicial ethics rest on the premise that any tribunal permitted by law to try cases and controversies not only must be unbiased but also must avoid even the appearance of bias. We cannot believe that it was the purpose of Congress to authorize litigants to submit their cases and controversies to arbitration boards that might reasonably be thought biased against one litigant and favorable to another.

Reversed.

Mr. Justice WHITE, with whom Mr. Justice MARSHALL joins, concurring.

While I am glad to join my Brother BLACK'S opinion in this case, I desire to make these additional remarks. The Court does not decide today that arbitrators are to be held to the standards of judicial decorum of Article III judges, or indeed of any judges. It is often because they are men of affairs, not apart from but of the marketplace, that they are effective in their adjudicatory function. . . . This does not mean the judiciary must overlook outright chicanery in giving effect to their awards; that would be an abdication of our responsibility. But it does mean that arbitrators are not automatically disqualified by a business relationship with the parties before them if both parties are informed of the relationship in advance, or if they are unaware of the facts but the relationship is trivial. I see no reason automatically to disqualify the best informed and most capable potential arbitrators.

The arbitration process functions best when an amicable and trusting atmosphere is preserved and there is voluntary compliance with the decree, without need for judicial enforcement. This end is best served by establishing an atmosphere of frankness at the outset, through disclosure by the arbitrator of any financial transactions which he has had or is negotiating with either of the parties. In many cases the arbitrator might believe the business relationship to be so insubstantial that to make a point of revealing it would suggest he is indeed easily swayed, and perhaps a partisan of that party. But if the law requires the disclosure, no such imputation can arise. And it is far better that the relationship be disclosed at the outset, when the parties are free to reject the arbitrator or accept him with knowledge of the relationship and continuing faith in his objectivity, than to have the relationship come to light after the arbitration, when a suspicious or disgruntled party can seize on it as a pretext for invalidating the award. The judiciary should minimize its role in arbitration as judge of the arbitrator's impartiality. That role is best consigned to the parties, who are the architects of their own arbitration process, and are far better informed of the prevailing ethical standards and reputations within their business.

Of course, an arbitrator's business relationships may be diverse indeed, involving more or less remote commercial connections with great numbers of people. He cannot be expected to provide the parties with his complete and unexpurgated business biography. But it is enough for present purposes to hold, as the Court does, that where the arbitrator has a substantial interest in a firm which has done more than trivial business with a party, that fact must be disclosed. If arbitrators err on the side of disclosure, as they should, it will not be difficult for courts to identify those undisclosed relationships which are too insubstantial to warrant vacating an award.

Mr. Justice FORTAS, with whom Mr. Justice HARLAN and Mr. Justice STEWART join, dissenting.

I dissent and would affirm the [lower court] judgment.

[. . .]

The arbitration was held pursuant to provisions in the contracts between the parties. It is not subject to the rules of the American Arbitration Association. It is governed by the United States Arbitration Act. . . .

[. . .]

The third arbitrator was not asked about business connections with either party. Petitioner's complaint is that he failed to volunteer information about professional services rendered by him to the other party to the contract, the most recent of which were performed over a year before the arbitration. Both courts below held, and petitioner concedes, that the third arbitrator was innocent of any actual partiality, or bias, or improper motive. There is no suggestion of concealment as distinguished from the innocent failure to volunteer information.

The third arbitrator is a leading and respected consulting engineer who has performed services for 'most of the contractors in Puerto Rico.' He was well known to petitioner's counsel and they were personal friends. Petitioner's counsel candidly admitted that if he had been told about the arbitrator's prior relationship 'I don't think I would have objected because I know Mr. Capacete (the arbitrator).'

Clearly, the District Judge's conclusion, affirmed by the Court of Appeals for the First Circuit, was correct, that "the arbitrators conducted fair, impartial hearings; that they reached a proper determination of the issues before them, and that plaintiff's objections represent a 'situation where the losing party to an arbitration is now clutching at straws in an attempt to avoid the results of the arbitration to which it became a party.' "

The Court nevertheless orders that the arbitration award be set aside. It uses this singularly inappropriate case to announce a *per se* rule that in my judgment has no basis in the applicable statute or jurisprudential principles: that, regardless of the agreement between the parties, if an arbitrator has any prior business relationship with one of the parties of which he fails to inform the other party, however innocently, the arbitration award is always subject to being set aside. This is so even where the award is unanimous; where there is no suggestion that the nondisclosure indicates partiality or bias; and where it is conceded that there was in fact no irregularity, unfairness, bias, or partiality. Until the decision today, it has not been the law that an arbitrator's failure to disclose a prior business relationship with one of the parties will compel the setting aside of an arbitration award regardless of the circumstances.

I agree that failure of an arbitrator to volunteer information about business dealings with one party will, *prima facie*, support a claim of partiality or bias. But where there is no suggestion that the nondisclosure was calculated, and where the complaining party disclaims any imputation of partiality, bias, or misconduct, the presumption clearly is overcome.

[. . .]

Arbitration is essentially consensual and practical. The United States Arbitration Act is obviously designed to protect the integrity of the process with a minimum of insistence upon set formulae and rules. The Court applies to this process rules applicable to judges and not to a system characterized by dealing on faith and reputation for reliability. Such formalism is not contemplated by the Act nor is it warranted in a case where no claim is made of partiality, of unfairness, or of misconduct in any degree.

NOTES AND QUESTIONS

1.   What rule does the majority adopt as to the impartiality of arbitrators? Does the rule alter the meaning of "evident partiality" in FAA § 10?

2.   You should recognize that arbitrator impartiality is linked to arbitrator disclosures. What objective is the Court endeavoring to achieve through its equation? Is there something magic about the supplying of information?

3.   Is the established standard too high? Is it impractical? Is it likely to frustrate the goals of the federal policy on arbitration?

4.   Is the dissent right to state that the facts of the case are a poor platform upon which to erect the rule propounded by the majority? Do the facts indicate integrity and solid professional judgment or insider dealings?

5.   *Commonwealth Coatings* is a plurality opinion and the only U.S. Supreme Court decision that places restrictions on the recourse to arbitration. Assess the impact of the Court's ruling on the regulation of arbitration. What best explains the ruling—the political make-up the Court, historical circumstances, or merits of the issue being debated? Why does the Court take this stance when it seems unable to muster a real majority? The Court has never confirmed the position it took so many years ago.

6.   The concurring opinion represents what the Court generally thinks and does in matters of arbitration. How would you describe the reasoning in the concurring opinion? What factors of analysis do Justice White and Justice Marshall emphasize? Is this opinion supported by the federal policy on

arbitration? Is practicality the dispositive factor? What is the concurring opinion's view of arbitrator impartiality?

7. What does the dissent mean when it says the arbitration took place "pursuant to provisions in the contracts between the parties. It is not subject to the rules of the American Arbitration Association. It is governed by the" FAA?

8. Who should pay arbitrators? How much? Are arbitrators already self-interested no matter their previous activities?

9. Should the same standard of impartiality apply to all arbitrators? Are party-designated arbitrators and the neutral indistinguishable for this purpose? Is tribunal-wide impartiality necessary, desirable, indispensable?

CROW CONSTR. CO. v. JEFFREY M. BROWN ASSOC. INC.

264 F.Supp.2d 217 (E.D. Pa. 2003).

NEWCOMER, Senior District Judge.

[. . .]

BACKGROUND

On August 17, 1994, . . . Crow Construction Company ("Crow") was hired by . . . general contractor Jeffrey M. Brown Associates, Inc. ("JMB"), to assist in completing a construction project. . . . When disputes arose between the two in 1995, pursuant to the parties' contractual agreement, JMB filed a Demand for Arbitration against Crow . . . seeking $1,319,880 in damages. Crow asserted a counterclaim for $1,883,074.

After settlement efforts proved unsuccessful, the arbitration became active in 1997. The American Arbitration Association ("AAA") three-arbitrator tribunal was seated after the parties had completed the arbitrator selection process. During this selection process the parties were given a list of eligible arbitrators and were asked to rank the arbitrators proposed by the AAA in their order of preference. . . . On November 16, 2000, during a short break from that day's hearings, Crow's lead attorney, Howard Rosen, overheard Arbitrators Meyer and Galante discussing the scheduling of another arbitration with JMB's lead attorney, Roy Cohen. It was at this time that the arbitrators disclosed to Crow, for the first time, that they had been selected to arbitrate another case in which JMB was a party, the JMB/Greenfield matter.

Crow immediately objected to the arbitrators' failure to disclose their other case involving Cohen and JMB. On November 20, 2000, pursuant to Crow's objections, the AAA sent a letter to Crow confirming that arbitrators Meyer and Galante were serving as arbitrators in another case involving JMB. In addition, the AAA disclosed for the first time that Cohen or his firm, Cohen, Seglias, Pallas & Furman, P.C. (Cohen Seglias), had selected Ms. Meyer through the AAA to mediate two cases involving one of Cohen Seglias' other clients. Crow subsequently requested further information from the AAA regarding these disclosures. Ms. Meyer then amended her disclosure to indicate that she was engaged by Cohen Seglias in two additional mediations (a total of four), one of which involved JMB, at the same time the arbitration hearings between JMB and Crow were taking place. Based on this new information, on November 30, 2000, and again on December 7, 2000, Crow formally objected to arbitrators Galante and Meyer's involvement in the JMB/Crow arbitration.

On April 13, 2001, the arbitrators published their findings in which they awarded JMB every dollar sought, exclusive of attorneys' fees and damages in a late claim JMB brought against Crow in the closing days of the arbitration. On September 10, 2001, this Court received Crow's Motion to Vacate the Arbitration Award which was originally filed in the Southern District of New York. This Court afforded the parties an opportunity to take discovery.... Some of the information uncovered during the discovery period concerning arbitrators Galante and Meyer had never been disclosed previously.

[. . .]

DISCUSSION

I.   Legal Standard

Congress vested the federal courts with power to vacate an arbitration award "[w]here there was evident partiality ... in the arbitrators...." ... The Petitioner relies on a United States Supreme Court holding that "evident partiality" is established when arbitrators fail to disclose "any dealings that might create an impression of possible bias." ... On the other hand, the Respondent relies on Third Circuit caselaw holding that evident partiality is present only when " 'a reasonable person would have to conclude that the arbitrator was partial' to the other party to the arbitration." ... The use of these seemingly contradictory interpretations illustrates what appears to be a fundamental misunderstanding concerning the complicated caselaw in this area. The following analysis sifts through this enigmatic area of law in an attempt to clarify these legal principles and determine which of these standards is appropriate for application here.

[. . .]

A.   Appearance of Bias Standard

The appearance of bias standard, the first of the two standards, was formed in 1968 when the United States Supreme Court considered *Commonwealth Coatings*. The *Commonwealth Coatings* Court was presented with a situation whereby a neutral arbitrator, that is, an arbitrator chosen not unilaterally by the plaintiff, defendant or by an outside party but rather directly or indirectly by both parties, held undisclosed business ties with one of the parties involved in the arbitration.... In what has been erroneously referred to as a plurality opinion, the Court vacated the arbitration award based on the neutral arbitrator's failure to "disclose to the parties any dealings that might create an impression of possible bias."

... The result is the appearance of bias standard which holds that evident partiality is established when arbitrators fail to disclose any relationships that might create an impression of possible bias.

B.   Actual Bias Standard

The Respondent argues strongly in favor of applying an actual bias standard. In doing so, the Respondent relies almost exclusively on *Kaplan's* footnote 30 where the Third Circuit borrows Sixth Circuit language to indicate that evident partiality is only present "when a reasonable person would have to conclude that an arbitrator was partial" to one of the parties. [*Kaplan v. First Options of Chicago, Inc.*, 19 F.3d 1503, 1523 n.30 (3d Cir. 1994).] In *Kaplan,* the Third Circuit's cursory mention of the evident partiality standard consists largely of a single sentence taken from the Sixth Circuit's *Apperson v. Fleet Carrier Corp.* [879 F.2d 1344, 1358 (6th Cir. 1989)]. The Sixth Circuit's approach in *Apperson* is directly taken from the Second Circuit's *Morelite Construction Corp. v. New York City District Council Carpenters Benefit Funds,* 748 F.2d 79 (2d Cir.1984). Thus, the origins of the actual bias standard can be traced directly to the Second Circuit's break from the *Commonwealth Coatings* holding in *Morelite.*

C.   Which Standard Should be Applied Here?

[. . .]

1.   *Problems with* Morelite

The *Morelite* Court was able to sidestep the *Commonwealth Coatings* holding and appearance of bias standard by declaring *Commonwealth Coatings* to be nothing more than a plurality opinion accompanied by an irreconcilable concurring opinion. . . . This Court respectfully disagrees with the Second Circuit's approach for the following four reasons.

First, "*Commonwealth Coatings* is not a plurality opinion." *Schmitz v. Zilveti,* 20 F.3d 1043, 1045 (9th Cir.1994). Even though Justice White wrote a concurring opinion, he clearly indicated that "he joined in the 'majority opinion' but wrote to make 'additional remarks.' " . . . Justice White's use of the term "majority opinion" speaks for itself. Without his vote, the opinion could have never been referred to as a majority opinion. In addition, with Justice White's vote, Justice Black's opinion had the five votes necessary to gain the moniker "opinion of the Court," which is clearly used by the Court in introducing the decision. . . .

Second, Justice White's concurring opinion is not irreconcilable with the Court's opinion as it does nothing to contradict the majority's stance. It is significant that in his concurrence, Justice White never even mentions the words "appearance of bias" or suggests in any way that the appearance of bias standard is inappropriate. Instead, in what the *Morelite* Court cites as language contradicting the Court's opinion, Justice White obviously accepts the Court's decision and the appearance of bias standard by issuing the following clarification, "arbitrators are not automatically disqualified by a business relationship with the parties before them if both parties are informed of the relationship in advance, or if they are unaware of the facts but the relationship is trivial." ... Rather than rejecting the appearance of bias standard Justice White clearly embraces it and attempts to refine it by more accurately defining its parameters. In addition, it should be noted that Justice White's narrowly tailored adjustment leaves the appearance of bias standard, as a whole, untouched.

Third, not only does Justice White's concurring opinion fail to contradict the Court's opinion, it actually complements it. The premise of the Court's opinion is that arbitrators shall "disclose to the parties any dealings that might create an impression of possible bias." ... Likewise, a great deal of Justice White's concurring opinion is dedicated to encouraging what he calls "frankness at the outset," or disclosure.... In this regard, both opinions share the same goal, disclosure. The two opinions work in unison to suggest that the arbitration process is most effective and less prone to judicial intervention when disclosure is made properly at the outset. If anything, Justice White's opinion strengthens the Court's opinion in this regard.

Fourth, and perhaps most notable, Justice White went to the trouble of drafting a concurring opinion. Presumably, if this was done with the intent to debunk the appearance of bias standard, Justice White would have expressly done so. Instead, as explained above, Justice White chose not only to embrace appearance of bias standard, but also chose to omit any mention of another possible standard, such as *Morelite's* actual bias standard or another similar standard.

2. Morelite *and its progeny are inapplicable here*

Even if this Court is mistaken in finding that *Morelite's* assessment of *Commonwealth Coatings* is in error, *Morelite* and its progeny do not apply here. In the wake of the *Morelite* Opinion a growing number of courts, including this one, have embraced the notion that *Morelite's* actual bias standard does not apply to all arbitration cases where evident partiality is alleged. Contained in the following analysis of *Morelite,* its progeny and the development of the actual bias standard is a crucial point which has gone unaddressed by the parties here as well as some other courts in similar cases. Regardless of whether a court considers the actual bias standard to be legitimate (this Court does not), such a standard does not apply in cases, such as this one, where (1) the parties have some influence in selecting their arbitrators and (2) an arbitrator failed to disclose information which may create a reasonable impression of the arbitrator's partiality. In situations where these two factors are present this Court, the Ninth Circuit and the Supreme Court of Texas have found that the *Commonwealth Coatings* appearance of bias standard should be applied. *Forest Electric Corporation v. HCB Contractors,* 1995 WL 37586, *3 (E.D.Pa.1995) (Padova, J.); *Schmitz,* 20 F.3d at 1047; *Burlington Northern Railroad Co. v. TUCO, Inc.* 960 S.W.2d 629, 636 (Tex.1997). The grounds for such a finding are largely based on the reasoning of the *Common-*

wealth Coatings Court. As discussed earlier, both Justice White's concurring opinion and the Court's opinion place a premium on disclosure and its importance in the arbitrator selection process. These opinions suggest that the parties are the best judge of bias and in order to be able to choose intelligently they must be made aware of all the facts showing potential partiality.... Thus, when an arbitrator is selected by the parties after having failed to disclose a fact which may create the appearance of bias, the selection process is prone to failure.

The *Morelite* actual bias standard was conceived in a case where the parties had no influence during the arbitrator selection process.... Moreover, the facts giving rise to the alleged impropriety in *Morelite* were fully disclosed to all parties involved at the outset of the arbitration.... Disclosure was never an issue.

Likewise, the Sixth Circuit faced a similar scenario in *Apperson* when it chose to adopt the *Morelite* actual bias standard. In *Apperson,* just as in *Morelite,* a collective bargaining agreement provided for preselected "arbitration committees" on the local, regional and national levels which excluded the parties from playing any role in selecting their arbitrators....

Finally, in *Kaplan,* the Third Circuit faced a similar scenario. Although the Court does not describe what the exact arbitration selection process was, it does indicate that the arbitration at issue was conducted under the rules of the Philadelphia Stock Exchange.... This Court's research failed to unearth what those rules were at the time in question. Presumably, the rules of the Exchange at that time, like the other corporate arbitration agreements considered here, offered the parties little or no input into the arbitrator selection process. Regardless, the significant point in our consideration of *Kaplan* is that the challenging party never alleged a failed disclosure as the basis for a finding of evident partiality. Instead, the Kaplans based their showing of evident partiality on the performance of the arbitrators during the arbitration process. Specifically, they allege "through a long series of irrational and unfair rulings, throughout the course of the [arbitration] proceedings, the arbitrators consistently (and without basis) disfavored the Kaplans and favored First Options." ...

Morelite, Apperson and *Kaplan* all have a common theme which distinguishes them from the case at hand as well as application of the actual bias standard. As we have seen in each of these cases, with the possible exception of *Kaplan,* the parties had no influence in the selection of their presiding arbitrators. More importantly, none of these cases involved a failed disclosure on behalf of an arbitrator.... As explained in the preceding, these significant differences with *Morelite* and its progeny suggest that even if this Court's consideration of *Morelite* is in error the actual bias standard is inapplicable and that the *Commonwealth Coatings* appearance of bias standard is the appropriate standard to apply here.

III. Application of the Appearance of Bias Standard

With the appropriate standard determined, the Court turns its attention to application of the appearance of bias standard. In support of its Petition to Vacate, the Petitioner raises a number of allegations concerning arbitrators Galante and Meyer's failure to disclose relationships. Petitioner argues that these failed disclosures amount to evident partiality.

This Court is unpersuaded by Petitioner's allegations in so far as they concern Mr. Cohen's or Cohen Seglias' representation of a party appearing before either arbitrator Galante or Meyer in a AAA sponsored arbitration or mediation before, during or after the JMB/Crow arbitration. These so called relationships appear to be exactly what Justice White was alluding to in his concurring opinion in *Commonwealth Coatings* when he cautioned against vacating an arbitration award based on undisclosed trivial business relationships. . . .

More troubling are Petitioner's remaining allegations concerning the arbitrators' more extensive undisclosed ties with JMB and Cohen Seglias. Specifically, Ms. Meyer's failure to disclose her role as a mediator in a case involving JMB, Mr. Galante's failure to disclose his private dealings with Cohen Seglias as a hired arbitrator in 1999 and both arbitrators' failure to disclose their roles in the JMB/Greenfield matter amount to nothing less than the appearance of bias.

There is no question that under AAA rules the arbitrators were required to disclose these dealings to JMB and Crow. . . . While this provision is not a governing standard here, it serves as a benchmark to assess the alleged failed disclosures under the appearance of bias standard and raises the question of the severity of these infractions.

Ms. Meyer's failure to disclose her prior dealing with JMB in a mediation which occurred at or about the same time as the JMB/Crow proceeding raises several concerns. First, since the two proceedings took place at roughly the same time there is little doubt that JMB's presence in both matters was not simply forgotten by Ms. Meyer. Given this fact it becomes difficult to account for the failure to disclose without considering the possibility of bias. Second, the obvious concern here is that information gleaned in the two hour review of the mediation case could prejudice Crow in the JMB/Crow arbitration by, among other things, not giving Crow a chance to respond to any information about JMB learned in the mediation and applied in the JMB/Crow matter. Disclosure is mandated to enable parties to proceedings, such as this one, to avoid such a scenario. Crow should have been notified of the potential conflict in order to have a chance to respond accordingly, or, at the very least, seek an alternate arbitrator. Ms. Meyer's failure to make the necessary disclosure gives rise to an obvious appearance of bias.

Mr. Galante's undisclosed work for Cohen Seglias is equally troublesome. The fact that at the time the JMB/Crow arbitration was proceeding Cohen Seglias selected Mr. Galante to arbitrate a matter and paid him, not under the auspices of AAA but rather directly, raises a number of obvious issues. Certainly any time money changes hands directly between an arbitrator and a representative of one of the parties involved in a pending arbitration before that arbitrator, disclosure must take place. Mr. Galante's failure to disclose this untimely transaction bears the appearance of bias.

Finally, perhaps most disturbing is the arbitrators' failure to disclose to Crow their role in the JMB/Greenfield arbitration. While the Respondent points out that the overlap between the two cases was minimal, this Court must point out that such an argument does little to explain the problems associated with such a situation. As indicated earlier, the arbitrators' hearing another case involving JMB could lead to consideration of facts about Plaintiff JMB which are largely irrelevant to the JMB/Crow matter. More importantly, any facts taken from the JMB/Greenfield matter either consciously or sub-consciously would go unaddressed by Crow....

When considered individually, any one of the above described failed disclosures constitutes an appearance of bias. Viewed together as a whole, they constitute not only the appearance of bias but, perhaps, a suggestion of bias. Regardless, the Petitioner has met the appearance of bias standard and therefore has proven ... that evident partiality is present thereby necessitating vacation of the arbitration award. The repeated failed disclosures in the arbitration process here resulted in a selection process whereby the Petitioner was not afforded a fair opportunity to make informed choices with regard to the arbitrators proposed by the AAA. Such a failure lies in direct contradiction with the spirit of *Commonwealth Coatings* and intent behind both the Court's opinion and Justice White's concurrence in that matter. Finally, such a failure ultimately fails the arbitration process as a whole.

[. . .]

NOTES AND QUESTIONS

1. What does the court finally say about *Commonwealth Coatings* and *Morelite*? Is there a true conflict between the opinions? Do factual differences prevent any real conflict?

2. Is the *Crow Constr. Co.* court accurate or persuasive in its assessment of Justice White's concurring opinion in *Commonwealth Coatings*?

3. What then is the applicable legal standard as to "evident partiality"?

4. Does the court's application of the standard for "evident partiality" comply with the federal policy on arbitration? Why and why not?

5. How would you argue against the court's application of the law?

SPHERE DRAKE INS. LTD. v. ALL AMERICAN LIFE INS. CO.

307 F.3d 617 (7th Cir. 2002).

EASTERBROOK, Circuit Judge.

Two underwriters cannot agree about whether seven policies of rein-surance are valid—or for that matter about who decides whether they are valid. All American, which contends that the contracts are effective, says that the dispute should be arbitrated. Sphere Drake, which denies the documents' binding quality, believes that a court should resolve the question. . . .

While litigating with respect to one of the seven policies, Sphere Drake submitted the other six to arbitration at All American's insistence. The arbitration was conducted under the auspices of the Association Internationale de Droits des Assurances ("AIDA") and its U.S. affiliate, the AIDA Reinsurance and Insurance Arbitration Society ("ARIAS i U.S."), which uses tripartite panels. Each insurer names one member of the panel, and these two choose a neutral (called the "umpire") to break ties. All American designated Robert M. Mangino, and Sphere Drake named Ronald A. Jacks. They chose Robert M. Huggins as the umpire. All three have considerable experience in international reinsurance arbitra-tion, having served on at least 35 panels. Mangino and Jacks are founding directors of ARIAS i U.S.; Jacks is a former president of the U.S. chapter of AIDA. All three have served as umpires; Jacks has been chosen for that duty more than 25 times by party-named arbitrators who relied on his reputation for legal acumen and impartiality. Huggins decided that Sphere Drake was entitled to victory on the ground that All American had disavowed Stirling Cooke Brown Reinsurance Brokers as its agent (a tactic apparently designed to avoid any risk that Stirling Cooke, which placed the reinsurance through EIU, would be found to know about EIU's limited authority). But Huggins concluded that if All American was not bound (because Stirling Cooke lacked authority to act on its behalf) then Sphere Drake could not be bound either. Jacks joined him to make a majority; Mangino dissented. Having demanded arbitration, All American decided that it did not like the result and asked a court to set aside the award—which it did, on the ground that Jacks displayed "evident partiali-ty," one of the few grounds for refusing to enforce an award. . . .

As far as we can see, this is the first time since the Federal Arbitra-tion Act was enacted in 1925 that a federal court has set aside an award because a party-appointed arbitrator on a tripartite panel, as opposed to a neutral, displayed "evident partiality." The lack of precedent is unsurpris-ing, because in the main party-appointed arbitrators are *supposed* to be advocates. In labor arbitration a union may name as its arbitrator the business manager of the local union, and the employer its vice-president for labor relations. Yet no one believes that the predictable loyalty of these designees spoils the award. . . . This is so because the parties are entitled to waive the protection of [FAA § 10(a)(2)], as they can waive almost any other statutory entitlement.... The Federal Arbitration Act makes arbitration agreements enforceable to the same extent as other contracts, so courts must "enforce privately negotiated agreements to arbitrate, like other contracts, in accordance with their terms." ...

Parties are free to choose for themselves to what lengths they will go in quest of impartiality. Section 10(a)(2) just states the presumptive rule, subject to variation by mutual consent. Industry arbitration, the modern law merchant, often uses panels composed of industry insiders, the better to understand the trade's norms of doing business and the consequences of proposed lines of decision.... The more experience the panel has, and the smaller the number of repeat players, the more likely it is that the panel will contain some actual or potential friends, counselors, or business rivals of the parties. Yet all participants may think the expertise-impartiality tradeoff worthwhile; the Arbitration Act does not fasten on every industry the model of the disinterested generalist judge.... To the extent that an agreement entitles parties to select interested (even beholden) arbitrators, § 10(a)(2) has no role to play.

There remains the question whether this was such an agreement, to which the answer is yes and no. Party-appointed arbitrators are entitled under the ARIAS i U.S. rules to engage in *ex parte* discussions with their principals until the case is taken under advisement, but they are supposed thereafter to be impartial adjudicators. The parties assume that as a result Sphere Drake could not have appointed one of its current employees as its arbitrator. (Whether that assumption is correct depends on ARIAS i U.S. rules and practices; we need not pursue the issue.) Still, Jacks was not, and never has been, one of Sphere Drake's employees. He is a retired lawyer, until recently a partner of Mayer, Brown & Platt (now Mayer, Brown, Rowe & Maw). The district court deemed Jacks "evidently partial" because four years before the arbitration, while still at Mayer Brown, Jacks had been engaged by the Bermuda subsidiary of Sphere Drake (a United Kingdom company) as counsel on an unrelated matter that landed in arbitration but was settled before decision. It emerged in discovery compelled by the district court that Jacks had billed about 380 hours for that matter. The judge deemed Sphere Drake (U.K.) his real client because its financial interests were at stake, even though the Bermuda subsidiary signed the engagement letter and paid the fees, and even though Jacks himself thought that most of his billable time related to corporate counseling rather than to the arbitration.

Let us suppose that the district judge's inferences are sound—that Jacks spent two months of equivalent full-time service as counsel for Sphere Drake in an international insurance arbitration, four years before the unrelated arbitration with All American. Even if Jacks had been the umpire, this would not have implied "evident partiality." Indeed, Jacks could have served as a federal judge in this case without challenge on grounds of partiality, and the scope of disqualification under § 10(a)(2) is considerably more confined than the rule applicable to judges.... "Evident partiality" under § 10(a)(2) is a subset of the conditions that disqualify a federal judge under 28 U.S.C. § 455(b). A judge can't hold even a single share of a party's stock, but this would not imply "evident partiality" for purposes of § 10(a)(2). The parties themselves evinced this understanding. Before the arbitration began, umpire Huggins revealed that he was an investor in American International Group, which recently had made a bid to acquire All American—yet neither side thought that this imperiled Huggins' ability to serve as the neutral.

A federal judge would be disqualified on account of prior legal work "[w]here in private practice he served as lawyer in the matter in controversy, or a lawyer with whom he previously practiced law served during such association as a lawyer concerning the matter, or the judge or such lawyer has been a material witness concerning it." 28 U.S.C. § 455(b)(2). Jacks fits none of these categories. The work he did for Sphere Drake was unrelated to the controversy with All American; no partner of Mayer Brown served "during such association" (that is, while Jacks also was a partner) as a lawyer in this dispute between Sphere Drake and All American (indeed, Sphere Drake has been represented throughout by a firm other than Mayer Brown); and neither Jacks nor any lawyer at Mayer Brown is a "material witness" in this case. Arbitration differs from adjudication, among many other ways, because the "appearance of partiality" ground of disqualification for judges does not apply to arbitrators; only *evident* partiality, not appearances or risks, spoils an award. Still, a judge's former representation of a litigant does not imply any need to disqualify under § 455(a) because "his impartiality might reasonably be questioned." . . . Nothing in the Code of Conduct for federal judges makes prior representation of a litigant a disqualifying event. The norm among new appointees to the bench is that once two years pass, perhaps even earlier, a judge is free to sit in controversies involving former clients. See Committee on Codes of Conduct, *Judicial Ethics Compendium* § 3.6–5.

If Jacks could have served as a federal judge in this case, it is impossible to see how his background could demonstrate "evident partiality" within the meaning of § 10(a)(2). . . .

[. . .]

Commonwealth Coatings observes that disclosure at the outset often avoids later controversies—as Huggins's disclosure did. One can only imagine what Sphere Drake would be saying now had Huggins kept his mouth shut and then supported All American's position. Disclosure in *Commonwealth Coatings* itself would have averted a problem that spoiled an award. The neutral in a tripartite arbitration was engaged in *ongoing* business relations with one of the parties, "and the relationship even went so far as to include the rendering of services on the very projects involved in this lawsuit." . . . The Court held that being on one side's payroll is a form of partiality condemned by § 10(a)(2). . . . The Justices urged arbitrators to disclose their business dealings so that similar problems would not recur.

Commonwealth Coatings did not hold, as All American would have it, that disclosure is compulsory for its own sake, and its absence fatal even if the arbitrator meets judicial standards of impartiality.... Nor did *Commonwealth Coatings* so much as hint that party-appointed arbitrators are governed by the norms under which neutrals operate. The point of *Commonwealth Coatings* is that the sort of financial entanglements that would disqualify a judge will cause problems for a neutral under § 10(a)(2) unless disclosure is made and the parties' consent obtained.

Disclosure by a neutral may serve purposes other than flagging potential conflicts. One gets to *be* a neutral only by agreement of the party-appointed arbitrators. A potential neutral may have contractual obligations to reveal information to those who select him. Failure to comply with a contractual requirement designed to facilitate the search for an acceptable neutral might imply that the neutral exceeded his authority, spoiling the award under 9 U.S.C. § 10(a)(4). But Mangino had no power to remove Jacks, and we have not been given any reason to think that umpire Huggins wanted more information from Jacks in order to know what to make of Jacks' arguments during the panel's deliberations. For someone in Jacks' position—a party-appointed arbitrator, and one who could have presided in court under the standards of § 455—failure to make a full disclosure may sully his reputation for candor but does not demonstrate "evident partiality" and thus does not spoil the award.

REVERSED.

NOTES AND QUESTIONS

1. Is Judge Easterbrook giving *Commonwealth Coatings* its due? Does he reinterpret the Court's holding in that case and render it less meaningful? In his view, what does *Commonwealth Coatings* require and what purpose does the holding in that case serve?

2. Is there any support in *Commonwealth Coatings* for the view that different standards of impartiality should apply to party-appointed arbitrators and the neutral? Is that distinction ever made or endorsed by the U.S. Supreme Court? How does the Seventh Circuit justify the distinction? Do you agree that party-appointed arbitrators are expected to be advocates for the appointing party? Why hire lawyers then to represent you?

3. Why does the Seventh Circuit give such importance in its reasoning to the ethical regulations that apply to federal judges? Is it simply a question of familiarity? Despite a general resemblance, do arbitrators and judges perform different tasks for different purposes?

4. How does the *Sphere Drake* court distinguish between "evident partiality" and the "appearance of bias"? Why is "evident partiality" the standard? If it is, is the "appearance" standard eliminated? What does *Commonwealth Coatings* say on that issue?

5. If there might be bias, does disclosure neutralize or eliminate it? What does it mean to be impartial or objective? Does the payment of money, or even the speculative prospect of a future payment, create a tilt in a

person's perspective? On the other hand, the proper compensation of arbitrators is a significant and important matter. Adequate payment may, in fact, be instrumental to good, impartial decision-making. How do you choose or intermediate between these differing perspectives?

6.   Was Jacks sufficiently impartial in your view? Why?

NATIONWIDE MUTUAL INS. CO. v. THE HOME INS. CO.
278 F.3d 621 (6th Cir. 2002).

GILMAN, Circuit Judge.

[. . .]

I.   BACKGROUND

Nationwide entered into a reinsurance agreement with Home in 1977. Under this agreement, Home undertook to cover certain claims that might be asserted against Nationwide. . . .

Nationwide sued Home . . . for breach of contract in 1995. Because the agreement between Home and Nationwide contained an arbitration clause, the district court entered a stay and ordered Home and Nationwide to submit the case to binding arbitration. . . .

Prior to the final resolution of their dispute, Nationwide filed a new lawsuit seeking confirmation of the interim decisions issued by the panel of arbitrators. Home filed cross-motions to stay confirmation or to vacate the decisions, and for additional discovery on whether the arbitrators were biased.

On March 30, 2000, the district court denied Home's motion for discovery on the issue of arbitral bias and confirmed all of the arbitration panel's interim decisions. . . . Home now appeals the district court's denial of its motion for additional discovery and the court's confirmation of the . . . three decisions by the arbitration panel. . . .

II.   ANALYSIS

[. . .]

Home . . . argues that the district court erred in not vacating the arbitration panel's rescission and costs decisions pursuant to 9 U.S.C. § 10(a)(2). Section 10(a)(2) provides that a district court may vacate an arbitration decision "[w]here there was evident partiality or corruption in the arbitrators, or either of them." Home cites the following five instances of purported "evident partiality": (1) arbitrator Hassard's undisclosed involvement in a dispute with Home; (2) arbitrator Twigden's marketing meetings with Nationwide; (3) collusion between Nationwide and the arbitration panel to insulate the security decision from review; (4) the arbitration panel's hostility toward Home; and (5) the arbitration panel's security decision.

This court has held that evident partiality "will be found only where a reasonable person would have to conclude that an arbitrator was partial to one party to the arbitration." ... "The alleged partiality must be direct, definite, and capable of demonstration, and the party asserting evident partiality must establish specific facts that indicate improper motives on the part of the arbitrator." ...

Home's first argument is that Hassard failed to disclose his involvement in a dispute with Home. It acknowledges, however, that during an organizational meeting of the arbitration panel with Home and Nationwide, Hassard disclosed that he served as Chairman of the Board for a company, Republic Financial Services, that had "a runoff relationship" with Home.... But Home claims that Hassard did not disclose that he was engaged in discussions concerning a dispute between Home and Republic regarding unpaid balances in the runoff account. Home also asserts that, contrary to the district court's $7,000 estimate, the amount of money involved in the dispute was $444,471.

The district court responded by noting that "Hassard disclosed the relationship between Home and Republic and described the ongoing runoff process," and that Home and Nationwide both stipulated that they waived subsequent objections as to bias or partiality stemming from matters disclosed at the organizational meeting.... Moreover, Hassard made a supplemental disclosure on October 28, 1998 that, based on his personal inquiry, Republic was claiming that Home owed it approximately $7,000.... The district court concluded that "the existence of a runoff relationship implies that a dispute could arise during the course of such relationship. Because such issues were clearly known to the parties before the arbitration began, Home cannot complain after the fact that the relationship exists." ...

The district court's finding that the net amount in dispute between Republic and Home was relatively small is not clearly erroneous. Although Republic purportedly owed Home $444,471, Home apparently owed Republic $455,672. The net amount in dispute, therefore, was only the difference of approximately $11,201. Furthermore ... Hassard disclosed the runoff relationship before arbitration commenced. These facts do not support Home's claim of "evident partiality" on the part of Hassard.

Home also asserts that Twigden's meetings with Nationwide were for the purpose of marketing his legal services. But the district court enumerated six reasons why the meetings did not justify vacatur: (1) Twigden fully disclosed the June 1998 and August 1998 meetings in advance, and Home did not timely object to them; (2) neither Twigden nor his firm has any business relationship with Nationwide; (3) Twigden did not discuss the arbitration with Nationwide during the meetings; (4) Home did not begin its attacks on Twigden's purported bias until after the arbitration panel issued the adverse rescission and security decisions; (5) Home agreed to submit this claim to members of a panel who were actively involved in the insurance industry; and (6) counsel for Home had also offered to meet Twigden socially.

Home challenges each of the district court's findings. First, Home claims that Twigden did not disclose a second meeting that he allegedly had with Nationwide in August of 1998. Although Home concedes that neither Twigden nor his firm had a business relationship with Nationwide, it asserts that Twigden was actively soliciting business from Nationwide. Home also argues that, in finding that Twigden did not discuss the arbitration with Nationwide, the district court improperly relied on Twigden's unsworn statement. Next, Home claims that the arbitration panel's adverse rulings had no bearing on the company's decision to attack Twigden's purported bias. Home further points out that it did not agree to submit the dispute to an arbitrator who was involved in marketing legal services to Nationwide. Finally, Home suggests that its own counsel was simply making a friendly gesture when he offered to meet Twigden socially.

The district court's findings that only one meeting took place between Twigden and Nationwide in August of 1998, and that the arbitration proceedings were not discussed at either of the meetings between Twigden and Nationwide, are not clearly erroneous. Although Home now complains that the district court relied on an unsworn statement by Twigden in finding that the arbitration was not discussed, Home failed to timely object to the statement in the court below. Moreover, Home used portions of the same unsworn statement to support its own submission to the district court. The district court also correctly pointed out that the arbitration agreement states that the panel members would be active members of the insurance industry. As a result, the parties should have expected that the business interests of the arbitrators might become entangled with those of the parties. That a representative of Home also made an offer to meet with Twigden socially further supports the conclusion that such meetings do not necessarily give rise to an inference of partiality. In sum, none of Home's objections have sufficient merit to warrant setting aside the district court's determination that Twigden's meetings with Nationwide do not justify vacatur of the awards in question.

Home next argues that the arbitration panel colluded with Nationwide in attempting to immunize the security decision from review. On September 11, 1998, the arbitration panel issued a "written confirmation" that its November 6, 1997 security decision was final as of the earlier date. Home claims that the ruling was designed to prevent vacatur of the decision because, under the FAA, a motion to vacate must be filed within three months from the date the decision is issued. . . . To the contrary, the district court found that the arbitration panel's September 1998 order was the result of Home having ignored the November 1997 order, and never posting the security awarded by the panel. The district court did not err in finding that the arbitration panel's "written confirmation" of the 1997 security decision was an effort to have Home comply with the panel's original ruling, not an attempt to collude with Nationwide.

Home also claims that the arbitration panel exhibited evident partiality in a series of letters criticizing Home's counsel. The district court found that this argument "borders on the frivolous," because Home's counsel had "engaged in an unrelenting, unremitting barrage of invectives impugning the integrity of the Panel members...." ... By comparison, the district court found the arbitration panel's responses to be "far more temperate, professional and appropriate." ... We agree with the district court's assessment that the letters to Home's counsel did not exhibit bias, particularly given that the letters were written in response to letters initiated by counsel for Home.

Home further suggests that the arbitration panel's security decision demonstrates evident partiality because: (1) the decision was based on spreadsheets that Nationwide unilaterally compiled, (2) the arbitration panel had not ruled on whether it had authority to order costs, (3) the amount of the security was grossly excessive, and (4) the arbitration panel did not allow discovery or hold a hearing. The district court rejected this claim because "[a]n adverse award ... is no evidence of bias absent some evidence of improper motivation." ...

Home claims that the district court erred because the arbitration panel's contemporaneous criticisms of Home provide independent evidence that the arbitration panel had an improper motive in making the security decision. We disagree. First, the panel's responses to the letters from Home's counsel were not inappropriate for the reasons stated above. Second, even the panel member selected by Home joined in the decision to order security for any damages that Nationwide might establish. Finally, the determination that the panel had the authority to make the security award was implicit in its decision on the merits. We therefore concur in the district court's finding that the arbitrators were not partial to Nationwide.

[. . .]

NOTES AND QUESTIONS

1. What standard does the court in *Nationwide* adopt in terms of establishing evident partiality? Does it comply with the holding in *Commonwealth Coatings*? If not, is it truly different? How?

2. What content would you attribute to the "reasonable person" standard in this context? How would you define "direct, definite, and capable of demonstration"? What do all of these words mean? Can you reformulate the rule for clarity, focus, and content?

3. The court engaged in a thorough examination of the facts pertaining to "evident partiality." How would you assess its evaluation of those facts? Is there a strong presumption against finding questionable circumstances?

4. How do you evaluate the circumstances described by the court?

5. Does the federal policy on arbitration influence the court's approach? If so, how?

6. In *JCI Communications, Inc. v. International Brotherhood of Electrical Workers, Local 103*, 324 F.3d 42 (1st Cir. 2003), the court referred to the *Nationwide* reasonable person standard and added that, "[a]bsent exceptional circumstances, a court 'will not entertain a claim of personal bias where it could have been raised at the arbitration proceedings but was not.' ..." Moreover, "[i]t would undermine the arbitration process to permit an employer with an industry-represented panel to await the outcome of an arbitration before deciding to cry bias." (*Citing Early*, 699 F.2d at 558 ["[W]e cannot accept that parties have a right to keep two strings to the bow—to seek victory before the tribunal and then, having lost, seek to overturn it for bias never before claimed."]). What do these rulings add to the discussion of evident partiality? Is *Commonwealth Coatings* still the law or more of a distant memory that is increasingly distorted? Which approach better supports the federal policy in favor of arbitration?

LUCENT TECHNOLOGIES INC. v. TATUNG CO.

379 F.3d 24 (2d Cir. 2004).

FEINBERG, Circuit Judge.

Respondent Tatung Co. appeals from a July 2003 judgment ... confirming an arbitral award in favor of petitioners Lucent Technologies Inc. and Lucent Technologies, GRL LLC (together, Lucent) and rejecting Tatung's arguments that the award should be vacated because of arbitrator bias. On appeal, Tatung argues that the court's judgment should be reversed and the award vacated because (1) Tatung never received the disclosure form submitted to the American Arbitration Association (AAA) by arbitrator J. David Luening; (2) Luening's service as an expert witness for Lucent in an unrelated matter constituted "evident partiality" requiring vacatur; and (3) Luening and fellow arbitrator Roger Smith failed to disclose their joint ownership of an airplane between 1974 and 1990. In the alternative, Tatung argues, this court should remand the case to the district court for discovery concerning the relationships between Luening, Lucent and Lucent's attorneys and between Luening and Smith. For reasons set forth below, we affirm the judgment of the district court.

I. BACKGROUND

In October 2000, Lucent initiated arbitration against Tatung, a Taiwanese corporation, because of Tatung's alleged failure to pay any of the royalties required by their patent licensing agreement with Lucent. Under the agreement, each party was to appoint one member of the arbitration panel. The two party-appointed panel members would then choose a third neutral member. The agreement also specified that the arbitration was to be governed by the International Rules of the American Arbitration Association (AAA). Pursuant to Article 7, paragraph 1 of those Rules:

> Prior to accepting appointment, a prospective arbitrator shall disclose to the administrator any circumstance likely to give rise to justifiable doubts as to the arbitrator's impartiality or independence.... Upon receipt of such information from an arbitrator or party, the administrator shall communicate it to the other parties and to the tribunal.

Moreover, arbitrators are required to file a "Notice of Appointment" form disclosing "any past or present relationship with the parties or their counsel, direct or indirect, whether financial, professional, social or of any other kind." The form explains that "[t]he AAA will call the facts to the attention of the parties' counsel."

On March 2, 2001, Lucent named J. David Luening as its choice for the panel of arbitrators. On his AAA disclosure form, Luening checked the box marked "I HEREBY DISCLOSE THE FOLLOWING" and wrote "SEE ATTACHED MEMORANDUM." In the attached memorandum, Luening explained that "[f]rom April, 1998, to December, 1999, I was retained by Lucent through their counsel, Kirkland and Ellis, as a litigation consultant and expert. That engagement has concluded and has no bearing on the subject arbitration." Luening's form was dated April 25, 2001. A fax line at the top of each page indicates that Luening faxed his materials to the AAA on April 30, 2001, and a date stamp indicates that the AAA received those materials that same day. Tatung alleges that it never received Luening's disclosure form from the AAA.

On March 2, 2001, Tatung named Ed Fiorito as its party-appointed arbitrator. On the disclosure form he filed with the AAA, Fiorito checked the box indicating he had nothing to disclose. Tatung apparently never received that form either. In May, Luening suggested Roger Smith as the third, neutral arbitrator, and Fiorito apparently agreed. On September 4, 2001, Smith was appointed to the arbitration panel. Smith disclosed to the AAA that he was of counsel to a firm that does work for Lucent. Tatung received Smith's disclosure form from the AAA. All three arbitrators were one-time employees of IBM. Tatung never asked about the missing disclosure forms and raised no objections concerning the arbitrators' identities until after it received notice that it had lost the arbitration.

... In October 2002, all three arbitrators found in favor of Lucent and voted to award it damages. The three disagreed only as to the amount. Luening and Smith awarded $12,665,639; Fiorito would have awarded $8,479,264. Pursuant to Tatung's request, the award was later lowered to $12,551,613 plus interest.

Thereafter, Lucent petitioned in the Southern District for confirmation of the award. In response, Tatung moved to vacate the award arguing, among other things, that Luening and Lucent had failed to disclose that Luening had been a paid patent license expert for Lucent in another case ... that was not yet final at the time the arbitration began. Tatung also complained that it was undisclosed that Luening and Smith had owned an airplane together from 1974 to 1990.

Tatung, which had apparently never asked the AAA about Luening's disclosure form, accused Lucent and Luening of intentionally hiding Luening's service as an expert witness for Lucent in the Delaware case.... Tatung argued that the failure of Luening and Lucent to disclose these facts constituted "evident partiality" under *Commonwealth Coatings* ... requiring vacatur of the award. Luening and Smith's failure to disclose their co-ownership of an airplane, Tatung added, also constituted "evident partiality" and required vacatur as well.

The district court rejected Tatung's arguments and confirmed the award. The court found that Luening had in fact disclosed his relationship with Lucent to the AAA and that his service as an expert witness had ended by November 1999, months before being selected as an arbitrator in this matter. Further, Judge Rakoff observed that Tatung could have discovered that relationship at any time had it simply asked the AAA, Luening or Lucent about the disclosure form Tatung must have known to have existed. This fact suggested to the court that Tatung's argument was a "classic example of a losing party seizing upon a pretext for invalidating the [arbitration] award."

Most important, the district court held that *Commonwealth Coatings* does not require vacatur where the arbitrator has disclosed potential conflicts of interest to the AAA but the AAA thereafter did not forward the information to a party. Judge Rakoff noted that requiring vacatur under such circumstances "would serve no public purpose." *Id*. Further, the court held, Luening's relationship with Lucent was not sufficiently suggestive of partiality to require vacatur under *Morelite*.... The judge also held that Luening and Smith's previous co-ownership of an airplane was " 'too insubstantial to warrant vacating an award,' "....

This appeal followed.

II. DISCUSSION

[...]

A. Should the Arbitration Award be Vacated Because of Nondisclosure?

1. Luening's expert testimony for Lucent

Tatung argues that under the Supreme Court's holding in *Commonwealth Coatings,* as well as this circuit's precedent interpreting it, an arbitration award must be vacated when one party is not informed of a material relationship between the other party and an arbitrator. Tatung claims that under this supposed rule it was Luening and Lucent's responsibility to guarantee that Tatung was informed of their relationship. According to Tatung, Lucent received copies of all correspondence between Tatung and the AAA and should thus have known that Tatung never received Luening's disclosure form.

Under the Federal Arbitration Act, an arbitration award should be vacated "[w]here there [is] evident partiality or corruption in the arbitrators, or either of them." 9 U.S.C. § 10(a)(2). In *Commonwealth Coatings,* the Supreme Court held that an arbitrator's failure to disclose a material relationship with one of the parties can constitute "evident partiality" requiring vacatur of the award.... Along with concerns about the appearance of bias that might result from such nondisclosure, ... the Court reasoned that the arbitration process would be best served by requiring early disclosure of any significant dealings between arbitrators and parties.... "The judiciary should minimize its role in arbitration as judge of the arbitrator's impartiality," and a policy of early disclosure would limit the opportunities for "a suspicious or disgruntled party [to] seize on [an undisclosed relationship] as a pretext for invalidating the award." ...

This court has, in turn, "viewed the teachings of *Commonwealth Coatings* pragmatically, employing a case-by-case approach in preference to dogmatic rigidity." *Andros Compania Maritima, S.A. v. Marc Rich & Co.*, 579 F.2d 691, 700 (2d Cir.1978). "[W]e have not been quick to set aside the results of an arbitration because of an arbitrator's alleged failure to disclose information." *Id.* In particular, we have declined to vacate awards because of undisclosed relationships where the complaining party should have known of the relationship, see *Cook Indus., Inc. v. C. Itoh & Co. (America)*, 449 F.2d 106, 107–08 (2d Cir.1971), or could have learned of the relationship "just as easily before or during the arbitration rather than after it lost its case." *Andros*, 579 F.2d at 702. We have also noted that "a principal attraction of arbitration is the expertise of those who decide the controversy," that "[e]xpertise in an industry is accompanied by exposure ... to those engaged in it, and the dividing line between innocuous and suspect relationships is not always easy to draw." *Id.* at 701.

Tatung cites no case from the Supreme Court or this court that has vacated an award for nondisclosure where the arbitrator has complied with his obligation to disclose potential sources of partiality.... If Tatung failed to receive Luening's disclosure form, the fault lies with the AAA and not with Luening or Lucent. The concern, noted in *Commonwealth Coatings*, that nondisclosure might create an appearance of bias or even be evidence of bias is simply not present in this case. There is no basis to argue that Luening and Lucent intended to hide their relationship from Tatung.

Furthermore, Tatung's proposed rule—that parties to an arbitration, in effect, guarantee that opposing parties obtain arbitrator disclosures— would make the results of arbitration less rather than more certain and would run counter to the general policy of encouraging and supporting arbitration....

Tatung's attempt to vacate the award here demonstrates the dangers of its proposed rule. Tatung seeks to set aside an arbitration that took nearly two years to conclude. Tatung argues that it reasonably relied on its failure to receive a copy of Luening's disclosure form as evidence that no relationship existed. However, there is no evidence that it so relied. Moreover, this argument was not made in any papers below and was barely mentioned in the district court at oral argument on Tatung's motion to vacate. Judge Rakoff obviously regarded the argument as unpersuasive. So do we. As the district court found, Tatung knew of the AAA rules requiring disclosure by arbitrators, must have known of the form filed by Fiorito, its party-appointed arbitrator, and knew of the AAA's disclosure form submitted by Smith and eventually forwarded to Tatung. There was no persuasive reason for Tatung to have assumed that Luening had not submitted a similar form, and Tatung could have inquired into it at any time before or during arbitration. Notably, the AAA rules strongly encourage early investigations and objections. Had Tatung asked the AAA for Luening's form or asked Luening himself about any relationship with Lucent, Tatung would have undoubtedly discovered the relationship now at issue—a relationship Luening and Lucent clearly had no intention of hiding—before the arbitration began. Instead, only after losing in arbitration and losing, on grounds different from those seized upon here, on a motion to dismiss Lucent's attempt to confirm the award, did Tatung "discover" Luening's relationship with Lucent and seek vacatur of the award on that ground. Even then, as the district court found, Tatung chose to remain ignorant of Luening's disclosure form. *Commonwealth Coatings* does not require vacatur of an award under circumstances such as these, and Tatung's proposed rule would prove inimical to the purposes of arbitration. Accordingly, we affirm the district court's decision on this issue.

2. *Luening and Smith's prior co-ownership of an airplane*

Tatung next argues that Luening and Smith's co-ownership of an airplane from 1974 to 1990, which was never disclosed to the parties, requires vacatur of the award under *Commonwealth Coatings*. Tatung cites no case where the *Commonwealth Coatings* rule has been applied to an undisclosed relationship between arbitrators rather than between an arbitrator and a party. Furthermore, *Commonwealth Coatings* does not establish a per se rule requiring vacatur of an award whenever an undisclosed relationship is discovered. Rather, the Court observed that some "undisclosed relationships ... are too insubstantial to warrant vacating the award." ... The Court explained that "an arbitrator's business relationships may be diverse indeed, involving more or less remote commercial connections with great numbers of people. He cannot be expected to provide the parties with his complete and unexpurgated business biography." ... We have further explained that "a principal attraction of arbitration is the expertise of those who decide the controversy," ... and that "[f]amiliarity with a discipline often comes at the expense of complete impartiality." .... "Moreover, specific areas tend to breed tightly knit professional communities. Key members are known to one another, and in fact may work with, or for, one another, from time to time." ...

Luening and Smith's co-ownership of an airplane ended more than a decade ago. As Judge Rakoff found, Tatung was on notice that both

Luening and Smith (along with Fiorito) had previously worked at IBM. Tatung did not object to that fact prior to arbitration, nor did it choose to investigate that relationship more deeply at that time. Even if an undisclosed relationship between arbitrators could be cause for vacatur under certain circumstances, an issue we do not resolve here, Luening and Smith's co-ownership of an airplane more than a decade ago is simply too insubstantial to require vacatur.

B.   Does Luening's Relationship with Lucent Require Vacatur of the Arbitration Award even though Luening Disclosed it to the AAA?

Relying on our opinion in *Morelite,* Tatung claims that Luening's relationship with Lucent is so strongly suggestive of bias that it warrants vacatur of the award even though it was disclosed by Luening to the AAA. Tatung argues that the district court thus erred by refusing to vacate the award.

In *Morelite,* after carefully weighing all the various interests at stake, we rejected both "appearance of bias" and "proof of actual bias" tests of evident partiality.... Instead we held that " 'evident partiality' within the meaning of 9 U.S.C. § 10 will be found where a reasonable person would have to conclude that an arbitrator was partial to one party to the arbitration." ... We added that "[i]n assessing a given relationship, courts must remain cognizant of peculiar commercial practices and factual variances." ... "In this way," we explained, "the courts may refrain from threatening the valuable role of private arbitration in the settlement of commercial disputes, and at the same time uphold their responsibility to ensure that fair treatment is afforded to those who come before them." . . .

In this case, Judge Rakoff found that Luening had completed his service as an expert witness for Lucent by November 1999 and had submitted his final invoice by January 2000. The judge thus found that "Luening's prior relationship with Lucent had terminated in all material respects before Lucent's counsel solicited" his services as an arbitrator in this matter.... Moreover, the court found that "Luening had no interest" in the outcome of the arbitration.... Accordingly, the court held that "[n]othing about the relationship 'provides strong evidence of partiality by the arbitrator' that would justify vacating the award." ...

... Moreover, accepting the court's finding that Luening's relationship with Lucent materially ended before Lucent appointed him as an arbitrator in this matter, we cannot say that "a reasonable person would have to conclude that an arbitrator was partial to one party to the arbitration." ... As we explained in *International Produce, Inc. v. A/S Rosshavet,* 638 F.2d 548, 552 (2d Cir. 1981), a shipping arbitration case in which we found no evident partiality, "arbitrators in important shipping arbitrations have typically participated in [many] prior maritime disputes, not only as arbitrators but also as parties and witnesses. They have therefore almost inevitably come into contact with a significant proportion of the relatively few lawyers who make up the New York admiralty bar."

[. . .]

III. CONCLUSION

We have considered all of Tatung's arguments and none justify reversal here. We affirm the judgment of the district court confirming the arbitration award in favor of Lucent.

NOTES AND QUESTIONS

1. Does *Lucent* establish that disclosure creates a nearly irrebutable presumption of arbitrator impartiality? Is that a fair reading of *Commonwealth Coatings*?

2. How does *Lucent* compare to *Sphere Drake*? Do the Seventh and Second Circuits agree on the applicable standard?

3. What impact does "dogmatic rigidity" and "expertise" within the business have upon the definition of impartiality?

4. What does the earlier decision in *Morelite* add to the continuing discussion of the applicable standard?

5. Is it likely that the Second Circuit will ever find an instance of arbitrator bias and partiality? In what circumstances?

6. How do you assess the relationships in *Lucent*?

7. Should impartiality be defined both in relation to the parties and the other arbitrators? Why and why not?

8. The court invokes disclosure, *ad hoc* rulings, reasonableness, and inside practices to justify its application of the standard. Are there other excuses it could have used?

9. Why is the AAA not criticized in *Lucent*?

OVITZ v. SCHULMAN

133 Cal.App.4th 830, 35 Cal.Rptr.3d 117 (2005).

WILLHITE, J.

The issues in this appeal involve the interplay of three arcane and technical areas of law: the California disclosure obligations in contractual arbitration; the California statute governing the vacating of arbitration awards; and the limited preemptive effect of the Federal Arbitration Act on state arbitration law.

. . . The [California] standards require arbitrators to make comprehensive disclosures of potential grounds for disqualification. On a showing that the arbitrator failed timely to disclose a ground for disqualification of which he or she was aware, the California Code of Civil Procedure requires the vacating of any award rendered by the arbitrator. . . .

By contrast, the Federal Arbitration Act employs a different standard: it permits the vacating of an arbitration award only on a showing of "evident partiality" by the arbitrator.... When the issue is the arbitrator's failure to disclose, the Ninth Circuit interprets "evident partiality" to mean that the undisclosed facts must create a "reasonable impression of partiality." (*Schmitz v. Zilveti* (9th Cir.1994) 20 F.3d 1043, 1046; *see also Commonwealth Coatings Corp. v. Continental Cas. Co.* (1968) 393 U.S. 145, 149, 89 S.Ct. 337, 21 L.Ed.2d 301.)

In this case, appellants Michael Ovitz, Artists Production Group, LLC, and five other business entities (we shall refer to all appellants collectively as "the APG parties") prevailed in an arbitration proceeding against respondent Cathy Schulman. The trial court, however, vacated the arbitration award under section 1286.2(a)(6)(A), finding that the arbitrator failed to comply with his disclosure obligation under standard 12(b) of the California Standards. The APG parties appeal from this ruling, as well as from the trial court's denial of their motion for reconsideration....

To resolve these issues, we examine the relevant disclosure requirements of the California Standards (past and present), and conclude that the arbitrator did not comply with his disclosure obligations. We further conclude that Schulman did not forfeit the right to vacate the arbitration award, and that the trial court properly denied reconsideration of the APG parties' forfeiture claim. Finally, after reviewing the language of the relevant sections of the FAA, the congressional purpose of that legislation, and the parties' arbitration agreement, we hold that the FAA does not preempt section 1286.2(a)(6)(A).

Factual And Procedural Background

In June 2001, respondent Schulman entered an employment agreement with one of the APG parties, a joint venture called the StudioCanal/APG Venture. Formed to produce 12 to 15 feature films over three years, the joint venture hired Schulman as President. The employment agreement contained an arbitration clause, which required arbitration before the American Arbitration Association (the "AAA") of "[a]ny controversy, claim or dispute arising out of or in any way relating to this agreement ... [or Schulman's] employment by [the joint venture]." In February 2002, simmering disputes between Schulman and others involved in the StudioCanal/APG Venture led to Schulman's departure. Schulman claimed that she was terminated without cause; the joint venture claimed that she resigned....

[...]

The APG parties appealed the trial court's ruling [compelling arbitration], but also moved forward with the arbitration. In a letter dated January 7, 2003, approved by Schulman's attorney, counsel for the APG parties informed the AAA that they and Schulman had agreed upon the appointment of Retired Justice Campbell Lucas ("the Arbitrator") as their arbitrator. The letter stated that "the designation of [the Arbitrator] is also subject to all of the disclosure requirements imposed on [him] by the American Arbitration Association and the California Code of Civil Procedure."

On January 14, 2003, the AAA faxed to counsel for Schulman and the APG parties a cover letter stating in part: "In accordance with the California Arbitration Law (C.C.P. Section 1281.9), the fully executed Arbitrator Disclosure form is enclosed for your review." The cover letter noted that the "response date" was January 29, 2003, and that "[a]bsent our receipt of a proper notice of disqualification within the time specified, the appointment of the proposed Arbitrator will be confirmed." ...

By the date specified in the AAA's cover letter, neither Schulman nor the APG parties filed a notice of disqualification, and the AAA confirmed the Arbitrator's appointment.... The claims to be arbitrated included not simply the claims alleged in Schulman's complaint and in the APG parties' arbitration demand, but all claims of any type. In relevant part, the agreement stated: "Such arbitration shall be final and binding, and judicial review shall be limited as provided by California Code of Civil Procedure § 1286.2 or other applicable law. The arbitrator shall apply, as applicable, federal or California substantive law and law of remedies. The arbitration shall be conducted in accordance with the AAA National Rules for the Resolution of Employment Disputes in effect at the time the Arbitration was initiated."

... On February 26, 2004, following closing arguments, the Arbitrator orally ruled in favor of the APG parties on certain of their claims, and awarded them approximately $1.5 million in damages. He found against Schulman on all of her claims. On May 12, 2004, the Arbitrator ruled that the APG parties were entitled to $1,878,739.15 in attorney fees and costs....

On May 27, 2004, ... the AAA faxed a letter to the attorneys for the APG parties and Schulman directing their attention to an enclosed "disclosure" from the Arbitrator. The disclosure was in the form of a letter dated May 26, 2004, from the Arbitrator to the AAA, regarding the Schulman arbitration, and a second arbitration entitled *California National Bank v. Kathleen Farnham and Farnham Security*. The Arbitrator wrote: "Pursuant to my telephone conversation with [two AAA representatives] this afternoon concerning the above cases, I am writing to you to clarify the disclosures made. In the *APG v. Cathy Schulman* case, I made a complete disclosure. In the California National Bank [case], I made a complete disclosure. In the APG case, the Claimant [APG parties] is represented by the Greenwald, Pauly firm, attorneys Andrew S. Pauly and Jeffrey J. Lewis [appearing]. In the California National Bank case, the Claimant is represented by the Greenwald, Pauly firm [the same firm representing the APG parties in the Schulman arbitration, but with], attorney Joshua D. Wayser [appearing]. [¶] Since I had made a complete disclosure in the California National Bank [case], including the fact that I was already in arbitration with the Greenwald, Pauly firm in the *APG v.*

Cathy Schulman case, I believed that the [AAA] case manager in the California National Bank case would send my disclosure to the case manager in the *APG v. Cathy Schulman* case to see if there were any objections to my accepting the California National Bank case. I received no objections in either case. I was appointed arbitrator in the California National Bank case and conducted a preliminary hearing on March 1, 2004. On May 19, 2004, the California National Bank case manager informed the parties that the case had been suspended since the deposits had not been paid pursuant to AAA rules.[¶] . . . In the event there is any problem, I would be willing to recuse myself from the California National Bank case without payment of any fee to me."

[. . .]

DISCUSSION

I. The Arbitrator Failed to Comply Timely with the Relevant Disclosure Obligations of California Standards 12 and 7

The APG parties contend that the Arbitrator's Disclosure Worksheet sent by the AAA on January 14, 2003, fully complied with the Arbitrator's disclosure obligations under the California Standards. . . . As we explain, the Worksheet did not contain the disclosure required by standard 12(b) of the California Standards. Further, without that disclosure, the Arbitrator's acceptance of employment in the California National Bank case violated a separate provision of the standards (standard 12(c)). Also, the Arbitrator's failure to disclose that employment within 10 calendar days violated two additional provisions (standards 7(c) and 7(d)(4)(A)(i)). We begin by summarizing the relevant provisions of the governing statutes and California Standards—provisions that are, to say the least, intricate.

A. The Requirements of the California Standards

Seeking to provide "minimum ethical standards and remedies for the arbitrator's failure to comply with existing disclosure requirements" . . . in 2001 the California legislature enacted revisions to the statutory duties of disclosure imposed on arbitrators in contractual arbitration. . . . As part of this revamping, the Legislature directed the California Judicial Council to "adopt ethical standards for all neutral arbitrators" effective July 1, 2002. . . . Further, the Legislature amended section 1281.9, subdivision (a) to provide that "[i]n any arbitration pursuant to an arbitration agreement, when a person is to serve as a neutral arbitrator, the proposed neutral arbitrator shall disclose all matters that could cause a person aware of the facts to reasonably entertain a doubt that the proposed neutral arbitrator would be able to be impartial." Among the statutory list of required disclosures in section 1281.9 is "[a]ny matters required to be disclosed by the ethics standards for neutral arbitrators adopted by the Judicial Council pursuant to this chapter." . . . Section 1281.9, subdivision (b) provides the statutory time period and method for the arbitrator's initial disclosure: "the proposed neutral arbitrator shall disclose all matters required to be disclosed pursuant to this section to all parties in writing within 10 calendar days of service of notice of the proposed nomination or appointment." . . .

The Judicial Council responded to the Legislature's mandate by adopting the California Standards effective July 1, 2002, later revised effective January 1, 2003. The standards "establish the minimum standards of conduct for neutral arbitrators" in contractual arbitration, and "are intended to guide the conduct of arbitrators, to inform and protect participants in arbitration, and to promote public confidence in the arbitration process." . . .

One concern the standards address is the "bias, or appearance of bias, that may flow from one side in an arbitration being a source or potential source of additional employment, and thus additional income, for the arbitrator." . . .

Standard 12 prohibits the arbitrator from entertaining or accepting an offer of employment "as a lawyer, an expert witness, or a consultant" from a party or lawyer in the pending arbitration. . . . However, it permits the arbitrator to entertain offers from the parties or their lawyers to serve in other capacities, if the arbitrator discloses that intent. Further, it grants the parties the right to disqualify the arbitrator based on such a disclosure. . . .

[. . .]

The primary disclosure provision of the California Standards is standard 7, which contains disclosure requirements applicable in all cases. As here relevant, it requires the arbitrator to disclose whether "[t]he arbitrator is serving . . . [a]s a neutral arbitrator in another prior *or pending* noncollective bargaining case involving a party to the current arbitration or a lawyer for a party." (Standard 7(d)(4)(A)(i), italics added.) As with all the topics covered by standard 7, this duty of disclosure is a continuing one. . . .

[. . .]

As pertinent to this case, the obligations imposed by these provisions may be summarized as follows: (1) if, while the current arbitration is pending, the arbitrator intends to entertain other offers of employment from the parties or their lawyers, the arbitrator must disclose that intention in writing within 10 calendar days of service of notice of the arbitrator's proposed nomination or appointment (standard 12(b)); (2) assuming this disclosure is made (and the arbitrator is not disqualified by a party), the arbitrator may accept such offers without the need for any further disclosure (standard 7(b)(2)); (3) assuming, however, that the arbitrator does *not* disclose an intent to entertain additional offers from the parties or their lawyers, the arbitrator *cannot* accept any such offer until the current arbitration is concluded (standard 12(c)); and (4) if, despite this prohibition, the arbitrator accepts such an offer, the arbitrator must disclose that fact to the parties in the current arbitration in writing (standard 7(d)(4)(A)(i)) within 10 calendar days (standard 7(c)).

[. . .]

C. The Arbitrator's Disclosure Worksheet Did Not Comply with Standard 12(b)

Missing from the Arbitrator's Disclosure Worksheet ... was any disclosure under standard 12(b)—that is, a declaration "if, while that arbitration is pending, [the arbitrator] will entertain offers of employment or new professional relationships ... from a party or a lawyer for a party." The document did contain the following instruction *to the arbitrator:* "You are not required to disclose an offer of employment or professional relationship from a party or lawyer in the arbitration or a lawyer or law firm that is currently associated in the private practice of law with a lawyer in the arbitration if you have informed the parties about the offer and have sought their consent as required by subdivision (d) of standard 10 of the Ethics Standards for Neutral Arbitrators."

The APG parties argue that the mere inclusion of this sentence adequately disclosed the Arbitrator's intent to accept future offers of employment from the parties or their lawyers while the Schulman arbitration was pending. As best we understand the logic, it is this: the sentence told the Arbitrator that he did not have to disclose offers from the parties or their lawyers if he complied with the consent procedure of former standard 10(d); FORMER STANDARD 10(d) applied only to "consumer arbitrations" as defined in the California Standards; Schulman's arbitration was *not* a consumer arbitration; therefore, by negative implication, Schulman should have understood that the Arbitrator *would* entertain offers of employment while *her* arbitration was pending.

[. . .]

Moreover, the California Standards "are to be construed and applied to further the[ir] purpose and intent ... and in conformance with all applicable law." (Standard 1(c).) The purpose and intent of the standards is "to guide the conduct of arbitrators, to inform and protect participants in arbitration, and to promote public confidence in the arbitration process." (Standard 1(a); see also *id.* at 1(b).) ... These objectives contemplate a disclosure under standard 12(b) that reasonably conveys the arbitrator's intent to entertain offers of employment from the parties or their lawyers. They do not contemplate the opaque, circuitous "disclosure" described by the APG parties....

D. The Arbitrator Did Not Comply with Standards 12(c), 7(c), and 7(d)(4)(A)(i)

Having failed to comply with standard 12(b), the Arbitrator was precluded from serving as an arbitrator in any other matter involving the parties or any lawyer for the parties until the Schulman arbitration was completed. (Standard 12(c).) However, apparently unaware of prohibition, the Arbitrator accepted appointment in the California National Bank case.... [W]hen appointed the Arbitrator knew that attorneys from the same law firm represented both California National Bank in its arbitration, and the APG parties in the Schulman arbitration. Further, as of his appointment in the California National Bank Case, the Schulman arbitration was still pending.... [H]e had not yet ruled on the APG parties' request for attorney fees or served his final arbitration award.

Besides being prohibited by standard 12(c), the Arbitrator's service in the California National Bank arbitration was a matter covered by the disclosure requirement of standard 7(d)(4)(A)(i)—service "[a]s a neutral arbitrator in another ... pending noncollective bargaining case [for] a lawyer for a party [to the current arbitration]." ... [T]he Arbitrator did not make any written disclosure until May 27, 2004, when the AAA faxed to the parties a copy of the Arbitrator's disclosure letter dated May 26, 2004, nearly three months after the date of the first hearing in the California National Bank case. By the date of the disclosure, the Arbitrator had orally ruled the APG parties were entitled to attorney fees, and had directed the APG parties to draft a proposed arbitration award.

II. *Section 1286.2 Requires the Vacating of the Arbitration Award*

Under California law, an arbitrator's failure to comply timely with his or her disclosure obligations risks a severe consequence: the vacating of any arbitration award rendered by the arbitrator. Section 1286.2(a)(6)(A) provides in relevant part that on a properly served and filed petition or response seeking to vacate an arbitration award ... "the court *shall* vacate the award if the court determines any of the following: [¶] ... [¶] (6) An arbitrator making the award ... (A) failed to disclose within the time required for disclosure a ground for disqualification of which the arbitrator was then aware." (Italics added.) On its face, the statute leaves no room for discretion. If a statutory ground for vacating the award exists, the trial court must vacate the award....

... These failures require that the arbitration award be vacated....

III. *Schulman Did Not Forfeit the Right to Vacate the Arbitration Award*

The APG parties contend that Schulman did not timely seek to disqualify the Arbitrator on the basis of his initial disclosure, and therefore forfeited her right to vacate the award based on any disclosure violation. The plain meaning of section 1281.91, which provides the statutory time frame for seeking disqualification of an arbitrator, defeats this contention.

[...]

Section 1281.91, subdivision (c) contains a limited provision under which a party is deemed to have waived the right to disqualify the arbitrator if the party fails to act within the 15–day time period provided in section 1281.91, subdivisions (a) or (b). Thus, section 1281.91, subdivision (c) provides in part: "The right of a party to disqualify a proposed neutral arbitrator pursuant to this section shall be waived if the party fails to serve the notice pursuant to the times set forth in this section [referring to the 15–calendar-day period of subds. (a) and (b)], *unless the proposed nominee or appointee makes a material omission or material misrepresentation in his or her disclosure.*" (Italics added.)

In the instant case, the Arbitrator's initial disclosure statement contained a material omission: it failed to disclose under standard 12(b) that he intended to entertain other offers of employment from the parties or their attorneys. Even if not initially material, it certainly became material when, in violation of standard 12(c), the Arbitrator accepted appointment in the California National Bank case, and failed timely to disclose it under standards 7(d)(4)(A)(i) and 7(c). Thus, although Schulman did not challenge the Arbitrator within 15 calendar days after the Arbitrator's initial disclosure, she did not waive her right to challenge him. The waiver rule of section 1281.91, subdivision (c) "manifestly applies only when the proposed arbitrator has made the requisite disclosure." . . .

[. . .]

V. The Federal Arbitration Act Does Not Preempt Section 1286.2(a)(6)(A)

The APG parties contend that even if the Arbitrator failed in his disclosure obligations, the failure does not require the vacating of the arbitration award. The reason: the FAA preempts California law governing the vacating of an arbitration award. We conclude, however, that a review of the relevant statutory language, the congressional purpose of the FAA, and the parties' arbitration agreement demonstrates that the FAA does not preempt section 1286.2(a)(6)(A).

"In 1925, Congress passed the FAA to 'overrule the judiciary's long-standing refusal to enforce agreements to arbitrate' and to place such agreements 'upon the same footing as other contracts, where it belongs.' "... The FAA applies to arbitrations held under arbitration clauses in written contracts "evidencing a transaction involving commerce." ... In the instant case, the parties agree that the FAA applies to the Schulman arbitration.

Section 10(a)(2) of the FAA provides in relevant part: "In any of the following cases the United States court in and for the district wherein the award was made may make an order vacating the award upon the application of any party to the arbitration—(2) Where there was *evident partiality* or corruption in the arbitrators, or either of them." (Italics added.) The APG parties contend that section 10(a)(2) of the FAA preempts application of section 1286.2(a)(6)(A) in two ways. First, according to the APG parties, the "evident partiality" standard of section 10(a)(2) of the FAA permits the vacating of an arbitration award for inadequate disclosure only if the undisclosed facts create a "reasonable impression of partiality." ... The APG parties assert that this standard preempts section 1286.2(a)(6)(A), which mandates the vacating of an arbitration award for *any* violation of California disclosure obligations, regardless of whether the undisclosed facts create a reasonable impression of partiality. Second, when a party has constructive knowledge of a ground for disqualification but remains silent, the APG parties argue that the waiver rule of *Fidelity Federal Bank, supra,* 386 F.3d at page 1313, preempts section 1286.2(a)(6)(A).

We quickly dispose of the second purported area of preemption—the Ninth Circuit's holding in *Fidelity.* It is not clear whether the *Fidelity* waiver rule has its roots in section 10(a)(2) of the FAA, or whether it is a judicially created procedural principle independent of the statute. Of course, if the rule is judicially created without a basis in the statute, it likely cannot be a predicate for federal preemption through the FAA.... Moreover, as the *Fidelity* opinion notes, "[s]everal federal courts hold that a party's failure to object to the real or evident partiality of an arbitrator before an award is issued does not waive the challenge *unless the party had real, actual knowledge of the conflict.*" ... Thus, even if the *Fidelity* rule of waiver based on constructive knowledge derives from section 10(a)(2) of the FAA, the rule is not a universally accepted principle. As we have noted, decisions of the Ninth Circuit are no more persuasive in California than decisions of other circuits.... More importantly, in the instant case, the only evidence that would arguably support application of *Fidelity* was presented in the declarations filed in support of the APG parties' motion for reconsideration. The trial court, however, declined to credit those declarations, and we will not set that determination aside.... Thus, deciding whether *Fidelity* preempts California law is of no consequence to this appeal.... Finally, even if the *Fidelity* waiver rule is a proper predicate for preemption deriving from section 10(a)(2) of the FAA, and even if it were material to this appeal, it could have no greater preemptive effect than section 10(a)(2) itself. For all these reasons, we decline to discuss *Fidelity* further. We will rest our decision on consideration of the preemptive effect of section 10(a)(2) alone.

A. *The Relevant Statutory Language of the FAA Applies to Federal District Courts*

Our discussion of the first ground of preemption asserted by the APG parties—preemption by the evident partiality standard of section 10(a)(2) of the FAA—requires some preliminary qualification. There is considerable debate among the federal circuits concerning the proper test of evident partiality under section 10(a)(2).... Understanding the uncertainty, we will assume that the Ninth Circuit's "reasonable impression of partiality" test is the correct definition.... That assumption in place, the answer to whether section 10(a)(2) of the FAA preempts California law lies in the relevant statutory language of the FAA, the purpose of that legislation, and the parties' arbitration agreement.

In cases to which it applies, the FAA has a "limited preemptive effect" on state law.... "'The FAA contains no express pre-emptive provision, nor does it reflect a congressional intent to occupy the entire field of arbitration.'" But even when Congress has not completely displaced state regulation in an area, state law may nonetheless be preempted to the extent that it actually conflicts with federal law—that is, to the extent that it "stands as an obstacle to the accomplishment and execution of the full purposes and objectives of Congress." . . .

One guide to congressional intent is the plain meaning of the federal statutory language. The language of the relevant sections of the FAA—sections 10 and 12—strongly suggest that they apply only in federal court proceedings. Section 10(a) states the statutory grounds under the FAA for vacating an arbitration award upon application of a party. It expressly refers to orders to vacate made by "the United States court in and for the district wherein the award was made." Similarly, subdivision (b) of section 10, which governs the vacating of an award issued under 5 United States Code section 580, provides that "[t]he United States district court for the district wherein the award was made" may vacate the award. Section 12 of the FAA provides the procedure for presenting a motion to vacate. . . .

B. Section 1286. 2(a)(6)(A) is not Inconsistent With the Purpose of the FAA

As the California Supreme Court has recognized, absent an express preemption provision, federal statutory language does not resolve the question of preemption. . . . Courts must also consider the broader objectives of the federal legislation.

Both the California and United States Supreme Courts have held that Congress intended the FAA to ensure that arbitration agreements are enforced according to their own terms, thereby encouraging the use of private arbitration as a means of resolving disputes. . . . Thus, the FAA "establishes that, as a matter of federal law, any doubts concerning the scope of arbitrable issues should be resolved in favor of arbitration, whether the problem at hand is the construction of the contract language itself or an allegation of waiver, delay, or a like defense to arbitrability." The policy of enforceability established by section 2 of the FAA is binding on state courts as well as federal courts. However, the FAA's purpose is not to provide special status for arbitration agreements, but only "to make arbitration agreements as enforceable as other contracts, but not more so." . . . Further, "[n]othing in the legislative reports and debates [concerning the FAA] evidences a congressional intention that postaward and state court litigation rules be preempted so long as the basic policy upholding the enforceability of arbitration agreements remained in full force and effect." . . .

By its terms, section 1286.2(a)(6)(A) does not undermine the enforceability of arbitration agreements. It neither limits the rights of contracting parties to submit disputes to arbitration, nor discourages persons from using arbitration. Section 1286.2(a)(6)(A) merely requires the vacating of an award if the arbitrator failed timely to disclose a ground for disqualification of which he was aware. Indeed, because it applies to vacating an arbitration award, section 1286.2(a)(6)(A) presupposes that the arbitration agreement has been enforced and the arbitration held. If an award is vacated, the result is not a preclusion of further arbitration, but rather a new arbitration held in accordance with the disclosure requirements.

[. . .]

The APG parties contend that section 1286.2(a)(6)(A) violates the purpose of the FAA because it "undermines the entire arbitration process, allowing a party to seize upon a technicality to vacate an arbitration award." In fashioning the disclosure requirements, however, the Judicial Council has made a reasoned effort to list matters that "could cause a person aware of the facts to reasonably entertain a doubt that the proposed neutral arbitrator would be able to be impartial." . . . Indeed, the declared legislative purpose of section 1286.2(a)(6)(A) is to give statutory voice to "existing case law which provides that an arbitration award may be vacated when a neutral arbitrator fails to disclose a matter that might cause a reasonable person to question the ability of the arbitrator to conduct the arbitration proceeding impartially." . . .

[. . .]

C. Application of Section 1286.2(a)(6)(A) is Not Inconsistent With The Parties' Arbitration Agreement

"There is no federal policy favoring arbitration under a certain set of procedural rules; the federal policy is simply to ensure the enforceability, according to their terms, of private agreements to arbitrate." . . . In the instant case, the vacating of the arbitration award is not inconsistent with the parties' objectively expressed intent in their correspondence and arbitration agreement. . . .

The trial court compelled arbitration of Schulman's claims against the StudioCanal/APG Venture, but not her claims against the other APG parties. In a letter dated January 7, 2003, Schulman and the APG parties informed the AAA that they accepted the Arbitrator's appointment "subject to all of the disclosure requirements imposed on [the Arbitrator] by the American Arbitration Association *and the California Code of Civil Procedure.*" (Italics added.) The AAA responded by forwarding to the parties a copy of the Arbitrator Disclosure Worksheet. The worksheet had been completed by the Arbitrator, and purported to comply with sections 1281.9 and 1281.95, as well as the California Standards. Thus, from the outset of the arbitration proceeding, the parties contemplated that the California disclosure requirements applied, in addition to AAA disclosure requirements.

[. . .]

The April 2003 arbitration agreement provided in relevant part: "Such arbitration shall be final and binding, *and judicial review shall be limited as provided by California Code of Civil Procedure § 1286.2 or other applicable law.*" (Italics added.) Of course, section 1286.2 prescribes the grounds on which an arbitration award shall be vacated, including the grounds of subdivision (a)(6)(A). Given the parties' expectation that California disclosure rules applied, they necessarily understood that the arbitration award could be vacated under section 1286.2(a)(6)(A) for a violation of the disclosure requirements.

The APG parties note that the April 2003 agreement also stated that the arbitration would be "conducted in accordance with the AAA National Rules for the Resolution of Employment Disputes in effect at the time the Arbitration was initiated." Because the AAA rules contain provisions governing disqualification of arbitrators, the APG parties contend that vacating the arbitration award under section 1286.2(a)(6)(A) for a violation of the California Standards would be inconsistent with the parties' contract. The relevant extrinsic evidence, however, does not support the contention. As we have discussed, that evidence shows that the parties contemplated that both AAA *and* California disclosure rules would apply. Further, the agreement provided that judicial review of the arbitration award would occur under section 1286.2 or other applicable law. To the extent there is any conflict on the subject of judicial review between this specific term and the more general provision that the arbitration would be governed by AAA rules, the specific provision controls. . . .

[. . .]

DISPOSITION

The orders vacating the arbitration award and denying reconsideration are *affirmed*.

NOTES AND QUESTIONS

1.   The opinion is characteristic of the rulings of California courts of appeal: Lengthy, thorough, and involved. The reasoning, however, is less than disinterested or detached. Do you agree with this assessment? Is there an underlying objective to how the court frames the issue and engages in the discussion of the law?

2.   Does the opinion indicate an anti-arbitration bias? Is the bias, if it does exist, commanded by the relevant legislation? Does that factor make it less of a bias and less prejudicial? Could the court reach another result in light of the applicable law?

3.   Is there any support for concluding that California disfavors the recourse to arbitration? Does the state in its laws and judicial rulings endorse arbitration? Explain your view.

4.   What is the gravamen of the regulations established by the California Judicial Council in regard to arbitrator disclosures. Is the approach drastic? Does it propound surreptitiously a particular ideology? Does it assume that California is forced to tolerate arbitration by federal law?

5.   To the extent that the arbitrator disclosure standards foster the vacatur of arbitral awards—or at least make that result more likely—they impinge upon FAA § 10 and also upon the "prime directive" of FAA § 2. Is it possible to allege with any credibility that the result under California law is not in conflict with the dictates of federal law?

6. How persuasive do you find the court's analysis of the federal preemption issue? Is the conclusion reached sustained principally or even exclusively by judicial fiat? The nonjudicial reality appears to be forcefully otherwise.

7. Can the California arbitrator disclosure standards be reconciled with FAA § 10 and the evident partiality ground? With *Commonwealth Coatings*? How? Is any possible accommodation likely to be strained and artificial? Does a state of belligerence exist between California law and federal law on this score? Is the belligerence both obdurate and characterized by irreconcilably different positions? Which side is likely to win when and if the skirmish escalates to actual warfare?

POSITIVE SOFTWARE SOLUTIONS, INC. v. NEW CENTURY MORTGAGE CORP.

436 F.3d 495 (5th Cir. 2006).

REAVLEY, Circuit Judge:

The question here is whether an arbitrator's failure to disclose that seven years before the arbitration, he and his former law firm were co-counsel in a lengthy litigation matter with one of the law firms and counsel in this matter, justifies vacating the award. We hold that the arbitrator was required to disclose the relationship because it might have created an impression of possible bias, and we affirm the district court's judgment vacating the arbitration award; but we vacate the portion of the district court's judgment that regulates a subsequent arbitration.

I.

A.

New Century Mortgage Corporation ("New Century") is in the mortgage business. It generates business through telephone contacts with prospective borrowers. Positive Software Solutions, Inc. ("Positive Software") develops, markets, and manufactures computer-software products for the mortgage industry. It developed "LoanForce," a software product that is a relational database for use in the mortgage lending business. Positive Software licensed LoanForce to New Century pursuant to a Software Subscription Agreement ("SSA"). Positive Software learned that New Century was allegedly copying LoanForce and was incorporating it into different software products. Thereafter, Positive Software filed this lawsuit alleging, *inter alia,* claims of copyright infringement, theft of trade secrets, breach of contract, seeking specific performance, money damages, and preliminary and permanent injunctive relief. The district court granted Positive Software's motion for a preliminary injunction enjoining New Century from using LoanForce. In addition, the district court compelled arbitration pursuant to the SSA.

B.

Arbitration of this matter took place under the auspices of the American Arbitration Association ("AAA"). Pursuant to AAA procedures, the AAA provided the parties with a list of candidate arbitrators, along with their *curricula vitae,* and requested that the parties rank the candidates. Both parties provided their lists of acceptable arbitrators to the AAA, ranking them in the order of preference as instructed. . . .

The AAA contacted [party chosen arbitrator] Shurn by letter to determine his availability. That letter listed the names of the parties and counsel, including designating Susman Godfrey L.L.P. ("Susman Godfrey") as the firm representing New Century, and one if its partners, Ophelia F. Camiña, as New Century's arbitration counsel. At the bottom of the letter, there was an "important reminder" advising arbitrators of their "obligation to disclose any circumstance likely to affect impartiality or create an appearance of partiality." The same "important reminder" appeared in two subsequent letters addressed to Shurn.

Shurn signed and returned the standard "Notice of Appointment" form to the AAA, which advised arbitrators to "please disclose any past or present relationship with the parties, their counsel, or potential witnesses, direct or indirect, whether financial, professional, social or any other kind. . . ." That letter included twelve questions to assist arbitrators in determining whether any "past or present relationship" required disclosure, including the following question, "Have you had any professional or social relationship with counsel for any party in this proceeding or with the firms for which they work?" Shurn indicated that he had nothing to disclose.

After a seven-day hearing, in a written ruling, Shurn found that New Century did not infringe Positive Software's copyrights, did not misappropriate Positive Software's trade secrets, did not breach the SSA, and did not defraud or conspire against Positive Software. Shurn ordered that Positive Software take nothing.

C.

Following the arbitration award, Positive Software conducted a detailed investigation into Shurn's background. It discovered that Shurn and his former law firm, Arnold White & Durkee ("Arnold White"), had been involved in a professional relationship with Susman Godfrey and Camiña, New Century's arbitration counsel, for a period of time.

Soon thereafter, Positive Software filed a motion to vacate the arbitration award. The district court granted Positive Software's motion on the ground that Shurn failed to disclose that he had "served as co-counsel with New Century's counsel over a period of years in significant litigation," and that this prior relationship "might create a reasonable impression of possible bias." Further, Shurn's "failure to disclose that relationship deprived Positive Software of the opportunity to make an informed choice of arbitrators and requires vacatur of the award."

[. . .]

The district court further found that had Positive Software been aware of Shurn's prior relationship with Susman Godfrey and Camiña, it would not have ranked Shurn highly, and he would not have been chosen as the arbitrator. The district court outlined the numerous reminders and opportunities that Shurn had to disclose his past professional relationship with Susman Godfrey and Camiña, and that he failed to do so.

The district court held that any reasonable lawyer selecting a sole arbitrator for arbitration would have wanted to know that the arbitrator chosen had a prior association with opposing counsel, given the contentious nature of the dispute between the parties and the duration and importance of the prior litigation with which both arbitrator and opposing counsel were associated. . . .

II.

We review a district court's decision to vacate an arbitration award under the same standard as any other district court decision. We accept findings of fact that are not clearly erroneous and decide questions of law *de novo*. We also review the application of law to fact *de novo*.

III.

A.

Congress promulgated the United States Arbitration Act . . . in 1925 to delineate the thorny relationship between the role of private arbitration and the federal courts. Section 10 of the Act provides the grounds upon which a court may vacate an arbitrator's award, and for our purposes, states that such a basis exists "[w]here there was evident partiality . . . in the arbitrator[ ] . . . ."

Deciding what constitutes "evident partiality" in an arbitrator and the use of "undue means" has proved troublesome. The case law in this area is confusing and complicated. While this court has not previously determined the scope of this standard,[20] numerous courts in other jurisdictions, including the Supreme Court, have done so. We analyze those cases.

The case of *Commonwealth Coatings Corp. v. Continental Cas. Co.* involved an arbitration panel composed of two arbitrators chosen by each of the parties and a third "neutral" arbitrator who had previously worked for one of the parties to the arbitration. The neutral arbitrator voted with the panel for an award in favor of the party with whom he had done business. Thereafter, the party that lost the arbitration challenged the award, claiming that the failure of the arbitrator to disclose his significant business relationship resulted in "evident partiality" under 9 U.S.C. § 10, warranting vacatur of the award.

Justice Black, in delivering the Court's opinion, concluded that the arbitrator's failure to disclose warranted vacating the award for evident

---

20. The closest this court came to addressing the "evident partiality" standard was in *Bernstein Seawell & Kove v. Bosarge,* 813 F.2d 726 (5th Cir.1987). There, this court stated in dicta that the "appearance of bias" is insufficient to warrant vacatur. *Id.* at 732. The standard for vacating an arbitration award for evident partiality has not been definitively addressed in this circuit.

partiality even though there was no evidence of actual bias. The Court noted that arbitrators are not expected to sever ties with the business world, but nevertheless, it must be scrupulous in safeguarding the impartiality of arbitrators, as they have "completely free rein to decide the law as well as the facts and are not subject to appellate review." As a result, the Court imposed "the simple requirement that arbitrators disclose to the parties any dealings that might create an impression of possible bias."

In a concurring opinion, Justice White, joined by Justice Marshall, specifically stated that he joined the Court's "majority opinion," and he emphasized that the parties must be cognizant of all non-trivial relationships in order to exercise full and fair judgment. Justice White agreed on a rule of full disclosure. . . .

Although Justice White indicated that he was "glad to join" Justice Black's opinion and that he desired to make "additional remarks," and Justice Black's opinion was designated the "opinion of the court," some lower federal courts have seen a conflict between the two writings. Accordingly, by treating Justice Black's opinion as a plurality opinion, some courts have felt free to reject Justice Black's statement that "evident partiality" is met by an "appearance of bias," and to apply a much narrower standard.

An early example of this occurred in *Morelite Constr. Corp* . . . . There, the court referred to Justice Black's opinion as a mere plurality of four justices and read much of that opinion as *dicta*. The court reasoned that something more than an "appearance of bias" was necessary to disqualify an arbitrator, but this was not a case of failure to disclose. Other federal circuits have adopted a similar "evident partiality" standard.[33]

Other federal circuits, centering on the need for full disclosure to parties who are choosing their own arbitrators, have adopted a much broader standard. One such case is *Schmitz,* wherein the Ninth Circuit held that an arbitrator had a duty to disclose that his law firm had represented the parent company of a party to the arbitration. After determining that Justice Black's opinion in *Commonwealth Coatings* was controlling precedent, the court stated that the "best expression" of the Supreme Court's holding is that evident partiality exists when "undisclosed facts show a reasonable impression of partiality." The court discussed the important distinction between cases in which actual bias is alleged and those involving allegations of failure to disclose, observing that

---

33. *See Peoples Sec. Life Ins. Co. v. Monumental Life Ins. Co.,* 991 F.2d 141, 146 (4th Cir.1993) (adopting the *Morelite* standard and holding that the arbitrator was unaware of the questioned relationship); *Apperson,* 879 F.2d at 1358 (adopting the *Morelite* standard and holding that the objection to the arbitrator had been waived); *Nationwide Mut. Ins. Co. v. Home Ins. Co.,* 429 F.3d 640 (6th Cir.2005) (declining to deviate from *Apperson*); *Health Servs. Mgmt. Corp. v. Hughes,* 975 F.2d 1253, 1264 (7th Cir.1992) (holding that the objection to the arbitrator was waived); *Ormsbee Dev. Co. v. Grace,* 668 F.2d 1140, 1147 (10th Cir.1982) ("only clear evidence of impropriety [ ] justifies the denial of summary confirmation of an arbitration award. . . . For an award to be set aside, the evidence of bias or interest of an arbitrator must be direct, definite and capable of demonstration rather than remote, uncertain or speculative.") (internal citations omitted); *ANR Coal Co., Inc. v. Cogentrix of N. Carolina, Inc.,* 173 F.3d 493, 500 (4th Cir.1999) (holding that mere nondisclosure does not itself justify vacatur).

although the "reasonable impression of partiality" standard may not be appropriate in actual bias cases (though it has, confusingly, been used by some courts in those cases), it is the correct standard for nondisclosure cases:

> The policies of 9 U.S.C. § 10 ... support the notion that the standard for nondisclosure cases should differ from that used in actual bias cases. In a nondisclosure case, the integrity of the process by which arbitrators are chosen is at issue. Showing a "reasonable impression of partiality" is sufficient in a nondisclosure case because the policy of section 10(a)(2) instructs that the parties should choose their arbitrators intelligently. The parties can choose their arbitrators intelligently only when facts showing potential partiality are disclosed. Whether the arbitrators' decision itself is faulty is not necessarily relevant. But in an actual bias determination, the integrity of the arbitrators' decision is directly at issue. That a reasonable impression of partiality is present does not mean the arbitration was the product of impropriety.

[. . .]

B.

Having analyzed the case law, we address what standard to apply in this case. This is a nondisclosure case in which the parties chose the arbitrator. Striking the balance of the competing goals of expertise and impartiality in the selection process, maintaining faithfulness to the Court's opinion in *Commonwealth Coatings,* and agreeing with the policy arguments set out in *Schmitz,* we hold that an arbitrator selected by the parties displays evident partiality by the very failure to disclose facts that might create a reasonable impression of the arbitrator's partiality. The evident partiality is demonstrated from the nondisclosure, regardless of whether actual bias is established.

Such a demanding disclosure rule ensures that the parties will be privy to a potential arbitrator's biases at the outset, when they are "free to reject the arbitrator or accept him with knowledge of the relationship and continuing faith in his objectivity," and allow the parties, who are "far better informed of the prevailing ethical standards and reputations within their business," to be the "architects of their own arbitration process." A simple disclosure requirement minimizes the role of the courts in weighing arbitrators' potential conflicts, and at the same time, minimizes the discretion of the arbitrators in determining what to reveal. In addition, as the district court stated, "the full disclosure rule of *Commonwealth Coatings* reinforces the parties' expectations that arbitrators will abide by the Rule of the American Arbitration Association (and related rules), which the Supreme Court deemed 'highly significant.'"

The standard we adopt comports with Canon II of the AAA's Code of Ethics for Arbitrators in Commercial Disputes ("Code of Ethics"), which provides, in relevant part:

A. Persons who are requested to serve as arbitrators should, before accepting, disclose:

* * *

(2) Any existing or past financial, business, professional, family or social relationships which are likely to affect impartiality or which might reasonably create any appearance of partiality or bias. . . .

* * *

B. The obligation to disclose interests or relationships described in the preceding paragraph A is a continuing duty which requires a person who accepts appointment as an arbitrator to disclose, at any stage of the arbitration, any such interests or relationships which may arise, or which are recalled or discovered.

We note that we are not adopting an inflexible *per se* rule in nondisclosure cases. While an arbitrator to be selected by the parties need not disclose relationships that are trivial, an arbitrator should always err in favor of disclosure.

C.

We now apply the standard we adopt to the facts of this case. Based on the facts of this case, New Century contends that no matter what standard this court adopts, including the standard above, Positive Software cannot meet that standard. We disagree.

[. . .]

After reviewing the facts, we hold, like the district court did, that Shurn's past professional relationship with Susman Godfrey and Camiña might have conveyed an impression of possible partiality to a reasonable person. It is important to remember that the issue is only whether Shurn's prior professional relationship might reasonably give someone who is considering his services as an arbitrator the impression that he might favor one litigant over the other. It is not hard to think that Positive Software might not want to employ his services in an arbitration hearing with New Century once it discovered his prior relationship with the law firm and counsel representing New Century. On the other hand, Positive Software might decide that Shurn's qualifications as an arbitrator outweigh whatever concerns it might have. The point is simply that the information should have been disclosed to Positive Software so that it could make that decision. The integrity of the arbitral process demands no less.

New Century argues that a finding of evident partiality under the facts of this case would make the job of finding a qualified arbitrator burdensome and would disqualify most attorneys from large firms from acting as arbitrators. We disagree. Qualified arbitrators would not be disqualified from acting as arbitrators, rather, they would merely have to disclose their past relationships, and then it would be for the parties to decide whether, based on the disclosure, the arbitrator merits objection.

We conclude that the district court properly vacated the arbitration award by reason of Shurn's failure to reveal to the parties his prior professional relationship with Susman Godfrey and Camiña. We hasten to add that we do not imply that Shurn was guilty of any wrongdoing or that he was in fact biased or influenced by reason of the relationship. Nevertheless, as Justice Black emphasized in *Commonwealth Coatings,* such relationships must be disclosed to the parties if the integrity and effectiveness of the arbitration process is to be preserved.

IV.

New Century maintains that Positive Software waived its nondisclosure objection by failing to raise the issue until after the arbitration award. The district court found that Positive Software was unaware of the undisclosed relationship until after the arbitration, and accordingly, held that Positive Software did not waive its objection to the nondisclosure.

This court has not considered the issue of waiver of a nondisclosure objection. Our sister circuits require *actual knowledge* of an arbitrator's potential partiality on the part of the complaining party prior to the arbitration proceeding as foundational to waiver.[50] We agree with our sister circuits and hold that one must have actual knowledge of the presence of a conflict of interest before one can waive the conflict. To hold otherwise, would turn the arbitration process on its head by shifting the onus from requiring an arbitrator to assume the duty of disclosure to requiring a party to assume a duty to investigate.

Turning to the facts of this case, there is no evidence that Positive Software had actual knowledge of Shurn's past professional relationship with Susman Godfrey and Camiña.... Based on these facts, we will not disturb the district court's finding that Positive Software did not learn of the professional relationship until after the arbitration, and therefore, did not waive its objection to the nondisclosure.

V.

In vacating the arbitration award, the district court ordered that in the second arbitration, the parties must refrain from certain practices, including referring to any ruling of the first arbitrator and advising the new arbitrator of the first arbitrator's award. New Century argues that the district court did not have the authority to dictate procedures for a second arbitration. We agree and hold that the district court erred in specifying procedures for the second arbitration. Here, the district court

---

50. *See, e.g., Apperson,* 879 F.2d at 1359 (affirming the district court's conclusion that, "as a general rule, a grievant must object to an arbitrator's partiality at the arbitration hearing before such an objection will be considered by the federal courts" but highlighting that "[t]he successful party ... may not rely on the failure to object for bias ... unless '[a]ll the facts now argued as to [the] alleged bias were known ... at the time the joint committee heard their grievances' "); *Middlesex,* 675 F.2d at 1204 ("Waiver applies only where a party has acted with full knowledge of the facts.").

lacked authority to go beyond vacating the award and dictating how the parties and the arbitrator should proceed in the second arbitration.

VI.

The district court's judgment vacating the arbitration award is modified to vacate the portion of the district court's judgment that regulates a subsequent arbitration and, as modified, is affirmed.

NOTES AND QUESTIONS

1. How does *Positive Software* compare to *Ovitz*, the preceding case? In light of the reasoning in *Positive Software*, do the California regulations on arbitrator disclosure still conflict, in your view, with the evident partiality ground in FAA § 10? Why or why not? Is the Fifth Circuit faithful to *Commonwealth Coating*? Is *Positive Software* an appearance of or actual bias case? Does the arbitrator fail to reveal relevant information in order to secure the appointment? Is that circumstance the true aim of evident partiality?

2. How do you assess the AAA's twelve-question form? What is the purpose of the document? Is it likely to be effective? How would you advise prospective arbitrators and clients?

3. In your evaluation of the case law, you should remember that the consequence of a finding of evident partiality results in the vacatur of the award. There is no possibility of retrieval or other means of lessening the consequences of the finding. The award is absolutely null and without effect. Also, there is no arbitrator malpractice. Therefore, the only available relief is to begin another arbitration and select more professional arbitrators.

4. Do you agree with the court's evaluation of the non-disclosure circumstances in *Positive Software*? Is the evaluation too dogmatic and doctrinaire? Does the court appear convinced that the flaw corrupted the entire process? Is the court applying *Commonwealth Coatings*? How? Does *ad hoc* circumstantial evaluation of the specific facts become a part of the applicable calculus?

5. Does the use of evident partiality become a means of post-award appeal? Does it allow a disappointed party to cover its initial gamble?

6. Did the challenging party wait too long to state its opposition to the arbitrator? When should such challenges be made?

7. How does the factor of the number of arbitrators work in the context of evident partiality? Are there, and should there be, different standards for different arbitrators and arbitral tribunals? Explain.

8. The case contains a good summary of the "complex" and "confusing" case law on this issue. Explain the law to a novice associate or client. Is the applicable standard statutory or decisional? Are disclosures instrumental? Do they, once made, absolve the arbitrator of any failing in regard to impartiality? How does the reasonable person gauge factor into the process? Do presumptions exist? Is timing important?

4. MANIFEST DISREGARD OF THE LAW

RODRIGUEZ v. PRUDENTIAL–BACHE SECURITIES, INC.

882 F.Supp. 1202, 1209 (D.P.R. 1995).

(footnotes omitted)

[. . .]

Prudential's next contention is that the award represents a manifest disregard of the law. In essence, Prudential argues that claimants were terminated for "just cause," in accordance with Commonwealth Law 80, . . . which provides the exclusive remedy for wrongfully discharged employees, and therefore are not entitled to any compensation. The "manifest disregard" language derives from *dicta* employed by the U.S. Supreme Court in *Wilko v. Swan* . . . . *See Advest, Inc.* at 9 n.5. "The lane of review that has opened out of this language is a judicially created one, not to be found in 9 U.S.C. § 10." *Id.*

In *Advest, Inc.*, the First Circuit identified two classes of cases where an arbitral award is subject to review under this standard. The first category, usually involving labor arbitration, is where an award is contrary to the plain language of the collective bargaining agreement. *Advest, Inc.* at 9. The second category involves instances where it is clear from the record that the arbitrator recognized the applicable law—and then ignored it. *Id.* As in *Advest*, Prudential is making a claim of the second type, asserting that the arbitrators' award is so irreconcilable with the provisions of Law 80 that the panel must have disregarded the law, and "embarked on a flight of fancy." *Id.* at 10. As expressly stated by the court in *Advest* however, the hurdle is a high one. In order to vacate an arbitration award, there must be some showing in the record, other than the result obtained, that the arbitrators knew the law and expressly disregarded it. *Id.* . . . . The court construed the term "disregard" to imply that the arbitrators appreciated the existence of a governing legal rule but willfully decided not to apply it. [*Id.*] As arbitrators need not explain the reasons justifying their award, and did not do so in this case, "it is no wonder that [Prudential] is hard pressed to satisfy the exacting criteria for invocation of the doctrine." *Id.*

Prudential's argument that it had just cause to terminate its relationship with claimants was considered and, judging from the award, rejected by the arbitrators. Furthermore, it is not disputed that Law 80 was not the only cause of action asserted by claimants in their quest for relief. Nor is it contested that claimants presented evidence regarding damages under Law 80 which directly contradicted that which was presented by Prudential. We therefore decline Prudential's invitation to revisit the merits of their factual contentions regarding just cause and the damages resulting from the termination of claimants.

[. . .]

NOTES AND QUESTIONS

1. The excerpt from *Rodriguez* provides a straightforward and basically accurate representation of the status and function of the "manifest disregard" basis for review. The reference to *Advest* explains the role of "manifest disregard" in the setting of labor arbitration and illustrates that it is available against any type of arbitral award "when it is clear from the record that the arbitrator recognized the applicable law—and then ignored it." Given this description of the means of recourse, the standard set of concerns surface. Should "manifest disregard" be available outside the context of labor arbitration, especially when the standard practice in nonlabor domestic arbitration is to render awards without opinions? Does the ground's origination in the *dicta* of *Wilko v. Swan* justify making it applicable in all arbitral contexts? Even assuming a wide application, shouldn't "manifest disregard" be employed only when the award involves the application of statutory law? What other rationale might there be for "manifest disregard" when the governing statute (Section Ten of the FAA) excludes any possibility of a review of the merits of awards?

2. In any event, the elements of the ground make it difficult to invoke: (1) there must be a record, and (2) that record must indicate clearly that the arbitrator (a) recognized the law and (b) disregarded it in reaching a determination. None of these elements is readily established. The award may not be accompanied by an opinion and usually there is no transcript of the proceedings. Few arbitrators are likely to provide a written statement of the applicable law and then reach a determination that completely ignores it as a guiding principle. Commercial arbitrators may describe the law or apply it in a judicially erroneous manner, but they are not likely simply to dismiss it once it has been presented and argued, unless they are authorized by the parties to rule as amiable compositors. Amiable compositors are given the right by the contract of arbitration to decide the matter according to their own sense of justice, provided they find the legal answer and then conclude it is unjust or untoward. Essentially, amiable compositors rule in equity after they discover the law and reject it. Outside the context of labor or maritime arbitration, "manifest disregard" appears to be misplaced and to have an obtuse function.

3. The *Advest* court notes that, if arbitrators do not render reasons with the award, the party challenging the award on the basis of "manifest disregard" is extremely unlikely to prevail. On this basis, the court in *Rodriguez* concludes that the attempt to vacate the award for "manifest disregard" constitutes an unwarranted invitation to the court to "revisit the merits" of the litigation. Do you agree with these assessments? How demanding is the court's scrutiny of the available record? Would you ever pursue "manifest disregard" as a remedy for your client?

BARAVATI v. JOSEPHTHAL, LYON & ROSS, INC.

28 F.3d 704, 706 (7th Cir. 1994).

[. . .]

Judicial review of arbitration awards is tightly limited; perhaps it ought not be called "review" at all. By including an arbitration clause in their contract the parties agree to submit disputes arising out of the contract to a nonjudicial forum, and we do not allow the disappointed party to bring his dispute into court by the back door, arguing that he is entitled to appellate review of the arbitrators' decision.... There are, nevertheless, limited grounds on which an arbitral award can be set aside, such as that the arbitrators "exceeded their powers."...

A number of courts, including our own, have said that they can set aside arbitral awards if the arbitrators exhibited a "manifest disregard of the law." ...Two courts, however, have declined to adopt this formula,...though without rejecting it. Two have criticized it.... This formula is dictum, as no one has found a case where, had it not been intoned, the result would have been different. It originated in *Wilko v. Swan*,...a case the Supreme Court first criticized for mistrust of arbitration and confined to its narrowest possible holding...and then overruled.... Created *ex nihilo* to be a nonstatutory ground for setting aside arbitral awards, the *Wilko* formula reflects precisely that mistrust of arbitration for which the Court in its two *Shearson/American* opinions criticized *Wilko*. We can understand neither the need for the formula nor the role that it plays in judicial review of arbitration (we suspect none—that it is just words). If it is meant to smuggle review for clear error in by the back door, it is inconsistent with the entire modern law of arbitration. If it is intended to be synonymous with the statutory formula that it most nearly resembles—whether the arbitrators "exceeded their powers"—it is superfluous and confusing. There is enough confusion in the law. The grounds for setting aside arbitration awards are exhaustively stated in the statute. Now that *Wilko* is history, there is no reason to continue to echo its gratuitous attempt at nonstatutory supplementation. So it will be enough in this case to consider whether the arbitrators exceeded their powers.

[. . .]

NOTES AND QUESTIONS

1. *Baravati* is one of the more interesting judicial variations on the theme of the judicial supervision of awards and on the concept of "manifest disregard." What do you think of the court's assertion that the judicial supervision of arbitral awards does not or should not constitute "judicial review"? What term or description do you think might be more appropriate or accurate?

2. The court justifies the limited availability of judicial scrutiny in terms of the need for arbitral autonomy. What are the other elements of its justification?

3.   The court then engages in a critical review of the origins and function of the "manifest disregard" basis for review. It not only emerged from a suspect source and in suspect circumstances, but is also useless, redundant, and confusing. Do you agree? Did "manifest disregard" die with the reversal of *Wilko* in *Rodriguez*?

PATTEN v. SIGNATOR INS. AGENCY, INC.

441 F.3d 230 (4th Cir.), *cert. denied* 127 S.Ct. 434 (2006).

KING, Circuit Judge:

Appellant Ralph F. Patten, Jr., appeals from the district court's denial of his motion to vacate an arbitration award rendered in favor of John Hancock Mutual Life Insurance Company, Signator Insurance Agency, Incorporated, and Signator Investors, Incorporated (collectively the "respondents").... By this appeal, Patten seeks only to vacate that aspect of the arbitration award dismissing as time-barred his claims against Signator Investors. Patten asserts that the arbitrator acted without authority when he unilaterally imposed an implied one-year limitations period onto the governing arbitration agreement between Patten and Signator Investors. As explained below, the arbitration agreement does not explicitly prescribe any limitations period with respect to an arbitration demand, and it supersedes all other agreements between the parties. In the circumstances presented, the arbitrator's ruling constituted a manifest disregard of the law and was not drawn from the essence of the governing arbitration agreement. As a result, we vacate the district court's refusal to vacate the arbitration award as to Signator Investors, and we remand for further proceedings.

I.

A.

Patten first began working as a sales agent for Hancock in the Washington, D.C. area in 1972. In 1989, he became a General Agent for Hancock in Bethesda, Maryland. In 1992, he entered into an agreement with Hancock and its affiliates, designated as a "Mutual Agreement to Arbitrate Claims" (the "Mutual Agreement"). The Mutual Agreement required, *inter alia*, that any claims arising between Patten and Hancock (or any of Hancock's affiliates or subsidiaries) were to be resolved by mandatory arbitration. The Mutual Agreement specifically provided, in a section captioned "Required Notice of all Claims and Statute of Limitations," that an "aggrieved party must give written notice of any claim to the other party within one (1) year of ... the event giving rise to the claim," or the claim would be deemed waived.... It is undisputed that Signator Investors was an "affiliate" of Hancock and thus a party to the Mutual Agreement.

In 1998, Patten entered into a new and superseding agreement with Signator Investors, to become its branch manager in Bethesda (the "Management Agreement"). The Management Agreement provided, *inter alia*, that "Signator [Investors] and Branch Manager [Patten] mutually consent to the resolution by arbitration of all claims or controversies." The Management Agreement was silent, however, on any requirements of timing or manner with respect to an arbitration demand. The Management Agreement also provided that it "supersedes all previous agreements, oral or written, between the parties hereto regarding the subject matter hereof." Finally, the Management Agreement mandated that it was to "be governed by and construed in accordance with the laws of the Commonwealth of Massachusetts."

On October 18, 1999, Hancock reprimanded Patten for alleged deficiencies in his performance as a General Agent—specifically, for advancing premiums on behalf of his clients, in violation of company policy. On December 13, 2000, the respondents each terminated Patten, effective January 2, 2001. On August 2, 2001, Patten sent a letter to the respondents advising them that he had been wrongfully terminated and discriminated against because of his age, and that he was preparing to file a lawsuit on the basis of these claims. The respondents, by letter of August 30, 2001, advised Patten that his allegations were "unequivocally denie[d]," and the parties then apparently entered into unsuccessful settlement negotiations.

On March 4, 2002, Patten forwarded the respondents a demand for arbitration, asserting claims of discrimination, wrongful termination, and breach of contract. On March 13, 2002, the respondents informed Patten by letter that they would not arbitrate because his demand for arbitration was made fourteen months after his termination, and thus was not "timely or proper" under the Mutual Agreement's one-year limitations period. On March 14, 2002, Patten replied that the Management Agreement (rather than the Mutual Agreement) governed his claims against Signator Investors, and that he would seek judicial enforcement of his rights if the respondents refused to arbitrate.

B.

On May 20, 2002, Patten filed a complaint for enforcement of arbitration in the District of Maryland, seeking to compel arbitration. The parties thereafter filed cross-motions for summary judgment and, on November 5, 2002, the court ruled in favor of Patten and directed the respondents to submit to arbitration.... Because the court concluded that arbitration should be compelled "under the Mutual Agreement, the Court [found] it unnecessary to address Plaintiff's argument regarding the Management Agreement." ... In its opinion, the court observed that all other questions concerning the arbitration—including the satisfaction of time and notice requirements—were "within the arbitrator's purview." *Id.* at 2.

The parties entered into arbitration in 2003 under the auspices of the American Arbitration Association (the "AAA"). On January 24, 2003, Patten filed a demand for arbitration with the AAA, making allegations of (1) wrongful termination, (2) breach of contract, (3) breach of the implied covenant of good faith and fair dealing, and (4) unlawful discrimination in violation of federal law as well as the law of Massachusetts and Maryland. After selecting an arbitrator under the procedures of the AAA, the parties engaged in discovery and exchanged witness lists. On December 8, 2003, the respondents filed a motion for summary judgment in the arbitration proceedings, asserting, *inter alia*, that Patten had failed to comply with the one-year notice provision of the Mutual Agreement. On December 18, 2003, Patten filed an opposition to the respondents' summary judgment request, asserting that the arbitration proceedings arose under both the Management Agreement and the Mutual Agreement. Patten contended that he had complied with the applicable notice requirements of each agreement—maintaining that his August 2, 2001 letter substantially complied with the one-year notice requirement in the Mutual Agreement, and that the Management Agreement contained no limitations period governing when an arbitration demand was to be made.

By his arbitration award of January 10, 2004, the arbitrator dismissed the arbitration proceedings as time-barred and entered summary judgment for the respondents, without conducting a hearing on the merits. As a preliminary matter, he determined that the arbitration proceedings were governed by both the Mutual Agreement and the Management Agreement. While the arbitrator accurately observed that the Management Agreement contained no notice requirement, he determined that it "necessarily contain[ed] an implied term limit." The arbitrator then "look[ed] to the Mutual Agreement for guidance," and "adopt[ed]" its one-year limitations period. Because Patten sent his demand for arbitration fourteen months after his termination in January 2001, the arbitrator dismissed Patten's claims "on the sole ground that Claimant's March 4, 2002 Demand for Arbitration is time-barred."

C.

On April 9, 2004, Patten filed a motion in the district court proceedings seeking to vacate the arbitration award's determination that the claims in arbitration under the Management Agreement were time-barred. By this motion, Patten contended that the arbitrator had acted in manifest disregard of the law, and had failed to draw his award from the essence of the agreement, by concluding that the Management Agreement contained an implied one-year limitations period on the filing of an arbitration demand. Patten asserted that the Management Agreement explicitly provided that it "supersede[d]" all previous agreements, and its lack of any limitations period had to be construed against Signator Investors, which had drafted it. On January 4, 2005, the district court denied the motion to vacate, concluding that the arbitrator had not ignored any governing legal principles, and that, in any event, an arbitrator's misinterpretation of an arbitration agreement is not a basis for vacating an arbitration award.... Patten has filed a timely notice of appeal, and we possess jurisdiction pursuant to 28 U.S.C. § 1291.

II.

The process and extent of federal judicial review of an arbitration award are substantially circumscribed. As a general proposition, a federal court may vacate an arbitration award only upon a showing of one of the grounds specified in the Federal Arbitration Act . . . or upon a showing of certain limited common law grounds. The permissible common law grounds for vacating such an award, which constitute the essential premises of this appeal, include those circumstances where an award fails to draw its essence from the contract, or the award evidences a manifest disregard of the law. . . . In reviewing a denial of a motion to vacate an arbitration award, we review the district court's determinations of law *de novo*. . . .

III.

A.

This dispute was submitted to arbitration pursuant to two separate agreements: first, the Mutual Agreement of 1992, which Patten entered into with Hancock and its affiliates (which included Signator Investors); and second, the Management Agreement, which Patten and Signator Investors entered into in 1998. On appeal, however, Patten seeks only to vacate the arbitrator's dismissal of his claims under the Management Agreement against Signator Investors. Importantly, he does not, in this appeal, take issue with those aspects of the arbitration award dismissing his claims against Hancock and Signator Insurance as time-barred under the Mutual Agreement. Thus, the governing arbitration agreement in this appeal is contained in Paragraph 11 of the Management Agreement between Patten and Signator Investors. That arbitration agreement provides, in pertinent part:

> Signator [Investors] and Branch Manager [Patten] mutually consent to the resolution by arbitration of all claims or controversies ("claims") . . . that Signator [Investors] may have against Branch Manager or that Branch Manager may have against Signator [Investors] . . . . The claims covered by this consent to arbitration include all claims arising out of or in connection with the business of Signator [Investors] . . . .

B.

Patten contends that the arbitration award should be vacated as to Signator Investors because the arbitrator's most crucial ruling—that the governing arbitration provision in the Management Agreement contained an implied time limitation on an arbitration demand—constituted a manifest disregard of the law, and failed to draw its essence from the agreement. In seeking to vacate an arbitration award, of course, an appellant "shoulders a heavy burden." . . . Put simply, an arbitrator's legal determination "may only be overturned where it is in manifest disregard of the law," and an arbitrator's interpretation of a contract must be upheld so long as it "draws its essence from the agreement." . . . Under our precedent, a manifest disregard of the law is established only where the "arbitrator[ ] understand [s] and correctly state[s] the law, but proceed[s] to disregard the same." ... Moreover, an arbitration award does not fail to draw its essence from the agreement merely because a court concludes that an arbitrator has "misread the contract." ... An arbitration award fails to draw its essence from the agreement only when the result is not "rationally inferable from the contract." ...

In supporting the district court's ruling on the motion to vacate, Signator Investors relies solely on the circumscribed scope of review which we are obliged to apply in assessing an arbitration award. And although the authority of an arbitrator is broad, and subject to great deference under the applicable standard of review, "it is not unlimited." ... For example, an arbitrator has acted in manifest disregard of the law if he "disregard[s] or modif[ies] unambiguous contract provisions." ... Moreover, an award fails to draw its essence from the agreement if an arbitrator has "based his award on his own personal notions of right and wrong." ... In such circumstances, a federal court has "no choice but to refuse enforcement of the award." *Int'l Union, United Mine Workers of Am. v. Marrowbone Dev. Co.*, 232 F.3d 383, 389 (4th Cir.2000) (internal quotation marks omitted) (affirming district court's vacatur of award where arbitrator refused to conduct hearing as required by agreement).

In this case, as explained below, the arbitrator disregarded the plain and unambiguous language of the governing arbitration agreement when he concluded that it included an implied one-year limitations period. In so doing, the arbitrator acted in manifest disregard of the law and failed to draw his award from the essence of the agreement.

C.

In assessing the timeliness of Patten's arbitration demand, the arbitrator correctly recognized that the Management Agreement contained no explicit time limitation. The arbitrator nonetheless determined, however, that the Management Agreement "necessarily contain[ed] an implied term limit." In certain instances, when the contracting parties have failed to specify a term that is essential to the determination of their rights and duties under an arbitration agreement, the arbitrator may supply a term that is "reasonable in the circumstances." ... In the circumstances of this case, however, the one-year limitations period imposed by the arbitrator was not reasonable, in that it contradicted the plain and unambiguous terms of the Management Agreement.

The Management Agreement unambiguously provided that, as to its parties (Patten and Signator Investors), it "supersede[d]" the Mutual Agreement.... Despite this clear repudiation of the Mutual Agreement by both Patten and Signator Investors, the arbitrator proceeded to "look to the Mutual Agreement for guidance" and "adopt[ed]" its one-year limitations period. In so doing, he failed to heed the plain and unambiguous terms of the Management Agreement—not only had Patten and Signator Investors contractually agreed that the Mutual Agreement was superseded, they had also chosen to omit certain of its terms from the Management Agreement, including the one-year limitations period.

Moreover, the arbitrator ignored the fact that the Management Agreement provided that it was to "be governed by and construed in accordance with the laws of the Commonwealth of Massachusetts." If the arbitrator felt the need to import a limitations period into the Management Agreement, the most obvious source was that which governed their agreement: Massachusetts law. And under Massachusetts law, claims of wrongful termination and discrimination are subject to a three-year statute of limitations . . . and contract claims must be filed within a six-year period. . . . Utilizing either of these limitations periods, Patten's March 2, 2002 demand for arbitration—submitted to Signator Investors within fourteen months of his termination—would have been timely.

Put succinctly, the arbitrator appears to have revised the governing arbitration agreement on the basis of his own "personal notions of right and wrong," and imposed a limitations period on the parties that they had specifically rejected. *See Upshur Coals,* 933 F.2d at 229; *see also U.S. Postal Serv.,* 204 F.3d at 527 ("When the arbitrator ignores the unambiguous language chosen by the parties, the arbitrator simply fails to do his job."). Consequently, this dispute does not fall into the category of awards based on "misapplication of principles of contractual interpretation [or] erroneous interpretation," which are not to be disturbed by judicial review. . . . Rather, the arbitrator in this instance simply "amend[ed] or alter[ed] the agreement," and thus he "act[ed] without authority." . . . The arbitrator's ruling thus resulted in an award that . . . simply was "not rationally inferable from the contract." . . .

Although our standard of review of an arbitration award is properly a limited and deferential one, it does not require that we affirm an award that contravenes the plain and unambiguous terms of the governing arbitration agreement. . . . In these circumstances, the arbitration award as to Patten and Signator Investors failed to draw its essence from the governing arbitration agreement and was made in manifest disregard of the law.

IV.

Pursuant to the foregoing, we vacate the district court's denial of Patten's motion to vacate the arbitration award as to Signator Investors. We remand for such other and further proceedings as may be appropriate.

VACATED AND REMANDED.

NOTES AND QUESTIONS

1. What does the choice-of-law provision in the contract say about the parties' *contractual* relationship? How does it factor into the court's reasoning in regard to manifest disregard? Is the court's assessment proper and persuasive?

2. You should examine the one-year provision in the first agreement. What requirement or contractual obligation does it establish? What is the purpose of the provision? What bearing does it have upon the arbitration agreement?

3. Can there be any dispute about whether Patten followed the precise language of the agreement in filing his compliant and demand for arbitration? Does the arbitrator misunderstand the facts? Does he engage in a creative interpretation of the applicable agreement? Is this fundamentally deviant? Has he "manifestly disregarded the law"? Is there any law at play? Was it stated and then ignored in the ruling ?

4. Given the succession of positions and agreements between the same parties, why is it wrong for the arbitrator to see the parties' relationship as a unitary transaction with an abstract overarching contract? How can it be wrong for the arbitrator to imply a term in the parties' contract relationship? How can gap-filling or boot-strapping constitute manifest disregard of the law?

5. What impact might *Howman* and *Bazzle* have upon the court's reasoning and the result it reaches? Is the question of what the contract provides a "gateway" issue to be decided by the arbitrator pursuant to his/her sovereign discretion?

6. The court also concludes in a parallel determination that the arbitrator's ruling that Patten's claims were prescribed could not be drawn from the essence of the contract. Can you explain the significance of this ruling? Is it a misplaced and ill-conceived conclusion? Is an employment contract equivalent to a collective bargaining agreement?

7. Does the result comply with the federal policy on arbitration? Is this an instance of judicial supervision at its doctrinal worse? Engaged in by an otherwise hospitable court? Where is the abuse or imperative in the circumstances?

GREENBERG v. BEAR, STEARNS & CO.
220 F.3d 22 (2d Cir. 2000).

JOHN M. WALKER, JR., Circuit Judge:

Petitioner-appellant Howard Greenberg appeals from the August 25, 1999 judgment of the United States District Court for the Southern District of New York ..., denying his petition to vacate an arbitration award that dismissed his securities fraud claims against respondents-appellees Bear, Stearns & Co., Inc., and Bear, Stearns Securities Corp. (collectively, "Bear Stearns"). On appeal, Greenberg argues that the district court's judgment should be reversed and the arbitration award against him vacated because the arbitrators manifestly disregarded federal law in rendering the award. Bear Stearns responds that there was no basis for federal subject matter jurisdiction in this case and that, in any event, the arbitral award easily withstands review.

This appeal squarely presents the question of whether and under what circumstances federal courts have jurisdiction to hear motions to vacate arbitration awards. We conclude that the district court had jurisdiction in this case because Greenberg challenged the award primarily on the grounds of manifest disregard of federal law. . . .

BACKGROUND

At the time of the events underlying Greenberg's claim, Bear Stearns (a "clearing broker") provided securities clearing services to Greenberg's primary broker, Sterling Foster (an "introducing broker"). According to Greenberg, Bear Stearns violated federal and state securities laws because it knew of and participated in a fraudulent scheme perpetrated by Sterling Foster; sent false and misleading confirmations in connection with this scheme; and failed to send out a required prospectus. We briefly discuss the facts and allegations pertinent to the appeal.

In 1996, Sterling Foster organized the initial public offering ("IPO") for a company called ML Direct. Under an agreement between Bear Stearns and Sterling Foster, the latter requested permission from the former to underwrite this sale. According to Sterling Foster's plan, ML Direct would make a public sale of 1.1 million shares, and Sterling Foster would sell short an additional 2.3 million shares, to be covered by shares it would obtain from existing shareholders. This scheme was fraudulent, alleged the plaintiff, because the prospectus distributed to purchasers of ML Direct stock stated that shares from the selling shareholders were subject to a lock-up agreement for 12 months and that there were "no agreements or understandings . . . with respect to release of the securities prior to [this time]." Bear Stearns employees admitted having seen the prospectus, but did not recall reading the sentences about the lock-up. Bear Stearns agreed to clear the transaction.

In September 1996, the IPO and stock sales proceeded as planned. Sterling Foster allegedly reaped an enormous profit at the expense of the selling shareholders by selling shares short and purchasing shares from those shareholders at a significantly lower price. . . .

In May 1997, the petitioner filed a claim with the National Association of Security Dealers ("NASD") against Bear Stearns alleging, among other things, fraud and market manipulation in connection with Bear Stearns's provision of securities clearing services to Sterling Foster. A panel of three arbitrators heard arguments and testimony through extensive briefing and seven days of hearings. The arbitrators first dismissed Greenberg's claim based on Bear Stearns's purported failure to send him a prospectus and thereafter dismissed his remaining claims. On March 9, 1999, the arbitrators issued a written award confirming their decision to dismiss.

On January 18, 1999, Greenberg moved in federal district court to vacate the award on the basis that it "violated public policy and manifestly disregarded the law." In an opinion and award dated August 23, 1999, the district court denied the motion on the grounds that the petitioner had failed to demonstrate manifest disregard of the law in the arbitrators' treatment of his claims. This appeal followed.

Discussion

I. Federal Jurisdiction

The principal question presented in this appeal is whether the district court had federal question jurisdiction over Greenberg's motion to vacate the arbitration award. Jurisdiction would plainly lie if, among other things, the parties were diverse, ... the claim arose in admiralty, ... or the dispute concerned the interpretation of a collective bargaining agreement.... However, we must decide whether and under what circumstances a federal court may entertain a motion to vacate an award where, as in this case, alternative bases for jurisdiction are absent. We conclude that: (1) the fact that the arbitration itself concerns issues of federal law does not, on its own, confer subject matter jurisdiction on a federal district court to review the award; but (2) federal jurisdiction may lie where the petitioner seeks to vacate the award primarily on the ground of manifest disregard of federal law.

Federal courts have jurisdiction over "all civil actions arising under the ... laws ... of the United States." ... Federal question jurisdiction exists where a well-pleaded complaint "establishes either that federal law creates the cause of action or that the plaintiff's right to relief necessarily depends on resolution of a substantial question of federal law." ...

Federal law plainly does not create the cause of action in this case. Greenberg filed his petition under § 10 of the Federal Arbitration Act ("FAA"), which authorizes "the United States court in and for the district wherein the [arbitration] award was made" to "make an order vacating the award" under certain circumstances.... However, it is well-settled that the FAA does not confer subject matter jurisdiction on the federal courts even though it creates federal substantive law.... Therefore, federal question jurisdiction does not arise simply because a petitioner brings a claim under § 10 of the FAA; there must be "an independent basis of jurisdiction" before district courts may entertain petitions to vacate....

Simply raising federal-law claims in the underlying arbitration is insufficient to supply this "independent basis." In the context of a motion to compel arbitration under § 4 of the FAA, ... we have specifically held that there is no federal subject matter jurisdiction "merely because the underlying claim raises a federal question." ... Petitions to compel arbitration "must be brought in state court unless some other basis for federal jurisdiction exists, such as diversity of citizenship or assertion of a claim in admiralty." ... Language in § 4 seemingly authorizing the federal courts to hear such petitions "is not intended to confer jurisdiction, but should instead be read as a response to the antiquated common law principle that an agreement to arbitrate would oust the federal courts of jurisdiction." ...

. . . As with a motion under § 4, the only federal rights that a motion under § 10 necessarily implicates are those created by the FAA itself, which rights do not give rise to federal question jurisdiction. In both contexts, there is no necessary link between the requested relief and the character of the underlying dispute. For example, a petition to compel arbitration because the dispute falls within the scope of an arbitration clause, or to vacate an award because the arbitrators exceeded their powers under that clause, will turn on the interpretation of the clause, regardless of whether the actual dispute implicates any federal laws. Accordingly, the fact that the arbitration concerns issues of federal law does not, standing alone, confer subject matter jurisdiction on a federal district court to review the arbitral award.

Nevertheless, federal jurisdiction may still lie if the ultimate disposition of the matter by the federal court "necessarily depends on resolution of a substantial question of federal law." . . . Thus we must decide whether the petition in this case to vacate an arbitral award presents a substantial question of federal law.

"[I]n determining federal question jurisdiction, courts must make principled, pragmatic distinctions, engaging in a selective process which picks the substantial causes out of the web and lays the other ones aside." . . . "[E]xamining only those allegations which are properly raised in a well-pleaded complaint, we look to the nature of the federal question raised in the claim to see if it is sufficiently substantial to warrant federal jurisdiction." . . . The greater the federal interest at stake, the more likely it is that federal jurisdiction will be found. . . .

In our view, under these standards, whether or not a petition to vacate under § 10 raises a substantial federal question turns on the ground for the petitioner's challenge to the award. The FAA and federal case law supply various bases for review of an arbitral award. Section 10 itself lists several grounds, including fraud in procuring the award; corruption, partiality, or prejudicial misconduct on the part of the arbitrators; abuse of power; and failure to render "a mutual, final, and definite award." 9 U.S.C. § 10(a). Judicial interpretation has added additional grounds, such that awards may be vacated under limited circumstances where the arbitrators manifestly disregarded the law . . . or where enforcement would violate a "well defined and dominant public policy," . . .

We hold that where, as here, the petitioner complains principally and in good faith that the award was rendered in manifest disregard of federal law, a substantial federal question is presented and the federal courts have jurisdiction to entertain the petition. In contrast to grounds of review that concern the arbitration process itself . . . such as corruption or abuse of power . . . review for manifest disregard of federal law necessarily requires the reviewing court to do two things: first, determine what the federal law is, and second, determine whether the arbitrator's decision manifestly disregarded that law. This process so immerses the federal court in questions of federal law and their proper application that federal question subject matter jurisdiction is present.

[. . .]

We note that, by and large, the rulings of other courts are not inconsistent with our holding here. Many courts have found the simple presence of federal claims in the arbitration itself insufficient as an independent basis for federal jurisdiction. These cases, however, generally did not involve a petition to vacate on the grounds of manifest disregard of federal law in the arbitrators' resolution of the underlying federal claims. *But see Manginelli,* 1999 WL 615096, at *2 (holding that the "limited application and interpretation of federal law" required to rule on a petition to vacate an award on the grounds of manifest disregard is insufficient to "provide an independent basis for federal jurisdiction"). Instead, the petitioners challenged arbitration awards on grounds that plainly did not require resolution of a uniquely federal issue, including perjury, *see Kasap,* 166 F.3d at 1245; "alleged misdeeds of the arbitrators," *Baltin v. Alaron Trading Corp.,* 128 F.3d 1466, 1472 (11th Cir. 1997); "fraud, corruption, undue means, evident partiality, and failure to consider pertinent and material evidence," *Minor v. Prudential Sec., Inc.,* 94 F.3d 1103, 1105–06 (7th Cir.1996); and manifest disregard of state law, *see Ford,* 29 F.3d at 258; *Lipton,* 934 F.Supp. at 639. The Seventh Circuit acknowledged that the federal courts might have jurisdiction if the motion to vacate involved, on its face, "the resolution of [the petitioner's] federal claims or some question of federal law." *Minor,* 94 F.3d at 1106. *But see Kasap,* 166 F.3d at 1247 (suggesting that review for fraud under § 10 implicates federal law but that this is insufficient to support federal jurisdiction). Where the petitioner seeks vacatur chiefly on the ground of manifest disregard of federal law, a federal question is plainly presented.

In this case, if it were not for the claim that vacatur is warranted because federal law was manifestly disregarded, we would find no jurisdiction. The simple fact that the underlying arbitration implicated federal questions would not be enough. But because the petition alleges primarily that the award was rendered in manifest disregard of the federal laws underpinning these claims, federal question jurisdiction is present.

Accordingly, the district court had jurisdiction to consider Greenberg's petition, and this appeal is properly before us. We turn now to the merits.

II. *Review of the Award for Manifest Disregard of the Law*

The district court held that the petitioner had failed to demonstrate that the arbitral award was rendered in manifest disregard of the law. Review for manifest disregard is "severely limited." *DiRussa,* 121 F.3d at 821. In order to vacate an award on these grounds, a reviewing court must find "both that (1) the arbitrators knew of a governing legal principle yet refused to apply it or ignored it altogether, and (2) the law ignored by the arbitrators was well defined, explicit, and clearly applicable to the case."

... The party seeking vacatur of the award bears the burden of showing manifest disregard under these standards.... A district court's application of the manifest disregard standard is a legal determination that we review *de novo* ....

The petitioner has failed to meet this very stringent burden with respect to any of his claims against Bear Stearns. First, Greenberg argues that the arbitrators manifestly disregarded federal law in denying his claim that Bear Stearns knew about Sterling Foster's fraudulent scheme and is therefore liable under § 10(b) of the Securities Exchange Act. Knowing participation in a fraudulent scheme may render a participant liable under § 10(b).... In this case, however, Bear Stearns employees testified that they did not know about Sterling Foster's fraud, and thus the arbitrators could reasonably have concluded that Bear Stearns lacked the knowledge required for § 10(b) liability. The petitioner argues that Bear Stearns should be deemed to have knowledge of the fraud because it had the necessary information before it, but it is by no means clear that the doctrine of imputed knowledge applies in this context.

Second, according to Greenberg, Bear Stearns violated federal securities law by sending knowingly false confirmations. The confirmations were allegedly misleading because, while they made certain disclosures, they failed to reveal that the transaction was an underwriting, not a market sale, and that Sterling Foster was reaping a 400% profit from the scheme. But the arbitrators could have concluded that the language was not actually false, since Sterling Foster, in fact, was a market maker in ML Direct securities at the time, although not for all transactions. In addition, there is no well-settled law imposing a duty upon a clearing broker, who is unaware of an introducing broker's undisclosed and excessive profit, to inquire into the matter and then inform the latter's customers of such self-dealing.

Third, Greenberg contends that Bear Stearns failed to comply with 17 C.F.R. § 230.174, which requires delivery of a prospectus in connection with the sale of newly issued securities. But the regulation imposes this requirement only on underwriters and dealers, not on clearing brokers, and nothing in the agreement between Bear Stearns and Sterling Foster unambiguously shifted the burden of complying with this requirement onto Bear Stearns.

Finally, Greenberg asserts that Bear Stearns should be held liable as an aider and abetter under New York law because it participated in the fraudulent scheme and provided substantial assistance to Sterling Foster.... However, there was ample basis for the arbitrators to conclude that Bear Stearns's participation was insufficient to constitute substantial assistance. "[T]he simple providing of normal clearing services to a primary broker who is acting in violation of the law does not make out a case of aiding and abetting against the clearing broker." ...

In sum, the arbitrators did not ignore or refuse to apply well-defined and clearly applicable law in rejecting any of the appellant's claims in such a way that would amount to manifest disregard.

Conclusion

For the foregoing reasons, we hold that: (1) where, as here, a § 10 petitioner complains principally and in good faith that an arbitration award was rendered in manifest disregard of federal law, the federal courts have jurisdiction to entertain the petition; and (2) the district court in this case properly rejected the petitioner's claim for failure to demonstrate that the arbitrators had manifestly disregarded the law in their treatment of his securities claims. We have considered the petitioner's other arguments and find them to be without merit. Accordingly, we affirm the judgment of the district court.

Notes and Questions

1. Does the FAA create federal rights and, therefore, federal jurisdiction whenever it applies? Given federal preemption, does the FAA apply whenever an arbitration matter is raised? What rights might exist in the FAA and in which provisions could they be found?

2. In the court's view, when does federal question jurisdiction arise in an arbitration? How else might federal jurisdiction arise in the context of an arbitration?

3. What is "an independent basis for federal jurisdiction"?

4. What does the court's holding add to the law interpreting manifest disregard of the law? Is there now a governing law component?

5. Is the court rigorous in its application of the law relating to manifest disregard?

6. In a controversial and highly visible opinion, the U.S. Court of Appeals for the Second Circuit vacated an arbitral award on the basis that the arbitrators presumptively disregarded the law or the evidence presented or both. *Halligan v. Piper Jaffray, Inc.*, 148 F.3d 197 (2d Cir. 1998), *cert. denied*, 526 U.S. 1034 (1999).

In *Halligan*, a salesman of equity investments submitted his ADEA and other claims against his employer, Piper Jaffray, Inc., to arbitration as required by the NASD Registration Form U–4. During the arbitration, Halligan presented evidence and testimonials of instances of age-based discrimination he allegedly had suffered. He had been hired by Piper in 1973. His employment was terminated in December 1992. At the time of his would-be resignation, Halligan was making nearly $500,000 per year and was ranked fifth of twenty-five institutional salesmen at Piper. Throughout his career, he apparently had been perceived as a top salesman at the firm. Halligan testified that the new senior management at Piper made "repeated discriminatory statements" based on his age prior to his resignation. Halligan's view that he was forced out of the firm because of his age was buttressed by notes he took after his discussions with senior management and by the testimony of other Piper employees. Halligan stated that he was unable to find employment after he left Piper in 1992. Since 1990, Halligan suffered from oral cancer and underwent several surgeries for the condition. He died during the arbitral proceedings.

In response to these allegations, Piper asserted that Halligan had chosen to retire from the firm. Moreover, Piper management questioned the quality of Halligan's performance as a salesman, arguing that his accounts had a built-in potential for profit and that other Piper employees contributed substantially to Halligan's success. Piper management also criticized Halligan's ability to develop new accounts and to use firm research. In effect, Piper contended that Halligan had taken the "option" of retirement because of his poor performance and health problems.

In March 1996, the arbitral tribunal rendered an award in which it rejected Halligan's claims. The award restated the parties' allegation and arguments and contained the arbitrators' determination, but it did not provide any explanation or reasoning for the result reached by the tribunal. The district court confirmed the award, concluding that there was "factual as well as legal support for the Panel's ultimate conclusion" and rejecting arguments that the arbitrators had "manifestly disregarded the law." The district court also noted that evaluating evidence for possible indications of discrimination was a "difficult" task and that "[c]rediting [the testimony of] one witness over another does not constitute manifest disregard of the law...." Finally, subscribing to the basic judicial position in matters of enforcement, the court stated that its "role is not to second-guess the fact-finding done by the Panel."

On appeal, the Second Circuit emphasized, at two different points in its brief opinion, that the "use of mandatory pre-dispute arbitration agreements to resolve statutory claims of employment discrimination...has caused increased controversy...[and] engendered greater [judicial] scrutiny...." According to the court, greater recourse to arbitration to resolve Title VII claims apparently has led to modifications in the standard law governing arbitration. First, "additional procedural requirements" may be necessary when using arbitration in this setting to effectuate the *Gilmer* mandate of allowing employees to " 'effectively...vindicate' " their statutory rights. Second, private ADR service providers have articulated due process protocols for application in this type of arbitration. Third, inside-the-industry SRO arbitration has come under increasing criticism because it is perceived as unfair and inadequate to deal with claims of statutory discrimination in employment. Finally, recent federal cases (*e.g., Cole v. Burns Int'l Security Services* and *Prudential Ins. Co. v. Lai*) have emphasized the specialty of Title VII claims and the need for greater judicial supervision of the employment arbitration process. Those four factors—indicating a change in the judicial regulation of arbitration—led the Second Circuit in *Halligan* to articulate a new interpretation and definition of the "manifest disregard" standard and to vacate the award in question.

The court found that the arbitrators were presented with convincing evidence of age discrimination and were correctly informed by the parties of the applicable legal standards. Because they did not reach a result that the court believed was commanded by the record, the court concluded "that they [the arbitrators] ignored the law or the evidence or both." Moreover, the failure of the arbitrators to include reasons with the award also appeared to be fatal to the enforceability of the award. While it recognized that awards with reasons were not legally mandated, the court stated that the *Gilmer* vindication of statutory rights corollary challenged the received wisdom in employment discrimination cases:

> At least in the circumstances here, we believe that when a reviewing court is inclined to hold that an arbitration panel manifestly disregarded the law, the failure of the arbitrators to explain the award can be taken into account. . . .
>
> . . . [W]here a reviewing court is inclined to find that arbitrators manifestly disregarded the law or the evidence and that an explanation, if given, would have strained credulity, the absence of explanation may reinforce the reviewing court's confidence that the arbitrators engaged in manifest disregard.

Notwithstanding the circularity and nonsense of the latter statement, the Second Circuit concluded that it was "left with the firm belief that the arbitrators here manifestly disregarded the law or the evidence or both."

7. As a result of the reasoning in *Halligan*, the "manifest disregard" standard now appears to be more flexible (at least, in employment discrimination cases) and to include a new element, *i.e.*, possible disregard of the evidence presented during the proceedings. Moreover, it seems that arbitrators ruling in Title VII employment discrimination cases should include reasons with their award whenever they hold against the plaintiff. The absence of reasons, it seems, creates a presumption of bias on the part of the arbitrators and of the misapplication of the law or misassessment of the evidence. The articulation of reasons by the tribunal, it appears, would have the effect of confirming what the court believes to be arbitrator bias, misapplication, and misassessment.

The opinion in *Halligan* constitutes one of the most striking examples of the judicial review of the merits of an arbitral award. The reviewing court thoroughly examines the factual record of the arbitration, assesses that evidence differently from the arbitrators, and substitutes its resolution of the adjudication for that of the arbitrators. By contrast, the district court opinion reflected the deferential approach that applies ordinarily in matters of enforcement, and that is commanded by law. The appellate court's perception of the specialty of employment discrimination claims may be accurate and has political appeal, but, no matter how controversial compulsory employment arbitration may be, it is difficult to understand how its controversial nature can justify a flagrant judicial intrusion into the adjudicatory jurisdiction and autonomy of arbitrators. This approach is all the more surprising given the settled character of current arbitration law and practice. It is an unfortunate and misguided means of achieving justice in the case.

WALLACE v. BUTTAR

378 F.3d 182 (2d Cir. 2004).

Pooler, Circuit Judge.

This case raises questions regarding the scope of federal court review of a decision issued by an arbitral panel. We resolve the case through the application of the familiar principle that the scope of such review is highly constrained. This is especially true with regard to an arbitral panel's assessment of whether the documentary and testimonial evidence presented to it is sufficient to satisfy a particular legal claim. Federal district judges are, of course, highly skilled in matters of weighing evidence. As illustrated by the result we reach here, however, district judges must put these skills aside when faced with the question of whether a decision issued by an arbitral panel should be confirmed.

Facts

A.   The Buttars' Claim

[...]

In July 1999, [Vermak] Verma persuaded Dr. Buttar to open the first of a series of investment accounts at the firm for which he worked, Montrose Capital Management ("Montrose"). The application signed by Dr. Buttar when he opened this account contains the following provision:

> All controversies which may arise between us concerning any transaction, or the construction, performance or breach of this or any other agreement between us, whether entered into prior, on, or subsequent to the date hereof, shall be determined by arbitration in accordance with the Federal Arbitration Act to the fullest extent permitted by law. The arbitration shall be determined only before and in accordance with the rules then in effect of either the New York Stock Exchange, Inc., or the National Association of Securities Dealers, Inc. or any other exchange or self-regulatory organization of which [Montrose is] a member as I may elect. The award of the arbitrators, or of the majority of them, shall be final....

We note that, immediately preceding the arbitration clause, the application sets forth the following "understanding" in bold lettering: **"The arbitrator's award is not required to include factual findings or legal reasoning and any party's right to appeal or to seek modification of rulings by arbitrators is strictly limited."**

Soon after opening this initial account, Dr. Buttar also began to discuss his investments with Robert Winston. Winston's actual responsibilities at Montrose are not entirely clear from the record, but Dr. Buttar testified that Winston "talked to me like he was the owner" of the firm. Verma himself testified that while he worked at Montrose he was under the impression that Winston ran the firm.

Verma and Winston successfully urged Dr. Buttar to make substantial investments in the securities of two firms: (1) Skynet Holdings, Inc.

("Skynet") and (2) CNF Technologies ("CNF"). Dr. Buttar was also persuaded to provide a "bridge loan" to CNF in the amount of $150,000.00. Eventually, Dr. Buttar alleges, Montrose "had invested virtually all of [his] liquid assets in CNF and Skynet." It is undisputed that Dr. Buttar suffered substantial losses as a result.

[. . .]

D.   The District Court's Decision

The Buttars filed an action on June 3, 2002 in the U.S. District Court for the Eastern District of North Carolina seeking confirmation of the Award. Four days later, Wallace, Jacaruso, and Scotti filed actions to vacate the Award in the U.S. District Court for the Southern District of New York. The Buttars thereupon voluntarily dismissed the North Carolina action, and crossed-moved for confirmation of the Award in the New York action. Winston filed no action to vacate the Award and has not filed any opposition the Buttars' cross-motion to confirm the Award.

The district court granted the motions to vacate the Award, and consequently denied the cross-motion to confirm the Award. . . . The district court took it to be "undisputed that Winston, a broker employed by Montrose, committed a primary violation of the securities laws, that Jacaruso and Scotti were directors and shareholders of Montrose and Wallace was its president." . . . The question then became whether the Panel could have properly found Wallace, Jacaruso, or Scotti in any way liable for Winston's acts.

The district court held that, in addition to the grounds for vacating an arbitration award set forth in the Federal Arbitration Act ("FAA"), . . . "the Second Circuit[ ] recognize[s] two additional bases for vacating arbitration awards: manifest disregard of the law and manifest disregard of the facts." . . . In the district court's view, the Panel could not have found Wallace, Jacaruso, or Scotti liable for the Buttars' losses without engaging in both sorts of disregard. First, secondary liability pursuant to the doctrine of respondeat superior could not lie because the doctrine "imposes liability on the employer of those committing fraud in their employment. The entity that could have been held liable for Winston's fraud under the doctrine . . . was Montrose, Winston's employer." . . . Second, Wallace, Jacaruso, and Scotti could not be found liable as co-participants in Winston's scheme to defraud the Buttars because "[i]n order to commit fraud, one must act with intent to defraud." . . .

Finally, the district court held that the Panel manifestly disregarded the law and the evidence by holding Wallace, Jacaruso, and Scotti liable as control persons because "[t]he Buttars rely solely on Wallace's status as President and Jacaruso and Scotti's designation as a control person of Montrose." . . . The district court observed, however, that status alone does not suffice to make one liable as a control person. Rather, "the control person must additionally possess the necessary mental culpability by either knowing, or failing to know due to their [sic] own recklessness or negligence, of the alleged wrongdoing." . . . Upon its review of the evidentiary record, the district court found "[n]o evidence [had been] adduced that the Petitioners were involved in the allegedly unsuitable and unauthorized transactions in the Buttars' accounts." . . . Therefore, a finding of intent as to Wallace, Jacaruso, and Scotti could only be the Panel's invention, made in disregard of the evidentiary record before it.

DISCUSSION

"When a party challenges the district court's review of an arbitral award under the manifest disregard standard, we review the district court's application of the standard *de novo.*" . . .

A.   *The Scope of Federal Court Review of an Arbitration Award.*

A motion to vacate filed in a federal court is not an occasion for *de novo* review of an arbitral award. "It is well established that courts must grant an arbitration panel's decision great deference. A party petitioning a federal court to vacate an arbitral award bears the heavy burden of showing that the award falls within a very narrow set of circumstances delineated by statute and case law." . . . The FAA sets forth certain grounds upon which a federal court may vacate an arbitral award, but "all of [these] involve corruption, fraud, or some other impropriety on the part of the arbitrators." . . . The district court did not hold, nor did it in any way imply, that the Award is the result of an act of corruption or unseemliness on the part of the Panel. We therefore immediately proceed to a consideration of the cases within our Circuit which have recognized grounds for vacating an arbitral award other than outright perfidy on the part of arbitrators. We conclude that the district court took too broad a view of these grounds for vacatur.

1.   *Manifest Disregard of the Law*

Our circuit has long held that "[a]n arbitration award may be vacated if it exhibits 'a manifest disregard of the law.'" *Goldman v. Architectural Iron Co.,* 306 F.3d 1214, 1216 (2d Cir.2002) (quoting *DiRussa v. Dean Witter Reynolds, Inc.,* 121 F.3d 818, 821 (2d Cir.1997)). But we have also been quick to add that "manifest disregard of law" as applied to review of an arbitral award is a "severely limited" doctrine. *Gov't of India v. Cargill Inc.,* 867 F.2d 130, 133 (2d Cir.1989) (internal quotation marks and citation omitted). Indeed, we have recently described it as "a doctrine of last resort—its use is limited only to those exceedingly rare instances where some egregious impropriety on the part of the arbitrators is apparent, but where none of the provisions of the FAA apply." *Duferco,* 333 F.3d at 389. Accordingly, we have said that the doctrine "gives extreme deference to arbitrators." *DiRussa,* 121 F.3d at 821.

An arbitral award may be vacated for manifest disregard of the law "only if 'a reviewing court . . . find[s] both that (1) the arbitrators knew of a governing legal principle yet refused to apply it or ignored it altogether, and (2) the law ignored by the arbitrators was well defined, explicit, and clearly applicable to the case.' "... We have emphasized that an arbitral panel's refusal or neglect to apply a governing legal principle " 'clearly means more than error or misunderstanding with respect to the law.' "... A federal court cannot vacate an arbitral award merely because it is convinced that the arbitration panel made the wrong call on the law. On the contrary, the award "should be enforced, despite a court's disagreement with it on the merits, if there is a *barely colorable justification* for the outcome reached." *Banco de Seguros del Estado*, 344 F.3d at 260 (emphasis added; citation and quotation marks omitted) ... *St. Mary Home, Inc. v. Service Employees Int'l Union, Dist. 1199*, 116 F.3d 41, 44–45 (2d Cir.1997) ("Internal inconsistencies in the [arbitrator's] opinion are not grounds to vacate the award notwithstanding the [movant's] plausible argument that the arbitrator's decision was misguided or our own concerns regarding the arbitrator's conclusion.")

In sum, a court reviewing an arbitral award cannot presume that the arbitrator is capable of understanding and applying legal principles with the sophistication of a highly skilled attorney. Indeed, this is so far from being the case that an arbitrator "under the test of manifest disregard is ordinarily assumed to be a blank slate unless educated in the law by the parties." ... There is certainly no requirement under the FAA that arbitrators be members of the bar and we have recognized "that arbitrators often are chosen for reasons other than their knowledge of applicable law." ... Further, "arbitrators are not required to provide an explanation for their decision." ... As already noted, the arbitration clause in this case explicitly informed the parties that they should not expect the Award to be accompanied by any explanation of the Panel's reasoning....

[...]

2. Manifest Disregard of the Evidence

Citing *Halligan v. Piper Jaffray, Inc.*, 148 F.3d 197, 202, 204 (2d Cir.1998), the district court held that an arbitral award may be vacated on the ground of "[m]anifest disregard of the facts" when the award "runs contrary to 'strong' evidence favoring the party bringing the motion to vacate." ... We note that a number of other district courts in our Circuit, directly relying on *Halligan* or on district court authority purporting to rely on that case, have asserted the same principle.... Such reliance is mistaken.

In *Halligan*, we reviewed a district court's confirmation of an arbitration award which rejected an employment discrimination claim. We reversed, finding that the award had been made in the face of "overwhelming evidence" that discriminatory conduct had occurred.... This evidence included the employer's admission that the claimant's "performance was not so unsatisfactory as to justify [his] discharge," and considerable circumstantial evidence that we found to be "consistent only with a finding that [the claimant] was pushed out of his job" by discriminatory animus. ... Further, the arbitration panel issued no explanation for its rejection of the claim, and we concluded that any explanation it could have given "would have strained credulity." . . . We held that the district court had erred in confirming the award because the evidence in the claimant's favor was so strong as to engender "the firm belief that the arbitrators here manifestly disregarded the law or the evidence or both." . . .

Our later cases, however, have cautioned against an over-broad reading of *Halligan.* In *GMS Group,* we noted that *Halligan* confronted "the unique concerns at issue with employment discrimination claims." . . . These concerns included "whether the composition of industry-specific panels were ill-suited to the nature of the claims, and whether employees were receiving due process in the course of arbitration." . . . We concluded, however, that "[t]hese concerns do not translate to the claims at issue in this case." . . . *GMS Group* dealt with a securities fraud claim, as does the instant case.

[. . .]

Moreover, if a federal court is convinced that an arbitral panel has reached a merely incorrect legal result—that is based upon an irrational application of a controlling legal principle—the court should not conduct an independent review of the factual record presented to the arbitral panel in order to achieve the "correct" result. In *Hardy,* as set forth above, an arbitral panel, which had provided no explanation of its award, found an employee, Skelly, to be secondarily liable "based upon the principles of respondeat superior," for primary acts of securities fraud committed by his fellow employee. . . . The district court, as did this Court, found this to be a patently illogical holding that could not be confirmed. The district court, however, conducted its own review of the evidentiary record and concluded that "a permissible view of the evidence" supported the conclusion that Skelly could be held primarily liable for securities fraud based upon his own conduct. . . . We held that the district court should not have undertaken such an assessment of the evidence. . . .

In sum, "the Second Circuit does not recognize manifest disregard of the evidence as proper ground for vacating an arbitrator's award." . . . We recognize only the doctrine of manifest disregard of the law, which doctrine holds that an arbitral panel's legal conclusions will be confirmed in all but those instances where there is no colorable justification for a conclusion. To the extent that a federal court may look upon the evidentiary record of an arbitration proceeding at all, it may do so *only* for the purpose of discerning whether a colorable basis exists for the panel's award so as to assure that the award cannot be said to be the result of the panel's manifest disregard of the law. A federal court may not conduct a reassessment of the evidentiary record, as did the district court here, upon the principle that an arbitral award may be vacated when it "runs contrary to 'strong' evidence favoring the party bringing the motion to vacate" the award. . . . Instead, whatever the weight of the evidence considered as a whole, "[i]f a ground for the arbitrator's decision can be inferred from the facts of the case, the award should be confirmed." . . .

Only this approach to the evidentiary record is consistent with the "great deference" which must be paid to arbitral panels by federal courts. . . .

B. Is the Award Supported by a Colorable Justification?

1. Control Person Liability

[. . .]

"We do not sit in judgment over the wisdom of [an] arbitrator's holdings." . . . We do, however, review an arbitral panel's decision to assure that it rests upon "a barely colorable justification for the outcome reached." . . . We conclude that North Carolina's control person statute, as it was explained to the Panel, provides such a justification for the Award. First, the Buttars directed the Panel's attention to case law which holds that "controlling shareholders, officers and directors . . . are . . . 'control persons' within the meaning of N.C.G.S. § 78A–56(c)." . . . As we have described, Wallace, Jacaruso, and Scotti are identified on numerous Securities and Exchange Commission filings as "control persons" of Montrose. Kavanagh testified that he directly informed Jacaruso of Winston's fraudulent activities and that he raised this same issue at numerous Montrose partner meetings. Collison, the Buttar's expert, opined that Jacaruso and Scotti, "as owners of the firm acquiesced, approved, sanctioned . . . the activities of Mr. Winston." Wallace, Jacaruso, and Scotti offered no expert testimony to counter Collison's opinion. Wallace testified that he "was in control of everybody performing their functions" at Montrose.

Considered as a whole, this evidence is sufficient to provide a colorable basis for control person liability under North Carolina law as that law was explained to the Panel by the parties. We therefore reject the contention of Wallace, Jacaruso, and Scotti that the Award was based on "the Panel's own brand of frontier justice without regard to the law or facts." Instead, we believe the Award is at least colorably based upon the facts and the law as presented to the Panel.

[. . .]

C. Confirmation of the Award as to Winston

Finally, the Buttars argue that the district court erred in declining to confirm the Award's finding of liability against Robert Winston. As already noted, Winston brought no action to vacate the Award and his time to do so has elapsed. . . . He has also filed no opposition to the Buttars' cross-motion to confirm the Award.

We have made clear that "a party may not raise a motion to vacate, modify or correct an arbitration award after the three month period has run, even when raised as a defense to a motion to confirm." . . . In their memorandum in support of their cross-motion to confirm the Award, the Buttars brought *Florasynth* to the attention of the district court, and argued that it required summary confirmation of the Award against Winston. . . . The district court, however, did not confirm the Award as to

Winston despite its statement that "[i]t is undisputed that Winston . . . committed a primary violation of the securities law . . . ." . . .

Winston was not a petitioner below, and he is not an appellee here. Indeed, it is unclear from the record whether the Buttars served Winston when they sought to have the Award confirmed. In its opinion, the district court made no statement as to whether the Award against Winston should be confirmed. Nevertheless, the Buttars' cross-motion below sought confirmation of the Award in full. In addition to granting appellees' motions to vacate, the district court denied the Buttars' cross-motion to confirm. Thus, the district court, at least implicitly, denied the cross-motion to confirm not merely as to appellees, but also as to Winston. To the extent that this is so, the district court erred. On remand, the district court should explicitly address the issue of the Award as it relates to Winston, and either confirm the Award as to him or explain why it is unnecessary or inappropriate to do so.

CONCLUSION

The decision of the district court is reversed. We remand the case for the entry of an order confirming the Award as to Wallace, Jacaruso, and Scotti and for consideration of the Award as to Winston.

NOTES AND QUESTIONS

1. In *Wallace*, the Second Circuit appears to have changed its attitude toward manifest disregard of the law. It seems to bury the common law ground in the shifting sands of exceptions, rendering it truly exceptional and extremely unlikely to be successfully invoked.

2. The court makes statements to the effect that vacatur proceedings are not a stepping stone to *de novo* court review; that the challenging party bears a substantial burden of proof; that judicial supervision is severely limited and very deferential; and that manifest disregard (like the other vacatur grounds) is intended to address the "outright perfidy" of the arbitrator or another "egregious impropriety." Moreover, the common law ground acted as a supplement to the statutory provisions when they did not cover the flagrant abuse.

3. The court makes clear that manifest disregard of the law is unavailable if a "barely colorable justification" for the result can be found. Substantive disagreements on the application of law between the court and the arbitrators are nowhere near sufficient to establish manifest disregard.

4. Do you accept the court's distinction between employment and securities arbitration and its impact on judicial supervision? Explain.

5. What are the consequences of having awards rendered without any explanation or reasons? What happens to judicial supervision?

* * *

In *Hall Street Associates, LLC v. Mattel, Inc.*, 552 U.S. ___, 128 S.Ct. 1396, 1404, 170 L.Ed.2d 254 (2008), the U.S. Supreme Court provided the following description of manifest disregard of the law:

Maybe the term 'manifest disregard' was meant to name a new ground for review, but maybe it merely referred to the § 10 grounds collectively, rather than adding to them. Or, as some courts have thought, 'manifest disregard' may have been shorthand for § 10 (a)(3) or § 10 (a)(4), the subsections authorizing vacatur when the arbitrators were 'guilty of misconduct' or 'exceeded their powers.'

The remark generated a flurry of activity and conclusions from lower courts. Some courts asserted that manifest disregard was a "judicial interpretation of the section 10 requirement, rather than ... a separate standard of review." *See Chase Bank USA, N.A. v. Hale*, 859 N.Y.S.2d 342, 349 (Sup. Ct. N.Y. 2008). Other courts concluded that the concept "is no longer an independent and proper basis under the [FAA] for vacating, modifying, or correcting an arbitrator's award." *See* Hereford v. D.R. Horton, Inc., 2009 WL 104666.

The following cases depict the range of reasoning and results on this question. Can you reconfigure the data into a coherent statement of doctrine? Which opinion best states what you believe to be true? Why? Which opinion is the least credible and persuasive? Explain. Has the U.S. Supreme Court done a service to U.S. arbitration law or simply created more confusion for no real purpose? How would you change the law on this score?

COMEDY CLUB, INC. v. IMPROV WEST ASSOCS.

553 F.3d 1277, 1282–1284, 1289–1290 (2009).

GOULD, Circuit Judge:

On June 13, 1999, Comedy Club, Inc. and Al Copeland Investments, Inc. (collectively "CCI") executed a Trademark License Agreement ("Trademark Agreement") with Improv West Associates ("Improv West") that granted CCI an exclusive nationwide license to use Improv West's trademarks. A few years later, CCI breached the agreement and sought to protect its interests in the trademarks in federal district court by filing a declaratory judgment action. After a complex procedural history, the parties were left with an arbitration award and two district court orders, one order compelling the parties to arbitrate, and another order confirming the arbitration award. CCI appealed both district court orders....

In a prior opinion,... we determined that we lacked jurisdiction to review the district court's order compelling arbitration. We affirmed in part and vacated in part the district court's order confirming the arbitration award. The Supreme Court vacated that opinion and remanded this case to us for reconsideration in light of *Hall Street Associates L.L.C. v. Mattel, Inc.,*.... We determine that *Hall Street Associates* does not undermine our prior precedent, *Kyocera Corp. v. Prudential–Bache T. Servs.,*.... As a result, in this circuit, an arbitrator's manifest disregard of the law remains a valid ground for vacatur of an arbitration award under § 10(a)(4) of the Federal Arbitration Act. Therefore, we adhere to the outcome in our prior decision.

I

Improv West is the founder of the Improv Comedy Club and the creator and owner of the "Improv" and "Improvisation" trademarks ("Improv marks"). CCI owns and operates restaurants and comedy clubs nationwide. On June 13, 1999, CCI and Improv West entered a Trademark Agreement [footnote omitted] that provided, *inter alia*: (1) that Improv West granted CCI an exclusive nationwide license to use the Improv marks in connection with the opening of new comedy clubs; (2) that, according to a development schedule, CCI was to open four Improv clubs a year in 2001 through 2003 [footnote omitted]; and (3) that CCI was prohibited from opening any non-Improv comedy clubs during the term of the Trademark Agreement. [Footnote omitted.] The Trademark Agreement also had an arbitration clause:

> All disputes relating to or arising under this Agreement or the Asset Purchase Agreement shall be resolved by arbitration in Los Angeles, California in accordance with the commercial arbitration rules of the American Arbitration Association. In any such arbitration, the parties shall be entitled to discovery in the same manner as if the dispute was being litigated in Los Angeles Superior Court. Notwithstanding this agreement to arbitrate, the parties, in addition to arbitration, shall be entitled to pursue equitable remedies and agree that the state and federal courts shall have exclusive jurisdiction for such purpose and for the purpose of compelling arbitration and/or enforcing any arbitration award. The parties agree to submit to the jurisdiction of such courts and agree that service of process in any such action may be made by certified mail. The prevailing party in any arbitration or action to enforce this Agreement or the Asset Purchase Agreement shall be entitled to its costs, including reasonable attorneys' fees.

CCI concedes that it failed to open eight Improv clubs by 2002, [footnote omitted] and that it was in default of amended § 12.a. of the Trademark Agreement. Consistent with Improv West's sole remedy, as stated in § 13.b., [footnote omitted] Improv West sent CCI a letter asserting that CCI was in default of the Trademark Agreement, withdrawing CCI's license to use the Improv marks and rights to open more Improv clubs, and informing CCI that Improv West intended to begin opening its own Improv clubs.

In response to Improv West's letter, CCI filed a complaint in federal district court seeking declaratory relief. CCI's complaint sought a declaration that the covenant that CCI could not open any non-Improv comedy clubs was void under California Business and Professions Code ("CBPC") § 16600, and that CCI's failure to meet the development schedule did not revoke CCI's license to the Improv marks or right to open Improv clubs. Improv West then filed a demand for arbitration seeking damages. [Footnote omitted.]

On August 2, 2004, the district court ordered the parties to arbitrate their dispute. CCI did not appeal that order until May 16, 2005. On February 28, 2005, the arbitrator entered a Partial Final Arbitration

Award that stated: (1) that CCI defaulted on the Trademark Agreement by failing to adhere to the development schedule listed in amended § 12.a.; (2) that CCI forfeited its rights to open Improv clubs and its use of the Improv marks license in connection with any clubs not open or under construction as of October 15, 2002; (3) that Improv West could open or license to third parties new Improv clubs; (4) that § 9.j. of the Trademark Agreement was "a valid and enforceable in-term covenant not to compete" and remained valid "for the remaining term of the Agreement"[footnote omitted]; (5) that CCI and its "Affiliates" [footnote omitted] were enjoined from opening or operating any other comedy clubs other than those open or under construction as of October 15, 2002 for the duration of the Trademark Agreement; (6) that neither CCI nor its Affiliates could change the name on any of its current clubs; and (7) that Improv West was entitled to attorneys fees and costs. On April 14, 2005, the district court confirmed the Partial Award. CCI timely appealed, tendering to us the issues addressed in this opinion. [Footnote omitted.]

In an opinion filed on September 7, 2007 and amended on January 23, 2008, we held that we did not have jurisdiction to review the district court's order compelling the parties to arbitrate; that the arbitrator did not exceed his authority by arbitrating the equitable claims; that the arbitrator did exceed his authority by issuing permanent injunctions that enjoined relatives who were not parties to the agreement; that the arbitrator's award was not completely irrational; and that the arbitrator's enforcement of the covenant not to compete was a manifest disregard of the law. The Supreme Court granted a petition for a writ of *certiorari*, vacated our prior opinion, and remanded this case to us to reconsider our decision in light of *Hall Street Associates v. Mattel*.

Both parties agree that this remand only affects the portion of the prior opinion in which we found the arbitrator acted with a "manifest disregard of the law." Therefore, we continue to hold that we do not have jurisdiction over the district court's order compelling arbitration. We also determine that the arbitrator did not exceed his authority when he arbitrated the equitable claims, but that he exceeded his authority regarding the permanent injunction that enjoined non-parties to the agreement. We also decide that the arbitrator's award was not completely irrational. Finally, addressing the issue raised by the Supreme Court's remand, we conclude that *Hall Street Associates* did not undermine the manifest disregard of law ground for vacatur, as understood in this circuit to be a violation of § 10(a)(4) of the Federal Arbitration Act, and that the arbitrator manifestly disregarded the law.

[. . .]

Finally, we address CCI's claim that the partial arbitration award should be vacated because it is in violation of CBPC § 16600. CCI argues that the arbitrator's validation of § 9.j. is in manifest disregard of the law. Improv West counters that after the recent Supreme Court case, *Hall Street Associates*, 128 S. Ct. 1396 (2008), manifest disregard of the law is not a valid ground for vacatur. In *Hall Street Associates*, the Supreme Court held that the FAA provided exclusive grounds to modify or vacate an arbitration award. *Id.* at 1404. Improv West argues that manifest disregard of the law is not among the statutory grounds for vacatur, and therefore we must amend our prior opinion that vacated this part of the arbitrator's award for that reason.

We have already determined that the manifest disregard ground for vacatur is shorthand for a statutory ground under the FAA, specifically 9 U.S.C. § 10(a)(4), which states that the court may vacate "where the arbitrators exceeded their powers." *Kyocera Corp. v. Prudential–Bache T. Servs.*, 341 F.3d 987, 997 (9th Cir. 2003) (en banc) (holding that "arbitrators 'exceed their powers' . . . when the award is 'completely irrational,' or exhibits a 'manifest disregard of law' ") (citations omitted). The Supreme Court did not reach the question of whether the manifest disregard of the law doctrine fits within §§ 10 or 11 of the FAA. *Hall Street Associates,* 128 S. Ct. at 1404. Instead, it listed several possible readings of the doctrine, including our own. *Id.* ("Or, as some courts have thought, 'manifest disregard' may have been shorthand for § 10(a)(3) or § 10(a)(4), the subsections authorizing vacatur when the arbitrators were 'guilty of misconduct' or 'exceeded their powers.' ") (*citing Kyocera,* 341 F.3d at 997). We cannot say that *Hall Street Associates* is "clearly irreconcilable" with *Kyocera* and thus we are bound by our prior precedent. . . . Therefore, we conclude that, after *Hall Street Associates*, manifest disregard of the law remains a valid ground for vacatur because it is a part of § 10(a)(4). We note that we join the Second Circuit in this interpretation of *Hall Street Associates. Stolt-Nielsen Transportation,* 548 F.3d 85, 96 (2d Cir. 2008). *But see Ramos–Santiago v. UPS,* 524 F.3d 120, 124 n.3 (1st Cir. 2004).

We have stated that for an arbitrator's award to be in manifest disregard of the law, "[i]t must be clear from the record that the arbitrator[ ] recognized the applicable law and then ignored it." *Mich. Mut. Ins. Co. v. Unigard Sec. Ins. Co.,* 44 F.3d 826, 832 (9th Cir. 1995).

[. . .]

CITIGROUP GLOBAL MKTS. INC. v. BACON

562 F.3d 349 (5th Cir. 2009).

E. GRADY JOLLY, Circuit Judge:

An arbitration panel ordered Citigroup Global Markets to pay Debra Bacon $256,000. Citigroup moved the district court to vacate the award, and the district court obliged on the basis that the arbitrators had manifestly disregarded the law. On appeal, we consider whether manifest disregard of the law remains a valid ground for vacatur of an arbitration award in the light of the Supreme Court's recent decision in *Hall Street Associates, L.L.C. v. Mattel, Inc.,* 128 S. Ct. 1396, 1403, 170 L. Ed. 2d 254 (2008). [Footnote omitted.] We conclude that *Hall Street* restricts the grounds for vacatur to those set forth in § 10 of the Federal Arbitration Act (FAA or Act), 9 U.S.C. § 1 et seq., and consequently, manifest disregard of the law is no longer an independent ground for vacating arbitration awards under the FAA. *Hall Street* effectively overrules our previous authority to the contrary, so we must VACATE the district court's judgment and REMAND for reconsideration in accord with the exclusivity of the statutory grounds.

I.

Debra Bacon's quarrel with Citigroup began in 2002 when she discovered that her husband had withdrawn funds from her Citigroup Individual Retirement Accounts without her permission. By forging her signature, he made five withdrawals totaling $238,000. As soon as Bacon discovered the unauthorized withdrawals, she notified Citigroup.

In 2004, Bacon submitted a claim in arbitration against Citigroup seeking reimbursement for the unauthorized withdrawals. The arbitration panel granted Bacon $218,000 in damages and $38,000 in attorneys' fees. Citing § 10 of the FAA, Citigroup made an application to the district court requesting vacatur of the award.

The district granted the motion to vacate, holding that the award was made in manifest disregard of the law. The court based its holding on three grounds: 1) Bacon was not harmed by the withdrawals because her husband used the money for her benefit and subsequently promised to pay her back; 2) Bacon's claims were barred by Texas law, which permits such claims only if the customer reports the unauthorized transaction within thirty days of the withdrawal; and 3) Texas law requires apportionment among the liable parties, which, in this case, includes Bacon's husband.

Bacon appeals. We review *de novo* the vacatur of an arbitration award. . . .

II

A.

Although *Hall Street* clearly has the effect of further restricting the role of federal courts in the arbitration process, there is nothing revolutionary about its holding.

Even before the enactment of the United States Arbitration Act in 1925, [footnote omitted] courts of equity would set aside an arbitration award only in narrowly defined circumstances. . . . If the arbitration award was "within the submission, and contain[ed] the honest decision of the arbitrators, after a full and fair hearing of the parties, a court of equity [would] not set it aside for error, either in law or fact." . . . This deference was appropriate because a submission agreement—a document executed by both parties and presented to the arbitrators in order to outline the dispute and the desired arbitration procedures—was a valid and enforceable contract. . . . Thus, a provision in the submission agreement requiring the parties to abide by the arbitrator's decision made the arbitration award binding. Even when a submission agreement did not contain an express agreement to adhere to the decision of the arbitrators, courts implied such an agreement and enforced the awards as binding. . . . Although arbitration was binding and final, awards could be set aside in the following circumstances: (1) where the arbitrators engaged in fraud, corruption, or improper conduct; (2) where the arbitrators failed to decide all of the issues submitted; (3) where the arbitrators exceeded their powers by deciding issues not submitted; and (4) where the award was not certain, final, and mutual. . . . These limited grounds are akin to the provisions of § 10 of the FAA.

Importantly, awards were affirmed even if based upon error in law or fact. . . . "A contrary course would be a substitution of the judgment of the chancellor in place of the judges chosen by the parties, and would make an award the commencement, not the end, of litigation." . . . [The case law] also cautioned against assuming improper conduct from mere error: "We are all too prone, perhaps, to impute either weakness of intellect or corrupt motives to those who differ with us in opinion." . . . The Supreme Court has continued to emphasize the importance of respecting the arbitration process. In *Hall Street,* the Court explained: permitting vacatur and modification of arbitration awards on more expansive grounds "opens the door to the full-bore legal and evidentiary appeals that can rende[r] informal arbitration merely a prelude to a more cumbersome and time-consuming judicial review process, and bring arbitration theory to grief in post-arbitration process." . . .

In short, strictly confining the perimeter of federal court review of arbitration awards is a widely accepted practice that runs throughout arbitration jurisprudence—from its early common law and equity days to the present.

B.

1.

Congress embraced this notion that arbitration awards should generally be upheld barring some sort of procedural injustice, and §§ 10 and 11 of the FAA enumerate the circumstances under which an award may be vacated, modified, or corrected when the action is one brought under the Act. . . .

[. . .]

Based both on the text and on the legislative history, *Hall Street* concluded that §§ 10 and 11 provide the exclusive regimes for review under the FAA. The Court reiterated this holding several times: "We hold that the statutory grounds are exclusive"; "We agree with the Ninth Circuit that they are [exclusive] . . ."; "We now hold that §§ 10 and 11 respectively provide the FAA's exclusive grounds for expedited vacatur and modification"; "In holding that §§ 10 and 11 provide exclusive regimes for the review provided by the statute. . . . "*Hall Street,* 128 S.Ct. at 1400, 1401, 1403, 1406. This rule, *Hall Street* determined, is consistent with the "national policy favoring arbitration with just the limited review needed to maintain arbitration's essential virtue of resolving disputes straightaway." ...

2.

[...]

... In short, *Hall Street* rejected manifest disregard as an independent ground for vacatur, and stood by its clearly and repeatedly stated holding, as noted in the earlier paragraph, that §§ 10 and 11 provide the exclusive bases for vacatur and modification of an arbitration award under the FAA.

C.

It is certainly true that over the years this circuit, like most other circuits, [footnote omitted] ultimately came to recognize manifest disregard of the law as a nonstatutory basis for vacatur.... Even so, manifest disregard of the law was defined as a standard difficult to satisfy. Manifest disregard of the law

> means more than error or misunderstanding with respect to the law. The error must have been obvious and capable of being readily and instantly perceived by the average person qualified to serve as an arbitrator. Moreover the term "disregard" implies that the arbitrator appreciates the existence of a clearly governing principle but decides to ignore or pay no attention to it.

... In addition, we have stated that an award may be vacated for manifest disregard of the law only when "the award resulted in, a 'significant injustice.'" ...

Our circuit did not accept manifest disregard of the law as a nonstatutory ground for vacatur with immediate confidence and certainty.... Indeed, manifest disregard of the law does not have a compelling origin as a ground for vacatur. Its modest debut occurs in a vague phrase found in *Wilko v. Swan*: "the interpretations of law by the arbitrators in contrast to manifest disregard are not subject, in the federal courts, to judicial review for error in interpretation." ... That is all *Wilko* said about it.

Thus, it is not surprising that the lower courts initially grappled with the uncertain implications of this clause.... Uncertain about the propriety of vacating an award for manifest disregard of the law, some courts avoided the issue by assuming, without deciding, that it was a valid ground for vacatur, but declining to vacate the award nonetheless.... Some circuits continued to maintain the exclusivity of the statutory grounds, in the face of *Wilko,* for decades.... However, despite its uncertain genesis, most circuits eventually accepted manifest disregard of the law as a valid extra statutory ground for vacatur....

We were among the very last to adopt manifest disregard.... But in *Williams v. CIGNA,* nearly fifty years after *Wilko,* we finally embraced manifest disregard as a nonstatutory ground for vacating arbitration awards.... We concluded that the departure from precedent was necessary and justified in the light of the Supreme Court's opinion in *First Options of Chicago, Inc. v. Kaplan,* which cited 9 U.S.C. § 10 and *Wilko* for the proposition that courts will set arbitration awards aside "only in very unusual circumstances." ...

III.

A.

The question before us now is whether, under the FAA, manifest disregard of the law remains valid, as an independent ground for vacatur, after *Hall Street.* The answer seems clear. *Hall Street* unequivocally held that the statutory grounds are the exclusive means for vacatur under the FAA. Our case law defines manifest disregard of the law as a *nonstatutory* ground for vacatur.... Thus, to the extent that manifest disregard of the law constitutes a nonstatutory ground for vacatur, it is no longer a basis for vacating awards under the FAA.

Four other circuits have considered this issue. The First Circuit, in dictum and with little discussion, concluded that *Hall Street* abolished manifest disregard of the law as a ground for vacatur.[Footnote omitted.] *See Ramos–Santiago v. United Parcel Serv.,* 524 F.3d 120, 124 n.3 (1st Cir. 2008) ("We acknowledge the Supreme Court's recent holding in *Hall Street Assocs., L.L.C. v. Mattel* that manifest disregard of the law is not a valid ground for vacating or modifying an arbitral award in cases brought under the [FAA].") .... The Sixth Circuit, in an unpublished opinion, reached the opposite conclusion by narrowly construing the holding of *Hall Street* to apply only to contractual expansions of the grounds for review. *Coffee Beanery, Ltd. v. WW, L.L.C.,* ... 2008 WL 4899478, at *4 (6th Cir. 2008). The Second Circuit has also held that manifest disregard survives *Hall Street. Stolt–Nielsen SA v. AnimalFeeds Int'l Corp.,* 548 F.3d 85, 93–95 (2d Cir. 2008). The court, however, recognized that *Hall Street's* holding was in direct conflict with the application of manifest disregard as a nonstatutory ground for review, but resolved the conflict by recasting manifest disregard as a shorthand for § 10(a)(4).... Finally, the Ninth Circuit has concluded that *Hall Street* did not abolish manifest disregard because its case law defined manifest disregard as shorthand for § 10(a)(4). *See Comedy Club Inc. v. Improv West Assocs.,* 553 F.3d 1277, 1290, ... (9th Cir. 2009) (*"Comedy Club II"*). We now turn to discuss the opinions of the Sixth, Second, and Ninth Circuits.

1.

Coffee Beanery only briefly considered the effect of *Hall Street* on manifest disregard of the law.... In what we view as an understatement, the Sixth Circuit acknowledged that *Hall Street* "significantly reduced the ability of federal courts to vacate arbitration awards for reasons other than those specified in 9 U.S.C. § 10...." Citing *Hall Street's* discussion of *Wilko,* which *Coffee Beanery* thought demonstrated a "hesitation to reject the 'manifest disregard' doctrine," and noting the acceptance of the standard by each and every court of appeals, the court concluded that it would be imprudent to cease vacating arbitration awards made in manifest disregard of the law. . . .

This decision suffers from two significant flaws. First, the opinion utterly fails to address *Hall Street*'s express holding that the grounds for vacatur found in § 10 are exclusive. Instead, the court narrowly construed *Hall Street* as applying only to contractual expansions of the grounds for vacatur. . . . In the light of *Hall Street*'s repeated statements that *"We hold* that the statutory grounds are exclusive," we think it incorrect so narrowly to construe *Hall Street*'s holding. 128 S. Ct. at 1400 (emphasis added).

Second, we believe that *Coffee Beanery* misread *Hall Street*'s discussion of *Wilko*. We do not see hesitation by *Hall Street* to reject manifest disregard of the law as an independent ground for vacating an award under the FAA; instead, *Hall Street's* discussion of *Wilko* demonstrates the Supreme Court's unwillingness to give any significant meaning to *Wilko's* vague language. *Hall Street* observed that *Wilko* dealt with an entirely separate issue and, noting the vagueness of *Wilko's* statement, concluded that: "When speaking as a Court, we have taken the *Wilko* language as we found it, without embellishment, and now that its meaning is implicated, we see no reason to accord it the significance that [the petitioner] urges." . . .

2.

Unlike *Coffee Beanery,* the Second Circuit in *Stolt-Nielsen* did not shy from *Hall Street*'s holding. The court acknowledged that *Hall Street* "held that the FAA sets forth the 'exclusive' grounds for vacating an arbitration award." . . . The court also recognized that this holding was in conflict with its own prior statements regarding manifest disregard, which the court discounted as *dicta*. . . . Instead of directly concluding that *Hall Street* eliminated manifest disregard as a ground for vacatur under the FAA, the court reasoned that manifest disregard of the law should be "reconceptualized as a judicial gloss on the specific grounds for vacatur enumerated in section 10 of the FAA. . . ."

Describing its "reconceptualization," the court stated:

> We must therefore continue to bear the responsibility to vacate arbitration awards in the rare instances in which "the arbitrator knew of the relevant [legal] principle, appreciated that this principle controlled the outcome of the disputed issue, and nonetheless willfully flouted the governing law by refusing to apply it." . . . At that point the arbitrators have "failed to interpret the contract at all," . . . for parties do not agree in advance to submit to arbitration that is carried out in manifest disregard of the law. Put another way, the arbitrators have thereby "exceeded their powers, or so imperfectly executed them that a mutual, final, and definite award upon the subject matter submitted was not made." . . .

Stolt-Nielsen, 548 F.3d at 95. Thus, the court seems to conclude that manifest disregard—as the court describes it—does not add to the statutory grounds. The court simply folds manifest disregard into § 10(a)(4).[1] In the full context of the Second Circuit's reasoning, this analysis is not inconsistent with *Hall Street's* speculation that manifest disregard may, among other things, "have been shorthand for § 10(a)(3) or § 10(a)(4)...." .....

We should be careful to observe, however, that this description of manifest disregard is very narrow. Because the arbitrator is fully aware of the controlling principle of law and yet does not apply it, he flouts the law in such a manner as to exceed the powers bestowed upon him. This scenario does not include an erroneous application of that principle. [Footnote omitted.]

3.

... In a decision issued prior to *Hall Street,* the Ninth Circuit found that the arbitration award at issue constituted a manifest disregard of the law.... The Supreme Court then vacated the decision in *Comedy Club I* and remanded for reconsideration in the light of its recently issued decision in *Hall Street*....

On remand, the Ninth Circuit, unlike the Second Circuit, had no need to reconceptualize manifest disregard because its own case law had already defined it as a shorthand for § 10(a)(4). *Comedy Club,* 553 F.3d at 1290. The court therefore held that manifest disregard of the law, as a shorthand for § 10(a)(4), survived *Hall Street.* ...

B.

In the light of the Supreme Court's clear language that, under the FAA, the statutory provisions are the exclusive grounds for vacatur, manifest disregard of the law as an independent, nonstatutory ground for setting aside an award must be abandoned and rejected. Indeed, the term itself, as a term of legal art, is no longer useful in actions to vacate arbitration awards. *Hall Street* made it plain that the statutory language means what it says: "courts *must* [confirm the award] unless the award is vacated, modified, or corrected as prescribed in sections 10 and 11 of this title," ... and there's nothing malleable about "must" ... Thus from this point forward, arbitration awards under the FAA may be vacated only for reasons provided in § 10.

To the extent that our ... precedent holds that nonstatutory grounds may support the vacatur of an arbitration award, it is hereby overruled.

IV.

The district court, which issued its opinion before *Hall Street,* held that the arbitrators in this case manifestly disregarded the law. The

---

1. The court relies heavily upon the Seventh Circuit's decision in *Wise v. Wachovia Securities, LLC,* which noted that the Seventh Circuit has defined manifest disregard "so narrowly that it fits comfortably under the first clause of the fourth statutory ground." 450 F.3d 265, 268 (7th Cir. 2006).

judgment of the district court is therefore VACATED. The court, however, did not consider whether the grounds asserted for vacating the award might support vacatur under any of the statutory grounds. Accordingly, we REMAND for further consideration not inconsistent with this opinion. The judgment of the district court is VACATED and the case REMANDED. . . .

STOLT-NIELSEN SA v. ANIMALFEEDS INT'L CORP.

548 F.3d 85, 91–96 (2d Cir. 2008).
(*certiorari* granted on June 15, 2009)

SACK, Circuit Judge:

The parties to this litigation are also parties to international maritime contracts that contain arbitration clauses. The contracts are silent as to whether arbitration is permissible on behalf of a class of contracting parties. The question presented on this appeal is whether the arbitration panel, in issuing a clause construction award construing that silence to permit class arbitration, acted in manifest disregard of the law. The United States District Court for the Southern District of New York (Jed S. Rakoff, *Judge*) answered that question in the affirmative and therefore vacated the award. We conclude to the contrary that the demanding "manifest disregard" standard has not been met. The judgment of the district court is therefore reversed and the cause remanded with instructions to deny the petition to vacate.

[. . .]

A. Legal Standards

The party seeking to vacate an award on the basis of the arbitrator's alleged "manifest disregard" of the law bears a "heavy burden." . . . "Our review under the [judicially constructed] doctrine of manifest disregard is 'severely limited.' ". . . . "It is highly deferential to the arbitral award and obtaining judicial relief for arbitrators' manifest disregard of the law is rare." . . . [Footnote omitted.] The "manifest disregard" doctrine allows a reviewing court to vacate an arbitral award only in "those exceedingly rare instances where some egregious impropriety on the part of the arbitrators is apparent." . . . .

Vacatur of an arbitral award is unusual for good reason: The parties agreed to submit their dispute to arbitration, more likely than not to enhance efficiency, to reduce costs, or to maintain control over who would settle their disputes and how—or some combination thereof. . . . "To interfere with this process would frustrate the intent of the parties, and thwart the usefulness of arbitration, making it 'the commencement, not the end, of litigation.' " . . . It would fail to "maintain arbitration's essential virtue of resolving disputes straightaway." . . .

In this light, "manifest disregard" has been interpreted "clearly [to] mean[] more than error or misunderstanding with respect to the law. . . ." We are not at liberty to set aside an arbitration panel's award because of an arguable difference regarding the meaning or applicability of laws urged upon it. . . .

[. . .]

In the context of contract interpretation, we are required to confirm arbitration awards despite "serious reservations about the soundness of the arbitrator's reading of th[e] contract." . . . "Whether the arbitrators misconstrued a contract is not open to judicial review." . . . "Whatever arbitrators' mistakes of law may be corrected, simple misinterpretations of contracts do not appear one of them." . . .

[. . .]

B.   The Effect of *Hall Street* on the "Manifest Disregard" Doctrine

We pause to consider whether a recent Supreme Court decision, *Hall Street Associates, L.L.C. v. Mattel, Inc.,* . . . affects the scope or vitality of the "manifest disregard" doctrine.

[. . .]

In the short time since *Hall Street* was decided, courts have begun to grapple with its implications for the "manifest disregard" doctrine. Some have concluded or suggested that the doctrine simply does not survive. . . . Others think that "manifest disregard," reconceptualized as a judicial gloss on the specific grounds for vacatur enumerated in section 10 of the FAA, remains a valid ground for vacating arbitration awards. . . .

We agree with those courts that take the latter approach. The *Hall Street* Court held that the FAA sets forth the "exclusive" grounds for vacating an arbitration award. . . . That holding is undeniably inconsistent with some *dicta* by this Court treating the "manifest disregard" standard as a ground for vacatur entirely separate from those enumerated in the FAA. . . . [Footnote omitted.] But the *Hall Street* Court also speculated that "the term 'manifest disregard' . . . merely referred to the § 10 grounds collectively, rather than adding to them"—or as "shorthand for § 10 (a)(3) or § 10 (a)(4)." . . . It did not, we think, abrogate the "manifest disregard" doctrine altogether. [Footnote omitted.]

We agree with the Seventh Circuit's view expressed before *Hall Street* was decided:

> It is tempting to think that courts are engaged in judicial review of arbitration awards under the Federal Arbitration Act, but they are not. When parties agree to arbitrate their disputes they opt out of the court system, and when one of them challenges the resulting arbitration award he perforce does so not on the ground that the arbitrators made a mistake but that they violated the agreement to arbitrate, as by corruption, evident partiality, exceeding their powers, etc.—conduct to which the parties did not consent when they included an arbitration clause in their contract. That is why in the typical arbitration . . . the issue for the court is not whether the contract interpretation is incorrect or even wacky but whether the arbitrators had failed to interpret the contract at all, for only then were they exceeding the authority granted to them by the contract's arbitration clause.

Wise v. Wachovia Sec., LLC, 450 F.3d 265, 269 (7th Cir.) (citations omitted), *cert. denied,* 549 U.S. 1047, 127 S. Ct. 582, 166 L. Ed. 2d 458 (2006). This observation is entirely consistent with *Hall Street.* And it reinforces our own *pre-Hall Street* statements that our review for manifest disregard is "severely limited," "highly deferential," and confined to "those exceedingly rare instances" of "egregious impropriety on the part of the arbitrators." . . .

Like the Seventh Circuit, we view the "manifest disregard" doctrine, and the FAA itself, as a mechanism to enforce the parties' agreements to arbitrate rather than as judicial review of the arbitrators' decision. We must therefore continue to bear the responsibility to vacate arbitration awards in the rare instances in which "the arbitrator knew of the relevant [legal] principle, appreciated that this principle controlled the outcome of the disputed issue, and nonetheless willfully flouted the governing law by refusing to apply it." . . . At that point the arbitrators have "failed to interpret the contract at all," . . . for parties do not agree in advance to submit to arbitration that is carried out in manifest disregard of the law. Put another way, the arbitrators have thereby "exceeded their powers, or so imperfectly executed them that a mutual, final, and definite award upon the subject matter submitted was not made." . . .

[. . .]

COFFEE BEANERY, LTD. v. WW, L.L.C.

300 Fed. Appx. 415, 416–419 (6th Cir. 2008).

AMENDED OPINION

COLE, Circuit Judge. Respondent–Appellant WW, L.L.C. and its two principal owners, Richard Welshans and Deborah Williams (collectively, "WW"), appeal the district court's denial of their motion to vacate an arbitration award. At issue is whether the Arbitrator showed a manifest disregard of the law when she issued her award. Because we conclude that the failure to disclose a prior felony conviction for grand larceny violates the Maryland Franchise Registration and Disclosure Law ("Franchise Act"), . . . and because the Arbitrator showed a manifest disregard of the law in concluding otherwise, we REVERSE the judgment of the district court and VACATE the Arbitrator's award.

I. BACKGROUND

Petitioner–Appellee, The Coffee Beanery Ltd., is a Michigan corporation with its principal place of business in Flushing, Michigan. Its primary business is to sell and operate Coffee Beanery franchises across the United States. The remaining Petitioners–Appellees . . . are officers of the company (collectively, "the Coffee Beanery"). WW, L.L.C. is a Maryland corporation with its principal place of business in Annapolis, Maryland.

This dispute arises out of a failed business agreement to license a Coffee Beanery Cafe. In Spring of 2003, Richard Welshans and Deborah

Williams, husband and wife, began researching the idea of opening a small coffee shop that would sell coffee and other beverages. The two arranged a meeting with Kevin Shaw, the Coffee Beanery's Vice President of Real Estate, to discuss the details of a purchase and a potential location for a store.

In June 2003, Richard and Deborah attended a Coffee Beanery "discovery day" at the headquarters in Flushing, Michigan to investigate the purchase of a franchise. During this trip, Coffee Beanery representatives took the two on a tour of the company-owned Coffee Beanery Cafe, where they met some employees and sampled food and beverages. That same day, Richard and Deborah agreed to license a Cafe Store in Annapolis, Maryland, and signed a franchise agreement to purchase and operate a store. With the consent of the Coffee Beanery, the rights, title and interest in and obligations under this agreement were later assigned to WW, L.L.C.

[. . .]

After its opening in 2003, WW's Cafe Store immediately encountered numerous difficulties. Spurned by significant losses, in January 2005, WW sent the American Arbitration Association ("AAA") and the Coffee Beanery a Demand for Mediation and Arbitration. The nature of the dispute, according to the demand, included fraud, negligent misrepresentation, fraudulent misrepresentation, fraudulent non-disclosure, breach of contract, breach of the covenant of good faith and fair dealing, violations of the Maryland Franchise Registration and Disclosure Law, Michigan Franchise Investment Law, and the Michigan Consumer Protection Act.

The arbitration process hit a snag when counsel for WW sent an email to AAA retracting its earlier demand for arbitration, because "the arbitration clause in the franchise agreement is limited to controversies between [the Coffee Beanery] and Store Owner." "The legal action that my clients are considering," the email explained, does not "fall within the scope of the arbitration agreement," and therefore "any arbitration requirement would also be of no force and effect." Based on those reasons, on December 15, 2005, WW abandoned arbitration altogether and filed suit in the United States District Court for the District of Maryland, alleging violations of the Maryland Franchise Act and seeking relief under other state-law claims for detrimental reliance, intentional misrepresentation, and negligent misrepresentation.

[. . .]

WW never accepted the rescission offer. Instead, in January 2007, it submitted its claims to arbitration in Ann Arbor, Michigan. Arbitrator JoAnne Barron presided over an eleven-day hearing that included testimony from WW, other Cafe Store owners, and representatives from the Coffee Beanery. On March 28, 2007, the Arbitrator issued an award finding in favor of the Coffee Beanery on all claims.

On April 18, 2007, WW filed a motion to vacate the arbitration award in the Eastern District of Michigan. The district court issued an order and opinion denying the motion to vacate and confirming the award.... The court found: that WW failed to establish "evident partiality" on the part of arbitrator as a ground to vacate the award; that the parties were not required to engage in mediation prior to proceeding to arbitration; that WW failed to establish fraud or perjury; and that the Arbitrator did not manifestly disregard either facts or laws when she ignored the findings made by the Commissioner....

On June 4, 2007, WW sought reconsideration of the district court's opinion and order, which the district court denied.... WW timely appealed.

II. ANALYSIS

[...]

"The Federal Arbitration Act ('FAA') expresses a presumption that arbitration awards will be confirmed." ... " 'When courts are called on to review an arbitrator's decision, the review is very narrow; [it is] one of the narrowest standards of judicial review in all of American jurisprudence.' " ... Section 10 of the FAA sets forth the statutory grounds to vacate an arbitration award; namely: (1) where the award was procured by corruption, fraud, or undue means; (2) where an arbitrator evidenced partiality or corruption; (3) where the arbitrators were guilty of misconduct; and (4) where the arbitrators exceeded their power....

This Court's ability to vacate an arbitration award is almost exclusively limited to these grounds, although it may also vacate an award found to be in manifest disregard of the law.... To constitute a manifest disregard for the law, "[a] mere error in interpretation or application of the law is insufficient. Rather, the decision must fly in the face of clearly established legal precedent." ... Thus, an arbitrator acts with manifest disregard if "(1) the applicable legal principle is clearly defined and not subject to reasonable debate; and (2) the arbitrators refused to heed that legal principle."

In *Hall Street Assocs., L.L.C. v. Mattel, Inc.*, 128 S.Ct. 1396, 170 L. Ed. 2d 254 (2008), the Supreme Court significantly reduced the ability of federal courts to vacate arbitration awards for reasons other than those specified in 9 U.S.C. § 10, but it did not foreclose federal courts' review for an arbitrator's manifest disregard of the law. The Court held that the FAA does not allow *private parties* to supplement by contract the FAA's statutory grounds for vacatur of an arbitration award.... Moreover, the Court rejected reading *Wilko* to allow any "general review for an arbitrator's legal errors." ... However, with respect to the judicially-invoked, narrow exception for an arbitrator's manifest disregard of the law, the Court acknowledged that "[m]aybe the term 'manifest disregard' [in *Wilko*] was meant to name a new ground for review," though it also suggested that narrower interpretations of *Wilko* were equally plausible.... The Court did not come to a conclusion regarding the precise meaning of *Wilko,* holding only that *Wilko* could not be read to allow parties to expand the scope of judicial review by their own agreement....

It is worth noting that since *Wilko,* every federal appellate court has allowed for the vacatur of an award based on an arbitrator's manifest disregard of the law.... In light of the Supreme Court's hesitation to reject the "manifest disregard" doctrine in all circumstances, we believe it would be imprudent to cease employing such a universally recognized principle. Accordingly, this Court will follow its well-established precedent here and continue to employ the "manifest disregard" standard.

[...]

5. EXCESS OF AUTHORITY AND ARBITRATOR MISCONDUCT

AGRAWAL v. AGRAWAL

775 F.Supp. 588, 591 (E.D.N.Y. 1991), *aff'd,* 969 F.2d 1041 (2d Cir. 1992).

[...]

Where the issue is whether the arbitrator properly exercised authority actually delegated to him, the Second Circuit has held that "if an arbitrator offers even a barely colorable justification for [the] decision, we will not vacate it on the basis of a claim [that] he exceeded his authority by misinterpreting the parties' contract." ...Such a holding reflects the rule that "arbitrators must have broad authority to interpret the contracts they apply."

[...]

NOTES AND QUESTIONS

1. *Agrawal* provides the generally operative definition of excess of authority under U.S. law. In most arbitration laws, excess of authority means that the arbitrators ruled on matters not submitted. They thereby exceeded their jurisdictional authority. How does that view of the basis for vacatur square with the definition in *Agrawal*? In your view, which approach is better? Why?

2. Is there a presumption against a finding of excessive use of authority by arbitrators? If so, how does it arise?

3. Does the excess authority ground merge with manifest disregard? If so, why tolerate the duplication? Does it serve any real purpose?

4. What factor in the excerpt might indicate that the ruling applies to a matter of labor arbitration? Is FAA arbitration coextensive with labor arbitration? Why and why not?

FAHNESTOCK & CO., INC. v. WALTMAN

935 F.2d 512, 515–17 (2d Cir. 1991).

[. . .]

DISCUSSION

I. *Compensatory Award*

An arbitration award may be vacated "[w]here the arbitrators exceeded their powers,". . .or where the arbitrators acted in "manifest disregard of the law." . . .Fahnestock asserts that the Arbitrators exceeded their powers and manifestly disregarded the law in granting an award for defamation based on its filing of the amended Form U–5. Fahnestock argues that, because it was required by law to file the form, the filing was subject to an absolute privilege. Therefore, it urges that the filing of the Form U–5 could not serve as a basis for an award for defamation. Fahnestock's arguments are without merit.

We have consistently accorded the narrowest reading to section 10(d), "especially when it 'has been invoked in the context of the arbitrators' alleged failure to correctly decide a question which all concede to have been properly submitted in the first instance.' ". . . Consequently, we have recognized that if arbitrators "rule[ ] on issues not presented to [them] by the parties, [they have] exceeded [their] authority and the award must be vacated." . . .Here, it is uncontested that the ruling of the Arbitrators was confined to the issues presented by the parties. Moreover, we have recognized that defamation claims based on statements in a Form U–5 are arbitrable. . . . Therefore, any argument that it is beyond the power of arbitrators to decide these types of claims is contrary to the law of this circuit. Nor are we persuaded that the Arbitrators manifestly disregarded the law in awarding Waltman damages for defamation. Judicial inquiry under the manifest disregard standard likewise is extremely limited. . . . We have held that there must be "something beyond and different from a mere error in the law or failure on the part of the arbitrators to understand or apply the law". . .in order to sustain a finding of manifest disregard of the law. Illustrative of the degree of "disregard" necessary to support vacatur under this standard is our holding that manifest disregard will be found where an "arbitrator 'understood and correctly stated the law but proceeded to ignore it.' ". . .

[. . .]

Here, the Arbitrators never indicated the reasons for the defamation award. However, it is axiomatic that arbitrators need not disclose the rationale for their award. . . . "[I]f a ground for the arbitrator's decision can be inferred from the facts of the case, the award should be confirmed." . . .Therefore, even though Fahnestock was protected by the qualified privilege in filing the amended form, based on the evidence, the arbitrators acted well within the bounds of their broad authority in making an award of compensatory damages in favor of Waltman.... The ample evidence of Fahnestock's flagrantly spiteful conduct, demonstrating its intent to simply injure Waltman's reputation, presented the Arbitrators with sufficient grounds to find that no qualified privilege attached to Fahnestock's filing of the amended form....

[...]

NOTES AND QUESTIONS

1. It is difficult to harness the revolving definitions and concepts that float through the opinion. How does the policy on arbitration help to resolve that problem and provide focus on the question of judicial supervision and vacatur?

2. Is excess of authority synonymous with manifest disregard? Is there a separate basis for each ground or are they fully interchangeable? Can one be constituted without the other?

3. How can the awarding of a specific type of damages constitute both excess authority and manifest disregard?

4. How does the provision of reasons or an explanation of the result fit into the discussion about excess of authority and judicial supervision?

5. How would you rewrite FAA § 10 to reform or codify the courts' approach to the confirmation or vacatur of arbitral awards?

6. Labor arbitrators are sometimes said to favor the unionized worker. They, therefore, approach the definition of "just cause" for termination under the collective bargaining agreement (CBA) with the worker's interests in mind. In many cases, they conclude that the imposition of discipline is warranted but not termination. In this framework, substance-abusing airline pilots, nuclear plant workers, and oil tanker captains have been reinstated to their positions. Whatever the merits of the practice, courts have been reluctant under FAA § 10 and the federal policy on arbitration to reverse the determinations and vacate the awards.

7. In *IMC–Agrico Co. v. International Chem. Workers Council of United Food and Commercial Workers Union, AFL-CIO*, 171 F.3d 1322 (11th Cir. 1999), an employee had a confrontation with her supervisor. IMC fired her for threatening the supervisor and for gross insubordination. In the eventual arbitration, Whitely alleged that IMC violated the CBA by terminating her without just cause. The arbitrator found that Whitely had been argumentative during the incident, used abusive language, threatened the supervisor, and refused to leave the premises when instructed to do so. The arbitrator ruled that, according to IMC's internal rules, major infractions could result in discharge or disciplinary leave. He concluded that IMC had just cause to impose a severe penalty, but not discharge. IMC objected to the reinstatement and filed an appeal to vacate the award. The district court vacated the award, but the U.S. Court of Appeals for the Eleventh Circuit upheld it, ruling that the Arbitrator "reasonably interpreted [the] collective bargaining agreement's...just-cause provisions...."

"A court may not vacate an arbitral award unless it is irrational, 'exceeds the scope of the arbitrator's authority,' or 'fails to draw its essence from the collective bargaining agreement.'" An arbitrator exceeds the scope of his authority and issues an award outside the essence of the agreement "when he issues an award that contradicts the express language of the agreement."

The issue presented to the arbitrator was not only whether Whitely engaged in a certain conduct, but also whether there was just cause for the discharge. The court recognized that courts give "great deference to an arbitrator's interpretation of the provisions of a collective bargaining agreement...It is not [the court's] role to review the merits of the arbitrator's interpretation, but only to ask whether it was arguably based on the language of the agreement."

The court rejected IMC's argument that, once an arbitrator finds that an employee engaged in prohibited conduct, it is an implicit finding of just cause for termination and any type of discipline imposed by the employer is beyond the scope of the arbitrator's adjudicatory powers. The court reasoned that

> [i]f the collective bargaining agreement confers on the employer the absolute right to discharge employees for certain types of conduct, then the inquiry of an arbitrator can be limited to whether or not the disciplined employee did or did not engage in the specific conduct which resulted in the disciplinary action.

Furthermore, "once an arbitrator implicitly finds that the employee engaged in conduct that is defined by a bargaining agreement to be an offense subjecting [the employee] to discharge, then that it is an implicit finding of just cause and the arbitrator's task is finished." The CBA, however, "[did] not clearly indicate whether the just-cause provision applies to the company's choice of a particular sanction" and did not contain a definition of just cause or any list of offenses that would automatically call for discharge.

VOLD v. BROIN & ASSOCIATES, INC.

699 N.W.2d 482 (S.D. 2005).

KONENKAMP, Justice.

In this appeal, we review a circuit court's decision to vacate an arbitration award. Because the arbitrator failed to follow his own order to issue a "reasoned award," we affirm.

BACKGROUND

Broin & Associates is a South Dakota corporation engaged in the business of designing and constructing ethanol production facilities. On November 2, 2000, Broin contracted to design and build a production plant known as Northern Lights Ethanol, L.L.C. Broin served as the general contractor for the project.

In April 2001, Broin signed a contract with Gregory Vold ... who would perform the site and grading work. From the beginning, there were difficulties. By December 2002, Vold had not completed much of the required work. As a result, on December 19, 2002, Broin terminated Vold's contract for cause.

In November 2003, Vold filed a demand for arbitration, seeking payment for unapproved change orders, alleged work stoppages, and other claims. Under their contract, "[a]ll claims, disputes, and other matters in question between Design/Builder and Contractor arising out of or relating to the Construction Agreement Documents or the breach thereof ... will be decided by binding arbitration in accordance with the Construction Industry Arbitration Rules of the American Arbitration Association [AAA]." Broin filed an answering statement with the AAA, denying liability on Vold's claims and seeking reimbursement for the costs and expenses sustained in connection with the remaining grading work on the construction project. Vold had thirteen claims, totaling more than $800,000. Broin had eleven claims, totaling approximately $500,000.

... [The arbitrator] conducted a telephonic preliminary hearing with the parties.... During the hearing, it was agreed that each side would submit a specification of claims to the AAA outlining their respective demands.... As the hearing progressed, Tim R. Shattuck, one of the attorneys for Broin, requested that the arbitrator issue a "reasoned award." According to another of Broin's attorneys, Daniel R. Harmelink, the attorney for Vold, Ron Schmidt, consented to the award being in the form of a "reasoned award." Attorney Ron Schmidt, however, denies that he agreed to a reasoned award. There was no verbatim record kept of the hearing.

After the preliminary hearing, the arbitrator prepared and signed a report and scheduling order indicating that the form of the award was to be a "reasoned award." ...

... On July 13, 2004, the arbitrator issued his decision awarding $267,298 in damages to Vold and denying Broin's counterclaims. The arbitrator's award consisted of two pages. It itemized the various dollar amounts allowed for each of Vold's claims, but gave no reason for each award and no reason for rejecting Broin's claims. The award did not mention any of the relevant contract provisions at issue, cite any law, or discuss any of the evidence admitted during the four day hearing.

Following the arbitrator's decision, Broin sought to vacate the award in circuit court. The court heard the matter on September 8, 2004, and thereafter issued its Findings of Fact and Conclusions of Law and Order Granting Motion to Vacate Arbitration Award and Denying Motion to Confirm Award. Several times in its "findings" the court noted ... that both Broin and Vold had agreed to a reasoned award during the telephonic preliminary hearing with the arbitrator on February 2, 2004. It is unclear how the court reached this factual, and perhaps, credibility, determination, since it appears that it heard no testimony during the hearing. Nonetheless, the court went on to conclude that "the parties had agreed to the issuance of a reasoned award" and "the arbitrator had exceeded the authority granted him by Broin and Vold by failing to issue a reasoned award." Accordingly, the court ruled that federal law required the award to be vacated.

[. . .]

ANALYSIS AND DECISION

In examining a circuit court's order vacating an arbitration award, we review the court's findings of fact under the clearly erroneous standard, but decide questions of law *de novo.* . . . "However, we must accord 'an extraordinary level of deference' to the underlying award itself." . . . "Indeed, we must confirm the award even if we are convinced that the arbitrator committed serious error, so 'long as the arbitrator is even arguably construing or applying the contract and acting within the scope of his authority.' " . . .

Arbitrators possess broad, but not unlimited, authority. . . . Section 10 of the FAA lists several bases for vacating an arbitration award. In addition, circuit courts may also vacate arbitration awards that are "completely irrational" or that "evidence a manifest disregard for the law." . . .

The arbitrator, Vold contends, was vested with discretion in how he handed down the final decision and award: the "arbitrator determined that he had no duty under the AAA Construction Industry Arbitration Rules to render a 'reasoned' award." Because the "parties did not request any reasoned award, in writing, prior to the appointment of the arbitrator," Vold argues that the arbitrator's decision to declare an award without a reasoned explanation was within his right. And, even if the agreement was changed to require a "reasoned award," Vold contends that the matter was one of procedure, rather than substance, precluding the circuit court from substituting its judgment for that of the arbitrator. As such, Vold argues that the circuit court's sole basis for vacating the arbitration award was procedural in nature, therefore constituting reversible error.

In addressing Vold's arguments, we first turn to the Construction Industry Arbitration Rules provided by the AAA. Rule R–1(a) states: " . . . The parties, by written agreement, may vary the procedures set forth in these rules. After appointment of the arbitrator, such modifications may be made only with the consent of the arbitrator." In accord with R–21(b), "the parties and the arbitrator," during the preliminary hearing, "should discuss the future conduct of the case, including clarification of the issues and claims, a schedule for the hearings and any other preliminary matters."

It is undisputed that no request for a reasoned award was made in writing prior to the arbitrator's appointment. At the preliminary hearing held on February 2, 2004, a request was made for a reasoned award by Broin's counsel. Vold's attorney denies that he consented to a reasoned award. After the preliminary hearing, nonetheless, the arbitrator prepared and signed a report and scheduling order, indicating that the form of the award was to be a "reasoned award." Vold contends that the parties did not agree to amend the form of the award. He also argues that the arbitrator's notation on the preliminary hearing report and scheduling order was merely suggestive, and thus the arbitrator was under no duty to issue a "reasoned award."

The preliminary hearing order, however, was then submitted to the AAA by the arbitrator. On February 10, 2004, the AAA case manager sent a letter to all parties, which reflected the terms of the arbitrator's preliminary hearing report and scheduling order. The letter indicated that "[t]he form of Award to be issued in the above matter will be a reasoned award," and that "[t]his order shall continue in effect unless and until amended by subsequent order by the arbitrator." No amendment was ever made or requested. Accordingly, the requirement of a reasoned award was apparently consented to by the arbitrator and confirmed and memorialized in writing under the terms of the preliminary hearing report and scheduling order and the letter issued by the AAA.

We now turn our analysis to the Federal Arbitration Act. "The Federal Arbitration Act (FAA) preempts state law and governs all written arbitration agreements in contracts involving interstate commerce." ... The FAA's expansive reach coincides with that of the Commerce Clause.... Therefore, when a dispute falls within the scope of the FAA, a contract that includes an arbitration clause is governed by federal law.... Here, because the contract and construction dispute involves residents from South Dakota and Minnesota, thereby implicating interstate commerce, we review the matter under controlling federal law.

Section 10 of the FAA sets forth the following four grounds for vacating an arbitration award. First, "the award was procured by corruption, fraud, or undue means...." ... Second, "there was evident partiality or corruption in the arbitrators, or either of them...." ... Third, "the arbitrators were guilty of misconduct in refusing to postpone the hearing, upon sufficient cause shown, or in refusing to hear evidence pertinent and material to the controversy; or of any other misbehavior by which the rights of any party have been prejudiced...." ... Fourth, "the arbitrators exceeded their powers, or so imperfectly executed them that a mutual, final, and definite award upon the subject matter submitted was not made." ...

The circuit court ruled that the "FAA requires a court to vacate an arbitration award in which 'the arbitrators exceeded their powers, or so imperfectly executed them that a mutual, final, and definite award upon the subject matter submitted was not made.' "... The court concluded that "[w]here parties to an arbitration have agreed and directed the arbitrator to issue a reasoned award, the arbitrator is obligated to conform to the parties' directive and issue a reasoned award." Thus, the "arbitrator's failure to issue a reasoned award when directed by the parties to do so [was] an act in excess of the arbitrator's power...." ...

In the absence of any credibility determination, we must label as spurious the circuit court's finding that the parties "agreed" to a reasoned award. Nonetheless, we conclude that the arbitrator violated the rule he consented to follow.... [W]hen a reasoned award is agreed to between the parties before selection of an arbitrator, or, after selection, when the arbitrator consents to give a reasoned award....

To emphasize the pertinent language [from the AAA rules], "[i]f requested in writing by all the parties prior to the appointment of the arbitrator, *or if the arbitrator believes it is appropriate to do so,* the arbitrator shall provide a written explanation of the award." R–43(b) (emphasis added.) The arbitrator must have determined that it was *appropriate* to give a reasoned award. This conclusion is unavoidable because his order states that the award will be "reasoned." ... Therefore, the question becomes whether the arbitrator exceeded his power by issuing an award inconsistent with his own order that he would render a reasoned award.

An arbitration award can be set aside when the arbitrator "exceeded [his] powers, or so imperfectly executed them that a mutual, final, and definite award upon the subject matter submitted was not made." ... This award exceeded the arbitrator's powers because the arbitrator violated the rules he agreed to follow. *See generally Gas Aggregation Serv., Inc. v. Howard Avista Energy, LLC,* 319 F.3d 1060, 1068–69 (8th Cir.2003) (stating that an arbitration decision evinces a manifest disregard for the law when it identifies a substantive rule and then proceeds to ignore it).... We must give greater deference to the arbitrator's decisions on procedural matters than those dealing with substantive questions....

Procedural questions involve matters that are "tangential to the main body of the arbitrable dispute.... A mere procedural irregularity provides no basis upon which to conclude that the [arbitrator] acted beyond its authority." ... "Procedural law" is defined as: "[t]he rules that prescribe the steps for having a right or duty judicially enforced, as opposed to the law that defines the specific rights or duties themselves." ...

"Substantive law" "creates, defines, and regulates the rights, duties, and powers of the parties." ... Vold contends that the "arbitrator determined that he had no duty under the AAA Construction Industry Arbitration Rules to render a 'reasoned' award." ... Once the arbitrator ordered that the award he would issue would be reasoned, his powers were defined. The arbitrator's decision to issue a reasoned award bestowed a substantive right on Broin and, at the same time, imposed a substantive duty upon the arbitrator. True, the arbitrator could have amended his written order with a subsequent order at any time. But he never did. The day he handed down his unreasoned award, his order requiring a reasoned award still stood. The arbitrator's disregard of his own order constituted a substantive error under the FAA and the AAA rules he operated under. Thus the unreasoned decision constituted a lack of a mutual, final, and definite award. For the foregoing reasons, we affirm the circuit court's decision vacating the arbitration award.

Affirmed.

ZINTER, Justice (dissenting).

I agree that the parties did not verbally "agree" to a "reasoned award." There is also no dispute that there was no *written* agreement for a reasoned award. Therefore, the right to require a reasoned award was lost by Broin under the American Arbitration Association's (AAA's) Construction Industry Arbitration Rules, which were incorporated into the parties' arbitration agreement. Under those rules, the arbitrator had express authority, in fact, unfettered discretion, to ultimately determine whether it was "appropriate" to render his decision in the form of a reasoned award. Because the arbitrator had express and absolute authority to determine whether a reasoned award was appropriate, this Court mistakenly concludes that "[t]his award exceeded the arbitrator's *powers*" and was not a "final and definite" award. (emphasis added).

Our standard of review of an arbitrator's decision concerning the form of the award is, like most arbitration matters, limited. Even if this Court is convinced that the arbitrator committed serious error, as "long as the arbitrator is even arguably construing or applying the contract and acting within the scope of his authority," arbitration awards must be confirmed. . . .

[. . .]

In this case, there was no written agreement, and therefore, the arbitrator was within the clear scope of his authority to issue a non-reasoned award. Simply stated, absent a written agreement, Rule R–43(b) gave the arbitrator absolute discretion to determine the form of the award he deemed "appropriate." Because the arbitrator possessed that authority, the arbitrator did not exceed his powers or so imperfectly execute them that a mutual, final, and definite award was not made. . . .

The Court concludes otherwise, reasoning that the arbitrator exceeded his powers because he "violated the rules *he agreed* to follow" and did not enter a final and definite award. (emphasis added). . . . The arbitrator's decision to issue a reasoned award bestowed a substantive right on Broin and, at the same time, "imposed a substantive duty upon the arbitrator." From this premise, the Court ultimately concludes that the arbitrator's change of decision and failure to amend the preliminary order "constituted a substantive error under the [Federal Arbitration Act] and the AAA rules he operated under." . . . However, the Court misinterprets Rule R–43(b) and the express language of the preliminary order. The Court fails to consider that an arbitrator, like any other comparable judicial officer, is authorized to change preliminary decisions that have not become final.

[. . .]

[Additionally, it] is specifically recognized that preliminary and inter-locutory orders do not bestow unalterable rights and duties. That is because the federal courts have recognized there is "inherent power to reconsider and modify an interlocutory order any time prior to entry of judgment." ... A departure from an earlier holding is allowed when the Court is "convinced that the holding is incorrect." ... Similarly, we have consistently held that "[a] trial court has the inherent power to reconsider and modify an order any time prior to entry of judgment." ... Therefore, it is no surprise that arbitrators also have this authority to reconsider their earlier rulings until the time they become final....

[...]

In the final analysis, the outcome of this case is controlled by the fact that there was no written agreement for a reasoned award. Therefore, this arbitrator had the sole authority to determine the form of the award. Moreover, his preliminary order was subject to change in the final award. Thus, after hearing the facts and law at the hearing, the arbitrator *had authority* to determine that the case only merited a non-reasoned award. I therefore dissent.

Notes and Questions

1. Does the majority ruling restrict the arbitrator's procedural discretion? The latter is usually absolute or nearly absolute. Why is the order binding upon the arbitrator?

2. What function does the parties' subscription to institutional rules play in resolving the conflict between the majority and dissent? What status do institutional rules have? Can the institutional administrator overrule the arbitrators? The parties? If so, in what circumstances? Does administration have a decisional impact?

3. In what way(s) does the decision in *Vold* uphold the federal policy on arbitration? How does it contradict and undermine that policy?

4. What is the nature of the factual controversy in the court's opinion and what role does it play?

5. Is the issue determining what the parties agreed to or whether the arbitrator can change his mind on procedural matters at will?

6. Why is providing an explanation of the ruling a matter of procedure? Are rights implicated?

HASBRO, INC. v. CATALYST USA, INC.
367 F.3d 689 (7th Cir. 2004).

Diane P. Wood, Circuit Judge.

Although companies often choose arbitration with the hope of avoiding the (presumed) greater time and expense of litigating in court, that was not the fate of the parties in this case. Hasbro, Inc. and Catalyst USA, Inc. waited more than two years for a final award from an arbitration panel that was adjudicating a dispute between them about a software license. After the award was finally issued, the losing party, Catalyst, asked the district court to vacate the arbitral award. The court agreed that this was appropriate on the ground that the arbitrators had exceeded their authority by waiting too long to issue their decision. While we appreciate the frustration caused by the delay, a closer look at the proceedings shows that no one objected at the crucial time to the panel's conduct of the proceedings. Whatever errors with respect to deadlines may have been committed were either waived or harmless. We therefore reverse and remand for entry of an order enforcing the award.

I

In 1993, Hasbro and Catalyst entered into a software licensing contract, in which they agreed to arbitrate any disputes that arose that could not be resolved amicably. Any such dispute was to be submitted to arbitration pursuant to the Federal Arbitration Act (FAA) and the rules of the American Arbitration Association (AAA).

Six years later, dissatisfied with the performance of Catalyst's software, Hasbro filed a demand for arbitration on October 8, 1999. A hearing was conducted in Milwaukee between October 2000 and March 2001 before a panel of arbitrators from the Commercial Arbitration Tribunal of the AAA. . . .

The parties did not hear again from the AAA or the panel until October 2, 2001, when the AAA sent a bill to the parties seeking compensation for the arbitrators' "post-hearing time" from July to September 2001. In response, Catalyst requested an explanation of the bill. On October 10, 2001, the AAA sent the parties an itemization of charges—a communication that raised red flags for Catalyst. Catalyst found questionable the hours and increased rate charged by the panel chair, Alan Wernick. The itemization of the charges also brought to light other key information. Among the many entries were ones that stated "review and revise damage calculations to provide interest" and "extended conferences with panel regarding damage calculations and award." Because only Hasbro had requested damages, Hasbro alleges that these references to damage calculations should have signaled to Catalyst that Hasbro was the prevailing party.

On October 26, 2001, Catalyst wrote to the AAA challenging the propriety of Wernick's charges. In that letter, it also asserted for the first time that under Rule 37 of the AAA rules, the hearing had been closed on July 10, 2001, "as of the final date set by the arbitrator for the receipt of briefs," and that under Rule 43, the arbitrator had until August 11, 2001, "30 days from the date of closing the hearing," to make the award. The panel's failure to issue the award by August 11, 2001, Catalyst charged, raised "serious questions about the validity of the entire process."

On November 8, 2001, Catalyst received additional information concerning the Wernick bills. Again it wrote to the AAA requesting further information that would help it to analyze the propriety of the charges. It also, at that point, inquired specifically about the status of the overdue award. Not receiving word from the AAA, on November 13, 2001, Catalyst formally objected to the untimeliness of the award. Perhaps prompted by this inquiry, or perhaps for their own reasons, the arbitrators declared the hearing closed on December 5, 2001, and issued their award on January 2, 2002. The panel awarded Hasbro $799,839.93, plus interest; denied Catalyst's counterclaims; and divided arbitration fees, expenses, and compensation equally between the two parties, requiring Hasbro to pay the remaining $2,083.63 and Catalyst the remaining $22,083.63 outstanding. It declined to award attorneys' fees to either side.

Catalyst moved in district court to vacate the arbitration award on the ground that the arbitrators exceeded their power by issuing an untimely award. The district court agreed, and this appeal followed.

II

Generally, a court will set aside an arbitration award only in "very unusual circumstances," ... Judicial review of arbitration awards is "tightly limited" ... and confirmation is "usually routine or summary." ... "With few exceptions, as long as the arbitrator does not exceed [her] delegated authority, her award will be enforced." ... This is so even if the arbitrator's award contains a serious error of law or fact.... We review the district court's decision to vacate the arbitration award *de novo,* ... accepting findings of fact that are not clearly erroneous....

The FAA makes arbitration agreements enforceable "to the same extent as other contracts, so courts must 'enforce privately negotiated agreements to arbitrate, like other contracts, in accordance with their terms.' "... Under Wisconsin law, which applies to this diversity action, ... untimely performance of a contractual obligation does not result in the harsh penalty of forfeiture or rescission, unless the parties agree that "time is [ ] of the essence." ... Thus, even assuming that the panel's performance was untimely, whether the arbitration agreement was thereby rendered unenforceable depends on whether the parties agreed that time would be of the essence.

Whether this was indeed the parties' agreement is generally a question of fact that, if there was some sign of a material dispute, we would need to remand to the district court as fact-finder....

Under Wisconsin law, time is generally not of the essence, "unless it is expressly made so by the terms of the contract, or by the conduct of the parties." ... In this case, nowhere either in the arbitration agreement or in the AAA rules does it expressly say that time was of the essence. Wisconsin law further indicates that the fact that the AAA rules specify a 30–day deadline is not enough to support the inference that time is of the essence....

Nor does the conduct of the parties in this case support a finding that time was of the essence.... Although Catalyst asserts that the hearing should have been declared closed on July 10, 2001, and an award should have been issued by August 11, 2001, Catalyst itself waited until October 26, 2001, before raising the issue of untimely performance, and until November 13, 2001, before formally objecting to the arbitrators' delay.

Indeed, all indications suggest that Catalyst, the party now complaining of untimely performance, benefited from the delay, given the fact that it was able to hold off payment to Hasbro for several months at no cost (apart from the questionable arbitrators' fees, which we discuss in a moment). A conclusion that time was not of the essence under these circumstances comports with Wisconsin's additional consideration of equity in construing the parties' agreement, by allowing Hasbro to avoid the harsh penalty of forfeiture when the delay caused no prejudice to Catalyst.

[. . .]

For these reasons, we find that time was not of the essence under this arbitration agreement. Therefore, the arbitrators did not exceed their authority by issuing an untimely award to the extent that the harsh penalty of forfeiture or rescission was warranted. . . .

This is not to say, obviously, that arbitrators may indefinitely delay issuance of an award, in open violation of the AAA rules, without the parties' consent. Under Wisconsin law, "time may be made of the essence after breach of the contract by reasonable notice to the person in default to perform." . . . But the prejudiced party must make its objection known, which Catalyst failed to do here. This entire problem stemmed from the panel's original failure to declare the hearing closed in accordance with Rule 37. Such a declaration would have triggered the 30–day deadline under Rule 43. From the time Catalyst gave notice of its position that the panel had breached Rule 37, however, there was no further delay or failure to perform to which Catalyst can point. . . . Upon receiving notice from Catalyst, the panel promptly invited Hasbro to respond. Soon after, it declared the hearing closed and issued an award within 30 days thereafter.

Notwithstanding our enforcement of the arbitral award, we do not condone the panel's substandard performance. The AAA (and judicial tribunals) have good reasons for rules that clarify when a proceeding is concluded. These rules allow all parties to know whether there is still time remaining to raise points with the original tribunal, whether the time has come to appeal, and how much time exists for all such steps. Just as Federal Rule of Civil Procedure 58, which requires a specific document memorializing a final judgment, avoids countless problems with the appellate process that arise when a separate final judgment is missing, the AAA's rules also structure the process so that parties will know at all times where they stand.

III

We therefore *vacate* the judgment of the district court and *remand* for enforcement of the arbitral award.

NOTES AND QUESTIONS

1. Is the court predisposed to upholding arbitration or is it right to minimize the arbitrators' blunder in these circumstances?

2. Given arbitrator and institutional administrator immunity, the parties are at the mercy of the arbitrators. Do you agree?

3. Should the nonobservance of the parties' agreement and the institutional rules result in a severe penalty?

4. Why should *post facto* pragmatism prevail here instead of doctrinal rectitude?

5. When should arbitrator delay result in vacatur?

6. Does the result fulfill the federal policy on arbitration?

UNITED STATES LIFE INS. CO. v. INSURANCE COMMISSIONER OF THE STATE OF CALIFORNIA

160 Fed. Appx. 559 (9th Cir. 2005).

KLEINFELD, Circuit Judge.

United States Life Insurance Company (U.S. Life) entered into a contract with Superior National Insurance Company and other insurers (collectively, Cedents) in May 1998, whereby U.S. Life agreed to reinsure insurance policies worth more than $1 billion issued by Cedents. U.S. Life allegedly discovered evidence of material nondisclosure by Cedents after entering into the reinsurance contract and requested arbitration. In the midst of arbitration, Cedents were judged insolvent and their assets were seized by the California Insurance Commissioner (Commissioner), who now appears as a party, in this suit as the statutory liquidator of Cedents. The arbitration panel reformed the reinsurance contract, reducing the liabilities ceded to U.S. Life by 10 percent. The district court denied U.S. Life's petition to vacate the arbitral award. We affirm....

I.

The Commissioner contends that the district court lacked jurisdiction over the petition for review of the arbitral award because (a) U.S. Life had "voluntarily invoked state court jurisdiction" before petitioning the federal district court and was bound to continue proceedings in state court, (b) a state court injunction prohibited the petition from being heard in district court and (c) the Commissioner is acting in his official capacity as the successor in title to the Cedents' assets and is immune from suit under the Eleventh Amendment of the United States Constitution. These arguments are without merit. We hold that the district court properly exercised jurisdiction over the petition for review of the arbitral award.

U.S. Life "invoked" state jurisdiction merely for the purpose of lifting a state injunction that had stayed ongoing arbitration proceedings. U.S.

Life did not petition a state court to vacate the arbitral award, and there is no danger that a federal and state court would adjudicate different portions of the same controversy as the Commissioner argues in reliance on a 1920s, out-of-circuit case. . . . Even if U.S. Life *had* challenged the arbitration award in parallel state court proceedings, when "federal courts and state courts . . . find themselves exercising concurrent jurisdiction over the same subject matter, . . . a federal court generally need neither abstain (*i.e.*, dismiss the case before it) nor defer to the state proceedings (*i.e.*, withhold action until the state proceedings have concluded)." . . .

In its November 13, 2000 order lifting the stay of proceedings with respect to the arbitration between U.S. Life and Cedents, the Los Angeles County Superior Court ordered that the prior stay of proceedings "shall not deprive U.S. Life of any of its rights or remedies in connection with the Arbitration." Petitioning the district court for review of the arbitral award is one of U.S. Life's rights in connection with the arbitration. We conclude that the district court was not precluded from hearing the petition for review by the California courts' general stays of proceedings against Cedents.

Lastly, Eleventh Amendment immunity does not apply where a state officer is being sued not for individual wrongdoing or in his official capacity, but only in his "representative capacity" as a receiver of assets formerly belonging to parties who would otherwise be the targets of a suit were they not insolvent. . . . Under California insurance law, "[w]hen the Commissioner takes title to the assets of an insolvent insurer . . . , he holds them as a trustee for the benefit of private parties, and they never become part of the public treasury." . . . Therefore, this suit is "truly one against the possessor, the government agent, and not against the sovereign, despite the fact that the agent purported to possess on behalf of the sovereign." . . . Because "the Eleventh Amendment does not apply in cases where the entity invoking the immunity is sued only in its *representative capacity*," . . . the district court properly exercised jurisdiction over the petition for review.

II.

U.S. Life contends that the arbitrators "exceeded their powers," 9 U.S.C. § 10(a)(4) (2005), because the arbitrators' reformation of the reinsurance contract exhibited a "manifest disregard of law" and was "completely irrational." *Kyocera Corp. v. Prudential–Bache Trade Servs., Inc.*, 341 F.3d 987, 997 (9th Cir.2003) (*en banc*). U.S. Life also contends in the alternative that the arbitral award should be vacated because "it is contrary to public policy." We disagree and affirm the district court's denial of U.S. Life's petition to review the arbitral award.

With the Federal Arbitration Act (FAA), . . . Congress has given federal courts "an extremely limited review authority" over arbitration proceedings. . . . "Neither erroneous legal conclusions nor unsubstantiated factual findings justify federal court review of an arbitral award . . ." . . .

"Congress' principal purpose [in passing the FAA was] ensuring that private arbitration agreements are enforced according to their terms." . . .

The arbitration clause of the reinsurance contract between U.S. Life and Cedents states in part:

> [I]n the event of any dispute or difference of opinion hereafter arising with respect to this Contract, it is hereby mutually agreed that such dispute or difference of opinion shall be submitted to arbitration. . . . The Arbiters shall consider this Contract as an honorable engagement rather than merely as a legal obligation and they are relieved of all judicial formalities and may abstain from following the strict rules of law.

The arbitration panel ruled that the contract was not to be rescinded, but was to be reformed to reduce U.S. Life's reinsurance obligations by 10 percent because "Cedents should have acted in a more open and forthright manner."

Given our deferential standard of review for arbitral awards and the terms of the contract voluntarily entered into by U.S. Life, its argument that the arbitrators' reformation remedy exhibits a "manifest disregard of law" must fail. . . . California Insurance Code Section 331 "entitles [an] injured party to rescind insurance" when there has been "concealment," defined in Section 330 as a "[n]eglect to communicate that which a party knows, and ought to communicate." We do not agree with U.S. Life's contention that the arbitrators' comment regarding Cedents's candor is the legal equivalent to a finding of "concealment" under Section 330. Rather, we agree with the district court that "[t]he statement falls conspicuously short of making any such finding." Furthermore, even if the arbitrators' statement did amount to a finding of "concealment," U.S. Life agreed that the arbitrators "shall consider th[e] [Reinsurance] Contract as an honorable engagement" and "may abstain from following the strict rules of law." The contract gave the arbitrators such wide latitude to resolve disputes that when combined with our inability to vacate even "erroneous legal conclusions" in an arbitral award, . . . we conclude that the arbitrators did not exhibit a "manifest disregard of law" . . . and acted well within the powers granted to them under the contract. . . .

U.S. Life's contention that the arbitral award was "completely irrational" . . . is without merit. U.S. Life asserts that Cedents failed to disclose that the reserves they held for the insurance policies they sought to have reinsured were short by $100 to $300 million. Therefore, it was rational for the arbitrators to accept the low end of that reserve shortfall as the measure of U.S. Life's actual economic injury and consequently reduce U.S. Life's approximately $1 billion reinsurance liability by 10[%].

Lastly, the arbitral award does not violate California's public policy "to promote full disclosure in reinsurance transactions." Although the Supreme Court has recognized in principle that an arbitral award that violates public policy may be vacated for that reason, "the public policy exception is narrow." . . . Even if we accept U.S. Life's characterization of California's public policy with respect to reinsurance transactions, we must also consider that the California "Legislature has expressed a strong public policy in favor of arbitration as a speedy and relatively inexpensive means of dispute resolution," and California "courts will indulge every intendment to give effect to such proceedings." *Moncharsh v. Heily & Blase,* 3 Cal.4th 1, 10 Cal.Rptr.2d 183, 832 P.2d 899, 902 (1992) (internal citations and quotations omitted). If we vacate the arbitral award as U.S. Life urges, we risk violating California's public policy to "indulge every intendment to give effect to" the arbitral award. Moreover, U.S. Life fails to show how the arbitrators' reformation of the contract, an award with a likely monetary value in excess of $100 million, violates California's public policy "to promote full disclosure in reinsurance transactions." Quite the opposite. The arbitral award in this case supports California's public policy by granting U.S. Life some relief even when the nondisclosure by Cedents stopped short of "concealment."

AFFIRMED.

NOTES AND QUESTIONS

1. The party in *United States Life* invokes a number of different bases for challenging the award. Are all these grounds equivalent and interchangeable?

2. How does public policy fit into the architecture of vacatur grounds? In arbitration, is there only one public policy?

3. How can reformation of a contract constitute excess of authority when the arbitrator is the sovereign interpreter of the contract? Manifest disregard and irrationality appear more suitable to the argument for vacatur.

4. Is the arbitrators' award characteristic of commercial justice?

5. When might an arbitrator exceed his/her interpretative authority and render an unenforceable award?

* * *

The following cases exemplify the various courts' assessment of allegations that the arbitrators engaged in misconduct in conducting the arbitral proceeding. Given that procedural informality and arbitrator discretion reign, it is very difficult to identify circumstances of misconduct. The courts can neither demand conformity to judicial practices nor require arbitrators to behave as judges. The agreement to arbitrate is a contract for private, informal adjudication.

As you assess the various excerpts, fashion a rule that encapsulates the decisional practice on this matter. Explain its underlying rationale. Should it discourage clients from agreeing to arbitrate disputes? Should there be a different approach? Is there abdication of judicial responsibility? A fundamental compromise of, and indifference to, legal rights?

AGRAWAL v. AGRAWAL

775 F.Supp. 588, 590–91 (E.D.N.Y. 1991), *aff'd*, 969 F.2d 1041 (2d Cir. 1992).

[. . .]

As noted above, the Act authorizes a court to vacate the arbitrator's award when the arbitrator is guilty of misconduct in refusing to "postpone the hearing upon sufficient cause shown. . . ." . . . A court's review on this basis is limited to a determination of whether the refusal to postpone was the result of misconduct by the arbitrator. . . . In addition, it is to be noted that "[t]he granting or denying of an adjournment falls within the broad discretion of appointed arbitrators." . . . In light of the considerable deference given to an arbitrator's decisions, . . . it is clear that a reasonable basis existed for the arbitrator's decision to deny the request for an adjournment.

[. . .]

BERLACHER v. PAINEWEBBER INC.

759 F.Supp. 21, 24 (D.D.C. 1991).

[. . .]

Berlacher argues that the arbitrators' refusal to postpone the May 21–22 hearings upon sufficient cause shown constituted misconduct and prejudiced his rights because he was unable to prepare his case.

"Arbitrators are to be accorded a degree of discretion in exercising their judgment with respect to a requested postponement. Therefore, assuming there exists a reasonable basis for the arbitrators' considered decision not to grant a postponement, the Court will be reluctant to interfere with the award on these grounds." . . . In this case, the arbitrators had a reasonable basis for denying Berlacher's request for a postponement. Throughout the proceeding, there had been problems in coordinating the schedule of all the parties, counsel and the arbitrators. The injury was never presented as a life-threatening situation, nor were any medical complications arising from the injury asserted. In addition, Berlacher knew about the claim months before the hearing and had ample time to prepare his case. Based upon this record, the arbitrators were not guilty of misconduct.

[. . .]

ROBBINS v. DAY

954 F.2d 679, 685 (11th Cir.), *cert. denied*, 506 U.S. 870 (1992).

[. . .]

A federal court may vacate an arbitrator's award under 9 U.S.C. § 10(a)(3) only if the arbitrator's refusal to hear pertinent and material evidence prejudices the rights of the parties and denies them a fair hearing. Further, an arbitration award must not be set aside for the arbitrator's refusal to hear evidence that is cumulative or irrelevant.... In the present case, it was within the arbitrator's broad discretion to accept the Trustees' representations that the Brokers' testimony was "unimportant" to their case and that if given would only provide cumulative evidence.

An arbitrator enjoys a wide latitude in conducting an arbitration hearing. Arbitration proceedings are not constrained by formal rules of procedure or evidence.... In applying the statutory grounds for the granting of a motion to vacate an award, we always bear in mind that the basic policy of conducting arbitration is to offer a means of deciding disputes expeditiously and at lower costs.... Thus, the Federal Arbitration Act allows arbitration to proceed with only a summary hearing and with restricted inquiry into factual issues.... The arbitrator is not bound to hear all the evidence tendered by the parties; he need only give each party the opportunity to present its arguments and evidence.... We will not undermine the expedience of arbitration to determine the materiality or pertinence of excluded evidence that the moving party agreed was unimportant....

[. . .]

HAYNE, MILLER & FARNI, INC. v. FLUME

888 F.Supp. 949, 952–53 (E.D. Wis. 1995).

[. . .]

HMF asserts that counsel for the Flumes introduced prejudicial evidence at the arbitration hearing which biased the arbitrators. Specifically, the plaintiff alleges that the Flumes' counsel introduced evidence of an FBI investigation of HMF with regard to HMF's alleged manipulation of Angeion Corporation's stock price. HMF maintains that the introduction of this evidence created an " 'aura of guilt' around HMF which could not be erased."

The plaintiff does not allege that the arbitrators engaged in misconduct.... Rather, HMF alleges that there was misconduct by the Flume's counsel at the arbitration hearing. Misconduct by a party can be a basis for setting aside an arbitration award.... However, the improper admission of evidence does not warrant vacation of the arbitration award. Arbitrators have wide latitude in conducting arbitration proceedings and are not bound by formal rules of evidence.... Arbitrators may admit evidence which would be unduly prejudicial if admitted in court....

An arbitrator need only provide the parties with a fundamentally fair hearing.... A fundamentally fair hearing "requires only notice, opportunity to be heard and to present relevant and material evidence and argument before the decision makers, and that the decision makers are not infected with bias." ... There is no substantial proof to support HMF's contention that the introduction of evidence by the Flumes' counsel denied the plaintiff a fundamentally fair hearing.

The plaintiff's reliance on cases involving the introduction of unfairly prejudicial evidence at a court trial is misplaced. Arbitration proceedings are fundamentally different than proceedings in federal court. Arbitration "is a private system of justice offering benefits of reduced delay and expense." ...The introduction of evidence of the FBI investigation by the Flume's counsel does not justify vacation of the arbitration award.

[. . .]

6. PUBLIC POLICY

BROWN v. RAUSCHER PIERCE REFSNES, INC.

994 F.2d 775, 782 (11th Cir. 1993).

[. . .]

The public policy exception to the enforcement of arbitration awards allows courts to refuse to enforce arbitration awards where enforcement "would violate 'some explicit public policy' that is 'well defined and dominant, and is to be ascertained by reference to the laws and legal precedents and not from general considerations of supposed public interests.' " [*Misco*]....

Typically, the public policy exception is implicated when enforcement of the award compels one of the parties to take action which directly conflicts with public policy....

[. . .]

RODRIGUEZ v. PRUDENTIAL–BACHE SECURITIES, INC.

882 F.Supp. 1202, 1208 (D.P.R. 1995).

[. . .]

The U.S. Supreme Court has made clear that a court's refusal to enforce an arbitrator's interpretation of a contract is limited to situations where the contract as interpreted would violate some explicit public policy that is well defined and dominant, and is to be ascertained by reference to the law and legal precedents, and not from general considerations of supposed public interests. *United Paper Workers' International Union, AFL–CIO v. Misco, Inc.*, 484 U.S. 29, 43, 108 S. Ct. 364, 373–74, 98 L. Ed. 2d 286 (1987). The Court's decision in *Misco, Inc.* forever dispelled any notion that its prior decision in *W.R. Grace,*...upon which Prudential relies, could be used to sanction a broad judicial power to set aside arbitration awards as against public policy. *Misco, Inc.*, 484 U.S. at 43, 108 S.Ct. at 373–74. Moreover, when reviewing an arbitration award being challenged on public policy grounds, the court must determine whether the arbitrator's interpretation of the contract runs afoul of a well-defined and dominant public policy, *taking the facts as found by the arbitrator*....

[. . .]

NOTES AND QUESTIONS

1. The foregoing excerpts illustrate the application of the public policy exception according to the ruling by the U.S. Supreme Court in the celebrated *Misco* opinion. *Misco* involved a labor arbitration, but its holding apparently has been generalized, like the public policy exception itself, to cover all forms of arbitration (labor, maritime, commercial, trade-sector, and consumer). In general, the courts ignore the decisional origins and intended specific application of the public policy exception, deeming it applicable in all cases involving the enforcement of arbitral awards. The courts have given no weight to the fact that FAA § 10 contains no reference to public policy.

2. *Misco* makes clear that the public policy exception cannot be applied lightly or on the basis of some diffuse judicial notion of the public interest. Although this interpretation is not expressly confirmed by the *Misco* formulation, the public policy exception, it seems, must emanate from and be embedded in a statute and articulated through express statutory language. Vacatur of the award would require the arbitrator to ignore conduct that specifically contravened a well-defined and identifiable congressional mandate. Not surprisingly, attesting to the labor specificity of the common law ground, the examples used by the court to illustrate the application of public policy to the enforcement of awards are drawn from labor arbitrations. They involve the reinstatement of employees by arbitrators despite a legal prohibition of reinstatement in the circumstances (*e.g.,* reinstating a pilot who had piloted airplanes while intoxicated). How might public policy then be applied in a nonlabor context?

3. The public policy exception, like the other common law grounds, appears difficult to establish. There is no "broad judicial power to set aside arbitration awards as against public policy" and it seems that the courts afford arbitrators every benefit of the doubt. Nonetheless, the practice does have its dangers. It invites greater judicial scrutiny that may not always result in a superficial examination of awards.

4. Was there an implied legislative intent in the FAA to exclude this basis for review in domestic law? How might the content of the FAA support that view? What might justify the courts' reintegration of public policy into the domestic law of arbitration? Should or can public policy considerations ever be excluded from a judicial determination?

UNITED PAPERWORKERS INT'L UNION, AFL–CIO v. MISCO, INC.

484 U.S. 29, 108 S.Ct. 364, 98 L.Ed.2d 286 (1987).

(footnotes omitted)

Justice WHITE delivered the opinion of the Court.

The issue for decision involves several aspects of when a federal court may refuse to enforce an arbitration award rendered under a collective-bargaining agreement.

I

Misco, Inc. (Misco, or the Company), operates a paper converting plant in Monroe, Louisiana. The Company is a party to a collective-bargaining agreement with the United Paperworkers International Union, AFL–CIO, and its union local (the Union); the agreement covers the production and maintenance employees at the plant. Under the agreement, the Company or the Union may submit to arbitration any grievance that arises from the interpretation or application of its terms, and the arbitrator's decision is final and binding upon the parties. The arbitrator's authority is limited to interpretation and application of the terms contained in the agreement itself. The agreement reserves to management the right to establish, amend, and enforce "rules and regulations regulating the discipline or discharge of employees" and the procedures for imposing discipline. Such rules were to be posted and were to be in effect "until ruled on by grievance and arbitration procedures as to fairness and necessity." For about a decade, the Company's rules had listed as causes for discharge the bringing of intoxicants, narcotics, or controlled substances on to plant property or consuming any of them there, as well as reporting for work under the influence of such substances. At the time of the events involved in this case, the Company was very concerned about the use of drugs at the plant, especially among employees on the night shift.

Isiah Cooper, who worked on the night shift for Misco, was one of the employees covered by the collective-bargaining agreement. He operated a slitter-rewinder machine, which uses sharp blades to cut rolling coils of paper. The arbitrator found that this machine is hazardous and had caused numerous injuries in recent years. Cooper had been reprimanded twice in a few months for deficient performance. On January 21, 1983, one day after the second reprimand, the police searched Cooper's house pursuant to a warrant, and a substantial amount of marijuana was found. Contemporaneously, a police officer was detailed to keep Cooper's car under observation at the Company's parking lot. At about 6:30 p.m., Cooper was seen walking in the parking lot during work hours with two other men. The three men entered Cooper's car momentarily, then walked to another car, a white Cutlass, and entered it. After the other two men later returned to the plant, Cooper was apprehended by police in the backseat of this car with marijuana smoke in the air and a lighted marijuana cigarette in the frontseat ashtray. The police also searched Cooper's car and found a plastic scales case and marijuana gleanings. Cooper was arrested and charged with marijuana possession.

On January 24, Cooper told the Company that he had been arrested for possession of marijuana at his home; the Company did not learn of the marijuana cigarette in the white Cutlass until January 27. It then investigated and on February 7 discharged Cooper, asserting that in the circumstances, his presence in the Cutlass violated the rule against having drugs on the plant premises. Cooper filed a grievance protesting his discharge the same day, and the matter proceeded to arbitration. The Company was not aware until September 21, five days before the arbitration hearing was scheduled, that marijuana had been found in Cooper's car. That fact did not become known to the Union until the hearing began. At the hearing it was stipulated that the issue was whether the Company had "just cause to discharge the Grievant under Rule II.1" and, "[i]f not, what if any should be the remedy." . . .

The arbitrator upheld the grievance and ordered the Company to reinstate Cooper with backpay and full seniority. The arbitrator based his finding that there was not just cause for the discharge on his consideration of seven criteria. In particular, the arbitrator found that the Company failed to prove that the employee had possessed or used marijuana on company property: finding Cooper in the backseat of a car and a burning cigarette in the front-seat ashtray was insufficient proof that Cooper was using or possessed marijuana on company property. . . . The arbitrator refused to accept into evidence the fact that marijuana had been found in Cooper's car on company premises because the Company did not know of this fact when Cooper was discharged and therefore did not rely on it as a basis for the discharge.

The Company filed suit in District Court, seeking to vacate the arbitration award on several grounds, one of which was that ordering reinstatement of Cooper, who had allegedly possessed marijuana on the plant premises, was contrary to public policy. The District Court agreed that the award must be set aside as contrary to public policy because it ran counter to general safety concerns that arise from the operation of dangerous machinery while under the influence of drugs, as well as to state criminal laws against drug possession. The Court of Appeals affirmed, with one judge dissenting. The court ruled that reinstatement would violate the public policy "against the operation of dangerous machinery by persons under the influence of drugs or alcohol." . . . The arbitrator had found that Cooper was apprehended on company premises in an atmosphere of marijuana smoke in another's car and that marijuana was found in his own car on the company lot. These facts established that Cooper had violated the Company's rules and gave the Company just cause to discharge him. The arbitrator did not reach this conclusion because of a "narrow focus on Cooper's procedural rights" that led him to ignore what he "knew was in fact true: that Cooper *did* bring marijuana onto his employer's premises." . . . Even if the arbitrator had not known of this fact at the time he entered his award, "it is doubtful that the award should be enforced today in light of what is now known." . . .

Because the Courts of Appeals are divided on the question of when courts may set aside arbitration awards as contravening public policy, we granted the Union's petition for a writ of *certiorari* . . . and now reverse the judgment of the Court of Appeals.

II

The Union asserts that an arbitral award may not be set aside on public policy grounds unless the award orders conduct that violates the positive law, which is not the case here. But in the alternative, it submits that even if it is wrong in this regard, the Court of Appeals otherwise exceeded the limited authority that it had to review an arbitrator's award entered pursuant to a collective-bargaining agreement. Respondent, on the other hand, defends the public policy decision of the Court of Appeals but alternatively argues that the judgment below should be affirmed because of erroneous findings by the arbitrator. We deal first with the opposing alternative arguments.

A

Collective-bargaining agreements commonly provide grievance procedures to settle disputes between union and employer with respect to the interpretation and application of the agreement and require binding arbitration for unsettled grievances. In such cases, and this is such a case, the Court made clear almost 30 years ago that the courts play only a limited role when asked to review the decision of an arbitrator. The courts are not authorized to reconsider the merits of an award even though the parties may allege that the award rests on errors of fact or on misinterpretation of the contract. "The refusal of courts to review the merits of an arbitration award is the proper approach to arbitration under collective bargaining agreements. The federal policy of settling labor disputes by arbitration would be undermined if courts had the final say on the merits of the awards." ... As long as the arbitrator's award "draws its essence from the collective bargaining agreement," and is not merely "his own brand of industrial justice," the award is legitimate....

The reasons for insulating arbitral decisions from judicial review are grounded in the federal statutes regulating labor-management relations. These statutes reflect a decided preference for private settlement of labor disputes without the intervention of government: The Labor Management Relations Act of 1947, 61 Stat. 154, 29 U.S.C. § 173(d), provides that "[f]inal adjustment by a method agreed upon by the parties is hereby declared to be the desirable method for settlement of grievance disputes arising over the application or interpretation of an existing collective-bargaining agreement." ... The courts have jurisdiction to enforce collective-bargaining contracts; but where the contract provides grievance and arbitration procedures, those procedures must first be exhausted and courts must order resort to the private settlement mechanisms without dealing with the merits of the dispute. Because the parties have contracted to have disputes settled by an arbitrator chosen by them rather than by a judge, it is the arbitrator's view of the facts and of the meaning of the contract that they have agreed to accept. Courts thus do not sit to hear claims of factual or legal error by an arbitrator as an appellate court does in reviewing decisions of lower courts. To resolve disputes about the application of a collective-bargaining agreement, an arbitrator must find facts and a court may not reject those findings simply because it disagrees with them. The same is true of the arbitrator's interpretation of the contract. The arbitrator may not ignore the plain language of the contract;

but the parties having authorized the arbitrator to give meaning to the language of the agreement, a court should not reject an award on the ground that the arbitrator misread the contract.... So, too, where it is contemplated that the arbitrator will determine remedies for contract violations that he finds, courts have no authority to disagree with his honest judgment in that respect. If the courts were free to intervene on these grounds, the speedy resolution of grievances by private mechanisms would be greatly undermined. Furthermore, it must be remembered that grievance and arbitration procedures are part and parcel of the ongoing process of collective bargaining. It is through these processes that the supplementary rules of the plant are established. As the Court has said, the arbitrator's award settling a dispute with respect to the interpretation or application of a labor agreement must draw its essence from the contract and cannot simply reflect the arbitrator's own notions of industrial justice. But as long as the arbitrator is even arguably construing or applying the contract and acting within the scope of his authority, that a court is convinced he committed serious error does not suffice to overturn his decision. Of course, decisions procured by the parties through fraud or through the arbitrator's dishonesty need not be enforced. But there is nothing of that sort involved in this case.

B

The Company's position, simply put, is that the arbitrator committed grievous error in finding that the evidence was insufficient to prove that Cooper had possessed or used marijuana on company property. But the Court of Appeals, although it took a distinctly jaundiced view of the arbitrator's decision in this regard, was not free to refuse enforcement because it considered Cooper's presence in the white Cutlass, in the circumstances, to be ample proof that Rule II.1 was violated. No dishonesty is alleged; only improvident, even silly, factfinding is claimed. This is hardly a sufficient basis for disregarding what the agent appointed by the parties determined to be the historical facts.

Nor was it open to the Court of Appeals to refuse to enforce the award because the arbitrator, in deciding whether there was just cause to discharge, refused to consider evidence unknown to the Company at the time Cooper was fired. The parties bargained for arbitration to settle disputes and were free to set the procedural rules for arbitrators to follow if they chose. Article VI of the agreement, entitled "Arbitration Procedure," did set some ground rules for the arbitration process. It forbade the arbitrator to consider hearsay evidence, for example, but evidentiary matters were otherwise left to the arbitrator.... Here the arbitrator ruled that in determining whether Cooper had violated Rule II.1, he should not consider evidence not relied on by the employer in ordering the discharge, particularly in a case like this where there was no notice to the employee or the Union prior to the hearing that the Company would attempt to rely on after-discovered evidence. This, in effect, was a construction of what the contract required when deciding discharge cases: an arbitrator was to look only at the evidence before the employer at the time of discharge. As the arbitrator noted, this approach was consistent with the practice followed by other arbitrators. And it was consistent with our observation in *John Wiley & Sons, Inc. v. Livingston,* 376 U.S. 543, 557, 84 S.Ct. 909, 918, 11 L.Ed.2d 898 (1964), that when the subject matter of a dispute is arbitrable, "procedural" questions which grow out of the dispute and bear on its final disposition are to be left to the arbitrator.

Under the Arbitration Act, the federal courts are empowered to set aside arbitration awards on such grounds only when "the arbitrators were guilty of misconduct ... in refusing to hear evidence pertinent and material to the controversy." ... If we apply that same standard here and assume that the arbitrator erred in refusing to consider the disputed evidence, his error was not in bad faith or so gross as to amount to affirmative misconduct. Finally, it is worth noting that putting aside the evidence about the marijuana found in Cooper's car during this arbitration did not forever foreclose the Company from using that evidence as the basis for a discharge.

Even if it were open to the Court of Appeals to have found a violation of Rule II.1 because of the marijuana found in Cooper's car, the question remains whether the court could properly set aside the award because in its view discharge was the correct remedy. Normally, an arbitrator is authorized to disagree with the sanction imposed for employee misconduct.... The parties, of course, may limit the discretion of the arbitrator in this respect; and it may be, as the Company argues, that under the contract involved here, it was within the unreviewable discretion of management to discharge an employee once a violation of Rule II.1 was found. But the parties stipulated that the issue before the arbitrator was whether there was "just" cause for the discharge, and the arbitrator, in the course of his opinion, cryptically observed that Rule II.1 merely listed causes for discharge and did not expressly provide for immediate discharge. Before disposing of the case on the ground that Rule II.1 had been violated and discharge was therefore proper, the proper course would have been remand to the arbitrator for a definitive construction of the contract in this respect.

C

The Court of Appeals did not purport to take this course in any event. Rather, it held that the evidence of marijuana in Cooper's car required that the award be set aside because to reinstate a person who had brought drugs onto the property was contrary to the public policy "against the operation of dangerous machinery by persons under the influence of drugs or alcohol." ... We cannot affirm that judgment.

A court's refusal to enforce an arbitrator's award under a collective-bargaining agreement because it is contrary to public policy is a specific application of the more general doctrine, rooted in the common law, that a court may refuse to enforce contracts that violate law or public policy.... That doctrine derives from the basic notion that no court will lend its aid to one who founds a cause of action upon an immoral or illegal act, and is further justified by the observation that the public's interests in confining the scope of private agreements to which it is not a party will go unrepresented unless the judiciary takes account of those interests when it considers whether to enforce such agreements. . . . In the common law of contracts, this doctrine has served as the foundation for occasional exercises of judicial power to abrogate private agreements.

In *W.R. Grace*, we recognized that "a court may not enforce a collective-bargaining agreement that is contrary to public policy," and stated that "the question of public policy is ultimately one for resolution by the courts." . . . We cautioned, however, that a court's refusal to enforce an arbitrator's *interpretation* of such contracts is limited to situations where the contract as interpreted would violate "some explicit public policy" that is "well defined and dominant, and is to be ascertained 'by reference to the laws and legal precedents and not from general considerations of supposed public interests.'" . . . In *W.R. Grace*, we identified two important public policies that were potentially jeopardized by the arbitrator's interpretation of the contract: obedience to judicial orders and voluntary compliance with Title VII of the Civil Rights Act of 1964. We went on to hold that enforcement of the arbitration award in that case did not compromise either of the two public policies allegedly threatened by the award. Two points follow from our decision in *W.R. Grace*. First, a court may refuse to enforce a collective-bargaining agreement when the specific terms contained in that agreement violate public policy. Second, it is apparent that our decision in that case does not otherwise sanction a broad judicial power to set aside arbitration awards as against public policy. Although we discussed the effect of that award on two broad areas of public policy, our decision turned on our examination of whether the award created any explicit conflict with other "laws and legal precedents" rather than an assessment of "general considerations of supposed public interests." . . . At the very least, an alleged public policy must be properly framed under the approach set out in *W.R. Grace*, and the violation of such a policy must be clearly shown if an award is not to be enforced.

As we see it, the formulation of public policy set out by the Court of Appeals did not comply with the statement that such a policy must be "ascertained 'by reference to the laws and legal precedents and not from general considerations of supposed public interests.'" . . . The Court of Appeals made no attempt to review existing laws and legal precedents in order to demonstrate that they establish a "well-defined and dominant" policy against the operation of dangerous machinery while under the influence of drugs. Although certainly such a judgment is firmly rooted in common sense, we explicitly held in *W.R. Grace* that a formulation of public policy based only on "general considerations of supposed public interests" is not the sort that permits a court to set aside an arbitration award that was entered in accordance with a valid collective-bargaining agreement.

Even if the Court of Appeals' formulation of public policy is to be accepted, no violation of that policy was clearly shown in this case. In pursuing its public policy inquiry, the Court of Appeals quite properly considered the established fact that traces of marijuana had been found in Cooper's car. Yet the assumed connection between the marijuana gleanings found in Cooper's car and Cooper's actual use of drugs in the workplace is tenuous at best and provides an insufficient basis for holding that his reinstatement would actually violate the public policy identified by the Court of Appeals "against the operation of dangerous machinery by persons under the influence of drugs or alcohol." . . . A refusal to enforce an award must rest on more than speculation or assumption.

In any event, it was inappropriate for the Court of Appeals itself to draw the necessary inference. To conclude from the fact that marijuana had been found in Cooper's car that Cooper had ever been or would be under the influence of marijuana while he was on the job and operating dangerous machinery is an exercise in factfinding about Cooper's use of drugs and his amenability to discipline, a task that exceeds the authority of a court asked to overturn an arbitration award. The parties did not bargain for the facts to be found by a court, but by an arbitrator chosen by them who had more opportunity to observe Cooper and to be familiar with the plant and its problems. Nor does the fact that it is inquiring into a possible violation of public policy excuse a court for doing the arbitrator's task. If additional facts were to be found, the arbitrator should find them in the course of any further effort the Company might have made to discharge Cooper for having had marijuana in his car on company premises. Had the arbitrator found that Cooper had possessed drugs on the property, yet imposed discipline short of discharge because he found as a factual matter that Cooper could be trusted not to use them on the job, the Court of Appeals could not upset the award because of its own view that public policy about plant safety was threatened. In this connection it should also be noted that the award ordered Cooper to be reinstated in his old job or in an equivalent one for which he was qualified. It is by no means clear from the record that Cooper would pose a serious threat to the asserted public policy in every job for which he was qualified.

The judgment of the Court of Appeals is reversed.

So ordered.

[. . .]

NOTES AND QUESTIONS

1. As noted earlier, *Misco* is the classic case on the public policy exception to the enforcement of arbitral awards. The Court makes clear in its reasoning that the applicable rule flows in part from the provisions of the Labor Management Relations Act of 1947. Does the rule in *Misco* also apply to FAA arbitration? Why and why not? What is the basis of your answer? Have you read other cases in which the court implies the holding in *Misco*?

2.   The lower court vacates the arbitral award because the arbitrator's ruling is self-evidently twisted to favor the interest of the unionized worker. Do you agree? Is the arbitrator's determination defensible? Is that an acceptable standard?

3.   Does the arbitrator's determination of reinstatement indicate partiality or irrationality? Why does the arbitrator apply a criminal law burden of proof standard? Are criminal sanctions contemplated or available? Is the arbitrator's reading of the CBA provision fair or accurate? Does the arbitrator dispense "his own brand of industrial justice"?

4.   Should the result remain the same if the conduct took place in another setting, like airport security, operation of machinery at a nuclear plant, public transport (train engineer)? How would you assess an arbitral award that reinstates a teacher accused, but not convicted, of pedophilia to an administrative position?

5.   The Court imposes a systemic discipline that fosters the operation of arbitration and defines the significance of the bargain for arbitration. Can you elaborate on the foregoing comment?

6.   The Court states, "The reasons for insulating arbitral decisions from juridical review are grounded in the federal statutes regulating labor-management relations." Explain.

7.   What balance does the Court establish between protecting the integrity of the workplace constitution and the autonomy of the arbitral process? Are the interests in protection and policy truly balanced? When might a court legitimately conclude that the arbitrator is rewriting the CBA?

8.   How is *Misco* public policy different from the diffuse sense of public policy that applies in tort litigation? Can you put content into the *W.R. Grace* adjectives? Is *Misco* public policy another way of saying subject-matter inarbitrability? When might public policy be breached?

9.   Is a criminal violation a breach of public policy? What about violating administrative regulations or municipal ordinances?

10.   Is public policy distinguishable from unconscionability?

11.   What result if the arbitrator in *Misco* had found "just cause" under the CBA and awarded the employer punitive damages and attorney's fees? Would such a ruling be compliant with public policy? Is it manifest disregard or irrationality?

12.   What result if an employer requires that each employment arbitral tribunal consist of a civil right lawyer and a member of the KKK, along with a true neutral? Is such a process legitimate? In conformity with public policy? Protected by the interest in arbitral autonomy?

EASTERN ASSOC. COAL CORP. v. UNITED MINE WORKERS OF AM., DIST. 17

531 U.S. 57, 121 S.Ct. 462, 148 L.Ed.2d 354 (2000).

Justice BREYER delivered the opinion of the Court.

A labor arbitrator ordered an employer to reinstate an employee truck driver who had twice tested positive for marijuana. The question before us is whether considerations of public policy require courts to refuse to enforce that arbitration award. We conclude that they do not. The courts may enforce the award. And the employer must reinstate, rather than discharge, the employee.

I

Petitioner, Eastern Associated Coal Corp., and respondent, United Mine Workers of America, are parties to a collective-bargaining agreement with arbitration provisions. The agreement specifies that, in arbitration, in order to discharge an employee, Eastern must prove it has "just cause." Otherwise the arbitrator will order the employee reinstated. The arbitrator's decision is final. . . .

James Smith worked for Eastern as a member of a road crew, a job that required him to drive heavy trucklike vehicles on public highways. As a truck driver, Smith was subject to Department of Transportation (DOT) regulations requiring random drug testing of workers engaged in "safety-sensitive" tasks. . . .

In March 1996, Smith tested positive for marijuana. Eastern sought to discharge Smith. The union went to arbitration, and the arbitrator concluded that Smith's positive drug test did not amount to "just cause" for discharge. Instead the arbitrator ordered Smith's reinstatement, provided that Smith (1) accept a suspension of 30 days without pay, (2) participate in a substance-abuse program, and (3) undergo drug tests at the discretion of Eastern (or an approved substance-abuse professional) for the next five years.

Between April 1996 and January 1997, Smith passed four random drug tests. But in July 1997 he again tested positive for marijuana. Eastern again sought to discharge Smith. The union again went to arbitration, and the arbitrator again concluded that Smith's use of marijuana did not amount to "just cause" for discharge, in light of two mitigating circumstances. First, Smith had been a good employee for 17 years. . . . And, second, Smith had made a credible and "very personal appeal under oath . . . concerning a personal/family problem which caused this one time lapse in drug usage." . . .

The arbitrator ordered Smith's reinstatement provided that Smith (1) accept a new suspension without pay, this time for slightly more than three months; (2) reimburse Eastern and the union for the costs of both arbitration proceedings; (3) continue to participate in a substance-abuse program; (4) continue to undergo random drug testing; and (5) provide Eastern with a signed, undated letter of resignation, to take effect if Smith again tested positive within the next five years. . . .

Eastern brought suit in federal court seeking to have the arbitrator's award vacated, arguing that the award contravened a public policy against the operation of dangerous machinery by workers who test positive for drugs. . . . The District Court, while recognizing a strong regulation-based public policy against drug use by workers who perform safety-sensitive functions, held that Smith's conditional reinstatement did not violate that policy.... And it ordered the award's enforcement....

The Court of Appeals for the Fourth Circuit affirmed on the reasoning of the District Court.... We granted *certiorari* in light of disagreement among the Circuits.... We now affirm the Fourth Circuit's determination.

II

Eastern claims that considerations of public policy make the arbitration award unenforceable. In considering this claim, we must assume that the collective-bargaining agreement itself calls for Smith's reinstatement. That is because both employer and union have granted to the arbitrator the authority to interpret the meaning of their contract's language, including such words as "just cause." ... They have "bargained for" the "arbitrator's construction" of their agreement.... And courts will set aside the arbitrator's interpretation of what their agreement means only in rare instances.... Of course, an arbitrator's award "must draw its essence from the contract and cannot simply reflect the arbitrator's own notions of industrial justice." ... "But as long as [an honest] arbitrator is even arguably construing or applying the contract and acting within the scope of his authority," the fact that "a court is convinced he committed serious error does not suffice to overturn his decision." ... Eastern does not claim here that the arbitrator acted outside the scope of his contractually delegated authority. Hence we must treat the arbitrator's award as if it represented an agreement between Eastern and the union as to the proper meaning of the contract's words "just cause." ... For present purposes, the award is not distinguishable from the contractual agreement.

We must then decide whether a contractual reinstatement requirement would fall within the legal exception that makes unenforceable "a collective-bargaining agreement that is contrary to public policy." ... The Court has made clear that any such public policy must be "explicit," "well defined," and "dominant." ... It must be "ascertained 'by reference to the laws and legal precedents and not from general considerations of supposed public interests.' "... And, of course, the question to be answered is not whether Smith's drug use itself violates public policy, but whether the agreement to reinstate him does so. To put the question more specifically, does a contractual agreement to reinstate Smith with specified conditions ... run contrary to an explicit, well-defined, and dominant public policy, as ascertained by reference to positive law and not from general considerations of supposed public interests? ...

III

Eastern initially argues that the District Court erred by asking, not whether the award is "contrary to" public policy "as ascertained by reference" to positive law, but whether the award "violates" positive law, a standard Eastern says is too narrow. We believe, however, that the District Court correctly articulated the standard set out in *W.R. Grace* and

Misco, see 66 F.Supp.2d, at 803 (quoting *Misco, supra,* at 43, 108 S.Ct. 364), and applied that standard to reach the right result.

We agree, in principle, that courts' authority to invoke the public policy exception is not limited solely to instances where the arbitration award itself violates positive law. Nevertheless, the public policy exception is narrow and must satisfy the principles set forth in *W.R. Grace* and *Misco.* Moreover, in a case like the one before us, where two political branches have created a detailed regulatory regime in a specific field, courts should approach with particular caution pleas to divine further public policy in that area.

Eastern asserts that a public policy against reinstatement of workers who use drugs can be discerned from an examination of that regulatory regime, which consists of the Omnibus Transportation Employee Testing Act of 1991 and DOT's implementing regulations. The Testing Act embodies a congressional finding that "the greatest efforts must be expended to eliminate the ... use of illegal drugs, whether on or off duty, by those individuals who are involved in [certain safety-sensitive positions, including] the operation of ... trucks." Pub.L. 102–143, § 2(3), 105 Stat. 953. The Act adds that "increased testing" is the "most effective deterrent" to "use of illegal drugs." § 2(5). It requires the Secretary of Transportation to promulgate regulations requiring "testing of operators of commercial motor vehicles for the use of a controlled substance." 49 U.S.C. § 31306(b)(1)(A) (1994 ed., Supp. III). It mandates suspension of those operators who have driven a commercial motor vehicle while under the influence of drugs. 49 U.S.C. § 31310(b)(1)(A) (requiring suspension of at least one year for a first offense); § 31310(c)(2) (requiring suspension of at least 10 years for a second offense). And DOT's implementing regulations set forth sanctions applicable to those who test positive for illegal drugs. 49 CFR § 382.605 (1999).

In Eastern's view, these provisions embody a strong public policy against drug use by transportation workers in safety-sensitive positions and in favor of random drug testing in order to detect that use. Eastern argues that reinstatement of a driver who has twice failed random drug tests would undermine that policy—to the point where a judge must set aside an employer-union agreement requiring reinstatement.

Eastern's argument, however, loses much of its force when one considers further provisions of the Act that make clear that the Act's remedial aims are complex. The Act says that "rehabilitation is a critical component of any testing program," § 2(7), 105 Stat. 953, that rehabilitation "should be made available to individuals, as appropriate," ... and that DOT must promulgate regulations for "rehabilitation programs," 49 U.S.C. § 31306(e). The DOT regulations specifically state that a driver who has tested positive for drugs cannot return to a safety-sensitive position until (1) the driver has been evaluated by a "substance abuse professional" to determine if treatment is needed, 49 CFR § 382.605(b) (1999); (2) the substance-abuse professional has certified that the driver has followed any rehabilitation program prescribed, § 382.605(c)(2)(i); and (3) the driver has passed a return-to-duty drug test, § 382.605(c)(1). In addition, the driver must be subject to at least six random drug tests during the first year after returning to the job. § 382.605(c)(2)(ii). Neither the Act nor the regulations forbid an employer to reinstate in a safety-sensitive position an employee who fails a random drug test once or twice. The congressional and regulatory directives require only that the above-stated prerequisites to reinstatement be met.

Moreover, when promulgating these regulations, DOT decided not to require employers either to provide rehabilitation or to "hold a job open for a driver" who has tested positive, on the basis that such decisions "should be left to management/driver negotiation." 59 Fed.Reg. 7502 (1994). That determination reflects basic background labor law principles, which caution against interference with labor-management agreements about appropriate employee discipline....

We believe that these expressions of positive law embody several relevant policies. As Eastern points out, these policies include Testing Act policies against drug use by employees in safety-sensitive transportation positions and in favor of drug testing. They also include a Testing Act policy favoring rehabilitation of employees who use drugs. And the relevant statutory and regulatory provisions must be read in light of background labor law policy that favors determination of disciplinary questions through arbitration when chosen as a result of labor-management negotiation.

The award before us is not contrary to these several policies, taken together. The award does not condone Smith's conduct or ignore the risk to public safety that drug use by truck drivers may pose. Rather, the award punishes Smith by suspending him for three months, thereby depriving him of nearly $9,000 in lost wages, ... it requires him to pay the arbitration costs of both sides; it insists upon further substance-abuse treatment and testing; and it makes clear (by requiring Smith to provide a signed letter of resignation) that one more failed test means discharge.

The award violates no specific provision of any law or regulation. It is consistent with DOT rules requiring completion of substance-abuse treatment before returning to work ... for it does not preclude Eastern from assigning Smith to a non-safety-sensitive position until Smith completes the prescribed treatment program. It is consistent with the Testing Act's 1–year and 10–year driving license suspension requirements, for those requirements apply only to drivers who, unlike Smith, actually operated vehicles under the influence of drugs.... The award is also consistent with the Act's rehabilitative concerns, for it requires substance-abuse treatment and testing before Smith can return to work.

The fact that Smith is a recidivist—that he has failed drug tests twice—is not sufficient to tip the balance in Eastern's favor. The award punishes Smith more severely for his second lapse. And that more severe punishment, which included a 90–day suspension, would have satisfied even a "recidivist" rule that DOT once proposed but did not adopt—a rule that would have punished two failed drug tests, not with discharge, but with a driving suspension of 60 days.... Eastern argues that DOT's withdrawal of its proposed rule leaves open the possibility that discharge is the appropriate penalty for repeat offenders. That argument fails, however, because DOT based its withdrawal, not upon a determination that a more severe penalty was needed, but upon a determination to leave in place, as the "only driving prohibition period for a controlled substances violation," the "completion of rehabilitation requirements and a return-to-duty test with a negative result." ...

Regarding drug use by persons in safety-sensitive positions, then, Congress has enacted a detailed statute. And Congress has delegated to the Secretary of Transportation authority to issue further detailed regulations on that subject. Upon careful consideration, including public notice and comment, the Secretary has done so. Neither Congress nor the Secretary has seen fit to mandate the discharge of a worker who twice tests positive for drugs. We hesitate to infer a public policy in this area that goes beyond the careful and detailed scheme Congress and the Secretary have created.

We recognize that reasonable people can differ as to whether reinstatement or discharge is the more appropriate remedy here. But both employer and union have agreed to entrust this remedial decision to an arbitrator. We cannot find in the Act, the regulations, or any other law or legal precedent an "explicit," "well defined," "dominant" public policy to which the arbitrator's decision "runs contrary." ... We conclude that the lower courts correctly rejected Eastern's public policy claim. The judgment of the Court of Appeals is

Affirmed.

Justice SCALIA, with whom Justice THOMAS joins, concurring in the judgment.

I concur in the Court's judgment, because I agree that no public policy prevents the reinstatement of James Smith to his position as a truck driver, so long as he complies with the arbitrator's decision, and with those requirements set out in the Department of Transportation's regulations. I do not endorse, however, the Court's statement that "[w]e agree, in principle, that courts' authority to invoke the public policy exception is not limited solely to instances where the arbitration award itself violates positive law." ... No case is cited to support that proposition, and none could be. There is not a single decision, since this Court washed its hands of general common-lawmaking authority, see *Erie R. Co. v. Tompkins,* 304 U.S. 64, 58 S.Ct. 817, 82 L.Ed. 1188 (1938), in which we have refused to enforce on "public policy" grounds an agreement that did not violate, or provide for the violation of, some positive law. See, *e.g., Hurd v. Hodge,* 334 U.S. 24, 68 S.Ct. 847, 92 L.Ed. 1187 (1948) (refusing to enforce under the public policy doctrine a restrictive covenant that violated Rev. Stat. § 1978, 42 U.S.C. § 1982).

After its dictum opening the door to flaccid public policy arguments of the sort presented by petitioner here, the Court immediately posts a giant "Do Not Enter" sign. "[T]he public policy exception," it says, "is narrow and must satisfy the principles set forth in *W.R. Grace*," . . . which require that the applicable public policy be "explicit," "well defined," "dominant," and "ascertained 'by reference to the laws and legal precedents and not from general considerations of supposed public interests.' " . . . It is hard to imagine how an arbitration award could violate a public policy, identified in this fashion, without actually conflicting with positive law. If such an award could ever exist, it would surely be so rare that the benefit of preserving the courts' ability to deal with it is far outweighed by the confusion and uncertainty, and hence the obstructive litigation, that the Court's Delphic "agree[ment] in principle" will engender.

The problem with judicial intuition of a public policy that goes beyond the actual prohibitions of the law is that there is no way of knowing whether the apparent gaps in the law are intentional or inadvertent. The final form of a statute or regulation, especially in the regulated fields where the public policy doctrine is likely to rear its head, is often the result of compromise among various interest groups, resulting in a decision to go so far and no farther. One can, of course, summon up a parade of horribles, such as an arbitration award ordering an airline to reinstate an alcoholic pilot who somehow escapes being grounded by force of law. But it seems to me we set our face against judicial correction of the omissions of the political branches when we declined the power to define common-law offenses. . . . Surely the power to invalidate a contract providing for actions that are not contrary to law (but "ought" to be) is less important to the public welfare than the power to prohibit harmful acts that are not contrary to law (but "ought" to be). And it is also less efficacious, since it depends upon the willingness of one of the parties to the contract to *assert* the public policy interest. (If the airline is not terribly concerned about reinstating an alcoholic pilot, the courts will have no opportunity to prevent the reinstatement.) The horribles that can be imagined—if they are really so horrible and ever come to pass—can readily be corrected by Congress or the agency, with no problem of retroactivity. Supervening law is always grounds for the dissolution of a contractual obligation. . . .

In sum, it seems to me that the game set in play by the Court's dictum endorsing "in principle" the power of federal courts to enunciate public policy is not worth the candle. Agreeing with the reasoning of the Court except insofar as this principle is concerned, I concur only in the judgment.

NOTES AND QUESTIONS

1. The Court in *Eastern Assoc. Coal Corp.* affirms the decisional law on public policy begun in *W.R. Grace* and continued in *Misco*. The content of the applicable rule does not vary in the three cases. Is the judicial application of the rule as consistent and predictable? Why and why not?

2. What is the principal consequence of the public policy exception to the enforcement of arbitral awards?

3. Does the arbitrator in *Eastern Assoc. Coal Corp.* take liberties with the applicable federal regulations on transportation? Does the award give effect to the regulatory regime?

4. Explain the Court's statement that, "the question to be answered is not whether Smith's drug use itself violates public policy, but whether the agreement to reinstate him does so."

5. Why is the employer impeded from terminating an employee for reasons of public safety? Does the circumstance affect the public welfare? Is self-regulation too expensive of a price for would-be industrial peace?

6. Can you explain the distinction between public policy and positive law? What is a "flaccid public policy argument"?

7. What is Justice Scalia's point? Can you restate his discussion in your own words?

EXXON SHIPPING CO. v. EXXON SEAMEN'S UNION

11 F.3d 1189, 1194–96 (3d Cir. 1993).

(footnotes omitted)

[. . .]

. . . [W]e agree with the district court that the award in question in this case violates a public policy that is both well-defined and dominant, *viz.*, that an owner or operator of an oil tanker should not be compelled to reinstate to a "safety-sensitive" position an individual who has been found to be intoxicated while on duty on that vessel.

Congress has expressly declared that it is "the policy of the United States that there should be no discharges of oil" into waters under federal jurisdiction. . . . Congress, moreover, has implemented this policy by enacting strong remedial and penalty provisions. Under the Clean Water Act, . . . the owner or operator of an oil tanker that causes a spill is liable for the costs of removal. Similarly, under the Oil Pollution Act of 1990, . . . an owner or operator may be liable for, among other things, removal costs, injury to natural resources, loss of the use of natural resources for subsistence, injury to real or personal property, loss of taxes by a government unit, loss of profits and earning capacity, and any increase in the cost of providing public services during removal. While there are limits on liability under both Acts, these limits do not apply if the spill was caused by gross negligence, willful misconduct, or, under the Oil Pollution Act, the violation of an applicable federal regulation. . . .

Not only has Congress enacted measures designed to prevent and deter oil spills, but Congress has also focused specifically on the risk that such spills may be caused by oil tanker personnel who are under the influence of alcohol or drugs. . . .

Consistent with these views, the Coast Guard has promulgated regulations permitting a marine employer to require crew members on commercial vessels to undergo a chemical test for alcohol or drugs when the crew member is involved in an accident or is suspected of being intoxicated. . . .

While we are aware of no statute or regulation that directly prohibits the owner or operator of an oil tanker from continuing to employ a crew member who is found to be intoxicated on duty, there can be no doubt that the statutes and regulations we have noted convey the unequivocal message that such an owner or operator should take every practicable step to ensure that an intoxicated crew member does not cause or contribute to an oil spill. . . .

[. . .]

Accordingly, based on our prior decision in *Exxon Shipping Co. I* and on the statutes, regulations, and expressions of congressional policy previously noted, we conclude that there is a well defined and dominant policy that owners and operators of oil tankers should be permitted to discharge crew members who are found to be intoxicated while on duty. An intoxicated crew member on such a vessel can cause loss of life and catastrophic environmental and economic injury. Some of this injury may not be reparable by money damages. Moreover, because of limitations on liability under the Clean Water Act and the Oil Pollution Act, it is entirely possible that much of the cost resulting from a major oil spill may fall on taxpayers and those who are injured by the accident. While the federal labor laws undoubtedly embody a strong policy favoring the settlement of labor disputes by arbitration, that policy must yield in the present context to the public policy favoring measures designed to avert potentially catastrophic oil spills. In *Exxon Shipping I*, we held that this policy precluded the reinstatement of a seaman who tested positive for marijuana. Consistency with this precedent dictates a similar result here.

[. . .]

NOTES AND QUESTIONS

1. The *Exxon* case deals with the arbitration of a labor law claim. The court identifies a specific congressional policy upon which to exercise its review and vacatur authority. Do you agree with the court's characterization of that policy? Is the policy expressly defined or diffuse? Although the case involves a labor award, the court finds the foundation of the annulling public policy in nonlabor statutes. Should such an approach be considered a problem? There seems to be some slope to the court's reasoning and it may eventually become more inclined and slippery in subsequent litigation.

2. Once the public policy exception is generalized to other contexts, could a court invalidate an award in the securities or RICO areas on the basis of public policy? Does the public policy exception amount to a determination of substantive inarbitrability or manifest disregard of the law? Once again, in

these exceptional circumstances of vacatur, does the court's action amount to a review of the merits of the awards? Such a result seems to be prohibited by the applicable statute in nonlabor matters.

3. In *Westvaco Corp. v. United Paperworkers Int'l Union, AFL–CIO,* 171 F.3d 971 (4th Cir. 1999), a district court held that an arbitrator's reinstatement of an employee who repeatedly violated the company's sexual harassment policy violated public policy.

On appeal, the court refused to enforce the award. It recognized that overturning an arbitrator's award is an extraordinary action, stating that "[a]n arbitration award may not be overturned unless the award 'violates well-settled and prevailing public policy, fails to draw its essence from the collective bargaining agreement or reflects the arbitrator's own notions of right and wrong.' " The court understood the judicial deference to the "federal policy of settling labor disputes by arbitration." The facts as found by the arbitrator, however, warranted vacatur of the award. Acknowledging that "the factual findings of an arbitrator are binding on a reviewing court," the court expressed its concern about allowing the arbitrator's decision to stand in light of those facts. The court linked this concern to the "public policy condemning sexual harassment in the workplace [that] is clearly defined and readily found in statutes, regulations, and judicial decisions."

The court noted that Westvaco would not be liable for Ravenscroft's actions if it took "immediate and appropriate corrective action." The court stated that the arbitrator's award "prevent[ed] the plaintiff from carrying out its explicit, dominant legal duty to eliminate sexual harassment from the workplace. Enforcement of this award would expose [Westvaco] to severe potential liability." Accordingly, the court held that "the arbitration award of reinstatement disregarded the public policy against sexual harassment in the workplace." The court concluded that

[We are] reluctant to overturn the award of a labor arbitrator, but cannot uphold an award which so plainly subverts the explicit policy of the United States. This case presents the aberration in which a court grants relief from an arbitration award, and may not be considered the norm. In this extreme case, based solely on the facts as found by the arbitrator, the [c]ourt must vacate the arbitration award of reinstatement.

On further appeal, the Fourth Circuit recognized that "the very purpose of arbitration procedures is to provide a mechanism for the expeditious settlement of industrial disputes without resort to strikes, lockouts, or other self-help measures." Additionally, "labor-management relations law reflect[s] a decided preference for private settlement of labor disputes without the intervention of government.... [E]ffective arbitration serves as 'the means of solving the unforeseeable by molding a system of private law for all the problems which may arise and to provide for their solution in a way which will generally accord with the variant needs and desires of the parties.' " Courts have recognized that arbitration "must be final to be effective.... Permitting judicial second-guessing of arbitral awards 'would transform a binding process into a purely advisory one, and ultimately impair the value of arbitration for labor and management alike.... Absent the most unusual of circumstances, courts must uphold and enforce arbitral awards.' "

After laying the foundation for the general acceptance of arbitration, the court rejected Westvaco's argument that the arbitrator exceeded the scope of his authority. The court reasoned that "the interpretation of a collective bargaining agreement is a matter left to the arbitrator." This is true even "when the arbitrator's interpretation resolves a question relating to the scope of the arbitrator's own authority.... [A]s long as the arbitrator is even arguably construing or applying the contract and acting within the scope of his authority, that a court is convinced he committed serious error does not suffice to overturn his decision." In reviewing an arbitrator's interpretation, a court examines only whether that interpretation "draw[s] its essence from the contract and [does not] simply reflect the arbitrator's own notions of industrial justice."

The court held that the interpretation did draw its essence from the CBA, noting that arbitrators have the power to disagree with a sanction imposed for certain employee misconduct. "By reinstating Ravenscroft, the arbitrator plainly substituted his own judgment for that of management"; the arbitrator, however, was empowered to do so under the CBA by determining "just cause." Westvaco was aware of Ravenscroft's misconduct, but did nothing to remedy the situation until it fired him. The arbitrator properly held that the company ignored the intermediary disciplinary steps and proceeded immediately to discharge Ravenscroft. By imposing the reinstatement of Ravenscroft, the arbitrator held that Westvaco violated the CBA by discharging an employee without "just cause." The court was not willing to address whether the arbitrator's interpretation was correct because it drew its essence from the CBA.

The court rejected Westvaco's argument that reinstatement violated public policy by hindering Westvaco's ability to remedy sexual harassment in the workplace. "All of the protections of a labor arbitration process would go for naught if they could be undone by a broad and amorphous public policy exception."

> [There is no] broad judicial power to set aside arbitration awards as against public policy.... If the contract as interpreted by [the arbitrator] violates some explicit public policy, [the court is] obliged to refrain from enforcing it. Such a public policy, however, must be well-defined and dominant, and is to be ascertained by reference to the laws and legal precedents and not from general considerations of supposed public interests.

The court noted that the district court overlooked three critical factors. First, it fashioned the public policy against sexual harassment in too general a fashion. "There is no public policy that every harasser must be fired." Instead, a company must exercise "reasonable care" to prevent sexual harassment in the workplace. Second, "the use of public policy to void written contracts is dangerous because public policy itself is often a two-edged sword." The public policy to remedy sexual harassment clashed in this case with the public policy to uphold written contracts. Third, the court recognized its "reluctance to invoke broad nostrums of public policy to void private bargains." The court reversed the district court's ruling and reinstated the arbitrator's award.

4. Which position in *Westvaco* would you endorse and why? Which position would you most readily reject and why?

5. Is there a U.S. public policy against sexual harassment that is equivalent to the public interest in antitrust or securities regulation?

7. ARBITRARY AND CAPRICIOUS OR IRRATIONAL AWARDS

BROWN v. RAUSCHER PIERCE REFSNES, INC.

994 F.2d 775, 781 (11th Cir. 1993).

[. . .]

. . . First, courts may vacate an award as arbitrary and capricious when the award exhibits a wholesale departure from the law. . . . Second, courts may vacate awards as being arbitrary and capricious when the award is not grounded in the contract which provides for the arbitration. . . .[6]

[. . .]

. . . For an award to be vacated as arbitrary and capricious, the Panel's award must contain more than an error of law or interpretation. . . . Rather, there must be no ground for the Panel's decision. . . .

[. . .]

AINSWORTH v. SKURNICK

960 F.2d 939, 941 (11th Cir. 1992), *cert. denied*, 507 U.S. 915 (1993).

[. . .]

Our cases do hold . . . that although great deference is normally accorded an arbitration award, an award that is arbitrary or capricious is not required to be enforced. . . . An award is arbitrary and capricious only if "a ground for the arbitrator's decision cannot be inferred from the facts of the case." . . .

Such is the case here. There is simply no explanation in the award itself why damages were not awarded. The award said that "the Claimant sustained no damages; [a]nd, therefore, we conclude [that the] Claimant is not entitled to recover" damages. This is a non-sequitur for which there is no basis. The arbitrators did not reflect any disagreement with the district court's statement of the law. . . . We have to assume that the arbitrators' decision was arbitrary or capricious for two reasons: first, it was a reasonable interpretation of the statute made by the district court in questioning the vagueness of the panel's first decision; and second, the district court told them what the law was, and their second award does

---

[6.] The First Circuit has commented that although the nomenclature varies from circuit to circuit, every circuit recognizes these two grounds—no basis in law or no basis in the contract—as non-statutory grounds for vacatur. *See Advest, Inc. v. McCarthy*, 914 F.2d 6, 9 (1st Cir. 1990).

not indicate that they differ with the point nor does it give any reason for not awarding mandatory damages. Since they knew the law required damages, their refusal to grant damages is clearly arbitrary. There was no reasonable basis upon which the panel may have acted. . . . In this case, it is not a question of deciding the law and getting it wrong or for some reason disregarding the law. The decision was simply an apparent arbitrary and capricious denial of relief with no factual or legal basis.

[. . .]

NOTES AND QUESTIONS

1. The excerpt from *Brown*, especially footnote six, demonstrates the labor arbitration origins and specificity of this additional common-law ground for policing the enforcement of arbitral awards. The basis for review appears to make little sense outside of the context of labor arbitration. Be that as it may, the majority of the decisional law uses the two labels—"arbitrary and capricious" and "irrational"—interchangeably. *See Drummond Coal Co. v. United Mine Workers of America, District 20*, 748 F.2d 1495, 1497 (11th Cir. 1984). Use of one label as opposed to the other varies among circuits for reasons unrelated to the substantive content of the terms. Their meaning is basically identical: The award is unenforceable because the arbitral determination cannot be even remotely sustained by the applicable labor statutes or collective bargaining agreement. The award contravenes expressly the applicable law.

2. Once again, it is difficult to ascribe any specific content to these two nonstatutory grounds and distinguish them meaningfully from the other nonstatutory grounds (especially manifest disregard) or even to distinguish them from the statutory grounds (here, FAA § 10[d]). Moreover, these definitional problems are hardly warranted by the laxity of review that is commanded by the statute and which generally prevails in vacatur actions. In addition, *Ainsworth* demonstrates the danger of having a generalized nonstatutory basis for the review of awards. There, the court, perhaps having a special knowledge of the applicable substantive law, makes use of the common law basis for review to express its disagreement with the arbitrator's application of the law and actually vacates the award. The arbitrators' determination, however, may not have deviated from standard arbitral practice, upheld by the courts in the vast majority of cases.

3. The vacatur in *Ainsworth* indicates the possible utilization of two equally unacceptable standards of review: (1) a thorough judicial examination of, and strong opposition to, the arbitrators' interpretation and application of law; or (2) a judicial reversal of the arbitrators' determination without a full examination of its underlying reasons. Neither approach conforms to the generally deferential and favorable standard of judicial review under FAA § 10. It appears that the reviewing court's disagreement with the arbitrators' application of law or with their exercise of decisional discretion constitutes a basis for characterizing their determination as an "arbitrary and capricious" award. *Ainsworth* thereby illustrates a substantial disparity and incompatibility between the statutory and nonstatutory grounds for review. The nonstatu-

tory grounds are directed to the substance of awards. The statutory grounds address primarily, if not exclusively, fundamental procedural lapses in the process. The reference to the district court's instructions to the arbitral panel makes the ruling in *Ainsworth* akin to the old case-stated procedure in English law. The court, in effect, is instructing the arbitral tribunal on how to rule on the legal question of damages. Should a court get that involved in the decision-making process?

4.   Given the origins and intended function of the common-law grounds for review, how might you clarify the confusion that appears to reign and remedy the inconsistencies of doctrine? Compare and contrast the statement of the applicable law in the excerpts from *Brown* and *Ainsworth*. Does the court in *Ainsworth* completely alter the content of the applicable legal rule while appearing to maintain it intact? Do you understand the *Ainsworth* court's objection to the award? Does it demand that the arbitrators state reasons or deliver an opinion with the award? Is the imposition of that obligation lawful?

5.   Consider the following excerpt from *Eljer* which states unequivocally that arbitrators are not required to state reasons for or even give an opinion with their awards. Are *Ainsworth* and *Eljer* consistent? If not, how do you accommodate the disparity? There appears to be a difference between the two cases in terms of the significance they attribute to alleged mistakes of law by the arbitrators. *Eljer* classifies the question as a "manifest disregard of the law," while *Ainsworth* invokes the "arbitrary and capricious" standard. Are both approaches sustainable within the same decisional law?

ELJER MFG., INC. v. KOWIN DEVELOPMENT CORP.

14 F.3d 1250, 1254–55 (7th Cir.), *cert. denied*, 512 U.S. 1205 (1994).

[. . .]

Eljer argues that the arbitrator's failure to articulate the grounds for his award prevented "meaningful judicial review" of his claim. Eljer's concern is that the arbitrator erroneously rejected some of its defenses and by shielding his decision from scrutiny, prevented reviewing courts from exposing those errors. Eljer asks that we remand the case to the arbitrator with instructions to clarify his award.

This argument fails for two reasons. First and most fundamentally, an arbitrator is simply not required to state the reasons for his decision. . . . Such a requirement would serve only to perpetuate the delay and expense which arbitration is meant to combat.

Eljer's requested remand must also be denied because errors of law alone do not constitute a sufficient basis for remanding the case. In its brief, Eljer goes to great lengths . . . to persuade us that various legal defenses it presented to the arbitrator should have prevailed. Eljer misses the point. Even if its legal defenses were dispositive, the fact that the arbitrator erroneously rejected them does not, by itself, provide grounds for a remand. The arbitrator must have deliberately disregarded what he knew to be the law. Eljer has not shown such disregard here.

[. . .]

* * *

The following excerpt from *Ainsworth* explains why the court chose to invoke the "arbitrary and capricious" standard instead of the "manifest disregard" ground for review. It also exhibits the decisional intricacy that accompanies the application of the common law recourse against awards, which contrasts with the judicial construction of the statutory grounds for the enforcement of arbitral awards.

AINSWORTH v. SKURNICK

960 F.2d 939, 940–41 (11th Cir. 1992), *cert. denied*, 507 U.S. 915 (1993).

[. . .]

Courts are generally prohibited from vacating an arbitration award on the basis of errors of law or interpretation, and the express terms of 9 U.S.C. §§ 10 and 11 have often been deemed the exclusive grounds for vacation or modification. . . . Several courts have discussed the use of a "manifest disregard of the law" standard to vacate an arbitration award. . . . This Circuit, however, has never adopted that standard as a ground for vacating an arbitration award. . . . The cases are unclear as to whether we have ever held that it would be error to vacate an arbitration award as being in manifest disregard of the law. . . .

* * *

8.   COMMENTARY: PUBLIC POLICY REVIEW AND THE *GARVEY* CASE

The U.S. Court of Appeals for the Ninth Circuit has rendered a number of decisions that deviate from the standard federal judicial practice on matters of arbitration. These decisions constrain the operation of arbitration and imperil its autonomy. One of the most long-standing and well-established rules of the federal common law on arbitration is that judicial review of arbitral awards should be severely limited and rarely—if ever—result in the vacatur of an award. In particular, a court should not reconsider the merits of an arbitrator's determination and substitute its judgment for that of the arbitrator. The rule of judicial deference remains unaltered even in the face of clear arbitrator error on the law or a tribunal's misunderstanding of the facts. A judicial revisiting and eventual revision of the merits of an award are antithetical to the gravamen of arbitral law, the content of the governing statute (FAA § 10), and the functionality of the arbitral process.

In *Garvey v. Roberts*, 203 F.3d 580 (9th Cir. 2000), the Ninth Circuit departed from the consecrated tradition of judicial deference to arbitration. It invoked several doctrines of labor arbitration to express its disagreement with the arbitrator's determinations in the award. It held that the arbitrator had engaged in "his own brand of industrial justice" and that would-be excess of authority warranted the vacatur of the award. The court was mindful of the unusual character of the result it reached. It recited the elements of the standard approach in such matters: "As long as the arbitrator is even arguably construing or applying the contract and acting within the scope of his authority, that a court is convinced he committed serious error does not suffice to overturn his decision." The court nonetheless found that the arbitrator's reliance on "perjurious" testimony in reaching his decision was so aberrant that it "surpasse[d] understanding." As the dissent pointed out, a more accurate and acceptable assessment of the facts would have been that the arbitrator simply chose to disbelieve recent testimony that conflicted with prior testimony: "It seems to me that the majority here quarrels with the arbitrator's fact finding rather than finding the award does not draw its essence from the collective bargaining agreement."

The power of courts to review arbitral awards on the merits, it appears, is a singular and unique feature of the Anglo–Saxon legal regulation of arbitration. Only English courts have equivalent authority under the "limited right of appeal to the High Court" and the current decisional and legislative practice in England is to permit such appeals only in truly exceptional cases. Moreover, the statutory grounds contained in FAA § 10 do not permit judicial supervision of the merits of awards; only the nonstatutory provisions, added to the statute by court decisions, countenance court review of the content of the arbitrator's determination. As noted in the foregoing material, the bargain for arbitration implies an acceptance of the limitations of the process, including periodic egregious arbitrator error. As the majority itself stated in the *Garvey* opinion: "We overturn an arbitrator's award only when it is clear from the arbitral opinion or award that the arbitrator did not base his decision on an interpretation of the collective bargaining agreement or that he disregarded what the parties put before him and instead followed his own whims or biases." Such immunity from judicial scrutiny is necessary to maintain arbitration's independence and its viability.

Labor arbitration is—in some respect—a unique form of arbitration. It is, for example, the type of arbitration that gave rise to the merits review of arbitral awards in U.S. law. Because labor arbitrators apply statutory provisions regulating labor relations and construe the provisions of collective bargaining agreements, the courts decided that some form of scrutiny was necessary to correct flagrant and abusive arbitrator interpretative error. One of the acknowledged grounds for effectuating this form of review is to supervise awards on the basis that the arbitrator strayed from the provisions of the collective bargaining agreement in reaching the determination. In effect, the arbitrator in the award rewrites the collective bargaining agreement and "dispenses his own brand of industrial justice." This is what the Ninth Circuit concluded had been done in the *Garvey* case.

It is increasingly difficult (even in labor arbitration) to reconcile the prospect of a judicial reconsideration of the merits with the continued efficacy of arbitration. Whether the rationale for the nonenforcement of an arbitral determination is expressed through the phrase of "not drawing the essence of the award from the provisions of the contract," "manifest disregard of the law," "manifest disregard of the law and facts," "capriciousness to the point of irrationality," or "the violation of a well-defined, dominant public policy," it appears that vacatur on any of these bases represents nothing more than the reviewing court's disagreement with the conclusions reached by the arbitrator or his methodology or both. In fact, the very act of reviewing aspects of the proceedings and the content of the determination in a thorough manner arguably breaches the rule and practice of judicial deference. Blatant procedural unfairness, evident partiality, or excessive use of adjudicatory authority are not buried in the details of the record. "Redoing" the arbitration (even if only as to its major aspects) gives the losing party another "bite at the apple"—a circumstance that is clearly not part of the standard bargain for arbitration. When the Ninth Circuit took strong exception to the arbitrator's assessment of an evidentiary element, it was disagreeing with the way the arbitrator performed his adjudicatory mission. It was not identifying a fundamental perversion of justice. The vital discipline of judicial deference failed in this case.

Although the court may be right on the result and the arbitrator wrong, the parties agreed to an arbitral determination. Unless the arbitrator commits or commands a profound illegality, the arbitral result should stand. The law protects the parties only from their choice of arbitration when the process constitutes a denial of justice. The Ninth Circuit here may have been influenced by the actors involved or the subject matter of the litigation. It might also have seen these circumstances as an opportunity to continue to express doubts about the range and suitability of arbitration in certain contexts. The Ninth Circuit's ruling emphasizes the need to have the arbitration bar reconsider a number of aspects of current arbitration law and practice.

First, *de novo* review of arbitrations in vacatur or confirmation proceedings should be eliminated. Losing parties should not be given the opportunity to hold the arbitral process and winning party hostage by making allegations that entail the *post facto* constitution of a record for the arbitration. The process of review, like the basic result of review, should be guided by a "hands-off" judicial policy. If the deficiency alleged does not appear on the face of the award or related documents, it should not be explored any further. Otherwise, arbitration is no longer private or confidential or subject to *pro forma* judicial supervision.

Second, the three or four nonstatutory grounds for the judicial supervision of awards need to be either eliminated or formally integrated into the statute or restricted to application in the labor arbitration area or—yet again—given a more precise general role and restricted content. At a minimum, there needs to be an accounting of the fact that FAA § 10 does not permit judicial supervision on the merits while the common-law grounds allow courts to scrutinize arbitral determinations. The mere possibility of a review of the merits of awards contradicts the policy directive of the relevant law and generates confusion and unpredictability in the area. Finally, the prospect of a merits review should not be used as a means by which courts can express their disagreement with the arbitrator's result and methodology of decision.

As stated in the case law, most courts see their review function as determining whether the arbitrators did their job—not that they did it well or accurately. The Third Circuit, in an opinion cited by the dissent in *Garvey*, described the applicable standard in the following terms: "Our review of the arbitrator's factual findings is not whether those findings were supported by the weight of the evidence or even whether they are clearly erroneous. All that is required is some support in the record. When the court finds some support, the inquiry is over."

Third, consideration should be given to the question of whether some form of judicial supervision of the merits is necessary when arbitrators apply or rule upon statutory law matters in employment or consumer arbitrations. Arguably, the courts should police arbitral determinations in circumstances in which arbitration can be imposed unilaterally by the stronger party and where the rulings have implications beyond the facts of the individual case. The Ninth Circuit decision in *Garvey* is unfortunate because it indicates how and why such a practice would be both difficult and dangerous to institute.

Finally, the practice of having an arbitral appellate level might obviate the need for and function of the common-law grounds for merits review even in the area of labor arbitration. Writing the possibility of internal arbitral appeal into collective bargaining agreements would give each party a chance to obtain a second look at the award and the process below. Having a procedural safeguard incorporated into the arbitral process would minimize the need to have recourse to courts. The possibility of internal arbitral appeal, however, should be confined to a limited number of grounds and circumstances. Arbitration should remain a process for expert, expedited justice in which the possibility of appeal is limited.

The U.S. Supreme Court, in an 8–1 decision, reversed the U.S. Court of Appeals for the Ninth Circuit in *Major League Baseball Players Ass'n v. Garvey*. *See* 532 U.S. 504 (2001). The Court stated that the appellate court ruling ran afoul of precedent that "courts are not authorized to review the arbitrator's decision on the merits despite allegations that the decision rests on factual errors or misinterprets the parties' agreement."

The Court noted that the prevailing decisional law regarding the judicial review of labor arbitration decisions pursuant to collective bargaining agreements makes clear that such review is very limited. Courts are not authorized to review the arbitrator's decision on the merits despite allegations that the decision rests on factual errors or misinterprets the parties' agreement. *United Paperworkers Int'l Union, AFL–CIO v. Misco,*

Inc., 484 U.S. 29, 36 (1987). The Court reiterated its recent holding that, if an arbitrator is even arguably construing or applying the contract and acting within the scope of his authority, the fact that a court is convinced he committed serious error does not suffice to overturn the decision. *Citing Eastern Associated Coal Corp. v. United Mine Workers of America, District 17*, 531 U.S. 57, 62 (2000), *quoting Misco, supra*, at 38. Only when the arbitrator strays from the interpretation and application of the agreement and effectively "dispense[s] his own brand on industrial justice" does his decision become unenforceable. *Citing United Steelworkers of America v. Enterprise Wheel & Car Corp.*, 363 U.S. 593, 597 (1960).

In analyzing the limited role of courts in reviewing the merits of arbitration awards, the Court noted that the Ninth Circuit recited these principles. The Court, however, found the circuit court's application of these principles "nothing short of baffling." The Court decided that the substance of the Ninth Circuit's opinion revealed that it overturned the arbitrator's decision because it disagreed with the arbitrator's factual findings, particularly those with respect to the credibility of witnesses. The appellate court rejected the arbitrator's findings and more, ultimately resolving the merits of the parties' dispute based on its own assessment of the record before the arbitrator. Because the appellate court vacated the arbitration for inappropriate reasons, the Court held that the Ninth Circuit erred in disturbing the arbitral award. It vacated the lower court decision and reinstated the arbitral award against Garvey.

NOTES AND QUESTIONS

1. Assess the introductory paragraph of the *Commentary*. Is it, in your view, a "fair and balanced" statement of the applicable law and judicial practice?

2. Why does the Ninth Circuit do what it does in *Garvey*? Is this an example of a judge or court becoming outraged by a facet of an arbitration and ranting at the arbitral result? Is it a more calculated and cold-blooded attack on the arbitral process? Explain your view.

3. It seems that every case of vacatur on the basis of a violation of a common law ground is embedded in a disagreement between the court and the arbitrators on a point of law or procedure. Is that accurate? Is it the purpose of the common law framework for review?

4. Why should the governing framework for vacatur maintain the possibility of judicial review of the merits? Appeal of the determination seems antithetical to the autonomy of arbitration. Evaluate the basis and impact of the practice.

5. Do you agree with the comment about *Garvey* that "[t]he vital discipline of judicial deference failed in this case"? Why and why not?

6. Define the concept of the "bargain for arbitration" and assess its role in the criticism of the Ninth Circuit opinion. When might the autonomy of the bargain be counterbalanced by a denial of justice? Was there a denial of justice in *Garvey*? Was there a "colorable basis" for the arbitrator's determination?

7. Is the U.S. Supreme Court assessment of the matter more persuasive?

8. Should statutory reform be instituted? What about statutory violations in employment arbitration cases? Should all appeals take place within the arbitration process? What about frivolous or losing appeals?

9. Having thus far surveyed the federal decisional law on the enforcement of arbitral awards, you should attempt to construct a legislative provision that would rationalize the current statutory framework. You should reconcile the original legislative intent underlying FAA § 10 with the common law contributions of the courts. The proposed substitute or amended version might recognize different forms of judicial supervision for different types of arbitral awards. The case for labor arbitration has been identified in the commentary, but there are other forms of arbitration that involve the application and interpretation of statutes that arguably present a need for a special form of judicial supervision. The arbitration of investor claims in securities arbitration is an obvious case in point and there are now other forms of consumer arbitration. Maritime arbitration is, in some respects, a *sui generis* form of arbitration and usually includes reasons or an opinion with the award. These circumstances might warrant a unique type of recourse to the courts.

10. One of the considerations that you might want to take into account in drafting the legislative provision is the need for economy, simplicity, and clarity in the directives you construct. These characteristics allow implementing courts and the affected parties to identify readily the objective of the legislation and to comply with it. The use of separate regimes for different types of arbitral awards, for example, will complicate the law and its application and eventually may result in conflict and confusion. A viable statutory framework will attempt to anticipate problems of implementation and avoid them. You might consider adding definitions to your statutory provision to achieve clarity.

11. As to matters of substance, a number of considerations need to be addressed. First, some definition of the type of judicial authority that will be exercised should be provided. Is it judicial review in the traditional sense? Is the term "judicial supervision" more appropriate? What does that term mean and how does it differ from judicial review? An express statutory statement of the relationship between courts and the arbitral process might be useful to clarify the judicial authority that is being invoked.

12. Also, the provision is intended to protect the rights of parties against arbitral awards that are fundamentally defective or contain other deficiencies that you believe makes them legally unenforceable. The judicial assessment of arbitral awards needs to balance these various factors: On the one hand, maintaining arbitration's necessary adjudicatory autonomy by limiting the availability of judicial supervision, and, on the other hand, providing parties with the prospect of real relief in the event that their interests are unlawfully harmed by the process.

13. Judicial second-guessing must be avoided, yet the statute must give the courts enough leeway to identify and remedy serious problems. In this connection, you need to consider the concept of the benefit of the bargain theory alluded to by some courts and the three nonstatutory grounds for review. The proposed statutory provision should make clear whether judicial

rescue from an agreement to arbitrate and its resulting award will be available only in the most exceptional circumstances and, relatedly, whether a court can ever vacate an award on the basis of the arbitral tribunal's interpretation and application of law. You should remember that FAA § 10 provides for judicial supervision primarily, if not exclusively, on the grounds of procedural irregularity. Should that approach be maintained and the common law grounds eliminated?

14. It may be possible to avoid these problems entirely by giving arbitral awards *res judicata* effect upon their rendition as a matter of law and provide for no judicial recourse at all. In effect, arbitral tribunals would act as courts of law for the particular dispute, the decisions of which are final and not subject to appeal. Is there any benefit to providing elaborate or inelaborate means of recourse that are generally applied in a perfunctory fashion? Why not exclude the reference to courts altogether if it is purely formalistic and may generate untoward accidents from time-to-time? If a reference to some form of subsequent consideration by another tribunal needs to be available, why not create a special court or private arbitration tribunal attached to an arbitral institution to supervise awards on a limited basis?

9. VENUE AND STATUTE OF LIMITATIONS

In *Cortez Byrd Chips, Inc. v. Bill Harbert Constr. Co.,* the U.S. Supreme Court held that the FAA's venue provisions, §§ 9–11, were permissive in character. The ruling allowed motions to confirm, vacate, or modify an arbitration award to be brought either in the district where the award had been rendered or in any proper district under the general venue statute. The general venue statute provides for venue in a diversity action in "a judicial district in which a substantial part of the events or omissions giving rise to the claim occurred, or a substantial part of property that is the subject of the action is situated." The Court explained that "the three venue sections of the FAA [were] best analyzed together, owing to their contemporaneous enactment and the similarity to their pertinent language."

CORTEZ BYRD CHIPS, INC. v. BILL HARBERT CONSTR. CO.

529 U.S. 193, 120 S.Ct. 1331, 146 L.Ed.2d 171 (2000).

(footnotes omitted)

Justice SOUTER delivered the opinion of the Court.

This case raises the issue whether the venue provisions of the Federal Arbitration Act (FAA or Act) ... are restrictive, allowing a motion to confirm, vacate, or modify an arbitration award to be brought only in the district in which the award was made, or are permissive, permitting such a motion either where the award was made or in any district proper under the general venue statute. We hold the FAA provisions permissive.

I

Petitioner Cortez Byrd Chips, Inc., and respondent Bill Harbert Construction Company agreed that Harbert would build a wood chip mill for Cortez Byrd in Brookhaven, Mississippi. One of the terms was that "[a]ll claims or disputes between the Contractor and the Owner arising out [of] or relating to the Contract, or the breach thereof, shall be decided by arbitration in accordance with the Construction Industry Arbitration Rules of the American Arbitration Association currently in effect unless the parties mutually agree otherwise." . . . The agreement went on to provide that "[t]he award rendered by the arbitrator or arbitrators shall be final, and judgment may be entered upon it in accordance with applicable law in any court having jurisdiction thereof," . . . that the agreement to arbitrate "shall be specifically enforceable under applicable law in any court having jurisdiction thereof," . . . and that the law of the place where the project was located, Mississippi, governed. . . .

After a dispute arose, Harbert invoked the agreement by a filing with the Atlanta office of the American Arbitration Association, which conducted arbitration in November 1997 in Birmingham, Alabama. The next month, the arbitration panel issued an award in favor of Harbert. . . .

In January 1998, Cortez Byrd filed a complaint in the United States District Court for the Southern District of Mississippi seeking to vacate or modify the arbitration award, which Harbert then sought to confirm by filing this action seven days later in the Northern District of Alabama. When Cortez Byrd moved to dismiss, transfer, or stay the Alabama action, the Alabama District Court denied the motion, concluding that venue was proper only in the Northern District of Alabama. . . .

The Court of Appeals for the Eleventh Circuit affirmed. It held itself bound by pre–1981 Fifth Circuit precedent . . . to the effect that under the Act's venue provisions . . . venue for motions to confirm, vacate, or modify awards was exclusively in the district in which the arbitration award was made. . . . The arbitration here having been held in Birmingham, the rule as so construed limited venue to the Northern District of Alabama.

We granted *certiorari* . . . to resolve a split among the Courts of Appeals over the permissive or mandatory character of the FAA's venue provisions. . . . We reverse.

II

Section 9 of the FAA governs venue for the confirmation of arbitration awards:

> "If the parties in their agreement have agreed that a judgment of the court shall be entered upon the award made pursuant to the arbitration, and shall specify the court, then at any time within one year after the award is made any party to the arbitration may apply to the court so specified for an order confirming the award, and thereupon the court must grant such an order unless the award is vacated, modified, or corrected as prescribed in sections 10 and 11 of this title. If no court is specified in the agreement of

the parties, then such application may be made to the United States court in and for the district within which such award was made." 9 U.S.C. § 9.

Section 10(a), governing motions to vacate arbitration awards, provides that

"the United States court in and for the district wherein the [arbitration] award was made may make an order vacating the award upon the application of any party to the arbitration [in any of five enumerated situations]."

And under § 11, on modification or correction,

"the United States court in and for the district wherein the award was made may make an order modifying or correcting the award upon the application of any party to the arbitration."

The precise issue raised in the District Court was whether venue for Cortez Byrd's motion under §§ 10 and 11 was properly laid in the southern district of Mississippi, within which the contract was performed. It was clearly proper under the general venue statute, which provides, among other things, for venue in a diversity action in "a judicial district in which a substantial part of the events or omissions giving rise to the claim occurred, or a substantial part of property that is the subject of the action is situated." 28 U.S.C. § 1391(a)(2). If §§ 10 and 11 are permissive and thus supplement, but do not supplant, the general provision, Cortez Byrd's motion to vacate or modify was properly filed in Mississippi, and under principles of deference to the court of first filing, the Alabama court should have considered staying its hand. . . . But if §§ 10 and 11 are restrictive, there was no Mississippi venue for Cortez Byrd's action, and the Northern District of Alabama correctly proceeded with the litigation to confirm. Although § 9 is not directly implicated in this action, since venue for Harbert's motion to confirm was proper in the northern district of Alabama under either a restrictive or a permissive reading of § 9, the three venue sections of the FAA are best analyzed together, owing to their contemporaneous enactment and the similarity of their pertinent language.

Enlightenment will not come merely from parsing the language, which is less clear than either party contends. Although "may" could be read as permissive in each section, as Cortez Byrd argues, the mere use of "may" is not necessarily conclusive of congressional intent to provide for a permissive or discretionary authority. . . . Cortez Byrd points to clearly mandatory language in other parts of the Act as some indication that "may" was used in a permissive sense. . . . Each party has a point, but neither point is conclusive. The answer is not to be had from comparing phrases.

Statutory history provides a better lesson, though, which is confirmed by following out the practical consequences of Harbert's position. When the FAA was enacted in 1925, it appeared against the backdrop of a considerably more restrictive general venue statute than the one current today. At the time, the practical effect of 28 U.S.C. § 112(a) was that a civil suit could usually be brought only in the district in which the defendant resided.... The statute's restrictive application was all the more pronounced due to the courts' general inhospitality to forum selection clauses.... Hence, even if an arbitration agreement expressly permitted action to be brought in the district in which arbitration had been conducted, the agreement would probably prove to be vain. The enactment of the special venue provisions in the FAA thus had an obviously liberalizing effect, undiminished by any suggestion, textual or otherwise, that Congress meant simultaneously to foreclose a suit where the defendant resided. Such a consequence would have been as inexplicable in 1925 as it would be passing strange 75 years later. The most convenient forum for a defendant is normally the forum of residence, and it would take a very powerful reason ever to suggest that Congress would have meant to eliminate that venue for postarbitration disputes.

The virtue of the liberalizing nonrestrictive view of the provisions for venue in the district of arbitration is confirmed by another obviously liberalizing venue provision of the Act, which in § 9 authorizes a binding agreement selecting a forum for confirming an arbitration award. Since any forum selection agreement must coexist with §§ 10 and 11, one needs to ask how they would work together if §§ 10 and 11 meant that an order vacating or modifying an arbitration award could be obtained only in the district where the award was made. The consequence would be that a proceeding to confirm the award begun in a forum previously selected by agreement of the parties (but outside the district of the arbitration) would need to be held in abeyance if the responding party objected. The objecting party would then have to return to the district of the arbitration to begin a separate proceeding to modify or vacate the arbitration award, and if the award withstood attack, the parties would move back to the previously selected forum for the confirming order originally sought. Harbert, naturally, is far from endorsing anything of the sort and contends that a court with venue to confirm under a § 9 forum selection clause would also have venue under a later filed motion under § 10. But the contention boils down to denying the logic of Harbert's own position. The regime we have described would follow from adopting that position, and the Congress simply cannot be tagged with such a taste for the bizarre.

Nothing, indeed, would be more clearly at odds with both the FAA's "statutory policy of rapid and unobstructed enforcement of arbitration agreements," ... or with the desired flexibility of parties in choosing a site for arbitration. Although the location of the arbitration may well be the residence of one of the parties, or have some other connection to a contract at issue, in many cases the site will have no relation whatsoever to the parties or the dispute. The parties may be willing to arbitrate in an inconvenient forum, say, for the convenience of the arbitrators, or to get a panel with special knowledge or experience, or as part of some compromise, but they might well be less willing to pick such a location if any future court proceedings had to be held there. Flexibility to make such practical choices, then, could well be inhibited by a venue rule mandating the same inconvenient venue if someone later sought to vacate or modify the award.

A restrictive interpretation would also place § 3 and §§ 9–11 of the FAA in needless tension, which could be resolved only by disrupting existing precedent of this Court. Section 3 provides that any court in which an action "referable to arbitration under an agreement in writing" is pending "shall on application of one of the parties stay the trial of the action until such arbitration has been had in accordance with the terms of the agreement." 9 U.S.C. § 3. If an arbitration were then held outside the district of that litigation, under a restrictive reading of §§ 9–11 a subsequent proceeding to confirm, modify, or set aside the arbitration award could not be brought in the district of the original litigation (unless that also happened to be the chosen venue in a forum selection agreement). We have, however, previously held that the court with the power to stay the action under § 3 has the further power to confirm any ensuing arbitration award. *Marine Transit Corp. v. Dreyfus*, 284 U.S. 263, 275–276, 52 S.Ct. 166, 76 L.Ed. 282 (1932) ("We do not conceive it to be open to question that, where the court has authority under the statute … to make an order for arbitration, the court also has authority to confirm the award or to set it aside for irregularity, fraud, *ultra vires* or other defect"). Harbert in effect concedes this point, acknowledging that "the court entering a stay order under § 3 retains jurisdiction over the proceeding and does not 'lose venue.'"… But that concession saving our precedent still fails to explain why Congress would have wanted to allow venue liberally where motions to confirm, vacate, or modify were brought as subsequent stages of actions antedating the arbitration, but would have wanted a different rule when arbitration was not preceded by a suit between the parties.

Finally, Harbert's interpretation would create anomalous results in the aftermath of arbitrations held abroad. Sections 204, 207, and 302 of the FAA together provide for liberal choice of venue for actions to confirm awards subject to the 1958 Convention on the Recognition and Enforcement of Foreign Arbitral Awards and the 1975 Inter–American Convention on International Commercial Arbitration…. But reading §§ 9–11 to restrict venue to the site of the arbitration would preclude any action under the FAA in courts of the United States to confirm, modify, or vacate awards rendered in foreign arbitrations not covered by either convention…. Although such actions would not necessarily be barred for lack of jurisdiction, they would be defeated by restrictions on venue, and anomalies like that are to be avoided when they can be….

Attention to practical consequences thus points away from the restrictive reading of §§ 9–11 and confirms the view that the liberalizing effect of the provisions in the day of their enactment was meant to endure through treating them as permitting, not limiting, venue choice today….

The judgment of the Court of Appeals is reversed, and the case is remanded for further proceedings consistent with this opinion.

It is so ordered.

NOTES AND QUESTIONS

1. Justice Souter delivered the opinion for a unanimous Court.

2. How does the reasoning and determination fit into the federal policy on arbitration? What are the practical advantages of the ruling?

3. What could be said in favor of a restrictive view of the venue provisions? What did Harbert argue?

4. How do the statutory provisions on international commercial arbitration influence the result in the case? How significant a factor are they?

5. Is the liberal tolerance espoused by the Court simply too much of a good thing? Is the permissiveness likely to generate adversarial litigation strategies and forum-shopping? How could that prospect be curtailed or eliminated?

PHOTOPAINT TECHN., LLC v. SMARTLENS CORP.

335 F.3d 152 (2d Cir. 2003).

JACOBS, Circuit Judge.

Photopaint Technologies, LLC, ("Photopaint") appeals from a final judgment entered in the United States District Court for the Southern District of New York ... denying Photopaint's motion to confirm an arbitration award under the Federal Arbitration Act ... and granting the cross-motion for summary judgment of Smartlens Corporation and Steven Hylen (collectively, "Smartlens") on the grounds that section 9 of the FAA imposes a one-year statute of limitations on an application for an order of confirmation and that Photopaint (which moved for confirmation more than one year after the award was made) was not entitled to relief from this limitation period....

We reverse, holding that the FAA does impose a one-year statute of limitations, but that Photopaint is entitled to relief from the statutory period. For the reasons that follow, the judgment of the district court is vacated and the case remanded for further proceedings not inconsistent with this opinion.

BACKGROUND

In December 1997, Photopaint and Smartlens entered into a license agreement containing a clause under which they agreed that their disputes would be submitted to arbitration. When a dispute arose in October 1999, they duly submitted it to an arbitrator selected by the American Arbitration Association ("AAA"). In an August 1999 "Partial/Interim Award," the arbitrator ruled largely in Photopaint's favor and ordered it to submit an accounting of costs associated with the license agreement. After reviewing these accounting submissions, the arbitrator signed a "Final Award" on May 26, 2000. The Final Award provided that the License Agreement was voidable; that either party could elect to rescind it within thirty days from receipt of the award; and that Smartlens would make a payment to Photopaint if either party elected to rescind. The amount of this payment was to depend on which party rescinded: if Smartlens rescinded first, it would pay approximately $384,000 plus Photopaint's share of the AAA costs; if Photopaint rescinded first, Smartlens would pay approximately $320,000.

Although the arbitrator signed the Final Award on May 26, 2000 and promptly sent it to the AAA for distribution, the AAA failed (for some reason) to deliver the award to the parties until October 3, 2000—more than four months later. The parties ultimately found out that the award had issued when Smartlens asked to have the arbitration hearing re-opened for additional submissions; in denying that request on October 23, 2000, the arbitrator treated it as one for modification of the Final Award, noting that this award had been rendered on May 26, 2000.

Since the Final Award provided that either party could rescind within thirty days of *receiving* the award, and since the parties first received it on October 3, 2000, the option to rescind was initially scheduled to expire on November 2, 2000. As this date neared, the parties entered into a series of letter agreements to allow for continued settlement discussions.

During the negotiations, Smartlens and Photopaint exchanged several drafts of a settlement agreement, in which they agreed that Smartlens would pay Photopaint a lump-sum of $360,000, but differed as to other provisions. In April, negotiations appeared close to resolution, and on April 16, 2001, Photopaint circulated a revised draft reflecting the $360,000 lump-sum payment and acceding to the remaining changes sought by Smartlens. Shortly afterward, however, Smartlens advised that, due to sharp financial reverses, it could offer no more than a lump-sum payment of $100,000, together with a promissory note. On May 1, Smartlens sought a further time extension "under exactly the same terms" as the parties' prior agreements, to "discuss [the] alternative proposal further and attempt to achieve a final resolution." Photopaint agreed. On the basis of this and subsequent letter agreements, the parties continued discussions into May, June, and July 2001—beyond the May 26 one-year anniversary of the rendering of the Final Award.

Negotiations broke down in July 2001, and on July 27, Photopaint rescinded the license agreement and demanded from Smartlens the $320,000 payment provided for under the terms of the Final Award. Smartlens refused to pay, and Photopaint filed this petition to confirm the Final Award pursuant to the FAA.

In the district court, Smartlens argued against confirmation on the ground that the application was time-barred, under section 9 of the FAA, because it was filed more than one year after the date the Final Award was made. The district court agreed, granted Smartlens summary judgment on this ground, and dismissed the petition. . . . Photopaint appealed.

DISCUSSION

We review *de novo* a ruling granting summary judgment ... construing the evidence in the light most favorable to the non-moving party (here, Photopaint) and drawing all reasonable inferences in that party's favor....

I

Section 9 of the FAA provides, in pertinent part:

> If the parties in their agreement have agreed that a judgment of the court shall be entered upon the award made pursuant to the arbitration, and shall specify the court, then *at any time within one year after the award is made* any party to the arbitration *may* apply to the court so specified for an order confirming the award, and thereupon the court *must* grant such an order [confirming the award] unless the award is vacated, modified, or corrected as prescribed in sections 10 and 11 of this title.

9 U.S.C. § 9 (emphasis added). The threshold question on appeal is whether this wording creates a one-year statute of limitations—a question of first impression in this Court.

As Photopaint emphasizes, the permissive verb "may," rather than the mandatory verb "must," is used in the clause affording one year to the party wishing to confirm an award, while "must" is used elsewhere in the same section and in other sections of the FAA. In section 12, for example, Congress used "must" in relation to the three-month period for filing a motion to vacate an arbitration award.[3]

We have recognized in another context that "when the same [statute] uses both 'may' and 'shall', the normal inference is that each is used in its usual sense—the one act being permissive, the other mandatory."... Both the Fourth and the Eighth Circuits have relied on this "normal inference" in holding that "may" in section 9 is permissive only, and that petitions to confirm arbitral awards under the FAA may be filed beyond the "one year" period. *See Sverdrup Corp. v. WHC Constructors, Inc.,* 989 F.2d 148, 151–56 (4th Cir.1993).... *But see In re Consol. Rail Corp.,* 867 F.Supp. 25, 30–32 (D.D.C.1994) (relying on considerations of finality to hold that section 9 imposes a mandatory one-year statute of limitations). In the Fourth Circuit's *Sverdrup* decision, which was relied on heavily by the Eighth Circuit in *Val-U Construction,* the court cited the ordinary permissive meaning of "may," as well as considerations of judicial economy, in holding that section 9's limitations period is not mandatory. *Sverdrup,* 989 F.2d at 151–52, 156; *accord Val–U Constr.,* 146 F.3d at 581.

We respectfully disagree, particularly in light of the Supreme Court's intervening decision in *Cortez Byrd Chips, Inc. v. Bill Harbert Construction Co.,* 529 U.S. 193, 120 S.Ct. 1331, 146 L.Ed.2d 171 (2000). *Cortez Byrd* considered whether the word "may" is used permissively in the

---

3. "Notice of a motion to vacate, modify, or correct an award *must* be served upon the adverse party or his attorney within three months after the award is filed or delivered." 9 U.S.C. § 12 (emphasis added).

context of the FAA's venue provisions, under which (whenever the parties do not specify otherwise) proceedings "may" be conducted in the district where the award was made.... Although the Court held that the venue provisions are permissive, it expressly declined to rely on the permissiveness of "may" as a matter of plain meaning.... Instead, *Cortez Byrd* relied on considerations particular to venue: the overall structure of the FAA (a narrow reading of the venue provisions would have created "needless tension" with other parts of the FAA, ... and the statutory history of the general federal venue provision ... (which was considerably more restrictive when the FAA was enacted, suggesting that Congress used "may" in § 9 to broaden venue under the FAA....)). And the Court rejected the idea that use of "may" in some provisions of the FAA (including § 9)—and not in others—carries definitive significance....

We therefore consider the text of section 9 without affording decisive effect to the ordinary permissive meaning of "may." Although the word "may" in a statute "usually implies some degree of discretion[, t]his common-sense principle of statutory construction ... can be defeated by indications of legislative intent to the contrary or by obvious inferences from the structure and purpose of the statute." ... One indication of legislative intent to the contrary here is that, unless the adverbial phrase beginning "at any time within one year" creates a time limitation within which one "may" apply for confirmation, the phrase lacks incremental meaning.... We read statutes to avoid rendering any words wholly superfluous.... Photopaint suggests that section 9 can be read to say that enforcement is mandatory if the application is made within one year, and that it is discretionary thereafter. We are unpersuaded. Photopaint gives no support for this reading, no explanation as to how such discretion would be guided, and no theory as to why Congress would want to do that.

In *Seetransport Wiking Trader Schiffarhtsgesellschaft MBH & Co. v. Navimpex Centrala Navala,* 989 F.2d 572 (2d Cir.1993), we construed section 207 of the International Convention on the Recognition and Enforcement of Foreign Arbitral Awards (the "Convention") ... which is analogous to section 9 of the FAA, and held that a clause using the word "may" created a statute of limitation notwithstanding that "shall" was used elsewhere in the same provision. *See Seetransport,* 989 F.2d at 580–81 (reversing judgment enforcing foreign arbitral award on ground that cause of action seeking enforcement of arbitral award under the convention was time-barred). *Seetransport* construed the Convention, not the FAA, but is otherwise difficult to distinguish.

Dicta in our previous cases is to the same effect. In *The Hartbridge,* 57 F.2d 672 (2d Cir.1932), we suggested that, even though section 9's language was permissive, "the privilege conferred by section 9" was a privilege "to move 'at any time' *within the year." Id.* at 673 (emphasis added). Similarly, in *Kerr-McGee Refining Corp. v. M/T Triumph,* 924 F.2d 467 (2d Cir.1991), we cited section 9 for the proposition that, "[u]nder the Arbitration Act, *a party has one year* to avail itself of summary proceedings for confirmation of an award." *Id.* at 471 (emphasis added).

In light of these authorities, we read the word "may" in section 9 as permissive, but only within the scope of the preceding adverbial phrase: "[a]t any time within one year after the award is made." We therefore hold that section 9 of the FAA imposes a one-year statute of limitations on the filing of a motion to confirm an arbitration award under the FAA. Our construction of the text is not inevitable, but it is intuitive: for example, tax returns may be filed anytime up to April 15, but one senses at once that the phrase is permissive only up to a point. Moreover, this result advances important values of finality:

> One of the FAA's purposes is to provide parties with an effective alternative dispute resolution system which gives litigants a sure and expedited resolution of disputes while reducing the burden on the courts. Arbitration should therefore provide not only a fast resolution but one which establishes conclusively the rights between the parties. A one year limitations period is instrumental in achieving this goal.

In re Consol. Rail, 867 F.Supp. at 31; *see also Young v. United States,* 535 U.S. 43, 47, 122 S.Ct. 1036, 152 L.Ed.2d 79 (2002) (describing the "basic policies [furthered by] all limitations provisions" as "repose, elimination of stale claims, and certainty about a plaintiff's opportunity for recovery and a defendant's potential liabilities" (modification in original)).

In arriving at an opposite conclusion, the Fourth Circuit's opinion in *Sverdrup* made contextual and policy arguments that merit consideration. The *Sverdrup* court noted that Congress used "may" in the section 9 context of the one-year period for filing a motion to confirm an award, and "must" in the section 12 context of the three-month period for filing a motion to vacate, modify, or correct an award. *Sverdrup,* 989 F.2d at 151. Concluding that these sections are otherwise parallel, the court concluded that Congress "understood the plain meaning of 'may' [in section 9] to be permissive," *id.* at 151, and that section 9 "must [therefore] be interpreted as its plain language indicates, as a permissive provision which does not bar the confirmation of an award beyond a one-year period." *Id.* at 156.

Sections 9 and 11, however, are not otherwise parallel. Sections 10 and 11 of the FAA govern the filing of motions to vacate or modify; both describe the circumstances under which a court "may" make an order vacating, modifying or correcting an award "upon the application of any party to the arbitration...." ... Because section 12 comes into play only in the event that a party makes such an application, "must" in section 12 unambiguously bears on *when* a party can file a motion to vacate, modify, or correct, and not *whether* the party has discretion to bring such a motion. (Such discretion is provided by the "may" in sections 10 and 11.) In section 9, by contrast, "may" *can* be read to reflect a party's discretion as to *whether* to "apply to the court ... for an order confirming the award." *See Kentucky River Mills v. Jackson,* 206 F.2d 111, 120 (6th Cir.1953) ("The language of [section 9] as to application to the court for an order is not mandatory, but permissive. A party may, therefore, apply to the court for an order confirming the award, but is not limited to such remedy.").

Sverdrup also relied on considerations of judicial economy: "[b]ecause remedies do exist outside the FAA's framework to enforce [an arbitral] award, reading § 9 as a strict statute of limitations would be an exercise in futility" because it would "merely encourage, at the expense of judicial economy, the use of another analogous method of enforcing awards." *Sverdrup*, 989 F.2d at 155. We agree with the Fourth Circuit that an action at law offers an alternative remedy to enforce an arbitral award, but we draw a different conclusion from the existence of that alternative. An action at law is not identical to the summary confirmation proceeding established by the FAA, which was intended to streamline the process and eliminate certain defenses. *See generally* Robert J. Gruendel, *Domestic Law and International Conventions, the Imperfect Overlay: The FAA as a Case Study,* Admiralty Law Institute Symposium: A Sea Chest for Sea Lawyers, 75 Tulane L.Rev. 1489, 1504–07 (2001) (noting that burdens and defenses available in an action at law to confirm an arbitration award differ from those in a statutory summary proceeding under the FAA). It was therefore not "futile" for Congress to have specified a statute of limitations for the filing of summary proceedings: consistent with the wording of the statute, a party to an arbitration is entitled to the benefits of the streamlined summary proceeding only if, as it may do, it files at any time within one year after the award is made.

II

It is undisputed in this case that Photopaint filed its motion to confirm the Final Award more than one year from the date on which the award was made, and that Photopaint's motion to confirm the award is therefore barred absent some relief from the limitations period. Photopaint asserts several grounds for such relief, largely framed in terms of equity. We need not consider, the availability of equitable relief, however, because the undisputed record establishes, as a matter of law, that Smartlens and Photopaint agreed to toll any applicable limitations periods imposed under the FAA.

It is undisputed that the parties entered into a series of agreements extending the time in which to conduct settlement negotiations; the parties, however, contest the scope of these agreements. The meaning of contract provisions is a question of law over which we exercise *de novo* review. . . . Under New York law, which applies here, judgment as a matter of law is appropriate if the contract language is unambiguous. . . . "Contract language is unambiguous when it has 'a definite and precise meaning, unattended by danger of misconception in the purport of the [contract] itself, and concerning which there is no reasonable basis for a difference of opinion.' " . . . Unambiguous contract language is not rendered ambiguous by competing interpretations of it urged in litigation. . . .

The letter agreements at issue were entered into after the parties received the Final Award, which provided that for a thirty day period, ending on November 2, 2000, either party could rescind the license agreement. In an October 31, 2000 letter memorializing previous oral discussions, however, the parties extended the rescission deadline as well as other (unspecified) dependent deadlines:

> [W]e both understand that the 30 day time period specified in section 2(A) of the Final Award would have required action by the parties on or before 2 November 2000. Our agreement to extend the time would therefore extend this date to on or before 16 November 2000. *All other dependent times, if any, would be extended a like amount. The agreed extension shall apply to all acts or failures to act permitted or required to or by either party.* (Emphasis added.)

Smartlens argues that this wording is insufficient to extend the statute of limitation under the FAA. But the scope of the extension is broad and undifferentiated—"all acts and failures to act permitted or required to or by either party"—and at oral argument, counsel for Smartlens was unable to come up with an alternative formulation that would have been any broader. Moreover, the letter agreement was drafted by counsel for Smartlens, and we generally interpret contractual ambiguities against the drafter. . . .

We need not rely on the breadth of this initial letter agreement, however, because the parties' intent was clarified in subsequent letter agreements—each of which recited that the extension of time is on the same terms as before. Specifically, the parties' November 13, 2000 letter extending their initial tolling agreement explicitly references the FAA: Smartlens, the drafter, warned that in the absence of a further extension of time, it would be forced "to complete the Motion [pursuant to section 12 of the FAA] to Vacate the Award and the Interpleader, both items [it] would like to avoid." Smartlens "therefore propose[d]" a further extension, "under exactly the same terms as were set out in [the] previous letter," emphasizing that the agreement would extend "the time within which action must be taken by either of us *to rescind the license, or otherwise*." (Emphasis added.) And Smartlens required that Photopaint sign an acknowledgment that "[t]he above terms accurately state[d]" the parties' agreement. More letter agreements followed, each expressly predicated on the ones before, and each extending the time within which the parties had "to rescind the license agreement, or otherwise." The initial series of letter agreements was followed by an "indefinite extension" for several months, and then by further periodic extensions.

This series of agreements and extensions, which continued until several months before Photopaint filed the instant petition for confirmation under the FAA, extended the one-year limitations period for filing the petition to confirm in this case.

It is undisputed that the period covered by the tolling agreements—the approximately nine months from October 31, 2000 through July 27, 2001—is long enough to make Photopaint's motion to confirm timely. Smartlens therefore cannot prevail on its statute of limitations defense.

CONCLUSION

For the reasons stated above, we agree with the district court's ruling that the FAA imposes a one-year statute of limitations, but reverse the judgment dismissing Photopaint's petition as untimely, and remand for further proceedings not inconsistent with this opinion.

NOTES AND QUESTIONS

1. How does the reasoning in *Cortez Byrd Chips, Inc.* influence the court in *Photopaint Techn.*? Is the language of the FAA subject to strict construction? When? What do you make of the court's distinction between an "inevitable" and "intuitive" interpretation of a statutory text?

2. Is the proceeding described in *Photopaint Techn.* an arbitration, an adjudication, arb-med, or a mini-trial—or even structured negotiation? Why? Why does the court not address that problem?

3. How many awards are rendered by the arbitrator in *Photopaint Techn.*? Is the ruling in the last award final and, therefore, binding? Why do the parties engage in post-award negotiations? Can their agreements at that stage of the process modify the award? Does freedom of contract govern the arbitrator's determinations as well as the post-award agreement? Can an award be open-ended?

4. What do you think of the interpretation of FAA § 9 that, before the lapsing of a one-year period, confirmation of the award is nearly automatic; after the one-year period, it is within the court's discretion? Is it wishful construction? Is it at all convincing? Explain.

5. Discuss and evaluate the use of express and implied extensions in the context of the facts and the court's reasoning.

6. Is the opinion's accommodative character likely to generate even more litigation about arbitration? Why is the court so reluctant to follow the stated rule and close the door? Is creative adaptation dangerous once again? How?

7. Is the federal policy on arbitration observed in the reasoning and result of *Photopaint Techn.*?

8. Why does the AAA escape retribution under these facts?

10. THE RIGHT TO SEEK A CLARIFICATION OF AN AWARD

M & C CORP. v. ERWIN BEHR GmbH & CO., KG

326 F.3d 772 (6th Cir. 2003).

OPINION

PER CURIAM.

This case is before us on appeal for the third time since an international arbitrator rendered an award in favor of the plaintiff, M & C

Corporation. That award was confirmed by the district court, and judgment was entered. The instant appeal arises from a dispute regarding enforcement of a specific portion of the award. The defendant, Erwin Behr GmbH & Co., KG, interprets the award one way, and the plaintiff interprets it another. The district court initially had found the award to be unambiguous but, after attempting to determine the precise amount owed under the award, held that the award was "unclear as to its application" and entered an order of remand to the original arbitrator to clear up the problem. Behr appeals from this order, arguing that remand is inappropriate and that it has satisfied the award. In response, M & C contends that the district court's order of remand is not a "final order" and that this court therefore has no jurisdiction over Behr's appeal. In addition, M & C argues that remand is appropriate.

For the reasons set out below, we conclude that we have jurisdiction over Behr's appeal but that we are unable to review the order of remand on its merits because the district court failed to identify in what respect(s) the arbitration award was ambiguous and in need of clarification. Without this guidance, we cannot determine whether remand is proper and, moreover, the arbitrator would be left to speculate about how to interpret the award. Hence, we find it necessary to remand this case to the district court for further clarification.

[. . .]

2. *Did The District Court Err By Entering Its Order Of Remand?*

The bulk of Behr's brief is spent making a complex, fact-intensive argument that it has paid M & C all commissions due under the Eighth Award. According to Behr, the district court's principal error was in failing to grant Behr's motion for partial satisfaction of the judgment. This argument is premature and, in our judgment, misses the point. The district court did not expressly *deny* Behr's motion for partial satisfaction of the judgment. Instead, it is apparent that the court was in the process of determining whether Behr had satisfied the judgment when it encountered an ambiguity in the award, necessitating a remand to the arbitrator. That brings us to the most pressing question raised by this appeal: whether that remand was proper. Behr argues that remand is inappropriate, while M & C disagrees.

"A remand is proper, both at common law and under the federal law of arbitration contracts, to clarify an ambiguous award or to require the arbitrator to address an issue submitted to him but not resolved by the award." *Green v. Ameritech Corp.,* 200 F.3d 967, 977 (6th Cir.2000). The authority to order a remand derives from a recognized exception to the *functus officio* doctrine, which holds that an arbitrator's duties are generally discharged upon the rendering of a final award, when the arbitral authority is terminated.... However, " '[w]here the award, although seemingly complete, leaves doubt whether the submission has been fully executed, an ambiguity arises which the arbitrator is entitled to clarify.' " *Id.* at 977 (quoting *La Vale Plaza, Inc. v. R.S. Noonan, Inc.,* 378 F.2d 569,

573 (3d Cir.1967)). *See also Hyle v. Doctor's Assoc.,* 198 F.3d 368, 370 (2d Cir.1999) ("[A] district court can remand an award to the arbitrator for clarification where an award is ambiguous.").

The propriety of remanding an ambiguous award to the arbitrator is reinforced by the strong federal policy favoring arbitration. *See Behr II,* 143 F.3d at 1041 (Daughtrey, J., dissenting) ("I am led to th[e] conclusion [that remand of ambiguous award was proper] by the Supreme Court's pronouncement that 'any doubts concerning the scope of arbitrable issues should be resolved in favor of arbitration'") (quoting *Moses H. Cone Memorial Hosp. v. Mercury Constr. Co.,* 460 U.S. 1, 24–25, 103 S.Ct. 927, 74 L.Ed.2d 765 (1983)); *Mutual Fire, Marine & Inland Ins. Co. v. Norad Reinsurance Co.,* 868 F.2d 52, 58 (3d Cir.1989) ("A district court itself should not clarify an ambiguous arbitration award but should remand it to the arbitration panel for clarification."). Of course it is true that "[w]hen possible, ... a court should avoid remanding a decision to the arbitrator because of the interest in prompt and final arbitration." *Publicis Communication v. True North Communications Inc.,* 206 F.3d 725, 730 (7th Cir.2000). At the same time, however, a court simply should not "engag[e] in impermissible interpretation" of an ambiguous award. *Tri-State Bus. Mach., Inc. v. Lanier Worldwide, Inc.,* 221 F.3d 1015, 1020 (7th Cir.2000) (reversing and remanding order executing post-arbitration judgment where district court erred in not remanding the ambiguous award to arbitration panel for clarification). *See also Americas Insurance Co. v. Seagull Compania Naviera, S.A.,* 774 F.2d 64, 67 (2d Cir.1985) ("An ambiguous award should be remanded to the arbitrators so that the court will know exactly what it is being asked to enforce."); *Ganey v. Raffone,* No. 90–00871, 1996 WL 382278, at *3 (6th Cir. July 5, 1996) ("There are limited circumstances under which a district court can remand a case to the arbitrators for clarification. While a remand is to be used sparingly, it may be employed to avoid judicial guessing of the meaning of arbitral awards.") (citations and quotations omitted). In short, for a court to engage in guesswork as to the meaning and application of an ambiguous arbitration award is inconsistent not only with federal policy, but also with the parties' own agreement to submit their dispute to arbitration.

In *Behr II,* the majority decided that remand was inappropriate because it determined that the award was *not* ambiguous. There, the portion of the arbitrator's award subject to dispute was easily identified: The district court determined that "Behr had raised a good faith issue of what constitutes an 'order' under the commission contract, and that the prior arbitration award had not addressed that issue." *Behr II,* 143 F.3d at 1036. Here, on the other hand, the district court's order lacks any indication of precisely how the Eighth Award is "unclear as to its application", or which issue submitted to the arbitrator was "not fully adjudicate[d]." Nor with any confidence can we divine the answers from the circumstances; prior to its remand order, the district court had expressly held that the arbitrator's opinion and award were *not* ambiguous with respect to Behr's obligation to pay commissions on the 1996 EK parts and 1997 K parts. If the district court has changed its mind about *this* issue, it needs to say so and explain it. If there is *another* ambiguity in the award that makes enforcement impossible, the district court needs to identify it. Until it does so, we cannot undertake a meaningful review of whether the award is ambiguous or whether the circumstances are appropriate for a remand to the arbitrator. Moreover, the district court's vague order creates a substantial risk that the arbitrator will have insufficient guidance as to how to clarify its award, creating the potential for yet another journey to the district court, to this court on appeal, and back yet again to the arbitrator. Accordingly, we find it necessary to remand this case to the district court for clarification of the precise issue or issues that remain for the arbitrator on remand.

Because the case will be remanded to the district court, two other issues raised by Behr merit discussion in the interest of judicial economy.

3. Should Remand Be To The Same Arbitrator?

Behr argues that, assuming remand was appropriate, it was error for the district court to remand the award to the original arbitrator rather than directing the parties to start the whole process over again before a brand new arbitrator. In making this argument, Behr fails to account for our observation in *Green* that "[c]ourts usually remand to the *original* arbitrator for clarification of an ambiguous award when the award fails to address a contingency that later arises or when the award is susceptible to more than one interpretation." *Green,* 200 F.3d at 977 (emphasis added). The district court characterized its remand order as "simply ... requir[ing the arbitrator] to complete his duties by applying his reasoning to the facts and ... not reopen[ing] the merits of the case." Assuming that the district court's revised order on remand is consistent with this characterization, remand to the original arbitrator is the right result.

4. Can This International Arbitration Be Remanded?

Hoping to avoid remand, Behr makes a two-pronged argument that remand is improper even if the award is ambiguous. First, Behr contends that the International Chamber of Commerce (ICC) Rules that govern this dispute pursuant to the parties' arbitration agreement do not expressly permit remand. Behr points out that the 1988 version of the ICC Rules "made no provision for reconsideration, reinterpretation, or remand." According to Behr, remand is therefore disallowed.

However, as M & C points out, Article 35 of the same rules demonstrates that a guiding principle behind the rules is to ensure that the award is ultimately susceptible of enforcement, providing, as it does, that "[i]n all matters not expressly provided for in these rules, the court and the Arbitral Tribunal shall act in the spirit of these Rules and shall make every effort to make sure that the Award is enforceable at law." We read this provision to permit remand in this case, given that clarification by the original arbitrator is critical in order to make the Eighth Award enforceable at law.

Moreover, as M & C indicates, the parties' terms of reference for the arbitration provide that "[w]here the Rules are silent then such rules shall apply as may be made from time to time by the Arbitrator consistent with any mandatory requirement of the law of the place of arbitration. . . ." The "place of arbitration" in this case was London, England, and English law appears to require remand under the circumstances presented by this case. In this regard, M & C points to the English Arbitration Act of 1996, in which Parliament provided that where there is "uncertainty or ambiguity as to the effect of the award," it may be "remit[ted] to the tribunal, in whole or in part." English Arbitration Act of 1996, 1996 Chapter 23, § 68(2)(f) and (3)(a). In the absence of a clear indication that remand is disallowed by the applicable rules, we find no merit to this argument by Behr.

Behr's final argument is based on the Convention on the Recognition and Enforcement of Foreign Arbitral Awards ("New York Convention"). *See* 9 U.S.C. § 201. Behr observes that "[t]he Convention makes no provision for a remand after an arbitration award is rendered." Making this same observation, the district court below concluded in a separate order entered almost six years ago that it had no authority to order a remand, saying that "[b]ecause the arbitration award is governed by the [New York Convention], and because that convention makes no provision for a remand after an arbitration award is rendered, there is no basis in law for this court to remand." In addition, Behr cites our holding in *Behr I* that the New York Convention applied to prevent a party from moving in the United States courts to *vacate* an arbitration award made in a foreign nation. 87 F.3d at 847.

Contrary to what Behr argues, however, neither the New York Convention itself nor our holding in *Behr I* compels a holding that the district court lacks authority to remand an ambiguous award. First, we note that the New York Convention is utterly silent on the issue, as it is on many other issues dealing with the nuts and bolts of international arbitration procedure. At bottom, a remand of an ambiguous award under the circumstances presented here is not inconsistent with any provision of the New York Convention, and we have been unable to locate any authority suggesting that it is. Moreover, our holding in *Behr I* is inapposite. There, we were faced with a motion to *vacate* a foreign arbitration award and held that the district court lacked jurisdiction to enter such an order because, "[p]ursuant to the Convention, an application for setting aside or suspending an arbitral award may be made only to a 'competent authority of the country in which, or under the law of which, that award was made.'" *Behr I*, 87 F.3d at 847 (quoting New York Convention, Art. VI). Here, by contrast, the parties do not seek to *vacate* the confirmed arbitration award, nor did the district court enter such an order. Rather, the district court ordered a remand so that an award that it determined to be ambiguous could be rendered enforceable.

CONCLUSION

The district court's order remanding this case to the original arbitrator for clarification of an apparent ambiguity fails to identify the issue or issues that supposedly need the arbitrator's attention. We cannot conduct a meaningful review of the propriety of the district court's order of remand without a statement by the district court of what it perceives to be the ambiguity in the award. In addition, the arbitrator's job on remand will be needlessly complicated in the absence of clear direction from the district court. Accordingly, we REMAND this case to the district court with instructions to enter an order specifying in what respects the Eighth Award is unclear as to its application.

NOTES AND QUESTIONS

1. Upon what source of law does the court ground its authority to order a remand?

2. Who or what created the "recognized exception to the *functus officio* doctrine"?

3. How does the right to seek a clarification buttress the federal policy on arbitration?

4. Do the parties have any role in making the determination? Should they?

5. Is the right of remand an implied addendum to FAA § 10? Where might it fit into the language of the provision?

6. Who determines ambiguity? Can the court and the arbitrators disagree on the issue? What result would such disagreement entail?

7. If the remand is submitted to a new arbitrator, does it then constitute appeal?

8. What role do foreign law and international treaties play in the court's reasoning? Why are they considered? Should there be different rules for domestic and international arbitration? Why or why not?

9. Explain the court's reference to the ICC Rules. How are they applicable? What light do they shed on the remand issue?

OFFICE & PROFESSIONAL EMPLOYEES INT'L UNION, LOCAL NO. 471 v. BROWNSVILLE GENERAL HOSPITAL

186 F.3d 326 (3d Cir. 1999).

OPINION OF THE COURT

SLOVITER, Circuit Judge.

It is both ironic and unfortunate that arbitration, a process designed to accomplish the peaceful and speedy resolution of labor disputes, should have devolved into the bitter impasse before us.

I.

Appellee, Local 471 of the Office and Professional Employees International Union ("Local 471" or "the Union"), brought this action in the United States District Court for the Western District of Pennsylvania against Brownsville General Hospital ("Brownsville" or "the Hospital") seeking enforcement of an arbitral award or, in the alternative, a remand to the arbitrator for clarification of the award. Local 471 invoked the District Court's jurisdiction under section 301 of the Labor Management Relations Act (LMRA), 29 U.S.C. § 185. The District Court denied Brownsville's motion for summary judgment and instead remanded the case to the arbitrator. Brownsville appeals. For the following reasons we will affirm the District Court's order as herein modified.

II.

This case arises out of an arbitral award entered on March 7, 1997, concerning Brownsville's decision to terminate David Abbadini, an employee represented by the Union.

Abbadini was an operating room technician at Brownsville for twenty-seven years. At all relevant times, he was a member of Local 471 and served as its president. On November 17, 1995, Brownsville suspended Abbadini pending its investigation of a sexual harassment complaint made by a housekeeping employee. Upon completion of the investigation approximately one month later, Brownsville's Board of Directors suspended Abbadini for sixty days and conditioned his return to work on his agreeing to undergo sexual harassment counseling under a program to be approved by Brownsville. Brownsville informed the Union of this condition in a letter stating: "If [Abbadini] refuses to undergo such counseling, his employment shall be terminated." ... Abbadini filed a grievance relating to this discipline but also agreed to undergo counseling. On January 24, 1996, Brownsville wrote to Abbadini, saying "we have made the necessary arrangements for you to enter counseling sessions with Michael Crabtree, Ph.D." ... The letter went on to direct that Abbadini "must agree to continue through the course of counseling as prescribed by Dr. Crabtree." ...

Abbadini then began the counseling sessions with Dr. Crabtree, attending eight sessions from February 1, 1996 to April 2, 1996. After the April 2 session, there was a breakdown in the counseling relationship. The parties dispute the reasons for and circumstances surrounding the breakdown. On June 25, 1996, Brownsville terminated Abbadini on the ground that the cessation of counseling sessions with Dr. Crabtree violated the condition upon which his reinstatement was based. Abbadini grieved this action as well.

The first grievance, that relating to Abbadini's suspension with its attendant counseling condition, culminated in an arbitral award dated October 18, 1996, which upheld Brownsville's action. This award is not challenged in the instant case.

The grievance pertaining to Abbadini's termination, the subject of this lawsuit, was heard by an arbitrator on November 18, 1996. At the hearing, the Hospital called Dr. Crabtree, who testified that until April 1996, Abbadini had regularly attended counseling sessions, but that on April 2, 1996, Abbadini called and asked to take one week off from counseling. When the Hospital's counsel asked why Abbadini made this request, Dr. Crabtree stated that he could not answer without revealing confidential details of the therapeutic relationship. Dr. Crabtree did, however, testify that he sent Abbadini a letter describing the one-week hiatus as a "cooling-off period," but when asked to specify what he meant by the description, Dr. Crabtree again declined. The Hospital introduced a June 13, 1996 letter from Dr. Crabtree to the Hospital, which Dr. Crabtree acknowledged authorship of, stating that he had agreed to Abbadini's request for a one-week cessation of counseling but that he believed that Abbadini had not finished his counseling sessions.

Abbadini testified that he was upset with Dr. Crabtree because Dr. Crabtree had billed Abbadini's wife's insurance carrier (which Abbadini considered to be a violation of confidentiality) and because he saw the counseling process as interminable. Abbadini's counsel, John Stember, testified about conversations that he had with Dr. Crabtree in which Dr. Crabtree agreed to suspend counseling until the arbitrator ruled on the termination grievance.

The arbitrator issued an award on March 7, 1997. In the opinion accompanying the award, the arbitrator declined to credit the Union's argument that there was an agreement between Dr. Crabtree, Abbadini, and Stember to defer the counseling process pending the outcome of the arbitration, finding instead that Dr. Crabtree agreed at most to a one-week cessation. With respect to Abbadini, the arbitrator found that although "the grievant had several problems with Dr. Crabtree ... this fact, in and of itself, did not justify the counseling process being stopped by the grievant in this circumstance." ... The arbitrator, however, also faulted both the Hospital for not taking more steps to monitor what was happening in counseling and Dr. Crabtree, who had, in the arbitrator's words, "failed miserably in his requirement to provide regular reports to the Hospital." ...

The opinion went on to conclude that "while the Hospital did not have just cause to terminate the employment of the grievant, it did have an absolute right to require him to continue with the counseling process.... Because the grievant made the determination, in conjunction with discussions with his psychologist to slow down the counseling process, does not eliminate the right of the Hospital to be sure that the grievant was counseled in the appropriate manner." ... Consequently, the arbitrator stated, "in this unique circumstance ... it is my determination that while the Hospital did not have a right to terminate the grievant, it was proper for the Hospital to keep the grievant from working until such time that he obtained proper counseling." ...

The award proper states in full:

The Hospital did not have the right to terminate the employment of the grievant. The Hospital was correct, however, when it determined that the grievant could not work because he was no longer receiving the counseling that was mandated in the January 24, 1996 letter. The grievant will be reinstated, without back pay, but only after he completes the course of counseling as prescribed by Dr. Crabtree, and after Dr. Crabtree advises the Hospital that the grievant has completed the required course of counseling. I will retain jurisdiction in this matter to resolve any issues that may arise related to the counseling and the possible return to work of the grievant.

. . . It is undisputed that shortly after the entry of this award, Abbadini contacted Dr. Crabtree to resume counseling and that Dr. Crabtree thereupon declined to continue counseling Abbadini. Dr. Crabtree included his explanation in a letter he sent Abbadini dated June 16, 1997, stating in relevant part: "I think it is appropriate that you seek a different therapist, given that at our last session together you threatened both a lawsuit against me and also to turn me into [sic] the licensing board. I feel that that threat makes it difficult to maintain a therapeutic relationship with you." . . . The letter went on to name a referral source for another counselor.

The Union then sought to resubmit Abbadini's grievance directly to the arbitrator. Brownsville resisted, arguing that the arbitrator was without authority to revisit the award. Thereupon, the arbitrator informed the parties that he would "make [him]self available to respond to the clarification or interpretation of my award, but only in the event that both parties consent. . . ." . . .

In early July 1997, Abbadini began seeing another counselor, Walter G. Golembiewski, a licensed therapist in private practice. Abbadini does not contend, nor does the record suggest, that he was referred to Golembiewski by the referral source recommended by Dr. Crabtree. The Union, by letter dated July 18, 1997, sought to secure Brownsville's agreement that this course of counseling would satisfy Abbadini's obligation under the arbitral award, given that Dr. Crabtree would no longer see him. The letter also stated: "If the Employer does not agree to the above proposal, then give us direction as to whether or not you can agree to Doctor Crabtree's referral as promptly as possible." . . . Responding by letter, Brownsville took the position that only counseling by Dr. Crabtree would satisfy the award and further stated: "Having made continued counseling by Dr. Crabtree impossible, Mr. Abbadini cannot now legitimately contend that the mention of an alternative counseling source constitute [sic] continuing treatment as prescribed by Dr. Crabtree." . . .

On September 23, 1997, counsel for the Union then forwarded to Brownsville a letter from Golembiewski expressing the opinion that in the course of more than fifteen counseling sessions, Abbadini had made "excellent progress," that "the issue of sexual harassment has been adequately addressed," and that there is "no threat to anyone from returning to his job." . . . The Union's cover letter reiterated its position that this course of counseling satisfied the arbitral award and requested reinstatement. Brownsville rejected the request, maintaining the position that the award contemplated counseling by Dr. Crabtree only.

The Union then filed the instant lawsuit, seeking enforcement of the award on the ground that Abbadini was in "substantial compliance" with its terms and, in the alternative, requesting a remand to the arbitrator for clarification of the award. The parties filed cross-motions for summary judgment. Brownsville contended that the Union's suit was barred by the doctrine of *functus officio,* the statute of limitations, and/or equitable estoppel. Rejecting Brownsville's arguments, the District Court nonetheless concluded that enforcement was not appropriate and consequently remanded the matter to the arbitrator. In so doing, the court reasoned that *"functus officio* does not preclude a remand because the arbitrator mistakenly assumed that Dr. Crabtree would agree to further sessions with Abbadini." *OPEIU, Local No. 471 v. Brownsville General Hosp.,* No. 97–1592, slip op. at 5 (E.D.Pa. May 5, 1998) ("Slip Op."). Brownsville timely appealed.

III.

Although Brownsville sets out six issues for review, they essentially reduce to the following four questions: whether the District Court erred in (1) concluding that the doctrine of *functus officio* did not bar remand to the arbitrator for clarification of the award, (2) stating that the arbitrator would not be free to revisit the merits or consider the reasons for the breakdown in the counseling relationship, (3) holding that the Union was not barred from relief under principles of equitable estoppel, and (4) concluding that the Union's suit was not barred by the statute of limitations.

A.

The principal issue in the case is whether the doctrine of *functus officio* bars the court from remanding the case for clarification of the award. *Functus officio* (Latin for "a task performed") is a shorthand term for a common-law doctrine barring an arbitrator from revisiting the merits of an award once it has issued. . . .

The common-law rule was summed up as follows in *Bayne v. Morris,* 68 U.S. (1 Wall.) 97, 99, 17 L.Ed. 495 (1863): "Arbitrators exhaust their power when they make a final determination on the matters submitted to them. They have no power after having made an award to alter it; the authority conferred on them is then at an end." The doctrine is motivated by a perception that arbitrators, lacking the institutional protection of judges, may be more susceptible to outside influences pressuring for a different outcome and also by the practical concern that the ad hoc nature of arbitral tribunals makes them less amenable to re-convening than a court. *See Matlack, Inc.,* 118 F.3d at 991. Although the doctrine was applied strictly at common law, following the Supreme Court's decision in *Textile Workers Union v. Lincoln Mills,* 353 U.S. 448, 77 S.Ct. 912, 1 L.Ed.2d 972 (1957), that section 301 of the LMRA directs the federal courts to create a common law of labor arbitration, "the federal courts have been less strict in applying the [doctrine] in reviewing labor disputes." *Matlack, Inc.,* 118 F.3d at 991.

We have consistently recognized that there are a number of exceptions to the *functus officio* rule and that those exceptions apply even in the non-labor arbitration arena, where *functus officio* can be said to have its strongest application. In *Colonial Penn Ins. Co. v. Omaha Indem. Co.,* 943 F.2d 327 (3d Cir.1991), a case governed by the Federal Arbitration Act, we summarized the three recognized exceptions to the general bar against remand as follows:

> (1) an arbitrator "can correct a mistake which is apparent on the face of his award"; (2) "where the award does not adjudicate an issue which has been submitted, then as to such issue the arbitrator has not exhausted his function and it remains open to him for subsequent determination"; and (3) "[w]here the award, although seemingly complete, leaves doubt whether the submission has been fully executed, an ambiguity arises which the arbitrator is entitled to clarify."

... Of interest to us in this case is the third exception, that pertaining to an ambiguity in the award. Discussing that exception in *Colonial Penn,* we explained that because of the "limited purpose" of a remand to clarify an ambiguity, "which serves the practical need for the district court to ascertain the intention of the arbitrators so that the award can be enforced, there is not even a theoretical inconsistency with the *functus officio* doctrine." ... We further explained that a remand for clarification under such conditions is consistent with the policy of judicial restraint that is the thrust of federal arbitral jurisprudence because it gives the arbitrator the opportunity to clarify an award with respect to which an ambiguity has arisen rather than forcing the court to interpolate its own estimate of the arbitrator's intent. Hence, although the merits of the controversy may not be revisited upon remand,

> when the remedy awarded by the arbitrators is ambiguous, a remand for clarification of the intended meaning of an arbitration award is appropriate.... Such a remand avoids the court's misinterpretation of the award and is therefore more likely to give the parties the award for which they bargained.

... Brownsville urges that this exception does not apply here. In its view, the award unambiguously directed Abbadini to complete counseling sessions with Dr. Crabtree, and Abbadini's failure to do so permitted the Hospital to terminate him. From the Hospital's perspective it is of no moment that Dr. Crabtree refused to treat Abbadini: "Abbadini's impossibility of performance under this private agreement does not render an arbitral decision requiring him to abide by it ambiguous. It is no different than if he had simply refused to see Dr. Crabtree." ... We disagree.

The situation encountered here fits within the ambiguity exception discussed in *Colonial Penn*. In that case, an arbitral panel entered a final award in a reinsurance dispute, ordering Omaha Indemnity to release all claims to reserves held by Colonial Penn Insurance. The award was entered on the assumption that some $8 million in reserves were so held, but after entry of the award Colonial Penn advised the arbitrators that no such reserves existed. In response, the arbitrators issued a second award purporting to "clarify" the first award, which deleted all mention of reserves and provided for a higher payment by Omaha to Colonial Penn. We held that the second award was barred by *functus officio* principles but also ruled that the district court was entitled to determine whether circumstances that became apparent after the first award rendered it sufficiently ambiguous that the arbitrator could revisit it without offending *functus officio* principles.

In holding that such a situation, if proved, would justify a remand to the arbitrators, we recognized that an award predicated upon a state of facts that prove, after the award, not to be true may be revisited on the ground of ambiguity: "Under such circumstances, the district court would be authorized to remand so that the arbitrators themselves could clarify their intent as to the remedy awarded. Put differently, the arbitral award would be deemed unenforceable if part of the consideration it awarded did not, in fact, exist." . . .

An essential element of the remedial scheme crafted by the arbitrator . . . proved unenforceable because after the entry of the award Dr. Crabtree declined to continue counseling. As the District Court noted, the arbitrator (though aware of tensions between Abbadini and Dr. Crabtree) entered his award on the assumption that Dr. Crabtree would continue to treat Abbadini. Because that assumption is no longer accurate, there is now an ambiguity, and the arbitrator should be permitted to revisit just so much of the award as pertains to the specific condition for re-employment in the light of this development.

To be sure, this ambiguity is not of the kind that is manifest on the face of the award. Rather, the ambiguity is more in the nature of a latent one, which is no less a reason for remand under our precedent. . . .

The necessity for a remand in this case is underscored by the limited options that were otherwise available to the District Court. Short of remand, that court could only grant or deny the Union's request for enforcement. The result of either action would be a *de facto* prognostication of what the arbitrator would have done had he been equipped with the information that has come to light after the award. That is, an order granting the Union's claim for enforcement would presuppose that the arbitrator intended to allow Abbadini unilaterally to choose his own therapist if Dr. Crabtree refused to treat him. Alternatively, an order denying the claim for enforcement would adopt the view of the Hospital that only counseling by Dr. Crabtree can satisfy the award, and the inability of Abbadini to obtain treatment from Dr. Crabtree, for whatever reason, is irrelevant.

In either scenario, the court would have to divine the intent of the arbitrator, a perilous endeavor. A remand, on the other hand, "avoids the court's misinterpretation of the award and is therefore more likely to give the parties the award for which they bargained." . . .

[. . .]

IV.

For the foregoing reasons, we will affirm the judgment of the District Court as herein modified. Each party to bear its own costs.

NOTES AND QUESTIONS

1. Does the rule on remand apply to both CBA and FAA arbitration? Why?

2. What are the historical origins of the *functus officio* doctrine? Are you persuaded that the statement is accurate? Does it, rather, address the absence of appeal in arbitration and *res judicata*?

3. Is surreptitious or stealth appeal a factor or consideration in *Brownsville*?

4. Is there an ambiguity in the award? Did the arbitrator simply fail to account for the circumstance that arose?

5. Why is it impermissible to let the company stand on its rights?

6. Is the conclusion that the award is unenforceable as written and rendered unacceptable? Why?

HARDY v. WALSH MANNING SECURITIES, LLC

341 F.3d 126 (2d Cir. 2003).

(footnotes omitted)

POOLER, Circuit Judge.

Respondent–Appellant Frank James Skelly, III appeals from the September 4, 2002 judgment of the U.S. District Court for the Southern District of New York (Lynch, J.), granting Petitioner–Appellee Warren A. Hardy's motion to confirm an arbitration award, and denying Skelly's and Respondent–Appellant Walsh Manning Securities, L.L.C.'s cross-motion to vacate the award. Skelly also appeals from the September 6, 2002 order denying his motion for reconsideration. Walsh Manning filed a Notice of Appeal, but has not pursued its appeal. We therefore affirm the district court's confirmation of the arbitration as it applies to Walsh Manning.

FACTS

Hardy, a British national, opened an investment account in 1997 at the Westbury, Long Island branch office of Walsh Manning, a New York

City brokerage firm. Skelly is Walsh Manning's "Chief Executive Officer," although it is uncontested that he is actually an employee of Walsh Manning, not an officer. Hardy's account was handled by Barry Cassese, who recommended stocks and made trades on Hardy's behalf.

In November 1998, Hardy filed a Statement of Claim with the National Association of Securities Dealers (NASD) claiming that Cassese, Skelly, and Walsh Manning, among others, engaged in various improprieties with regard to his account. In brief, Hardy charged that the respondents had misrepresented the fiscal health of certain companies whose stock Hardy was urged to buy, and did not disclose that these securities were "house stocks," which Walsh Manning had an interest in selling.

Before Hardy's claim proceeded to arbitration, Cassese agreed to settle with Hardy for $250,000.00. The settlement agreement also provided that Cassese would testify at any subsequent arbitration hearing with respect to Hardy's claims against the other respondents.

The NASD arbitration panel ("the Panel") consisted of three members, only one of whom is an attorney. The Panel's award was based upon an extensive documentary record and twenty-five days of testimony. Cassese testified extensively, charging that the malfeasance with respect to Hardy's account was undertaken at the behest, or with the connivance, of Walsh Manning and Skelly.

The Panel issued its award on February 2, 2002 ("the Award"). In the section of the Award relevant to this appeal, the Panel stated as follows:

> After considering the pleadings, the testimony and evidence presented at the hearing, and the post-hearing submissions, the Panel has decided in full and final resolution of the issues submitted for determination as follows:
>
> 1.   Respondents Walsh Manning and Skelly be and hereby are jointly and severally liable for and shall pay to Claimant compensatory damages in the amount of $2,217,241.00 **based upon the principles of respondeat superior.** It is noted that this amount reflects deductions for the amounts previously paid by settling respondents.
>
> 2.   Respondents Walsh Manning and Skelly be and hereby are jointly and severally liable for and shall pay to Claimant interest in the amount of $548,767.00.
>
> 3.   Respondents Walsh Manning and Skelly be and hereby are jointly and severally liable for and shall pay to Claimant the sum of $250.00 to reimburse Claimant for the non-refundable filing fee previously paid to NASD Dispute Resolution, Inc. (emphasis added)

The Award is problematic. In addition to asserting various grounds of primary liability as to Skelly, Hardy asserted in his Statement of Claim that Skelly was liable to him "in [Skelly's] capacity as the Chief Executive Officer and Manager of Walsh Manning, under Section 20 of the Securities & Exchange Act [sic] of 1934 and under the common law theory of respondeat superior." But in their post-hearing brief, the respondents argued that Skelly could not be liable to Hardy under respondeat superior because of the undisputed fact that Skelly is an employee, not an officer, of Walsh Manning. In his own post-hearing brief, Hardy asserts respondeat superior as a ground for liability *only* with respect to Walsh Manning, but he does not explicitly repudiate the assertion of respondeat superior as to Skelly. Confusingly, Hardy also asserts in his post-hearing brief that Skelly and others "are secondarily liable for Cassese's misconduct. Such secondary liability is based on Section 20 of the Securities Exchange Act of 1934 and agency law." In any event, the only basis of liability as to Walsh Manning and Skelly stated in the Award is secondary liability pursuant to respondeat superior.

Hardy moved in the district court to confirm the Award, and Walsh Manning and Skelly cross-moved to vacate the Award. Judge Lynch found all of Walsh Manning's and Skelly's claims to be wholly without merit except for the application of respondeat superior liability to Skelly. Judge Lynch held that although "Skelly was the CEO of Walsh Manning, he was technically only an employee, and vicarious personal liability cannot be imposed on individual supervisors based solely on the conduct of their underlings, when both are fellow employees of a common employer." ... Judge Lynch nevertheless concluded that the language employed by the Panel in the Award as to Skelly's liability can be read to mean that the Panel did not find Skelly liable pursuant to respondeat superior alone:

> It is possible to find that the phrase "based upon ... respondeat superior" refers not to the finding of *liability* of each respondent, but to the conclusion that both respondents are "jointly and severally liable." This is essentially the reading adopted by petitioner, who would read the sentence as saying, "[Skelly is liable in damages, based on his own conduct, and] both respondents are jointly and severally liable, based on respondeat superior." While the words chosen may not be the most direct or grammatical way of expressing this thought, it is worth noting that the sentence ("Respondents ... be and hereby are ... liable") isn't grammatical in the first place.

... Finding therefore that Hardy's reading of the Award was "a plausible one ... supported by a permissible view of the evidence," Judge Lynch ordered that the Award should be enforced as written. ...

Skelly immediately moved for reconsideration, asserting that the Award should be remanded to the Panel for an explanation of the grounds of his liability. In his unreported denial of the motion, Judge Lynch held it would not be proper to remand the Award to the Panel for clarification as to its intent regarding Skelly's liability. Such action might be warranted, Judge Lynch held, if there were ambiguities in the nature and extent of the relief awarded. Here, however, "[t]he arbitrators were crystal clear in directing the respondents to pay a sum certain."

DISCUSSION

I. *Was the District Court Correct in Holding That the Panel's Award Should Be Confirmed as Written?*

As a general matter, "[a]rbitration awards are subject to very limited review in order to avoid undermining the twin goals of arbitration, namely, settling disputes efficiently and avoiding long and expensive litigation." ... It is nevertheless the case that an arbitration award should not be confirmed where it can be shown that the arbitration panel acted in "manifest disregard of the law" to such an extent that "(1) the arbitrators knew of a governing legal principle yet refused to apply it or ignored it altogether and (2) the law ignored by the arbitrators ... [was] well defined, explicit, and clearly applicable." ...

We are fully aware that this is not an easy standard to meet for a party challenging confirmation of an arbitration award.... In *Duferco International Steel Trading v. T. Klaveness Shipping A/S,* 333 F.3d 383, 389 (2d Cir.2003), it was calculated that "since 1960 we have vacated some part or all of an arbitral award for manifest disregard in ... four out of at least 48 cases where we applied the standard." (collecting cases) Yet, even though this standard "gives extreme deference to arbitrators," ... we believe that it is satisfied here, at least to the extent of warranting a remand of the Award to the Panel for clarification of what it intended regarding Skelly's liability.

It is certainly possible to find that the Panel disregarded the principles of respondeat superior, the same principles that it purported to apply. Although the Panel did not explicitly say so, it is agreed by all parties that these are meant to be the principles of New York law. The principle that respondeat superior is a form of secondary liability that cannot be imposed upon the fellow employee of a wrongdoer is certainly well-defined and explicit in New York.... Indeed, it has been noted that the very possibility of liability *between* employees for acts committed in connection with their employment was an anomalous development in New York's tort law meant as a means of limiting the reach of respondeat superior liability. That is, "[t]he onerous 'fellow-servant' rule, [was] developed at common law to preclude respondeat superior claims against an employer by an employee injured in the workplace due to the negligence of a co-worker."

. . .

As already noted, the Panel was made aware of the argument that Skelly could not be found liable for the acts of Cassese because both men were employees of Walsh Manning. Walsh Manning explicitly made this argument in their post-hearing brief, and Hardy impliedly agreed by raising respondeat superior as to Walsh Manning, but remaining silent as to Skelly's liability pursuant to the doctrine....

Judge Lynch asserts that the Award can be read as holding that Skelly is liable "based on his own conduct." This reading reduces the Panel's explicit reference to respondeat superior to "a stray and unnecessary remark," as Judge Lynch terms it. But this reading is simply untenable. The Award is *silent* as to the issue of Skelly's primary wrongdoing, and it states no other ground of liability but respondeat superior. The untenability is implicitly confirmed by Hardy himself. He asserts that "[t]he Panel elected not to discuss the rationale for its finding of primary wrongdoing." ... But he later acknowledges that "[t]he Award is completely silent regarding the primary wrongdoer." Hardy Brief at 14. Hardy gets it right the second time. The Panel made no finding of primary wrongdoing.

Judge Lynch himself acknowledges that "[t]he arbitrators nowhere made a finding that Skelly had committed no misconduct." ... He nevertheless asserts that it is proper to infer that the arbitrators concluded that Skelly *had* committed misconduct because this is "a permissible view of the evidence." ... But this "permissible" view is by no means necessarily equivalent to the view of the evidence actually taken by the Panel and ... the latter view is dispositive. That is, a reviewing court is bound to accept the facts considered by an arbitrator "*as those facts have been determined by the arbitrator.*" ...

Indeed, Judge Lynch found that Walsh Manning's assertion that *it* could not properly be found liable under respondeat superior is without merit because the assertion "ask[ed] the Court to reassess the evidence." ... But what is Judge Lynch's holding that Skelly was found to be primarily liable? It is an assessment of the evidence. We note also that Hardy's brief is largely devoted to assessing the evidence so as to assure this Court that there is indeed substantial evidence in the record to find that Skelly is primarily liable. Such evidence may exist. But since the award makes no mention of it, we will not assess this evidence.

Judge Lynch is correct that "[t]he arbitrators were crystal clear in directing the respondents to pay petitioner a sum certain." But, once again, it is also crystal clear that the award states no other basis for liability than respondeat superior. The district court correctly found that a court must "confirm [an arbitrator's] award if [it is] able to discern any colorable justification for the arbitrator's judgment, even if that reasoning would be based on an error of fact or law." ... There may indeed be more than enough evidence in the record to find that Skelly should have been found primarily liable. But that is not what "the arbitrator's judgment" is in the instant case. The arbitrator's judgment is that Skelly was liable "upon the principles of respondeat superior," and no one points us to any evidence in the record that provides a colorable justification for this conclusion.

[. . .]

Finally, we disagree with Judge Lynch's contention that there is anything relevant in the fact that the Award "isn't grammatical." ... The Award may fail in terms of usage, but it succeeds in stating a ground of liability in a manner that is manifestly intelligible.

It is true that the Award does not contain anything that can be termed "legal reasoning." But it *does* contain an explicit legal conclusion. To this extent, the award is not ambiguous and is not susceptible to more than one plausible reading. Nor does it rest on "a colorable interpretation of the law." ... The award indeed contains a fundamental mistake of law.

II. Since This Court Holds That the Award Cannot Be Enforced as Written, What Should Be Done?

Voiding an award because an arbitration panel acted in manifest disregard of the law "requires more than a mistake of law or a clear error in fact finding." . . . We are reluctant to announce that the Award is void outright as written.

Although certainly not the normal course of things, we do have the authority to remand to the Panel for purposes broader than a clarification of the terms of a specific remedy. That is, we have the authority to seek a clarification of whether an arbitration panel's intent in making an award "evidence[s] a manifest disregard of the law." . . . The Panel should be afforded such an opportunity. . . .

. . . In this case, the Panel chose to make an explicit legal conclusion in the award, a conclusion that may very well be wrong. It should be given the opportunity to explain themselves. We are emphatically opening no floodgates here. We simply wish for more clarity because we think that substantial financial liability should not be imposed upon an individual without a clear basis in law.

The inquiries to the Panel on remand are not extensive and its response need not be, and should not be, detailed. We merely ask the Panel to do the following: (1) Confirm that Skelly is liable only under the principles of respondeat superior because there are indeed facts which have not been brought to our attention which support this holding; (2) In the alternative, assert that some other ground of secondary liability applies to Skelly; or (3) Failing both of these, acknowledge that it erred in finding Skelly secondarily liable and that the record does or does not support a finding that Skelly is primarily liable to Hardy.

CONCLUSION

The judgment of the district court is AFFIRMED in so far as the award applies to Walsh Manning. In so far as the award applies to Skelly, the district court's judgment is VACATED and REMANDED for proceedings consistent with this opinion.

STRAUB, Circuit Judge, dissenting.

By remanding to the arbitration panel for clarification as to the underlying legal basis for liability, the majority, in my most respectful view, disregards the well-settled precedent establishing our severely limited review of arbitration awards. It is precisely because arbitration is designed to provide parties with an expedited process for conclusively resolving their disputes, that judicial review of arbitration awards is so narrow. . . . Accordingly, I dissent.

While the majority fully recognizes that substantial deference must be given to the arbitrator's finding of liability under the governing manifest disregard standard, it fails to acknowledge that equal deference must be accorded in interpreting the arbitration award itself. As this Court has recently reaffirmed, "where an arbitral award contains more than one plausible reading, manifest disregard cannot be found if at least one of the readings yields a legally correct justification for the outcome." ... Thus, mere ambiguity in the award itself is not a basis for denying confirmation, so long as the award can be interpreted as having a colorable factual or legal basis.... Moreover, in interpreting an arbitration award, deference mandates that "we look only to *plausible* readings of the award, and not to *probable* readings of it." ... Our goal, then, is not to discern the actual subjective intent of the arbitration panel, but only to determine if the award can be sustained under any plausible reading....

Although the majority suggests that this is somehow an extraordinary case, we are presented at most with an arbitration award that is ambiguous and susceptible of more than one plausible reading. Because the award need not be read as stating that respondeat superior is the sole basis for Skelly's primary liability, affirmance is required under the established standard of this Circuit. Even if the majority is correct that there is no ambiguity, and the award must be read as erroneously holding Skelly liable under the principles of respondeat superior, then the appropriate remedy is to vacate the judgment of the District Court and remand for vacatur of the arbitration award. To suggest that we may remand for clarification despite finding that the arbitrator has manifestly disregarded the law has little support in prior precedent. Indeed, such a rule fatally frustrates the very goals which arbitration seeks to advance: the efficient resolution of disputes and the avoidance of prolonged expensive litigation.

I.

In this case, the disputed portion of the arbitrators' decision simply states: "Walsh Manning and Skelly be and hereby are jointly and severally liable ... based upon the principles of respondeat superior." The majority's interpretation, while conceivable, ignores the fact that the critical phrase "based upon the principles of respondeat superior" may simply explain the basis for Walsh Manning's joint and several liability, without referring to the basis for Skelly's primary liability. Indeed, the phrase may indicate Walsh Manning's liability for *Skelly's* actions, not just Cassese's wrongful conduct, based upon the theory of respondeat superior. In other words, the award may specify the form of liability, joint and several, while remaining completely silent as to the underlying claims on which Skelly was actually found liable.

Not only is this a *plausible* interpretation of the decision, but also a completely *probable* one, for Hardy presented substantial evidence during the arbitration hearing that Skelly, who was Cassese's direct supervisor, failed to properly supervise Cassese, that Skelly was personally aware of Cassese's unauthorized trading, and that Skelly violated federal securities laws by engaging in direct market manipulation. In addition, as the majority points out, Hardy did not argue that Skelly faced direct liability on the basis of respondeat superior in his post-hearing brief, an argument, which nonetheless, Skelly directly refuted in his opposing brief. Finally, although Walsh Manning and Skelly did request that the Panel specify the damages awarded as to each particular claim for indemnification purposes, arbitrators have no obligation to provide such explanations for their decisions. . . .

[. . .]

III.

In sum, in "wish[ing] for more clarity," the majority's decision overlooks our limited role in reviewing arbitration decisions and encourages the very type of protracted litigation that arbitration seeks to avoid.

For all of the foregoing reasons, I respectfully dissent and would affirm the decision of the District Court.

NOTES AND QUESTIONS

1. There are three competing interpretations of the NASD award in *Hardy*: The district court's, the majority, and the dissent. Which do you find most persuasive? Why?

2. Is the majority's construction of the facts the least plausible interpretation of what the NASD tribunal intended to rule? Why?

3. How does the majority align the remand with manifest disregard of the law? Is this a legitimate use of the manifest disregard ground? Is the court using remand as a veiled threat to have the arbitrators rule the way it believes the law should be applied?

4. In your view, did the arbitrators get the law wrong? What might constitute a legally correct determination? Is plausibility a more realistic standard than correctness? Can you distinguish objective error from opinion? Illustrate your answer.

5. Does the court's reasoning comply with the dictates of the federal policy on arbitration? Is the district court's ruling more acceptable from this perspective?

6. Is there any confidentiality left to the arbitration?

11.   PENALTIES FOR FRIVOLOUS VACATUR ACTIONS

B.L. HARBERT INTERNATIONAL, LLC v. HERCULES STEEL CO.

441 F.3d 905 (11th Cir. 2006).

CARNES, Circuit Judge:

The Federal Arbitration Act (FAA) liberally endorses and encourages arbitration as an alternative to litigation. . . .

The laudatory goals of the FAA will be achieved only to the extent that courts ensure arbitration is an alternative to litigation, not an additional layer in a protracted contest. If we permit parties who lose in arbitration to freely relitigate their cases in court, arbitration will do nothing to reduce congestion in the judicial system; dispute resolution will be slower instead of faster; and reaching a final decision will cost more instead of less. This case is a good example of the poor loser problem and it provides us with an opportunity to discuss a potential solution.

I.

B.L. Harbert International, LLC, is a Delaware corporation based in Birmingham, Alabama, which makes money in large construction projects including some done for the government. Hercules Steel Company is a North Carolina corporation based in Fayetteville, North Carolina, that manufactures steel used in construction.

On August 25, 2000, the United States Army Corp of Engineers, Savannah District, awarded Harbert a contract to construct an office complex for the Special Operations Forces at Fort Bragg, North Carolina. Harbert, in turn, awarded Hercules a $1,197,000 steel fabrication and erection subcontract on September 21, 2000.

The subcontract between the parties includes a provision that disputes between them will be submitted to binding arbitration under the auspices of the American Arbitration Association, using the Construction Industry Arbitration Rules. Later, the parties executed a separate Agreement to Arbitrate, which recognizes that the Federal Arbitration Act, 9 U.S.C. § 1, would control arbitration proceedings.

The subcontract further provides that Harbert will issue a "Progress Schedule" for the project and will provide a copy to each subcontractor. It states that the subcontractor must perform all work "in accordance with Progress Schedule as prepared by [Harbert] and as it may be revised from time to time with the Subcontractor's input." . . .

Harbert's failure to define those terms might have gone unnoticed if it had created only one schedule for the project, but Harbert developed two, which it referred to as the 2000 and 3000 schedules. . . . [N]either schedule is mentioned in the subcontract.

The dispute-generating problem is that the 2000 schedule contained earlier completion dates than the 3000 one. According to the 2000 schedule, Hercules was to begin work on March 5, 2001, and finish it by June 6, 2001. That did not happen. Hercules began work in April of 2001, and did not finish it until January of 2002. That completion of the work was, however, within the more lenient deadlines of the 3000 schedule.

[. . .]

After considering the parties' opposing arguments and a voluminous record, the arbitrator issued his "Award of Arbitrator" on September 8, 2004. That award denied Hercules' delay damages claim, denied all of Harbert's counterclaims, denied both parties' claims for attorney's fees, and awarded Hercules $369,775, representing the subcontract balance and the interest on that sum. Because the award, not counting interest, was nearly $100,000 less than the amount the parties had agreed was the subcontract balance, Hercules believed that the arbitrator had made a scrivener's or mathematical error. It submitted a request for clarification which pointed out the problem.

[. . .]

On October 18, 2004, the arbitrator issued his "Disposition for Application of Modification/Clarification of the Award," a decision document which corrected the scrivener's error by increasing the award from $369,775 to $469,775. The document also revealed the arbitrator's findings on the six issues, stating in answer to the first one that Hercules was contractually bound to the more generous "project schedule submitted to the Corps of Engineers which was used to build the project [the 3000 schedule] . . . not the sixteen week schedule unilaterally set by Harbert [the 2000 schedule]." The arbitrator stated in answer to another of the six issues that Harbert was not entitled to any damages because "[t]he delay and acceleration damages are necessarily dependent on the claimed project schedule which has been found not applicable."

On November 18, 2004, Harbert filed in the district court a motion to vacate the arbitration award, contending that the arbitrator's rationale reflected a manifest disregard of the applicable law. Hercules opposed Harbert's motion with one of its own, asking the court to confirm the award pursuant to 9 U.S.C. § 9.

On February 7, 2005, the district court entered an order denying Harbert's motion to vacate the award and granting Hercules' motion to confirm it. . . .

[. . .]

II.

Judicial review of commercial arbitration awards is narrowly limited under the Federal Arbitration Act. . . . The FAA presumes the confirmation of arbitration awards . . . and federal courts should defer to an arbitrator's decision whenever possible. . . . The FAA sets out four narrow bases for vacating an award, none of which are even remotely applicable in this case.

In addition to those four statutory grounds for vacatur, we have said that there are three non-statutory grounds. An award may be vacated if it is arbitrary and capricious, . . . if enforcement of the award is contrary to public policy . . . or if the award was made in manifest disregard for the law. . . .

Harbert's challenge to the arbitrator's award rests solely on its contention that the arbitrator acted in manifest disregard of the law. This ground for vacating an arbitration award requires clear evidence that the arbitrator was "conscious of the law and deliberately ignore[d] it." . . . A showing that the arbitrator merely misinterpreted, misstated, or misapplied the law is insufficient.... .. We review *de novo* the district court's legal conclusions on this issue.... ..

This Court first adopted manifest disregard for the law as a basis for challenging an arbitration award in the *Montes* case. 128 F.3d at 1461. It remains the only case in which we have ever found the exceptional circumstances that satisfy the exacting requirements of this exception. ...

The *Montes* litigation arose out of a dispute between an employer and employee about overtime pay.... The controlling law, the Fair Labor Standards Act, was against the employer's position, and during the arbitration proceedings its attorney repeatedly urged the arbitrators to disregard the requirements of the Act and rule for the employer on the basis of equitable considerations.... He told the arbitrators that: "you as an arbitrator are not guided strictly to follow case law precedent ... you can also do what's fair and just and equitable and that is what [my client] is asking you to do in this case." ... Instead of contending that the law could be applied favorably to his client's position, the attorney argued to the arbitrators that "in this case this law is not right," and "[t]he law says one thing. What equity demands and requires and is saying is another." ... He explicitly asked the arbitrators not to follow the law....

The arbitrators in *Montes* found in favor of the employer, and in their award they repeated the plea of the employer's attorney that they disregard the law.... There was nothing in the transcript of the proceedings or the award itself to indicate that the arbitrators had not heeded that plea, and the evidence and law did not support the award....

In holding that the arbitrators had acted in manifest disregard of the law in *Montes,* we disavowed any notion that an arbitrator's decision "can be reviewed on the basis that its conclusion or reasoning is legally erroneous." *Id.* at 1461; *accord id.* at 1460 ("This does not mean that arbitrators can be reversed for errors or misinterpretations of law."). And we emphasized the rare nature of the circumstances in that case. *Id.* at 1461–62. Four facts came together in *Montes* and will seldom recur:

> Those facts are that: 1) the party who obtained the favorable award had conceded to the arbitration panel that its position was not supported by the law, which required a different result, and had urged the panel not to follow the law; 2) that blatant appeal to disregard the law was explicitly noted in the arbitration panel's award; 3) neither in the award itself nor anywhere else in the record is there any indication that the panel disapproved or rejected the suggestion that it rule contrary to law; and 4) the evidence to support the award is at best marginal.

... While *Montes* shows the exception, the rule is shown in every other case where we have decided if the arbitration loser had established manifest disregard of the law. In all of those other cases the loser in arbitration was the loser in our decision....

The facts of this case do not come within shouting distance of the *Montes* exception. This is a typical contractual dispute in which the parties disagree about the meaning of terms of their agreement. There are arguments to be made on both sides of the contractual interpretation issue, and they were made to the arbitrator before being made to the district court and then to us. Even if we were convinced that we would have decided this contractual dispute differently, that would not be nearly enough to set aside the award. *See Peebles,* 431 F.3d at 1326 ("[A] litigant arguing that an arbitrator acted in manifest disregard of the law must show something more than a misinterpretation, misstatement, or misapplication of the law."); *Brown,* 211 F.3d at 1223 ("Arbitration awards will not be reversed due to an erroneous interpretation of law by the arbitrator."); *Montes,* 128 F.3d at 1461 ("An arbitration board that incorrectly interprets the law has not manifestly disregarded it. It has simply made a legal mistake.").

Harbert's argument that the arbitration award clearly contradicts an express term of the contract is simply another way of saying that the arbitrator clearly erred, and even a showing of a clear error on the part of the arbitrator is not enough. The arbitration loser must establish more than that in order to have the award set aside, the more being that the arbitrator actually recognized a clear rule of law and deliberately chose to ignore it. *Peebles,* 431 F.3d at 1326 ("A manifest disregard for the law involves a conscious and deliberate decision to ignore the applicable law."); *id.* at 1327.... On the record before us, we cannot find proof that the arbitrators recognized a clear rule of law and chose to ignore it....

[...]

There is no evidence that the attorney for Hercules urged the arbitrator to disregard the law, and Harbert does not even suggest that happened. There is no evidence that the arbitrator decided the dispute on the basis of anything other than his best judgment—whether right or wrong—of how the law applies to the facts of the case. There is, in short, no evidence that the arbitrator manifestly disregarded the law. The only manifest disregard of the law evident in this case is Harbert's refusal to accept the law of this circuit which narrowly circumscribes judicial review of arbitration awards. By attacking the arbitration award in this case Harbert has shown at best an indifference to the law of our circuit governing the subject. Harbert's refusal to accept that there is no basis in the law for attacking the award has come at a cost to the party with whom Harbert entered into the arbitration agreement and to the judicial system.

In litigating this case without good basis through the district court and now through this Court, Harbert has deprived Hercules and the judicial system itself of the principal benefits of arbitration. Instead of costing less, the resolution of this dispute has cost more than it would have had there been no arbitration agreement. Instead of being decided sooner, it has taken longer than it would have to decide the matter without arbitration. Instead of being resolved outside the courts, this dispute has required the time and effort of the district court and this Court.

When a party who loses an arbitration award assumes a never-say-die attitude and drags the dispute through the court system without an objectively reasonable belief it will prevail, the promise of arbitration is broken. Arbitration's allure is dependent upon the arbitrator being the last decision maker in all but the most unusual cases. The more cases there are, like this one, in which the arbitrator is only the first stop along the way, the less arbitration there will be. If arbitration is to be a meaningful alternative to litigation, the parties must be able to trust that the arbitrator's decision will be honored sooner instead of later.

Courts cannot prevent parties from trying to convert arbitration losses into court victories, but it may be that we can and should insist that if a party on the short end of an arbitration award attacks that award in court without any real legal basis for doing so, that party should pay sanctions. A realistic threat of sanctions may discourage baseless litigation over arbitration awards and help fulfill the purposes of the pro-arbitration policy contained in the FAA. It is an idea worth considering.

We have considered ordering Harbert and its counsel to show cause why sanctions should not be imposed in this case, but have decided against doing so. That decision is the product of the combined force of three reasons, which we list in reverse order of weight. First, there is speculative dicta in the *University Commons* opinion that provided Harbert with a little cover for its actions, although this factor alone does not carry much weight. The rule that prior panel precedent trumps later decisions, to say nothing of later dicta, is so well known and well established that lawyers and their clients should be held responsible for knowing that rule and acting accordingly. Second, Hercules did not move for sanctions against Harbert in either the district court or in this Court. While we can raise and consider the issue of sanctions on our own, after giving the parties notice and an opportunity to be heard, the lack of interest in sanctions shown by the party to whom any monetary sanctions would be paid is a factor to consider.

Third, and most importantly, when Harbert took its arbitration loss into the district court and then pursued this appeal, it did not have the benefit of the notice and warning this opinion provides. The notice it provides, hopefully to even the least astute reader, is that this Court is exasperated by those who attempt to salvage arbitration losses through litigation that has no sound basis in the law applicable to arbitration awards. The warning this opinion provides is that in order to further the purposes of the FAA and to protect arbitration as a remedy we are ready, willing, and able to consider imposing sanctions in appropriate cases. While Harbert and its counsel did not have the benefit of this notice and warning, those who pursue similar litigation positions in the future will.

Affirmed.

NOTES AND QUESTIONS

1.   Are sanctions for perfunctory, speculative, or frivolous vacatur litigation a good idea? How might the prospect of legal malpractice affect the imposition of sanctions? How onerous do sanctions need to be?

2.   How does the court assess the downside of due process in arbitration? Do you agree?

3.   In your view, is manifest disregard far-fetched in the *B.L. Harbert* circumstances?

4.   Will the decision have a chilling impact on vacatur actions? How will or might the bar respond to this development?

Conclusions

Enforcement is the stage at which the force of law meets arbitration head-on. The topic, therefore, warrants thorough treatment. Legal issues here may render an entire arbitration useless. Without voluntary compliance, the law is necessary to give operative effect to the arbitral process.

While the objective of FAA § 10 is limpid, its construction by courts attests to a surfeit of disfiguring judicial interest. With an abundance of judicial pronouncements, FAA § 10 has mutated into a complex regime. Despite the activity, the presumption in favor of enforcement remains generally steadfast. The proclamation of a common law basis for judicial supervision complicated the matter of enforcement, if only by generating ambiguity and indecision in applicable concepts. The basic result was never really in doubt no matter how it was reached. There have been periodic glitches—cases in which the courts take on the arbitrators—but those episodes are true abnormalities.

The newer assaults upon arbitral autonomy are also devoid of impact in the end. They, however, trigger a clash of systems. The federal circuits dealt well with the emergence of opt-in provisions by underscoring how much such agreements reflect an abusive and perverse use of contract freedom in arbitration. Tolerance and self-regulation, if unguided, can readily be transformed into license. The action to clarify awards poses a more substantial challenge because it plays simultaneously to legitimate practical needs and the ends of adversarial representation. Unlike the misplaced and elusive common law grounds for vacatur, these developments compelled courts to debate the core attributes of arbitration and its relationship to the law and the judiciary. What privilege must now be associated with party choice, independence, correct legal results, reviewability, the protection of rights, and practicality? The expansive application of arbitration has given these concerns a more vital and critical contemporary concern. Does the autonomy of the arbitral process demand absolute obeisance to the rulings of the arbitrator?

The Eleventh Circuit in *B.L. Harbert* endorses the traditional answer to the insoluble problems of the arbitration process, *i.e.*, to reinforce the meaning of the bargain for arbitration by nearly eliminating any basis for judicial reconsideration of awards. The revitalization of the evident partiality ground through arbitrator disclosures makes the traditional answer less available as a means of disciplining the process. Evident partiality is now a possibly potent means of challenge. The standard of tribunal-wide neutrality places the entire result of the arbitration at risk and may be an overly exuberant correction to the prospect of unfettered arbitrator discretion.

What impact should these developments in the enforcement of awards have upon your advice to clients? Is arbitration more or less attractive? Why? If you were a federal judge, how would you assess these developments if they arose in the litigation you were hearing? What distinctions, if any, would you establish between the common law grounds, opt-in provisions, and an action to clarify awards? Explain your choices. How would your choices further the law of arbitration or the protection of legal rights?

Chapter Nine

International Commercial Arbitration

■ ■ ■

1. INTRODUCTION

The rise of arbitration in domestic U.S. law is related to the dysfunction of the domestic judicial process. In fact, one of the primary objectives of the federal policy on arbitration is to minimize public expenditures on adjudicatory services and achieve efficiency in and accessibility to these services. The prominence of arbitration in international commercial transactions also can be explained in terms of the deficiencies of the process of judicial adjudication. In transnational commercial relations, arbitration is a means by which international merchants avoid the ineffectiveness of national legal systems and by which trade policymakers cope with a rule of unbending national political sovereignty.

Whenever a commercial transaction goes beyond national territorial boundaries, it inevitably encounters either a conflict-of-law problem or the barrier of sovereignty, if not both. Transborder transactional settings are varied but can be grouped into paradigmatic categories. The most commonplace transaction consists of the standard sales agreement between parties of different nationalities who reside in different countries. Another category encompasses mixed commercial and political circumstances in which a private investor enters into, for instance, a construction project with an agency of a foreign government. Finally, the political conduct or policies of a host State can affect the embedded economic interests of foreign nationals. In all of these typical circumstances, the resolution of claims can be subject to a wide range of sometimes insurmountable problems that defeat the rule of law. At the very least, a transborder contractual or transactional dispute can raise choice-of-forum, venue, jurisdictional, choice-of-law, proof and interpretation of foreign law, and enforcement of judgment problems. Moreover, the fear of foreign law and of foreign judicial bias compels the parties to file suit in their respective national jurisdictions, to pursue parallel actions in the two fora simultaneously, and to arrive at the stalemate of having two judgments that are equally unenforceable.

The conduct of business across national boundaries already involves a high level of risk: Compliance with custom regulations, obtaining government permissions and licenses, coping with the hazards of international transport, negotiating the special labor law regimes in foreign countries, and grappling with the variability and complexity of national import-export regulation. It is unlikely, therefore, that transborder commerce would take place at all if there were no effective adjudicatory mechanism for resolving the basic problems of commercial contracts (defining breach, establishing performance, enforcing delivery, and other requirements). Arbitration has made global business transactions possible despite the inadequacies and inability of domestic legal processes to fashion a rule of law for international business.

When a government is implicated in either a business transaction or commercial dispute, the pattern of complex and unworkable conflicts is augmented by the "trump card" of sovereignty. The government, as political actor or transactional participant, can simply refuse to be held accountable under its law, or any other law, because of its sovereign status. The foreign investor has little or no recourse against the imposition of the sovereign will. Even the use of political risk insurance can result in complex and dysfunctional litigation against the insurer. Along with more liberal laws on sovereign immunity, arbitration has made inroads into the "lawlessness" of sovereignty by providing a reasonably functional, albeit imperfect, mechanism for adjudicating foreign investor claims against national governments.

Many national laws recognize an arbitration agreement as an implied waiver of sovereign immunity (*i.e.*, as sovereign consent to be sued before the arbitral tribunal). These legal provisions thereby minimize sovereignty as a defense to the enforcement of arbitral awards. Moreover, ICSID arbitration—a specialized form of institutional arbitration—is intended to respond to the special circumstances of adjudicating disputes between foreign investors and host States. Finally, arbitral proceedings can serve indirectly as a forum through which governments and business parties can negotiate their commercial disputes. In a word, arbitration makes foreign investment palatable and allows States to participate in international business as commercial rather than political actors.

When purely political conduct or events affect international commercial interests, a customized form of arbitration can become part of an agreed-upon framework by which States engage in dispute resolution. The Iran–U.S. Claims Tribunal, established by the Algiers Accord of 1979, illustrates the use of arbitration to resolve some of the intractable problems that followed in the wake of the Iranian Revolution. President Carter had frozen Iranian assets in the United States and the revolution resulted in the destruction or confiscation of U.S. commercial assets in Iran as well as the disruption of numerous U.S. business transactions. The tribunal and its arbitral procedure became a neutral, non-political means of resolving the commercial claims that attended the political events in Iran. The Tribunal apparatus "privatized" and "de-politicized" the dispute between the U.S. and Iranian governments by vesting authority to resolve the commercial claims in a proven and functional mechanism for adjudicating transborder commercial claims.

The use of arbitration as part of a treaty framework to resolve mixed public and private disputes has also been employed in less dramatic political circumstances. Both the Canada–U.S. Free Trade Agreement and the subsequent North American Free Trade Agreement (NAFTA) between Mexico, Canada, and the United States contain a self-defining arbitral process by which trade policy disagreement among the various national governments can be submitted for resolution to a panel of arbitrators. In effect, the exercise of political authority is delegated to a group of private trade experts when governmental negotiations reach an impasse. The arbitral mechanism is accompanied by bi-national panels that hear disputes of private individuals that involve NAFTA. NAFTA arbitration is an unconventional use of the arbitral methodology. On the one hand, it reflects the traditional ideology associated with arbitration: International commercial relations should not be hampered by political disagreements between governments. On the other hand, it allows private commercial experts to engage in political decision-making and establish (to some degree, at least) national trade policy. There are obvious questions about the propriety of using arbitration in this manner both from a political and arbitral perspective. Determining trade policy is not equivalent to adjudicating individual cases under a commercially adapted procedure. Although NAFTA arbitration has a limited track-record, it seems that it would operate as a type of stop-gap measure in the traditional sense of public international law: To adjust highly charged political disagreements between the contracting States.

The U.S. ratification of the New York Convention in 1970 inspired the U.S. Supreme Court to elaborate a set of decisional principles on international commercial arbitration. The series of cases, ranging from *Bremen v. Zapata* through *Scherk* and *Mitsubishi* and ending with *Vimar v. Sky Reefer*, initially seeks to fashion legal rules that accommodate the process of international commercial arbitration. They eventually establish broad legal deference to arbitral jurisdiction in international matters, and lead to a merger of the domestic and international case law. In the end, the rulings create an unitary U.S. judicial policy on arbitration. Throughout the Court's development of law in this area, the "emphatic federal policy on arbitration" overwhelms juridical considerations and constantly moves the decisional rulings in the direction of eliminating any legal constraint that might hinder or impede arbitration. The lower federal courts' rulings on enforcement matters were crafted, in large measure, from the Court's holdings in the landmark cases on international commercial arbitration. The litigation in each of the landmark cases deals with an issue vital to the autonomy of the international arbitral process. Finally, each decision addresses the status and role of national law in the regulation of international arbitration.

Bremen v. Zapata is not, strictly speaking, an arbitration case. It deals with the validity of forum-selection clauses in international contracts. Arbitration is a type of forum-selection clause that provides not only a venue, but also a mode, of litigation. Nonetheless, the Court's reasoning regarding party autonomy and the needs of international commerce in *Bremen* reverberates through *Scherk* and *Mitsubishi* as well as other cases on transnational litigation not considered in these materials (*e.g., Carnival Cruise Lines, Inc. v. Shute*, 499 U.S. 585 [1991], and *Asahi Metal Indus. Co., Ltd. v. Superior Court of California, Solano County*, 480 U.S. 102 [1987]).

Scherk and *Mitsubishi* address the question of substantive inarbitrability: Whether rights established by national statutes can be adjudicated by international arbitrators. The doctrine in *Scherk* and *Mitsubishi* practically extinguished the role of national law in regulating the process of international arbitration. The ruling that statutory claims can be submitted to international arbitration redefines the adjudicatory mission of arbitration by attributing quasi-legislative powers to international arbitrators. As explained previously, it also spawned new principles in domestic U.S. arbitration law.

Finally, the Court in *Vimar* engages in an elaborate exercise of interpretative logic to skirt a basic conflict between treaty and statutory law. The *Vimar* litigation raised the question of the compatibility of a provision in the Carriage of Goods by Sea Act (COGSA) with the policy underlying the federal legislation on arbitration. Ostensibly, the case required the Court to confront a choice between upholding maritime interests or the policy on arbitration. Had the Court addressed the issue directly, its holding would have created a parallel between its decisional law on international arbitration and its domestic rulings on the federalism question. The Court, however, chose to ignore rather than decide the conflict.

2. THE ENFORCEMENT OF FORUM-SELECTION CLAUSES

THE BREMEN v. ZAPATA OFF–SHORE CO.
407 U.S. 1, 92 S.Ct. 1907, 32 L.Ed.2d 513 (1972).

(footnotes omitted)

MR. CHIEF JUSTICE BURGER delivered the opinion of the Court.

We granted certiorari to review a judgment of the United States Court of Appeals for the Fifth Circuit declining to enforce a forum-selection clause governing disputes arising under an international towage contract between petitioners and respondent. The circuits have differed in their approach to such clauses. For the reasons stated hereafter, we vacate the judgment of the Court of Appeals.

In November 1967, respondent Zapata, a Houston-based American corporation, contracted with petitioner Unterweser, a German corporation, to tow Zapata's ocean-going, self-elevating drilling rig *Chaparral* from Louisiana to a point off Ravenna, Italy, in the Adriatic Sea, where Zapata had agreed to drill certain wells.

Zapata had solicited bids for the towage, and several companies including Unterweser had responded. Unterweser was the low bidder and Zapata requested it to submit a contract, which it did. The contract submitted by Unterweser contained the following provision, which is at issue in this case:

> "Any dispute arising must be treated before the London Court of Justice."

In addition the contract contained two clauses purporting to exculpate Unterweser from liability for damages to the towed barge.

After reviewing the contract and making several changes, but without any alteration in the forum-selection or exculpatory clauses, a Zapata vice president executed the contract and forwarded it to Unterweser in Germany, where Unterweser accepted the changes, and the contract became effective.

On January 5, 1968, Unterweser's deep sea tug *Bremen* departed Venice, Louisiana, with the *Chaparral* in tow bound for Italy. On January 9, while the flotilla was in international waters in the middle of the Gulf of Mexico, a severe storm arose. The sharp roll of the *Chaparral* in Gulf waters caused its elevator legs, which had been raised for the voyage, to break off and fall into the sea, seriously damaging the *Chaparral*. In this emergency situation Zapata instructed the *Bremen* to tow its damaged rig to Tampa, Florida, the nearest port of refuge.

On January 12, Zapata, ignoring its contract promise to litigate "any dispute arising" in the English courts, commenced a suit in admiralty in the United States District Court at Tampa, seeking $3,500,000 in damages against Unterweser *in personam* and the *Bremen in rem*, alleging negligent towage and breach of contract. Unterweser responded by invoking the forum clause of the towage contract, and moved to dismiss for lack of jurisdiction or on *forum non conveniens* grounds, or in the alternative to stay the action pending submission of the dispute to the "London Court of Justice." Shortly thereafter, in February, before the District Court had ruled on its motion to stay or dismiss the United States action, Unterweser commenced an action against Zapata seeking damages for breach of the towage contract in the High Court of Justice in London, as the contract provided. Zapata appeared in that court to contest jurisdiction, but its challenge was rejected, the English courts holding that the contractual forum provision conferred jurisdiction.

In the meantime, Unterweser was faced with a dilemma in the pending action in the United States court at Tampa. The six-month period for filing action to limit its liability to Zapata and other potential claimants was about to expire, but the United States District Court in Tampa had not yet ruled on Unterweser's motion to dismiss or stay Zapata's action. On July 2, 1968, confronted with difficult alternatives, Unterweser filed an action to limit its liability in the District Court in Tampa. That court entered the customary injunction against proceedings outside the limitation court, and Zapata refiled its initial claim in the limitation action.

It was only at this juncture, on July 29, after the six-month period for filing the limitation action had run, that the District Court denied Unterweser's January motion to dismiss or stay Zapata's initial action. In denying the motion, that court relied on the prior decision of the Court of Appeals in *Carbon Black Export, Inc. v. The Monrosa*.... In that case the Court of Appeals had held a forum-selection clause unenforceable, reiterating the traditional view of many American courts that "agreements in advance of controversy whose object is to oust the jurisdiction of the courts are contrary to public policy and will not be enforced." ...Apparently concluding that it was bound by the *Carbon Black* case, the District Court gave the forum-selection clause little, if any, weight. Instead, the court treated the motion to dismiss under normal *forum non conveniens* doctrine applicable in the absence of such a clause.... Under that doctrine "unless the balance is strongly in favor of the defendant, the plaintiff's choice of forum should rarely be disturbed." ...The District Court concluded: "The balance of conveniences here is not strongly in favor of [Unterweser] and [Zapata's] choice of forum should not be disturbed."

[...]

On appeal, a divided panel of the Court of Appeals affirmed, and on rehearing *en banc* the panel opinion was adopted, with six of the 14 *en banc* judges dissenting. As had the District Court, the majority rested on the *Carbon Black* decision, concluding that "at the very least" that case stood for the proposition that a forum-selection clause "will not be enforced unless the selected state would provide a more convenient forum than the state in which suit is brought." From that premise the Court of Appeals proceeded to conclude that, apart from the forum-selection clause, the District Court did not abuse its discretion in refusing to decline jurisdiction on the basis of forum non conveniens. It noted that (1) the flotilla never "escaped the Fifth Circuit's mare nostrum, and the casualty occurred in close proximity to the district court"; (2) a considerable number of potential witnesses, including Zapata crewmen, resided in the Gulf Coast area; (3) preparation for the voyage and inspection and repair work had been performed in the Gulf area; (4) the testimony of the *Bremen* crew was available by way of deposition; (5) England had no interest in or contact with the controversy other than the forum-selection clause. The Court of Appeals majority further noted that Zapata was a United States citizen and "[t]he discretion of the district court to remand the case to a foreign forum was consequently limited," especially since it appeared likely that the English courts would enforce the exculpatory clauses. In the Court of Appeals' view, enforcement of such clauses would be contrary to public policy in American courts under *Bisso v. Inland Waterways Corp*.... Therefore, "[t]he district court was entitled to consider that remanding Zapata to a foreign forum, with no practical contact with the controversy, could raise a bar to recovery by a United States citizen which its own convenient courts would not countenance."

We hold, with the six dissenting members of the Court of Appeals, that far too little weight and effect were given to the forum clause in resolving this controversy. For at least two decades we have witnessed an expansion of overseas commercial activities by business enterprises based in the United States. The barrier of distance that once tended to confine a business concern to a modest territory no longer does so. Here we see an American company with special expertise contracting with a foreign company to tow a complex machine thousands of miles across seas and oceans. The expansion of American business and industry will hardly be encouraged if, notwithstanding solemn contracts, we insist on a parochial concept that all disputes must be resolved under our laws and in our courts. Absent a contract forum, the considerations relied on by the Court of Appeals would be persuasive reasons for holding an American forum convenient in the traditional sense, but in an era of expanding world trade and commerce, the absolute aspects of the doctrine of the *Carbon Black* case have little place and would be a heavy hand indeed on the future development of international commercial dealings by Americans. We cannot have trade and commerce in world markets and international waters exclusively on our terms, governed by our laws, and resolved in our courts.

Forum-selection clauses have historically not been favored by American courts. Many courts, federal and state, have declined to enforce such clauses on the ground that they were "contrary to public policy," or that their effect was to "oust the jurisdiction" of the court. Although this view apparently still has considerable acceptance, other courts are tending to adopt a more hospitable attitude toward forum-selection clauses. This view, advanced in the well-reasoned dissenting opinion in the instant case, is that such clauses are prima facie valid and should be enforced unless enforcement is shown by the resisting party to be "unreasonable" under the circumstances. We believe this is the correct doctrine to be followed by federal district courts sitting in admiralty.... Not surprisingly, foreign businessmen prefer, as do we, to have disputes resolved in their own courts, but if that choice is not available, then in a neutral forum with expertise in the subject matter. Plainly, the courts of England meet the standards of neutrality and long experience in admiralty litigation. The choice of that forum was made in an arm's-length negotiation by experienced and sophisticated businessmen, and absent some compelling and countervailing reason it should be honored by the parties and enforced by the courts.

The argument that such clauses are improper because they tend to "oust" a court of jurisdiction is hardly more than a vestigial legal fiction. It appears to rest at core on historical judicial resistance to any attempt to reduce the power and business of a particular court and has little place in an era when all courts are overloaded and when businesses once essentially local now operate in world markets. It reflects something of a provincial attitude regarding the fairness of other tribunals.... The threshold question is whether that court should have exercised its jurisdiction to do more than give effect to the legitimate expectations of the parties, manifested in their freely negotiated agreement, by specifically enforcing the forum clause.

There are compelling reasons why a freely negotiated private international agreement, unaffected by fraud, undue influence, or overweening bargaining power, such as that involved here, should be given full effect. In this case, for example, we are concerned with a far from routine transaction between companies of two different nations contemplating the tow of an extremely costly piece of equipment from Louisiana across the Gulf of Mexico and the Atlantic Ocean, through the Mediterranean Sea to its final destination in the Adriatic Sea. In the course of its voyage, it was to traverse the waters of many jurisdictions. The *Chaparral* could have been damaged at any point along the route, and there were countless possible ports of refuge. That the accident occurred in the Gulf of Mexico and the barge was towed to Tampa in an emergency were mere fortuities. It cannot be doubted for a moment that the parties sought to provide for a neutral forum for the resolution of any disputes arising during the tow. Manifestly much uncertainty and possibly great inconvenience to both parties could arise if a suit could be maintained in any jurisdiction in which an accident might occur or if jurisdiction were left to any place where the *Bremen* or Unterweser might happen to be found. The elimination of all such uncertainties by agreeing in advance on a forum acceptable to both parties is an indispensable element in international trade, commerce, and contracting. There is strong evidence that the forum clause was a vital part of the agreement, and it would be unrealistic to think that the parties did not conduct their negotiations, including fixing the monetary terms, with the consequences of the forum clause figuring prominently in their calculations. . . .

Thus, in the light of present-day commercial realities and expanding international trade we conclude that the forum clause should control absent a strong showing that it should be set aside. Although their opinions are not altogether explicit, it seems reasonably clear that the District Court and the Court of Appeals placed the burden on Unterweser to show that London would be a more convenient forum than Tampa, although the contract expressly resolved that issue. The correct approach would have been to enforce the forum clause specifically unless Zapata could clearly show that enforcement would be unreasonable and unjust, or that the clause was invalid for such reasons as fraud or overreaching. Accordingly, the case must be remanded for reconsideration.

We note, however, that there is nothing in the record presently before us that would support a refusal to enforce the forum clause. The Court of Appeals suggested that enforcement would be contrary to the public policy of the forum under *Bisso* . . . because of the prospect that the English courts would enforce the clauses of the towage contract purporting to exculpate Unterweser from liability for damages to the *Chaparral*. A contractual choice-of-forum clause should be held unenforceable if enforcement would contravene a strong public policy of the forum in which suit is brought, whether declared by statute or by judicial decision.... It is clear, however, that whatever the proper scope of the policy expressed in *Bisso*, it does not reach this case. *Bisso* rested on considerations with respect to the towage business strictly in American waters, and those considerations are not controlling in an international commercial agreement....

[...]

This case...involves a freely negotiated international commercial transaction between a German and an American corporation for towage of a vessel from the Gulf of Mexico to the Adriatic Sea. As noted, selection of a London forum was clearly a reasonable effort to bring vital certainty to this international transaction and to provide a neutral forum experienced and capable in the resolution of admiralty litigation. Whatever "inconvenience" Zapata would suffer by being forced to litigate in the contractual forum as it agreed to do was clearly foreseeable at the time of contracting. In such circumstances it should be incumbent on the party seeking to escape his contract to show that trial in the contractual forum will be so gravely difficult and inconvenient that he will for all practical purposes be deprived of his day in court. Absent that, there is no basis for concluding that it would be unfair, unjust, or unreasonable to hold that party to his bargain.

[...]

The judgment of the Court of Appeals is vacated and the case is remanded for further proceedings consistent with this opinion.

Vacated and remanded.

[...]

MR. JUSTICE DOUGLAS, dissenting.

[...]

Respondent is a citizen of this country. Moreover, if it were remitted to the English court, its substantive rights would be adversely affected. Exculpatory provisions in the towage [contract] provide (1) that petitioners, the masters and the crews "are not responsible for defaults and/or errors in the navigation of the tow" and (2) that "(d)amages suffered by the towed object are in any case for account of its Owners."

Under our decision in *Dixilyn Drilling Corp.*,..."a contract which exempts the tower from liability for its own negligence" is not enforceable, though there is evidence in the present record that it is enforceable in England. That policy was first announced in *Bisso*.... Although the casualty occurred on the high seas, the *Bisso* doctrine is nonetheless applicable....

Moreover, the casualty occurred close to the District Court, a number of potential witnesses, including respondent's crewmen, reside in that area, and the inspection and repair work were done there. The testimony of the tower's crewmen, residing in Germany, is already available by way of depositions taken in the proceedings.

All in all, the District Court judge exercised his discretion wisely in enjoining petitioners from pursuing the litigation in England.

[. . .]

NOTES AND QUESTIONS

1. The loss in *Zapata* was substantial. When *The Bremen* was arrested in Tampa, it was released upon Unterweser's provision of $3,500,000 as security. Moreover, the limitation fund in the Tampa federal district court was $1,390,000 while its counterpart in England contained only $80,000. In all likelihood, the damage to the *Chaparral* and to Zapata's business represented a multimillion dollar loss. The prospect of recovery was more likely in the United States than England. In addition, although Unterweser's bid included an offer to arrange for insurance coverage, Zapata decided to self-insure. This was Zapata's general policy regarding all its rigs. The two exculpatory clauses in "The General Towage Conditions" of the contract transferred all the risk of loss to the owners of the rig and held Unterweser harmless for any acts of negligence by its employees.

How do, or should, these factors have influenced the Court's reasoning and determination? Should the quantum of actual damages determine the legality of the contractual allocation of risk? Is this a "bad deal" for Zapata warranting judicial intervention after the fact? Upon what legal basis might the court intervene? Did Zapata enter into the transaction assuming that the special protections of U.S. law would apply, perhaps unbeknownst to its co-contractant? Should the Court take such a circumstance into account?

2. Relief for Zapata is less likely, or perhaps unavailable, in England. The exculpatory clauses probably would be enforced by English courts, resulting in a dismissal of the action against Unterweser. *See* 407 U.S. at 8 n.8. Moreover, even if Unterweser were held liable, the limitation fund in England, as noted in the foregoing, was modest. Why shouldn't these factors, in addition to the public policy against exculpatory clauses in maritime transactions articulated in *Bisso*, be sufficient to place the litigation within the jurisdiction of U.S. courts and law? Moreover, the incident occurred near a U.S. jurisdiction, involved directly the business assets of a U.S. national, and generally implicated U.S. interests. Why should English courts and law have exclusive jurisdiction over a matter that has no connection or proximity to England or English interests?

3. The Court finds both the policy in *Bisso* and the *Carbon Black* doctrine on forum-selection clauses inapplicable to a transborder commercial agreement. The Court, in effect, reverses the rule of *Carbon Black*, holding that forum-selection clauses are presumptively enforceable in international contracts. The adverse party can rebut the presumption by establishing that enforcement would result in debilitating inconvenience or a denial of justice. In his dissent, Justice Douglas takes a more insidious view of the interplay between the forum-selection clause and the *Bisso* policy against exculpatory

clauses. Read the following excerpt from Justice Douglas' dissent and contrast it to the majority's reasoning:

> It is said that because these parties specifically agreed to litigate their disputes before the London Court of Justice, the District Court, absent "unreasonable" circumstances, should have honored that choice by declining to exercise its jurisdiction. The forum-selection clause, however, is part and parcel of the exculpatory provisions in the towing agreement which, as mentioned in the text, is not enforceable in American courts. For only by avoiding litigation in the United States could petitioners hope to evade the *Bisso* doctrine. Judges in this country have traditionally been hostile to attempts to circumvent the public policy against exculpatory agreements. For example, clauses specifying that the law of a foreign place (which favors such releases) should control have regularly been ignored. Thus, in *The Kensington*, . . . the Court held void an exemption from liability despite the fact that the contract provided that it should be construed under Belgian law[,] which was more tolerant. . . .
>
> The instant stratagem of specifying a foreign forum is essentially the same as invoking a foreign law of construction except that the present circumvention also requires the American party to travel across an ocean to seek relief. Unless we are prepared to overrule *Bisso* we should not countenance devices designed solely for the purpose of evading its prohibition. It is argued, however, that one of the rationales of the *Bisso* doctrine, "to protect those in need of goods or services from being overreached by others who have power to drive hard bargains," . . . does not apply here because these parties may have been of equal bargaining stature. Yet we have often adopted prophylactic rules rather than attempt to sort the core cases from the marginal ones. In any event, the other objective of the *Bisso* doctrine, to "discourage negligence by making wrongdoers pay damages," . . . applies here and in every case regardless of the relative bargaining strengths of the parties.

407 U.S. at 24 n.*.

What are the primary and most persuasive arguments in favor of the assertion of U.S. court jurisdiction and the application of existing U.S. law?

4. You should examine the content of the applicable forum selection clause carefully. Are there problems with its construction? For example: (1) to what subject areas does the phrase "any dispute arising" refer; (2) "arising" how and where; (3) what does "treated" mean—adjudication, processing, acknowledgment, or settlement; and (4) what is "the London Court of Justice"? It appears that those sophisticated commercial parties agreed to have "any dispute arising" "treated" before a court in London that does not exist. Don't these problems reveal that the parties failed to consider, or to agree upon, an appropriate situs for dispute resolution, and that these failures mean that choice-of-law considerations should dictate which court has jurisdiction? Why should the Court remedy the parties' contractual ineptitudes and deficiencies in these circumstances? Isn't the contractual failing a proper foundation for applying the standard doctrines in *Bisso* and *Carbon Black*?

5. The objections in the foregoing notes notwithstanding, it is now clear that the majority opinion in *Zapata* is good law and acts as the foundation for

the Court's progressive articulation of a judicial policy on transborder litigation and international arbitration. *Zapata* is the first case in which the Court establishes a marked boundary between law for domestic and international matters, holding that domestic rules may be inapposite in the international sector and that they need to be disregarded or amended for application in that sector. With *Zapata*, the Court begins the process of elaborating normative rules of private international law that generally reject the extraterritorial application of domestic law as a source of law for transborder commercial ventures.

6. Key phrases in the new judicial policy, applicable to forum-selection and arbitral clauses alike, include: "The expansion of American business...will hardly be encouraged if, notwithstanding solemn contracts, we insist on a parochial concept that all disputes must be resolved under our laws and in our courts." "We cannot have trade and commerce in world markets and international waters exclusively on our terms, governed by our laws, and resolved in our courts." "There are compelling reasons why a freely negotiated private international agreement...should be given full effect." "The elimination of...uncertainties by agreeing in advance on a forum acceptable to both parties is an indispensable element in international trade, commerce, and contracting."

Do these statements constitute a rule of law? Do they amount to judicial legislation? How might the Court be in a better position than the Congress to elaborate a framework for regulating international business transactions?

You should isolate the various tenets of the Court's doctrine on matters of transborder litigation and international contracts. They will be echoed, *in haec verba*, in the rulings that deal specifically with international commercial arbitration.

3. THE ARBITRABILITY OF CLAIMS ARISING UNDER THE 1934 SECURITIES AND EXCHANGE ACT

SCHERK v. ALBERTO-CULVER CO.

417 U.S. 506, 94 S.Ct. 2449, 41 L.Ed.2d 270, *reh'g denied*,
419 U.S. 885, 95 S.Ct. 157, 42 L.Ed.2d 129 (1974).

(footnotes omitted)

MR. JUSTICE STEWART delivered the opinion of the Court.

Alberto–Culver Co., the respondent, is an American company incorporated in Delaware with its principal office in Illinois. It manufactures and distributes toiletries and hair products in this country and abroad. During the 1960's Alberto–Culver decided to expand its overseas operations, and as part of this program it approached the petitioner Fritz Scherk, a German citizen residing at the time of trial in Switzerland. Scherk was the owner of three interrelated business entities, organized under the laws of Germany and Liechtenstein, that were engaged in the manufacture of toiletries and the licensing of trademarks for such toiletries. An initial contact with Scherk was made by a representative of Alberto–Culver in Germany in June 1967, and negotiations followed at further meetings in both Europe and the United States during 1967 and 1968. In February 1969[,] a contract was signed in Vienna, Austria, which provided for the transfer of the ownership of Scherk's enterprises to Alberto–Culver, along with all rights held by these enterprises to trademarks in cosmetic goods. The contract contained a number of express warranties whereby Scherk guaranteed the sole and unencumbered ownership of these trademarks. In addition, the contract contained an arbitration clause providing that "any controversy or claim [that] shall arise out of this agreement or the breach thereof" would be referred to arbitration before the International Chamber of Commerce in Paris, France, and that "[t]he laws of the State of Illinois, U.S.A. shall apply to and govern this agreement, its interpretation and performance."

The closing of the transaction took place in Geneva, Switzerland, in June 1969. Nearly one year later Alberto–Culver allegedly discovered that the trademark rights purchased under the contract were subject to substantial encumbrances that threatened to give others superior rights to the trademarks and to restrict or preclude Alberto–Culver's use of them. Alberto–Culver thereupon tendered back to Scherk the property that had been transferred to it and offered to rescind the contract. Upon Scherk's refusal, Alberto–Culver commenced this action for damages and other relief in a Federal District Court in Illinois, contending that Scherk's fraudulent representations concerning the status of the trademark rights constituted violations of 10(b) of the Securities Exchange Act of 1934...and Rule 10b–5 promulgated thereunder....

In response, Scherk filed a motion to dismiss the action for want of personal and subject-matter jurisdiction as well as on the basis of *forum non conveniens*, or, alternatively, to stay the action pending arbitration in Paris pursuant to the agreement of the parties. Alberto–Culver, in turn, opposed this motion and sought a preliminary injunction restraining the prosecution of arbitration proceedings. On December 2, 1971, the District Court denied Scherk's motion to dismiss, and, on January 14, 1972, it granted a preliminary order enjoining Scherk from proceeding with arbitration. In taking these actions the court relied entirely on this Court's decision in Wilko v. Swan,...which held that an agreement to arbitrate could not preclude a buyer of a security from seeking a judicial remedy under the Securities Act of 1933, in view of the language of 14 of that Act, barring "[a]ny condition, stipulation, or provision binding any person acquiring any security to waive compliance with any provision of this subchapter...." ...The Court of Appeals for the Seventh Circuit, with one judge dissenting, affirmed, upon what it considered the controlling authority of the *Wilko* decision.... Because of the importance of the question presented we granted Scherk's petition for a writ of certiorari....

I.

The United States Arbitration Act,...reversing centuries of judicial hostility to arbitration agreements, was designed to allow parties to avoid "the costliness and delays of litigation," and to place arbitration agreements "upon the same footing as other contracts...." ...Accordingly the Act provides that an arbitration agreement such as is here involved "shall be valid, irrevocable, and enforceable, save upon such grounds as exist at law or in equity for the revocation of any contract." ...The Act also provides in § 3 for a stay of proceedings in a case where a court is satisfied that the issue before it is arbitrable under the agreement, and § 4 of the Act directs a federal court to order parties to proceed to arbitration if there has been a "failure, neglect, or refusal" of any party to honor an agreement to arbitrate.

In *Wilko v. Swan*,...this Court acknowledged that the Act reflects a legislative recognition of the "desirability of arbitration as an alternative to the complications of litigation,"...but nonetheless declined to apply the Act's provisions....

The Court found that "[t]wo policies, not easily reconcilable, are involved in this case." ...On the one hand, the Arbitration Act stressed "the need for avoiding the delay and expense of litigation,"...and directed that such agreements be "valid, irrevocable, and enforceable" in federal courts. On the other hand, the Securities Act of 1933 was "[d]esigned to protect investors"...by creating "a special right to recover for misrepresentation...." ...In particular, the Court noted that § 14 of the Securities Act...provides:

> Any condition, stipulation, or provision binding any person acquiring any security to waive compliance with any provision of this subchapter or of the rules and regulations of the Commission shall be void.

The Court ruled that an agreement to arbitrate "is a 'stipulation,' and [that] the right to select the judicial forum is the kind of 'provision' that cannot be waived under § 14 of the Securities Act." ...Thus, Wilko's advance agreement to arbitrate any disputes subsequently arising out of his contract to purchase the securities was unenforceable under the terms of § 14 of the Securities Act of 1933.

Alberto–Culver, relying on this precedent, contends that the District Court and Court of Appeals were correct in holding that its agreement to arbitrate disputes arising under the contract with Scherk is similarly unenforceable in view of its contentions that Scherk's conduct constituted violations of the Securities Exchange Act of 1934 and rules promulgated thereunder. For the reasons that follow, we reject this contention and hold that the provisions of the Arbitration Act cannot be ignored in this case.

At the outset, a colorable argument could be made that even the semantic reasoning of the *Wilko* opinion does not control the case before us. *Wilko* concerned a suit brought under § 12(2) of the Securities Act of 1933, which provides a defrauded purchaser with the "special right" of a private remedy for civil liability.... There is no statutory counterpart of § 12(2) in the Securities Exchange Act of 1934, and neither § 10(b) of that Act nor Rule 10b–5 speaks of a private remedy to redress violations of the kind alleged here. While federal case law has established that § 10(b) and

Rule 10b–5 create an implied private cause of action...the Act itself does not establish the "special right" that the Court in *Wilko* found significant. Furthermore, while both the Securities Act of 1933 and the Securities Exchange Act of 1934 contain sections barring waiver of compliance with any "provision" of the respective Acts, certain of the "provisions" of the 1933 Act that the Court held could not be waived by Wilko's agreement to arbitrate find no counterpart in the 1934 Act. In particular, the Court in *Wilko* noted that the jurisdictional provision of the 1933 Act...allowed a plaintiff to bring suit "in any court of competent jurisdiction—federal or state—and removal from a state court is prohibited." ...The analogous provision of the 1934 Act, by contrast, provides for suit only in the federal district courts that have "exclusive jurisdiction,"...thus significantly restricting the plaintiff's choice of forum.

Accepting the premise, however, that the operative portions of the language of the 1933 Act relied upon in *Wilko* are contained in the Securities Exchange Act of 1934, the respondent's reliance on *Wilko* in this case ignores the significant and, we find, crucial differences between the agreement involved in *Wilko* and the one signed by the parties here. Alberto–Culver's contract to purchase the business entities belonging to Scherk was a truly international agreement. Alberto–Culver is an American corporation with its principal place of business and the vast bulk of its activity in this country, while Scherk is a citizen of Germany whose companies were organized under the laws of Germany and Liechtenstein. The negotiations leading to the signing of the contract in Austria and to the closing in Switzerland took place in the United States, England, and Germany, and involved consultations with legal and trademark experts from each of those countries and from Liechtenstein. Finally, and most significantly, the subject matter of the contract concerned the sale of business enterprises organized under the laws of and primarily situated in European countries, whose activities were largely, if not entirely, directed to European markets.

Such a contract involves considerations and policies significantly different from those found controlling in *Wilko*. In *Wilko*, quite apart from the arbitration provision, there was no question but that the laws of the United States generally, and the federal securities laws in particular, would govern disputes arising out of the stock-purchase agreement. The parties, the negotiations, and the subject matter of the contract were all situated in this country, and no credible claim could have been entertained that any international conflict-of-laws problems would arise. In this case, by contrast, in the absence of the arbitration provision considerable uncertainty existed at the time of the agreement, and still exists, concerning the law applicable to the resolution of disputes arising out of the contract.

Such uncertainty will almost inevitably exist with respect to any contract touching two or more countries, each with its own substantive laws and conflict-of-laws rules. A contractual provision specifying in advance the forum in which disputes shall be litigated and the law to be applied is, therefore, an almost indispensable precondition to achievement of the orderliness and predictability essential to any international business transaction. Furthermore, such a provision obviates the danger that a dispute under the agreement might be submitted to a forum hostile to the interests of one of the parties or unfamiliar with the problem area involved.

A parochial refusal by the courts of one country to enforce an international arbitration agreement would not only frustrate these purposes, but would invite unseemly and mutually destructive jockeying by the parties to secure tactical litigation advantages. In the present case, for example, it is not inconceivable that if Scherk had anticipated that Alberto–Culver would be able in this country to enjoin resort to arbitration he might have sought an order in France or some other country enjoining Alberto–Culver from proceeding with its litigation in the United States. Whatever recognition the courts of this country might ultimately have granted to the order of the foreign court, the dicey atmosphere of such a legal no-man's-land would surely damage the fabric of international commerce and trade, and imperil the willingness and ability of businessmen to enter into international commercial agreements.

The exception to the clear provisions of the Arbitration Act carved out by *Wilko* is simply inapposite to a case such as the one before us. In *Wilko* the Court reasoned that "[w]hen the security buyer, prior to any violation of the Securities Act, waives his right to sue in courts, he gives up more than would a participant in other business transactions. The security buyer has a wider choice of courts and venue. He thus surrenders one of the advantages the Act gives him...." ...In the context of an international contract, however, these advantages become chimerical since, as indicated above, an opposing party may by speedy resort to a foreign court block or hinder access to the American court of the purchaser's choice.

Two Terms ago in *The Bremen v. Zapata Off–Shore Co.*,...we rejected the doctrine that a forum-selection clause of a contract, although voluntarily adopted by the parties, will not be respected in a suit brought in the United States "unless the selected state would provide a more convenient forum than the state in which suit is brought." ...Rather, we concluded that a "forum clause should control absent a strong showing that it should be set aside.". . .

An agreement to arbitrate before a specified tribunal is, in effect, a specialized kind of forum-selection clause that posits not only the situs of suit but also the procedure to be used in resolving the dispute. The invalidation of such an agreement in the case before us would not only allow the respondent to repudiate its solemn promise but would, as well, reflect a "parochial concept that all disputes must be resolved under our laws and in our courts.... We cannot have trade and commerce in world markets and international waters exclusively on our terms, governed by our laws, and resolved in our courts.". . .

[. . .]

Accordingly, the judgment of the Court of Appeals is reversed and the case is remanded to that court with directions to remand to the District Court for further proceedings consistent with this opinion.

It is so ordered.

MR. JUSTICE DOUGLAS, with whom MR. JUSTICE BRENNAN, MR. JUSTICE WHITE, and MR. JUSTICE MARSHALL concur, dissenting.

[. . .]

The basic dispute between the parties concerned allegations that the trademarks which were basic assets in the transaction were encumbered and that their purchase was induced through serious instances of fraudulent representations and omissions by Scherk and his agents within the jurisdiction of the United States. If a question of trademarks were the only one involved, the principle of *The Bremen v. Zapata Off-Shore Co.* . . . .would be controlling.

We have here, however, questions under the Securities Exchange Act of 1934. . . .

[. . .]

. . .§ 29(b). . .[of the 1934 Act provides] that "[e]very contract" made in violation of the Act "shall be void." No exception is made for contracts which have an international character.

The Securities Act of 1933. . .has a like provision in its § 14:

Any condition, stipulation, or provision binding any person acquiring any security to waive compliance with any provision of this subchapter or of the rules and regulations of the Commission shall be void.

In *Wilko v. Swan*. . .[t]he Court held that an agreement for arbitration was a "stipulation" within the meaning of § 14 which sought to "waive" compliance with the Securities Act. We accordingly held that the courts, not the arbitration tribunals, had jurisdiction over suits under that Act. The arbitration agency, we held, was bound by other standards which were not necessarily consistent with the 1933 Act. . . .

Wilko was held by the Court of Appeals to control this case—and properly so.

[. . .]

It could perhaps be argued that *Wilko* does not govern because it involved a little customer pitted against a big brokerage house, while we deal here with sophisticated buyers and sellers: Scherk, a powerful German operator, and Alberto–Culver, an American business surrounded and protected by lawyers and experts. But that would miss the point of the problem. The Act does not speak in terms of "sophisticated" as opposed to "unsophisticated" people dealing in securities. The rules when the giants play are the same as when the pygmies enter the market.

If there are victims here, they are not Alberto–Culver the corporation, but the thousands of investors who are the security holders in Alberto–

Culver. If there is fraud and the promissory notes are excessive, the impact is on the equity in Alberto–Culver.

Moreover, the securities market these days is not made up of a host of small people scrambling to get in and out of stocks or other securities. The markets are overshadowed by huge institutional traders. The so-called "off-shore funds," of which Scherk is a member, present perplexing problems under both the 1933 and 1934 Acts. The tendency of American investors to invest indirectly as through mutual funds may change the character of the regulation but not its need.

There has been much support for arbitration of disputes; and it may be the superior way of settling some disagreements. If A and B were quarreling over a trademark and there was an arbitration clause in the contract, the policy of Congress in implementing the United Nations Convention on the Recognition and Enforcement of Foreign Arbitral Awards...would prevail. But the Act does not substitute an arbiter for the settlement of disputes under the 1933 and 1934 Acts....

But § 29(a) of the 1934 Act makes agreements to arbitrate liabilities under § 10 of the Act "void" and "inoperative" [under Article II(3) of the Convention]. Congress has specified a precise way whereby big and small investors will be protected and the rules under which the Alberto–Culvers of this Nation shall operate. They or their lawyers cannot waive those statutory conditions, for our corporate giants are not principalities of power but guardians of a host of wards unable to care for themselves. It is these wards that the 1934 Act tries to protect. Not a word in the Convention governing awards adopts the standards which Congress has passed to protect the investors under the 1934 Act. It is peculiarly appropriate that we adhere to *Wilko,* more so even than when *Wilko* was decided. Huge foreign investments are being made in our companies. It is important that American standards of fairness in security dealings govern the destinies of American investors until Congress changes these standards.

The Court finds it unnecessary to consider Scherk's argument that this case is distinguishable from *Wilko* in that *Wilko* involved parties of unequal bargaining strength.... Instead, the Court rests its conclusion on the fact that this was an "international" agreement, with an American corporation investing in the stock and property of foreign businesses, and speaks favorably of the certainty which inheres when parties specify an arbitral forum for resolution of differences in "any contract touching two or more countries."

This invocation of the "international contract" talisman might be applied to a situation where, for example, an interest in a foreign company or mutual fund was sold to an utterly unsophisticated American citizen, with material fraudulent misrepresentations made in this country. The arbitration clause could appear in the fine print of a form contract, and still be sufficient to preclude recourse to our courts, forcing the defrauded citizen to arbitration in Paris to vindicate his rights.

It has been recognized that the 1934 Act, including the protections of Rule 10b–5, applies when foreign defendants have defrauded American investors, particularly when, as alleged here, they have profited by virtue of proscribed conduct within our boundaries. This is true even when the defendant is organized under the laws of a foreign country, is conducting much of its activity outside the United States, and is therefore governed largely by foreign law. The language of § 29 of the 1934 Act does not immunize such international transactions, and the United Nations Convention provides that a forum court in which a suit is brought need not enforce an agreement to arbitrate which is "void" and "inoperative" as contrary to its public policy. When a foreign corporation undertakes fraudulent action which subjects it to the jurisdiction of our federal securities laws, nothing justifies the conclusion that only a diluted version of those laws protects American investors.

Section 29(a) of the 1934 Act provides that a stipulation binding one to waive compliance with "any provision" of the Act shall be void, and the Act expressly provides that the federal district courts shall have "exclusive jurisdiction" over suits brought under the Act.... The Court appears to attach some significance to the fact that the specific provisions of the 1933 Act involved in *Wilko* are not duplicated in the 1934 Act, which is involved in this case. While Alberto–Culver would not have the right to sue in either a state or federal forum as did the plaintiff in *Wilko*...the Court deprives it of its right to have its Rule 10b–5 claim heard in a federal court. We spoke at length in *Wilko* of this problem, elucidating the undesirable effects of remitting a securities plaintiff to an arbitral, rather than a judicial, forum. Here, as in *Wilko*, the allegations of fraudulent misrepresentation will involve "subjective findings on the purpose and knowledge" of the defendant, questions ill-determined by arbitrators without judicial instruction on the law.... An arbitral award can be made without explication of reasons and without development of a record, so that the arbitrator's conception of our statutory requirement may be absolutely incorrect yet functionally unreviewable, even when the arbitrator seeks to apply our law. We recognized in *Wilko* that there is no judicial review corresponding to review of court decisions.... The extensive pretrial discovery provided by the Federal Rules of Civil Procedure for actions in district court would not be available. And the wide choice of venue provided by the 1934 Act...would be forfeited.... The loss of the proper judicial forum carries with it the loss of substantial rights.

When a defendant, as alleged here, has, through proscribed acts within our territory, brought itself within the ken of federal securities regulation, a fact not disputed here, those laws including the controlling principles of *Wilko,* apply whether the defendant is foreign or American, and whether or not there are transnational elements in the dealings. Those laws are rendered a chimera when foreign corporations or funds unlike domestic defendants, can nullify them by virtue of arbitration clauses, which send defrauded American investors to the uncertainty of arbitration on foreign soil, or, if those investors cannot afford to arbitrate their claims in a far-off forum, to no remedy at all.

Moreover, the international aura which the Court gives this case is ominous. We now have many multinational corporations in vast operations around the world, Europe, Latin America, the Middle East, and Asia. The investments of many American investors turn on dealings by these companies. Up to this day, it has been assumed by reason of *Wilko* that they were all protected by our various federal securities Acts. If these guarantees are to be removed, it should take a legislative enactment. I would enforce our laws as they stand, unless Congress makes an exception.

The virtue of certainty in international agreements may be important, but Congress has dictated that when there are sufficient contacts for our securities laws to apply, the policies expressed in those laws take precedence. Section 29 of the 1934 Act, which renders arbitration clauses void and inoperative, recognizes no exception for fraudulent dealings which incidentally have some international factors. The Convention makes provision for such national public policy in Art. II(3). Federal jurisdiction under the 1934 Act will attach only to some international transactions, but when it does, the protections afforded investors such as Alberto–Culver can only be full-fledged.

NOTES AND QUESTIONS

1. The *Scherk* opinion specifically incorporates the *Zapata* doctrine into the area of international commercial arbitration. The majority's determination that the *Wilko* ruling is either irrelevant or inapplicable to international business transactions attests to the Court's intent to restrict the extraterritorial reach of U.S. domestic law and devise special rules for transnational litigation. The majority determination also provides a forceful illustration of the conflict that is emerging between the judicial policy on arbitration and the domain of law, in particular, sectors of regulatory activity with public importance. For example, although it is never stated in these terms, the question in *Scherk* centers upon subject-matter inarbitrability: Whether securities claims, specifically those arising under the 1934 Securities Exchange Act, can be submitted to arbitration as a matter of law. The resolution of that question also involves another vital, and equally understated, aspect of arbitration law, namely, the role of contract rights in defining arbitration's scope of application and their impact upon the legal regulation of arbitration. The decision ignores both considerations and places nearly exclusive emphasis upon the judicial policy on transnational litigation and the perceived needs of international commerce.

There is, therefore, some incongruity between the statement of policy and the analytical questions and doctrinal considerations that are raised in *Scherk*. In fact, it is possible to agree with the Court's internationalist policy (the rejection of extraterritoriality and the recognition of the need for the global regulation of commerce) and disagree with the conclusions it reaches on the questions of law that are presented. The policy appears to be unnecessarily intolerant of legal restrictions on arbitration. While the New York Convention obligates contracting States to enforce international arbitral awards on a nondiscriminatory basis and with only a modicum of judicial supervision, it allows them to refuse to enforce arbitral agreements and awards that pertain to an inarbitrable subject matter under their law or which violate national public policy. The balance between arbitral autonomy and national legal interests achieved in the Convention simply does not factor into the Court's reasoning and elaboration of policy. The Court's view seems to be that any legal curtailment of arbitration *per force* invites greater restrictions, leading inevitably to the collapse of world trade and financial markets. The hyperbole is manifest, but to what effect is the policy exaggerated?

The Court may be concerned about the influence of its ruling upon lower federal courts or about the effect of the U.S. decisional law upon courts in other national jurisdictions. The discipline of an unequivocal policy and clear doctrine avoids the undermining reference to exceptions or the *ad hoc* invocation of *sui generis* rules. It is also possible that the Court's policy on arbitration reflects systemic concerns: The congressional ratification of the New York Convention establishes law which the Court is obligated to enforce and to safeguard against the historical menace of judicial hostility to arbitration. None of these rationales is particularly convincing or explains how the right to arbitration acquires a constitutional status nearly equivalent to the right of freedom of expression. Despite its many allusions to a congressional mandate, the Court's policy exceeds any legislative endorsement of arbitration and constitutes an example of how the Court fashions law on its own. There are, for example, no congressional statutes that consecrate the importance to the United States of international business transactions or transborder commerce.

The consistency and unequivocal character of the Court's policy on international arbitration, as well as its eventual merger with the policy on domestic arbitration, perhaps can best be explained by the Court's need to manage judicial dockets and administer the federal court system. Because transnational litigation imposes an additional and more complex burden upon the federal courts, it is critical to make arbitration agreements and awards effective to avoid placing inordinate demands upon national judicial resources. The same "managerial" rationale explains the compromise of rights that occurred in the federalization of domestic U.S. arbitration law and the extension of domestic arbitration to statutory conflicts.

Do you agree with the foregoing construction of *Scherk*? What parts of the interpretation do you or might you find problematic? Do you believe that *Scherk* is a statement of pure judicial policy? Is it also a distorted policy? Does the rights protection argument undermine the reasoning in the *Scherk* decision?

2.   In the remaining notes, we will examine the more technical aspects of the decision. You should observe that, unlike some other arbitration rulings, *Scherk* emanated from a divided Court. The vote was 5 to 4. The opposition came primarily from the liberal wing of the Court (Justices Douglas, Brennan, Marshall, and—to some extent—White), although neither the majority nor

dissenting opinion fits neatly into their presumed ideological pattern. In fact, with the exception of *Volt Information Sciences, Inc.*, none of the Court's rulings on arbitration appear to be motivated to any significant extent by its members' ideological convictions. *Scherk*, therefore, appears to be an initial step at a critical juncture in the direction of a judicial policy on arbitration that espouses most, if not all, the tenets of "a-national" arbitration, but for the name.

3.   The applicable arbitral clause in *Scherk* provided:

"The parties agree that if any controversy or claim shall arise out of this agreement or the breach thereof and either party shall request that the matter shall be settled by arbitration, the matter shall be settled exclusively by arbitration in accordance with the rules then obtaining of the International Chamber of Commerce, Paris, France, by a single arbitrator, if the parties shall agree upon one, or by one arbitrator appointed by each party and a third arbitrator appointed by the other arbitrators. In case of any failure of a party to make an appointment referred to above within four weeks after notice of the controversy, such appointment shall be made by said chamber. All arbitration proceedings shall be held in Paris, France, and each party agrees to comply in all respects with any award made in any such proceeding and to the entry of a judgment in any jurisdiction upon any award rendered in such proceeding. The laws of the State of Illinois, U.S.A. shall apply to and govern this agreement, its interpretation and performance."

417 U.S. at 508 n.1.

The *Scherk* agreement should give you a sense of the content, structure, and function of an international agreement to arbitrate. In light of the circumstances of the case, do you believe the foregoing provision is an appropriate representation of the parties' dispute resolution needs and interests? Despite its length and deviation from the standard clause, it appears to leave gaps and fails to provide for many reasonably foreseeable contingencies. Can you identify and cure the agreement's deficiencies? In what respects is it a good provision for arbitration? The parties appear to have "traded-off" Paris-based ICC arbitration for the application of Illinois state law to the contract. Is the exchange equally beneficial to the parties? Does the exchange reveal that one party had the upper hand or was a more able negotiator? What comfort should Alberto–Culver derive from the application of Illinois law by ICC arbitrators? According to the arbitration agreement, which national law of arbitration governs the arbitral proceeding? Does the phrase "if any controversy or claim shall arise out of this agreement or the breach thereof" cover claims arising under the 1934 Securities Exchange Act? Who should decide that matter? Why doesn't the Court focus upon that question?

4.   Both sides of the Court view the question of *Scherk* as a conflict of statutes, whether the obligations under the New York Arbitration Convention will prevail over the rights contained in the 1934 Act. As has just been suggested, another perspective that could have been adopted by the Court would look to whether the parties intended in their arbitral compact to submit both contractual and statutory claims to arbitration. If the contract provision as such is interpreted to limit the reference to arbitration to

contractual claims or if the Court determines that the reference to arbitration is always limited to contract disputes as a matter of law, then the question of statutory conflict does not need to be addressed because the litigation is resolved on other, less dramatic grounds.

Do you find this approach to be analytically sound? What advantages does it have over the Court's methodology and conceptualization of the case? What if the ICC arbitrators rule that the contract of arbitration does not allow them to rule on noncontractual claims or that they have no authority to rule on a dispute involving the application of the 1934 Act? Would that award be enforceable in the United States? Could Scherk seek an injunction from a U.S. federal court, or an Austrian, German, Swiss, French, or Liechtenstein court, ordering the arbitrators to rule on the statutory cause of action? Would it be proper and lawful for the ICC arbitrators to rule that the 1934 Act has no bearing upon the controversy between Scherk and Alberto–Culver and to dismiss that part of the cause of action? Would that award be enforceable in the United States? Could Alberto–Culver's grievance be reviewed in an enforcement proceeding?

In a footnote to his dissent, Justice Douglas observes that the choice-of-law provision may not lead the arbitrators to apply federal law. Even if it does, the arbitral tribunal may misapply or misinterpret the legislation, and review of the determination would be unavailable. "Even if the arbitration court should read this clause to require application of Rule 10b–5's standards, Alberto–Culver's victory would be Pyrrhic." See 417 U.S. at 532 n.11. Lack of discovery would compromise Alberto–Culver's right to redress of its grievances.

5.   The arbitrability of statutory rights is never expressly mentioned in *Scherk*, although that issue will preoccupy the Court in *Mitsubishi* ten years later. In *Scherk*, the issue never escalates beyond the applicability of domestic precedents and statutes in the context of international business transactions. The question centers upon the *Wilko* bar to arbitration in securities matters. The Court quickly determines that *Wilko* is inoperative in litigation dealing with international arbitration. It initially makes a number of technical distinctions to support its determination: *Wilko* addressed a conflict between the FAA and the 1933 Securities Act, while *Scherk* pits the codification of the New York Convention in Title 9 against the 1934 Securities Exchange Act. Moreover, despite the enormous similarities between the statutes, "[t]here is no statutory counterpart of 12(2) in the Securities Exchange Act of 1934, and neither 10(b) of that Act nor Rule 10(b)-(5) speaks of a private remedy to redress violations of the kind alleged here." While 10(b)(5) creates "an implied private cause of action," it "does not establish the 'special right' that the Court in *Wilko* found significant." Moreover, the Court identifies a lack of concordance between the jurisdictional "provisions" of the Acts. See 417 U.S. at 513–14. Accordingly, these distinctions create "a colorable argument" for sustaining the view that the *Wilko* bar to predispute arbitration agreements in securities contracts does not apply to the international contract in *Scherk*.

How persuasive is the Court's reasoning on these points? Is the "colorable" logic of its argument persuasive? Do the Acts not provide for exclusive judicial jurisdiction in terms of the adjudication of claims arising under their provisions? In comparing section 14 of the 1933 Act and section 29(a) of the 1934 Act, the Court concludes in a footnote that "[w]hile the two sections are not identical, the variations in their wording seem irrelevant to the issue presented in this case." *See* 417 U.S. at 514 n.7. Isn't this a more plausible account of the significance and content of the securities laws? Isn't the legislation necessary to maintain the integrity of the financial market? Also the Court advanced a different interpretation of the provisions in *Rodriguez*, *supra*.

6. Having established these technical distinctions, the Court turns to the elaboration of its now celebrated language on the international contract and the significance of arbitration to transborder commerce. There is no doubt that an international commercial divorce can be acrimonious, and that the parties, in all likelihood, will have recourse to all the adversarial and choice-of-law devices at their disposal to hamper the effort at resolution. Arbitration does stabilize international commercial dispute resolution and allows the avoidance of jurisdictional and conflicts issues. It provides neutrality, predictability, expertise, and enforceability where organized litigious chaos would otherwise reign. You should isolate the most meaningful phrases from the majority opinion's proclamation of its internationalist policy on arbitration and international contracts. They echo the essence of the policy elaborated in *Zapata*.

Of what analytical relevance is this eloquent language to the issue involving the applicability of national law, the provision for exclusive domestic court jurisdiction over securities disputes, and the arbitrability of statutory disputes that arise pursuant to a contract relationship? The admonition against parochialism, the need to avoid the uncertainty of resolution that proceeds from the entanglements of conflicts and forum-shopping strategies, and the rejection of extraterritoriality in transborder litigation appear to have little to do with whether securities claims arising under the 1934 Act can be submitted to arbitration. Federal statutory law is applicable because Scherk chose to engage in a business transaction with a U.S. party covered by the provisions of the statute. The facts involve not only a breach of contract, but implicate directly the regulation of commercial conduct for the benefit of society. It is not the character of the contract that is at issue, but rather how the behavior of the parties affected larger U.S. juridical interests.

The majority responds to these arguments in a footnote:

> This case...provides no basis for a judgment that only United States laws and United States courts should determine this controversy in the face of a solemn agreement between the parties that such controversies be resolved elsewhere. The only contact between the United States and the transaction involved here is the fact that Alberto–Culver is an American corporation and the occurrence of some—but by no means the greater part, of the pre-contract negotiations in this country. To determine that "American standards of fairness"...must nonetheless govern the controversy demeans the standard of justice elsewhere in the world, and unnecessarily exalts the primacy of United States law over the laws of other countries.

417 U.S. at 517 n.11.

Again, the brief against extraterritoriality is admirable, but is it germane to the issues and facts of the case? Is the ICC a sovereign national entity? Didn't the parties agree to the application of U.S. law? What other laws would be displaced by the application of U.S. law? Didn't the Congress define the scope of application of the statute in question to cover foreign commerce?

You should attempt to choose the better analysis and approach to the litigation in light of the foregoing discussion.

7. The majority uses the ratification of the New York Arbitration Convention as a justifying foundation for its policy. "Our conclusion today is confirmed by international developments and domestic legislation in the area of commercial arbitration subsequent to the *Wilko* decision. In 1970 the United States acceded to the [Convention]...and Congress passed Chapter 2 of the United States Arbitration Act.... [W]e think that this country's...ratification of the Convention...provide[s] strongly persuasive evidence of congressional policy consistent with the decision we reach today." 417 U.S. at 520 n.15.

Do you believe that the Convention supports or dictates the result in *Scherk*? Would a different determination have contravened either the spirit or the letter of the Convention? In the same passage, the Court describes the essential purpose of the Convention: "to encourage the recognition and enforcement of commercial arbitration agreements in international contracts and to unify the standards by which agreements to arbitrate are observed and arbitral awards are enforced...." *Id.* Is this an accurate appraisal? Does *Scherk* affect this objective? Might the decision undermine it?

The dissent responds to this reasoning in its own footnote: "Neither § 29 [of the Securities Exchange Act], nor the Convention on international arbitration, nor *The Bremen* justifies abandonment of a national public policy that securities claims be heard by a judicial forum simply because some international elements are involved in a contract." 417 U.S. at 532 n.10. Do these comments constitute an effective argument against the majority position?

8. Read the dissenting opinion carefully, identifying its basic points and the elements of its reasoning. Justice Douglas' objections to the majority's judicial policy are both useful and prophetic. They anticipate, for example, the more ambitious doctrinal content of the later Court opinion in *Mitsubishi Motors, Inc. v. Soler*. They also clarify the legal issues and interests that are at stake in *Scherk* through the haze of the majority's high-minded rhetoric. The concept of the "international contract talisman" is a reminder of the dangers of creating legal policy without regard to substantive analytical considerations. Justice Douglas argues that the issues in *Scherk* are not a matter of contract, but rather a matter of law—that rights established by Congress are substantially compromised by the reference of disputes to arbitration. Although there may not be much sympathy for rescuing Alberto–Culver from its unfortunate circumstances, the rule of decision involves more than the immediate circumstances of the litigation. It calls into question the very "fabric" of securities regulation.

You should remember that *Scherk* begins a progression toward a more far-reaching judicial arbitral policy. The Court eventually will decide that all statutory claims arising under national law are arbitrable in transborder arbitration and that the reference to arbitration represents a mere choice of trial procedure, having no impact upon the substantive rights at issue. The integration of these internationalist doctrines into the domestic law of arbitration and the reversal of *Wilko v. Swan* also will become part of the judicial policy set in motion in *Scherk*.

4. THE ARBITRABILITY OF U.S. ANTITRUST CLAIMS

MITSUBISHI MOTORS CORP. v. SOLER CHRYSLER–PLYMOUTH, INC.

473 U.S. 614, 105 S.Ct. 3346, 87 L.Ed.2d 444 (1985).

(footnotes omitted)

JUSTICE BLACKMUN delivered the opinion of the Court.

The principal question presented by these cases is the arbitrability, pursuant to the Federal Arbitration Act...and the Convention on the Recognition and Enforcement of Foreign Arbitral Awards,...of claims arising under the Sherman Act...and encompassed within a valid arbitration clause in an agreement embodying an international commercial transaction.

I.

Petitioner-cross-respondent Mitsubishi Motors Corporation ... is a Japanese corporation...and has its principal place of business in Tokyo, Japan. Mitsubishi is the product of a joint venture between, on the one hand, Chrysler International, S.A. (CISA), a Swiss corporation registered in Geneva and wholly owned by Chrysler Corporation, and, on the other, Mitsubishi Heavy Industries, Inc., a Japanese corporation. The aim of the joint venture was the distribution through Chrysler dealers outside the continental United States of vehicles manufactured by Mitsubishi and bearing Chrysler and Mitsubishi trademarks. Respondent-cross-petitioner Soler Chrysler–Plymouth, Inc....is a Puerto Rico corporation with its principal place of business in Pueblo Viejo, Guaynabo, Puerto Rico.

On October 31, 1979, Soler entered into a Distributor Agreement with CISA which provided for the sale by Soler of Mitsubishi-manufactured vehicles within a designated area, including metropolitan San Juan.... On the same date, CISA, Soler, and Mitsubishi entered into a Sales Procedure Agreement...which, referring to the Distributor Agreement, provided for the direct sale of Mitsubishi products to Soler and governed the terms and conditions of such sales.... Paragraph VI of the Sales Agreement, labeled "Arbitration of Certain Matters," provides:

"All disputes, controversies or differences which may arise between [Mitsubishi] and [Soler] out of or in relation to Articles I–B through V of this Agreement or for the breach thereof, shall be finally settled by arbitration in

Japan in accordance with the rules and regulations of the Japan Commercial Arbitration Association.''. . .

Initially, Soler did a brisk business in Mitsubishi-manufactured vehicles. . . . In early 1981, however, the new-car market slackened. Soler ran into serious difficulties in meeting the expected sales volume, and by the spring of 1981 it felt itself compelled to request that Mitsubishi delay or cancel shipment of several orders. . . . About the same time, Soler attempted to arrange for the transshipment of a quantity of its vehicles for sale in the continental United States and Latin America. Mitsubishi and CISA, however, refused permission for any such diversion, citing a variety of reasons, and no vehicles were transshipped. Attempts to work out these difficulties failed. Mitsubishi eventually withheld shipment of 966 vehicles, apparently representing orders placed for May, June, and July 1981 production, responsibility for which Soler disclaimed in February 1982. . . .

The following month. . .Mitsubishi sought an order, pursuant to 9 U.S.C. 4 and 201, to compel arbitration in accord with. . .the Sales Agreement. . . . Shortly after filing the complaint, Mitsubishi filed a request for arbitration before the Japan Commercial Arbitration Association. . . .

Soler denied the allegations and counterclaimed against both Mitsubishi and CISA. . . . In the counterclaim premised on the Sherman Act, Soler alleged that Mitsubishi and CISA had conspired to divide markets in restraint of trade. To effectuate the plan, according to Soler, Mitsubishi had refused to permit Soler to resell to buyers in North, Central, or South America vehicles it had obligated itself to purchase from Mitsubishi; had refused to ship ordered vehicles or the parts, such as heaters and defoggers, that would be necessary to permit Soler to make its vehicles suitable for resale outside Puerto Rico; and had coercively attempted to replace Soler and its other Puerto Rico distributors with a wholly owned subsidiary which would serve as the exclusive Mitsubishi distributor in Puerto Rico. . . .

After a hearing, the District Court ordered Mitsubishi and Soler to arbitrate each of the issues raised in the complaint and in all the counterclaims save two and a portion of a third. With regard to the federal antitrust issues, it recognized that the Courts of Appeals, following *American Safety Equipment Corp. v. J.P. Maguire & Co.*, 391 F.2d 821 (2d Cir. 1968), uniformly had held that the rights conferred by the antitrust laws were '' 'of a character inappropriate for enforcement by arbitration.' '' . . .The District Court held, however, that the international character of the Mitsubishi–Soler undertaking required enforcement of the agreement to arbitrate even as to the antitrust claims. It relied on *Scherk v. Alberto–Culver Co*. . . .

The United States Court of Appeals for the First Circuit affirmed in part and reversed in part. 723 F.2d 155 (1983). . . .

Finally, after endorsing the doctrine of *American Safety*, precluding arbitration of antitrust claims, the Court of Appeals concluded that neither this Court's decision in *Scherk* nor the Convention required abandonment of that doctrine in the face of an international transaction.... Accordingly, it reversed the judgment of the District Court insofar as it had ordered submission of "Soler's antitrust claims" to arbitration....

We granted certiorari primarily to consider whether an American court should enforce an agreement to resolve antitrust claims by arbitration when that agreement arises from an international transaction....

II.

[...]

...[W]e find no warrant in the Arbitration Act for implying in every contract within its ken a presumption against arbitration of statutory claims. The Act's centerpiece provision makes a written agreement to arbitrate "in any maritime transaction or a contract evidencing a transaction involving commerce...valid, irrevocable, and enforceable, save upon such grounds as exist at law or in equity for the revocation of any contract." ...The "liberal federal policy favoring arbitration agreements," *Moses H. Cone Memorial Hospital*,...manifested by this provision and the Act as a whole, is at bottom a policy guaranteeing the enforcement of private contractual arrangements: the Act simply "creates a body of federal substantive law establishing and regulating the duty to honor an agreement to arbitrate."...

Accordingly, the first task of a court asked to compel arbitration of a dispute is to determine whether the parties agreed to arbitrate that dispute.... Thus, as with any other contract, the parties' intentions control, but those intentions are generously construed as to issues of arbitrability.

There is no reason to depart from these guidelines where a party bound by an arbitration agreement raises claims founded on statutory rights.... [W]e are well past the time when judicial suspicion of the desirability of arbitration and of the competence of arbitral tribunals inhibited the development of arbitration as an alternative means of dispute resolution.... Of course, courts should remain attuned to well-supported claims that the agreement to arbitrate resulted from the sort of fraud or overwhelming economic power that would provide grounds "for the revocation of any contract." ...But, absent such compelling considerations, the Act itself provides no basis for disfavoring agreements to arbitrate statutory claims by skewing the otherwise hospitable inquiry into arbitrability.

That is not to say that all controversies implicating statutory rights are suitable for arbitration. There is no reason to distort the process of contract interpretation, however, in order to ferret out the inappropriate.... For that reason, Soler's concern for statutorily protected classes provides no reason to color the lens through which the arbitration clause is read. By agreeing to arbitrate a statutory claim, a party does not forgo the substantive rights afforded by the statute; it only submits to their resolution in an arbitral, rather than a judicial, forum. It trades the procedures and opportunity for review of the courtroom for the simplicity, informality, and expedition of arbitration. We must assume that if Congress intended the substantive protection afforded by a given statute to include protection against waiver of the right to a judicial forum, that intention will be deducible from text or legislative history.... Having made the bargain to arbitrate, the party should be held to it unless Congress itself has evinced an intention to preclude a waiver of judicial remedies for the statutory rights at issue. Nothing, in the meantime, prevents a party from excluding statutory claims from the scope of an agreement to arbitrate....

[...]

III.

We now turn to consider whether Soler's antitrust claims are nonarbitrable even though it has agreed to arbitrate them. In holding that they are not, the Court of Appeals followed the decision of the Second Circuit in *American Safety Equipment Corp. v. J.P. Maguire & Co.*, 391 F.2d 821 (1968). Notwithstanding the absence of any explicit support for such an exception in either the Sherman Act or the Federal Arbitration Act, the Second Circuit there reasoned that "the pervasive public interest in enforcement of the antitrust laws, and the nature of the claims that arise in such cases, combine to make...antitrust claims...inappropriate for arbitration." ...We find it unnecessary to assess the legitimacy of the *American Safety* doctrine as applied to agreements to arbitrate arising from domestic transactions. As in *Scherk v. Alberto–Culver Co.,*...we conclude that concerns of international comity, respect for the capacities of foreign and transnational tribunals, and sensitivity to the need of the international commercial system for predictability in the resolution of disputes require that we enforce the parties' agreement, even assuming that a contrary result would be forthcoming in a domestic context.

[...]

The Bremen and *Scherk* establish a strong presumption in favor of enforcement of freely negotiated contractual choice-of-forum provisions. Here, as in *Scherk*, that presumption is reinforced by the emphatic federal policy in favor of arbitral dispute resolution. And at least since this Nation's accession in 1970 to the Convention,...that federal policy applies with special force in the field of international commerce. Thus, we must weigh the concerns of *American Safety* against a strong belief in the efficacy of arbitral procedures for the resolution of international commercial disputes and an equal commitment to the enforcement of freely negotiated choice-of-forum clauses.

At the outset, we confess to some skepticism of certain aspects of the *American Safety* doctrine. As distilled by the First Circuit,...the doctrine comprises four ingredients. First, private parties play a pivotal role in aiding governmental enforcement of the antitrust laws by means of the private action for treble damages. Second, "the strong possibility that contracts which generate antitrust disputes may be contracts of adhesion militates against automatic forum determination by contract." Third, antitrust issues, prone to complication, require sophisticated legal and economic analysis, and thus are "ill-adapted to strengths of the arbitral process, i.e., expedition, minimal requirements of written rationale, simplicity, resort to basic concepts of common sense and simple equity." Finally, just as "issues of war and peace are too important to be vested in the generals,...decisions as to antitrust regulation of business are too important to be lodged in arbitrators chosen from the business community—particularly those from a foreign community that has had no experience with or exposure to our law and values."...

Initially, we find the second concern unjustified. The mere appearance of an antitrust dispute does not alone warrant invalidation of the selected forum on the undemonstrated assumption that the arbitration clause is tainted. A party resisting arbitration of course may attack directly the validity of the agreement to arbitrate.... Moreover, the party may attempt to make a showing that would warrant setting aside the forum-selection clause, that the agreement was "[a]ffected by fraud, undue influence, or overweening bargaining power"; that "enforcement would be unreasonable and unjust"; or that proceedings "in the contractual forum will be so gravely difficult and inconvenient that [the resisting party] will for all practical purposes be deprived of his day in court." ...But absent such a showing—and none was attempted here—there is no basis for assuming the forum inadequate or its selection unfair.

Next, potential complexity should not suffice to ward off arbitration. We might well have some doubt that even the courts following *American Safety* subscribe fully to the view that antitrust matters are inherently insusceptible to resolution by arbitration, as these same courts have agreed that an undertaking to arbitrate antitrust claims entered into after the dispute arises is acceptable.... And the vertical restraints which most frequently give birth to antitrust claims covered by an arbitration agreement will not often occasion the monstrous proceedings that have given antitrust litigation an image of intractability. In any event, adaptability and access to expertise are hallmarks of arbitration. The anticipated subject matter of the dispute may be taken into account when the arbitrators are appointed, and arbitral rules typically provide for the participation of experts either employed by the parties or appointed by the tribunal. Moreover, it is often a judgment that streamlined proceedings and expeditious results will best serve their needs that causes parties to agree to arbitrate their disputes; it is typically a desire to keep the effort and expense required to resolve a dispute within manageable bounds that prompts them mutually to forgo access to judicial remedies. In sum, the factor of potential complexity alone does not persuade us that an arbitral tribunal could not properly handle an antitrust matter.

For similar reasons, we also reject the proposition that an arbitration panel will pose too great a danger of innate hostility to the constraints on business conduct that antitrust law imposes. International arbitrators frequently are drawn from the legal as well as the business community; where the dispute has an important legal component, the parties and the arbitral body with whose assistance they have agreed to settle their dispute can be expected to select arbitrators accordingly. We decline to indulge the presumption that the parties and arbitral body conducting a proceeding will be unable or unwilling to retain competent, conscientious, and impartial arbitrators.

We are left, then, with the core of the *American Safety* doctrine—the fundamental importance to American democratic capitalism of the regime of the antitrust laws.... Without doubt, the private cause of action plays a central role in enforcing this regime.... As the Court of Appeals pointed out:

> "A claim under the antitrust laws is not merely a private matter. The Sherman Act is designed to promote the national interest in a competitive economy; thus, the plaintiff asserting his rights under the Act has been likened to a private attorney-general who protects the public's interest."...

The treble-damages provision wielded by the private litigant is a chief tool in the antitrust enforcement scheme, posing a crucial deterrent to potential violators....

The importance of the private damages remedy, however, does not compel the conclusion that it may not be sought outside an American court. Notwithstanding its important incidental policing function, the treble-damages cause of action conferred on private parties by § 4 of the Clayton...Act and pursued by Soler here by way of its third counterclaim, seeks primarily to enable an injured competitor to gain compensation for that injury.

[...]

There is no reason to assume at the outset of the dispute that international arbitration will not provide an adequate mechanism. To be sure, the international arbitral tribunal owes no prior allegiance to the legal norms of particular states; hence, it has no direct obligation to vindicate their statutory dictates. The tribunal, however, is bound to effectuate the intentions of the parties. Where the parties have agreed that the arbitral body is to decide a defined set of claims which includes, as in these cases, those arising from the application of American antitrust law, the tribunal therefore should be bound to decide that dispute in accord with the national law giving rise to the claim.... And so long as the prospective litigant effectively may vindicate its statutory cause of action in the arbitral forum, the statute will continue to serve both its remedial and deterrent function.

Having permitted the arbitration to go forward, the national courts of the United States will have the opportunity at the award-enforcement stage to ensure that the legitimate interest in the enforcement of the antitrust laws has been addressed. The Convention reserves to each signatory country the right to refuse enforcement of an award where the "recognition or enforcement of the award would be contrary to the public policy of that country." ...While the efficacy of the arbitral process requires that substantive review at the award-enforcement stage remain minimal, it would not require intrusive inquiry to ascertain that the tribunal took cognizance of the antitrust claims and actually decided them.

As international trade has expanded in recent decades, so too has the use of international arbitration to resolve disputes arising in the course of that trade. The controversies that international arbitral institutions are called upon to resolve have increased in diversity as well as in complexity. Yet the potential of these tribunals for efficient disposition of legal disagreements arising from commercial relations has not yet been tested. If they are to take a central place in the international legal order, national courts will need to "shake off the old judicial hostility to arbitration"...and also their customary and understandable unwillingness to cede jurisdiction of a claim arising under domestic law to a foreign or transnational tribunal. To this extent, at least, it will be necessary for national courts to subordinate domestic notions of arbitrability to the international policy favoring commercial arbitration.

Accordingly, we "require this representative of the American business community to honor its bargain"...by holding this agreement to arbitrate "enforce[able]...in accord with the explicit provisions of the Arbitration Act."...

The judgment of the Court of Appeals is affirmed in part and reversed in part, and the cases are remanded for further proceedings consistent with this opinion.

It is so ordered.

JUSTICE POWELL took no part in the decision of these cases.

JUSTICE STEVENS, with whom JUSTICE BRENNAN joins, and with whom JUSTICE MARSHALL joins except as to Part II, dissenting.

[...]

...This Court's holding rests almost exclusively on the federal policy favoring arbitration of commercial disputes and vague notions of international comity arising from the fact that the automobiles involved here were manufactured in Japan. Because I am convinced that the Court of Appeals' construction of the arbitration clause is erroneous, and because I strongly disagree with this Court's interpretation of the relevant federal statutes, I respectfully dissent. In my opinion, (1) a fair construction of the language in the arbitration clause in the parties' contract does not encompass a claim that auto manufacturers entered into a conspiracy in violation of the antitrust laws; (2) an arbitration clause should not normally be construed to cover a statutory remedy that it does not expressly identify; (3) Congress did not intend § 2 of the Federal Arbitration Act to apply to antitrust claims; and (4) Congress did not intend the Convention on the Recognition and Enforcement of Foreign Arbitral Awards to apply to disputes that are not covered by the Federal Arbitration Act.

I.

On October 31, 1979, respondent, Soler Chrysler–Plymouth, Inc. (Soler), entered into a "distributor agreement" to govern the sale of Plymouth passenger cars to be manufactured by petitioner, Mitsubishi Motors Corporation of Tokyo, Japan (Mitsubishi). Mitsubishi, however, was not a party to that agreement. Rather the "purchase rights" were granted to Soler by a wholly owned subsidiary of Chrysler Corporation that is referred to as "Chrysler" in the agreement. The distributor agreement does not contain an arbitration clause. Nor does the record contain any other agreement providing for the arbitration of disputes between Soler and Chrysler.

Paragraph 26 of the distributor agreement authorizes Chrysler to have Soler's orders filled by any company affiliated with Chrysler, that company thereby becoming the "supplier" of the products covered by the agreement with Chrysler. Relying on paragraph 26 of their distributor agreement, Soler, Chrysler, and Mitsubishi entered into a separate Sales Procedure Agreement designating Mitsubishi as the supplier of the products covered by the distributor agreement. The arbitration clause the Court construes today is found in that agreement. As a matter of ordinary contract interpretation, there are at least two reasons why that clause does not apply to Soler's antitrust claim against Chrysler and Mitsubishi.

First, the clause only applies to two-party disputes between Soler and Mitsubishi. The antitrust violation alleged in Soler's counterclaim is a three-party dispute. Soler has joined both Chrysler and its associated company, Mitsubishi, as counterdefendants. The pleading expressly alleges that both of those companies are "engaged in an unlawful combination and conspiracy to restrain and divide markets in interstate and foreign commerce, in violation of the Sherman Antitrust Act and the Clayton Act."... It is further alleged that Chrysler authorized and participated in several overt acts directed at Soler. At this stage of the case we must, of course, assume the truth of those allegations. Only by stretching the language of the arbitration clause far beyond its ordinary meaning could one possibly conclude that it encompasses this three-party dispute.

Second, the clause only applies to disputes "which may arise between MMC and BUYER out of or in relation to Articles I–B through V of this Agreement or for the breach thereof...." ...Thus, disputes relating to only 5 out of a total of 15 Articles in the Sales Procedure Agreement are arbitrable. Those five Articles cover: (1) the terms and conditions of direct sales (matters such as the scheduling of orders, deliveries, and payment); (2) technical and engineering changes; (3) compliance by Mitsubishi with customs laws and regulations, and Soler's obligation to inform Mitsubishi of relevant local laws; (4) trademarks and patent rights; and (5) Mitsubishi's right to cease production of any products. It is immediately obvious that Soler's antitrust claim did not arise out of Articles I–B through V and it is not a claim "for the breach thereof." The question is whether it is a dispute "in relation to" those Articles.

Because Mitsubishi relies on those Articles of the contract to explain some of the activities that Soler challenges in its antitrust claim, the Court of Appeals concluded that the relationship between the dispute and those Articles brought the arbitration clause into play. I find that construction of the clause wholly unpersuasive. The words "in relation to" appear between the references to claims that arise under the contract and claims for breach of the contract; I believe all three of the species of arbitrable claims must be predicated on contractual rights defined in Articles I–B through V.

The federal policy favoring arbitration cannot sustain the weight that the Court assigns to it. A clause requiring arbitration of all claims "relating to" a contract surely could not encompass a claim that the arbitration clause was itself part of a contract in restraint of trade. ... Nor in my judgment should it be read to encompass a claim that relies, not on a failure to perform the contract, but on an independent violation of federal law. The matters asserted by way of defense do not control the character, or the source, of the claim that Soler has asserted. Accordingly, simply as a matter of ordinary contract interpretation, I would hold that Soler's antitrust claim is not arbitrable.

II.

Section 2 of the Federal Arbitration Act describes three kinds of arbitrable agreements. Two—those including maritime transactions and those covering the submission of an existing dispute to arbitration—are not involved in this case. ... The plain language of this statute encompasses Soler's claims that arise out of its contract with Mitsubishi, but does not encompass a claim arising under federal law, or indeed one that arises under its distributor agreement with Chrysler. Nothing in the text of the 1925 Act, nor its legislative history, suggests that Congress intended to authorize the arbitration of any statutory claims.

Until today all of our cases enforcing agreements to arbitrate under the Arbitration Act have involved contract claims. In one, the party claiming a breach of contractual warranties also claimed that the breach amounted to fraud actionable under 10(b) of the Securities Exchange Act of 1934. *Scherk v. Alberto–Culver Co*. ... But this is the first time the Court has considered the question whether a standard arbitration clause referring to claims arising out of or relating to a contract should be construed to cover statutory claims that have only an indirect relationship to the contract. In my opinion, neither the Congress that enacted the Arbitration Act in 1925, nor the many parties who have agreed to such standard clauses, could have anticipated the Court's answer to that question.

On several occasions we have drawn a distinction between statutory rights and contractual rights and refused to hold that an arbitration barred the assertion of a statutory right. Thus, in *Alexander v. Gardner–Denver Co.*, ... we held that the arbitration of a claim of employment discrimination would not bar an employee's statutory right to damages under Title VII of the Civil Rights Act of 1964 ... notwithstanding the strong federal policy favoring the arbitration of labor disputes.... In addition, the Court noted that the informal procedures which make arbitration so desirable in the context of contractual disputes are inadequate to develop a record for appellate review of statutory questions. Such review is essential on matters of statutory interpretation in order to assure consistent application of important public rights.

In *Barrentine v. Arkansas–Best Freight System, Inc.*, ... we reached a similar conclusion with respect to the arbitrability of an employee's claim based on the Fair Labor Standards Act, 29 U.S.C. 201–219. We again noted that an arbitrator, unlike a federal judge, has no institutional obligation to enforce federal legislative policy....

... In view of the Court's repeated recognition of the distinction between federal statutory rights and contractual rights, together with the undisputed historical fact that arbitration has functioned almost entirely in either the area of labor disputes or in "ordinary disputes between merchants as to questions of fact," ... it is reasonable to assume that most lawyers and executives would not expect the language in the standard arbitration clause to cover federal statutory claims. Thus, in my opinion, both a fair respect for the importance of the interests that Congress has identified as worthy of federal statutory protection, and a fair appraisal of the most likely understanding of the parties who sign agreements containing standard arbitration clauses, support a presumption that such clauses do not apply to federal statutory claims.

III.

The Court has repeatedly held that a decision by Congress to create a special statutory remedy renders a private agreement to arbitrate a federal statutory claim unenforceable. Thus, ... the express statutory remedy provided in the Ku Klux Act of 1871, the express statutory remedy in the Securities Act of 1933, the express statutory remedy in the Fair Labor Standards Act, and the express statutory remedy in Title VII of the Civil Rights Act of 1964, each provided the Court with convincing evidence that Congress did not intend the protections afforded by the statute to be administered by a private arbitrator. The reasons that motivated those decisions apply with special force to the federal policy that is protected by the antitrust laws.

... The Sherman and Clayton Acts reflect Congress' appraisal of the value of economic freedom; they guarantee the vitality of the entrepreneurial spirit. Questions arising under these Acts are among the most important in public law.

The unique public interest in the enforcement of the antitrust laws is repeatedly reflected in the special remedial scheme enacted by Congress. Since its enactment in 1890, the Sherman Act has provided for public enforcement through criminal as well as civil sanctions. The pre-eminent federal interest in effective enforcement once justified a provision for special three-judge district courts to hear antitrust claims on an expedited basis, as well as for direct appeal to this Court bypassing the courts of appeals. . . .

The special interest in encouraging private enforcement of the Sherman Act has been reflected in the statutory scheme ever since 1890. Section 7 of the original Act[ ] used the broadest possible language to describe the class of litigants who may invoke its protection. . . .

The provision for mandatory treble damages—unique in federal law when the statute was enacted—provides a special incentive to the private enforcement of the statute, as well as an especially powerful deterrent to violators. What we have described as "the public interest in vigilant enforcement of the antitrust laws through the instrumentality of the private treble-damage action" . . . is buttressed by the statutory mandate that the injured party also recover costs, "including a reasonable attorney's fee.". . . The interest in wide and effective enforcement has thus, for almost a century, been vindicated by enlisting the assistance of "private Attorneys General"; we have always attached special importance to their role because "[e]very violation of the antitrust laws is a blow to the free-enterprise system envisaged by Congress.". . .

There are, in addition, several unusual features of the antitrust enforcement scheme that unequivocally require rejection of any thought that Congress would tolerate private arbitration of antitrust claims in lieu of the statutory remedies that it fashioned. . . . [A]n antitrust treble-damages case "can only be brought in a District Court of the United States." The determination that these cases are "too important to be decided otherwise than by competent tribunals" surely cannot allow private arbitrators to assume a jurisdiction that is denied to courts of the sovereign States.

[. . .]

In view of the history of antitrust enforcement in the United States, it is not surprising that all of the federal courts that have considered the question have uniformly and unhesitatingly concluded that agreements to arbitrate federal antitrust issues are not enforceable. . . .

This Court would be well advised to endorse the collective wisdom of the distinguished judges of the Courts of Appeals who have unanimously concluded that the statutory remedies fashioned by Congress for the enforcement of the antitrust laws . . . render an agreement to arbitrate antitrust disputes unenforceable. Arbitration awards are only reviewable for manifest disregard of the law and the rudimentary procedures which make arbitration so desirable in the context of a private dispute often mean that the record is so inadequate that the arbitrator's decision is virtually unreviewable. Despotic decisionmaking of this kind is fine for parties who are willing to agree in advance to settle for a best approximation of the correct result in order to resolve quickly and inexpensively any contractual dispute that may arise in an ongoing commercial relationship. Such informality, however, is simply unacceptable when every error may have devastating consequences for important businesses in our national economy and may undermine their ability to compete in world markets. Instead of "muffling a grievance in the cloakroom of arbitration," the public interest in free competitive markets would be better served by having the issues resolved "in the light of impartial public court adjudication." . . .

IV.

The Court assumes for the purposes of its decision that the antitrust issues would not be arbitrable if this were a purely domestic dispute, . . . but holds that the international character of the controversy makes it arbitrable. The holding rests on vague concerns for the international implications of its decision and a misguided application of *Scherk v. Alberto–Culver, Co* . . . .

International Obligations of the United States

[. . .]

. . . [T]he United States, as *amicus curiae*, advises the Court that the Convention "clearly contemplates" that signatory nations will enforce domestic laws prohibiting the arbitration of certain subject matters. . . . The construction is beyond doubt.

[. . .]

. . . Thus, reading Articles II and V together, the Convention provides that agreements to arbitrate disputes which are nonarbitrable under domestic law need not be honored, nor awards rendered under them enforced.

This construction is also supported by the legislative history of the Senate's advice and consent to the Convention. . . .

International Comity

It is clear then that the international obligations of the United States permit us to honor Congress' commitment to the exclusive resolution of antitrust disputes in the federal courts. The Court today refuses to do so, offering only vague concerns for comity among nations. The courts of other nations, on the other hand, have applied the exception provided in the Convention, and refused to enforce agreements to arbitrate specific subject matters of concern to them.

It may be that the subject-matter exception to the Convention ought to be reserved—as a matter of domestic law—for matters of the greatest public interest which involve concerns that are shared by other nations. The Sherman Act's commitment to free competitive markets is among our most important civil policies. . . . This commitment, shared by other nations which are signatory to the Convention, is hardly the sort of parochial concern that we should decline to enforce in the interest of international comity. Indeed, the branch of Government entrusted with the conduct of political relations with foreign governments has informed us that the "United States' determination that federal antitrust claims are nonarbitrable under the Convention . . . is not likely to result in either surprise or recrimination on the part of other signatories to the Convention.". . .

[. . .]

. . . [I]t is especially distressing to find that the Court is unable to perceive why the reasoning in *Scherk* is wholly inapplicable to Soler's antitrust claims against Chrysler and Mitsubishi. The merits of those claims are controlled entirely by American law. It is true that the automobiles are manufactured in Japan and that Mitsubishi is a Japanese corporation, but the same antitrust questions would be presented if Mitsubishi were owned by two American companies instead of by one American and one Japanese partner. When Mitsubishi enters the American market and plans to engage in business in that market over a period of years, it must recognize its obligation to comply with American law and to be subject to the remedial provisions of American statutes.

The federal claim that was asserted in *Scherk*, unlike Soler's antitrust claim, had not been expressly authorized by Congress. Indeed, until this Court's recent decision in *Landreth Timber Co. v. Landreth*, . . . the federal cause of action asserted by Scherk would not have been entertained in a number of Federal Circuits because it did not involve the kind of securities transaction that Congress intended to regulate when it enacted the Securities Exchange Act of 1934. The fraud claimed in *Scherk* was virtually identical to the breach of warranty claim; arbitration of such claims arising out of an agreement between parties of equal bargaining strength does not conflict with any significant federal policy.

In contrast, Soler's claim not only implicates our fundamental antitrust policies . . . but also should be evaluated in the light of an explicit congressional finding concerning the disparity in bargaining power between automobile manufacturers and their franchised dealers. In 1956, when Congress enacted special legislation to protect dealers from bad-faith franchise terminations, it recited its intent "to balance the power now heavily weighted in favor of automobile manufacturers." . . . The special federal interest in protecting automobile dealers from overreaching by car manufacturers, as well as the policies underlying the Sherman Act, underscore the folly of the Court's decision today.

V.

The Court's repeated incantation of the high ideals of "international arbitration" creates the impression that this case involves the fate of an institution designed to implement a formula for world peace. But just as it is improper to subordinate the public interest in enforcement of antitrust policy to the private interest in resolving commercial disputes, so is it equally unwise to allow a vision of world unity to distort the importance of the selection of the proper forum for resolving this dispute. Like any other mechanism for resolving controversies, international arbitration will only succeed if it is realistically limited to tasks it is capable of performing well, the prompt and inexpensive resolution of essentially contractual disputes between commercial partners. As for matters involving the political passions and the fundamental interests of nations, even the multilateral convention adopted under the auspices of the United Nations recognizes that private international arbitration is incapable of achieving satisfactory results.

In my opinion, the elected representatives of the American people would not have us dispatch an American citizen to a foreign land in search of an uncertain remedy for the violation of a public right that is protected by the Sherman Act. This is especially so when there has been no genuine bargaining over the terms of the submission, and the arbitration remedy provided has not even the most elementary guarantees of fair process. Consideration of a fully developed record by a jury, instructed in the law by a federal judge, and subject to appellate review, is a surer guide to the competitive character of a commercial practice than the practically unreviewable judgment of a private arbitrator.

Unlike the Congress that enacted the Sherman Act in 1890, the Court today does not seem to appreciate the value of economic freedom. I respectfully dissent.

Notes and Questions

1. The *Mitsubishi* opinion introduces a more detailed substantive focus in the Court's decisional law on international commercial arbitration. From the outset of the opinion, Justice Blackmun recognizes arbitrability as the principal question of the case. In keeping with *Scherk*, a domestic law precedent is on point and is determined to be inapplicable in the context of international commercial arbitration. Also, the decision, as in *Scherk*, includes a forceful dissent authored by a member of the Court with long-standing expertise in the area deemed arbitrable by the majority. Unlike *Scherk*, the dissent in *Mitsubishi* does not harness the allegiance of a substantial minority of the Court. Finally, the Court in *Mitsubishi* begins to commingle its rulings on domestic and international arbitration. The majority makes significant reference to the federalism trilogy in supporting its conclusions on the question of arbitrability. Although the ruling is still couched in terms of the needs of transborder commerce, a unitary policy on arbitration begins to emerge. As has already been noted, the Court will simply have forgotten the international specialty of the rule of statutory arbitrability once it decides *McMahon* and *Rodriguez*. There had been an expectation that *Mitsubishi* would provide the Court with the opportunity to refine and contain its judicial policy on international commerce and arbitration. This expectation, needless to say, was disappointed by the opinion.

2. From the facts recited in the opinion, how would you characterize the dispute between Soler and Mitsubishi? Is it exclusively a commercial or

contractual dispute—a breach of contract and nothing more? Is it more accurate to represent the conflict as a private contractual dispute with some public law implications? When should a "mixed" dispute become inarbitrable and who should make that decision? Why not sever the private and public law claims, and have separate adjudications apply to them? Would such a procedure raise *res judicata* and collateral estoppel problems? Is the result in *Mitsubishi* the best solution, especially in the transborder context? Should questions pertaining to important jurisdictional matters be resolved exclusively from the perspective of practicality?

In assessing these questions, you should note that, to justify its refusal to allow Soler to trans-ship some of the vehicles, Mitsubishi alleges that a diversion of the vehicles to Houston, Texas, for example, could have had a negative impact upon U.S.-Japan trade relations. Moreover, some vehicles were unsuitable for sale in other locales because of manufacturing specifications (*e.g.*, type of gas required, availability of heaters and defoggers) and an inability to service the vehicles in these locations. Mitsubishi's claim against Soler stated that Soler did not pay for the 966 vehicles it had ordered or for the cost of storage and financial charges. Moreover, Soler failed to fulfill warranty obligations to customers, thereby harming Mitsubishi's commercial reputation. Soler allegedly also did not obtain the agreed-upon financing. Soler's counterclaim against Mitsubishi and CISA included a series of contract breaches (wrongful refusal to ship vehicles and parts, failure to pay for warranty work and rebates, bad faith in determining sales volume); two defamation claims; and violations of two federal and two Puerto Rican statutes.

In this context, you should attempt to determine whether Soler's antitrust claim constituted a legitimate cause of action under the applicable statute? Was Soler simply "blowing smoke" in an attempt to complicate the litigation and avoid the arbitral proceeding? Moreover, Soler's desire to avoid arbitration may have been linked to Mitsubishi's decision to invoke that remedy. If the antitrust allegation was indeed bogus and amounted to a dilatory tactic, would that factor explain or account for the content of the majority opinion?

3.   In Part II of the majority opinion, the Court elaborates the doctrinal framework that is now generally applicable in matters of arbitration, making extensive reference to the FAA and domestic law precedent (*Moses H. Cone*, *Byrd*, *Keating*, *Prima Paint*, and even labor arbitration cases like *Steelworkers v. Warrior & Gulf Navigation Co.*). Is this an appropriate methodology? What role does freedom of contract play in the doctrine? Is it meant to eradicate judicial hostility to arbitration? Does the Court give any importance to the character and quality of the arbitration contract? Was adhesion involved in *Mitsubishi*? In your view, does the FAA foster the arbitration of statutory claims? Following *Mitsubishi*, which "controversies implicating statutory rights" cannot be submitted to arbitration?

At the end of Part II, the Court argues that the submission of claims to arbitration has no impact upon substantive rights, and that the arbitration agreement reflects a mere choice of remedy or forum of litigation. Do you agree? The Court then establishes two defenses to the arbitrability of claims based upon statutory rights: (1) an express or implied congressional provision in the statute for exclusive judicial recourse; and (2) a provision in the arbitral clause which excludes such claims from the arbitrators' jurisdiction. Given the content of the case law, is it likely that even an express congressional directive for the exclusive judicial resolution of disputes would be sufficient? The Court could require that arbitral adjudication be specifically disallowed or that the statutory or contractual exclusion of arbitration conform to the Court's assessment of the adjudicatory viability of arbitration in the particular setting. In any event, given the current climate, it is unlikely that specific congressional proscriptions of arbitration will be forthcoming.

The Court then places the burden of defining subject-matter inarbitrability upon the parties and their lawyers. This, in effect, is the practical contribution of the *Mitsubishi* decision: To avoid surprises and potential malpractice, lawyers must advise their clients to decide whether the reference to "disputes" includes both contractual and statutory conflicts that might arise between the parties during the course of their transaction. If clients want to conserve some ability to seek judicial relief, their agreement to arbitrate must specify that the arbitral clause only provides for the arbitral adjudication of ordinary contractual disputes (such as disagreements about performance, delivery, payment, or the interpretation of the contract). The Court, in effect, anticipates the contractualist theory of arbitration in *Kaplan*: "Nothing...prevents a party from excluding statutory claims from the scope of an agreement to arbitrate." How comprehensive can the exclusion of law and of the legal process become in an arbitration agreement? Can the parties agree to eliminate all forms of judicial supervision, even those specifically mandated by the governing law? Can they agree to eliminate the inarbitrability defense and the public policy exception to enforcement for purposes of their arbitration? Why should the parties be invested with such law-making authority even for purposes of their particular transaction?

Filing a petition for bankruptcy may be the only way to defeat the presumption that statutory claims are arbitrable. Soler did participate in the arbitration, but later filed a petition for bankruptcy reorganization under Chapter 11. The filing of a petition for bankruptcy "halted" the arbitration. Bankruptcy reorganization is perhaps the most effective defense to the obligation to arbitrate claims that a party believes to be unwarranted. In these circumstances, the question becomes whether Soler initiated the filing simply for litigious purposes, whether the bankruptcy resulted from Mitsubishi's failure to seek accommodations within the context of the transaction and from its refusal to allow trans-shipment, or whether Soler—as an economic actor—simply poorly assessed its abilities, misjudged the market, and entered into a transaction that was economically misguided. The filing for bankruptcy protection confirms the evident and substantial disparity of position between the parties both within the transaction and the litigation. It also illustrates that recourse to the courts and the application of antitrust statutes might have redressed the disparity somewhat and salvaged the economic viability of the weaker party, and provided consumers with a local distributor of goods. However interpreted, the petition for bankruptcy arguably may not have constituted a mandatory barrier to the continuation of the arbitral proceedings.

4. Part III of the majority opinion recites the reasoning and doctrine previously established in *Scherk* and *Zapata*. The Court remains committed to the elaboration of bifurcated rules on domestic and international arbitration, although its determination appears to be wavering: "We find it unnecessary [not inapposite or inapplicable] to assess the legitimacy of the *American Safety* doctrine as applied to agreements to arbitrate arising from domestic transactions." The Court's ambivalence (demonstrated again by its further conditional qualification: ". . . even assuming that a contrary result would be forthcoming in a domestic context") anticipates the abandonment of the bifurcated doctrine in *McMahon* and *Rodriguez* where the specialty of transborder circumstances, the gravamen of the holding both in *Scherk* and *Mitsubishi*, is simply cast aside.

The Court devotes a good deal of its considerations in Part III to eviscerating the holding and essential rationale of *American Safety*. The Court notes the four reasons the First Circuit identified to deny submission of antitrust claims to arbitration in domestic litigation. The *American Safety* doctrine still holds sway upon a number of lower federal courts despite the ruling in *Mitsubishi*. The Court has not had occasion to rule on the domestic arbitrability of antitrust disputes. The Court responds to the *American Safety* doctrine by an unwavering proclamation of faith in arbitration. You should evaluate *American Safety* on your own and then assess the Court's critique of the *American Safety* doctrine. Which version has the greater appeal? Wasn't the transaction in *Mitsubishi* troubled by a disparity between the parties and an arbitration agreement that was one-sided on its face? How sympathetic or sensitive do you think the Japanese arbitrators were to Soler's antitrust assertions?

The arbitral tribunal actually consisted of three Japanese lawyers: A former law school dean, a former judge, and a practicing lawyer who had some U.S. legal training and had written on Japanese antitrust law. Would the arbitral litigation in Japan at all resemble a trial proceeding in the United States? Do you believe that the regulatory culture and the antitrust laws in Japan bear any equivalency to their U.S. counterparts? What about the concern regarding private attorneys-general, treble damages, and the discovery features of the applicable U.S. statute? Isn't the Court right to focus upon the nonnational and private character of arbitration? Don't those additional features argue for the inarbitrability of statutory claims? Is the Court being flippant in its assessment of the situation? Is it at all possible that "the statute will continue to serve both its remedial and deterrent function"? Can there be any doubt that the reference of the antitrust claims to arbitration results in a deprivation of rights? Would the Court's reasoning be more plausible in a domestic context in which arbitrators might have the requisite adjudicatory experience and legal and cultural knowledge? Doesn't the reasoning in *Mitsubishi per force* entail a substantial diminution of the status of the antitrust legislation and of law itself? While the implied rejection of extraterritoriality is admirable, is it feasible—politically or legally—when it entails a unilateral divestiture of legal authority in circumstances in which there is no international regime of antitrust regulation to fill the void?

5. There are two technical arguments that appear at the end of Part III of the majority opinion. First, the Court states in a footnote: "[I]n the event

the choice-of-forum and choice-of-law clauses operated in tandem as a prospective waiver of a party's right to pursue statutory remedies for antitrust violations, we would have little hesitation in condemning the agreement as against public policy." Second, in the text of the opinion, the Court observes: "[T]he national courts of the United States will have the opportunity at the award-enforcement stage to ensure that the legitimate interest in the enforcement of the antitrust laws has been addressed."

Both remarks are intended to allay fears that all legal authority in matters of antitrust has been abdicated to international arbitrators. How do you assess the meaning and significance of what the Court is saying in these two passages? Do they constitute effective judicial supervision? Are they intended to do so? As to the first passage, how does it square with the contractualist theory of arbitration? As to the second passage, known as the "second look" doctrine, does it coincide with the obligations contained in Articles III and V of the New York Convention? How do you evaluate the general impact of *Mitsubishi* upon the Convention? The majority states: "The utility of the Convention in promoting the process of international commercial arbitration depends upon the willingness of national courts to let go of matters they normally would think of as their own." What does that remark signify?

6. As noted earlier, Justice Stevens' dissent reflects his extensive acquaintance with and knowledge of the antitrust laws. Toward the end of his dissent, he compares *Mitsubishi* and *Scherk*, stating that *Scherk* involved basically a nonstatutory fraud claim that was "virtually identical to the breach of warranty claim...." Stevens, a Seventh Circuit judge at the time, dissented in *Scherk* at the appellate level. His dissent coincided with the result later reached by the Court. As to *Mitsubishi*, Justice Stevens states that it "implicates our fundamental antitrust policies...." Do you agree with his comparative evaluation of the statutory significance of the two cases? Is there simply a difference in expertise that dictates a different appraisal? Does Justice Stevens inadequately evaluate the international dimension of the two cases?

7. How persuasive is Justice Stevens in arguing that the arbitral clause does not apply to the dispute between Soler and Mitsubishi on the basis of contractual interpretation? Isn't he right that the contract itself limits the scope of the arbitral clause to technical and business disputes where commercial expertise and adjudicatory informality are especially useful and relevant? Which parties in fact have agreed to arbitration? Which contract contains the arbitral clause? Is there a free-floating agreement to arbitrate? Why do you think the majority avoids these considerations? Which methodology makes for good or legitimate law?

8. Justice Stevens notes a reference made by Justice Black in his dissent in *Prima Paint*. According to Cohen and Dayton, *The New Federal Arbitration Law*, 12 VA. L. REV. 265, 281 (1926):

> Not all questions arising out of contracts ought to be arbitrated. It is a remedy peculiarly suited to the disposition of the ordinary disputes between merchants as to questions of fact—quantity, quality, time of delivery, compliance with terms of payment, excuses for non-performance.... It has

a place also in the determination of the simpler questions of law—the questions of law which arise out of these daily relations between merchants as to the passage of title, the existence of warranties, or the questions of law which are complementary to the questions of fact which we have just mentioned. . . .

The foregoing excerpt characterizes, to some degree, Justice Stevens' view of arbitration—at least as it relates to the arbitrability of antitrust claims. Is that assessment an accurate reading of the work of arbitration in the transborder context? What degree of national law and national court intervention should be permitted in the operation of the process of international commercial arbitration? What does the New York Arbitration Convention provide on this question? How do the realities of transborder commercial litigation affect your thinking? Is the majority right? Would a system of advisory opinions between arbitral tribunals and national courts be preferable as a mode of operation? Does or should engaging in international commercial transactions imply a loss of rights created by national law as enforced by national courts? Is this a peculiarly American problem? Are U.S. parties the only international merchants subject to this regime?

9. The domestic case law on arbitration has created a very different adjudicatory role for the process of arbitral adjudication than the one described in Cohen and Dayton's 1926 article. As noted earlier, *McMahon* and *Rodriguez*, for example, have transformed arbitration into a private court system for resolving securities claims. Moreover, Justice Stevens refers to domestic cases decided by the Court that hold Title VII claims and disputes under the Fair Labor Standards Act to be quasi-inarbitrable, *i.e.*, the arbitration of the grievance does not preclude subsequent court action to vindicate statutory rights. These cases describe the operation of the judicially created public policy defense in labor arbitration cases. Although it could be argued that this litigation deals only with domestic matters, the real problem with the example is that the Court has subsequently reversed its position, holding Title VII, RICO, and securities claims under both the 1933 and 1934 Act to be arbitrable. In addition, there has been a corresponding diminution of the effectiveness of the public policy defense in the review of labor arbitral awards. The enabling statutes have not changed, but the Court's reading of congressional intent has been altered considerably in light of the evolving doctrine on arbitration. Arbitration plays a much more fundamental role in the operation of U.S. civil justice than it did in 1985.

Justice Stevens believes that these examples explain the reasons for inarbitrability and that they "apply with special force to the federal policy that is protected by the antitrust laws." The Sherman Antitrust Act has been described by the Court as "a charter of freedom," as a statute with an "extraordinary 'magnitude' of . . . value choices," and as "the Magna Carta of free enterprise." Are these descriptions still applicable in either the domestic or international context? Is there a "unique public interest in the enforcement of antitrust laws"?

The majority opinion notes that federal courts that hold domestic antitrust claims as inarbitrable allow such claims to go to arbitration under a submission agreement. Justice Stevens responds to this point by stating that arbitration may be a "permissible" remedy when the parties have agreed that an antitrust problem exists and when they have had an opportunity "to evaluate the strength of their position." Nonetheless, isn't the majority's reference a particularly damaging blow to the position that the "collective wisdom" of the federal courts is that antitrust laws are vital to the U.S. system and can only be interpreted and applied by courts of law? Aren't general settlement practices that apply in the U.S. system also a strong argument against that position? Does Justice Stevens fail to distinguish the mythology of law from the enforcement of law or does the majority's commitment to the defense of arbitration encourage administrative considerations to be mistaken for high-minded internationalism and fealty to congressional directives?

10. You should also examine and ponder several other features of Justice Stevens' dissent: (1) his reference to arbitral adjudication as "[d]espotic decisionmaking" and the general tenor of his view of arbitration that follows; (2) his assessment of the significance of the New York Convention to the resolution of the issue in *Mitsubishi*; (3) his willingness to apply U.S. antitrust laws extraterritorially; (4) his view that the majority distorts the purposes and function of arbitration through its "repeated incantation of the high ideals of 'international arbitration' "; and (5) his characterization at the end of his opinion of the plight of a U.S. national who is "dispatched" to arbitrate a public law claim in a foreign land under an alien procedure.

11. The ruling in *Mitsubishi* generated considerable commentary. One exchange involved substantial disagreement not only about the outcome, but also about its purported meaning. The initial commentator criticized the content, reasoning, and determination in the case—not unlike some of the remarks contained in these notes and questions. Even if the internationalism espoused by the Court were attractive as a foundation for articulating legal rules, it was argued, the Court did a disservice to law and the process of international commercial arbitration by failing to establish constraints upon the jurisdictional and subject-matter reach of the arbitral process. *Scherk*, in effect, compelled the Court to decide *Mitsubishi* with a sense of balance and a measure of restraint. The compromise of rights and extinguishment of national regulatory authority over arbitration and substantive priority areas contributed to the "lawlessness" of the transborder environment and certainly was not commanded by treaty obligations. The Court's would-be fixation on arbitration induced a wrong-headed determination.

There were two responses, each authored by a distinguished international lawyer with substantial credentials in the law and practice of international commercial arbitration. The first response saw the criticism of the *Mitsubishi* decision as contrary to the reigning spirit of internationalism and to the operative realities of the international arbitral process. The Court's reliance upon the skills and expertise of international arbitrators, it was argued, was not misplaced; these arbitrators could evaluate the pertinent statutes, and the character of the claims, and provide determinations that were reflective of the interests of international commercial justice. Disrupting the operation of the process of transborder commercial adjudication by the reference of statutory claims to national courts would undermine the arbitral process and global commerce. The process works and its self-regulatory character prevents abuse.

The second response added yet another and highly provocative dimension to the debate. The third commentator argued that the interpretation of the Court's holding in *Mitsubishi* had been overstated. The Court did not hold that antitrust claims were arbitrable in international contracts, but rather that statutory claims made as a counterclaim to contractual liability could be disregarded by international arbitrators who would rule only upon the principal contractual claims. This interpretation represented the most lucid and ingenious disposition of the question that was presented to the Court in *Mitsubishi*. It accounts for the sometimes "wayward" litigious strategies in which desperate or recalcitrant parties engage to find some basis for defense. It is proportionate to the objectives of the arbitral process (the resolution of contractual liabilities) and to the need to find a commercial rule of decision. Finally, it protects the integrity of the process by having it avoid the taint of usurping public legal authority and it thereby safeguards the autonomy and international commercial mission of the process.

You should consider these three different positions on the meaning and significance of the *Mitsubishi* opinion. Do you identify more readily with one and not the others? Is the reality of the situation so complex that no one interpretation can account for all of the ramifications of the decision? Does the doctrinal embellishment simply cloud the issue? Is there any mistaking the result or the Court's direction? What advice would you give a client in light of the ruling in and commentary on *Mitsubishi*?

On the debate, *see* Thomas Carbonneau, *The Exuberant Pathway to Quixotic Internationalism: Assessing the Folly of Mitsubishi*, 19 VAND. J. TRANS L. 265 (1986); Andreas Lowenfeld, *The Mitsubishi Case: Another View*, 2 ARB. INT'L 178 (1986); Hans Smit, *Mitsubishi: It is Not What it Seems To Be*, 4 J. INT'L ARB. 7 (1987).

12. The Court's "in tandem" and "prospective waiver" argument in *Mitsubishi*, along with the influence of its *Mitsubishi* holding in *McMahon* and *Rodriguez*, have generated some complicated propositions in subsequent decisions by the lower federal courts. The excerpt from *Roby* is illustrative of this development. Does the Second Circuit properly understand the Court's "second look" doctrine? Does the court apply the doctrine as intended to the facts of *Roby*? Is the court raising a straw argument that it proceeds to knock down as soon as it is raised? Although the plaintiffs or "names" in *Roby* are not deprived of remedies or even the opportunity for possible substantial relief, aren't they just as evidently deprived of the special protections and rights guaranteed by the U.S. securities laws to American investors? What about the testimony of the English expert who opines that English conflict rules prohibit the recourse to foreign statutory law? Why doesn't the court make more of this seemingly centrally-important factor? Why should English law and remedies, and not U.S. statutes, set the standard for adjudicating international securities claims involving a large number of U.S. investors? English law appears much less tolerant and internationalist on this score. Does the Second Circuit's reasoning call into question the Court's decisional law on transborder litigation, from *The Bremen* to *Mitsubishi*? Why is the

Second Circuit so solicitous of Lloyd's interest and position in the circumstances?

ROBY v. CORPORATION OF LLOYD'S

996 F.2d 1353, 1356–57, 1361–66 (2d Cir. 1993).

(footnotes omitted)

[. . .]

Appellants, all American citizens or residents, are more than one hundred "Names" in the Corporation of Lloyd's (Lloyd's). Loosely speaking, Names are investors in Lloyd's syndicates, the entities that nominally underwrite insurance risk. . . . Appellant Names (Roby Names) alleged in their consolidated complaint that they have suffered severe financial loss as a result of appellees' violations of the Securities Act of 1933 . . . , the Securities Exchange Act of 1934 . . . , and the Racketeer Influenced and Corrupt Organizations Act. . . . This opinion, however, addresses only the Roby Names' contention on appeal that their disputes with Lloyd's and Lloyd's entities should be litigated in the United States despite a host of contract clauses that appear to bind them to arbitrate in England under English law. The district court held that those contract clauses must be enforced and therefore dismissed the Roby Names' complaint for improper venue. The Roby Names contend that the district court erred because (1) the clauses by their very terms do not protect certain defendants and do not cover the substance of appellants' complaints, and (2) the clauses are unenforceable because they effectively waive compliance with the United States securities laws, contrary to the antiwaiver provisions of those laws and the public policy reflected by them. . . .

[. . .]

II. *Application of the Securities Laws*

The Roby Names argue that the public policy codified in the antiwaiver provisions of the securities laws renders unenforceable any agreement that effectively eliminates compliance with those laws. . . . According to the undisputed testimony of a British attorney, neither an English court nor an English arbitrator would apply the United States securities laws, because English conflict of law rules do not permit recognition of foreign tort or statutory law. From this, the Roby Names conclude that the contract clauses work to waive compliance with the securities laws and therefore are void.

We note at the outset that *Wilko v. Swan* . . . has been squarely overruled. . . . *Wilko* held that an agreement to arbitrate future controversies was void under the antiwaiver provision of the Securities Act. We do not doubt that judicial hostility to arbitration has receded dramatically since 1953 and that the arbitral forum is perfectly competent to protect litigants' substantive rights. In the words of the *Mitsubishi* Court, quoted by both the *Rodriguez* and *McMahon* Courts, "[b]y agreeing to arbitrate a statutory claim, a party does not forgo the substantive rights afforded by the statute; it only submits to their resolution in an arbitral, rather than a judicial, forum." ... If the Roby Names objected merely to the choice of an arbitral rather than a judicial forum, we would reject their claim immediately, citing *Rodriguez* and *McMahon*. However, the Roby Names argue that they have been forced to forgo the *substantive* protections afforded by the securities laws, not simply the judicial forum. We therefore do not believe that *Rodriguez* and *McMahon* are controlling and must look elsewhere to determine whether parties may contract away their substantive rights under the securities laws.

The Tenth Circuit recently addressed this exact issue in a similar context in *Riley v. Kingsley Underwriting Agencies, Ltd.* ... [T]he *Riley* Court concluded that "[w]hen an agreement is truly international, as here, and reflects numerous contacts with the foreign forum, the Supreme Court has quite clearly held that the parties' choice of law and forum selection provisions will be given effect." ... While we agree with the ultimate result in *Riley*, we are reluctant to interpret the Supreme Court's precedent quite so broadly.

A. *Presumption of Validity*

The Supreme Court certainly has indicated that forum selection and choice of law clauses are presumptively valid where the underlying transaction is fundamentally international in character....

This presumption of validity may be overcome, however, by a clear showing that the clauses are " 'unreasonable' under the circumstances." ... The Supreme Court has construed this exception narrowly: forum selection and choice of law clauses are "unreasonable" (1) if their incorporation into the agreement was the result of fraud or overreaching ...; (2) if the complaining party "will for all practical purposes be deprived of his day in court," due to the grave inconvenience or unfairness of the selected forum ...; (3) if the fundamental unfairness of the chosen law may deprive the plaintiff of a remedy ...; or (4) if the clauses contravene a strong public policy of the forum state....

In this case, we can easily dispose of the first two factors. The Roby Names do not contend that they were fraudulently induced into agreeing to the forum selection, choice of law or arbitration clauses. Nor do we believe it gravely inconvenient for the Roby Names to litigate in London; they found it convenient enough to travel there for their mandatory interviews, and, in any event, many of them presently are prosecuting actions there. Moreover, nothing in the record suggests that the English courts would be biased or otherwise unfair, and United States courts consistently have found them to be neutral and just forums.... Finally, the Roby Names have not presented any convincing evidence that the chosen arbitral forum would be biased in any way.

As to the third factor, we note that it is not enough that the foreign law or procedure merely be different or less favorable than that of the

United States. . . . Instead, the question is whether the application of the foreign law presents a danger that the Roby Names "will be deprived of *any* remedy or treated unfairly." . . . As we explain below in section C, we believe the Roby Names have ample remedies under English law.

B.   Public Policy

We depart somewhat from the *Riley* Court with respect to the fourth factor. We believe that there is a serious question whether United States public policy has been subverted by the Lloyd's clauses. In this section we explain our concerns; in section C below we resolve those concerns. Ultimately, we hold that the presumption of validity has not been overcome.

The Supreme Court in *The Bremen* wrote, "[a] contractual choice-of-forum clause should be held unenforceable if enforcement would contravene a strong public policy of the forum in which suit is brought." . . . By including antiwaiver provisions in the securities laws, Congress made clear its intention that the public policies incorporated into those laws should not be thwarted.

The framers of the securities laws were concerned principally with reversing the common law rule favoring "caveat emptor." . . . To this end, the securities laws are aimed at prospectively protecting American investors from injury by demanding "full and fair disclosure" from issuers. . . . Private actions exist under the securities laws not because Congress had an overwhelming desire to shift losses after the fact, but rather because private actions provide a potent means of deterring the exploitation of American investors. . . . We believe therefore that the public policies of the securities laws would be contravened if the applicable foreign law failed adequately to deter issuers from exploiting American investors.

In this sense, the securities laws somewhat resemble the antitrust laws at issue in *Mitsubishi*. The *Mitsubishi* Court enforced a clause providing that all disputes arising under a contract between a Puerto Rican corporation and a Japanese corporation be submitted for arbitration by the Japan Commercial Arbitration Association. The Court recognized that private actions under the Sherman Act . . . play a "central role" in promoting the national interest in a competitive economy. . . . Like private actions in the securities context, private actions under the Sherman Act serve primarily a deterrent purpose. . . . Nevertheless, the *Mitsubishi* Court held that a Japanese arbitration panel, *applying United States antitrust law*, adequately would further the deterrent purpose of the Sherman Act, despite the panel's lack of allegiance to United States' interests. . . . The Court indicated quite clearly in dicta, however, that "in the event the choice-of-forum and choice-of-law clauses operated in tandem as a prospective waiver of a party's right to pursue statutory remedies for antitrust violations, we would have little hesitation in condemning the agreement as against public policy." . . .

We are concerned in the present case that the Roby Names' contract clauses may operate "in tandem" as a prospective waiver of the statutory remedies for securities violations, thereby circumventing the strong and expansive public policy in deterring such violations. We are cognizant of the important reasons for enforcing such clauses in Lloyd's' agreements. Lloyd's is a British concern which raises capital in over 80 nations. Its operations are clearly international in scope. There can be no doubt that the contract clauses mitigate the uncertainty regarding choice of law and forum inherent in the multinational affairs of Lloyd's. Comity also weighs in favor of enforcing the clauses. Yet we do not believe that a United States court can in good conscience enforce clauses that subvert a strong national policy, particularly one that for over fifty years has served as the foundation for the United States financial markets and business community. In this case, the victims of Lloyd's' alleged securities violations are hundreds of individual American investors, most of whom were actively solicited in the United States by Lloyd's representatives. We believe that if the Roby Names were able to show that available remedies in England are insufficient to deter British issuers from exploiting American investors through fraud, misrepresentation or inadequate disclosure, we would not hesitate to condemn the choice of law, forum selection and arbitration clauses as against public policy. For the reasons set forth in section C below, however, we conclude that the Roby Names have failed to make such a showing.

C. Availability of Adequate Remedies

We are satisfied not only that the Roby Names have several adequate remedies in England to vindicate their substantive rights, but also that in *this* case the policies of ensuring full and fair disclosure and deterring the exploitation of United States investors have not been subverted. We address the fraud and misrepresentation claims first.

1. Fraud and Misrepresentation

English common law provides remedies for knowing or reckless deceit, negligent misrepresentation, and even innocent misrepresentation. Moreover, the Misrepresentation Act of 1967 provides some additional statutory remedies.... While the Roby Names might have been able to sue "controlling persons" under the United States securities laws and establish liability without proving reliance, it certainly is not unfair for English law to require proof of actual misconduct and reliance. Furthermore we are skeptical that "controlling person" liability could be established against many of the defendants here....

In any event, the available remedies are adequate and the potential recoveries substantial. This is particularly true given the low scienter requirements under English misrepresentation law (*e.g.*, negligence, "innocence"). Moreover, together with the contractual obligations imposing certain fiduciary and similar duties on Members and Managing Agents, we believe that the available remedies and potential damages recoveries suffice to deter deception of American investors.

In this context we also note that many of the so-called "misrepresentations" the Roby Names allege are really complaints about the conduct of Lloyd's' affairs rather than complaints about fraudulent reporting. Thus, for instance, while it may be true that the defendants kept insufficient reserves and permitted "questionable accounting practices," failure to convey this information to the Roby Names is more a violation of the letter of the securities laws than their spirit, because the complaints really address Lloyd's' misconduct *after* securities are sold. We do not believe that these complaints implicate the public policy of the securities laws.

Finally, although, as the Roby Names observe, section 14 of the Lloyd's Act of 1982 exempts the Corporation of Lloyd's (and its officers and employees) from liability, no other entity within Lloyd's is exempt. Moreover, even the Corporation of Lloyd's is not exempt for acts "done in bad faith." Furthermore, as a self-regulating organization, we cannot say that Lloyd's' own bylaws will not insure the honesty and forthrightness that American investors deserve and expect. We conclude that the Roby Names have adequate remedies in England to vindicate their statutory fraud and misrepresentation claims.

2. *Disclosure*

[. . .]

While we do not doubt that the United States securities laws would provide the Roby Names with a greater variety of defendants and a greater chance of success due to lighter scienter and causation requirements, we are convinced that there are ample and just remedies under English law. Moreover, we cannot say that the policies underlying our securities laws will be offended by the application of English law. In this case, the Roby Names have entered into contracts that require substantial disclosure by both the Members' and Managing Agents. The specter of liability for breach of contract should act as an adequate deterrent to the exploitation of American investors. The well developed English law of fraud and misrepresentation likewise adequately requires that the disclosure be "fair."

III. *APPLICATION OF RICO*

That RICO provides treble damages and seeks to deter persistent misconduct does not dissuade us from our view that the Roby Names' contract clauses must be enforced. As we have explained, the Roby Names have adequate potential remedies in England and there are significant disincentives to deter English issuers from unfairly exploiting American investors. Although the remedies and disincentives might be magnified by the application of RICO, we cannot say that application of English law would subvert the policies underlying that statute.

CONCLUSION

For the foregoing reasons we hold that the Roby Names' contract clauses cover the scope of, and the parties named in, the complaint and that the Roby Names have remedies under English law adequate not only to vindicate their substantive rights but also to protect the public policies established by the United States securities laws.

[...]

* * *

The Ninth Circuit's holding in *Simula, Inc. v. Autoliv, Inc.*, 175 F.3d 716 (9th Cir. 1999), is in keeping with the views advanced in *Roby*. It is unlikely that the deprivation of rights under foreign law will ever be significant enough to allow the courts to refuse enforcement to an arbitration agreement, consented to in some fashion by the parties.

In 1992, Simula invented the Inflatable Tubular Structure (ITS), a side impact protection air bag system for automobiles. In 1993, Simula approached BMW about purchasing the ITS. BMW instructed Simula to work through Autoliv to present its technology and consider its integration into BMW cars. Simula and Autoliv signed a nondisclosure agreement whereby Simula agreed to disclose to Autoliv confidential, proprietary, and trade secret information regarding the ITS. Under the contract, Simula was to manufacture the ITS and give a conditional license to Autoliv, who would integrate the ITS into the BMW automobile. In 1994, Autoliv (with Simula's permission) presented the Simula ITS to Mercedes Benz—a competitor of BMW. Thereafter, at Mercedes–Benz's suggestion, Autoliv began to develop an inflatable product of its own. According to Simula, Autoliv began to disparage the ITS and promote its own product. Simula filed suit and Autoliv moved to compel arbitration. The district court held that all of Simula's claims against Autoliv were subject to the arbitration clause in their contract because they all related to, derived from, and arose in connection with that contract.

The court recognized that the FAA governed the question of arbitrability, and that "[a]ny doubts concerning the scope of arbitrable issues should be resolved in favor of arbitration." In this case, the scope of the arbitration clause was at issue. The arbitration agreement stated that "[a]ll disputes arising in connection with th[e] Agreement [should] be finally settled [by arbitration]." The Ninth Circuit had previously held that an arbitration clause stating that "any and all disputes arising under the arrangements contemplated hereunder" must be interpreted liberally. "Every court that has construed the phrase 'arising in connection with' in an arbitration clause has interpreted that language broadly." The court likewise held that the phrase "reaches every dispute between the parties having a significant relationship to the contract and all disputes having their origin or genesis in the contract."

"To require arbitration, Simula's factual allegations need[ed] only 'touch matters' covered by the contract containing the arbitration clause."

Both the U.S. Supreme Court and the Ninth Circuit previously held that antitrust violations such as the ones at issue here were arbitrable. "[T]he most minimal indication of the parties' intent to arbitrate must be given full effect, especially in international disputes [such as the one at issue here]." The resolution of Simula's antitrust claims "necessitate[d] interpreting the 1995 Agreement to determine its meaning and whether the contracts between Autoliv and Simula actually [did] suppress competition as alleged."

The court rejected Simula's argument that the enforcement of the arbitration clause would deprive it of remedies provided solely by antitrust law, declining to follow the dictum footnote in *Mitsubishi* that stated that, "in the event the choice-of-forum and choice-of-law clauses operate[ ] in tandem as a prospective waiver of a party's right to pursue statutory remedies for antitrust violations, [the court] would have little hesitation in condemning the agreement as against public policy." The court noted that it had previously transferred a dispute to a British court, despite the fact that the plaintiff's statutory rights would not be expressly available under British law. "[T]he applicable standard should be whether the law of the transferee court is so deficient that the plaintiffs would be deprived of any reasonable recourse." The court held that the law applied by the arbitration panel in this case "would afford sufficient antitrust remedies." "[R]emedies in a foreign forum need not be identical [to United States remedies]; to require that 'American standards of fairness ... must govern the controversy demeans the standards of justice elsewhere in the world, and unnecessarily exalts the primacy of United States law over the laws of other countries.' "

5. A CONFLICT BETWEEN THE FAA AND COGSA?

VIMAR SEGUROS Y REASEGUROS, S.A. v. M/V SKY REEFER

515 U.S. 528, 115 S.Ct. 2322, 132 L.Ed.2d 462 (1995).

(footnotes omitted)

JUSTICE KENNEDY delivered the opinion of the Court.

This case requires us to interpret the Carriage of Goods by Sea Act (COGSA) ... as it relates to a contract containing a clause requiring arbitration in a foreign country. The question is whether a foreign arbitration clause in a bill of lading is invalid under COGSA because it lessens liability in the sense that COGSA prohibits. Our holding that COGSA does not forbid selection of the foreign forum makes it unnecessary to resolve the further question whether the Federal Arbitration Act ... would override COGSA were it interpreted otherwise. In our view, the relevant provisions of COGSA and the FAA are in accord, not in conflict.

I.

The contract at issue in this case is a standard form bill of lading to evidence the purchase of a shipload of Moroccan oranges and lemons. The purchaser was Bacchus Associates (Bacchus), a New York partnership that distributes fruit at wholesale throughout the Northeastern United States. Bacchus dealt with Galaxie Negoce, S.A. (Galaxie), a Moroccan fruit supplier. Bacchus contracted with Galaxie to purchase the shipload of fruit and chartered a ship to transport it from Morocco to Massachusetts. The ship was the M/V Sky Reefer, a refrigerated cargo ship owned by M.H. Maritima, S.A., a Panamanian company, and time-chartered to Nichiro Gyogyo Kaisha, Ltd., a Japanese company. Stevedores hired by Galaxie loaded and stowed the cargo. As is customary in these types of transactions, when it received the cargo from Galaxie, Nichiro as carrier issued a form bill of lading to Galaxie as shipper and consignee. Once the ship set sail from Morocco, Galaxie tendered the bill of lading to Bacchus according to the terms of a letter of credit posted in Galaxie's favor.

Among the rights and responsibilities set out in the bill of lading were arbitration and choice-of-law clauses. Clause 3, entitled "Governing Law and Arbitration," provided:

"(1) The contract evidenced by or contained in this Bill of Lading shall be governed by the Japanese law.

"(2) Any dispute arising from this Bill of Lading shall be referred to arbitration in Tokyo by the Tokyo Maritime Arbitration Commission (TO-MAC) of The Japan Shipping Exchange, Inc., in accordance with the rules of TOMAC and any amendment thereto, and the award given by the arbitrators shall be final and binding on both parties." . . .

When the vessel's hatches were opened for discharge in Massachusetts, Bacchus discovered that thousands of boxes of oranges had shifted in the cargo holds, resulting in over $1 million damage. Bacchus received $733,442.90 compensation from petitioner Vimar Seguros y Reaseguros (Vimar Seguros), Bacchus' marine cargo insurer that became subrogated pro tanto to Bacchus' rights. Petitioner and Bacchus then brought suit against Maritima in personam and M/V Sky Reefer in rem in the District Court for the District of Massachusetts under the bill of lading. These defendants, respondents here, moved to stay the action and compel arbitration in Tokyo under clause 3 of the bill of lading and § 3 of the FAA, which requires courts to stay proceedings and enforce arbitration agreements covered by the Act. Petitioner and Bacchus opposed the motion, arguing the arbitration clause was unenforceable under the FAA both because it was a contract of adhesion and because it violated COGSA § 3(8). The premise of the latter argument was that the inconvenience and costs of proceeding in Japan would "lesse[n] . . . liability" as those terms are used in COGSA.

[. . .]

II.

The parties devote much of their argument to the question whether COGSA or the FAA has priority.... There is no conflict unless COGSA by its own terms nullifies a foreign arbitration clause, and we choose to address that issue rather than assume nullification *arguendo....* We consider the two arguments made by petitioner. The first is that a foreign arbitration clause lessens COGSA liability by increasing the transaction costs of obtaining relief. The second is that there is a risk foreign arbitrators will not apply COGSA.

A

The leading case for invalidation of a foreign forum selection clause is ... *Indussa Corp. v. S.S. Ranborg,* 377 F.2d 200 (1967) (en banc). The court there found that COGSA invalidated a clause designating a foreign judicial forum because it "puts 'a high hurdle' in the way of enforcing liability, and thus is an effective means for carriers to secure settlements lower than if cargo [owners] could sue in a convenient forum".... The court observed "there could be no assurance that [the foreign court] would apply [COGSA] in the same way as would an American tribunal subject to the uniform control of the Supreme Court." ... Following *Indussa,* the Courts of Appeals without exception have invalidated foreign forum selection clauses under § 3(8).... As foreign arbitration clauses are but a subset of foreign forum selection clauses in general, ... the *Indussa* holding has been extended to foreign arbitration clauses as well.... The logic of that extension would be quite defensible, but we cannot endorse the reasoning or the conclusion of the *Indussa* rule itself.

The determinative provision in COGSA, examined with care, does not support the arguments advanced first in *Indussa* and now by the petitioner. Section 3(8) of COGSA provides as follows:

> "Any clause, covenant, or agreement in a contract of carriage relieving the carrier or the ship from liability for loss or damage to or in connection with the goods, arising from negligence, fault, or failure in the duties or obligations provided in this section, or lessening such liability otherwise than as provided in this chapter, shall be null and void and of no effect."...

The liability that may not be lessened is "liability for loss or damage ... arising from negligence, fault, or failure in the duties or obligations provided in this section." The statute thus addresses the lessening of the specific liability imposed by the Act, without addressing the separate question of the means and costs of enforcing that liability. The difference is that between explicit statutory guarantees and the procedure for enforcing them, between applicable liability principles and the forum in which they are to be vindicated.

The liability imposed on carriers under COGSA 3 is defined by explicit standards of conduct, and it is designed to correct specific abuses by carriers. In the 19th century it was a prevalent practice for common carriers to insert clauses in bills of lading exempting themselves from liability for damage or loss, limiting the period in which plaintiffs had to present their notice of claim or bring suit, and capping any damages awards per package.... Thus, § 3 ... requires that the carrier "exercise due diligence to ... [m]ake the ship seaworthy" and "[p]roperly man, equip, and supply the ship" before and at the beginning of the voyage, § 3(1), "properly and carefully load, handle, stow, carry, keep, care for, and discharge the goods carried," § 3(2), and issue a bill of lading with specified contents, § 3(3).... Section 3(6) allows the cargo owner to provide notice of loss or damage within three days and to bring suit within one year. These are the substantive obligations and particular procedures that § 3(8) prohibits a carrier from altering to its advantage in a bill of lading. Nothing in this section, however, suggests that the statute prevents the parties from agreeing to enforce these obligations in a particular forum. By its terms, it establishes certain duties and obligations, separate and apart from the mechanisms for their enforcement.

Petitioner's contrary reading of § 3(8) is undermined by the Court's construction of a similar statutory provision in *Carnival Cruise Lines, Inc. v. Shute*.... There a number of Washington residents argued that a Florida forum selection clause contained in a cruise ticket should not be enforced because the expense and inconvenience of litigation in Florida would "caus[e] plaintiffs unreasonable hardship in asserting their rights" ... in violation of the Limitation of Vessel Owner's Liability Act.... We observed that the clause "does not purport to limit petitioner's liability for negligence" ... and enforced the agreement over the dissent's argument, based in part on the *Indussa* line of cases, that the cost and inconvenience of traveling thousands of miles "lessens or weakens [plaintiffs'] ability to recover."...

If the question whether a provision lessens liability were answered by reference to the costs and inconvenience to the cargo owner, there would be no principled basis for distinguishing national from foreign arbitration clauses. Even if it were reasonable to read § 3(8) to make a distinction based on travel time, airfare, and hotel bills, these factors are not susceptible of a simple and enforceable distinction between domestic and foreign forums. Requiring a Seattle cargo owner to arbitrate in New York likely imposes more costs and burdens than a foreign arbitration clause requiring it to arbitrate in Vancouver. It would be unwieldy and unsupported by the terms or policy of the statute to require courts to proceed case by case to tally the costs and burdens to particular plaintiffs in light of their means, the size of their claims, and the relative burden on the carrier.

Our reading of "lessening such liability" to exclude increases in the transaction costs of litigation also finds support in the goals of the Brussels Convention for the Unification of Certain Rules Relating to Bills of Lading ... on which COGSA is modeled. Sixty-six countries, including the United States and Japan, are now parties to the Convention ... and it appears that none has interpreted its enactment of § 3(8) of the Hague Rules to prohibit foreign forum selection clauses.... In light of the fact that COGSA is the culmination of a multilateral effort "to establish uniform ocean bills of lading to govern the rights and liabilities of carriers and shippers *inter se* in international trade,"... we decline to interpret our version of the Hague Rules in a manner contrary to every other nation to have addressed this issue....

It would also be out of keeping with the objects of the Convention for the courts of this country to interpret COGSA to disparage the authority or competence of international forums for dispute resolution. Petitioner's skepticism over the ability of foreign arbitrators to apply COGSA or the Hague Rules, and its reliance on this aspect of *Indussa* ... must give way to contemporary principles of international comity and commercial practice. As the Court observed in *The Bremen v. Zapata Off–Shore Co.* ... the historical judicial resistance to foreign forum selection clauses "has little place in an era when ... businesses once essentially local now operate in world markets."... "The expansion of American business and industry will hardly be encouraged," we explained, "if, notwithstanding solemn contracts, we insist on a parochial concept that all disputes must be resolved under our laws and in our courts." ... *See Mitsubishi Motors Corp. v. Soler Chrysler–Plymouth, Inc.* ... (if international arbitral institutions "are to take a central place in the international legal order, national courts will need to 'shake off the old judicial hostility to arbitration,' and also their customary and understandable unwillingness to cede jurisdiction of a claim arising under domestic law to a foreign or transnational tribunal")...; *Scherk v. Alberto–Culver Co*.... ("A parochial refusal by the courts of one country to enforce an international arbitration agreement" would frustrate "the orderliness and predictability essential to any international business transaction")....

That the forum here is arbitration only heightens the irony of petitioner's argument, for the FAA is also based in part on an international convention.... If the United States is to be able to gain the benefits of international accords and have a role as a trusted partner in multilateral endeavors, its courts should be most cautious before interpreting its domestic legislation in such manner as to violate international agreements. That concern counsels against construing COGSA to nullify foreign arbitration clauses because of inconvenience to the plaintiff or insular distrust of the ability of foreign arbitrators to apply the law.

B

Petitioner's second argument against enforcement of the Japanese arbitration clause is that there is no guarantee foreign arbitrators will apply COGSA. This objection raises a concern of substance. The central guarantee of § 3(8) is that the terms of a bill of landing [sic] may not relieve the carrier of the obligations or diminish the legal duties specified by the Act. The relevant question, therefore, is whether the substantive law to be applied will reduce the carrier's obligations to the cargo owner below what COGSA guarantees....

Petitioner argues that the arbitrators will follow the Japanese Hague Rules, which, petitioner contends, lessen respondents' liability in at least one significant respect. The Japanese version of the Hague Rules, it is said, provides the carrier with a defense based on the acts or omissions of the stevedores hired by the shipper, Galaxie ... [while COGSA] ... makes nondelegable the carrier's obligation to "properly and carefully ... stow ... the goods carried[.]" ...

Whatever the merits of petitioner's comparative reading of COGSA and its Japanese counterpart, its claim is premature. At this interlocutory stage it is not established what law the arbitrators will apply to petitioner's claims or that petitioner will receive diminished protection as a result. The arbitrators may conclude that COGSA applies of its own force or that Japanese law does not apply so that, under another clause of the bill of lading, COGSA controls. Respondents seek only to enforce the arbitration agreement. The district court has retained jurisdiction over the case and "will have the opportunity at the award-enforcement stage to ensure that the legitimate interest in the enforcement of the ... laws has been addressed." *Mitsubishi Motors*.... Were there no subsequent opportunity for review and were we persuaded that "the choice-of-forum and choice-of-law clauses operated in tandem as a prospective waiver of a party's right to pursue statutory remedies ..., we would have little hesitation in condemning the agreement as against public policy." *Mitsubishi Motors*.... [M]ere speculation that the foreign arbitrators might apply Japanese law which, depending on the proper construction of COGSA, might reduce respondents' legal obligations, does not in and of itself lessen liability under COGSA § 3(8).

Because we hold that foreign arbitration clauses in bills of lading are not invalid under COGSA in all circumstances, both the FAA and COGSA may be given full effect. The judgment of the Court of Appeals is affirmed, and the case is remanded for further proceedings consistent with this opinion.

It is so ordered.

JUSTICE BREYER took no part in the consideration or decision of this case.

JUSTICE O'CONNOR, concurring in the judgment.

I agree with what I understand to be the two basic points made in the Court's opinion. First, I agree that the language of ... COGSA ... and our decision in *Carnival Cruise Lines* ... preclude a holding that the increased cost of litigating in a distant forum, without more, can lessen liability within the meaning of COGSA § 3(8).... Second, I agree that, because the District Court has retained jurisdiction over this case while the arbitration proceeds, any claim of lessening of liability that might arise out of the arbitrators' interpretation of the bill of lading's choice of law clause, or out of their application of COGSA, is premature.... Those two points suffice to affirm the decision below.

Because the Court's opinion appears to do more, however, I concur only in the judgment. Foreign arbitration clauses of the kind presented here do not divest domestic courts of jurisdiction, unlike true foreign forum selection clauses such as that considered in *Indussa*.... That difference is an important one—it is, after all, what leads the Court to dismiss much of petitioner's argument as premature—and we need not decide today whether *Indussa*, insofar as it relied on considerations other than the increased cost of litigating in a distant forum, retains any vitality in the context of true foreign forum selection clauses.... As the Court notes, "[f]ollowing *Indussa*, the Courts of Appeals without exception have invalidated foreign forum selection clauses under § 3(8)[.]" ... I would prefer to disturb that unbroken line of authority only to the extent necessary to decide this case.

JUSTICE STEVENS, dissenting.

The Carriage of Goods by Sea Act (COGSA), enacted in 1936 as a supplement to the 1893 Harter Act, regulates the terms of bills of lading issued by ocean carriers transporting cargo to or from ports of the United States....

Petitioners in this case challenge the enforceability of a foreign arbitration clause, coupled with a choice-of-foreign-law clause, in a bill of lading.... The bill, issued by the Japanese carrier, provides (1) that the transaction " 'shall be governed by Japanese law,' " and (2) that any dispute arising from the bill shall be arbitrated in Tokyo.... Under the construction of COGSA that has been uniformly followed by the Court[s] of Appeals and endorsed by scholarly commentary for decades, both of those clauses are unenforceable against the shipper because they "relieve" or "lessen" the liability of the carrier. Nevertheless, relying almost entirely on a recent case involving a domestic forum selection clause that was not even covered by COGSA, *Carnival Cruise Lines*..., the Court today unwisely discards settled law and adopts a novel construction of § 3(8).

I.

In the 19th century it was common practice for ship owners to issue bills of lading that included stipulations exempting themselves from liability for losses occasioned by the negligence of their employees. Because a bill of lading was (and is) a contract of adhesion, which a shipper must accept or else find another means to transport his goods, shippers were in no position to bargain around these no-liability clauses. Although the English courts enforced the stipulations, ... this Court concluded, even prior to the 1893 enactment of the Harter Act, that they were "contrary to public policy, and consequently void."...

Section 1 of the Harter Act makes it unlawful for the master or owner of any vessel transporting cargo between ports of the United States and foreign ports to insert in any bill of lading any clause whereby the carrier "shall be relieved from liability for loss or damage arising from negligence." In *Knott v. Botany Mills*, 179 U.S. 69, 21 S.Ct. 30, 45 L.Ed. 90 (1900), we were presented with the question whether that prohibition applied to a bill of lading containing a choice-of-law clause designating British law as controlling. . . .

The Court's holding that the choice-of-law clause was invalid rested entirely on the Harter Act's prohibition against relieving the carrier from liability. . . . Since *Knott*, courts have consistently understood the Harter Act to create a flat ban on foreign choice-of-law clauses in bills of lading. . . . Courts have also consistently found such clauses invalid under COGSA, which embodies an even broader prohibition against clauses "relieving" or "lessening" a carrier's liability. . . .

[. . .]

. . . In *Indussa*, the bill of lading contained a provision requiring disputes to be resolved in Norway under Norwegian law. Judge Friendly first remarked on the harsh consequence of "requiring an American consignee claiming damages in the modest sum of $2600 to journey some 4200 miles to a court having a different legal system and employing another language." . . . The decision, however, rested not only on the impact of the provision on a relatively small claim, but also on a fair reading of the broad language in COGSA. Judge Friendly explained:

> "[Section] 3(8) of COGSA says that 'any clause, covenant, or agreement in a contract of carriage * * * lessening [the carrier's liability for negligence, fault, or dereliction of statutory duties] otherwise than as provided in this Act, shall be null and void and of no effect.' From a practical standpoint, to require an American plaintiff to assert his claim only in a distant court lessens the liability of the carrier quite substantially, particularly when the claim is small. Such a clause puts 'a high hurdle' in the way of enforcing liability . . . and thus is an effective means for carriers to secure settlements lower than if cargo could sue in a convenient forum. A clause making a claim triable only in a foreign court would almost certainly lessen liability if the law which the court would apply was neither the Carriage of Goods by Sea Act nor the Hague Rules. Even when the foreign court would apply one or the other of these regimes, requiring trial abroad might lessen the carrier's liability since there could be no assurance that it would apply them in the same way as would an American tribunal subject to the uniform control of the Supreme Court, and § 3(8) can well be read as covering a potential and not simply a demonstrable lessening of liability." . . .

As the Court notes, . . . the Courts of Appeals without exception have followed *Indussa*. In the 1975 edition of their treatise, Gilmore and Black also endorsed its holding, adding this comment:

> "Cogsa allows a freedom of contracting out of its terms, but only in the direction of increasing the shipowner's liabilities, and never in the direction of diminishing them. This apparent onesidedness is a commonsense recognition of the inequality in bargaining power which both Harter and Cogsa were designed to redress, and of the fact that one of the great objectives of both Acts is to prevent the impairment of the value and

negotiability of the ocean bill of lading. Obviously, the latter result can never ensue from the increase of the carrier's duties."...

Thus, our interpretation of maritime law prior to the enactment of the Harter Act, our reading of that statute in *Knott*, and the federal courts' consistent interpretation of COGSA, buttressed by scholarly recognition of the commercial interest in uniformity, demonstrate that the clauses in the Japanese carrier's bill of lading purporting to require arbitration in Tokyo pursuant to Japanese law both would have been held invalid under COGSA prior to today.

The foreign arbitration clause imposes potentially prohibitive costs on the shipper, who must travel—and bring his lawyers, witnesses and exhibits—to a distant country in order to seek redress. The shipper will therefore be inclined either to settle the claim at a discount or to forgo bringing the claim at all. The foreign-law clause leaves the shipper who does pursue his claim open to the application of unfamiliar and potentially disadvantageous legal standards, until he can obtain review (perhaps years later) in a domestic forum under the high standard applicable to vacation of arbitration awards.... Yet this Court today holds that carriers may insert foreign-arbitration clauses into bills of lading, and it leaves in doubt the validity of choice-of-law clauses.

Although the policy undergirding the doctrine of *stare decisis* has its greatest value in preserving rules governing commercial transactions, particularly when their meaning is well understood and has been accepted for long periods of time, the Court nevertheless has concluded that a change must be made. Its law-changing decision is supported by three arguments: (1) the statutory reference to "lessening such liability" has been misconstrued; (2) the prior understanding of the meaning of the statute has been "undermined" by the *Carnival Cruise* case; and (3) the new rule is supported by our obligation to honor the 1924 "Hague Rules." None of these arguments is persuasive.

II.

The Court assumes that the words "lessening such liability" must be narrowly construed to refer only to the substantive rules that define the carrier's legal obligations.... Under this view, contractual provisions that lessen the amount of the consignee's net recovery, or that lessen the likelihood that it will make any recovery at all, are beyond the scope of the statute.

In my opinion, this view is flatly inconsistent with the purpose of COGSA § 3(8). That section responds to the inequality of bargaining power inherent in bills of lading and to carriers' historic tendency to exploit that inequality whenever possible to immunize themselves from liability for their own fault. A bill of lading is a form document prepared by the carrier, who presents it to the shipper on a take-it-or-leave-it basis.... Characteristically, there is no arm's-length negotiation over the bill's terms; the shipper must agree to the carrier's standard-form language, or else refrain from using the carrier's services. Accordingly, if courts were to enforce bills of lading as written, a carrier could slip in a clause relieving itself of all liability for fault, or limiting that liability to a fraction of the shipper's damages, and the shipper would have no recourse. COGSA represents Congress' most recent attempt to respond to this problem. By its terms, it invalidates any clause in a bill of lading "relieving" or "lessening" the "liability" of the carrier for negligence, fault, or dereliction of duty.

When one reads the statutory language in light of the policies behind COGSA's enactment, it is perfectly clear that a foreign forum selection or arbitration clause "relieves" or "lessens" the carrier's liability. The transaction costs associated with an arbitration in Japan will obviously exceed the potential recovery in a great many cargo disputes. As a practical matter, therefore, in such a case no matter how clear the carrier's formal legal liability may be, it would make no sense for the consignee or its subrogee to enforce that liability. It seems to me that a contractual provision that entirely protects the shipper from being held liable for anything should be construed either to have "lessened" its liability or to have "relieved" it of liability.

Even if the value of the shipper's claim is large enough to justify litigation in Asia, contractual provisions that impose unnecessary and unreasonable costs on the consignee will inevitably lessen its net recovery. If, as under the Court's reasoning, such provisions do not affect the carrier's legal liability, it would appear to be permissible to require the consignee to pay the costs of the arbitration, or perhaps the travel expenses and fees of the expert witnesses, interpreters, and lawyers employed by both parties. Judge Friendly and the many other wise judges who shared his opinion were surely correct in concluding that Congress could not have intended such a perverse reading of the statutory text.

More is at stake here than the allocation of rights and duties between shippers and carriers. A bill of lading, besides being a contract of carriage, is a negotiable instrument that controls possession of the goods being shipped. Accordingly, the bill of lading can be sold, traded, or used to obtain credit as though the bill were the cargo itself. Disuniformity in the interpretation of bills of lading will impair their negotiability.... Thus, if the security interests in some bills of lading are enforceable only through the courts of Japan, while others may be enforceable only in Liechtenstein, the negotiability of bills of lading will suffer from the uncertainty. COGSA recognizes that this negotiability depends in part upon the financial community's capacity to rely on the enforceability, in an accessible forum, of the bills' terms. Today's decision destroys that capacity.

The Court's reliance on its decision in *Carnival Cruise Lines, Inc.* ... is misplaced. That case held that a domestic forum selection clause in a passenger ticket was enforceable. As no carriage of goods was at issue, COGSA did not apply to the parties' dispute. Accordingly, the enforceability of the ticket's terms did not implicate the commercial interests in uniformity and negotiability that are served by the statutory regulation of bills of lading. Moreover, the *Carnival Cruise* holding is limited to the enforceability of domestic forum selection clauses. The Court in that case pointedly refused to respond to the concern expressed in my dissent that a wooden application of its reasoning might extend its holding to the selection of a forum outside of the United States. . . . The wooden reasoning that the Court adopts today does make that extension, but it is surely not compelled by the holding in *Carnival Cruise*.

Finally, I am simply baffled by the Court's implicit suggestion that our interpretation of the Harter Act (which preceded the Hague Rules), and the federal courts' consistent interpretation of COGSA since *Indussa* was decided in 1967, has somehow been unfaithful to our international commitments. . . . The concerns about invalidating freely negotiated forum selection clauses that this Court expressed in *The Bremen v. Zapata Off– Shore Co* . . . .have no bearing on the validity of the provisions in bills of lading that are commonly recognized as contracts of adhesion. Our international obligations do not require us to enforce a contractual term that was not freely negotiated by the parties. Much less do they require us to ignore the clear meaning of COGSA—itself the product of international negotiations—which forbids enforcement of clauses lessening the carrier's liability. . . .

The majority points to several foreign statutes, passed by other signatories to the Hague Rules, that make foreign forum selection clauses unenforceable in the courts of those countries. . . . The majority assumes (without citing any evidence) that these statutes were passed in order to depart from the Hague Rules, and that COGSA, our Nation's enactment of the Hague Rules, should therefore be read to mean something different from these statutes. I think the opposite conclusion is at least as plausible: these foreign nations believed nonenforcement of foreign forum selection clauses was consistent with their international obligations, and they passed these statutes to make that explicit. If anything, then, these statutes demonstrate that several foreign countries agree that the United States courts' consistent interpretation of COGSA does not contravene our mutual treaty obligations. . . .

III.

Lurking in the background of the Court's decision today is another possible reason for holding, despite the clear meaning of COGSA and decades of precedent, that a foreign arbitration clause does not lessen liability. It may be that the Court does violence to COGSA in order to avoid a perceived conflict with another federal statute, the Federal Arbitration Act (FAA). . . . The FAA requires that courts enforce arbitration clauses in contracts—including those requiring arbitration in foreign countries—the same way they would enforce any other contractual clause. . . . According to the Court of Appeals, reading COGSA to invalidate foreign arbitration clauses would conflict directly with the terms and policy of the FAA.

Unfortunately, in adopting a contrary reading to avoid this conflict, the Court has today deprived COGSA § 3(8) of much of its force. Its narrow reading of "lessening [of] liability" excludes more than arbitration; it apparently covers only formal, legal liability.... Although I agree with the Court that it is important to read potentially conflicting statutes so as to give effect to both wherever possible, I think the majority has ignored a much less damaging way to harmonize COGSA with the FAA.

Section 2 of the FAA ... intends to place arbitration clauses upon the same footing as all other contractual clauses. Thus, like any clause, an arbitration clause is enforceable, "save upon such grounds" as would suffice to invalidate any other, non-arbitration clause. The FAA thereby fulfills its policy of jettisoning the prior regime of hostility to arbitration. Like any other contractual clause, then, an arbitration clause may be invalid without violating the FAA if, for example, it is procured through fraud or forgery; there is mutual mistake or impossibility; the provision is unconscionable; or, as in this case, the terms of the clause are illegal under a separate federal statute which does not evidence a hostility to arbitration. Neither the terms nor the policies of the FAA would be thwarted if the Court were to hold today that a foreign arbitration clause in a bill of lading "lessens liability" under COGSA. COGSA does not single out arbitration clauses for disfavored treatment; it invalidates any clause that lessens the carrier's liability. Illegality under COGSA is therefore an independent ground "for the revocation of any contract," under FAA § 2. There is no conflict between the two federal statutes.

The correctness of this construction becomes even more apparent when one considers the policies of the two statutes. COGSA seeks to ameliorate the inequality in bargaining power that comes from a particular form of adhesion contract. The FAA seeks to ensure enforcement of freely-negotiated agreements to arbitrate.... [F]oreign arbitration clauses in bills of lading are not freely-negotiated. COGSA's policy is thus directly served by making these clauses illegal; and the FAA's policy is not disserved thereby. In contrast, allowing such adhesionary clauses to stand serves the goals of neither statute.

IV.

The Court's decision in this case is an excellent example of overzealous formalism. By eschewing a commonsense reading of "lessening [of] liability," the Court has drained those words of much of their potency. The result compounds, rather than contains, the Court's unfortunate mistake in the *Carnival Cruise* case.

I respectfully dissent.

NOTES AND QUESTIONS

1. *Vimar* is a recent expression of the Court's policy on arbitration. It is a decision on international commercial arbitration in that it involves a maritime transaction, the application of maritime statutory law to the trans-

border transport of goods, and treaty law. It is also characteristic of the litigation on domestic arbitration in that it involves an alleged conflict between the legislation on arbitration and another regulatory statute. Given the merger of arbitral judicial policy, however, the precise character of the litigation may not be very significant: What applies internationally also governs purely domestic arbitral matters.

2.   The majority believes that COGSA and the FAA are not in conflict because the reference of a COGSA dispute to arbitration is permissible under Section 3(8) of COGSA. The dissent believes that the contractual reference to arbitration in the bill of lading violates the letter and spirit of Section 3(8) and is, therefore, invalid. The majority takes exception with "the reasoning" and "the conclusion" of the Second Circuit Court of Appeals decision in *Indussa* by drawing a distinction between the substantive obligations under the legislation and the procedure for the enforcement of these obligations. How characteristic is this distinction of the Court's general decisional law methodology on arbitration? Where else has the Court made such a distinction? Justice Stevens is highly critical of the majority opinion on this point, but didn't he deploy the same logic when he authored the majority opinion in *Mastrobuono* on the issue of punitive damages and the applicable state law?

3.   The precedential significance and relevance of *Carnival Cruise* is another area of disagreement between the majority and dissenting opinions. Which side of the Court has it right? From the perspective of logic and analysis? From the vantage point of policy? Which appraisal is likely to generate the better arbitration law? If Justice Stevens' evaluation is at all convincing, will the logical gaps and tendentious determinations in the majority opinion discredit the U.S. law on arbitration? Why then do so few justices join the minority in these cases?

4.   How do you assess the majority's derisory comments concerning the transaction costs of litigation abroad? Isn't the dissent correct in arguing that the increased costs of litigation are a means of discounting or eliminating liability, a consequence prohibited by the legislation? Doesn't the customarily unilateral character of the contract and the foregoing factor amount to undermining the legislative regulation? Is the majority invoking the defense of the sophisticated merchant and simply acquiescing to the self-regulating practice of international merchants? If it is, should it?

5.   How do the practice of other nations, the Court's other rulings on international commercial arbitration, and the New York Arbitration Convention fit into the majority's determination? How "wooden," "mechanical," or "formalistic" is the majority reasoning on this score? How distinguishable is the question in *Vimar* from the issues in *Scherk* and *Mitsubishi*? Justice Stevens observed in *Mitsubishi* that the dispute in *Scherk* was more of a breach of contractual warranty claim than a statutory claim. How might that reasoning be applied to *Vimar*? Is Justice Stevens right when he asserts: "Nothing in ... [the New York Convention] even remotely suggests an intent to enforce arbitration clauses that constitute a 'lessening' of liability under COGSA or the Hague Rules"? 515 U.S. at 554 n.14.

6.   How does the "second look" doctrine factor into the majority analysis and determination? How does Justice Stevens respond? Can the international

adjudicatory mechanism be trusted? Is that consideration relevant in the nonconflictualist, post-modern, and nonextraterritorial era?

7. Gilmore and Black's treatise on admiralty law plays a prominent role in the dissenting opinion as a voice of experience and reason in evaluating the rules of maritime law. The dissent finds a great deal of support in this distinguished scholarly source. The majority relies very little upon secondary sources or the recognized academic bible on maritime law. What does that factor say about the majority opinion? Is the majority correct in its concluding assertion that its determination gives full effect to both COGSA and the FAA? Or, is the U.S. version of maritime regulation determined by whatever tribunal is designated by a unilateral provision for dispute resolution in an international contract? Does the majority opinion create new law that, in every respect, privileges the rule of the FAA?

6. THE 1958 NEW YORK ARBITRATION CONVENTION

The Convention on the Recognition and Enforcement of Foreign Arbitral Awards is probably one of the most successful United Nations efforts at establishing a rule of law in the community of nations. The Convention has been ratified by more than one hundred countries (138 at last count) and generally receives a uniformly favorable construction in the national courts of the ratifying States. Its success reflects the breadth and depth of the world community perception that transborder commerce is vital to national interests and that arbitration is indispensable to the operation of international business. The New York Arbitration Convention replaces several prior international agreements on arbitration and is intended to function as the "universal charter" on international commercial arbitration. To some extent, the New York Arbitration Convention has superseded its own content and legislative history. It has become a juridical vehicle for the elaboration of a transborder law on international commercial arbitration.

The United States was initially reluctant to adhere to the Convention. The lack of enthusiasm reflected in part the traditional U.S. skepticism about participation in international instruments, namely, that they create an obligation to abide by non-national rules of conduct and amount to a relinquishment of national legal authority to govern. It also demonstrated the power of U.S. business interests following the Second World War; there was no need to acquiesce to a system of private international adjudicatory mechanisms when transborder contract disputes could be resolved according to our laws and before our courts. These various factors delayed United States adhesion to the emerging world community perception of the need to establish an autonomous rule of transborder commercial law.

The United States ratified the Convention in December 1970, some twelve years after the Convention had been opened for signature. Once ratification had been achieved, the United States began playing a central role, primarily through U.S. Supreme Court decisions, in legitimizing and promoting international commercial arbitration. In fact, ratification provided a juridical foundation upon which the Court elaborated not only a judicial doctrine on international commercial arbitration, but also a larger U.S. private international law on transborder litigation. The Court's rulings on international commercial arbitration are among the most liberal and supportive judicial pronouncements on arbitration. The U.S. law on arbitration now directs the global consensus on arbitration.

The foregoing materials include four separate documents. The first document is the text of the 1958 New York Arbitration Convention ratified by the United States through Public Law 91–368 of July 31, 1970. *See* 84 Stat. 692. The Convention entered into force for the United States on December 29, 1970. The second document is the text of 9 U.S.C. §§ 201–08, which contains provisions integrating the ratification into the U.S. legal system. The various sections of Title 9 deal with jurisdictional and venue questions that might arise under federal and state law in matters of international arbitration. Despite this oblique codification under Title 9, the text of the Convention constitutes the law applicable to matters of international commercial arbitration.

The third and fourth documents are the text of the Inter–American Convention on International Commercial Arbitration and the Title 9 codification pertaining to the ratification of the 1975 Inter–American Convention. The Inter–American Convention came into force on August 15, 1990 through Public Law No. 101–369. *See* 104 Stat. 448. These documents are included primarily to provide a complete list of major multilateral treaty obligations of the United States in the area of arbitration. There is no significant difference between the New York and Inter–American Conventions. The Inter–American Convention, ratified by eleven Latin American States, is the regional counterpart of the New York Arbitration Convention and was intended to symbolize the unity of the Americas on the historically difficult topic of international claims settlement through arbitration. The Title 9 codification does not reproduce the text of the Convention and fulfills the same integrative function it does with the New York Arbitration Convention.

CONVENTION ON THE RECOGNITION AND ENFORCEMENT OF FOREIGN ARBITRAL AWARDS,

opened for signature June 10, 1958, 21 U.S.T. 2517, T.I.A.S. No. 6997, 330 U.N.T.S. 3, *codified in* 9 U.S.C.A. §§ 201–08 (1970).

ARTICLE I

1.   This Convention shall apply to the recognition and enforcement of arbitral awards made in the territory of a State other than the State where the recognition and enforcement of such awards are sought, and arising out of differences between persons, whether physical or legal. It shall also apply to arbitral awards not considered as domestic awards in the State where their recognition and enforcement are sought.

2. The term "arbitral awards" shall include not only awards made by arbitrators appointed for each case but also those made by permanent arbitral bodies to which the parties have submitted.

3. When signing, ratifying or acceding to this Convention, or notifying extension under article X hereof, any State may on the basis of reciprocity declare that it will apply the Convention to the recognition and enforcement of awards made only in the territory of another Contracting State. It may also declare that it will apply the Convention only to differences arising out of legal relationships, whether contractual or not, which are considered as commercial under the national law of the State making such declaration.

ARTICLE II

1. Each Contracting State shall recognize an agreement in writing under which the parties undertake to submit to arbitration all or any differences which have arisen or which may arise between them in respect of a defined legal relationship, whether contractual or not, concerning a subject matter capable of settlement by arbitration.

2. The term "agreement in writing" shall include an arbitral clause in a contract or an arbitration agreement, signed by the parties or contained in an exchange of letters or telegrams.

3. The court of a Contracting State, when seized of an action in a matter in respect of which the parties have made an agreement within the meaning of this article, shall, at the request of one of the parties, refer the parties to arbitration, unless it finds that the said agreement is null and void, inoperative or incapable of being performed.

ARTICLE III

Each Contracting State shall recognize arbitral awards as binding and enforce them in accordance with the rules of procedure of the territory where the award is relied upon, under the conditions laid down in the following articles. There shall not be imposed substantially more onerous conditions or higher fees or charges on the recognition or enforcement of arbitral awards to which this Convention applies than are imposed on the recognition or enforcement of domestic arbitral awards.

ARTICLE IV

1. To obtain the recognition and enforcement mentioned in the preceding article, the party applying for recognition and enforcement shall, at the time of the application, supply:

> (a) The duly authenticated original award or a duly certified copy thereof;

> (b) The original agreement referred to in article II or a duly certified copy thereof.

2.　If the said award or agreement is not made in an official language of the country in which the award is relied upon, the party applying for recognition and enforcement of the award shall produce a translation of these documents into such language. The translation shall be certified by an official or sworn translator or by a diplomatic or consular agent.

ARTICLE V

1.　Recognition and enforcement of the award may be refused, at the request of the party against whom it is invoked, only if that party furnishes to the competent authority where the recognition and enforcement is sought, proof that:

> (a) The parties to the agreement referred to in article II were, under the law applicable to them, under some incapacity, or the said agreement is not valid under the law to which the parties have subjected it or, failing any indication thereon, under the law of the country where the award was made; or

> (b) The party against whom the award is invoked was not given proper notice of the appointment of the arbitrator or of the arbitration proceedings or was otherwise unable to present his case; or

> (c) The award deals with a difference not contemplated by or not falling within the terms of the submission to arbitration, or it contains decisions on matters beyond the scope of the submission to arbitration, provided that, if the decisions on matters submitted to arbitration can be separated from those not so submitted, that part of the award which contains decisions on matters submitted to arbitration may be recognized and enforced; or

> (d) The composition of the arbitral authority or the arbitral procedure was not in accordance with the agreement of the parties, or, failing such agreement, was not in accordance with the law of the country where the arbitration took place; or

> (e) The award has not yet become binding on the parties, or has been set aside or suspended by a competent authority of the country in which, or under the law of which, that award was made.

2.　Recognition and enforcement of an arbitral award may also be refused if the competent authority in the country where recognition and enforcement is sought finds that:

> (a) The subject matter of the difference is not capable of settlement by arbitration under the law of that country; or

> (b) The recognition or enforcement of the award would be contrary to the public policy of that country.

ARTICLE VI

If an application for the setting aside or suspension of the award has been made to a competent authority referred to in article V(1)(e), the authority before which the award is sought to be relied upon may, if it considers it proper, adjourn the decision on the enforcement of the award and may also, on the application of the party claiming enforcement of the award, order the other party to give suitable security.

ARTICLE VII

1. The provisions of the present Convention shall not affect the validity of multilateral or bilateral agreements concerning the recognition and enforcement of arbitral awards entered into by the Contracting States nor deprive any interested party of any right he may have to avail himself of an arbitral award in the manner and to the extent allowed by the law or the treaties of the country where such award is sought to be relied upon.

2. The Geneva Protocol on Arbitration Clauses of 1923 and the Geneva Convention on the Execution of Foreign Arbitral Awards of 1927 shall cease to have effect between Contracting States on their becoming bound and, to the extent that they become bound, by this Convention.

ARTICLE VIII

1. This Convention shall be open until 31 December 1958 for signature on behalf of any Member of the United Nations and also on behalf of any other State which is or hereafter becomes a member of any specialized agency of the United Nations, or which is or hereafter becomes a party to the Statute of the International Court of Justice, or any other State to which an invitation has been addressed by the General Assembly of the United Nations.

2. This Convention shall be ratified and the instrument of ratification shall be deposited with the Secretary–General of the United Nations.

ARTICLE IX

1. This Convention shall be open for accession to all States referred to in Article VIII.

2. Accession shall be effected by the deposit of an instrument of accession with the Secretary–General of the United Nations.

[. . .]

NOTES AND QUESTIONS

1. The New York Arbitration Convention is the central focus of consideration. It is an exemplary treaty; a model of modern arbitration legislation. The force of its authority is based upon its codification of the international consensus on arbitration. Also, rather than attempt to regulate all aspects of the arbitral process, the New York Convention focuses directly upon two vital elements of arbitral procedure (the validity of arbitration agreements and the enforcement of arbitral awards), leaving a more comprehensive regulatory scheme to be implied from its express principles.

The Convention's objective is to unify national laws on the enforcement of foreign arbitral awards and to establish a transnational rule of law that favors the recourse to arbitral adjudication. For example, Article II(1) provides that the Contracting States shall recognize an agreement to submit disputes to arbitration. The purpose of this article is to eradicate systemic hostility to arbitration—hostility stemming from the view that arbitration amounts to a usurpation of judicial adjudicatory authority. Consequently, by adhering to the Convention, Contracting States agree to recognize the arbitral process as a legitimate means of resolving disputes. Under Article II(3), a motion to compel arbitration can be defeated only by establishing that the arbitration agreement was null and void, inoperative, or incapable of being performed. Decisional interpretations of the Convention demonstrate that these grounds were meant to function as ordinary contract defenses to the enforcement of an agreement. Arbitration agreements, therefore, are valid contractual arrangements and do not, *per se*, violate principles of public policy. They symbolize party use of contractual rights—rights the assertion of which can be defeated only by a deficiency in contractual intent, capacity, or language. Accordingly, courts in the Contracting States are under a legal obligation to enforce arbitration agreements if they meet the ordinary requirements of contractual validity.

The text of the Convention proposes a unified transnational rule of law not only in regard to the validity of arbitration agreements, but also concerning the enforcement of foreign arbitral awards. The systemic viability of any nonjudicial adjudicatory process is dependent both upon the legal system's recognition of the validity of agreements to enter into such processes and its willingness to give binding effect to its determinations. The seven grounds for the judicial supervision of awards contained in Article V can be grouped into two broad categories: First, the procedural requirements that dictate compliance with basic adjudicatory standards. The parties must have had the contractual capacity to enter into an arbitration agreement; they must have been afforded proper notice of the proceeding; the arbitrators must not have exceeded the jurisdictional authority conferred upon them by the agreement; the composition of the arbitral tribunal and the appointment of arbitrators must reflect the provisions of the agreement; and the award must have been binding in the jurisdiction in which it was rendered.

Second, national courts can deny recognition and enforcement to a foreign arbitral award upon the basis of two broad substantive law grounds. The dispute which the award settles must be arbitrable under the law of the requested jurisdiction; moreover, recognition and enforcement of the award must not be contrary to the requested jurisdiction's public policy. To some extent, the inarbitrability defense and public policy exception overlap. For example, as a general rule, disputes relating to the status and capacity of persons are inarbitrable. An award relating to a person's status and capacity, if recognized and enforced, could also be contrary to the public policy of the requested jurisdiction.

The Convention's truly international stature and law-making capacity are built upon two factors: First, its symbolic function of codifying an existing and emerging international consensus on arbitration. Second, its endorsement by national legal systems which seek to affirm and integrate the Convention's content and underlying intent, and thereby entrench the transnational recognition of and support for arbitration.

2. The text of the Convention and its continued interpretation by national courts raise three questions pertaining to the Convention's current status and meaning. First, in light of the development of the law and practice of international commercial arbitration since 1958, is it still accurate to refer to the Convention as a regime for the enforcement of "foreign" rather than "international" arbitral awards? Second, and relatedly, in terms of the specific language of the Convention, does the application of national law remain relevant under the provisions of the Convention? Has the movement toward an "a-national" regime of transborder arbitration superseded the Convention's reference to national law? Third, also in keeping with the foregoing considerations, do the substantive law limits on arbitration under the Convention—the inarbitrability defense and the public policy exception to enforcement—retain any vitality given the evolution of law in the area?

3. These questions warrant systematic consideration and analysis. Commentators are likely to argue that national courts must apply the provisions of the Convention as written, and that would-be trends and developments cannot repeal or amend the content of an international treaty. Therefore, the law of the place of arbitration, the parties' national law, and the law of the place of enforcement still play a significant role in validating arbitration agreements and awards. Private international adjudications are still dependent upon national legal authority. Coercive enforcement cannot be achieved without invoking the laws of the requested territorial jurisdiction.

There is, however, another view of the Convention's law-making status—one that relies upon a sense of the realities of litigation practices and which ignores, rightly or wrongly, considerations of legal formalism. The provisions of the Convention are not static, but rather reflect law-in-the-making. They are primarily responsive to the policy imperative that underlies the Convention. The references to the application of national law within the Convention may have been necessary to create an international movement toward ratification. Events, however, have outpaced that original purpose. International commercial arbitration has become an "a-national" phenomenon. Although transborder adjudication can acquire the force of law only through national legal authority, arbitration—once the Convention gained universal adherence—transcended the need for continued national legal approval.

National courts and legislation, in effect, relinquished their authority to regulate arbitration and permitted it to function autonomously. As a result, considerations pertaining to the parties' national law, the law of the place of arbitration, and even the law of the place of enforcement are relevant only to the extent that they converge with the norms generated by the process of "a-national" arbitration.

4. In light of the foregoing considerations, you should consider the language of the following articles of the Convention: Article I(1), Article V(1)(a), Article V(1)(d), Article V(1)(e), and V(2)(a) & (b). What role does, should, or can national law play in the interpretation and application of the Convention?

It should be noted that the movement toward uniform national laws on arbitration has undercut much of the debate about the impact of national sovereignty and national law in the implementation of the Convention. In fact, the continuing global ratification of the Convention has reversed the traditional tendency of States to make local exceptions to an agreed-upon international regime. Moreover, States appear to be competing to enact the most liberal laws on international commercial arbitration. The UNCITRAL Model Law and Rules on Arbitration also indicate a trend toward "a-national" uniformity. Parties seeking to enforce arbitration agreements and awards, of course, are always subject to the particularities of their case and a given national law and judiciary. By and large, however, national law is no longer a constraint upon arbitration. States understand the international commercial importance of arbitration and actively promote themselves as venues for international arbitral proceedings. The "deregulatory" movement and the State acquiescence to the rise of arbitration are motivated in large measure by the desire to sell professional and infrastructure services to the international business community.

5. The Convention has created an effective and functional rule of law in the international community. Its textual provisions are neither numerous nor complex. The economy of the Convention's text is as remarkable as its international force. Of the sixteen articles that constitute the Convention, only Articles I, II, III, and V contain law-making content; other articles deal with formal procedural concerns. We now examine the salient provisions of the Convention.

Article I establishes the Convention's scope of application. You should note that the provision first establishes a territorial definition of "foreign" arbitral awards and then refers, as a secondary matter, to definitions of "nondomestic" awards under the national law of the requested States. Accordingly, a ratifying State can apply the provisions of the Convention to the enforcement of arbitral awards rendered outside its territory or which it deems as a matter of law not to be domestic awards. The Convention's proffered definition is objective (territory of rendition) and its secondary definition (national legal definitions of "foreign") is more subjective and variable. The Convention's tolerance for individual national variations on its scope of application, necessary for wide ratification, could have created problems for its subsequent uniform application.

Some States, like France, adopted a broad subject matter definition of the term "foreign" arbitral award or arbitration. Under French law, an award is foreign, international, or nondomestic whenever it implicates the interests of international commerce. Accordingly, an arbitration between two French nationals taking place in France could still be considered "foreign" despite the linkage to France because the transaction giving rise to the arbitration may have had a bearing upon or contained elements of international business. Prior to and under the legislation enacted in 1996, the English position on this question focuses in major part upon nationality (Section 85 of the 1996 Arbitration Act). A "nondomestic" arbitral award is one which does not involve British nationality. Therefore, a commodities transaction between a U.S. and a British national, involving transport between three different countries, leading to an arbitral award might not be considered as "nondomestic" for purposes of enforcement in the United Kingdom.

The U.S. position on the Convention's scope of application intermediates between the French and English views. Under 9 U.S.C. § 202, an award has the requisite foreign character when it pertains to a transaction that involves some "reasonable" relationship or connection "with one or more foreign States." A transaction that lacks foreign nationality and that gives rise to an award will not fall under the jurisdiction of the Convention unless it has other ties to transborder commerce. U.S. law also requires that the award resolve commercial differences between the parties.

The question of the Convention's scope of application is significant only if there is a substantial disparity between the Convention's enforcement provisions and the national provisions on the enforcement of domestic or international arbitral awards. The purpose of the Convention was to establish a hospitable regime for the enforcement of foreign arbitral awards in the ratifying States by exempting foreign awards from restrictive domestic requirements for the enforcement of arbitral awards. Allowing States to apply a narrow definition of "nondomestic" awards could have undermined the underlying intent of the Convention regime.

Modern arbitration statutes tend to minimize the difference between the enforcement of domestic and international arbitral awards, making the problem of distinguishing between domestic and "nondomestic" awards moot to some extent. In fact, it appears that, under U.S. law, it is easier to enforce a domestic award under Section Ten of the FAA than an international award under Article V of the Convention. Section Ten, as noted earlier, contains no mention of the inarbitrability defense and public policy exception to enforcement, while Article V(2)(a) & (b) includes both grounds. The equivalency of regimes and the alignment of arbitral policy have lessened the importance of the issue and transformed it primarily into a legalistic concern.

Do you agree with this assessment of the problem? Doesn't a determination that the award is domestic eliminate the application of the policy favoring the enforcement of international arbitral awards? Do all jurisdictions have an equally favorable policy on the enforcement of domestic arbitral awards? How do you know? What makes an arbitral award international or non-domestic in your view? Do you believe your definition would persuade a U.S. court or a foreign tribunal? Why do you believe the Convention has survived this knotty problem of definition?

You should also note that Article I(3) allows States to declare that their ratification of the Convention is subject to two reservations: (1) reciprocity—the Convention shall apply only to awards rendered in the territory of another ratifying State; and (2) the commercial relationships qualification—the Convention shall apply only to awards that resolve commercial disputes (as defined by national law) between the parties. Reservations are hold-backs or a form of qualified acceptance. The State accedes to or ratifies the treaty with qualifications. The instrument permits this form of acquiescence to its provisions. The purpose of reservations is to increase the pool of likely adherents. The United States ratified the Convention with the two reservations. Of what significance are the two reservations? How do they protect the sovereign interests of the ratifying State? In particular, what does the commercial relationship qualification achieve? Given the depicted evolution of law under the Convention, do these reservations have any but a formalistic meaning? Finally, are there in your view other interpretative difficulties with the text of Article I that have not been identified in the discussion?

Article II establishes the legal obligations of ratifying States in regard to arbitration. By ratifying the Convention, States agree to recognize the submission and the arbitral clause as valid contractual undertakings and to enforce them as they would ordinary contracts. What specific problems of arbitration law are these obligations intended to cure? What parallel can you establish between the Convention and the FAA on this question? Article II(1), establishing the States' obligation to recognize arbitration agreements, refers at the end of its formulation to restrictions upon the States' obligation, namely, that the arbitration agreement relates to "a defined legal relationship, whether contractual or not" and to "a subject matter capable of settlement by arbitration." What do these restrictions mean, especially the latter reference to the subject matter of the contract or dispute? Do you find any parallel between the Convention and the FAA on this question? When can a ratifying State refuse to recognize an arbitration agreement as a valid "agreement in writing"?

Article II(2) defines the "in writing" requirement broadly and by reference to commercial practices rather than legal requirements. This provision reveals aspects of the underlying ideology of the Convention, namely, that it is meant to codify the dispute resolution practices of the international commercial community rather than establish a legal regime for its governance. Courts have recognized that new technological means of communication also satisfy the "in writing" requirement.

Finally, Article II(3) establishes the duty of national courts in the ratifying States to compel arbitration in the appropriate circumstances. The obligation is triggered upon the request of a contracting party when it can establish that an arbitration agreement exists. The motion can be denied only if the court finds that the agreement to arbitrate is deficient as a contract. The parallelism to the FAA is evident; both statutes require a cooperative relationship between the judicial and arbitral process. Moreover, the parties have the right to enter into arbitration agreements; that right can be defeated only when the requirements of contractual validity are not satisfied. Would the language of Article II(3) authorize a U.S. court to compel arbitration in a foreign jurisdiction between foreign nationals? How would you formulate a basis for responding to that question?

Having established its jurisdictional application and the State obligation to recognize and enforce arbitration agreements, the Convention then provides, in *Article III*, that contracting States also are under an obligation to recognize and enforce foreign arbitral awards. In the second sentence, the language of the provision expresses the concern that foreign arbitral awards not be subject to discriminatory treatment, that they should be treated in a manner similar to domestic arbitral awards. The content of the provision testifies to the enormous distance that has been traveled since 1958. The actual effect of the Convention has been to establish an enforcement regime that distinctly favors international, non-domestic, or foreign arbitral awards and exempts them from any rigorous domestic law scrutiny. You should also note the brevity and focus of the regulatory framework; in three relatively short articles, the Convention has addressed all of the fundamental stages of the legal process regulating arbitration.

Article V is a critical provision. It outlines the grounds upon which a national court in a contracting State can deny recognition and enforcement to an international, non-domestic, or foreign arbitral award. There are five procedural grounds and two other grounds based upon substantive law considerations. Although the references within the article to national law have already been discussed, you should be aware of and evaluate the role of local law in challenging the enforceability of an award under the Convention. Moreover, you should compare and contrast the content of Article V with Section Ten of the FAA. There appears to be a general convergence between the two statutory frameworks on the question of enforcement. According to the Convention, an award can be challenged on the basis of contractual deficiency of the arbitration agreement, lack of notice or of an opportunity to be heard, excess of arbitral authority (with a severance caveat), and failure to abide by the agreement in matters of procedure. Is the same regime applicable under the FAA? Are there any substantial differences? Are the FAA grounds more rooted in a past of judicial hostility and juridical distrust of arbitration? Has the coexistence of the two regimes for enforcement in effect modified the content of Section Ten?

Article V(1)(e) adds a traditional private international law consideration to the enforcement regime under the Convention, namely, *res judicata* and the conflict of judgment. This provision forcefully puts into play the national law question and brings the text of the Convention into direct conflict with the tenets of "a-national" arbitration. It provides that an award can be denied recognition or enforcement if it is not final or has been set aside by a court in another jurisdiction with contacts to the arbitration. The courts having jurisdiction to set aside an award are courts in the place of arbitration or courts in the jurisdiction the law of which governed the making of the award. This part of the provision, in effect, restates the problem of the "double *exequatur*" in a diluted form. Although an award need not be enforceable both at the place of rendition and at the place of enforcement, it must not have been rendered unenforceable at the place of rendition in order to be legally enforceable at the place of enforcement.

There are significant interpretative difficulties with the language of Article V(1)(e). For example, it is unclear what the wording "[t]he award has not yet become binding on the parties" actually means. Have the arbitrators failed to rule upon some submitted claims? Is it a partial award? Do damages remain to be assessed? Is there something in the arbitral procedure that remains incomplete? Under French law, a domestic arbitral award has *res judicata* effect upon its rendition. Therefore, once the arbitrators have ruled, the resulting award, like a court judgment, is binding upon the parties. Appeals can delay the enforcement of a judicial judgment, but the right of appeal is very limited in arbitration and ordinarily confined to the grounds that apply in an enforcement proceeding.

It is also difficult to interpret the meaning of the binding requirement because it is linked by the disjunctive "or" to the setting aside procedure. The disjunction denotes two separate rather than related actions. It seems, therefore, that, unlike the situation in French law, an award under the Convention is not legally binding until the adverse party has exercised its right to relief from the enforcement of the award either at the place of rendition, the place of the law governing the merits or the arbitration, or the place of actual enforcement. A denial of recognition or enforcement (setting aside the award) at the place of rendition or at the place of the governing law cripples its enforceability under the Convention at the place of intended enforcement.

There is a further ambiguity in the reference to "the country . . . under the law of which . . . [the] award was made." The designation could mean the jurisdiction the substantive law of which was applied by the arbitrators to the merits of the dispute or the jurisdiction the arbitration law of which controlled the arbitral proceeding or, albeit more unlikely, the jurisdiction the procedural law of which controlled the proceeding. Depending upon the complexity of the parties' choice of applicable law, an award could be subject to the scrutiny of four different national courts (place of rendition, place of substantive governing law, place of governing arbitration law, place of governing trial law) before any action was brought at the place of intended enforcement. Moreover, the reference to an award being "set aside or suspended" entails further problems of construction. Are the two actions equivalent or do they refer to independent means by which to challenge an award at any one of the four possible jurisdictions?

Article V(1)(e) squarely places the enforcement of international, non-domestic, or foreign arbitral awards under the Convention into a complex choice-of-law framework. It contradicts the liberal policy on arbitration that animates the other provisions of the Convention and undermines the effort to establish a functional transborder regime for the enforcement of arbitral awards. In particular, it invites lawyers to engage in forum-shopping strategies to protect the interests of their award-averse clients by using disparate national laws to frustrate the process of international commercial accountability and justice. Article V(1)(e) is expressly at odds with the central premise of "a-national" arbitration that the only national law of any consequence in an enforcement action is the law of the place of intended enforcement (where assets exist to satisfy the award). Laws or venues selected for transactional or contractual convenience should not impinge upon the legitimacy of awards. Considerations of territoriality have little relevance to global commerce. Moreover, the emerging view of "a-national" arbitration is that the local law of the place of intended enforcement should have a bearing on the award only to the extent that it conforms with the "a-national" transborder norms on arbitration.

In light of the foregoing remarks, how do you evaluate the content and implications of Article V(1)(e)? Do you believe the provision is no longer applicable law and has been written out of the Convention by subsequent events and practice? Has the would-be uniformity of national laws on arbitration made the language of ground "e" perfunctory? Are the conflict-of-law problems likely to arise in the more modern and developed climate of international commercial arbitration? Consider these problems in light of the U.S. Supreme Court's federalism decisions on arbitration. Would the Court allow any state law to imperil the operation of arbitration? Are there any differences between the operation of arbitration in the two sectors?

Article V(2)(a) & (b) establishes the substantive law grounds for opposing the enforcement of an award under the Convention: (1) subject-matter inarbitrability (ground a); and (2) public policy (ground b). Both concepts expressly rely upon the local law of the enforcement jurisdiction for their content; according to the Convention, it is the national law version of inarbitrability and public policy that governs. As noted previously, there is some unavoidable overlap between the two grounds: More than likely, a subject area will be deemed inarbitrable because its importance to the State makes it part of national public policy. The public policy exception to enforcement, however, can include matters that have no linkage to the inarbitrability defense. An award could violate local public policy for reasons of trial procedure or for its conflict with other fundamental legal norms of the jurisdiction. A vigorous application of the public policy exception to enforcement could come close in some instances to a judicial review of the merits of the award.

For example, the requested court might determine that the arbitrators misapplied a provision of law or awarded excessively generous damages and that "misconduct" violates local public policy. This is precisely what the Convention intended to eradicate: Arbitral awards are presumptively enforceable unless they represent a fundamental miscarriage of procedural justice or are juridically repugnant to the requested jurisdiction. National courts are precluded from revisiting the litigation on any other ground, especially as to the determination on the merits. Otherwise, the prospect of judicial second-guessing would rob the process of arbitral adjudication of its viability.

The deference paid to national law in Article V(2)(a) & (b) again points to the danger of acknowledging the role of national law in the regulation of international commercial arbitration and of inviting choice-of-law considerations to have a bearing upon the operation of a transborder regime for arbitration. Practice under the Convention since 1958 has largely eliminated the possibility of national law interference. In applying the Convention, national courts have responded to the underlying spirit rather than the technical letter of the Convention and Article V(2)(a) & (b). In fact, they have devised the notion of an "international" public policy that applies under Article V(2)(b) and which replaces the application of domestic notions of public policy to guard against unwarranted national law intrusion upon the transborder regime of arbitration. Also, through the efforts primarily of the U.S. Supreme Court, the inarbitrability defense has waned considerably in significance and operation. The emerging position under many national laws of arbitration is that international arbitrators have the right, if not the obligation, to rule upon disputes that involve rights created by statute rather than through contract. Both of these developments attest to the fact that, through its application before national courts, the Convention has generated legal norms that transcend the specific language of its provisions, and that it stands as the foundation of a transborder law on arbitration in constant adaptation.

In light of the foregoing remarks, can you make the case for retaining some national law reach in matters of international commercial arbitration through the inarbitrability defense or the public policy exception to enforcement? Is a more moderate position possible, desirable, or workable? Why should international arbitrators be authorized to apply national or regional regulatory law? Is there a difference between "unlimited" arbitration in the domestic and international sectors?

CHAPTER 2 OF THE FAA: CONVENTION ON THE RECOGNITION AND ENFORCEMENT OF FOREIGN ARBITRAL AWARDS

9 U.S.C. Ch. 2 (§§ 201–08).

§ 201. ENFORCEMENT OF CONVENTION

The Convention on the Recognition and Enforcement of Foreign Arbitral Awards of June 10, 1958, shall be enforced in United States courts in accordance with this chapter.

§ 202. AGREEMENT OR AWARD FALLING UNDER THE CONVENTION

An arbitration agreement or arbitral award arising out of a legal relationship, whether contractual or not, which is considered as commercial, including a transaction, contract, or agreement described in section 2 of this title, falls under the Convention. An agreement or award arising out of such a relationship which is entirely between citizens of the United States shall be deemed not to fall under the Convention unless that relationship involves property located abroad, envisages performance or enforcement abroad, or has some other reasonable relation with one or more foreign states. For the purpose of this section a corporation is a citizen of the United States if it is incorporated or has its principal place of business in the United States.

§ 203. JURISDICTION; AMOUNT IN CONTROVERSY

An action or proceeding falling under the Convention shall be deemed to arise under the laws and treaties of the United States. The district courts of the United States (including the courts enumerated in section 460 of title 28) shall have original jurisdiction over such an action or proceeding, regardless of the amount in controversy.

§ 204. VENUE

An action or proceeding over which the district courts have jurisdiction pursuant to section 203 of this title may be brought in any such court in which save for the arbitration agreement an action or proceeding with respect to the controversy between the parties could be brought, or in such court for the district and division which embraces the place designated in the agreement as the place of arbitration if such place is within the United States.

§ 205. REMOVAL OF CASES FROM STATE COURTS

Where the subject matter of an action or proceeding pending in a State court relates to an arbitration agreement or award falling under the

Convention, the defendant or the defendants may, at any time before the trial thereof, remove such action or proceeding to the district court of the United States for the district and division embracing the place where the action or proceeding is pending. The procedure for removal of causes otherwise provided by law shall apply, except that the ground for removal provided in this section need not appear on the face of the complaint but may be shown in the petition for removal. For the purposes of Chapter 1 of this title any action or proceeding removed under this section shall be deemed to have been brought in the district court to which it is removed.

§ 206. ORDER TO COMPEL ARBITRATION; APPOINTMENT OF ARBITRATORS

A court having jurisdiction under this chapter may direct that arbitration be held in accordance with the agreement at any place therein provided for, whether that place is within or without the United States. Such court may also appoint arbitrators in accordance with the provisions of the agreement.

§ 207. AWARD OF ARBITRATORS; CONFIRMATION; JURISDICTION; PROCEEDING

Within three years after an arbitral award falling under the Convention is made, any party to the arbitration may apply to any court having jurisdiction under this chapter for an order confirming the award as against any other party to the arbitration. The court shall confirm the award unless it finds one of the grounds for refusal or deferral of recognition or enforcement of the award specified in the said Convention.

§ 208. CHAPTER 1; RESIDUAL APPLICATION

Chapter 1 applies to actions and proceedings brought under this chapter to the extent that that chapter is not in conflict with this chapter or the Convention as ratified by the United States.

NOTES AND QUESTIONS

1. 9 U.S.C. §§ 202–208 implement the Convention in U.S. law. Section 202 defines the scope of application of the Convention or its jurisdictional reach in U.S. law. The significance of the provision has already been discussed, but you should be attentive to the requirements for determining when an award becomes subject to the Convention. Given the liberal enforcement regime that generally applies to arbitral awards, however, there is no real doctrinal or practical handicap associated with the enforcement of non-Convention arbitral agreements or awards.

2. Section 203 establishes that the application of the Convention raises federal-question jurisdiction that cannot be defeated by the amount in controversy requirement. Sections 204 and 205 are largely self-explanatory. Section 206 gives U.S. courts extraterritorial powers to sustain the reference to arbitration. Does this exceed the mandate in the Convention? Is the use of this authority likely to work? Would a foreign court need to approve the order?

3. Section 207 establishes both a three-year statute of limitation period for bringing an enforcement action under the Convention and an obligation upon courts to confirm awards that do not violate the grounds for enforcement. The three-year limit tolls from the date of the award's rendition. *See Seetransport Wiking Trader Schiffarhtsgesellschaft MBH & Co., Kommanditgesellschaft v. Navimpex Centrala Navala*, 989 F.2d 572, 580–81 (2d Cir. 1993). Section 208 is largely self-explanatory.

INTER-AMERICAN CONVENTION ON INTERNATIONAL COMMERCIAL ARBITRATION

9 U.S.C.A. Ch. 3, at 346 (1996 Ann. Poc. Pt.),
reprinted in 14 I.L.M. 336 (1975).

The Governments of the Member States of the Organization of American States, desirous of concluding a convention on international commercial arbitration, have agreed as follows:

ARTICLE 1

An agreement in which the parties undertake to submit to arbitral decision any differences that may arise or have arisen between them with respect to a commercial transaction is valid. The agreement shall be set forth in an instrument signed by the parties, or in the form of an exchange of letters, telegrams, or telex communications.

ARTICLE 2

Arbitrators shall be appointed in the manner agreed upon by the parties. Their appointment may be delegated to a third party, whether a natural or juridical person.

Arbitrators may be nationals or foreigners.

ARTICLE 3

In the absence of an express agreement between the parties, the arbitration shall be conducted in accordance with the rules of procedure of the Inter–American Commercial Arbitration Commission.

ARTICLE 4

An arbitral decision or award that is not appealable under the applicable law or procedural rules shall have the force of a final judicial judgment. Its execution or recognition may be ordered in the same manner as that of decisions handed down by national or foreign ordinary courts, in accordance with the procedural laws of the country where it is to be executed and the provisions of international treaties.

ARTICLE 5

1. The recognition and execution of the decision may be refused, at the request of the party against which it is made, only if such party is able

to prove to the competent authority of the State in which recognition and execution are requested:

    a.   That the parties to the agreement were subject to some incapacity under the applicable law or that the agreement is not valid under the law to which the parties have submitted it, or, if such law is not specified, under the law of the State in which the decision was made; or

    b.   That the party against which the arbitral decision has been made was not duly notified of the appointment of the arbitrator or of the arbitration procedure to be followed, or was unable, for any other reason, to present his defense; or

    c.   That the decision concerns a dispute not envisaged in the agreement between the parties to submit to arbitration; nevertheless, if the provisions of the decision that refer to issues submitted to arbitration can be separated from those not submitted to arbitration, the former may be recognized and executed; or

    d.   That the constitution of the arbitral tribunal or the arbitration procedure has not been carried out in accordance with the terms of the agreement signed by the parties or, in the absence of such agreement, that the constitution of the arbitral tribunal or the arbitration procedure had not been carried out in accordance with the law of the State where the arbitration took place; or

    e.   That the decision is not yet binding on the parties or has been annulled or suspended by a competent authority of the State in which, or according to the law of which, the decision has been made.

    2.   The recognition and execution of an arbitral decision may also be refused if the competent authority of the State in which the recognition and execution is requested finds:

    a.   That the subject of the dispute cannot be settled by arbitration under the law of that State; or

    b.   That the recognition or execution of the decision would be contrary to the public policy (*"ordre public"*) of that State.

ARTICLE 6

If the competent authority mentioned in Article 5.1.e has been requested to annul or suspend the arbitral decision, the authority before which such decision is invoked may, if it deems it appropriate, postpone a decision on the execution of the arbitral decision and, at the request of the party requesting execution, may also instruct the other party to provide appropriate guaranties.

ARTICLE 7

This Convention shall be open for signature by the Member States of the Organization of American States.

[. . .]

NOTES AND QUESTIONS

1. You should examine the text of the Inter–American Convention. Does it fit into the common mold of uniform law on arbitration?

2. In addition to the United States, it has been ratified by eleven Latin American States (Chile, Columbia, Costa Rica, El Salvador, Guatemala, Honduras, Mexico, Panama, Paraguay, Uruguay, and Venezuela).

3. Are there any differences between the text of the Inter–American and New York Conventions? How meaningful are those differences? The 1975 Inter–American Convention is a more recent articulation of transborder standards on arbitration than the New York Convention. Does the Inter–American Convention deal more appropriately with the role of national law in the process of international commercial arbitration? Look in particular at Articles 4, 5(1)(a), 5(1)(e), and 5(2)(a) & (b).

CHAPTER 3 OF THE FAA: INTER-AMERICAN CONVENTION ON INTERNATIONAL COMMERCIAL ARBITRATION

9 U.S.C. Ch. 3 (§§ 301–07).

§ 301. ENFORCEMENT OF CONVENTION

The Inter–American Convention on International Commercial Arbitration of January 30, 1975, shall be enforced in United States courts in accordance with this chapter.

§ 302. INCORPORATION BY REFERENCE

Sections 202, 203, 204, 205, and 207 of this title shall apply to this chapter as if specifically set forth herein, except that for the purposes of this chapter "the Convention" shall mean the Inter–American Convention.

§ 303. ORDER TO COMPEL ARBITRATION; APPOINTMENT OF ARBITRATORS; LOCALE

(a) A court having jurisdiction under this chapter may direct that arbitration be held in accordance with the agreement at any place therein provided for, whether that place is within or without the United States. The court may also appoint arbitrators in accordance with the provisions of the agreement.

(b) In the event the agreement does not make provision for the place of arbitration or the appointment of arbitrators, the court shall direct that the arbitration shall be held and the arbitrators be appointed in accordance with Article 3 of the Inter–American Convention.

§ 304. RECOGNITION AND ENFORCEMENT OF FOREIGN ARBITRAL DECISIONS AND AWARDS; RECIPROCITY

Arbitral decisions or awards made in the territory of a foreign State shall, on the basis of reciprocity, be recognized and enforced under this chapter only if that State has ratified or acceded to the Inter–American Convention.

§ 305. RELATIONSHIP BETWEEN THE INTER–AMERICAN CONVENTION AND THE CONVENTION ON THE RECOGNITION AND ENFORCEMENT OF FOREIGN ARBITRAL AWARDS OF JUNE 10, 1958

When the requirements for application of both the Inter–American Convention and the Convention on the Recognition and Enforcement of Foreign Arbitral Awards of June 10, 1958, are met, determination as to which Convention applies shall, unless otherwise expressly agreed, be made as follows:

(1) If a majority of the parties to the arbitration agreement are citizens of a State or States that have ratified or acceded to the Inter–American Convention and are member States of the Organization of American States, the Inter–American convention shall apply.

(2) In all other cases the Convention on the Recognition and Enforcement of Foreign Arbitral Awards of June 10, 1958, shall apply.

§ 306. APPLICABLE RULES OF INTER–AMERICAN COMMERCIAL ARBITRATION COMMISSION

(a) For the purposes of this chapter the rules of procedure of the Inter–American Commercial Arbitration Commission referred to in Article 3 of the Inter–American Convention shall, subject to subsection (b) of this section, be those rules as promulgated by the Commission on July 1, 1988.

(b) In the event the rules of procedure of the Inter–American Commercial Arbitration Commission are modified or amended in accordance with the procedures for amendment of the rules of that Commission, the Secretary of State, by regulation in accordance with section 553 of title 5, consistent with the aims and purposes of this Convention, may prescribe that such modifications or amendments shall be effective for purposes of this chapter.

§ 307. CHAPTER 1: RESIDUAL APPLICATION

Chapter 1 applies to actions and proceedings brought under this chapter to the extent chapter 1 is not in conflict with this chapter or the Inter–American Convention as ratified by the United States.

NOTES AND QUESTIONS

1.   In many respects, especially in the content of Article 5, the Inter–American Convention closely parallels the New York Convention. The Inter–American Convention was designed to act as a type of New York Convention for the Americas and the Organization of American States (OAS). Why was that necessary?

2.   What would happen if the two Conventions could apply simultaneously in a particular case? The United States responded to the latter eventuality by conditioning its ratification upon the following reservation:

Unless there is an express agreement among the parties to an arbitration agreement to the contrary, where the requirements for application of both the Inter–American Convention on International Commercial Arbitration and the Convention on the Recognition and Enforcement of Foreign Arbitral Awards are met, if a majority of such parties are citizens of a state or states that have ratified or acceded to the Inter–American Convention and are member states of the Organization of American States, the Inter–American Convention shall apply. In all other cases, the Convention on the Recognition and Enforcement of Foreign Arbitral Awards shall apply.

3.   The United States also made two other reservations:

The United States of America will apply the rules of procedure of the Inter–American Commercial Arbitration Commission which are in effect on the date that the United States of America deposits its instrument of ratification, unless the United States of America makes a later official determination to adopt and apply subsequent amendments to such rules.

    The United States of America will apply the Convention, on the basis of reciprocity, to the recognition and enforcement of only those awards made in the territory of another Contracting State.

These reservations are reflected in 9 U.S.C. §§ 304, 305, 306.

You should note that 9 U.S.C. § 15 is relevant to the present considerations. Under Section 15 of the FAA, the Act of State doctrine cannot be invoked to frustrate the enforcement of arbitration agreements or arbitral awards. As was discussed in the section on domestic law, it is curious that this provision was added to the domestic legislation on arbitration and was not integrated into the codification of the New York Convention in Chapter Two of the same title. The content of the provision can only be germane to international arbitration, although it could also apply to non-Convention awards that involve State parties. It would, however, be difficult to imagine a situation involving a foreign State party that does not satisfy the definition of 9 U.S.C. § 202—unless the State party has not ratified the Convention (also an unlikely circumstance). Section 15 does make clear, nonetheless, that the Act of State doctrine cannot defeat the recourse to arbitration or the enforcement of an otherwise valid arbitral award.

The Courts and the New York Arbitration Convention

This section contains excerpts from a number of landmark and more recent cases that involve the application and interpretation of the New York Arbitration Convention by U.S. courts. This abbreviated, albeit representative, survey of the federal decisional law reveals a singularity of position that is characteristic of the federal court policy on arbitration— both domestic and international. The courts appear to be mindful of the underlying policy of the Convention, the U.S. Supreme Court's unfailing support of the right to arbitrate, and arbitration's international mandate and mission. The case law generally conveys an impression that the federal courts take a very flexible view of the requirements for the enforceability of awards under the Convention, and that standard legal arguments are unavailing in attempting to challenge awards.

As you read through the cases, imagine circumstances in which procedural deficiencies, inarbitrability, or public policy might be invoked to defeat the enforcement of an international arbitral award. What could constitute a sufficient denial of justice to trigger negative judicial scrutiny? Are political or diplomatic circumstances relevant to the application of the public policy exception? Would a foreign national court judgment on the same issue between the same parties be entitled to the same deference? Why does the judicial position on arbitration have to be so unequivocal and uni-dimensional?

PARSONS & WHITTEMORE OVERSEAS CO., INC. v. SOCIÉTÉ GÉNÉRALE DE L'INDUSTRIE DU PAPIER (RAKTA)

508 F.2d 969 (2d Cir. 1974).

(footnotes omitted)

[. . .]

Parsons & Whittemore Overseas Co., Inc., (Overseas), an American corporation, appeals from the entry of summary judgment ... on the counter-claim by Société Générale de L'Industrie du Papier (RAKTA), an Egyptian corporation, to confirm a foreign arbitral award holding Overseas liable to RAKTA for breach of contract.... We affirm the district court's confirmation of the foreign award....

In November 1962, Overseas consented by written agreement with RAKTA to construct, start up and, for one year, manage and supervise a paperboard mill in Alexandria, Egypt. The Agency for International Development (AID), a branch of the United States State Department, would finance the project by supplying RAKTA with funds with which to purchase letters of credit in Overseas' favor. Among the contract's terms was an arbitration clause, which provided a means to settle differences arising in the course of performance, and a "force majeure" clause, which excused delay in performance due to causes beyond Overseas' reasonable capacity to control.

Work proceeded as planned until May, 1967. Then, with the Arab–Israeli Six Day War on the horizon, recurrent expressions of Egyptian hostility to Americans—nationals of the principal ally of the Israeli enemy—caused the majority of the Overseas work crew to leave Egypt. On June 6, the Egyptian government broke diplomatic ties with the United States and ordered all Americans expelled from Egypt except those who would apply and qualify for a special visa.

Having abandoned the project for the present with the construction phase near completion, Overseas notified RAKTA that it regarded this postponement as excused by the force majeure clause. RAKTA disagreed and sought damages for breach of contract. Overseas refused to settle and RAKTA, already at work on completing the performance promised by Overseas, invoked the arbitration clause. Overseas responded by calling into play the clause's option to bring a dispute directly to a three-man arbitral board governed by the rules of the International Chamber of Commerce. After several sessions in 1970, the tribunal issued a preliminary award, which recognized Overseas' force majeure defense as good only during the period from May 28 to June 30, 1967. In so limiting Overseas' defense, the arbitration court emphasized that Overseas had made no more than a perfunctory effort to secure special visas and that AID's notification that it was withdrawing financial backing did not justify Overseas' unilateral decision to abandon the project. After further hearings in 1972, the tribunal made its final award in March, 1973: Overseas was held liable to RAKTA for $312,507.45 in damages for breach of contract and $30,000 for RAKTA's costs; additionally, the arbitrators' compensation was set at $49,000, with Overseas responsible for three-fourths of the sum.

Subsequent to the final award, Overseas in the action here under review sought a declaratory judgment to prevent RAKTA from collecting the award out of a letter of credit issued in RAKTA's favor by Bank of America at Overseas' request. The letter was drawn to satisfy any "penalties" which an arbitral tribunal might assess against Overseas in the future for breach of contract. RAKTA contended that the arbitral award for damages met the letter's requirement of "penalties" and counterclaimed to confirm and enter judgment upon the foreign arbitral award. Overseas' defenses to this counterclaim, all rejected by the district court, form the principal issues for review on this appeal. Four of these defenses are derived from the express language of the applicable United Nations Convention on the Recognition and Enforcement of Foreign Arbitral Awards ... and a fifth is arguably implicit in the Convention. These include: enforcement of the award would violate the public policy of the United States; the award represents an arbitration of matters not appropriately decided by arbitration; the tribunal denied Overseas an adequate opportunity to present its case; the award is predicated upon a resolution of issues outside the scope of contractual agreement to submit to arbitration; and the award is in manifest disregard of law. In addition to disputing the district court's rejection of its position on the letter of credit, RAKTA seeks on appeal modification of the court's order to correct an arithmetical error in the sum entered for judgment, as well as an assessment of damages and double costs against Overseas for pursuing a frivolous appeal.

I.   OVERSEAS' DEFENSES AGAINST ENFORCEMENT

[...]

A. *Public Policy*

[...]

We conclude ... that the Convention's public policy defense should be construed narrowly. Enforcement of foreign arbitral awards may be denied on this basis only where enforcement would violate the forum state's most basic notions of morality and justice. . . .

Under this view of the public policy provision in the Convention, Overseas' public policy defense may easily be dismissed. Overseas argues that various actions by United States officials subsequent to the severance of American–Egyptian relations—most particularly, AID's withdrawal of financial support for the Overseas–RAKTA contract—required Overseas, as a loyal American citizen, to abandon the project. Enforcement of an award predicated on the feasibility of Overseas' returning to work in defiance of these expressions of national policy would therefore allegedly contravene United States public policy. In equating "national" policy with United States "public" policy, the appellant quite plainly misses the mark. To read the public policy defense as a parochial device protective of national political interests would seriously undermine the Convention's utility. This provision was not meant to enshrine the vagaries of international politics under the rubric of "public policy." Rather, a circumscribed public policy doctrine was contemplated by the Convention's framers and every indication is that the United States, in acceding to the Convention, meant to subscribe to this supranational emphasis. . . .

To deny enforcement of this award largely because of the United States' falling out with Egypt in recent years would mean converting a defense intended to be of narrow scope into a major loophole in the Convention's mechanism for enforcement. We have little hesitation, therefore, in disallowing Overseas' proposed public policy defense.

B.   Nonarbitrability

Article V(2)(a) authorizes a court to deny enforcement, on a defendant's or its own motion, of a foreign arbitral award when "the subject matter of the difference is not capable of settlement by arbitration under the law of that [the forum] country." Under this provision, a court sitting in the United States might, for example, be expected to decline enforcement of an award involving arbitration of an antitrust claim in view of domestic arbitration cases which have held that antitrust matters are entrusted to the exclusive competence of the judiciary. . . . On the other hand, it may well be that the special considerations and policies underlying a "truly international agreement" . . . call for a narrower view of nonarbitrability in the international than the domestic context. . . .

. . . Overseas' argument, that "United States foreign policy issues can hardly be placed at the mercy of foreign arbitrators 'who are charged with the execution of no public trust' and whose loyalties are to foreign interests" . . . plainly fails to raise so substantial an issue of arbitrability. The mere fact that an issue of national interest may incidentally figure into the resolution of a breach of contract claim does not make the dispute not arbitrable. Rather, certain categories of claims may be non-arbitrable because of the special national interest vested in their resolution. . . . Simply because acts of the United States are somehow implicated in a case one cannot conclude that the United States is vitally interested in its outcome.

[. . .]

C. *Inadequate Opportunity to Present Defense*

Under Article V(1)(b) of the Convention, enforcement of a foreign arbitral award may be denied if the defendant can prove that he was "not given proper notice ... or was otherwise unable to present his case." This provision essentially sanctions the application of the forum state's standards of due process. . . .

Overseas seeks relief under this provision for the arbitration court's refusal to delay proceedings in order to accommodate the speaking schedule of one of Overseas' witnesses. . . . This attempt to state a due process claim fails for several reasons. First, inability to produce one's witnesses before an arbitral tribunal is a risk inherent in an agreement to submit to arbitration. By agreeing to submit disputes to arbitration, a party relinquishes his courtroom rights—including that to subpoena witnesses—in favor of arbitration "with all of its well known advantages and drawbacks." . . . Secondly, the logistical problems of scheduling hearing dates convenient to parties, counsel and arbitrators scattered about the globe argues against deviating from an initially mutually agreeable time plan unless a scheduling change is truly unavoidable. . . . Finally, Overseas cannot complain that the tribunal decided the case without considering evidence critical to its defense and within only Mr. Nes' ability to produce. In fact, the tribunal did have before it an affidavit by Mr. Nes. . . .

The arbitration tribunal acted within its discretion in declining to reschedule a hearing for the convenience of an Overseas witness. Overseas' due process rights under American law, rights entitled to full force under the Convention as a defense to enforcement, were in no way infringed by the tribunal's decision.

D. *Arbitration in Excess of Jurisdiction*

Under Article V(1)(c), one defending against enforcement of an arbitral award may prevail by proving that:

> The award deals with a difference not contemplated by or not falling within the terms of the submission to arbitration, or it contains decisions on matters beyond the scope of the submission to arbitration. . . .

This provision tracks in more detailed form § 10(d) of the Federal Arbitration Act, ... which authorizes vacating an award "where the arbitrators exceeded their powers." Both provisions basically allow a party to attack an award predicated upon arbitration of a subject matter not within the agreement to submit to arbitration. This defense to enforcement of a foreign award, like the others already discussed, should be construed narrowly. Once again a narrow construction would comport with the enforcement-facilitating thrust of the Convention. In addition, the caselaw under the similar provision of the Federal Arbitration Act strongly supports a strict reading. . . .

In making this defense as to three components of the award, Overseas must therefore overcome a powerful presumption that the arbitral body acted within its powers. . . .

The appellant's attack on the $60,000 awarded for start-up expenses and $30,000 in costs cannot withstand the most cursory scrutiny. In characterizing the $60,000 as "consequential damages" (and thus proscribed by the arbitration agreement), Overseas is again attempting to secure a reconstruction in this court of the contract . . . an activity wholly inconsistent with the deference due arbitral decisions on law and fact. . . .

Although the Convention recognizes that an award may not be enforced where predicated on a subject matter outside the arbitrator's jurisdiction, it does not sanction second-guessing the arbitrator's construction of the parties' agreement. The appellant's attempt to invoke this defense, however, calls upon the court to ignore this limitation on its decision-making powers and usurp the arbitrator's role. The district court took a proper view of its own jurisdiction in refusing to grant relief on this ground.

E.   Award in "Manifest Disregard" of Law

Both the legislative history of Article V . . . and the statute enacted to implement the United States' accession to the Convention are strong authority for treating as exclusive the bases set forth in the Convention for vacating an award. On the other hand, the Federal Arbitration Act, specifically 9 U.S.C. § 10, has been read to include an implied defense to enforcement where the award is in "manifest disregard" of the law. . . .

This case does not require us to decide, however, whether this defense . . . obtains in the international arbitration context. For even assuming that the "manifest disregard" defense applies under the Convention, we would have no difficulty rejecting the appellant's contention that such "manifest disregard" is in evidence here. Overseas in effect asks this court to read this defense as a license to review the record of arbitral proceedings for errors of fact or law—a role which we have emphatically declined to assume in the past and reject once again. . . .

Insofar as this defense to enforcement of awards in "manifest disregard" of law may be cognizable under the Convention, it, like the other defenses raised by the appellant, fails to provide a sound basis for vacating the foreign arbitral award. We therefore affirm the district court's confirmation of the award.

[. . .]

II.   TECHNICAL CORRECTION OF THE JUDGMENT AND SUPPLEMENTAL AWARD TO PENALIZE PURSUIT OF FRIVOLOUS APPEAL

[. . .]

RAKTA ... requests that this court award it damages and double costs as a penalty against Overseas for pursuing an allegedly frivolous appeal for purposes of delay. It is true that such an award has been made where an appellant presses a case of unquestionable frivolity, particularly where "the inference of an intent to delay is plausible." ... But although we are not persuaded by any of the appellant's numerous defenses to enforcement of the arbitral award, we would consider it harsh indeed to penalize by damages and double costs an effort of apparent honesty to explore the defense possibilities presented by a new and largely untested statute. We therefore reject RAKTA's invitation to supplement its judgment with the type of award reserved for fundamentally insincere appeals.

We affirm the district court's confirmation of the foreign arbitral award. Since the latter affirmance renders academic the validity of the court's disposition of RAKTA's letter of credit claim, we do not rule on RAKTA's appeal from that part of the order below. Additionally, we find no error in the court's computation of Overseas' liability to RAKTA and deny RAKTA's request to assess damages and double costs against Overseas for bringing an allegedly frivolous appeal.

Affirmed.

NOTES AND QUESTIONS

1. How do you evaluate Overseas' arguments against enforcement of the award? Do you find the court's appraisal of the effectiveness of those arguments harsh? Wasn't Overseas indeed being a loyal U.S. citizen, or is Overseas simply exploiting political circumstances to a commercial end? What is the court's primary basis for rejecting Overseas' arguments? What policy does the court espouse? Is the court right about the question of subpoena powers?

2. Consider and assess the implications for the enforcement of the Convention and the evolving judicial doctrine on arbitration of the following statements in the court's opinion:

a) "To read the public policy defense as a parochial device protective of national political interests would seriously undermine the Convention's utility."

b) "...[T]he United States, in acceding to the Convention, meant to subscribe to this supranational emphasis."

c) "The mere fact that an issue of national interest may incidentally figure into the resolution of a breach of contract claim does not make the dispute not arbitrable."

3. What level of scrutiny do you believe is available under the Convention against international arbitral awards after *Parsons*? Does the court deal effectively and appropriately with the merits review question in this case?

FOTOCHROME, INC. v. COPAL CO., LTD.

517 F.2d 512 (2d Cir. 1975).

(footnotes omitted)

[. . .]

The parties to this appeal present some interesting questions concerning the impact of the United Nations Convention on the Recognition and Enforcement of Foreign Arbitral Awards . . . upon the provisions of the Bankruptcy Act. We find that there is no conflict between the Convention and the Act on the facts of this case. We accordingly affirm the order . . . which held that a Bankruptcy Court does not have the power in a Chapter XI arrangement to relitigate the merits of a contract dispute which has been resolved by binding arbitration in a foreign forum, commenced before the filing of the Chapter XI petition and concluded thereafter by an arbitral award in the foreign country.

Fotochrome, Inc. ("Fotochrome"), a Delaware corporation with offices in the Eastern District of New York, and Copal Company, Ltd. ("Copal"), a Japanese corporation, neither present nor doing business in the United States, entered into a contract in 1966 under which Copal would manufacture cameras in Japan according to specifications provided by Fotochrome, and Fotochrome would purchase the cameras for distribution in the United States. A dispute arose in which each party charged the other with failure to abide by the terms of the contract. . . .

The parties had agreed in their contract that final settlement of any disputes arising out of the contract would be reached by arbitration in Tokyo, Japan. In 1967, Copal filed a petition for arbitration with the Japan Commercial Arbitration Association ("JCAA"); Fotochrome filed a formal answer on July 31, 1967. The first of seventeen arbitral sessions was held by the JCAA on December 21, 1967. Fotochrome participated with Japanese counsel in all sessions except the last. Copal presented its evidence in sixteen sessions over the course of twenty-five months.

At the fourteenth session on October 1, 1969, Fotochrome's counsel asked to be allowed to examine two witnesses on his client's behalf. The tribunal scheduled examinations on October 31 and November 5, but the witnesses were not produced. Sessions were rescheduled for December 4 and, later, for January 27, but on each occasion, Fotochrome failed to produce its witnesses. On January 27, 1970 the arbitrators informed Fotochrome's counsel that if the witnesses did not appear at the next session, the arbitration might be terminated. The session was scheduled for March 31.

On March 26, 1970, Fotochrome filed a petition for an arrangement under Chapter XI of the Bankruptcy Act . . . in the Eastern District of New York. Referee Sherman Warner issued an order on March 27 continuing Fotochrome as debtor in possession and enjoining "all creditors of the debtor . . . from commencing or continuing any actions, suits, arbitrations,

or the enforcement of any claim in any Court against this debtor...." ...
The restraining order, in terms, applied only to creditors, not to the
debtor in possession. In any event, Fotochrome did not seek the court's
permission to continue to participate in the JCAA arbitration, although it
knew it was scheduled to present its case in Tokyo four days later.

On March 31, at the JCAA arbitral session, counsel for Fotochrome
notified the tribunal that the petition had been filed in the United States
District Court and that the stay had issued. He did not present the two
witnesses as scheduled. On April 8, Fotochrome's counsel informed the
JCAA that he had been discharged by his client. On April 9, the JCAA
panel convened to consider the effect of Fotochrome's withdrawal and the
stay order of the United States District Court. Copal urged the tribunal to
proceed. On July 2, the tribunal decided that the bankruptcy court's stay
was not effective with respect to it, and ordered the sessions terminated.

On September 18, the arbitral panel issued an award in favor of
Copal.... The tribunal resolved both Copal's claim and Fotochrome's
counterclaim, which it dismissed, considering evidence supplied by both
parties; it was unable, of course, to consider evidence that might have
been supplied by the two witnesses Fotochrome had intended to present....

On October 21, Copal filed the arbitral award with the Tokyo District
Court. As of that time, under Article 800 of the Japan Code of Civil
Procedure, the award became in effect a final and conclusive judgment
settling the rights and obligations of the parties in Japan.

On October 22, Copal filed a proof of claim in Fotochrome's bankruptcy proceedings in the amount of the arbitral award. Apparently in the
belief that the Referee's stay would operate to bar proceedings to enforce
the Japanese award in this country, Copal did not seek confirmation of the
Japanese judgment either in the New York courts under the Act for the
Recognition of Foreign Money Judgments ... or in a federal court under
the Arbitration Act ... or the Convention....

Fotochrome, as debtor in possession, challenged the claim presented
to the Bankruptcy Court, and requested a hearing on the merits of Copal's
underlying claim. Referee Parente, after a preliminary hearing, held that
the Japanese award could not be treated as a final judgment in the
bankruptcy proceeding and that the bankruptcy court would reconsider
the merits of the underlying dispute. The Referee reasoned that under
Section 2a(15) of the Bankruptcy Act, ... the restraining order of March
27 "effectively imposed [the Bankruptcy Court's] paramount authority
over the estate of the debtor in possession ousting the jurisdiction of the
Japan CAA." He ruled that the Japanese arbitral award, obtained after
the filing of the petition for an arrangement, without authority of the
Bankruptcy Court, was not binding on the debtor in possession and could
be reopened for consideration on the merits in the Chapter XI proceeding.

Judge Weinstein reversed the Referee's order, holding that the restraining order of the Bankruptcy Court had no extraterritorial effect as

such, Japan not being within the territorial limits subject to the jurisdiction of the Bankruptcy Court, ... and because Copal did not have the requisite minimum contacts with the United States to render it subject to the in personam jurisdiction of the Bankruptcy Court; that the award was a final judgment under Japanese law; and that the provisions of the bilateral treaty on Friendship, Commerce and Navigation between the United States and Japan ... and the Convention entitled Copal to seek confirmation of its award as a judgment in the United States.

[. . .]

The public policy in favor of international arbitration is strong .... And we have recently indicated that the "public policy" limitation on the Convention is to be construed narrowly to be applied only where enforcement would violate the forum state's most basic notions of morality and justice. *Parsons & Whittemore*....

[. . .]

The conclusion that we must enforce the award as a valid determination on the merits is mandated by the United Nations Convention.... Under ... Article [III], equal treatment of foreign awards is the minimum required of a Contracting State. Foreign awards are vulnerable to attack only on the grounds expressed in other articles of the Convention, particularly Article V....

Under the Convention it seems quite clear that enforcement may be refused at the instance of the losing party only on proof of specified conditions, one of which is that "[t]he party against whom the award is invoked was not given proper notice of the appointment of the arbitrator or of the arbitration proceedings or was otherwise unable to present his case."...

These provisions of the Convention are made effective by the statute which implements the Convention. 9 U.S.C. § 207 provides in part: "The court shall confirm the award unless it finds one of the grounds for refusal or deferral of recognition or enforcement of the award specified in the said Convention."

At this point we must, however, recognize another difficulty. We have recently held that if the arbitral award actually results in a judgment in the foreign country, it may be enforced as a foreign money judgment in the State of New York, regardless of the limiting provisions of the Convention and subject only to the non-enforcement provisions of Article 53 of the New York C.P.L.R .. ...

This raises the question whether the Japanese arbitration award has, *ipso facto*, the status of a judgment, in which event arguments against enforcement would be limited to those provided in Article 53 of the C.P.L.R. if enforcement is sought in the state courts of New York. If it is not equivalent to a judgment, enforcement is governed by the provisions of the Convention.

It is true that, in literal terms, as Judge Weinstein noted, Article 800 of the Japanese Code of Civil Procedure provides: "An [arbitral] award shall have the same effect as a judgment which is final and conclusive between the parties." The Judge stated that the Japanese award may be recognized pursuant to New York's statute on recognition of foreign country money judgments, ... but also noted the provision for removal from state to federal court in actions relating to the Convention.... He carefully refrained from a definitive choice between state and federal courts, declaring that "Copal is now free to seek recognition of its award as an American judgment. Fotochrome may prove grounds for nonrecognition." We think that Judge Weinstein was right in concluding that the Japanese arbitral award may not itself be treated as a foreign money judgment.

Under the Convention, enforcement of an arbitral award may be refused at the instance of the losing party on proof of specified conditions.... There is, in addition, a requirement in Article III of the Convention, as we have seen, that each contracting state shall enforce arbitral awards in accordance with the rules of procedure of the territory where the award is relied upon. Since under our procedure the losing party may object to confirmation on limited grounds that are specified in the Convention, we cannot treat the Japanese arbitral award as equivalent to a final judgment barring such recourse by the losing party when enforcement is sought. We need not rely on theories of territorial jurisdiction to conclude that a foreign award can never be self-executing in the forum state but must be merged in a local judgment to be effective as a matter of domestic law.... The Convention itself makes a distinction between recognition and enforcement of an arbitral award. And when grounds are specified for nonenforcement, such a provision necessarily implies a remedy for its assertion.

The award, on this analysis, is therefore not a judgment under Section 63a(5) of the Bankruptcy Act ... and its filing as a proof of claim was premature. Copal must seek a judgment based on the award in a District Court of the United States under 9 U.S.C. § 207. Fotochrome must, in turn, be given the right to assert the non-enforceability of the award under conditions specified in Article V of the Convention. The determination of the enforcement of the award is a matter not before us on this appeal.

The restraining order of the Bankruptcy Court must be vacated with respect to Copal to allow it to secure a judgment. Both the Supreme Court ... and this court ... have stressed the need for encouraging international arbitration and for putting no roadblocks in its way.

[. . .]

NOTES AND QUESTIONS

1. *Fotochrome* adds little to the discussion of policy articulated in *Parsons*. It deals with and responds to more technical matters. In addition to

conveying a sense of the complexity and hazards of transnational litigation, the case raises a number of doctrinal and practical problems associated with the implementation of the Convention's enforcement provisions. The court's discussion does not elaborate upon the significance of the provision in the arbitral clause for arbitration in Tokyo under Japanese arbitration rules. The impression that is conveyed is that the Japanese arbitration process is equivalent to arbitration in the United States or Europe under AAA or ICC rules of arbitration. That impression, however, is erroneous.

The Japanese attitude toward arbitration is not as favorable as that of their Western counterparts. Japanese culture generally disfavors the recourse to judicial litigation and strongly prefers to have disputes resolved by the parties themselves through negotiations or secondarily with the assistance of a mediator or conciliator. The Japanese see arbitration as an unauthorized form of dispute resolution in which a third party performs the role of a judge without official sanction. Arbitration, in effect, is even more unacceptable to Japanese cultural assumptions than judicial proceedings.

As a result, arbitrations often are conducted as a framework for negotiation or mediation. The arbitral tribunal attempts to get the parties to reach their own settlement. The arbitral tribunal will delay and prolong the proceedings to achieve that objective. This factor may explain why the JCAA proceeding in *Fotochrome* was so protracted, especially in terms of the number of sessions. Also, one wonders why the U.S. company would have agreed to such a one-sided and non-nationality-neutral arbitral procedure?

2. The opinion addresses a number of technical problems. First, it implies a distinction between recognition and enforcement. The New York Convention deals with both the recognition and enforcement of international, nondomestic, or foreign arbitral awards and conditions both determinations on the same grounds. Recognition involves an acknowledgment or a confirmation by a U.S. court of a foreign juridical act—here an arbitral award rendered in Japan. This entitles the award, for example, to be introduced into a domestic legal proceeding and to act as evidence in that proceeding. The introduction of an award that has been given recognition could act as the material foundation for a collateral estoppel defense. Enforcement involves the coercive implementation of the arbitrators' decision within the United States. The arbitral award is converted into a court judgment that is enforceable by all ordinary legal means against the assets of the defendant. The distinction thus far has not given rise to any reported litigation and does not involve a point of significant practical interest.

3. Second, the court notes that international, nondomestic, or foreign awards are not self-executing within the United States. They are subject to an action based on the Convention, unless there is voluntary compliance. If, however, the award is confirmed by the courts in the place of rendition (as it was in *Fotochrome*), the confirmation may convert the award into a foreign judicial act or a foreign court judgment for purposes of enforcement. In that event, the award no longer is an arbitral award, but rather a foreign court judgment. Enforcement would not take place under the Convention, but rather pursuant to the law that governs the enforcement of foreign judgments. Presumably, given its liberal policy, the Convention is more favorable

to enforcement than other legal regimes. In any event, this circumstance could lead to a situation in which a federal court, hearing the litigation on the basis of diversity, applies the state law on the enforcement of foreign judgments to a foreign court judgment recognizing or enforcing an international, nondomestic, or foreign arbitral award. To some degree, this situation may contradict the provisions of 9 U.S.C. §§ 203 & 205, undermining to some extent the authority of federal law in the area and the implementation of the Convention.

4. Third, the court appears to imply that the mere confirmation of an award does not convert it into a foreign court judgment for purposes of enforcement. Accordingly, the award in *Fotochrome* is enforceable by the federal courts under the framework of the Convention. The award, as a private foreign juridical act, is entitled to legal enforcement once it satisfies the conditions of the Convention. At that point, it is converted into a domestic court judgment. That judgment should be final and binding. Even though it provides for the domestic enforcement of an arbitral award, recourse should not be available against it under Section Ten of the FAA. The Convention grounds constitute a *res judicata* resolution of all enforcement questions. If prior foreign court action on the award does amount to a foreign judgment, even federal courts would be obligated to apply state law on the enforcement of foreign judgments. If such laws contain restrictions, they indirectly constrain the recourse to arbitration, thereby raising obliquely issues of federalism in the inapposite context of transborder litigation.

5. The foregoing issues are complex and uncertain both of definition and resolution. They raise speculative difficulties that have not surfaced in the litigation dealing with the Convention. If compelled or invoked, they could do substantial damage to the straightforward and favorable federal policy on arbitration. The *Fotochrome* opinion adumbrates these potential problems and then leaves them in abeyance. The policy on arbitration "for encouraging international arbitration and for putting no roadblocks in its way," 517 F.2d at 519, appears to be the final response of the *Fotochrome* and subsequent courts to the legalistic problems raised by the Convention and the enforcement of international arbitral awards.

NATIONAL OIL CORP. v. LIBYAN SUN OIL CO.

733 F.Supp. 800 (D. Del. 1990).

(footnotes omitted)

[. . .]

FACTUAL BACKGROUND

NOC is a corporation organized under the laws of . . . [Libya] and wholly owned by the Libyan Government. . . . Sun Oil is a Delaware corporation and a subsidiary of Sun Company, Inc. . . . The dispute currently before the Court stems from an Exploration and Production Sharing Agreement ("EPSA") entered into by the parties on November 20, 1980. . . . The EPSA provided, *inter alia*, that Sun Oil was to carry out and fund an oil exploration program in Libya.

Sun Oil began exploration activities in the first half of 1981. On December 18, 1981, Sun Oil invoked the *force majeure* provision contained in the EPSA and suspended performance.... Sun Oil claimed that a State Department order prohibiting the use of United States passports for travel to Libya prevented its personnel, all of whom were U.S. citizens, from going to Libya.... Thus, Sun Oil believed it could not carry out the EPSA "in accordance with the intentions of the parties to the contract." ... NOC disputed Sun Oil's claim of *force majeure* and called for continued performance....

In March of 1982, the U.S. Government banned the importation into the United States of any oil from Libya and severely restricted exports from the United States to Libya.... Export regulations issued by the U.S. Department of Commerce required a license for the export of most goods, including all technical information. Because it "had planned to export substantial quantities of technical data and oil technology to Libya in connection with the exploration program," Sun Oil claims that it filed for such an export license "so as to be prepared to resume operations in Libya promptly in the event the U.S. Government lifted the passport prohibition." ... The application for a license was denied.... Thereafter, in late June of 1982, Sun Oil notified NOC that it was claiming the export regulations as an additional event of *force majeure*....

On July 19, 1982, NOC filed a request for arbitration with the Court of Arbitration of the International Chamber of Commerce ("the ICC") in Paris, France, pursuant to the arbitration provision contained in the EPSA.... The members of the arbitration panel ("the Arbitral Tribunal") were chosen in accordance with the arbitration clause....

The arbitration proceedings were held in Paris, France. In May and June of 1984, the Arbitral Tribunal held hearings on the issue of *force majeure*. It issued an initial award on May 31, 1985, that stated there had been no *force majeure* within the meaning of the EPSA.... The Arbitral Tribunal later held further hearings, and on February 23, 1987, it rendered a second and final award in favor of NOC and against Sun Oil in the amount of twenty million U.S. dollars.... NOC has since been unable to collect payment from Sun Oil....

[...]

THE MOTION TO DISMISS

Sun Oil makes numerous arguments regarding why NOC's petition for recognition of this arbitral award should be dismissed. For the reasons stated below, the Court will deny Sun Oil's motion.

I. Recognition as Prerequisite for Access to U.S. Courts

In support of its motion to dismiss NOC's petition, Sun Oil first advances the argument that NOC, as an arm of the Libyan Government, is not entitled to access to U.S. courts because of the status of U.S.-Libyan relations. NOC counters that it is an entity owned by a foreign government which is recognized by the U.S., and is thus entitled to access to our courts regardless of the present state of diplomatic relations between the U.S. and Libya. The Court agrees with NOC that it should not be barred from U.S. courts merely because of poor U.S.-Libyan relations.

[. . .]

The Supreme Court more recently reaffirmed, in dictum, its adherence to this recognition-access principle. "It has long been established," stated the Court, "that only governments recognized by the United States and at peace with us are entitled to access to our courts. . . ." . . . In sum, under existing case law it is clear that NOC should not be barred from this Court unless the United States either does not recognize the Qadhafi Government, or is at war with Libya.

. . . Sun Oil further argues that the appropriate inquiry, for determining whether a foreign government should be denied access to U.S. courts based on foreign policy concerns, is no longer whether a government is "recognized." . . . Therefore, after detailing the decline of U.S.-Libyan relations, Sun Oil concludes that the resulting breakdown in diplomatic relations bars the Libyan Government's access to U.S. courts. . . .

Nevertheless, Libya is still "recognized" by the U.S., albeit perhaps only "technically" given the unfriendly state of relations. . . . [I]t seems clear that however poor relations with Qadhafi may be today, relations with Castro when *Sabbatino* was decided were at least equally strained. Thus, under the Supreme Court's *Sabbatino* analysis, the currently unfriendly state of diplomatic relations with Libya would not appear to be sufficient to bar the Libyan Government from U.S. courts.

A second reason why the Libyan Government should not be barred from our courts because of the state of its diplomatic relations with the U.S. is that the Executive Branch has indicated its preference that the Libyan Government should be given access by granting NOC a license to initiate these proceedings. . . .

[. . .]

Regardless of how repugnant the current Libyan Government may be to this Court and the American public, President Bush has not derecognized it. Instead, his Administration has seen fit to issue NOC a license to bring this suit. The Court has no choice here but to defer to the foreign policy wisdom of the Executive Branch.

[. . .]

THE MOTION TO ENFORCE THE ARBITRAL AWARD

The Convention on the Recognition and Enforcement of Foreign Arbitral Awards attempts "to *encourage* the recognition and enforcement of commercial arbitration agreements in international contracts and to unify the standards by which agreements to arbitrate are observed and arbitral awards are enforced in the signatory countries." . . . This Court must recognize the award rendered by the ICC Arbitral Tribunal in NOC's favor unless Sun Oil can successfully assert one of the seven defenses enumerated in Article V of the Convention. . . . Sun Oil has invoked three of the seven defenses against recognition. . . . It bears the burden of proving that any of these defenses is applicable. . . .

After considering the evidence and arguments of the parties, this Court, for the reasons outlined below, rejects Sun Oil's defenses and concludes that the arbitral award is entitled to recognition and enforcement under the Convention.

I.   Use of "False and Misleading" Testimony

Sun Oil's first ground for asserting that the arbitral award should not be recognized revolves around the Arbitral Tribunal's reliance on the testimony of a Mr. C. James Blom, a witness for NOC. Essentially, Sun Oil claims that Mr. Blom's testimony was false and misleading, that this testimony was critical to the Arbitral Tribunal's decision, and, therefore, that recognition of the award would violate Sun Oil's due process rights. . . .

Intentionally giving false testimony in an arbitration proceeding would constitute fraud. . . . But "in order to protect the finality of arbitration decisions, courts must be slow to vacate an arbitral award on the ground of fraud." . . . Accordingly, "[t]he fraud must not have been discoverable upon the exercise of due diligence prior to the arbitration." . . . The alleged fraud must also relate to a material issue. . . .

a.   Mr. Blom's Credentials

Sun Oil's first challenge, regarding the alleged misrepresentation of Mr. Blom's credentials, borders on the frivolous. It is true that the Tribunal appears to have misunderstood the extent of Mr. Blom's actual duties. But there is no reason to conclude that NOC was at fault for this misapprehension.

Mr. Blom's testimony was completely accurate. . . . If the Tribunal got the wrong impression about Mr. Blom's relationship with Occidental's Libyan operations or the meaning of his area of responsibility (the "Eastern Hemisphere"), it is Sun Oil's own fault.

Counsel for Sun Oil had ample opportunity to cross-examine Mr. Blom regarding the extent of his duties. . . . Counsel simply chose not to do so. Moreover, Mr. Blom's appearance as a witness was not a surprise. NOC had provided Sun Oil with its list of witnesses over six months before Mr. Blom testified. . . . That list not only identified Mr. Blom as an NOC witness, but also noted his credentials and relationship to Occidental, and stated as to which matters he would testify. . . .

[. . .]

b.   Alleged Use of Canadian Personnel

Sun Oil's second challenge to Mr. Blom's testimony has more force, but is nonetheless not sufficient to warrant nonrecognition of the Tribunal's award. Mr. Blom's statement that Occidental replaced its American personnel with Canadians does in fact appear to have been inaccurate.... But, as with its first challenge, Sun Oil has not produced any evidence to show that this inaccuracy was anything other than unintentional.

[...]

The most important consideration of all, however, is that Sun Oil was able to present all of these arguments to the Arbitral Tribunal.... Mr. Blom's affidavit, which recounts what transpired during his second appearance before the Tribunal in June of 1986, attests to the fact that all of Sun Oil's current arguments were made to, and hence implicitly rejected by, the Tribunal.... Sun Oil has not exactly offered an alternate picture of what occurred during this second hearing. Its few comments on this issue are rather ambiguous and are not supported by any affidavits or other evidence.

The Court therefore accepts Mr. Blom's description of the second hearing, and concludes that Sun Oil was not prevented from presenting its case.... In addition, Sun Oil has not proven fraud. Alternatively, even assuming the alleged fraud did occur, it did not relate to a material issue in the arbitration, and Sun Oil could have discovered it during the proceedings.

II.   *Damage Award Not Supported by the Evidence*

Sun Oil's second challenge to confirmation of the award focuses on the $20 million the Tribunal granted in damages. According to Sun Oil, confirmation of the award should be denied based on article V, section 1(c), because the arbitrators exceeded their authority, and based on article V, section 2(b), the Convention's public policy defense, because confirmation would violate due process. Sun Oil argues that the Tribunal exceeded its authority because it did not base its damage award on the evidence presented and instead acted as an *amiable compositeur*, which tries to reach merely an equitable, and not necessarily legal, result. Sun Oil also argues that the Tribunal did not have jurisdiction to consider NOC's claims based on Article 8.2 of the EPSA because such claims were outside the scope of the Terms of Reference to which the parties agreed before submitting their dispute to arbitration.

Article V, section (1)(c) of the Convention, on which Sun Oil relies, "tracks in more detailed form § 10(d) of the Federal Arbitration Act, ... which authorizes vacating an award '[w]here the arbitrators exceeded their powers.'" ...Like other Convention defenses to enforcement of a foreign arbitral award, this defense "should be construed narrowly." ... Its counterpart, section 10(d) of the Federal Arbitration Act, has also been given a narrow reading....

The Third Circuit recently addressed a claim that an arbitral award should be vacated because the arbitrators exceeded their powers in violation of section 10(d) of the Federal Arbitration Act.... [There, the court] ... describes the inquiry a court should undertake as follows:

It is ... well established that the "court's function in confirming or vacating a commercial [arbitration] award is severely limited." In conducting our review we must examine both the form of relief awarded by the arbitrator as well as the terms of that relief. We must determine if the form of the arbitrators' award can be *rationally derived* either from the agreement between the parties or from the parties submissions to the arbitrators. In addition, the terms of the arbitral award will not be subject to judicial revision unless they are *"completely irrational."* ...

... For the reasons stated below, the Court finds that the Tribunal's award of damages was "rationally derived" from the parties' agreement and that the terms of the award are not "completely irrational."

a. Jurisdiction of the Tribunal

The arbitration clause contained in the EPSA is very broad. It provides, *inter alia*, that "[a]ny *controversy or claim* arising out of or relating to this Agreement, or breach thereof, shall, in the absence of an amicable arrangement between the Parties, be settled by arbitration...."
... The Terms of Reference, pursuant to which the dispute underlying this case was submitted to arbitration, specifically state that one of the "issues to be determined" at arbitration was "[t]o what relief, if any, is each party entitled?" ... In addition, as stated in the Terms of Reference, NOC's claims included the allegation that Sun Oil was "liable to NOC for all remedies and amounts available under the EPSA and the applicable law...." ... Thus, the issue of damages, under Article 8.2 or any other provision of the EPSA, was properly before the arbitrators.

b. The Tribunal's Rationale for Damages

After evaluating whether and to what extent Sun Oil was liable for damages, the Arbitral Tribunal concluded that Article 8.2 of the EPSA constituted a liquidated damages provision.... The Tribunal found that this language in the contract made Sun Oil liable "for the costs of the uncompleted part of the exploration program ... [without any] finding that the First Party [NOC] suffered actual loss." ... The Tribunal went on, however, to consider the effects of Libyan law, which governs the EPSA.

The Tribunal noted that, under Libyan law, liquidated damages provisions are valid; however, "damages fixed in advance by such [liquidated damages] clauses are not due 'if the debtor establishes that the creditor has not suffered any loss'[ ]" whatsoever.... The Tribunal concluded that "the debtor," Sun Oil, failed to establish that NOC had not suffered a loss....

Having concluded that Sun Oil failed to make out the requisite showing under Libyan law that NOC did not suffer any loss at all, the Tribunal then went on to consider whether the entire sum called for by the contract as liquidated damages should in fact be awarded. The Tribunal focused again on Libyan law, which provides that "[t]he Judge may reduce the amount of these [liquidated] damages if the debtor establishes that the amount fixed was grossly exaggerated or that the principal obligation has been partially performed." ... For several reasons—including its conclusions that Sun Oil, although incorrect in claiming *force majeure*, nevertheless acted in good faith, that NOC did not make reasonable efforts to mitigate its loss, and that the cost of NOC's actual loss decreased because of the drop in global crude oil prices—the Tribunal found that NOC's recovery of liquidated damages should be limited to $20 million....

In fashioning its damages award, the Tribunal carefully considered both the EPSA and Libyan law, as well as the submissions and arguments of the parties. The Court finds that there is nothing "completely irrational" about the Tribunal's award or its reading of the parties' contract. Thus, mindful of the fact that "[i]t is not this Court's role ... to sit as the panel did and reexamine the evidence under the guise of determining whether the arbitrators exceeded their powers," ... the Court will not inquire any further.

c.   *Sun Oil's Due Process Rights*

Sun Oil argues that its due process rights would be violated by confirmation of this damages award. Hence, it asks that the award not be recognized based on the Convention's public policy defense. Because the Court has already concluded that the Tribunal's award is rationally derived from the language contained in the EPSA and Libyan law, Sun Oil's due process argument does not have any merit.

III.   *Violation of U.S. Public Policy*

Sun Oil's final challenge to confirmation of the award rests solely on the public policy exception contained in article V, section 2(b), of the Convention. Both parties in this case agree that the public policy defense "should be construed narrowly," and that confirmation of a foreign award should be denied on the basis of public policy "only where enforcement would violate the forum state's most basic notions of morality and justice." ... Not too surprisingly, however, the parties do not agree as to whether this particular case fits within such a definition of the public policy defense.

Sun Oil argues that confirmation of the award in this case would violate the public policy of the United States for three reasons. First, Sun Oil contends that because confirmation would "penalize Sun for obeying and supporting the directives and foreign policy objectives of its government," other companies and individuals would be less likely to support U.S. sanctions programs, thereby diminishing "[t]he ability of the U.S. government to make and enforce policies with economic costs to U.S. citizens and corporations...." ... Secondly, Sun Oil contends that confirming the award would simply be "inconsistent with the substance of United States antiterrorism policy" ... and thirdly, that it would also "undermine the internationally-supported antiterrorism policy...by sending a contradictory signal concerning U.S. commitment to this policy and by making possible the transfer to . . . Libya . . . [of] funds which could be employed to finance its continuing terrorist activities." . . .

The problem with Sun Oil's arguments is that "public policy" and "foreign policy" are not synonymous. For example, in *Parsons & Whittemore* . . . the Second Circuit addressed this very issue, saying: "To read the public policy defense as a parochial device protective of national political interests would seriously undermine the Convention's utility. This provision was not meant to enshrine the vagaries of international politics under the rubric of 'public policy.'"

[. . .]

Despite Sun Oil's attempts to distinguish *Parsons*, it is clear that the policy objectives at issue here and the ones at issue in *Parsons* differ, at most, in degree and not in kind. This Court does not doubt that the ugly picture of the Qadhafi Government painted by Sun Oil's papers is accurate. The Court is similarly cognizant of the fact that Libya itself is not a signatory to the Convention; and hence, "if the tables were turned," as Sun Oil points out, a U.S. company would not necessarily be able to enforce an arbitral award against NOC in the Libyan courts. . . . But Libya's terrorist tactics and opportunistic attitude towards international commercial arbitration are simply *beside the point*.

[. . .]

CONCLUSION

The Court will recognize and enforce the Tribunal's award in favor of NOC and against Sun Oil in the amount of 20 million U.S. dollars, with prejudgment and postjudgment interest as described above.

A final judgment will be entered in accordance with this opinion; but execution on the judgment will be stayed, and the judgment may not be registered and transferred in accordance with 28 U.S.C. § 1963 unless the Libyan Sanctions Regulations are complied with. . . .

[. . .]

NOTES AND QUESTIONS

1.   The court in *Sun Oil* goes through an extensive review of various segments of the arbitral proceeding and determination. The adverse party, in effect, wants the court to second-guess the arbitral tribunal on various matters (*e.g.*, conduct of the proceeding as to witness testimony and as to the assessment of damages). Is it appropriate for the court even to consider such claims? Doesn't this amount to a review of the merits of the proceeding and of the determination? Although the court eventually rules in favor of sustaining the arbitrators' determinations, a more adaptive position might have consisted of refusing to entertain the arguments in the first place. They go directly to the merits of the case. Do you agree? Is the court engaging in a form of merits review with the caveat that it will always affirm the conclusions and conduct of the arbitral tribunal? Is this the most sensible position that could be adopted in these circumstances?

2. *Sun Oil* is an excellent illustration of the overlap between a political and a commercial dispute. It illuminates the dangers associated with foreign investment and the conduct of transborder business with foreign State-owned entities. The composition of the arbitral tribunal reflected the elevated status of the parties and the amount of the claim. The tribunal consisted of a former U.S. Senator and Secretary of State, Edmund Muskie, a distinguished German legal scholar, and the former Chief Justice of the French Court of Cassation. Although the tribunal members had the experience and skill to deal with the complex layers of the litigation, is a standard ICC arbitral procedure the appropriate vehicle by which to address the resolution of the claim? The parties themselves chose the process, but would you have advised them to consider other options? Libyan law governs the contract, but there was no Libyan law expert or lawyer on the tribunal. Is this a patent deficiency or does the law applicable have little impact upon the process? Is it likely that any court but a Libyan court would challenge the ability of the tribunal members to dispense justice in this case? Isn't Sun Oil wasting its money on lawyer fees?

3. You should assess the process of scrutiny that is available under the Convention for challenging international arbitral awards. What is the meaning and purpose of the public policy exception to enforcement in light of *Sun Oil*? What arguments are likely to work under Article V of the Convention?

4. Should the concept of reciprocity have been relevant to the determination?

In the Matter of *Chromalloy Aeroservices*

The decision in the *Chromalloy* case addresses the question of whether a U.S. court—applying the New York Arbitration Convention—should enforce an international arbitral award that has been set aside by a court at the place of rendition. The question involves an apparent conflict between Articles V and VII of the New York Arbitration Convention. Generally, it implicates the functioning of the process of international commercial arbitration and of the New York Arbitration Convention.

The approving view argues that *Chromalloy* adds to the autonomy of international commercial arbitration by insulating it from arbitrary national idiosyncrasies on arbitration:

> By limiting the ability of courts in the countries of origin to thwart enforcement abroad through the use of their nullification powers, the court's decision sends a message to business, governments, and arbitrators that they can rely on international arbitration for final and binding resolution of the merits of disputes.

Sampliner, *Enforcement of Foreign Arbitral Awards After Annulment in Their Country of Origin*, 11–9 MEALEY'S INT'L ARB REP. 22, 28 (1996). The disapproving interpretation criticizes the U.S. court's disregard of treaty obligations and its creation of potential inconsistencies in enforcement:

> Enforcing set aside awards may result in the coexistence of two conflicting awards concerning the same issues between the same parties, and thus

violate the intended uniformity of the Convention and damage the image of international commercial arbitration.

Gharavi, *Chromalloy: Another View*, 12–1 MEALEY'S INT'L ARB. REP. 21, 23 (1997).

Another commentator sees *Chromalloy* as providing support for the position that the New York Arbitration Convention establishes a permissive set of guidelines for enforcement matters:

> ... I propose here to demonstrate that the leading commentator on the New York Convention, Prof. van den Berg, is wrong when he contends that Article V(1)(e) of the New York Convention precludes the enforcement of an award set aside in its country of origin. The fact is that courts of a State bound by the Convention *cannot violate it by enforcing a foreign award*. Rather, a violation would occur if such a court were to *refuse* enforcement in the absence of one of the limited exceptions defined in Article V(1).
>
> This brings us to a core objective of the New York Convention: to free the international arbitral process from the domination of the law of the place of arbitration.

Paulsson, *Rediscovering the N.Y. Convention: Further Reflections on Chromalloy*, 12–4 MEALEY'S INT'L ARB. REP. 20, 24 (1997).

The federal court action was echoed in at least one major European arbitration jurisdiction. The Paris Court of Appeals upheld a lower court decision granting enforcement to the *Chromalloy* award in France. *See* 12–4 MEALEY'S INT'L ARB. REP. 5 (1997). The court reasoned that, under the 1982 Franco–Egyptian Treaty of Judicial Cooperation, domestic French law applied pursuant to Article VII of the New York Arbitration Convention. In matters of enforcement, French law (which does not include foreign annulment of the award as a ground for nonenforcement) is less restrictive than the Convention.

Apparently, this position is not new among French courts. According to Gharavi, "[f]or more than a decade, French courts have held that the setting aside of a foreign arbitral award in the rendering country is not a ground for refusing enforcing of the award in France." Gharavi, *Chromalloy: Another View*, *supra*, at 25, n. 8. *See also* Gharavi, *Enforcing Set Aside Arbitral Awards: France's Controversial Steps Beyond The New York Convention*, 6 J. TRANSNAT'L L. & POL'Y 93 (1996). In a reply to Paulsson, Gharavi states pointedly that "[t]he fact that the award was also enforced in France does not make *Chromalloy* immune from criticism." Gharavi, *The Legal Inconsistencies of Chromalloy*, 12–5 MEALEY'S INT'L ARB. REP. 21, 22 (1997).

The text of the *Chromalloy* decision is reproduced below. It should be evaluated by reference generally to the basic U.S. judicial policy on arbitration and more specifically as it relates to the enforcement question. Do you find the court's reasoning persuasive? Is there no textual conflict between the various provisions of the New York Arbitration Convention? Is Paulsson's construction of the Convention plausible in light of the court's opinion? Is Gharavi's view more prudent and practical?

IN THE MATTER OF THE ARBITRATION
OF CERTAIN CONTROVERSIES BETWEEN
CHROMALLOY AEROSERVICES AND
THE ARAB REPUBLIC OF EGYPT

939 F.Supp. 907 (D. D.C. 1996).

(footnotes omitted)

[...]

II. BACKGROUND

This case involves a military procurement contract between a U.S. corporation, Chromalloy Aeroservices, Inc., [(CAS)], and the Air Force of the Arab Republic of Egypt.

On June 16, 1988, Egypt and CAS entered into a contract under which CAS agreed to provide parts, maintenance, and repair for helicopters belonging to the Egyptian Air Force.... On December 2, 1991, Egypt terminated the contract by notifying CAS representatives in Egypt.... On December 4, 1991, Egypt notified CAS headquarters in Texas of the termination.... On December 5, 1991, CAS notified Egypt that it rejected the cancellation of the contract "and commenced arbitration proceedings on the basis of the arbitration clause contained in Article XII and Appendix E of the Contract."... Egypt then drew down CAS' letters of guarantee in an amount totaling some $11,475,968....

On February 23, 1992, the parties began appointing arbitrators, and shortly thereafter, commenced a lengthy arbitration.... On August 24, 1994, the arbitral panel ordered Egypt to pay to CAS the sums of $272,900 plus 5 percent interest from July 15, 1991, (interest accruing until the date of payment), and $16,940,958 plus 5 percent interest from December 15, 1991, (interest accruing until the date of payment).... The panel also ordered CAS to pay to Egypt the sum of 606,920 pounds sterling, plus 5 percent interest from December 15, 1991, (interest accruing until the date of payment)....

On October 28, 1994, CAS applied to this Court for enforcement of the award. On November 13, 1994, Egypt filed an appeal with the Egyptian Court of Appeal, seeking nullification of the award. On March 1, 1995, Egypt filed a motion with this Court to adjourn CAS's [sic] Petition to enforce the award. On April 4, 1995, the Egyptian Court of Appeal suspended the award, and on May 5, 1995, Egypt filed a Motion in this Court to Dismiss CAS's [sic] petition to enforce the award. On December 5, 1995, Egypt's Court of Appeal at Cairo issued an order nullifying the award....

Egypt argues that this Court should deny CAS' Petition to Recognize and Enforce the Arbitral Award out of deference to its court.... CAS argues that this Court should confirm the award because Egypt "does not present any serious argument that its court's nullification decision is consistent with the New York Convention or United States arbitration law.''...

III. DISCUSSION

A. *Jurisdiction*

[...]

CAS brings this action to confirm an arbitral award made pursuant to an agreement to arbitrate any and all disputes arising under a contract between itself and Egypt, a foreign state, concerning a subject matter capable of settlement by arbitration under U.S. law.... Enforcement of the award falls under the Convention on Recognition and Enforcement of Foreign Arbitral Awards, (''Convention''), ... which grants ''[t]he district courts of the United States ... original jurisdiction over such an action or proceeding, regardless of the amount in controversy.''...

B. *Chromalloy's Petition for Enforcement*

A party seeking enforcement of a foreign arbitral award must apply for an order confirming the award within three years after the award is made.... The award in question was made on August 14, 1994. CAS filed a Petition to confirm the award with this Court on October 28, 1994, less than three months after the arbitral panel made the award. CAS's [sic] Petition includes a ''duly certified copy'' of the original award as required by Article IV(1)(a) of the Convention, translated by a duly sworn translator, as required by Article IV(2) of the Convention, as well as a duly certified copy of the original contract and arbitration clause, as required by Article IV(1)(b) of the Convention.... CAS's Petition is properly before this Court.

1. *The Standard under the Convention*

This Court *must* grant CAS's [sic] Petition to Recognize and Enforce the arbitral ''award unless it finds one of the grounds for refusal ... of recognition or enforcement of the award specified in the ... Convention.''... Under the Convention, ''Recognition and enforcement of the award *may* be refused'' if Egypt furnishes to this Court ''proof that ... [t]he award has ... been set aside ... by a competent authority of the country in which, or under the law of which, that award was made.'' ... In the present case, the award was made in Egypt, under the laws of Egypt, and has been nullified by the court designated by Egypt to review arbitral awards. Thus, the Court *may*, at its discretion, decline to enforce the award.

While Article V provides a discretionary standard, Article VII of the Convention *requires* that, ''The provisions of the present Convention *shall not* ... deprive any interested party of any right he may have to avail himself of an arbitral award in the manner and to the extent allowed by the law ... of the count[r]y where such award is sought to be relied upon.'' ... In other words, under the Convention, CAS maintains all rights to the enforcement of this Arbitral Award that it would have in the absence of the Convention. Accordingly, the Court finds that, if the Convention did not exist, the Federal Arbitration Act ("FAA") would provide CAS with a legitimate claim to enforcement of this arbitral award. . . . Jurisdiction over Egypt in such a suit would be available under 28 U.S.C. §§ 1330 (granting jurisdiction over foreign states "as to any claim for relief in personam with respect to which the foreign state is not entitled to immunity . . . under sections 1605–1607 of this title") and 1605(a)(2) (withholding immunity of foreign states for "an act outside . . . the United States in connection with a commercial activity of the foreign state elsewhere and that act causes a direct effect in the United States"). . . . Venue for the action would lie with this Court under 28 U.S.C. § 1391(f) & (f)(4) (granting venue in civil cases against foreign governments to the United States District Court for the District of Columbia).

2. *Examination of the Award under 9 U.S.C. § 10*

[. . .]

The Court's analysis thus far has addressed the arbitral award, and, as a matter of U.S. law, the award is proper. . . . The Court now considers the question of whether the decision of the Egyptian court should be recognized as a valid foreign judgment.

As the Court state earlier, this is a case of first impression. There are no reported cases in which a court of the United States has faced a situation, under the Convention, in which the court of a foreign nation has nullified an otherwise valid arbitral award. This does not mean, however, that the Court is without guidance in this case. . . .

In *Scherk*, the Court forced a U.S. corporation to arbitrate a dispute arising under an international contract containing an arbitration clause. . . . In so doing, the Court relied upon the FAA, but took the opportunity to comment upon the purposes of the newly acceded-to Convention:

> The delegates to the Convention voiced frequent concern that courts of signatory countries in which an agreement to arbitrate is sought to be enforced should not be permitted to decline enforcement of such agreements on the basis of parochial views of their desirability or in a manner that would diminish the mutually binding nature of the agreements. . . . [W]e think that this country's adoption and ratification of the Convention and the passage of Chapter 2 of the United States Arbitration Act provide strongly persuasive evidence of congressional policy consistent with the decision we reach today.

. . . The Court finds this argument equally persuasive in the present case, where Egypt seeks to repudiate its solemn promise to abide by the results of the arbitration.

C. The Decision of Egypt's Court of Appeal

1. The Contract

[. . .]

. . . Article XII of the contract requires that the parties arbitrate all disputes that arise between them under the contract. Appendix E, which defines the terms of any arbitration, forms an integral part of the contract. The contract is unitary. Appendix E to the contract defines the "Applicable Law Court of Arbitration." The clause reads, in relevant part:

> It is . . . understood that both parties have irrevocably agreed to apply Egypt (sic) Laws and to choose Cairo as seat of the court of arbitration.

> * * *

> The decision of the said court shall be final and binding and cannot be made subject to any appeal or other recourse. . . .

This Court may not assume that the parties intended these two sentences to contradict one another, and must preserve the meaning of both if possible. . . . Egypt argues that the first quoted sentence supersedes the second, and allows an appeal to an Egyptian court. Such an interpretation, however, would vitiate the second sentence, and would ignore the plain language on the face of the contract. The Court concludes that the first sentence defines choice of law and choice of forum for the hearings of the arbitral panel. The Court further concludes that the second quoted sentence indicates the clear intent of the parties that any arbitration of a dispute arising under the contract is not to be appealed to any court. This interpretation, unlike that offered by Egypt, preserves the meaning of both sentences in a manner that is consistent with the plain language of the contract. The position of the latter sentence as the seventh and final paragraph, just before the signatures, lends credence to the view that this sentence is the final word on the arbitration question. In other words, the parties agreed to apply Egyptian Law to the arbitration, but, more important, they agreed that the arbitration ends with the decision of the arbitral panel.

2. The Decision of the Egyptian Court of Appeal

The Court has already found that the arbitral award is proper as a matter of U.S. law, and that the arbitration agreement between Egypt and CAS precluded an appeal in Egyptian courts. The Egyptian court has acted, however, and Egypt asks this Court to grant *res judicata* effect to that action.

The "requirements for enforcement of a foreign judgment . . . are that there be 'due citation' [*i.e.*, proper service of process] and that the original claim not violate U.S. public policy." . . . The Court uses the term "public policy" advisedly, with a full understanding that, "[J]udges have no license to impose their own brand of justice in determining applicable public policy." . . . Correctly understood, "[P]ublic policy emanates [only] from clear statutory or case law, 'not from general considerations of supposed public interest.' " . . .

The U.S. public policy in favor of final and binding arbitration of commercial disputes is unmistakable, and supported by treaty, by statute, and by case law. The Federal Arbitration Act "and the implementation of the Convention in the same year by amendment of the Federal Arbitration Act," demonstrate that there is an "emphatic federal policy in favor of arbitral dispute resolution," particularly "in the field of international commerce." . . . A decision by this Court to recognize the decision of the Egyptian court would violate this clear U.S. public policy.

3.   *International Comity*

"No nation is under an unremitting obligation to enforce foreign interests which are fundamentally prejudicial to those of the domestic forum." . . . "[C]omity *never* obligates a national forum to ignore 'the rights of its own citizens or of other persons who are under the protection of its laws.' " . . . Egypt alleges that, "Comity is the chief doctrine of international law *requiring* U.S. courts to respect the decisions of competent foreign tribunals." However, comity does not and may not have the preclusive effect upon U.S. law that Egypt wishes this Court to create for it.

[. . .]

4.   *Choice of Law*

Egypt argues that by choosing Egyptian law, and by choosing Cairo as the sight [sic] of the arbitration, CAS has for all time signed away its rights under the Convention and U.S. law. This argument is specious. When CAS agreed to the choice of law and choice of forum provisions, it waived its right to sue Egypt for breach of contract in the courts of the United States in favor of final and binding arbitration of such a dispute under the Convention. Having prevailed in the chosen forum, under the chosen law, CAS comes to this Court seeking recognition and enforcement of the award. The Convention was created for just this purpose. It is untenable to argue that by choosing arbitration under the Convention, CAS has waived rights specifically guaranteed by that same Convention.

5.   *Conflict between the Convention & the FAA*

As a final matter, Egypt argues that, "Chromalloy's use of [A]rticle VII [to invoke the Federal Arbitration Act] contradicts the clear language of the Convention and would create an impermissible conflict under 9 U.S.C. § 208," by eliminating all consideration of Article V of the Convention. . . . As the Court has explained, however, Article V provides a permissive standard, under which this Court *may* refuse to enforce an award. Article VII, on the other hand, mandates that this Court *must* consider CAS' claims under applicable U.S. law.

Article VII of the Convention provides:

The provisions of the present Convention shall not ... deprive any interested party of any right he may have to avail himself of an arbitral award in the manner and to the extend allowed by the law ... of the count[r]y where such award is sought to be relied upon.

9 U.S.C. § 201 note. Article VII does not eliminate all consideration of Article V; it merely requires that this Court protect any rights that CAS has under the domestic laws of the United States. There is no conflict between CAS' use of Article VII to invoke the FAA and the language of the Convention.

IV. CONCLUSION

The Court concludes that the award of the arbitral panel is valid as a matter of U.S. law. The Court further concludes that it need not grant *res judicata* effect to the decision of the Egyptian Court of Appeal at Cairo. Accordingly, the Court GRANTS Chromalloy Aeroservices' Petition to Recognize and Enforce the Arbitral Award, and DENIES Egypt's Motion to Dismiss that Petition.

NOTES AND QUESTIONS

1.   In related litigation, the U.S. District Court of the Southern District of New York recently refused to enforce an arbitral award rendered in Italy because the award had been nullified by an Italian court of first instance, and the nullification had been upheld by Italy's highest court. The trial court in Italy ruled that the arbitrators had exceeded their authority because they conferred a "bonus" on the petitioner that had not been authorized by the parties' contract. The petitioner sought to enforce the award in the district court in New York while his opponent challenged the award before the Italian courts. The district court deferred judgment until after a decision by the Italian trial court, at which time the petitioner renewed his petition. The district court denied the petition. The court stated that, under the Convention on the Recognition and Enforcement of Foreign Arbitral Awards, the State (in this case, Italy) where an award is rendered is free to set aside an arbitral award in accordance with its own law. Moreover, a foreign court decision setting aside an award should not be ignored simply because a national court would have reached a different result with respect to the enforcement of the award under an application of domestic law. *See Spier v. Calzaturificio Tecnica, S.p.A.*, 77 F.Supp.2d 405 (S.D.N.Y. 1999).

2.   Martin Spier, an engineer and U.S. citizen, entered into a contract with Calzaturificio Tecnica S.p.A. ("Tecnica"), an Italian corporation, to provide expertise for the manufacture, by Tecnica, of various hard boots. The contract was executed in Italy and included an agreement to arbitrate any disputes arising between the two parties concerning the contract. A dispute arose between Tecnica and Spier over compensation for a line of footwear allegedly created with the help of Spier's expertise. The dispute went to arbitration. During the arbitration, the arbitrators retained a technical consultant who advised them on the disputed issue. The arbitrators declined to follow the consultant's opinion. The arbitrators awarded Spier monetary

damages—an award that Spier would not have received had the arbitrators followed the consultant's opinion. Tecnica appealed the award to an Italian court.

The Italian court of first instance entered judgment nullifying the award. The court of appeals of Venice affirmed the judgment, which was in turn affirmed by Italy's highest court, the Court of Cassation. In its decision, the Court of Cassation stated that the arbitrators exceeded their authority by rendering an award that was unrelated to the content of the arbitration agreement. While the challenge to the award was being made in Italy, Spier petitioned the U.S. district court in New York to enforce the award. The court deferred the U.S. enforcement proceedings, pending the outcome of the appeals in Italy. When Spier renewed his petition, the district court denied it on the basis of the provisions in the Convention on the Recognition and Enforcement of Foreign Arbitral Awards.

3. Article I(1) of the Convention states that "this Convention shall apply to the recognition and enforcement of arbitral awards made in the territory of a State other than the State where the recognition and enforcement of such awards are sought, and arising out of differences between persons, whether physical or legal." In general, the Convention requires the recognition of foreign arbitral awards. Article V(1)(e), however, provides an exception to the rule. A court may refuse enforcement of an award that "has been set aside or suspended by a competent authority of the country in which, or under the law of which, the award was made." On these grounds, the U.S. district court denied Spier's petition for enforcement of the arbitration award.

4. Spier made three arguments in favor of enforcement. First, he argued that U.S. law required enforcement. The court rejected this argument stating that, when under the Convention, an arbitration that takes place in another State such as Italy, the arbitral proceeding is subject to the laws of that State, unless otherwise provided. Spier also argued that, under Article V(1) of the Convention, a court may overturn a foreign court's denial of enforcement to an arbitration award for adequate reasons. The court found that Spier presented no adequate reason why it should overturn the Italian courts' decisions. Finally, Spier argued that, under *In re Chromalloy Aeroservices*, 939 F.Supp. 907 (D.D.C. 1996), the FAA required the U.S. policy in favor of arbitration to override the decisions of the Italian courts. The district court disagreed. *Chromalloy* was distinguishable in that, there, the Egyptian government, a party to the arbitration, had blatantly disregarded its contractual agreement not to appeal the arbitral award. No such agreement was present in the case before the court. The court noted further that, even if the decision had been subject to the laws of the United States, the result may not have been different. All three Italian courts nullified the arbitral award on the ground that, in making their decision, the arbitrators had exceeded their authority, a specific ground for vacatur under the FAA. The court, therefore, denied the petition to enforce the arbitral award.

5. The district court's opinion in *Spier* is in line with the standard approach to the application and interpretation of the New York Arbitration Convention on the question of the effect of a setting aside of an award at the place of rendition. Despite the court's statements on this matter, it is

difficult—if not, impossible—to reconcile the reasoning in *Spier* with its counterpart in *Chromalloy*. In his argument to the court, Spier had the proper characterization of the *Chromalloy* holding: The U.S. policy favoring arbitration overrides the express provisions of the Convention and decisions of parallel foreign tribunals. The district court's attempt to distinguish the cases is neither persuasive nor responsive to the clash of doctrine that separates the decisions. In addition, it is not necessarily true that vacatur would have resulted under an application of U.S. domestic arbitration law in these or similar facts. The Italian courts appear to have scrutinized the arbitrator's determination with an over-abundance of judicial zeal. In any event, the district court decision provides for the unwholesome result of allowing national law to block the enforcement of an international arbitral award on the basis of a judicial review of the merits of the arbitrator's determination. Despite its foibles, *Chromalloy* established a much sounder policy on the enforcement of awards under the New York Convention.

EPILOGUE

ISSUES ON THE "CUSP"

■ ■ ■

The final section describes issues and developments that may move the law of arbitration in a different direction. These issues and developments respond to the constant opposition in arbitration law between rights protection and the functionality and effectiveness of the arbitral process. For example, the contemporary development of arbitration includes the integration of lawyers into the process. The participation of attorneys has led to the importation of adversarial litigation devices into arbitral proceedings. Should the hearings in an arbitration include discovery and other evidence-gathering trial techniques? Should some form of reconsideration be available for the arbitrators' conduct of the proceedings or their rulings on the merits? Is any measure of judicialization useful or tenable in arbitration?

The judicial litigation on arbitration includes a large number of decisions on the arbitration agreement's scope of application—whether a nonsignatory party can be bound to arbitrate and whether that party can obligate a signatory party to arbitrate under the agreement. This litigation challenges the contract foundation of the obligation to arbitration. Is there, or should there be, elasticity to the scope of the contract of arbitration? Can a noncontracting party be held to an agreement or avail itself of the agreement? Can the agreement be stretched to circumstances in which a court implies an agreement to arbitrate because it is convenient or conventional?

Finally, the political reconfiguration of the U.S. Congress and the White House has encouraged the critics of arbitration to become more vocal and energetic. They have proposed legislation that will invalidate arbitral clauses in adhesionary transactions. The latter include consumer and employment contracts. Such legislation could undo arbitration and the best interests of American citizens.

1. THE "JUDICIALIZATION" OF ARBITRATION

The domestic and international growth of arbitration has had a number of consequences for the arbitral process and the practice of arbitration. First, the U.S. Supreme Court's endorsement and sponsorship of arbitration (along with the activity of the international mercantile community and foreign States) not only has legitimated the right of contractual recourse to arbitration, but also has established the arbitral process as a *bona fide* means of adjudicating disputes. Arbitral adjudication has become part of the adjudicatory mainstream. Second, as a consequence, lawyers were required to abandon their disparagement of the process as a "bastardized" approximation of the judicial trial. Too much of the business of litigation had shifted to the domain of arbitration for lawyers to continue to view the process of arbitral adjudication with hostility and contempt. Third, the integration of lawyers into the conduct of arbitral proceedings and the development of an arbitral practice of law had an impact upon the adjudicatory character of the process. As a "mainstream" remedy servicing the dispute resolution needs of domestic societies and the international community, arbitration underwent a number of transformations.

The following materials advance one interpretation of the adjustments that have been made to the process of arbitral adjudication. It vigorously critiques both the perceived necessity of the changes and the changes themselves, arguing for the maintenance of the original attributes and ideology of the arbitral process. Complaints of "over-adversarialization" have surfaced in securities arbitration and the standard practice in AAA arbitration is heading in the direction of greater procedural formality. The importation of adversarial techniques into the arbitral process is seen as antithetical to the adjudicatory identity, mission, and function of arbitration. The materials represent a minoritarian evaluation of the evolution of the process. What they advance in terms of international arbitration applies with roughly equal force to the current U.S. domestic usage of the arbitral remedy.

T. CARBONNEAU, *DARKNESS AND LIGHT IN THE SHADOWS OF INTERNATIONAL ARBITRAL ADJUDICATION*

in FACT-FINDING BEFORE INTERNATIONAL TRIBUNALS 153
[Eleventh Sokol Colloquium] [R. Lillich ed. 1991].

(footnotes omitted)

[. . .]

The traditional gravamen of arbitral procedure—born of its contractual origins and of its operation in a primarily commercial setting—is to have arbitral tribunals render their rulings on the basis of supple procedure and according to relatively fluid substantive standards. Moreover, under the received wisdom, arbitrating parties—despite their conflict— conserve a willingness to cooperate with each other and with the tribunal, and impliedly have agreed to abide by the dictates of good faith and basic fairness during the proceeding. In regard to fact-finding, each side is afforded a reasonable opportunity to present evidence and is expected to provide the other side with adequate notice and comply with document requests and discovery orders. Flexibility and informality—the hallmarks of arbitral adjudicatory ideology—make stringent rules of evidence unnecessary. Party cooperation and arbitrator expertise allow for the general admissibility and free evaluation of evidence. When a party fails to comply or is otherwise recalcitrant, the tribunal may take the party's lack of cooperation into account in rendering the award.

The precepts of this prosaic world may no longer correspond to the sobering reality of disagreement and to the significance of the interests at stake. The simplicity of the arbitral procedural framework—its reliance upon party cooperation and sound arbitrator discretion—creates companion dangers: first, that arbitral awards will be rendered on the basis of misinformation or a lack of information; and, second, that the content of such awards will become the basis for international law-making. Arbitration, as presently conceived and practiced, then could undermine the international rule of law and destabilize the process of international adjudication. In order to preserve the integrity of the international community and of international law, therefore, it has been suggested that arbitration should be informed by more traditional lawyerly values, including formal adjudicatory procedures that guarantee extensive fact-finding.

[. . .]

Arbitration is neither a primitive nor a wayward form of adjudication, despite its operation in the twilight of official authority. Arbitral Systems acknowledge the importance of fact-finding, having developed procedures that generate sufficient facts to sustain adjudicatory determinations and that nonetheless remain faithful to the ideology of arbitral adjudication. Due process is not arbitration's only religion. Arbitration achieves results that simply are not possible in more formalized proceedings subject to public exposure and to constant contentious debate. The concern for fact-finding and for the integrity of law-making determinations should result in a redefinition, not of arbitral practices, but of the parties' role in the proceeding and of the concept of adjudication itself. International adjudication should be aligned with the values that have long guided arbitration rather than being placed at the mercy of the vicissitudes of adversarial advocacy.

2. FACT-FINDING AND THE ADVOCATE

For advocates, fact-finding is the lifeblood of adjudication. Lawyers commonly maintain that facts propel or "drive" the process of adjudication. The craft of litigation logically dictates that outcomes (in the form of judgments, awards, or advisory opinions) reflect substantial information and knowledge of the material elements of the case. Whether the tribunal is domestic or international in scope, a judicial or an arbitral body, concerned with matters of sovereign relations or commercial conduct, fact-finding and the constitution of a thorough and precise record, so the argument goes, are its most critical functions. The pleading and proof of facts necessarily precedes (and, in effect, subsumes) all other aspects of adjudication. Evidence-gathering in the form of discovery, interrogatories, and depositions dominate[s] the process and [is] its principal preoccupation. Judges and arbitrators simply cannot decide without acquiring a comprehensive and an accurate understanding of the events and deeds that engendered the parties' conflict. The tribunal's true function is to supervise the parties' gathering of facts and to identify those facts that are decisive to the eventual application of legal principles.

Not unsurprisingly, the advocates' insistence upon fact-finding also makes them the centerpiece of the adjudicatory process. It is through their adversarial confrontation that the "true" facts eventually appear and permit the tribunal to rule on the merits. The lawyer's hard-headed pragmatism and unrelenting attention to detail are critical to a full and accurate record. Advocates bear the burden of bringing forth relevant information and of expounding upon its significance. Sound adjudication, therefore, consists in thorough fact-finding by lawyers and the use of their advocacy skills in the presentation and evaluation of facts.

This concept of fact-finding in adjudication recommends itself by its simplicity and clarity. It conveys a single, focused, and coherent insight into the process, logically emphasizing the importance of first principles. Ignorant decision-makers can achieve only misguided resolutions. Material knowledge, reasonably certain and complete, is a necessary foundation for articulating sound determinations and maintaining the integrity of the adjudicatory process. The clarity of the advocate's perception, however, is both sustained and diminished by its simplicity. It promises more than it actually delivers.

The single-minded and unequivocal concentration upon facts, the touting of lawyerly skills, and the assumption that a preordained "right answer" is buried in the facts and need only be discovered by the careful advocate are, upon reflection, mere ploys of advocacy—hyperbolic renderings bound in a tissue of oratorical and illusory realities. Surely, other actors and elements in the process have a role, perhaps even one of equal importance. Law-making through adjudication must be more than mere investigation; the discovery of "factual" truth does not necessarily reconcile the contending interests. The adversarial depiction of the facts and of discovery, on the one hand, rightly signals their importance in the process of adjudication, but, on the other hand, it fails to communicate—perhaps because of its anti-normative bias—any understanding of the process' true nature or underlying dynamic. The clarity of the advocate's insight pales in the face of the larger complexity and ambiguities of adjudicatory practice.

3. ADJUDICATION: CHARACTER, MISSION, AND REALITY

In the context of adjudication, the advocate's ideal of "objective" facts that once established can command particular determinations are resistant to definition and are rare. The adversarial method is itself testimony to the underlying ambiguity of all adjudicatory elements, even the most material. Moreover, purely factual elements cannot be readily identified or separated from the legal questions that attend their evaluation. Efforts to segregate questions of fact from questions of law always are futile. For example, whether the elements of a particular behavior constitute negligence or a breach of contract is inextricably tied to the abstract definition of the applicable legal rule. Interpretative judgment cannot be artificially held in abeyance until the final constitution of the record and the end of the proceeding. Throughout the process, adjudicators will see and advocates will present facts from the vantage point of the potentially governing legal predicate; even decisions on the type of investigatory procedures and practice to be used, taken during the proceeding, reflect choices as to applicable norms and standards. From the very outset, a particular view of the circumstances, of acceptable behavior, and of the governing rules already is being formulated.

It is often impossible, moreover, to establish incontrovertibly what happened. The tribunal is obliged to weigh circumstantial evidence, to use presumptions, and to draw inferences from the circumstances. The parties will advance arguments on these issues, all of which demand the exercise of judgment by the tribunal. Experts sometimes are called upon to assist the tribunal in clarifying the meaning of factual allegations. Finally, unstated but deep-seated assumptions, cultural or otherwise, permeate adjudication as they do any other human activity. A process cleansed of any baggage is as elusive as the "objective" facts are themselves.

There are, therefore, no facts without judgment any more than there are judgments without facts. Adjudication includes an irreducible normative and subjective dimension at every stage of its operation that transforms all considerations into mixed questions of fact and law. Facts inexorably coexist and are closely intertwined with norms. Adjudication is a complex bundle (and sometimes jumble) of elements, not easily separated from each other, that coalesce in a process that wants an objective appearance but is, in reality, [diffuse] and fluid. This is only when determinations separate themselves from a basic rule of reason and fairness that their inherently subjective nature becomes fundamentally arbitrary and unacceptable.

A realistic appraisal of adjudication recognizes the uncertainty and approximations created by its multifarious components and the gap that often exists between its purported and actual operation. The process does not function in a vacuum or exist on an independent plane of reality; its objectives are necessarily subject to both human and physical constraints. No one factor explains the process or harmonizes its elements. Fact-finding, as important as it may be, is only one of many components that seek to accomplish the larger goal of fairness and reason in dispute resolution. Disputes are not resolved by invoking the platitudes of self-contained "right answers," but rather by an always imperfect exercise of judgment in the face of highly competitive, sometimes equally sympathetic, but conflicting interests.

Unequivocal precision and exactitude are not the order of the day in justice determinations. If the mere discovery of what actually transpired were enough to resolve the problem, the conflict never would have gone to adjudication. Controversies submitted to adjudication defy easy solution and necessarily involve making difficult choices that the parties are unable to arrive at on their own.

[...]

5. THE "ADVERSARIALIZATION" OF INTERNATIONAL ARBITRATION AND ADJUDICATION

International adjudication through arbitration now reaches a larger volume of claims and increasingly significant financial and commercial interests. The privatization of state political conflicts that touch upon commercial interests and sovereign trade policy disputes and the elaboration of a transnational commercial law through arbitration are testimony to the emerging significance and status of the international arbitration process. Lawyers must now take this process seriously and learn to participate in it; their clients must be able to live with its determinations. The wholesale removal of issues of international litigation from the province of national laws and domestic courts has required attorneys trained in the unique American brand of adversarial litigation to leave their "friendly confines" and to acknowledge the jurisdiction of emerging transnational arbitral adjudicatory bodies.

Their acknowledgment has been partial, however; while removal to different fora was tolerable (perhaps unavoidable), adversarially trained lawyers have found it more difficult to adapt to the strange procedural mores of the new adjudicatory land. Old debates about common law and civil law concepts of procedure have been revitalized. These attorneys, in effect, have attempted to "adapt" to the alien surroundings of international adjudication simply by transplanting their unique procedural methodology into these new frameworks. Their objectives include making fact-finding, in the form of discovery and other means of evidence-gathering, the core facet of the proceedings.

This attempted imposition obviously risks undermining the efficiency and integrity of the established and emerging international process. Transnational adjudicatory bodies, especially arbitral tribunals, could become victim and prisoner of adversarial practices. Adversarial importations threaten to undermine the gravamen of arbitration. A struggle between discordant adjudicatory ideologies for the control of international procedure and proceedings is clearly being undertaken.

Arbitration's keynote features have been flexibility, informality, and trust—trust of arbitrator fairness on the basic questions of procedure and substance. The need to avoid the entanglements of legal technicalities motivated parties to rely upon a process that was fair, reasonable, and relatively expeditious. Indeed, the use of arbitration to resolve State conflicts bespeaks a similar desire to avoid the intractable dimension of formal litigation and to create a process that, while safeguarding sovereign dignity, still allows for functional conflict resolution. The so-called civilian model of adjudicatory procedure, which attributes a more active role to the tribunal in terms of both constituting the record and applying law, best describes the essential features of the arbitral adjudicatory methodology. "Civil law" procedure applies in most European legal systems, and, although it includes an adversarial component, that component is not the centerpiece of the process. The application of law is not subordinated to debates about procedural or factual elements. What may appear to adversarial advocates as laxity and a lack of rigor in procedure is to most jurists a sensible means of avoiding unfairness and abuse while providing parties with a workable process.

Arbitration's expanding mission may invite the increased participation of adversarial advocates, but it does not mandate an alteration of its procedural ethic or adjudicatory *raison d'être*. The volume of business, the larger financial interests, or the implicated State interests will not receive more thorough consideration or better protection by the infusion of adversarial fact-finding or discovery into international arbitration. The adversarial approach's sole objective is to have the client's interests triumph essentially without regard to the financial, ethical, and human costs that might accompany the litigation. It is not merely a form of debate or a means of expressing disagreement, but rather a single-minded, unrelenting, and strident advocacy for the unilateral disposition of the case. It breeds distrust among all the actors involved, and—as a consequence—demands elaborate procedures and numerous opportunities for challenge.

Disagreement often is so pervasive that trial proceedings rarely get beyond the facts; inordinate time and energy are spent on discovery, not for the sake of fact-finding but to guarantee that the opposing party does not get an advantage or the client (if ultimately disappointed) an opportunity to sue for professional malpractice. Adversarial proceedings are tailored exclusively to the needs of the advocate and amount to senseless combat—a war of attrition and of irreducible opposition that seeks to dictate, postpone, or eliminate the exercise of judgment or normative decision-making. The aim is not to achieve the lofty goals of truth and justice or the more modest objective of rational dispute resolution but to win.

This unique brand of trial procedures has literally paralyzed the administration of justice in the United States. It has made justice financially prohibitive and inaccessible, and has undermined the integrity of law and of the legal profession. United States attorneys, however, generally are critical of arbitration. It represents the antithesis of their professional training. Rules that vest ultimate procedural authority either in the parties or in the arbitrators are simply too general and permissive. Too few opportunities are available for formal opposition and appeal. The reliance upon the integrity of the arbitrators and the process is not, in their view, a substitute for rules that provide specifically for a means of defense or retaliation.

For example, despite their wide acceptance and use, the UNCITRAL arbitration rules on fact-finding and evidence-gathering are perceived by advocates as too broad and open-ended. The rules governing the admissibility and weighing of evidence, the credibility and examination of witnesses, the use of experts, and notice requirements are inelaborate. They provide insufficient guidance. The advocate may be unfairly surprised by the other side or may not know what multinational arbitrators require as evidence. The indeterminacy of procedural rules can make parties vulnerable to arbitrator activism and to inconsonant results. Advocates further argue that, as a practical matter and in terms of legitimacy, it is better to have an award based upon a surplus of evidence rather than a lack of it. Therefore, some type of international consensus on arbitral procedure should be articulated, especially when arbitration is used to resolve public law issues.

The argument is subtle and appealing but short-sighted. It represents a first step in the direction of acquiescing to the adversarial ethic's insatiable and self-aggrandizing logic. The UNCITRAL rules were the product of an already existing international consensus on arbitral procedure[s] and were informed by a wide and diverse body of international experts. The plea for more refined rules of procedure then reflects an attempt, *sub silen[c]io,* to align arbitral proceedings with adversarial practices. The argument leaves a number of salient questions unanswered: When will the applicable rules be sufficient to meet the requirements of the international consensus? How will the latter be established and who will define it? When will notice avoid unfair surprise? How precisely must arbitrators communicate their expectations as to evidence? The argument smacks of a strategy to open the door for a complete reconsideration of arbitral procedure, to have international arbitral proceedings function in keeping with the basic tenets of the Federal Rules of Civil Procedure.

Once the proposition for change is admitted, the tendency—either in terms of regulation or proceedings—will be to permit the parties unlimited opportunities for fact-finding, allowing them to gorge the tribunal with facts and evidence. Refined, albeit even more permissive, predicates for advocates' behavior and exceptions thereto will become the central focus of consideration, eliminating the particularity of and rationale for the arbitral process. The advocates will have arbitration right where they wanted it originally: caught in the maze of procedural obfuscation, completely dependent upon the requirements of advocacy, and forced to privilege fact-finding and evidence over the interests of the parties and integrity of the process.

Dispute resolution processes cannot function without an eventual reference to systemic balance and rationality. Maintaining a functional and fair process is as critical as avoiding abuse and protecting rights. Indeed, all of these factors must be conjoined into a single, functional system. There is no persuasive empirical or logical reason to have international arbitration fall victim to the American-born due process cancer and to have international arbitrators, like U.S. federal judges, become mere managers of the parties' adversarial disagreement. There is a substantial track record of arbitral performance, showing that the civilian concept of sound procedural judgment is a sufficient standard to allow for justice determinations. Abuses in terms of discovery, fact-finding, and awards have been neither manifest nor common. Decisions as to the credibility of witnesses, the probative value of circumstantial or written evidence, [and] the need for special masters or on-site inspections can be made without erecting a framework that is literally paralyzed by safeguards. The fact that arbitration functions and functions well while maintaining an essential link to common sense, rationality, and fairness should not disqualify it as a legitimate adjudicatory mechanism for international dispute resolution.

A more cynical appraisal would hold that adjudication is essentially an exercise in deception and approximation. The advocates attempt to deceive each other and the tribunal by unequivocal statements of position. In turn, the tribunal will engage in its own deception or metaphorical discourse by expressing its sense of what happened and of justice through legal reasoning and doctrines. The malleability of logic, factual elements, legal rules, and [ ] the process itself allows the tribunal's collective intuition to stand as an adjudicated outcome—the application and creation of legal norms. Adjudication, therefore, has an intractably human quality to it that is difficult to conceal with procedural trappings, no matter how intricate.

According to one arbitration expert [the late J. Wetter], "formalities are not nearly [as] important as the impression conveyed to the arbitrators of the justness of a party's case and the fairness of his business dealings." This human quality is given more forthright expression in the civilian evidentiary standard of *"la conviction intime du juge"* than by the arcane and brutal intricacies of adversarial procedure. Although it may be an inevitable part of the rhetoric of adjudication, deception should not be allowed to seep to its very core.

The critical objective of adjudication is to remain functional and avoid flagrantly arbitrary determinations and patent injustice. Despite its imperfections and approximations, the process remains legitimate [as] long as it operates in concert with reason and basic fairness. Arbitral proceedings and awards are more akin to justice than an ironclad but inaccessible procedural framework that disguises both the truth and its own frailties.

6. REFORMING ADJUDICATION THROUGH ARBITRATION

[. . .]

How should arbitrators deal with recalcitrant parties in the fact-finding phase of the proceeding? Do the arbitrators have the jurisdictional authority to compel evidence deemed necessary to the adjudication of issues? If so, what constraints apply to the exercise of such authority? If not, does the inability to obtain necessary evidence paralyze the proceeding or lead to a misinformed or uninformed adjudicatory determination?

How does the arbitral tribunal resolve a situation of procedural conflict between the parties—through the exclusive use of its unfettered discretion, or by reference to established rules? If through the latter, who attributes an established status or content to these rules?

If the growing scope of international adjudication requires a consideration of procedural reforms, prospective changes should intermediate between creating a more elaborate factual predicate and maintaining a procedure faithful to arbitration's original adjudicatory design. Integrating different adjudicatory values into the established ideology of arbitration could impede or extinguish the viability of the process rather than adapt it to changing circumstances. Tinkering with the tried and true, a workable and working process, is a hazardous undertaking. Imposing new procedures upon the process may not be appropriate at all. Rather, a clarification and an expansion of the role of the arbitrating parties within the proceeding may achieve more salutary results.

The agreement to arbitrate is a type of solemn adjudicatory contract to which the parties consent in order to benefit mutually from and abide by certain adjudicatory values, distinct from those that prevail in judicial processes. To achieve more thorough fact-finding and to avoid an impasse on questions it might generate, arbitral procedures could be interpreted to include—because of the parties' consent to arbitrate—a duty of good faith cooperation on matters of discovery and evidence-gathering. A party's breach of duty could be penalized by a damage award (applied to a bond deposited for this purpose prior to the hearing) or by the tribunal's drawing of negative inferences from the recalcitrant conduct. The duty gives the parties an incentive to participate fully in discovery, resolves problems of noncompliance with reasonable effectiveness and efficiency, and aligns itself with the general arbitral ideology of fair dealing, cooperation, and reasonableness in adjudication.

[. . .]

Particular aspects of United States arbitral practice . . . provide support for the creation of a good faith duty. A 1987 survey conducted by the American Bar Association reveals that attorneys who participated in arbitral proceedings favored both preliminary conferences and greater arbitrator authority "to order pre-hearing discovery and to establish hearing schedules." This development converges with new guidelines issued by the American Arbitration Association (AAA) encouraging recourse to preliminary and prearbitration conferences. The AAA guidelines recommend that, prior to the hearing, parties establish the specific issues in dispute and the amounts of their claims. Moreover, at this time, arbitrators should schedule the evidentiary hearings, organize the procedure for document exchange, and further oblige the parties to share their lists of witnesses and outlines of prospective testimony. Preliminary conferences are meant to make for more expeditious hearings and to foster basic cooperation among the parties, thereby allowing them and the process to focus upon the real issues of disagreement.

In 1985, the National Futures Association (NFA) adopted a rule providing for pre-hearing discovery procedures. The rule not only emphasizes but mandates cooperation and voluntary exchange among the parties in the gathering of evidence and the collection of documents. Section 8 of the NFA's Code of Arbitration provides in pertinent part:

> The parties shall cooperate...in the voluntary exchange of documents and information (reasonably in advance of the hearing) which may serve to facilitate a fair, equitable, and expeditious hearing.

The rule is designed to be implemented "without resort to issuance of subpoenas."

The decision to submit commodities disputes to arbitration then presupposes a commitment to a particular form and ideology of adjudication. To resolve the conflict, strident opposition does not need to take place between the parties at every stage of the proceeding or upon every issue. The material elements supporting the parties' respective positions first need to be established so that neither party is surprised by the other's allegations and the hearing can actually focus upon the areas of true disagreement. Adversarial exchange, therefore, can be used to elucidate the cardinal points of conflict rather than take place through[out] the proceeding. The dedramatization or de-adversarialization of the discovery and fact-finding process is meant to create a more professional and realistic attitude toward dispute resolution and to have conflict resolved upon the basis of competent knowledge rather than oratory or tactical warfare.

Also, formal coercion, *i.e.*, the use of subpoenas, is expressly excluded from the NFA prehearing discovery process. This provision recognizes that good faith cooperation cannot be compelled and should not be implemented through contentious means. The penalties for engaging in uncooperative behavior and refusing to participate in voluntary document exchange—in effect, for disrupting the agreed-upon arbitral process—center upon the adjudicatory consequences of the recalcitrant conduct. The arbitral tribunal may at its discretion:

    1.   presume that the other party's factual allegations are established as stated;

    2.   refuse to hear the non-complying party's arguments on the matter;

    3.   dismiss the action, parts of it, or render an award in default.

The NFA rule brings to the fore an understated, often neglected facet of arbitration, namely, its ideological content. That ideology is rooted in both pragmatism and rationality—in a sense of the reach and limits of human experience. Arbitration is an alternative approach to the resolution of conflict that attends usually specialized areas of human activity. At best, it is only a quasi-judicial, quasi-juridical instrument for choosing between countervailing interests. It relies upon a clear jurisdictional base, expertise, flexibility, and essential non-reviewability to achieve its ends. The practical purpose of arbitration is to streamline adjudication and to make dispute resolution quicker and less costly. These attributes, however, are merely the surface manifestations of the institution. In the American experience, especially, arbitration redefines adjudication by countermanding the techniques of and rationale for adversarial adjudication. The streamlining of adjudication is achieved by a deliberate elimination or severe constraint of adversarial histrionics, by keeping the parties focused on their real—as opposed to postured—conflicts, by obliging the parties and their representatives, in a word, not to abandon their rationality and common sense in their struggle for decision and to pursue a course of conduct in the proceeding that is disciplined by reason and a sense of the ultimate resolutory objective.

Arbitral proceedings do not lose their sense of adjudicatory identity in a maze of contentious exchange or in advocates' rankings. Arbitrators do not abnegate their responsibility to direct the proceeding in accordance with its mission and toward a reasonably fair termination. Rights are not allowed to evaporate in the heat of perpetual argumentation or in a process commanded by the insufferable foolishness of interminable opposition. More than a change of procedures, arbitration forces adjudicating parties to quit the scholastic exercise of adversarial discourse and to adopt an attitude of responsibility and maturity in dispute resolution. The adjudicatory consensus, implied by arbitration and expressly codified in the NFA rule but conspicuously absent in the deliberate irrationality of adversarial proceedings, acts as an essential *garde-fou*, that prevents the parties from committing procedural suicide or otherwise self-destructing in the infantile logic of single-minded adversarial confrontation.

[. . .]

. . .Adjudicatory concerns that reflect an adversarial tradition hostile to arbitration and to other dispute resolution alternatives cannot redefine the underpinnings of arbitration, but rather must adapt to them. More intricate procedures are not the answer. Parties must themselves assume responsibility and cooperate to constitute a sufficiently accurate and comprehensive record, relegating their contentious exchange to the principled phases of the proceeding. Finally, trust must be vested in the arbitrators to control the process and to provide sanctions for a party's breach of its adjudicatory commitment and duty.

The reference to such general principles and values is probably too simplistic to persuade holders of the adversarial flame. Compared to the intricate dogmas of their procedural religion, arbitration is mere child's play, or some form of play, that is neither sufficiently ponderous nor mysterious to be the instrument of professional adjudicatory determinations. Theirs is a vision of justice submerged in detail and counter-detail, where rhetoric eventually triumphs over other rhetoric and extinguishes the light of substance and reason. Unlike the simplicity of the advocate's insight, the simplicity of the arbitral solution is anchored in an authentic understanding and consensus about the human experience with conflict— not the deceptive persuasion of rhetoric. Because it mirrors this human reality, arbitration provides a sound architecture for dispute resolution. Aesthetic appeal and beauty, however, are not the only attributes of its simplicity—wisdom and truth are as well.

[. . .]

NOTES AND QUESTIONS

1. Does this contrarian position make sense to you? Are there real dangers in the adjustments that have been made to the arbitral process? Should lawyers dominate the arbitral process with their ideology and practice of dispute resolution or should they adapt and be dominated by arbitration?

2. Why would an arbitration agreement be the best means of dealing with these concerns? If you want simplicity, could you just provide for it in the agreement?

3. Doesn't the adversarial methodology best reflect and respond to the circumstances of conflict?

4. Is this discussion an academic "tempest in a teapot" with few, if any, significant practical ramifications?

5. You should investigate how you might best protect the client's interest in light of these considerations.

* * *

The U.S. Court of Appeals for the Fifth Circuit recently rendered an opinion in *Barousse v. Paper, Allied–Industrial, Chemical & Energy Workers Int'l Union*, 265 F.3d 1059 (5th Cir. 2001). The case raises a novel and difficult issue of arbitration law: To what extent arbitral awards can be interpreted and clarified, once they have been rendered.

The facts of the case pit the interest of the union against that of its members. The employer instituted a mandatory "day off" program for its employees, and the union claimed that the program violated the collective bargaining agreement. The union represented the employees as a class in its dispute with the company regarding how the collective bargaining agreement should be construed. The employees worked at the Westwego, Louisiana plant of the National Gypsum Company. The parties submitted the matter to binding arbitration. The arbitrator ruled in favor of the employees, ordering the company to pay both compensatory and punitive damages (as well as attorney's fees, costs, and interest). The punitive damages were in the amount of $100,000.

The controversy submitted to the district court involved "the proper distribution of the punitive damage portion of the award." While it was clear that the employees were entitled to the compensatory damages, the union and its members disagreed about which was entitled to the punitive damage award. The union's executive board contended that the punitive damages were for the union as a whole, not the individual members who grieved. The affected members opposed that interpretation and demanded a clarification of the award.

Nearly two years after the award was rendered and following the distribution of the compensatory damages for back pay to the grieving members, the union wrote to the arbitrator and asked him to clarify the award as to entitlement to punitive damages. The arbitrator answered, stating that $90,000 should be distributed to the affected membership as "further compensation for their wage loss" and the union should received $10,000 "for its admirable prosecution of the case." Moreover, "any surplus remaining after the employees have been made whole...should go to the Union." The union then notified the affected members, "stating that they may be entitled to a portion of the punitive damages award." The notice "advised that the employees must prove entitlement...."

The parties continued to dispute the matter of the "rightful recipient" of the exemplary relief. Their "differences became irreconcilable" and legal action was commenced. The union argued, *inter alia*, that the arbitrator's clarification of the award on the punitive damage matter was "a non-binding advisory opinion" and, as such, "should...be disregarded." The members asserted that the issue should be "remand[ed]...to the arbitrator to determine the proper method of distributing the award."

These circumstances warrant a number of observations. First, the attitude of the union on the allocation of punitive damages appears to be quite litigious. The union's initial resolve to lay claim to punitive damages in their entirety, and—later—its characterization of the arbitrator's unfavorable clarification as "a non-binding advisory opinion" reflect an obdurate and unbending approach to the matter. The judicial skepticism regarding union representation of members expressed in *Pryner v. Tractor Supply Co.* and later reaffirmed in *Cole v. Burns Int'l Security Services* and *Wright v. Universal Maritime Service Corp.* is certainly borne out in the circumstances of the instant case. *See Pryner*, 109 F.3d 354 (7th Cir.), *cert. denied*, 522 U.S. 912 (1997); *Cole*, 105 F.3d 1465 (D.C. Cir. 1997); *Wright*, 525 U.S. 70 (1998). The collective organizational interest here was at odds with the interest of the individual grievants. There was no fiduciary dimension to the union representation. But for its specific implementation, the arbitrator's clarification was free of ambiguity. The award of punitive damages was and remained intended in principal part for the individually affected workers. The union retained a small and subsidiary claim to those damages, the extent of which could only be fully determined once the workers' claims have been satisfied.

Second, the circumstances raise doctrinal questions pertaining to the *functus officio* doctrine and the right of a party to seek a clarification of the award under Federal Arbitration Act (FAA) Section Eleven. They also raise a problem of possible judicial interference with the arbitration process. As noted in the chapter on enforcement, it is well-established that, once an arbitrator renders a final award, his/her authority to rule in the matter ceases. The arbitrator becomes *functus officio*; his/her mandate has been fulfilled and is, therefore, extinguished. Under the applicable federal statute, the arbitrator retains the authority to correct evident mistakes, to complete an incomplete award, and to clarify ambiguities in the award. The prerogative of clarification, however, does not allow the matter to be relitigated or the arbitrator to receive new arguments on the matters that were submitted and to change his/her mind and revise the ruling. Once rendered, an award is final and binding. Moreover, if the award is incomprehensible in some of its particulars or as a whole, it may be subject to vacatur under FAA Section Ten for the arbitrator's imperfect or highly defective execution of his/her mission. When a basic clarification cannot be achieved, vacatur—it seems—becomes the appropriate remedy.

The problematic consideration, obviously, is determining when an attempt at clarification becomes a readjudication of the matter. Moreover, who decides whether the line has been crossed in the specific circumstances? Finally, does clarification become a means for a losing party to obfuscate and delay resolution of a matter? Can sanctions be imposed for bad faith conduct—antagonistic not only to the interests of the other party, but also to the proper operation of the arbitral process?

The union's litigious disposition in the *Barousse* case seems to push this matter beyond the existing framework of rules. Having received a clarification unfavorable to its interests, the union argued that the clarification was not a clarification and/or was barred by *functus officio* (even though it was the union which requested the arbitrator to clarify his ruling). Once it was established that the punitive damages were intended principally to compensate the individual workers, the only question—as the court determined—should have been as to the method for specific distribution. The sovereignty of the arbitrator—as the court also acknowledged—should have prevailed. The law applied by the arbitrator was the standard predicate of decision: The defendant company had engaged in bad faith behavior toward its workers by instituting its mandatory "day off" program and in the arbitration by "trash[ing] its scheduling records" and misplacing other documents. Therefore, both compensatory and punitive damages were warranted and represented an amount that would punish the defendant and provide a windfall recovery to the primary victims of the conduct.

The court affirmed the arbitrator's clarification, but added that the clarification did not "finaliz[e] his opinion" because it did not address how much additional money each employee was to receive or how the employees were to establish their losses. The court remanded the award to the arbitrator for further clarification of these issues, citing a "policy in favor of clear final awards that completely resolve the dispute originally submitted to the arbitrator." The court appeared anxious to avoid criticism of judicial interference with the arbitration, stating:

> It is not the court's place to determine the intent of an arbitrator when the award fails to make the arbitrator's intent clear.... Consistent with the case law and federal statutes, a court should not undertake to construe the meaning of arbitration awards where they are unclear.... This would only serve to undermine the authority of arbitrators.... Where parties have elected to submit their disputes to arbitration, they should be completely resolved by arbitration rather than only partially resolved.... Court clarifica-

tion would amount to preemption of the arbitrator's fact-finding function, and this Court declines to do so . . . .

The critical issue raised in *Barousse* is the use by the union of litigious practices to delay and undermine the arbitration process. The union used the problem of clarity to express its disagreement with the arbitrator's conclusions on the matter of the allocation of punitive damages. This adversarial approach can only do damage to the arbitration process and its function in a workplace and other arenas of dispute resolution. It creates the need to elaborate further law and establish and justify distinctions. Measures should be available to sanction and discourage this type of conduct. Such behavior should not be allowed to create circumstances that lead an arbitrator to alter or change his determination on the matter. The result would be much more than a clarification.

Some time later, the arbitrator issued a second clarification in the matter pursuant to the Fifth Circuit's affirmance of the district court order. On August 8, 2001, the arbitrator awarded all of the punitive damages to the workers and directed the union to pay interest on the $100,000 for the period of time during which those funds were improperly held. In this "final resolution," the arbitrator further ruled that the "affected class of thirty-two (32) union members shall share equally the $100,000 . . . [,] each of the thirty-two (32) members shall receive an equally proportionate share in the amount of $3,125.00 . . . ." The same allocation principle would apply to the interest to be paid by the union. The arbitrator also stated that the union had "suffered no harm" due to the company's "illicit actions."

Thus far, the union, it seems, has shown no interest in settling or resolving the matter. The arbitrator's second clarification raises a host of new problems—for example, the second clarification contradicts the disposition on the issue of the allocation of punitive damages in the first clarification. Although the court asked the arbitrator to provide a method of distribution for the award, it did not request that he redo the basic allocation. Do these circumstances constitute a revision of the award and an excess of authority or do they represent the arbitrator's final sovereign disposition in the matter?

Also, the dispute now is no longer between the company and the union, but rather between the employees and the union. Is that dispute separable from the initial claim and subject to arbitration? If so, what is the authority of this arbitrator? Does the dispute raise a *res nova*? Moreover, can the arbitrator award judicial interest in light of the content of the initial award and the generally applicable law?

The union can take, and appears to be taking, advantage of these problematic circumstances to delay the ultimate resolution of the matter. It thereby continues to deprive its members of what the arbitrator believes to rightfully belong to them. "The object of the arbitration was vindication of the harm suffered by the thirty-two (32) members." The union's posture thwarts the strong judicial policy in favor of arbitration and should be emphatically discouraged by the courts.

2. JUDICIAL EXPANSION OF THE AGREEMENT TO ARBITRATE

When can a court alter the terms or effect of an arbitration agreement? Judicial intervention in this form may be intended to favor arbitration and advance the policy on arbitration. Under Sections Two, Three, and Four of the FAA, a party can be compelled to arbitrate only when it has agreed to a valid contract of arbitration. That rule is a cornerstone principle of U.S. arbitration law. It epitomizes contract freedom. *Mastrobuono*, however, suggests that absolute contract freedom is not operative. What matters the most is securing the recourse to arbitration and achieving the efficiency and access it provides. As a result, non-contracting parties can be bound by an arbitration agreement or avail themselves of it.

Consider, for example, the following circumstances. "A" agrees to supply "B" with a given quantity of retail products at a particular price and at a fixed time. In order to fulfill its obligations under the supply contract with "B," "A" enters into an agreement with "C" for the assembly of the component parts, and "C" agrees to buy the component parts from "D" who, in turn, signs a shipping contract with "E" for transport of the parts. The various segments of this interrelated transaction are governed by separate bilateral contracts, and only "A" and "C" and "D" and "E" have included arbitral clauses in their agreements. As a matter of commercial reality, a party's failure to perform, or inadequate performance, in one branch of the transaction will affect the other branches and the rights and obligations of all actors. When a dispute emerges between "D" and "E" for the loss or damage of goods during transport, should the other participants, whose interests and positions are affected by the alleged breach, also be obligated to arbitrate the ensuing disputes?

The "blackletter" answer is clear. Only those parties who have expressly agreed to arbitrate their disputes are under a legal obligation to engage in arbitration. Therefore, only "D" and "E" and "A" and "C" must submit their breach of contract claims to arbitration. The other parties to the transaction have retained their right to file suit. They are entitled to bring an action against those parties who are bound to arbitrate with other parties. Other remedial approaches, of course, are possible. The parties not bound to arbitrate could enter into a submission agreement, and those parties who have agreed to arbitrate could always rescind the arbitration agreement by mutual consent. The parties also could have provided for commercial risk insurance, thereby lessening or eliminating the economic impact of a breach. Finally, they might prefer to accept substitute performance rather than litigate or arbitrate the matter.

If the parties undertake adjudicatory recourse, however, a number of considerations apply. First, the transaction and breach are characteristically commercial. The recourse to arbitration, therefore, is both sensible and appropriate. The prospective adjudication will not involve the interpretation of statutes or implementation of social policy, but rather will treat allegations of contractual breach and its implications upon a transaction. Second, resorting to parallel adjudicatory systems and filing separate actions in different jurisdictions will create duplicative proceedings and possibly conflicting determinations. A unitary approach to dispute resolution could avoid such administrative problems. Finally, the parties appear to be experienced commercial parties. They should have been aware of the special dispute resolution needs of an interdependent commercial transaction and devised a commercially appropriate framework for anticipated problems.

These factors might induce a court to find that the separate provisions for arbitration, one of which relates to the main commercial relationship in the transaction, are adequate to create a general, implied agreement to arbitrate on all parties to the transaction. Further support could be found in the view that arbitration is recognized as a particularly suitable remedy for commercial disputes and in the need to foster efficient commercial adjudication. It is clear that some of the parties to the transaction did not agree to arbitrate and that the judicial discovery of a general arbitration agreement constitutes a *post facto* revision of the various commercial agreements. Such a result is tenable in light of the case law.

As you should recall, the Court in *Moses H. Cone* expressed the view that mere adjudicatory efficiency and the avoidance of duplicative proceedings were not sufficient considerations for defeating the recourse to arbitration. Moreover, in several subsequent cases, like *Volt* and *Kaplan*, the Court affirmed that arbitration agreements would be enforced as written. Given the imperative judicial policy on arbitration, those rulings, however, appear to be applicable only if they achieve a result favorable to arbitration. While the considerations in *Moses H. Cone* and *Kaplan* are relevant in a case for upholding an inefficient reference to arbitration, they may not be controlling when the issue of litigation is to find a basis for compelling arbitration. In a word, considerations of adjudicatory inefficiency may not defeat the agreed-upon reference to arbitration, but considerations of adjudicatory efficiency could be used to compel arbitration—even though the contract of arbitration does not specifically reach some of the parties to the transaction. The question of whether an arbitration agreement can be implied from the commercial circumstances of an interdependent transaction in which there is some reference to arbitration remains open and unresolved.

The federal decisional law has addressed the more standard questions: Whether a noncontracting party can be bound to arbitrate by the contractual conduct of a third party and, more interestingly, whether a noncontracting party can obligate a contracting party to arbitrate. The following cases establish the substantive rules that apply to these questions. After reading the various passages in the two cases, you should consider how you might best protect your client against the "surprise" of a judicial order to arbitrate or to extend its arbitral obligations under the contract. How damaging are these decisions to the integrity of arbitration and to its institutional legitimacy? Should the courts confine their supervision to questions relating to the existence or validity of arbitration agreements? Does the case law point to a need for statutory revisions or additions?

THOMSON–CSF, S.A. v. AMERICAN ARBITRATION ASS'N

64 F.3d 773, 776–79 (2d Cir. 1995).

[. . .]

DISCUSSION

Arbitration is contractual by nature—"a party cannot be required to submit to arbitration any dispute which he has not agreed so to submit." . . . Thus, while there is a strong and "liberal federal policy favoring arbitration agreements," . . . such agreements must not be so broadly construed as to encompass claims and parties that were not intended by the original contract. "It does not follow, however, that under the [Federal Arbitration] Act an obligation to arbitrate attaches only to one who has personally signed the written arbitration provision." . . . This Court has made clear that a nonsignatory party may be bound to an arbitration agreement if so dictated by the "ordinary principles of contract and agency." . . .

I. Traditional Bases for Binding Nonsignatories

This Court has recognized a number of theories under which nonsignatories may be bound to the arbitration agreements of others. Those theories arise out of common law principles of contract and agency law. Accordingly, we have recognized five theories for binding nonsignatories to arbitration agreements: 1) incorporation by reference; 2) assumption; 3) agency; 4) veil-piercing/alter ego; and 5) estoppel. . . .

A. Incorporation by Reference

A nonsignatory may compel arbitration against a party to an arbitration agreement when that party has entered into a separate contractual relationship with the nonsignatory which incorporates the existing arbitration clause. . . .

B. Assumption

In the absence of a signature, a party may be bound by an arbitration clause if its subsequent conduct indicates that it is assuming the obligation to arbitrate. . . .

C. Agency

Traditional principles of agency law may bind a nonsignatory to an arbitration agreement....

D. Veil Piercing/Alter Ego

In some instances, the corporate relationship between a parent and its subsidiary are sufficiently close as to justify piercing the corporate veil and holding one corporation legally accountable for the actions of the other. As a general matter, however, a corporate relationship alone is not sufficient to bind a nonsignatory to an arbitration agreement.... Nonetheless, the courts will pierce the corporate veil "in two broad situations: to prevent fraud or other wrong, or where a parent dominates and controls a subsidiary."...

Veil piercing determinations are fact specific and "differ[ ] with the circumstances of each case." ...This Court has determined that a parent corporation and its subsidiary lose their distinct corporate identities when their conduct demonstrates a virtual abandonment of separateness....

[...]

E. Estoppel

This Court has also bound nonsignatories to arbitration agreements under an estoppel theory. In *Deloitte Noraudit A/S v. Deloitte Haskins & Sells*, 9 F.3d 1060, 1064 (2d Cir. 1993), a foreign accounting firm received a settlement agreement concerning the use of the trade name "Deloitte" in association with accounting practices. Under the agreement—containing an arbitration clause—local affiliates of the international accounting association Deloitte Haskins & Sells International were entitled to use the trade name "Deloitte" in exchange for compliance with the dictates of the agreement. A Norwegian accounting firm received the agreement, made no objection to the terms of the agreement, and proceeded to utilize the trade name. This Court held that by knowingly exploiting the agreement, the accounting firm was estopped from avoiding arbitration despite having never signed the agreement....

[...]

Several courts of appeal have recognized an alternative estoppel theory requiring arbitration between a signatory and nonsignatory.... In these cases, a signatory was bound to arbitrate with a nonsignatory at the nonsignatory's insistence because of "the close relationship between the entities involved, as well as the relationship of the alleged wrongs to the nonsignatory's obligations and duties in the contract...and [the fact that] the claims were 'intimately founded in and intertwined with the underlying contract obligations.'"...

As these cases indicate, the circuits have been willing to estop a signatory from avoiding arbitration with a nonsignatory when the issues the nonsignatory is seeking to resolve in arbitration are intertwined with the agreement that the estopped party has signed.... Arbitration is strictly a matter of contract; if the parties have not agreed to arbitrate, the courts have no authority to mandate that they do so.... In the line of cases discussed above, the courts held that the parties were estopped from avoiding arbitration because they had entered into written arbitration agreements, albeit with the affiliates of those parties asserting the arbitration and not the parties themselves....

Moreover, these estoppel cases all involve claims which are integrally related to the contract containing the arbitration clause....

[. . .]

NOTES AND QUESTIONS

1. In *Grigson v. Creative Artists Agency LLC*, 210 F.3d 524 (5th Cir.), *cert. denied*, 531 U.S. 1013 (2000), the Fifth Circuit assessed the role of equitable estoppel in an action to compel arbitration. The case involved allegations of tortious interference with contract. The contract was a movie distribution agreement that provided for the allocation of revenues and disputes to be settled by arbitration. The nonsignatories filed a demand for arbitration because their complaint was intertwined with the contract. The signatories opposed arbitration because the nonsignatories had not agreed to arbitrate and the circumstances did not warrant the application of equitable estoppel.

The federal district court disagreed, holding that "because the claims are so intertwined with, and dependent upon, the distribution agreement," signatories were equitably estopped from relying upon the plaintiffs' status as nonsignatories. The district court ruled that the arbitration provision in the distribution agreement was enforceable.

The appellate court first addressed the questions relating to the doctrine of equitable estoppel. It determined that MS Dealer Serv. Corp. v. Franklin, 177 F.3d 942, 947 (11th Cir. 1999), provided the most cogent test for determining when equitable estoppel can be used to compel arbitration in circumstances involving non-signatory parties:

> Existing case law demonstrates that equitable estoppel allows a non-signatory to compel arbitration in two different circumstances. First, equitable estoppel applies when the signatory to a written agreement containing an arbitration clause must rely on the terms of the written agreement in asserting its claim against the non-signatory...[s]econd, application of equitable estoppel is warranted when the signatory to the contract containing an arbitration clause raises allegations substantially interdependent and concerted misconduct by both the non-signatory and one or more of the signatories to the contract.

The court adopted the *Franklin* test, and found that the doctrine of equitable estoppel could compel arbitration when a signatory to the agreement sought to "have it both ways: [a signatory] cannot...seek to hold the non-signatory liable pursuant to duties imposed by the agreement, which contains an arbitration agreement, but...deny arbitration's applicability because the defendant is a non-signatory."

The appellate court then considered whether the district court abused its discretion in the instant case when it applied the doctrine of equitable estoppel to compel arbitration. "The district court did not abuse its discretion by concluding that [Grigson's] claims [were] so intertwined with and dependent upon the Distribution Agreement that the arbitration agreement within the Distribution Agreement should be given effect." The court stated that its "conclusion [was] compelled" by a comparison of Grigson's allegations to the terms of the Distribution Agreement.

In a lengthy dissent, Judge Dennis argued that application of the doctrine of equitable estoppel to compel arbitration between two parties, one of whom is a non-signatory to the contract containing the arbitration provision, is in conflict with the U.S. Supreme Court's opinion in *First Options of Chicago, Inc. v. Kaplan*, 514 U.S. 938 (1995):

> "Nearly anything can be called estoppel. When a lawyer or a judge does not know what other name to give for his decision to decide a case in a certain way, he says there is an estoppel." The trouble with that kind of use of the estoppel label by the majority in this case making circuit precedent is that it will seriously hinder this court in upholding the basic principle that a person has a right to a court's decision about the merits of a dispute unless he has agreed to submit it to arbitration. Because the majority decision conflicts with the Supreme Court's recent emphatic affirmations of that principle, and the precedents of this circuit, I respectfully dissent.

> [. . .]

> As a general rule, an arbitration clause cannot be invoked by a non-party to the arbitration contract, and only parties to the arbitration agreement are bound to arbitrate...The federal policy favoring arbitration is strong, but it alone cannot authorize a non-party to invoke arbitration or requiring a non-signatory to arbitrate...*Nonetheless, a non-signatory may be bound by or acquire rights under an arbitration agreement under ordinary state-law principles of agency or contract.* . . .

> Courts have recognized a number of theories arising out of common law principles of contract and agency law under which non-signatories may be bound to the arbitration agreements of others. For example, 1) incorporation by reference; 2) assumption by conduct; 3) agency; 4) veil-piercing/alter ego; and 5) estoppel. . . .

> In theory, under ordinary state-law principles of equitable and promissory estoppel, a non-party to a contract containing an arbitration clause may invoke the clause and compel a signatory party to arbitrate when the signatory reasonably should have expected that, because of his statements or conduct, the non-signatory would be induced to rely justifiably on the contract and would be injured thereby if the signatory refused to recognize the non-signatory's rights or entitlements with respect to the contract. However, there have been few, if any, cases in which a non-signatory has successfully invoked an arbitration clause against a party signatory to the contract under ordinary equitable or promissory estoppel principles. In a relatively few arbitration cases, a non-signatory to the arbitration agreement has been allowed to compel arbitration under a spurious estoppel theory when the peculiar integrated or interlocking circumstances of the parties'

relationships, related contracts, contractually assigned responsibilities, conduct and disputes would allow the inference that the signatory and non-signatory parties have by an agreement implied in fact become bound reciprocally by the arbitration clause or the contract of which it is a part. . . .

Which position is most convincing to you? When should a party not bound by the contract be obligated by it or benefit from it? Is there any warrant for widespread flexibility in commercial circumstances? Can you restate the rule that applies in regard to equitable estoppel? How does it square with the federal policy on arbitration?

2. In *Smith/Enron Cogeneration Ltd. Partnership, Inc. v. Smith Cogeneration Int'l, Inc.*, 198 F.3d 88 (2d Cir. 1999), *cert. denied*, 531 U.S. 815 (2000), the U.S. Court of Appeals for the Second Circuit held that a non-signatory assignee of the original party to the arbitration clause may compel the signatory to arbitrate. The court found no reason to allow the signatory to avoid arbitration on the ground that the parties had not agreed to arbitrate. When the issues the non-signatory is seeking to resolve in arbitration are intertwined with the agreement containing the arbitral clause, the signatory party is estopped from avoiding arbitration. Furthermore, the avoiding party also is estopped from pleading a lack of agreement where it previously referred to the non-signatory party and the original signatory as one entity in prior litigation and business practice.

Does this mean that there are "shadow" contracts and "shadow" contracts of arbitration? Can you explain the court's holding by reference to practicality? Is the result commanded by policy? Is the result fair? Is it justified?

* * *

The question of whether an arbitration agreement can be implied from the commercial circumstances of a transaction has not been addressed directly in the U.S. decisional law. It appears, however, to have both a statutory and decisional law answer in German law. The following article evaluates a German case on the question and points to the danger of adopting such a rule in U.S. law.

T. CARBONNEAU, "A–LEGALITY" AND ARBITRATION: THE GERMAN SUPREME COURT JOINS THE FRAY

4 AM. REV. INT'L ARB. 217 (1993).

(footnotes omitted)

I. PREFACE

. . .I undertook this comment upon a recent German Supreme Court case because I found the language of the Court's opinion, as reported in summary through unofficial translations, to have a potentially revolutionary impact upon arbitration law. After completing the analysis, I did find the opinion extraordinary. I remain a steadfast supporter of arbitration, but I am firmly convinced that the opinion and the decisional law to which it can be aligned constitute a wrong-headed approach to arbitration and to the definition of its relationship to the law and of its role in legal order.

It should also be underscored at the outset that the opinion is characteristically civilian: anonymous as to the parties, cryptic in the reporting of facts and in elucidating the Court's reasoning, and containing no indicia of counterpoint or dissent. Moreover, in terms of the procedural status of the decision, the opinion is merely a remand of the case to the lower appellate court for reconsideration in light of the higher court's admonitions. In a formal sense, the opinion is not a decision establishing doctrine.

I believe, however, that the mere pronouncement of these views by such an elevated tribunal, regardless of the qualified language of the opinion and its instructional character, gives them precedential value. They fit perfectly into the trend of eliminating all legal constraints on arbitration and parallel recent, equally radical developments in U.S. law. Procedural and technical considerations aside, this is a landmark opinion once it is integrated into the transborder context of the world law on arbitration.

II. THE OPINION AND ITS SETTING

The German Supreme Court for Civil, Commercial, and Criminal Matters (the Federal Court of Justice) recently made an extraordinary contribution (albeit, of dubious doctrinal merit) to the developing world law on arbitration. The Court remanded a case to the rendering appellate court with instructions suggesting, subtly but firmly, that an arbitration agreement can be implied in a contract as a result of customary commercial usage. . . .

[. . .]

Despite the understated tone of the language of the opinion, the German Supreme Court chose to address the arbitration issue raised in the litigation in a highly creative fashion. The Court appears to have pitched its decision at a precedent-setting level. Whatever its ultimate fate in a procedural sense, the content of the opinion makes German law nearly automatically a player in the elaboration of a transborder law on arbitration. The pronouncement quietly binds itself with and rivals the anational liberalism of both French and American law. More importantly, it creates the image of a German jurisdiction that is very hospitable to arbitration and able to compete with its neighbors as a center for European and international arbitral practice.

The price for this accomplishment, however, is yet another substantial departure from the traditional legal basis for arbitration; it is another example of unlimited and uncontained arbitral deregulation in-the-making. Prior to this decision, despite the favorable attitude (both legislative and judicial) toward arbitration in many jurisdictions, courts at least required contracts to contain some semblance of an arbitration agreement before compelling the recourse to arbitration. Moreover, although U.S.

decisions on arbitrability appeared to confound the basic limits of arbitral jurisdiction, courts in civil law jurisdictions, France especially, recognized the necessary contractual foundation of arbitration, allowing the party autonomy principle to reign provided it manifested itself in the transaction.

The German Supreme Court opinion potentially violates this basic legal principle in a manner unthinkable for a civil law court and even for its more pugnacious U.S. counterpart. The world law on arbitration now has been introduced to the view that the transactional context and its accepted bargaining patterns are a proper foundation for implying the existence of an arbitration agreement as a matter of law when the parties fail to make provision for arbitration.

III.   The Facts

The decisional content of the opinion far exceeds the commonplace circumstances of the transaction or of the litigation. The dispute arose in the setting of a typical brokered sale. The broker sent a telegram to a supplier on behalf of a buyer, offering to purchase a large quantity of Wetblue–Sheepskins. In the telegram, the broker specified the use of a particular standard contract that did not contain an arbitration clause. The supplier responded, agreeing to supply the goods; however, it referred to another standard contract by which to memorialize the agreement and that contract did contain an arbitration clause.

Thereafter, the broker instructed the buyer that he had purchased the sheepskins, and sent him, to complete the transaction, the standard contract omitting the arbitral clause. The buyer approved the terms of the agreement. Thereupon, the broker sent the supplier the same contract. Several days later, the supplier confirmed the terms of the agreement, and requested that the provisions of the standard contract it had referred to in its acceptance be modified to conform to the contract used by the broker and agreed upon by the buyer. The supplier then sent the buyer an invoice for the goods that made reference to the standard contract containing an arbitration clause. The buyer paid the invoice a few weeks later, but then sued the supplier to recover its payment. The supplier responded with a demand for arbitration, with which the buyer refused to comply.

IV.   An Assessment of the Facts

[. . .]

. . .[T]here appears to be a good deal of confusion among the parties as to which contract form codifies and regulates the sale. The broker appeared intent upon using his standard form (contract no. 3132) that apparently did not contain a provision for arbitral dispute resolution (otherwise the litigation would not have occurred). The supplier made initial reference in its acceptance to another standard form (contract no. 7297) that provided for arbitration, but the facts later indicate that the supplier was willing to be bound by contract 3132 in its confirmation of the terms of the agreement. It is not clear from the Court's recitation of the facts whether or how contracts 3132 and 7297 differed in other respects or whether the supplier believed the reference to arbitration was a material part of the bargain.

It does seem clear, however, that the supplier was willing to go along with contract 3132 at the conclusion of the agreement and presumably (albeit, perhaps unwittingly) forego arbitration. Also, the purchaser never saw contract 7297, *i.e.*, the form contract referring to arbitration. It seems that each merchant party, the broker and supplier, wanted to have the transaction governed by standard contracts with which they were familiar, and that the supplier ultimately acquiesced to the broker's habits. The reference in the invoice to the other standard form may have been a clerical mistake and may not have been noticed or appreciated by the buyer....

[...]

The facts as reported reveal that the buyer and seller agreed to the sale, that the goods were paid for, and that the buyer was unhappy with the transaction and wanted to recover his money. The preliminary question of the litigation, central to this analysis and to the importance of the case, was what form of justice, arbitral or judicial, was commanded by the contract. Was there a valid agreement to arbitrate disputes? The exchange of contracts through the broker constituted a valid sales agreement; the only issue centers upon whether the governing agreement contained an arbitration provision. The facts further indicate that contract 3132 did not contain a reference to arbitration.

V.   Procedural History

The various courts that considered the case disagreed...upon a proper resolution of the question. At the trial level, the district court held that it lacked jurisdiction by virtue of an agreement to arbitrate, and concluded that the matter should go to arbitration. That determination was reversed on appeal by two courts; these appellate courts determined that the contract did not contain an arbitration agreement. The defendant filed a special appeal on legal questions (*révision*) against the appellate determination to the Supreme Court. The Court criticized the federal appellate court for failing to consider trade usages and their potential impact upon the litigation, implying that the parties could be bound to arbitrate by standard practices in the trade sector.

According to the Court: In the absence of special circumstances, implying an arbitral clause into the contract might be justified even when such a provision had not been expressly included in the contract. Further paraphrasing, usages in the trade could be used to fill gaps in contracts and to supplement existing contractual duties because such usages can have a normative character. Therefore, a usage could be the vehicle for a "tacit arbitration agreement" in a particular trade sector—especially if the parties participated regularly in this area of business.

VI. The Opinion

In characteristically brief, but perplexing reasoning, the Court opined that the very nature of the parties' transaction could imply as a matter of law the existence of an arbitration agreement in the contract. In reaching this determination, the Court not only minimized, but eliminated the relevance of which contract form governed, what the governing contract actually provided, and what the parties intended by their conduct.

In the Court's view, the consideration of significant moment ignored by the appellate court was the standard practice that prevailed in the trade sector. It concluded that the recourse to arbitration appeared to be the standard "business usage," and could bind the parties to arbitration. It faulted the decision on appeal because the issuing court failed to acknowledge or give sufficient weight to the existence of special arbitral courts for the skins and hides trade that dealt with the adjudication of contract claims in this area. These international and domestic arbitral mechanisms and the predominance of arbitral clauses in the general contract practice of the sector were enough to warrant consideration of the governing business usage or trade practice to submit disputes to arbitral resolution.

In light of standard industry practice, the Court stated that the express content of the actual contract might have little bearing upon the question of what had been agreed to by the parties. Any divergence in the parties' intent would void the entire contract, not just the would-be arbitral clause. There clearly had been a sale. The provision for arbitral dispute resolution was standard practice. The failure of an actual provision then might be simply a lacuna that could be supplied by the courts.

In effect, the Court impliedly invited the appellate court upon reconsideration to create a nearly irrebuttable presumption that standard commercial agreements within certain specialized trade sectors contain arbitration clauses. The absence of an arbitration agreement apparently is not sufficient to rebut the presumption. Indeed, in order to avoid the automatic reference to arbitration, a party doing business in the area would need to include express language in the contract rejecting the arbitral remedy. Therefore, on remand, the appellate court should probably conclude that arbitral provisions exist as a matter of law in standard contracts, unless they contain express language rejecting arbitration.

Finally, the Court alluded to the German procedural law on arbitration. . . . The [C]ourt does point to a provision of German law that provides some support for the proposition that it advances. Article 1027 (1) and (2) of the German Code of Civil Procedure provides that arbitration agreements must be "concluded expressly" and must be "in writing," unless "the arbitration agreement is a business transaction for both parties." The content of the article appears to state that less formality can accompany the conclusion of arbitration agreements in commercial matters and it also might sustain the view that arbitration agreements can be implied from usages in particular commercial sectors.

The latter position, however, extends considerably the actual content of the provision. Paragraph (3) of the article, for example, merely states that such "agreements" do not "require a form" but that either party "may demand the drawing up of a written document concerning the agreement." This additional statement does not clarify the import of the provision except to emphasize that the usual contract formalities need not be fully observed in the commercial context. Although the Court's expertise on its national law cannot be questioned, Article 1027 does not appear to provide unambiguous support, if any, for the Court's view that trade usages can serve as a basis for implying an arbitration agreement—even in a commercial context.

[. . .]

VII. A WIDER ASSESSMENT

The opinion, if adopted by a lower court, is at odds with the traditional approach of civil law courts to arbitration—at least, the civil law approach represented by some judicial rulings in France. One of the basic tenets of the French decisional law on arbitration, presumably applicable in other civil law countries, is that arbitration is a creature of contract. The right to have recourse to arbitration is a consequence of the parties' freedom of contract—in civil law terms, the right to arbitrate is a function of the parties' will and is restricted only by the relatively inconsequential limits of public policy (as defined by contemporary decisional and statutory law). The parties can create their own system of justice to resolve their private law claims. The State's adjudicatory interests extend to disputes directly implicating the public interest, and its vigilance in the private setting is confined to assuring that non-judicial proceedings conform to the dictates of essential fairness.

[. . .]

. . . To force parties to arbitration when, in fact, they have not agreed to it, however, is violative of the very foundation of contract law. The valuable lessons of the civil law contractualism appear to have been lost on the German Supreme Court. According to its opinion, the law of arbitration is not an architecture of rules and principles meant to intermediate between private contractual rights and the public functions of adjudication. The Court's suggested disposition of the matter is more in keeping with the decisional law of the U.S. Supreme Court on arbitration. . . .

After *McMahon* and *Rodriguez*, in which the U.S. Supreme Court ignored the adhesionary character of the implicated contracts, one wondered what the next step might be in the development of the "emphatic [U.S.] federal policy" supporting arbitration. Arbitration had just become viable, by judicial fiat, in the context of consumer transactions involving a substantial disparity of bargaining position. It seemed that the only possible progression in the liberal U.S. decisional law on arbitration was to have U.S. federal courts rule that arbitration agreements were implied in certain types of transactions as a matter of law. They could declare arbitration to be the exclusive remedial recourse in whatever context considerations of federal arbitral policy dictated.

That prospect was the logical next step in an uncompromising policy of support for arbitration, but it was unthinkable, the height of absurdity, a circumstance in which logic was not informed by experience, reason or the reality of professional decision-making. That development, thus far resisted by the U.S. Supreme Court, could become the result propounded by German law.

[. . .]

* * *

Finally, the reasoning and result in *Jain v. de Méré*, 51 F.3d 686 (7th Cir.), *cert. denied*, 516 U.S. 914 (1995), illustrate that federal courts are predisposed to a favorable interpretation of arbitration agreements. The predisposition could lead them either to imply arbitration agreements or extend their effects beyond the legal perimeters of the contract. In *Jain*, a French and an Indian national found themselves before a federal court in Illinois for a dispute involving the payment of a commission for the brokering of a licensing agreement. Their agreement contained a dispute resolution clause which provided that "[a]ny disagreement arising out of this contract may only be presented to an arbitrary commission applying French laws." *Id.* at 688. Jain, the Indian national, served de Méré with a demand for arbitration in Illinois under AAA rules, and brought an action to compel arbitration before a federal district court in Illinois. On appeal, the motion to compel arbitration was upheld.

Apart from the complex questions pertaining to the propriety of the federal court's jurisdiction in this case, there are substantial problems with the content of the would-be arbitration clause. The clause appears to confer exclusive jurisdiction to hear contract "disagreements" upon "an arbitrary commission." While the phrasing reflects clear problems of translation from the French, what is "an arbitrary commission"? Does it mean arbitral tribunal? How do you know? Moreover, what does to "present" disagreements in the arbitral clause mean? Does it refer to adjudication or mediation or something else? It is clear that de Méré wanted whatever it was and whatever it was doing to apply French law. How does a demand for AAA arbitration in Illinois comport with that clear requirement of the so-called arbitral clause? How should the court's order to compel arbitration read in light of this provision? If you were a federal judge hearing this case, how would you rule on the arbitration questions?

* * *

In matters of ordinary litigation, the federal courts have the power to consolidate separate actions. Under Rule 42(a) of the Federal Rules of Civil Procedure,

> When actions involving a common question of law or fact are pending before the court, it may order a joint hearing or trial of any or all the matters

in issue in the actions; it may order all the actions consolidated; and it may make such orders concerning proceedings therein as may tend to avoid unnecessary costs or delay.

The purpose of the provision is to promote judicial economy and efficient management and to avoid conflicting determinations in related litigation. Although the FAA does not contain any authorizing language, some federal courts have applied their authority to consolidate arbitrations.

The question of consolidating arbitral proceedings raises many of the same issues that were discussed in the foregoing sections. The judicial consolidation of separate but related arbitral proceedings, in effect, can represent a *post facto* rewriting of the parties' agreement to arbitrate. The judicial order requires the parties to arbitrate with noncontracting parties and extends the effect of the agreement. The action, however, is not undertaken with an antagonistic motivation. The courts are attempting to promote what they believe is the best interest of arbitration—its institutional welfare depends in part upon the efficiency of its operation and the consistency of its determinations. Consolidation generates analytical and practical problems. A number of critical issues can be identified: Is the court engaging in judicial supervision or interference when it orders the consolidation of arbitral proceedings? Is the ordering of consolidation a lawful exercise of its judicial authority? What problems of administration are likely to arise when proceedings are consolidated? The number and designation of arbitrations? The applicable procedure? The form of the award? Is the award rendered in a consolidated proceeding the result of an arbitration agreement? Is it enforceable under Section Ten of the FAA?

The federal circuits generally do not favor consolidation. The Second, Fifth, Eighth, Ninth, and Eleventh Circuits have taken the position that consolidations cannot be ordered unless the parties have consented and the arbitration agreement provides for multiparty arbitration. The Fourth Circuit intermediates by stating that an agreement to allow consolidation can be inferred from the parties' agreement. *See* Thomas Stipanowich, *Arbitration and the Multiparty Dispute: The Search for Workable Solutions,* 72 IOWA L. REV. 473 (1987); Schaeffer, Comment, *Compulsory Consolidation of Commercial Arbitration Disputes,* 33 ST. LOUIS U. L.J. 495 (1989).

The central issue is whether judicial consolidation is legitimate in the context of arbitration. Is consolidation entirely inapposite in regard to arbitral proceedings? Is the agreement to arbitrate the only legitimate source of authorizing authority for consolidation in the setting of arbitration? What role should institutional arbitral rules play in the development of a suitable approach? Do the arbitrators have the power to consolidate different but related arbitral proceedings? Would an award ordering consolidation need to be unanimous among the various sets of arbitrators? Must all of the parties agree? Should the FAA be amended to include a provision on consolidation in which courts can order consolidation only in the most exceptional circumstances? How might such a provision read?

Other national laws on arbitration also recognize the process of consolidation. Australia, Canada, Ecuador, England, Hong Kong, and the Netherlands provide for consolidation. The English practice requires the consent of both parties; Hong Kong law gives the courts wide discretion to order consolidation with or without party consent; while Australia follows the English practice of consensual consolidation. The Netherlands Arbitration Act of 1986 allows a party to seek an order of consolidation, "unless the parties have agreed otherwise." One party may seek consolidation and the decision is within the court's discretion. *See* The Netherlands Arbitration Act 1986, art. 1046(1), *translated in* P. SANDERS & A. JAN VAN DEN BERG, THE NETHERLANDS ARBITRATION ACT 1986, at 26 (1987). *See generally* I. DORE, THEORY AND PRACTICE OF MULTIPARTY COMMERCIAL ARBITRATION (1990).

GOVERNMENT OF THE UNITED KINGDOM v. BOEING CO.

998 F.2d 68 (2d Cir. 1993).

(footnotes omitted)

MESKILL, Chief Judge:

This is an appeal from a judgment...granting the motion of petitioner-appellee Government of the United Kingdom...to consolidate an American Arbitration Association (AAA) arbitration proceeding between the United Kingdom and respondent-appellant The Boeing Company (Boeing) with a separate AAA arbitration proceeding between the United Kingdom and respondent Textron, Inc. (Textron). The district court held that it has the authority pursuant to the Federal Arbitration Act...and the Federal Rules of Civil Procedure to compel consolidation of separate arbitration proceedings when the proceedings involve the same questions of fact and law, even in the absence of the parties' consent to consolidation.

We hold that a district court cannot order consolidation of arbitration proceedings arising from separate agreements to arbitrate absent the parties' agreement to allow such consolidation. Therefore, we reverse the district court.

BACKGROUND

This case, filed under seal, arises from a January 1989 ground testing incident in which a military helicopter owned by the United Kingdom was damaged. The incident occurred during Boeing's testing of a new electronic fuel control system (FADEC) that had been designed by Textron and installed in the helicopter by Boeing. The helicopter had been manufactured by Boeing and its engine had been manufactured by Textron.

Boeing and Textron have separate contracts with the United Kingdom governing long-standing relationships that each company has with the United Kingdom on a variety of military projects. The relevant arbitration agreement between the United Kingdom and Boeing is contained in a 1981 base contract for certain services. The relevant arbitration agreement between the United Kingdom and Textron is contained in a 1985 contract relating specifically to the design and development of FADEC. The contracts contain identical arbitration clauses which read:

> Any controversy or claim arising out of or relating to this contract, or the breach thereof, shall be settled by arbitration in New York City by three Arbitrators in accordance with the Rules of the American Arbitration Association, and judgment upon the award rendered by the Arbitrator(s) may be entered in any court having jurisdiction thereof.

Boeing and Textron also are parties to a separate Interface Agreement between them which defines their respective responsibilities for the FADEC project.

On July 18, 1991, the United Kingdom filed Demands for Arbitration with the AAA against Boeing and Textron for its losses resulting from the January 1989 ground testing incident. Both before and after filing the Demands for Arbitration, the United Kingdom requested that Boeing and Textron consent to consolidation of the arbitration proceedings. Boeing refused, alleging that consolidation would lead to undue expense and effort on its behalf because of the alleged simplicity of the issues involved in its arbitration with the United Kingdom compared to those in the United Kingdom/Textron arbitration. The AAA informed the United Kingdom that it would not order consolidation of arbitration proceedings without the consent of all parties.

On October 1, 1991, the United Kingdom filed a Petition to Compel Consolidated Arbitration in the United States District Court for the Southern District of New York. All parties agreed that both arbitrations would be stayed pending disposition of the United Kingdom's petition. On October 14, 1992, Judge Stanton issued a Memorandum Endorsement in which he granted the United Kingdom's Petition to Compel Consolidated Arbitration and denied Boeing's Motion to Dismiss....

DISCUSSION

I

The United Kingdom urges, and the district court held, that our decision in *Compania Espanola de Petroleos, S.A. v. Nereus Shipping, S.A.*....definitively established in this Circuit the district courts' authority pursuant to the FAA and the Federal Rules of Civil Procedure to consolidate arbitration proceedings that turn on the same questions of fact and law. As we describe in greater detail below, the facts in *Nereus* were much different than the facts in this case, and the district court erred in applying the *Nereus* holding.

[. . .]

Nereus is distinguishable from the case before us. In *Nereus*, all three parties signed Addendum No. 2, which incorporated the provisions of the Charter Party, including the arbitration provision. We held that in signing the addendum, Cepsa had agreed to "assume the rights and obligations" of Hideca, including the obligation to participate in arbitration over any disputes. . . . Thus all three parties were in arbitration pursuant to a single arbitration agreement. We determined that the intention of the signatories to Addendum No. 2 would be most closely adhered to with a single arbitration proceeding. In contrast, in the case before us, Boeing and Textron are in arbitration with the United Kingdom pursuant to two distinct agreements to arbitrate contained in two distinct contracts. Neither agreement contains any provision for consolidation. Boeing never agreed to participate in arbitration with Textron, and vice versa. We simply have no grounds to conclude that the parties consented to consolidated arbitration. The district court is without authority to consolidate the two actions based upon the mere fact that the disputes contain similar or identical issues of fact and law. *See Volt Info. Sciences v. Board of Trustees,* . . . ("[The FAA] simply requires courts to enforce privately negotiated agreements to arbitrate, like other contracts, in accordance with their terms.").

II

As the district court and the United Kingdom point out, in our holding in *Nereus* we also relied on the Federal Rules of Civil Procedure and the "liberal purposes" of the FAA. . . . Subsequent to our decision in *Nereus*, several district courts in this Circuit have determined that they have the authority to compel consolidated arbitration in cases involving separate agreements to arbitrate but similar or identical factual circumstances and questions of law. However, as we explain below, recent Supreme Court case law has undermined our previous conclusion that the FAA's "liberal purposes" and the Federal Rules of Civil Procedure allow us to consolidate arbitration proceedings absent consent. To the extent that *Nereus* relied on that conclusion it is no longer good law.

A

[. . .]

. . . Cases decided in the Supreme Court since our decisions in *Robert Lawrence* and *Nereus* have undermined our interpretation of the purposes of the FAA. *See Volt Info. Sciences,* . . . *Dean Witter Reynolds Inc. v. Byrd,* . . . *Moses H. Cone Memorial Hosp. v. Mercury Constr. Corp.* . . . These cases concluded that the FAA was intended merely to assure the enforcement of privately negotiated arbitration agreements, despite possible inefficiencies created by such enforcement.

The Supreme Court affirmed an order requiring enforcement of an arbitration agreement in *Moses H. Cone Memorial Hosp.*, even though arbitration would result in bifurcated proceedings because not all of the parties to the dispute were parties to the arbitration agreement. In words quite relevant to the case at hand, the Supreme Court stated that "[u]nder the [FAA], an arbitration agreement must be enforced notwithstanding the presence of other persons who are parties to the underlying dispute but not to the arbitration agreement." . . . Subsequently in *Byrd,* the Supreme Court explained in detail the limited purposes behind the FAA:

> The legislative history of the [FAA] establishes that the purpose behind its passage was to ensure judicial enforcement of privately made agreements to arbitrate. We therefore reject the suggestion that the overriding goal of the [FAA] was to promote the expeditious resolution of claims. The [FAA], after all, does not mandate the arbitration of all claims, but merely the enforcement—upon the motion of one of the parties—of privately negotiated arbitration agreements. The House Report accompanying the [FAA] makes clear that its purpose was to place an arbitration agreement "upon the same footing as other contracts, where it belongs,"...and to overrule the judiciary's longstanding refusal to enforce agreements to arbitrate.

> [...]

> The preeminent concern of Congress in passing the [FAA] was to enforce private agreements into which parties had entered, and that concern requires that we rigorously enforce agreements to arbitrate, even if the result is "piecemeal" litigation, at least absent a countervailing policy manifested in another federal statute.

...Four years later the Supreme Court reemphasized its position by stating that the FAA "simply requires courts to enforce privately negotiated agreements to arbitrate, like other contracts, in accordance with their terms." *Volt Info. Sciences,*....

Each of our sister circuit courts that has considered the question since these Supreme Court decisions has held that district courts do not have the authority under the FAA to consolidate arbitrations absent the parties' consent. In *Weyerha[e]user Co. v. Western Seas Shipping Co.,*...the Ninth Circuit declined to compel consolidation.... Similarly, the Sixth Circuit has made clear that "a court is not permitted to interfere with private arbitration arrangements in order to impose its own view of speed and economy. This is the case even where the result would be the possibly inefficient maintenance of separate proceedings." *American Centennial Ins. Co. v. National Casualty Co.,* 951 F.2d 107, 108 (6th Cir. 1991); *see also Baesler v. Continental Grain Co.,* 900 F.2d 1193, 1195 (8th Cir. 1990) ("The Supreme Court has explicitly rejected the assertion that the overriding goal of the [FAA] is to promote the expeditious resolution of claims."); *Protective Life Ins. Corp. v. Lincoln Nat'l Life Ins. Corp.,* 873 F.2d 281, 282 (11th Cir. 1989) (per curiam) ("Parties may negotiate for and include provisions for consolidation of arbitration proceedings in their arbitration agreements, but if such provisions are absent, federal courts may not read them in."); *Del E. Webb Constr. v. Richardson Hosp. Auth.,* 823 F.2d 145, 150 (5th Cir. 1987) ("[U]nder § 4 of the [FAA] the sole question for the district court is whether there is a written agreement among the parties providing for consolidated arbitration."). One district court in this Circuit has held that it was without authority to consolidate arbitrations in light of *Byrd. Ore & Chemical Corp. v. Stinnes Interoil,* 606

F.Supp. 1510, 1513 (S.D.N.Y.1985) ("the Second Circuit's reliance in *Nereus* on the 'liberal purposes' of the [FAA] was misplaced").

B

The United Kingdom also claims that the district court has the authority to compel consolidation of the United Kingdom/Boeing and United Kingdom/Textron arbitrations pursuant to the Federal Rules of Civil Procedure, Rules 42(a) and 81(a)(3). The United Kingdom and the district court point out that in *Nereus*, we specifically stated that Rules 42(a) and 81(a)(3) were applicable.... We hold that these rules are not applicable to the case before us.

Rule 42(a) provides, in pertinent part, that "[w]hen actions involving a common question of law or fact are pending before the court...it may order all the actions consolidated." Rule 81(a)(3) provides, in pertinent part, that "[i]n proceedings under Title 9, U.S.C., relating to arbitration,...[the Federal Rules of Civil Procedure] apply only to the extent that matters of procedure are not provided for in those statutes." The United Kingdom asserts that Rule 42(a) as incorporated through Rule 81(a)(3) allows, or at least "provide[s] valuable guidance" to, the district court to consolidate private arbitration proceedings in appropriate situations. We reject this argument. Rule 81(a)(3) merely allows the application of the Federal Rules of Civil Procedure to judicial proceedings that are before a court pursuant to U.S.C. Title 9, to the extent that Title 9 does not provide appropriate procedural rules. Rule 81(a)(3) clearly does not import the Federal Rules of Civil Procedure to the private arbitration proceedings that underlie the Title 9 proceedings pending before a court. *See* 4 C. Wright & A. Miller, *Federal Practice and Procedure* § 1015, at 66–67 (1987) ("It is only the judicial proceedings under the [FAA]...that are subject to the rules. The federal rules do not govern the procedure in the hearings before the arbitrators.") (footnote omitted); *Washington-Baltimore Newspaper Guild v. The Washington Post Co.*, 442 F.2d 1234, 1239 (D.C. Cir. 1971) ("[None] of the Federal Rules of Civil Procedure was ever designed to apply to proceedings in other than the United States District Courts.") (citation omitted); *Foremost Yarn Mills v. Rose Mills*, 25 F.R.D. 9, 11 (E.D. Pa. 1960) ("it is clearly evident that the [FAA] itself does not in any wise attempt to regulate the procedures before the arbitrators or prescribe rules or regulations with respect to hearings before arbitrators"). Therefore, although a district judge considering related petitions to compel arbitration can have all of the petitions heard at once pursuant to Rule 42(a), he or she could not use Rule 42(a) to order that the underlying arbitrations, once compelled, be conducted together.

The United Kingdom also makes much of the inefficiencies and possible inconsistent determinations that may result if the United Kingdom/Boeing and United Kingdom/Textron arbitrations are allowed to proceed separately. Although these may be valid concerns to the United Kingdom, they do not provide us with the authority to reform the private contracts which underlie this dispute. If contracting parties wish to have all disputes that arise from the same factual situation arbitrated in a single proceeding, they can simply provide for consolidated arbitration in the arbitration clauses to which they are a party. *See Volt Info. Sciences*...("Arbitration under the [FAA] is a matter of consent, not coercion, and parties are generally free to structure their arbitration agreements as they see fit. Just as they may limit by contract the issues which they will arbitrate,...so too may they specify by contract the rules under which that arbitration will be conducted.") (citation omitted).

Conclusion

We reverse the judgment of the district court granting the United Kingdom's Petition to Compel Consolidated Arbitration and we hold that the district court cannot consolidate arbitration proceedings arising from separate agreements to arbitrate, absent the parties' agreement to allow such consolidation. To the extent our decision in *Nereus* is based on the Federal Rules of Civil Procedure and the "liberal purposes" of the Federal Arbitration Act, we hold that it is no longer good law. We do not disturb *Nereus* to the extent it is based on the general equitable powers of the court and principles of contract law.

Notes and Questions

1. Despite a strongly favorable statutory and decisional disposition toward arbitration in French law, the French Court of Cassation has refused to allow the consolidation of arbitral proceedings solely on the basis of a court order—especially when the administration of the consolidated proceeding engendered a violation of the principle of the equal treatment of the parties. *See* Decision of Jan. 7, 1992, *reported in* 7 Mealey's Int'l Arb. Rep. 20 (Feb. 1992) ("the *Dutco* case"). The critical consideration appears to reside in the Court's view of the contractual foundation of arbitration and of the dictates of procedural fairness in arbitration. Judicial authority cannot be superimposed upon the mechanism of arbitration without challenging the systemic autonomy and legitimacy of the arbitral process. As the Second Circuit notes in *Boeing*, courts have the power to manage litigation dockets, but their power cannot simply be transferred to the administration of private arbitral proceedings without blurring essential distinctions between the judicial and arbitral processes. Subject to the judicial supervision of arbitral awards and court assistance of the arbitral process, the contract of arbitration establishes the reach and the limits of arbitral justice.

2. The foregoing decisions provide that judicial consolidation should be avoided, unless the parties specifically provide for it in their agreement. That position appears to fit perfectly within the doctrinal circumference of the *Kaplan* holding. In effect, lawyers and clients will determine the availability and suitability of consolidation in the negotiating and contract-drafting stage of the transaction. Do you agree with the doctrine and its practical implementation? Is this the best way to address the problem? Given the disparity of position in various national laws, is there a likelihood of disrupting arbitration

through the emergence of conflict problems? Is doctrine or practicality the controlling consideration on this question?

3. PROPOSED ANTI-ARBITRATION LEGISLATION

Thomas Carbonneau, *"ARBITRACIDE": THE STORY OF ANTI-ARBITRATION SENTIMENT IN THE U.S. CONGRESS*

18 AM. REV. INT'L ARB. 233 (2007).

(footnotes and headers omitted)

PROPOSED ANTI-ARBITRATION LEGISLATION

The Court's policy on arbitration avoided serious objections until the development of employment and consumer arbitration in the late 1980s and early 1990s. The emergence of disparate-party arbitration generated some dissension among lower courts centering upon the enforceability of adhesion contracts. The Court itself basically shunned the matter. In several landmark opinions, it provided an oblique response by holding fast to the position that the statutory duty of courts was to enforce arbitration contracts. In effect, the Court was saying that would-be contract unfairness did not alter the "prime directive" of the governing statute. Displaying its allegiance to the contract foundation of arbitration, the Seventh Circuit provided an unequivocal justification for tolerating inequity in contract formation. It declared that adhesion contracts were legitimate contracts, as long as they gave each side to the transaction significant benefits that were desirable and in furtherance of their individual interests. In effect, the Seventh Circuit advanced a new perspective on contract formation, one which minimized and superseded the requirement of bilaterality and freely given consent, and focused upon the "benefits of the bargain."

When a merchant or employer imposed the obligation to arbitrate upon a customer or employee as a condition of doing business or employment, the unilateral character of the imposition, in addition to its origin in power of the economically superior party, did not necessarily nullify the "agreement." These circumstances merely demonstrated a substantial imbalance in the negotiation of the agreement, so-called procedural unconscionability. The critical question was whether the terms and condition of the "bargain" actually oppressed the weaker party. Would an "objective and rational" consumer or employee, empowered with choice, reject or accept the transaction with its contingencies? In a more populous world in which regulatory conflicts can readily flare and in which markets were ever more competitive, the traditional contract, like the concept of judicial litigation as the mainstay of adjudication, needed to be adapted and reformulated.

[. . .]

This refashioning of arbitration and contract doctrine was not received with universal enthusiasm and approval. The Ninth Circuit frequently expressed opposition to the Supreme Court's doctrine on arbitration, especially in cases involving disparate-party transactions. For example, it held that the employment contract exclusion generally prohibited the FAA from applying to employment arbitrations and that weaker transactional parties could not be obligated by unconsented-to provisions, no matter how much federal policy favored arbitration. In fact, the Ninth Circuit rendered several decisions that conflicted directly with the precepts of the U.S. Supreme Court's arbitration doctrine. Eventually, the lower court strayed frequently and far enough to justify the reversal of most of its contrarian rulings.

The federal bench was not the sole source of opposition in California to the federal revitalization and transformation of arbitration. The California state Supreme Court and the California state courts of appeal evinced reluctance, and then outright opposition, to the unequivocally favorable position on arbitration, especially in the transactional circumstances of adhesion. Time and again, California state high court rulings came close to the very edge of the federal preemptive doctrine. In *Southland*, the central case in the federalism trilogy, the U.S. Supreme Court proclaimed that California decisional law and legislation on arbitration must respect the dictates of federal policy. Because of the costs [of appeal] to litigants and the Court's crowded agenda, other non-conforming California rulings escaped the Court's scrutiny and correction. Despite a few reprimands and the unmistakable clarity of the federal position, the California high court remained intent upon rectifying the perceived unfairness of arbitration in situations in which the parties were not at economic parity and the contract was a unilateral, all-or-nothing proposition.

In its ruling in *Armendariz*, the California state Supreme Court established a minimum standard of validity for arbitral provisions relating to disparate-party arbitrations. The court held that validity depended in part upon maintaining the judicial protection of legal rights in the arbitral proceeding (the right to discovery, the provision of a written decision to enable judicial review, and the availability of standard relief). Moreover, the economic burden for the weaker party forced to arbitrate needed to be circumscribed and modest. The costs of arbitration for that party could not exceed the fare for judicial proceedings. Finally, the court emphasized that the agreement to arbitrate must exhibit "a modicum of bilaterality," meaning that each party to the transaction had to be equally obligated to arbitrate disputes. As a consequence, "carve-outs" or "hold-backs" created a strong presumption that the agreement was oppressive and, therefore, unenforceable.

The *Armendariz* ruling and its impact upon subsequent cases raised a number of concerns. Although the holding has never been challenged, it is likely that it violates the federal preemption doctrine. In effect, it represents a rewriting of the contract validity requirements contained in FAA

§ 2. It certainly conflicts with the federal judicial policy underlying that section of the governing law. At least potentially, the ruling frustrates the objective of achieving "unobstructed recourse" to arbitration through the unimpeded enforcement of agreements to arbitrate. In effect, the California high court ruling invites courts to mandate the judicialization of arbitration and to use the unconscionability defense to privilege contract fairness above all other juridical considerations in the context of disparate-party arbitration. Subsequent cases demonstrate that the California state courts of appeal, upon a finding of unconscionability, do not favor the use of the severance doctrine to salvage the recourse to arbitration—even when the would-be problem with the contract does not permeate all aspects of the agreement. In effect, such determinations exemplify the type of judicial prejudice that the FAA was intended to remedy and eradicate.

It would be panglossian to maintain that the California judiciary, either at the federal or state level, is anything but hostile to arbitration and to its present-day function in the American legal system. While courts in other federal circuits and in other states have occasionally aligned themselves with the California position on arbitration, California is the principal source of resistance to the empathic federal judicial policy on arbitration. Over the years, there have been skirmishes and a few major battles relating to the federal policy. An all-out war has yet to take place. The hostility is nonetheless palatable and undeniable.

With the development of disparate party arbitration and the Court's proclamation of the domestic arbitrability of statutory claims in the landmark securities cases, a trend developed in the U.S. Congress and some state legislatures to propose legislation to oppose arbitration's increasing range of application and its influence upon the protection of legal rights. [*See* Bill to Restore, Reaffirm, and Reconcile Legal Rights and Remedies under Civil Rights Statutes, S. 2554, 110th Cong. 2d sess. (Jan. 24, 2008) (Title VII, Subtitle C., § 423: Unenforceability of Arbitration Clauses in Employment Contracts—"Notwithstanding any other provision of law, any clause of any agreement between an employer and an employee that requires arbitration of a dispute arising under the Constitution or laws of the United States shall not be enforceable ... [The foregoing provision] shall not apply with respect to any dispute if, after such dispute arises, the parties involved knowingly and voluntarily consent to submit such dispute to arbitration ... [Moreover the foregoing provision] shall not preclude the enforcement of any of the rights or terms of a valid collective bargaining agreement.").

Bill to Amend Certain Federal Civil Rights Statutes to Prevent the Involuntary Application of Arbitration to Claims that Arise from Unlawful Employment Discrimination Based on Race, Color, Religion, Sex, National Origin, Age, or Disability ... H.R. 4981, 103d Cong. 2d sess. (Aug. 17, 1994) (§ 2: "Title VII of the Civil Rights Act of 1964...is amended by adding at the end of the following: 'Exclusivity of Powers and Procedures Sec. 719. Notwithstanding any Federal statute of general applicability that would modify any powers and procedures expressly applicable to a claim arising under this title, such powers and procedures shall be the exclusive powers and procedures applicable to such claim unless after such claim arises the claimant voluntarily enters into an agreement to resolve such claim through arbitration or another procedure.' "). Also amends in the same way The Rehabilitation Act of 1973, Americans with Disabilities Act of 1990, the Family and Medical Leave Act of 1993, and other federal statutes.

The Civil Rights Procedures Protection Act of 1994, S. 2405, 103d Cong. 2d sess. (Aug. 18, 1994) (also designed to prevent involuntary arbitration in discrimination cases) ("General prohibition reads: 'Sec. 719. Notwithstanding any Federal statute of general applicability that would modify any of the powers and procedures expressly applicable to a claim arising under this title, such powers and procedures shall be the exclusive powers and procedures applicable to such claim unless after such claim arises the claimant voluntarily enters into an agreement to resolve such claims through arbitration or another procedure.' ") (Applies to a variety of federal social welfare statutes).

H.R. 3748, 104th Cong. 2d sess. (June 27, 1996) (Prohibits involuntary arbitration in discrimination case and contains standard exclusivity of powers and procedures provision). *See also*, S. 366, 104th Cong. 1st sess. (Jan. 30, 1995); H.R. 983 105th Cong. 1st sess. (Mar. 6, 1997); S. 63, 105th Cong. 1st sess. (Jan. 21, 1997); H.R. 872 106th Cong. 1st sess. (Feb. 25, 1999); S. 121, 106th Cong. 2d sess. (Jan. 19, 1999); H.R. 1489 107th Cong. 1st sess. (April 4, 2001); S. 163, 107th Cong. 1st sess. (Jan. 24, 2001); H.R. 5182, 108th Cong. 2d sess. (Sept. 29, 2004).

See Congressional Legislation to Amend the FAA is Proposed, 15 WORLD ARBITRATION & MEDIATION REPORT 97 (2004)..]

To the power brokers in society—at least to a vocal minority among them—the privatization of the adjudication of public law rights was an unacceptable development in the law of arbitration. The statutory regulation of commercial conduct in a form of antitrust and security laws and the guarantees of citizenship in terms of civil rights, equal protection, and due process needed to be addressed in public proceedings by duly designated public servants who rendered published determinations reasoned according to well-settled law.

In fact, these opponents of arbitration suspected that, despite the diversity of its membership, the Court possessed an underlying sympathy for business interests and commercial lawyers. It was using arbitration to facilitate capitalism and business activity. While such a policy (whether true or not) hardly contravenes the ethos of America, the opponents pursued their New Dealesque criticism. They believed that arbitration and the Court's support of it would deprive workers and consumers of their most important legal rights and thereby reduce operational costs and yield greater resource efficiencies. Further, the avoidance of protracted legal proceedings would enhance profits and strengthen the economic enterprise. Finally, arbitration relegated disputed matters to decision by private and essentially unaccountable adjudicators whose only loyalty was to the contract that authorized them to act, not the law, society, or a public institution. Coercing people generally into such a process was bad enough; coercing the weaker actors in society in particular added insult to injury.

Arbitral proceedings are akin to judicial bench trials. Participating eliminates any right to a civil jury trial. Moreover, arbitration, by definition, extinguishes the consumer's ability to engage in class action litigation. The agreement to arbitrate forecloses judicial recourse and the bilateral character of the contract precludes the aggregation of claims. At this stage of the elaboration of law, there was some question as to what type of relief was available in arbitration. It was unclear whether arbitrators could award attorney's fees (often provided for by statutory regulations) or punitive damages. Moreover, weaker parties might be discouraged or prevented from arbitrating by high up-front costs in the form of deposits for arbitrator fees and administrative costs. Additionally, the selection of arbitrators or arbitral service providers could favor the interests of the stronger party simply because it was a more frequent participant in the process. Finally, the possibility of appeal—especially on legal questions—was severely limited in arbitration. To some, arbitration appeared to be an adjudicatory dictatorship, controlled by like-minded players who operated in the shadows to advance exclusively the interests of their kind. Although most, if not all, of this criticism was unfounded and, in many instances, maligned arbitration, it gave rise to annual anti-arbitration bills in the U.S. Congress. The proposed legislation was intended primarily, it seems, to thwart arbitration's infringement upon the public law jurisdiction of courts and its perceived unfairness to traditional political constituencies. . . .

The "Arbitration Fairness Act" of 2007, S. 1782 and H.R. 3010, 110th Cong. 1st sess. (July 12, 2007), continues this tradition but in a less symbolic way. It was introduced in the 110th Congress as H.R. 3010 and S. 1782. The House and Senate versions of the proposed legislation are identical; they, therefore, can be assessed in a single commentary. The principal sponsors of the legislation appear to be Representative Henry C. "Hank" Johnson, Jr. (Ga.) (along with 103 co-sponsors) and Senator Russell D. Feingold (Wis.) (along with seven co-sponsors). The configuration of sponsorships indicate that the proposed legislation is a Democrat party measure that reflects the interests of its traditional constituencies, especially the American Trial Lawyers Association ("ATLA").

The stated purpose of the bills is to dismantle the process of coerced arbitration in disparate-party transactional circumstances: "[N]o predispute arbitration agreement shall be valid or enforceable if it requires arbitration of: (1) an employment, consumer, or franchise dispute, or (2) a dispute arising under any statute intended to protect civil rights or to regulate contracts or transactions between parties of unequal bargaining power." It also eliminates, apparently in all arbitration circumstances, the jurisdictional or *kompetenz-kompetenz* powers of the arbitrator: "[T]he

validity or enforceability of an agreement to arbitrate shall be determined
by a court, under federal law, rather than an arbitrator, irrespective of
whether the party resisting arbitration challenges the arbitration agreement specifically or in conjunction with other terms of the contract
containing such agreement." The latter provision reverses or eliminates
the effect of the separability doctrine. It also seems to eliminate any
reference to state contract law and to create a complete federal law of
contracts applying exclusively to arbitration agreements. This federal
contract law for arbitration propounds the limited validity of arbitration
contracts and places particular encumbrances upon their range of application. In effect, if the bill is enacted into law, the U.S. Congress will
discriminate against arbitration as a form of contract by placing disabling
requirements upon it in certain transactions. By so doing, the Congress
will be engaging in conduct that the U.S. Supreme Court forbade to the
states for years through the federal preemption doctrine.

Finally, in keeping with Justice Douglas' legacy on arbitration, the
proposed legislation "exempts arbitration in collective bargaining agreements from the regulation established in the legislation." Justice Douglas
was a virulent critic of arbitration in all circumstances but those of labor-
management relations. Like Justice Douglas, the proponents of the legislation approve of the traditional role of arbitration in achieving industrial
self-governance in the unionized workplace. In their view, union representation establishes a sufficient level of protection to guarantee the essential
fairness of this application of arbitration. It is again interesting to note
that the federal decisional law, especially the rulings of the U.S. Supreme
Court, arrives at a diametrically opposed conclusion. In the latter, the
Court believed that the union's collective interest prevented union members from asserting their personal acquiescence to the arbitrability of their
individual statutory rights through the union. As a result, the individual
union member needed to affirm personally the arbitrability of disputes
involving citizenship guarantees. In the final analysis, it is difficult to
comprehend why an employee's interests are seen as advantaged in one
form of arbitration and not the other.

It should be emphasized that the stated purpose of the proposed
legislation not only bans arbitral clauses in the identified transactional
circumstances, but it also prohibits the arbitrability of civil rights disputes
on a subject-matter basis. Both aspects of the bills stand in contradiction
to the U.S. Supreme Court's long-standing decisional law on arbitration.
[In its very recent opinion in *14 Penn Plaza v. Pyett*, the Court affirmed
the arbitrability of civil rights claims.] The latter provides for a wide, if
not unlimited, rule of arbitrability that is not constrained by subject-
matter considerations or transactional inequality. The Court's objective in
devising this law was to guarantee citizen access to a functional and
effective process of adjudication. The proposed law simply bans arbitration
without creating more courts, naming judges to unfilled positions, or
correcting the abuses and dysfunctionality of judicial litigation.

The bills contain a section of "findings" about arbitration, the law, and the need for reform. The statements made in this section of the proposed legislation constitute a veritable "manifesto" against arbitration that distorts the current law and its impact. The declarations are built upon a set of false and conclusory assumptions about the functioning of the court system, unabashed ideological and political convictions, and an ill-concealed objective of advancing the individual self-interests of favored groups. The alleged contractual unfairness of arbitration proceeds from a misconception about the purpose and reality of dispute resolution. It is anchored in the contrived reality of an ideological vision and world. The would-be abuse is at best theoretical. The legislative critique mouths the criticism of arbitration advanced by the ATLA. Regardless of how justice is defined, arbitration undeniably depreciates the business interest, adversarial skills, and the professional necessity of ATLA members by creating a more effective and efficient civil dispute resolution process. Eliminating the option for arbitration is equivalent to relegating American citizens to the emergency room for their health care needs.

Section 2(1) describes the historical origins and purpose of the FAA but with a self-evident twist to support the objective of the proposed legislation. The section reads: "The Federal Arbitration Act (now enacted as chapter 1 of title 9 of the United States Code) was intended to apply to disputes between commercial entities of generally similar sophistication and bargaining power." It is one thing to state—accurately—that the FAA was enacted at the behest of commercial interests to guarantee that arbitration would be available for commercial transactions. It is quite another matter to describe the statute's scope of application as limited to parties of generally similar sophistication and bargaining power. The latter statement emphasizes an aspect of contemporary arbitration law that was never considered or mentioned in the original legislation or its legislative history. It establishes a false link between the proposed legislation and the origins of the governing statute. It essentially distorts the special-interest character of the FAA to justify the bills' content.

Disparate-party arbitration arose much later in the development of arbitration through the decisional law. It had not been conceived or even contemplated in 1925. In 1988, the U.S. Congress added content to the FAA, thereby tacitly approving the decisional alteration of the statute over the years and ignoring the emerging use of arbitration in disparate-party circumstances. The bill's description of the historical origins of the FAA ignores completely (probably, deliberately) the judicial adaptation of the statutory text over a forty-year period. It is entirely reasonable to argue that the FAA's present-day gravamen is a hybrid of its original historical intendment and how the courts have construed it during an extensive period of time. The judicial performance of a legislative function was done with the Congress' implied approbation.

Section 2(2) contains a more accurate account of the evolution and development of U.S. arbitration law. It reads:

A series of United States Supreme Court decisions have changed the meaning of the Act so that it now extends to disputes between parties of greatly disparate economic power, such as consumer disputes and employment disputes. As a result, a large and rapidly growing number of corporations are requiring millions of consumers and employees to give up their right to have disputes resolved by a judge or jury, and instead submit their claims to binding arbitration.

It is true that the Court instituted disparate-party arbitration through a number of landmark decisions. Whether the latter "changed the meaning of the Act" is at least analytically debatable. It could be argued, entirely justifiably, that the case law simply is of a piece with FAA § 2, which creates a judicial duty to enforce arbitration agreements. It is also incontestable that *McMahon, Rodriguez*, and *Gilmer* have allowed entire service and manufacturing sectors, along with employers in the non-unionized workplace, to require weaker party acquiescence to the recourse to arbitration. It is also true that these practices are becoming more (rather than less) widespread. These transactions unquestionably represent situations in which the stronger, more sophisticated party imposes the obligation to arbitrate upon the economically weaker and less savvy party unilaterally on an all-or-nothing basis. The adhesionary character of these transactions is undeniable. Whether this circumstance results in unacceptable inequity and whether "consumers and employees [are forced] to give up their right to have disputes resolved by a judge or jury..." is at least a matter of opinion, if not a matter of political predilection, rather than a matter of fact. From the perspective of the U.S. Supreme Court, the mission of erecting a private civil justice process could not be accomplished if uninformed parties, distrustful of corporate practices, were allowed to reject the arbitral alternative on the basis of misconceptions. The simple lack of familiarity would be sufficient to thwart the overriding goal.

The recourse to arbitration may, in fact, be a more effective remedy for the weaker party and a better vehicle for protecting the weaker party's legal rights. The potential superiority of arbitration becomes manifest when the obligor pays the costs of arbitration, is equally subject to the duty to submit disputes to arbitration, and includes all the forms of relief available in court, including class action litigation, attorney's fees, and punitive damages. The proposed legislation assumes that there is supreme virtue to participation in the process of judicial litigation and that the affected parties surrender rather than forego their right of recourse to that "mystical" mechanism. The courts are seen as 'the one true religion.' There is, in fact, a great deal of *trompe l'oeil* to the judicial process; for example, court dockets are overwhelmed, access is difficult and expensive, outcomes are difficult to predict, and the availability of appeal can transform a victory at the trial level into a financially driven defeat through appeal. These disadvantages are accompanied by the foibles of the jury, relentless efforts to forum-shop and argue about jurisdiction, and gaming the system through choice-of-law puzzles and the intricate rules of evidence.

The failures of the court trial, over the years, have been the *raison d'être* of arbitration's success. The stronger party seems to have the better position in the litigious realities of the judicial process. "Referee" judges can hardly direct the conduct of party-driven proceedings. The litigation process, in fact, was conceived for lawyers, not for the client's interests. In effect, only the mythology of outdated belief systems could sustain the view that coerced participation of employees and consumers in arbitration constitutes a denial of justice. In point of fact, the weaker party should rationally seek to avail itself of a more user-friendly dispute resolution process that provides for acceptable final results. Prospective harm is not actual harm or the negation of actual benefit. The assessment in the proposed legislation ignores (probably, deliberately) the advances and adjustments that have been made to disparate-party arbitration in the case law.

Section 2(3) lists all of the transactional aspects that contribute to the contractual unfairness of adhesion contracts for arbitration:

> Most consumers and employees have little or no meaningful option whether to submit their claims to arbitration. Few people realize, or understand the importance of the deliberately fine print that strips them of rights; and because entire industries are adopting these clauses, people increasingly have no choice but to accept them. They must often give up their rights as a condition of having a job, getting necessary medical care, buying a car, opening a bank account, getting a credit card, and the like. Often times, they are not even aware that they have given up their rights.

There is no doubt that disparate-party arbitration is coerced and a prerequisite to the sale and purchase of necessary commodities and the supply of indispensable social services. As noted earlier, the infringement of choice results in benefits for both parties. Suppliers lessen their operating costs and can become more profitable; consumers have increased market choice, lower prices, and greater convenience. For both consumers and employees, grievances are brought to a more available, functional, and effective process of adjudication. In fact, true unfairness to the weaker party may well reside in not compelling the recourse to arbitration given the realities of the judicial processing of claims. The weaker party's real disadvantage is its lack of familiarity with arbitration. Courts are pervasive in American society and a core part of constitutional governance. The realities of adversarial justice, however, long ago ceased to fulfill the convictions of the American political tradition and forced litigation to promote the self-serving indecision of advocate justice and to become part of the business of law. The would-be ideals associated with judicial justice are as corroded as the "dream" of home ownership after the subprime mortgage loan fiasco. The greed and perverse ambition of the celebrants of the cult falsified the faith in higher beliefs. The lawyers who propound adversarial justice are merely expressing their financial self-interest, not rendering (in most cases) a public service.

While weaker parties know more about courts, they probably do not understand the process of judicial litigation any more than arbitral adjudication. It seems that a legal counselor is needed to understand and negotiate either process. Arbitration, in fact, is more flexible and adjustable than the judicial trial; the arbitral proceeding rarely, if ever, exceeds the economic significance of the parties' dispute. Court trials can overwhelm the facts of the dispute through legal considerations and the construction of legal provisions. The drafters of the proposed legislation might have rendered a more essential public service by mandating greater public education about arbitration and its role in the resolution of the daily and commonplace disputes of contemporary society. They would have done better to consider the view that not every dispute deserves or requires the unfurling of elaborate constitutional protections and strident adversarial representation.

Section 2(4) defames the community of arbitral service providers by portraying them as greed-driven entities servilely at the mercy of their well-heeled customers' corrupt demands: "Private arbitration companies are sometimes under great pressure to devise systems that favor the corporate repeat players who decide whether those companies will receive their lucrative business." According to the remark, there is a type of implied collusion between the service providers and their corporate clients to fix the arbitral proceedings. The service providers get paid and the corporate clients win or at least these actors are under "great pressure" to conduct themselves in a corrupt and self-interested way.

These statements again substantially misrepresent the actual operation of the arbitral process, the parties' conduct, and the applicable decisional law. In fact, service providers have recently spearheaded a successful movement to establish tribunal-wide neutrality for arbitral tribunals. This effort was not directed to actual abuse, but rather to the avoidance of any potential abuse. The objective was to reinforce arbitration's image as legitimate adjudication. The statements also fail to account for the work of the case law. In a set of *Ryan's Family Steak House, Inc.* cases, the federal courts thwarted an attempt by an employer to avoid the mutuality of the obligation to arbitrate by requiring its employees to enter into a contract with a compromised service provider. The courts are fully capable of rectifying the occasional misuse of the arbitral process.

The repeat player phenomenon to which the provision refers describes an intractable problem in the disparate-party arbitration process that is difficult to minimize or eliminate. That corporate entities appear more frequently in the designated arbitral process does not give rise to collusion between the corporate parties and the arbitral administrators, but rather it creates a level of familiarity between the companies and the arbitrators. It also gives companies a greater knowledge of the applicable arbitral process. Familiarity can be a double-edged sword; it can also breed contempt. The factor of increased presence is also a part of judicial proceedings. Familiarity with a judge is not any different from familiarity with an arbitrator. There may not be any way to remedy the repeat player problem (but to weight the tribunal) because it is endemic to the reality of the parties' positions. Weighted tribunals are, by definition, a form of corruption no matter which side is advantaged. The statement in the findings makes a poor and calculated use of the concept and fails to provide any useful insight by which to resolve the problem.

Section 2(5) demonstrates a complete misunderstanding of the arbitral process and its need for autonomy, as well as its emerging law-making function:

> Mandatory arbitration undermines the development of public law for civil rights and consumer rights, because there is no meaningful judicial review of arbitrators' decisions. With the knowledge that their rulings will not be seriously examined by a court applying current law, arbitrators enjoy near complete freedom to ignore the law and [invent] their own rules.

It is axiomatic that "judicial review"—meaningful or otherwise—is antithetical to the viability of arbitration. Inviting courts into the procedural or decisional operation of the arbitral process will render it ineffective and essentially counterproductive and useless. There is no data to indicate that arbitrators engage in arbitrary and capricious decision-making; in fact, their marketplace interest is to decide cases in the most professional manner possible. Party respect for impartiality, expertise, and judgment determines reappointment. Unless they are empowered by the parties to rule in equity, arbitrators are no more likely (in fact, less—given the marketplace factor) to take liberties with the law. Arbitrators generally have substantial expertise in the field—generally more than judges. Their knowledge may cause them to apply governing legal rules with greater intelligence. The drafters of the proposed legislation assumed that the law contains objective answers that are susceptible of rigorous scientific application and that judges never construe the law by exercising their personal judgment. The existence of dissents and reversals demonstrate unquestionably that so-called legal rules are extremely variable and that judges are hardly uniform in their appraisals of them. As Cardoro stated, adjudicators are intermediaries between history, society, and private interests; they, therefore, frequently invent rules to achieve resolution in individual cases. This is the bargain for judicial and arbitral justice alike. Arbitrators have a greater incentive to avoid being characterized as arbitrary decision-makers.

When domestic arbitration first began to flourish and the Court instituted its liberal policy on statutory (or subject-matter) arbitrability, few domestic arbitrations resulted in significantly reasoned determinations or published awards. The Court's ruling, however, made arbitral decisions into more significant pronouncements. Arbitrators not only were authorized by contract to resolve the parties' dispute, but now the law regulating arbitration invested them with the power to address and rule upon statutory claims. This wider range of arbitral jurisdiction would apply unless the parties provided otherwise in their agreement. To some degree, therefore, the Court's decisional pronouncement attributed public law-making authority to the arbitrators. They ruled primarily pursuant to contract, but acquired (as a matter of law) some of the responsibility of the public servant because they were performing the same function as a judge.

Given their enhanced jurisdiction, the determinations reached by arbitrators became both more voluminous and significant. As in matters of transborder arbitrations involving large sums of money, domestic arbitrators asked to resolve workplace discrimination claims, issues relating to the public regulation of commerce (like antitrust or securities regulation), or to apply consumer protection legislation (e.g., truth-in-lending) felt obligated to contribute to the *gravitas* of their larger mission by engaging in statutory analysis and consulting the case law. They produced judge-like opinions that were introduced in subsequent proceedings by lawyers and were eventually (in some cases) made available to the public through the internet or publication. Increasingly, the publication of arbitral awards included commentary and assessment by specialists in the field. Succinctly stated, the proposed legislation is again a vehicle of disinformation. Disparate-party arbitration has not stunted the discussion of public law issues, but rather shifted the discussion to a more accessible and effective adjudicatory mechanism. On this score as well, the development of arbitration has demonstrated its creative ability to adjust and adapt to its changing mandate.

Section 2(6) disfigures the reality of arbitration with even greater intemperance and unfounded assumptions:

> Mandatory arbitration is a poor system for protecting civil rights and consumer rights because it is not transparent. While the American civil justice system features publicly accountable decision makers who generally issue written decisions that are widely available to the public, arbitration offers none of these features.

An adjudicatory process that is efficient, effective, and accessible can hardly be described as incapable of protecting rights. The expense and indecision associated with protracted adversarial proceedings before courts do not protect citizen rights, but rather promote the attorneys' combat and embellish their fees. Lawyers, of course, tendentiously assert that participation in their battleground is synonymous with rights protection. The argument ignores the impact of litigation warfare on the litigants' lives and interests. The lack of transparency criticism was also leveled at NAFTA arbitration a few years ago on the basis of the fabricated outcry that corporations and corporate lawyers were colluding in NAFTA arbitral proceedings to advance their interests with little, if any, public accountability. Once the public was afforded full access to the NAFTA arbitrations, even the complaining journalists quickly abandoned their surveillance of the process. The matters being decided, the reasoning employed, and the discourse leading to decision had none of the appeal of a political sex scandal or the lure of destroying a humanly flawed celebrity's reputation or privacy.

Sunshine is an invaluable tool to democracy precisely because it promotes accountability and prevents sweetheart deals and self-dealing. Mandating that all consumer and employment arbitrations be open to the public would not hinder the process of disparate-party arbitration. To some degree, the openness of such proceedings is already achieved (albeit in a delayed fashion) by vacatur actions and the periodic publication of awards. The need for confidentiality is much greater in commercial proceedings because of the parties' need to preserve business advantage and reputation. Further, reform of disparate-party arbitration can be readily achieved by altering the governing procedure to provide for written opinions that contain reasons and are published. These are generally facile and innocuous modifications that are responsive to the public law character of the implicated disputes.

Section 2(7) is literally a diatribe, a form of infantile temper tantrum against arbitration; it borrows a page out of ATLA's book of litigious distortions:

> Many corporations add to their arbitration clauses unfair provisions that deliberately tilt the systems against individuals, including provisions that strip individuals of substantive statutory rights, ban class actions, and force people to arbitrate their claims hundreds of miles from their homes. While some courts have been protective of individuals, too many courts have upheld even egregiously unfair mandatory arbitration clauses in deference to a supposed Federal policy favoring arbitration over the constitutional rights of individuals.

It is difficult to identify the circumstances the drafters contemplated when they articulated their proverbial parade of horribles. The general claim that corporations "tilt" arbitrations "against individuals" is opaque, although—by making the accusation—the drafters clearly are seeking to engender a populist maelstrom against adhesionary corporate practices. The message conveyed is that these "mean" companies, proprietors of much of America's wealth, acquire it in part by forcing their employees to arbitrate and then subjugating them in slanted and biased arbitral proceedings. The statement seeks to induce instantaneous hatred of arbitration as a device of overwhelming economic oppression of the weak and disenfranchised.

[. . .]

NOTES AND QUESTIONS

1. How would you explain the California or western United States position on arbitration? Is it rational, political, practical, or cultural and ideological? What purpose does it serve?

2. The unfairness of adhesionary arbitration agreements appears to be at the heart of the debate and controversy. Would a guarantee that the stronger party would pay not only the arbitral costs, but also a portion of the weaker party's attorney's fees remedy the inequity sufficiently? What about internal arbitral merits review through another tribunal?

3. Do you think the proposed legislation is too draconian? Why and why not?

4. Does the judicial system meet the demands of the critics of arbitration?

5. Why is *kompetenz-kompetenz* targeted in the proposed legislation?

6. Why is CBA or labor arbitration attributed a special status?

7. How would you rule if a judge and vote if a legislator?

INDEX

References are to Pages

References are to Pages

†